PRENTICE

LITERATURE

Timeless Voices, Timeless Themes

THE AMERICAN EXPERIENCE

PEARSON

Prentice
Hall

Upper Saddle River, New Jersey

Needham, Massachusetts

ISBN 0-13-180436-7
7 8 9 10   09 08 07 06 05

Cover: *Travel by Ox-Drawn Covered Wagons,* Artist unknown, Courtesy of the Bancroft Library, University of California, Berkeley

ACKNOWLEDGMENTS

Grateful acknowledgment is made to the following for copyrighted material:

Amistad Research Center, administered by Thompson and Thompson "From the Dark Tower" by Countee Cullen published in *Copper Sun*, Harper & Bros., © 1927, renewed 1954 by Ida Cullen. Copyrights held by the Amistad Research Center, administered by Thompson and Thompson, New York, NY. Used by permission.

Arte Público Press "To Walt Whitman" by Angela de Hoyos from *In Other Words: Literature by Latinas of the United States* (Houston: Arte Público Press, University of Houston, 1994).

The James Baldwin Estate "The Rockpile" is collected in *Going to Meet the Man,* (c) 1965 by James Baldwin. Copyright renewed. Published by Vintage Books. Used by arrangement with the James Baldwin Estate.

Peter Basch, Literary Agent "When Grizzlies Walked Upright" (Modoc) from *American Indian Myths and Legends,* selected and edited by Richard Erdoes and Alfonso Ortiz, published by Pantheon Books. Copyright © 1984 by Richard Erdoes and Alfonso Ortiz.

Susan Bergholz Literary Services "Antojos" by Julia Alvarez, copyright © 1991 by Julia Alvarez. Later published in slightly different form in *How the Garcia Girls Lost Their Accents,* copyright © 1991 by Julia Alvarez. Published by Plume, an imprint of Dutton Signet, a division of Penguin USA, Inc., and originally in hardcover by Algonquin Books of Chapel Hill. "Straw into Gold" by Sandra Cisneros. Copyright © 1987 by Sandra Cisneros. First published in *The Texas Observer,* September 1987. Reprinted by permission of Susan Bergholz Literary Services, New York. All rights reserved.

(Acknowledgments continue on page R58, which constitutes an extension of this copyright page.)

PRENTICE HALL
LITERATURE

Timeless Voices, Timeless Themes

COPPER

BRONZE

SILVER

GOLD

PLATINUM

THE AMERICAN EXPERIENCE

THE BRITISH TRADITION

CONTRIBUTING AUTHORS

The contributing authors guided the direction and philosophy of *Prentice Hall Literature: Timeless Voices, Timeless Themes*. Working with the development team, they helped to build the pedagogical integrity of the program and to ensure its relevance for today's teachers and students.

Kate Kinsella

Kate Kinsella, Ed.D., is a faculty member in the Department of Secondary Education at San Francisco State University. A specialist in second-language acquisition and adolescent reading and writing, she teaches coursework addressing language and literacy development across the secondary curricula. She has taught high-school ESL and directed SFSU's *Intensive English Program* for first-generation bilingual college students. She maintains secondary classroom involvement by teaching an academic literacy class for second-language learners through the University's *Step to College* partnership program. A former Fulbright lecturer and perennial institute leader for TESOL, the California Reading Association, and the California League of Middle Schools, Dr. Kinsella provides professional development nationally on topics ranging from learning-style enhancement to second-language reading. Her scholarship has been published in journals such as the *TESOL Journal*, the *CATESOL Journal*, and the *Social Studies Review*. Dr. Kinsella earned her M.A. in TESOL from San Francisco State University and her Ed.D. in Second Language Acquisition from the University of San Francisco.

Kevin Feldman

Kevin Feldman, Ed.D., is the Director of Reading and Early Intervention with the Sonoma County Office of Education (SCOE). His career in education spans thirty-one years. As the Director of Reading and Early Intervention for SCOE, he develops, organizes, and monitors programs related to K–12 literacy and prevention of reading difficulties. He also serves as a Leadership Team Consultant to the California Reading and Literature Project and assists in the development and implementation of K–12 programs throughout California. Dr. Feldman earned his undergraduate degree in Psychology from Washington State University and has a Master's degree in Special Education, Learning Disabilities, and Instructional Design from U.C. Riverside. He earned his Ed.D. in Curriculum and Instruction from the University of San Francisco.

Colleen Shea Stump

Colleen Shea Stump, Ph.D., is a Special Education Supervisor in the area of Resource and Inclusion for Seattle Public Schools. She has served as a professor and chairperson for the Department of Special Education at San Francisco State University. She continues as a lead consultant in the area of collaboration for the California State Improvement Grant and travels the state of California providing professional development training in the areas of collaboration, content literacy instruction, and inclusive instruction. Dr. Stump earned her doctorate at the University of Washington, her M.A. in Special Education from the University of New Mexico, and her B.S. in Elementary Education from the University of Wisconsin–Eau Claire.

Joyce Armstrong Carroll

In her forty-year career, Joyce Armstrong Carroll, Ed. D., has taught on every grade level from primary to graduate school. In the past twenty years, she has trained teachers in the teaching of writing. A nationally known consultant, she has served as president of TCTE and on NCTE's Commission on Composition. More than fifty of her articles have appeared in journals such as *Curriculum Review, English Journal, Media & Methods, Southwest Philosophical Studies, English in Texas,* and the *Florida English Journal.* With Edward E. Wilson, Dr. Carroll co-authored *Acts of Teaching: How to Teach Writing* and co-edited *Poetry After Lunch: Poetry to Read Aloud.* She co-directs the New Jersey Writing Project in Texas.

Edward E. Wilson

A former editor of *English in Texas,* Edward E. Wilson has served as a high-school English teacher and a writing consultant in school districts nationwide. Wilson has served on both the Texas Teacher Professional Practices Commission and NCTE's Commission on Composition. Wilson's poetry appears in Paul Janeczko's anthology *The Music of What Happens.* With Dr. Carroll, he co-wrote *Acts of Teaching: How to Teach Writing* and co-edited *Poetry After Lunch: Poetry to Read Aloud.* Wilson co-directs the New Jersey Writing Project in Texas.

PROGRAM ADVISORS

The program advisors provided ongoing input throughout the development of *Prentice Hall Literature: Timeless Voices, Timeless Themes*. Their valuable insights ensure that the perspectives of the teachers throughout the country are represented within this literature series.

Diane Cappillo
English Department Chair
Barbara Goleman Senior High School
Miami, Florida

Anita Clay
Language Arts Instructor
Gateway Institute of Technology
St. Louis, Missouri

Ellen Eberly
Language Arts Instructor
Catholic Memorial High School
West Roxbury, Massachusetts

Nancy Fahner
L.A.M.P. Lansing Area Manufacturing
   Partnership
Ingham Intermediate School District
Mason, Michigan

Terri Fields
Instructor of Language Arts,
   Communication Arts, and Author
Sunnyslope High School
Phoenix, Arizona

Susan Goldberg
Language Arts Instructor
Westlake Middle School
Thornwood, New York

Margo L. Graf
English Department Chair, Speech,
   Yearbook, Journalism
Lane Middle School
Fort Wayne, Indiana

Christopher E. Guarraia
Language Arts Instructor
Lakewood High School
Saint Petersburg, Florida

V. Pauline Hodges
Teacher, Educational Consultant
Forgan High School
Forgan, Oklahoma

Karen Hurley
Language Arts Instructor
Perry Meridian Middle School
Indianapolis, Indiana

Lenore D. Hynes
Language Arts Coordinator
Sunman-Dearborn Community
   Schools
Sunman, Indiana

Linda Kramer
Language Arts Instructor
Norman High School North
Norman, Oklahoma

Thomas S. Lindsay
Assistant Superintendent of Schools
Manheim District 83
Franklin Park, Illinois

Agathaniki (Niki) Locklear
English Department Chair
Simon Kenton High School
Independence, Kentucky

Ashley MacDonald
Language Arts Instructor
South Forsyth High School
Cumming, Georgia

Mary Ellen Mastej
Language Arts Instructor
Scott Middle School
Hammond, Indiana

Nancy L. Monroe
English, Speed Reading Teacher
Bolton High School
Alexandria, Louisiana

Jim Moody
Language Arts Instructor
Northside High School
Fort Smith, Arkansas

David Morris
Teacher of English, Writing,
   Publications, Yearbook
Washington High School
South Bend, Indiana

Rosemary A. Naab
English Department Chair
Ryan High School
Archdiocese of Philadelphia
Philadelphia, Pennsylvania

Ann Okamura
English Teacher
Laguna Creek High School
Elk Grove, California

Tucky Roger
Coordinator of Languages
Tulsa Public Schools
Tulsa, Oklahoma

Jonathan L. Schatz
English Teacher/Team Leader
Tappan Zee High School
Orangeburg, New York

John Scott
Assistant Principal
Middlesex High School
Saluda, Virginia

Ken Spurlock
Assistant Principal, Retired
Boone County High School
Florence, Kentucky

Dr. Jennifer Watson
Secondary Language Arts
   Coordinator
Putnam City Schools
Oklahoma City, Oklahoma

Joan West
Assistant Principal
Oliver Middle School
Broken Arrow, Oklahoma

UNIT 1

Beginnings–1750

PART 3   The Puritan Influence

SKILLS WORKSHOPS

UNIT 2

A Nation Is Born (1750–1800)

PART 3   Defining an American

UNIT 4

Division, Reconciliation, and Expansion (1850–1914)

UNIT 5

Disillusion, Defiance, and Discontent (1914–1946)

PART 3   From Every Corner of the Land

(continued)

UNIT 5

Disillusion, Defiance, and Discontent (1914–1946) (continued)

SKILLS WORKSHOPS

Prosperity and Protest (1946–Present)

(continued)

UNIT 6

Prosperity and Protest (1946–Present) (continued)

SKILLS WORKSHOPS

Resources

COMPARING LITERARY WORKS

READING INFORMATIONAL MATERIALS

CONNECTIONS: LITERATURE PAST AND PRESENT

WRITING WORKSHOPS

LISTENING AND SPEAKING WORKSHOPS

ASSESSMENT WORKSHOPS

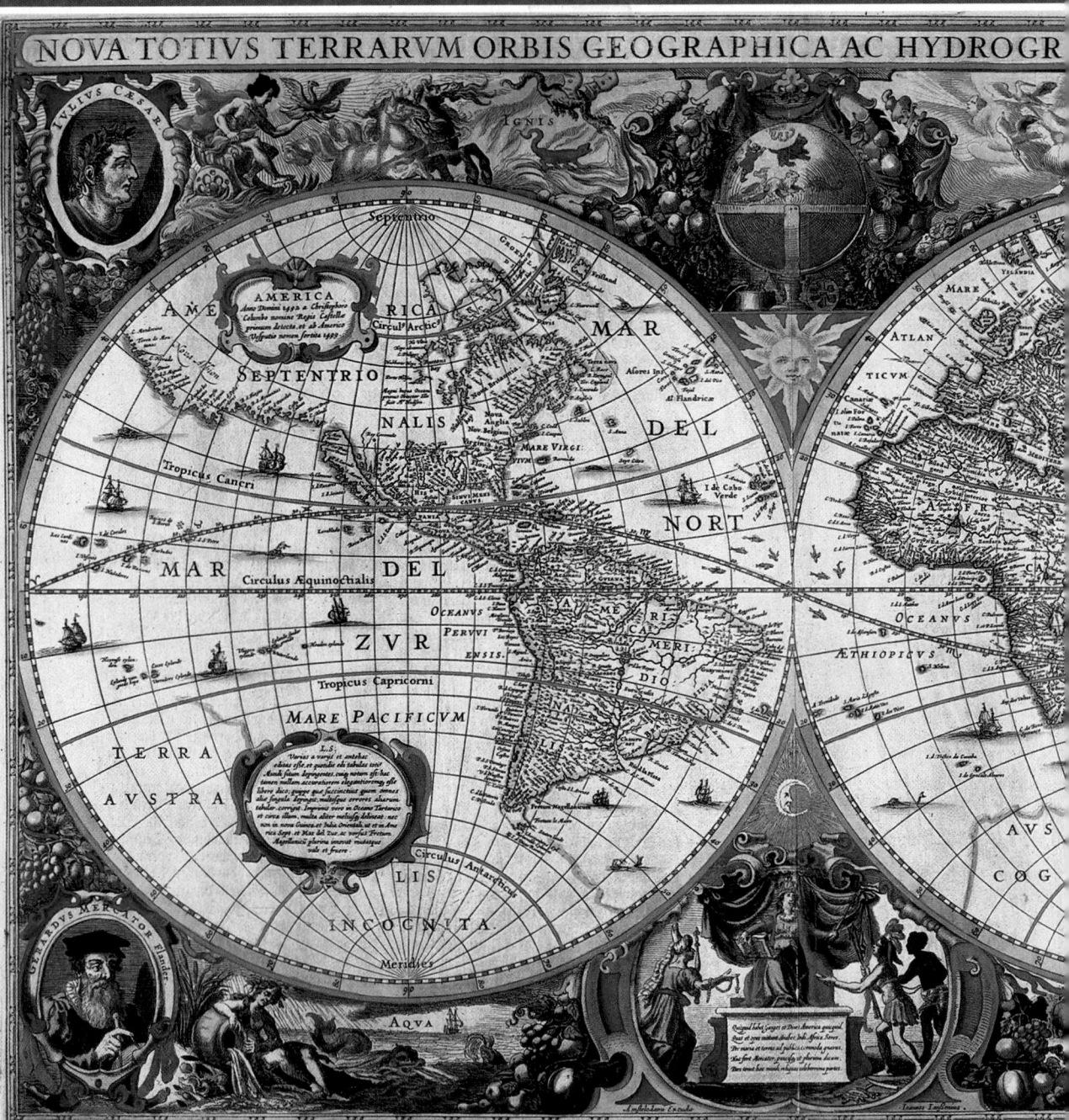

> 66 *We shall be as a City upon a Hill, the eyes of all people are upon us; so that if we shall deal falsely with our God in this work we have undertaken and so cause him to withdraw his present help from us, we shall be made a story and a by-word through the world.* 99

—John Winthrop,
Governor of the Massachusetts
Bay Colony

Timeline 1490–1750

1490   1542   1594

American Events

- **1492** Christopher Columbus lands in the Bahamas. ▼

- **1513** Juan Ponce de Léon lands on the Florida peninsula.
- **1515** Vasco Núñez de Balboa reaches the Pacific Ocean.
- **1540** Francisco Vázquez de Coronado explores the Southwest.

- **1565** St. Augustine, Florida: First permanent settlement in U.S., founded by Pedro Menendez.
- **1586** English colony at Roanoke Island disappears; known as the Lost Colony.
- **1590** Iroquois Confederacy established to stop warfare among the Five Nations.

- **1607** First permanent English settlement at Jamestown, Virginia.
- **1608** Captain John Smith writes *A True Relation . . . of Virginia*. ◄
- **1620** Pilgrims land at Plymouth, Massachusetts. ▼

- **1636** Harvard College founded in Massachusetts.
- **1639** First printing press in English-speaking North America arrives in Massachusetts.
- **1640** *Bay Psalm Book* published; first book printed in the colonies.

World Events

- **1499** England: 20,000 die in London plague.
- **1503** Italy: Leonardo da Vinci paints the *Mona Lisa*.
- **1508** Italy: Michelangelo paints ceiling of Sistine Chapel.
- **1518** Africa: Barbarossa drives the Spanish from most of Algeria.
- **1519** Spain: Chocolate introduced to Europe.
- **1520** Magellan sails around the world.
- **1520** Mexico: Cortez conquers Aztecs.
- **1531** Peru: Pizarro conquers Incas.

- **1558** England: Elizabeth I inherits throne. ►
- **1560** Brazil: Smallpox epidemic kills millions.
- **1566** Belgium: Bruegel paints *The Wedding Dance*.
- **1580** France: Montaigne's *Essays* published.

- **1595** England: Shakespeare completes *A Midsummer Night's Dream*.
- **1605** Spain: Cervantes publishes Part I of *Don Quixote*.
- **1609** Italy: Galileo builds first telescope.
- **1630** Japan: All Europeans expelled.
- **1639** India: English establish settlement at Madras.
- **1642** Holland: Rembrandt paints *The Nightwatch*.
- **1642** England: Civil War begins.
- **1644** China: Ming Dynasty ends.

American and World Events

- **1647** Massachusetts establishes free public schools.
- **1650** Publication (in London) of Anne Bradstreet's *The Tenth Muse . . .*, a collection of poems.

- **1675** King Philip, chief of the Wampanoags, begins raiding New England frontier towns. ▲
- **1692** Salem witchcraft trials result in the execution of twenty people.

- **1652** South Africa: First Dutch settlers arrive.
- **1664** France: Molière's *Tartuffe* first performed.
- **1667** England: Milton publishes *Paradise Lost*.
- **1683** China: All ports opened to foreign trade.
- **1690** India: Calcutta founded by British.

- **1735** John Peter Zenger acquitted of libel, furthering freedom of the press.
- **1741** Great Awakening, a series of religious revivals, begins to sweep the colonies. ▼

- **1741** Jonathan Edwards first delivers his sermon *Sinners in the Hands of an Angry God.*

- **1702** England: First daily newspaper begins publication.
- **1719** England: Daniel Defoe publishes *Robinson Crusoe*.
- **1721** Germany: Bach composes *Brandenburg Concertos*.
- **1726** England: Jonathan Swift publishes *Gulliver's Travels*.
- **1727** Brazil: First coffee plants cultivated. ◄
- **1748** France: Montesquieu publishes *The Spirit of Laws*.

Beginnings to 1750

More than a century after European explorers first landed in North America, there were still no permanent settlements in the Western Hemisphere north of St. Augustine, Florida. By 1607, however, a small group of English settlers was struggling to survive on a marshy island in the James River in the present state of Virginia. In 1611, Thomas Dale, governor of the colony, wrote a report to the king expressing the colonists' determination to succeed. Despite disease and starvation, Jamestown did survive.

The first settlers were entranced by the native inhabitants they met. They did not at first realize that these earlier Americans, like Europeans, had cultural values and literary traditions of their own. Their literature was entirely oral, for the tribes of North America had not yet developed writing systems. This extensive oral literature, along with the first written works of the colonists, forms the beginning of the American literary heritage.

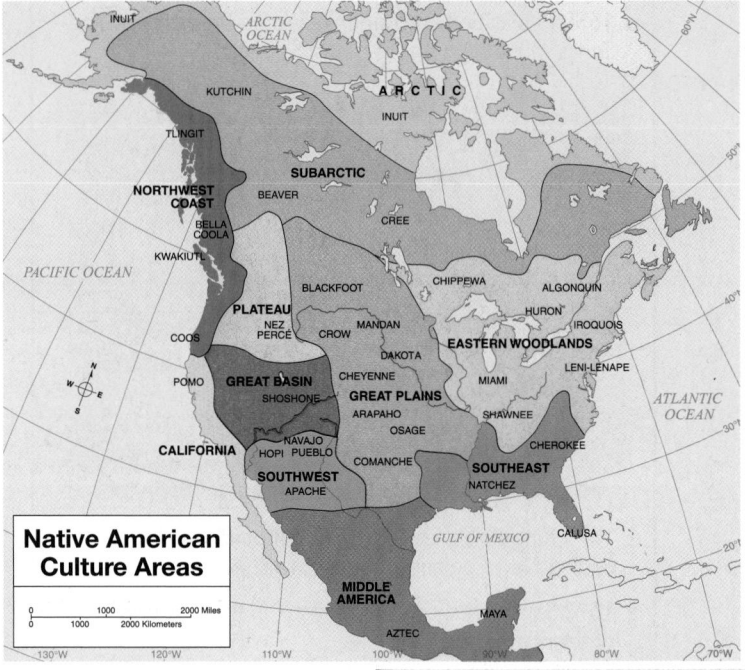

Native American Culture Areas

Historical Background

When Christopher Columbus reached North America in 1492, the continent was already populated, though sparsely, by several hundred Native American tribes. Europeans did not encounter these tribes all at one time. Explorers from different nations came into contact with them at different times. As we now know, these widely dispersed tribes of Native Americans differed greatly from one another in language, government, social organization, customs, housing, and methods of survival.

The Native Americans No one knows for certain when or how the first Americans arrived in what is now the United States. It may have been as recently as 12,000 years ago or as long ago as 70,000 years. Even if the shorter estimate is correct, Native Americans have been on the continent thirty times longer than the Europeans. Colonists from Europe did not begin arriving on the east coast of North America until the late 1500s.

What were the earliest Americans doing for those many centuries? To a great extent, the answer is shrouded in mystery. No written story of the

▲ **Critical Viewing**
As Native Americans spread out to populate North America, they developed varied cultures.
(a) Name two tribes in the Southwest culture area.
(b) What geographic features might have led to the development of different ways of life?
[Interpret]

Native Americans exists. Archaeologists have deduced a great deal from artifacts, however, and folklorists have recorded a rich variety of songs, legends, and myths.

What we do know is that the Native Americans usually, but by no means always, greeted the earliest European settlers as friends. They instructed the newcomers in their agriculture and woodcraft and introduced them to maize, beans, squash, maple sugar, snowshoes, toboggans, and birch bark canoes. Indeed, many more of the European settlers would have succumbed to the bitter northeastern winters had it not been for the help of these first Americans.

▲ **Critical Viewing**
What Puritan values does this painting illustrate?
[Interpret]

Pilgrims and Puritans A small group of Europeans sailed from England on the *Mayflower* in 1620. The passengers were religious reformers—Puritans who were critical of the Church of England. Having given up hope of "purifying" the Church from within, they chose instead to withdraw from the Church. This action earned them the name Separatists; we know them as the Pilgrims. They landed in North America and established a settlement at what is now Plymouth, Massachusetts. With help from friendly tribes of Native Americans, the Plymouth settlement managed to survive the rigors of North America. The colony never grew very large, however. Eventually, it was engulfed by the Massachusetts Bay Colony, the much larger settlement to the north.

Like the Plymouth Colony, the Massachusetts Bay Colony was founded by religious reformers. These reformers, however, did not withdraw from the Church of England. Unlike the Separatists, they were Puritans who intended instead to reform the Church from within. In America, the Puritans hoped to establish what John Winthrop, governor of the Colony, called a "city upon a hill," a model community guided in all aspects by the Bible. Their form of government would be a theocracy, a state under the immediate guidance of God.

Among the Puritans' central beliefs were the ideas that human beings exist for the glory of God and that the Bible is the sole expression of God's will. They also believed in predestination—John Calvin's doctrine that God has already decided who will achieve salvation and who will not. Nevertheless, those who are to be saved cannot take their salvation for granted. For that reason, all devout Puritans searched their souls with great rigor and frequency for signs of grace. The Puritans felt that they could accomplish good only through continual hard work and self-discipline, a principle known today as the "Puritan ethic."

Puritanism was in decline throughout New England by the early 1700s, as more liberal Protestant congregations attracted followers. A reaction against this new freedom, however, set in around 1720. The Great Awakening, a series of religious revivals led by such eloquent ministers as Jonathan Edwards and George Whitefield, swept through the colonies. The Great Awakening attracted thousands of converts to many Protestant groups, but it did little to revive old-fashioned Puritanism. Nevertheless, Puritan ideals of hard work, frugality, self-improvement, and self-reliance are still regarded as basic American virtues.

The Southern Planters The Southern Colonies differed from New England in climate, crops, social organization, and religion. Prosperous coastal cities grew up in the South, just as in the North, but beyond the southern cities lay large plantations, not small farms. Despite its romantic image, the plantation was in fact a large-scale agricultural enterprise and a center of commerce. Up to a thousand people, many of them enslaved, might live and work on a single plantation.

The first black slaves were brought to Virginia in 1619, a year before the Pilgrims landed at Plymouth. The plantation system and the institution of slavery were closely connected from the very beginning, although slavery existed in every colony, including Massachusetts.

Most of the plantation owners were Church of England members who regarded themselves as aristocrats. The first generation of owners, the men who established the great plantations, were ambitious, energetic, self-disciplined, and resourceful, just as the Puritans were. The way of life on most plantations, however, was more sociable and elegant than that of any Puritan. By 1750, Puritanism was in decline everywhere, and the plantation system in the South was just reaching its peak.

▲ **Critical Viewing** These exhibition rooms in Colonial Williamsburg illustrate the living quarters of African slaves and white landowners. (a) What do these rooms have in common? (b) What are the major differences? **[Compare and Contrast]**

Literature of the Period

It was an oddly assorted group that established the foundations of American literature: the Native Americans with their oral traditions, the Puritans with their preoccupation with sin and salvation, enslaved and free African Americans, and the southern planters with their busy social lives. Indeed, much of the literature that the colonists read was not produced in the colonies—it came from England. Yet, by 1750, there were the clear beginnings of a native literature that would one day be honored throughout the English-speaking world.

Native American Tradition For a long time, Native American literature was viewed mainly as folklore. The consequence was that song lyrics, hero tales, migration legends, and accounts of the creation were studied more for their content than for their literary qualities. In an oral tradition, the telling of a tale may change with each speaker, and the words are almost sure to change over time. Thus, no fixed versions of such literary works exist. Still, in cases where the words of Native American lyrics or narratives have been captured in writing, the language is often poetic and moving. As might be expected in an oral setting, oratory was much prized among Native Americans. The names of certain orators, such as Logan and Red Jacket, were widely known.

The varied Native American cultures produced a diverse body of literature. However, while the myths, legends, and folk tales vary greatly, one common characteristic is the deep respect that Native American literature generally shows for nature. Tales and chants celebrate the wonders of the natural world and its interconnectedness with the world of the spirit.

The samples of Native American literature in this unit reveal the depth and power of those original American voices.

Explorers' Accounts No one knows when the first Europeans came to the Americas. However, archaeological evidence suggests that the seafaring northern Europeans known as Vikings set up small encampments on the islands of northeastern Canada beginning some time around A.D. 1000. Still, our knowledge about Viking settlements is largely speculative. Not until the late fifteenth century did Europe inaugurate an Age of Exploration in which its journeys to the Americas were well documented.

Christopher Columbus, an Italian living in Portugal, was convinced that he could reach Asia by sailing west. After receiving financial backing from Spain's Queen Isabella, he set sail in August of 1492 and landed on October 12 on an island in what is now the Bahamas. He wrote about his experience in his Journal of the First Voyage to America, in which he stressed the rich potential of the new lands that he still regarded as part of Asia.

Other explorers who wrote accounts of their voyages were the Spaniards Alvar Núñez Cabeza de Vaca and García López de Cárdenas. Cabeza de Vaca was one of four survivors of a 400-man expedition to Texas. In his narrative, he describes a wilderness that is sometimes bountiful and sometimes very harsh. López de Cárdenas was the first European to see and describe the Grand Canyon, as we learn from Pedro de Castañeda's retelling.

Slave Narrative Olaudah Equiano, who lived about two hundred years later than these European explorers, came to America against his will as an enslaved African. However, he later purchased his freedom, settled in England, and worked to abolish slavery. As part of this effort, he wrote a two-volume autobiography entitled *The Interesting Narrative of the Life of Olaudah Equiano*. It contains a vivid and horrifying account of slaves journeying to America.

"In Adam's Fall/We Sinned All" Just as religion dominated the lives of the Puritans, it also dominated their writings—most of which would not be considered literary works by modern standards. Typically, the Puritans wrote theological studies, hymns, histories, biographies, and autobiographies. The purpose of such writing was to provide spiritual insight and instruction. When Puritans wrote for themselves in journals or diaries, their aim was the serious kind of self-examination they practiced in other aspects of their lives. The Puritans produced neither fiction nor drama because they regarded both as sinful.

A Writer's Voice

Lucy Terry, Earliest Known African American Poet

If Olaudah Equiano wrote the first slave narrative, Lucy Terry wrote what Henry Louis Gates, Jr., and Nellie Y. McKay have called "the earliest known poem by an African American." Like Equiano, Terry was kidnapped from Africa to serve as a slave in America. Also like him, she eventually gained her freedom.

Her 28-line poem entitled "Bars Fight" is the only poem she is known to have written. It describes an ambush by Indians of white families in a place in Massachusetts called "the Bars," meaning "meadows." Its rhythm indicates that it was probably meant to be sung. Transmitted orally for many years, the poem was finally published in 1855. Its first stanza appears below.

from "Bars Fight," by Lucy Terry

August, 'twas the twenty-fifth,
Seventeen hundred forty-six,
The Indians did in ambush lay,
Some very valiant° men to slay,   °valiant
5 The names of whom I'll not leave out:
Samuel Allen like a hero fout,°   °fought
And though he was so brave and bold,
His face no more shall we behold. . . .

The Puritans did write poetry, however, as a vehicle of spiritual enlightenment. Although they were less concerned with a poem's literary form than with its message, some writers were more naturally gifted than others. A few excellent Puritan poets emerged in the 1600s, among them Anne Bradstreet and Edward Taylor. Anne Bradstreet's moving, personal voice and Edward Taylor's devotional intensity shine through the conventional Puritanism of their themes.

The Puritans had a strong belief in education for both men and women. In 1636, they founded Harvard College to ensure a well-educated ministry. Three years later, they set up the first printing press in the colonies. In 1647, free public schools were established in Massachusetts. *The New England Primer*, first published around 1690, combined instruction in spelling and reading with moralistic teachings, such as "In Adam's fall/We sinned all."

▲ Critical Viewing
The Puritans founded Harvard College at Newtowne in 1636. Three years later, they renamed the city Cambridge to honor the British city where many of the colonists had studied. What does this fact reveal about the group who fled England? [Draw Conclusions]

One of the first books printed in the colonies was the *Bay Psalm Book*, the standard hymnal of the time. Richard Mather, one of the book's three authors, was the father of Increase Mather, who served for many years as pastor of the North Church in Boston. Increase Mather was also the author of more than 130 books. *Cases of Conscience Concerning Evil Spirits*, published in 1693, was a discourse on the Salem witchcraft trials of the previous year. The trials, conducted in an atmosphere of hysteria, resulted in the hanging of twenty people as witches.

Increase's eldest son, Cotton Mather, far exceeded his father's literary output, publishing at least 400 works in his lifetime. Cotton Mather, like his father, is remembered in part because of his connection with the Salem witchcraft trials. Although he did not actually take part in the trials, his works on witchcraft had helped to stir up some of the hysteria. Still, Cotton Mather was one of the most learned men of his time, a power in the state and a notable author. Although his writing was multifaceted, his theory of writing was simple: The more information a work contains, the better its style.

In fact, the Puritans in general had a theory about literary style. They believed in a plain style of writing, one in which clear statement is the highest goal. An ornate or clever style would be a sign of vanity and, as such, would not be in accordance with God's will. Despite the restrictions built into their life and literature, the Puritans succeeded in producing a small body of excellent writing.

Southern Writers Considering the number of brilliantly literate statesmen who would later emerge in the South, especially in Virginia, it seems surprising that only a few notable southern writers appeared prior to 1750. As in Puritan New England, those who were educated produced a substantial amount of writing, but it was mostly of a practical nature. For example, John Smith, the leader of the settlement at Jamestown, Virginia, wrote *The General History of Virginia* to describe his experiences for Europeans. In addition to accounts like Smith's, letters written by southern planters also provide insight into this time period. Unlike the Puritans, southerners did not oppose fiction or drama, and the first theater in America opened in Williamsburg, Virginia, in 1716.

A Living Tradition

John Berryman and Anne Bradstreet

In the 1950s, the American poet John Berryman responded powerfully to the life and work of Puritan poet Anne Bradstreet, who had lived 300 years earlier. He wrote her a long poem of praise entitled "Homage to Mistress Bradstreet." In this adventurous poem, Berryman speaks both in his own voice and in the voice of Bradstreet herself. He also uses unusual sentence structures that seem to suggest the difficulty in contacting Bradstreet and the difficulty of life in the New World.

Speaking as himself in the beginning of the poem, he imagines the terrible "New World winters" that must have "stunned" Bradstreet and her Puritan companions. Berryman also addresses Bradstreet directly, indicating that he is more sympathetic to her poetry than was her busy husband, Simon Bradstreet.

from "Homage to Mistress Bradstreet" by John Berryman

Outside the New World winters in grand dark
white air lashing high thro' the virgin stands°   °unexplored forests

foxes down foxholes sigh,
surely the English heart quails, stunned.
5 I doubt if Simon than this blast, that sea,
spares from his rigor for your poetry
more. We are on each other's hands
who care. Both of our worlds unhanded us.
  Lie stark,

thy eyes look to me mild. Out of maize° & air   °Corn
10 your body's made, and moves. I summon, see,
from the centuries it. . . .

The Planter From Westover

The important literature of the pre-Revolutionary South can be summed up in one name: William Byrd. Byrd lived at Westover, a magnificent plantation on the James River bequeathed to him by his wealthy father. Commissioned in 1728 to survey the boundary line between Virginia and North Carolina, Byrd kept a journal of his experiences. That journal served as the basis for his book, *The History of the Dividing Line*, which was circulated in manuscript form among Byrd's friends in England. Published nearly a century after Byrd's death, the book was immediately recognized as a minor humorous masterpiece. More of Byrd's papers were published later, establishing his reputation as the finest writer in the pre-Revolutionary South.

THE FIRST PRINTING PRESS BROUGHT TO AMERICA.

The writers whose work appears in this unit are not the great names in American literature. They are the founders, the men and women who laid the groundwork for the towering achievements that followed. The modest awakening of American literature seen in this unit had repercussions that echoed down the years.

▲ **Critical Viewing**
This is a picture of the first printing press in English-speaking North America. Judging by its appearance, how do you think it worked? **[Infer]**

A Writer's Voice

William Byrd, Writer with a Sense of Humor

Byrd's humor comes through in this anecdote he passes on to readers. It tells about a man from the north of England who out of curiosity explored the Dismal swamp, where Byrd later did his surveying.

from *The History of the Dividing Line* by William Byrd

. . . he, having no compass nor seeing the sun for several days together, wandered about till he was almost famished: but at last he bethought himself of a secret his countrymen make use of to pilot themselves in a dark day. He took a fat louse out of his collar and exposed it to the open day on a piece of white paper which he brought along with him for his journal. The poor insect, having no eyelids, turned himself about till he found the darkest part of the heavens and so made the best of his way toward the north. By this direction he steered himself safe out and gave such a frightful account of the monsters he saw and the distresses he underwent that no mortal since has been hardy enough to go upon the like dangerous discovery.

THE DEVELOPMENT OF AMERICAN ENGLISH

Our Native American Heritage

BY RICHARD LEDERER

If you had been one of the early explorers or settlers of North America, you would have found many things in your new environment unknown to you. The handiest way of filling voids in your vocabulary would have been to ask local Native Americans what words they used. The early colonists began borrowing words from friendly Native Americans almost from the moment of their first contact, and many of those shared words have remained in our everyday language.

ANGLICIZING

Pronouncing many of the Native American words was difficult for the early explorers and settlers. In many instances, they shortened and simplified the names. For example, *otchock* became "woodchuck," *rahaugcum* turned to "raccoon," and the smelly *segankw* transformed into a "skunk." The North American menagerie brought more new words into the English language, including caribou (Micmac), chipmunk (Ojibwa), moose (Algonquian), muskrat (Abenaki), and porgy (Algonquian).

THE POETRY OF PLACE NAMES

William Penn said he did not know "a language spoken in Europe that hath words of more sweetness and greatness." To Walt Whitman, *Monongahela* "rolls with venison richness upon the palate." Some of our loveliest place names— *Susquehanna, Shenandoah, Rappahannock*—began life as Native American words. Such names are the stuff of poetry.

If you look at a map of the United States, you will realize how freely settlers used words of Indian origin to name our states, cities, towns, mountains, lakes, rivers, and ponds. Five of our six Great Lakes and exactly half of our states have names that were borrowed from Native American words. Many other bodies of water and land have taken on names we have come to know as part of the American language.

Food

squash (Natick)	pecan (Algonquian)
hominy (Algonquian)	pone (Algonquian)
pemmican (Cree)	succotash (Narraganset)

People

sachem (Narraganset)	papoose (Narraganset)
squaw (Massachuset)	mugwump (Natick)

Native American life

moccasin (Chippewa)	toboggan (Algonquian)
tomahawk (Algonquian)	wigwam (Abenaki)
tepee (Dakota)	caucus (Algonquian)
pow-wow (Narraganset)	wampum (Massachuset)
bayou (Choctaw)	potlatch (Chinook)
hogan (Navajo)	hickory (Algonquian)
kayak (Inuit)	totem (Ojibwa)

ACTIVITY

1. Brainstorm for a list of the states that have Native American names. Research the origin of each name.
2. With help from an encyclopedia or other source, find out which Native American tribes live—or once lived—in your part of the country. Do their languages survive in many place names? Pick out ten names of places in your state—cities, towns, mountains, or bodies of water—that have Native American names. Try to find their exact origins. What can you find out about the history of your state that will help explain why these names were chosen?

Meeting of Cultures

Prepare to Read

The Earth on Turtle's Back ◆ When Grizzlies Walked Upright ◆ *from* The Navajo Origin Legend ◆ *from* The Iroquois Constitution

Onondaga

As one of the original five member nations, the Onondaga were an influential force in the Iroquois Confederation, a league of Iroquoian-speaking Native Americans in what is now the northeastern United States. The Onondaga lived in what is now central New York State, in villages of wood-and-bark long houses occupied by related families. The Onondaga were originally from Canada, where they acquired the French language. They practiced hospitality toward all people and did not believe in fighting. Following the breakup of the Iroquois Confederation after the American Revolution, factions of Onondaga scattered to various parts of the country, but the majority returned to their ancestral valley in New York where the Onondaga reservation now exists.

Modoc

The Modoc once lived in villages in the area of Oregon and Northern California, where they farmed, fished, and hunted. They also had a highly developed method of weaving. Though each village was independent and had its own leaders, in times of war they would band together. In the mid-nineteenth century, the Modoc were forced onto a reservation in Oregon. A band of Modoc, under the leadership of a subchief known as Captain Jack, later fled the reservation. The result was several years of hostilities with United States troops and the eventual relocation of Captain Jack's followers to Oklahoma. They were later allowed to return to the Oregon reservation, since dissolved.

Navajo

Today, the Navajo nation is the largest Native American nation in the United States and has more than 100,000 members. Many live on the Navajo reservation, which covers 24,000 square miles of Arizona, Utah, and New Mexico. Fierce warriors and hunters, the ancient Navajo settled in the Southwest about 1,000 years ago and eventually intermarried with the peaceful Pueblo people, who taught them to weave and raise crops. In 1864, after decades of fighting off encroaching American settlers, the Navajo were driven from their territory by the United States Army. They were eventually allowed to return to a reservation on Navajo land. Many Navajo still carry on native customs, living in earth-and-log structures and practicing the tribal religion.

Iroquois

The powerful Iroquois nation lived in what is now central New York State in the northeastern United States. During the sixteenth century, an Iroquoian mystic and prophet named Dekanawidah traveled from village to village urging the Iroquois-speaking people to stop fighting and band together in peace and brotherhood. Dekanawidah's efforts led to the formation of the Iroquois Confederation of the Five Nations, a league of five Iroquois tribes: Mohawk, Oneida, Seneca, Cayuga, and Onondaga. These tribes were democratic in process and composition, with leaders elected by their own people. The Iroquois tribes still exist today as self-governing bodies.

Preview

Connecting to the Literature

Just as you collect stories of your family history, cultures create stories to explain their world and place themselves in it. We share a fundamental desire to understand our origins—where we came from and our place in the world. In these stories, different cultures explain the world as they know it.

Literary Analysis

Origin Myths

The need to explain how life began gave birth to myths and traditional stories that were passed down from generation to generation. These stories are called **origin myths.** Myths explain phenomena, including:

- customs, institutions, or religious rites;
- natural landmarks such as a great mountain;
- events beyond people's control.

Look for the roles that nature and animals play in Native American life, and note who or what is responsible for the start of life on Earth.

Comparing Literary Works

In cultures without a written language, the **oral tradition** captures a group's ideals. Stories, poems, and songs convey a people's values, concerns, and history by word of mouth. As you read these selections, compare the worlds they describe. Note what each culture values, fears, or determines important to pass on to its next generation.

Reading Strategy

Recognizing Cultural Details

The Navajo Origin Legend excerpt opens with an image of the spirit men and women drying themselves with cornmeal. They call upon the gods, who appear carrying ears of corn. The references to corn reflect corn's importance to Navajo life.

Literature mirrors the culture that produces it. As you read, **recognize cultural details** by noticing references to objects, animals, or practices that signal how the people of a culture live, think, or worship. Use a chart like the one shown to record the details you find.

Details that signal how each group lives, thinks, or worships	
Onondaga	
Modoc	
Navajo	
Iroquois	

Vocabulary Development

ablutions (ab lōō′ shənz) *n.* cleansing the body as part of a religious rite (p. 22)

protruded (prō trōōd′ id) *v.* jutted out (p. 23)

confederate (kən fed′ ər it) *adj.* united with others for a common purpose (p. 24)

disposition (dis′ pə zish′ ən) *n.* an inclination or tendency (p. 24)

deliberation (di lib′ ər ā′ shən) *n.* careful consideration (p. 26)

The Earth on Turtle's Back

(Onondaga-Northeast Woodlands)

Retold by Michael J. Caduto and Joseph Bruchac

Background

Native Americans have great respect for the natural world. They believe that each creature has its own power by which it maintains itself and affects others. Each Native American culture has its own name for this power, but many Native American cultures recognize a Great Spirit—an invisible power that is the source of life and good for humans. Many of the animals that helped feed and clothe the early Native Americans are also highly revered. Native American folklore, much of which portrays animals, reflects this great respect.

Before this Earth existed, there was only water. It stretched as far as one could see, and in that water there were birds and animals swimming around. Far above, in the clouds, there was a Skyland. In that Skyland there was a great and beautiful tree. It had four white roots which stretched to each of the sacred directions,[1] and from its branches all kinds of fruits and flowers grew.

There was an ancient chief in the Skyland. His young wife was expecting a child, and one night she dreamed that she saw the Great Tree uprooted. The next day she told her husband the story.

He nodded as she finished telling her dream. "My wife," he said, "I am sad that you had this dream. It is clearly a dream of great power and, as is our way, when one has such a powerful dream we must do all we can to make it true. The Great Tree must be uprooted."

Then the Ancient Chief called the young men together and told them that they must pull up the tree. But the roots of the tree were so deep, so strong, that they could not budge it. At last the Ancient Chief himself came to the tree. He wrapped his arms around it, bent his knees and strained. At last, with one great effort, he uprooted the tree and placed it on its side. Where the tree's roots had gone deep into the Skyland there was now a big hole. The wife of the chief came close and leaned over to look down, grasping the tip of one of the Great Tree's branches to steady her. It seemed as if she saw something down there, far below, glittering like water. She leaned out further to look and, as she leaned, she lost her balance and fell into the hole. Her grasp slipped off the tip of the branch, leaving her with only a handful of seeds as she fell, down, down, down, down.

Far below, in the waters, some of the birds and animals looked up.

"Someone is falling toward us from the sky," said one of the birds.

"We must do something to help her," said another. Then two Swans flew up. They caught the Woman From The Sky between their wide wings. Slowly, they began to bring her down toward the water, where the birds and animals were watching.

"She is not like us," said one of the animals. "Look, she doesn't have webbed feet. I don't think she can live in the water."

"What shall we do, then?" said another of the water animals.

"I know," said one of the water birds. "I have heard that there is Earth far below the waters. If we dive down and bring up Earth, then she will have a place to stand."

So the birds and animals decided that someone would have to bring up Earth. One by one they tried.

The Duck dove first, some say. He swam down and down, far beneath the surface, but could not reach the bottom and floated back up. Then the Beaver tried. He went even deeper, so deep that

---

1. **the sacred directions** North, South, East, and West.

◀ **Critical Viewing** What characteristics of this turtle are explained in this origin myth? **[Connect]**

Literary Analysis
Origin Myths How do the opening words of this story identify it as an origin myth?

Reading Strategy
Recognizing Cultural Details What do the chief's words to his wife tell you about the beliefs of the Onondaga?

?? WHY SAVE HER

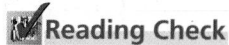
Reading Check

What does the Skyland Chief's wife dream?

it all was dark, but he could not reach the bottom, either. The Loon tried, swimming with his strong wings. He was gone a long long time, but he, too, failed to bring up Earth. Soon it seemed that all had tried and all had failed. Then a small voice spoke.

"I will bring up Earth or die trying."

They looked to see who it was. It was the tiny Muskrat. She dove down and swam and swam. She was not as strong or as swift as the others, but she was determined. She went so deep that it was all dark, and still she swam deeper. She swam so deep that her lungs felt ready to burst, but she swam deeper still. At last, just as she was becoming unconscious, she reached out one small paw and grasped at the bottom, barely touching it before she floated up, almost dead.

When the other animals saw her break the surface they thought she had failed. Then they saw her right paw was held tightly shut.

"She has the Earth," they said. "Now where can we put it?"

"Place it on my back," said a deep voice. It was the Great Turtle, who had come up from the depths.

They brought the Muskrat over to the Great Turtle and placed her paw against his back. To this day there are marks at the back of the Turtle's shell which were made by the Muskrat's paw. The tiny bit of Earth fell on the back of the Turtle. Almost immediately, it began to grow larger and larger and larger until it became the whole world.

Then the two Swans brought the Sky Woman down. She stepped onto the new Earth and opened her hand, letting the seeds fall onto the bare soil. From those seeds the trees and the grass sprang up. Life on Earth had begun.

Literary Analysis

Origin Myths and the Oral Tradition In oral literature, why might characters have generic names like "Loon" or "Muskrat"?

Review and Assess

Thinking About the Selection

1. **Respond:** If you had been the Great Chief, would you have pulled up the Great Tree? Explain your answer.

2. **(a) Recall:** Explain what happened to the wife of the chief when the young men uprooted the Great Tree. **(b) Interpret:** Why did this action generate concern among the animals?

3. **(a) Recall:** Describe the actions of the swans, the beaver, and the duck. **(b) Analyze:** How do these actions exhibit the best aspects of human nature?

4. **(a) Infer:** Whom do the Onondaga credit with bringing Earth into existence? **(b) Analyze:** From this myth, what can you conclude about the relationship between the Onondaga and their natural environment? Explain your answer.

5. **Generalize:** Muskrat makes a risky and desperate swim. How does society benefit from brave actions like this?

When Grizzlies Walked Upright

Modoc

Retold by Richard Erdoes and Alfonso Ortiz

Before there were people on earth, the Chief of the Sky Spirits grew tired of his home in the Above World, because the air was always brittle with an icy cold. So he carved a hole in the sky with a stone and pushed all the snow and ice down below until he made a great mound that reached from the earth almost to the sky. Today it is known as Mount Shasta.

Then the Sky Spirit took his walking stick, stepped from a cloud to the peak, and walked down to the mountain. When he was about halfway to the valley below, he began to put his finger to the ground here and there, here and there. Wherever his finger touched, a tree grew. The snow melted in his footsteps, and the water ran down in rivers.

The Sky Spirit broke off the small end of his giant stick and threw the pieces into the rivers. The longer pieces turned into beaver and otter; the smaller pieces became fish. When the leaves dropped from the trees, he picked them up, blew upon them, and so made the birds. Then he took the big end of his giant stick and made all the animals that walked on the earth, the biggest of which were the grizzly bears.

Now when they were first made, the bears were covered with hair and had sharp claws, just as they do today, but they walked on two feet and could talk like people. They looked so fierce that the Sky Spirit sent them away from him to live in the forest at the base of the mountain.

Pleased with what he'd done, the Chief of the Sky Spirits decided to bring his family down and live on earth himself. The mountains of snow and ice became their lodge. He made a big fire in the center of the mountain and a hole in the top so that the smoke and sparks could fly out. When he put a big log on the fire, sparks would fly up and the earth would tremble.

Late one spring while the Sky Spirit and his family were sitting round the fire, the Wind Spirit sent a great storm that shook the top of the mountain. It blew and blew and roared and roared. Smoke blown back into the lodge hurt their eyes, and finally the Sky Spirit

Literary Analysis
Origin Myths What natural phenomenon is explained here?

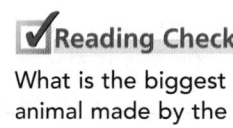
Reading Check

What is the biggest animal made by the Sky Spirit?

Dreamwalker, Nancy Wood Taber

said to his youngest daughter, "Climb up to the smoke hole and ask the Wind Spirit to blow more gently. Tell him I'm afraid he will blow the mountain over."

As his daughter started up, her father said, "But be careful not to stick your head out at the top. If you do, the wind may catch you by the hair and blow you away."

The girl hurried to the top of the mountain and stayed well inside the smoke hole as she spoke to the Wind Spirit. As she was about to climb back down, she remembered that her father had once said you could see the ocean from the top of their lodge. His daughter wondered what the ocean looked like, and her curiosity got the better of her. She poked her head out of the hole and turned toward the west, but before she could see anything, the Wind Spirit caught her long hair, pulled her out of the mountain, and blew her down over the snow and ice. She landed among the scrubby fir trees at the edge of the timber and snow line, her long red hair trailing over the snow.

There a grizzly bear found the little girl when he was out hunting food for his family. He carried her home with him, and his wife brought her up with their family of cubs. The little red-haired girl and the cubs ate together, played together, and grew up together.

When she became a young woman, she and the eldest son of the grizzly bears were married. In the years that followed they had many children, who were not as hairy as the grizzlies, yet did not look exactly like their spirit mother, either.

All the grizzly bears throughout the forests were so proud of these new creatures that they made a lodge for the red-haired mother and her children. They placed the lodge near Mount Shasta—it is called Little Mount Shasta today.

After many years had passed, the mother grizzly bear knew that she would soon die. Fearing that she should ask of the Chief of the Sky Spirits to forgive her for keeping his daughter, she gathered all the grizzlies at the lodge they had built. Then she sent her eldest grandson in a cloud to the top of Mount Shasta, to tell the Spirit Chief where he could find his long-lost daughter.

When the father got this news he was so glad that he came down the mountainside in giant strides, melting the snow and tearing up the land under his feet. Even today his tracks can be seen in the rocky path on the south side of Mount Shasta.

As he neared the lodge, he called out, "Is this where my little daughter lives?"

He expected his child to look exactly as she had when he saw her last. When he found a grown woman instead, and learned that the strange creatures she was taking care of were his grandchildren, he became very angry. A new race had been created that was not of his making! He frowned on the old grandmother so sternly that she promptly fell dead. Then he cursed all the grizzlies:

"Get down on your hands and knees. You have wronged me, and from this moment all of you will walk on four feet and never talk again."

He drove his grandchildren out of the lodge, put his daughter over his shoulder, and climbed back up the mountain. Never again did he come to the forest. Some say that he put out the fire in the center of his lodge and took his daughter back up to the sky to live.

Those strange creatures, his grandchildren, scattered and wandered over the earth. They were the first Indians, the ancestors of all the Indian tribes.

That's why the Indians living around Mount Shasta would never kill a grizzly bear. Whenever a grizzly killed an Indian, his body was burned on the spot. And for many years all who passed that way cast a stone there until a great pile of stones marked the place of his death.

Reading Strategy
Recognizing Cultural Details What detail about the way Native American women wear their hair is revealed here?

Reading Strategy
Recognizing Cultural Details What does the mother grizzly bear's decision reveal about the culture's view of responsibility or guilt?

✓**Reading Check**
What is the Spirit Chief's reaction to the mother grizzly bear's confession?

When Grizzlies Walked Upright ◆ 21

from The Navajo Origin Legend

Navajo

Retold by Washington Matthews

On the morning of the twelfth day the people washed themselves well. The women dried themselves with yellow cornmeal; the men with white cornmeal. Soon after the <u>ablutions</u> were completed they heard the distant call of the approaching gods.[1] It was shouted, as before, four times—nearer and louder at each repetition—and, after the fourth call, the gods appeared. Blue Body and Black Body each carried a sacred buckskin. White Body carried two ears of corn, one yellow, one white, each covered at the end completely with grains.

The gods laid one buckskin on the ground with the head to the west: on this they placed the two ears of corn, with their tips to the east, and over the corn they spread the other buckskin with its head to the east; under the white ear they put the feather of a white eagle, under the yellow ear the feather of a yellow eagle. Then they told the people to stand at a distance and allow the wind to enter. The white wind blew from the east, and the yellow wind blew from the west, between the skins. While the wind was blowing, eight of the Mirage People[2] came and walked around the objects on the ground four

<aside>
ablutions (ab lōō´ shənz) *n.* cleansing the body as part of a religious rite

Reading Strategy
Recognizing Cultural Details What does this description suggest about the role of deer in Navajo life?
</aside>

---

1. **the approaching gods** the four Navajo gods: White Body, Blue Body, Yellow Body, and Black Body.
2. **Mirage People** mirages personified.

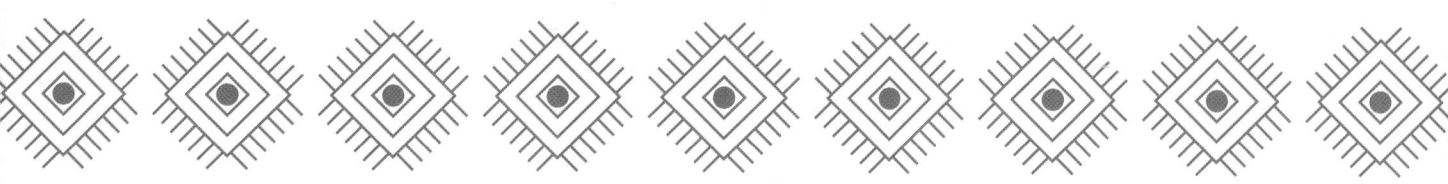

times, and as they walked the eagle feathers, whose tips <u>protruded</u> from between the buckskins, were seen to move. When the Mirage People had finished their walk the upper buckskin was lifted; the ears of corn had disappeared, a man and a woman lay there in their stead.

The white ear of corn had been changed into a man, the yellow ear into a woman. It was the wind that gave them life. It is the wind that comes out of our mouths now that gives us life. When this ceases to blow we die. In the skin at the tips of our fingers we see the trail of the wind; it shows us where the wind blew when our ancestors were created.

The pair thus created were First Man and First Woman (Atsé Hastin and Atsé Estsán). The gods directed the people to build an enclosure of brushwood for the pair. When the enclosure was finished, First Man and First Woman entered it, and the gods said to them: "Live together now as husband and wife."

protruded (prō trōōd´ id) v. jutted out

Literary Analysis
Origin Myths Why might the Navajo have viewed the wind as the source of life?

Review and Assess

Thinking About the Selections

1. **Respond:** What words would you use to describe the images in these tales and the impression they made on you?

2. **(a) Recall:** What do the grizzly bears do that angers the Chief of the Sky Spirit? **(b) Analyze:** What does his reaction tell you about him?

3. **(a) Recall:** What punishment does the Chief of the Sky Spirits levy against the grizzlies? **(b) Analyze Cause and Effect:** How does this action affect his grandchildren, the people of the Earth?

4. **(a) Recall:** Identify the stages of the Navajo creation ceremony. **(b) Analyze:** What do the order and ritual of the ceremony tell you about the Navajo people?

5. **(a) Recall:** What is the wind's role in the ceremony? **(b) Contrast:** How does the wind's role contrast with the order and ritual of the ceremony?

6. **(a) Compare and Contrast:** In what ways do the two tales differ in their attitude toward nature? **(b) Evaluate:** With which attitude do you most identify? Why?

from

The Iroquois Constitution

Iroquois

Translated by Arthur C. Parker

I am Dekanawidah and with the Five Nations[1] <u>confederate</u> lords I plant the Tree of the Great Peace. I name the tree the Tree of the Great Long Leaves. Under the shade of this Tree of the Great Peace we spread the soft white feathery down of the globe thistle as seats for you, Adodarhoh, and your cousin lords.

We place you upon those seats, spread soft with the feathery down of the globe thistle, there beneath the shade of the spreading branches of the Tree of Peace. There shall you sit and watch the council fire of the confederacy of the Five Nations, and all the affairs of the Five Nations shall be transacted at this place before you.

Roots have spread out from the Tree of the Great Peace, one to the north, one to the east, one to the south and one to the west. The name of these roots is the Great White Roots and their nature is peace and strength.

If any man or any nation outside the Five Nations shall obey the laws of the Great Peace and make known their <u>disposition</u> to the lords of the confederacy, they may trace the roots to the tree and if their minds are clean and they are obedient and promise to obey the wishes of the confederate council, they shall be welcomed to take shelter beneath the Tree of the Long Leaves.

We place at the top of the Tree of the Long Leaves an eagle who is able to see afar. If he sees in the distance any evil approaching or any

confederate (kən fed′ ər it) *adj.* united with others for a common purpose

Literary Analysis
Origin Myths and the Oral Tradition How would this visual description facilitate the oral transmission of this constitution?

disposition (dis′ pə zish′ ən) *n.* an inclination or tendency

---

1. **Five Nations** the Mohawk, Oneida, Onondaga, Cayuga, and Seneca tribes. Together, these tribes formed the Iroquois Confederation.

danger threatening he will at once warn the people of the confederacy.

The smoke of the confederate council fire shall ever ascend and pierce the sky so that other nations who may be allies may see the council fire of the Great Peace . . .

Whenever the confederate lords shall assemble for the purpose of holding a council, the Onondaga lords shall open it by expressing their gratitude to their cousin lords and greeting them, and they shall make an address and offer thanks to the earth where men dwell, to the streams of water, the pools, the springs and the lakes, to the maize and the fruits, to the medicinal herbs and trees, to the forest trees for their usefulness, to the animals that serve as food and give their pelts for clothing, to the great winds and the lesser winds, to the thunderers, to the sun, the mighty warrior, to the moon, to the messengers of the Creator who reveal his wishes and to the Great Creator who dwells in the heavens above, who gives all the things useful to men, and who is the source and the ruler of health and life.

Then shall the Onondaga lords declare the council open . . .

All lords of the Five Nations' Confederacy must be honest in all things . . . It shall be a serious wrong for anyone to lead a lord into trivial affairs, for the people must ever hold their lords high in estimation out of respect to their honorable positions.

When a candidate lord is to be installed he shall furnish four strings of shells (or wampum)[2] one span in length bound together at one end. Such will constitute the evidence of his pledge to the confederate lords that he will live according to the constitution of the Great Peace and exercise justice in all affairs.

When the pledge is furnished the speaker of the council must hold the shell strings in his hand and address the opposite side of the council fire and he shall commence his address saying: "Now behold him. He has now become a confederate lord. See how splendid he looks." An address may then follow. At the end of it he shall send the bunch of shell strings to the opposite side

Red Jacket, George Catlin, The Thomas Gilcrease Institute of American History and Art, Tulsa, Oklahoma

▲ **Critical Viewing**
What details or features of this portrait reflect a belief in the dignity and nobility of the Native Americans? **[Analyze]**

☑ **Reading Check**
What does the speaker say is the nature of the Great White Roots?

---

2. **wampum** (wäm´ pəm) *n.* small beads made of shells.

and they shall be received as evidence of the pledge. Then shall the opposite side say:

"We now do crown you with the sacred emblem of the deer's antlers, the emblem of your lordship. You shall now become a mentor of the people of the Five Nations. The thickness of your skin shall be seven spans—which is to say that you shall be proof against anger, offensive actions and criticism. Your heart shall be filled with peace and good will and your mind filled with a yearning for the welfare of the people of the confederacy. With endless patience you shall carry out your duty and your firmness shall be tempered with tenderness for your people. Neither anger nor fury shall find lodgement in your mind and all your words and actions shall be marked with calm deliberation. In all of your deliberations in the confederate council, in your efforts at law making, in all your official acts, self-interest shall be cast into oblivion. Cast not over your shoulder behind you the warnings of the nephews and nieces should they chide you for any error or wrong you may do, but return to the way of the Great Law which is just and right. Look and listen for the welfare of the whole people and have always in view not only the present but also the coming generations, even those whose faces are yet beneath the surface of the ground—the unborn of the future nation."

Reading Strategy
Recognizing Cultural Details What can you learn about the Iroquois culture from the items mentioned here?

deliberation (di lib´ ər ā´ shən) *n.* careful consideration

Review and Assess

Thinking About the Selection

1. **Respond:** If you were the chief of a Native American nation, would this speech persuade you to join the Confederation? Explain.

2. **(a) Recall:** What do the lords plant to commemorate their meeting? **(b) Analyze:** What do the roots of this plant symbolize?

3. **(a) Recall:** According to the Constitution, what must confederate lords do to open a council meeting?
   (b) Infer: What does this decree suggest about the Iroquois?

4. **(a) Analyze:** What three images from nature does Dekanawidah use in the Iroquois Constitution? **(b) Infer:** What do these references tell you about the Iroquois?

5. **(a) Summarize:** Summarize the qualities and conduct required of council lords by the Iroquois Constitution.
   (b) Synthesize: How well do these qualities apply to leaders in the modern world?

6. **Take a Position:** Do you agree with and support the ideas presented in *The Iroquois Constitution*? Why or Why not?

Review and Assess

Literary Analysis

Origin Myths

1. According to the Modoc **origin myth,** who formed the landscape and the creatures of the Earth?
2. (a) Review the selections and use a chart like the one shown here to record the roles nature plays in explaining and maintaining Native American life.

Aspect of Nature	Connection to Native American Life

    (b) What can you conclude from the details you have collected?
3. How do animals and natural objects portray aspects of human nature in these origin myths?
4. Origin myths explain natural phenomena, customs, and specific characteristics of animals. Cite examples from the myths.

Comparing Literary Works

5. In cultures with **oral traditions** such as these, in what ways do myths and stories instruct or share important values?
6. (a) Which culture sees the spirits as generous and kind? Explain. (b) Which culture sees them as vengeful? Explain.
7. (a) In what way does the language of the Iroquois Constitution differ from that of the other selections? (b) How does this contrast reflect the Constitution's purpose?

Reading Strategy

Recognizing Cultural Details

8. Identify two **cultural details** you learned from each selection. Then, describe what each selection reveals about the culture that created it.
9. What do the prevalent attitudes in the Iroquois Constitution reveal about the culture behind the literature?

Extend Understanding

10. **Social Studies Connection:** In what ways is the United States Constitution similar to the Iroquois Constitution? In what ways is it different?

Integrate Language Skills

Vocabulary Development Lesson

Word Analysis: Latin Suffix *-tion*

The word *deliberation* contains the Latin suffix *-tion,* which forms a noun when added to a verb. The literal meaning of *deliberation* is "the act of deliberating." Change the following verbs to nouns by adding the suffix *-tion*. Then, use each new word in a sentence.

1. constitute: to set up in a legal or official form; establish
2. estimate: to form an opinion or judgment based on preliminary information
3. dispose: to tend or incline; to place in a certain order
4. hesitate: to stop because of indecision; pause or delay
5. inoculate: to provide a vaccine that creates immunity

Concept Development: Synonyms

For each grouping, identify the word whose meaning does not match the other two.

1. (a) cleansings, (b) imaginings, (c) ablutions
2. (a) deliberation, (b) consideration, (c) commotion
3. (a) protruded, (b) dangled, (c) jutted
4. (a) disposition, (b) inclination, (c) assumption
5. (a) varied, (b) confederate, (c) united

Spelling Strategy

When you add the suffix *-tion* to a verb that ends in *te*, drop the *te*: deliberate + *-tion* = *deliberation*. Add *-tion* to the following verbs. Use the resulting nouns in sentences.

1. locate   2. insulate   3. excavate

Grammar and Style Lesson

Compound Sentences

A main clause is a complete thought that contains a subject that tells who or what the sentence is about and a predicate that tells what the subject is or does.

In oral and written language, compound sentences provide a natural way to link ideas. A **compound sentence** has two or more main clauses linked by a semicolon or a comma and a coordinating conjunction such as *and*, *or*, or *but*. In the example, subjects are underlined and predicates are italicized.

> **Example:** <u>Muskrat</u> *dove down and brought up Earth*, and <u>Earth</u> *was placed on Turtle's back.*

Practice Rewrite the following paragraph so that it contains at least three compound sentences. You may need to add or change some words. Then, underline the subject and predicate in each clause.

> Then the Beaver tried. He went deeper into the darkness. He could not reach the bottom. Next, the loon dove into the water. Even he could not reach the bottom. He floated back up. Then a voice spoke, "I will bring up Earth or die trying."

Writing Application Write a paragraph about a natural landmark such as a river, cliff, or mountain in your state. In your writing, use at least two compound sentences.

W̶G̶ Prentice Hall Writing and Grammar Connection: Chapter 19, Section 4

Writing Lesson

Retelling of a Story

Storytellers add something of their own when repeating stories. Select one of the myths presented here and retell it. Keep the structure and sequence of events, but rewrite the tale to appeal to your audience. For example, you might update the setting.

Prewriting   Create a rough story outline based on the myth. Then, using a chart like the one shown, list elements of the myth that you will retain and elements that you will adapt.

Model: Gathering Details from the Original

Food	Clothing	Beliefs	Environment

Drafting   Following your outline, create a rough draft. Consider using repetition of actions, phrases, or words to create drama and to heighten suspense.

Revising   Read your tale aloud, listening carefully to your repetition. Make sure it includes vibrant words and dynamic actions that create dramatic and memorable effects.

Prentice Hall Writing and Grammar Connection: Chapter 5, Section 3

Extension Activities

Listening and Speaking With a group, develop a **dramatic reenactment** of a council meeting called to install a new Iroquois lord.

- Create the roles outlined in *The Iroquois Constitution*.
- Plan the staging to determine the physical movement of the reenactment.
- Rehearse your reenactment several times to learn your roles.

When you are ready, present your reenactment to the class. Then answer audience questions about the Constitution or reenactment. **[Group Activity]**

Research and Technology Using the images contained in *The Iroquois Constitution* for inspiration, design a **logo** representing the Iroquois Confederation. Be sure to include details in your design that relate to the culture and history of the Iroquois. Produce your logo, write a brief explanation of it, and share your work with classmates.

 **Take It to the Net**   www.phschool.com

Go online for an additional research activity using the Internet.

Prepare to Read

A Journey Through Texas ◆
Boulders Taller Than the Great Tower of Seville

Alvar Núñez Cabeza de Vaca (1490?–1557?)

In 1528, Pánfilo de Narváez and 400 Spanish soldiers landed near Tampa Bay and set out to explore Florida's west coast. Alvar Núñez Cabeza de Vaca (äl′ bär nōōn′ yes kä bā′ sä dä bä′ kä) was second in command. Beset by hostile natives, illness, and the prospect of starvation, Narváez and his men then set sail for Mexico in five flimsy boats, but he and most of the men drowned. Cabeza de Vaca and a party of about sixty survived and reached the Texas shore near present-day Galveston.

Shipwrecked without supplies, only fifteen of the group lived through the winter. In the end, Cabeza de Vaca and three others survived. They were captured by natives and spent the next several years in captivity. During that time, Cabeza de Vaca gained a reputation as a medicine man and trader. The four Spaniards finally escaped and wandered for eighteen months across the Texas plains. In 1536, the survivors finally reached Mexico City.

Invitation to Others Cabeza de Vaca's adventures and his reports on the richness of Texas sparked exploration of the region. In "A Journey Through Texas," he speaks of Estevanico, the first African to set foot in Texas.

In 1541, Cabeza de Vaca also led a 1,000-mile expedition through the south of present day Brazil to Asunción, the capital of Río de la Plata. He was appointed governor of the Río de la Plata region (now Paraguay), but he was ousted two years later as a result of revolt.

Through his journals, Cabeza de Vaca encouraged others, including Francisco Vásquez de Coronado, to explore America.

García López de Cárdenas (c. 1540)

García López de Cárdenas (gär sē′ ä lō′ pes dā kär′ dā näs) is best remembered as the first European to visit the Grand Canyon. As a leader of Francisco Vásquez de Coronado's expedition to New Mexico (1540–1542), Cárdenas was dispatched from Cibola (Zuni) in western New Mexico to see a river that the Moqui Native Americans of northeastern Arizona had described to one of Coronado's captains. The river was the Colorado. López de Cárdenas departed on August 25, 1540, reaching the Grand Canyon after a westward journey of about twenty days. He became the first explorer to view the canyon and its river, which from the vantage of the canyon's rim appeared to be a stream merely six feet wide! Unable to descend to the river, they took back to Europe descriptions that attempted to record the magnitude of the sight. López de Cárdenas reported that boulders in the Grand Canyon were taller than the 300-foot high Great Tower of Seville, one of the world's tallest cathedrals.

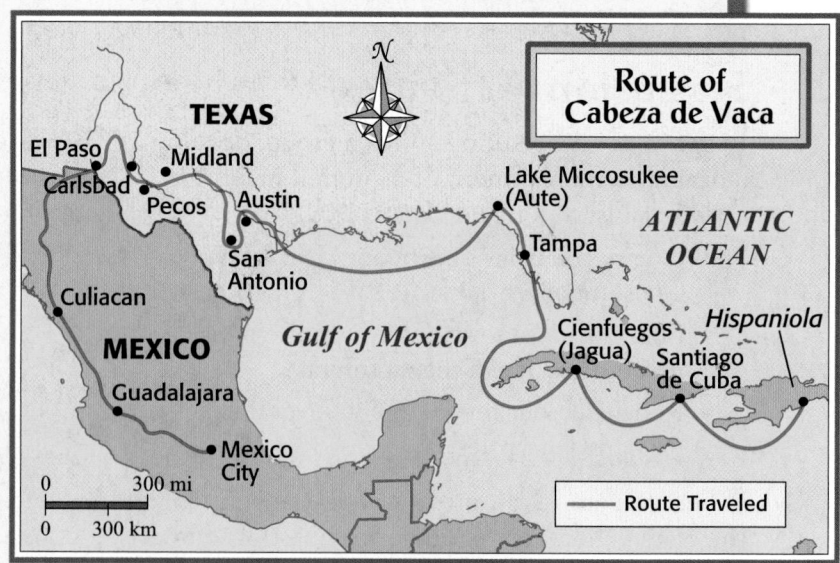

Route of Cabeza de Vaca

TEXAS · El Paso · Midland · Carlsbad · Pecos · Austin · San Antonio · Culiacan · MEXICO · Guadalajara · Mexico City · Lake Miccosukee (Aute) · Tampa · Cienfuegos (Jagua) · Santiago de Cuba · Hispaniola · ATLANTIC OCEAN · Gulf of Mexico

0 — 300 mi
0 — 300 km

— Route Traveled

Preview

Connecting to the Literature

The writers of these historical accounts describe places their readers could barely imagine. Think of the tales you would have told had you been among the first Europeans to travel to the southwest region of North America to meet the natives.

Literary Analysis

Exploration Narratives

The Europeans who trailblazed the Americas recounted their experiences in **exploration narratives**—firsthand accounts of their travels. These accounts provided information to the people back home in Europe, so the explorers were careful to record in detail what they observed. For example, López de Cárdenas gives these details about the region.

> This region was high and covered with low and twisted pine trees; it was extremely cold, being open to the north . . .

As you read, look for details that provide descriptive images and insights about the regions these men explored.

Comparing Literary Works

These exploration narratives reflect two distinctly different **authors' styles,** or choices of words, details, and focus. Cabeza de Vaca uses descriptive details in his narrative. In contrast, López de Cárdenas avoids description and instead provides a detailed explanation of events. Create a Venn diagram like the one shown to compare and contrast the authors' styles.

Reading Strategy

Recognizing Signal Words

To follow the order of events, pay close attention to **signal words**—words that highlight the relationships among ideas. Look at these examples:

- **time:** *After five days,* they had not *yet* returned.
- **contrast:** . . . *although* this was the warm season, no one could live in this canyon because of the cold.

As you read, take note of signal words and the relationships they indicate.

Cabeza de Vaca's Style

López de Cárdenas's Style

Vocabulary Development

entreated (en trēt′ id) *v.* begged; pleaded (p. 33)

feigned (fānd) *v.* pretended; faked (p. 33)

mortality (môr tal′ ə tē) *n.* death on a large scale (p. 34)

subsisted (səb sist′ id) *v.* remained alive; were sustained (p. 35)

traversed (trə vʉrst′) *v.* moved over, across, or through (p. 36)

dispatched (di spacht′) *v.* sent off on a specific assignment (p. 37)

A Journey Through Texas

Alvar Núñez Cabeza de Vaca

Background

Alvar Núñez Cabeza de Vaca and three countrymen wandered for months through Texas as they journeyed toward the Spanish settlement in Mexico City. In the course of his travels, Cabeza de Vaca healed a Native American by performing the first recorded surgery in Texas. His resulting fame attracted so many followers that Cabeza de Vaca noted in his journal, "The number of our companions became so large that we could no longer control them." As they continued traveling westward, the group was well received by the Native Americans they encountered.

▼ **Critical Viewing**
What details of a landscape like this one might pose difficulty for the expeditions that explored it? **[Speculate]**

The same Indians led us to a plain beyond the chain of mountains, where people came to meet us from a long distance. By those we were treated in the same manner as before, and they made so many presents to the Indians who came with us that, unable to carry all, they left half of it. . . . We told these people our route was towards sunset, and they replied that in that direction people lived very far away. So we ordered them to send there and inform the inhabitants that we were coming and how. From this they begged to be excused, because the others were their enemies, and they did not want us to go to them. Yet they did not venture to disobey in the end, and sent two women, one of their own and the other a captive. They selected women because these can trade everywhere, even if there be war.

We followed the women to a place where it had been agreed we should wait for them. After five days they had not yet returned, and the Indians explained that it might be because they had not found anybody. So we told them to take us north, and they repeated that there were no people, except very far away, and neither food nor water. Nevertheless we insisted, saying that we wanted to go there, and they still excused themselves as best they could, until at last we became angry.

One night I went away to sleep out in the field apart from them; but they soon came to where I was, and remained awake all night in great alarm, talking to me, saying how frightened they were. They <u>entreated</u> us not to be angry any longer, because, even if it was their death, they would take us where we chose. We <u>feigned</u> to be angry still, so as to keep them in suspense, and then a singular[1] thing happened.

On that same day many fell sick, and on the next day eight of them died! All over the country, where it was known, they became so afraid that it seemed as if the mere sight of us would kill them. They besought[2] us not to be angry nor to procure the death of any

---

1. **singular** *adj.* strange.
2. **besought** *v.* (be sôt′) pleaded with.

Literary Analysis
Exploration Narratives
Why does Cabeza de Vaca include such detail about the conversation with the Indians in his narrative?

entreated (en trēt′ id) *v.* begged; pleaded

feigned (fānd) *v.* pretended; faked

Reading Check
Why do the Indians fear going on ahead?

Painting of Cabeza de Vaca, Esteban, and their companions among various Texas Indian tribes, Tom Mirrat, The Institute of Texan Cultures, San Antonio, Texas

▲ **Critical Viewing** What does this painting suggest about the relationship between Cabeza de Vaca and the Native Americans? Why? **[Infer]**

more of their number, for they were convinced that we killed them by merely thinking of it. In truth, we were very much concerned about it, for, seeing the great <u>mortality</u>, we dreaded that all of them might die or forsake us in their terror, while those further on, upon learning of it, would get out of our way hereafter. We prayed to God our Lord to assist us, and the sick began to get well. Then we saw something that astonished us very much, and it was that, while the parents, brothers and wives of the dead had shown deep grief at their illness, from the moment they died the survivors made no demonstration whatsoever, and showed not the slightest feeling; nor did they dare to go near the bodies until we ordered their burial. . . .

The sick being on the way of recovery, when we had been there already three days, the women whom we had sent out returned, saying that they had met very few people, nearly all having gone after the cows, as it was the season. So we ordered those who had been sick to remain, and those who were well to accompany us, and that, two days' travel from there, the same women should go with us and get people to come to meet us on the trail for our reception.

mortality (môr tal′ ə tē) *n.* death on a large scale, as from disease or war

Reading Strategy
Recognizing Signal Words What words signal time or other relationships in this paragraph?

The next morning all those who were strong enough came along, and at the end of three journeys we halted. Alonso del Castillo and Estevanico,[3] the negro, left with the women as guides, and the woman who was a captive took them to a river that flows between mountains, where there was a village, in which her father lived, and these were the first abodes we saw that were like unto real houses. Castillo and Estevanico went to these and, after holding parley[4] with the Indians, at the end of three days Castillo returned to where he had left us, bringing with him five or six of the Indians. He told how he had found permanent houses, inhabited, the people of which ate beans and squashes, and that he had also seen maize.

Of all things upon earth this caused us the greatest pleasure, and we gave endless thanks to our Lord for this news. Castillo also said that the negro was coming to meet us on the way, near by, with all the people of the houses. For that reason we started, and after going a league and a half met the negro and the people that came to receive us, who gave us beans and many squashes to eat, gourds to carry water in, robes of cowhide, and other things. As those people and the Indians of our company were enemies, and did not understand each other, we took leave of the latter, leaving them all that had been given to us, while we went on with the former and, six leagues beyond, when night was already approaching, reached their houses, where they received us with great ceremonies. Here we remained one day, and left on the next, taking them with us to other permanent houses, where they <u>subsisted</u> on the same food also, and thence on we found a new custom.

The people who heard of our approach did not, as before, come out to meet us on the way, but we found them at their homes, and they had other houses ready for us. . . . There was nothing they would not give us. They are the best formed people we have seen, the liveliest and most capable; who best understood us and answered our questions. We called them "of the cows," because most of the cows die near there, and because for more than fifty leagues up that stream they go to kill many of them. Those people go completely naked, after the manner of the first we met. The women are covered with deerskins, also some men, especially the old ones, who are of no use any more in war.

The country is well settled. We asked them why they did not raise maize, and they replied that they were afraid of losing the crops, since for two successive years it had not rained, and the seasons were so dry that the moles had eaten the corn, so that they did not dare to plant any more until it should have rained very hard. And they also begged us to ask Heaven for rain, which we promised to do. We also wanted to know from where they brought their maize, and they said it came from where the sun sets, and that

---

3. **Estevanico** (es´ tä vä nē´ kō) Of Moorish extraction, Estevanico was the first African man to set foot in Texas.
4. **holding parley** (pär´ lē) conferring.

Literary Analysis
Exploration Narratives
What specific details about the region does the writer provide here?

subsisted (səb sist´ id) v. remained alive; were sustained

Reading Check
What prevents some of the expedition group from completing the planned trip?

it was found all over that country, and the shortest way to it was in that direction. We asked them to tell us how to go, as they did not want to go themselves, to tell us about the way.

They said we should travel up the river towards the north, on which trail for seventeen days we would not find a thing to eat, except a fruit called *chacan*, which they grind between stones; but even then it cannot be eaten, being so coarse and dry; and so it was, for they showed it to us and we could not eat it. But they also said that, going upstream, we could always travel among people who were their enemies, although speaking the same language, and who could give us no food, but would receive us very willingly, and give us many cotton blankets, hides and other things; but that it seemed to them that we ought not to take that road.

In doubt as to what should be done, and which was the best and most advantageous road to take, we remained with them for two days. They gave us beans, squashes, and calabashes.[5] Their way of cooking them is so new and strange that I felt like describing it here, in order to show how different and queer are the devices and industries of human beings. They have no pots. In order to cook their food they fill a middle-sized gourd with water, and place into a fire such stones as easily become heated, and when they are hot to scorch they take them out with wooden tongs, thrusting them into the water of the gourd, until it boils. As soon as it boils they put into it what they want to cook, always taking out the stones as they cool off and throwing in hot ones to keep the water steadily boiling. This is their way of cooking.

After two days were past we determined to go in search of maize, and not to follow the road to the cows, since the latter carried us to the north, which meant a very great circuit, as we held it always certain that by going towards sunset we should reach the goal of our wishes.

So we went on our way and <u>traversed</u> the whole country to the South Sea,[6] and our resolution was not shaken by the fear of great starvation, which the Indians said we should suffer (and indeed suffered) during the first seventeen days of travel. All along the river, and in the course of these seventeen days we received plenty of cowhides, and did not eat of their famous fruit (*chacan*), but our food consisted (for each day) of a handful of deer-tallow, which for that purpose we always sought to keep, and so endured these seventeen days, at the end of which we crossed the river and marched for seventeen days more. At sunset, on a plain between very high mountains, we met people who, for one-third of the year, eat but powdered straw, and as we went by just at that time, had to eat it also, until, at the end of that journey we found some permanent houses, with plenty of harvested maize, of which and of its meal they gave us great quantities, also squashes and beans, and blankets of cotton. . . .

Literary Analysis
Exploration Narratives and Author's Style What might readers in Europe have thought about the group's determination to find maize?

traversed (trə vʉrst´) v. moved over, across, or through

---

5. **calabashes** (kal´ ə bash´ əz) *n.* dried, hollow shells of gourds used to hold food or beverages.
6. **the South Sea** the Gulf of Mexico.

Boulders Taller Than the Great Tower of Seville

From an account by García López de Cárdenas
Retold by Pedro de Castañeda

Information was obtained of a large river and that several days down the river there were people with very large bodies. As Don Pedro de Tovar had no other commission, he returned from Tusayán and gave his report to the general. The latter at once <u>dispatched</u> Don García López de Cárdenas there with about twelve men to explore this river. When he reached Tusayán he was well received and lodged by the natives. They provided him with guides to proceed on his journey. They set out from there laden with provisions, because they had to travel over some uninhabited land before coming to settlements, which the Indians said were more than twenty days away. Accordingly when they had marched for twenty days they came to gorges of the river, from the edge of which it looked as if the opposite side must have been more than three or four leagues[1] away by air. This region was high and covered with low and twisted pine trees; it was extremely cold, being open to the north, so that, although this was the warm season, no one could live in this canyon because of the cold.

The men spent three days looking for a way down to the river; from the top it looked as if the water were a fathom[2] across. But, according to the information supplied by the Indians, it must have been half a league wide. The descent was almost impossible, but, after these three days, at a place which seemed less difficult, Captain Melgosa, a certain Juan Galeras, and another companion, being the most agile, began to go down. They continued descending within view of those on top until they lost sight of them, as they could not be seen from the top. They returned about four o'clock in the afternoon, as they could not reach the bottom because of the many obstacles they met, for

---

1. **leagues** (lēgz) *n.* units of measurement of approximately 3 miles.
2. **fathom** (fath′ əm) *n.* a unit of measurement of six feet.

dispatched (di spacht′) *v.* sent off on a specific assignment

Literary Analysis
Exploration Narratives
What impression of the group's efforts is López de Cárdenas trying to convey in his narrative?

✓**Reading Check**
Who is dispatched to explore the river?

what from the top seemed easy, was not so, on the contrary, it was rough and difficult. They said that they had gone down one-third of the distance and that, from the point they had reached, the river seemed very large, and that, from what they saw, the width given by the Indians was correct. From the top they could make out, apart from the canyon, some small boulders which seemed to be as high as a man. Those who went down and who reached them swore that they were taller than the great tower of Seville.[3]

The party did not continue farther up the canyon of the river because of the lack of water. Up to that time they had gone one or two leagues inland in search of water every afternoon. When they had traveled four additional days the guides said that it was impossible to go on because no water would be found for three or four days, that when they themselves traveled through that land they took along women who brought water in gourds, that in those trips they buried the gourds of water for the return trip, and that they traveled in one day a distance that took us two days.

This was the Tizón river, much closer to its source than where Melchior Díaz and his men had crossed it. These Indians were of the same type, as it appeared later. From there Cárdenas and his men turned back, as that trip brought no other results.

Reading Strategy
Recognizing Signal Words What change do the words "up to that time" signal?

---

3. **great tower of Seville** The Giralda, the tower on the Cathedral of Seville in Spain, rises above the cathedral more than twice its height.

Review and Assess

Thinking About the Selections

1. **Respond:** How does López de Cárdenas's description compare with your knowledge of the Grand Canyon?

2. **(a) Recall:** Why do the Spaniards in "A Journey Through Texas" order the Native Americans to travel with them? **(b) Infer:** Why do the Native Americans obey the orders?

3. **(a) Recall:** In "A Journey Through Texas," why do the Spaniards become fearful when the Native Americans in their company die? **(b) Draw Conclusions:** What do the Native Americans believe is the cause of the sickness?

4. **(a) Recall:** What are López de Cárdenas and his men expecting to explore? **(b) Infer:** Why does Coronado send the group on this mission?

5. **(a) Recall:** How wide does the river appear from the edge? **(b) Hypothesize:** Why does the river seem narrow from above?

6. **Extend:** How might these accounts have been different if they had been written to secure further funding?

Review and Assess

Literary Analysis

Exploration Narratives

1. Why is the image of the great tower of Seville used to convey the size of the boulders?
2. How do López de Cárdenas's experiences with the rough Grand Canyon terrain affect which details he includes in his **narrative**?

Comparing Literary Works

3. Compare and contrast the reactions of Cabeza de Vaca and López de Cárdenas to the Native American culture they encounter in their explorations. Record them in a chart like the one shown here.

Writer	Landscape and Cultural Details	Writer's Reaction
Cabeza de Vaca		
López de Cárdenas		

4. (a) How are the **authors' styles** similar? (b) How do they differ?
5. Which narrative do you think is more effective? Explain.

Reading Strategy

Recognizing Signal Words

6. Determine the type of relationship (time, reason, or contrast) in each of the italicized **signal words** in these passages.
   a. *Nevertheless* we insisted, saying that we wanted to go there, and they still excused themselves as best they could, *until* at last we became angry.
   b. We feigned to be angry still, *so as* to keep them in suspense, and *then* a singular thing happened.
   c. The party did not continue farther up the canyon of the river *because of* a lack of water.

Extend Understanding

7. **Social Studies Connection:** What other searches have led to settlement of specific areas of what is now the United States?

Quick Review

Exploration narratives recount the firsthand expedition experiences of their authors.

An **author's style** reflects his choice and arrangement of words and details.

Signal words indicate relationships of time, reason, or contrast among ideas or events in a narrative.

 **Take It to the Net**
www.phschool.com
Take the interactive self-test online to check your understanding of these selections.

Integrate Language Skills

Vocabulary Development Lesson

Word Analysis: Latin Root -mort-

The word *mortality* includes the Latin root *-mort-*, meaning "death." With a small group, develop a paragraph about a modern-day space explorer who dies during the landing of a dangerous mission. Use the following words in your description.

mortally   mortuary

mortician   immortalized

Spelling Strategy

Prefixes do not change spellings. When you add a prefix to a word, keep all the letters of the original word: *im-* + mortality = immortality.

Add a prefix such as *in-*, *im-*, or *dis-* to each of the words listed below to create a new word.

1. __ direct   3. __ dependent

2. __ proper   4. __ honest

Fluency: Words in Context

Choose the word from the vocabulary list on page 31 that best completes each sentence.

1. The soldiers were ___?___ by the expedition leader to find the river.
2. The Spaniards ___?___ their guides to continue leading the way.
3. When pleading didn't work, they ___?___ anger in order to intimidate their guides.
4. In the course of their seventeen-day march, they ___?___ a barren stretch of land.
5. The starving travelers ___?___ on mouthfuls of deer tallow.
6. The conquistadors were alarmed by the ___?___ that befell the natives.

Grammar and Style Lesson

Past and Perfect Verb Tenses

The **past tense** of a verb shows an action that began and ended at a given time in the past. The **past perfect tense** indicates an action that ended before another past action began. Verbs in the past perfect consist of *had*, followed by the past participle. In this example, the past tense verbs are in italicized text and the past perfect verbs are underlined.

After five days they <u>had</u> not <u>returned</u> and the Indians *explained* that it might be because they <u>had</u> not <u>found</u> anybody.
(The explorers *had not returned* and *had not found* before the Indians *explained*.)

Practice Identify the tense of the italicized verb where appropriate, and then indicate the sequence of the action.

1. We *followed* the woman to a place where it *had been agreed* we should wait for them.
2. Many *fell* sick.
3. On the next day, eight of them *died*!
4. They *had gone* down one third of the distance.
5. Until then, they *had gone* one or two leagues inland in search of water.

Writing Application Write a description of an activity that you had worked on for some time. Use both the past and past perfect tenses.

W̷G *Prentice Hall Writing and Grammar Connection: Chapter 21, Section 2*

Writing Lesson

Explorer's Journal

Imagine that like Cabeza de Vaca and López de Cárdenas, you have begun to explore a territory where no one has gone before. Write a journal entry that provides precise details about your discoveries.

Prewriting   Choose a location to explore. Gather specific details, through research if necessary, so that your description will help others follow in your footsteps.

Drafting   Use precise details, identifying items as clearly and exactly as you can. Remember, your audience may be unfamiliar with these objects.

Revising   Ask a friend to read your draft. If your reader cannot "see" your description, highlight vague words and replace them with more precise details.

Model: Revising to Add Precise Details

stretched out   *Evergreen*

The narrow valley was nearly a mile from end to end. Trees dotted the

laurel

upper mountain slopes, giving way first to bushes and then to grassy

granite

areas pierced by outcroppings.

> Words like *evergreen, laurel,* and *granite* identify details with more precision.

W̶G̶ Prentice Hall Writing and Grammar Connection: Chapter 6, Section 4

Extension Activities

Listening and Speaking   As a member of the party that explored the Grand Canyon with López de Cárdenas, give a **speech** to convince Coronado that the entire expedition should travel to view the canyon. Use these tips.

- Incorporate your personal experiences.
- Blend vivid description with well-supported persuasion.

Present your speech to the class.

Research and Technology   In a group, create an **exploration booklet** covering either the Grand Canyon or the area between Austin and El Paso, Texas. Gather information from the selections and Internet sources. Use a desktop publishing program to blend these with your text.

 **Take It to the Net**   www.phschool.com

Go online for an additional research activity using the Internet.

Prepare to Read

from The Interesting Narrative of the Life of Olaudah Equiano

Olaudah Equiano (1745–1797)

When published in 1789, the autobiography of Olaudah Equiano (ō lä ōō´ dä ek´ wē än´ ō) created a sensation. It was so widely acclaimed that by 1794 it had run through eight editions in England and one in the United States. *The Interesting Narrative of the Life of Olaudah Equiano* made society face the cruelties of slavery and contributed to the banning of the slave trade in both the United States and England.

Born to Leadership The son of a tribal elder in the powerful kingdom of Benin, Equiano might have followed in his father's footsteps had he not been sold into slavery. When Equiano was eleven years old, he and his sister were kidnapped from their home in West Africa and sold to British slave traders. Their circumstance was not unusual. About 15 million Africans were captured between 1500 and 1800 and shipped to the Western Hemisphere, where they became slaves. Historians estimate that nearly two million slaves died before reaching their destination.

The Middle Passage As Equiano reports, the conditions of the Atlantic voyage were atrocious. For six to ten weeks, the slaves were crammed below deck in spaces sometimes less than five feet high. Families were torn apart, with men and women placed in separate holds. The men were often shackled together in pairs. Because Equiano was so young at the time of his capture, however, he was allowed to remain on deck, unshackled. There, he observed the mariners using a compass-like instrument to determine the ship's heading.

Seeing Equiano's fascination with the device, the mariners allowed him to get a closer look. It was on that deck, perhaps, that Equiano first gained an interest in the sea.

The ship first anchored in Bridgetown, the capital of Barbados in the West Indies. Separated from his sister, Equiano was taken to Virginia, where he was purchased by a British captain and employed at sea.

Saving to Buy Liberty Renamed Gustavus Vassa, Equiano was enslaved for nearly ten years. After managing his Philadelphia master's finances and making his own money in the process, Equiano amassed enough to buy his freedom. In later years, he settled in England and devoted himself to the abolition of slavery. In 1787, he was named commissary of the slave ship *Vernon*, which held more than five hundred freed slaves who were taken to Freetown, Sierra Leone, to establish a settlement there.

Telling the Tale To publicize the plight of slaves, Equiano wrote his two-volume autobiography, *The Interesting Narrative.* . . . Although his writing raised concerns about the inhumane conditions of slavery, the U.S. slave trade was not abolished by law until 1808, nearly twenty years after its publication. In addition to his writings on American slavery, Equiano also lectured and rallied against the cruelty of British slave owners in Jamaica.

Equiano's writing demonstrates the important influence slave narratives have in documenting historic events. Encouraged by abolitionists, many other freed or escaped slaves published narratives in the years before the Civil War. Others told their stories in the first part of the twentieth century. Henry Louis Gates, Jr., professor of English and African American studies, notes that "No other group of slaves anywhere, at any other period in history, has left such a large repository of testimony about the horror of becoming the legal property of another human being."

Preview

Connecting to the Literature

Imagine knowing that members of your family are valuable merchandise and could be shipped to a distant land to perform forced labor! If you lived in a world where slavery exists, you might develop a new attitude about the sweetness of freedom and the value of life.

Literary Analysis

Slave Narratives

A uniquely American literary genre, a **slave narrative** is an autobiographical account of life as a slave. Often written to expose the horrors of human bondage, it documents a slave's experiences from his or her own point of view. In this example, Equiano describes the conditions on the ship.

> The shrieks of the women, and the groans of the dying, rendered the whole a scene of horror almost inconceivable.

As you read, look for other details that describe the horrors of the voyage.

Connecting Literary Elements

Equiano's narrative speaks persuasively against the slave trade by using deliberate **emotional appeals** to strengthen its impact. Writers create emotional appeals with words, such as "groans" and "shrieks," and details that trigger feelings of sympathy or outrage. For example, when Equiano describes the Africans begging for food, readers who have experienced hunger can likely sympathize with their plight. Notice how Equiano appeals to readers' emotions.

Reading Strategy

Summarizing

As you read material published in another time period or written in an unfamiliar style, it is often helpful to **summarize** the main points. When you summarize, you state briefly in your own words the main ideas and key details of the text. Use a chart like the one shown which summarizes Equiano's first paragraph. As you read, write notes like these to help you summarize Equiano's ideas.

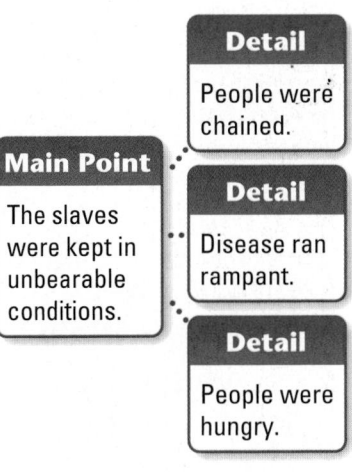

Vocabulary Development

loathsome (lōth′ səm) *adj.* hateful; detestable (p. 45)

pestilential (pes′ tə len′ shəl) *adj.* likely to cause disease (p. 45)

copious (kō′ pē əs) *adj.* plentiful; abundant (p. 45)

improvident (im präv′ ə dənt) *adj.* shortsighted (p. 45)

avarice (av′ ə ris) *n.* greed for riches (p. 45)

pacify (pas′ ə fī′) *v.* calm; soothe (p. 48)

from The Interesting Narrative of the Life of Olaudah Equiano

Olaudah Equiano

*Slaves **Below Deck** (detail),* Lt. Francis Meynell, National Maritime Museum, Greenwich

▲ **Critical Viewing** The artist portrays conditions on a slave ship.
Compare and contrast this image with the one that Equiano describes.
[Compare and Contrast]

Background

In the first several chapters of his narrative, Olaudah Equiano describes how he and his sister were kidnapped by slave traders from their home in West Africa and transported to the African coast. During this six- or seven-month journey, Equiano was separated from his sister and held at a series of way stations. After reaching the coast, Equiano was shipped with other slaves to North America. The following account describes this horrifying journey.

At last when the ship we were in, had got in all her cargo, they made ready with many fearful noises, and we were all put under deck, so that we could not see how they managed the vessel. But this disappointment was the least of my sorrow. The stench of the hold while we were on the coast was so intolerably <u>loathsome</u>, that it was dangerous to remain there for any time, and some of us had been permitted to stay on the deck for the fresh air; but now that the whole ship's cargo were confined together, it became absolutely <u>pestilential</u>. The closeness of the place, and the heat of the climate, added to the number in the ship, which was so crowded that each had scarcely room to turn himself, almost suffocated us. This produced <u>copious</u> perspirations, so that the air soon became unfit for respiration, from a variety of loathsome smells, and brought on a sickness among the slaves, of which many died—thus falling victims to the <u>improvident avarice</u>, as I may call it, of their purchasers. This wretched situation was again aggravated by the galling of the chains, now become insupportable, and the filth of the necessary tubs, into which the children often fell, and were almost suffocated. The shrieks of the women, and the groans of the dying, rendered the whole a scene of horror almost inconceivable. Happily perhaps, for myself, I was soon reduced so low here that it was thought necessary to keep me almost always on deck; and from my extreme youth I was not put in fetters.[1] In this situation I expected every hour to share the fate of my companions, some of whom were almost daily brought upon deck at the point of death, which I began to hope would soon put an end to my miseries. Often did I think many of the inhabitants of the deep much more happy than myself. I envied them the freedom they enjoyed, and as often wished I could change my condition for theirs. Every circumstance I met with, served only to render my state more painful, and heightened my apprehensions, and my opinion of the cruelty of the whites.

---

1. **fetters** (fet´ ərz) *n.* chains.

loathsome (lōth´ səm) *adj.* hateful; detestable

pestilential (pes´ tə len´ shəl) *adj.* likely to cause disease

copious (kō´ pē əs) *adj.* plentiful; abundant

improvident (im präv´ ə dənt) *adj.* shortsighted

avarice (av´ ə ris) *n.* greed for riches

✔**Reading Check**

What conditions on the ship caused many of the slaves to die?

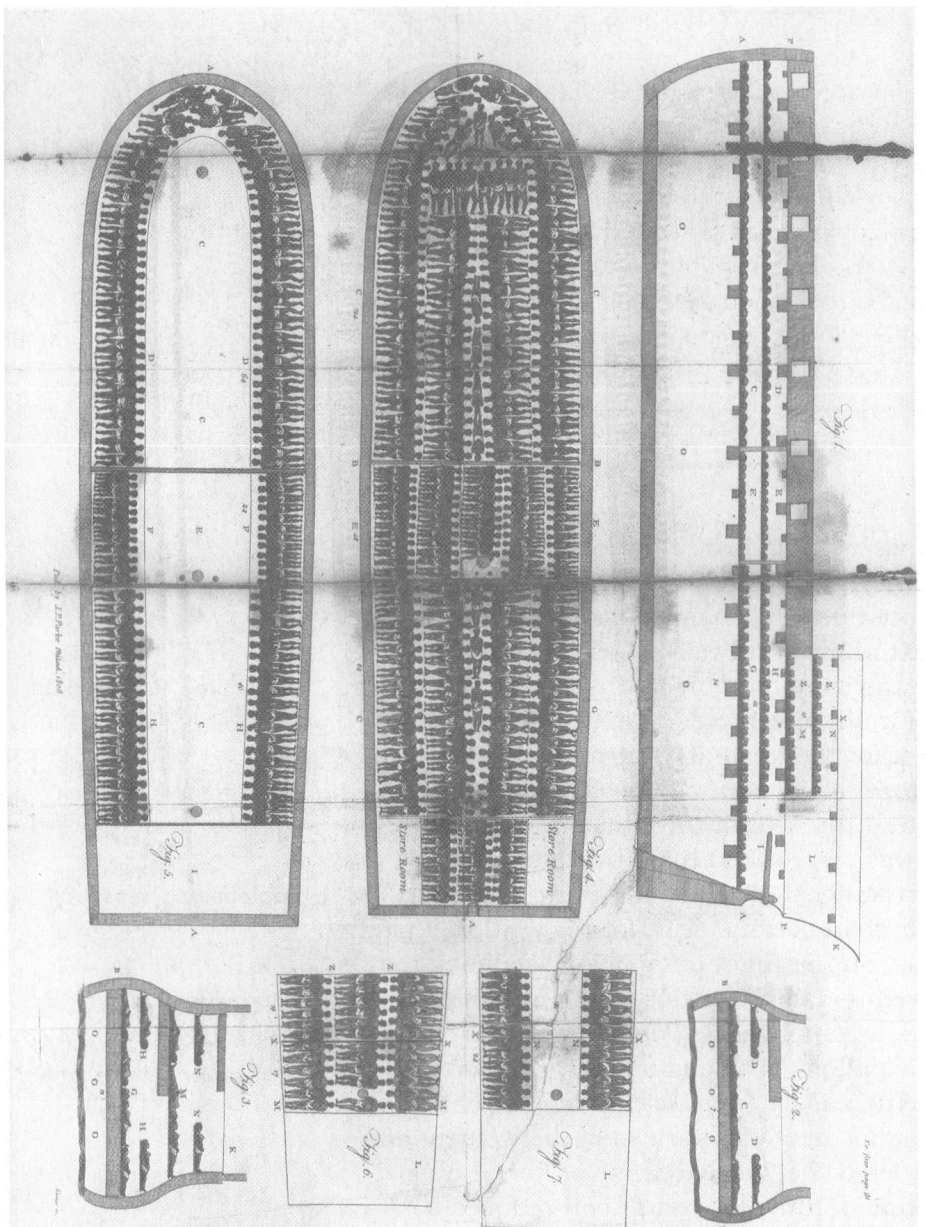

◀ **Critical Viewing**
Estimate the number
of slaves that this ship
can carry. What do the
drawings suggest about
the ship designer's
attitude toward slavery?
[Draw Conclusions]

One day they had taken a number of fishes; and when they had
killed and satisfied themselves with as many as they thought fit, to
our astonishment who were on deck, rather than give any of them to
us to eat, as we expected, they tossed the remaining fish into the sea
again, although we begged and prayed for some as well as we could,
but in vain; and some of my countrymen, being pressed by hunger,
took an opportunity, when they thought no one saw them, of trying
to get a little privately; but they were discovered, and the attempt
procured them some very severe floggings. One day, when we had
a smooth sea and moderate wind, two of my wearied countrymen who
were chained together (I was near them at the time), preferring death

Literary Analysis
Slave Narratives What
is the effect of these
floggings on the reader's
emotions?

to such a life of misery, somehow made through the nettings and jumped into the sea; immediately, another quite dejected fellow, who, on account of his illness, was suffered to be out of irons, also followed their example; and I believe many more would very soon have done the same, if they had not been prevented by the ship's crew, who were instantly alarmed. Those of us that were the most active, were in a moment put down under the deck; and there was such a noise and confusion amongst the people of the ship as I never heard before, to stop her, and get the boat out to go after the slaves. However, two of the wretches were drowned, but they got the other, and afterwards flogged him unmercifully, for thus attempting to prefer death to slavery. In this manner we continued to undergo more hardships than I can now relate, hardships which are inseparable from this accursed trade. Many a time we were near suffocation from the want of fresh air, which we were often without for whole days together. This, and the stench of the necessary tubs, carried off many.

During our passage, I first saw flying fishes, which surprised me very much; they used frequently to fly across the ship, and many of them fell on the deck. I also now first saw the use of the quadrant;[2] I had often with astonishment seen the mariners make observations with it, and I could not think what it meant. They at last took notice of my surprise; and one of them, willing to increase it, as well as to gratify my curiosity, made me one day look through it. The clouds appeared to me to be land, which disappeared as they passed along. This heightened my wonder; and I was now more persuaded than ever, that I was in another world, and that every thing about me was magic. At last, we came in sight of the island of Barbados, at which the whites on board gave a great shout, and made many signs of joy to us. We did not know what to think of this; but as the vessel drew nearer, we plainly saw the harbor, and other ships of different kinds an sizes, and we soon anchored amongst them, off Bridgetown.[3] Many merchants and planters now came on board, though it was in the evening. They

Literature in context   Economics

The Slave Trade

While many people came to the new world in search of riches, many others were brought against their will to the Western Hemisphere to be sold as slaves. The map below indicates the major slave trade routes.

The Atlantic crossing, known as "the middle passage," was atrocious. For six to ten weeks, Africans were chained below decks in cramped, confining spaces. Overcrowding, disease, and despair claimed many lives. Some Africans mutinied, and others tried to starve themselves or jump overboard. Equiano's narrative describes his middle-passage experience.

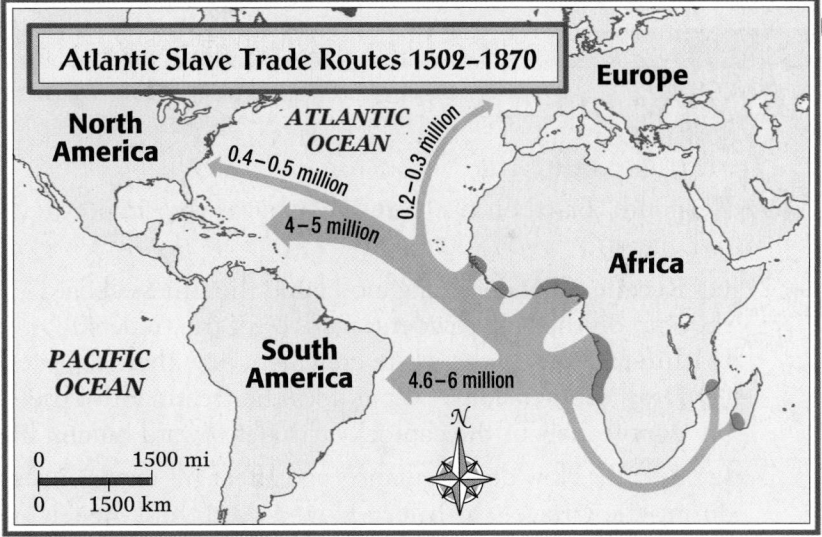

Atlantic Slave Trade Routes 1502–1870

North America

ATLANTIC OCEAN

Europe

0.4–0.5 million

0.2–0.3 million

4–5 million

Africa

PACIFIC OCEAN

South America

4.6–6 million

0   1500 mi
0   1500 km

N

✓ Reading Check

What do some slaves do to escape the misery of the middle passage?

---

2. **quadrant** (kwä´ drənt) n. an instrument used by navigators to determine the position of a ship.
3. **Bridgetown** n. the capital of Barbados.

from *The Interesting Narrative of the Life of Olaudah Equiano* ◆ 47

put us in separate parcels,[4] and examined us attentively. They also made us jump, and pointed to the land, signifying we were to go there. We thought by this, we should be eaten by these ugly men, as they appeared to us; and, when soon after we were all put down under the deck again, there was much dread and trembling among us, and nothing but bitter cries to be heard all the night from these apprehensions, insomuch, that at last the white people got some old slaves from the land to pacify us. They told us we were not to be eaten, but to work, and were soon to go on land, where we should see many of our country people. This report eased us much. And sure enough, soon after we were landed, there came to us Africans of all languages.

We were conducted immediately to the merchant's yard, where we were all pent up together, like so many sheep in a fold, without regard to sex or age. . . . We were not many days in the merchant's custody, before we were sold after their usual manner, which is this: On a signal given (as the beat of a drum), the buyers rush at once into the yard where the slaves are confined, and make choice of that parcel they like best. . . .

pacify (pas´ ə fī´) v. calm; soothe

[handwritten: ?? trick]

---

4. parcels (pär´ səlz) n. groups.

Review and Assess

Thinking About the Selection

1. **Respond:** Based on his narrative, what is your impression of Equiano?

2. **(a) Recall:** Why does Equiano blame the illness aboard the ship on the "improvident avarice" of the traders?
   (b) Infer: How do the white crewmen view their captives?
   (c) Draw Conclusions: What does the treatment of the slaves reveal about the captors' attitudes toward human life?

3. **(a) Recall:** How does Equiano's age affect his experiences during the voyage? **(b) Infer:** How do you think he felt about his experience compared to the fate of other slaves on the ship?

4. **(a) Recall:** Why do some of the slaves jump overboard?
   (b) Infer: Why do you suppose the slaves who were rescued after jumping overboard got flogged?

5. **Analyze:** How does Equiano prove his great zest for life despite his assertion that he wants to die? Provide examples from the story.

6. **Generalize:** Why is it important for people who are victims of such human injustices to record their experiences?

Review and Assess

Literary Analysis

Slave Narratives

1. According to Equiano's **slave narrative,** what was the general feeling of the slaves toward their situation?
2. Cite two examples of the slave traders' cruelty to the slaves.
3. Cite two examples that show the traders' concern for the slaves' well-being.
4. What might have motivated the traders' behavior toward their human cargo? Explain.

Connecting Literary Elements

5. (a) Using a chart like the one shown here, identify three examples of **emotional appeal** in Equiano's narrative. (b) What is the effect of these appeals on the reader?

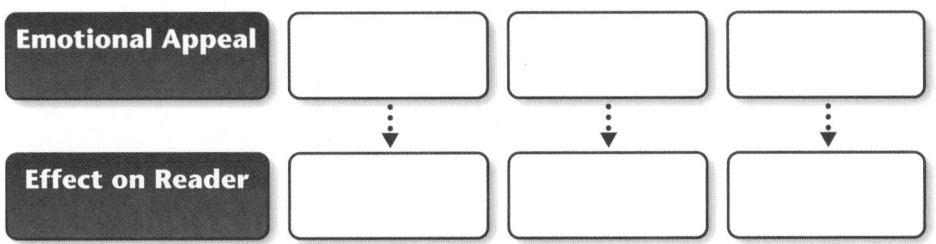

6. What aspect of the conditions aboard ship does Equiano stress in his account?
7. Explain how emotional appeals might strengthen Equiano's position against the slave trade.

Reading Strategy

Summarizing

8. Identify at least three main ideas the author conveys about the voyage.
9. Summarize the events that occur after the ship reached Bridgetown.

Extend Understanding

10. **Social Studies Connection:** How does Equiano's voyage compare with those of explorers and colonists?

Integrate Language Skills

Vocabulary Development Lesson

Word Analysis: Latin Root -vid-

The Latin root -vid-, from *videre*, means "to see." The word *provident* means "to have foresight." Considering the meaning of the root -vid-, answer these questions:

1. Why is *evidence* useful in establishing guilt?
2. How would *video* technology change telephone habits?

Spelling Strategy

Change the spelling of *in-*, a common prefix meaning "not," to *im-* when you add it to words beginning with *b*, *m*, or *p* (as in *improvident*). Using this strategy, spell the words described below:

1. not mortal
2. not balanced
3. not possible
4. not precice

Concept Development: Synonym or Antonym

Review the list of vocabulary words on page 43. Then, analyze the relationship between the words in each of the following pairs. Indicate whether the words are synonyms (words with similar meanings) or antonyms (words with opposite meanings).

1. loathesome, hateful
2. pestilential, sanitary
3. copious, sparse
4. improvident, cautious
5. avarice, greed
6. pacify, torment

Grammar and Style Lesson

Active and Passive Voice

A verb is in the **active voice** when the subject of the sentence performs the action. A verb is in the **passive voice** when the subject receives the action.

> **Active Voice:** <u>They</u> *tossed* the remaining fish into the sea.
> (The subject, *they*, performs the action of the verb *tossed*.)
>
> **Passive Voice:** This <u>situation</u> *was aggravated* by the galling of the chains.
> (The subject, *situation*, receives the action of the verb *was aggravated*.)

Practice Rewrite the following sentences using the active voice. You may need to add words to indicate who performed the action.

1. Some of us had been permitted to stay on the deck for fresh air.
2. I was soon reduced so low here.
3. It was thought necessary to keep me almost always on deck.
4. They were discovered.
5. Flying fish were seen.

Looking at Style Find three examples of the passive voice in the final paragraph of the selection. What effect does the style have on your understanding of the slaves' experiences?

 Prentice Hall Writing and Grammar Connection: Chapter 21, Section 4

Writing Lesson

Museum Placard

To educate today's audiences, museums present exhibits that document the slave trade of the 1800s. Write the introductory information for a large placard that visitors will read at an exhibit's beginning. Explain the sequence of events of the slave trade, from capture to slave auction.

Prewriting   Use library sources to gather facts. Organize your findings in sequence, perhaps by drawing a map to trace the routes or marking dates and other key details on a timeline.

Drafting   Create a timeline like the one shown to organize the events that occurred, listing them in chronological order. Begin with what happens first, and then continue in time order.

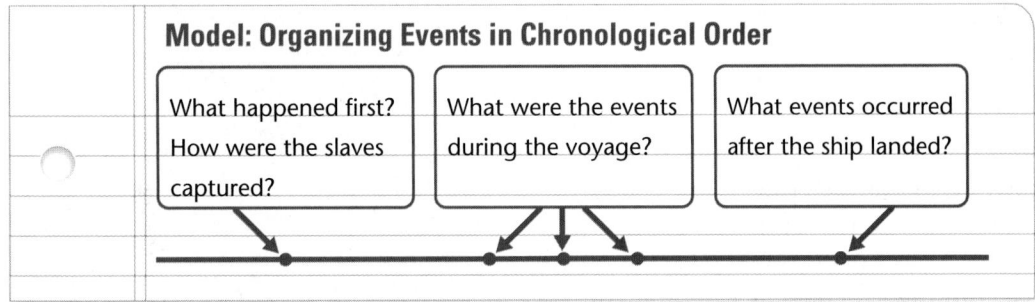

Model: Organizing Events in Chronological Order

| What happened first? How were the slaves captured? | What were the events during the voyage? | What events occurred after the ship landed? |

Revising   Check that your placard highlights the important stages of the slave trade. Eliminate any confusing shifts in time sequence, and add transitions to sharpen that sequence.

W̶G Prentice Hall Writing and Grammar Connection: Chapter 10, Section 3

Extension Activities

Listening and Speaking Can slavery exist in today's society? In a **debate** argue this question with a group of classmates, using these tips:

- Create "pro" and "con" teams.
- Develop key arguments.
- Find supporting evidence.
- Assign positions for introductory arguments, rebuttal and conclusion.

Stage the debate for the class, responding to questions from your audience. **[Group Activity]**

Research and Technology Modern organizations such as Amnesty International work to increase awareness of injustices around the world. Use the Internet or the library to research the causes it publicizes. Develop charts or diagrams and give a **research presentation.**

 **Take It to the Net**   www.phschool.com

Go online for an additional research activity using the Internet.

CONNECTIONS
Literature Past and Present
Meeting of Cultures

Though each is quite different, the works in Part 1 share one thing in common: They record impressions of the world, new experiences, and new people seen through the filter of the writers' experiences and cultures. The Native Americans saw nature as the source of earthly life. The conquistadors viewed new lands and people within the framework of European values. Olaudah Equiano vividly portrayed the consequences of one culture's belief in its right to dominate another.

Each of their stories contributes uniquely to our understanding of the country that would become the United States of America. Today, the distinct lines that separated these cultures have blurred into a shared "American experience." America is still celebrated as a melting pot of cultures from around the world, but there are those who feel that some of the values that once shaped the nation are in danger of being left behind.

Keeping the Flame Alive The last two centuries have also seen the gradual disappearance of many of the cultures and customs of Native American peoples. Darryl Babe Wilson preserves in writing the memories of Native American elders. He confronts the elders' fear that the younger generation of Native Americans is unenlightened about its ancestral heritage. Wilson strives to bring about a "meeting of cultures."

Photo of a Native American male (Wailaki tribe), Edward S. Curtis, Southwest Museum, Los Angeles

▶ Critical Viewing
In what way does this portrait convey the wisdom of the grandfather in the story? **[Connect]**

Diamond Island: ALCATRAZ

Allisti Ti-Tanin-Miji (Rock Rainbow)

Darryl Babe Wilson

There was a single letter in the mailbox. Somehow it seemed urgent. The address, although it was labored over, could hardly be deciphered—square childlike print that did not complete the almost individual letters. Inside, five pages written on both sides. Blunt figures. Each word pressed heavily into the paper. I could not read it but I could feel the message. "Al traz" was in the first paragraph, broken and scattered, but there. At the very bottom of the final page—running out of space—he scrawled his name. It curved down just past the right-hand corner. The last letter of his name, *n,* did not fit: *Gibso.* It was winter, 1971. I hurried to his home.

Grandfather lived at Atwam, 100 miles east of Redding, California, in a little shack out on the flat land. His house was old and crooked just like in a fairy tale. His belongings were few and they, too, were old and worn. I always wanted to know his age and often asked some of the older of our people if they could recall when Grandfather was born. After silences that sometimes seemed more than a year, they always shook their silver-gray heads and answered: "I dunno. He was old and wrinkled with white hair for as long as I can remember. Since I was just a child." He must have been born between 1850 and 1870.

Thanksgiving weekend, 1989. It is this time of the year when I think about Grandfather and his ordeal. I keep promising myself that I will write his story down because it is time to give the island of Alcatraz a proper identity and a "real" history. It is easy for modern people to think that the history of Alcatraz began when a foreign ship sailed into the bay and a stranger named Don Juan Manuel de Ayala[1] observed the "rock" and recorded "Alcatraz" in a log book in 1775. That episode, that sailing and that recording was only moments ago.

Grandfather said that long ago the Sacramento Valley was a huge freshwater lake, that it was "as long as the land" (from the northern

Thematic Connection
Why might the writer want to write his grand-father's story down?

---

1. **Don Juan Manuel de Ayala** (dän hwän män wel´ dä ä yä´ lä) an eighteenth-century Spanish explorer who was the first European to enter San Francisco Bay.

part of California to the southern), and that a great shaking of an angry spirit within the earth caused part of the coastal range to crumble into the outer-ocean. When the huge lake finally drained and the waves from the earthquake finally settled, there was the San Francisco Bay, and there, in isolation and containing a "truth," was Diamond Island (Alcatraz).

He told me the story one winter in his little one-room house in Atwam. It is bitter cold there during winters. I arrived late in the evening, tires of my truck spinning up his driveway. The driveway was a series of frozen, broken mudholes in a general direction across a field to his home. The headlights bounced out of control.

My old 1948 Chevy pickup was as cold inside as it was outside. The old truck kept going, but it was a fight to make it go in the winter. It was such a struggle that we called it "Mr. Miserable." Mr. Miserable and I came to a jolting halt against a snowbank that was the result of someone shoveling a walk in the front yard. We expended our momentum. The engine died with a sputtering cough. Lights flopped out.

It was black outside but the crusted snow lay like a ghost upon the earth and faded away in every direction. The night sky trembled with the fluttering of a million stars—all diamond blue. Wind whipped broken tumbleweeds across his neglected yard. The snow could not conceal the yard's chaos.

The light in the window promised warmth. Steam puffing from every breath, I hurried to his door. The snow crunched underfoot, sounding like a horse eating a crisp apple. The old door lurched open with a complaint. Grandfather's fatigued, centenarian[2] body a black silhouette against the brightness—bright although he had but a single shadeless lamp to light the entire house. I saw a skinned bear once. It looked just like Grandfather. Short, stout arms and bowed legs. Compact physique. Muscular—not fat. Thick chest. Powerful. Natural.

Old powder-blue eyes strained to see who was out there in the dark. "Hallo. You're just the man I'm lookin' for." Coffee aroma exploded from the open door. Coffee. Warmth!

Grandfather stood back and I entered the comfort of his jumbled little bungalow. It was cozy in there. He was burning juniper wood. Juniper, cured for a summer, has a clean, delicate aroma—a perfume. After a healthy handshake we huddled over steaming cups of coffee. Grandfather looked long at me. I think that he was not totally convinced that I was there. The hot coffee was good. It was not a fancy Colombian, aromatic blend, but it was so good!

We were surrounded by years of Grandfather's collections. It was like a museum. Everything was very old and worn. It seemed that every part of the clutter had a history—sometimes a history that remembered the origin of the earth, like the bent pail filled with

Thematic Connection
In what way does the author's inclusion of Grandfather's description of the creation of San Francisco Bay represent a meeting of cultures?

expended (ek spend′ id) *v.* to have spent or used by consuming

---

2. **centenarian** (sen′ tə ner′ ē ən) *adj.* at least one hundred years old.

obsidian[3] that he had collected from Glass Mountain many summers before, "just in case."

He also had a radio that he was talked into purchasing when he was a young working man in the 1920's. The radio cost $124. I think he got conned by that merchant and the episode magnified in mystery when he recalled that it was not until 1948 before he got the electric company to put a line to his home. By that time he forgot about the radio and he did not remember to turn it on until 1958. It worked. There was an odor of oldness—like a mouse that died then dried to a stiffness through the years—a <u>redolence</u> of old neglected newspapers.

The old person in the old house under the old moon began to tell the story of his escape from "the rock" long ago. He gathered himself together and reached back into a painful past. The silence was long and I thought that he might be crying silently. Then, with a quiver in his voice, he started telling the story that he wanted me to know:

"Alcatraz Island. Where the Pit River runs into the sea is where I was born, long ago. *Alcatraz,* that's the white man's name for it. To our people, in our legends, we always knew it as *Allisti Ti-tanin-miji* [Rock Rainbow], Diamond Island. In our legends, that's where the Mouse Brothers, the twins, were told to go when they searched for a healing treasure for our troubled people long, long ago. They were to go search at the end of *It A-juma* [Pit River]. They found it. They brought it back. But it is lost now. It is said, the 'diamond' was to bring goodness to all our people, everywhere.

"We always heard that there was a 'diamond' on an island near the great salt water. We were always told that the 'diamond' was a thought, or a truth. Something worth very much. It was not a jewelry. It sparkled and it shined, but it was not a jewelry. It was more. Colored lights came from inside it with every movement. That is why we always called it [Alcatraz] *Allisti Ti-Tanin-miji."* With a wave of an ancient hand and words filled with enduring knowledge, Grandfather spoke of a time long past.

In one of the many raids upon our people of the Pit River country, his pregnant mother was taken captive and forced, with other Indians, to make the long and painful march to Alcatraz in the winter. At that same time, the military was "sweeping" California. Some of our people were "removed" to the Round Valley Reservation at Covelo; others were taken east by train in open cattle cars during the winter to Quapa, Oklahoma. Still others were taken out into the ocean at Eureka and thrown overboard into icy waters.

Descendants of those that were taken in chains to Quapa are still there. Some of those cast into the winter ocean at Eureka made it back to land and returned to Pit River country. A few of those defying confinement, the threat of being shot by "thunder sticks," and

redolence (red´ əl əns)
n. scent; smell

Thematic Connection
What kind of meeting of cultures is described here?

---

3. obsidian (əb sid´ ē ən) *n.* hard, dark-colored or black volcanic glass.

dark winter nights of a cold Alcatraz-made-deadly by churning, freezing currents, made it back to Pit River country, too.

Grandfather said, "I was very small, too small to remember, but my grandmother remembered it all. The guards allowed us to swim around the rock. Every day, my mother swam. Every day, the people swam. We were not just swimming. We were gaining strength. We were learning the currents. We had to get home.

"When it was time, we were ready. We left at darkness. Grandmother said that I was a baby and rode my mother's back, clinging as she swam from Alcatraz to solid ground in night. My Grandmother remembered that I pulled so hard holding on that I broke my mother's necklace. It is still there in the water . . . somewhere." With a pointing of a stout finger southward, Grandfather indicated where "there" was.

Quivering with emotion, he hesitated. He trembled. "I do not remember if I was scared," Grandfather said, crooked, thick fingers rubbing a creased and wrinkled chin covered with white stubble. "I must have been."

When those old, cloudy eyes dripped tears down a leathery, crevassed[4] face, and long silences were between his sentences, often I trembled too. He softly spoke of his memory.

Our cups were long empty; *maliss* (fire) needed attention. The moon was suspended in the frozen winter night—round, bright, scratched and scarred—when Grandfather finally paused in his thinking. The old castiron heater grumbled and screamed when I slid open the top to drop in a fresh log. Sparks flew up into the darkness then disappeared. I slammed the top closed. Silence, again.

Grandfather continued, "There was not real diamonds on the island. At least I don't think so. I always thought the diamonds were not diamonds but some kind of understanding, some kind of good thought—or something." He shook a white, shaggy head and looked off into the distance into a time that was so long ago that the mountains barely remembered. For long moments he reflected, he gathered his thoughts. He knew that I "wrote things down on paper."

The night was thick. To the north a coyote howled. Far to the west an old coyote rasped a call to the black wilderness, a supreme presence beneath starry skies with icy freedom all around.

"When first I heard about the 'diamond,' I thought it might be a story of how we escaped. But after I heard that story so many times, I don't think so. I think there was a truth there that the Mouse Brothers were instructed to get and bring back long ago to help our people. I don't think that I know where that truth is now. Where can it be? It must be deep *inside Axo-Yet* [Mount Shasta][5] or *Sa Titt* [Medicine Lake]. It hides from our people. The truth

San Francisco, 1849, Attributed to Joshua Pierce

▲ **Critical Viewing**
This painting shows Alcatraz as seen from a San Francisco hilltop at twilight. What mood is created by this depiction of the island? **[Describe]**

---

4. **crevassed** (krə vast´) *adj.* deeply cracked.
5. **Mount Shasta** (shas´ tə) a volcanic mountain in northern California.

hides from us. It must not like us. It denies us."

The One-as-Old-as-the-Mountains made me wonder about this story. It seems incredible that there was such an escape from Alcatraz. Through American propaganda I have been trained to believe that it was impossible to escape from that isolated rock because of the currents and because of the freezing temperature as the powerful ocean and the surging rivers merged in chaos. I was convinced—until I heard Grandfather's story and until I realized that he dwelled within a different "time," a different "element." He dwelled within a spirituality of a natural source. In his world, I was only a foreign infant. It is true today that when I talk with the old people I feel like *nilladuwi*—(a white man). I feel like some domesticated creature addressing original royalty—knowing that the old ones were pure savage, born into the wild, free.

Thematic Connection
Why do you think it is so difficult for the writer to believe the story?

In his calm manner, Grandfather proceeded. "We wandered for many nights. We hid during the day. It is said that we had to go south for three nights before we could turn north. [My people landed at San Francisco and had to sneak to what is now San Jose, traveling at night with no food until they could turn northward.] They [the U.S. Army] were after us. They were after us all. We had to be careful. We had to be careful and not make mistakes. We headed north for two nights.

"We came to a huge river. We could not cross it. It was swift. My mother walked far upstream then jumped in. Everybody followed. The river washed us to the other shore [possibly the Benicia Straits]. We rested for two days eating dead fish that we found along the river. We could not build a fire because they would see the smoke and catch us so we must eat it [fish] raw. At night we traveled again. Again we traveled, this time for two nights also.

"There is a small island of mountains in the great valley [Sutter Buttes]. When we reached that place one of the young men climbed the highest peak. He was brave. We were all brave. It was during the sunlight. We waited for him to holler as was the plan. We waited

Thematic Connection
How does the language of Grandfather's story compare and contrast with García López de Cárdenas's account of the explanation of the Grand Canyon?

a long, long time. Then we heard: '*Axo-Yet! Axo-Yet! To-ho-ja-toki! To-ho-ja-toki Tanjan*' [Mount Shasta! Mount Shasta! North direction!]. Our hearts were happy. We were close to home. My mother squeezed me to her. We cried. I know we cried. I was there. So was my mother and grandmother."

Grandfather has been within the earth for many snows now. The volumes of knowledge that were buried with him are lost to my generation, a generation that needs original knowledge now more than ever, if we are to survive as a distinct and <u>autonomous</u> people. Perhaps a generation approaching will be more aware, more excited with tradition and custom and less satisfied to being off balance somewhere between the world of the "white man" and the world of the "Indian," and will seek this knowledge.

It is nearing winter, 1989. Snows upon *Axo-Yet* (Mount Shasta) are deep. The glaring white makes Grandfather's hair nearly yellow—now that I better recall the coarse strands that I often identified as "silver." That beautiful mountain. The landmark that caused the hunted warrior 140 years ago to forget the tragic episode that could have been the termination of our nation, and, standing with the sun shining full upon him, hollered to a frightened people waiting below: "*Axo-Yet! Axo-Yet! To-ho-ja-toki Tanjan!*"

Perhaps the approaching generation will seek and locate *Allisti Ti-tanin-miji* within the mountains. Possibly that generation will reveal many truths to this world society that is immense and confused in its immensity. An old chief of the Pit River country, "Charlie Buck," said often: "Truth. It is truth that will set us free." Along with Grandfather, I think that it was a "truth" that the Mouse Brothers brought to our land from Diamond Island long ago. A truth that needs to be understood, appreciated, and acknowledged. A truth that needs desperately to be found and known for its value.

Grandfather's letter is still in my files. I still can't read it, but if I could, I am sure that the message would be the same as this story that he gave to me as the moon listened and the winds whispered across a frozen Atwam, during a sparkling winter night long ago.

autonomous (ô tän´ ə məs) *adj.* independent

Darryl Babe Wilson

(b. 1939)

Darryl Babe Wilson is a Native American and short-story writer. He lives in California's San Francisco Bay area and teaches writing at two local colleges. Before moving to California in 1997, Wilson taught Native American studies at the University of Arizona, where he earned his Ph.D. in Comparative Culture and Literary Studies. Wilson often writes about the struggles of his people. For his book *Voices From the Earth*, he interviewed Native Americans from Barrow, Alaska, to the Mayan Peninsula of Mexico and Guatemala.

Connecting Literature Past and Present

1. (a) Why do you think Wilson says he feels like a domesticated creature or "white man" when he talks to the elders of his people? (b) In what way does Wilson's narrative account compare with the meeting of different cultures described by Alvar Núñez Cabeza de Vaca and García López de Cárdenas?

2. Describe a situation from your own life or observations that you feel represents a "meeting of cultures." (a) What are the "cultures" involved? (b) Is the meeting characterized by friendly exchange, or is it more a clash of cultures? Explain.

Focus on Literary Forms: Narrative Accounts

Building the Fort, Julien Binford,
The Jamestown/Yorktown Educational Trust

The settlers who journeyed across a hostile ocean and forged homes in a new land were generally far too busy just surviving to create poems and other types of literature that matched those of other areas of the world. The early settlers did succeed, however, in writing vivid narrative accounts—a literary form that has remained popular to this day.

Prepare to Read

from Journal of the First Voyage to America

Christopher Columbus (1451–1506)

Not much is known about the early life of Christopher Columbus, one of history's most famous explorers. In the late 1400s, Europeans had little knowledge about world geography, but Columbus left his home in Genoa, Italy, at a young age and went to sea. At age 25, he was shipwrecked off the coast of Portugal. Once back on land, Columbus studied mapmaking and navigation. He also learned Latin and read Marco Polo's account of the riches of Asia. Between 1480 and 1482, Columbus sailed to the Azores and to the Canary Islands off Africa. He then began to dream of more challenging voyages. Within ten years, he embraced the idea that led to his lifelong goal: reaching the fabled cities of Asia by sailing westward around the world.

First, Columbus tried to convince King John II of Portugal to fund a westward voyage. When his request was rejected there, he sought funding from other European rulers. After a series of unsuccessful attempts, Columbus won the support of Queen Isabella of Spain.

A Hard Bargain Queen Isabella and her husband, King Ferdinand, agreed to finance Columbus's first voyage in 1492. In forging the agreement, Columbus negotiated favorable terms. In addition to funding, he asked for and received the right to rule any lands he conquered. The agreement also noted that he would be entitled to 10 percent of all wealth from those lands.

The Famous Voyage On August 3, 1492, Columbus set sail from Palos, a small port in southwestern Spain, with his three ships—the *Niña*, the *Pinta*, and the *Santa Maria*. Although he knew how to measure latitude by using the North Star, Columbus had no navigational instruments. He used a compass to determine direction and an hourglass to estimate time. After more than a month at sea, his crews became disillusioned when they did not reach the islands Columbus had led them to expect. However, soon signs of life such as coastal seaweed and birds flying overhead indicated land was near, and the crew members' hopes were renewed. On October 12, Columbus reached one of the islands of Bahama, which he mistook for an island off India. He named the island San Salvador; he then continued to explore the Caribbean.

Linking East and West When Columbus reached these islands he had no idea there were millions of people living a short distance away in North and South America. He faced many challenges sailing the largely uncharted waters, but his voyages linked the Eastern and Western hemispheres. Over the next twelve years, he made three more transatlantic journeys, ever convinced that he had reached Asia and always hopeful of finding Marco Polo's fabled cities.

His Final Years Columbus was driven by his unrelenting desire to discover new territories, and he continued to sail until nearly the end of his life. His goal in his final voyage was to find a passage to the mainland of China. He set out from Cadiz, Spain, in 1502, traveling to Martinique and later east and south to the coasts of Honduras, Nicaragua, Costa Rica, Panama, and Jamaica. Suffering from exhaustion and malaria, he abandoned his search for China and returned to Spain in 1504. Although many scholars believe Columbus was poor at the time of his death, others say he died a wealthy man at the age of 54 in 1506. Today, he is recognized as one of the greatest mariners of all time.

Preview

Connecting to the Literature

Fulfilling the desire to circle the globe in a boat or discovering the cure for a deadly disease takes more than sheer will. A dreamer needs financial resources. To achieve his dream of circling the globe, Christopher Columbus had to persuade others to provide the funding. More often than not, people did not think it was worth the expense.

Literary Analysis

Journal

The European expeditions in the Americas are recorded in the journals of the explorers. A **journal** is an individual's day-by-day account of events. As the example below shows, a journal provides valuable details that only a participant or an eyewitness can supply.

> . . . the inhabitants on discovering us abandoned their houses, and took to flight, carrying off their goods to the mountains.

As a record of personal reactions, a journal reveals as much about the writer as it does about events. As you read, look for details that reveal Columbus's values, hopes, and reactions.

Connecting Literary Elements

A journal is not necessarily a reliable record of the facts. The **author's point of view,** or attitudes about the topic or audience, may color the telling of events, particularly when the writer is a participant. Journals written for publication rather than private use are even less likely to be objective. While reading Columbus's journal, look for evidence that he was writing for an audience.

Reading Strategy

Recognizing Author's Purpose

Columbus's purpose for writing his journal was to convince Queen Isabella and King Ferdinand to continue funding his explorations. **Recognizing the author's purpose** will help you to understand why a work was written, and it will also help you to understand Columbus's careful choice of words, details, and events to include in his journal. As you read, use a chart like this one to record Columbus's favorable descriptions and events. Then, explain his purpose for describing it that way.

Favorable Descriptions	Author's Purpose

Vocabulary Development

exquisite (eks´ kwi zit) *adj.* very beautiful; delicate; carefully wrought (p. 62)

affliction (ə flik´ shən) *n.* something causing pain or suffering (p. 63)

indications (in´ di kā´ shənz) *n.* signs; things that point out or signify (p. 64)

abundance (ə bun´ dəns) *n.* a great supply; more than enough (p. 64)

FROM JOURNAL OF THE FIRST VOYAGE TO AMERICA

CHRISTOPHER COLUMBUS

Background

In the 1450s, the only way to India from Europe involved traveling through Turkey, but explorers in Portugal and Spain began to look at alternate sea routes. Columbus's search brought Europe into contact with North and South America. His voyages took him from Lisbon, Portugal, to Palos, Spain, and the Canary Islands before he crossed the Atlantic. He landed first on the island of San Salvador. This account begins nine days after Columbus landed there.

SUNDAY, OCT. 21ST [1492]. At 10 o'clock, we arrived at a cape of the island,[1] and anchored, the other vessels in company. After having dispatched a meal, I went ashore, and found no habitation save a single house, and that without an occupant; we had no doubt that the people had fled in terror at our approach, as the house was completely furnished. I suffered nothing to be touched, and went with my captains and some of the crew to view the country. This island even exceeds the others in beauty and fertility. Groves of lofty and flourishing trees are abundant, as also large lakes, surrounded and overhung by the foliage, in a most enchanting manner. Everything looked as green as in April in Andalusia.[2] The melody of the birds was so <u>exquisite</u> that one was never willing to part from the

---

1. **the island** San Salvador.
2. **Andalusia** (an′ də lōō′ zhə) a region of Spain.

Writing Lesson

Oral Report on the Voyage

Columbus's funding depended on his ability to sell his experiences to an audience of readers who had not seen the lands he explored. Imitating Columbus's writing style, write an oral report that you would give to the king and queen of Spain upon your return to Europe.

Prewriting Imagine the landscape of the island Columbus visited. List the tropical sights, sounds, textures, smells, and tastes that he may have encountered.

Drafting As you describe the island, elaborate by including as many sensory details as you can. Instead of telling how lovely the island is, describe what you see, hear, feel, touch, or smell. Strive to imitate Columbus's style by choosing ornate words.

Model: Elaborating for Vividness

As we sailed the ocean, the sun sparkled on the water like translucent prisms of color. Yonder, we could see the different shades of lush, green foliage on the beach surrounded by many flowers of every hue.

> Sensory details such as *translucent prisms of color* and *different shades of lush green foliage* help readers imagine what they have never experienced.

Revising Add details to strengthen your images. Add smells to descriptions that appeal only to sight and sound; consider adding details about texture or taste where appropriate.

Prentice Hall Writing and Grammar Connection: Chapter 8, Section 2

Extension Activities

Listening and Speaking Many Native American cultures have artistic traditions. For a **humanities presentation** find pictures of Native American art forms, and compare them to European art from the same time period.

- Consider art, music, and dance.
- Determine the historical influences on the cultures.

Share your analysis with your class, including samples of the art you discuss.

Research and Technology With a group, use online newspapers and data banks for Columbus's presence in today's world. Create a **chart** of parks and public places named after him. Present your findings to the class. **[Group Activity]**

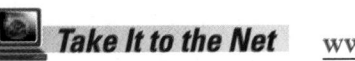 **Take It to the Net** www.phschool.com

Go online for an additional research activity using the Internet.

A Closer Look

Captivity Narratives: Colonial Pulp Fiction

Mary Rowlandson was taken captive by Wampanoag Indians in 1676. The result was America's first bestseller, and a glimpse at Native American life.

Tensions were high in the Massachusetts Bay Colony near the end of the seventeenth century. The once-friendly relations between Native Americans and European settlers had broken down. While the peaceful Wampanoag tribe had shared its land and resources with the Massachusetts colonists for almost forty years, by the 1670s, cooperation between the two groups had failed.

Colonial troops began driving the Wampanoag from their land. As the winter of 1676 approached, the Wampanoag were cut off from the food they had stored for the harsh, snowy months. They were in desperate need of supplies, and they were angered by an attack on Wampanoag Indians in Rhode Island the previous December.

The Town Falls At sunrise on February 10, 1676, a group of Wampanoag Indians stormed the English frontier settlement of Lancaster, Massachusetts. It was perfect timing. Most of Lancaster's leaders were in Boston, seeking help in their struggle with the Indians from the royal governor. When gunshots rang out on that February morning, the settlement was virtually unguarded.

Mary Rowlandson, the forty-year-old wife of a Lancaster minister, huddled in her house and watched the battle. She saw friends and family cut down by gunfire. "The attack was launched not by human contestants in a struggle for land and power but by wolves . . . ," she later wrote. In all, twenty colonists were killed and twenty-four were taken captive, including Rowlandson and her son and daughter.

Thus began Rowlandson's three-month odyssey among the Wampanoag Indians. In May, Rowlandson and her children were ransomed back to her husband. After their release, she wrote an account of her captivity. The book, which has come to be called *A Narrative of the Captivity*, was originally published with a much longer title: *The Sovereignty & Goodness of God, Together with the Faithfulness of His Promises Displayed; Being a Narrative of the Captivity and Restauration of Mrs. Mary Rowlandson*. It was the first American bestseller written by a woman.

Rowlandson's book was so successful it spawned dozens of imitations. These other captivity narratives were largely fictional, though they claimed to be true. Immensely popular, they portrayed Native Americans as brutal savages, contributing to a stereotype that persisted for hundreds of years.

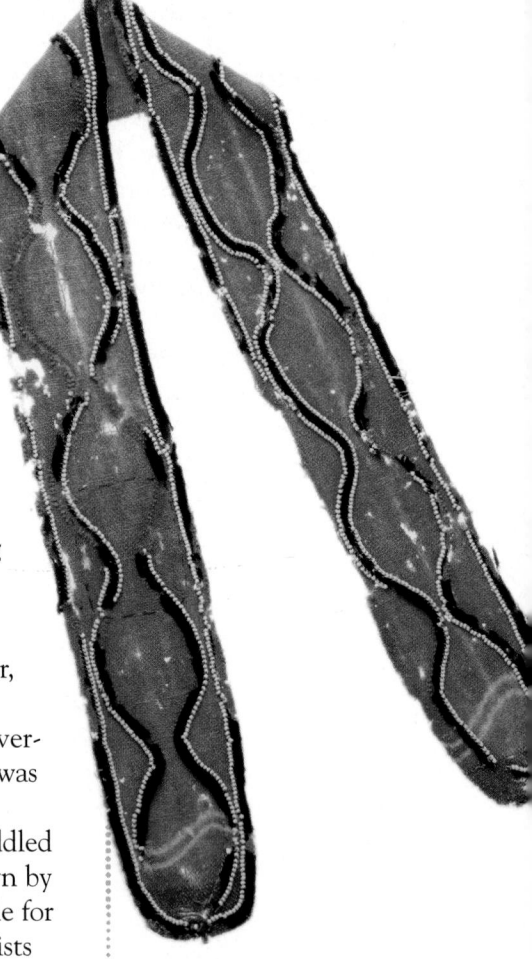

▲ **Critical Viewing** What does the beautiful bead work and design of this sash belonging to Wampanoag leader King Philip suggest about his status in his society? **[Interpret]**

A Different Culture Ironically, though Rowlandson's book offered a one-sided and often negative view of Native Americans, her observations helped explain Indian culture to colonists. Native Americans had a rich oral tradition, but they had no literary tradition. They communicated their history, family genealogies, and religious beliefs through the spoken word. In most Native American communities, certain people were the designated storytellers. They learned all the tales that served as a repository for their tribe's traditions, values, and beliefs. They also chose and trained their successors. If there was one break in the cycle between generations, these stories—and the worldview they depicted—could vanish completely.

Rowlandson's narrative gave Europeans their first peek into Native American beliefs. Much of her story concerned details of the Indians' struggle for survival—how they ate beaver, foraged for other wild foods, and constructed rafts to cross rivers. Rowlandson describes how she knitted and sewed in exchange for food and asserted herself to receive better treatment. Some of the Indians were kind to her. She calls one of her captors her "best friend." Another found a Bible to comfort her.

Eventually, Rowlandson came to respect aspects of Native American culture. She admired their reverence for their elders, was impressed by the high status of women, and commended the close bonds between members of their community. She also noted details about Indian social hierarchy and government, reporting how the Indians credited their chief, or *sachem*, with great authority, but also used a "General Court to consult and determine."

In the latter years of her life, Rowlandson was widowed, and then remarried. She died in 1711. The Wampanoag, meanwhile, came close to extinction. By the summer of 1676, most of their warriors had been killed and their families sold into slavery. By the nineteenth century, the U.S. government abolished the tribe as a legal entity. Still, efforts were made to maintain Wampanoag traditions. Today, Rhode Island's Native American community has managed to preserve much of the tribe's culture, history, and language.

▼ **Critical Viewing**
What details on this early edition of Mary Rowlandson's book would be regarded as one-sided or inflammatory today? **[Analyze]**

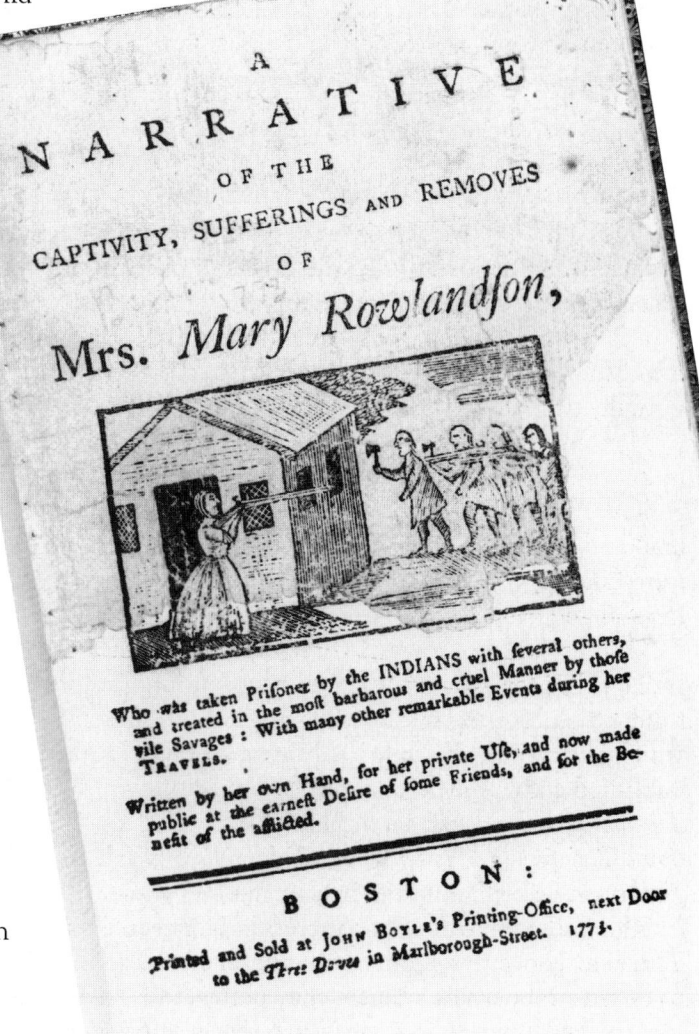

A
NARRATIVE
OF THE
CAPTIVITY, SUFFERINGS AND REMOVES
OF
Mrs. *Mary Rowlandson*,

Who was taken Prisoner by the INDIANS with several others, and treated in the most barbarous and cruel Manner by those vile Savages : With many other remarkable Events during her Travels.

Written by her own Hand, for her private Use, and now made public at the earnest Desire of some Friends, and for the Benefit of the afflicted.

BOSTON :
Printed and Sold at JOHN BOYLE's Printing-Office, next Door to the Three Doves in Marlborough-Street. 1773.

Prepare to Read

from The General History of Virginia ◆
from Of Plymouth Plantation

John Smith (1580–1631)

If John Smith were alive today, he would probably be starring opposite Arnold Schwarzenegger in blockbuster adventure films—at least, that might be where he would see himself. Adventurer, poet, mapmaker, and egotist are just a few of the labels that apply to Smith, who earned a reputation as one of England's most famous explorers by helping to lead the first successful English colony in America. Stories of his adventures, often embellished by his own pen, fascinated readers of his day and continue to provide details about the early exploration of the Americas.

Smith and a group of colonists landed in Virginia in 1607 and founded Jamestown. As president of the colony from 1608 to 1609, Smith helped to obtain food, enforce discipline, and deal with the local Native Americans. Although Smith returned to England in 1609, he made two more voyages to America and, in 1614, explored what he called New England. Using his skills as a mapmaker to chart his course, Smith mapped out the coast from Penobscot Bay, Maine, to Cape Cod, Massachusetts.

On a second voyage to further carve out new and chartered lands, Smith found himself in the dangerous company of pirates who held him against his will. Although Smith managed to escape, he returned to England without any money. In 1617, he made one final colonizing effort, but his ship was held back by wind gusts that lasted three months. After that, he never had a chance to set sail. Smith published several works in the course of his life, including *The General History of Virginia, New England, and the Summer Isles* (1624).

William Bradford (1590–1657)

Survival in North America was a matter of endurance, intelligence, and courage. William Bradford had all three. Thirteen years after the first permanent English settlement was established in Jamestown, Virginia, Bradford helped lead the Pilgrims to what is now Massachusetts.

Seeking Freedom Bradford, who was born in Yorkshire, England, joined a group of Puritans who believed that the Church of England was corrupt. This group wished to separate from the church. In the face of stiff persecution, they eventually fled to Holland and from there sailed to North America. In *Of Plymouth Plantation*, Bradford provides an account of the experiences of these early settlers. Historians consider this account to be accurate.

A Long Leadership After the death of the colony's first leader, the Pilgrims elected William Bradford governor. He was reelected thirty times. During his tenure, he organized the repayment of debts to financial backers, encouraged new immigration, and established good relations with the Native Americans, without whose help the colony never would have survived. He also instituted the town meeting within the colonies, a democratic process that continues to take place in state government today. Bradford was largely responsible for leading the infant colony through many hardships to success.

In 1630, Bradford began writing *Of Plymouth Plantation*, a firsthand account of the Pilgrims' struggle to endure, sustained only by courage and unbending faith. The work, written in the simple language known as Puritan Plain Style, was not published until 1856.

Preview

Connecting to the Literature

You may remember a point in your life when you kept going even when everything seemed to be going against you. Consider the difficulties the early American colonists faced when they fought against all odds in their determination to cross the ocean and find a new homeland.

Literary Analysis

Narrative Accounts

Narrative accounts tell the story of real-life events. Some historical narratives, including these, are firsthand accounts by people who lived through significant historic events. Others are secondhand accounts, written by people who researched the events but did not experience them. In the following passage, William Bradford provides a firsthand description.

> . . . after long beating at sea they fell with that land which is called Cape Cod; the which being made and certainly known to be it, they were not a little joyful.

Because of the writer's personal involvement, firsthand accounts are sometimes subjective.

Comparing Literary Works

John Smith and the settlers at Jamestown came to the New World in search of wealth. In contrast, Bradford and the Pilgrims sought religious freedom. As you read, compare and contrast the experiences of the two groups, and note how the different purposes of the two groups are reflected in the presentation of events.

Reading Strategy

Breaking Down Sentences

You can analyze meaning by **breaking down sentences** and considering one section at a time. Look at a complex sentence, and separate its essential parts (the *who* and *what*) from the difficult language until you get to the main idea. As you read, use a diagram like the one shown to help you analyze and interpret the meaning of complex sentences.

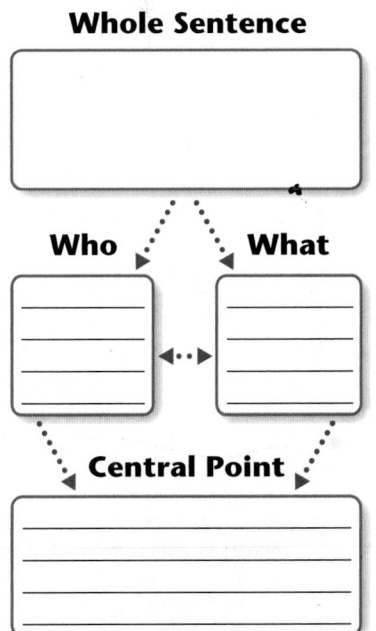

Whole Sentence

Who   **What**

Central Point

Vocabulary Development

pilfer (pil´ fər) *v.* steal (p. 72)

palisades (pal´ə sādz´) *n.* large, pointed stakes set in the ground to form a fence used for defense (p. 73)

conceits (kən sēts´) *n.* strange or fanciful ideas (p. 73)

mollified (mäl´ ə fīd´) *v.* soothed; calmed (p. 76)

peril (per´əl) *n.* danger (p. 78)

loath (lōth) *adj.* reluctant, unwilling (p. 79)

sundry (sun´ drē) *adj.* various; different (p. 79)

recompense (rek´ əm pens´) *n.* reward; repayment (p. 81)

from The General History of Virginia

John Smith

The First Day at Jamestown, 14th May 1607, Augustus L. Mason, Library of Congress, Washington, D.C.

What Happened Till the First Supply

Being thus left to our fortunes, it fortuned[1] that within ten days, scarce ten amongst us could either go[2] or well stand, such extreme weakness and sickness oppressed us. And thereat none need marvel if they consider the cause and reason, which was this: While the ships stayed, our allowance was somewhat bettered by a daily proportion of biscuit which the sailors would <u>pilfer</u> to sell, give, or exchange with us for money, sassafras,[3] or furs. But when they departed, there remained neither tavern, beer house, nor place of relief but the common kettle.[4] Had we been as free from all sins as gluttony and drunkenness we might have been canonized for saints, but our President[5] would never have been admitted for engrossing to

▲ **Critical Viewing**
Contrast the feeling this image evokes with the details of the first sentence of Smith's account. **[Connect]**

pilfer (pil′ fər) *v.* steal

---

1. **fortuned** *v.* happened.
2. **go** *v.* be active.
3. **sassafras** (sas′ ə fras′) *n.* a tree, the root of which was valued for its supposed medicinal qualities.
4. **common kettle** communal cooking pot.
5. **President** Wingfield, the leader of the colony.

his private,[6] oatmeal, sack,[7] oil, aqua vitae,[8] beef, eggs, or what not but the kettle; that indeed he allowed equally to be distributed, and that was half a pint of wheat and as much barley boiled with water for a man a day, and this, having fried some twenty-six weeks in the ship's hold, contained as many worms as grains so that we might truly call it rather so much bran than corn; our drink was water, our lodgings castles in the air.

With this lodging and diet, our extreme toil in bearing and planting <u>palisades</u> so strained and bruised us and our continual labor in the extremity of the heat had so weakened us, as were cause sufficient to have made us as miserable in our native country or any other place in the world.

From May to September, those that escaped lived upon sturgeon and sea crabs. Fifty in this time we buried; the rest seeing the President's projects to escape these miseries in our pinnace[9] by flight (who all this time had neither felt want nor sickness) so moved our dead spirits as we deposed him and established Ratcliffe in his place . . .

But now was all our provision spent, the sturgeon gone, all helps abandoned, each hour expecting the fury of the savages; when God, the patron of all good endeavors, in that desperate extremity so changed the hearts of the savages that they brought such plenty of their fruits and provision as no man wanted.

And now where some affirmed it was ill done of the Council[10] to send forth men so badly provided, this incontradictable reason will show them plainly they are too ill advised to nourish such ill <u>conceits</u>: First, the fault of our going was our own; what could be thought fitting or necessary we had, but what we should find, or want, or where we should be, we were all ignorant and supposing to make our passage in two months, with victual to live and the advantage of the spring to work; we were at sea five months where we both spent our victual and lost the opportunity of the time and season to plant, by the unskillful presumption of our ignorant transporters that understood not at all what they undertook.

Such actions have ever since the world's beginning been subject to such accidents, and everything of worth is found full of difficulties, but nothing so difficult as to establish a commonwealth so far remote from men and means and where men's minds are so untoward[11] as neither do well themselves nor suffer others. But to proceed.

The new President and Martin, being little beloved, of weak judgment in dangers, and less industry in peace, committed the managing of all things abroad[12] to Captain Smith, who, by his own example,

---

6. **engrossing to his private** taking for his own use.
7. **sack** *n.* type of white wine.
8. **aqua vitae** (ak′ wə vī′ tə) brandy.
9. **pinnace** (pin′ is) *n.* small sailing ship.
10. **Council** the seven persons in charge of the expedition.
11. **untoward** *adj.* stubborn.
12. **abroad** *adv.* outside the palisades.

palisades (pal′ ə sādz′) *n.* large, pointed stakes set in the ground to form a fence used for defense

Reading Strategy
Breaking Down Sentences
In the long sentence beginning "But now" there is an important turn of events. Break the sentence down to understand its meaning.

conceits (kən sētz′) *n.* strange or fanciful ideas

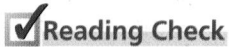
Reading Check

Where do the pilgrims get food, once their supply runs out?

Founding of the First Permanent English Settlement in America, A. C. Warren, New York Public Library

good words, and fair promises, set some to mow, others to bind thatch, some to build houses, others to thatch them, himself always bearing the greatest task for his own share, so that in short time he provided most of them lodgings, neglecting any for himself. . . .

⇒◆⇐

Leading an expedition on the Chickahominy River, Captain Smith and his men are attacked by Indians, and Smith is taken prisoner.

⇒◆⇐

When this news came to Jamestown, much was their sorrow for his loss, few expecting what ensued.

Six or seven weeks those barbarians kept him prisoner, many strange triumphs and conjurations they made of him, yet he so demeaned himself amongst them, as he not only diverted them from surprising the fort, but procured his own liberty, and got himself and his company such estimation amongst them, that those savages admired him.

▲ Critical Viewing
What can you infer about the artist's attitude toward Native Americans from the way he depicts them? **[Infer]**

Literary Analysis
Narrative Accounts
Which words in this paragraph alert you to the fact that Smith's account is not completely objective?

The manner how they used and delivered him is as followeth:

The savages having drawn from George Cassen whither Captain Smith was gone, prosecuting that opportunity they followed him with three hundred bowmen, conducted by the King of Pamunkee,[13] who in divisions searching the turnings of the river found Robinson and Emry by the fireside; those they shot full of arrows and slew. Then finding the Captain, as is said, that used the savage that was his guide as his shield (three of them being slain and divers[14] others so galled),[15] all the rest would not come near him. Thinking thus to have returned to his boat, regarding them, as he marched, more than his way, slipped up to the middle in an oozy creek and his savage with him; yet dared they not come to him till being near dead with cold he threw away his arms. Then according to their compositions[16] they drew him forth and led him to the fire where his men were slain. Diligently they chafed his benumbed limbs.

He demanding for their captain, they showed him Opechancanough, King of Pamunkee, to whom he gave a round ivory double compass dial. Much they marveled at the playing of the fly and needle,[17] which they could see so plainly and yet not touch it because of the glass that covered them. But when he demonstrated by that globe-like jewel the roundness of the earth and skies, the sphere of the sun, moon, and stars, and how the sun did chase the night round about the world continually, the greatness of the land and sea, the diversity of nations, variety of complexions, and how we were to them antipodes[18] and many other such like matters, they all stood as amazed with admiration.

Nothwithstanding, within an hour after, they tied him to a tree, and as many as could stand about him prepared to shoot him, but the King holding up the compass in his hand, they all laid down their bows and arrows and in a triumphant manner led him to Orapaks where he was after their manner kindly feasted and well used. . . .

At last they brought him to Werowocomoco, where was Powhatan, their Emperor. Here more than two hundred of those grim courtiers stood wondering at him, as he had been a monster, till Powhatan and his train had put themselves in their greatest braveries. Before a fire upon a seat like a bedstead, he sat covered with a great robe made of raccoon skins and all the tails hanging by. On either hand did sit a young wench of sixteen or eighteen years and along on each side the house, two rows of men and behind them as many women, with all their heads and shoulders painted red, many of their heads bedecked

---

13. **Pamunkee** Pamunkee River.
14. **divers** (dī´ vərz) *adj.* several.
15. **galled** *v.* wounded.
16. **compositions** *n.* ways.
17. **fly and needle** *n.* parts of a compass.
18. **antipodes** (an tip´ ə dēz´) *n.* two places on opposite sides of the Earth.

Reading Strategy
Breaking Down Sentences
Analyze the first sentence in this paragraph to determine who was killed.

Literary Analysis
Narrative Accounts
How does Smith portray himself in this description?

Reading Check

What saves Smith from death after he is tied to a tree?

from *The General History of Virginia* ◆ 75

with the white down of birds, but every one with something, and a great chain of white beads about their necks.

At his entrance before the King, all the people gave a great shout. The queen of Appomattoc was appointed to bring him water to wash his hands, and another brought him a bunch of feathers, instead of a towel, to dry them; having feasted him after their best barbarous manner they could, a long consultation was held, but the conclusion was, two great stones were brought before Powhatan: then as many as could, laid hands on him, dragged him to them, and thereon laid his head and being ready with their clubs to beat out his brains, Pocahontas,♦ the King's dearest daughter, when no entreaty could prevail, got his head in her arms and laid her own upon his to save him from death; whereat the Emperor was contented he should live to make him hatchets, and her bells, beads, and copper, for they thought him as well of all occupations as themselves.[19] For the King himself will make his own robes, shoes, bows, arrows, pots; plant, hunt, or do anything so well as the rest.

Two days after, Powhatan, having disguised himself in the most fearfulest manner he could, caused Captain Smith to be brought forth to a great house in the woods and there upon a mat by the fire to be left alone. Not long after, from behind a mat that divided the house, was made the most dolefulest noise he ever heard; then Powhatan more like a devil than a man, with some two hundred more as black as himself, came unto him and told him now they were friends, and presently he should go to Jamestown to send him two great guns and a grindstone for which he would give him the country of Capahowasic and forever esteem him as his son Nantaquond.

So to Jamestown with twelve guides Powhatan sent him. That night they quartered in the woods, he still expecting (as he had done all this long time of his imprisonment) every hour to be put to one death or other, for all their feasting. But almighty God (by His divine providence) had mollified the hearts of those stern barbarians with compassion. The next morning betimes they came to the fort, where Smith having used the savages with what kindness he could, he showed Rawhunt, Powhatan's trusty servant, two demiculverins[20] and a millstone to carry Powhatan; they found them somewhat too heavy, but when they did see him discharge them, being loaded with stones, among the boughs of a great tree loaded with icicles, the ice and branches came so tumbling down that the poor savages ran away half dead with fear. But at last we regained some conference with them and gave them such toys and sent to Powhatan, his women, and children such presents as gave them in general full content.

___

19. as well . . . themselves capable of making them just as well as they could themselves.
20. demiculverins (dem´ ē kul´ vər inz) large cannons.

Literature in context Social Studies Connection

♦ Pocahontas

Throughout American history, there has been much speculation about Pocahontas and John Smith. Smith's story of Pocahontas raises questions because of the subjectivity of his relationship with her and because there is no other documentation that substantiates his writing.

In early accounts of his capture, Smith never mentions that Pocahontas is only twelve or thirteen years old. He was twenty-eight at the time. In addition, Smith also speaks of other similar adventures with admiring women. This has led historians to question the accuracy of his account of Pocahontas. In addition, Smith wrote in third person. Historians suggest he may have chosen this style to distance himself from the writing and make it more believable.

mollified (mäl´ ə fīd´) *v.* soothed; calmed

Literary Analysis
Narrative Accounts and Historical Influences
What do you notice about the writer's attitudes toward people who are different from Europeans?

Now in Jamestown they were all in combustion,[21] the strongest preparing once more to run away with the pinnace; which, with the hazard of his life, with saker falcon[22] and musket shot, Smith forced now the third time to stay or sink.

Some, no better than they should be, had plotted with the President the next day to have him put to death by the Levitical law,[23] for the lives of Robinson and Emry; pretending the fault was his that had led them to their ends: but he quickly took such order with such lawyers that he laid them by their heels till he sent some of them prisoners for England.

Now every once in four or five days, Pocahontas with her attendants brought him so much provision that saved many of their lives, that else for all this had starved with hunger.

His relation of the plenty he had seen, especially at Werowocomoco, and of the state and bounty of Powhatan (which till that time was unknown), so revived their dead spirits (especially the love of Pocahontas) as all men's fear was abandoned.

Thus you may see what difficulties still crossed any good endeavor; and the good success of the business being thus oft brought to the very period of destruction; yet you see by what strange means God hath still delivered it.

---

21. **combustion** (kəm bus′ chən) *n.* tumult.
22. **saker falcon** small cannon.
23. **Levitical law** "He that killeth man shall surely be put to death" (Leviticus 24:17).

Reading Strategy
Breaking Down Sentences
Break down the long sentence beginning "Now in Jamestown" to interpret its meaning.

Review and Assess

Thinking About the Selection

1. **Respond:** If you faced a situation similar to Smith's, would you have returned to England at the earliest opportunity or stayed on at Jamestown? Why?

2. **(a) Recall:** Give one example of the way Smith praises his own good qualities. **(b) Infer:** What impression of Smith do you get from this account?

3. **(a) Recall:** What words does Smith use when he refers to himself? **(b) Draw Conclusions:** Why do you think he does this?

4. **(a) Interpret:** What is Smith's attitude toward the Native Americans? **(b) Analyze:** Do you think Smith's attitude changes after he gets to know them and they help him? Explain.

5. **Evaluate:** Do you think Smith's account is accurate? Why or why not?

6. **Take a Position:** Do you admire Smith? Why or why not?

from
P Of Plymouth Plantation

William Bradford

Background

In 1620, the Pilgrims made the difficult voyage to America aboard the tiny *Mayflower*. After fierce storms and the loss of lives, the Pilgrims landed near Cape Cod, Massachusetts, not in Virginia as intended. It was mid-December before they could build shelters and move ashore. Once ashore, the Pilgrims found the hardships of settling in a strange land worsened by a harsh winter. They struggled to make a new life in America.

Of Their Voyage and How They Passed the Sea; and of Their Safe Arrival at Cape Cod

After they had enjoyed fair winds and weather for a season, they were encountered many times with cross winds and met with many fierce storms with which the ship was shroudly[1] shaken, and her upper works made very leaky; and one of the main beams in the midships was bowed and cracked, which put them in some fear that the ship could not be able to perform the voyage. So some of the chief of the company, perceiving the mariners to fear the sufficiency of the ship as appeared by their mutterings, they entered into serious consultation with the master and other officers of the ship, to consider in time of the danger, and rather to return than to cast themselves into a desperate and inevitable <u>peril</u>. And truly there was great distraction and difference of opinion amongst the mariners themselves: fain

---

1. **shroudly** (shrōōd´ lē) *adv.* wickedly.

would they do what could be done for their wages' sake (being now near half the seas over) and on the other hand they were <u>loath</u> to hazard their lives too desperately. But in examining of all opinions, the master and others affirmed they knew the ship to be strong and firm under water; and for the buckling of the main beam, there was a great iron screw the passengers brought out of Holland, which would raise the beam into his place; the which being done, the carpenter and master affirmed that with a post put under it, set firm in the lower deck and otherways bound, he would make it sufficient. And as for the decks and upper works, they would caulk them as well as they could, and though with the working of the ship they would not long keep staunch, yet there would otherwise be no great danger, if they did not overpress her with sails. So they committed themselves to the will of God and resolved to proceed.

In <u>sundry</u> of these storms the winds were so fierce and the seas so high, as they could not bear a knot of sail, but were forced to hull[2] for divers days together. And in one of them, as they thus lay at hull

save boat

---

2. hull *v.* drift with the wind.

loath (lōth) *adj.* reluctant; unwilling

sundry (sun´ drē) *adj.* various; different

✔**Reading Check**
What happens to the ship in the storm?

The Coming of the Mayflower, N. C. Wyeth, from the Collection of the Metropolitan Life Insurance Company, New York City

▲ **Critical Viewing** Is this an idealized or a realistic depiction of the *Mayflower's* Atlantic crossing? Explain your decision. **[Judge; Support]**

in a mighty storm, a lusty[3] young man called John Howland, coming upon some occasion above the gratings was, with a seel[4] of the ship, thrown into sea; but it pleased God that he caught hold of the topsail halyards[5] which hung overboard and ran out at length. Yet he held his hold (though he was sundry fathoms under water) till he was hauled up by the same rope to the brim of the water, and then with a boat hook and other means got into the ship again and his life saved. And though he was something ill with it, yet he lived many years after and became a profitable member both in church and commonwealth. In all this voyage there died but one of the passengers, which was William Butten, a youth, servant to Samuel Fuller, when they drew near the coast.

But to omit other things (that I may be brief) after long beating at sea they fell with that land which is called Cape Cod; the which being made and certainly known to be it, they were not a little joyful. After some deliberation had amongst themselves and with the master of the ship, they tacked about and resolved to stand for the southward (the wind and weather being fair) to find some place about Hudson's River for their habitation. But after they had sailed that course about half the day, they fell amongst dangerous shoals and roaring breakers, and they were so far entangled therewith as they conceived themselves in great danger; and the wind shrinking upon them withal,[6] they resolved to bear up again for the Cape and thought themselves happy to get out of those dangers before night overtook them, as by God's good providence they did. And the next day they got into the Cape Harbor[7] where they rid in safety.

Being thus arrived in a good harbor, and brought safe to land, they fell upon their knees and blessed the God of Heaven who had brought them over the vast and furious ocean, and delivered them from all the perils and miseries thereof, again to set their feet on the firm and stable earth, their proper element.

The Starving Time

But that which was most sad and lamentable was, that in two or three months' time half of their company died, especially in January and February, being the depth of winter, and wanting houses and

---

3. **lusty** *adj.* strong; hearty.
4. **seel** *n.* rolling.
5. **halyards** (hal′ yərdz) *n.* ropes for raising or lowering sails.
6. **withal** (with ôl′) *adv.* also.
7. **Cape Harbor** now Provincetown Harbor.

other comforts: being infected with the scurvy[8] and other diseases which this long voyage and their inaccommodate[9] condition had brought upon them. So as there died sometimes two or three of a day in the foresaid time, that of one hundred and odd persons, scarce fifty remained. And of these, in the time of most distress, there was but six or seven sound persons who to their great commendations, be it spoken, spared no pains night or day, but with abundance of toil and hazard of their own health, fetched them wood, made them fires, dressed them meat, made their beds, washed their loathsome clothes, clothed and unclothed them. In a word, did all the homely[10] and necessary offices for them which dainty and queasy stomachs cannot endure to hear named; and all this willingly and cheerfully, without any grudging in the least, showing herein their true love unto their friends and brethren; a rare example and worthy to be remembered. Two of these seven were Mr. William Brewster, their reverend Elder, and Myles Standish, their Captain and military commander, unto whom myself and many others were much beholden in our low and sick condition. And yet the Lord so upheld these persons as in this general calamity they were not at all infected either with sickness or lameness. And what I have said of these I may say of many others who died in this general visitation,[11] and others yet living: that whilst they had health, yea, or any strength continuing, they were not wanting to any that had need of them. And I doubt not but their recompense is with the Lord.

But I may not here pass by another remarkable passage not to be forgotten. As this calamity fell among the passengers that were to be left here to plant, and were hasted ashore and made to drink water that the seamen might have the more beer, and one[12] in his sickness desiring but a small can of beer, it was answered that if he were their own father he should have none. The disease began to fall amongst them also, so as almost half of their company died before they went away, and many of their officers and lustiest men, as the boatswain, gunner, three quartermasters, the cook and others. At which the Master was something strucken and sent to the sick ashore and told the Governor he should send for beer for them that had need of it, though he drunk water homeward bound.

But now amongst his company there was far another kind of carriage[13] in this misery than amongst the passengers. For they that before had been boon[14] companions in drinking and jollity in the time of their health and welfare, began now to desert one another in this calamity, saying they would not hazard their lives for them, they

---

8. **scurvy** (skur´ vē) *n.* disease caused by vitamin C deficiency.
9. **inaccommodate** (in´ ə käm´ ə dāt´) *adj.* unfit.
10. **homely** (hōm´ lē) *adj.* domestic.
11. **visitation** *n.* affliction.
12. **one** William Bradford.
13. **carriage** *n.* behavior.
14. **boon** *adj.* close.

recompense (rek´ əm pens´) *n.* reward; repayment

Literary Analysis
Narrative Accounts
Do you think Bradford's illness would have been included in a secondhand narrative account? Explain.

✔**Reading Check**
What did people like William Brewster and Miles Standish do to earn Bradford's respect?

should be infected by coming to help them in their cabins; and so, after they came to lie by it, would do little or nothing for them but, "if they died, let them die." But such of the passengers as were yet aboard showed them what mercy they could which made some of their hearts relent, as the boatswain (and some others) who was a proud young man and would often curse and scoff at the passengers. But when he grew weak, they had compassion on him and helped him; then he confessed he did not deserve it at their hands, he had abused them in word and deed. "Oh!" (saith he) "you, I now see, show your love like Christians indeed one to another, but we let one another lie and die like dogs." Another lay cursing his wife, saying if it had not been for her he had never come this unlucky voyage, and anon cursing his fellows, saying he had done this and that for some of them; he had spent so much and so much amongst them, and they were now weary of him and did not help him, having need. Another gave his companion all he had, if he died, to help him in his weakness; he went and got a little spice and made him a mess[15] of meat once or twice. And because he died not so soon as he expected, he went amongst his fellows and swore the rogue would cozen[16] him, he would see him choked before he made him any more meat; and yet the poor fellow died before morning.

Indian Relations

All this while the Indians came skulking about them, and would sometimes show themselves aloof off, but when any approached near them, they would run away; and once they stole away their tools where they had been at work and were gone to dinner. But about the sixteenth of March, a certain Indian came boldly amongst them and spoke to them in broken English, which they could well understand but marveled at it. At length they understood by discourse with him, that he was not of these parts, but belonged to the eastern parts where some English ships came to fish, with whom he was acquainted and could name sundry of them by their names, amongst whom he had got his language. He became profitable to them in acquainting them with many things concerning the state of the country in the east parts where he lived, which was afterwards profitable unto them; as also of the people here, of their names, number and strength, of their situation and distance from this place, and who was chief amongst them. His name was Samoset. He told them also of another Indian whose name was Squanto, a native of this place, who had been in England and could speak better English than himself.

---

15. **mess** *n.* meal.
16. **cozen** (kuz′ ən) *v.* cheat.

Literary Analysis
Narrative Accounts
What is revealed here about the Pilgrims' religious beliefs?

Being, after some time of entertainment and gifts dismissed, a while after he came again, and five more with him, and they brought again all the tools that were stolen away before, and made way for the coming of their great Sachem,[17] called Massasoit. Who, about four or five days after, came with the chief of his friends and other attendance, with the aforesaid Squanto. With whom, after friendly entertainment and some gifts given him, they made a peace with him (which hath now continued this twenty-four years) in these terms:

1. That neither he nor any of his should injure or do hurt to any of their people.

---

17. Sachem (sā´ chəm) Chief.

▲ **Critical Viewing**
What can you learn about the lifestyle at Plymouth Plantation from this photograph of an authentic re-creation of the settlement? **[Infer]**

☑**Reading Check**

Who is Samoset, and how do the Pilgrims meet him?

2. That if any of his did hurt to any of theirs, he should send the offender, that they might punish him.

3. That if anything were taken away from any of theirs, he should cause it to be restored; and they should do the like to his.

4. If any did unjustly war against him, they would aid him; if any did war against them, he should aid them.

5. He should send to his neighbors confederates to certify them of this, that they might not wrong them, but might be likewise comprised in the conditions of peace.

6. That when their men came to them, they should leave their bows and arrows behind them.

After these things he returned to his place called Sowams, some 40 miles from this place, but Squanto continued with them and was their interpreter and was a special instrument sent of God for their good beyond their expectation. He directed them how to set their corn, where to take fish, and to procure other commodities, and was also their pilot to bring them to unknown places for their profit, and never left them till he died.

Literary Analysis
Narrative Accounts
What does Bradford reveal about his religious beliefs in this description of Squanto as a "special instrument"?

Review and Assess

Thinking About the Selection

1. **Respond:** If you had been making the journey on the *Mayflower*, what would you have done to prepare for life in America?

2. **(a) Recall:** What were some of the hardships the Pilgrims faced during their trip across the Atlantic and their first winter at Plymouth? **(b) Interpret:** What do their troubles suggest about the climate and landscape of Plymouth?

3. **(a) Recall:** How do the Pilgrims explain Squanto's role in their experience? **(b) Interpret:** What does this explanation suggest about the Pilgrims' religious convictions?

4. **(a) Draw Conclusions:** What do you think is the message that Bradford tries to convey in this narrative? **(b) Apply:** How might the message have meaning for people today?

5. **Hypothesize:** In what ways might this account have been different if the Pilgrims had successfully settled farther south?

6. **Evaluate:** How has this account changed your impression of the Pilgrims? Explain.

Review and Assess

Literary Analysis

Narrative Accounts

1. Use a chart like the one shown to find examples of the key characteristics of **narrative accounts** in the selections.

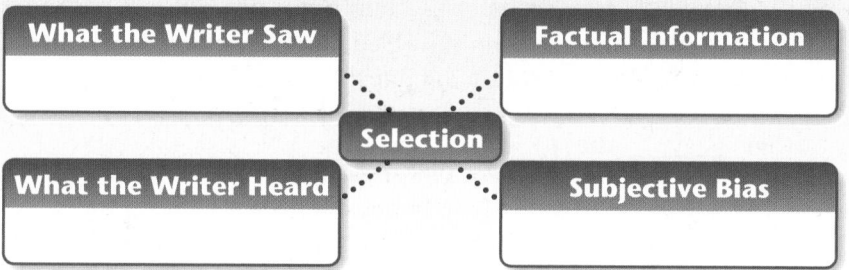

What the Writer Saw	Factual Information

Selection

What the Writer Heard	Subjective Bias

2. (a) What do you think Smith's purpose was in writing his narrative? (b) In what way was Bradford's purpose different?

Comparing Literary Works

3. Compare and contrast the relationship Smith and the Pilgrims had with the Native Americans.

4. In what way might political concerns have played a part in shaping John Smith's account of the Jamestown Colony's early days?

5. How might the Puritans' religious beliefs have influenced Bradford's account of the first experiences of the Massachusetts settlers?

6. (a) In what ways do the authors' presentations of events and the impressions they convey differ? (b) How do these differences reflect the purpose of each group's settlement?

7. Which account seems more reliable to you? Explain.

Reading Strategy

Breaking Down Sentences

8. Scan the narratives for three sentences that you found particularly challenging to interpret. Separating the complex language from the essential parts, analyze the sentences. Then, write the meaning of the sentences as you understand them.

Extend Understanding

9. **Social Studies Connection:** Do you feel that the changing attitudes of the settlers and the Native Americans reflect typical experiences with newcomers? Why or why not?

Integrate Language Skills

Vocabulary Development Lesson

Word Analysis: Related Forms of *Peril*

The word *peril* comes from the Latin word *periculum*, which means "danger." Using your knowledge of the base word, fill in each blank with the word that best completes the sentence.

a. perilous   **b.** perilously   **c.** imperiled

1. Undertaking the risky voyage ___?___ the Pilgrims' lives.
2. The ship tossed ___?___ in the waves.
3. Building a new home in the wilderness was ___?___ as well.

Spelling Strategy

When you add *-ed* to a word that ends in the letters *-ify*, change the *y* to *i* before adding the suffix. For example, *mollify* becomes *mollified*. Write sentences using the past tense of each word.

1. pacify   2. modify   3. testify

Concept Development: Antonyms and Synonyms

Antonyms are words that have opposite meanings. **Synonyms** are words that have similar meanings. Decide whether the words in each of following pairs are antonyms or synonyms. Write A for *Antonym* or S for *Synonym*.

1. pilfer, donate
2. palisades, fences
3. conceits, fantasies
4. mollified, angered
5. peril, safety
6. loath, willing
7. sundry, single
8. recompense, reward

Grammar and Style Lesson

Singular and Plural Possessive Nouns

The **possessive** form of nouns indicates kinship and ownership. Add an apostrophe and *-s* to form the **possessive singular** of most nouns. Add an apostrophe to form the **possessive of plural** nouns that end in *-s* or *-es*.

> **Singular:** The *passenger's* spirits were low.
>
> **Plural:** The *passengers'* spirits were low.

Do not use an apostrophe for simple plurals that do not show possession. Do not add an extra *s* for the possessive of plural nouns ending in *-s*.

Practice Rewrite this paragraph, correcting any mistakes in italicized plurals or possessives.

> Much to *Bradfords* amazement, Samoset spoke to the *Pilgrims* in broken English. Samoset convinced his fellow *Indians'* to return the *settler's* tools. He persuaded Massasoit to pay his *respects* to the *Pilgrims* and introduced them to one of his *friend's*, Squanto.

Writing Application Write a paragraph about the Pilgrims' arrival in Plymouth, using at least five plural and possessive nouns.

WG Prentice Hall Writing and Grammar Connection: Chapter 27, Section 6

Writing Lesson

Comparison of Narratives

These narratives leave readers with the impression that Smith and Bradford held distinctly different outlooks on life. Write a comparison of these firsthand accounts.

Prewriting Review the two narratives, noting each author's style, purpose, and objectivity. To help you gather and organize details, use a Venn diagram like the one shown.

Model: Gathering Details

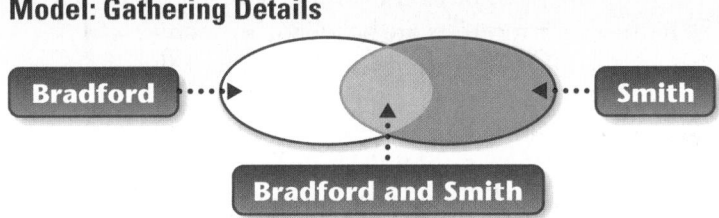

Drafting To keep your ideas clear for readers, choose a method of organization. You might discuss each aspect of your subjects in turn. For example, you could discuss Smith's tone and immediately contrast it with Bradford's tone. Alternatively, you might discuss all the qualities of one subject and then all the qualities of the other.

Revising To clarify your comparison and contrast, consider transitions, such as *similarly* and *equally, to compare* and *in contrast,* and *instead* and *to contrast.* Be sure your conclusion effectively reinforces your ideas.

Prentice Hall Writing and Grammar Connection: Chapter 9, Section 3

Extension Activities

Listening and Speaking As Samoset, deliver a **persuasive speech** to make the case for fostering peace between the settlers and your tribe. Make your speech dramatic and convincing. To prepare, consider these questions:

- What personal experiences can you relate?
- What events prove your point?
- What are your greatest concerns?

Organize and review your notes before presenting your speech to your class.

Research and Technology Many Pilgrims suffered from scurvy, a disease caused by a diet lacking in vitamin C. Research to learn about the foods the colonists ate and the crops they planted. Check the Internet or the library for colonial recipes. Then, plan a historically accurate **menu** for a typical day in the life of an early American colonist.

 ***Take It to the Net*** www.phschool.com

Go online for an additional research activity using the Internet.

READING INFORMATIONAL MATERIALS

Web Sites

About Web Sites

A **Web site** is a collection of Web pages—text and graphics on a topic, accessible over the Internet through browser software. Each page has its own URL, or "address." Web sites feature underlined words that serve as links to other sites or pages. By clicking on these words, you can find more information.

The Web can be a wonderful tool. You can perform business transactions on the Web—for example, trading stocks or buying clothing. The Web also offers great ways to learn. Whether your interests are academic or recreational, you probably can locate several Web sites devoted to each of them.

Reading Strategy

Locating Appropriate Information

To get the most out of Internet research, learn how to locate appropriate information. Familiarize yourself with search engines on the Web. These services will list any page on the Web that contains text matching the search term that you type in. To use a search engine effectively, you need to select search terms with care. For instance, if you are looking for information on the Puritans who settled in America, you might use the word *Pilgrim*. Too broad a term, such as *colony*, will produce a list that is unmanageably long and cluttered with irrelevant listings, such as pages on space colonies.

Even a focused search term may yield irrelevant results. To further narrow down the list of sites, review the name of the sponsor that is listed on the search engine list, along with the brief excerpt from the site. You can eliminate sites in languages you do not speak, sites on unrelated topics, and, depending on your requirements, personal home pages.

When you arrive at a Web site, you usually will find that it offers many features. The box at right lists just a few of these elements. Not every feature will be appropriate to your search, so keep your purpose in mind as you explore.

Elements of Web Sites

- **Hotspotted text**, **buttons**, and other **navigation elements** help you move around the site quickly. Click on any area of the page over which your cursor changes to a hand, and you will be brought to a linked page.

- **A SEARCH function** helps you locate information anywhere on the site, using search terms.

- **Photos, videos, and audio clips** enrich many sites, providing audiovisual information or entertainment. You may need to download additional software to use these resources.

- **Links** connect you to related Web sites.

- **Contact information** tells you who sponsored the site. An e-mail address to which you may send questions or comments may be included.

Home Page

A home page is the "front door" of a Web site. It provides an overview of the site's information and features. From this home page of the Plimoth Plantation Web site, a user can learn about the museum in Plymouth, Massachusetts, that is devoted to the colonial history of the town. Using the home page, visitors can "navigate," or move to other pages within the site.

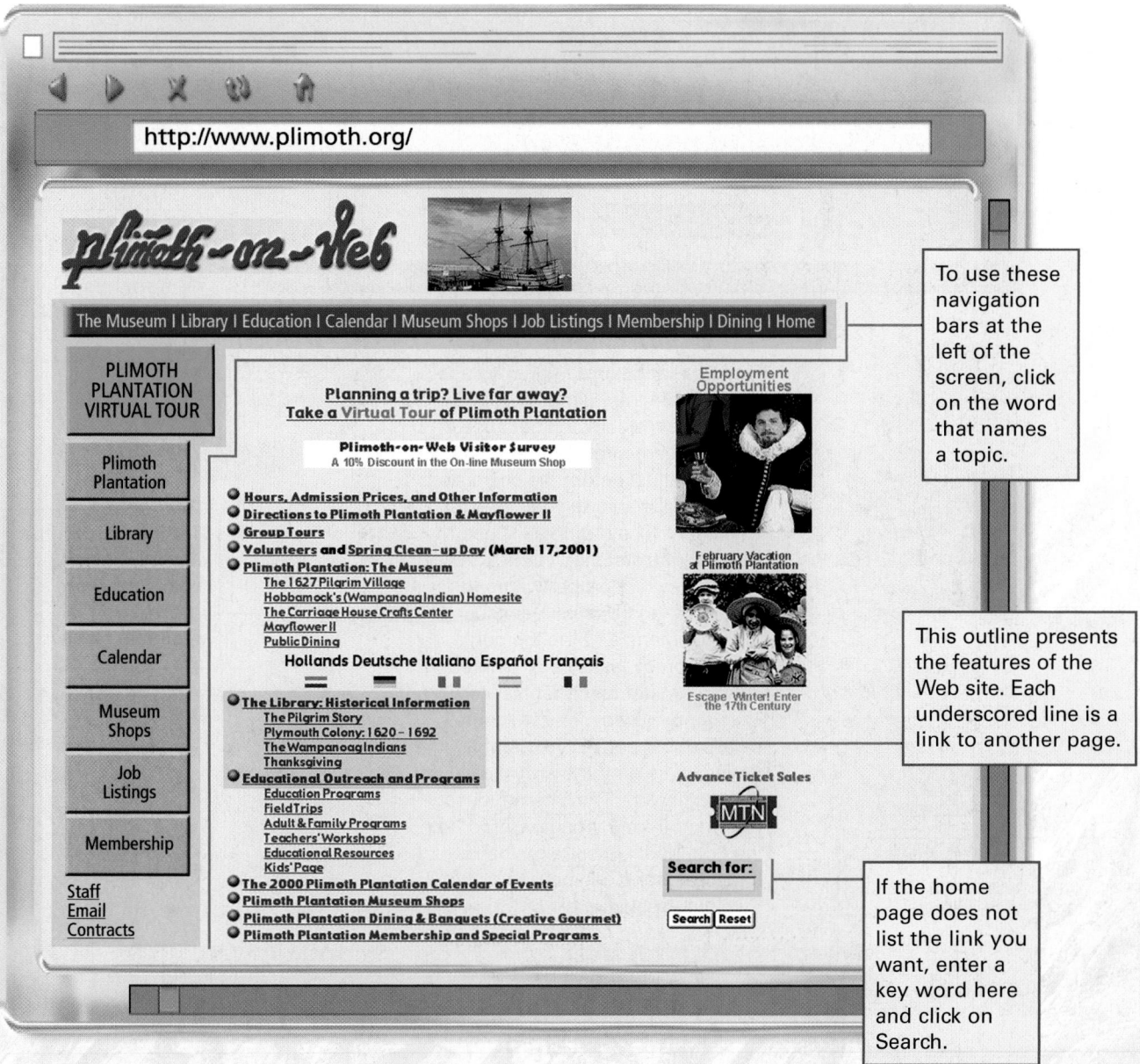

http://www.plimoth.org/

plimoth-on-web

The Museum | Library | Education | Calendar | Museum Shops | Job Listings | Membership | Dining | Home

PLIMOTH PLANTATION VIRTUAL TOUR

Plimoth Plantation

Library

Education

Calendar

Museum Shops

Job Listings

Membership

Staff
Email
Contracts

Planning a trip? Live far away?
Take a Virtual Tour of Plimoth Plantation

Plimoth-on-Web Visitor Survey
A 10% Discount in the On-line Museum Shop

- **Hours, Admission Prices, and Other Information**
- **Directions to Plimoth Plantation & Mayflower II**
- **Group Tours**
- **Volunteers and Spring Clean-up Day (March 17, 2001)**
- **Plimoth Plantation: The Museum**
  - The 1627 Pilgrim Village
  - Hobbamock's (Wampanoag Indian) Homesite
  - The Carriage House Crafts Center
  - Mayflower II
  - Public Dining

Hollands Deutsche Italiano Español Français

- **The Library: Historical Information**
  - The Pilgrim Story
  - Plymouth Colony: 1620–1692
  - The Wampanoag Indians
  - Thanksgiving
- **Educational Outreach and Programs**
  - Education Programs
  - Field Trips
  - Adult & Family Programs
  - Teachers' Workshops
  - Educational Resources
  - Kids' Page
- **The 2000 Plimoth Plantation Calendar of Events**
- **Plimoth Plantation Museum Shops**
- **Plimoth Plantation Dining & Banquets (Creative Gourmet)**
- **Plimoth Plantation Membership and Special Programs**

Employment Opportunities

February Vacation at Plimoth Plantation

Escape Winter! Enter the 17th Century

Advance Ticket Sales

MTN

Search for:

Search   Reset

To use these navigation bars at the left of the screen, click on the word that names a topic.

This outline presents the features of the Web site. Each underscored line is a link to another page.

If the home page does not list the link you want, enter a key word here and click on Search.

Interior Page

Various pages within a Web site may offer passages of text, photographs, audio and video clips, and other related information. The page shown here presents an essay about the re-created village at Plimoth.

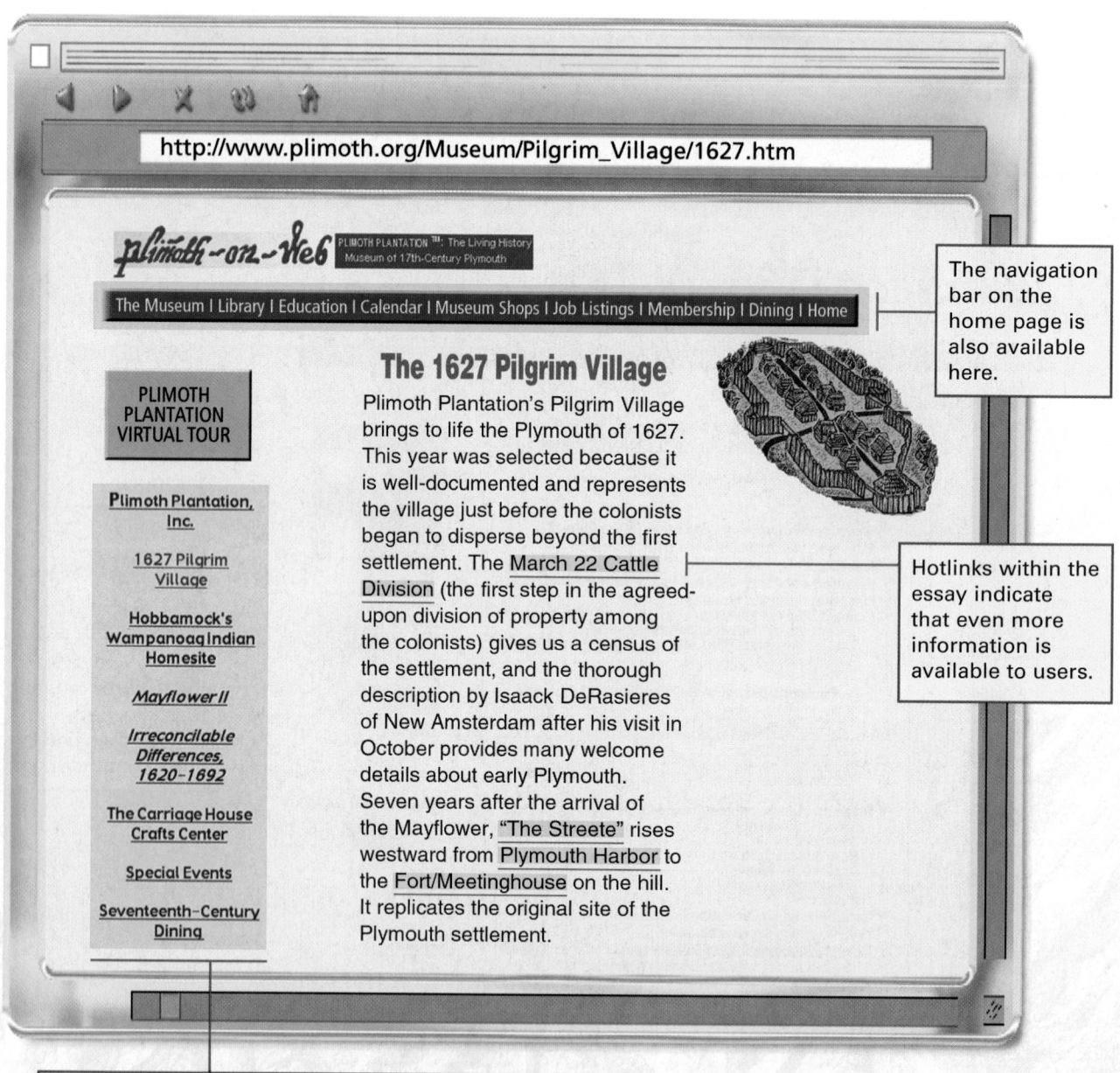

http://www.plimoth.org/Museum/Pilgrim_Village/1627.htm

plimoth~on~web

PLIMOTH PLANTATION ™: The Living History Museum of 17th-Century Plymouth

The Museum | Library | Education | Calendar | Museum Shops | Job Listings | Membership | Dining | Home

PLIMOTH PLANTATION VIRTUAL TOUR

Plimoth Plantation, Inc.

1627 Pilgrim Village

Hobbamock's Wampanoag Indian Homesite

Mayflower II

Irreconcilable Differences, 1620-1692

The Carriage House Crafts Center

Special Events

Seventeenth-Century Dining

The 1627 Pilgrim Village

Plimoth Plantation's Pilgrim Village brings to life the Plymouth of 1627. This year was selected because it is well-documented and represents the village just before the colonists began to disperse beyond the first settlement. The March 22 Cattle Division (the first step in the agreed-upon division of property among the colonists) gives us a census of the settlement, and the thorough description by Isaack DeRasieres of New Amsterdam after his visit in October provides many welcome details about early Plymouth. Seven years after the arrival of the Mayflower, "The Streete" rises westward from Plymouth Harbor to the Fort/Meetinghouse on the hill. It replicates the original site of the Plymouth settlement.

The navigation bar on the home page is also available here.

Hotlinks within the essay indicate that even more information is available to users.

This list of topics on the left margin uses a design similar to the one on the home page, but the content is different.

Check Your Comprehension

1. From the home page, what tool can you use to find Plimoth Plantation's calendar of events without knowing the URL for that page?
2. In the essay, why are the words *Plymouth Harbor* and *Fort / Meeting House* underlined and printed in blue?

Applying the Reading Strategy

Locating Appropriate Information

3. Using a chart like the one shown, indicate where you would expect to find the answers to each question—on the home page, the interior page, or in material found through a link from one of those pages.

Question	Location
When will the Holiday Fair at Plimouth be held?	
Do any early documents contain a census of the village?	
Why did the Pilgrims come to North America?	
What purpose or purposes did the Meetinghouse serve?	

Activity

Evaluating Information Online

Locate and explore another Web site relating to Plymouth Colony or the Pilgrims. Then, write an evaluation. Use these questions to guide you:

- What is the purpose of the site?
- Who are the site authors and what are the credentials of its sponsor? (Was the site developed by a university? A historical society? A college student?)
- What information and features does the site offer?
- Does the design complement the site's purpose and contents?

Compile your evaluation with those that classmates have completed. Together, prepare an annotated list of sites that you would recommend.

Contrasting Informational Materials

Web Sites and Other Reference Sources

What is the value of visiting a site like the one pictured in this feature instead of reading a book about Plymouth Colony? Jot down your ideas about the advantages and disadvantages of Web sites and more traditional reference sources, such as encyclopedias, atlases, and books. Then, write a conclusion based on your notes.

The Pioneer Spirit

The early American settlers struggled through rough seas, sickness, and starvation to carve out a home in a new land. The hunger for uncharted territory drove them to sail across the ocean and set foot on a forbidding continent. They were risking their lives for such things as religious freedom, economic opportunity, and political autonomy. That spirit kept Americans going for three more centuries as pioneers continued westward, blazing trails across the continent.

The New Pioneers In the new millennium, the frontier has given way to a network of highways, airports, and shopping malls. When the frontier disappeared, the pioneer spirit had nowhere to go but up. In the twentieth century, this spirit pushed Americans into tiny, cramped capsules. The new pioneers defied gravity and leapt upward into space. Tom Wolfe's book *The Right Stuff* documents this new American exploration.

Narrative Accounts John Smith, William Bradford, and Tom Wolfe all wrote historical narrative accounts—factual reports of notable events. You will notice clear differences between Wolfe's twentieth-century account of John Glenn's brief zooms around the planet and Smith's and Bradford's seventeenth-century chronicles of the colonists' struggles to survive. One obvious difference is in the style—the shift from the formal religious vocabulary of seventeenth-century men of authority to the more casual, slang-filled language of a twentieth-century journalist.

from
The Right Stuff

Tom Wolfe

Here he is!—within twenty seconds of lift-off, and the only strange thing is how little adrenaline[1] is pumping when the moment comes . . . He can hear the rumble of the Atlas engines building up down there below his back. All the same, it isn't terribly loud. The huge squat rocket shakes a bit and struggles to overcome its own weight. It all happens very slowly in the first few seconds, like an extremely heavy elevator rising. They've lit the candle and there's no turning back, and yet there's no surge inside him. His pulse rises only to 110, no more than the minimum rate you should have if you have to deal with a sudden emergency. How strange that it should be this way! He has been more wound up for a takeoff in an F-102.[2]

"The clock is operating," he said, "We're underway."

It was all very smooth, much smoother than the centrifuge[3] . . . just as Shepard and Grissom said it would be. He had gone through the same g-forces[4] so many times . . . he hardly noticed them as they built up. It would have bothered him much more if they had been less. Nothing novel! No excitement, please! It took thirteen seconds for the huge rocket to reach

---

1. **adrenaline** (ə dren´ ə lin´) *n.* stress-related hormone secreted by the adrenal gland. When released, it increases heartbeat and raises blood pressure.
2. **F-102** U.S. Air Force fighter plane.
3. **centrifuge** (sen´ trə fyoō j´) *n.* a machine using force to pull a rotating object outward from a center. This type of machine was used to train the astronauts for the effects of spaceflight.
4. **g-forces** *n.* units measuring inertial pressure on a body during rapid acceleration. Units represent multiples of the acceleration of gravity.

◀ **Critical Viewing**
In what ways might the astronauts' impressions of a liftoff differ from the views of spectators?
[Hypothesize]

transonic speed. The vibrations started. It was just as Shepard and Grissom said: it was much gentler than the centrifuge. He was still lying flat on his back, and the g-forces drove him deeper and deeper into the seat, but it all felt so familiar. He barely noticed it. He kept his eyes on the instrument panel the whole time . . . All quite normal, every little needle and switch in the right place . . . No <u>malevolent</u> instructor feeding *Abort* problems into the loop . . . As the rocket entered the transonic zone, the vibration became intense. The vibrations all but <u>obliterated</u> the roar of the engines. He was entering the area of "*max q*," maximum aerodynamic pressure, in which the pressure of the shaft of the Atlas forcing its way through the atmosphere at supersonic speed would reach almost a thousand pounds per square foot. Through the cockpit window he could see the sky turning black. Almost 5 g's were driving him back into his seat. And yet . . . *easier than the centrifuge* . . . All at once he was through *max q*, as if through a turbulent strait, and the <u>trajectory</u> was smooth and he was supersonic and the rumble of the rocket engines was more muffled than ever and he could hear all the little fans and recorders and the busy little kitchen, the humming little shop . . . . The pressure on his chest reached 6 g's. The rocket pitched down. For the first time he could see clouds and the horizon. In a moment—*there it was*—the Atlas rocket's two booster engines shut down and were <u>jettisoned</u> from the side of the shaft and his body was slammed forward, as if he were screeching to a halt, and the g-forces suddenly dropped to 1.25, almost as if he were on earth and not accelerating at all, but the central sustainer engine and two smaller engines were still driving him up through the atmosphere . . . A flash of white smoke went up past the window. . . . *No! The escape tower was firing early—but the* JETTISON TOWER *light wasn't on!* . . . He didn't see the tower go . . . Wait a minute . . . There went the tower, on schedule . . . The JETTISON TOWER light came on green . . . The smoke must have been from the booster rockets as they left the shaft . . . The rocket pitched back up . . . going straight up . . . The sky was very black now . . . The g-forces began pushing him back into his seat again . . . 3 g's . . . 4 g's . . . 5 g's . . . Soon he would be forty miles up . . . the last critical moment of powered flight, as the capsule separated from the rocket and went into its orbital trajectory . . . or didn't . . . *Hey!* . . . All at once the whole capsule was whipping up and down, as if it were tied to the end of a diving board, a springboard. The g-forces built up and the capsule whipped up and down. Yet no sooner had it begun than Glenn knew what it was. The weight of the rocket on the launch pad had been 260,000 pounds, practically all of it rocket fuel, the liquid oxygen. This was being consumed at such a furious rate, about one ton per second, that the rocket was becoming merely a skeleton with a thin skin of metal stretched over it, a tube so long and light that it was flexing. The g-forces reached six and then he was weightless, just like that. The sudden release made him feel as if he were tumbling head over heels, as if he had been catapulted off the end of that same

malevolent (mə lev′ ə lənt) *adj.* mean-spirited; showing ill will

obliterated (ə blit′ ər āt′ id) *v.* blotted out; destroyed

trajectory (trə jek′ tə rē) *n.* the curved path of an object hurtling through space

jettisoned (jet′ ə sənd) *v.* thrown overboard to lighten the weight of a ship

▶ **Critical Viewing**
President John F. Kennedy inspects the Friendship 7 capsule in 1962. What effect would a president's interest in the space program have on its success? [Analyze Cause and Effect]

springboard and was falling through the air doing forward rolls. But he had felt this same thing on the centrifuge when they ran the g-forces up to seven and then suddenly cut the speed. At the same moment, right on schedule . . . a loud report . . . the posigrade rockets fired, throwing the capsule free of the rocket shaft . . . the capsule began its automatic turnabout, and all the proper green lights went on in front of him, and he knew he was "through the gate," as they said.

"Zero-g and I feel fine," he said. "Capsule is turning around . . ."

Glenn knew he was weightless. From the instrument readings and through sheer logic he knew it, but he couldn't feel it, just as Shepard and Grissom had never felt it. The turnaround brought him up to a sitting position, vertical to the earth, and that was the way he felt. He was sitting in a chair, upright, in a very tiny cramped quiet little cubicle 125 miles above the earth, a little metal closet, silent except for the humming of its electrical system, the inverters, the gyros, the cameras, the radio . . . *the radio* . . . He had been specifically instructed to violate the Fighter Jock code of No Chatter. He was supposed to radio back every sight, every sensation, and otherwise give the taxpayers the juicy stuff they wanted to hear. Glenn, more than any of the others, was fully capable of doing the job. Yet it was an awkward thing. It seemed unnatural.

"Oh!" he said. "That view is tremendous!"

Well, it was a start. In fact, the view was not particularly extraordinary. It was extraordinary that he was up here in orbit about the earth. He could see the exhausted Atlas rocket following him. It was tumbling end over end from the force of the small rockets throwing the capsule free of it.

He could hear Alan Shepard, who was serving as capcom[5] in the Mercury Control Center at the Cape. His voice came in very clearly. He was saying, "You have a go, at least seven orbits."

"Roger," said Glenn. "Understand Go for at least seven orbits . . . This is *Friendship 7*. Can see clear back, a big cloud pattern way back across toward the Cape. Beautiful sight."

---

5. **capcom** (kap′ käm) *n. jargon* capsule communicator; person speaking directly to astronaut.

Connecting Literature Past and Present

1. In what ways is John Glenn's experience similar to that of the Europeans who crossed the Atlantic Ocean and settled in America?

2. (a) In what ways do twentieth-century advances make Glenn's experience different from that of the colonists? (b) Do you think these advances enhance Glenn's experience or diminish it? Why?

3. What takes more courage: riding in a capsule into space like the astronauts or making a new life in an uncharted land like the early settlers? Why?

Tom Wolfe

(b. 1930)
Born in a Virginia far different from the one that John Smith knew, Tom Wolfe began his writing career working as a reporter and Latin America correspondent for the *Washington Post*. He then turned to magazine writing and eventually published essays, articles, and, later, full-length books that focused on the contemporary American scene. He described elements of popular culture in *The Kandy-Kolored Tangerine Flake Streamline Baby* and dissected the art world in *The Painted Word*. Many critics regard *The Right Stuff*, an account of the Mercury space program, as Wolfe's best work.

The Puritan Influence

Pilgrims Going to Church (detail)
George Henry Boughton
© Collection of The New York Historical Society

Prepare to Read

Huswifery ◆ To My Dear and Loving Husband

Edward Taylor (1642–1729)

Puritanism was a religious reform movement that began in England in the sixteenth century. The Puritans sought to reform the Church of England, and to reshape English society according to their beliefs. These efforts led to both civil strife, and to government persecution of the Puritans. In response, many Puritans, including Edward Taylor, fled to the American colonies.

Before his emigration to America, Edward Taylor worked as a teacher in England. Upon arriving in Boston in 1668, Taylor entered Harvard College, graduating in 1671. He accepted the position of minister and physician in the small farming community of Westfield, Massachusetts, and then walked more than one hundred miles, much of it through snow, to his new home.

Harsh Life in a New World Life in Westfield was filled with hardships. Fierce battles between the Native Americans and the colonists left the community in constant fear. Taylor also experienced many personal tragedies. Five of his eight children died in infancy; then, his wife died while still a young woman. He remarried and had five or six more children. (Biographers differ on the exact number.)

Edward Taylor is now generally regarded as the best of the colonial poets. Yet, because Taylor thought of his poetry as a form of personal worship, he allowed only two stanzas to be published during his lifetime. In 1833, one of his descendants gave Taylor's writings to Yale University, and, in 1939, *The Poetical Works of Edward Taylor* was published. Most of Taylor's poetry, including "Huswifery," uses extravagant comparisons, intellectual wit, and subtle argument to explore religious faith and affection.

Anne Bradstreet (1612–1672)

Anne Bradstreet and her husband, Simon, arrived in the Massachusetts Bay Colony in 1630, when she was only eighteen. Armed with the convictions of her Puritan upbringing, she left behind her hometown of Northampton, England, to start afresh in America. It was not an easy life for Bradstreet, who raised eight children and faced many hardships.

A Private Writer Made Public Despite the difficulties she endured, Bradstreet was able to devote her spare moments to the very "unladylike" occupation of writing. She wrote for herself, not for publication. Nevertheless, in 1650, John Woodbridge, her brother-in-law, arranged for the publication in England of a collection of her scholarly poems, *The Tenth Muse Lately Sprung Up in America, By a Gentlewoman of Those Parts*. Generally considered to be the first collection of original poetry written in colonial America, the book examined the rights of women to learn and express themselves. Bradstreet's later poems, such as "To My Dear and Loving Husband," are more personal, expressing her feelings about the joys and difficulties of everyday Puritan life. In one, she wrote about her thoughts before giving birth. In another, she wrote about the death of a grandchild.

Bradstreet's poetry reflects the Puritans' knowledge of the stories and language of the Bible, as well as their concern for the relationship between earthly and heavenly life. Her work also exhibits some of the characteristics of the French and English poetry of her day.

In 1956, the poet John Berryman wrote "Homage to Mistress Bradstreet," a long poem that pays tribute to this first American poet.

Preview

Connecting to the Literature

Unlike most of us today, the Puritans had few possessions, dressed uniformly, and frowned on creative expression. Because they left so few personal belongings behind, they remain a mystery. These poems provide us with glimpses into the poets' inner lives and show the universal emotions individual Puritans experienced within the confines of their culture.

Literary Analysis

The Puritan Plain Style

The Puritans' writing style reflected the plain style of their lives—spare, simple, and straightforward. The **Puritan Plain Style** is characterized by short words, direct statements, and references to ordinary, everyday objects. Puritans believed that poetry should serve God by clearly expressing only useful or religious ideas. Poetry appealing to the senses or emotions was viewed as dangerous.

Comparing Literary Works

The poems by Taylor and Bradstreet are both expressions of devotion, but they are very different in the way they address the beloved. Taylor uses an **apostrophe**—a figure of speech in which a speaker directly addresses an absent person or a personified object, quality, or idea. For example:

Line 1: Make me, O Lord, Thy spinning wheel complete.

Line 8: And make Thy holy spirit, Lord, wind quills:

By contrast, the title of Bradstreet's poem indicates that the speaker is addressing her husband, but the poem contains no apostrophes. As you read, look for ways in which each poem reflects a distinct relationship between the speaker and his or her object of affection.

Reading Strategy

Paraphrasing

Although these poems capture the simplicity of Puritan life, they are not necessarily simple to understand. To help you better absorb the meaning of each poem, take time to **paraphrase,** or restate in your own words, the ideas expressed by each poet. Because it helps to clarify meaning, paraphrasing will allow you to make accurate statements about each poet's ideas. Use a chart like the one shown to organize your paraphrases.

Vocabulary Development

recompense (rek´ əm pens´) *n.* repayment; something given or done in return for something else (p. 102)

manifold (man´ ə fōld´) *adv.* in many ways (p. 102)

persevere (pʉr´ sə vir´) *v.* persist; be steadfast in purpose (p. 102)

Poet's Version

My love is such that rivers cannot quench, Nor ought but love from thee, give recompense.

Restatement

My love is so strong that rivers cannot relieve its thirst; only your love will satisfy me.

Huswifery

Edward Taylor

Crewel work chair seat cover, Gift of Samuel Bradstreet, Museum of Fine Arts, Boston

▲ **Critical Viewing** What makes this sampler an effective illustration to accompany Taylor's poem? **[Make a Judgment]**

Background

Edward Taylor's work was generally unknown during his lifetime. Some believe that he chose not to publish his poems because their joyousness and delight in sensory experience ran counter to Puritan attitudes that poetry be for moral instruction only. The discovery in the 1930s of a stash of Taylor's poetry, including the poem that appears here, is considered one of the major literary finds of the twentieth century.

Although there were many writers of verse in Puritan times, few were women. Anne Bradstreet knew that writing was considered an unacceptable activity for women, but she persevered nonetheless, writing while children slept or in moments between household chores.

Make me, O Lord, Thy spinning wheel complete.
Thy holy word my distaff[1] make for me.
Make mine affections[2] Thy swift flyers[3] neat
And make my soul Thy holy spoole to be.
5   My conversation make to be Thy reel
And reel the yarn thereon spun of Thy wheel.

Make me Thy loom then, knit therein this twine:
And make Thy holy spirit, Lord, wind quills:[4]
Then weave the web Thyself. The yarn is fine.
10   Thine ordinances[5] make my fulling mills.[6]
Then dye the same in heavenly colors choice.
All pinked[7] with varnished flowers of paradise.

Then clothe therewith mine understanding, will,
Affections, judgment, conscience, memory
15   My words, and actions, that their shine may fill
My ways with glory and Thee glorify.
Then mine apparel shall display before Ye
That I am clothed in holy robes for glory.

Literary Analysis
Puritan Plain Style In what sense are the words *spinning wheel, distaff, flyers, spoole, reel,* and *yarn* symbolic of the Puritan Plain Style?

---

1. **distaff** (dis´ taf´) *n.* staff on which flax or wool is wound for use in spinning.
2. **affections** (ə fek´ shənz) *n.* emotions.
3. **flyers** *n.* part of a spinning wheel that twists fibers into yarn.
4. **quills** *n.* weaver's spindles or bobbins.
5. **ordinances** (ôrd´ nəns əz) *n.* sacraments or religious rites.
6. **fulling mills** *n.* machines that shrink and thicken cloth to the texture of felt.
7. **pinked** *v.* decorated.

Review and Assess

Thinking About the Selection

1. **Respond:** *Huswifery* means "housekeeping." Given the title, were you surprised by the content of this poem? Explain.

2. **(a) Recall:** To what household objects and activities is the speaker compared in the first two stanzas? **(b) Analyze:** How do the images in the first two stanzas contribute to the idea of being "clothed in holy robes for glory," stated in the third stanza?

3. **(a) Interpret:** What images in this poem may have contradicted the Puritan requirement that clothing be dark and undecorated? **(b) Deduce:** What do these images suggest about the speaker's feelings about God?

4. **(a) Interpret:** What details in the final two lines convey Taylor's belief that religious grace comes as a gift from God? **(b) Analyze:** What seems to be the poem's overall purpose?

5. **Synthesize:** What household task or process might Taylor describe if he were writing this poem today?

To My Dear and Loving Husband

Anne Bradstreet

If ever two were one, then surely we.
If ever man were lov'd by wife, then thee;
If ever wife was happy in a man,
Compare with me ye women if you can.

5   I prize thy love more than whole mines of gold,
Or all the riches that the East doth hold.
My love is such that rivers cannot quench,
Nor ought[1] but love from thee, give <u>recompense</u>.
Thy love is such I can no way repay,

10   The heavens reward thee <u>manifold</u>, I pray.
Then while we live, in love let's so <u>persevere</u>,[2]
That when we live no more, we may live ever.

---

1. **ought** (ôt) *n.* anything whatever.
2. **persevere** pronounced *per se´ ver* in the seventeenth century, and thus rhymed with the word ever.

Reading Strategy
Paraphrasing How would you paraphrase these first two lines?

recompense (rek´ əm pens´) *n.* repayment; something given or done in return for something else

manifold (man´ ə fōld´) *adv.* in many ways

persevere (pur´ sə vir´) *v.* persist; be steadfast in purpose

Review and Assess

Thinking About the Selection

1. **Respond:** What is your image of Anne Bradstreet after reading this poem? Does she fit your concept of a Puritan? Explain.

2. **(a) Recall:** Note where Bradstreet uses repetition in the first stanza. **(b) Analyze:** How does her use of repetition suggest a growing emotional intensity?

3. **(a) Recall:** What does the speaker value more than "whole mines of gold"? **(b) Distinguish:** What other images suggest the richness and abundance of the love the speaker and her husband share?

4. **(a) Analyze:** What is the apparent contradiction in the last two lines? **(b) Draw Conclusions:** What does the last stanza reveal about Puritan beliefs in the afterlife?

5. **Apply:** Do you think personal devotion is as much esteemed today as it was in Bradstreet's day? Support your answer.

Review and Assess

Literary Analysis

Puritan Plain Style

1. Which words, phrases, and references in each poem reflect the plainness of the Puritans' lives? Use a chart like the one shown to organize your perceptions.

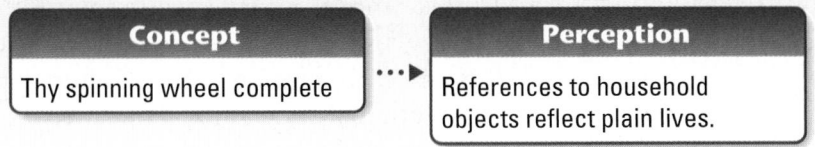

Concept	Perception
Thy spinning wheel complete	References to household objects reflect plain lives.

2. Which aspects of each poem are not typical of the **Puritan Plain Style**? Explain.

3. Compared to other poetry you know, how would you describe the effect of the Puritan Plain Style?

Comparing Literary Works

4. (a) Compare and contrast the emotions each of these speakers directs toward his or her subject. (b) What do these speakers want from the objects of their devotion? Explain.

5. How do both of these poems express emotions that are distinctly Puritan yet universally human?

6. Cite two lines from each of these poems that may have violated the Puritan prohibition against personal expression.

7. A **conceit** is an elaborate comparison between two very different subjects. (a) How does Taylor's use of conceit help to structure his poem? (b) By contrast, how does Bradstreet build the ideas in her poem?

Reading Strategy

Paraphrasing

8. **Paraphrase** these passages from the poems as though you were explaining their meaning to a friend: (a) "To My Dear and Loving Husband," lines 9–12, (b) "Huswifery," lines 9–12.

Extend Understanding

9. **History Connection:** (a) What was the Puritan attitude toward material wealth and spirituality? (b) In our culture today, what is the general view of the relationship between the two?

Quick Review

The **Puritan Plain Style** is a simple, direct style of writing characterized by the use of short, easily understood words common to seventeenth-century conversation.

When you **paraphrase**, you restate important ideas in your own words.

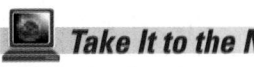 **Take It to the Net**

www.phschool.com

Take the interactive self-test online to check your understanding of these selections.

Integrate Language Skills

Vocabulary Development Lesson

Word Analysis: Anglo-Saxon Suffix *-fold*

The Anglo-Saxon suffix *-fold*, meaning "a specific number of times or ways," is used to form both adjectives and adverbs. *Tenfold* means "ten times." Replace the italicized phrases with a word containing the suffix *-fold*.

1. Since having quadruplets, Sandy's laundry has grown *by four times*.
2. The savvy investor watched the value of his stock increase to *three times its size*.

Spelling Strategy

When the unvoiced *th* sound occurs at the end of a word, spell it with the letters *th*. When the voiced *th* sound occurs, include a final *e*. Find examples of each of these rules in these poems.

Fluency: Word Meaning

Identify the letter of the situation that best demonstrates the meaning of the italicized word or phrase.

1. *well-deserved recompense:* (a) getting a flat tire while taking your grandmother to the doctor, (b) getting a day off after working overtime, (c) cleaning a messy room after a long day
2. *increase manifold:* (a) to receive a twenty percent raise, (b) to add a drop of water to a full bucket, (c) to get a 300 percent return on an investment
3. *to persevere:* (a) to quit when you get tired, (b) to practice until you improve, (c) to argue with a referee

Grammar and Style Lesson

Direct Address

When the speaker in a poem talks directly to someone or something, the form of speech is called a **direct address.** Commas are used to separate the word or phrase of the direct address from the rest of the sentence, regardless of its position in the sentence.

> **Middle:** Make me, O *Lord*, Thy spinning wheel complete.
>
> **End:** May you be rewarded for your love, *dear husband*.

Practice Identify the word or phrase of direct address. Add punctuation where needed.

1. I beseech you O Muse to bring me inspiration!
2. And make Thy holy spirit Lord wind quills: / Then weave the web Thyself.
3. I could not love thee dear so much, / Loved I not honor more.
4. How can I repay my love the love you have given to me?
5. I see you in the holy work I strive to perform Lord.

Writing Application Write a letter to a political figure explaining your opinion about a subject of your choice. Use at least one direct address.

W̶G Prentice Hall Writing and Grammar Connection: Chapter 27, Section 2

Writing Lesson

Reflective Essay

To write his poem, Edward Taylor had to understand the process by which clothes were made, from the spinning of the yarn to the sewing of a garment. The poem works on two different levels—as a description of an ordinary activity and as a comparison between that task and religious devotion. In an essay, describe a common household chore and then explain how that task suggests a larger meaning.

Prewriting   Identify a task to be completed in the average household. Note the steps involved in the process and the tools that might be used.

Drafting   Describe the task from beginning to end, incorporating details that appeal to the senses. Write a brief conclusion to address the larger meaning within this ordinary activity.

> ### Model: Providing Descriptive Details
>
> When I sort the clothes into darks and lights, I feel the roughness of denim and the smoothness of cotton. I smell the grass from mowing the lawn and pick out bits of leaves that found their way into folds of the cloth.

> Specific details like *roughness of denim* and the smell of the grass help make writing vivid.

Revising   Invite a classmate to judge the vividness of your writing and to identify any points where the process is not described clearly. Evaluate whether or not the larger meaning makes sense.

W/G Prentice Hall Writing and Grammar Connection: Chapter 6, Section 2

Extension Activities

Listening and Speaking Foremost among the Puritan values were a strong work ethic and devotion to God and family. Stage an **informal debate** to argue whether these values exist in today's society. Use these tips to prepare:

- Review a range of sources for evidence supporting either a pro or con stance.
- Anticipate opponents' arguments and prepare your defenses in advance.

When debating, speak clearly and slowly to make sure your ideas are heard. **[Group Activity]**

Research and Technology Research the process of spinning yarn and weaving cloth as it was practiced in the colonial era. Using available computer graphics, produce a **graphic display** that identifies the steps and tools referenced in "Huswifery," and write the corresponding line(s) of verse next to each.

 **Take It to the Net**   www.phschool.com

Go online for an additional research activity using the Internet.

Prepare to Read

from Sinners in the Hands of an Angry God

Jonathan Edwards (1703–1758)

The sermons of Jonathan Edwards were so filled with "fire and brimstone"—a phrase symbolizing the torments of hell endured by sinners—that his name alone was enough to make many eighteenth-century Puritans shake in their shoes. Yet, Edwards was not merely a stone-faced religious zealot. He was also a man who believed in science and reason and who saw in the physical world the proof of God's presence and will.

A Preacher Born and Raised This great American theologian and powerful Puritan preacher was born in East Windsor, Connecticut, where he grew up in an atmosphere of devout discipline. As a young boy, he is said to have demonstrated his religious devotion by preaching sermons to his playmates from a makeshift pulpit he built behind his home. Edwards also displayed academic brilliance at an early age. By the time he was twelve, he had learned to speak Latin, Greek, and Hebrew and had written numerous philosophical and scientific essays. These essays, which include "Of Insects," and "Of the Rainbow," display Edwards's remarkable powers of observation and analysis. Edwards entered the Collegiate School of Connecticut (now Yale University) at the age of thirteen and graduated four years later as the valedictorian of his class. He went on to earn his master's degree in theology.

The Great Awakening Edwards began his preaching career in 1727 as assistant to his grandfather, Solomon Stoddard, pastor of the church at Northampton, Massachusetts, one of the largest and wealthiest Puritan congregations. Edwards became the church pastor two years later when his grandfather died. He also began preaching throughout New England. Committed to a return to the orthodoxy and fervent faith of the Puritan past, Edwards became one of the leaders of the Great Awakening, a religious revival that swept the colonies in the 1730s and 1740s. His sermons stimulated religious zeal and sparked conversions, often in a frenzied atmosphere.

Changing Attitudes As Pastor of the church at Northampton, Edwards had instituted disciplinary proceedings against members of his congregation for reading what he considered improper books. In his sermons he denounced by name those he considered sinners. Such actions, combined with the severity of his views, drew criticism. In 1750, a council representing ten congregations in the region dismissed Edwards as pastor.

Fall from Favor Edwards then moved to Stockbridge, Massachusetts, where he preached to the Native Americans. While in Stockbridge, Edwards wrote his most important theological works, including "A Careful and Strict Enquiry into . . . Notions of . . . Freedom of Will" (1754), in which he argued that human beings do not possess self-determination. The essay remains one of the most famous theological works ever written in America. Edwards continued to preach and write until his death in 1758, shortly after becoming president of the College of New Jersey (now Princeton University).

Although in most of his sermons, books, and essays Edwards appeals to reason and logic, his highly emotional sermon "Sinners in the Hands of an Angry God" is by far his most famous work. This sermon, which was delivered to a congregation in Enfield, Connecticut, in 1741 and is said to have caused listeners to rise from their seats in a state of hysteria, demonstrates Edwards's tremendous powers of persuasion and captures the religious fervor of the Great Awakening.

Preview

Connecting to the Literature

Suppose a friend is involved with the "wrong crowd" and you are concerned about his or her awful future. Jonathan Edwards had such concerns about his congregation. To turn his congregants toward repentance, Edwards filled his sermons with descriptions of the horrors that awaited those who did not mend their ways.

Literary Analysis

Sermon

A **sermon** is broadly defined as a speech given from a pulpit in a house of worship. Like its written counterpart, the essay, a sermon conveys to an audience the speaker's message or point of view. In colonial America's religious atmosphere, the sermon flourished as a popular literary form.

Connecting Literary Elements

Sermons are one example of **oratory,** or formal public speaking. The best oratory almost always displays the following elements:

- It is persuasive, inspiring listeners to take action.
- It is emotionally appealing.
- It addresses the needs and concerns of its audience.
- It involves the use of colorful or rhythmic language.

Although oratory has become less common in American society, its lofty tones can still be heard in Senate chambers, courtrooms, and houses of worship. In Edwards's time, oratory played an important role in the lives of nearly all citizens of a community.

Reading Strategy

Using Context Clues

Searching the **context**—the surrounding words, phrases, and sentences—for clues can help you understand the meaning of unfamiliar words. For example, look at the word *abominable* in this passage:

> You are ten thousand times more *abominable* in his [God's] eyes, than the most hateful venomous serpent is in ours. . . .

Edwards likens the way the sinner appears in God's eyes with our view of a snake. From this clue, you can determine that *abominable* must be close in meaning to *disgusting* or *horrible*. Use a chart like the one shown to define other difficult words by using context clues.

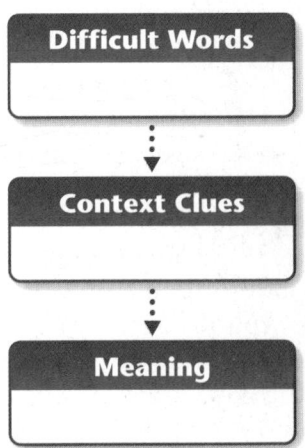

Difficult Words

↓

Context Clues

↓

Meaning

Vocabulary Development

omnipotent (äm nip´ ə tənt) *adj.* all-powerful (p. 109)

ineffable (in ef´ ə bəl) *adj.* inexpressible (p. 110)

dolorous (dō´ lər əs) *adj.* sad; mournful (p. 110)

from Sinners in the Hands of an Angry God

Jonathan Edwards

Background

Surprisingly, Jonathan Edwards preached this famous fire-and-brimstone sermon in a quiet, restrained style. According to one account, he read the six-hour work in a level voice, staring over the heads of his congregation at the bell rope that hung against the back wall "as if he would stare it in two." Despite his calm demeanor, his listeners are said to have groaned and screamed in terror, and Edwards stopped several times to ask for silence.

This is the case of every one of you that are out of Christ:[1] That world of misery, that lake of burning brimstone, is extended abroad under you. There is the dreadful pit of the glowing flames of the wrath of God; there is Hell's wide gaping mouth open; and you have nothing to stand upon, nor anything to take hold of; there is nothing between you and Hell but the air; it is only the power and mere pleasure of God that holds you up.

You probably are not sensible of this; you find you are kept out of Hell, but do not see the hand of God in it; but look at other things, as the good state of your bodily constitution, your care of your own life, and the means you use for your own preservation. But indeed these things are nothing; if God should withdraw his hand, they would avail no more to keep you from falling than the thin air to hold up a person that is suspended in it.

---

1. out of Christ not in God's grace.

Your wickedness makes you as it were heavy as lead, and to tend downwards with great weight and pressure towards Hell; and if God should let you go, you would immediately sink and swiftly descend and plunge into the bottomless gulf, and your healthy constitution, and your own care and prudence, and best contrivance, and all your righteousness, would have no more influence to uphold you and keep you out of Hell, than a spider's web would have to stop a fallen rock. Were it not for the sovereign pleasure of God, the earth would not bear you one moment . . . The world would spew you out, were it not for the sovereign hand of Him who hath subjected it in hope. There are black clouds of God's wrath now hanging directly over your heads, full of the dreadful storm, and big with thunder; and were it not for the restraining hand of God, it would immediately burst forth upon you. The sovereign pleasure of God, for the present, stays[2] his rough wind; otherwise it would come with fury, and your destruction would come like a whirlwind, and you would be like the chaff of the summer threshing floor.

The wrath of God is like great waters that are dammed for the present; they increase more and more, and rise higher and higher, till an outlet is given; and the longer the stream is stopped, the more rapid and mighty is its course, when once it is let loose. It is true, that judgment against your evil works has not been executed hitherto; the floods of God's vengeance have been withheld; but your guilt in the meantime is constantly increasing, and you are every day treasuring up more wrath; the waters are constantly rising, and waxing more and more mighty; and there is nothing but the mere pleasure of God, that holds the waters back, that are unwilling to be stopped, and press hard to go forward. If God should only withdraw his hand from the floodgate, it would immediately fly open, and the fiery floods of the fierceness and wrath of God, would rush forth with inconceivable fury, and would come upon you with <u>omnipotent</u> power; and if your strength were ten thousand times greater than it is, yea, ten thousand times greater than the strength of the stoutest, sturdiest devil in Hell, it would be nothing to withstand or endure it.

The bow of God's wrath is bent, and the arrow made ready on the string, and justice bends the arrow at your heart, and strains the bow, and it is nothing but the mere pleasure of God, and that of an angry God, without any promise or obligation at all, that keeps the arrow one moment from being made drunk with your blood. Thus all you that never passed under a great change of heart, by the mighty power of the spirit of God upon your souls; all you that were never

The Puritan, 1898, Frank E. Schoonover, Collection of the Brandywine River Museum

▲ **Critical Viewing**
What words from the text would you apply to describe the mood of this painting? **[Analyze]**

Literary Analysis
Sermon In what ways do these images of the fury of water help convey Edwards's message?

omnipotent (äm nip´ ə tənt) *adj.* all-powerful

✓**Reading Check**
What does Edwards say is the state of his congregation?

---

2. **stays** (stāz) *v.* restrains.

born again, and made new creatures, and raised from being dead in sin, to a state of new, and before altogether unexperienced light and life, are in the hands of an angry God. However you may have reformed your life in many things, and may have had religious affections, and may keep up a form of religion in your families and closets,[3] and in the house of God, it is nothing but His mere pleasure that keeps you from being this moment swallowed up in everlasting destruction. However unconvinced you may now be of the truth of what you hear, by and by you will be fully convinced of it.

Those that are gone from being in the like circumstances with you, see that it was so with them; for destruction came suddenly upon most of them; when they expected nothing of it, and while they were saying, peace and safety: now they see, that those things on which they depended for peace and safety, were nothing but thin air and empty shadows.

The God that holds you over the pit of Hell, much as one holds a spider, or some loathsome insect over the fire, abhors you, and is dreadfully provoked: his wrath towards you burns like fire; he looks upon you as worthy of nothing else, but to be cast into the fire; he is of purer eyes than to bear to have you in his sight; you are ten thousand times more abominable in his eyes, than the most hateful venomous serpent is in ours. . . .

O sinner! Consider the fearful danger you are in: it is a great furnace of wrath, a wide and bottomless pit, full of the fire of wrath, that you are held over in the hand of that God, whose wrath is provoked and incensed as much against you, as against many of the damned in Hell. You hang by a slender thread, with the flames of divine wrath flashing about it, and ready every moment to singe it, and burn it asunder; and you have no interest in any mediator, and nothing to lay hold of to save yourself, nothing to keep off the flames of wrath, nothing of your own, nothing that you ever have done, nothing that you can do, to induce God to spare you one moment. . . .

When God beholds the ineffable extremity of your case, and sees your torment to be so vastly disproportioned to your strength, and sees how your poor soul is crushed, and sinks down, as it were, into an infinite gloom; he will have no compassion upon you, he will not forbear the executions of his wrath, or in the least lighten his hand; there shall be no moderation or mercy, nor will God then at all stay his rough wind; he will have no regard to your welfare, nor be at all careful lest you should suffer too much in any other sense, than only that you shall *not suffer beyond what strict justice requires.* . . .

God stands ready to pity you; this is a day of mercy; you may cry now with some encouragement of obtaining mercy. But once the day of mercy is past, your most lamentable and dolorous cries and shrieks will be in vain; you will be wholly lost and thrown away of

---

3. **closets** *n.* small, private rooms for meditation.

3. **closets** *n.* small, private rooms for meditation.

Biblical Imagery

Jonathan Edwards's frightening imagery of God's potential for wrath and destruction recalls stories of fires, floods, and divine retribution in the Old Testament of the King James Bible. While this imagery terrified Edwards's audience, they would have found it quite familiar. In fact, in 1741, when Edwards delivered this sermon, the King James Bible had been in wide circulation for 130 years. The first English version of the Bible to include both the Old and New Testaments, the King James Bible had been produced at the express request of the Puritans in England in 1611. This Bible, with its haunting language and powerful imagery, would have been common daily reading for most of Edwards's listeners.

ineffable (in ef´ ə bəl) *adj.* inexpressible

dolorous (dō´ lər əs) *adj.* sad; mournful

God, as to any regard to your welfare. God will have no other use to put you to, but to suffer misery; you shall be continued in being to no other end; for you will be a vessel of wrath fitted to destruction; and there will be no other use of this vessel, but to be filled full of wrath. . . .

Thus it will be with you that are in an unconverted state, if you continue in it; the infinite might, and majesty, and terribleness of the omnipotent God shall be magnified upon you, in the ineffable strength of your torments. You shall be tormented in the presence of the holy angels, and in the presence of the Lamb,[4] and when you shall be in this state of suffering, the glorious inhabitants of Heaven shall go forth and look on the awful spectacle, that they may see what the wrath and fierceness of the Almighty is; and when they have seen it, they will fall down and adore that great power and majesty. . . .

It would be dreadful to suffer this fierceness and wrath of Almighty God one moment; but you must suffer it to all eternity. There will be no end to this exquisite horrible misery. When you look forward, you shall see a long forever, a boundless duration before you, which will swallow up your thoughts and amaze your soul; and you will absolutely despair of ever having any deliverance, any end, any mitigation, any rest at all. . . .

How dreadful is the state of those that are daily and hourly in the danger of this great wrath and infinite misery! But this is the dismal case of every soul in this congregation that has not been born again, however moral and strict, sober and religious, they may otherwise be. Oh that you would consider it, whether you be young or old! . . . Those of you that finally continue in a natural condition, that shall keep you out of Hell longest will be there in a little time! Your damnation does not slumber; it will come swiftly, and, in all probability, very suddenly upon many of you. You have reason to wonder that you are not already in Hell. It is doubtless the case of some whom you have seen and known, that never deserved Hell more than you, and that heretofore appeared as likely to have been now alive as you. Their case is past all hope; they are crying in extreme misery and perfect despair; but here you are in the land of the living and in the house of God, and have an opportunity to obtain salvation. What would not those poor damned hopeless souls give for one day's opportunity such as you now enjoy!

And now you have an extraordinary opportunity, a day wherein Christ has thrown the door of mercy wide open, and stands in calling and crying with a loud voice to poor sinners; a day wherein many are flocking to him, and pressing into the kingdom of God. Many are daily coming from the east, west, north and south; many that were very lately in the same miserable condition that you are in, are now in a happy state, with their hearts filled with love to him who has loved them, and washed them from their sins in his own blood, and

4. **the Lamb** Jesus.

Literary Analysis
Sermon and Oratory
What action is this passage beginning "But this is the dismal case" designed to inspire?

✔**Reading Check**

What does Edwards say will happen when the day of mercy has passed?

rejoicing in hope of the glory of God. How awful is it to be left behind at such a day! To see so many others feasting, while you are pining and perishing! To see so many rejoicing and singing for joy of heart, while you have cause to mourn for sorrow of heart, and howl for vexation of spirit! . . .

Therefore, let everyone that is out of Christ now awake and fly from the wrath to come. The wrath of Almighty God is now undoubtedly hanging over a great part of this congregation: let everyone fly out of Sodom.[5] "Haste and escape for your lives, look not behind you, escape to the mountain, lest you be consumed."[6]

---

5. **Sodom** (säd´ əm) In the Bible, a city destroyed by fire because of the sinfulness of its people.
6. **"Haste . . . consumed"** from Genesis 19:17, the angels' warning to Lot, the only virtuous man in Sodom, to flee the city before they destroy it.

Review and Assess

Thinking About the Selection

1. **Respond:** How might you have reacted to this sermon if you had been **(a)** a "Puritan," **(b)** a Native American, **(c)** another leader of the Great Awakening? Explain.

2. **(a) Recall:** According to the opening paragraph, what keeps sinners from falling into hell? **(b) Interpret:** According to Edwards, what do his listeners mistakenly feel keeps them from falling into hell?

3. **(a) Recall:** What words in the sermon's title suggest the emotional focus of Edwards's message? **(b) Analyze:** What additional traits does Edwards attribute to God as the sermon progresses?

4. **(a) Recall:** Toward the end of the sermon, what does Edwards say sinners can obtain? **(b) Analyze Cause and Effect:** What must sinners do to obtain these things?

5. **(a) Classify:** Note at least two images of natural destruction that Edwards uses to depict the wrath of God. **(b) Evaluate:** Why would images of the power of nature be particularly appropriate to Edwards's message?

6. **Evaluate:** Given his purpose and the audience of worshipers to whom he spoke, do you think Edwards's sermon was effective? Why or why not?

7. **(a) Extend:** For what other types of subjects might an appeal to an audience's fears be an effective persuasive technique? **(b) Judge:** Do you think it is right for a speaker to appeal to an audience's fears? Why or why not?

Review and Assess

Literary Analysis

Sermon

1. What point of view or message is Edwards conveying in this **sermon**?
2. (a) To what emotion does Edwards primarily appeal in his effort to motivate his congregation? (b) Considering Edwards's purpose, why is this an appropriate choice? Explain your answer.
3. (a) Use the chart shown here to identify the many symbols and images Edwards uses to describe God's wrath.

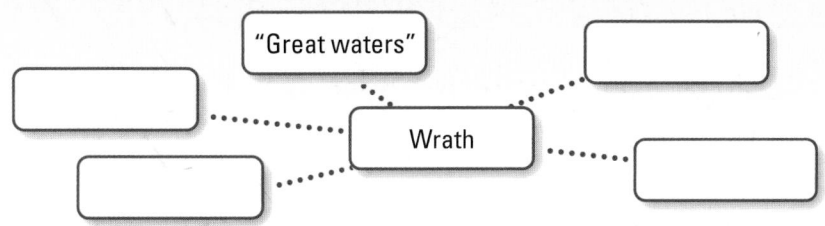

   (b) How do these symbols and images add to the impact of Edwards's message?
4. What does Edwards seem to feel about those who maintain a "form of religion" or who seem "moral and strict"?

Connecting Literary Elements

5. What statements does Edwards make that indicate an understanding of the people he is addressing?
6. Why might Edwards's **oratory** have been less effective if he had not had a reputation as a brilliant spiritual leader?

Reading Strategy

Using Context Clues

7. Use **context clues** to define the italicized words:
   (a) "you are every day treasuring up more wrath; the waters are constantly rising, and *waxing* more and more mighty. . . ."
   (b) "The God that holds you over the pit of Hell, much as one holds a spider, or some loathsome insect over the fire, *abhors* you, and is dreadfully provoked. . . ."

Extend Understanding

8. **Cultural Connection:** In which situations, if any, is it justifiable to use fear to get a person to improve his or her behavior? Explain.

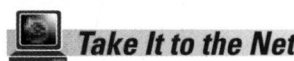

Integrate Language Skills

Vocabulary Development Lesson

Word Analysis: Latin Prefix *omni-*

The Latin prefix *omni-* means "all" or "every." *Omnipotent,* then, means "all-powerful." Each of the adjectives below contains the prefix *omni-*. Use the information in parentheses to match each adjective with the situation to which it best applies.

1. omniscient (*sciens* = knowing)
2. omnivorous (*vor* = to eat)
3. omnipotent (*potent* = powerful)

a. how a zoologist might describe an animal that eats both meat and plants
b. how a student might describe a brilliant teacher
c. how a prisoner might describe his jailer

Concept Development: Context

Fill each blank in the following sentence with the appropriate word from the vocabulary list on page 107.

The citizens of Oz sighed with a ___?___ air, indicating their ___?___ sadness at learning that the Wizard they considered ___?___ was just an ordinary man, hiding behind a curtain.

Spelling Strategy

To decide how to spell the unstressed vowel sound represented by a schwa (ə), think of another form of the word in which the vowel is stressed. Then, use the same vowel. For example, think of *morality,* and you will know to use an *a* in *moral.* Correct the following misspelled words.

1. provacation   2. prefarable   3. oppasite

Grammar and Style Lesson

Forms of Adjectives and Adverbs

The **comparative** form of adjectives and adverbs is used to compare two things or ideas; the **superlative** form is used to compare more than two things or ideas. Many words follow the pattern below to indicate comparative and superlative degrees:

Regular form: Ann is *tall.*

Comparative: Yvette is *taller.*

Superlative: Miku is the *tallest.*

Other adjectives and adverbs use the words *more* or *most,* as in, "Ann is *more punctual* than Joe. Mina is the *most punctual* of all."

Finally, some forms such as "good, better, best" are irregular.

Practice Rewrite the following paragraph, correcting all errors in comparisons:

When we think of great preachers, Edwards is the name that quickliest comes to mind. Of the many Puritan sermonizers who rose to fame during the Great Awakening, Edwards is considered the more influential. Most of his writing appealed to reason; "Sinners" is his most emotional and more famous work.

Looking at Style Review the sermon, and find an adjective and an adverb in each form. Explain how Edwards uses each one to create a powerful image.

W͞G Prentice Hall Writing and Grammar Connection: Chapter 24, Section 1

Writing Lesson

Evaluation of Persuasion

A speaker's choice of persuasive techniques should depend on the audience and the occasion. Write an evaluation of the persuasive techniques of imagery and theme that Edwards uses. Discuss the response he evokes and the ways he achieves it. Your evaluation will have greater clarity and strength if its elements work together to form a unified effect.

Prewriting To help focus your writing, jot down examples of Edwards's uses of imagery and identify his specific themes. Then, evaluate their effectiveness in a clearly defined statement.

Drafting Use the statement you wrote as the basis for a strong, focused opening paragraph. Support your main point in the paragraphs that follow.

Model: Building Unity

Jonathan Edwards appealed to his audience's vulnerability by using powerful, elemental images of nature run amok. His images of air, water, and fire terrified his audience by summoning up mental pictures of unlimited natural destruction.

> A general statement followed by specific examples builds unity.

Revising Read your evaluation as though you were seeing it for the first time. Eliminate any information that is unrelated to the main idea.

W͟G Prentice Hall Writing and Grammar Connection: Chapter 14, Section 3

Extension Activities

Listening and Speaking Sermons like those of Dr. Martin Luther King, Jr., still have the power to inspire us. With a group, research Dr. King's sermons and their role in the civil rights movement. Give a brief **oral report** on your findings. To increase your listeners' interest, include the following:

- direct quotes from Dr. King's sermons
- quotes from reports in the media.

If possible, include a short video or audio tape of Dr. King as part of your report. **[Group Activity]**

Research and Technology Because of their religious beliefs, Puritans developed a strong sense of the importance of work. Gather information about Puritan doctrine and the famous "work ethic." Create a **handbook** that includes guidelines and rules for living and working as a proper Puritan.

 **Take It to the Net**   www.phschool.com

Go online for an additional research activity using the Internet.

Writing About Literature

Analyze Literary Periods

Although the forms and context of earliest American literature are diverse, much of it deals with people's attempts to cope with the world around them. Strategies included everything from trying to overcome hunger and disease, to trying to set up a workable government, to trying to please an angry God. Writers' concerns reflected both their own belief systems and the circumstances in which they found themselves. Using the assignment outlined in the yellow box, write an analytical essay about this period in American literature.

Prewriting

Review the selections. Look for ways in which the writers try to cope with the world. Use these questions as a guide:

- Does the writer focus on the physical world?
- Does the writer focus on other people?
- Does the writer discuss political and social systems?
- Does the writing explain how the world was created?

Use index cards to note details of people's efforts to cope. On each card, identify the title of the selection and the page number, details describing people's actions or reactions, and the conclusions you draw from these details.

Assignment: Living in This World

Write an analytical essay that explores the way the earliest Americans (both Native Americans and European immigrants) tried to cope with their world.

Criteria:

- Include a thesis statement that draws on information from at least three different selections in the unit.
- Support your thesis with details from specific selections.
- Approximate length: 1,500 words.

Conclusion: The urge to explore was limited by obstacles within the environment. This account shows that some newcomers survived by following the advice of local inhabitants.

Model: Drawing Conclusions Based on Evidence

"Boulders Taller Than the Great Tower of Seville"

p. 34 Two of the explorers descend the canyon, determining that the terrain is rough and the river is as wide as was previously reported by Indians.

p. 34 The explorers do not travel farther up the canyon because of the lack of water reported by their Indian guides.

Find a focus. Review your notes to find a working thesis that expresses the main idea you want to explore. Write the idea in one sentence, and use this sentence as a working thesis.

Gather details. Once you have your working thesis, focus on the relevant selections. Return to your index cards to gather more details. Then, identify the ideas that will best support your thesis statement.

Read to Write

Reread the texts and focus on the motivation behind the individuals' questions, explanations, and struggles. Take notes to discover how those individuals attempted to cope with the world.

Drafting

Organize into paragraphs. You might want to write a separate paragraph for each selection that illustrates your thesis, or you might choose to devote each paragraph to a unique concept that all the selections you have identified support.

Two Approaches to Paragraph Organization

By Selection		Selection One	Selection Two
Survival required • getting food and shelter. • overcoming enemy attacks.	····▶	Discuss all the ways in which this selection supports your thesis.	Discuss all the ways in which this selection supports your thesis.

By Subject		Aspect One	Aspect Two
Survival was threatened by hostilities between old and new arrivals.	····▶	Analyze all of the selections that illustrate this idea.	Analyze all of the selections that illustrate this idea.

Develop each paragraph. Develop each paragraph, supplying details from the selections that clearly support your ideas.

Revising and Editing

Review content: Check the relevance of details. Review each paragraph, evaluating the connection between the main idea and the support. Confirm that details are relevant, and delete those that do not further your analysis.

Review style and format: Replace unclear pronouns. Improve your writing by checking for unclear pronouns. Review your essay, circling each pronoun and checking that the word to which it refers will be clear to your readers.

Vague Referent: The *guides* told the *Spaniards* that the terrain was dry and difficult, so they turned back.

Clarify the sentence above by replacing the pronoun with a noun that clearly refers to the Spaniards, such as *the European explorers.*

Publishing and Presenting

Hold a panel discussion. In today's world, we still have to figure out how to adapt to our environment and one another if we are to live successfully. Hold a panel discussion in which you and your classmates identify the selections that had the wisest lessons for today's reader.

W/G Prentice Hall Writing and Grammar Connection: Chapter 14

Write to Learn
Writing can help you transform vague ideas into a clear analysis.

Write to Explain
Help your reader understand your reasoning by making clear connections between details from the selections and the conclusions you have drawn.

Writing WORKSHOP

Narration: Autobiographical Narrative

An **autobiographical narrative** is a work in which a writer relates an experience from his or her life. In this workshop, you will write an autobiographical narrative that tells a story from your life.

Assignment Criteria Your autobiographical narrative should have the following characteristics:

- The writer as the main character
- A sequence of events that leads to an insight gained by the writer
- Action that incorporates shifts in time and mood
- Concrete details that locate and describe the sights, sounds, and smells of scenes and incidents
- Personal feelings, thoughts, and views of the writer

To preview the criteria on which your autobiographical narrative may be assessed, see the Rubric on page 121.

Prewriting

Choose a topic. For an entire day, keep an **idea notebook** that records your activities and thoughts. Consider these personal experiences as possible topics for exploration in your autobiographical narrative.

Isolate an episode. Once you have chosen your topic, list all the events related to it. Review the list, and choose a significant moment that you can develop into an effective piece of autobiographical narrative.

Add factual information. Some autobiographical incidents may require more information than is available to you through your memory or powers of observation. For such incidents, you will need to conduct research. For example, if you are describing an incident in a region or climate unknown to most people, you may have to add facts that place your experience in context. In the example shown here, factual details are italicized.

> **Example:** We flew *200 miles* to the nearest village. Throughout Antarctica, *planes are the primary mode of transportation*. I shook with fear for most of the flight.

Model: Isolating an Episode

- My mother's nocturnal schedule.
- The effect of the schedule on our relationship: We watched old TV shows, I saw mom reading books.
- I asked about a book of poems.
- I experienced "Patty Poem."
- I discovered the power of poetry.
- This event changed my life.

Student Model

Before you begin to write, read this student model and review the characteristics of effective autobiographical narrative.

Branden Boyer-White
Palm Springs, California

Discovering Poetry

My mother was a night owl. She worked nights as a nurse at the hospital. She liked it; the schedule suited her. The nights she was off, she maintained her nocturnal routine—active at night and asleep in the early part of the day.

One early morning, I went into the living room to find my mother reading a thick book called *Best Loved Poems to Read Again and Again.* My interest was piqued solely by the fact that the word *Poems* appeared in big, hot pink letters.

"Is it good?" I asked her.

"Yeah," she answered. "There's one you'll really like."

She began to thumb through the grainy white pages. She finally stopped and asked, "Ready?" I certainly was! I leaned forward.

"'Patty Poem,'" she read the title. *Who is Patty?* my mind buzzed. The poem began:

> She never puts her toys away,
> Just leaves them scattered where they lay, . . .

The poem was just three short stanzas. The final one came quickly:

> When she grows and gathers poise,
> I'll miss her harum-scarum noise,
> And look in vain for scattered toys,
>   And I'll be sad.

A terrible sorrow washed over me. Whoever Patty was, she was a dreadful, mean girl. Then, the bombshell.

"It's you, honey," my mother sentimentalized.

To my mother, the poem captured a parent's nostalgic love when her child grows up and leaves. To me, the "she" in the poem was a horror. It was *my* mama who would be sad. It was so terrible I burst into tears.

"What's wrong?" my mother asked.

"Oh Mama," I babbled. "I don't want to grow up *ever*!"

She smiled. "Honey, it's okay. You're not growing up anytime soon. And when you do, I'll still love you, okay?"

"Okay," I hiccuped. My panic had subsided. But I could not stop thinking about that silly poem. After what seemed like a safe amount of time, I read the poem again, and was mystified. It all fit so well together, like a puzzle. The language was simple, so simple I could plainly understand its meaning, yet it was still beautiful. I was now transfixed by the idea of poetry, words that had the power to make or break a person's world. . . .

I have since fallen in love with other poems, but "Patty Poem" remains my poem. It was my first, and it will be mine to the end, because it brought me my love for poetry. This is a great testimony to the poignancy of the art. After all, "Patty Poem" gave me my love for poetry not because it was the verse that lifted my spirits, but because it was the one that hurt me the most.

Branden uses concrete details to set the scene.

The inclusion of excerpts from the poem allows readers to understand the writer's emotional reaction.

Dialogue makes the narrative more realistic and poignant.

Branden clearly demonstrates the importance of this experience.

Drafting

Organize significant events. As you write, add the most significant events to your story, and order them in a logical sequence. Identify the climax, or point of highest interest. Then, arrange the other events to fit the structure of an event diagram as shown here.

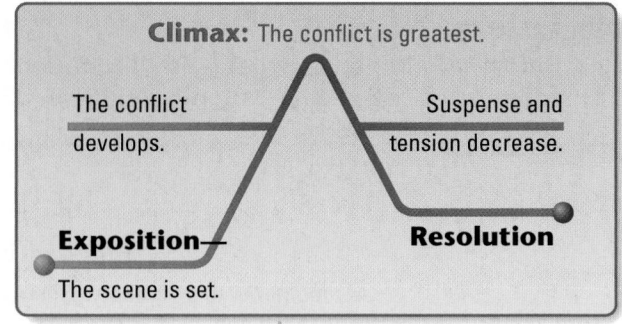

Climax: The conflict is greatest.

The conflict develops.

Suspense and tension decrease.

Exposition—
The scene is set.

Resolution

Provide details. For each event in your narrative, provide concrete details that enrich the story and make it more vivid. Types of details include the following:

- Sights, sounds, and smells of a scene or incident
- Specific actions, movements, and gestures of key characters
- Locations where events occurred

Elaborate your feelings. As you draft, note where you could include more information about your thoughts or feelings at the time of the event. Jot these ideas down. If necessary, you can incorporate such details later, when you revise.

Revising

Revise to add dialogue and description. Read your draft, and highlight points in the narrative that might be made clearer or more emotionally effective with the inclusion of dialogue or description. Pay special attention to those parts of your story in which emotions are most intense, as well as to points at which one character's actions directly affect another character. Jot down these details on a separate piece of paper, and incorporate them into your revised draft.

Model: Adding Dialogue

To my mother, the poem captured a parent's nostalgic love

when her child grows up and leaves. To me, the "she" in the poem

was a horror. It was *my* mama who would be sad. It was so terrible

I burst into tears.

"What's wrong?" my mother asked.

~~My mother seemed concerned, and asked me what was wrong.~~

"Oh, Mama," I babbled. "I don't want to grow up ever!"

~~I told her that I did not want to grow up.~~

> The use of dialogue makes a narrative more vivid and interesting to read.

Revise word choice. To bring your narrative to life for your readers, use active language rather than vague or general words. Choose vivid action verbs, precise adjectives, and specific nouns to convey your meaning.

Vague: There *were* lightning and wind all night.

Vivid: Lightning *crashed,* and wind *gusted* all night.

Compare the model and the non-model. Why is the model more effective than the non-model?

Nonmodel	Model
"Okay," I said. My fear had gone. But I could not stop thinking about that poem.	"Okay," I hiccuped. My panic had subsided. But I could not stop thinking about that silly poem.

Publishing and Presenting

Share your writing with a wider audience by presenting your narrative to your classmates.

Deliver an oral presentation. Practice reading your autobiographical narrative aloud. Mark a copy of your finished draft, underlining any dialogue, thoughts, quotations, or descriptions. As you present the narrative to your classmates, emphasize those passages.

Produce an Illustrated Anthology. With classmates, combine several essays in a single binder. To enhance each narrative, include photographers or artwork that capture the mood the writing achieves.

𝒲𝒢 *Prentice Hall Writing and Grammar Connection: Chapter 4*

Rubric for Self-Assessment

Evaluate your autobiographical narrative using the following criteria and rating scale:

Criteria	Rating Scale Not very				Very
How well established is the writer as the main character?	1	2	3	4	5
How effectively organized is the sequence of events?	1	2	3	4	5
How well does the action accommodate shifts in time and mood?	1	2	3	4	5
How powerfully are concrete and sensory details used to describe events?	1	2	3	4	5
How well does the narrative convey the feelings of the writer?	1	2	3	4	5

Listening and Speaking WORKSHOP

Delivering a Speech

Whether you are recounting an autobiographical incident while accepting an award or explaining the new student-government rules, delivering speeches offers a unique opportunity to convey ideas. The following speaking strategies can help you master the components of **speech delivery**.

Organizing Content

Before you begin rehearsing your speech, spend time planning and refining the content you will present.

Focus on purpose. Determine whether your purpose is narrative or informative. Then, choose and develop main points and details that suit your purpose.

Modify to fit your audience. Keep the knowledge level and interest of your audience in mind when you organize content. With a general audience, for example, plan frequent pauses to refer to explanatory visual material. Choose examples and illustrations, such as personal anecdotes and common experiences, that will draw your audience in.

Craft the speech. Using numbered index cards like the ones shown here, outline your main ideas. Then, choose from techniques such as rhetorical questions, figurative language, and dialogue to convey your ideas. You can keep the interest level high by choosing and combining informal expressions, Standard English, and technical language as dictated by your material.

I NEW STUDENT GOVERNMENT

Announce new government

A. Format and Rules
B. Offices

II GOALS FOR SCHOOL YEAR

A. Develop priorities and clear vision
B. Focus on 5 key projects
C. Raise necessary funds

III HOW TO GET INVOLVED

A. Come to meetings
B. Join project committees
C. Help raise funds

Giving the Speech

Effective speakers use appropriate rehearsal and delivery strategies to keep audiences engaged.

- **Performance details** Memorize main ideas so that you can refer only briefly to notes, and maintain eye contact with the audience.
- **Special effects** Use sound or visual effects, graphics, and background music to enhance your presentation.
- **Artistic staging** Choose movements and gestures that support the speech content and suit the occasion.

Activity:
Prepare and Deliver a Speech Choose a situation, audience, and purpose for which you might deliver a speech. Then, prepare, rehearse, and deliver a three-minute speech. Use index cards to highlight and sequence key ideas. Ask classmates for feedback so you can improve your public speaking skills.

Assessment WORKSHOP

Summaries of Written Texts

The reading sections of some tests often require you to identify the implied main idea in a passage. They may also require you to choose the best summary of a passage. Use these strategies to help you answer test questions on these skills:

- As you read, identify the sentence in the text that best expresses the main idea of the passage.
- If you are having difficulty identifying the implied main idea, ask yourself, "What general idea is the writer expressing?"

Test Taking Strategies

- Look for the details in the passage that will help you identify the main idea.
- Taking notes as you read is an active way to organize and condense the material.

Sample Test Item

Directions: Read the passage, and then answer the question that follows.

Haiku are three-line poems in which the first and third lines contain five syllables and the second line contains seven syllables. This form of poetry, which originated in Japan, reflects Japanese views of simplicity and nature. Matsuo Bashō, a seventeenth-century Japanese poet, is credited with making haiku an important art form.

1. Which of the following choices best expresses the main idea implied in the first paragraph?

   A Haiku originated in Japan.

   B Bashō was the first great haiku poet.

   C Haiku is a unique and important art form in Japan.

   D People have been writing haiku for 300 years.

Answer and Explanation

The correct answer is *C*. Answers A, B, and D give background information. C contains the implied main idea.

Practice

Directions: Read the passage, and then answer the question that follows.

Born into a wealthy family in the seventeenth century, Bashō left home to study Zen Buddhism, history, and classical Chinese poetry. His nomadic life increased the popularity of haiku—a concise style of lyric poetry—as he shared his verse in the communities through which he passed. Most literary historians agree that he was influential in building the recognition of haiku as a poetic form.

1. Which of the following is the best summary of this paragraph?

   A Uniquely Japanese, haiku is a concise poetic form popularized by the seventeenth-century poet Bashō.

   B Most literary historians agree that Bashō was an important poet.

   C Haiku would never have developed as a separate form were it not for wandering poets.

   D Bashō, a seventeenth-century poet, popularized haiku.

Washington Crossing the Delaware, Emanuel Gottlieb Leutze, Metropolitan Museum of Art

66 *The fate of unborn millions will now depend, under God, on the courage and conduct of this army. Our cruel and unrelenting enemy leaves us only the choice of brave resistance, or the most abject submission. We have, therefore, to resolve to conquer or die.* 99

—George Washington,
addressing the Continental Army before
the battle of Long Island, August 27, 1776

Timeline 1750–1800

American Events

- **1748** Benjamin Franklin retires from the printing business after 26 years. ▶

- **1752** Benjamin Franklin conducts his kite-and-key experiment with lightning. ▲

- **1753** African American Benjamin Banneker constructs the first striking clock with all parts made in America.

- **1754** French and Indian War begins.

Poor Richard, 1733.
AN
Almanack
For the Year of Chrift
1733,
Being the Firft after LEAP YEAR:

And makes fince the Creation	Years
By the Account of the Eaftern Greeks	7241
By the Latin Church, when ☉ ent. ♈	6932
By the Computation of W.W.	5742
By the Roman Chronology	5682
By the Jewiſh Rabbies	5494

Wherein is contained
The Lunations, Eclipfes, Judgment of the Weather, Spring Tides, Planets Motions & mutual Afpects, Sun and Moon's Rifing and Setting, Length of Days, Time of High Water, Fairs, Courts, and obfervable Days.
Fitted to the Latitude of Forty Degrees, and a Meridian of Five Hours Weft from London, but may without fenfible Error, ferve all the adjacent Places, even from Newfoundland to South-Carolina.
By RICHARD SAUNDERS, Philom.
PHILADELPHIA:
Printed and fold by B. FRANKLIN, at the New Printing-Office near the Market.

- **1759–63** France gives up claims to North American territory.

- **1765** Stamp Act passed by British Parliament; colonists protest bitterly

- **1767** Townshend Acts impose new taxes, angering colonists further.

- **1773** Parliament's Tea Act prompts Boston Tea Party.

- **1773** Phillis Wheatley's *Poems on Various Subjects* published in England. ▶

- **1774** First Continental Congress meets in Philadelphia.

- **1775** The American Revolution begins.

- **1776** Second Continental Congress adopts Declaration of Independence. ▼

World Events

- **1755** France: School for deaf opens in Paris.

- **1755** England: Samuel Johnson publishes *Dictionary of the English Language.*

- **1759** France: Voltaire publishes *Candide,* satirizing optimism of the philosopher Leibniz.

- **1762** France: Jean Jacques Rousseau states his political philosophy in *The Social Contract.*

- **1763** Seven Years' War ends.

- **1769** Scotland: James Watt invents an improved steam engine.

- **1769** England: Richard Arkwright invents a frame for spinning; helps bring about factory system.

- **1770** Germany: Ludwig von Beethoven is born.

- **1774** England: Joseph Priestley discovers oxygen, named later by Lavoisier.

- **1779** South Africa: First of Kaffir wars between blacks and whites breaks out.

American and World Events

■ **1781** General Cornwallis surrenders British army to George Washington at Yorktown. ▼

■ **1790** First federal U.S. census shows approximately 757,208 blacks in the U.S., nearly 20% of the total population. 59,557 are free.

■ **1800** Second U.S. census shows a total population of 5,308,483.

■ **1801** Thomas Jefferson, principal author of Declaration of Independence, elected President.

■ **1804** Federalist leader Alexander Hamilton killed in a duel with Aaron Burr.

■ **1783** Noah Webster's *Spelling Book* first appears; 60 million copies would be sold.

■ **1783** Revolutionary War ends.

■ **1787** Constitutional Convention meets in Philadelphia to draft Constitution.

■ **1789** George Washington elected first President of United States.

■ **1793** Eli Whitney invents cotton gin. ▶

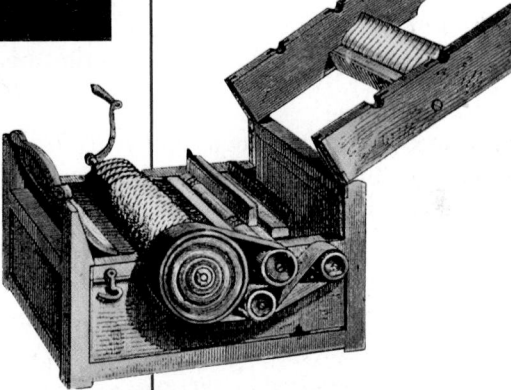

■ **1781** England: William Herschel discovers planet Uranus.

■ **1786** Scotland: Robert Burns is widely acclaimed for his first book of poems.

■ **1786** Austria: Wolfgang Amadeus Mozart creates the comic opera *The Marriage of Figaro*.

■ **1789** France: Storming of Bastille in Paris sets off French Revolution.

■ **1791** England: James Boswell publishes *The Life of Samuel Johnson*.

■ **1793** France: King Louis XVI and Marie Antoinette executed.

■ **1796** France: Napoleon Bonaparte comes to power in France. ▶

■ **1798** England: William Wordsworth and Samuel Taylor Coleridge publish *Lyrical Ballads*.

■ **1800** Germany: Ludwig von Beethoven composes *First Symphony*.

A Nation Is Born
(1750–1800)

Historical Background

It is easy to forget how long the thirteen original states had been colonies. By 1750, there were fourth- and fifth-generation Americans of European descent living in Virginia and New England. These people were English subjects, and, on the whole, they were well satisfied with that status. In fact, as late as the early 1760s, few Americans had given much thought to the prospect of independence.

Between the mid-1760s and the mid-1770s, however, attitudes changed dramatically. King George III and Parliament imposed a number of regulations that threatened the liberties of the colonists. With each succeeding measure, the outrage in America grew, finally erupting into war.

The Age of Reason Great upheavals in history occur when circumstances are ripe. The American Revolution was such an upheaval, and the groundwork for it had been laid by European writers and thinkers as well as by the English king and Parliament. The eighteenth century is often characterized as the Enlightenment, or the Age of Reason. Spurred by the work of many seventeenth-century thinkers— such as scientists Galileo and Sir Isaac Newton, philosophers Voltaire and Jean-Jacques Rousseau, and political theorist John Locke—the writers and thinkers of the Enlightenment valued reason over faith. Unlike the Puritans, they had little interest in the hereafter, believing instead in the power of reason and science to further human progress. They spoke of a social contract that forms the basis of government. Above all, they believed that people are by nature good, not evil. A perfect society seemed to them to be more than just an idle dream.

The American statesmen of the Revolutionary period were themselves figures of the Enlightenment. No history of the period would be complete without mention of the ideas and writings of Benjamin Franklin, Thomas Paine, and Thomas Jefferson. These Americans not only expressed the ideas of the Age of Reason but also helped to put them spectacularly into practice.

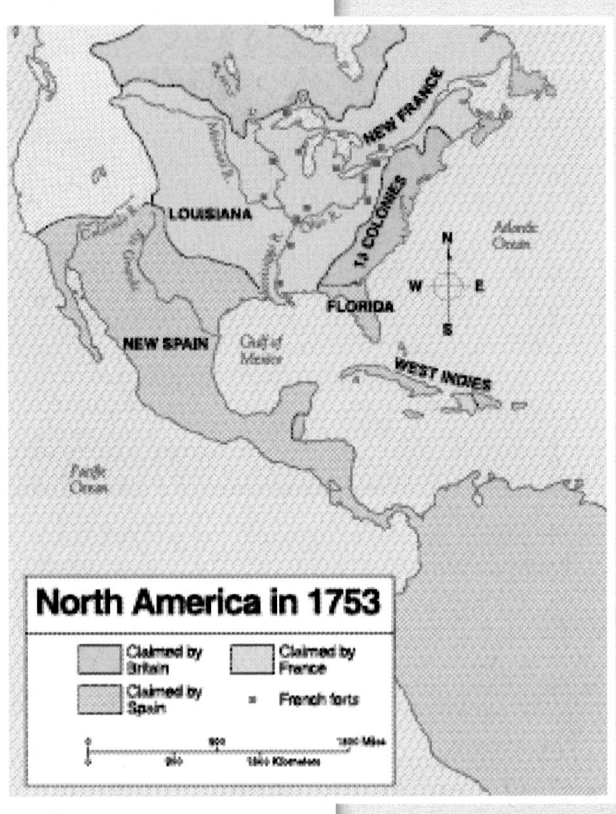

North America in 1753

Claimed by Britain
Claimed by Spain
Claimed by France
◼ French forts

▲ **Critical Viewing** On the eve of the French and Indian War, France still had claim to a majority of the interior of North America. What strategic advantage did the thirteen colonies enjoy because of their geographic location? **[Interpret]**

Toward a Clash of Arms The American Revolution was preceded by the French and Indian War, a struggle between England and France for control of North America. The conflict broke out in 1754 and continued for nearly a decade. When the war officially ended in 1763, defeated France gave up its claims to North American territory. There was general jubilation in the thirteen English colonies.

The good feelings were short-lived, however. The British government, wanting to raise revenue in the colonies to pay its war debt, passed the Stamp Act in 1765. Colonial reaction to the Stamp Act, which required the buying and affixing of stamps to each of 54 ordinary items, was swift and bitter. Stamps were burned. Stamp distributors were beaten and their shops destroyed. Eventually, the Stamp Act was repealed.

Other acts and reactions followed. The Townshend Acts of 1767 taxed paper, paint, glass, lead, and tea. When the colonists organized a boycott, the British dissolved the Massachusetts legislature and sent two regiments of British troops to Boston. In 1770, these Redcoats fired into a taunting mob, causing five fatalities. This so-called Boston Massacre further inflamed colonial passions. Parliament repealed the Townshend duties except for the tax on tea, but a separate Tea Act giving an English company a virtual monopoly soon greeted the colonists. Furious, a group of Bostonians dressed as Mohawks dumped a shipment of tea into Boston harbor. As punishment for this Boston Tea Party, the English Parliament passed the Coercive Acts. Because these laws shut down the port of Boston, forbade meetings other than annual town meetings, and insisted that British troops could be housed in colonists' homes, colonists immediately dubbed them the Intolerable Acts.

In September 1774, colonial leaders, although not speaking openly of independence, met in Philadelphia for the First Continental Congress. The British, their authority slipping away, appointed General Thomas Gage governor of Massachusetts. The stage was set for war.

"The Shot Heard Round the World" On April 19, 1775, 700 British troops met some 70 colonial minutemen on the Lexington green. A musket shot was fired (from which side, no one knows), and before the shooting that followed was over, eight Americans lay dead. The British marched west to Concord, where another skirmish took place. The encounters at Lexington and Concord, a landmark in American history, have been referred to as "the shot heard round the world." The American Revolution had begun, and there would be no turning back.

▲ **Critical Viewing**
Paul Revere's engraving of the Boston Massacre played a major role in whipping up colonial fury against the British. Revere purposefully distorted the events. Which details suggest the artist was pro-colonist? **[Analyze]**

In June, the Americans killed or wounded more than a thousand British soldiers at the Battle of Bunker Hill. Although the fighting up to this point had taken place in Massachusetts, the revolt involved all the colonies. Two days before Bunker Hill, the Second Continental Congress, meeting in Philadelphia, had named a commander in chief of the official American army. He was George Washington of Virginia.

More than a year would pass before the colonies declared their independence. More than six years would pass before the war ended, although the Battle of Saratoga, in the fall of 1777, marked a turning point. At Saratoga, in upstate New York, the British were surrounded and 5,700 of them were forced to surrender. When news of the American victory reached Paris, the government of France formally recognized the independence of the United States. Soon afterward, France began to commit troops to aid the American cause.

After six years of fighting, the war finally came to an end at Yorktown, Virginia, on October 19, 1781. Aided by the French army and navy, and enlisting the service of African American soldiers, General Washington's army bottled up the 8,000-man British force under General Cornwallis. Seeing that escape was impossible, General Cornwallis surrendered.

Close-up on History

African Americans and Women in the Revolution

In 1776, more than a half million African Americans lived in the colonies. At first, the Continental Congress did not permit enslaved or free African Americans to join the American army. However, when the British offered to free any male slave who fought for the king, George Washington changed American policy and allowed free African Americans to enlist.

About 5,000 African Americans fought against the British. As this eyewitness account demonstrates, they fought with great courage:

> Three times in succession, [African American soldiers] were attacked . . . by well-disciplined and veteran [British] troops, and three times did they successfully repel the assault, and thus preserve our army from capture.

Women also helped in the struggle for independence. When men went off to war, they took on added work. They planted and harvested the crops that fed the army. They also made shoes and wove cloth for blankets and uniforms. Many women joined their soldier-husbands at the front, where they washed, cooked, and cared for the wounded.

A few women actually took part in battle. In 1778, Mary Ludwig Hays carried water to her husband and other soldiers. The soldiers called her Moll of the Pitcher or Molly Pitcher. When her husband was wounded, she took his place, loading and firing a cannon. Another woman, Deborah Sampson of Massachusetts, dressed as a man and fought in several battles. Later, she wrote about her experiences in the army.

The New Nation The path to self-government was not always smooth. After the Revolution, the Articles of Confederation established a "league of friendship" among the new states. This arrangement did not work well. The federal Constitution that replaced the Articles required many compromises and was ratified only after a long fight. Even then, a Bill of Rights had to be added to placate those who feared the centralized power that the Constitution conferred.

The old revolutionaries, by and large, remained true to their principles and continued their public duties. George Washington became the nation's first president. John Adams, a signer of the Declaration of Independence, succeeded him in that office. Then, in 1800, Americans elected as their president the brilliant statesman who had drafted the Declaration, one of the heroes of the Enlightenment, Thomas Jefferson.

▲ Critical Viewing Patrick Henry criticized the Stamp Act in the Virginia House of Burgesses, and Virginia became the first colony officially to protest the new tax law. Based on this painting, what type of citizen do you think was generally elected to serve in the Virginia House of Burgesses? **[Draw Conclusions]**

Literature of the Period

A Time of Crisis In contrast to the private soul-searching of the Puritans of New England, much of what was produced during the Revolutionary period was public writing. By the time of the War for Independence, nearly thirty newspapers had been established in the coastal cities. At the time of Washington's inauguration, there were nearly forty magazines. Almanacs were popular from Massachusetts to Georgia.

The mind of the nation was on politics. Journalists and printers provided a forum for the expression of ideas. After 1763, those ideas were increasingly focused on relations with Great Britain and, more broadly, on the nature of government. As the literature presented in this unit testifies, the writing of permanent importance from the Revolutionary era is mostly political writing.

Politics as Literature The writing and speaking of American statesmen in two tumultuous decades, the 1770s and 1780s, helped to reshape not only the nation but also the world. James Otis of Massachusetts defended colonial rights vigorously in speeches and pamphlets. Otis is credited with giving Americans their rallying cry: "Taxation without representation is tyranny."

Patrick Henry was a spellbinding orator whose speech against the Stamp Act in the Virginia House of Burgesses brought cries of "Treason!" Ten years later, his electrifying speech to the Virginia Convention expressed the rising sentiment for independence.

Thomas Paine was perhaps more influential than any other in swaying public opinion in favor of independence. His 1776 pamphlet *Common Sense* swept the colonies, selling 100,000 copies in three months.

A Writer's Voice

Thomas Paine and the Age of Reason

The Age of Reason was not necessarily reasonable or moderate. Indeed, a chief characteristic of reason during this era was that it led some writers very far past old customs and institutions. Questioning the way things were, these writers reasoned their way to revolution.

You can see this link between reason and revolution in Thomas Paine's *Common Sense*. Even the title is an appeal to everyday logic, and throughout this pamphlet, Paine uses what George Washington called "unanswerable reasoning" to make the case for dramatic political changes.

from *Common Sense*

In the following pages I offer nothing more than simple facts, plain arguments, and common sense; and have no other preliminaries to settle with the reader than that he will divest himself of prejudice and prepossession [preconceived ideas] and suffer [allow] his reason and his feelings to determine for themselves. . . .

. . . it is not in the power of Britain to do this continent justice: The business of it will soon be too weighty, and intricate, to be managed with any tolerable degree of convenience, by a power so distant from us, and so very ignorant of us; for if they cannot conquer us, they cannot govern us. To be always running 3000 or 4000 miles with a tale or a petition, waiting four or five months for an answer, which when obtained required five or six more to explain it in, will in a few years be looked upon as folly and childishness—there was a time when it was proper, and there is a proper time for it to cease. . . .

The Declaration of Independence was first drafted by Thomas Jefferson in June 1776. The finished document is largely his work, although a committee of five statesmen, including Benjamin Franklin, was involved in its creation. The Declaration, despite some exaggerated charges against King George III, is one of the most influential political statements ever made.

Another Revolutionary-period document written by committee that has stood the test of time is the Constitution of the United States, drafted in 1787. The framers, whose new nation boasted about four million people, hoped that the Constitution would last at least a generation. It still survives, amended only 27 times, as the political foundation of a superpower of 50 states and more than 250 million people. However, not everyone in 1787 was pleased with the Constitution. Alexander Hamilton called it a "weak and worthless fabric," and Benjamin Franklin supported it only because, as he said, "I expect no better."

The doubts of the framers were reflected in the controversy over ratification. Delaware ratified the Constitution within three months, thus becoming the first state in the Union. However, the ratification of nine states was necessary before the document could go into effect. The last few states proved difficult. The contest between supporters and opponents was especially hard-fought in New York. Alexander Hamilton, who did not think highly of the Constitution, nevertheless wanted to see it pass in his home state. With James Madison and John Jay, he wrote a series of essays that were first published as letters to three New York newspapers. These essays, collected as *The Federalist*, served their immediate purpose. New York ratified the Constitution by a vote of 30 to 27. Over time, these essays have come to be recognized as authoritative statements on the principles of American government.

The Cultural Scene While politics dominated the literature of the Revolutionary period, not every writer of note was a statesman. Verse appeared in most of the newspapers, and numerous broadside ballads were published. (A broadside ballad is a single sheet of paper, printed on one or both sides, dealing with a current topic.) One of the most popular broadside ballads was called "The Dying Redcoat," supposedly written by a British sergeant mortally wounded in the Revolution. The sergeant in the ballad realizes too late that his sympathy lies with the American cause:

> Fight on, America's noble sons,
> Fear not Britannia's thundering guns:
> Maintain your cause from year to year,
> God's on your side, you need not fear.

One poet of the time whose works were more sophisticated than the broadside ballads was Philip Freneau, a 1771 graduate of Princeton. A journalist and newspaper editor, Freneau wrote poetry throughout his life. Several of his poems, such as "The Indian Burying Ground," earned him a reputation as America's earliest important lyric poet.

Two other poets of the day were Joel Barlow and Phillis Wheatley. Barlow, a 1778 Yale graduate, is best remembered for "The Hasty Pudding," a mock-heroic tribute to cornmeal mush. Phillis Wheatley, born in Africa and brought to Boston in childhood as a slave, showed early signs of literary genius. A collection of her poems was published in England while she was still a young woman.

Another writer of the Revolutionary period recorded his impressions of everyday American life. Born into an aristocratic French family, Michel-Guillaume Crèvecoeur became a soldier of fortune, a world traveler, and a farmer. For fifteen years, he owned a plantation in Orange County, New York, and his impressions of life there were published in London in 1782 as *Letters From an American Farmer*.

▲ **Critical Viewing** This painting captures the writing of the Declaration of Independence. What do the many papers on the floor of the room suggest about the writing of the document? **[Draw Conclusion]**

Perhaps the best-known writing of the period outside the field of politics was done by Benjamin Franklin. His *Poor Richard's Almanack* became familiar to most households in the colonies. In addition to information on the calendar and the weather common to most almanacs, it contained such sayings as these:

No man e'er was glorious, who was not laborious.
Make haste slowly.
Little Strokes, fell great Oaks.

A statesman, printer, author, inventor, and scientist, Franklin was a true son of the Enlightenment. His *Autobiography*, covering only his early years, is regarded as one of the finest autobiographies in any language.

Culture and Art During the Revolutionary period, America began to establish a cultural identity of its own. Theaters were built from New York to Charleston. Yet despite the energy invested in these enterprises, the plays produced were often little more than pale imitations of dramas that had achieved success in Britain. The first play written by an author born in America was Thomas Godfrey's tragedy *The Prince of Parthia* (1767). However, no truly American characters appeared in a play before Royall Tyler featured American types in his comedy *The Contrast* (1787). That play also dealt with a theme that would be popular in many early American dramas: the victory of honest Americans over deceitful foreigners. It is not hard to see how that theme might appeal to audiences who had lived through the Revolution.

A number of new colleges were established after the war, especially in the South. For example, what is today the University of Tennessee, Knoxville, was founded in 1794 as Blount College, and the University of North Carolina, Chapel Hill, opened its doors in 1795.

Several outstanding painters were at work in the colonies and the young republic. Among them were John Singleton Copley, Gilbert Stuart, John Trumbull, and Charles Willson Peale. Patience Wright, famous in the colonies as a sculptor of wax portraits, moved to London before the war. While there, she acted as a Revolutionary spy. In music, William Billings produced *The New England Psalm-Singer* and a number of patriotic hymns. Billings earned his living as a tanner and taught himself music. Among his friends were such revolutionary activists as Samuel Adams and Paul Revere. This was a turbulent time—a time of action—and its legacy was cultural as well as political.

▼ **Critical Viewing**
As the first secretary of the treasury, Alexander Hamilton had to develop a financial plan for the government. (a) What was the government's income in 1789? (b) How much did it owe? **[Analyze]**

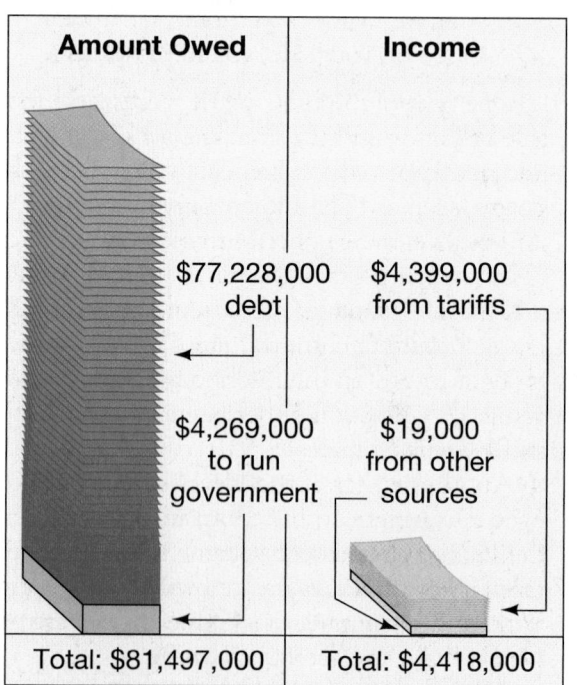

Money Problems of the New Nation, 1789–1791

Amount Owed	Income
$77,228,000 debt	$4,399,000 from tariffs
$4,269,000 to run government	$19,000 from other sources
Total: $81,497,000	Total: $4,418,000

Source: *Historical Statistics of the United States*

Art in the Historical Context

Gilbert Stuart, Portraitist

After Americans won the Revolution in 1781, one might have expected to see painters portray some of the most dramatic battle scenes—for example, the Battle of Bunker Hill or the surrender at Yorktown, Virginia. Most of the country's best-known painters, however, produced portraits.

Gilbert Stuart was among the most distinguished of these portraitists. He had studied with Benjamin West, a famous American painter who lived and worked in London. When Stuart did several paintings of the country's first citizen, George Washington, it was as if he were painting a portrait of the Revolution itself. Perhaps believing that the ideals of that struggle could be read in Washington's features and personality, Stuart focused on the upper part of Washington's body, especially his face, and he did not include any props or scenery.

► **Make an Inference** What impression of Washington—and, by extension, of the American Revolution—does this portrait convey? Explain.

George Washington (Vaughan portrait), Gilbert Stuart, Photograph © Board of Trustees, National Gallery of Art, Washington, D.C.

American Literature at Daybreak By the early 1800s, America could boast a small body of national literature. The Native Americans had contributed haunting poetry and legends through their oral traditions. The Puritans had written a number of powerful, inward-looking works. The statesmen of the Revolutionary period had produced political documents for the ages. A few poets and essayists had made a permanent mark on the literature of the young republic. There were, however, no American novels or plays of importance, and the modern short story had yet to be invented.

As the eighteenth century came to a close, however, the raw materials for a great national literature were at hand, waiting to be used. The nation stood on the threshold of a territorial and population explosion unique in the history of the world. It would take almost exactly a century to close the frontier of the vast and varied continent beyond the Appalachians. During that century, American literature would burst forth with a vitality that might have surprised even the farsighted founders of the nation. The colonial age ended with a narrow volume of memorable literature. The nineteenth century would close with a library of works that form a major part of America's literary heritage.

THE DEVELOPMENT OF AMERICAN ENGLISH

Noah Webster and the American Language

BY RICHARD LEDERER

Travel back in time to May 1787 to the city of Philadelphia. It is thronged with important visitors, including Benjamin Franklin, Alexander Hamilton, James Madison, and the brightest of these luminaries—George Washington. They have come to attend the Constitutional Convention "in order to form a more perfect Union" of states that have recently won a surprising military victory.

On the evening of May 26, 1787, General Washington pays a visit to talk about education with a 28-year-old New Englander who is teaching school in Philadelphia. His name is Noah Webster.

AMERICA'S SCHOOLMASTER

Why did Washington call on a young man scarcely half his age who was neither a Revolutionary War hero nor a Convention delegate? One reason was that Noah Webster was the author, publisher, and salesman of *The Blue-Backed Speller*, a book that was then more widely read in the United States than any other except the Bible.

WEBSTER AND THE AMERICAN DICTIONARY

On top of such an amazing achievement, Webster devoted thirty years to creating the first great American dictionaries. The fact that the name *Webster* and the word *dictionary* are practically syn-onymous indicates the enduring brightness of Webster's reputation.

Throughout his life, Noah Webster was afire with the conviction that the United States should have its own version of the English language. In 1789, he wrote:

As an independent nation, our honor requires us to have a system of our own, in language as well as government. Great Britain, whose children we are and whose language we speak, should no longer be our standard.

In putting this theory into practice, Noah Webster traveled throughout the East and South, listening to the speech of American people, and taking endless notes. He included in his dictionaries an array of shiny new American words, among them *applesauce, bullfrog, chowder, handy, hickory, succotash, tomahawk*—and *skunk*: "a quadruped remarkable for its smell."

In shaping the American language, Noah Webster also taught a new nation a new way to spell.

British	Webster's
honour	honor
humour	humor
musick	music
publick	public
centre	center
theatre	theater
plough	plow

ACTIVITY

1. Dictionary-makers are the biographers of words. Pick a word from the *Oxford English Dictionary* and write its "biography"—when the word was born and how it acquired new meanings over the course of its life.
2. Give the American equivalent of each of the following British words:
   (a) braces, (b) lift, (c) lorry, (d) petrol, (e) telly.
   Identify additional words that distinguish Americans from British citizens.

Voices for Freedom

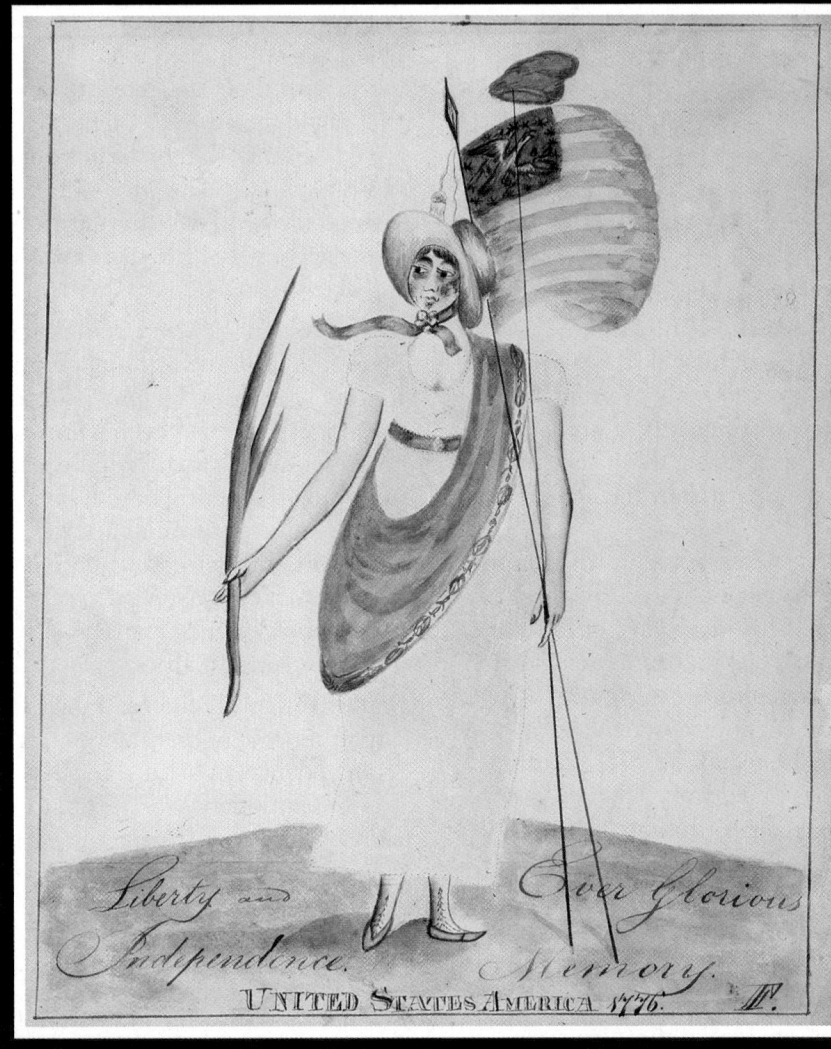

Miss Liberty, artist unknown, Abby Aldrich Rockefeller Folk Art Center, Williamsburg, VA

Prepare to Read

from The Autobiography ◆ *from* Poor Richard's Almanack

Benjamin Franklin
(1706–1790)

From his teen years until his retirement at forty-two, Benjamin Franklin worked as a printer. Franklin got his start as an apprentice to his brother, James Franklin, a Boston printer. By the time he was sixteen, he was not only printing, but writing parts of his brother's newspaper. Using the name "Silence Dogood," Franklin satirized daily life and politics in Boston.

When he was seventeen, Franklin left Boston and traveled to Philadelphia, intending to open his own print shop. This move gave birth to one of Franklin's most popular and enduring contributions to American culture, *Poor Richard's Almanack*. This annual publication, which Franklin published from 1732 to 1757, contained information, observations, and advice and was very popular with readers of his day.

The "Write Reputation" Just as he had signed "Silence Dogood" to the letters he wrote for his brother's paper, Franklin created for the *Almanack* a fictitious author/editor, the chatty Richard Saunders (and his wife, Bridget). Although Poor Richard's early appearances in the *Almanack* present him as a dull and foolish astronomer, his character developed over the years, becoming more thoughtful, pious, and humorous. Despite the fact that Franklin published under a pseudonym, the *Almanack* earned him a reputation as a talented writer.

Secret to Success Like most almanacs, Franklin's contained practical information about the calendar, the sun and moon, and the weather. *Poor Richard's Almanack* also featured a wealth of homespun sayings and observations, many of which are still quoted today. It was these aphorisms, with their characteristic moral overtones, that made the *Almanack* a bestseller. Franklin put an aphorism at the top or bottom of most pages of his almanacs. The wit and brevity of these sayings allowed Franklin to include many moral messages in very little space, while also entertaining his readers.

Man of Science When Franklin was forty-two, he retired from the printing business to devote himself to science. He proved to be as successful a scientist as he had been a printer. Over the course of his lifetime, Franklin was responsible for inventing the lightning rod, bifocals, and a new type of stove; confirming the laws of electricity; and contributing to the scientific understanding of earthquakes and ocean currents. In spite of all these achievements, Franklin is best remembered for his career in politics.

Statesman and Diplomat Franklin played an important role in drafting the Declaration of Independence, enlisting French support during the Revolutionary War, negotiating a peace treaty with Britain, and drafting the United States Constitution. In his later years, he was ambassador first to England and then to France. Even before George Washington, Franklin was considered to be "the father of his country."

The Story Behind the Story Franklin wrote the first section of *The Autobiography* in 1771 at the age of sixty-five. At the urging of friends, he wrote three more sections—the last shortly before his death—but succeeded in bringing the account of his life only to the years 1757 to 1759. Though never completed, his *Autobiography*, filled with his opinions and suggestions, provides not only a record of his achievements but also an understanding of his character.

Preview

Connecting to the Literature

Autobiographies of historical figures such as Franklin allow us a closer look at world-shaping events and can be just as gripping as great fiction.

Literary Analysis

Autobiography

Benjamin Franklin's *Autobiography* set the standard for what was then a new genre. Usually written in the first person, **autobiographies** present life events as the writer sees them. They also provide a view of history that is more personal than accounts in history books. Use a chart like the one shown to record details from Franklin's *Autobiography* that paint a portrait of the man, his attitudes, and the world he inhabited.

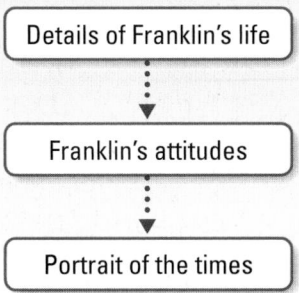

Comparing Literary Works

Franklin's interest in self-improvement is evident both in this excerpt from *The Autobiography* and in the **aphorisms**—short sayings with a message—he wrote for the *Almanack:*

> If you would know the value of money, try to borrow some.

In *The Autobiography*, Franklin examines his own life and applies higher standards to his behavior. By contrast, the aphorisms offer witty advice to the general public. As you read these selections, examine how they each convey messages of moral self-improvement, but with very different effects.

Reading Strategy

Drawing Conclusions

Franklin vividly describes his life and goals, letting you form an impression of his character. To form an impression, **draw conclusions** based on evidence from the text and your own experience. For example:

> **Detail:** Franklin makes lists to organize his plan.
>
> **Personal Experience:** You make "to do" lists, too.
>
> **Conclusion:** Franklin likes to plan ahead.

Draw conclusions about Franklin's character as you read these works.

Vocabulary Development

arduous (är′ jōō əs) *adj.* difficult (p. 141)

avarice (av′ ə ris) *n.* greed (p. 141)

vigilance (vij′ ə ləns) *n.* watchfulness (p. 142)

disposition (dis′ pə zish′ ən) *n.* management (p. 144)

foppery (fäp′ ər ē) *n.* foolishness (p. 145)

felicity (fə lis′ i tē) *n.* happiness; bliss (p. 145)

squander (skwän′ dər) *v.* spend or use wastefully (p. 147)

fasting (fast′ iŋ) *v.* eating very little or nothing (p. 148)

from *The Autobiography*

Benjamin Franklin

Background

Benjamin Franklin arrived in the city of Philadelphia in 1723 at the age of 17. He knew no one, and he had little money and fewer possessions. However, his accomplishments shaped the city in ways that are still visible today. He helped establish Philadelphia's public library and fire department, as well as its first college. In addition, through his efforts, Philadelphia became the first city in the colonies to have street lights. While Franklin was a brilliant man, some of his success can be attributed to sheer self-discipline, which is evident in this excerpt from his *Autobiography*.

Quaker Meeting, British, fourth quarter 18th century or first quarter 19th century, Museum of Fine Arts, Boston

▲ **Critical Viewing** Relate this picture to *The Autobiography*. What does each suggest about discipline and order? **[Draw Conclusions]**

It was about this time I conceived the bold and <u>arduous</u> project of arriving at moral perfection. I wished to live without committing any fault at any time; I would conquer all that either natural inclination, custom, or company might lead me into. As I knew, or thought I knew, what was right and wrong, I did not see why I might not always do the one and avoid the other. But I soon found I had undertaken a task of more difficulty than I had imagined. While my care was employed in guarding against one fault, I was often surprised by another; habit took the advantage of inattention; inclination was sometimes too strong for reason. I concluded, at length, that the mere speculative conviction that it was our interest to be completely virtuous was not sufficient to prevent our slipping; and that the contrary habits must be broken, and good ones acquired and established, before we can have any dependence on a steady, uniform rectitude of conduct. For this purpose I therefore contrived the following method.

In the various enumerations of the moral virtues I had met with in my reading, I found the catalog more or less numerous, as different writers included more or fewer ideas under the same name. Temperance, for example, was by some confined to eating and drinking, while by others it was extended to mean the moderating every other pleasure, appetite, inclination, or passion, bodily or mental, even to our <u>avarice</u> and ambition. I proposed to myself, for the sake of clearness, to use rather more names, with fewer ideas annexed to each, than a few names with more ideas; and I included under thirteen names of virtues all that at that time occurred to me as necessary or desirable, and annexed to each a short precept, which fully expressed the extent I gave to its meaning.

These names of virtues, with their precepts, were:

1. TEMPERANCE Eat not to dullness; drink not to elevation.
2. SILENCE Speak not but what may benefit others or yourself; avoid trifling conversation.
3. ORDER Let all your things have their places; let each part of your business have its time.
4. RESOLUTION Resolve to perform what you ought; perform without fail what you resolve.
5. FRUGALITY Make no expense but to do good to others or yourself; i.e., waste nothing.
6. INDUSTRY Lose no time; be always employed in something useful; cut off all unnecessary actions.
7. SINCERITY Use no hurtful deceit; think innocently and justly, and, if you speak, speak accordingly.
8. JUSTICE Wrong none by doing injuries, or omitting the benefits that are your duty.
9. MODERATION Avoid extremes; forebear resenting injuries so much as you think they deserve.
10. CLEANLINESS Tolerate no uncleanliness in body, clothes, or habitation.

arduous (är´ jōō əs) *adj.* difficult

Literary Analysis
Autobiography What does Franklin's goal of moral "perfection" suggest about the values of the time period?

avarice (av´ ə ris) *n.* greed

**Reading Check**

What prompts Franklin to make his list?

11. TRANQUILLITY Be not disturbed at trifles, or at accidents common or unavoidable.
12. CHASTITY
13. HUMILITY Imitate Jesus and Socrates◆.

My intention being to acquire the *habitude* of all these virtues, I judged it would be well not to distract my attention by attempting the whole at once but to fix it on one of them at a time; and, when I should be master of that, then to proceed to another, and so on, till I should have gone through the thirteen; and, as the previous acquisition of some might facilitate the acquisition of certain others, I arranged them with that view, as they stand above. *Temperance* first, as it tends to procure that coolness and clearness of head, which is so necessary where constant vigilance was to be kept up, and guard maintained against the unremitting attraction of ancient habits and the force of perpetual temptations. This being acquired and established, *Silence* would be more easy; and my desire being to gain knowledge at the same time that I improved in virtue, and considering that in conversation it was obtained rather by the use of the ears than of the tongue, and therefore wishing to break a habit I was getting into of prattling, punning, and joking, which only made me acceptable to trifling company, I gave *Silence* the second place. This and the next, *Order*, I expected would allow me more time for attending to my project and my studies. *Resolution*, once become habitual, would keep me firm in my endeavors to obtain all the subsequent virtues; *Frugality* and *Industry* freeing me from my remaining debt and producing affluence and independence, would make more easy the practice of *Sincerity* and *Justice*, etc., etc. Conceiving then, that, agreeably to the advice of Pythagoras[1] in his *Golden Verses*, daily examination would be necessary, I contrived the following method for conducting that examination.

I made a little book, in which I allotted a page for each of the virtues. I ruled each page with red ink, so as to have seven columns, one for each day of the week, marking each column with a letter for the day. I crossed these columns with thirteen red lines, marking the beginning of each line with the first letter of one of the virtues, on which line and in its proper column I might mark, by a little black spot, every fault I found upon examination to have been committed respecting that virtue upon that day.

I determined to give a week's strict attention to each of the virtues successively. Thus, in the first week, my great guard was to avoid every[2] the least offense against *Temperance*, leaving the other virtues

---

1. **Pythagoras** (pi *thag´* ə rəs) Greek philosopher and mathematician who lived in the sixth century B.C.
2. **every** even.

Literature in context History Connection

◆ *Socrates*
A Greek philosopher and teacher who lived in the fifth century B.C., Socrates pioneered the kind of self-reflection that Benjamin Franklin undertakes with his moral improvement plan. Socrates held self-knowledge dear, believing that only through knowledge can people achieve moral virtue. He led many in Athens in searching for moral truth and defining rules for right conduct. Nonetheless, Socrates' criticism of Athenian government resulted in his execution.

vigilance (vij´ ə ləns) *n.* watchfulness

Reading Strategy
Drawing Conclusions
What does Franklin's methodical approach, described in this passage, suggest about his dedication to his plan for self-improvement?

to their ordinary chance, only marking every evening the faults of the day. Thus, if in the first week I could keep my first line, marked *T.* clear of spots, I supposed the habit of that virtue so much strengthened, and its opposite weakened, that I might venture extending my attention to include the next, and for the following week keep both lines clear of spots. Proceeding thus to the last, I could go through a course complete in thirteen weeks, and four courses in a year. And like him who, having a garden to weed, does not attempt to eradicate all the bad herbs at once, which would exceed his reach and his strength, but works on one of the beds at a time, and, having accomplished the first, proceeds to a second, so I should have, I hoped, the encouraging pleasure of seeing on my pages the progress I made in virtue, by clearing successively my lines of their spots, till in the end, by a number of courses, I should be happy in viewing a clean book, after a thirteen weeks' daily examination. . . .

The precept of *Order* requiring that *every part of my business should have its allotted time*, one page in my little book contained the following scheme of employment for the twenty-four hours of a natural day.

Literary Analysis
Autobiography What insight into Franklin's character does this list provide?

THE MORNING.	5	Rise, wash, and
Question. What good shall I do this day?	6	address *Powerful Goodness!* Contrive day's business, and take the resolution of the day;
	7	prosecute the present study, and breakfast.
	8	
	9	Work.
	10	
	11	
NOON.	12	Read, or overlook
	1	my accounts, and dine.
	2	
	3	Work.
	4	
	5	
EVENING.	6	Put things in their places. Supper.
Question. What good have I done today?	7	Music or diversion, or conversation.
	8	Conversation. Examination of
	9	the day.
	10	
	11	
	12	
NIGHT.	1	Sleep.
	2	
	3	
	4	

✔**Reading Check**

Which virtue did Franklin hope to achieve by planning each day's activities?

I entered upon the execution of this plan for self-examination, and continued it with occasional intermissions for some time. I was surprised to find myself so much fuller of faults than I had imagined; but I had the satisfaction of seeing them diminish. To avoid the trouble of renewing now and then my little book, which, by scraping out the marks on the paper of old faults to make room for new ones in a new course, became full of holes, I transferred my tables and precepts to the ivory leaves of a memorandum book, on which the lines were drawn with red ink that made a durable stain, and on those lines I marked my faults with a black-lead pencil, which marks I could easily wipe out with a wet sponge. After a while I went through one course only in a year, and afterward only one in several years, till at length I omitted them entirely, being employed in voyages and business abroad, with a multiplicity of affairs that interfered; but I always carried my little book with me.

My scheme of *Order* gave me the most trouble; and I found that, though it might be practicable where a man's business was such as to leave him the <u>disposition</u> of his time, that of a journeyman printer, for instance, it was not possible to be exactly observed by a master, who must mix with the world and often receive people of business at their own hours. *Order*, too, with regard to places for things, papers, etc., I found extremely difficult to acquire. I had not been early accustomed to it, and, having an exceeding good memory, I was not so sensible of the inconvenience attending want of method. This article, therefore, cost me so much painful attention, and my faults in it vexed me so much, and I made so little progress in amendment, and had such frequent relapses, that I was almost ready to give up the attempt, and content myself with a

Benjamin Franklin as a Young Printer in Philadelphia, The Granger Collection, New York

▲ **Critical Viewing**
What does the expression on Franklin's face suggest about his personality? **[Infer]**

disposition (dis´ pə zish´ ən) *n.* management

faulty character in that respect, like the man who, in buying an ax of a smith, my neighbor, desired to have the whole of its surface as bright as the edge. The smith consented to grind it bright for him if he would turn the wheel; he turned, while the smith pressed the broad face of the ax hard and heavily on the stone, which made the turning of it very fatiguing. The man came every now and then from the wheel to see how the work went on, and at length would take his ax as it was, without farther grinding. "No," said the smith, "turn on, turn on; we shall have it bright by and by; as yet, it is only speckled." "Yes," says the man, "*but I think I like a speckled ax best.*" And I believe this may have been the case with many, who, having, for want of some such means as I employed, found the difficulty of obtaining good and breaking bad habits in other points of vice and virtue, have given up the struggle, and concluded that "*a speckled ax was best*"; for something, that pretended to be reason, was every now and then suggesting to me that such extreme nicety as I exacted of myself might be a kind of <u>foppery</u> in morals, which, if it were known, would make me ridiculous; that a perfect character might be attended with the inconvenience of being envied and hated; and that a benevolent man should allow a few faults in himself, to keep his friends in countenance.

In truth, I found myself incorrigible with respect to *Order*; and now I am grown old, and my memory bad, I feel very sensibly the want of it. But, on the whole, though I never arrived at the perfection I had been so ambitious of obtaining, but fell far short of it, yet I was, by the endeavor, a better and a happier man than I otherwise should have been if I had not attempted it; as those who aim at perfect writing by imitating the engraved copies, though they never reached the wished-for excellence of those copies, their hand is mended by the endeavor, and is tolerable while it continues fair and legible.

It may be well my posterity should be informed that to this little artifice, with the blessing of God, their ancestor owed the constant <u>felicity</u> of his life, down to his seventy-ninth year in which this is written. What reverses may attend the remainder is in the hand of Providence; but, if they arrive, the reflection on past happiness enjoyed ought to help his bearing them with more resignation. To *Temperance* he ascribes his long-continued health, and what is still left to him of a good constitution; to *Industry* and *Frugality*, the early easiness of his circumstances and acquisition of his fortune, with all that knowledge that enabled him to be a useful citizen, and obtained for him some degree of reputation among the learned; to *Sincerity* and *Justice*, the confidence of his country, and the honorable employs it conferred upon him; and to the joint influence of the whole mass of the virtues, even in the imperfect state he was able to acquire them, all that evenness of temper, and that cheerfulness in conversation, which makes his company still sought for, and agreeable even to his younger acquaintance. I hope, therefore, that some of my descendants may follow the example and reap the benefit.

Literary Analysis
Autobiography What does this anecdote about the man with the axe reveal about Franklin's sense of humor?

foppery (fäp′ ər ē) *n.* foolishness

felicity (fə lis′ i tē) *n.* happiness; bliss

**Reading Check**
Did Franklin consider his moral improvement plan successful? Explain.

from Poor Richard's Almanack

Benjamin Franklin

Poor Richard, 1733.

AN

Almanack

For the Year of Christ

1733,

Being the First after LEAP YEAR:

And makes since the Creation
	Years
By the Account of the Eastern Greeks	7241
By the Latin Church, when ☉ ent. ♈	6932
By the Computation of W.W.	5742
By the Roman Chronology	5682
By the Jewish Rabbies	5494

Wherein is contained

The Lunations, Eclipses, Judgment of
the Weather, Spring Tides, Planets Motions &
mutual Aspects, Sun and Moon's Rising and Setting, Length of Days, Time of High Water,
Fairs, Courts, and observable Days.
Fitted to the Latitude of Forty Degrees,
and a Meridian of Five Hours West from London,
but may without sensible Error, serve all the adjacent Places, even from Newfoundland to South-
Carolina.

By RICHARD SAUNDERS, Philom.

PHILADELPHIA:

Printed and sold by B. FRANKLIN, at the New
Printing-Office near the Market.

Poor Richard's Almanack, The Granger Collection, New York

► **Critical Viewing** The abbreviation "Philom.," short for *philomath*, follows Ben Franklin's pseudonym Richard Saunders. Can you guess the meaning of the word *philomath*? **[Speculate]**

Fools make feasts, and wise men eat them.

Be slow in choosing a friend, slower in changing.

Keep thy shop, and thy shop will keep thee.

Early to bed, early to rise, makes a man healthy,
    wealthy, and wise.

Three may keep a secret if two of them are dead.

God helps them that help themselves.

The rotten apple spoils his companions.

An open foe may prove a curse; but a pretended
    friend is worse.

Have you somewhat to do tomorrow, do it today.

A true friend is the best possession.

A small leak will sink a great ship.

No gains without pains.

'Tis easier to prevent bad habits than to break them.

Well done is better than well said.

Dost thou love life? Then do not <u>squander</u> time; for
    that's the stuff life is made of.

Write injuries in dust, benefits in marble.

A slip of the foot you may soon recover, but a
    slip of the tongue you may never get over.

If your head is wax, don't walk in the sun.

A good example is the best sermon.

Hunger is the best pickle.

Genius without education is like silver in the mine.

Literature in context — Cultural Connection

Proverbs

Most of Franklin's aphorisms are adapted from traditional or folk sayings, known as proverbs. Franklin, who believed that clarity and brevity were two of the most important characteristics of good prose, rewrote many proverbs, crafting short, witty sayings that taught a lesson.

Proverbs are nearly as old as language itself, and exist in all societies. They reflect each culture's view of the world, conveying feelings about fate, the seasons, the natural world, work and effort, love, death, and other universal experiences. These memorable bits of wisdom have survived for centuries, perhaps because they reflect unchanging truths about human nature.

squander (skwän´ dər) v.
spend or use wastefully

 **Reading Check**

Which aphorisms offer advice about using time wisely?

For want of a nail the shoe is lost; for want of a shoe
the horse is lost; for want of a horse the rider is lost.

Haste makes waste.

The doors of wisdom are never shut.

Love your neighbor; yet don't pull down your hedge.

He that lives upon hope will die <u>fasting</u>.

fasting (fast′ iŋ) v. eating very little or nothing

Review and Assess

Thinking About the Selections

1. **Respond:** Which virtue on Franklin's list strikes you as being the most important? Explain.

2. **(a) Recall:** According to his *Autobiography*, what efforts does Franklin make to become more orderly? **(b) Infer:** Is he successful? Explain. **(c) Analyze:** What aspect of his attempt to become more orderly is illustrated by the anecdote of the man with the speckled ax?

3. **(a) Interpret:** When Franklin began his project, he was a young man. How do you think he felt at the time about his chances of attaining moral "perfection"? **(b) Compare and Contrast:** What insights does Franklin gain about the importance of achieving moral perfection as he gets older? **(c) Take a Position:** Do you think the goal of achieving moral perfection is reasonable? Explain.

4. **(a) Recall:** Note three aphorisms that deal directly with friendship. **(b) Analyze:** Is Franklin's message about friendship consistent? Explain.

5. **(a) Recall:** According to the aphorisms from *Poor Richard's Almanack*, what happens to a person who "lives upon hope"? **(b) Infer:** Why might Franklin see hope as impractical or even dangerous? **(c) Speculate:** What more reliable value would Franklin say a person can successfully "live upon"?

6. **Generalize:** In what ways can analyzing one's own behavior contribute to personal growth?

7. **(a) Generalize:** Which of Franklin's aphorisms express values that are still widely held in America? Explain. **(b) Evaluate:** With which of Franklin's aphorisms do you most strongly agree? Why? **(c) Evaluate:** With which of Franklin's aphorisms do you disagree? Why?

Review and Assess

Literary Analysis

Autobiography

1. What does Franklin's concern with moral virtue reveal about the period in which he lived?
2. (a) Do you think Franklin achieved the virtue of humility? (b) Do you find any evidence of pride—humility's opposite—in this account of his life?
3. How do you think the *Autobiography* would be different if it were written about Franklin rather than by him?

Comparing Literary Works

4. (a) Are Franklin's struggles to improve himself related to the advice he offers in the **aphorisms**? (b) Do these aphorisms seem to be written by the same person who wrote the *Autobiography*? Why, or why not?
5. Use a chart like the one below to match aphorisms with virtues from the *Autobiography*. Explain each choice.

Reading Strategy

Drawing Conclusions

6. Franklin made adjustments to his record-keeping system as his plan progressed. What **conclusion** can you draw about his character from these adjustments? Explain.
7. (a) What conclusions can you draw from Franklin's statement that people dislike perfection in others? (b) Do you agree? Explain.

Extend Understanding

8. **Cultural Connection:** Franklin's aphorism, "If your head is wax, don't walk in the sun," is similar to a Russian proverb that advises, "One who sits between two chairs may easily fall down." (a) What do these proverbs mean? (b) How are they similar? (c) Why do different cultures preserve similar kinds of wisdom?

Quick Review

An **autobiography** is a person's account of his or her own life, usually written in the first person.

An **aphorism** is a short saying with a message.

A **conclusion** is a reasonable statement you develop from details in the text and your own life experience.

 Take It to the Net
www.phschool.com
Take the interactive self-test online to check your understanding of these selections.

Integrate Language Skills

Vocabulary Development Lesson

Word Analysis: Word Root -vigil-

The word *vigilance*, meaning "watchfulness," contains the root *-vigil-*, which means "the act or period of remaining awake so as to guard or observe something." Write a definition of the italicized word in each sentence below.

1. He was *vigilant* in his efforts to reform.
2. To restore safety, members of a *vigilante* group patrolled the streets at night.

Spelling Strategy

When you add a suffix that begins with a vowel to a one-syllable word that ends with a consonant, double the consonant: *fop + -ery = foppery*. Add the indicated suffixes to the following words.

1. fad + -ish
2. pun + -ing
3. snob + -ery
4. map + -ed

Concept Development: Analogies

In each item, match the relationship between the first two words by selecting a word from the vocabulary list on page 139.

1. *Permission* is to *authorization* as ____?____ is to *greed*.
2. *Danger* is to *peril* as ____?____ is to *silliness*.
3. *Tragedy* is to *comedy* as ____?____ is to *negligence*.
4. *Order* is to *chaos* as ____?____ is to *sadness*.
5. *Rare* is to *common* as ____?____ is to *easy*.
6. *Error* is to *mistake* as ____?____ is to *arrangement*.
7. *Cruelty* is to *kindness* as ____?____ is to *generosity*.
8. *Sloth* is to *industry* as ____?____ is to *indulgence*.

Grammar and Style Lesson

Pronoun Case

Pronouns are words that replace nouns. **Pronoun case** refers to the form that a pronoun takes to indicate its function in a sentence. Always use pronouns in the case reflecting their function.

Subjective case pronoun, also called **nominative** pronouns—*I, we, you, he, she, it, they*, are used when the pronoun is the subject of the sentence.

Objective case pronouns—*me, us, him, her, it, them*—are used when the pronoun receives the action of the verb or is the object of a preposition.

SUBJ. CASE		OBJ. CASE
I always carried my little book with *me*.		

Practice Choose the correct pronoun to complete each sentence below.

1. At length a fresh difference arose between my brother and (I, me).
2. It was time for (we, us) to leave that place.
3. Though I did not give them any dissatisfaction, (they, them) dismissed me from my position.
4. (We, Us) two undertook to move to Boston.
5. Wilson and (he, him) took care to prevent my getting employment anywhere else.

Writing Application Write an account of a time when you made a conscious effort at self-improvement, using pronoun cases correctly.

*W*G *Prentice Hall Writing and Grammar Connection: Chapter 22, Section 1*

Writing Lesson

Autobiographical Account

With your activities, friendships, family and school events, successes and failures, you have a vast amount of material to build your autobiography. Choose an important experience and discuss it. Tell what made this experience memorable and describe what you have learned from it.

Prewriting   Brainstorm for a list of details from the experience. Note what happened, what you felt, and what you learned. Include specific details that will help your readers understand your experience better.

Drafting   As you draft, incorporate details that will make the event and its significance clear to readers. Remember to show the cause-and-effect relationship between the event or experience and your life.

Revising   When you revise, pay attention to cause-and-effect relationships. Add transition words to make these relationships more obvious.

Model: Revising to Show Cause and Effect

I pivoted the wrong way. The ball bounced off Alec's back, and

ricocheted into the goal. I had scored a goal for the other team!

as a result of my mistake

The buzzer sounded. The game was over, we had lost.

> Transition words and phrases such as *as a result* highlight cause-and-effect relationships.

---

*W**G* *Prentice Hall Writing and Grammar Connection: Chapter 4, Section 4*

Extension Activities

Listening and Speaking Think of a few areas in which the students in your class would like to improve. In small groups, consider specific action steps you can take, and write a **class improvement plan.** Be sure to identify the following elements of a plan:

- how you will define the steps to be taken
- how you will record your efforts
- what your time frame will be

Each group should then present its plan in brief oral reports. [**Group Activity**]

Research and Technology With a group, create a **travel brochure** for tourists visiting Philadelphia. Use the Internet and electronic reference sources to gather information and obtain appropriate pictures, maps, or lists. If possible, blend your text and images in one file using a desktop publishing program.

 **Take It to the Net**   www.phschool.com

Go online for an additional research activity using the Internet.

A Closer Look

All the News That's Fit to Print

Colonial Newspapers Paved the Way for a Free Press

"EXTRA! EXTRA! Read all about it! Newspapers banned! Journalists Jailed! Americans Fight for a Free Press!" Those might have been the headlines blaring from a local newspaper if you had lived in America in the eighteenth century. Might have been, that is, if colonial newspapers had headlines. America's earliest newspapers bore little resemblance to the publications we know today. They were crudely printed on wooden hand presses, and contained only a clumsy illustration or two. Most were just one or two pages, and their stories were often no more involved than a listing of ship arrivals. Despite the primitive character of these early newspapers, they laid the groundwork for a uniquely American phenomenon: a free press that could criticize the government.

▲ **Critical Viewing** In this image portraying the trial of Peter Zenger, with what emotions does the audience seem to be reacting to the lawyer's argument? **[Interpret]**

Trailblazers The first American newspaper was printed on September 25, 1690. Titled *Publick Occurrences, Both Foreign and Domestick*, the Boston-based paper filled three of four pages, leaving the last page blank for readers' notes. It contained no headlines, and mixed news and editorials into the same stories. The remarkable thing about *Publick Occurrences* was that it existed at all. England had no history of a free and independent press. All British publications were licensed by the King. If a newspaper criticized the crown, it could be shut down with no legal recourse. Yet *Publick Occurrences* was published without British approval, and printed stories that the Massachusetts royal governor found offensive. As a result, it lasted exactly one issue.

Americans waited 14 more years for another newspaper. In 1704, the Boston *News-Letter*, appeared. The *News-Letter* contained financial and foreign news as well as records of births and deaths. Approved by the governor of the Massachusetts Bay Colony, the *News-Letter* was little more than a British mouthpiece, careful not to offend colonial authorities.

The Franklin Brothers In contrast, other papers sought controversy. For example, the New England *Courant*, first published in 1721 by James Franklin, appeared without British approval. The paper jabbed mercilessly at the royal governor, and eventually landed Franklin in jail. While serving his sentence,

JOIN, or DIE.

James Franklin handed control of the paper to his 16-year-old brother, Benjamin—someone who would play his own significant role in our nation's history. The following year, Ben ran away to New York, and later to Philadelphia.

In 1729, Benjamin Franklin founded another newspaper, the Pennsylvania *Gazette*. The *Gazette* was the first newspaper to carry weather reports, interviews, and cartoons, and it immediately became the most successful publication of its kind in the colonies.

Freedom of the Press is Born A landmark legal case helped establish freedom of the press in America. In 1733, John Peter Zenger, a German immigrant, began publishing the *New York Weekly Journal*. The paper immediately ran afoul of the royal governor by publishing articles critical of his policies. One year after the newspaper was founded, Zenger was thrown in jail for libel.

In his 1735 trial, Zenger's lawyer, Andrew Hamilton, argued that while Zenger had indeed printed material offensive to the governor, the material was true and, therefore, not libelous. Under British law, such a concept had never been argued. British law held that even true statements against the government could be legally silenced. Hamilton made an impassioned plea to the jury to defend the "cause of liberty . . . the liberty both of exposing and opposing arbitrary power . . . by speaking and writing truth."

The jury found Zenger innocent. As a result of the Zenger case, the British refrained from prosecuting American journalists, even when their criticisms of the government grew intense in the years leading up to the American Revolution.

Revolutionary Journalists Most historians agree that the American Revolution would not have happened when it did without the efforts of colonial newspapers. Newspapers stoked the flames of revolution, coining phrases like "taxation without representation" and influencing public perception of England as an enemy. When the British Stamp Act of 1765 imposed a heavy tax on all printed materials, the press denounced the legislation and refused to pay the tax. Even though the Stamp Act was repealed in 1766, it united editors and publishers in support of independence. Indeed, in 1776, most newspapers printed the Declaration of Independence on their front page.

During the Revolution, newspapers brought accounts of military developments to an eager readership. By the time the war was over, newspapers had gained enormous strength. American newspapers represented something the world had never before seen: a press committed to telling the truth, not pleasing the government.

▲ **Critical Viewing** This image was created by Benjamin Franklin for his newspaper in 1754. What does it suggest about the impact of the French war on colonial unity? **[Analyze]**

▼ **Critical Viewing** What does this image of Ben Franklin's printing press show about the physical labor of printing in colonial America? **[Infer]**

Prepare to Read

The Declaration of Independence ◆ *from* The Crisis, Number 1

Thomas Jefferson (1743–1826)

When you look at all of Thomas Jefferson's achievements, it seems there was virtually nothing that he couldn't do. Not only did he help our nation win its independence and serve as its third president, but he also founded the University of Virginia, helped establish the public school system, designed his own home, invented a type of elevator for sending food from floor to floor, and created the decimal system for American money. He was a skilled violinist, an art enthusiast, and a brilliant writer.

Revolutionary Leader Born into a wealthy Virginia family, Jefferson attended the College of William and Mary and went on to earn a law degree. While serving in the Virginia House of Burgesses, he became an outspoken defender of American rights. When conflict between the colonists and the British erupted into revolution, Jefferson emerged as a leader in the effort to win independence.

Valued Statesman When the war ended, Jefferson served as the American minister to France for several years. He then served as the nation's first secretary of state and second vice president before becoming president in 1801. While in office, Jefferson nearly doubled the size of the nation by authorizing the purchase of the Louisiana Territory from France.

On the morning of July 4, 1826, the fiftieth anniversary of the Declaration of Independence, Jefferson died at the age of 83. John Adams, Jefferson's fellow contributor to the Declaration of Independence, died only several hours after his longtime friend. Adams's last words were "Thomas Jefferson still survives."

Thomas Paine (1737–1809)

Thomas Paine met Benjamin Franklin in London, and the introduction changed his life—and American history. Paine emigrated to the colonies from England in 1774. With a letter of introduction from Franklin, Paine began a career as a journalist. In January 1776, he published *Common Sense*, in which he argued that Americans must fight for independence. The pamphlet created a national mood for revolution.

Inspiring Essayist Paine enlisted in the American army toward the end of 1776. At that time, the army had just suffered a crushing defeat by the British in New Jersey and had retreated into Pennsylvania. The soldiers were suffering from freezing weather, a shortage of provisions, and low morale. Paine was writing the first of a series of essays entitled *The American Crisis*. Washington ordered Paine's essay read to his troops before they crossed the Delaware River to defeat the Hessians at the Battle of Trenton.

In 1787, several years after the end of the American Revolution, Paine traveled to Europe and became involved with the French Revolution. Though he wrote in support of the revolutionary cause in *The Rights of Man* (1791–1792), he was imprisoned for pleading against the execution of the overthrown French king. While in prison, he began writing *The Age of Reason* (1794), an attack on organized religion. The book turned American public opinion against him, and when he died in 1809, he was a broken man. Years later, however, Paine was once again recognized as a hero of the Revolution.

Preview

Connecting to the Literature

Today, we witness armed struggles for freedom through reports in the news media. The best way to experience what our own revolution was like, however, is to read documents, like these by Jefferson and Paine.

Literary Analysis

Persuasion

Persuasion is writing meant to convince readers to think or act in a certain way. A persuasive writer appeals to emotions or reason, offers opinions, and urges action. The writer must also back up his or her points with evidence. For example, to support his argument for independence, Jefferson presents a list of offenses committed by the British king.

> He has dissolved representative houses repeatedly, for opposing with manly firmness his invasions of the rights of the people.

In these works, notice how each writer appeals to both reason and emotion to persuade readers of the rightness of his position.

Comparing Literary Works

Jefferson's and Paine's writings argue in support of independence. They were, however, written for different **audiences**. Jefferson wrote to the British king, while Paine wrote for a broad colonial readership. As you read, look for the ways in which different audiences shape each document's message.

Reading Strategy

Recognizing Charged Words

Charged words are likely to produce a strong emotional response. For example, a word like *tyranny*, which means "oppressive power," may evoke feelings of outrage. To avoid being swayed by charged words, look for support to back up the words. Use a chart like the one shown to record charged words and their connotations, or the ideas they suggest.

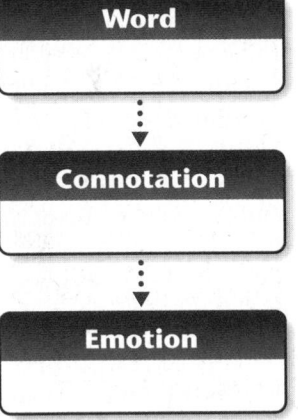

Vocabulary Development

unalienable (un āl´ yən ə bəl) *adj.* not to be taken away (p. 156)

usurpations (yo͞o´ sər pā´ shənz) *n.* unlawful seizures of rights or privileges (p. 156)

perfidy (pur´ fə dē) *n.* betrayal of trust (p. 158)

redress (ri dres´) *n.* compensation for a wrong done (p. 158)

magnanimity (mag´ nə nim´ ə tē) *n.* ability to rise above pettiness or meanness (p. 158)

acquiesce (ak´ wē es´) *v.* agree without protest (p. 159)

consanguinity (kän´ saŋ gwin´ ə tē) *n.* kinship (p. 159)

impious (im´ pē əs) *adj.* lacking reverence for God (p. 161)

infidel (in´ fə dəl´) *n.* person who holds no religious belief (p. 161)

The Declaration of Independence

Thomas Jefferson

Background

In 1776, Jefferson was chosen (with Franklin, Adams, and others) to write a declaration of the colonies' independence. The draft presented to the Second Continental Congress was largely Jefferson's work. To his disappointment, however, Congress made changes before approving the document. They dropped Jefferson's condemnation of the British for tolerating a corrupt Parliament, and they struck out a strong statement against slavery.

When in the course of human events, it becomes necessary for one people to dissolve the political bands which have connected them with another, and to assume among the powers of the earth, the separate and equal station to which the laws of nature and of nature's God entitle them, a decent respect to the opinions of mankind requires that they should declare the causes which impel them to the separation.

We hold these truths to be self-evident: that all men are created equal; that they are endowed by their Creator with certain <u>unalienable</u> rights; that among these are life, liberty and the pursuit of happiness; that to secure these rights, governments are instituted among men, deriving their just powers from the consent of the governed; that whenever any form of government becomes destructive of these ends, it is the right of the people to alter or to abolish it, and to institute new government, laying its foundation on such principles and organizing its powers in such form, as to them shall seem most likely to effect their safety and happiness. Prudence, indeed, will dictate that governments long established should not be changed for light and transient causes; and accordingly all experience hath shown, that mankind are more disposed to suffer while evils are sufferable than to right themselves by abolishing the forms to which they are accustomed. But when a long train of abuses and <u>usurpations</u>, pursuing invariably the same object, evinces a design to reduce them under absolute despotism,[1] it is their

unalienable (un āl′ yən ə bəl) *adj.* not to be taken away

Literary Analysis
Persuasion Why does Jefferson introduce the idea that one does not change a government for "light" causes?

usurpations (yōō′ sər pā′ shənz) *n.* unlawful seizures of rights or privileges

---

1. despotism (des′ pət iz′ əm) *n.* tyranny.

right, it is their duty, to throw off such government, and to provide new guards for their future security. Such has been the patient sufferance of these colonies; and such is now the necessity which constrains them to alter their former systems of government. The history of the present king of Great Britain is a history of repeated injuries and usurpations, all having in direct object the establishment of an absolute tyranny over these states. To prove this, let facts be submitted to a candid world.

He has refused his assent to laws the most wholesome and necessary for the public good.

He has forbidden his governors to pass laws of immediate and pressing importance, unless suspended in their operation till his assent should be obtained; and when so suspended, he has utterly neglected to attend to them.

He has refused to pass other laws for the accommodation of large districts of people, unless those people would relinquish the right of representation in the legislature, a right inestimable to them and formidable to tyrants only.

He has called together legislative bodies at places unusual, uncomfortable, and distant from the depository of their public records, for the sole purpose of fatiguing them into compliance with his measures.

He has dissolved representative houses repeatedly, for opposing with manly firmness his invasions on the rights of the people.

He has refused for a long time after such dissolutions to cause others to be elected, whereby the legislative powers, incapable of annihilation, have returned to the people at large for their exercise, the state remaining in the mean time exposed to all the dangers of invasion from without, and convulsions within.

He has endeavored to prevent the population of these states; for that purpose obstructing the laws for naturalization of foreigners, refusing to pass others to encourage their migration hither, and raising the conditions of new appropriations of lands.

He has obstructed the administration of justice, by refusing his assent to laws for establishing judiciary powers.

He has made judges dependent on his will alone, for the tenure of their offices, and the amount and payment of their salaries.

He has erected a multitude of new offices, and sent hither swarms of officers to harass our people and eat out their substance.

He has kept among us in times of peace standing armies without the consent of our legislatures.

Literary Analysis

Persuasion What does the statement about submitting facts to a "candid world" suggest about the intended audience?

▲ **Critical Viewing**
What is the mood of this painting? In what ways does the mood suit the occasion? **[Relate]**

✔ **Reading Check**

Why did Jefferson write this long list of facts?

He has affected to render the military independent of, and superior to, the civil power.

He has combined with others to subject us to a jurisdiction foreign to our constitution and unacknowledged by our laws, giving his assent to their acts of pretended legislation: for quartering large bodies of armed troops among us; for protecting them by a mock trial from punishment for any murders which they should commit on the inhabitants of these states; for cutting off our trade with all parts of the world; for imposing taxes on us without our consent; for depriving us, in many cases, of the benefits of trial by jury; for transporting us beyond seas to be tried for pretended offenses; for abolishing the free system of English laws in a neighboring province,[2] establishing therein an arbitrary government, and enlarging its boundaries, so as to render it at once an example and fit instrument for introducing the same absolute rule into these colonies; for taking away our charters, abolishing our most valuable laws, and altering fundamentally the forms of our governments; for suspending our own legislatures, and declaring themselves invested with power to legislate for us in all cases whatsoever.

He has abdicated government here, by declaring us out of his protection and waging war against us.

He has plundered our seas, ravaged our coasts, burned our towns, and destroyed the lives of our people.

He is at this time transporting large armies of foreign mercenaries to complete the works of death, desolation, and tyranny, already begun with circumstances of cruelty and <u>perfidy</u> scarcely paralleled in the most barbarous ages, and totally unworthy the head of a civilized nation.

He has constrained our fellow citizens taken captive on the high seas to bear arms against their country, to become the executioners of their friends and brethren, or to fall themselves by their hands.

He has excited domestic insurrections amongst us, and has endeavored to bring on the inhabitants of our frontiers, the merciless Indian savages, whose known rule of warfare is an undistinguished destruction of all ages, sexes, and conditions.

In every stage of these oppressions we have petitioned for <u>redress</u> in the most humble terms. Our repeated petitions have been answered only by repeated injury.

A prince whose character is thus marked by every act which may define a tyrant is unfit to be the ruler of a free people.

Nor have we been wanting in attentions to our British brethren. We have warned them from time to time of attempts by their legislature to extend an unwarrantable jurisdiction over us. We have reminded them of the circumstances of our emigration and settlement here. We have appealed to their native justice and <u>magnanimity</u> and we

2. **neighboring province** Quebec.

The American Experience

Jefferson, Locke, and the Social Contract

In writing the Declaration of Independence, Jefferson drew on a theory of government devised by earlier European political thinkers, especially the Englishman John Locke (1632–1704). Locke argued that all people are born with certain *natural rights*. According to Locke, these rights are not the property of governments. Rather, these rights belong to people simply because they are human. Locke's ideas also contributed to Jefferson's notion that governments derive their power from "the consent of the governed." Locke called this concept the *social contract*. According to Locke, and Jefferson after him, when a ruler like King George III breaks the social contract by acting abusively, the people have the right to revolt against his unjust rule. In 1776, that is what the American colonists did.

perfidy (pur´ fə dē) n. betrayal of trust

redress (ri dres´) n. compensation for a wrong done

Literary Analysis
Persuasion What support does this catalog of offenses provide for Jefferson's argument?

magnanimity (mag´ nə nim´ ə tē) n. ability to rise above pettiness or meanness

have conjured[3] them by the ties of our common kindred to disavow these usurpations which would inevitably interrupt our connections and correspondence. They too have been deaf to the voice of justice and of <u>consanguinity</u>. We must therefore <u>acquiesce</u> in the necessity which denounces our separation and hold them, as we hold the rest of mankind, enemies in war, in peace friends.

We, therefore, the representatives of the United States of America in general congress assembled, appealing to the Supreme Judge of the world for the rectitude of our intentions, do in the name and by authority of the good people of these colonies, solemnly publish and declare that these united colonies are and of right ought to be free and independent states; that they are absolved from all allegiance to the British Crown, and that all political connection between them and the state of Great Britain is and ought to be totally dissolved; and that as free and independent states, they have full power to levy war, conclude peace, contract alliances, establish commerce, and to do all other acts and things which independent states may of right do.

And for the support of this declaration, with a firm reliance on the protection of divine providence, we mutually pledge to each other our lives, our fortunes and our sacred honor.

consanguinity (kän´ saŋ gwin´ ə tē) *n.* kinship

acquiesce (ak´ wē es´) *v.* agree without protest

---

3. conjured *v.* solemnly appealed to.

Review and Assess

Thinking About the Selection

1. **Respond:** How would you have responded to the Declaration if you were (a) the king of England, (b) someone from a nation lacking in human rights, or (c) a Native American?

2. **(a) Recall:** What points about human rights does Jefferson make at the beginning of the Declaration? **(b) Analyze:** Why does he begin with these observations before addressing the colonists' situation?

3. **(a) Recall:** What does Jefferson claim has happened at "every stage of these oppressions"? **(b) Interpret:** What is Jefferson's purpose in presenting this information?

4. **(a) Evaluate:** What is the most convincing evidence that Jefferson cites to support his points? Explain. **(b) Evaluate:** How would you rate the overall effectiveness of his argument? Why?

5. **Synthesize:** The period in which this document was written is often referred to as the Age of Reason because of the emphasis on logic and discipline at the time. What elements of Jefferson's Declaration reflect a faith in reason?

from *The Crisis* Number 1

Thomas Paine

Recruiting for the Continental Army, c. 1857–59, William T. Ranney, Munson-Williams-Proctor Institute, Museum of Art, Utica, New York

These are the times that try men's souls.

The summer soldier and the sunshine patriot will in this crisis, shrink from the service of his country; but he that stands it now, deserves the love and thanks of man and woman. Tyranny, like hell, is not easily conquered; yet we have this consolation with us, that the harder the conflict, the more glorious the triumph. What we obtain too cheap, we esteem too lightly; 'tis dearness only that gives everything its value. Heaven knows how to put a proper price upon its goods; and it would be strange indeed, if so celestial an article as FREEDOM should not be highly rated. Britain, with an army to enforce

▲ **Critical Viewing**
What details in this image capture the patriotic fervor of Paine's essay? **[Connect]**

her tyranny, has declared that she has a right (*not only* to TAX) but "to BIND us in ALL CASES WHATSOEVER," and if being *bound in that manner*, is not slavery, then is there not such a thing as slavery upon earth. Even the expression is <u>impious</u>, for so unlimited a power can belong only to God . . .

I have as little superstition in me as any man living, but my secret opinion has ever been, and still is, that God Almighty will not give up a people to military destruction, or leave them unsupportedly to perish, who have so earnestly and so repeatedly sought to avoid the calamities of war, by every decent method which wisdom could invent. Neither have I so much of the <u>infidel</u> in me, as to suppose that he has relinquished the government of the world, and given us up to the care of devils; and as I do not, I cannot see on what grounds the king of Britain can look up to heaven for help against us: a common murderer, a highwayman, or a housebreaker, has as good a pretense as he . . .

I once felt all that kind of anger, which a man ought to feel, against the mean[1] principles that are held by the Tories:[2] a noted one, who kept a tavern at Amboy, was standing at his door, with as pretty a child in his hand, about eight or nine years old, as I ever saw, and after speaking his mind as freely as he thought was prudent, finished with this unfatherly expression, "*Well! give me peace in my day.*" Not a man lives on the continent but fully believes that a separation must some time or other finally take place, and a generous parent should have said, "*If there must be trouble let it be in my day, that my child may have peace*"; and this single reflection, well applied, is sufficient to awaken every man to duty. Not a place upon earth might be so happy as America. Her situation is remote from all the wrangling world, and she has nothing to do but to trade with them. A man can distinguish himself between temper and principle, and I am as confident, as I am that God governs the world, that America will never be happy till she gets clear of foreign dominion. Wars, without ceasing, will break out till that period arrives, and the continent must in the end be conqueror; for though the flame of liberty may sometimes cease to shine, the coal can never expire . . .

I turn with the warm ardor of a friend to those who have nobly stood, and are yet determined to stand the matter out: I call not upon a few, but upon all; not on *this* state or *that* state, but on *every* state; up and help us; lay your shoulders to the wheel; better have too much force than too little, when so great an object is at stake. Let it be told to the future world, that in the depth of winter, when nothing but hope and virtue could survive, that the city and the country, alarmed at one common danger, came forth to meet and to repulse it. Say not that thousands are gone, turn out your tens of thousands; throw not the burden of the day upon Providence, but "*show your faith by your*

---

1. **mean** *adj.* here, small-minded.
2. **Tories** colonists who remained loyal to Great Britain.

impious (im′ pē əs) *adj.* lacking reverence for God

infidel (in′ fə dəl′) *n.* a person who holds no religious belief

Reading Strategy
Recognizing Charged Words In what ways might the word "foreign" help Paine inspire the colonists to fight against Great Britain?

✔**Reading Check**
Whom does Paine call to arms?

works," that God may bless you. It matters not where you live, or what rank of life you hold, the evil or the blessing will reach you all. The far and the near, the home counties and the back, the rich and the poor, will suffer or rejoice alike. The heart that feels not now, is dead: the blood of his children will curse his cowardice, who shrinks back at a time when a little might have saved the whole, and made *them* happy. (I love the man that can smile at trouble; that can gather strength from distress, and grow brave by reflection.) 'Tis the business of little minds to shrink; but he whose heart is firm, and whose conscience approves his conduct, will pursue his principles unto death. My own line of reasoning is to myself as straight and clear as a ray of light. Not all the treasures of the world, so far as I believe, could have induced me to support an offensive war, for I think it murder; but if a thief breaks into my house, burns and destroys my property, and kills or threatens to kill me, or those that are in it, and to "*bind me in all cases whatsoever*," to his absolute will, am I to suffer it? What signifies it to me, whether he who does it is a king or a common man: my countryman, or not my countryman; whether it be done by an individual villain or an army of them? If we reason to the root of things we shall find no difference; neither can any just cause be assigned why we should punish in the one case and pardon in the other.

Review and Assess

Thinking About the Selection

1. **Respond:** If you were a colonist who had remained loyal to the British how would you react to Paine's argument?

2. **(a) Recall:** In the second paragraph, what terms does Paine use to describe the British king? **(b) Analyze:** Is this description realistic or exaggerated? Explain. **(c) Draw Conclusions:** Is Paine trustworthy as a reporter of historical events? Explain.

3. **(a) Recall:** In the first paragraph, with what ideas does the author justify the struggle of revolution? **(b) Interpret:** What does Paine mean when he refers to "the summer soldier" and the "sunshine patriot"?

4. **(a) Classify:** Name two emotions to which Paine appeals in this essay. **(b) Make a Judgment:** Does Paine appeal more to emotion or to reason in this essay? Support your answer.

5. **(a) Interpret:** What is the main idea of this essay? **(b) Support:** What persuasive techniques does Paine use to develop his main idea? **(c) Evaluate:** In your opinion, how persuasive is Paine's essay?

6. **Connect:** Which of Paine's images of the American Revolution still hold true today? Why?

Review and Assess

Literary Analysis

Persuasion

1. (a) Why does Jefferson present such a long list of grievances?
   (b) Does this list make his argument more or less convincing? Why?
2. What strategy does Jefferson use to organize his list of grievances—for example, time order, order of severity, or order of importance—and why do you think he chose this organization?
3. An **aphorism** is a brief, pointed statement expressing a wise or clever observation. Use a chart like the one shown to identify three aphorisms Paine uses and to analyze how each one contributes to his overall message.

Aphorism	Meaning	Purpose
What we obtain too cheap, we esteem too lightly.	We value only those things that cost us dearly.	to emphasize the point that the struggle for freedom is worth it

Comparing Literary Works

4. (a) Who is the intended **audience** for each of these works? (b) What kinds of supporting evidence would you expect to see in writing meant for each audience? (c) Does each writer offer the type of support that is most convincing for his audience? Explain.
5. In what ways does the language of each document reflect its intended audience?

Reading Strategy

Recognizing Charged Words

6. These authors carefully selected **charged words** to stir readers' emotions. What responses do each of these words evoke in you?

   a. liberty **b.** justice **c.** honor **d.** barbarous

7. In describing the colonists' British rulers, how does Paine's use of the word *thief* evoke a different response than would the word *supporters*?

Extend Understanding

8. **Social Studies Connection:** The Declaration of Independence has been a source of inspiration throughout the world, and Paine's essay contains many frequently quoted sayings. Why do you think these documents have had such a lasting impact?

Quick Review

Persuasion is writing meant to convince readers to think or act in a certain way.

The **audience** of a literary work is the person or group of people the author intends to reach.

Charged words contain strong connotations likely to produce an emotional response.

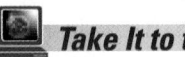 **Take It to the Net**
www.phschool.com
Take the interactive self-test online to check your understanding of these selections.

Integrate Language Skills

Vocabulary Development Lesson

Word Analysis: Latin Root *-fid-*

The Latin root *-fid-* means "faith" or "trust." An *infidel* is a person without faith, and *perfidy* is a betrayal of trust. Use your understanding of this root to define the following words.

1. confident   **2.** fidelity   **3.** confidential

Spelling Strategy

When you join the prefix *ac-* to a word or root beginning with *q*, *k*, or hard *c*, retain the *c*, as in *acclaim*. Add *ac-* to each of the words or roots below.

1. -quaint
2. -knowledge
3. -quittal
4. -quire
5. -quiesce

Fluency: True or False

Indicate which of the statements below are true and which are false. Explain your answers.

1. If a child *acquiesces* about being put to bed, she accepts her bedtime.
2. Leaders should have *magnanimity*.
3. There is no need for *redress* if no wrong has been committed.
4. American citizens would not be right to protest *usurpations* of their property.
5. Enemies have *consanguinity* toward one another.
6. The quality of *perfidy* is honorable.
7. *Unalienable* rights must be agreed upon annually.
8. *Infidels* observe certain religious holidays.
9. A pastor's *impious* behavior would be celebrated by his parishioners.

Grammar and Style Lesson

Parallelism

Parallelism refers to the repeated use of phrases, clauses, or sentences that are similar in structure or meaning.

> **Example:** He has *plundered our seas, ravaged our coasts, burned our towns,* and *destroyed the lives of our people.* (parallel verb phrases: *verb-our-object*)

Practice Rewrite each sentence to correct errors in parallel structure.

1. Jefferson was patriotic, intelligent, imaginative, and he had courage.
2. He wrote the Declaration, designed his home, and was one of the people who founded a university.
3. Henry was a great speaker, Jefferson was a gifted writer, and the talented military leader was Washington.
4. Paine was passionate, eloquent, inspiring, and he was persuasive.
5. The Declaration accused King George III of tyranny, of unfair taxation, of military occupation, and it said he bullied the legislature.

Writing Application Write your opinion on an issue about which you have strong feelings. Use two examples of parallelism to emphasize ideas.

W̶G̶ Prentice Hall Writing and Grammar Connection: Chapter 20, Section 6

Writing Lesson

A Proposal to the Principal

Like Jefferson and Paine, you can change your world with the persuasive use of words. Choose a problem or troubling situation in your school. Then, draft a proposal to the principal explaining why the situation needs attention and how you think it should be corrected. Use parallelism to emphasize your ideas.

Prewriting List the reasons that the situation in your school should be changed. Write details—facts, examples, explanations—supporting each reason. Keep word connotations in mind as you choose evidence.

Drafting Use language with positive connotations to present ideas you would like your audience to accept; use language with negative connotations to present ideas you would like your audience to reject. Remember, however, that because you are writing for the principal, you should demonstrate respect.

Model: Drafting with Forceful Language

Separate lounges for upper-and lowerclassmen reflect superior planning. Wise thinkers recognize that each group needs a place to pursue age-appropriate activities.

> Terms such as *superior* and *wise* reinforce the soundness of this proposal.

Revising Review your proposal and revise any statements that seem unreasonable. Check that you have offered evidence in addition to using forceful language to support your argument.

WG Prentice Hall Writing and Grammar Connection: Chapter 7, Section 4

Extension Activities

Listening and Speaking With a group, write and deliver two **news reports**. First, recount the signing of the Declaration. Then, present the version of the story that might have appeared on London television. For each, remember these tips:

- Include the facts of the events.
- Consider what the news means to each specific audience.

Present both reports to classmates. [**Group Activity**]

Research and Technology A **précis** is a concise summary of essential points or statements. Research Thomas Paine's life, using library and Internet sources to gather information about his philosophies and activities. Then, write a précis detailing Paine's contributions to the Revolutionary cause.

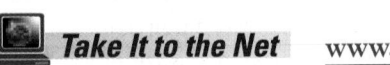 **Take It to the Net** www.phschool.com

Go online for an additional research activity using the Internet.

READING INFORMATIONAL MATERIALS

Newspaper Editorials

About Newspaper Editorials

In addition to the news, newspapers also offer opinions on the issues they report. Opinions appear primarily on the editorial page and may include political cartoons, letters to the editor, and editorials.

An **editorial** is a persuasive essay that addresses a current topic on which public opinion may be divided, and it presents the editor's or publisher's point of view. Occasionally, a newspaper may pair two editorials representing opposing points of view, creating a debate of sorts. In the editorials you are about to read, the newspaper presents two opposing viewpoints on the benefits of *pro bono* work—services donated "for the public good."

Reading Strategy

Analyzing Logical and Faulty Modes of Persuasion

To achieve its persuasive purpose, an editorial's argument requires factual support. Such support may include:

- *statistics*, or numerical data.
- *anecdotes*, or brief stories that illustrate the writer's point.
- *quotations* from expert sources.
- *facts* that are well researched and that support the writer's view.

Faulty modes of persuasion, on the other hand, twist facts or use nonfactual methods in an attempt to persuade. Review the chart below for a list of these commonly used—but faulty—techniques.

Faulty Modes of Persuasion

Type	Definition	Example
loaded language	using words with strongly negative or positive connotations	"The firm's *horse-and-buggy* attitudes *tyrannize* mothers."
bandwagon appeal	urging readers to adopt a course of action because "everyone is doing it"	"*Every other high school* in the county has a soccer team; we need one, too."
circular reasoning	supporting a point by merely stating it in other words	"The law *should be amended* because it needs *changing*."
post hoc, ergo propter hoc argument	assuming that because one event occurs after another, the first causes the second	"Since she became CEO, the value of our stock has fallen. It's time for her to resign."

Lawyers Leave Poor Behind

Our View: Volunteerism in legal profession drops as salaries rise.

For weeks, the head of the Arizona Civil Liberties Union has been asking law firms to represent, on a volunteer basis, a client in a free-speech case against the state government. And for weeks, Eleanor Eisenberg has been turned down.

Eisenberg knows firsthand what national statistics are now showing: Law firms are bucking the national trend toward charity and doing less "pro bono" work than in the past. As a result, there aren't enough lawyers willing to represent the poor and disenfranchised when they have legal trouble.

According to a recent survey by *The American Lawyer* magazine, lawyers average 40 minutes of pro bono work per week on lawsuits. That's 35% less unpaid legal work than in 1992.

Lawyers aren't even keeping their own standards. During the same period that 20% more Americans took up volunteer work, attorneys at 82 of the USA's top 100 law firms averaged fewer than the 50 hours a year of pro bono that the American Bar Association (ABA) recommends.

But instead of offering solutions for the disenfranchised, the bar association gives excuses. ABA pro bono committee chairman Robert Weiner says the top firms' record isn't as bad as it looks, and predicts it will improve as young, idealistic new hires demand to do charitable work and change the culture of their offices.

That view glibly skips over the real problem: To cover wildly increasing salaries, lawyers at many firms have been told to work more hours—2,000 per year in some cases—to bring in more revenue, according to findings from the Pro Bono Institute at Georgetown University.

Some firms in Washington, D.C., Texas, and California have stopped or cut back on counting pro bono hours as part of their lawyers' work time, institute president Esther Lardent says. With management creating that sort of an atmosphere, it's no surprise that charitable work at all but a dozen of the nation's biggest firms gets short shrift.

The ABA's own statistics show that 80% of the nation's poor are forced to go without legal help when they really need it. And the association is in the perfect position to lead efforts to ensure that the poor are treated equally.

For a start, it should encourage greater donations to legal-aid charities and insist that pro bono hours be counted as part of a lawyer's performance. A toughly worded rule could influence state bar associations, which often have the power to enforce standards.

Last winter, the Minnesota state bar was defeated in its effort to force lawyers to report fully the amount of pro bono work they do. Similar measures in Massachusetts and Colorado were also defeated.

Yet reforms do work. In Florida, a court forced lawyers to disclose their pro bono hours, and the ABA says their record subsequently improved.

The late Supreme Court Justice Louis Brandeis once noted that the legal profession "is an occupation which is pursued largely for others and not merely for one's self."

The ABA needs to remind law firms of that standard—forcefully.

An editorial expresses the official view of the publication.

In order to be persuasive, editorials often include factual support, such as statistics (numerical data).

As a part of its persuasive strategy, this editorial anticipates and answers opposition arguments.

This quote by a revered member of the legal profession eloquently supports the editorial position.

Pro Bono Work Still Valued

Opposing View:
Idealistic new lawyers will lead way in boosting service to poor.

By Robert N. Weiner

The great judge, Learned Hand, once identified the central commandment in a democracy, "Thou shalt not ration justice." As caretakers of our system of justice, lawyers have a special obligation to ensure access to justice for those who cannot afford legal fees.

The legal profession has embraced its obligation to serve the poor. Our model code of ethics instructs that "A lawyer should aspire to render at least 50 hours of pro bono public legal services per year," primarily to persons of limited means.

The legal profession can be proud of its record. The recent survey indicating a drop in pro bono hours covers only some large firms, not the profession as a whole. The largest 500 firms donated more than 2 million pro bono hours in 1999. Moreover, the vast majority of lawyers do not practice in large firms. These lawyers, including government attorneys and corporate counsel, also do valuable pro bono work, serving as the last best hope of the least fortunate among us.

Indeed, many lawyers, from every corner of the profession, have toiled with great dedication on behalf of the poor. The American Bar Association (ABA), for example, launched an effort to obtain representation for disabled children denied Social Security benefits. Thousands of lawyers responded. In addition, with numerous projects ranging from rural pro bono to child custody to immigration and asylum, ABA has worked with state and local programs linking many thousands of lawyers with even more clients.

Nonetheless, we meet less than 20% of the legal needs of the poor, far short of ensuring access to justice. In addition to pro bono efforts, federal funding of the Legal Services Corp. remains critical.

The paradox here is that prosperity—higher billable hours—indeed has put pressure on pro bono time. But this will not last. Firms must compete for the best law students. They remain idealistic, and a prime area of competition is the firms' pro bono programs. We expect that this new generation of lawyers will reinforce our profession's commitment to its most basic values.

Robert N. Weiner is chairman of the American Bar Association's Standing Committee on Pro Bono and Public Service.

The writer begins with a quote from an expert source that will frame the ideas to follow.

This editorial writer uses numerical data to support his argument.

The writer answers critics by noting that the issue is more complex than it seems at first glance.

The editorial also uses anecdotal information that illustrates the writer's position.

Check Your Comprehension

1. According to the first editorial, how well do lawyers meet the standard for *pro bono* work set by the American Bar Association?
2. According to the second editorial, how should the legal profession feel about its record regarding *pro bono* work?
3. What does the writer of that editorial believe will increase law firms' involvement in *pro bono* work?

Apply the Reading Strategy

Analyzing Logical and Faulty Modes of Persuasion

4. Using a chart like the one shown here, analyze the persuasive techniques at work in each editorial.

Mode of Persuasion	Editorial 1	Editorial 2
Statistics		
Quotations		
Anecdotes		
Faulty Modes?		

5. Which editorial is more persuasive? Explain your response.

Activity

Evaluating Editorials

In a group, read and analyze several newspaper editorials on an issue that interests you. Use these questions to guide your analysis:

- What is the proposition or main idea that each editorial supports?
- What supporting evidence does each writer provide?
- What arguments, facts, or details are omitted? Why?

To complete your evaluation, rate the editorials from most to least persuasive. Explain your ratings to the class.

Comparing Informational Materials

Editorials and Advertisements

Like an editorial, an advertisement often includes factual details to support its "pitch." Look through a magazine or newspaper, and find three advertisements that catch your attention. Then, analyze their persuasive approaches. For each advertisement, decide whether the central persuasive technique is logical or faulty.

Prepare to Read

An Hymn to the Evening ◆
To His Excellency, General Washington

Phillis Wheatley
(1753?–1784)

Although she was an enslaved African whose native language was not English, Phillis Wheatley achieved success as a poet at an early age and went on to become one of the finest American poets of her day. This was an amazing feat, considering that few women in the colonies and even fewer slaves could read or write.

Born in West Africa, Wheatley was brought to America on a slave ship when she was about eight years old. She was purchased by John Wheatley, a Boston merchant, in 1761, probably as a gift for his wife Susannah. The Wheatleys gave Phillis their name and converted her to Christianity. They also recognized the girl's high intelligence and taught her to read and write. She avidly read the Bible, Latin and Greek classics, and works by contemporary English poets. At age thirteen, she saw her first poem published.

Fame Abroad at an Early Age In 1770, when she published a poem about the death of George Whitehead, a celebrated English clergyman, Wheatley became famous. Two years later, Wheatley met several British aristocrats who admired her poetry and helped her to publish *Poems on Various Subjects: Religious and Moral* in London in 1773. This was probably the first published work by an African in the colonies.

In a foreword to the book, the publisher claimed that persons who had read the poems felt that "Numbers would be ready to suspect they were not really the Writings of Phillis."

Therefore, he offered an "attestation" to their authorship, which was signed by eighteen prominent Massachusetts men, among them John Hancock. Phillis Wheatley was well received by London society, and Benjamin Franklin visited her there. However, *Poems on Various Subjects: Religious and Moral* was not published in the United States until 1786, two years after her death.

The Story Behind the Poem During the Revolutionary War, Wheatley wrote a poem addressed to the commander of the American forces, George Washington. In October 1775, Wheatley sent the poem to Washington. He responded:

I thank you most sincerely for your polite notice of me in the elegant lines you enclosed; and however undeserving I may be of such encomium [high praise] and panegyric [tribute], the style and manner exhibit a striking proof of your poetical talents; in honor of which, and as a tribute justly due you, I would have published the poem, had I not been apprehensive that, while I only meant to give the world this new instance of your genius, I might have incurred the imputation of vanity. . . .

Slide From Glory Though she was freed in 1773, the last several years of Wheatley's life were filled with hardship and sorrow. Three of her children died in infancy, her husband was jailed for debt, and she fell into obscurity as a poet. Though she assembled a second collection of her poetry, the manuscript was lost before it could be published. With her husband in jail and her fame having faded, Phillis Wheatley died alone and impoverished in 1784.

In the centuries since Wheatley's death, her star has again risen. She is now seen as an important forerunner—the first writer of African origin to gain a voice in the United States.

Preview

Connecting to the Literature

A movie, a haircut, a joke—you may informally praise several things or people every day. At times you may express praise in a more formal way—in a song, essay, or poem—as Phillis Wheatley does in these selections.

Literary Analysis

Personification

Personification is the attribution of human powers or qualities to something that is not human, such as an inanimate object, an aspect of nature, or an abstract idea. For instance, note the way Phillis Wheatley describes the ocean in these lines:

> Enwrapp'd in tempest and a night of storms;
> Astonish'd ocean feels the wild uproar . . .

Here, the poet personifies the sea by giving it a human emotion and sensibility. In both poems, notice how Wheatley uses personification to portray her subjects in human terms.

Comparing Literary Works

Beginning with the earliest epic poems, the **poem of praise** has had a long history in literature. Some poems of praise celebrate the deeds of a hero, others celebrate the natural world, and others celebrate ordinary objects. Though both of Wheatley's poems are tributes, their subjects are very different. As you read, think about how the subject matter leads Wheatley to use distinct descriptive language and to create very different moods and meaning in each poem.

Reading Strategy

Clarifying Meaning

When reading poetry, you may need to **clarify the meaning** of passages that at first seem unclear. In these poems, Wheatley often inverts common sentence order by placing a verb before its subject. Clarify meaning by rephrasing unusual word orders and checking the definitions of unfamiliar words. Use a chart like the one shown to aid your understanding.

Original Sentence
See mother earth her offspring's fate bemoan.

↓

Define Words

↓

offspring=children bemoan=grieve

↓

Reordered and Clarified Sentence
See mother earth grieve over her children's fate.

Vocabulary Development

placid (plas´ id) *adj.* tranquil; calm; quiet (p. 172)

scepter (sep´ tər) *n.* a rod or staff held by rulers as a symbol of sovereignty (p. 172)

celestial (sə les´ chəl) *adj.* of the heavens (p. 175)

refulgent (ri ful´ jənt) *adj.* radiant; shining (p. 175)

propitious (prō pish´ əs) *adj.* favorably inclined or disposed (p. 175)

refluent (ref´ loo ənt) *adj.* flowing back (p. 175)

pensive (pen´ siv) *adj.* thinking deeply or seriously (p. 176)

An Hymn to the Evening

Phillis Wheatley

Soon as the sun forsook the eastern main
The pealing thunder shook the heav'nly plain;
Majestic grandeur! From the zephyr's[1] wing,
Exhales the incense of the blooming spring.
5 Soft purl[2] the streams, the birds renew their notes,
And through the air their mingled music floats.

Through all the heav'ns what beauteous dyes are spread!
But the west glories in the deepest red:
So may our breasts with ev'ry virtue glow,
10 The living temples of our God below!

Filled with the praise of him who gives the light;
And draws the sable curtains of the night,
Let <u>placid</u> slumbers soothe each weary mind,
At morn to wake more heav'nly, more refined;
15 So shall the labours of the day begin
More pure, more guarded from the snares of sin.

Night's leaden <u>scepter</u> seals my drowsy eyes,
Then cease, my song, till far *Aurora* rise.

placid (plas´ id) *adj.*
tranquil; calm; quiet

scepter (sep´ tər) *n.* a rod
or staff held by rulers as
a symbol of sovereignty

---

1. zephyr's (zef´ ərz) *n.* belonging to the west wind.
2. purl (pʉrl) *v.* to move in ripples or with a murmuring sound.

Review and Assess

Thinking About the Selection

1. **Respond:** This poem contains many descriptive details about the natural world. Would it be possible to praise evening using details of an urban setting? Why, or why not?

2. **(a) Recall:** What natural events happen in the first stanza? **(b) Interpret:** What specific words suggest the speaker's feelings about the scene she observes?

3. **(a) Recall:** What natural phenomenon does the poet describe in lines 7–8? **(b) Analyze:** What image does the poet use to make a transition from describing the natural world to describing a spiritual state of being? **(c) Draw Conclusions:** According to the poet, what are the "living temples of our God below"?

4. **(a) Recall:** What descriptive details does Wheatley use to describe the evening? **(b) Recall:** What details does she use to describe the morning? **(c) Compare and Contrast:** What mood or feeling does the poet connect with each time of day?

5. **(a) Recall:** When, according to Wheatley, are human beings more pure? **(b) Evaluate:** In your view, how accurate is Wheatley's contrast of a person's state of mind at night and in the morning?

To His Excellency, General Washington

PHILLIS WHEATLEY

Liberty and Washington, New York State Historical Association, Cooperstown

FIRST in WAR, FIRST in PEACE, & FIRST in the HEARTS OF HIS COUNTRYMEN.

◀ **Critical Viewing**
Noting the symbols of the Revolutionary conflict, explain the action of the painting. **[Interpret]**

Background

Phillis Wheatley was the first poet to personify America as the goddess Columbia. By giving the country's muse a name based on the explorer Columbus, Wheatley added to the new nation's mythology. The image caught on. In fact, a statue of Columbia sits atop the dome of the Capitol building in Washington, D.C.

Celestial choir! enthron'd in realms of light,
    Columbia's scenes of glorious toils I write.
While freedom's cause her anxious breast alarms,
She flashes dreadful in refulgent arms.
5 See mother earth her offspring's fate bemoan,
And nations gaze at scenes before unknown!
See the bright beams of heaven's revolving light
Involved in sorrows and the veil of night!
    The goddess comes, she moves divinely fair,
10 Olive and laurel binds her golden hair:
Wherever shines this native of the skies,
Unnumber'd charms and recent graces rise.
    Muse![1] bow propitious while my pen relates
How pour her armies through a thousand gates,
15 As when Eolus[2] heaven's fair face deforms,
Enwrapp'd in tempest and a night of storms;
Astonish'd ocean feels the wild uproar,
The refluent surges beat the sounding shore;
Or thick as leaves in Autumn's golden reign,
20 Such, and so many, moves the warrior's train.
In bright array they seek the work of war,
Where high unfurl'd the ensign[3] waves in air.
Shall I to Washington their praise recite?
Enough thou know'st them in the fields of fight.
25 Thee, first in peace and honors,—we demand
The grace and glory of thy martial band.
Fam'd for thy valor, for thy virtues more,
Hear every tongue thy guardian aid implore!

---

1. **Muse** A Greek goddess, in this case Erato, who is thought to inspire poets. She is one of nine muses presiding over literature, the arts, and the sciences.
2. **Eolus** (ē´ ə ləs) the Greek god of the winds.
3. **ensign** (en´ sin) flag.

celestial (sə les´ chəl) *adj.* of the heavens

refulgent (ri ful´ jənt) *adj.* radiant; shining

propitious (prō pish´ əs) *adj.* favorably inclined or disposed

refluent (ref´ lōō ənt) *adj.* flowing back

Reading Check
What army is the poet celebrating?

One century scarce perform'd its destined round,

30 When Gallic[4] powers Columbia's fury found;
And so may you, whoever dares disgrace
The land of freedom's heaven-defended race!
Fix'd are the eyes of nations on the scales,
For in their hopes Columbia's arm prevails.

35 Anon Britannia[5] droops the <u>pensive</u> head,
While round increase the rising hills of dead.
Ah! cruel blindness to Columbia's state!
Lament thy thirst of boundless power too late.
      Proceed, great Chief, with virtue on thy side,

40 Thy ev'ry action let the goddess guide.
A crown, a mansion, and a throne that shine,
With gold unfading, WASHINGTON! be thine.

pensive (pen´ siv) *adj.*
thinking deeply or
seriously

---

4. **Gallic** (gal´ ik) French. The colonists, led by Washington, defeated the French in the
French and Indian War (1754–1763).
5. **Britannia** England.

Review and Assess

Thinking About the Selection

1. **Respond:** Do you think that Columbia and General
   Washington are worthy subjects of the poet's praise? Explain.

2. **(a) Recall:** In lines 9–12, how is Columbia described?
   (b) Deduce: What does this image of Columbia suggest
   about the speaker's view of America?

3. **(a) Recall:** In lines 13–20, to what natural phenomenon is
   the American army compared? **(b) Interpret:** What does this
   comparison suggest about the power of American military forces
   in battle?

4. **(a) Recall:** Note three instances where Wheatley indicates
   a relationship between God and the American cause.
   (b) Analyze: What is the nature of this relationship?

5. **(a) Infer:** What details in the last two lines reflect the influence
   of the British political system? **(b) Deduce:** What position in a
   new government does the speaker assume Washington will
   occupy? **(c) Synthesize:** Which details in this depiction of
   Washington suggest the debate about the kind of government
   to be established after the war?

6. **(a) Relate:** If you were to write a poetic tribute, how would you
   personify the spirit of the United States today? **(b) Synthesize:**
   Whom would you choose for the subject of such a poetic tribute?
   Explain your choice.

Review and Assess

Literary Analysis

Personification

1. (a) In lines 9–12 of "To His Excellency, General Washington," how does the poet characterize Columbia? (b) What details does she use to describe Columbia's appearance?

2. Use a chart like the one shown to analyze other examples of **personification** that appear in "To His Excellency . . .".

Object/Idea	Human Qualities		Poet's Meaning
Eolus heaven's fair face deforms	The sky has a face.	···▶	Wind makes the sky turbulent

3. Compare and contrast Wheatley's personification of America as the goddess Columbia with the common personification of the United States as Uncle Sam.

Comparing Literary Works

4. Compare the two poems in this section. Without seeing her name, could you tell they are by the same poet? Explain.

5. In what ways does the descriptive language and mood of each **poem of praise** reflect its distinct subject?

6. Both of these poems are written in **couplets**—two consecutive lines of poetry that rhyme. Do you think the couplet works equally well in both of these poems? Why, or why not?

Reading Strategy

Clarifying Meaning

7. **Clarify** lines 11–14 of "To His Excellency, General Washington" by explaining the meaning of *unnumber'd* and *graces* and reordering the sentence parts.

8. What effect does the inverted subject and verb order have on the reader of today?

Extend Understanding

9. **Social Studies Connection:** How might a historian's treatment of the British-American conflict differ from Wheatley's treatment of the same subject in "To His Excellency, General Washington"?

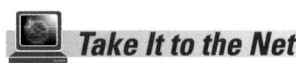

Integrate Language Skills

Vocabulary Development Lesson

Word Analysis: Latin Prefix *re-*

The prefix *re-*, which means "again" or "back," can help you define many words. The Latin word *fluere* means "to flow," and *refluent* can be defined as "flowing back." *Refulgent*, from the Latin word *refulgere*—"to flash back"—means "brilliant." Match each word in the left column with its definition in the right column.

1. revolve   **a.** repeat from memory
2. relate   **b.** link back to; connect
3. recite   **c.** turn or roll again and again

Spelling Strategy

The *-re* ending in British words like *sceptre* is usually spelled *-er* in American English: *scepter*. Rewrite each of these words with the correct American English spelling.

1. theatre   2. centre   3. meagre

Concept Development: Antonyms

Identify the word whose meaning is most nearly opposite that of the first word:

1. celestial: (a) heavenly, (b) earthbound, (c) windy
2. refulgent: (a) tarnished, (b) sparkling, (c) colorful
3. propitious: (a) evil, (b) lucky, (c) inopportune
4. refluent: (a) surging, (b) stagnant, (c) ebbing
5. pensive: (a) reflective, (b) mournful, (c) carefree
6. placid: (a) unfettered, (b) agitated, (c) generous
7. scepter: (a) trinket, (b) emblem, (c) wand

Grammar and Style Lesson

Subject and Verb Agreement

Even in poetry, the rules of **subject-verb agreement** apply. Verbs become either singular or plural to agree with their subject in number. Singular subjects take singular verb forms; plural subjects take plural verb forms.

> **Singular:** *She* <u>flashes</u> dreadful . . .
>
> **Plural:** And *nations* <u>gaze</u> at scenes . . .

Practice Identify the subject in each sentence. Then, choose the correct form of the verb in parentheses.

1. The thunder (shake, shakes) the heavenly plain.
2. When Gallic powers Columbia's fury (find, finds).
3. So may our breasts with every virtue (glow, glows).
4. Slumbers (soothe, soothes) each weary mind.
5. While round (increase, increases) the rising hills of dead.

Writing Application Write a paragraph describing a visit you made to a site of historic importance. Circle at least three instances where you use correct subject-verb agreement.

Prentice Hall Writing and Grammar Connection: Chapter 23, Section 1

Writing Lesson

Inscription for a Monument

Choose a figure from history whom you admire. Imagine you have been hired to write an inscription for a monument honoring this individual. Using Wheatley's poems as a model, convey the heroic qualities of this historical figure.

Prewriting Briefly research your chosen historical subject. Make a list of specific accomplishments and notable qualities—personal and professional—to persuade readers of your subject's historical importance.

Drafting Choose language that emphasizes the subject's greatness. Use forceful nouns (*trailblazer* instead of *worker*) and adjectives (*tireless* in place of *good*) that have positive connotations.

Model: Drafting with a Persuasive Tone

A man of supreme courage and skill, George

Washington was an inspiring general, a true patriot,

and a fearless leader. . . .

> Charged words like *supreme* and *patriot* emphasize heroic qualities.

Revising Look for opportunities to be more economical, precise, and persuasive with word choices. Check to be sure you have included the figure's most important accomplishments.

W̶G̶ Prentice Hall Writing and Grammar Connection: Chapter 7, Section 4

Extension Activities

Listening and Speaking When read aloud, poems gain richness because sound devices such as rhyme, meter, alliteration, and assonance become fully animated. Choose one of Wheatley's poems and prepare a **dramatic reading.** Use these tips to guide your rehearsal:

- Read the poem several times aloud to hear and identify the elements that make it musical.
- Mark a copy of the poem with notes about where to pause, and where to change the tone of your voice.

As you present the poem to classmates, use body language and eye contact for dramatic effect.

Research and Technology Team up with two classmates to research George Washington's military career, political life, and youth. Using computer graphics software, create a **graphic display** that highlights important events from his life. With your classmates, integrate the displays into a fold-out presentation poster.
[Group Activity]

 **Take It to the Net**   www.phschool.com

Go online for an additional research activity using the Internet.

The voices that cried out for freedom during the revolutionary period began a tradition that has carried on to this day. In recent years, Americans have raised insistent voices in the name of personal, social, and political freedoms. Among the most eloquent voice for freedom was that of Martin Luther King, Jr.

Twentieth-Century Echoes Martin Luther King, Jr. and other American civil rights leaders of the 1950s and 1960s shared similar ideas of freedom expressed by early Americans such as Thomas Paine, Thomas Jefferson, and Phillis Wheatley. King addressed some of the same themes as did his revolutionary forebears—freedom, the fundamental importance of justice, and strategies for fighting oppression. Like Paine's, King's language was vivid; like Wheatley's, his words alluded to deities and heroes; and like Jefferson's, his voice called for boldness, wisdom, and morality.

In 1963, King was arrested for protesting racial segregation in Birmingham, Alabama. As he sat in jail, he read a newspaper article in which eight white clergymen chastised him for "unwise and untimely" demonstrations. Without proper writing paper, King drafted a response—the "Letter from Birmingham City Jail"—in the cramped margins of that newspaper. A few months later, King led the March on Washington. On this occasion, more than 200,000 Americans of all races gathered around the Lincoln Memorial and heard his voice ring out again for the causes of racial justice and freedom.

from Letter from Birmingham City Jail

Dr. Martin Luther King, Jr.

I hope the church as a whole will meet the challenge of this decisive hour. But even if the church does not come to the aid of justice, I have no despair about the future. I have no fear about the outcome of our struggle in Birmingham, even if our <u>motives</u> are presently misunderstood. We will reach the goal of freedom in Birmingham and all over the nation, because the goal of America is freedom. Abused and scorned though we may be, our destiny is tied up with the destiny of America. Before the Pilgrims landed at Plymouth we were here. Before the pen of Jefferson etched across the pages of history the majestic words of the

motives (mōt´ ivz) *n.* reasons for action; inner drives

Declaration of Independence, we were here. For more than two centuries our foreparents labored in this country without wages; they made cotton king; and they built the homes of their masters in the midst of brutal injustice and shameful humiliation—and yet out of a bottomless <u>vitality</u> they continued to thrive and develop. If the inexpressible cruelties of slavery could not stop us, the opposition we now face will surely fail. We will win our freedom because the sacred heritage of our nation and the eternal will of God are embodied in our echoing demands.

I must close now. But before closing I am <u>impelled</u> to mention one other point in your statement that troubled me profoundly. You warmly commended the Birmingham police force for keeping "order" and "preventing violence." I don't believe you would have so warmly commended the police force if you had seen its angry violent dogs literally biting six unarmed, nonviolent Negroes. I don't believe you would so quickly commend the policemen if you would observe their ugly and inhuman treatment of Negroes here in the city jail; if you would watch them push and curse old Negro women and young Negro girls; if you would see them slap and kick old Negro men and young Negro boys; if you will observe them, as they did on two occasions, refuse to give us food because we wanted to sing our grace together. I'm sorry that I can't join you in your praise for the police department.

It is true that they have been rather disciplined in their public handling of the demonstrators. In this sense they have been rather publicly "nonviolent." But for what purpose? To preserve the evil system of segregation. Over the last few years I have consistently preached that nonviolence demands that the means we use must be as pure as the ends we seek. So I have tried to make it clear that it is wrong to use immoral means to attain moral ends. But now I must affirm that it is just as wrong, or even more so, to use moral means to preserve immoral ends. Maybe Mr. Connor and his policemen have been rather publicly nonviolent, as Chief Pritchett was in Albany, Georgia, but they have used the moral means of nonviolence to maintain the immoral end of <u>flagrant</u> racial injustice. T. S. Eliot has said that there is no greater treason than to do the right deed for the wrong reason.

I wish you had commended the Negro sit-inners and demonstrators of Birmingham for their sublime courage, their willingness to suffer and their amazing discipline in the midst of the most inhuman provocation. One day the South will recognize its real heroes. They will be the James Merediths, courageously and with a majestic sense of purpose facing jeering and hostile mobs and the agonizing loneliness that characterizes the life of the pioneer. They will be old, oppressed, battered Negro women, symbolized in a seventy-two-year-old woman of Montgomery, Alabama, who rose up with a sense of dignity and with her people decided not to ride the segregated buses, and responded to one who inquired about

vitality (vī tal′ ə tē) n. power to endure or survive; life force

impelled (im peld′) v. moved; forced

flagrant (flā′ grənt) adj. glaring, outrageous

▼ Critical Viewing
To prevent others from joining this African American sitting at a "whites only" lunch counter, the other seats were piled with linen supplies. Basing your response on their posture and activity, what might the customer and the waitress be feeling? **[Hypothesize]**

her tiredness with ungrammatical <u>profundity</u>: "My feet is tired, but my soul is rested." They will be the young high school and college students, young ministers of the gospel and a host of their elders courageously and nonviolently sitting-in at lunch counters and willingly going to jail for conscience's sake. One day the South will know that when these disinherited children of God sat down at lunch counters they were in reality standing up for the best in the American dream and the most sacred values in our Judeo-Christian heritage, and thusly, carrying our whole nation back to those great wells of democracy which were dug deep by the Founding Fathers in the formulation of the Constitution and the Declaration of Independence.

Never before have I written a letter this long (or should I say a book?). I'm afraid that it is much too long to take your precious time. I can assure you that it would have been much shorter if I had been writing from a comfortable desk, but what else is there to do when you are alone for days in the dull <u>monotony</u> of a narrow jail cell other than write long letters, think strange thoughts, and pray long prayers?

If I have said anything in this letter that is an overstatement of the truth and is indicative of an unreasonable impatience, I beg you to forgive me. If I have said anything in this letter that is an understatement of the truth and is indicative of my having a patience that makes me patient with anything less than brotherhood, I beg God to forgive me.

I hope this letter finds you strong in the faith. I also hope that circumstances will soon make it possible for me to meet each of you, not as an integrationist or a civil rights leader, but as a fellow clergyman and a Christian brother. Let us all hope that the dark clouds of racial prejudice will soon pass away and the deep fog of misunderstanding will be lifted from our fear-drenched communities and in some not too distant tomorrow the radiant stars of love and brotherhood will shine over our great nation with all of their <u>scintillating</u> beauty.

> Yours for the cause of Peace
> and Brotherhood,
> Martin Luther King, Jr.

profundity (prō fun′ də tē) *n.* intellectual depth

monotony (mə nät′ ən ē) *n.* tiresome, unchanging sameness; lack of variety

scintillating (sint′ əl āt′ iŋ) *adj.* sparkling

Martin Luther King, Jr.

(1929–1968)

A charismatic Baptist minister and civil rights leader, Martin Luther King, Jr. struggled to bring African Americans into the political and economic mainstream of American life in the 1950s and 1960s. King drew inspiration from Christian ideals and insisted, like Indian leader Mohandas K. Gandhi, that political and social freedoms were attainable through nonviolent actions.

King led boycotts, marches, and sit-ins to protest segregation and organized the March on Washington, speaking out against discrimination. Although King stressed nonviolence, he became an American martyr for freedom when he was assassinated at the age of 39. His widow, Coretta Scott King, works to keep King's message and achievements alive.

Connecting Literature Past and Present

1. How is King's imprisonment related to "those great wells of democracy which were dug deep by the founding fathers in the formulation of the Constitution and the Declaration of Independence"?

2. Both "Letter from Birmingham City Jail" and "To His Excellency, General Washington" glorify freedom. What similarities and differences can you identify between the war for independence and the struggle for civil rights?

George Washington Standing on the Platform,
Pennsylvania State Capitol, Harrisburg

The colonial period of American history witnessed speeches and oratory powerful enough to start the Revolution. In speeches that rang through the halls of government, speakers such as Patrick Henry and Benjamin Franklin turned away from colonial loyalty toward a spirit of independence.

Prepare to Read

Speech in the Virginia Convention ◆
Speech in the Convention

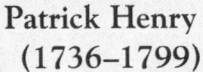

Patrick Henry
(1736–1799)

It was said that Patrick Henry could move his listeners to anger, fear, or laughter more easily than the most talented actor. Remembered most for his fiery battle cry— "Give me liberty or give me death"—Henry is considered to be the most powerful orator of the American Revolution. He helped to inspire colonists to unite in an effort to win their independence from Britain.

Voice of Protest In 1765, Henry was elected to the Virginia House of Burgesses. Shortly after his election, he delivered one of his most powerful speeches, declaring his opposition to the Stamp Act. The Stamp Act, which was passed by the British Parliament, required American colonists to pay a tax on every piece of printed paper they used. Legal documents, newspapers, and even playing cards were all subject to the tax. Over the protests of some of its most influential members, the Virginia House adopted Henry's resolutions.

A Call to Arms In 1775, Henry delivered his most famous speech at the Virginia Provincial Convention. While most of the speakers that day argued that the colony should seek a compromise with the British, Henry boldly urged armed resistance to England. His speech had a powerful impact on the audience, feeding the revolutionary spirit that led to the signing of the Declaration of Independence.

In the years that followed, Henry continued to be an important political leader, serving as governor of Virginia and member of the Virginia General Assembly.

Benjamin Franklin
(1706–1790)

No other colonial American better embodied the promise of America than Benjamin Franklin. Through hard work, dedication, and ingenuity, Franklin was able to rise out of poverty to become a wealthy, famous, and influential person. Although he never received a formal education, Franklin made important contributions in the fields of literature, journalism, science, diplomacy, education, and philosophy.

A Persuasive Diplomat Franklin was a leader in the movement for independence. In 1776, Congress sent him to France to enlist aid for the American Revolution. Franklin's persuasive powers proved effective, as he was able to achieve his goal—a pivotal breakthrough that may have been the deciding factor in the war.

Helping Forge a Nation In 1783, Franklin signed the peace treaty that ended the war and established the new nation. He returned home to serve as a delegate to the Constitutional Convention in Philadelphia. There, as politicians clashed over plans for the new government, Franklin worked to resolve conflicts and ensure ratification of the Constitution.

In spite of his other contributions, Franklin is best remembered as a statesman and diplomat. He was the only American to sign all four documents that established the nation: the Declaration of Independence, the treaty of alliance with France, the peace treaty with England, and the Constitution. (For more on Franklin, see p. 138.)

Preview

Connecting to the Literature

Speeches, like Martin Luther King's "I have a dream," have helped to shape the American identity by expressing our goals as a people. As you read these speeches, think about the vital American principles they express.

Literary Analysis

Speeches

Speeches are written works that are delivered orally. An effective speaker uses a variety of techniques to emphasize key points:

- *Restatement:* repeating an idea in a variety of ways
- *Repetition:* restating an idea using the same words
- *Parallelism:* repeating grammatical structures
- *Rhetorical question:* asking a question whose answer is self-evident

Watch for examples of these techniques in these speeches.

Comparing Literary Works

Speeches from the same time period, even those addressing related topics, may sound very different. One reason for this is that a speaker's **diction**—the choice and arrangement of words—creates a personal stamp. Diction may be casual, formal, simple, or sophisticated, and is often altered to address the aims of the speech. Compare the diction of these speeches, evaluating how well each speaker's word choices support his purposes.

Reading Strategy

Evaluating Persuasive Appeals

To stir an audience, speakers may appeal to people's emotions, or to a sense of reason. When you read a persuasive speech, **evaluate** the **persuasive appeals** that the speaker makes. Assess the speaker's motivation in evoking emotions. Note the arguments and evidence offered, and evaluate how well the appeals suit the audience and occasion. Use a diagram like the one shown to record each speaker's persuasive appeals.

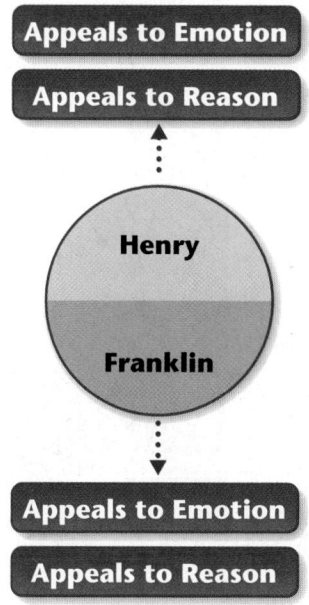

Vocabulary Development

arduous (är′ jōō əs) *adj.* difficult (p. 188)

insidious (in sid′ ē əs) *adj.* deceitful; treacherous (p. 188)

subjugation (sub′ jə gā′ shən) *n.* the act of conquering (p. 188)

vigilant (vij′ ə lənt) *adj.* alert to danger (p. 189)

infallibility (in fal′ ə bil′ ə tē) *n.* inability to be wrong; reliability (p. 191)

despotism (des′ pət iz′ əm) *n.* absolute rule; tyranny (p. 191)

salutary (sal′ yoo ter′ ē) *adj.* beneficial; promoting a good purpose (p. 192)

unanimity (yoo′ nə nim′ ə tē) *n.* complete agreement (p. 192)

posterity (päs ter′ ə tē) *n.* all succeeding generations (p. 192)

manifest (man′ ə fest′) *adj.* evident; obvious; clear (p. 192)

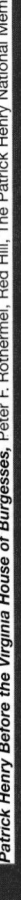

Patrick Henry Before the Virginia House of Burgesses, Peter F. Rothermel, Red Hill, The Patrick Henry National Memorial

▲ **Critical Viewing** Patrick Henry's dramatic speeches swayed sentiment away from loyalty to the British crown and toward armed resistance. What details in this painting convey the power of Henry's oratory? **[Analyze]**

Speech in the Virginia Convention

Patrick Henry

Background

In this speech, delivered in 1775, Patrick Henry publicly denounces the British king and urges the colonists to fight for independence. Making such a declaration took tremendous bravery. England was the world's most powerful country at the time, and the odds against the colonists were overwhelming. If the colonies had failed to win independence, Henry could have been executed for treason.

Mr. President: No man thinks more highly than I do of the patriotism, as well as abilities, of the very worthy gentlemen who have just addressed the house. But different men often see the same subject in different lights; and, therefore, I hope it will not be thought disrespectful to those gentlemen, if, entertaining, as I do, opinions of a character very opposite to theirs, I shall speak forth my sentiments freely and without reserve. This is no time for ceremony. The question before the house is one of awful moment[1] to this country. For my own part, I consider it as nothing less than a question of freedom or slavery. And in proportion to the magnitude of the subject ought to be the freedom of the debate. It is only in this way that we can hope to arrive at truth, and fulfill the great responsibility which we hold to God and our country. Should I keep back my opinions at such a time, through fear of giving offense, I should consider myself as guilty of treason toward my country, and of an act of disloyalty toward the Majesty of Heaven, which I revere above all earthly kings.

Literary Analysis
Speeches and Diction
Identify three phrases from this section that show Henry's use of sophisticated diction.

✓**Reading Check**
Does Henry agree or disagree with those who spoke before him?

---

1. **moment** importance.

Mr. President, it is natural to man to indulge in the illusions of hope. We are apt to shut our eyes against a painful truth, and listen to the song of that siren till she transforms us into beasts.[2] Is this the part of wise men, engaged in a great and <u>arduous</u> struggle for liberty? Are we disposed to be of the number of those who having eyes see not, and having ears hear not,[3] the things which so nearly concern their temporal salvation? For my part, whatever anguish of spirit it may cost, I am willing to know the whole truth; to know the worst and to provide for it.

I have but one lamp by which my feet are guided, and that is the lamp of experience. I know of no way of judging of the future but by the past. And judging by the past, I wish to know what there has been in the conduct of the British ministry for the last ten years to justify those hopes with which gentlemen have been pleased to solace themselves and the house? Is it that <u>insidious</u> smile with which our petition has been lately received? Trust it not, sir; it will prove a snare to your feet. Suffer not yourselves to be betrayed with a kiss.[4] Ask yourselves how this gracious reception of our petition comports with those warlike preparations which cover our waters and darken our land. Are fleets and armies necessary to a work of love and reconciliation? Have we shown ourselves so unwilling to be reconciled that force must be called in to win back our love? Let us not deceive ourselves, sir. These are the implements of war and <u>subjugation</u>—the last arguments to which kings resort.

I ask gentlemen, sir, what means this martial array, if its purpose be not to force us to submission? Can gentlemen assign any other possible motive for it? Has Great Britain any enemy in this quarter of the world, to call for all this accumulation of navies and armies? No, sir, she has none. They are meant for us: they can be meant for no other. They are sent over to bind and rivet upon us those chains which the British ministry have been so long forging.

And what have we to oppose to them? Shall we try argument? Sir, we have been trying that for the last ten years. Have we anything new to offer upon the subject? Nothing. We have held the subject up in every light of which it is capable; but it has been all in vain. Shall we resort to entreaty and humble supplication? What terms shall we find which have not been already exhausted? Let us not, I beseech you, sir, deceive ourselves longer. Sir, we have done everything that could be done to avert the storm which is now coming on. We have petitioned; we have remonstrated; we have supplicated; we have prostrated ourselves before the throne, and have implored its interposition[5] to arrest the tyrannical hands of the ministry and Parliament. Our petitions

arduous (är´ jŏŏ əs) *adj.* difficult

insidious (in sid´ ē əs) *adj.* deceitful; treacherous

subjugation (sub´ jə gā´ shən) *n.* the act of conquering

Literary Analysis
Speeches What is the effect of the five rhetorical questions in this paragraph?

---

2. **listen . . . beasts** In Homer's *Odyssey*, the enchantress Circe transforms men into swine after charming them with her singing.
3. **having eyes . . . hear not** In Ezekiel 12:2, those "who have eyes to see, but see not, who have ears to hear, but hear not" are addressed.
4. **betrayed with a kiss** In Luke 22:47–48, Jesus is betrayed with a kiss.
5. **interposition** intervention.

have been slighted; our remonstrances have produced additional violence and insult; our supplications have been disregarded; and we have been spurned with contempt from the foot of the throne! In vain, after these things, may we indulge the fond[6] hope of peace and reconciliation. There is no longer any room for hope. If we wish to be free, if we mean to preserve inviolate those inestimable privileges for which we have been so long contending, if we mean not basely to abandon the noble struggle in which we have been so long

AMERICA TRIUMPHANT and BRITANNIA in DISTRESS

EXPLANATION.

I America fitting on that quarter of the globe with the Flag of the United States difplayed over her head; holding in one hand the Olive branch, inviting the fhips of all nations to partake of her commerce, and in the other hand fupporting the Cap of Liberty.

II Fame proclaiming the joyful news to all the world.

III Britannia weeping at the lofs of the trade of America, attended with an evil genius.

IV The British flag ftruck, on her ftrong Fortreffes.

V French, Spanifh, Dutch, &c fhipping in the harbours of America.

VI A view of New-York, wherein is exhibited the Traitor Arnold, taken with remorfe for felling his country, and Judas like hanging himfelf.

engaged, and which we have pledged ourselves never to abandon until the glorious object of our contest shall be obtained—we must fight! I repeat it, sir, we must fight! An appeal to arms and to the God of Hosts is all that is left us!

They tell us, sir, that we are weak—unable to cope with so formidable an adversary. But when shall we be stronger? Will it be the next week, or the next year? Will it be when we are totally disarmed, and when a British guard shall be stationed in every house? Shall we gather strength by irresolution and inaction? Shall we acquire the means of effectual resistance by lying supinely on our backs and hugging the delusive phantom of hope until our enemies shall have bound us hand and foot? Sir, we are not weak, if we make a proper use of those means which the God of nature hath placed in our power. Three millions of people, armed in the holy cause of liberty, and in such a country as that which we possess, are invincible by any force which our enemy can send against us. Besides, sir, we shall not fight our battles alone. There is a just God who presides over the destinies of nations and who will raise up friends to fight our battles for us. The battle, sir, is not to the strong alone;[7] it is to the <u>vigilant</u>, the active, the brave. Besides,

---

6. **fond** foolish.
7. **The battle . . . alone** "The race is not to the swift, nor the battle to the strong." (Ecclesiastes 9:11)

▲ **Critical Viewing**
What details in this political cartoon convey the artist's opinion? **[Analyze]**

vigilant (vij´ ə lənt) *adj.* alert to danger

☑ **Reading Check**
What measures, short of war, have the colonists tried?

sir, we have no election;[8] if we were base enough to desire it, it is now too late to retire from the contest. There is no retreat but in submission and slavery! Our chains are forged! Their clanging may be heard on the plains of Boston! The war is inevitable—and let it come! I repeat it, sir, let it come!

It is in vain, sir, to extenuate the matter. Gentlemen may cry, "Peace, peace"—but there is no peace. The war is actually begun! The next gale that sweeps from the north[9] will bring to our ears the clash of resounding arms! Our brethren are already in the field! Why stand we here idle? What is it that gentlemen wish? What would they have? Is life so dear, or peace so sweet, as to be purchased at the price of chains and slavery? Forbid it, Almighty God! I know not what course others may take; but as for me, give me liberty or give me death!

---

8. **election** choice.
9. **The next gale . . . north** In Massachusetts, some colonists had already shown open resistance to the British.

Review and Assess

Thinking About the Selection

1. **Respond:** If you had been in the audience, how would you have responded to Henry's speech? Why?

2. **(a) Recall:** What does Henry say about the previous speakers? **(b) Infer:** What does he hope to accomplish by commenting on the earlier speakers?

3. **(a) Recall:** What measures does Henry say the colonists have already tried in their dealings with England? **(b) Analyze:** What examples does Henry provide to support his position that compromise with the British is not a workable solution?

4. **(a) Infer:** What course of action does Henry want the colonists to take? **(b) Draw Conclusions:** What is Henry's answer to the objection that the colonists are not ready to fight against the British?

5. **(a) Speculate:** Do you think Henry was prepared to stand behind his words when he exclaimed, "Give me liberty or give me death"? Why, or why not? **(b) Deduce:** What does his willingness to make such an assertion reveal about his character? **(c) Extend:** If you had been in his place, would you have made such an assertion? Why, or why not?

6. **Speculate:** What types of people living in the colonies at the time of Henry's speech might have reacted negatively to his words? Why?

Speech in the Convention

Benjamin Franklin

Mr. President,

I confess, that I do not entirely approve of this Constitution at present; but, Sir, I am not sure I shall never approve it; for, having lived long, I have experienced many instances of being obliged, by better information or fuller consideration, to change my opinions even on important subjects, which I once thought right, but found to be otherwise. It is therefore that, the older I grow, the more apt I am to doubt my own judgment of others. Most men, indeed, as well as most sects in religion, think themselves in possession of all truth, and that wherever others differ from them, it is so far error. . . . Though many private Persons think almost as highly of their own infallibility as of that of their Sect, few express it so naturally as a certain French Lady, who, in a little dispute with her sister, said, "But I meet with nobody but myself that is *always* in the right." "*Je ne trouve que moi qui aie toujours raison.*"

In these sentiments, Sir, I agree to this Constitution, with all its faults,—if they are such; because I think a general Government necessary for us, and there is no form of government but what may be a blessing to the people, if well administered; and I believe, farther, that this is likely to be well administered for a course of years, and can only end in despotism, as other forms have done before it, when the people shall become so corrupted as to need despotic government, being incapable of any other. I doubt, too, whether any other Convention we can obtain, may be able to make a better constitution; for, when you assemble a number of men, to have the advantage of their joint wisdom, you inevitably assemble with those men all their prejudices, their passions, their errors of opinion, their local interests, and their selfish views. From such an assembly can a *perfect* production be expected? It therefore astonishes me, Sir, to find this system approaching so near to perfection as it does; and I think it will astonish our enemies, who are waiting with confidence to hear, that our councils are confounded like those of the builders of Babel, and that our States are on the point of separation, only to meet hereafter for the purpose of cutting one another's throats. Thus I consent, Sir, to this Constitution, because I expect no better, and because I am

infallibility (in faľ ə biľ ə tē) *n.* inability to be wrong; reliability

despotism (desʹ pət izʹ əm) *n.* absolute rule; tyranny

✔**Reading Check**

Why is Franklin so astonished by the high quality of the Constitution?

not sure that it is not the best. The opinions I have had of its *errors* I sacrifice to the public good. I have never whispered a syllable of them abroad. Within these walls they were born, and here they shall die. If every one of us, in returning to our Constituents, were to report the objections he has had to it, and endeavour to gain Partisans in support of them, we might prevent its being generally received, and thereby lose all the <u>salutary</u> effects and great advantages resulting naturally in our favour among foreign nations, as well as among ourselves, from our real or apparent <u>unanimity</u>. Much of the strength and efficiency of any government, in procuring and securing happiness to the people, depends on *opinion*, on the general opinion of the goodness of that government, as well as of the wisdom and integrity of its governors. I hope, therefore, for our own sakes, as a part of the people, and for the sake of our <u>posterity</u>, that we shall act heartily and unanimously in recommending this Constitution, wherever our Influence may extend, and turn our future thoughts and endeavors to the means of having it *well administered*.

On the whole, Sir, I cannot help expressing a wish, that every member of the Convention who may still have objections to it, would with me on this occasion doubt a little of his own infallibility, and, to make <u>*manifest*</u> our *unanimity*, put his name to this Instrument.

salutary (sal′ yoo ter′ ē)
adj. beneficial; promoting a good purpose

unanimity (yoo′ nə nim′ ə tē)
n. complete agreement

posterity (päs ter′ ə tē)
n. all succeeding generations

manifest (man′ ə fest′) *adj.* evident; obvious; clear

Review and Assess

Thinking About the Selection

1. **Respond:** Based on Franklin's argument, would you have ratified the Constitution? Why or why not?

2. **(a) Recall:** What confession does Franklin make in the first paragraph? **(b) Interpret:** What effect does Franklin achieve with this "confession"?

3. **(a) Recall:** Why does Franklin feel that unanimity among the delegates is essential to the success of the United States? **(b) Analyze:** What is Franklin's purpose in suppressing his "opinions" for the "public good"?

4. **(a) Recall:** Why, according to Franklin, would any document created by a committee be faulty? **(b) Draw Conclusions:** What is Franklin implying about human nature?

5. **(a) Recall:** What three reasons does Franklin give for finally agreeing to accept the Constitution? **(b) Evaluate:** How effectively does he convey the thought process that brought him from doubt about the Constitution to a decision to accept it? Explain.

6. **Take a Position:** Franklin says that government depends in part on the wisdom and integrity of its leaders. Do you agree? Explain.

Review and Assess

Literary Analysis

Speeches

1. Use a chart like the one shown to analyze each speaker's use of persuasive techniques.

	Example	Effect
Restatement		
Repetition		
Parallelism		

2. In what way does each speaker use "concession," or the acknowledgment of opposition arguments, to advance his position?
3. Based on this **speech,** do you think Henry's reputation as a great orator was deserved? Explain.

Comparing Literary Works

4. (a) To analyze the **diction** used by each speaker, find an example of ornate language from each speech. (b) Rewrite the passage in plain language. (c) Explain how the diction helps convey the message.
5. (a) Compare and contrast the endings of these speeches and weigh their impact on an audience. (b) Which do you think is more effective? Explain.
6. (a) What words does each speaker use to refer to the country's future? (b) How does each man see his responsibility—and that of his audience—to that future?
7. (a) How is Franklin's experience as a diplomat reflected in his speech? (b) How is Henry's experience as a lawyer reflected in his?

Reading Strategy

Evaluating Persuasive Appeals

8. Considering the purpose of Henry's speech, why are **persuasive appeals** to both emotions and reason appropriate?
9. What arguments does Franklin use to back up his emotional appeals?

Extend Understanding

10. **Social Studies Connection:** At times of crisis, what role can political speeches like those of Henry and Franklin play in public life? Explain.

Integrate Language Skills

Vocabulary Development Lesson

Word Analysis: Latin Suffix -ity

The Latin suffix -ity turns adjectives into nouns. Added to the adjective *infallible*, meaning "incapable of error," it creates the noun *infallibility*, meaning "the state of being infallible."

Define each of the following words:

1. complexity   3. anonymity
2. flexibility   4. adaptability

Spelling Strategy

When you add the suffix -ity to a word that ends in -able or -ible, drop the final e and insert i between the b and l (infallible + -ity = infallibility).

Add the suffix -ity to each word below.

1. legible   2. acceptable   3. reliable

Fluency: Definitions

Match the vocabulary word with its definition.

1. insidious   a. evident; clear
2. subjugation   b. deceitful; treacherous
3. vigilant   c. complete agreement
4. infallibility   d. tyranny
5. despotism   e. the act of conquering
6. salutary   f. alert to danger
7. unanimity   g. reliability
8. manifest   i. beneficial
9. arduous   j. succeeding generations
10. posterity   k. very difficult

Grammar and Style Lesson

Double Negatives

Although it is no longer considered acceptable style, orators in the Revolutionary period sometimes used **double negatives**—two negatives where only one is needed—to stress their opinions. Look at these incorrect and correct examples. In both, the negatives are italicized:

Incorrect:	I *don't hardly* know where to begin.
Correct:	I *don't* know where to begin.

In the first example, there are two negatives. Remember to use only one negative to make a negative sentence.

Practice Revise each sentence that contains a double negative. If a sentence is correct, write "correct."

1. Don't sign nothing until you hear from me.
2. You don't have enough information.
3. I don't think you'll want hardly anything from me.
4. I didn't have any idea that he wouldn't show up.
5. It wouldn't make no difference to me if they cancelled the meeting.

Writing Application Write a paragraph in which you explain how the spirit of revolutionary Americans like Henry and Franklin does or does not still exist today. Use double negatives at least three times. Then, exchange your speech with a classmate and correct each other's mistakes.

W͟G Prentice Hall Writing and Grammar Connection: Chapter 25, Section 1

Writing Lesson

Commentary on a Speech

Choose a speech by a skilled modern orator and write a commentary that evaluates the way in which the speaker leads an audience to agree with his or her ideas.

Prewriting Review the speech to outline the speaker's key points and to note the persuasive techniques used. Then, critically analyze how well the speaker has supported his or her key points and how effectively he or she has used persuasive techniques.

Drafting Focus each paragraph on a single point—for example, one paragraph might focus on the speaker's appeals to emotions, another on the speaker's appeals to reason.

Revising Review your commentary to make sure you have adequately supported your ideas. Identify places in your draft where you might strengthen your analysis with direct quotations from the speech.

Model: Revising to Add Quotations

In his speech on the occasion of the Challenger space shuttle

(add quote)

disaster, President Reagan spoke first as a private man, and

(add quote)

second as a political leader.

> A caret identifies places where direct quotation would support the thesis.

 Prentice Hall Writing and Grammar Connection: Chapter 28, Section 1

Extension Activities

Listening and Speaking With a group, prepare a **debate** about the value of independence or the ratification of the Constitution. Keep the following tips in mind:

- Choose evidence that supports your persuasive purpose.
- Include logical, ethical, and emotional appeals.

Present the debate to classmates.

Research and Technology Using electronic and online encyclopedias as sources, collect speeches from different periods of history. Incorporate photographs and audiotaped recordings of the speeches. Create a **display** highlighting key passages from the speeches.

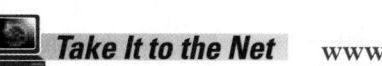 **Take It to the Net**   www.phschool.com

Go online for an additional research activity using the Internet.

American Speechmaking

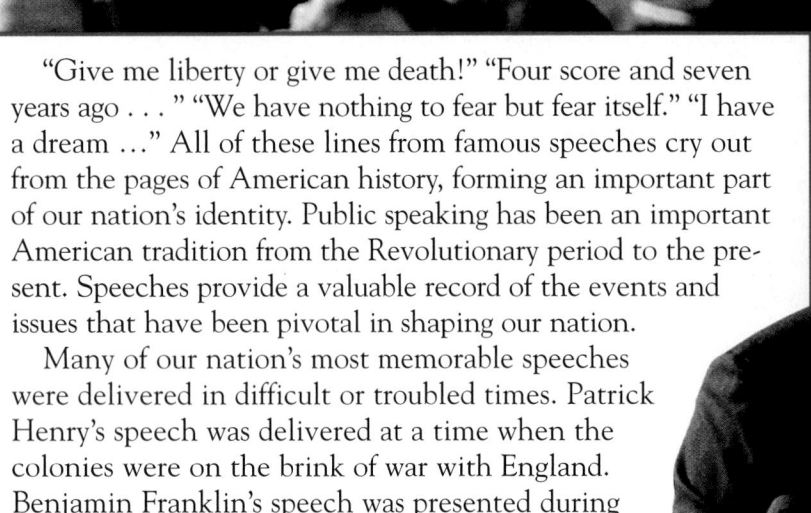

"Give me liberty or give me death!" "Four score and seven years ago . . . " "We have nothing to fear but fear itself." "I have a dream …" All of these lines from famous speeches cry out from the pages of American history, forming an important part of our nation's identity. Public speaking has been an important American tradition from the Revolutionary period to the present. Speeches provide a valuable record of the events and issues that have been pivotal in shaping our nation.

Many of our nation's most memorable speeches were delivered in difficult or troubled times. Patrick Henry's speech was delivered at a time when the colonies were on the brink of war with England. Benjamin Franklin's speech was presented during the heated struggle to forge our Constitution.

A Modern Orator When John F. Kennedy took office in 1961, the United States was locked in a potentially explosive stalemate with the Soviet Union and its allies. Fierce adversaries, the United States and the Soviet Union were stockpiling nuclear weapons, creating the possibility of a disastrous war that could destroy the Earth. In his now-famous inaugural address, Kennedy addressed our nation's fears and reached out to our adversaries, while reaffirming our nation's strength.

Inaugural Address

John F. Kennedy

Vice President Johnson, Mr. Speaker, Mr. Chief Justice, President Eisenhower, Vice President Nixon, President Truman,[1] *reverend clergy, fellow citizens,* we observe today not a victory of party, but a celebration of freedom—symbolizing an end, as well as a beginning—signifying renewal, as well as change. For I have sworn before you and Almighty God the same solemn oath our forebears prescribed nearly a century and three quarters ago.

The world is very different now. For man holds in his mortal hands the power to abolish all forms of human poverty and all forms of human life. And yet the same revolutionary beliefs for which our forebears fought are still at issue around the globe—the belief that the rights of man come not from the generosity of the state, but from the hand of God.

We dare not forget today that we are the <u>heirs</u> of that first revolution. Let the word go forth from this time and place, to friend and foe alike, that the torch has been passed to a new generation of Americans—born in this century, tempered by war, disciplined by a hard and bitter peace, proud of our ancient heritage—and unwilling to witness or permit the slow undoing of those human rights to which this Nation has always been committed, and to which we are committed today at home and around the world.

Let every nation know, whether it wishes us well or ill, that we shall pay any price, bear any burden, meet any hardship, support any friend, oppose any foe, in order to assure the survival and the success of liberty.

This much we pledge—and more.

To those old allies whose cultural and spiritual origins we share, we pledge the loyalty of faithful friends. United, there is little we cannot do in a host of cooperative ventures. Divided, there is little we can do—for we dare not meet a powerful challenge at odds and split asunder.[2]

heirs (erz) *n.* people who carry on the tradition of predecessors

Thematic Connection
What characteristics of this sentence echo Patrick Henry's and Benjamin Franklin's speeches?

---

1. **Vice President . . . Truman** Present at Kennedy's inauguration were Lyndon B. Johnson, Kennedy's vice president; 34th president Dwight D. Eisenhower and his vice president, Richard M. Nixon; and 33rd president Harry S. Truman.
2. **United . . . Divided . . . split asunder** Kennedy echoes the famous lines from Abraham Lincoln's second inaugural address: "United we stand . . . divided we fall."

To those new States whom we welcome to the ranks of the free, we pledge our word that one form of colonial control shall not have passed away merely to be replaced by a far more iron <u>tyranny</u>. We shall not always expect to find them supporting our view. But we shall always hope to find them strongly supporting their own freedom—and to remember that, in the past, those who foolishly sought power by riding the back of the tiger ended up inside.

To those peoples in the huts and villages across the globe struggling to break the bonds of mass misery, we pledge our best efforts to help them help themselves, for whatever period is required—not because the Communists may be doing it, not because we seek their votes, but because it is right. If a free society cannot help the many who are poor, it cannot save the few who are rich.

To our sister republics south of our border, we offer a special pledge—to convert our good words into good deeds—in a new <u>alliance</u> for progress—to assist free men and free governments in casting off the chains of poverty. But this peaceful revolution of hope cannot become the prey of hostile powers. Let all our neighbors know that we shall join with them to oppose aggression or subversion anywhere in the Americas. And let every other power know that this Hemisphere intends to remain the master of its own house.

To that world assembly of sovereign states, the United Nations, our last best hope in an age where the instruments of war have far outpaced the instruments of peace, we renew our pledge of support—to prevent it from becoming merely a forum for <u>invective</u>—to strengthen its shield of the new and the weak—and to enlarge the area in which its writ may run.

Finally, to those nations who would make themselves our <u>adversary</u>, we offer not a pledge but a request: that both sides begin anew the quest for peace, before the dark powers of destruction[3] unleashed by science engulf all humanity in planned or accidental self-destruction.

We dare not tempt them with weakness. For only when our arms are sufficient beyond doubt can we be certain beyond doubt that they will never be employed.

But neither can two great and powerful groups of nations take comfort from our present course—both sides overburdened by the cost of modern weapons, both rightly alarmed by the steady spread of the deadly atom, yet both racing to alter that uncertain balance of terror that stays the hand of mankind's final war.

So let us begin anew—remembering on both sides that civility is not a sign of weakness, and sincerity is always subject to proof. Let us never negotiate out of fear. But let us never fear to negotiate.

Let both sides explore what problems unite us instead of belaboring those problems which divide us.

---

tyranny (tir′ ə nē) *n.* oppressive and unjust government

alliance (ə lī′ əns) *n.* union of nations for a specific purpose

invective (in vek′ tiv) *n.* verbal attack; strong criticism

adversary (ad′ vər ser′ ē) *n.* opponent; enemy

Thematic Connection
In what way does the reference to "fear" compare with Henry's statement, "Give me liberty or give me death"?

---

3. **dark powers of destruction** nuclear war.

◀ **Critical Viewing**
What do the images in this montage—and the unfinished quality of the upper right corner—suggest about Kennedy? [Infer]

Let both sides, for the first time, formulate serious and precise proposals for the inspection and control of arms—and bring the absolute power to destroy other nations under the absolute control of all nations.

Let both sides seek to <u>invoke</u> the wonders of science instead of its terrors. Together let us explore the stars, conquer the deserts, <u>eradicate</u> disease, tap the ocean depths, and encourage the arts and commerce.

Let both sides unite to heed in all corners of the earth the command of Isaiah—to "undo the heavy burdens . . . and to let the oppressed go free."[4]

And if a beachhead of cooperation may push back the jungle of suspicion, let both sides join in creating a new endeavor, not a new balance of power, but a new world of law, where the strong are just and the weak secure and the peace preserved.

invoke (in vōk´) *v.* call on for help, inspiration, or support

eradicate (e rad´ i kāt´) *v.* get rid of; wipe out; destroy

---

4. Isaiah the quotation refers to the passage in Isaiah 58:6.

All this will not be finished in the first 100 days. Nor will it be finished in the first 1,000 days, nor in the life of this Administration, nor even perhaps in our lifetime on this planet. But let us begin.

In your hands, my fellow citizens, more than in mine, will rest the final success or failure of our course. Since this country was founded, each generation of Americans has been summoned to give testimony to its national loyalty. The graves of young Americans who answered the call to service surround the globe.

Now the trumpet summons us again—not as a call to bear arms, though arms we need; not as a call to battle, though embattled we are—but a call to bear the burden of a long twilight struggle, year in and year out, "rejoicing in hope, patient in tribulation"[5]—a struggle against the common enemies of man: tyranny, poverty, disease, and war itself.

Can we forge against these enemies a grand and global alliance, North and South, East and West, that can assure a more fruitful life for all mankind? Will you join in that historic effort?

In the long history of the world, only a few generations have been granted the role of defending freedom in its hour of maximum danger. I do not shrink from this responsibility—I welcome it. I do not believe that any of us would exchange places with any other people or any other generation. The energy, the faith, the devotion which we bring to this endeavor will light our country and all who serve it—and the glow from that fire can truly light the world.

And so, my fellow Americans: ask not what your country can do for you—ask what you can do for your country.

My fellow citizens of the world: ask not what America will do for you, but what together we can do for the freedom of man.

Finally, whether you are citizens of America or citizens of the world, ask of us the same high standards of strength and sacrifice which we ask of you. With a good conscience our only sure reward, with history the final judge of our deeds, let us go forth to lead the land we love, asking His blessing and His help, but knowing that here on earth God's work must truly be our own.

---

5. **"rejoicing . . . tribulation"** from Romans 12:12. In Paul's letter to the Romans, he enjoins people to work together in love and mutual respect.

Connecting Literature Past and Present

1. Henry and Franklin gave speeches that were heard only by an immediate audience. What advances in technology have changed the way speeches like Kennedy's are received? Explain.

2. How does setting—the Oval Office, the Capitol steps, or the halls of Congress—affect the way a speech is prepared and received?

3. Do you think a sense of history influenced Henry's, Franklin's, and Kennedy's speech writing? Explain.

John F. Kennedy

(1917–1963)
Elected thirty-fifth president of the United States, John Fitzgerald Kennedy was the youngest person ever to serve in that office. The era over which Kennedy presided during his brief presidency witnessed events as diverse as the launch of the first communication satellite, Telstar, and the signing of the first nuclear nonproliferation treaty with the Soviet Union. The United States teetered on the brink of nuclear war during the Cuban missile crisis and put its first astronaut into orbit around the Earth. Tragically, Kennedy was assassinated on November 22, 1963, after serving only two years and ten months in office.

Defining an American

Eighteenth-century New England needlework Colonial Williamsburg Foundation

Prepare to Read

Letter to Her Daughter From the New White House ◆ *from* Letters From an American Farmer

Abigail Smith Adams (1744–1818)

Wife, mother, writer, first lady, revolutionary, women's rights pioneer—Abigail Smith Adams was all these and more. As the intelligent, outspoken wife of John Adams, the second president of the United States, and the mother of John Quincy Adams, the sixth president, Abigail Adams was one of the most influential women of her time.

Unequal Education Abigail Smith was born in Weymouth, Massachusetts. Although her father was a well-to-do minister and her mother came from an upper-class family, Abigail had no formal schooling. She often excused this shortcoming by saying that she was ill as a child. However, as a mother, she made sure that her daughter received as thorough an education as her four sons did—a privilege allotted to few American girls. Throughout her life, Adams vigorously supported women's rights to an education equal to the one men received.

A Political Wife At the age of twenty, Abigail married John Adams, whose political duties during and after the Revolution kept him from home for the better part of ten years. Abigail, therefore, became an avid correspondent, penning hundreds of letters to her husband and relatives and discussing everything from her opposition to slavery to her belief in women's rights. During the war, she even kept her husband posted on the movements of British troops.

Abigail Adams died in 1818. Twenty-two years after her death, her letters were collected and published. Today, she is a celebrated writer who is widely recognized as a pioneer of the American women's movement.

Michel-Guillaume Jean de Crèvecoeur (1735–1813)

The first writer to compare America to a melting pot, French aristocrat Michel-Guillaume Jean de Crèvecoeur (mē shel′ gē yōm zhän də krev kʉr) chronicled his experiences as a European immigrant adjusting to life in America. His idealistic descriptions confirmed a common vision of America as a land of great promise.

A Famous Farmer Born into a wealthy French family, Crèvecoeur emigrated to Canada and served for several years as a member of the French army in Quebec. After spending ten years traveling the colonies as a land surveyor and Indian trader, he married and settled on a farm in New York, where he began writing about his experiences in America. In 1780, Crèvecoeur sailed to London, where his *Letters From an American Farmer* was published two years later. This book, which was translated into several languages, made Crèvecoeur famous.

Returning To America In 1783, after visiting France, Crèvecoeur returned to America as a French Consul. Upon his return, he discovered that his farm had been burned, his wife killed, and his children sent to live with foster parents. When the French Revolution began in 1789, Crèvecoeur was obliged to return to Paris. He later fled to his family home in Normandy, where he continued to write about the adoptive country that he would never see again.

As France and the rest of Europe descended into the turmoil of the Napoleonic Wars, interest in the New World waned. Crèvecoeur spent the last years of his life largely forgotten amid the political turbulence.

Preview

Connecting to the Literature

Today, fewer and fewer people reach for pen and paper when they want to get in touch with someone. These selections, however, come from an era when letters were the only means of communicating over distances.

Literary Analysis

Private and Public Letters (Epistles)

Personal or **private letters** tend to be spontaneous, conversational, and intended only for the reader(s) to whom they are addressed. For example, Abigail Adams's language is conversational in this letter to her daughter:

> You must keep all this to yourself, and when asked how I like it, say that I write you the situation is beautiful, which is true.

By contrast, Crèvecoeur's *Letters* are **public letters** intended for a wide audience. Such literary works—essays written in letter form—are called **epistles.** By writing his essays in this form, Crèvecoeur maintains a personal approach while arguing public ideas.

Comparing Literary Works

The letters by Adams and the epistle by Crèvecoeur are both **primary source documents**—nonfiction accounts that reflect and comment upon the era in which they are written. Some primary source documents, like the Declaration of Independence, speak solely to issues of public concern. Others reveal information about the private life of the writer. Compare and contrast the ways in which these letters detail the challenges of life in a new country.

Reading Strategy

Distinguishing Between Fact and Opinion

- A **fact** is something that can be proved or observed.
- An **opinion** is a personal belief that can be supported but not proved. Opinions are usually indicated by words like "I think" or "it seems," suggesting individual judgment.

By **distinguishing between fact and opinions,** you can interpret the meaning of a literary work with greater accuracy. Use a chart like the one shown to record your observations about facts and opinions in these letters.

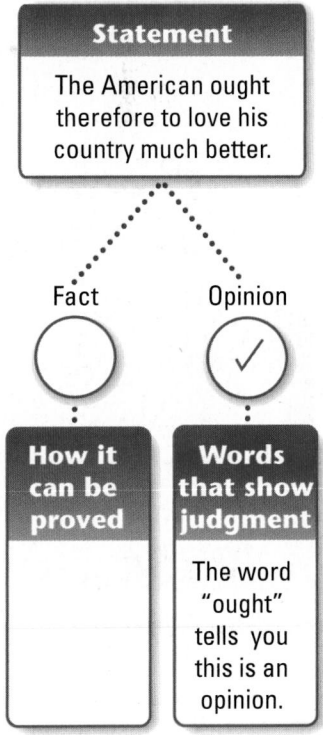

Vocabulary Development

extricate (eks´ tri kāt´) *v.* set free (p. 205)

agues (ā´ gyo͞oz) *n.* fits of shivering (p. 206)

asylum (ə sī´ ləm) *n.* place of refuge (p. 208)

penury (pen´ yə rē) *n.* lack of money, property, or necessities (p. 208)

despotic (des pät´ ik) *adj.* harsh; cruel; unjust (p. 210)

subsistence (səb sis´ təns) *n.* means of support (p. 210)

BUILDING THE FIRST WHITE HOUSE

WASHINGTON D.C. 1798

Building the First White House, N. C. Wyeth, White House Historical Association

▲ **Critical Viewing** With what emotions might Abigail Adams have reacted to this scene? **[Speculate]**

Letter to Her Daughter from the New White House

ABIGAIL ADAMS

Background

When John Adams was elected president of the United States, he and Abigail became the first couple to live in the White House. At the time, the city of Washington consisted of a few public buildings and a scattered collection of crude residences. This letter to Adams's daughter describes the unfinished White House and captures the essence of life in the new nation.

Washington, 21 November, 1800

My Dear Child:

I arrived here on Sunday last, and without meeting with any accident worth noticing, except losing ourselves when we left Baltimore and going eight or nine miles on the Frederick road, by which means we were obliged to go the other eight through woods, where we wandered two hours without finding a guide or the path. Fortunately, a straggling black came up with us, and we engaged him as a guide to extricate us out of our difficulty; but woods are all you see from Baltimore until you reach the *city*, which is only so in name. Here and there is a small cot, without a glass window, interspersed amongst the forests, through which you travel miles without seeing any human being. In the city there are buildings enough, if they were

extricate (eks´ tri kāt´) *v.* set free

Reading Check

What kind of terrain does Adams encounter on her trip?

compact and finished, to accommodate Congress and those attached to it; but as they are, and scattered as they are, I see no great comfort for them. The river, which runs up to Alexandria,[1] is in full view of my window, and I see the vessels as they pass and repass. The house is upon a grand and superb scale, requiring about thirty servants to attend and keep the apartments in proper order, and perform the ordinary business of the house and stables; an establishment very well proportioned to the President's salary. The lighting of the apartments, from the kitchen to parlors and chambers, is a tax indeed; and the fires we are obliged to keep to secure us from daily agues is another very cheering comfort. To assist us in this great castle, and render less attendance necessary, bells are wholly wanting, not one single one being hung through the whole house, and promises are all you can obtain. This is so great an inconvenience, that I know not what to do, or how to do. The ladies from Georgetown[2] and in the city have many of them visited me. Yesterday I returned fifteen visits—but such a place as Georgetown appears—why, our Milton is beautiful.

But no comparisons—if they will put me up some bells and let me have wood enough to keep fires, I design to be pleased. I could content myself almost anywhere three months; but, surrounded with forests, can you believe that wood is not to be had because people cannot be found to cut and cart it? Briesler entered into a contract with a man to supply him with wood. A small part, a few cords only, has he been able to get. Most of that was expended to dry the walls of the house before we came in, and yesterday the man told him it was impossible for him to procure it to be cut and carted. He has had recourse to coals; but we cannot get grates made and set. We have, indeed, come into a *new country*.

You must keep all this to yourself, and, when asked how I like it, say that I write you the situation is beautiful, which is true. The house is made habitable, but there is not a single apartment finished, and all withinside, except the plastering, has been done since Briesler came. We have not the least fence, yard, or other convenience without and the great unfinished audience room I make a drying-room of, to hang up the clothes in. The principal stairs are not up, and will not be this winter. Six chambers are made comfortable; two are occupied by the President and Mr. Shaw; two lower rooms, one for a common parlor, and one for a levee room. Upstairs there is the oval room, which is designed for the drawing room, and has the crimson furniture in it. It is a very handsome room now; but, when completed, it will be beautiful. If the twelve years, in which this place has been considered as the future seat of government had been improved, as they would have been if in New England, very many of the present inconveniences would have been removed. It is a beautiful spot,

---

1. **Alexandria** city in northeastern Virginia.
2. **Georgetown** section of Washington, D.C.

agues (ā´ gyo͞oz) *n.* fits of shivering

Literary Analysis
Private and Public Letters (Epistles) Why would this comment about "ladies" be found only in a private letter, never in an epistle?

Literary Analysis
Letters and Primary Source Documents In what ways does this statement about coming into a "new country" suggest a moment in time that is both historically and personally significant?

capable of every improvement, and, the more I view it, the more I am delighted with it.

Since I sat down to write, I have been called down to a servant from Mount Vernon,[3] with a billet[4] from Major Custis, and a haunch of venison, and a kind, congratulatory letter from Mrs. Lewis, upon my arrival in the city, with Mrs. Washington's love, inviting me to Mount Vernon, where, health permitting, I will go before I leave this place.

Affectionately, your mother,

Abigail Adams

---

3. **Mount Vernon** home of George Washington, located in northern Virginia.
4. **billet** (bil′ it) *n.* brief letter.

Review and Assess

Thinking About the Selection

1. **Respond:** What, if anything, surprised you about Adams's description of the White House and the surrounding area?

2. **(a) Recall:** What details does Adams use to describe the area surrounding the White House? **(b) Generalize:** What does Adams's letter suggest about the difficulties facing those who were setting up a centralized national government?

3. **(a) Recall:** What does Adams instruct her daughter to tell those who ask about the White House? **(b) Speculate:** Why might Adams be greatly concerned about the opinions of others?

4. **(a) Classify:** Name two character traits that Adams exhibits as she faces the difficulties of life in her new home. **(b) Evaluate:** Adams is often referred to as a remarkable figure in our nation's history. Which character traits exhibited in this letter contribute to that assessment?

5. **(a) Apply:** Today, how are the White House and the city of Washington, D.C., different from the way they were when Adams lived there? **(b) Synthesize:** What do these differences tell you about changes in the United States since the eighteenth-century?

6. **Analyze:** In what ways does the construction of a home for its Presidents help the young nation to establish (a) its identity on the world stage, (b) symbolism, (c) tradition?

7. **Evaluate:** Is the continuity of the Presidential residence—the fact that every U.S. President lives in the White House—valuable? Explain.

from Letters from an American Farmer

Michel-Guillaume Jean de Crèvecoeur

Independence (Squire Jack Porter), 1858, Frank Blackwell Mayer, National Museum of American Art, Smithsonian Institution

▲ **Critical Viewing** What connections do you see between this painting and Crèvecoeur's *Letters from an American Farmer*? **[Connect]**

In this great American <u>asylum</u>, the poor of Europe have by some means met together, and in consequence of various causes; to what purpose should they ask one another what countrymen they are? Alas, two thirds of them had no country. Can a wretch who wanders about, who works and starves, whose life is a continual scene of sore affliction or pinching <u>penury</u>, can that man call England or any other kingdom his country? A country that had no bread for him, whose fields

asylum (ə sī´ ləm) *n.* place of refuge

penury (pen´ yə rē) *n.* lack of money, property, or necessities

procured him no harvest, who met with nothing but the frowns of the rich, the severity of the laws, with jails and punishments; who owned not a single foot of the extensive surface of this planet? No! Urged by a variety of motives, here they came. Everything has tended to regenerate them; new laws, a new mode of living, a new social system; here they are become men: in Europe they were as so many useless plants, wanting vegetative mold[1] and refreshing showers; they withered, and were mowed down by want, hunger, and war; but now by the power of transplantation, like all other plants they have taken root and flourished!

Formerly they were not numbered in any civil lists[2] of their country, except in those of the poor; here they rank as citizens. By what invisible power has this surprising metamorphosis been performed? By that of the laws and that of their industry. The laws, the indulgent laws, protect them as they arrive, stamping on them the symbol of adoption; they receive ample rewards for their labors; these accumulated rewards procure them lands; those lands confer on them the title of freemen, and to that title every benefit is affixed which men can possibly require. This is the great operation daily performed by our laws. From whence proceed these laws? From our government. Whence the government? It is derived from the original genius and strong desire of the people ratified and confirmed by the crown. . . .

What attachment can a poor European emigrant have for a country where he had nothing? The knowledge of the language, the love of a few kindred as poor as himself, were the only cords that tied him: his country is now that which gives him land, bread, protection, and consequence: *Ubi panis ibi patria*[3] is the motto of all emigrants. What then is the American, this new man? He is either a European, or the descendant of a European, hence that strange mixture of blood, which you will find in no other country. I could point out to you a family whose grandfather was an Englishman, whose wife was Dutch, whose son married a French woman, and whose present four sons have now four wives of different nations. *He* is an American, who, leaving behind him all his ancient prejudices and manners, receives new ones from the new mode of life he has embraced, the new government he obeys, and the new rank he holds. He becomes an American by being received in the broad lap of our great *Alma Mater.*[4] Here individuals of all nations are melted into a new race of men, whose labors and posterity will one day cause great changes in the world. Americans are the western pilgrims, who are carrying along with them that great mass of arts, sciences, vigor, and industry which began long since in the east; they will finish the great circle. The Americans were once scattered all over Europe: here they

---

1. **vegetative mold** enriched soil.
2. **civil lists** lists of distinguished persons.
3. **Ubi . . . patria** (ü´ bē pä nis ib´ ē pä´ trē ə) "Where there is bread, there is one's fatherland" (Latin).
4. **Alma Mater** (al´ mə mät´ ər) "Fostering mother." Here, referring to America; usually used in reference to a school or college (Latin).

Reading Strategy
Distinguishing Between Fact and Opinion By referencing a family with roots in many nations, does the writer present a fact or an opinion? Explain.

✔**Reading Check**
What kind of lives did Europeans have in their homelands?

are incorporated into one of the finest systems of population which has ever appeared, and which will hereafter become distinct by the power of the different climates they inhabit. The American ought therefore to love this country much better than that wherein either he or his forefathers were born. Here the rewards of his industry follow with equal steps the progress of his labor; his labor is founded on the basis of nature, *self-interest*; can it want a stronger allurement? Wives and children, who before in vain demanded of him a morsel of bread, now, fat and frolicsome, gladly help their father to clear those fields whence exuberant crops are to arise to feed and to clothe them all; without any part being claimed, either by a <u>despotic</u> prince, a rich abbot,[5] or a mighty lord. Here religion demands but little of him; a small voluntary salary to the minister, and gratitude to God; can he refuse these? The American is a new man, who acts upon new principles; he must therefore entertain new ideas, and form new opinions. From involuntary idleness, servile dependence, penury, and useless labor, he has passed to toils of a very different nature, rewarded by ample <u>subsistence</u>—This is an American.

despotic (des pät′ ik) *adj.* harsh; cruel; unjust

subsistence (səb sis′ təns) *n.* means of support

---

5. **abbot** *n.* the head of a monastery.

Review and Assess

Thinking About the Selection

1. **Respond:** If you were an eighteenth-century European, would this essay motivate you to relocate to the United States? Why or why not?

2. **(a) Recall:** To what natural objects does Crèvecoeur compare impoverished Europeans? **(b) Assess:** What is suggested through this imagery about Europeans' capacity to thrive in a new environment?

3. **(a) Recall:** What are the sources of the "invisible power" that is responsible for transforming humble Europeans into esteemed American "citizens"? **(b) Define:** How do you think Crèvecoeur would define a "citizen"?

4. **(a) Compare and Contrast:** How does the American population differ from that of Europe? **(b) Explain:** In what ways does Crèvecoeur believe the world will be invigorated by Americans?

5. **(a) Define:** How would you summarize Crèvecoeur's definition of an American? **(b) Evaluate:** Does Crèvecoeur's definition still hold true today? Explain. **(c) Take a Position:** Do you think that there can be a single definition of an American? Why or why not?

6. **Apply:** Do you think that eighteenth-century immigrants to America had the same goals as immigrants of today? Explain.

Review and Assess

Literary Analysis

Private and Public Letters (Epistles)

1. Use a chart like the one shown to explore ways in which you might rewrite Adams's **private letter** for a public audience.

Letter
Surrounded with forests, can you believe that wood is not to be had?

···▶

Words suggesting private purpose
Can you believe

···▶

Revision
We are surrounded by dense forest, but wood is not readily available.

2. What kinds of information would Crèvecoeur have included in a private letter to a friend that are inappropriate for an **epistle**?

3. How does the epistle form allow Crèvecoeur to be more persuasive than a regular essay would permit?

Comparing Literary Works

4. (a) What character traits does Crèvecoeur hold up as being both typically American and admirable? (b) Are these character traits evident in Adams's descriptions? Explain.

5. (a) Which writer presents a more idealized view of America? Explain. (b) Which presents a more realistic view? Explain.

Reading Strategy

Distinguishing Between Fact and Opinion

6. Identify the **facts** and **opinions** in this statement.

   "The house is made habitable, but there is not a single apartment finished, and all withinside, except the plastering, has been done since Briesler came."

7. Identify at least one fact Crèvecoeur uses to support the following opinion: "here they are become men: in Europe they were as so many useless plants."

Extend Understanding

8. **Social Studies Connection:** Crèvecoeur implies that self-interest is valuable because it motivates people to work harder. Does modern society regard self-interest as a desirable quality? Explain your answer.

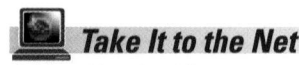

Integrate Language Skills

Vocabulary Development Lesson

Word Analysis: Etymologies

You can learn how words evolved by using a dictionary that shows etymologies, or word histories. Use this etymology for the word *interspersed* to answer the questions that follow.

> < *interspersus*, pp. of *interspergere* <
> *inter-*, among + *spargere*, to scatter

1. *Interspersed* can be traced back to what two words or word parts?

2. What is the meaning of *interspersed*?

Spelling Strategy

The suffixes *-ance* and *-ence* are used to form nouns from adjectives. *Evident* becomes *evidence*, and *significant* becomes *significance*. Write the noun form of each adjective:

1. observant   2. confident   3. intelligent

Fluency: Word Matching

Match each numbered word with the best lettered description.

1. extricate
2. agues
3. asylum
4. penury
5. subsistence
6. despotic

a. a minimal income
b. what people who live in drafty houses suffer from
c. how you might describe an evil dictator
d. the quiet privacy of your room
e. to work your way out of an argument
f. the condition in which most homeless people live

Grammar and Style Lesson

Semicolons

The **semicolon** can replace a comma and a coordinating conjunction to signal closely connected ideas. The semicolon can also be used to join independent clauses separated by a conjunctive adverb or a transitional expression.

> **Semicolon with conjunctive adverb:**
> Crèvecoeur was the first to express the concept of America as a melting pot; **however,** the term was not used until the twentieth century.

Practice Rewrite the following sentences, adding semicolons where needed.

1. The travelers sought help finding Baltimore the woods blocked their view of the city.

2. Six rooms were completed two were not.

3. Adams thought she could be happy however, the shortages caused her distress.

4. Crèvecoeur presents America as a land of opportunity in fact he shows how European immigrants have prospered.

5. Crèvecoeur wrote convincingly about the land nevertheless some felt he created an unrealistic picture of the quality of life.

Writing Application Write four sentences reflecting on what America means to you. Use a semicolon in each sentence.

W͟G Prentice Hall Writing and Grammar Connection: Chapter 27, Section 3

Writing Lesson

Personal Letter

In a personal letter to either Adams or Crèvecoeur, provide an update on how an area of interest to the recipient has changed since his or her lifetime. Like a foreign pen pal, your reader lives in a different country—the country of the past—and will need help understanding your world.

Prewriting Decide on an appropriate subject for your letter. Outline the developments you will cover. Then, decide what background information your reader will need to understand your points.

Drafting Make sure to address the person to whom you are writing. You will need to include necessary context and background—the information a reader needs in order to make sense of the information you provide.

> ### Model: Providing Context and Background
>
> Unlike your contemporaries, who rarely worked outside
> the home, women today have many choices, Ms.
> Adams. While some stay home to raise children,
> others have full-time jobs.

Comparison-and-contrast examples establish context.

Revising Review your letter and decide whether the recipient would be able to understand the references you make. If necessary, add more detail to explain and prove your point.

W̶G Prentice Hall Writing and Grammar Connection: Chapter 9, Section 2

Extension Activities

Research and Technology With a group of your classmates, use a drawing software program to design **advertisements** that might have attracted immigrants to America in the late eighteenth century. As you plan, think about these questions:

- Who would have been the target group for such ads?
- What messages and images would have convinced them to make the journey to a new land?

Display your ads for the class. **[Group Activity]**

Listening and Speaking Interview a recent immigrant to find out why and how he or she came to this country. Prepare your questions in advance, and ask follow-up questions as the interview progresses. With your subject's permission, you might take photographs of him or her as well. Record your **interview,** and then share it with your class.

 **Take It to the Net** www.phschool.com

Go online for an additional research activity using the Internet.

CONNECTIONS
Literature Past and Present
Defining an American

What is an American? The works in Part 3 offer a telling look at a young nation consciously struggling with this question. At the time, neither Abigail Adams, nor Michel-Guillaume Jean de Crèvecoeur could have foreseen the impact that descendants of enslaved Africans would one day have on America's answer. Those writers could not have known that a book written by an African American in the twentieth-century would influence the way in which millions of Americans defined their identities. That book is *Roots*.

An Educational Blockbuster Published in 1976 and followed by a television miniseries of the same name, *Roots* changed the nation's perception of itself as only very powerful events can. A fictionalized tale of the author Alex Haley's search for his African ancestors and the story of his family's history from their beginnings in Africa to emancipation, the book focused America's attention on the richness of the African cultural heritage. Civil rights leader Vernon Jordan called the television miniseries based on Haley's book "the single most spectacular educational experience in race relations in America." African Americans everywhere followed Haley's example by renewing ties with their African ancestry. Thanks to a single book, the identities of millions of Americans expanded to include a new awareness of rich roots firmly planted in another time and place.

from
ROOTS

Alex Haley

*Alex Haley's search for his African roots takes him to the small vil-
lage of Juffure, located in the country in western Africa now known as
The Gambia. The elderly village historian honors the American visitor
by relating for him the ancestral history of the Kinte clan.*

The old *griot*[1] had talked for nearly two hours up to then, and
perhaps fifty times the narrative had included some detail
about someone whom he had named. Now after he had just
named those four sons, again he appended a detail, and the interpreter translated—

"About the time the King's soldiers came"—another of the *griot's*
time-fixing references— "the oldest of these four sons, Kunta, went
away from his village to chop wood . . . and he was never seen again.
. . ." And the *griot* went on with his narrative.

I sat as if I were carved of stone. My blood seemed to have congealed.
This man whose lifetime had been in this back-country African village
had no way in the world to know that he had just echoed what I had
heard all through my boyhood years on my grandma's front porch in
Henning, Tennessee . . . of an African who always had insisted that
his name was "Kin-tay"; who had called a guitar a *"ko,"* and a river
within the state of Virginia, "Kamby Bolongo";[2] and who had been
kidnaped into slavery while not far from his village, chopping wood,
to make himself a drum.

I managed to fumble from my duffelbag my basic notebook, whose
first pages containing grandma's story I showed to an interpreter.
After briefly reading, clearly astounded, he spoke rapidly while showing it to the old *griot,* who became agitated; he got up, exclaiming to
the people, gesturing at my notebook in the interpreter's hands, and
they all got agitated.

congealed (kən jēld´) *v.*
thickened or solidified

Thematic Connection
How might growing up
with this story have
influenced Haley's
perception of his
American identity?

---

1. **griot** (grē´ ō) *n.* the village oral historian, generally an elderly man who recites
   histories of famous heroes and families on special occasions.
2. **"Kamby Bolongo"** (käm´ bē bō lôŋ´ gō) "Gambia River" in the Mandinka language
   of western Africa.

I don't remember hearing anyone giving an order, I only recall becoming aware that those seventy-odd people had formed a wide human ring around me, moving counterclockwise, chanting softly, loudly, softly; their bodies close together, they were lifting their knees high, stamping up reddish puffs of the dust. . . .

The woman who broke from the moving circle was one of about a dozen whose infant children were within cloth slings across their backs. Her jet-black face deeply contorting, the woman came charging toward me, her bare feet slapping the earth, and snatching her baby free, she thrust it at me almost roughly, the gesture saying "Take it!" . . . and I did, clasping the baby to me. Then she snatched away her baby; and another woman was thrusting her baby, then another, and another . . . until I had embraced probably a dozen babies. I wouldn't learn until maybe a year later, from a Harvard University professor, Dr. Jerome Bruner, a scholar of such matters, "You didn't know you were participating in one of the oldest ceremonies of humankind, called 'The laying on of hands'! In their way, they were telling you 'Through this flesh, which is us, we are you, and you are us!'"

Later the men of Juffure[3] took me into their mosque[4] built of bamboo and thatch, and they prayed around me in Arabic. I remember thinking, down on my knees, "After I've found out where I came from, I can't understand a word they're saying." Later the <u>crux</u> of their prayer was translated for me: "Praise be to Allah for one long lost from us whom Allah has returned."

crux (kruks) *n.* essential point

Since we had come by the river, I wanted to return by land. As I sat beside the wiry young Mandingo driver who was leaving dust pluming behind us on the hot, rough, pitted, back-country road toward Banjul, there came from somewhere into my head a staggering awareness . . . that *if* any black American could be so blessed as I had been to know only a few ancestral clues—could he or she know *who* was either the paternal or maternal African ancestor or ancestors, and about *where* that ancestor lived when taken, and finally about *when* the ancestor was taken—then only those few clues might well see that black American able to locate some wizened old black *griot* whose narrative could reveal the black American's ancestral clan, perhaps even the very village.

Dance Africa, Synthia Saint James, Third World Art Exchange

▲ **Critical Viewing**
What details of this image suit Haley's description of the African village he visits? **[Connect]**

In my mind's eye, rather as if it were mistily being projected on a screen, I began envisioning descriptions I had read of how collectively millions of our ancestors had been enslaved. Many thousands were individually kidnaped, as my own forebear Kunta had been, but into the millions had come awake screaming in the night, dashing out into

---

3. **Juffure** (jōō´ fōō rā)
4. **mosque** (mäsk) *n.* Muslim temple or place of worship.

the bedlam of raided villages, which were often in flames. The captured able survivors were linked neck-by-neck with thongs into processions called "coffles," which were sometimes as much as a mile in length. I envisioned the many dying, or left to die when they were too weak to continue the torturous march toward the coast, and those who made it to the beach were greased, shaved, probed in every orifice, often branded with sizzling irons; I envisioned them being lashed and dragged toward the longboats; their spasms of screaming and clawing with their hands into the beach, biting up great choking mouthfuls of the sand in their desperation efforts for one last hold on the Africa that had been their home; I envisioned them shoved, beaten, jerked down into slave ships' stinking holds and chained onto shelves, often packed so tightly that they had to lie on their sides like spoons in a drawer. . . .

My mind reeled with it all as we approached another, much larger village. Staring ahead, I realized that word of what had happened in Juffure must have left there well before I did. The driver slowing down, I could see this village's people thronging the road ahead; they were weaving, amid their <u>cacophony</u> of crying out something; I stood up in the Land-Rover, waving back as they seemed grudging to open a path for the Land-Rover.

I guess we had moved a third of the way through the village when it suddenly registered in my brain what they were all crying out . . . the wizened, robed elders and younger men, the mothers and the naked tar-black children, they were all waving up at me; their expressions buoyant, beaming, all were crying out together, *"Meester Kinte! Meester Kinte!"*

Let me tell you something: I am a man. A sob hit me somewhere around my ankles; it came surging upward, and flinging my hands over my face, I was just bawling, as I hadn't since I was a baby. *"Meester Kinte!"* I just felt like I was weeping for all of history's incredible atrocities against fellowmen, which seems to be mankind's greatest flaw. . . .

Flying homeward from Dakar, I decided to write a book. My own ancestors would automatically also be a symbolic saga of all African-descent people—who are without exception the seeds of someone like Kunta who was born and grew up in some black African village, someone who was captured and chained down in one of those slave ships that sailed them across the same ocean, into some succession of plantations, and since then a struggle for freedom.

cacophony (kə kăf´ ə nē) *n.* harsh, jarring sound

Alex Haley

(1921–1992)
Alex Haley spent twenty years in the Coast Guard as a journalist before deciding to become a freelance writer. His first big success came with his highly praised *The Autobiography of Malcolm X.* His greatest and best-known accomplishment, however, is *Roots: The Saga of an American Family.* The book was an immediate bestseller and within two years had won more than 200 awards. The television miniseries based on the book was viewed by 130 million people. About the success of *Roots,* Haley said, "When you start talking about family, about lineage and ancestry, you are talking about every person on earth. We all have it; it's a great equalizer. . . . I think the book has touched a strong, subliminal chord."

Connecting Literature Past and Present

1. How do you think Alex Haley might answer the question, What is an American?

2. Which of the beliefs expressed by other writers in this section do you think Haley might share? Why?

Writing About Literature

Evaluate Literary Themes

The writers of the Revolutionary period believed that they could—and should—take control of their destinies, both as individuals and as Americans. Belief in personal and political freedom gave these writers an enormous sense of optimism and energy. They saw all problems, from those of poor personal habits to those of political tyranny, as obstacles to be overcome rather than as circumstances to accept. In many respects, this sense of revolutionary optimism continues to characterize American political discourse. Review the literature in this unit to complete the assignment outlined in the box at right.

Prewriting

Judge the selections. To evaluate literary works, follow these steps:

- First, determine the criterion upon which to base the evaluation.
- Second, analyze the authors' messages and methods.
- Finally, make judgments about the works in light of the stated criterion.

In this essay, your criterion is the success of the author's arguments in favor of freedom. Therefore, when you analyze each selection, focus on references to personal and political liberty.

Formulate a thesis. Use a chart like the one shown to organize your analysis of the references to freedom made by a number of authors. Then, state your judgment about the success with which the authors have argued for the rights of individuals to direct their own lives. Write your assessment in one sentence. Use this sentence as a working thesis.

> **Assignment:**
> **A Matter of Persuasion**
>
> Write an analytical essay that evaluates the success with which the authors in this unit make their cases for personal and/or political freedom.
>
> **Criteria:**
> - Include a thesis statement that states your opinion.
> - Support your opinion with examples from the selections.
> - Approximate length: 1,500 words.

**Read to Write**

Reread the texts, looking for the precise methods that the writers use to make their points about personal liberty.

Model: Charting to Develop a Thesis

Thesis: Jefferson and his colleagues are cautious men moved to radical action by extreme circumstances.

Selection	Reference	Method/Message
The Declaration of Independence	"Prudence, indeed, will dictate that governments long established should not be changed for light and transient causes."	Jefferson highlights idea of prudence, implying that reasons for declaring independence are not trivial.

Select powerful examples. Some of the selections you have analyzed will support your thesis better than others will. Pick the examples that most powerfully support your thesis statement.

Drafting

Write an introduction. In your introduction, state your subject matter and purpose, and identify the works you will be evaluating—in this case, literature from the formative years of the United States. Then, assert your opinion of the success or failure of this literature in its argument that individuals should determine their own futures.

Present examples in order. Follow your introduction with the example that best supports your opinion. For example, if you think the writers in this unit fail to make a strong case for individual liberty, quote the argument that most clearly supports your point. Then, explain the reasons for your opinion.

Revising and Editing

Review content: Make sure that you are evaluating your material. To be successful, an evaluative essay must assert a judgment about a subject, not just report on it. To make sure you are actually evaluating the literature, review each paragraph of your essay. Jot down the ideas you present in each paragraph. Then, use a highlighter to mark the sentences that contain evaluations. If you see too few highlighted sentences, go back and add well-supported judgments.

	Model: Revising to Add Evaluation
Paragraph	1. Jefferson wrote the Declaration as a message to the British king.
	2. He portrays the colonists as cautious men who do not want to rebel, but feel they have no choice.
	3. He says that the signers of the Declaration stake their lives and sacred honors on this document.
	4. This strategy is persuasive because it shows that freedom matters more than anything, including wealth or life itself.

Review style: Use a variety of evaluative terms. An evaluative essay contains value-laden terms such as *effective, clear, convincing,* and *persuasive.* Review your draft, and underline your use of such terms. Replace vague adjectives, such as *good,* with more precise alternatives. If you have used certain words too often, replace them with synonyms.

Publishing and Presenting

Generate a literary magazine. With classmates, publish your essays in a literary magazine. Select a title for your magazine that indicates the scope and subject matter of the essays.

W̧ Prentice Hall Writing and Grammar Connection: Chapter 14

Write to Learn
You may find a selection to be more or less effective than you had originally thought. Allow for such changes in opinion; the writing process has given you a new perspective.

Write to Explain
It is not sufficient to judge a work in a casual way. Instead, justify your evaluations with examples from the selection.

Writing WORKSHOP

Exposition: Problem-and-Solution Essay

A **problem-and-solution essay** identifies and explains a problem and then offers a practical solution. In this workshop, you will plan, draft, and revise a problem-and-solution essay.

Assignment Criteria Your problem-and-solution essay should have the following characteristics:

- A statement of a problem that is clear enough to develop fully and support in an essay
- A proposed solution that is practical
- Facts, statistics, or expert testimony that illustrates the scope of the problem and the practicality of the solution
- Language appropriate to the knowledge level of the audience
- A logical organization that establishes the relationship between problem and solution

To preview the criteria on which your problem-and-solution essay may be assessed, refer to the Rubric on page 223.

Prewriting

Choose a topic. Write your problem-and-solution essay about an issue of interest to you. To find a subject, **watch or listen to the news** on television or radio, and create a chart like the one shown to assess the problems reported. Then, review your chart to select a problem for which you can offer a viable solution.

Problem List

Problem	Personal Experience	Can I Provide a Solution?
Forest Fires	No direct experience.	No.
Pedestrian traffic accidents	Yes. Sister almost hit by car on Main Street.	Yes, but not that interested.
Teen Stress	A lot of personal experience	Yes. I could use my own advice.

Analyze your audience. When you write a problem-and-solution essay, keep a specific audience in mind: readers who have the ability to implement your suggestions. Ask yourself the following questions to customize your essay to your audience's needs:

- Who is my audience?
- What does my audience already know about my topic?
- What information do I need to provide?
- In what ways can I stir my audience's interest in this problem?
- Does my audience have the power and authority to implement the solution I suggest?

Gather details. To collect the information you will need, make a list of details, facts, and examples that prove there is a problem. To gather additional information, conduct interviews with people who have been frustrated by the situation your essay will address.

Student Model

Before you begin writing, read this student model and review the characteristics of an effective problem-and-solution essay.

Katie Burcham
Florence, Kentucky

Rat Race Tips: Surviving Student Stress

William Henry Davies once wrote, "A poor life this is, full of care; we have no time to stand and stare." Due to the high amount of stress our society creates, this quotation accurately portrays the quality of life for many teenagers. Stress is a leading cause of health problems, including depression, a major issue among teenagers.

> Katie tells readers why they should care about her subject.

A recent study by Reuters [http://www.intelihealth.com, 27 Oct. 1999] reported that one third of American teens say they feel "stressed out" every day. The study also reports that one source of all this stress is unrealistic expectations which parents have for their children.

> She then provides evidence attesting to the magnitude of the problem.

Parental Expectations Parental stress can play out in comparisons that make teens feel inadequate. For me, parental stress means comparison to siblings. One sister was valedictorian, and another sister was salutatorian. An air of expectation returns every time my report card arrives: "Will Katie do as well as her sisters?" This motivates me, but it creates stress.

College Admissions Teens know that college admissions are more competitive than ever. However, paying for college can place financial pressures on a family. Teens become frantic to create the type of profile that scholarship committees love—one packed with activities, top grades, volunteer jobs, and part-time work. These activities create an unmanageable schedule, and a lot of stress.

> This logical point-by-point form of organization, with main points called out by subheads, is effective in a problem-and-solution essay.

Self-Inflicted Stress Often, students will overextend themselves, resolving to stay up longer and study harder. But the "cramming" that overachievers resort to—an activity that can involve pulling all-nighters, and skipping meals—usually backfires. Studies show that the stress linked with this frenzied preparation actually impairs the memory [http:///www.cgi.cnn.com/HEALTH/9808/19/stress.memory, Aug. 19, 1998].

Solutions How can teenagers combat stress? Experts have these suggestions:

- *Learn relaxation and breathing techniques.* When the body relaxes, the emotions follow [http://www.aacap.org/publications/factsfam/66.htm, 21 Jan. 2001].
- *Say no.*
- *Take one thing at a time.*
- *Have fun!* Laughter is a proven stress reducer.

> Katie provides reasonable solutions supported by evidence.

Some might say that if teens do not push themselves, they will lose out on opportunities, and that stress is just a part of striving. To that, I can only say that everything suffers when an individual is overextended, and eventually the teen will burn out, not achieve. Instead, by being selective about their activities, approaching projects in small steps, and learning to laugh, teenagers can live rewarding lives—not stress free, but manageable.

> Katie anticipates and answers possible objections.

Drafting

Choose an organization. Your problem-and-solution essay must achieve two goals: It must define a problem, and it must identify and develop a workable solution. Review the following forms of organization and determine which will work best for the problem you have chosen:

- **Point-by-Point:** This organizational strategy breaks down the main problem into an array of smaller problems, and then addresses each one, point by point, offering small-scale solutions.

- **Block:** This organizational strategy lays out the problem as a whole, and then proposes a comprehensive solution to the entire problem.

Provide evidence. Support all statements with facts, statistics, personal experiences, and any other documentation that will persuade your audience of the soundness of your ideas. Use a chart like the one shown to guide your selection of evidence.

Address readers' concerns. Convince those who may not approve of your solution by anticipating objections and demonstrating that you have taken them into account. Address each objection with explanations and evidence that prove your solution is the best plan.

Collect Types of Evidence	
Type of Evidence	
Fact	Anxiety obstructs memory.
Statistic	One third of American teens say they feel "stressed out" on a daily basis.
Anecdote	I am compared to my high-achieving sisters.
Expert Testimony	Teens should learn to say "no."

Revising

Revise by taking the opposing view. Look for places where a critic might disagree with your ideas, and answer their likely objections. A few common objections are listed below, along with strategies that may be used to answer them. Use these strategies to guide your revision.

- **Why should I care?** Include information to show how the problem affects your audience.

- **Why should I do it?** Use language that makes your audience see that their participation is a critical part of the solution.

- **This solution is too difficult.** Show how the solution can be completed easily, or stress that a complicated solution is necessary because of the complexity of the problem.

Model: Address the Opposition

Stress is a leading cause of health problems, including depression, a major issue among teenagers.

Due to the high amount of stress our society creates, this quotation accurately portrays the quality of life for many teenagers.

Katie added information to reinforce the importance of her topic.

Revise for word choice. Review your draft as if you were a member of your intended audience. Circle terms that need to be defined, or vocabulary that seems too easy for your readers. For example, in the following passage, the word *hybridization* is defined to make sense to a general audience.

Without definition: The plants feature a genetic *hybridization* that modifies their color.

With definition: The plants feature a genetic hybridization, or *blending,* that modifies their color.

Compare the model and the non-model. Why is the model more effective?

Nonmodel	Model
But the "cramming" that overachievers resort to usually backfires.	But the "cramming" that overachievers resort to—an activity that can involve pulling all-nighters, and skipping meals—usually backfires.

Publishing and Presenting

Consider the following activity to share your writing with classmates or a wider audience.

Deliver an oral presentation. Read your problem-and-solution essay aloud for your class. When you have finished, invite comments and questions. Determine whether or not your classmates are convinced that your solution is the best answer to the problem.

WG Prentice Hall Writing and Grammar Connection: Chapter 11

Rubric for Self-Assessment

Evaluate your problem-and-solution essay using the following criteria and rating scale:

Criteria	Rating Scale Not very				Very
Is the problem stated clearly enough to be fully developed and supported?	1	2	3	4	5
How practical is the suggested solution?	1	2	3	4	5
How effective are facts, statistics, and details that illustrate the problem and the solution?	1	2	3	4	5
Is the language appropriate to the audience's knowledge level?	1	2	3	4	5
How well is the material organized?	1	2	3	4	5

Listening and Speaking WORKSHOP

Analyze Persuasive Techniques

When speakers want to convince you to accept their ideas, they can use a variety of **persuasive techniques**. The strategies noted below will help you recognize and evaluate four kinds of speech.

Analyze Persuasive Purposes

Persuasive speakers seek to convince audiences using one or more of these four types of ideas:

- **Proposition of fact:** The speaker wants listeners to accept a claim as either true or false.
- **Proposition of value:** The speaker wants listeners to accept a claim as either good or bad.
- **Proposition to illuminate a problem:** The speaker asks listeners to share a concern.
- **Proposition of policy:** The speaker wants listeners to agree to a change in policy regarding an issue.

As you listen to a persuasive speech, identify the speaker's main purpose.

Identify evidence. Each type of persuasive speech offers distinct kinds of evidence: For a proposition of fact, evidence should include hard data, examples, or testimony. For a proposition of value, evidence should include both facts and appeals to emotion, and will indicate the speaker's sense of values. For a proposition to illuminate a problem, the speaker must establish the existence of a threat or obstacle. Lastly, in a proposition of policy, the speaker must persuade listeners to take specific action.

As you listen to a speech, identify the evidence presented, note whether it is suited to the speaker's purpose, and weigh its strength.

Evaluating Persuasive Techniques

Rating System

+ = excellent   ✔ = average   − = weak

Goals and Organization

Purpose clearly presented _____
Thesis statement is clear _____
Logical organization of supporting material _____
Clear link to audience _____

Support

Proofs match speech type _____
Proofs support thesis _____
Language is compelling _____
Language is persuasive _____
Reasoning is sound _____

Answer the following questions:

Which type of persuasive speech did you find most compelling?

Which persuasive techniques did you find most effective?

Evaluate Support

Use these questions to evaluate the support a speaker provides:

- **Proof:** Does the speaker's proof pertain directly to the thesis?
- **Persuasive Language:** Does the speaker use strong language that urges agreement, and clear language that ensures understanding?
- **Reasoning:** Is the speaker's reasoning sound and logical?

Use a form like the one shown to assess the effectiveness of a speech.

Activity:
Speak and Respond   In a group of four, present speeches of each type on a topic familiar to group members. Evaluate the effectiveness of each speech's organization and support.

Assessment WORKSHOP

Cause-and-Effect Relationships

The reading sections of some tests often require you to recognize cause-and-effect relationships and to predict probable outcomes based on the content of a passage. Use the following strategies to answer test questions on these skills:

- As you read, clarify the connections among events to help you identify the cause-and-effect relationships.
- Remember that a single cause can have many effects, and a single effect can have many causes.
- While other causes may be stated or implied, concentrate on the cause that has the most direct influence on the outcome.
- Look for words that indicate cause and effect, such as *causes, produces, affects, because of, as a result,* or *for this reason.*

Sample Test Item

Directions: Read the passage, and then answer the question that follows.

The increasing growth of weeds in Cabot Lake threatens to turn it into a stagnant swamp. Ira North, a researcher for the Cabot Institute, cites an increase in phosphorus-based lawn fertilizers as the primary factor in the growth of lake weeds. "When it rains, fertilizer runs into the lake, causing aquatic plants to grow rapidly. Phosphorus-laden water from washing machines and dishwashers also contributes to the problem."

1. What is the main cause of weed over-growth in Cabot Lake?

   A the fertilizing properties of phosphorus

   B rainwater runoff

   C lawn fertilizers

   D dishwashers and washing machines

Answer and Explanation

The correct answer is *C.* Answers *A, B,* and *D* all play a role in lake weed growth. *C,* however, is the "primary factor."

▶ Practice

Directions: Read the passage, and then answer the question that follows.

At this point, more than one third of Cabot Lake is overrun by lake weeds and is unsuitable for swimming. North says that as more people build homes in the area, the use of phosphorus-based lawn fertilizers will increase dramatically. The number of dishwashers and washing machines in use will also go up, putting additional strain on the ecosystem. North predicts that if nothing is done to control development and fertilizer use, the lake will be fully overrun with weeds within twenty-five years.

1. Why is one third of Cabot Lake unsuitable for swimming?

   A an increased number of lawns in the area

   B an overgrowth of weeds in the lake

   C more roads, increasing rainwater runoff

   D more people buying fertilizer for their lawns

Niagara Falls, Thomas Chambers, Wadsworth Atheneum, Hartford, Connecticut

66 *America is a land of wonders, in which everything is in constant motion and every change seems an improvement. . . . No natural boundary seems to be set to the efforts of man; and in his eyes what is not yet done is only what he has not yet attempted to do* **99**

— Alexis de Tocqueville

Timeline 1800–1870

1800   1810   1820

American Events

- **1803** Louisiana Purchase extends nation's territory to the Rocky Mountains.
- **1804** Lewis and Clark begin expedition exploring and mapping vast regions of the West. ▼

- **1807** Robert Fulton's steamboat makes first trip from New York City to Albany.

- **1812** U.S. declares war on Great Britain; early battles in War of 1812 are at sea.
- **1814** Bombardment of Fort McHenry inspires Francis Scott Key to write "The Star-Spangled Banner." ▼

- **1817** William Cullen Bryant publishes early draft of "Thanatopsis" in a Boston magazine.

- **1820** Missouri Compromise bans slavery in parts of new territories.

- **1825** Completion and success of Erie Canal spurs canal building throughout the nation. ▲
- **1827** Edgar Allan Poe publishes *Tamerlane*, his first collection of poems.

World Events

- **1804** France: Napoleon Bonaparte proclaims himself emperor. ▼

- **1813** England: Jane Austen publishes *Pride and Prejudice*.
- **1815** Belgium: French army under Napoleon routed at Waterloo.
- **1815** Austria: Congress of Vienna redraws map of Europe following Napoleon's downfall.
- **1816** France: René Läennec invents the stethoscope.
- **1818** England: Mary Wollstonecraft Shelley creates a legend with *Frankenstein*.

- **1829** England: George Stephenson perfects a steam locomotive for Liverpool-Manchester Railway. ▼

American and World Events

- **1831** Cyrus McCormick invents mechanical reaper. ▼

MᶜCORMICK.

REAPING MACHINE.

- **1837** Samuel F. B. Morse patents electromagnetic telegraph.
- **1838** U.S. Army marches Cherokees of Georgia on long "Trail of Tears" to Oklahoma. ▶

- **1846** Mexican War begins.
- **1846** Abraham Lincoln first elected to Congress.
- **1848** Mexican War ends; United States expands borders.
- **1848** California Gold Rush begins.
- **1848** Women's Rights Convention held in Seneca Falls, New York.

- **1850** Nathaniel Hawthorne publishes *The Scarlet Letter*.
- **1850** California admitted to the Union. ▼

- **1851** Herman Melville publishes *Moby-Dick*.
- **1851** Nathaniel Hawthorne publishes *The House of the Seven Gables*.
- **1852** Harriet Beecher Stowe publishes *Uncle Tom's Cabin*.

- **1831** France: Victor Hugo publishes *Notre Dame de Paris*. ▼

- **1841** Antarctica: First explored by Englishman James Ross.
- **1842** Asia: Hong Kong becomes a British colony.
- **1845** Ireland: Famine results from failure of potato crop.
- **1847** Italy: Verdi's opera *Macbeth* first performed.
- **1847** England: Emily Brontë publishes *Wuthering Heights*.
- **1848** Belgium: Karl Marx and Friedrich Engels publish *The Communist Manifesto*.

- **1850** France: Life insurance introduced.
- **1850** England: Elizabeth Barrett Browning publishes *Sonnets from the Portuguese*.
- **1851** Australia: Gold discovered in New South Wales.
- **1853** Europe: Crimean War begins.
- **1854** Japan: Ports open to trade.
- **1855** England: Robert Browning publishes *Men and Women*.
- **1856** Crimean War ends.

A Growing Nation

(1800–1870)

In 1831, the Frenchman Alexis de Tocqueville, sent to report on America's prisons, ultimately wrote about something far more interesting: a bustling new nation full of individuals optimistically pursuing their destinies. His *Democracy in America* observed that Americans had "a lively faith in the perfectibility of man," believing "what appears to them today to be good may be superseded by something better tomorrow."

The bustling spirit that had enchanted Tocqueville in 1831 would make for a turbulent "tomorrow" in the decades to come: By 1870, industrialism, explosive population and economic growth, and the Civil War had all aged the nation's spirit. American literature also matured during this time. In 1831, Tocqueville wrote, "America has produced very few writers of distinction. . . . [The literature of England] still darts its rays into the forests of the New World." By 1870, America had produced many "writers of distinction": Irving, Cooper, Bryant, Poe, Emerson, Thoreau, Hawthorne, Melville, Dickinson, and Whitman—all of whom eventually shone their unmistakably American light into and far beyond "the forests of the New World."

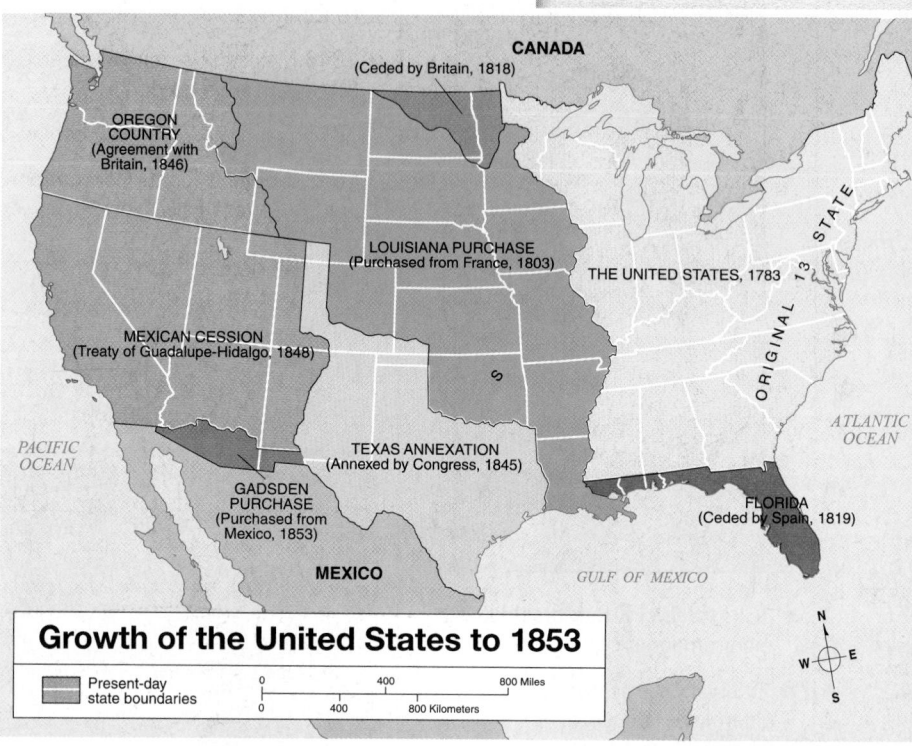

Growth of the United States to 1853

CANADA (Ceded by Britain, 1818)

OREGON COUNTRY (Agreement with Britain, 1846)

LOUISIANA PURCHASE (Purchased from France, 1803)

THE UNITED STATES, 1783

ORIGINAL 13 STATE

MEXICAN CESSION (Treaty of Guadalupe-Hidalgo, 1848)

MEXICAN CESSION

TEXAS ANNEXATION (Annexed by Congress, 1845)

GADSDEN PURCHASE (Purchased from Mexico, 1853)

PACIFIC OCEAN

MEXICO

GULF OF MEXICO

FLORIDA (Ceded by Spain, 1819)

ATLANTIC OCEAN

Present-day state boundaries

0   400   800 Miles
0   400   800 Kilometers

Historical Background

In 1800, the United States consisted of sixteen states clustered near the east coast. In 1803, Thomas Jefferson doubled the nation's size by signing the Louisiana Purchase. The rapid growth of the nation inspired an upsurge in national pride and self-awareness. Improved transportation helped bind the old and the new states together. Canals, turnpikes, and railroads boomed during this period. Steamboats and sailing packets helped speed people and goods to their destinations.

▲ **Critical Viewing**
By 1848, the United States stretched from the Atlantic Ocean to the Pacific Ocean. What region of the map was the last to be added to the United States?
[Read a Map]

The Growth of Democracy at Home: 1800–1840 As the nation expanded, Americans began to take more direct control of their government. The 1828 election of Andrew Jackson, "the People's President," ushered in the era of the common man, as property requirements for voting began to be eliminated. The democratic advances of the time, however, were confined to white males. Scant political attention was paid to women, and most African Americans remained enslaved. One of the most tragic policies of this period was "Indian removal," the forced westward migration of Native Americans from confiscated tribal lands—as in the 1838 "Trail of Tears," in which 4,000 of 15,000 Cherokee perished on the trek from Georgia to Oklahoma.

Young Nation on the World Stage Despite all this, the first decades of the 1800s were, on the whole, hopeful ones. The young republic seemed able to weather any storm.

The War of 1812 convinced Europeans that the United States was on the world stage to stay. In the Monroe Doctrine of 1823, President James Monroe warned Europe not to intervene in the new Latin American nations. In the 1830s, the U.S. became embroiled in a conflict over the secession of Texas from Mexico; in 1836, the Mexican Army made its

Close-up on History

Sacajawea, Guide for Lewis and Clark

Here is a sad contradiction: A Shoshone Indian woman named Sacajawea helped Lewis and Clark explore the territories bought in the Louisiana Purchase, but the westward movement inspired by this expedition eventually led to "Indian removal" and the confiscation of Indian lands.

In 1804, Sacajawea was staying with the Mandan Indians near present-day Bismarck, North Dakota. Meriwether Lewis and William Clark, who had been asked by President Thomas Jefferson to explore the new western lands, were overwintering with the Mandans. They worried about how they would cross the Rocky Mountains when they continued the expedition in the spring. Fortunately, Sacajawea offered to guide them. The Shoshones lived in the Rockies, and she knew the region well. She could also translate for them in their encounters with different Indian tribes.

Sacajawea contributed greatly to the success of the expedition, gathering wild vegetables and advising the men where to fish and hunt game. She also knew about the healing qualities of different herbs. When the party reached the mountains, Sacajawea recognized the lands of her people. Soon, she was reunited with her brother, and she persuaded her relatives to support the expedition with the food and horses it needed to continue.

After successfully crossing the Rockies, the explorers reached the west coast and returned to St. Louis in 1806. Thanks in large part to Sacajawea, their relations with Indians had been almost entirely peaceful. However, in the westward expansion to come, such peaceful relations were an early casualty.

famous assault on the Alamo, in which every Texan defender was killed. When Texas was admitted to the Union in 1845, the resulting war with Mexico (1846–1848) ended in a U.S. victory, which added more territory to the nation, including California. Soon after, the Gold Rush of 1849 drew hundreds of thousands to this new land of promise.

The Way West and Economic Growth

In a sense, the entire course of American history can be seen as a pageant rolling ever westward, as new territories opened up and transportation improved. The first white settlers sailed west from Europe, establishing their homes on the East Coast of the New World. All thirteen original states were on the eastern seaboard, hemmed in by mountain barriers blocking easy access to the interior. As late as 1845 the most western state in the Union was Texas. The last of the fifty states, Hawaii, lying far to the west of the North American continent, was at the time an independent kingdom.

During the early decades of the 1800s, transportation was steadily changing and improving. The Erie Canal, completed in New York in 1825, set off a wave of canal building. In the 1850s, the "iron horse"—the railroad—began to dominate long-distance American travel; by 1869, rail lines linked east and west coasts.

Advances in technology spurred social change. Factories sprang up all over the Northeast. The steel plow and reaper encouraged frontier settlement by making farming practical on the vast, sod-covered grasslands. The telegraph facilitated almost instant communication across great distances. Inventor Samuel F. B. Morse's message from Washington to Baltimore in 1844 could serve as the motto for this era: "What hath God wrought!"

Winds of Change

It was evident to even the most cheerful observer that the United States at mid-century faced trouble as well as bright promise. The new prosperity unleashed fierce competition, leading to the creation of factories scarred by child labor and unsafe working conditions. In 1840, most women could not vote or file a lawsuit. The 1840s and 1850s saw an outburst of efforts promoting women's rights, notably the 1848 Seneca Falls Convention. Above all, the centuries-old institution of slavery bitterly divided the nation. The conflict between abolitionists, who opposed slavery, and the advocates of states' rights, who argued that the federal government could not bend states to its will, sharpened in the 1850s. The gathering storm finally burst into war in 1861, but it was a storm that had been building for 250 years, ever since the first slave was brought in chains to this continent.

▲ **Critical Viewing** Harriet Beecher Stowe's novel *Uncle Tom's Cabin* (1851–1852) stirred anti-slavery sentiment in the North. What message regarding slavery is conveyed by this poster for an 1881 theatrical production of the novel? **[Analyze]**

Literature of the Period

American Literature Comes of Age Before 1800, American writers were not widely read—not even in America—but that situation soon began to change. The writers of this period would define the American voice—personal, idiosyncratic, bold—and its primary theme: the quest of the individual to define him- or herself.

Romanticism Despite their unmistakable differences, the writers of the early nineteenth century—Washington Irving, James Fenimore Cooper, William Cullen Bryant, and Edgar Allan Poe—can all be described as Romantics.

Romanticism was an artistic movement that dominated Europe and America during the nineteenth century. The name Romanticism can be a bit misleading because Romantics do not necessarily write about love. Romantic writers elevated the imagination over reason and intuition over fact. Washington Irving, the first American to be read widely overseas, made his mark with his *History of New York* (1809), which is not a dry historical record but a rollicking narrative that alters facts at will.

Point /Counterpoint

Edgar Allan Poe, Immature Genius or Mature Craftsman?

Was Edgar Allan Poe an immature genius who appeals to our childish love of mysteries and puzzles, or was he a mature craftsman who knew exactly what he wanted to achieve with every effect? Two critics—one of them, T.S. Eliot, a major poet himself—disagree about Poe's worth and craftsmanship.

An Immature Genius "That Poe had a powerful intellect is undeniable: but it seems to me the intellect of a highly gifted young person before puberty. The forms which his lively curiosity takes are those in which a pre-adolescent mentality delights: . . . puzzles and labyrinths, mechanical chess players . . . The variety and ardor of his curiosity delight and dazzle; yet in the end the eccentricity and lack of coherence of his interests tire. There is just that lacking which gives dignity to the mature man: a consistent view of life."

—**T.S. Eliot**, *To Criticize the Critic*

A Mature Craftsman "In the new picture of Poe, then, . . . we see somewhat less 'mad genius' and somewhat more 'commercial craftsman.' More wit, erudition, and philosophical consistency are evident in the new Poe, and far less compulsion. If we cannot entirely do away with the popular image of guttering candles and circling bats, in short, we should at least be able to point to craftsmanship, detachment, and humor . . . his brilliance is indisputable and his contribution to American and world literature, enormous."

—**Stuart Levine**, Introduction to *The Short Fiction of Edgar Allan Poe*

The Romantics reveled in nature. William Cullen Bryant is best known for his lyric poems rejoicing in the healing powers of nature. Irving's "Rip Van Winkle" and "The Legend of Sleepy Hollow" sparked an interest in his beloved Hudson River Valley. James Fenimore Cooper's four *Leatherstocking Tales* feature the exploits of Natty Bumppo in the frontier forests of upstate New York. A man of absolute moral integrity, Natty Bumppo preferred nature over civilization, establishing the pattern for countless American heroes to come.

Romantic writing often accented the fantastic aspects of human experience. The tortured genius Edgar Allan Poe remains popular to this day for his haunting poems and suspenseful stories whose characters, as one biographer has said, "are either grotesques or the inhabitants of another world than this."

New England Renaissance: 1840–1855 In 1837, Ralph Waldo Emerson, a former Boston minister, delivered his famous oration "The American Scholar," calling for American intellectual independence from Europe. Emerson believed that American writers should begin to interpret their own culture in new ways. As if in response to Emerson's call, an impressive burst of literary activity took place in and around Boston between 1840 and 1855. This "flowering of New England" would produce an array of great writers and enduring literature.

Transcendentalism Most, if not all, of these writers were influenced by the Transcendental movement then flourishing in New England. Emerson and Thoreau were the best-known Transcendentalists, but the ferment of Transcendental ideas affected many other writers.

Transcendentalism demands careful definition, yet it is very hard to define. It has many facets, many sources, and encompasses a range of beliefs whose specific principles depend on the individual writer or thinker. The term itself and some of the ideas came from the German philosopher Immanuel Kant. In his *Critique of Practical Reason* (1788), Kant defines the "transcendental" as the understanding a person gains intuitively because it lies beyond direct experience. American Transcendentalism drew on other thinkers as well: the ancient Greek philosopher Plato, the French mathematician Pascal,

▲ **Critical Viewing**
Above is a ticket to Charles Willson Peale's museum, which he ran to teach Americans how to learn by observing nature. How does this effort reflect Transcendentalist beliefs? **[Connect]**

the Swedish mystic and scientist Swedenborg, and the anti-materialism of Buddhist thought. Philosophy, religion, and literature all merged in New England Transcendentalism producing a native blend that was romantic, intuitive, mystical, and considerably easier to recognize than to explain.

For Transcendentalists the point was that the real truths, the most fundamental truths lie outside the experience of the senses, residing instead, as Emerson put it, in the "Over-Soul . . . a universal and benign omnipresence. . . ." If that seems a bit obscure, so did the essays in *The Dial*, the quarterly magazine of New England Transcendentalism. Published from 1840 to 1844, *The Dial* was first edited by Margaret Fuller, a dominant personality and zealous feminist who was an accepted member of the Transcendentalist group.

Walden The most influential expression of Transcendental philosophy came from Emerson and his younger friend and protégé, Henry David Thoreau, who withdrew from society to live by himself on the shores of Walden Pond. Thoreau undertook this way of life because he felt intensely the Transcendentalists' reverence for nature. He begins *Walden*, his account of this experience, by writing, "When I wrote the following pages . . . I lived alone, in the woods, a mile from any neighbor, in a house which I had built myself, on the shore of Walden Pond, in Concord, Massachusetts, and earned my living by the labor of my hands only." Published in 1854, *Walden* consists of eighteen essays about matters ranging from a battle between red and black ants to the individual's relation to society. Thoreau's observations of nature reveal his philosophy of individualism, simplicity, and passive resistance to injustice.

A Living Tradition

Walden Pond and Tinker Creek

About 120 years after Thoreau set himself the experiment of living "alone, in the woods . . . on the shore of Walden Pond," Annie Dillard undertook a similar experiment with nature and solitude: "I live by a creek, Tinker Creek, in a valley in Virginia's Blue Ridge." Just as Thoreau wrote *Walden* to describe his experiences, she, too, wrote a book about what she saw and thought, the best-selling *Pilgrim at Tinker Creek*. Near the beginning of the book, she describes the home base for her observations:

"An anchorite's hermitage [hermit's secluded retreat] is called an anchor-hold; some anchor-holds were simple sheds clamped to the side of a church like a barnacle to a rock. I think of this house clamped to the side of Tinker Creek as an anchor-hold. It holds me at anchor to the rock bottom of the creek itself and it keeps me steadied in the current, as a sea anchor does, facing the stream of light pouring down. It's a good place to live; there's a lot to think about. The creeks—Tinker and Carvin's—are an active mystery, fresh every minute."

The Possibility of Evil Not everyone shared the Transcendentalists' optimistic views. Nathaniel Hawthorne and Herman Melville expressed the darker vision of those who, in Hawthorne's words, "burrowed into the depths of our common nature" and found the area not always shimmering, but often "dusky." Hawthorne's Puritan heritage was never far from his consciousness. His masterpiece, *The Scarlet Letter* (1850), set in Boston in the seventeenth century, deals with sin, concealed guilt, hypocrisy, and humility. In *The House of the Seven Gables*, he delves into seventeenth-century witchcraft, insanity, and a legendary curse.

Hawthorne became a kind of mentor to Melville. Depressed about the negative critical response to his novel *Moby-Dick* (1851), Melville approached the older, more successful writer. Both men saw human life in grim terms, but their personalities were quite different. Hawthorne, despite a tendency toward solitude, was stable and self-possessed, a shrewd man without illusions. Melville, by contrast, was a man at odds with the world, a tortured and cryptic personality. For a large part of his career, he raged against his fate, much as Captain Ahab in *Moby-Dick* unleashed his fury against the white whale that had maimed him.

At Home in Amherst While Thoreau was planting beans next to Walden Pond, Emily Dickinson was growing up in the nearby town of Amherst, Massachusetts. Her startling, intensely focused poetry catapulted her into the company of the greatest American poets—although not in her lifetime. A recluse for the second half of her life, Dickinson did not write for publication, or even for her family, but rather from a personal need to wrestle with questions about death, immortality, and the soul—questions unresolved by conventional religion.

Beyond New England Meanwhile, the quintessential American poet was tramping about the countryside, laboring at odd jobs to finance his poetry. In 1855, New Yorker Walt Whitman published his groundbreaking series of poems, *Leaves of Grass*, proudly broadcasting his "barbaric yawp" from Brooklyn to the universe. Most American readers ignored the irregular forms and frank language of this revolutionary poet, but Emerson knew an American original when he saw one and praised Whitman's work. Of all the poets of the period between 1800 and 1870, Whitman would have the most lasting effect on American literature—despite the fact that the first edition of *Leaves* sold fewer than twenty copies.

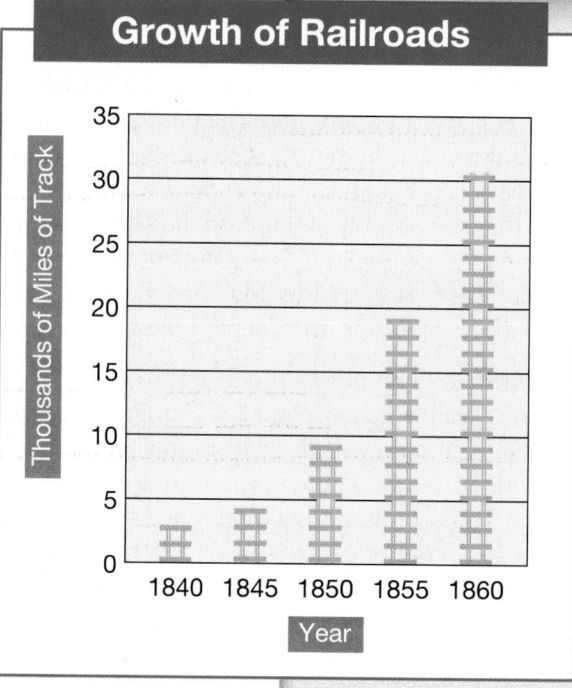

Growth of Railroads

▲ **Critical Viewing** Railroads expanded rapidly after 1840. According to this graph, what five-year period saw the greatest growth in railroads? **[Read a Graph]**

Fireside Poets Those were the literary giants of the period, as singled out by twentieth-century scholars. In 1850, however, the American reading public would probably have pointed instead to four other New England writers, known as the Fireside Poets: Henry Wadsworth Longfellow, a Harvard professor and tremendously popular poet; John Greenleaf Whittier, from a hardworking Quaker farm family; James Russell Lowell, born to wealth and position; and Oliver Wendell Holmes, a poet-physician and the unofficial laureate of the group.

After the Flowering As the war clouds gathered, the great burst of creativity in the Northeast began to subside. Antislavery writers, such as Emerson, Melville, Whittier, and Lowell, strongly supported the northern effort in the Civil War. Thoreau and Hawthorne died before the war ended. Whitman worked as a nurse in the war and incorporated war poems in his later editions of *Leaves of Grass*. Dickinson ignored the war in her poetry.

Oliver Wendell Holmes, energetic and cheerful, outlasted the rest of his renowned generation. He became "the last leaf upon the tree," to quote words he himself had written about Melville's grandfather, an old Revolutionary War veteran, in a poem published in 1831, when the poet and his country were still young.

▼ **Critical Viewing** In this image, a freight train delivers ore to a foundry where it will be turned into steel. The railroad was a key to the growth of industry in the North. What other effects do you think the growth of the railroads had on northern life? **[Form a Hypothesis]**

The Truth About O.K.

BY RICHARD LEDERER

We Americans seem to have a passion for stringing initial letters together. We use *a.m.* and *p.m.* to separate light from darkness and B.C. and A.D. to identify vast stretches of time. We may listen to a deejay or veejay on *ABC, CBS, NBC,* or *MTV* or a crusading *DA* on *CNN, NPR,* or *PBS.*

Perhaps the most widely understood American word in the world is O.K. The explanations for its origin have been as imaginative as they have been various. Some have claimed that O.K. is a version of the Chocktaw affirmative *okeh.* Others have asserted that it is short for the Greek *olla kalla* ("all good") or *Orrin Kendall* crackers or *Aux Kayes* rum, or the name of chief *Old Keokuk.*

The truth is more politically correct than any of these theories.

In the 1830s in New England, there was a craze for initialisms, in the manner of the currently popular *T.G.I.F.* and *F.Y.I.* The fad went so far as to generate letter combinations of intentional misspellings: *K.G.* for "know go," *K.Y.* for "know use," and *O.W.* for "oll wright." *O.K.* for "oll korrect" naturally followed.

Of all the loopy initialisms and misspellings of the time, *O.K.* alone survived. That's because of a presidential nickname that consolidated the letters in the national memory.

Martin Van Buren, elected our eighth president in 1836, was born in Kinderhook, New York, and, early in his political career, was dubbed "Old Kinderhook." Echoing the "Oll Korrect" initialism, *O.K.* became the rallying cry of the Old Kinderhook Club, a political organization supporting Van Buren during the 1840 campaign.

The coinage did Van Buren no good, and he was defeated in his bid for reelection. But the word honoring his name today remains what H. L. Mencken identified as "the most shining and successful Americanism ever invented."

Martin Van Buren

ACTIVITIES

1. In a dictionary, research what each of these initialisms stand for:
   (a) A.D./B.C.
   (b) aka
   (c) GOP
   (d) A.M./F.M.
   (e) CD
   (f) ERA
   (g) a.m./p.m.
   (h) IQ
   (i) PS
   (j) RIP
   (k) RSVP
   (l) UFO

2. Identify ten additional initialisms and the words each represents.

Fireside and Campfire

Fredericksburg Refugee Family at Campfire, D. E. Henderson, Gettysburg National Military Park Museum

Prepare to Read

The Devil and Tom Walker

Washington Irving (1783–1859)

Named after President George Washington, Washington Irving became the first American writer to achieve an international reputation. He was born into a wealthy family and began studying law at the age of sixteen. Although he had planned to be a lawyer, he found he was more interested in travel and writing. He spent a great deal of time exploring New York's Hudson Valley. He also traveled throughout Europe and enjoyed European literature.

A Writing Career Blooms Irving wrote satirical essays using the pen name Jonathan Oldstyle. When he was twenty-four, he and his brother anonymously began publishing the magazine *Salmagundi* (the name of a spicy appetizer), which carried humorous sketches and essays about New York society.

In 1809, using the pseudonym Diedrich Knickerbocker, he published his first major work, *A History of New York From the Beginning of the World to the End of the Dutch Dynasty*. The book, a humorous examination of New York during colonial times, was well received and made Irving famous.

Tour of Europe From 1815 to 1832, Irving lived in Europe. There, he traveled extensively and learned about European customs, traditions, and folklore. Inspired by the European folk heritage, Irving created two of his most famous stories, "The Legend of Sleepy Hollow" and "Rip Van Winkle." Both stories transform two traditional German tales into distinctly American narratives set in the Hudson Valley. Both Ichabod Crane, the nervous school teacher who hunts the headless horseman in Sleepy Hollow, and Rip Van Winkle, the colonist who sleeps for decades, have become classic figures of American literature. When Irving published these two stories in the *Sketchbook* (1820) under the pseudonym Geoffrey Crayon, writers and critics throughout Europe and United States responded enthusiastically.

While in Europe, Irving completed three other books, including *Tales of a Traveler*, which contains "The Devil and Tom Walker." In this story ill-gotten wealth, Irving reshaped a German folk tale about a man who sells his soul to the Devil for earthly gain. Irving's adaptation of the story was timely in New England during the 1720s when the Puritan belief of devoting one's life to God was being replaced by materialism and the desire for personal gain.

A Devoted American Because of the amount of time he spent abroad, some questioned Irving's patriotism. Irving offered this response:

> I am endeavoring to serve my country. Whatever I have written has been written with the feelings and published as the writing of an American. Is that renouncing my country? How else am I to serve my country—by coming home and begging an office of it: which I should not have the kind of talent or the business habits requisite to fill?—If I can do any good in this world it is with my pen.

Irving continued to publish after returning to the United States, and, like the original folk tales which inspired his work, his stories have remained popular for generations. His writing has become an important part of the American literary heritage.

Preview

Connecting to the Literature

Most of us know people who are consumed with making money. In this story, you will meet a character who is so filled with the desire for wealth that he will do virtually anything to attain it.

Literary Analysis

Third-Person Omniscient Point of View

"The Devil and Tom Walker" uses a **third-person omniscient point of view** in which an all-knowing narrator relates the events of the story. Stories told using this perspective have the following characteristics:

- A narrator who stands outside the action
- Details about the thoughts and feelings of all the characters
- The narrator's commentary about the events of the story

As you read the story, notice how Irving's use of the omniscient narrator allows you to see the conflicts in the story from several angles.

Connecting Literary Elements

Irving uses **characterization** to reveal the personality traits of his characters. In stories told using the third-person point of view, characterization is achieved in two primary ways.

- In **direct characterization,** the narrator tells the reader what the character is like.
- In **indirect characterization,** personality traits are revealed through the words, thoughts, and actions of the characters.

Notice how Irving makes use of both characterization methods.

Reading Strategy

Inferring Cultural Attitudes

This story reveals the **cultural attitudes** of New Englanders during the 1720s. Irving suggests these attitudes through descriptive details, the narrator's comments, and dialogue, and leaves it up to you to **make inferences,** or draw conclusions, based on these elements. For example, the colonists' belief in the Devil and the reference to Native Americans as "savages" reveal cultural attitudes. As you read, record details in a chart like the one shown, and draw conclusions about the cultural attitudes they represent.

Detail	Cultural Attitude

Vocabulary Development

avarice (av′ ər is) *n.* greed (p. 246)

usurers (yōō′ zhər rərz) *n.* money-lenders who charge very high interest (p. 249)

extort (eks tôrt′) *v.* to obtain by threat or violence (p. 249)

ostentation (äs′ tən tā′ shən) *n.* boastful display (p. 250)

parsimony (pär′ sə mō′ nē) *n.* stinginess (p. 250)

The Devil and Tom Walker

Washington Irving

Background

"The Devil and Tom Walker" is a variation of the Faust legend—a tale about a man who sells his soul to the Devil for earthly benefits. The legend was inspired by a real person, a wandering scholar and conjurer named Faust who lived in early sixteenth-century Germany. *Faustbach*, the first printed version of a Faust legend, was published in 1587. That story proposed that Faust had made a pact with the Devil for knowledge and power on Earth. Over the years, many variations of the Faust legend have appeared. Each retelling involves a person who trades his soul for experience, knowledge, or treasure. Adaptations do not share the same ending—in some, the protagonist is doomed; in others, he is redeemed.

A few miles from Boston in Massachusetts, there is a deep inlet, winding several miles into the interior of the country from Charles Bay, and terminating in a thickly wooded swamp or morass. On one side of this inlet is a beautiful dark grove; on the opposite side the land rises abruptly from the water's edge into a high ridge, on which grow a few scattered oaks of great age and immense size. Under one of these gigantic trees, according to old stories, there was a great amount of treasure buried by Kidd the pirate.[1] The inlet allowed a facility to bring the money in a boat secretly and at night to the very foot of the hill; the elevation of the place permitted a good look-out to be kept that no one was at hand; while the remarkable trees formed good landmarks by which the place might easily be found again. The old stories add, moreover,

---

1. Kidd the pirate Captain William Kidd (1645-1701).

that the Devil presided at the hiding of the money, and took it under his guardianship; but this it is well known he always does with buried treasure, particularly when it has been ill-gotten.

Be that as it may, Kidd never returned to recover his wealth; being shortly after seized at Boston, sent out to England, and there hanged for a pirate.

About the year 1727, just at the time that earthquakes were prevalent in New England, and shook many tall sinners down upon their knees, there lived near this place a meager, miserly fellow, of the name of Tom Walker. He had a wife as miserly as himself: they were so miserly that they even conspired to cheat each other. Whatever the woman could lay hands on, she hid away; a hen could not cackle but she was on the alert to secure the new-laid egg. Her husband was continually prying about to detect her secret hoards, and many and fierce were the conflicts that took place about what ought to have been common property. They lived in a forlorn-looking house that stood alone, and had an air of starvation. A few straggling savin trees, emblems of sterility, grew near it; no smoke ever curled from its chimney; no traveler stopped at its door. A miserable horse, whose ribs were as articulate as the bars of a gridiron, stalked about a field, where a thin carpet of moss, scarcely covering the ragged beds of puddingstone, tantalized and balked his hunger; and sometimes he would lean his head over the fence, look piteously at the passerby, and seem to petition deliverance from this land of famine.

The house and its inmates had altogether a bad name. Tom's wife was a tall termagant,[2] fierce of temper, loud of tongue, and strong of arm. Her voice was often heard in wordy warfare with her husband; and his face sometimes showed signs that their conflicts were not confined to words. No one ventured, however, to interfere between them. The lonely wayfarer shrunk within himself at the horrid clamor and clapperclawing;[3] eyed the den of discord askance; and hurried on his way, rejoicing, if a bachelor, in his celibacy.

One day that Tom Walker had been to a distant part of the neighborhood, he took what he considered a shortcut homeward, through the swamp. Like most shortcuts, it was an ill-chosen route. The swamp was thickly grown with great gloomy pines and hemlocks, some of them ninety feet high, which made it dark at noonday, and a retreat for all the owls of the neighborhood. It was full of pits and quagmires, partly covered with weeds and mosses, where the green surface often betrayed the traveler into a gulf of black, smothering mud; there were also dark and stagnant pools, the abodes of the tadpole, the bullfrog, and the watersnake; where the trunks of pines and hemlocks lay half-drowned, half-rotting, looking like alligators sleeping in the mire.

Tom had long been picking his way cautiously through this treacherous forest; stepping from tuft to tuft of rushes and roots, which

---

2. **termagant** (tur′ mə gənt) *n.* quarrelsome woman.
3. **clapperclawing** (klap′ ər klô′ iŋ) *n.* clawing or scratching.

Literary Analysis
Third-Person Omniscient Point of View What do you learn about Tom and his wife through this description?

✓**Reading Check**
Summarize what you have learned about the Walkers.

afforded precarious footholds among deep sloughs; or pacing carefully, like a cat, along the prostrate trunks of trees; startled now and then by the sudden screaming of the bittern, or the quacking of a wild duck, rising on the wing from some solitary pool. At length he arrived at a piece of firm ground, which ran out like a peninsula into the deep bosom of the swamp. It had been one of the strongholds of the Indians during their wars with the first colonists. Here they had thrown up a kind of fort, which they had looked upon as almost impregnable, and had used as a place of refuge for their squaws and children. Nothing remained of the old Indian fort but a few embankments, gradually sinking to the level of the surrounding earth, and already overgrown in part by oaks and other forest trees, the foliage of which formed a contrast to the dark pines and hemlocks of the swamp.

It was late in the dusk of evening when Tom Walker reached the old fort, and he paused there awhile to rest himself. Anyone but he would have felt unwilling to linger in this lonely, melancholy place, for the common people had a bad opinion of it, from the stories handed down from the time of the Indian wars; when it was asserted that the savages held incantations here, and made sacrifices to the evil spirit.

Tom Walker, however, was not a man to be troubled with any fears of the kind. He reposed himself for some time on the trunk of a fallen hemlock, listening to the boding cry of the tree toad, and delving with his walking staff into a mound of black mold at his feet. As he turned up the soil unconsciously, his staff struck against something hard. He raked it out of the vegetable mold, and lo! a cloven skull, with an Indian tomahawk buried deep in it, lay before him. The rust on the weapon showed the time that had elapsed since this deathblow had been given. It was a dreary memento of the fierce struggle that had taken place in this last foothold of the Indian warriors.

"Humph!" said Tom Walker, as he gave it a kick to shake the dirt from it.

"Let that skull alone!" said a gruff voice. Tom lifted up his eyes, and beheld a great black man seated directly opposite him, on the stump of a tree. He was exceedingly surprised, having neither heard nor seen anyone approach; and he was still more perplexed on observing, as well as the gathering gloom would permit, that the stranger was neither Negro nor Indian. It is true he was dressed in a rude half-Indian garb, and had a red belt or sash swathed round his body; but his face was neither black nor copper color, but swarthy and dingy, and begrimed with soot, as if he had been accustomed to toil among fires and forges. He had a shock of coarse black hair, that stood out from his head in all directions, and bore an ax on his shoulder.

He scowled for a moment at Tom with a pair of great red eyes.

"What are you doing on my grounds?" said the black man, with a hoarse growling voice.

"Your grounds!" said Tom with a sneer, "no more your grounds than mine; they belong to Deacon Peabody."

Reading Strategy
Inferring Cultural Attitudes What does the sentence begining "Anyone but he" reveal about the colonists' attitudes toward Native Americans?

Literary Analysis
Third-Person Omniscient Point of View Whose thoughts and feelings—if anyone's—are revealed in this paragraph?

"Deacon Peabody be d—d," said the stranger, "as I flatter myself he will be, if he does not look more to his own sins and less to those of his neighbors. Look yonder, and see how Deacon Peabody is faring."

Tom looked in the direction that the stranger pointed, and beheld one of the great trees, fair and flourishing without, but rotten at the core, and saw that it had been nearly hewn through, so that the first high wind was likely to blow it down. On the bark of the tree was scored the name of Deacon Peabody, an eminent man, who had waxed wealthy by driving shrewd bargains with the Indians. He now looked round, and found most of the tall trees marked with the name of some great man of the colony, and all more or less scored by the ax. The one on which he had been seated, and which had evidently just been hewn down, bore the name of Crowninshield: and he recollected a mighty rich man of that name, who made a vulgar display of wealth, which it was whispered he had acquired by buccaneering.

"He's just ready for burning!" said the black man, with a growl of triumph. "You see I am likely to have a good stock of firewood for winter."

"But what right have you," said Tom, "to cut down Deacon Peabody's timber?"

"The right of a prior claim," said the other. "This woodland belonged to me long before one of your white-faced race put foot upon the soil."

"And pray, who are you, if I may be so bold?" said Tom.

"Oh, I go by various names. I am the wild huntsman in some countries; the black miner in others. In this neighborhood I am known by the name of the black woodsman. I am he to whom the red men consecrated this spot, and in honor of whom they now and then roasted a white man, by way of sweet-smelling sacrifice. Since the red men have been exterminated by you white savages, I amuse myself by presiding at the persecutions of Quakers and Anabaptists;[4] I am the great patron and prompter of slave dealers, and the grandmaster of the Salem witches."

"The upshot of all which is, that, if I mistake not," said Tom, sturdily, "you are he commonly called Old Scratch."

---

4. **Quakers and Anabaptists** two religious groups that were persecuted for their beliefs.

The Devil and Tom Walker, 1856, John Quidor, The Cleveland Museum of Art

▲ **Critical Viewing**
This painting is called *The Devil and Tom Walker.* In what ways do the lighting and details reflect the mood of Irving's story? **[Analyze]**

**Reading Check**

Who does Tom encounter in the woods?

"The same, at your service!" replied the black man, with a half-civil nod.

Such was the opening of this interview, according to the old story; though it has almost too familiar an air to be credited. One would think that to meet with such a singular personage, in this wild, lonely place, would have shaken any man's nerves; but Tom was a hard-minded fellow, not easily daunted, and he had lived so long with a termagant wife, that he did not even fear the Devil.

It is said that after this commencement they had a long and earnest conversation together, as Tom returned homeward. The black man told him of great sums of money buried by Kidd the pirate, under the oak trees on the high ridge, not far from the morass. All these were under his command, and protected by his power, so that none could find them but such as propitiated his favor. These he offered to place within Tom Walker's reach, having conceived an especial kindness for him; but they were to be had only on certain conditions. What these conditions were may easily be surmised, though Tom never dis-closed them publicly. They must have been very hard, for he required time to think of them, and he was not a man to stick at trifles where money was in view. When they had reached the edge of the swamp, the stranger paused—"What proof have I that all you have been telling me is true?" said Tom. "There is my signature," said the black man, pressing his finger on Tom's forehead. So saying, he turned off among the thickets of the swamp, and seemed, as Tom said, to go down, down, down, into the earth, until nothing but his head and shoulders could be seen, and so on, until he totally disappeared.

When Tom reached home, he found the black print of a finger, burnt, as it were, into his forehead, which nothing could obliterate.

The first news his wife had to tell him was the sudden death of Absalom Crowninshield, the rich buccaneer. It was announced in the papers with the usual flourish, that "A great man had fallen in Israel."[5]

Tom recollected the tree which his black friend had just hewn down, and which was ready for burning, "Let the freebooter roast," said Tom, "who cares!" He now felt convinced that all he had heard and seen was no illusion.

He was not prone to let his wife into his confidence; but as this was an uneasy secret, he willingly shared it with her. All her <u>avarice</u> was awakened at the mention of hidden gold, and she urged her husband to comply with the black man's terms and secure what would make them wealthy for life. However Tom might have felt disposed to sell himself to the Devil, he was determined not to do so to oblige his

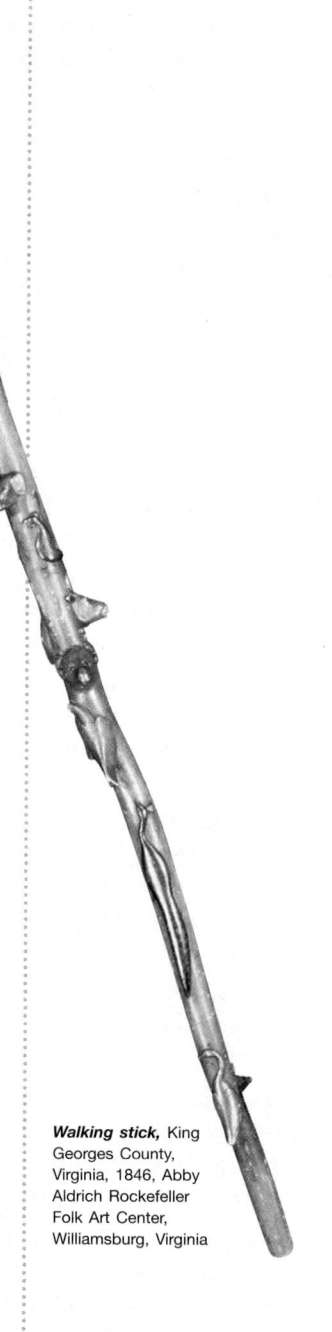

Walking stick, King Georges County, Virginia, 1846, Abby Aldrich Rockefeller Folk Art Center, Williamsburg, Virginia

avarice (av´ ə ris) *n.* greed

---

5. **A . . . Israel** a reference to II Samuel 3:38 in the Bible. The Puritans often called New England "Israel."

wife; so he flatly refused, out of the mere spirit of contradiction. Many and bitter were the quarrels they had on the subject, but the more she talked, the more resolute was Tom not to be damned to please her.

At length she determined to drive the bargain on her own account, and if she succeeded, to keep all the gain to herself. Being of the same fearless temper as her husband, she set off for the old Indian fort towards the close of a summer's day. She was many hours absent. When she came back, she was reserved and sullen in her replies. She spoke something of a black man, whom she had met about twilight, hewing at the root of a tall tree. He was sulky, however, and would not come to terms: she was to go again with a propitiatory offering, but what it was she forbore to say.

The next evening she set off again for the swamp, with her apron heavily laden. Tom waited and waited for her, but in vain; midnight came, but she did not make her appearance: morning, noon, night returned, but still she did not come. Tom now grew uneasy for her safety, especially as he found she had carried off in her apron the silver teapot and spoons, and every portable article of value. Another night elapsed, another morning came; but no wife. In a word, she was never heard of more.

What was her real fate nobody knows, in consequence of so many pretending to know. It is one of those facts which have become confounded by a variety of historians. Some asserted that she lost her way among the tangled mazes of the swamp, and sank into some pit or slough; others, more uncharitable, hinted that she had eloped with the household booty, and made off to some other province; while others surmised that the tempter had decoyed her into a dismal quagmire, on the top of which her hat was found lying. In confirmation of this, it was said a great black man, with an ax on his shoulder, was seen late that very evening coming out of the swamp, carrying a bundle tied in a checked apron, with an air of surly triumph.

The most current and probable story, however, observes that Tom Walker grew so anxious about the fate of his wife and his property, that he set out at length to seek them both at the Indian fort. During a long summer's afternoon he searched about the gloomy place, but no wife was to be seen. He called her name repeatedly, but she was nowhere to be heard. The bittern alone responded to his voice, as he flew screaming by; or the bullfrog croaked dolefully from a neighboring pool. At length, it is said, just in the brown hour of twilight, when the owls began to hoot, and the bats to flit about, his attention was attracted by the clamor of carrion crows hovering about a cypress tree. He looked up, and beheld a bundle tied in a checked apron, and hanging in the branches of the tree, with a great vulture perched hard by, as if keeping watch upon it. He leaped with joy; for he recognized his wife's apron, and supposed it to contain the household valuables.

Literary Analysis
Third-Person Omniscient Point of View What does the narrator reveal about Mrs. Walker's thoughts and feelings here?

Teapot, Yale University Art Gallery, New Haven

▲ **Critical Viewing**
Tom Walker's wife packs up her valuables to take into the forest. Why might a teapot like this one be considered valuable? **[Support]**

✔ **Reading Check**
What action does Tom's wife take?

"Let us get hold of the property," said he, consolingly to himself, "and we will endeavor to do without the woman."

As he scrambled up the tree, the vulture spread its wide wings, and sailed off screaming into the deep shadows of the forest. Tom seized the checked apron, but woeful sight! found nothing but a heart and liver tied up in it!

Such, according to the most authentic old story, was all that was to be found of Tom's wife. She had probably attempted to deal with the black man as she had been accustomed to deal with her husband; but though a female scold is generally considered a match for the Devil, yet in this instance she appears to have had the worst of it. She must have died game, however; for it is said Tom noticed many prints of cloven feet deeply stamped about the tree, and found handfuls of hair, that looked as if they had been plucked from the coarse black shock of the woodsman. Tom knew his wife's prowess by experience. He shrugged his shoulders, as he looked at the signs of a fierce clapperclawing. "Egad," said he to himself, "Old Scratch must have had a tough time of it!"

Tom consoled himself for the loss of his property, with the loss of his wife, for he was a man of fortitude. He even felt something like gratitude towards the black woodsman, who, he considered, had done him a kindness. He sought, therefore, to cultivate a further acquaintance with him, but for some time without success; the old blacklegs played shy, for whatever people may think, he is not always to be had for calling for: he knows how to play his cards when pretty sure of his game.

At length, it is said, when delay had whetted Tom's eagerness to the quick, and prepared him to agree to anything rather than not gain the promised treasure, he met the black man one evening in his usual woodsman's dress, with his ax on his shoulder, sauntering along the swamp, and humming a tune. He affected to receive Tom's advances with great indifference, made brief replies, and went on humming his tune.

By degrees, however, Tom brought him to business, and they began to haggle about the terms on which the former was to have the pirate's treasure. There was one condition which need not be mentioned, being generally understood in all cases where the Devil grants favors; but there were others about which, though of less importance, he was inflexibly obstinate. He insisted that the money found through his means should be employed in his service. He proposed, therefore, that Tom should employ it in the black traffic; that is to say, that he should

▲ **Critical Viewing**
The narrator describes "a great vulture perched hard by" and a checked apron hanging in the tree. What do you think happened to Tom Walker's wife? **[Infer]**

fit out a slave ship. This, however, Tom resolutely refused: he was bad enough in all conscience, but the Devil himself could not tempt him to turn slave-trader.

Finding Tom so squeamish on this point, he did not insist upon it, but proposed, instead, that he should turn usurer; the Devil being extremely anxious for the increase of usurers, looking upon them as his peculiar[6] people.

To this no objections were made, for it was just to Tom's taste.

"You shall open a broker's shop in Boston next month," said the black man.

"I'll do it tomorrow, if you wish," said Tom Walker.

"You shall lend money at two per cent a month."

"Egad, I'll charge four!" replied Tom Walker.

"You shall extort bonds, foreclose mortgages, drive the merchant to bankruptcy—"

"I'll drive him to the D——l," cried Tom Walker.

"You are the usurer for my money!" said the blacklegs with delight. "When will you want the rhino?"[7]

"This very night."

"Done!" said the Devil.

"Done!" said Tom Walker. So they shook hands and struck a bargain.

A few days' time saw Tom Walker seated behind his desk in a countinghouse in Boston.

His reputation for a ready-moneyed man, who would lend money out for a good consideration, soon spread abroad. Everybody remembers the time of Governor Belcher,[8] when money was particularly scarce. It was a time of paper credit. The country had been deluged with government bills; the famous Land Bank[9] had been established; there had been a rage for speculating; the people had run mad with schemes for new settlements, for building cities in the wilderness; land jobbers[10] went about with maps of grants, and townships, and El Dorados,[11] lying nobody knew where, but which everybody was ready to purchase. In a word, the great speculating fever which breaks out every now and then in the country, had raged to an alarming degree, and everybody was dreaming of making sudden fortunes from nothing. As usual the fever had subsided; the dream had gone off, and the imaginary fortunes with it; the patients were left in doleful plight, and the whole country resounded with the consequent cry of "hard times."

At this propitious time of public distress did Tom Walker set up as usurer in Boston. His door was soon thronged by customers. The needy

---

6. **peculiar** particular; special.
7. **rhino** (rīˊnō) slang term for money.
8. **Governor Belcher** Jonathan Belcher, the governor of Massachusetts Bay Colony from 1730 through 1741.
9. **Land Bank** a bank that financed transactions in real estate.
10. **land jobbers** people who bought and sold undeveloped land.
11. **El Dorados** (elˊ də räˊ dōz) n. places that are rich in gold or opportunity. El Dorado was a legendary country in South America sought by early Spanish explorers for its gold and precious stones.

usurers (yo͞oˊ zhər ərz) n. moneylenders who charge very high interest

extort (eks tôrtˊ) v. to obtain by threat or violence

Reading Check

What is Tom's new occupation?

and adventurous, the gambling speculator, the dreaming land jobber, the thriftless tradesman, the merchant with cracked credit, in short, everyone driven to raise money by desperate means and desperate sacrifices, hurried to Tom Walker.

Thus Tom was the universal friend of the needy, and acted like a "friend in need"; that is to say, he always exacted good pay and good security. In proportion to the distress of the applicant was the hardness of his terms. He accumulated bonds and mortgages; gradually squeezed his customers closer and closer, and sent them at length, dry as a sponge, from his door.

In this way he made money hand over hand, became a rich and mighty man, and exalted his cocked hat upon 'Change.[12] He built himself, as usual, a vast house, out of <u>ostentation</u>; but left the greater part of it unfinished and unfurnished, out of <u>parsimony</u>. He even set up a carriage in the fullness of his vainglory, though he nearly starved the horses which drew it; and as the ungreased wheels groaned and screeched on the axletrees, you would have thought you heard the souls of the poor debtors he was squeezing.

As Tom waxed old, however, he grew thoughtful. Having secured the good things of this world, he began to feel anxious about those of the next. He thought with regret on the bargain he had made with his black friend, and set his wits to work to cheat him out of the conditions. He became, therefore, all of a sudden, a violent churchgoer. He prayed loudly and strenuously, as if heaven were to be taken by force of lungs. Indeed, one might always tell when he had sinned most during the week, by the clamor of his Sunday devotion. The quiet Christians who had been modestly and steadfastly traveling Zionward,[13] were struck with self-reproach at seeing themselves so suddenly outstripped in their career by this new-made convert. Tom was as rigid in religious as in money matters; he was a stern supervisor and censurer of his neighbors, and seemed to think every sin entered up to their account became a credit on his own side of the page. He even talked of the expediency of reviving the persecution of Quakers and Anabaptists. In a word, Tom's zeal became as notorious as his riches.

Still, in spite of all this strenuous attention to forms, Tom had a lurking dread that the Devil, after all, would have his due. That he might not be taken unawares, therefore, it is said he always carried a small Bible in his coat pocket. He had also a great folio Bible on his countinghouse desk, and would frequently be found reading it when people called on business; on such occasions he would lay his green spectacles in the book, to mark the place, while he turned round to drive some usurious bargain.

Some say that Tom grew a little crackbrained in his old days, and that fancying his end

---

ostentation (äs´ tən tā´ shən) *n.* boastful display

parsimony (pär´ sə mō´ nē) *n.* stinginess

Reading Strategy
Inferring Cultural Attitudes From the paragraph beginning "As Tom waxed old," what can you infer about the attitudes of the day about money?

Literary Analysis
Third-person Omniscient Point of View and Characterization What do you learn about Tom's character from the narrator's description of his religious zeal?

---

12. **'Change** exchange where bankers and merchants did business.
13. **Zionward** (zī´ ən wərd) toward heaven.

approaching, he had his horse newly shod, saddled and bridled, and buried with his feet uppermost; because he supposed that at the last day the world would be turned upside down, in which case he should find his horse standing ready for mounting, and he was determined at the worst to give his old friend a run for it. This, however, is probably a mere old wives' fable. If he really did take such a precaution, it was totally superfluous; at least so says the authentic old legend, which closes his story in the following manner.

One hot summer afternoon in the dog days, just as a terrible black thunder-gust was coming up, Tom sat in his counting-house in his white linen cap and India silk morning gown. He was on the point of foreclosing a mortgage, by which he would complete the ruin of an unlucky land speculator for whom he had professed the greatest friendship. The poor land jobber begged him to grant a few months' indulgence. Tom had grown testy and irritated, and refused another day.

"My family will be ruined and brought upon the parish," said the land jobber.

"Charity begins at home," replied Tom; "I must take care of myself in these hard times."

"You have made so much money out of me," said the speculator.

Tom lost his patience and his piety—"The Devil take me," said he, "if I have made a farthing!"

Just then there were three loud knocks at the street door. He stepped out to see who was there. A black man was holding a black horse, which neighed and stamped with impatience.

"Tom, you're come for," said the black fellow, gruffly. Tom shrunk back, but too late. He had left his little Bible at the bottom of his coat pocket, and his big Bible on the desk buried under the mortgage he was about to foreclose: never was sinner taken more unawares. The black man whisked him like a child into the saddle, gave the horse the lash, and away he galloped, with Tom on his back, in the midst of the thunderstorm. The clerks stuck their pens behind their ears, and stared after him from the windows. Away went Tom Walker, dashing down the streets, his white cap bobbing up and down, his morning gown fluttering in the wind, and his steed striking fire out of the pavement at every bound. When the clerks turned to look for the black man he had disappeared.

Tom Walker never returned to foreclose the mortgage. A countryman who lived on the border of the swamp, reported that in the height of the thunder-gust he had heard a great clattering of hoofs and a howling along the road, and running to the window caught sight of a figure, such as I have described, on a horse that galloped like mad across the fields, over the hills and down into the black hemlock swamp towards the old Indian fort; and that shortly after a thunderbolt falling in that direction seemed to set the whole forest in a blaze.

✓ Reading Check

According to legend, how does the Devil catch up with Tom?

The good people of Boston shook their heads and shrugged their shoulders, but had been so much accustomed to witches and goblins and tricks of the Devil, in all kind of shapes from the first settlement of the colony, that they were not so much horror struck as might have been expected. Trustees were appointed to take charge of Tom's effects. There was nothing, however, to administer upon.

On searching his coffers all his bonds and mortgages were found reduced to cinders. In place of gold and silver his iron chest was filled with chips and shavings; two skeletons lay in his stable instead of his half-starved horses, and the very next day his great house took fire and was burned to the ground.

Such was the end of Tom Walker and his ill-gotten wealth. Let all griping money brokers lay this story to heart. The truth of it is not to be doubted. The very hole under the oak trees, whence he dug Kidd's money, is to be seen to this day; and the neighboring swamp and old Indian fort are often haunted in stormy nights by a figure on horseback, in morning gown and white cap, which is doubtless the troubled spirit of the usurer. In fact, the story has resolved itself into a proverb, and is the origin of that popular saying, so prevalent throughout New England, of "The Devil and Tom Walker."

Review and Assess

Thinking About the Selection

1. **Respond:** Were you surprised by Tom's actions in this story? Why or why not?

2. **(a) Recall:** What does the Devil offer Tom Walker?
   (b) Analyze: What factors contribute to Tom's initial refusal?

3. **(a) Recall:** What happens to Tom's wife? **(b) Interpret:** What do you learn about Tom, based on his reaction to the loss of his wife?

4. **(a) Recall:** What agreement does Tom Walker ultimately make with the Devil? **(b) Draw Conclusions:** As the story progresses, why do you think Tom begins to go to church and carry a Bible around with him at all times?

5. **(a) Recall:** What does Tom do to cause the narrator to call him a "violent churchgoer"? **(b) Interpret:** In what way is Tom's approach to religion similar to his approach to financial dealings?

6. **Evaluate:** What kind of people do you think Tom Walker and his wife are? Explain.

7. **(a) Take a Position:** Do you feel that Tom Walker deserved his fate? Why or why not? **(b) Defend:** Would you have felt more sympathy for Tom if he had sold his soul for knowledge instead of money? Explain.

Review and Assess

Literary Analysis

Third-Person Omniscient Point of View

1. Using a diagram like the one shown, give two examples in which the **third-person omniscient point of view narrator** reveals the thoughts and feelings of the characters in the story.

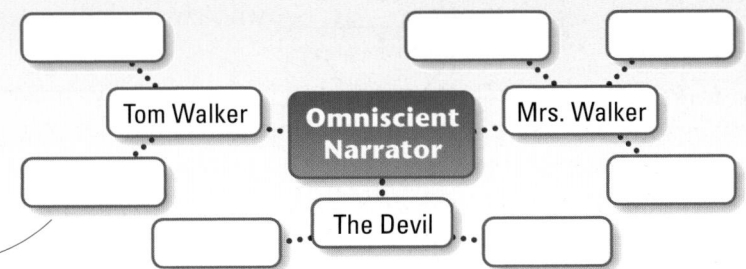

2. Find two places in the story where the narrator reveals Tom Walker's plans.
3. Find one place in the story where the narrator reveals the thoughts or unspoken plans of Tom Walker's wife.

Connecting Literary Elements

4. Identify three things you learn about Tom through **direct characterization.**
5. (a) Characterize Tom's wife based on the narrator's comments. (b) What do you learn about the relationship of Tom and his wife through **indirect characterization**? Explain.
6. What does the narrator's description of the Walker's house and the condition of their horse tell you about their personalities?

Reading Strategy

Inferring Cultural Details

7. What inferences can you draw about the **cultural attitudes** of New Englanders during the 1720s, especially in the area of religion? Explain.
8. (a) What can you infer about the attitudes of people toward moneylenders in Tom Walker's time? (b) Which details in the story lead you to draw this inference?

Extend Understanding

9. **Career Connection:** In what way might a banker today respond to Irving's suggestion that moneylenders are greedy?

Quick Review

In a story told through **third-person omniscient point of view,** a narrator is all-knowing, stands outside the action, and relates the thoughts and feelings of all the characters.

Characterization is the art of revealing character. With **direct characterization,** a writer simply states what a character is like. With **indirect characterization,** a writer reveals personality traits through the characters' thoughts, words, and actions, and through what other characters say about them.

By drawing conclusions about the details describing people in a story, you can **infer cultural attitudes.**

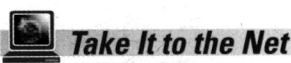 **Take It to the Net**
www.phschool.com
Take the interactive self-test online to check your understanding of the selection.

Integrate Language Skills

Vocabulary Development Lesson

Word Analysis: Latin Prefix *ex-*

The Latin prefix *ex-* means "out," as in *extort*, which means "to squeeze out." Match the words on the left with their definitions on the right.

1. exceed   **a.** elevate; glorify
2. exact   **b.** go beyond normal limits
3. exalt   **c.** look out; look forward
4. expedite   **d.** wring; pry out
5. expect   **e.** speed up; hasten

Spelling Strategy

When the prefix *ex-* means "out," do not use a hyphen after it: *extort, export, extract*. When it means "former," use a hyphen: *ex-president, ex-wife*. Add the prefix *ex-* to the following words, using a hyphen if it is needed.

1. cerpt   2. marine   3. cavate

Grammar and Style Lesson

Adjective Clauses

An **adjective clause** is a subordinate clause that modifies a noun or a pronoun. Adjective clauses are introduced with relative pronouns: *who* or *whom*, *whose*, *which*, or *that*.

> Adjective Clause
>
> **Example:** A miserable horse, <u>whose ribs stuck out,</u> stalked about a field. (modifies *horse*)

Practice Identify the adjective clause and the word it modifies in each of the following sentences.

1. At length he arrived at a piece of firm ground, which ran out like a peninsula into the . . . deep bosom of the swamp.

Fluency: Words in Context

Select the word from the vocabulary list on page 241 that best completes each sentence.

1. Unfortunately, we had borrowed money from ___?___, who charged an excessive rate of interest.
2. He would ___?___ money by threatening to harm victims if they did not pay.
3. Her ___?___ led her to refuse to send for a doctor—even when she was ill.
4. The house was such a model of ___?___ that visitors speculated about its excessive cost.
5. A main characteristic of Mrs. Walker's personality was ___?___ .

2. His reputation for a ready-moneyed man, who would lend money out for a good consideration, soon spread abroad.
3. She spoke something of a black man, whom she had met about twilight . . .
4. He had a shock of coarse black hair, that stood out from his head in all directions . . .
5. The . . . swamp and the old Indian fort are often haunted . . . by a figure on horseback, which is doubtless the troubled spirit of the usurer.

Writing Application Write a paragraph about another character who makes a deal at a high price. Use three adjective clauses that contain the relative pronouns *who, whom, whose, which,* or *that.*

W͏G Prentice Hall Writing and Grammar Connection: Chapter 19, Section 3

Writing Lesson

Modern Retelling of a Story

Write an updated version of Irving's story with new plot elements and character details. Use your story to convey the same message as Irving, but in a way that addresses a modern audience.

Prewriting   Outline the plot of the original story. Consider the best way to update each plot event you list. For example, instead of meeting in a forest, Tom Walker might encounter the Devil at the mall.

Drafting   Write your story, making sure your characters' dialogue, dress, and actions reflect modern times. Include references to food, clothes, and current events.

Writing Model: Updating a Story

Tom sitting at his computer, and downloading promissory notes. Suddenly, he saw a pair of beady eyes glaring at him from the screen. Then, pixel by pixel, a strange-looking face took shape.

> While maintaining the intent of the story, modern elements such as "pixel" and "computer" update the setting.

Revising   Confirm that your draft balances the original story elements with the new details that update it. Check to see that the conflict and the message are the same, but make sure the language and setting reflect today's world.

 Prentice Hall Writing and Grammar Connection: Chapter 5, Section 2

Extension Activities

Listening and Speaking Speculate about what happens when Mrs. Walker meets the Devil. Prepare an **enactment** of the scene as you think it would occur.

- Write dialogue to show what might take place between the two characters.
- Choose a classmate to perform the scene with you.

Practice the scene; then perform it for your class. **[Group Activity]**

Research and Technology In addition to providing the basis for this story, the Faust legend has inspired plays, operas, and even a Broadway musical. Research these works, and write an **essay** reporting your findings. Include photographs, illustrations, and other art with your essay.

 **Take It to the Net**   www.phschool.com

Go online for an additional research activity using the Internet.

Prepare to Read

A Psalm of Life ◆ The Tide Rises, the Tide Falls

Henry Wadsworth Longfellow (1807–1882)

Henry Wadsworth Longfellow once wrote, "Music is the universal language of mankind—poetry their universal pastime and delight." During the latter half of the nineteenth century, Longfellow's poetry certainly was a "universal pastime and delight"; his work was translated into two dozen languages and read by millions.

The Teaching Years Longfellow was born and raised in Portland, Maine. He attended Bowdoin College, where one of his classmates was Nathaniel Hawthorne. After graduating in 1825, Longfellow spent three years in Europe before returning to Bowdoin as a professor of modern languages. After five years, he left the college to spend another year in Europe before accepting a position at Harvard University, where he taught for eighteen years.

A Teacher and an Editor Longfellow often wrote and published his own textbooks since no others were available. The translation of foreign literature, especially poetry, was very important to him. For many years, his translations outnumbered his original poems. Although Longfellow began translating to provide material for his college students, it is clear that he also found in the foreign poetry inspirational models for his own work.

Tragedy Strikes Longfellow suffered the tragic deaths of two wives. His first wife, Mary, died in Europe in 1835 from an infection following a miscarriage. Eight years later, after a long courtship, Longfellow married Frances Appleton of Boston. Their happy marriage ended tragically when Frances was fatally burned in a household accident. Longfellow's attempts to beat out the flames left him badly burned. The resulting scars prevented him from shaving, and he grew the long, flowing beard so familiar to generations of his readers.

Poet to the People Longfellow enjoyed a long and successful career as a poet, publishing his first collection of poems, *Voices in the Night*, in 1839. By writing poetry that soothed and encouraged readers, Longfellow became the first American poet to reach a wide audience and create a national interest in poetry. His popular anthology *The Poets and Poetry of Europe*, published in 1845, accomplished his goal of bringing non-English poetry to the ordinary American reader.

Longfellow experimented with adapting traditional European verse forms and themes to uniquely American subjects. Many of his narrative poems, such as *Evangeline* (1847), *The Song of Hiawatha* (1855), *The Courtship of Miles Standish* (1858), and "Paul Revere's Ride" (1860), gave a romanticized view of America's early history and democratic ideals.

Longfellow's Legacy Longfellow's poetry has been criticized for being overly optimistic and sentimental. Yet it was his optimism and sentimentality that made Longfellow the most popular poet of his time. He became known as one of the "Fireside Poets." Families gathered around the fireplace would spend evenings reading and discussing their favorite poems by Longfellow, just as many of today's families are likely to gather around the television set to watch a favorite program.

Longfellow was so popular in his time that his seventy-fifth birthday was celebrated as if it were a national holiday. Indeed, the last years of Longfellow's life were filled with honors, both in the United States and abroad. He was given honorary degrees at Oxford and Cambridge, and invited to audiences with royalty. "Of all the suns of the New England morning," wrote the literary historian Van Wyck Brooks after the poet's death, "he was the largest in his golden sweetness."

Preview

Connecting to the Literature

In each stage of our lives, we leave marks by which others remember us: breaking a school basketball record, performing acts of charity, or even establishing close friendships. In these poems, Longfellow explores the passage of time and the human desire to leave a mark on the world.

Literary Analysis

Stanza Form

Longfellow wrote his poems in **stanzas**—units of two or more lines arranged in patterns of rhythm (or meter) and rhyme. Like a paragraph, each stanza develops a single main idea. Unlike paragraphs, however, stanzas are often a fixed length and share the same rhythm. Stanzas are named according to the number of lines they contain.

- A two-line stanza is a **couplet.**
- A four-line stanza is a **quatrain.**
- A five-line stanza is a **cinquain.**

Note which stanza form Longfellow uses in each poem.

Comparing Literary Works

In these poems, Longfellow reflects on two different periods of his life. "A Psalm of Life" was written when he was thirty-one years old, after the tragic death of his wife and child. In contrast, "The Tide Rises, The Tide Falls" was written nearly forty years later, when Longfellow was in his seventies. By this time, he had endured many hardships and learned many of life's lessons. As you read, compare the two poems and look for the prevailing **mood** and sentiment in each of them to see how they represent a difference of forty years.

Reading Strategy

Associating Images With Life

Poets often use images that take on greater significance when we consider them as symbols of the journey of life. To **associate images with life,** think about what each image means in a broader context. For example, when Longfellow describes the end of the day with "The twilight darkens, the curlew calls," he may also be describing the end of a life. Use a chart like the one shown to help you interpret images in these poems.

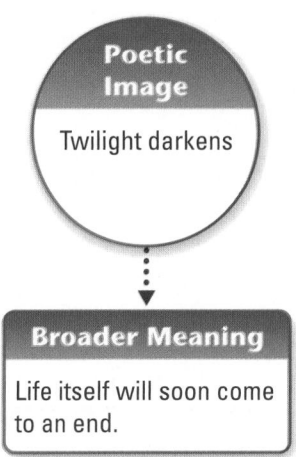

Poetic Image

Twilight darkens

Broader Meaning

Life itself will soon come to an end.

Vocabulary Development

bivouac (biv′ wak) *n.* temporary encampment (p. 259)

sublime (sə blīm′) *adj.* noble; inspiring (p. 259)

efface (ə fās′) *v.* erase; wipe out (p. 260)

A Psalm of Life

Henry Wadsworth Longfellow

Background

Longfellow wrote "A Psalm of Life" in 1838 after suffering through the tragic death of his first wife, Mary, coupled with the loss of the baby they were happily expecting. Longfellow intended the poem as an inspiration to himself and others to overcome the misfortunes of the past and to live productively in the present. In contrast, "The Tide Rises, The Tide Falls" was penned when Longfellow was in his early seventies. That poem reveals the poet's acceptance of the inevitability of death.

Tell me not, in mournful numbers,[1]
    Life is but an empty dream!—
For the soul is dead that slumbers,
    And things are not what they seem.

5   Life is real! Life is earnest!
    And the grave is not its goal:
Dust thou art, to dust returnest,
    Was not spoken of the soul.

Not enjoyment, and not sorrow,
10   Is our destined end or way;
But to act, that each tomorrow
    Find us farther than today.

Art is long, and Time is fleeting,
    And our hearts, though stout and brave,
15   Still, like muffled drums, are beating
    Funeral marches to the grave.

Literary Analysis
Stanza Form Identify the stanza form used in this poem.

---

1. numbers verses.

In the world's broad field of battle,
    In the <u>bivouac</u> of Life,
Be not like dumb, driven cattle!
20   Be a hero in the strife!

Trust no Future, howe'er pleasant!
    Let the dead Past bury its dead!
Act—act in the living Present!
    Heart within, and God o'erhead!

25 Lives of great men all remind us
    We can make our lives <u>sublime</u>,
And, departing, leave behind us
    Footprints on the sands of time;

Footprints, that perhaps another,
30   Sailing o'er life's solemn main,[2]
A forlorn and shipwrecked brother,
    Seeing, shall take heart again.

Let us, then, be up and doing,
    With a heart for any fate;
35 Still achieving, still pursuing,
    Learn to labor and to wait.

---

2. **main** open sea.

bivouac (biv´ wak´) *n.* temporary encampment

sublime (sə blīm´) *adj.* noble; inspiring

Reading Strategy
Associating Images With Life What does the poet mean by encouraging people to "leave behind us / Footprints in the sands of time"?

Review and Assess

Thinking About the Selection

1. **Respond:** What "footprints" would you like to leave "on the sands of time"?

2. **(a) Recall:** What attitude or idea does the speaker challenge in the first two stanzas? **(b) Evaluate:** Is the attitude the poet expresses positive or negative?

3. **(a) Recall:** In the third stanza, what does the speaker warn against? **(b) Interpret:** What is the speaker's attitude concerning individuality and self-reliance?

4. **(a) Recall:** According to the poem, how can our lives influence future generations? **(b) Interpret:** What is the poet calling readers to do?

5. **(a) Draw Conclusions:** Summarize the speaker's view of life. **(b) Evaluate:** What is the message of this poem? Do you agree with the poet's ideas?

The Tide Rises, The Tide Falls

Henry Wadsworth Longfellow

The tide rises, the tide falls.
The twilight darkens, the curlew[1] calls;
Along the sea sands damp and brown
The traveler hastens toward the town,
5   And the tide rises, the tide falls.

Darkness settles on roofs and walls,
But the sea, the sea in the darkness calls:
The little waves, with their soft, white hands,
<u>Efface</u> the footprints in the sands,
10   And the tide rises, the tide falls.

The morning breaks; the steeds in their stalls
Stamp and neigh, as the hostler[2] calls:
The day returns, but nevermore
Returns the traveler to the shore,
15   And the tide rises, the tide falls.

efface (ə fās´) v. erase; wipe out

---

1. **curlew** (kur´ loō´) n. large wading bird associated with the evening.
2. **hostler** (häs´ lər) n. person who tends horses at an inn or stable.

Review and Assess

Thinking About the Selection

1. **Respond:** What images did this poem evoke for you?
2. **(a) Recall:** Which events occur in the first stanza? **(b) Interpret:** Which details suggest that the traveler is nearing death? **(c) Support:** Which details suggest that he has died?
3. **(a) Recall:** Which line does the speaker repeat throughout the poem? **(b) Evaluate:** What effect does this repetition have on the message of the poem?
4. **(a) Contrast:** In the third stanza, what is the difference between the traveler and the day? **(b) Draw Conclusions:** What does the poem suggest about humanity and nature?
5. **Evaluate:** What do you think Longfellow's outlook on life and death was when he wrote this poem? Explain.

Review and Assess

Literary Analysis

Stanza Forms

1. Describe the **stanza form** of (a) "A Psalm of Life" and (b) "The Tide Rises, The Tide Falls."

2. With only one exception, every stanza in "A Psalm of Life" develops a separate idea and can stand alone. Which stanza is dependent on the one before for its meaning?

3. How does the stanza form in "The Tide Rises, The Tide Falls" allow Longfellow to emphasize the repetition of nature's cycles?

Comparing Literary Works

4. (a) Describe the overall **mood** in "A Psalm of Life." (b) Describe the mood in "The Tide Rises, The Tide Falls."

5. In what ways, if any, does Longfellow's attitude toward life change between the first poem and the one he wrote forty years later?

6. In what ways do the images in each poem and the moods they evoke connect with the circumstances of Longfellow's life? Explain.

Reading Strategy

Associating Images With Life

7. Identify three **images** in these poems that suggest a broader meaning about the journey of life.

8. How do the images contribute to the overall meaning of each poem? Using a chart like the one shown, select five images and explain how they relate to life.

Image	How It Relates to Life
1. Footprints on the sands of time	

Extend Understanding

9. **Philosophy Connection:** What are the similarities and differences in the philosophies of life expressed in both poems?

Quick Review

A **stanza** is a unit of two or more lines arranged in a pattern of rhythm (or meter) and rhyme.

The **mood** is the overall tone or feeling evoked from a literary work.

To **associate images with life,** discover a deeper meaning by thinking about the image in the broader context of life.

 Take It to the Net
www.phschool.com
Take the interactive self-test online to check your understanding of these selections.

Integrate Language Skills

Vocabulary Development Lesson

Word Analysis: Latin Root *-face-*

The root *-face-* means "appearance or outward aspect." To *efface* a footprint is to remove any trace of its presence. Use your knowledge of the meaning of the root *-face-* to match each word with its definition. Then, use a dictionary to check your answers.

1. facade   **a.** to ruin the appearance of

2. interface   **b.** the front of a building

3. deface   **c.** the exterior of an object

4. surface   **d.** to precede or come before

5. preface   **e.** to come in contact with

Concept Development: Analogies

Complete each analogy with a word from the vocabulary list on page 257. Write your answers on a separate sheet of paper.

1. *Raise* is to *lower* as *inscribe* is to ___?___ .
2. *Hut* is to *shack* as *campsite* is to ___?___ .
3. *Aggravated* is to *calm* as *humble* is to ___?___ .

Spelling Strategy

Several English words that come from Greek roots begin with a silent *p* before the *s*, as in *psalm* or *psychiatrist*. It is best simply to memorize these spellings. Complete each of the following words.

1. A __altery is a flat, stringed instrument.
2. A false or fictitious name is a __eudonym.
3. __ychology is the science of the mind.

Grammar and Style Lesson

Inverted Word Order

To achieve a rhyme or maintain a rhythm, poets may **invert** the normal English word order of subject-verb-complement. Longfellow sometimes used inverted word order for effect, as in this example from "The Tide Rises, The Tide Falls":

> **Example:** ". . . nevermore / Returns the traveler to the shore."

Longfellow places the verb, *returns*, before the subject, *the traveler*, which is an inversion of typical subject-verb order.

You can also invert the structure of a prose sentence to emphasize a particular word or idea.

Looking at Style Answer these questions about lines 9 and 10 of "A Psalm of Life."

> Not enjoyment, and not sorrow,
> Is our destined end or way

1. What word order is shown in these lines?
2. What effect does the word order have on the meaning of the lines? Explain.
3. Rewrite the lines in conventional order.
4. What do you notice about the rhythm of the new lines when read aloud?
5. What imagery does the new order create?

Writing Application Using inverted word order, write a stanza describing how you would like to leave your mark on the world.

*W*G *Prentice Hall Writing and Grammar Connection: Chapter 20, Section 3*

Writing Lesson

Analytical Essay

A German proverb says: "Look not mournfully into the Past. It comes not back again. Wisely improve the Present. It is thine. Go forth to meet the shadowy Future, without fear, and with a manly heart." Write an essay that explains whether "A Psalm of Life" reflects these sentiments, comparing the poem to the proverb.

Prewriting   Reread the poem and the proverb, looking for similar symbols, imagery, or messages. Use a chart like the one shown to note words, lines, and stanzas you will compare, with the poem on one side and the proverb on the other.

Model: Gathering Details

A Psalm of Life	German Proverb
For the soul is dead that slumbers . . . Be a hero in the strife!	Go forth to meet the shadowy Future, without fear, and with a manly heart.

Drafting   Organize your comparison, analyzing each section of the poem against the relevant portion of the proverb. Consider including paraphrases of both to ensure readers' understanding. Quote accurately to make logical comparisons.

Revising   Review your essay and make sure you have presented your ideas convincingly. Review your conclusion to determine whether you have made a strong connection between the poem and the proverb.

W͞G Prentice Hall Writing and Grammar Connection: Chapter 9, Section 3

Extension Activities

Listening and Speaking Play a **recording** of ocean sounds for the class. Discuss the ideas and emotions you associate with the sea. Consider the following questions:

- What images do crashing waves convey?
- What do you associate with the ocean?
- Does the recording enhance the poem?

Follow by having classmates discuss why Longfellow selected ocean imagery to communicate his ideas. [**Group Activity**]

Research and Technology Use library resources and the Internet to gather information about Henry Wadsworth Longfellow and his life, family, and children. Write a **research essay,** comparing the circumstances of his life to his writing to see whether there is a relationship between the two. Present your essay to the class.

 **Take It to the Net**   www.phschool.com

Go online for an additional research activity using the Internet.

Prepare to Read

Thanatopsis ◆ Old Ironsides ◆
The First Snowfall ◆ *from* Snowbound

William Cullen Bryant
(1794–1878)

As a journalist and political activist, William Cullen Bryant fought to ensure that industrialization did not obscure America's democratic values. Bryant began writing poetry at the age of nine and drafted the first version of "Thanatopsis," his most famous poem, when he was only nineteen. To support himself, Bryant practiced law for ten years while continuing to write poetry in his spare time. In 1825, he moved to New York City and became a journalist; by 1829, he had become editor-in-chief and part owner of the New York newspaper the *Evening Post*.

Voice for Justice Bryant used his position as an influential journalist to defend human rights and personal freedoms. He was an outspoken advocate of women's rights and a passionate foe of slavery. Bryant was the first American poet to win worldwide critical acclaim, and his work helped establish the Romantic Movement in America.

Oliver Wendell Holmes
(1809–1894)

Oliver Wendell Holmes made important contributions to both literature and medicine. A descendant of seventeenth-century poet Anne Bradstreet (p. 98), he briefly studied law and then moved on to study medicine. Holmes completed a medical degree at Harvard University in 1836, the same year his first collection of poetry, *Poems,* was published.

Holmes enjoyed a long teaching career at Harvard, becoming a leading medical researcher and continuing his literary pursuits. Along with James Russell Lowell, Holmes founded *The Atlantic Monthly*. His love of exaggeration, colorful expressions, and quotable statements made his essays popular with readers.

In 1830, Holmes wrote "Old Ironsides" to protest the planned destruction of the battleship *Constitution*, nicknamed "Old Ironsides" for its ability to withstand British attacks during the War of 1812. The poem saved the ship and earned Holmes national recognition as a poet.

James Russell Lowell
(1819–1891)

James Russell Lowell may have been the most talented of the Fireside Poets. However, his literary career was disrupted by personal tragedies, including the deaths of three of his four children. Following the death of his wife in 1853, he lost much of his focus and was never able to match his earlier work, but he still made important literary contributions as a poet, editor, and critic.

Lowell published his first book of poetry, *A Year's Life*, in 1841. His literary career reached its peak in 1848 with the publication of three highly successful works—*A Fable for Critics*, *The Bigelow Papers*, and *The Vision of Sir Launfal*—that gained him international fame.

Later in his life, Lowell pursued other interests. He wrote editorials supporting the abolition of slavery. He succeeded Longfellow as professor of languages at Harvard, and he helped found *The Atlantic Monthly*, serving as its first editor.

John Greenleaf Whittier (1807–1892)

John Greenleaf Whittier was born in poverty. As a child, he worked on his family's debt-ridden farm near Haverhill, Massachusetts and received virtually no formal education. As a Quaker, Whittier believed in hard work, simplicity, pacifism, religious devotion, and social justice.

Whittier was more deeply involved in the social issues of his day than were his fellow poets. He was elected to the Massachusetts State Legislature in 1835. For twenty-five years, he worked diligently for the abolition of slavery. Because of his devotion to the abolitionist cause, he did not gain national prominence until after the Civil War. When the Civil War ended, Whittier focused on writing poetry, earning national fame with the 1866 publication of *Snowbound*, which depicts the simple warmth of rural New England life. In the poem, Whittier remembers with fondness the life he spent as a boy in his family's farmhouse. As the way of life captured in Whittier's poetry disappeared, the popularity of his poems grew.

Background

Until the third decade of the nineteenth century, America had little real literature to call its own. The Fireside Poets—Henry Wadsworth Longfellow, Oliver Wendell Holmes, James Russell Lowell, and John Greenleaf Whittier—represented a literary coming of age for the young country. This first generation of acclaimed American poets took their name from the popularity of their works, which were widely read both as fireside family entertainment and in the schoolroom, where generations of children memorized them.

The four poets—all New England born and bred—chose uniquely American settings and subjects. Their themes, meter, and imagery, however, borrowed heavily from the English tradition. Though their reliance on conservative literary styles prevented them from being truly innovative, the Fireside Poets were literary giants of their day. In their own time, and for decades afterward, they ranked as America's most read and best-loved poets.

The Four Seasons of Life, Currier & Ives

Preview

Connecting to the Literature

Do the lyrics or attitudes of your favorite musicians reflect *your* feelings, and *your* views? Gifted musicians and writers often give voice to a generation. Similarly, in the early nineteenth century, the Fireside Poets gave voice to the sentiments of their age.

Literary Analysis

Meter

In poetry, a systematic arrangement of stressed (´) and unstressed (˘) syllables is called **meter.** The basic unit of meter is the foot, which usually consists of one stressed and one or more unstressed syllables. The most frequently used foot in American verse is the *iamb*—one unstressed syllable followed by a stressed syllable. The type and number of feet in the lines of a poem determine its meter. For example, a pattern of four iambs per line, as in this excerpt from *Snowbound,* is known as iambic tetrameter.

Thĕ sún thăt bríef Dĕcémbĕr dáy
Rŏse cheérleš óvĕr hílls ŏf gráy

Read each poem aloud to discover its meter, listening for metrical patterns that repeat.

Comparing Literary Works

While these poems were written during the same period in history, they each present a different mood. **Mood,** or atmosphere, is the feeling created in a reader by a literary work or passage. Setting, tone, subject, or events can influence mood. As you read, notice the similarities and differences in the mood of each poem and how each poem makes you feel.

Reading Strategy

Summarizing

To check your understanding of what you have read, **summarize** the work or parts of the work by briefly stating the main ideas and supporting details in your own words. Use an organizer like the one shown to summarize each poem.

Vocabulary Development

sepulcher (sep´əl kər) *n.* tomb (p. 268)

pensive (pen´ siv) *adj.* expressing deep thoughtfulness (p. 268)

venerable (ven´ ər ə bəl) *adj.* worthy of respect (p. 268)

gloaming (glōm´ iŋ) *n.* evening dusk; twilight (p. 272)

ominous (äm´ ə nəs) *adj.* threatening (p. 275)

querulous (kwer´ yoo ləs) *adj.* complaining (p. 276)

patriarch (pā´ trē ärk´) *n.* the father and ruler of a family or tribe (p. 278)

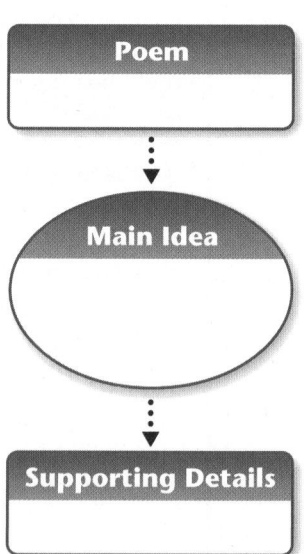

Thanatopsis

William Cullen Bryant

Kindred Spirits, Asher B. Durand, New York Public Library

To him who in the love of Nature holds
Communion with her visible forms, she speaks
A various language; for his gayer hours
She has a voice of gladness, and a smile

5 And eloquence of beauty, and she glides
Into his darker musings, with a mild
And healing sympathy, that steals away
Their sharpness, ere[1] he is aware. When thoughts
Of the last bitter hour come like a blight

10 Over thy spirit, and sad images
Of the stern agony, and shroud, and pall,
And breathless darkness, and the narrow house,[2]
Make thee to shudder, and grow sick at heart—
Go forth, under the open sky, and list

15 To Nature's teachings, while from all around—
Earth and her waters, and the depths of air—

---

1. **ere** before.
2. **narrow house** coffin.

▲ **Critical Viewing** This painting pays tribute to the friendship between the poet Bryant and landscape painter Thomas Cole. What does the painting suggest about the two men's shared interests? **[Infer]**

✓**Reading Check**

Who has "a voice of gladness" and a "healing sympathy"?

Comes a still voice—Yet a few days, and thee
The all-beholding sun shall see no more
In all his course; nor yet in the cold ground,
20 Where thy pale form was laid, with many tears,
Nor in the embrace of ocean, shall exist
Thy image. Earth, that nourished thee, shall claim
Thy growth, to be resolved to earth again,
And, lost each human trace, surrendering up
25 Thine individual being, shalt thou go
To mix forever with the elements,
To be a brother to the insensible rock
And to the sluggish clod, which the rude swain[3]
Turns with his share,[4] and treads upon. The oak
30 Shall send his roots abroad, and pierce thy mold.

      Yet not to thine eternal resting place
Shalt thou retire alone, nor couldst thou wish
Couch[5] more magnificent. Thou shalt lie down
With patriarchs of the infant world—with kings,
35 The powerful of the earth—the wise, the good,
Fair forms, and hoary seers of ages past,
All in one mighty <u>sepulcher</u>. The hills
Rock-ribbed and ancient as the sun—the vales
Stretching in <u>pensive</u> quietness between;
40 The <u>venerable</u> woods—rivers that move
In majesty, and the complaining brooks
That make the meadows green; and, poured round all,
Old Ocean's gray and melancholy waste—
Are but the solemn decorations all
45 Of the great tomb of man. The golden sun,
The planets, all the infinite host of heaven,
Are shining on the sad abodes of death,
Through the still lapse of ages. All that tread
The globe are but a handful to the tribes
50 That slumber in its bosom. Take the wings
Of morning,[6] pierce the Barcan[7] wilderness,
Or lose thyself in the continuous woods
Where rolls the Oregon,[8] and hears no sound,
Save his own dashings—yet the dead are there:
55 And millions in those solitudes, since first
The flight of years began, have laid them down

3. **swain** country youth.
4. **share** plowshare.
5. **couch** bed.
6. **Take . . . morning** allusion to Psalm 139:9.
7. **Barcan** (bär´ kən) referring to Barca, a desert region in North Africa.
8. **Oregon** river flowing between Oregon and Washington, now known as the Columbia River.

Reading Strategy
Summarizing Summarize the meaning of lines 22–30.

Literary Analysis
Meter and Mood Describe the shift in mood in lines 31–35.

sepulcher (sep´əl kər) *n.* tomb

pensive (pen´ siv) *adj.* expressing deep thoughtfulness

venerable (ven´ər ə bəl) *adj.* worthy of respect

In their last sleep—the dead reign there alone.
So shalt thou rest, and what if thou withdraw
In silence from the living, and no friend
60 Take note of thy departure? All that breathe
Will share thy destiny. The gay will laugh
When thou art gone, the solemn brood of care
Plod on, and each one as before will chase
His favorite phantom; yet all these shall leave
65 Their mirth and their employments, and shall come
And make their bed with thee. As the long train
Of ages glide away, the sons of men,
The youth in life's green spring, and he who goes
In the full strength of years, matron and maid,
70 The speechless babe, and the gray-headed man—
Shall one by one be gathered to thy side,
By those, who in their turn shall follow them.

　　　So live, that when thy summons comes to join
The innumerable caravan, which moves
75 To that mysterious realm, where each shall take
His chamber in the silent halls of death,
Thou go not, like the quarry-slave at night,
Scourged to his dungeon, but, sustained and soothed
By an unfaltering trust, approach thy grave,
80 Like one who wraps the drapery of his couch
About him, and lies down to pleasant dreams.

Reading Strategy
Summarizing How would you restate the poet's message in the final stanza?

Review and Assess

Thinking About the Selection

1. **Respond:** Did this poem make you think of nature in a new way? Explain.

2. **(a) Recall:** Identify the various languages Nature speaks to those who love her. **(b) Interpret:** How does the speaker find comfort in Nature's "various language"?

3. **(a) Recall:** According to the "still voice" introduced in line 17 what will happen to the individual being? **(b) Interpret:** In what ways do the images in lines 27–30 reinforce this idea?

4. **(a) Recall:** In the end, who shares the individual being's destiny? **(b) Draw Conclusions:** How would you summarize the poet's attitudes toward life and death?

5. **(a) Connect:** The title combines the Greek words *thanatos* (death) and *opsis* (a vision). Explain the title's connection to the poem. **(b) Apply:** In what ways can Nature provide insight into the mysteries of life and death?

OLD IRONSIDES

Oliver Wendell Holmes

▲ **Critical Viewing** To celebrate the 200th anniversary of her October 1797 launch, the U.S.S. *Constitution* took a five-hour sail around Massachusetts Bay in July 1997. Before that date, the ship had not sailed under its own power in more than 116 years. Which lines from the poem still apply to "Old Ironsides" today? **[Connect]**

Ay, tear her tattered ensign down!
    Long has it waved on high,
And many an eye has danced to see
    That banner in the sky;
5   Beneath it rung the battle shout,
    And burst the cannons roar;—
The meteor of the ocean air
    Shall sweep the clouds no more.

Her deck, once red with heroes' blood,
10   Where knelt the vanquished foe,
When winds were hurrying o'er the flood,
    And waves were white below,
No more shall feel the victor's tread,
    Or know the conquered knee;—
15   The harpies[1] of the shore shall pluck
    The eagle of the sea!

Oh, better that her shattered hulk
    Should sink beneath the wave;
Her thunders shook the mighty deep,
20   And there should be her grave;
Nail to the mast her holy flag.
    Set every threadbare sail,
And give her to the god of storms,
    The lightning and the gale!

---

1. **harpies** (här´ pēz) In Greek mythology, hideous, half-woman, half bird monsters.

Literary Analysis
Meter Why do you think Holmes occasionally alters the meter in "Old Ironsides"?

Reading Strategy
Summarizing Summarize the last stanza of the poem.

Review and Assess

Thinking About the Selection

1. **Respond:** If you had been alive in 1830, would this poem have inspired you to protest the ship's demolition? Explain.

2. **(a) Recall:** In the first stanza, what does the speaker suggest doing with the ship? **(b) Infer:** Is he being sincere?

3. **(a) Recall:** By what names does the speaker refer to the ship? **(b) Infer:** What do these names imply?

4. **(a) Draw Conclusions:** Which do you think is more important to the speaker—the ship itself or its historic role? Explain. **(b) Analyze:** In what ways does the poet appeal to the American sense of patriotism?

5. **Evaluate:** This poem was instrumental in saving *Old Ironsides*. Could a poem have such an effect today? Explain.

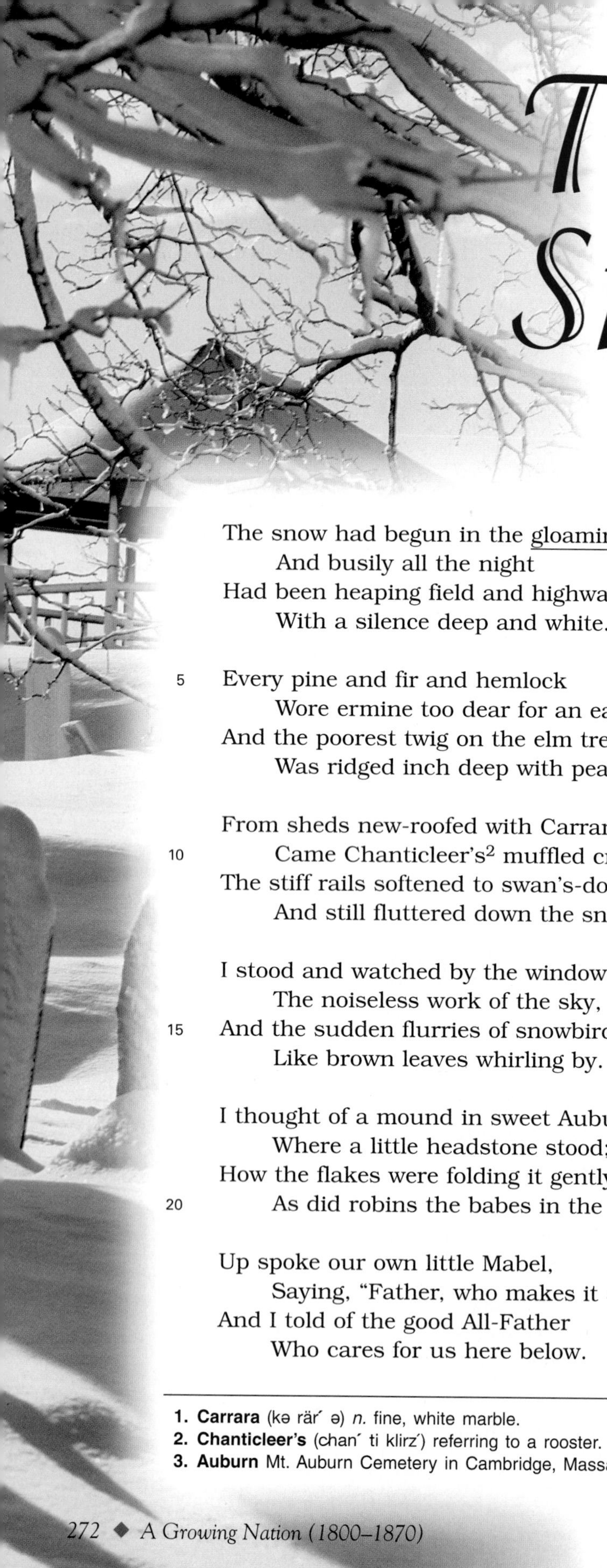

The First Snowfall

James Russell Lowell

The snow had begun in the <u>gloaming</u>,
    And busily all the night
Had been heaping field and highway
    With a silence deep and white.

5 Every pine and fir and hemlock
    Wore ermine too dear for an earl
And the poorest twig on the elm tree
    Was ridged inch deep with pearl.

From sheds new-roofed with Carrara[1]
10   Came Chanticleer's[2] muffled crow
The stiff rails softened to swan's-down,
    And still fluttered down the snow.

I stood and watched by the window
    The noiseless work of the sky,
15 And the sudden flurries of snowbirds.
    Like brown leaves whirling by.

I thought of a mound in sweet Auburn[3]
    Where a little headstone stood;
How the flakes were folding it gently,
20   As did robins the babes in the wood.

Up spoke our own little Mabel,
    Saying, "Father, who makes it snow?"
And I told of the good All-Father
    Who cares for us here below.

gloaming (glōm´ iŋ) *n.*
evening dusk; twilight

Literary Analysis
Meter In what way does
the meter of this poem
help to convey the
speaker's feelings?

---

1. Carrara (kə rär´ ə) *n.* fine, white marble.
2. Chanticleer's (chan´ ti klirz´) referring to a rooster.
3. Auburn Mt. Auburn Cemetery in Cambridge, Massachusetts.

25 Again I looked at the snowfall,
        And thought of the leaden sky
    That arched o'er our first great sorrow,
        When that mound was heaped so high.

    I remembered the gradual patience
30   That fell from that cloud like snow,
    Flake by flake, healing and hiding
        The scar that renewed our woe.

    And again to the child I whispered,
        "The snow that husheth all,
35 Darling, the merciful Father
        Alone can make it fall!"

    Then, with eyes that saw not, I kissed her:
        And she, kissing back, could not know
    That my kiss was given to her sister,
40   Folded close under deepening snow.

Literary Analysis
Meter and Mood What mood is conveyed in the stanza beginning "Again I looked at the snowfall"? Explain.

Review and Assess

Thinking About the Selection

1. **Respond:** Which natural events trigger personal memories for you? Explain.

2. **(a) Recall:** Of what does the snowfall make the speaker think? **(b) Draw Conclusions:** Why do you think the snowfall reminds the speaker of this event?

3. **(a) Recall:** How does the speaker first respond to his daughter's question about the snow? **(b) Connect:** What does he later add to his response?

4. **(a) Analyze:** In lines 29–32, in what way does the snowfall act as a healer? **(b) Infer:** What do lines 34–36 suggest about the source of emotional healing?

5. **(a) Analyze:** What does the falling snow symbolize, or represent? **(b) Extend:** In what way could such symbolism provide comfort for someone grieving the loss of a loved one?

6. **Speculate:** How might the high infant mortality rate of the nineteenth century have affected the attitudes and values of the day?

7. **Evaluate:** Do you think this poem realistically conveys a parent's pain over a lost child? Explain.

Old Holley House, Cos Cob, John Henry Twachtman, Cincinnati Art Museum

▲ **Critical Viewing** At the end of this poem, the speaker describes the inside of his home. Contrast that interior with the exterior of the house in this painting. **[Contrast]**

from SNOWBOUND

John Greenleaf Whittier

A Winter Idyll

The sun that brief December day
Rose cheerless over hills of gray,
And, darkly circled, gave at noon
A sadder light than waning moon.
5   Slow tracing down the thickening sky
Its mute and <u>ominous</u> prophecy,

A portent seeming less than threat,
It sank from sight before it set.
A chill no coat, however stout,
10 Of homespun stuff could quite shut out,
A hard, dull bitterness of cold,
That checked, mid-vein, the circling race
Of lifeblood in the sharpened face,
The coming of the snowstorm told.
15 The wind blew east; we heard the roar
Of Ocean on his wintry shore,
And felt the strong pulse throbbing there
Beat with low rhythm our inland air.

Meanwhile we did our nightly chores—
20 Brought in the wood from out of doors,
Littered the stalls, and from the mows
Raked down the herd's-grass for the cows:
Heard the horse whinnying for his corn;
And, sharply clashing horn on horn,
25 Impatient down the stanchion[1] rows
The cattle shake their walnut bows;
While, peering from his early perch

ominous (äm´ ə nəs) *adj.*
threatening

---

1. stanchion (stan´ chən) restraining device fitted around the neck
of a cow to confine it to its stall.

☑ **Reading Check**

What signals the coming
of the snowstorm?

Upon the scaffold's pole of birch,
The cock his crested helmet bent

30 And down his <u>querulous</u> challenge sent.

Unwarmed by any sunset light
The gray day darkened into night,
A night made hoary with the swarm
And whirl-dance of the blinding storm,

35 As zigzag, wavering to and fro,
Crossed and recrossed the winged snow:
And ere the early bedtime came
The white drift piled the window frame,
And through the glass the clothesline posts

40 Looked in like tall and sheeted ghosts.

So all night long the storm roared on:
The morning broke without a sun;
In tiny spherule[2] traced with lines
Of Nature's geometric signs,

45 in starry flake, and pellicle,[3]
All day the hoary meteor fell;

---

2. **spherule** (sfer´ o͞ol) small sphere.
3. **pellicle** (pel´ i kəl) thin film of crystals.

querulous (kwer´ ə ləs) *adj.*
complaining

Literary Analysis
Meter The pattern of the meter changes at lines 35 and 36. In what ways does this change correspond with the action described in these lines?

And, when the second morning shone,
We looked upon a world unknown,
On nothing we could call our own.
50 Around the glistening wonder bent
The blue walls of the firmament,
No cloud above, no earth below—
A universe of sky and snow!
The old familiar sights of ours
55 Took marvelous shapes; strange domes and towers
Rose up where sty or corncrib stood,
Or garden wall, or belt of wood;
A smooth white mound the brush pile showed,
A fenceless drift what once was road;
60 The bridle post an old man sat
With loose-flung coat and high cocked hat;
The wellcurb had a Chinese roof;
And even the long sweep,[4] high aloof,
In its slant splendor, seemed to tell
65 Of Pisa's leaning miracle.[5]

A prompt, decisive man, no breath
Our father wasted: "Boys, a path!"
Well pleased (for when did farmer boy
Count such a summons less than joy?)
70 Our buskins[6] on our feet we drew;
With mittened hands, and caps drawn low,
To guard our necks and ears from snow,

---

4. **sweep** pole with a bucket at one end, used for raising water from a well.
5. **Pisa's leaning miracle** famous leaning tower of Pisa in Italy.
6. **buskins** high-cut leather shoes or boots.

Literary Analysis
Meter and Mood What mood is conveyed in the morning light? Which words create this mood?

Reading Strategy
Summarizing Why are the boys so excited by their father's order to make a path through the snow?

✔ **Reading Check**
What does the family discover on the second morning?

We cut the solid whiteness through.
And, where the drift was deepest, made
75 A tunnel walled and overlaid
With dazzling crystal: we had read
Of rare Aladdin's[7] wondrous cave,
And to our own his name we gave,
With many a wish the luck were ours
80 To test his lamp's supernal powers.
We reached the barn with merry din,
And roused the prisoned brutes within,
The old horse thrust his long head out,
And grave with wonder gazed about;
85 The cock his lusty greeting said,
And forth his speckled harem led;
The oxen lashed their tails, and hooked,
And mild reproach of hunger looked;
The hornèd patriarch of the sheep,
90 Like Egypt's Amun[8] roused from sleep,
Shook his sage head with gesture mute,
And emphasized with stamp of foot.

All day the gusty north wind bore
The loosening drift its breath before:
95 Low circling round its southern zone,
The sun through dazzling snow-mist shone.
No church bell lent its Christian tone
To the savage air, no social smoke
Curled over woods of snow-hung oak
100 A solitude made more intense
By dreary-voicèd elements,
The shrieking of the mindless wind,
The moaning tree boughs swaying blind,
And on the glass the unmeaning beat
105 Of ghostly fingertips of sleet.
Beyond the circle of our hearth
No welcome sound of toil or mirth
Unbound the spell, and testified
Of human life and thought outside.
110 We minded that the sharpest ear
The buried brooklet could not hear,
The music of whose liquid lip
Had been to us companionship,
And, in our lonely life, had grown
115 To have an almost human tone.

patriarch (pā′ trē ärk′) *n.*
the father and ruler of a
family or tribe

Reading Strategy
Summarizing How do
the sounds of the world
change as a result of the
snowstorm?

---

7. **Aladdin's** referring to Aladdin, a boy in *The Arabian Nights* who found a magic lamp
and through its powers discovered a treasure in a cave.
8. **Amun** Egyptian god with a ram's head.

As night drew on, and, from the crest
Of wooded knolls that ridged the west,
The sun, a snow-blown traveler, sank
From sight beneath the smothering bank,
120   We piled, with care, our nightly stack
Of wood against the chimney back—
The oaken log, green, huge, and thick,
And on its top the stout backstick;
The knotty forestick laid apart,
125   And filled between with curious art
The ragged brush; then, hovering near,
We watched the first red blaze appear,
Heard the sharp crackle, caught the gleam
On whitewashed wall and sagging beam,
130   Until the old, rude-furnished room
Burst, flowerlike, into rosy bloom;
While radiant with a mimic flame
Outside the sparkling drift became,
And through the bare-boughed lilac tree
135   Our own warm hearth seemed blazing free.
The crane and pendent trammels[9] showed,
The Turks' heads[10] on the andirons glowed;
While childish fancy, prompt to tell
The meaning of the miracle,
140   Whispered the old rhyme: *"Under the tree,*
When fire outdoors burns merrily,
There the witches are making tea."

The moon above the eastern wood
Shone at its full; the hill range stood
145   Transfigured in the silver flood,
Its blown snows flashing cold and keen,
Dead white, save where some sharp ravine
Took shadow, or the somber green
Of hemlocks turned to pitchy black
150   Against the whiteness at their back.
For such a world and such a night
Most fitting that unwarming light,
Which only seemed where'er it fell
To make the coldness visible.

155   Shut in from all the world without,
We sat the clean-winged hearth[11] about,

---

9. **trammels** (tram′ əlz) *n.* adjustable pothooks hanging from the movable arm, or crane, attached to the hearth.
10. **Turks' heads** turbanlike knots at the top of the andirons.
11. **clean-winged hearth** a turkey wing was used for the hearth broom.

Literary Analysis
Meter and Mood What mood is conveyed by nightfall, the crackling fire, and the warm hearth?

Reading Strategy
Summarizing Summarize the action in lines 116–142

☑**Reading Check**

What is the "mimic flame" outside?

Content to let the north wind roar
In baffled rage at pane and door,
While the red logs before us beat
160   The frost line back with tropic heat;
And ever, when a louder blast
Shook beam and rafter as it passed,
The merrier up its roaring draft
The great throat of the chimney laughed;
165   The house dog on his paws outspread
Laid to the fire his drowsy head.
The cat's dark silhouette on the wall
A couchant tiger's seemed to fall:
And, for the winter fireside meet,
170   Between the andirons' straddling feet.
The mug of cider simmered slow.
The apples sputtered in a row.
And, close at hand, the basket stood
With nuts from brown October's wood.

Review and Assess

Thinking About the Selection

1. **Respond:** Would you find it pleasant to be isolated, like the narrator and his family, by a powerful snowstorm? Why or why not?

2. **(a) Recall:** What weather conditions forewarn the narrator of the approaching snowstorm? **(b) Connect:** In what way do these "previews" build suspense in the poem?

3. **(a) Recall:** In what ways does the family prepare for and cope with the storm? **(b) Draw Conclusions:** What do these responses to the storm suggest about the family's relationship with nature?

4. **(a) Recall:** Which details in the poem convey a sense of warmth, security, and family closeness? **(b) Analyze:** Which descriptive details in lines 47–80 convey the narrator's sense of wonder upon viewing the snow-covered landscape? **(c) Infer:** What are the family's feelings about being snowbound?

5. **(a) Assess:** In what ways has life changed since *Snowbound* was written in 1865? **(b) Extend:** Today, influenced as we are by modern technologies, how would people cope with the consequences such a storm could pose? **(c) Take a Position:** Are people still at the mercy of nature, as they were in Whittier's day? Explain your answer.

Review and Assess

Literary Analysis

Meter

1. Copy these lines from "Thanatopsis" and mark the stressed and unstressed syllables of the **meter:** So shalt thou rest, and what if thou withdraw / In silence from the living, and no friend.

2. Copy these lines from *Snowbound*. Mark the stressed and unstressed syllables: Beyond the circle of our hearth / No welcome sound of toil or mirth.

3. (a) In the second stanza of "Old Ironsides," which lines are in iambic tetrameter (four iambs)? (b) Which are iambic trimeter (three iambs)?

Comparing Literary Works

4. (a) Contrast the **moods** of the two poems set in winter—"The First Snowfall" and the excerpt from *Snowbound*. (b) How does the situation in each poem contribute to these moods?

5. (a) What shift in mood occurs in line 31 of "Thanatopsis"? (b) How does this mood shift offer comfort?

6. Which of the other poems in this grouping best matches the mood of "Thanatopsis"? Why?

Reading Strategy

Summarizing

7. Using a chart like the one shown, write a **summary** of the first two stanzas of the excerpt from *Snowbound*.

Key Details		Summary
Stanza 1		
Stanza 2		

8. Summarize the main idea of "Thanatopsis." Consider your summary as a prereading guide for someone who is unfamiliar with the poem.

Extend Understanding

9. **Cultural Connection:** What value do historical monuments and symbols have to American society?

Integrate Language Skills

Vocabulary Development Lesson

Word Analysis: Latin Root -patr-

The Latin root -patr-, comes from the word *pater*, meaning "father." This root is found in many English words, including *patriarch*. Complete each sentence by writing one of the -patr- words listed below in the blank.

patronage   paternal   patriot

1. People who love their fatherland are called ___?___.
2. My father's mother is my ___?___ grandmother.
3. The mayor has the authority to give out certain ___?___ jobs to his supporters.

Concept Development: Antonyms or Synonyms?

Decide whether the words in each pair are *antonyms* (opposites) or *synonyms* (similar).

1. sepulcher, tomb
2. pensive, frivolous
3. venerable, contemptible
4. gloaming, sunlight
5. ominous, forbidding
6. querulous, content
7. patriarch, father

Spelling Strategy

The suffix -able / -ible is used to form adjectives, such as *biodegradable* and *visible*. Use the roots below to write adjectives that end with -able / -ible.

1. divide   2. sense   3. use

Grammar and Style Lesson

Participles as Adjectives

A **participle** is a verb form that can act as an adjective and answers the question *What kind?* or *Which one?* about the noun or pronoun it modifies. **Present participles** end in -ing, as in *dazzling*. **Past participles,** like *walled* and *overlaid*, may end in -ed, -d, -t, or -en. Notice the participles in this example.

> **Example:** "A tunnel *walled* and *overlaid* / With *dazzling* crystal . . . "

Practice Identify the participles in each item, along with the noun each participle modifies.

1. The sun . . . / Rose cheerless . . . , / And, darkly circled, gave at noon / A sadder light than waning moon.

2. Yet not to thine eternal resting place / Shalt thou retire alone, . . .
3. Into his darker musings, with a mild / And healing sympathy, . . .
4. . . . Yet a few days, and thee / The all-beholding sun shall see no more / In all his course; . . .
5. Oh, better that her shattered hulk / Should sink beneath the wave; . . .

Writing Application Write three sentences describing a snow-covered landscape. Use participial forms of the following verbs as adjectives: *dazzle, coat, crust, drift, chill.* Draw arrows from the participles to the words they modify.

𝒲𝒢 *Prentice Hall Writing and Grammar Connection: Chapter 19, Section 2*

Writing Lesson

Précis

Write a précis (prā sē′)—a concise abridgment or brief summary of a longer work—of the selection from *Snowbound*. Include all the main ideas and key details a reader would need in order to understand the events in the poem. Your summary should have a clear beginning, middle, and end.

Prewriting For each stanza of the poem, list the main ideas and key details you will include in your précis. Try to convey a series of details with a single phrase or sentence.

Model: Identifying Beginning, Middle, and End

Beginning	Middle	End
Darkening December sky, cold, windy . . .	Chores, blizzard starts, roars through night . . .	

> A clear beginning, middle, and end are especially important to a précis, which should reflect the structure or progression of the original work.

Drafting Set the mood for the poem's impending storm by summarizing the poem's opening stanza. Refer to your prewriting notes to avoid confusing the sequence of events as you draft the middle and end.

Revising Evaluate whether your précis accurately reflects the phases of the storm. Add details to convey the wonder of the snowy landscape and the coziness of the farmhouse hearth.

Prentice Hall Writing and Grammar Connection: Chapter 31, Section 1

Extension Activities

Listening and Speaking Convey Holmes's patriotic fervor in a **dramatic reading** of "Old Ironsides." As you rehearse:

- Work to achieve command of text and meter.
- Use a tone and pace suited to the work.
- Present the poem in a way that will persuade and move the audience.

Ask classmates to critique your reading.

Research and Technology The painting on page 267 depicts William Cullen Bryant and Thomas Cole. Research Cole and the Hudson River School of artists to determine the basis for Cole's claim to kinship with Bryant. Present your findings in an **oral presentation.**

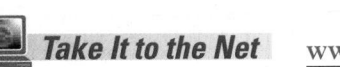 **Take It to the Net**   www.phschool.com

Go online for an additional research activity using the Internet.

Prepare to Read

Crossing the Great Divide ◆ The Most Sublime Spectacle on Earth

Meriwether Lewis (1774–1809)

Meriwether Lewis, along with William Clark and a team of hearty former soldiers, completed a two-year, 8,000-mile expedition across the uncharted territory that the United States acquired in the Louisiana Purchase. Between 1804 and 1806, Lewis and Clark traveled from St. Louis up the Missouri River to its source, then across Rocky Mountain passes to the Pacific coast. When they returned to St. Louis, they brought back valuable information about the Pacific Northwest and the other lands through which they had passed.

An American Expedition Captain Lewis's efforts were sponsored by President Thomas Jefferson, for whom Lewis had served as personal secretary. Jefferson gave Lewis and his team a rigorous assignment: map a passage to the Pacific Ocean, collect scientific information about the regions he traveled, trace the boundaries of the Louisiana territory, and claim the Oregon territory for the United States.

Along his journey, Lewis documented plants, animals, and minerals. To complement Lewis's naturalist interests, Clark provided strong map skills and created detailed sketches of the regions they crossed. The men also encountered a variety of Indian nations on the frontier with whom they traded gifts and information.

Mixed Results When Meriwether Lewis returned to Washington, D.C., after the expedition had concluded, he was received as a national hero. However, because he had not found what Jefferson sought—an all-water route to the Pacific Ocean— he himself thought the journey was a failure.

John Wesley Powell (1834–1902)

As a Union soldier fighting in the Civil War, John Wesley Powell lost an arm at the Battle of Shiloh. Despite this injury, he was the first to navigate and chart the Colorado River and the Grand Canyon.

Exploring the Grand Canyon Powell was a geologist who conducted a daring and dangerous three-month journey on the Colorado River in 1869. Financed by the Smithsonian Institution and Congress, Powell led a party of ten men in four boats. In a reflective moment before he entered the canyon, Powell described the experience ahead of him as "an unknown distance yet to run; an unknown river yet to explore." Entering the Grand Canyon by boat, the explorers faced raging rapids, towering waterfalls, and dangerously sharp rock formations. Once in the canyon, Powell's expedition party split up. Those who had become too terrified of the river went overland at "Separation Rapids" and eventually perished. Powell and the others who remained on the river survived and completed the expedition.

An Early Conservationist Later, in other expeditions, Powell surveyed the Rocky Mountains and the canyons of the Green River. In the 1870s, he directed a federal geographic survey of western lands in the public domain, urging the government to develop plans for using the land. Powell had a profound understanding of the American West, and he warned the government of the hazards of economic exploitation of the region. He spent the rest of his life trying to communicate his message of responsible development of that magnificent but arid, unpredictable, and fragile land.

Preview

Connecting to the Literature

If you have ever had an outdoor adventure while backpacking or mountain climbing, you know how exciting it is to experience the power of nature. Imagine what it would have been like to chart new territory like the adventurers who blazed a trail across the western frontier.

Literary Analysis

Description

Description in writing captures the physical sensations of sight, sound, smell, taste, and touch. Consider this example from Powell's journal:

> But form and color do not exhaust all the divine qualities of the Grand Canyon. It is the land of music. The river thunders in perpetual roar . . .

Look for similar examples of descriptive language that bring scenes to life in these selections. Use a chart like the one shown to record descriptive details.

Descriptions	
Sight	
Sound	
Smell	
Taste	
Touch	

Comparing Literary Works

Both of the men who wrote these selections were working under government commissions to explore uncharted lands. In writing these journals, both explorers sought to describe the amazing sights and experiences of their expeditions to readers in cities and towns far away. While their motives for writing were similar, their styles differ greatly. As you read, note the effects of each **writer's style**—word choice, level of formality, and imagery—on your perception of his experiences.

Reading Strategy

Noting Spatial Relationships

Noting spatial relationships as you read can help to clarify the size, distance, and location of the features being described. Using this information will help you form an accurate mental picture of the subject. Note the spatial relationships in these selections to gain a better understanding of the features they describe.

Vocabulary Development

conspicuous (kən spik´ yōō əs) *adj.* obvious; easy to see or perceive (p. 288)

sublime (sə blīm´) *adj.* inspiring awe or admiration through grandeur or beauty (p. 289)

labyrinth (lab´ə rinth´) *n.* intricate network of winding passages; maze (p. 289)

excavated (eks´ kə vāt´ id) *v.* dug out; made a hole (p. 289)

demarcation (dē´ mär kā´ shən) *n.* separation (p. 290)

multifarious (mul´ tə far´ ē əs) *adj.* having many parts; diverse (p. 291)

multitudinous (mul´ tə tōōd´ 'n əs) *adj.* numerous (p. 291)

Crossing the Great Divide

August 17–20, 1805
Meriwether Lewis

Lewis and Clark With Sacagawea at the Great Falls of the Missouri,
Olaf Seltzer, The Thomas Gilcrease Institute of Art, Tulsa, Oklahoma

▲ **Critical Viewing** What does this picture of Lewis and Clark with Sacagawea suggest about the relationship among the people in it? Does Lewis's journal support the suggestion? **[Infer; Support]**

Background

In 1803, the United States doubled the amount of territory it controlled with a single purchase of land from the French. Looking for money to finance its wars against other European nations, France sold land to the United States for a total price of $15 million—less than three cents an acre. Known as the Louisiana Purchase, the acquisition began an era of westward expansion that lasted for nearly a century. These accounts detail what the explorers found in the newly purchased territory.

Saturday, August 17th, 1805

This morning I arose very early and dispatched Drewyer and the Indian down the river. Sent Shields to hunt. I made McNeal cook the remainder of our meat which afforded a slight breakfast for ourselves and the Chief. Drewyer had been gone about 2 hours when an Indian who had straggled some little distance down the river returned and reported that the white men were coming, that he had seen them just below. They all appeared transported with joy, and the chief repeated his fraternal hug. I felt quite as much gratified at this information as the Indians appeared to be. Shortly after Capt. Clark arrived with the Interpreter Charbono, and the Indian woman, who proved to be a sister of the Chief Cameahwait. The meeting of those was really affecting, particularly between Sah-ca-ga-we-ah and an Indian woman, who had been taken prisoner at the same time with her, and who had afterwards escaped from the Minnetares and rejoined her nation. At noon the canoes arrived, and we had the satisfaction once more to find ourselves all together, with a flattering prospect of being able

◀ **Critical Viewing** What do visuals like maps and illustrations add to the narrative of exploration accounts? **[Interpret]**

▲ **Critical Viewing**
What does the placement and size of this sketch in Clark's journal reveal about his purpose in creating it? **[Infer]**

☑ **Reading Check**

What information does the Indian bring to Lewis and his group?

to obtain as many horses shortly as would enable us to prosecute our voyage by land should that by water be deemed unadvisable.

We now formed our camp just below the junction of the forks on the Lard. side[1] in a level smooth bottom covered with a fine turf of greensward. Here we unloaded our canoes and arranged our baggage on shore; formed a canopy of one of our large sails and planted some willow brush in the ground to form a shade for the Indians to sit under while we spoke to them, which we thought it best to do this evening. Accordingly about 4 P.M. we called them together and through the medium of Labuish, Charbono and Sah-ca-ga-we-ah, we communicated to them fully the objects which had brought us into this distant part of the country, in which we took care to make them a <u>conspicuous</u> object of our own good wishes and the care of our government. We made them sensible of their dependence on the will of our government for every species of merchandise as well for their defense and comfort; and apprised them of the strength of our government and its friendly dispositions towards them. We also gave them as a reason why we wished to penetrate the country as far as the ocean to the west of them was to examine and find out a more direct way to bring merchandise to them. That as no trade could be carried on with them before our return to our homes that it was mutually advantageous to them as well as to ourselves that they should render us such aids as they had it in their power to furnish in order to hasten our voyage and of course our return home.

---

1. **Lard. side** abbreviation for larboard, the port side of a ship. From their perspective, they camped on the left side of the river.

Reading Strategy
Noting Spatial Relationships Which words help readers gain a clearer picture of the campsite?

conspicuous (kən spik´ yoo əs) *adj.* obvious; easy to see or perceive

Review and Assess

Thinking About the Selection

1. **Respond:** What did you think of the way Lewis negotiated with the Indians? Explain.

2. **(a) Recall:** How did Lewis feel about being reunited with his party? **(b) Analyze:** What were his reasons for feeling as he did?

3. **(a) Recall:** What did Lewis tell the Indians was the reason for the expedition? **(b) Infer:** Was he being candid in his explanation? Explain.

4. **(a) Recall:** What did Lewis tell the Indians to expect from the United States government? **(b) Speculate:** Why do you think he told the Indians the things he did?

5. **(a) Generalize:** What did Lewis expect from the Indians? **(b) Evaluate:** How would you rate Lewis as a negotiator?

The Most Sublime Spectacle on Earth

John Wesley Powell

The Grand Canyon of the Colorado is a canyon composed of many canyons. It is a composite of thousands, of tens of thousands, of gorges. In like manner, each wall of the canyon is a composite structure, a wall composed of many walls, but never a repetition. Every one of these almost innumerable gorges is a world of beauty in itself. In the Grand Canyon there are thousands of gorges like that below Niagara Falls, and there are a thousand Yosemites. Yet all these canyons unite to form one grand canyon, the most <u>sublime</u> spectacle on the earth. Pluck up Mt. Washington by the roots to the level of the sea and drop it headfirst into the Grand Canyon, and the dam will not force its waters over the walls. Pluck up the Blue Ridge and hurl it into the Grand Canyon, and it will not fill it.

The carving of the Grand Canyon is the work of rains and rivers. The vast <u>labyrinth</u> of canyon by which the plateau region drained by the Colorado is dissected is also the work of waters. Every river has <u>excavated</u> its own gorge and every creek has excavated its gorge. When a shower comes in this land, the rills carve canyons—but a little at each storm; and though storms are far apart and the heavens above are cloudless for most of the days of the year, still, years are plenty in the ages, and an intermittent rill called to life by a shower can do much work in centuries of centuries.

sublime (sə blīm´) *adj.* inspiring admiration

labyrinth (lab´ ə rinth´) *n.* network of passages; maze

excavated (eks´ kə vāt´ id) *v.* dug out; made a hole

✔Reading Check

What is "the most sublime spectacle" on Earth?

The erosion represented in the canyons, although vast, is but a small part of the great erosion of the region, for between the cliffs blocks have been carried away far superior in magnitude to those necessary to fill the canyons. Probably there is no portion of the whole region from which there have not been more than a thousand feet degraded, and there are districts from which more than 30,000 feet of rock have been carried away. Altogether, there is a district of country more than 200,000 square miles in extent from which on the average more than 6,000 feet have been eroded. Consider a rock 200,000 square miles in extent and a mile in thickness, against which the clouds have hurled their storms and beat it into sands and the rills have carried the sands into the creeks and the creeks have carried them into the rivers and the Colorado has carried them into the sea. We think of the mountains as forming clouds about their brows, but the clouds have formed the mountains. Great continental blocks are upheaved from beneath the sea by internal geologic forces that fashion the earth. Then the wandering clouds, the tempest-bearing clouds, the rainbow-decked clouds, with mighty power and with wonderful skill, carve out valleys and canyons and fashion hills and cliffs and mountains. The clouds are the artists sublime.

In winter some of the characteristics of the Grand Canyon are emphasized. The black gneiss[1] below, the variegated quartzite, and the green or alcove sandstone form the foundation for the mighty red wall. The banded sandstone entablature is crowned by the tower limestone. In winter this is covered with snow. Seen from below, these changing elements seem to graduate into the heavens, and no plane of <u>demarcation</u> between wall and blue firmament[2] can be seen. The heavens constitute a portion of the facade and mount into a vast dome from wall to wall, spanning the Grand canyon with empyrean blue. So the earth and the heavens are blended in one vast structure.

When the clouds play in the canyon, as they often do in the rainy season, another set of effects is produced. Clouds creep out of canyons and wind into other canyons. The heavens seem to be alive, not moving as move the heavens over a plain, in one direction with the wind, but following the multiplied courses of these gorges. In this manner the little clouds seem to be individualized, to have wills and souls of their own, and to be going on diverse errands—a vast assemblage of self-willed clouds, faring here and there, intent upon purposes hidden in their own breasts. In the imagination the clouds belong to the sky, and when they are in the canyon the skies come

demarcation (dē′ mär kā′ shən) *n.* separation

---

1. **gneiss** (nīs) *n.* coarse-grained metamorphic rock resembling granite, consisting of alternating layers of minerals such as feldspar, quartz, and mica and having a banded appearance.
2. **firmament** (furm′ ə mənt) *n.* sky.

down into the gorges and cling to the cliffs and lift them up to immeasurable heights, for the sky must still be far away. Thus they lend infinity to the walls.

The wonders of the Grand Canyon cannot be adequately represented in symbols of speech, nor by speech itself. The resources of the graphic art are taxed beyond their powers in attempting to portray its features. Language and illustration combined must fail. The elements that unite to make the Grand Canyon the most sublime spectacle in nature are <u>multifarious</u> and exceedingly diverse. The Cyclopean forms which result from the sculpture of tempests through ages too long for man to compute, are wrought into endless details, to describe which would be a task equal in magnitude to that of describing the stars of the heavens or the <u>multitudinous</u> beauties of the forest with its traceries of foliage presented by oak and pine and poplar, by beech and linden and hawthorn, by tulip and lily and rose, by fern and moss and lichen. Besides the elements of form, there are elements of color, for here the colors of the heavens are rivaled by the colors of the rocks. The rainbow is not more replete with hues. But form and color do not exhaust all the divine qualities of the Grand Canyon. It is the land of music. The river thunders in perpetual roar, swelling in floors of music when the storm gods play upon the rocks and fading away in soft and low murmurs when the infinite blue of heaven is unveiled. With the melody of the great tide rising and falling, swelling and vanishing forever, other melodies are heard in the gorges of the lateral[3] canyons, while the waters plunge in the rapids among the rocks or leap in great cataracts. Thus the Grand Canyon is a land of song. Mountains of music swell in the rivers, hills of music billow in the creeks, and meadows of music murmur in the rills that ripple over the rocks. Altogether it is a symphony of multitudinous melodies. All this is the music of waters. The adamant foundations of the earth have been wrought into a sublime harp, upon which the clouds of the heavens play with mighty tempests or with gentle showers.

The glories and the beauties of form, color, and sound unite in the Grand Canyon—forms unrivaled even by the mountains, colors that

Grand Canyon With Rainbow, 1912 (detail), Thomas Moran, Fine Arts Museum of San Francisco

▲ **Critical Viewing**
Compare Powell's description with the painter's interpretation of the same natural wonder. **[Compare]**

multifarious (mul′ tə far′ ē əs) *adj.* having many parts; diverse

multitudinous (mul′ tə to͞od′ ′n əs) *adj.* numerous

☑️ **Reading Check**

Why does Powell describe the Grand Canyon as the "land of song"?

---

3. lateral (lat′ ər əl) *adj.* of, from, or at the sides.

vie with sunsets, and sounds that span the diapason[4] from tempest to tinkling raindrop, from cataract to bubbling fountain. But more: it is a vast district of country. Were it a valley plain it would make a state. It can be seen only in parts from hour to hour and from day to day and from week to week and from month to month. A year scarcely suffices to see it all. It has infinite variety, and no part is ever duplicated. Its colors, though many and complex at any instant, change with the ascending and declining sun; lights and shadows appear and vanish with the passing clouds, and the changing seasons mark their passage in changing colors. You cannot see the Grand Canyon in one view, as if it were a changeless spectacle from which a curtain might be lifted, but to see it you have to toil from month to month through its labyrinths. It is a region more difficult to traverse than the Alps or the Himalayas, but if strength and courage are sufficient for the task, by a year's toil a concept of sublimity can be obtained never again to be equaled on the hither side of Paradise.

---

4. **diapason** (dī´ ə pā´ zən) *n.* entire range of a musical instrument.

Review and Assess

Thinking About the Selection

1. **Respond:** (a) Why do you think Powell says much about the Grand Canyon but almost nothing about his journey? (b) What do you think that says about him?

2. (a) **Recall:** List three aspects of the Grand Canyon that Powell describes at length. (b) **Analyze:** To what senses does Powell appeal in those descriptions?

3. (a) **Recall:** Powell describes two special visual effects that are produced seasonally. What are they? (b) **Evaluate:** What is effective about the descriptions?

4. (a) **Interpret:** What point does he make when he writes that, in portraying the Grand Canyon, "Language and illustration combined must fail"? (b) **Draw Conclusions:** What do you think it meant to Powell to explore the Grand Canyon?

5. (a) **Compare and Contrast:** What might a painting of the Grand Canyon show that a description cannot? (b) **Compare and Contrast:** What can a description include that a painting cannot?

6. (a) **Assess:** If you were reading this description without any prior knowledge of the Grand Canyon, what would Powell's words effectively convey? (b) **Criticize:** What further questions might you have?

Review and Assess

Literary Analysis

Description

1. (a) Choose three passages of **description** in "The Most Sublime Spectacle on Earth." (b) What makes each one effective?
2. Lewis is not as descriptive as Powell, but he does include some descriptive elements in his writing. Identify a passage in Lewis's journal that helps readers see his camp.

Comparing Literary Works

3. Based on these accounts, what differences do you see in the **writers' styles**?
4. Judging by the amount of description each writer includes, what would you guess is the purpose of each piece? Support your answer with references from the selections.
5. Considering Lewis's word choice, tone, and level of formality, how would you categorize his style of writing?
6. Which of the two accounts do you find more effective, and why? Support your answer with evidence from the selections.

Reading Strategy

Noting Spatial Relationships

7. **Noting relationships** of space and size as Powell describes them, determine which is greater—the erosion of the canyons or the erosion of the region? Explain.
8. Using a chart like the one shown, note details that indicate size and spatial relationships of the Grand Canyon. Then, describe these relationships in your own words.

Description	Spatial Relationships	In My Own Words

Extend Understanding

9. **Social Studies Connection:** Where are some unexplored areas in the world today? Upon which of these do you think we should focus the most attention? Why?

Quick Review

Description is language or writing that uses sensory details to create a word picture.

A **writer's style** includes such elements as word choice, tone, level of formality, figurative language, imagery, and sentence structure.

To **note spatial relationships,** pay attention to the description of sizes, distances, and locations of features.

 Take It to the Net
www.phschool.com

Take the interactive self-test online to check your understanding of these selections.

Integrate Language Skills

Vocabulary Development Lesson

Word Analysis: Latin Prefix *multi-*

The word *multitudinous* contains the common Latin prefix *multi-*, which means "many" or "much." The word "multitudinous" means "numerous." Write definitions for each of the following words.

1. multiply
2. multicultural
3. multimedia

Spelling Strategy

In general, use *-tion* to spell the sound of *shun*, as in *portion*. Use *-sion* to spell the sound of *zhun*, as in *erosion*. Complete each word with: *-tion* or *-sion*.

1. *vi__*   3. *examina__*   5. *dimen__*
2. *explo__*   4. *situa__*   6. *explana__*

Fluency: Clarify Word Meaning

Review the vocabulary list on p. 285. Then, answer the following questions. Explain each answer, referring to the meaning of italicized word in the question.

1. Are *conspicuous* omissions easy to find?
2. Is a graduation-day rainstorm a *sublime* experience?
3. How would you prepare before entering an unexplored *labyrinth*?
4. What tools are used to *excavate* a sandbox?
5. Is a fence a sign of *demarcation*?
6. Is your wardrobe *multifarious*?
7. Are the inhabitants of an anthill *multitudinous*?

Grammar and Style Lesson

Participial Phrases

A **participial phrase** consists of a participle (a verb form used as an adjective to modify a noun or pronoun) and its complements and modifiers. Participial phrases can add details to descriptions.

> **Past Participle:** The Grand Canyon is a canyon composed of many canyons. (modifies *canyon*)

Practice Identify each participial phrase, and explain the word it modifies.

1. Sights described by Powell can be seen today.

2. Lewis's expedition would fail without the woman known as Sacagawea.
3. Begun in 1804, the expedition to explore uncharted territories of the United States took two years.
4. Deeply moved by what he saw, Powell produced a poetic description.
5. Powell's description of the Grand Canyon, published years after his visit, set off a wave of tourism.

Writing Application Write a paragraph describing something that you recently witnessed. In your writing, include sensory images and at least three participial phrases.

W̶G̶ Prentice Hall Writing and Grammar Connection: Chapter 19, Section 2

Writing Lesson

Description of a Natural Wonder

Have you ever seen a natural wonder—something so amazing that it leaves you searching for words to describe it? Choose a natural wonder that you have observed directly, learned about through research, or seen on film. Like Powell, write a description of it, using sensory images so that your readers can share your experience.

Prewriting   Picture the natural wonder you are going to describe. Create a rough sketch of your subject, and jot down some details. Also jot down the feelings your subject evoked in you.

Drafting   Decide which feature you will describe first, and continue logically and spatially from that point. Use transitions such as *behind*, *next to*, *in front of*, or *at the bottom* to show the relationship of details in your description.

> ### Model: Using Transitions to Show Place
>
> The solitary rock, as tall as a skyscraper, stood guard *at the foot* of the canyon, *just to the east* of the rushing river. We looked past the lone sentinel, *up the canyon,* to the plateau *in the distance.*

> The transitions *at the foot, just to the east, past, up,* and *in the distance* aid and enhance the description by clarifying spatial relationships.

Revising   Review your work, adding or changing your sensory details to make the description more clear. Look for places where you can add transitions to clarify the spatial relationships.

 Prentice Hall Writing and Grammar Connection: Chapter 6, Section 2

Extension Activities

Listening and Speaking In a small group, create a **tourism presentation** about a Grand Canyon sightseeing tour by raft. Address the following aspects of the tour:

- Present a vivid description of the sights.
- Provide an explanation of what rafting through the Grand Canyon will be like.
- Offer a list of the clothing and equipment to take along.

Use slides and photos of the canyon to enrich your presentation. [**Group Activity**]

Research and Technology Prepare a map showing Lewis and Clark's expedition route from its start in St. Louis, Missouri, to its conclusion at the Oregon coast. Use the Internet to gather details about the journey. If possible, use a desktop publishing program to produce an **expedition map** and an informative brochure to accompany it.

 Take It to the Net   www.phschool.com

Go online for an additional research activity using the Internet.

READING INFORMATIONAL MATERIALS

Memorandums

About Memorandums

You may already have a job, or you may be planning for your career. Either way, you are likely to read memorandums, or memos, in your workplace.

In today's workplace, the average memorandum is brief and rather informal in tone. It usually contains a heading beginning with these recognizable lines:

TO: (naming the recipient (s) of the memo)

FROM: (naming the sender)

DATE:

TOPIC:

The body of the note contains only a few facts—for example, an announcement of a time change for a staff meeting or a reminder about a deadline.

The memorandums that you read today may differ from those written in the past. Historical memorandums may be more formal, longer, and more detailed. You will find these qualities in the following memorandum, written by President Thomas Jefferson when he assigned Meriwether Lewis to undertake the exploration of the Missouri River.

Reading Strategy

Analyzing Text Structures: Patterns of Organization

Informative writing of any length can follow several different patterns of organization. Three patterns are described below.

Common Patterns of Organization

Pattern of Organization	Structure	Type of writing in which it is found
Chronological Order	Details appear in the sequence in which they occur.	do-it-yourself instructions
Order of Importance	Information is arranged so that ideas flow from most to least important, or build from least to most important.	persuasive writing
Enumeration	Supporting details are provided in list form.	brochures or sales documents

Commission of Meriwether Lewis

Thomas Jefferson
Historic memorandum

June 20, 1803

To Meriwether Lewis, esquire, captain of the first regiment of infantry of the United States of America: Your situation as secretary of the president of the United States, has made you acquainted with the objects of my confidential message of January 18, 1803, to the legislature; you have seen the act they passed, which, though expressed in general terms, was meant to sanction those objects, and you are appointed to carry them into execution.

. . .

The object of your mission is to explore the Missouri river, and such principal streams of it, as, by its course and communication with the waters of the Pacific ocean, whether the Columbia, Oregan [*sic*], Colorado, or any other river, may offer the most direct and practicable water-communication across the continent, for the purposes of commerce.

Beginning at the mouth of the Missouri, you will take observations of latitude and longitude, at all remarkable points on the river, and especially at the mouths of rivers, at rapids, at islands, and other places and objects distinguished by such natural marks and characters, of a durable kind, as that they may with certainty be recognized hereafter. The courses of the river between these points of observation may be supplied by the compass, the log-line, and by time, corrected by the observations themselves. The variations of the needle, too, in different places, should be noticed.

The interesting points of the portage between the heads of the Missouri, and of the water offering the best communication with the Pacific Ocean, should also be fixed by observation; and the course of that water to the ocean, in the same manner as that of the Missouri.

Your observations are to be taken with great pains and accuracy; to be entered distinctly and intelligibly for others as well as yourself; to comprehend all the elements necessary, with the aid of the usual tables, to fix the latitude and longitude of the places at which they were taken; and are to be rendered to the war-office, for the purpose of having the calculations made concurrently by proper persons within the United States. Several copies of these, as well as of your other notes, should be made at leisure times, and put into the care of the most trustworthy of your attendants to guard, by multiplying them against the accidental losses to which they will be exposed. A further guard would be, that one of these copies be on the cuticular membranes of the paper-birch, as less liable to injury from damp than common paper.

The commerce which may be carried on with the people inhabiting the line you will pursue, renders a knowledge of those people important. You will therefore endeavor to make yourself acquainted, as far as a diligent pursuit of your journey shall admit, with the names of the nations and their numbers;

The extent and limits of their possessions;

Their relations with other tribes or nations;

Their language, traditions, monuments;

Their ordinary occupations in agriculture, fishing, hunting, war, arts, and the implements for these;

Their food, clothing, and domestic accommodations;

The diseases prevalent among them, and the remedies they use;

Moral and physical circumstances which distinguish them from the tribes we know;

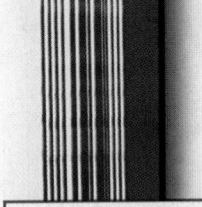

Although this historical memorandum does not have the same format as a modern memorandum, it still begins with the date and the name of the recipient.

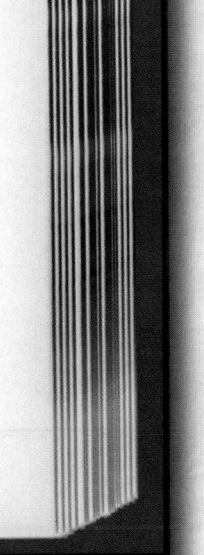

Jefferson takes the time in this memorandum to explain not only what is required but also why it is required.

Peculiarities in their laws, customs, and dispositions;

And articles of commerce they may need or furnish, and to what extent.

And, considering the interest which every nation has in extending and strengthening the authority of reason and justice among the people around them, it will be useful to acquire what knowledge you can of the state of morality, religion, and information among them; as it may better enable those who may endeavor to civilize and instruct them, to adapt their measures to the existing notions and practices of those on whom they are to operate.

Other objects worthy of notice will be—The soil and face of the country, its growth and vegetable productions, especially those not of the United States;

The animals of the country generally, and especially those not known in the United States;

The remains and accounts of any which may be deemed rare or extinct;

The mineral productions of every kind, but more particularly metals, limestone, pit-coal, and saltpeter; salines and mineral waters, noting the temperature of the last, and such circumstances as may indicate their character;

Volcanic appearances;

Climate, as characterized by the thermo-meter, by the proportion of rainy, cloudy, and clear days; by lightning, hail, snow, ice; by the access and recess of frost; by the winds prevailing at different seasons; the dates at which particular plants put forth, or lose their flower or leaf; times of appearance of particular birds, reptiles or insects.. . . .

In all your [dealings] with the natives, treat them in the most friendly and conciliatory manner which their own conduct will admit; allay all jealousies as to the object of your journey; satisfy them of its innocence; make them acquainted with the position, extent, character, peaceable and commercial dispositions of the United States; of our wish to be neighborly, friendly, and useful to them, and of our dispositions to a commercial [relationship] with them; confer with them on the points most convenient as mutual emporiums, and the articles of most desirable interchange for them and us. If a few of their influential chiefs, within practicable distance, wish to visit us, arrange such a visit with them, and furnish them with authority to call on our officers on their entering the United States, to have them conveyed to this place at the public expense. If any of them should wish to have some of their young people brought up with us, and taught such arts as may be useful to them, we will receive, instruct, and take care of them. Such a mission, whether of influential chiefs, or of young people, would give some security to your own party. Carry with you some matter of the kine-pox; inform those of them with whom you may be of its efficacy as a preservative from the small-pox, and instruct and encourage them in the use of it. This may be especially done wherever you winter.

As it is impossible for us to foresee in what manner you will be received by those people, whether with hospitality or hostility, so is it impossible to prescribe the exact degree of perseverance with which you are to pursue your journey. We value too much the lives of citizens to offer them to probable destruction. Your numbers will be sufficient to secure you against the unauthorized opposition of individuals, or of small parties; but if a superior force, authorized, or not authorized, by a nation, should be arrayed against your further passage, and inflexibly determined to arrest it, you must decline its further pursuit and return. In the loss of yourselves we should lose also the information you will have acquired. By returning safely with that, you may enable us to renew the essay with better calculated means. To your own discretion, therefore, must be left the degree of danger you may risk, and the point at which you should decline, only saying, we wish you to err on the side of your safety, and to bring back your party safe, even if it be with less information. . . .

Like today's memorandums, this historical memorandum focuses on precise facts.

Check Your Comprehension

1. Why does Jefferson want Lewis to explore the Missouri River?
2. What information does Jefferson consider so important that he wants Lewis to make multiple copies of it?
3. How is Lewis to treat Native Americans whom he meets?

Applying the Reading Strategy

Analyzing Text Structures: Patterns of Organization

4. Copy this chart below, leaving room to make notes. Complete the chart by naming one example of each type of organization in this historical memorandum.

Pattern of Organization	Examples
Chronological Order	
Order of Importance	
Enumeration	

Activity

Writing a Modern Memorandum

In Jefferson were to write "Commission of Meriwether Lewis" today, he probably would compose several different memorandums, each with its own date and special focus. Choose one topic that Jefferson covers and write one such memorandum. Use modern language to share the information clearly and concisely, following the format shown in the example.

TO:	Meriwether Lewis
FROM:	Thomas Jefferson
DATE:	June 15, 1803
TOPIC:	Animals and Vegetables

Contrasting Informational Materials

Patterns of Organization

Part of Lewis's job would have been to turn Jefferson's commission into day-to-day instructions for the expedition. Today, a handbook would present such material. If Lewis had prepared a handbook, what kind of information would he have presented in chronological order? In order of importance? Through enumeration? Give an example of each.

CONNECTIONS
Literature Past and Present

Fireside and Campfire: Views of Nature

The world of nature takes on a different meaning for just about every person. Henry Wadsworth Longfellow looked at the eternal flow of the ocean's tides and saw a reminder of our mortality. William Cullen Bryant found comfort in nature's never-ending cycle of life and death. For James Russell Lowell, snow symbolized emotional healing, while John Greenleaf Whittier saw a force with the power to transform the landscape. John Wesley Powell encountered awesome majesty. What do you see?

A New Perspective In an effort to find new ways to view nature, contemporary writer and naturalist Annie Dillard lived for a year in a small cabin next to Tinker Creek in the Blue Ridge Mountains of Virginia. Her only companion was a goldfish named Ellery Channing. Dillard described her life and thoughts there in the award-winning book *Pilgrim at Tinker Creek,* published in 1974, from which this excerpt is taken. As "Seeing" reveals, Dillard's experiences in the Virginia wilderness reshaped the way she viewed nature and led her to find underlying meaning in her observations of trees, water, animals, and the changing seasons.

Seeing

from Pilgrim at Tinker Creek

Annie Dillard

When I was six or seven years old, growing up in Pittsburgh, I used to take a precious penny of my own and hide it for someone else to find. It was a curious compulsion; sadly, I've never been seized by it since. For some reason I always "hid" the penny along the same stretch of sidewalk up the street. I would cradle it at the roots of a sycamore, say, or in a hole left by a chipped-off piece of sidewalk. Then I would take a piece of chalk and, starting at either end of the block, draw huge arrows leading up to the penny from both directions. After I learned to write I labeled the arrows: SURPRISE AHEAD or MONEY THIS WAY. I was greatly excited, during all this arrow drawing, at the thought of the first lucky passerby who would receive in this way, regardless of merit, a free gift from the universe. But I never lurked about, I would go straight home and not give the matter another thought until, some months later, I would be gripped by the impulse to hide another penny.

It is still the first week in January, and I've got great plans. I've been thinking about seeing. There are lots of things to see, unwrapped gifts and free surprises. The world is fairly studded and strewn with pennies cast broadside from a generous hand. But—and this is the point—who gets excited by a mere penny? If you follow one arrow, if you crouch motionless on a bank to watch a tremulous ripple thrill on the water and are rewarded by the sight of a muskrat kit paddling from its den, will you count that sight a chip of copper only, and go your rueful way? It is dire poverty indeed when a man is so malnourished and fatigued that he won't stoop to pick up a penny. But if you cultivate a healthy poverty and simplicity, so that finding a penny will literally make your day, then, since the world is in fact planted in pennies, you have with your poverty bought a lifetime of days. It is that simple. What you see is what you get.

I used to be able to see flying insects in the air. I'd look ahead and see, not the row of hemlocks across the road, but the air in front of it. My eyes would focus along that column of air, picking out flying insects. But I lost interest, I guess, for I dropped the habit. Now I can see birds.

> **✓ Reading Check**
>
> What did Dillard do when she was a child?

Probably some people can look at the grass at their feet and discover all the crawling creatures. I would like to know grasses and sedges—and care. Then my least journey into the world would be a field trip, a series of happy recognitions. Thoreau, in an expansive mood, exulted, "What a rich book might be made about buds, including, perhaps, sprouts!" It would be nice to think so. I cherish mental images of three perfectly happy people. One collects stones. Another—an Englishman, say—watches clouds. The third lives on a coast and collects drops of seawater, which he examines microscopically and mounts. But I don't see what the specialist sees, and so I cut myself off, not only from the total picture, but from the various forms of happiness.

Unfortunately, nature is very much a now-you-see-it, now-you-don't affair. A fish flashes, then dissolves in the water, before my eyes like so much salt. Deer apparently ascend bodily into heaven; the brightest oriole fades into leaves. These disappearances stun me into stillness and concentration; they say of nature that it conceals with a grand nonchalance, and they say of vision that it is a deliberate gift, the revelation of a dancer who for my eyes only flings away her seven veils. For nature does reveal as well as conceal: now you don't see it, now you do. For a week last September, migrating red-winged blackbirds were feeding heavily down by the creek at the back of the house. One day I went out to investigate the racket; I walked up to a tree, an Osage orange, and a hundred birds flew away. They simply materialized out of the tree. I saw a tree, then a whisk of color, then a tree again. I walked closer, and another hundred blackbirds took flight. Not a branch, not a twig budged: the birds were apparently weightless as well as invisible. Or it was as if the leaves of the Osage orange had been freed from a spell in the form of red-winged blackbirds: they flew from the tree, caught my eye in the sky, and vanished. When I looked again at the tree, the leaves had reassembled as if nothing had happened. Finally I walked directly to the trunk of the tree, and a final hundred, the real diehards, appeared, spread, and vanished. How could so many hide in the tree without my seeing them? The Osage orange, unruffled, looked just as it had looked from the house, when three hundred red-winged blackbirds cried from its crown. I looked downstream where they flew, and they were gone. Searching, I couldn't spot one. I wandered downstream to force them to play their hand, but they'd crossed the creek and scattered. One show to a customer. These appearances catch at my throat; they are the free gifts, the bright coppers at the roots of trees.

It's all a matter of keeping my eyes open. Nature is like one of those line drawings of a tree that are puzzles for children: Can you find hidden in the leaves a duck, a house, a boy, a bucket, a zebra, and a boot? Specialists can find the most incredibly well-hidden things. A book I read when I was young recommended an easy way to

Thematic Connection
Compare Dillard's message of "seeing" with Bryant's "visible forms" in the first two lines of "Thanatopsis."

find caterpillars to rear: you simply find some fresh caterpillar droppings, look up, and there's your caterpillar. Most recently an author advised me to set my mind at ease about those piles of cut stems on the ground in grassy fields. Field mice make them; they cut the grass down by degrees to reach the seeds at the head. It seems that when the grass is tightly packed, as in a field of ripe grain, the blade won't topple at a single cut through the stem; instead the cut stem simply drops vertically, held in the crush of grain. The mouse severs the bottom again and again, the stem keeps dropping an inch at a time, and finally the head is low enough for the mouse to reach the seeds. Meanwhile, the mouse is positively littering the field with its little piles of cut stems, into which, presumably, the author of the book is constantly stumbling.

If I can't see these minutiae,[1] I still try to keep my eyes open. I'm always on the lookout for ant lion traps in sandy soil, monarch pupae near milkweed, skipper larvae in locust leaves. These things are utterly common, and I've not seen one. I bang on hollow trees near water, but so far no flying squirrels have appeared. In flat country I watch every sunset in hopes of seeing the green ray. The green ray is a seldom-seen streak of light that rises from the sun like a spurting fountain at the moment of sunset; it throbs into the sky for two seconds and disappears. One more reason to keep my eyes open.

A photography professor at the University of Florida just happened to see a bird die in midflight; it jerked, died, dropped, and smashed on the ground. I squint at the wind because I read Stewart Edward White: "I have always maintained that if you looked closely enough you could *see* the wind—the dim, hardly-made-out, fine débris fleeing high in the air." White was an excellent observer, and devoted an entire chapter of *The Mountains* to the subject of seeing deer: "As soon as you can forget the naturally obvious and construct an artificial obvious, then you too will see deer."

Thematic Connection
Compare Dillard's message about observing nature with John Wesley Powell's success in doing so.

But the artificial obvious is hard to see. My eyes account for less than one percent of the weight of my head; I'm bony and dense; I *see* what I expect. I once spent a full three minutes looking at a bullfrog that was so unexpectedly large I couldn't see it even though a dozen enthusiastic campers were shouting directions.

Finally I asked, "What color am I looking for?" and a fellow said, "Green." When at last I picked out the frog, I saw what painters are up against: the thing wasn't green at all, but the color of wet hickory bark.

The lover can see, and the knowledgeable. I visited an aunt and uncle at a quarter-horse ranch in Cody, Wyoming. I couldn't do much of anything useful, but I could, I thought, draw. So as we all sat around the kitchen table after supper, I produced a sheet of paper and drew a horse. "That's one lame horse," my aunt volunteered. The rest of the family joined in: "Only place to saddle that one is his neck"; "Looks like we better shoot the poor thing, on account of those terrible growths."

---

1. minutiae (mi noo′ shē ĭ) *n.* small or relatively unimportant details.

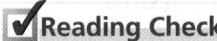

Reading Check

According to the author, how does one see nature?

Meekly, I slid the pencil and paper down the table. Everyone in that family, including my three cousins, could draw a horse. Beautifully. When the paper came back, it looked as though five shining, real quarter horses had been corraled by mistake with a papier-mâché moose; the real horses seemed to gaze at the monster with a steady, puzzled air. I stay away from horses now, but I can do a creditable goldfish. The point is that I just don't know what the lover knows; I just can't see the artificial obvious that those in the know construct. The herpetologist[2] asks the native, "Are there snakes in the ravine?" "Nosir." And the herpetologist comes home with, yessir, three bags full. Are there butterflies on that mountain? Are the bluets in bloom, are there arrowheads here, or fossil shells in the shale?

Peeping through my keyhole, I see within the range of only about 30 percent of the light that comes from the sun; the rest is infrared and some little ultraviolet, perfectly apparent to many animals, but invisible to me. A nightmare network of ganglia,[3] charged and firing without my knowledge, cuts and splices what I do see, editing it for my brain. Donald E. Carr points out that the sense impressions of one-celled animals are not edited for the brain: "This is philosophically interesting in a rather mournful way, since it means that only the simplest animals perceive the universe as it is."

A fog that won't burn away drifts and flows across my field of vision. When you see fog move against a backdrop of deep pines, you see not the fog itself but streaks of clearness floating across the air in dark shreds. So I see only tatters of clearness through a pervading obscurity. I can't distinguish the fog from the overcast sky; I can't be sure if the light is direct or reflected. Everywhere darkness and the presence of the unseen appalls. We estimate now that only one atom dances alone in every cubic meter of intergalactic space. I blink and squint. What planet or power yanks Halley's Comet out of orbit? We haven't seen that force yet; it's a question of distance, density, and the pallor of reflected light. We rock, cradled in the swaddling band of darkness. Even the simple darkness of night whispers suggestions to the mind.

---

2. **herpetologist** (hŭr′ pə täl′ ə jist) one who practices the study of reptiles and amphibians.
3. **ganglia** (gaŋ′ glē ə) masses of nerve cells that serve as centers from which nerve impulses are transmitted.

Connecting Literature Past and Present

1. What does Dillard see when she looks at nature?
2. What enables some people to see things in nature that go unnoticed by others? Name two poems in Part 1 in which the speakers share the appreciation of nature expressed in "Seeing." Explain your choices.

Annie Dillard

(b. 1945)

As a child in Pittsburgh, Pennsylvania, Annie Dillard loved reading, drawing, and observing the natural world.

She attended Hollins College in Roanoke, Virginia, and graduated with a B.A. and later an M.A in English. Her exploration of a Virginia valley during her years at Hollins led to the publication of *Pilgrim at Tinker Creek* (1974), which won the Pulitzer Prize for Nonfiction in 1975. Since then, she has published ten other books, including the memoir *An American Childhood* (1987) and *The Living* (1992), a novel.

PART 2

Shadows of the Imagination

Mysterious Night, ca. 1895, Daingerfield, Morris Museum of Art, Georgia

Prepare to Read

The Fall of the House of Usher ◆ The Raven

Edgar Allan Poe (1809–1849)

When Edgar Allan Poe died, Rufus Griswold wrote a slanderous obituary of the eccentric writer. He claimed that Poe had been expelled from college, that he had neither good friends nor good qualities, and that he committed flagrant acts of plagiarism. Suspicious of this unconventional obituary, some have speculated that Poe orchestrated the death notice himself to keep his name in the public eye. Yet, Poe's real life was almost as dark and dismal as the possibly false obituary described it.

A Troubled Childhood Poe was born in Boston in 1809, the son of impoverished traveling actors. Shortly after Poe's birth, his father deserted the family; a year later, his mother died. Young Edgar was taken in—though never formally adopted—by the family of John Allan, a wealthy Virginia merchant. Poe lived with the Allans in England from 1815 to 1820, when they returned to the United States. It was from John Allan that Poe received his middle name. The Allans also provided for Poe's education; however, when his stepfather refused to pay Poe's large gambling debts at the University of Virginia, the young man was forced to leave the school.

Building a Literary Career In 1827, after joining the army under an assumed name, Poe published his first volume of poetry, *Tamerlane and Other Poems*. Two years later, he published a second volume, *Al Aaraaf*. In 1830, John Allan helped Poe win an appointment to the United States Military Academy at West Point. Within a year, however, Poe was expelled for academic violations,

and his dismissal resulted in an irreparable break with his stepfather.

An Unhappy Ending During the second half of his short life, Poe pursued a literary career in New York, Richmond, Philadelphia, and Baltimore, barely supporting himself by writing and working as an editor for several magazines. After his third volume of poetry, *Poems* (1831), failed to bring him either money or acclaim, he turned from poetry to fiction and literary criticism. Five of his short stories were published in newspapers in 1832, and in 1838 he published his only novel, *The Narrative of Arthur Gordon Pym*. Although his short stories gained him some recognition and his poem "The Raven" (1845) was greeted with enthusiasm, Poe could never escape from poverty. He suffered from bouts of depression and madness. Then, in 1849, two years after the death of his beloved wife, Virginia, Poe died in Baltimore, alone and unhappy.

A Legacy Since his death, Poe's work has been a magnet for attention. Poe is widely accepted as the inventor of the detective story, and his psychological thrillers have been imitated by scores of modern writers. His work has been translated into nearly every language, and dozens of film adaptations have been made of his stories. Although critics have not always agreed about Poe, the Mystery Writers of America have honored their best and brightest by conferring upon them the "Edgar" award for great achievement in mystery writing.

Poe's work has provoked intense critical debate. Some scholars have harshly criticized his writing, while others have celebrated his use of vivid imagery and sound effects, as well as his tireless exploration of altered mental states and the dark side of human nature. Despite Poe's uncertain status among critics, his work has remained extremely popular among generations of American readers.

Preview

Connecting to the Literature

It is natural to feel anxiety, but in extreme circumstances, "nerves" can become a destructive part of a person's personality. Such is the case for the characters in the selections that follow.

Literary Analysis

Single Effect

Poe argued that a short story should be constructed to achieve "a certain unique or **single effect.**" He believed that every character, incident, and detail should contribute to this effect. As you read, examine the ways in which Poe heeds his own advice.

Comparing Literary Works

Although one is a story and the other a poem, both "The Fall of the House of Usher" and "The Raven" exemplify the literary genre known as **gothic.** The gothic style is characterized by the following elements:

- The story is set in bleak or remote places.
- The plot involves macabre or violent incidents.
- Characters are in psychological and/or physical torment.
- A supernatural or otherworldly element is often present.

As you read, examine how both the story and the poem emphasize different elements of the gothic style.

Reading Strategy

Breaking Down Long Sentences

Long, intricate sentences can challenge your understanding. It may help to **break down long sentences** into logical parts. First, look for a sentence's core: its subject and verb. Then, look for clues in punctuation, conjunctions, and modifying words. Use a chart like the one shown to break down Poe's lengthy sentences into more manageable parts.

Vocabulary Development

importunate (im pôr′ chōō nit) *adj.* insistent (p. 310)

munificent (myōō nif′ ə sənt) *adj.* generous (p. 310)

equivocal (ē kwiv′ ə kəl) *adj.* having more than one possible interpretation (p. 311)

appellation (ap′ ə lā′ shən) *n.* name or title (p. 311)

specious (spē′ shəs) *adj.* seeming to be good or sound without actually being so (p. 311)

anomalous (ə näm′ ə ləs) *adj.* abnormal (p. 314)

sentience (sen′ shəns) *n.* capacity of feeling (p. 318)

obeisance (ō bā′ səns) *n.* gesture of respect (p. 327)

craven (krā′ vən) *adj.* very cowardly (p. 327)

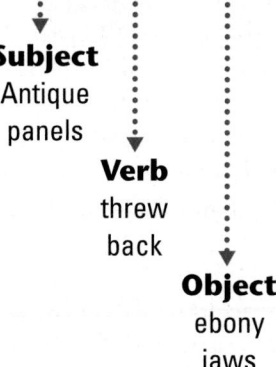

Sentence

As if . . . there had been found the potency of a spell, the huge antique panels to which the speaker pointed threw slowly back, upon the instant, their ponderous and ebony jaws.

Subject
Antique panels

Verb
threw back

Object
ebony jaws

The Fall of the House of Usher

Edgar Allan Poe

Background

In 1839, Poe lived in Philadelphia and became coeditor of *Burton's Gentleman's Magazine*, a journal that published essays, fiction, reviews, and poems, as well as articles on sailing, hunting, and cricket. Poe's articles ran the gamut of topics. He explained the parallel bars, mused about the mysteries of Stonehenge, and reviewed more than eighty books on a variety of topics. It was in this magazine, in 1839, that Poe first published "The Fall of the House of Usher."

*Son Coeur est un luth suspendu:
Sitôt qu'on le touche il résonne.*[1]

During the whole of a dull, dark, and soundless day in the autumn of the year, when the clouds hung oppressively low in the heavens, I had been passing alone, on horseback, through a singularly dreary tract of country, and at length found myself, as the shades of evening drew on, within view of the melancholy House of Usher. I know not how it was—but, with the first glimpse of the building, a sense of insufferable gloom pervaded my spirit. I say insufferable; for the feeling was unrelieved by any of that half-pleasurable, because poetic, sentiment, with which the mind usually receives even the sternest natural images of the desolate or terrible. I looked upon the scene before me—upon the mere house, and the simple landscape features of the domain—upon the bleak walls—upon the vacant eyelike windows—upon a few rank sedges[2]—and upon a few white trunks of decayed trees—with an utter

Literary Analysis
Single Effect What single effect does Poe create in the very first sentence?

---

1. **Son . . . résonne** "His heart is a lute strung tight: As soon as one touches it, resounds." From "Le Refus" by Pierre Jean de Béranger (1780–1857).
2. **sedges** (sej´ iz) *n.* grasslike plants.

"I at length...," Edgar Allan Poe's Tales of Mystery and Imagination, Arthur Rackham, The New York Public Library

▲ **Critical Viewing** What mood does the artist's choice of shapes and colors create in this painting? Which details of the story's opening paragraph does the painter convey? **[Analyze]**

depression of soul, which I can compare to no earthly sensation more properly than to the afterdream of the reveler upon opium—the bitter lapse into everyday life—the hideous dropping off of the veil. There was an iciness, a sinking, a sickening of the heart—an unredeemed dreariness of thought which no goading of the imagination could torture into aught[3] of the sublime. What was it—I paused to think—what was it that so unnerved me in the contemplation of the House of Usher? It was a mystery all insoluble; nor could I grapple with the shadowy fancies that crowded upon me as I pondered. I was forced to fall back upon the unsatisfactory conclusion, that while, beyond doubt, there are combinations of very simple natural objects which have the power of thus affecting us, still the analysis of this power lies among considerations beyond our depth. It was possible, I reflected, that a mere different arrangement of the particulars of the scene, of the details of the picture, would be sufficient to modify, or perhaps to annihilate its capacity for sorrowful impression; and, acting upon this idea, I reined my horse to the precipitous brink of a black and lurid tarn[4] that lay in unruffled luster by the dwelling, and gazed down—but with a shudder even more thrilling than before—upon the remodeled and inverted images of the gray sedge, and the ghastly tree stems, and the vacant and eyelike windows.

Reading Strategy
Breaking Down Long Sentences What is the subject and what are the verbs in the sentence beginning "It was possible, I reflected"?

Nevertheless, in this mansion of gloom I now proposed to myself a sojourn of some weeks. Its proprietor, Roderick Usher, had been one of my boon companions in boyhood; but many years had elapsed since our last meeting. A letter, however, had lately reached me in a distant part of the country—a letter from him—which, in its wildly importunate nature, had admitted of no other than a personal reply. The MS[5] gave evidence of nervous agitation. The writer spoke of acute bodily illness—of a mental disorder which oppressed him—and of an earnest desire to see me, as his best and indeed his only personal friend, with a view of attempting, by the cheerfulness of my society, some alleviation of his malady. It was the manner in which all this, and much more, was said—it was the apparent *heart* that went with his request—which allowed me no room for hesitation; and I accordingly obeyed forthwith what I still considered a very singular summons.

importunate (im pôr′ chə nit) *adj.* insistent

Reading Strategy
Breaking Down Long Sentences What is the core of the sentence beginning "It was the manner"?

Although, as boys, we had been even intimate associates, yet I really knew little of my friend. His reserve had been always excessive and habitual. I was aware, however, that his very ancient family had been noted, time out of mind, for a peculiar sensibility of temperament, displaying itself, through long ages, in many works of exalted art, and manifested, of late, in repeated deeds of munificent yet unobtrusive charity, as well as in a passionate devotion to the intricacies, perhaps even more than to the orthodox and easily recognizable

munificent (myo͞o nif′ ə sənt) *adj.* generous

---

3. **aught** (ôt) anything.
4. **tarn** (tärn) *n.* small lake.
5. **MS.** *abbr.* manuscript.

beauties, of musical science. I had learned, too, the very remarkable fact, that the stem of the Usher race, all time-honored as it was, had put forth, at no period, any enduring branch: in other words, that the entire family lay in the direct line of descent, and had always, with very trifling and very temporary variations, so lain. It was this deficiency, I considered, while running over in thought the perfect keeping of the character of the premises with the accredited character of the people, and while speculating upon the possible influence which the one, in the long lapse of centuries, might have exercised upon the other—it was this deficiency, perhaps of collateral issue,[6] and the consequent undeviating transmission, from sire to son, of the patrimony[7] with the name, which had, at length, so identified the two as to merge the original title of the estate in the quaint and equivocal appellation of the "House of Usher"—an appellation which seemed to include, in the minds of the peasantry who used it, both the family and the family mansion.

I have said that the sole effect of my somewhat childish experiment—that of looking down within the tarn—had been to deepen the first singular impression. There can be no doubt that the consciousness of the rapid increase of my superstition—for why should I not so term it?—served mainly to accelerate the increase itself. Such, I have long known, is the paradoxical law of all sentiments having terror as a basis. And it might have been for this reason only, that, when I again uplifted my eyes to the house itself, from its image in the pool, there grew in my mind a strange fancy—a fancy so ridiculous, indeed, that I but mention it to show the vivid force of the sensations which oppressed me. I had so worked upon my imagination as really to believe that about the whole mansion and domain there hung an atmosphere peculiar to themselves and their immediate vicinity—an atmosphere which had no affinity with the air of heaven, but which had reeked up from the decayed trees, and the gray wall, and the silent tarn—a pestilent and mystic vapor, dull, sluggish, faintly discernible and leaden-hued.

Shaking off from my spirit what *must* have been a dream, I scanned more narrowly the real aspect of the building. Its principal feature seemed to be that of an excessive antiquity. The discoloration of ages had been great. Minute fungi overspread the whole exterior, hanging in a fine tangled web-work from the eaves. Yet all this was apart from any extraordinary dilapidation. No portion of the masonry had fallen; and there appeared to be a wild inconsistency between its still perfect adaptation of parts, and the crumbling condition of the individual stones. In this there was much that reminded me of the specious totality of old woodwork which has rotted for long years in some neglected vault, with no disturbance from the breath of the

---

6. **collateral** (kə lat´ ər əl) **issue** descended from the same ancestors but in a different line.
7. **patrimony** (pat´ rə mō´ nē) *n.* property inherited from one's father.

equivocal (i kwiv´ ə kəl) *adj.* having more than one possible interpretation

appellation (ap´ ə lā´ shən) *n.* name or title

specious (spē´ shəs) *adj.* seeming to be good or sound without actually being so

✔**Reading Check**

What is the physical condition of the House of Usher?

external air. Beyond this indication of extensive decay, however, the fabric gave little token of instability. Perhaps the eye of a scrutinizing observer might have discovered a barely perceptible fissure, which, extending from the roof of the building in front, made its way down the wall in a zigzag direction, until it became lost in the sullen waters of the tarn.

Noticing these things, I rode over a short causeway to the house. A servant in waiting took my horse, and I entered the Gothic[8] archway of the hall. A valet, of stealthy step, then conducted me, in silence, through many dark and intricate passages in my progress to the studio of his master. Much that I encountered on the way contributed, I know not how, to heighten the vague sentiments of which I have already spoken. While the objects around me—while the carvings of the ceilings, the somber tapestries of the walls, the ebon blackness of the floors, and the phantasmagoric[9] armorial trophies which rattled as I strode, were but matters to which, or to such as which, I had been accustomed from my infancy—while I hesitated not to acknowledge how familiar was all this—I still wondered to find how unfamiliar were the fancies which ordinary images were stirring up. On one of the staircases, I met the physician of the family. His countenance, I thought, wore a mingled expression of low cunning and perplexity. He accosted me with trepidation and passed on. The valet now threw open a door and ushered me into the presence of his master.

The room in which I found myself was very large and lofty. The windows were long, narrow, and pointed, and at so vast a distance from the black oaken floor as to be altogether inaccessible from within. Feeble gleams of encrimsoned light made their way through the trellised panes, and served to render sufficiently distinct the more prominent objects around; the eye, however, struggled in vain to reach the remoter angles of the chamber, or the recesses of the vaulted and fretted[10] ceiling. Dark draperies hung upon the walls. The general furniture was profuse, comfortless, antique, and tattered. Many books and musical instruments lay scattered about, but failed to give any vitality to the scene. I felt that I breathed an atmosphere of sorrow. An air of stern, deep, and irredeemable gloom hung over and pervaded all.

Upon my entrance, Usher arose from a sofa on which he had been lying at full length, and greeted me with a vivacious warmth which had much in it, I at first thought, of an overdone cordiality—of the constrained effort of the *ennuyé*[11] man of the world. A glance, however, at his countenance convinced me of his perfect sincerity.

---

8. **Gothic** high and ornate.
9. **phantasmagoric** (fan taz´ mə gôr´ ik) *adj.* fantastic or dreamlike.
10. **fretted** (fret´ id) *v.* ornamented with a pattern of small, straight, intersecting bars.
11. *ennuyé* (än´ wē ā´) *adj.* bored (French).

We sat down; and for some moments, while he spoke not, I gazed upon him with a feeling half of pity, half of awe. Surely, man had never before so terribly altered, in so brief a period, as had Roderick Usher! It was with difficulty that I could bring myself to admit the identity of the wan being before me with the companion of my early boyhood. Yet the character of his face had been at all times remarkable. A cadaverousness of complexion; an eye large, liquid, and luminous beyond comparison; lips somewhat thin and very pallid, but of a surpassingly beautiful curve; a nose of a delicate Hebrew model, but with a breadth of nostril unusual in similar formations; a finely molded chin, speaking, in its want of prominence, of a want of moral energy; hair of a more than weblike softness and tenuity— these features, with an inordinate expansion above the regions of the temple, made up altogether a countenance not easily to be forgotten. And now in the mere exaggeration of the prevailing character of these features, and of the expression they were wont to convey, lay so much of change that I doubted to whom I spoke. The now ghastly pallor of the skin, and the now miraculous luster of the eye, above all things startled and even awed me. The silken hair, too, had been suffered to grow all unheeded, and as, in its wild gossamer texture, it floated rather than fell about the face, I could not, even with effort, connect its Arabesque[12] expression with any idea of simple humanity.

In the manner of my friend I was at once struck with an incoherence—an inconsistency; and I soon found this to arise from a series of feeble and futile struggles to overcome an habitual trepidancy—an excessive nervous agitation. For something of this nature I had indeed been prepared, no less by his letter than by reminiscences of certain boyish traits, and by conclusions deduced from his peculiar physical conformation and temperament. His action was alternately vivacious and sullen. His voice varied rapidly from a tremulous indecision (when the animal spirits seemed utterly in abeyance) to that species of energetic concision—that abrupt, weighty, unhurried, and hollow-sounding enunciation—that leaden, self-balanced, and perfectly modulated guttural utterance, which may be observed in the lost drunkard, or the irreclaimable eater of opium, during the periods of his most intense excitement.

It was thus that he spoke of the object of my visit, of his earnest desire to see me, and of the solace he expected me to afford him. He entered, at some length, into what he conceived to be the nature of his malady. It was, he said, a constitutional and a family evil and one for which he despaired to find a remedy—a mere nervous affection,[13] he immediately added, which would undoubtedly soon pass off. It displayed itself in a host of unnatural sensations. Some of these, as he detailed them, interested and bewildered me; although, perhaps, the terms and the general manner of their narration had their weight. He

---

12. **Arabesque** (ar´ ə besk´) *adj.* of complex and elaborate design.
13. **affection** affliction.

Reading Strategy
Breaking Down Long Sentences In your own words, restate the meaning of the sentence beginning "His voice varied."

✓**Reading Check**

In what ways has Roderick Usher changed since the speaker last saw him?

suffered much from a morbid acuteness of the senses; the most insipid food was alone endurable; he could wear only garments of certain texture; the odors of all flowers were oppressive; his eyes were tortured by even a faint light; and there were but peculiar sounds, and these from stringed instruments, which did not inspire him with horror.

To an <u>anomalous</u> species of terror I found him a bounden slave. "I shall perish," said he, "I *must* perish in this deplorable folly. Thus, thus, and not otherwise, shall I be lost. I dread the events of the future, not in themselves, but in their results. I shudder at the thought of any, even the most trivial, incident, which may operate upon this intolerable agitation of soul. I have, indeed, no abhorrence of danger, except in its absolute effect—in terror. In this unnerved, in this pitiable, condition I feel that the period will sooner or later arrive when I must abandon life and reason together, in some struggle with the grim phantasm, FEAR."

I learned, moreover, at intervals, and through broken and equivocal hints, another singular feature of his mental condition. He was enchained by certain superstitious impressions in regard to the dwelling which he tenanted, and whence, for many years, he had never ventured forth—in regard to an influence whose supposititious[14] force was conveyed in terms too shadowy here to be restated—an influence which some peculiarities in the mere form and substance of his family mansion had, by dint of long sufferance, he said, obtained over his spirit—an effect which the physique of the gray walls and turrets, and of the dim tarn into which they all looked down, had at length, brought about upon the morale of his existence.

He admitted, however, although with hesitation, that much of the peculiar gloom which thus afflicted him could be traced to a more natural and far more palpable origin—to the severe and long-continued illness—indeed to the evidently approaching dissolution—of a tenderly beloved sister, his sole companion for long years, his last and only relative on earth. "Her decease," he said, with a bitterness which I can never forget, "would leave him (him, the hopeless and the frail) the last of the ancient race of the Ushers." While he spoke, the lady Madeline (for so was she called) passed through a remote portion of the apartment, and, without having noticed my presence, disappeared. I regarded her with an utter astonishment not unmingled with dread; and yet I found it impossible to account for such feelings. A sensation of stupor oppressed me as my eyes followed her retreating steps. When a door, at length, closed upon her, my glance sought instinctively and eagerly the countenance of the brother; but he had buried his face in his hands, and I could only perceive that a far more than ordinary wanness had overspread the emaciated fingers through which trickled many passionate tears.

The disease of the lady Madeline had long baffled the skill of her physicians. A settled apathy, a gradual wasting away of the person,

anomalous (ə näm′ ə ləs) *adj.* abnormal

Literary Analysis
Single Effect and Gothic Style In what ways do Usher's mental state and the house itself typify a work of gothic literature?

---

14. supposititious (sə päz′ ə tish′ əs) *adj.* supposed.

and frequent although transient affections of a partially cataleptical[15] character were the unusual diagnosis. Hitherto she had steadily borne up against the pressure of her malady, and had not betaken herself finally to bed; but on the closing in of the evening of my arrival at the house, she succumbed (as her brother told me at night with inexpressible agitation) to the prostrating power of the destroyer; and I learned that the glimpse I had obtained of her person would thus probably be the last I should obtain—that the lady, at least while living, would be seen by me no more.

Literary Analysis
Single Effect In what way does Madeline's surrender on this night contribute to a single effect?

For several days ensuing, her name was unmentioned by either Usher or myself; and during this period I was busied in earnest endeavors to alleviate the melancholy of my friend. We painted and read together, or I listened, as if in a dream, to the wild improvisations of his speaking guitar. And thus, as a closer and still closer intimacy admitted me more unreservedly into the recesses of his spirit, the more bitterly did I perceive the futility of all attempt at cheering a mind from which darkness, as if an inherent positive quality, poured forth upon all objects of the moral and physical universe in one unceasing radiation of gloom.

I shall ever bear about me a memory of the many solemn hours I thus spent alone with the master of the House of Usher. Yet I should fail in any attempt to convey an idea of the exact character of the studies, or of the occupations, in which he involved me, or led me the way. An excited and highly distempered ideality[16] threw a sulfureous[17] luster over all. His long improvised dirges will ring forever in my ears. Among other things, I hold painfully in mind a certain singular perversion and amplification of the wild air of the last waltz of von Weber.[18] From the paintings over which his elaborate fancy brooded, and which grew, touch by touch, into vaguenesses at which I shuddered the more thrillingly, because I shuddered knowing not why—from these paintings (vivid as their images now are before me) I would in vain endeavor to educe more than a small portion which should lie within the compass of merely written words. By the utter simplicity, by the nakedness of his designs, he arrested and overawed attention. If ever mortal painted an idea, that mortal was Roderick Usher. For me at least, in the circumstances then surrounding me, there arose out of the pure abstractions which the hypochondriac contrived to throw upon his canvas, an intensity of intolerable awe, no shadow of which felt I ever yet in the contemplation of the certainly glowing yet too concrete reveries of Fuseli.[19]

---

15. **cataleptical** (kat′ əl ep′ tik əl) *adj.* in a state in which consciousness and feeling are suddenly and temporarily lost and the muscles become rigid.
16. **ideality** (ī dē al′ i tē) *n.* something that is ideal and has no reality.
17. **sulfureous** (sul fyoor′ ē əs) *adj.* greenish-yellow.
18. **von Weber** (fôn vā′ bər) Karl Maria von Weber (1786–1826), a German Romantic composer whose music was highly emotional and dramatic.
19. **Fuseli** (foo ze′ lē) Johann Hinrich Fuseli (1741–1825), also known as Henry Fuseli, Swiss-born painter who lived in England and was noted for his depictions of dreamlike and sometimes nightmarish images.

**Reading Check**

What conclusion does the narrator draw about Usher's mental state?

One of the phantasmagoric conceptions of my friend, partaking not so rigidly of the spirit of abstraction, may be shadowed forth, although feebly, in words. A small picture presented the interior of an immensely long and rectangular vault or tunnel, with low walls, smooth, white and without interruption or device. Certain accessory points of the design served well to convey the idea that this excavation lay at an exceeding depth below the surface of the earth. No outlet was observed in any portion of its vast extent, and no torch or other artificial source of light was discernible; yet a flood of intense rays rolled throughout, and bathed the whole in a ghastly and inappropriate splendor.

I have just spoken of that morbid condition of the auditory nerve which rendered all music intolerable to the sufferer, with the exception of certain effects of stringed instruments. It was, perhaps, the narrow limits to which he thus confined himself upon the guitar which gave birth, in great measure, to the fantastic character of his performances. But the fervid facility of his impromptus could not be so accounted for. They must have been, and were, in the notes, as well as in the words of his wild fantasias (for he not unfrequently accompanied himself with rhymed verbal improvisations), the result of that intense mental collectedness and concentration to which I have previously alluded as observable only in particular moments of the highest artificial excitement. The words of one of these rhapsodies I have easily remembered. I was, perhaps, the more forcibly impressed with it as he gave it because, in the under or mystic current of its meaning, I fancied that I perceived, and for the first time, a full consciousness on the part of Usher of the tottering of his lofty reason upon her throne. The verses, which were entitled "The Haunted Palace," ran very nearly, if not accurately, thus:

▲ **Critical Viewing** In what ways do the colors and shapes in this image suggest Roderick Usher's tormented mental condition? **[Interpret]**

I

> *In the greenest of our valleys,*
> *By good angels tenanted,*
> *Once a fair and stately palace—*
> *Radiant palace—reared its head.*
> *In the monarch Thought's dominion—*
> *It stood there!*
> *Never seraph[20] spread a pinion*
> *Over fabric half so fair.*

---

20. **seraph** (ser´ əf) angel.

II

Banners yellow, glorious, golden,
    On its roof did float and flow
(This—all this—was in the olden
    Time long ago)
And every gentle air that dallied,
    In that sweet day,
Along the ramparts plumed and pallid,
    A winged odor went away.

III

Wanderers in that happy valley
    Through two luminous windows saw
Spirits moving musically
    To a lute's well-tunéd law;
Round about a throne, where sitting
    (Porphyrogene!)²¹
In state his glory well befitting,
    The ruler of the realm was seen.

Literary Analysis
Single Effect Which details of this poem contribute to the story's style effect?

IV

And all with pearl and ruby glowing
    Was the fair palace door,
Through which came flowing, flowing, flowing
    And sparkling evermore,
A troop of Echoes whose sweet duty
    Was but to sing,
In voices of surpassing beauty,
    The wit and wisdom of their king.

V

But evil things, in robes of sorrow,
    Assailed the monarch's high estate;
(Ah, let us mourn, for never morrow
    Shall dawn upon him, desolate!)
And, round about his home, the glory
    That blushed and bloomed
Is but a dim-remembered story
    Of the old time entombed.

VI

And travelers now within that valley,
    Through the red-litten²² windows see

---

21. Porphyrogene (pôr fər ō jēn´) born to royalty or "the purple."
22. litten lighted.

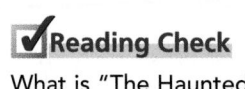

Reading Check

What is "The Haunted Palace"?

> Vast forms that move fantastically
> To a discordant melody;
> While, like a rapid ghastly river,
> Through the pale door,
> A hideous throng rush out forever,
> And laugh—but smile no more.

I well remember that suggestions arising from this ballad led us into a train of thought wherein there became manifest an opinion of Usher's which I mention not so much on account of its novelty (for other men have thought thus), as on account of the pertinacity with which he maintained it. This opinion, in its general form, was that of the <u>sentience</u> of all vegetable things. But, in his disordered fancy the idea had assumed a more daring character, and trespassed, under certain conditions, upon the kingdom of inorganization.[23] I lack words to express the full extent, or the earnest abandon of his persuasion. The belief, however, was connected (as I have previously hinted) with the gray stones of the home of his forefathers. The conditions of the sentience had been here, he imagined, fulfilled in the method of collocation of these stones—in the order of their arrangement, as well as in that of the many fungi which overspread them, and of the decayed trees which stood around—above all, in the long undisturbed endurance of this arrangement, and in its reduplication in the still waters of the tarn. Its evidence—the evidence of the sentience—was to be seen, he said (and I here started as he spoke), in the gradual yet certain condensation of an atmosphere of their own about the waters and the walls. The result was discoverable, he added, in that silent yet importunate and terrible influence which for centuries had molded the destinies of his family, and which made him what I now saw him—what he was. Such opinions need no comment, and I will make none.

Our books—the books which, for years, had formed no small portion of the mental existence of the invalid—were, as might be supposed, in strict keeping with this character of phantasm. We pored together over such works as the *Ververt et Chartreuse*[24] of Gresset; the *Belphegor* of Machiavelli; the *Heaven and Hell* of Swedenborg; the *Subterranean Voyage of Nicholas Klimm* by Holberg; the *Chiromancy* of Robert Flud, of Jean D'Indaginé and of De la Chambre; the *Journey into the Blue Distance* of Tieck; and the *City of the Sun* of Campanella. One favorite volume was a small octavo edition of the *Directorium Inquisitorium*, by the Dominican Eymeric de Gironne; and there were passages in Pomponius Mela, about the old African Stayrs and Œgipans, over which Usher would sit dreaming for hours. His chief delight, however, was found in the perusal of an exceedingly rare and curious book in quarto

---

sentience (sen´ shəns) *n.* capacity of feeling

Literary Analysis
Single Effect Which details of this philosophical discussion contribute to the story's single effect?

---

23. **inorganization** (in´ ôr gə ni zā´ shən) *n.* inanimate objects.
24. ***Ververt et Chartreuse,* etc.** All the books listed deal with magic or mysticism.

Gothic—the manual of a forgotten church—the *Vigilae Mortuorum secundum Chorum Ecclesiae Maguntinae.*

I could not help thinking of the wild ritual of this work, and of its probable influence upon the hypochondriac, when, one evening, having informed me abruptly that the lady Madeline was no more, he stated his intention of preserving her corpse for a fortnight (previously to its final interment), in one of the numerous vaults within the main walls of the building. The worldly reason, however, assigned for this singular proceeding, was one which I did not feel at liberty to dispute. The brother had been led to his resolution (so he told me) by consideration of the unusual character of the malady of the deceased, of certain obtrusive and eager inquiries on the part of her medical men, and of the remote and exposed situation of the burial ground of the family. I will not deny that when I called to mind the sinister countenance of the person whom I met upon the staircase, on the day of my arrival at the house, I had no desire to oppose what I regarded as at best but a harmless, and by no means an unnatural precaution.

At the request of Usher, I personally aided him in the arrangements for the temporary entombment. The body having been encoffined, we two alone bore it to its rest. The vault in which we placed it (and which had been so long unopened that our torches, half smothered in its oppressive atmosphere, gave us little opportunity for investigation) was small, damp, and entirely without means of admission for light; lying, at great depth, immediately beneath that portion of the building in which was my own sleeping apartment. It had been used, apparently, in remote feudal times, for the worst purposes of a donjon-keep, and, in later days, as a place of deposit for powder, or some other highly combustible substance, as a portion of its floor, and the whole interior of a long archway through which we reached it, were carefully sheathed with copper. The door, of massive iron, had been, also, similarly protected. Its immense weight caused an unusually sharp, grating sound, as it moved upon its hinges.

Having deposited our mournful burden upon trestles within this region of horror, we partially turned aside the yet unscrewed lid of the coffin, and looked upon the face of the tenant. A striking similitude between the brother and sister now first arrested my attention; and Usher, divining, perhaps, my thoughts, murmured out some few words from which I learned that the deceased and himself had been twins, and that sympathies of a scarcely intelligible nature had always existed between them. Our glances, however, rested not long upon the dead—for we could not regard her unawed. The disease which had thus entombed the lady in the maturity of youth, had left, as usual in all maladies of a strictly cataleptical character, the mockery of a faint blush upon the bosom and the face, and that suspiciously lingering smile upon the lip which is so terrible in death. We replaced and screwed down the lid, and, having secured the door of iron, made our way, with toil, into the scarcely less gloomy apartments of the upper portion of the house.

Reading Strategy
Breaking Down Long Sentences Clarify the main idea of the sentence beginning "The vault in which we placed it."

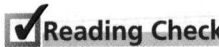**Reading Check**

What does the narrator notice about Madeline's appearance in her coffin?

And now, some days of bitter grief having elapsed, an observable change came over the features of the mental disorder of my friend. His ordinary manner had vanished. His ordinary occupations were neglected or forgotten. He roamed from chamber to chamber with hurried, unequal, and object-less step. The pallor of his countenance had assumed, if possible, a more ghastly hue—but the luminousness of his eye had utterly gone out. The once occasional huskiness of his tone was heard no more; and a tremulous quaver, as if of extreme terror, habitually characterized his utterance. There were times, indeed, when I thought his unceasingly agitated mind was laboring with some oppressive secret, to divulge which he struggled for the necessary courage. At times, again, I was obliged to resolve all into the mere inexplicable vagaries[25] of madness, for I beheld him gazing upon vacancy for long hours, in an attitude of the profoundest attention, as if listening to some imaginary sound. It was no wonder that his condition terrified—that it infected me. I felt creeping upon me, by slow yet uncertain degrees, the wild influences of his own fantastic yet impressive superstitions.

It was, especially, upon retiring to bed late in the night of the seventh or eighth day after the placing of the lady Madeline within the donjon, that I experienced the full power of such feelings. Sleep came not near my couch—while the hours waned and waned away. I struggled to reason off the nervousness which had dominion over me. I endeavored to believe that much, if not all of what I felt, was due to the bewildering influence of the gloomy furniture of the room—of the dark and tattered draperies, which, tortured into motion by the breath of a rising tempest, swayed fitfully to and fro upon the walls, and rustled uneasily about the decorations of the bed. But my efforts were fruitless. An irrepressible tremor gradually pervaded my frame; and, at length, there sat upon my very heart an incubus[26] of utterly causeless alarm. Shaking this off with a gasp and a struggle, I uplifted myself upon the pillows, and, peering earnestly within the intense darkness of the chamber, hearkened—I know not why, except that an instinctive spirit prompted me—to certain low and indefinite sounds which came, through the pauses of the storm, at long intervals, I knew not whence. Overpowered by an intense sentiment of horror, unaccountable yet unendurable, I threw on my clothes with haste (for I felt that I should sleep no more during the night), and endeavored to arouse myself from the pitiable condition into which I had fallen by pacing rapidly to and fro through the apartment.

I had taken but few turns in this manner, when a light step on an adjoining staircase arrested my attention. I presently recognized it as that of Usher. In an instant afterward he rapped, with a gentle touch, at my door, and entered, bearing a lamp. His countenance was, as usual, cadaverously wan—but, moreover, there was a species of mad hilarity in his eyes—an evidently restrained hysteria in his whole demeanor. His

Literary Analysis
Single Effect and Gothic Style Which elements of gothic literature does the narrator's physical and mental state reflect?

---

25. **vagaries** (vā´ ger ēz) *n.* odd, unexpected actions or notions.
26. **incubus** (iŋ´ kyə bəs) *n.* something nightmarishly burdensome.

air appalled me—but anything was preferable to the solitude which I had so long endured, and I even welcomed his presence as a relief.

"And you have not seen it?" he said abruptly, after having stared about him for some moments in silence—"you have not then seen it?—but, stay! you shall." Thus speaking, and having carefully shaded his lamp, he hurried to one of the casements, and threw it freely open to the storm.

The impetuous fury of the entering gust nearly lifted us from our feet. It was, indeed, a tempestuous yet sternly beautiful night, and one wildly singular in its terror and its beauty. A whirlwind had apparently collected its force in our vicinity; for there were frequent and violent alterations in the direction of the wind; and the exceeding density of the clouds (which hung so low as to press upon the turrets of the house) did not prevent our perceiving the lifelike velocity with which they flew careering from all points against each other, without passing away into the distance. I say that even their exceeding density did not prevent our perceiving this—yet we had no glimpse of the moon or stars, nor was there any flashing forth of the lightning. But the under surfaces of the huge masses of agitated vapor, as well as all terrestrial objects immediately around us, were glowing in the unnatural light of a faintly luminous and distinctly visible gaseous exhalation which hung about and enshrouded the mansion.

Literary Analysis
Single Effect In what way does the description of the storm contribute to the growing sense of terror?

"You must not—you shall not behold this!" said I, shuddering, to Usher, as I led him, with a gentle violence, from the window to a seat. "These appearances, which bewilder you, are merely electrical phenomena not uncommon—or it may be that they have their ghastly origin in the rank miasma[27] of the tarn. Let us close this casement:—the air is chilling and dangerous to your frame. Here is one of your favorite romances. I will read, and you shall listen:—and so we will pass away this terrible night together."

The antique volume which I had taken up was the *Mad Trist* of Sir Launcelot Canning;[28] but I had called it a favorite of Usher's more in sad jest than in earnest; for, in truth, there is little in its uncouth and unimaginative prolixity which could have had interest for the lofty and spiritual ideality of my friend. It was, however, the only book immediately at hand; and I indulged a vague hope that the excitement which now agitated the hypochondriac, might find relief (for the history of mental disorder is full of similar anomalies) even in the extremeness of the folly which I should read. Could I have judged, indeed, by the wild overstrained air of vivacity with which he hearkened, or apparently hearkened, to the words of the tale, I might well have congratulated myself upon the success of my design.

I had arrived at that well-known portion of the story where Ethelred, the hero of the Trist, having sought in vain for peaceable admission into the dwelling of the hermit, proceeds to make good an

✓**Reading Check**

Which odd or unnatural sight does the narrator see when the curtains are opened?

---

27. miasma (mī az´ mə) *n.* unwholesome atmosphere.
28. *Mad Trist* of Sir Launcelot Canning fictional book and author.

entrance by force. Here, it will be remembered, the words of the narrative run thus:

"And Ethelred, who was by nature of a doughty heart, and who was now mighty withal, on account of the powerfulness of the wine which he had drunken, waited no longer to hold parley with the hermit, who, in sooth, was of an obstinate and maliceful turn, but feeling the rain upon his shoulders, and fearing the rising of the tempest, uplifted his mace outright, and, with blows, made quickly room in the plankings of the door for his gauntleted hand; and now pulling therewith sturdily, he so cracked, and ripped, and tore all asunder, that the noise of the dry and hollow-sounding wood alarumed and reverberated throughout the forest."

At the termination of this sentence I started and, for a moment, paused; for it appeared to me (although I at once concluded that my excited fancy had deceived me)—it appeared to me that, from some very remote portion of the mansion, there came, indistinctly to my ears, which might have been, in its exact similarity of character, the echo (but a stifled and dull one certainly) of the very cracking and ripping sound which Sir Launcelot had so particularly described. It was, beyond doubt, the coincidence alone which had arrested my attention; for, amid the rattling of the sashes of the casements, and the ordinary commingled noises of the still increasing storm, the sound, itself, had nothing, surely, which should have interested or disturbed me. I continued the story:

"But the good champion Ethelred, now entering within the door, was sore enraged and amazed to perceive no signal of the maliceful hermit; but, in the stead thereof, a dragon of a scaly and prodigious demeanor, and of a fiery tongue, which sate in guard before a palace of gold, with a floor of silver; and upon the wall there hung a shield of shining brass with this legend enwritten—

> Who entereth herein, a conqueror
>   hath bin;
> Who slayeth the dragon, the shield
>   he shall win.

And Ethelred uplifted his mace, and struck upon the head of the dragon, which fell before him, and gave up his pasty breath, with a shriek so horrid and harsh, and withal so piercing, that Ethelred had fain to close his ears with his hands against the dreadful noise of it, the like whereof was never before heard."

Here again I paused abruptly, and now with a feeling of wild amazement—for there could be no doubt whatever that, in this instance, I did actually hear (although from what direction it proceeded I found it impossible to say) a low and apparently distant, but harsh, protracted, and most unusual screaming or grating sound—the exact counterpart of what my fancy had already conjured up for the dragon's unnatural shriek as described by the romancer.

Literary Analysis
Single Effect Which words and details from this description of the unusual sounds add to the single effect?

Separation, 1896, Edvard Munch, Munch Museet, Oslo, Norway

Oppressed, as I certainly was, upon the extraordinary coincidence, by a thousand conflicting sensations, in which wonder and extreme terror were predominant, I still retained sufficient presence of mind to avoid exciting, by an observation, the sensitive nervousness of my companion. I was by no means certain that he had noticed the sounds in question; although, assuredly, a strange alteration had, during the last few minutes, taken place in his demeanor. From a position fronting my own, he had gradually brought round his chair; so as to sit with his face to the door of the chamber; and thus I could but partially perceive his features, although I saw that his lips trembled as if he were murmuring inaudibly. His head had dropped upon his breast—yet I knew that he was not asleep, from the wide and rigid opening of the eye as I caught a glance of it in profile. The motion of his body, too, was at

▲ **Critical Viewing**
Describe the ways in which this painting conveys the same unnatural sense of terror Poe creates in the story. **[Analyze]**

✔ **Reading Check**

What unusual sounds does the narrator hear?

variance with this idea—for he rocked from side to side with a gentle yet constant and uniform sway. Having rapidly taken notice of all this, I resumed the narrative of Sir Launcelot, which thus proceeded:

"And now, the champion, having escaped from the terrible fury of the dragon, bethinking himself of the brazen shield, and of the breaking up of the enchantment which was upon it, removed the carcass from out of the way before him, and approached valorously over the silver pavement of the castle to where the shield was upon the wall; which in sooth tarried not for his full coming, but fell down at his feet upon the silver floor, with a mighty great and terrible ringing sound."

No sooner had these syllables passed my lips, than—as if a shield of brass had indeed, at the moment, fallen heavily upon a floor of silver—I became aware of a distinct, hollow, metallic, and clangorous, yet apparently muffled, reverberation. Completely unnerved, I leaped to my feet; but the measured rocking movement of Usher was undisturbed. I rushed to the chair in which he sat. His eyes were bent fixedly before him, and throughout his whole countenance there reigned a stony rigidity. But, as I placed my hand upon his shoulder, there came a strong shudder over his whole person; a sickly smile quivered about his lips; and I saw that he spoke in a low, hurried, and gibbering murmur, as if unconscious of my presence. Bending closely over him I at length drank in the hideous import of his words.

"Not hear it?—yes, I hear it, and have heard it. Long—long—long— many minutes, many hours, many days, have I heard it—yet I dared not—oh, pity me, miserable wretch that I am!—I *dared* not—I dared not speak! *We have put her living in the tomb!* Said I not that my senses were acute? I *now* tell you that I heard her first feeble movement in the hollow coffin. I heard them—many, many days ago—yet I dared not—*I dared not speak!* and now—tonight—Ethelred—ha! ha!—the breaking of the hermit's door, and the death cry of the dragon, and the clangor of the shield—say, rather, the rending of her coffin, and the grating of the iron hinges of her prison, and her struggles within the coppered archway of the vault! Oh! wither shall I fly? Will she not be here anon? Is she not hurrying to upbraid me for my haste? Have I not heard her footstep on the stair? Do I not distinguish that heavy and horrible beating of her heart? Madman!"—here he sprang furiously to his feet, and shrieked out his syllables, as if in the effort he were giving up his soul—"*Madman! I tell you that she now stands without the door!*"

As if in the superhuman energy of his utterance there had been found the potency of a spell, the huge antique panels to which the speaker pointed threw slowly back, upon the instant, their ponderous and ebony jaws. It was the work of the rushing gust—but then without those doors there *did* stand the lofty and enshrouded figure of the lady Madeline of Usher. There was blood upon her white robes, and the evidence of some bitter struggle upon every portion of her emaciated frame. For a moment she remained trembling and reeling to and fro upon the threshold—then, with a low moaning cry, fell heavily inward upon the person of her brother, and in her violent and now final

Reading Strategy
Breaking Down Long Sentences Summarize the action of the paragraph-long sentence beginning "And now, the champion."

Literary Analysis
Single Effect and Gothic Style Which elements of gothic literature are evident in this passage about Madeline Usher?

death agonies, bore him to the floor a corpse, and a victim to the terrors he had anticipated.

From that chamber, and from that mansion, I fled aghast. The storm was still abroad in all its wrath as I found myself crossing the old causeway. Suddenly there shot along the path a wild light, and I turned to see whence a gleam so unusual could have issued; for the vast house and its shadows were alone behind me. The radiance was that of the full, setting, and bloodred moon, which now shone vividly through that once barely discernible fissure, of which I have before spoken as extending from the roof of the building, in a zigzag direction, to the base. While I gazed, this fissure rapidly widened—there came a fierce breath of the whirlwind—the entire orb of the satellite burst at once upon my sight—my brain reeled as I saw the mighty walls rushing asunder—there was a long tumultuous shouting sound like the voice of a thousand waters—and the deep and dank tarn at my feet closed sullenly and silently over the fragments of the *"House of Usher."*

Review and Assess

Thinking About the Selection

1. **Respond:** In this story, the narrator barely escapes being drawn into Roderick's fantasy world. Were you drawn into the fantasy world of the story? Explain.

2. **(a) Recall:** Why has the narrator gone to visit Usher?
   (b) Assess: Does the narrator succeed in his purpose?
   (c) Analyze: What is the significance of the detail that the narrator finds himself becoming affected by Usher's condition?

3. **(a) Analyze:** In the description of the exterior of the house, which words suggest the presence of decay in the structure itself? **(b) Connect:** In what ways does this description foreshadow, or hint at, the ending of the story?

4. **(a) Interpret:** Which descriptive details of the interior of the house suggest that the narrator has entered a realm that is quite different from the ordinary world? **(b) Infer:** Which details in Usher's appearance suggest that he has been cut off from the outside world for many years? **(c) Connect:** In what ways is the appearance of the interior of the house related to Usher's appearance and to the condition of his mind?

5. **(a) Speculate:** Poe chose to characterize Roderick and Madeline as twins, not simply as brother and sister. Why do you think he made this choice? **(b) Support:** What evidence is there to support the claim of some critics who have argued that Madeline and Roderick are actually physical and mental components of the same being?

THE RAVEN

Edgar Allan Poe

Once upon a midnight dreary, while I pondered, weak and weary,
Over many a quaint and curious volume of forgotten lore—
While I nodded, nearly napping, suddenly there came a tapping,
As of some one gently rapping, rapping at my chamber door.
5 "'Tis some visitor," I muttered, "tapping at my chamber door—
            Only this, and nothing more."

Ah, distinctly I remember it was in the bleak December;
And each separate dying ember wrought its ghost upon the floor.
Eagerly I wished the morrow;—vainly I had sought to borrow
10 From my books surcease[1] of sorrow—sorrow for the lost Lenore—
For the rare and radiant maiden whom the angels name Lenore—
            Nameless *here* for evermore.

And the silken, sad, uncertain rustling of each purple curtain
Thrilled me—filled me with fantastic terrors never felt before;
15 So that now, to still the beating of my heart, I stood repeating
"'Tis some visitor entreating entrance at my chamber door—

Literary Analysis
Single Effect In what ways does Poe's use of sound devices contribute to the creation of a single effect?

---

1. **surcease** (sʉr sēs´) end.

Some late visitor entreating entrance at my chamber door;—
        This it is and nothing more."

Presently my soul grew stronger; hesitating then no longer,
20 "Sir," said I, "or Madam, truly your forgiveness I implore;
But the fact is I was napping, and so gently you came rapping,
And so faintly you came tapping, tapping at my chamber door,
That I scarce was sure I heard you"—here I opened wide the door;—
        Darkness there and nothing more.

25 Deep into that darkness peering, long I stood there wondering,
     fearing,
Doubting, dreaming dreams no mortal ever dared to dream before;
But the silence was unbroken, and the stillness gave no token,
And the only word there spoken was the whispered word, "Lenore?"
This I whispered, and an echo murmured back the word, "Lenore!"
30   Merely this and nothing more.

Back then into the chamber turning, all my soul within me
     burning,
Soon again I heard a tapping somewhat louder than before.
"Surely," said I, "surely that is something at my window lattice;
Let me see, then, what thereat is, and this mystery explore—
35 Let my heart be still a moment and this mystery explore;—
        'Tis the wind and nothing more!"

Open here I flung the shutter, when, with many a flirt and flutter,
In there stepped a stately Raven of the saintly days of yore;
Not the least <u>obeisance</u> made he; not a minute stopped or
     stayed he;
40 But, with mien of lord or lady, perched above my chamber door—
Perched upon a bust of Pallas[2] just above my chamber door—
        Perched, and sat, and nothing more.

Then this ebony bird beguiling[3] my sad fancy into smiling,
By the grave and stern decorum of the countenance[4] it wore,
45 "Though thy crest be shorn and shaven, thou," I said, "art sure
     no <u>craven</u>,
Ghastly grim and ancient Raven wandering from the Nightly shore—
Tell me what thy lordly name is on the Night's Plutonian[5] shore!"
        Quoth the Raven, "Nevermore."

Reading Strategy
Breaking Down Long Sentences Summarize the action of the stanza-long sentence beginning "Presently my soul grew stronger."

obeisance (ō bā′ səns) *n.* gesture of respect

craven (krā′ vən) *adj.* very cowardly

---

2. **Pallas** (pal′ əs) Pallas Athena, the ancient Greek goddess of wisdom.
3. **beguiling** (bi gīl′ iŋ) *part.* charming.
4. **countenance** (koun′ tə nəns) *n.* facial expression.
5. **Plutonian** (ploo tō′ nē ən) *adj.* like the underworld or infernal regions; refers to Pluto, Greek and Roman god of the underworld.

Reading Check

What is the speaker's first reaction to the Raven?

The Raven, Edmund Dulac

Much I marveled this ungainly fowl to hear discourse so plainly,
50 Though its answer little meaning—little relevancy bore;
For we cannot help agreeing that no living human being
Ever yet was blessed with seeing bird above his chamber door—
Bird or beast upon the sculptured bust above his chamber door,
With such name as "Nevermore."

55 But the Raven, sitting lonely on the placid bust, spoke only
That one word, as if his soul in that one word he did outpour.
Nothing farther than he uttered—not a feather then he fluttered—
Till I scarcely more than muttered, "Other friends have flown
before—
On the morrow *he* will leave me, as my Hopes have flown before."
60 Then the bird said, "Nevermore."

▲ **Critical Viewing**
Explain the effect produced by the lines and shading of this drawing. Does the mood of the illustration match that of the poem? Explain.
[Assess]

Startled at the stillness broken by reply so aptly spoken,
"Doubtless," said I, "what it utters is its only stock and store
Caught from some unhappy master whom unmerciful Disaster
Followed fast and followed faster till his songs one burden bore—
65 Till the dirges of his Hope that melancholy burden bore
                          Of 'Never—nevermore.'"

But the Raven still beguiling my sad fancy into smiling,
Straight I wheeled a cushioned seat in front of bird, and bust
      and door;
Then, upon the velvet sinking, I betook myself to linking
70 Fancy unto fancy, thinking what this ominous[6] bird of yore—
What this grim, ungainly, ghastly, gaunt, and ominous bird of yore
                    Meant in croaking "Nevermore."

This I sat engaged in guessing, but no syllable expressing
To the fowl whose fiery eyes now burned into my bosom's core;
75 This and more I sat divining, with my head at ease reclining
On the cushion's velvet lining that the lamp-light gloated o'er,
But whose velvet-violet lining with the lamp-light gloating o'er,
               She shall press, ah, nevermore!

Then, methought, the air grew denser, perfumed from an unseen
      censer
80 Swung by seraphim whose foot-falls tinkled on the tufted floor.
"Wretch," I cried, "thy God hath lent thee—by these angels he
      hath sent thee
Respite—respite and nepenthe[7] from thy memories of Lenore;
Quaff, oh quaff this kind nepenthe and forget this lost Lenore!"
               Quoth the Raven, "Nevermore."

85 "Prophet!" said I, "thing of evil!—prophet still, if bird or devil!—
Whether Tempter sent, or whether tempest tossed thee here
      ashore,
Desolate yet all undaunted, on this desert land enchanted—
On this home by Horror haunted—tell me truly, I implore—
Is there—*is* there balm in Gilead?[8]—tell me—tell me, I implore!"
90   Quoth the Raven, "Nevermore."

"Prophet!" said I, "thing of evil!—prophet still, if bird or devil!
By that Heaven that bends above us—by that God we both adore—
Tell this soul with sorrow laden if, within the distant Aidenn,[9]

Literary Analysis
Single Effect and Gothic Style Which aspects of the gothic style are evident in the speaker's relationship to the Raven?

---

6. **ominous** (äm´ ə nəs) *adj.* threatening; sinister.
7. **nepenthe** (ni pen´ thē) *n.* drug that the ancient Greeks believed could relieve sorrow.
8. **balm in Gilead** (gil´ ē əd) in the Bible, a healing ointment made in Gilead, a region of ancient Palestine.
9. **Aidenn** (ā´ den) Arabic for Eden or heaven.

✓ Reading Check

What does the speaker want the Raven to tell him?

It shall clasp a sainted maiden whom the angels name Lenore—
95 Clasp a rare and radiant maiden whom the angels name Lenore."
Quoth the Raven, "Nevermore."

"Be that word our sign of parting, bird or fiend!" I shrieked,
    upstarting—
"Get thee back into the tempest and the Night's Plutonian shore!
Leave no black plume as a token of that lie thy soul hath spoken!
100 Leave my loneliness unbroken!—quit the bust above my door!
Take thy beak from out my heart, and take thy form from off
    my door!"
Quoth the Raven, "Nevermore."

And the Raven, never flitting, still is sitting, *still* is sitting
On the pallid bust of Pallas just above my chamber door;
105 And his eyes have all the seeming of a demon's that is dreaming;
And the lamp-light o'er him streaming throws his shadow on
    the floor;
And my soul from out that shadow that lies floating on the floor
Shall be lifted—nevermore!

Review and Assess

Thinking About the Selection

1. **Respond:** This poem has been popular for more than one hundred years. Explain why you think the poem does or does not merit this continued attention.

2. **(a) Recall:** Why is the speaker reading at the beginning of the poem? **(b) Assess:** What is his emotional state as the poem begins?

3. **(a) Recall:** With what emotion does the speaker first greet the Raven? **(b) Interpret:** During the course of the poem, how does the speaker's attitude toward the Raven change? **(c) Analyze Cause and Effect:** In what way is the word *nevermore* related to these emotional changes?

4. **(a) Recall:** What does the speaker eventually order the Raven to do? **(b) Analyze:** At the end of the poem, what does the speaker mean when he says the Raven "still is sitting" above the door?

5. **(a) Interpret:** What is the relationship between the raven's shadow and the speaker's soul at the end of the poem? **(b) Analyze:** What does the Raven finally come to represent?

6. **Apply:** Do you think grief can truly cause a person to permanently lose the ability to reason? Explain.

Review and Assess

Literary Analysis

Single Effect

1. Describe the ways in which the following elements contribute to the **single effect** of a growing sense of terror in "The Fall of the House of Usher": (a) the description of the house, (b) Madeline's entombment, (c) the storm.

2. In "The Raven," how do both the tapping and the Raven's fiery eyes contribute to the speaker's deteriorating emotional state?

Comparing Literary Works

3. Use a chart like the one shown to compare the **gothic** elements in both the story and the poem. Is one of these works more typical of the gothic style than the other? Explain.

Gothic Element	House of Usher	Raven
Setting		
Violence		
Characterization		
The Supernatural		

4. Are the narrators of these works reliable or unreliable? Explain.

5. (a) When Madeline appears at the end of the story, is she there in actuality or is she a hallucination? Explain. (b) At the end of "The Raven," do you think the bird is actually still in the room? Why or why not?

Reading Strategy

Breaking Down Long Sentences

6. Break down this sentence from the story and restate it in your own words.

    At times, again, I was obliged to resolve all into the mere inexplicable vagaries of madness, for I beheld him gazing upon vacancy for long hours, in an attitude of the profoundest attention, as if listening to some imaginary sound.

Extend Understanding

7. **Psychology Connection:** Both this story and this poem suggest that the imagination is capable of producing false perceptions of reality. Do you agree with this suggestion? Why or why not?

Quick Review

In writing constructed to achieve a **single effect**, every character, incident, and detail contributes to an overall impression.

The **gothic style** is characterized by remote settings, violent or macabre acts, tormented characters, and, often, the presence of supernatural elements.

To **break down a long sentence**, identify logical parts and analyze the relationship of these parts.

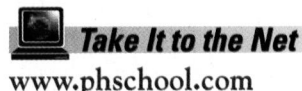 **Take It to the Net**
www.phschool.com

Take the interactive self-test online to check your understanding of these selections.

Integrate Language Skills

Vocabulary Development Lesson

Word Analysis: Latin Root -voc-

The word *equivocal* contains the Latin root *-voc-*, which derives from the Latin word *vox*, meaning "voice." *Equivocal* can be defined as "equal voices" or "having two or more interpretations."

Explain how the root *-voc-* influences the meaning of each of the following words.

1. vocal
2. equivocate
3. vociferous
4. vocation

Spelling Strategy

The sound of *sh* is sometimes spelled *ci*, as in *specious*, or *ti*, as in *sentience*. Complete each word with the correct spelling of the *sh* sound.

1. gra__ous
2. men__on
3. suspi__on
4. mali__ous

Concept Development: Synonyms or Antonyms?

Identify each of the following pairs of words as either synonyms (words with similar meanings) or antonyms (words with opposite meanings).

1. anomalous, normal
2. appellation, title
3. craven, weak
4. equivocal, ambiguous
5. importunate, yielding
6. munificent, charitable
7. obeisance, reverence
8. specious, sound
9. sentience, emotion

Grammar and Style Lesson

Coordinate Adjectives

Coordinate adjectives are adjectives of equal rank that separately modify the noun they precede. They should always be separated by commas. To determine whether adjectives are coordinate, switch their order or add *and* between them. If the sentence still makes sense, the adjectives are coordinate.

> **Example:** During the whole of a *dull, dark,* and *soundless* day . . .
>
> **Example:** . . . about the whole mansion and domain there hung an atmosphere . . . a pestilent and mystic vapor, *dull, sluggish, faintly discernible*, and *leaden-hued*.

Practice In each item, identify which adjectives are coordinate. Then, insert commas where necessary. If a sentence needs no commas, write *Correct*.

1. I was his only personal friend.
2. He gazed longingly at the clear placid lake.
3. She marveled at the low smooth white walls of the tunnel.
4. The guests noticed her wild theatrical manner.
5. The dry hollow-sounding wood splintered and crashed.

Writing Application Write an obituary of Roderick Usher. Include at least two sentences that contain coordinate adjectives.

WG *Prentice Hall Writing and Grammar Connection: Chapter 27, Section 2*

Writing Lesson

Literary Criticism

Since its publication in 1839, "The Fall of the House of Usher" has prompted many critical views. Some say it is the narrator who is insane, not Usher. Others say that each character represents a separate aspect of human psychology—the conscious mind, the unconscious mind, and the soul. Write an essay in which you defend or refute one of these critical views.

Prewriting   Reread the story, noting passages and details that support your critical interpretation.

Drafting   In your introduction, note the critical viewpoint you will address, and state whether or not you agree with it. Elaborate upon your reasoning in each body paragraph, using details from the text.

Model: Refuting an Argument

The idea that the narrator of Poe's famous story is himself insane is compelling. After all, that would explain the story's strangeness: It is all in the narrator's mind. Unfortunately, that view is unconvincing.

> The writer shows an understanding of the opinion being critiqued. The essay to follow will support the analysis.

Revising   Review your draft, making sure you have supported your ideas with details from the text. Note places where you might address readers who hold opposing viewpoints.

Prentice Hall Writing and Grammar Connection: Chapter 14, Section 2

Extension Activities

Listening and Speaking Present a **dramatic reading** of "The Raven" that captures the poem's tension and brings to life its unique rhymes and rhythms. Use the following technique to prepare:

- Record yourself on audio- or videotape, and review your presentation for possible lack of clarity or dramatic effect.
- Use body language to help convey the poems meaning.

As you perform, speak clearly, and allow your voice to reflect the poem's rising emotion.

Research and Technology In a group, watch a film by director Alfred Hitchcock. Then, lead a **discussion** in which you analyze the techniques Hitchcock uses to produce suspense and fear, and compare Hitchcock's techniques with Poe's. With classmates, discuss whether print or film is a better medium for horror. **[Group Activity]**

 **Take It to the Net** www.phschool.com

Go online for an additional research activity using the Internet.

Prepare to Read

The Minister's Black Veil

Nathaniel Hawthorne (1804–1864)

Along with Herman Melville, Nathaniel Hawthorne is sometimes referred to as an Anti-Transcendentalist. Although he lived at a time when many intellectuals glorified the power of the human spirit, as it was described by Transcendentalists like Ralph Waldo Emerson, Hawthorne found it impossible to adopt such an optimistic worldview. Despite his admiration for Emerson, Hawthorne believed that evil was a dominant force in the world, and his fiction expresses a gloomy vision of human affairs.

Inherited Guilt Born in Salem, Massachusetts, Hawthorne was descended from a prominent Puritan family. One of Hawthorne's ancestors was a Puritan judge who played a key role in the Salem witchcraft trials. Another ancestor was a judge known for his persecution of Quakers. Both Hawthorne's character and his focus as a writer were shaped by a sense of inherited guilt. He was haunted by the intolerance and cruelty of these ancestors, even though he himself was not a Puritan and was born 112 years after the Salem witchcraft trials.

The Long Seclusion After graduation from Maine's Bowdoin College in 1825, Hawthorne secluded himself at his mother's house in Salem and wrote a novel, *Fanshawe*. Soon after the book's anonymous publication in 1828, the young author was seized by shame and abruptly burned most available copies of it. During the nine years that followed, Hawthorne single-mindedly honed his writing skills, working in a room he called "the dismal chamber" on the third floor of his mother's house. These labors resulted in a collection of stories entitled *Twice-Told Tales*, which was published in 1837. Although the book sold poorly, it established Hawthorne as a respected writer and gave him sufficient resources and encouragement to continue his writing.

Moving in Transcendentalist Society After moving out of his mother's house, Hawthorne lived briefly at Brook Farm, the utopian community designed by the Transcendentalists. Then, in 1842, he married Sophia Peabody and moved to the Old Manse at Concord, Massachusetts, where Emerson had once lived. During his years in Concord, Hawthorne spent time with both Emerson and Henry David Thoreau, but their vastly different spiritual philosophies remained an obstacle to deeper friendship. While in Concord, Hawthorne published a second collection of stories, *Mosses From an Old Manse* (1846), and celebrated the birth of his first daughter, Una.

Man of Letters When he was appointed surveyor at the Salem customhouse, Hawthorne moved with his family back to his birthplace. In 1850, after a change in administration forced him out of office, he published his masterpiece, *The Scarlet Letter*, a powerful novel about sin and guilt among early Puritans. The book was extremely successful, earning its author international fame. He soon wrote two more novels, *The House of the Seven Gables* (1851) and *The Blithedale Romance* (1852).

When his college friend Franklin Pierce became president, Hawthorne was named the American consul at Liverpool, England. He spent several years in England and traveled through Italy before returning to Massachusetts. He used his Italian experiences in the novel *The Marble Faun* (1860). Hawthorne died in his sleep four years later, while on a walking tour in New Hampshire. He left four unfinished novels among his belongings.

Preview

Connecting to the Literature

A secret, when kept too long, can take on mysterious significance. If unrevealed, it can cause people to fill in the missing story and draw their own untrue conclusions. In "The Minister's Black Veil," a Puritan parson keeps a secret from an entire village for his whole life.

Literary Analysis

Parable

A **parable** is a simple, usually brief, story that teaches a moral lesson. Unlike a fable, which features animal characters, a parable is populated by human beings. In subtitling this story "A Parable," Hawthorne indicates that the moral message it conveys is important. As you read, think about the lesson Hawthorne wants his story to communicate.

Connecting Literary Elements

The veil that Mr. Hooper vows never to remove is a **symbol**—something that has meaning in itself while also standing for something greater. To understand the message expressed in Hawthorne's parable, you must analyze the veil's symbolic meaning, which is revealed through the responses of the parishioners and in the minister's own deathbed explanation:

> "I look around me, and, lo! on every visage a Black Veil!"

To discover the veil's symbolic meaning, notice Hawthorne's descriptions of the veil and its effects on the characters in the story.

Reading Strategy

Drawing Inferences About Meaning

When the message of a work of fiction is conveyed indirectly, as it is in this symbolic story, the reader must **draw inferences,** or conclusions, by looking closely at details, especially description and dialogue. Use a chart like the one shown to draw inferences about the story's characters and events.

Description/ Dialogue

"He has changed himself into something awful, only by hiding his face."

↓

Inference

Villagers are frightened by the veil.

Vocabulary Development

venerable (ven´ ər ə bəl) *adj.* commanding respect (p. 338)

iniquity (i nik´ wi tē) *n.* sin (p. 339)

indecorous (in dek´ ə rəs) *adj.* improper (p. 339)

ostentatious (äs´ tən tā´ shəs) *adj.* intended to attract notice (p. 339)

sagacious (sə gā´ shəs) *adj.* shrewd (p. 339)

vagary (və ger´ ē) *n.* unpredictable occurrence (p. 340)

tremulous (trem´ yoo ləs) *adj.* characterized by trembling (p. 341)

waggery (wag´ ər ē) *n.* mischievous humor (p. 341)

impertinent (im purt´ ən ənt) *adj.* not showing proper respect (p. 342)

obstinacy (äb´ stə nə sē) *n.* stubbornness (p. 343)

THE MINISTER'S BLACK VEIL

A PARABLE

Nathaniel Hawthorne

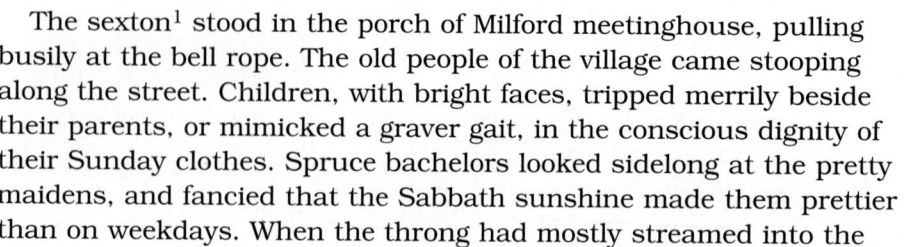

Background

Set in the 1600s, in a typical village of Puritan New England, this story reflects Hawthorne's deep awareness of his Puritan ancestry. The Puritans lived stern lives, emphasizing hard work and religious devotion. They believed that only certain people were predestined by God to go to heaven. This belief led Puritans to search their souls continually for signs that God had chosen them. At the same time, those who behaved unusually were often thought to be controlled by evil forces. This attitude contributed to the Salem witchcraft trials of 1692, during which at least twenty accused witches were executed. In this story, Hawthorne explores how such attitudes probably led to other, more commonplace acts of cruelty.

The sexton[1] stood in the porch of Milford meetinghouse, pulling busily at the bell rope. The old people of the village came stooping along the street. Children, with bright faces, tripped merrily beside their parents, or mimicked a graver gait, in the conscious dignity of their Sunday clothes. Spruce bachelors looked sidelong at the pretty maidens, and fancied that the Sabbath sunshine made them prettier than on weekdays. When the throng had mostly streamed into the porch, the sexton began to toll the bell, keeping his eye on the

---

1. **sexton** (seks´ tən) *n.* person in charge of the maintenance of a church.

Reverend Mr. Hooper's door. The first glimpse of the clergyman's figure was the signal for the bell to cease its summons.

"But what has good Parson Hooper got upon his face?" cried the sexton in astonishment.

All within hearing immediately turned about, and beheld the semblance of Mr. Hooper, pacing slowly his meditative way towards the meetinghouse. With one accord they started, expressing more wonder than if some strange minister were coming to dust the cushions of Mr. Hooper's pulpit.

"Are you sure it is our parson?" inquired Goodman[2] Gray of the sexton.

"Of a certainty it is good Mr. Hooper," replied the sexton. "He was to have exchanged pulpits with Parson Shute, of Westbury; but Parson Shute sent to excuse himself yesterday, being to preach a funeral sermon."

---

2. **Goodman** title of respect similar to "Mister."

✔**Reading Check**

As the story begins, what weekly event is about to take place?

▼ **Critical Viewing**
Identify the elements or details of this painting that correspond to those in Hawthorne's story. **[Connect]**

Winter Sunday in Norway, Maine, Unidentified artist, New York State Historical Association, Cooperstown

The cause of so much amazement may appear sufficiently slight. Mr. Hooper, a gentlemanly person, of about thirty, though still a bachelor, was dressed with due clerical neatness, as if a careful wife had starched his band, and brushed the weekly dust from his Sunday's garb. There was but one thing remarkable in his appearance. Swathed about his forehead, and hanging down over his face, so low as to be shaken by his breath, Mr. Hooper had on a black veil. On a nearer view it seemed to consist of two folds of crape,[3] which entirely concealed his features, except the mouth and chin, but probably did not intercept his sight, further than to give a darkened aspect to all living and inanimate things. With this gloomy shade before him, good Mr. Hooper walked onward, at a slow and quiet pace, stooping somewhat, and looking on the ground, as is customary with abstracted men, yet nodding kindly to those of his parishioners who still waited on the meetinghouse steps. But so wonderstruck were they that his greeting hardly met with a return.

"I can't really feel as if good Mr. Hooper's face was behind that piece of crape," said the sexton.

"I don't like it," muttered an old woman, as she hobbled into the meetinghouse. "He has changed himself into something awful, only by hiding his face."

"Our parson has gone mad!" cried Goodman Gray, following him across the threshold.

A rumor of some unaccountable phenomenon had preceded Mr. Hooper into the meetinghouse, and set all the congregation astir. Few could refrain from twisting their heads towards the door; many stood upright, and turned directly about; while several little boys clambered upon the seats, and came down again with a terrible racket. There was a general bustle, a rustling of the women's gowns and shuffling of the men's feet, greatly at variance with that hushed repose which should attend the entrance of the minister. But Mr. Hooper appeared not to notice the perturbation of his people. He entered with an almost noiseless step, bent his head mildly to the pews on each side, and bowed as he passed his oldest parishioner, a white-haired great-grandsire, who occupied an armchair in the center of the aisle. It was strange to observe how slowly this venerable man became conscious of something singular in the appearance of his pastor. He seemed not fully to partake of the prevailing wonder, till Mr. Hooper had ascended the stairs, and showed himself in the pulpit, face to face with his congregation, except for the black veil. That mysterious emblem was never once withdrawn. It shook with his measured breath, as he gave out the psalm; it threw its obscurity between him and the holy page, as he read the Scriptures; and while he prayed, the veil lay heavily on his uplifted countenance. Did he seek to hide it from the dread Being whom he was addressing?

Such was the effect of this simple piece of crape, that more than one woman of delicate nerves was forced to leave the meetinghouse.

---

3. **crape** (krāp) *n.* piece of black cloth worn as a sign of mourning.

Yet perhaps the palefaced congregation was almost as fearful a sight to the minister, as his black veil to them.

Mr. Hooper had the reputation of a good preacher, but not an energetic one: he strove to win his people heavenward by mild, persuasive influences, rather than to drive them thither by the thunders of the Word. The sermon which he now delivered was marked by the same characteristics of style and manner as the general series of his pulpit oratory. But there was something, either in the sentiment of the discourse itself, or in the imagination of the auditors, which made it greatly the most powerful effort that they had ever heard from their pastor's lips. It was tinged, rather more darkly than usual, with the gentle gloom of Mr. Hooper's temperament. The subject had reference to secret sin, and those sad mysteries which we hide from our nearest and dearest, and would fain conceal from our own consciousness, even forgetting that the Omniscient[4] can detect them. A subtle power was breathed into his words. Each member of the congregation, the most innocent girl, and the man of hardened breast, felt as if the preacher had crept upon them, behind his awful veil, and discovered their hoarded iniquity of deed or thought. Many spread their clasped hands on their bosoms. There was nothing terrible in what Mr. Hooper said, at least, no violence; and yet, with every tremor of his melancholy voice, the hearers quaked. An unsought pathos came hand in hand with awe. So sensible were the audience of some unwonted attribute in their minister, that they longed for a breath of wind to blow aside the veil, almost believing that a stranger's visage would be discovered, though the form, gesture, and voice were those of Mr. Hooper.

At the close of the services, the people hurried out with indecorous confusion, eager to communicate their pent-up amazement, and conscious of lighter spirits the moment they lost sight of the black veil. Some gathered in little circles, huddled closely together, with their mouths all whispering in the center; some went homeward alone, wrapt in silent meditation; some talked loudly, and profaned the Sabbath day with ostentatious laughter. A few shook their sagacious heads, intimating that they could penetrate the mystery; while one or two affirmed that there was no mystery at all, but only that Mr. Hooper's eyes were so weakened by the midnight lamp, as to require a shade. After a brief interval, forth came good Mr. Hooper also, in the rear of his flock. Turning his veiled face from one group to another, he paid due reverence to the hoary heads, saluted the middle-aged with kind dignity as their friend and spiritual guide, greeted the young with mingled authority and love, and laid his hands on the little children's heads to bless them. Such was always his custom on the Sabbath day. Strange and bewildered looks repaid him for his courtesy. None, as on former occasions, aspired to the honor of walking by their pastor's side. Old Squire Saunders, doubtless by an

---

4. **Omniscient** (äm niˊ shǝnt) all-knowing God.

iniquity (i nikˊ wi tē) *n.* sin

indecorous (in dekˊ ǝ rǝs) *adj.* improper

ostentatious (äsˊ tǝn tāˊ shǝs) *adj.* intended to attract notice

sagacious (sǝ gāˊ shǝs) *adj.* shrewd

✓**Reading Check**

What change has occurred in Mr. Hooper's appearance?

accidental lapse of memory, neglected to invite Mr. Hooper to his table, where the good clergyman had been wont to bless the food, almost every Sunday since his settlement. He returned, therefore, to the parsonage, and, at the moment of closing the door, was observed to look back upon the people, all of whom had their eyes fixed upon the minister. A sad smile gleamed faintly from beneath the black veil, and flickered about his mouth, glimmering as he disappeared.

"How strange," said a lady, "that a simple black veil, such as any woman might wear on her bonnet, should become such a terrible thing on Mr. Hooper's face!"

"Something must surely be amiss with Mr. Hooper's intellects," observed her husband, the physician of the village. "But the strangest part of the affair is the effect of this vagary, even on a sober-minded man like myself. The black veil, though it covers only our pastor's face, throws its influence over his whole person, and makes him ghostlike from head to foot. Do you not feel it so?"

"Truly do I," replied the lady; "and I would not be alone with him for the world. I wonder he is not afraid to be alone with himself!"

"Men sometimes are so," said her husband.

The afternoon service was attended with similar circumstances. At its conclusion, the bell tolled for the funeral of a young lady. The relatives and friends were assembled in the house, and the more distant acquaintances stood about the door, speaking of the good qualities of the deceased, when their talk was interrupted by the appearance of Mr. Hooper, still covered with his black veil. It was now an appropriate emblem. The clergyman stepped into the room where the corpse was laid, and bent over the coffin, to take a last farewell of his deceased parishioner. As he stooped, the veil hung straight down from his forehead, so that, if her eyelids had not been closed forever, the dead maiden might have seen his face. Could Mr. Hooper be fearful of her glance, that he so hastily caught back the black veil? A person who watched the interview between the dead and living, scrupled not to affirm, that, at the instant when the clergyman's features were disclosed, the corpse had slightly shuddered, rustling the shroud and muslin cap, though the countenance retained the composure of death. A superstitious old woman was the only witness of this prodigy. From the coffin Mr. Hooper passed into the chamber of the mourners, and thence to the head of the staircase; to make the funeral prayer. It was a tender and heart-dissolving prayer, full of sorrow, yet so imbued with celestial hopes, that the music of a heavenly harp, swept by the fingers of the dead, seemed faintly to be heard among the saddest accents of the minister. The people trembled, though they but darkly understood him when he prayed that they, and himself, and all of mortal race, might be ready,

Jonathan Edwards, Puritans, and Sermons of Fear

The congregation's fear of Mr. Hooper's veil recalls Jonathan Edwards, one of the greatest preachers of the colonial period. Edwards used his sermons to inspire fear of eternal damnation in the minds of his listeners. He insisted that the evidence they saw as proof of God's grace in their lives was false. According to Edwards, personal comfort, success, health, and a sense of being a good person were no proof that one was saved. Rather, these satisfactions in the earthly realm were mere distractions, providing comfort, but no substance, to the ignorant.

Though Hawthorne describes Mr. Hooper as a mild and benevolent preacher—certainly no spouter of fire-and-brimstone like Edwards—his veil inspires a similar fear and trembling among the villagers. You can read an excerpt of Jonathan Edwards's "Sinners in the Hands of an Angry God" on page 106.

vagary (və ger′ ē) n. unpredictable occurrence

as he trusted this young maiden had been, for the dreadful hour that should snatch the veil from their faces. The bearers went heavily forth, and the mourners followed, saddening all the street, with the dead before them, and Mr. Hooper in his black veil behind.

"Why do you look back?" said one in the procession to his partner.

"I had a fancy," replied she, "that the minister and the maiden's spirit were walking hand in hand."

"And so had I, at the same moment," said the other.

That night, the handsomest couple in Milford village were to be joined in wedlock. Though reckoned a melancholy man, Mr. Hooper had a placid cheerfulness for such occasions, which often excited a sympathetic smile where livelier merriment would have been thrown away. There was no quality of his disposition which made him more beloved than this. The company at the wedding awaited his arrival with impatience, trusting that the strange awe, which had gathered over him throughout the day, would now be dispelled. But such was not the result. When Mr. Hooper came, the first thing that their eyes rested on was the same horrible black veil, which had added deeper gloom to the funeral, and could portend nothing but evil to the wedding. Such was its immediate effect on the guests that a cloud seemed to have rolled duskily from beneath the black crape, and dimmed the light of the candles. The bridal pair stood up before the minister. But the bride's cold fingers quivered in the tremulous hand of the bridegroom, and her deathlike paleness caused a whisper that the maiden who had been buried a few hours before was come from her grave to be married. If ever another wedding were so dismal, it was that famous one where they tolled the wedding knell.[5] After performing the ceremony, Mr. Hooper raised a glass of wine to his lips, wishing happiness to the new-married couple in a strain of mild pleasantry that ought to have brightened the features of the guests, like a cheerful gleam from the hearth. At that instant, catching a glimpse of his figure in the looking glass, the black veil involved his own spirit in the horror with which it overwhelmed all others. His frame shuddered, his lips grew white, he spilt the untasted wine upon the carpet, and rushed forth into the darkness. For the Earth, too, had on her Black Veil.

The next day, the whole village of Milford talked of little else than Parson Hooper's black veil. That, and the mystery concealed behind it, supplied a topic for discussion between acquaintances meeting in the street, and good women gossiping at their open windows. It was the first item of news that the tavernkeeper told to his guests. The children babbled of it on their way to school. One imitative little imp covered his face with an old black handkerchief, thereby so affrighting his playmates that the panic seized himself, and he well nigh lost his wits by his own waggery.

---

5. **If . . . knell** reference to Hawthorne's short story "The Wedding Knell." A knell is the slow ringing of a bell, as at a funeral.

It was remarkable that of all the busybodies and <u>impertinent</u> people in the parish, not one ventured to put the plain question to Mr. Hooper, wherefore he did this thing. Hitherto, whenever there appeared the slightest call for such interference, he had never lacked advisers, nor shown himself averse to be guided by their judgment. If he erred at all, it was by so painful a degree of self-distrust that even the mildest censure would lead him to consider an indifferent action as a crime. Yet, though so well acquainted with this amiable weakness, no individual among his parishioners chose to make the black veil a subject of friendly remonstrance. There was a feeling of dread, neither plainly confessed nor carefully concealed, which caused each to shift the responsibility upon another, till at length it was found expedient to send a deputation of the church, in order to deal with Mr. Hooper about the mystery, before it should grow into a scandal. Never did an embassy so ill discharge its duties. The minister received them with friendly courtesy, but became silent, after they were seated, leaving to his visitors the whole burden of introducing their important business. The topic, it might be supposed, was obvious enough. There was the black veil swathed round Mr. Hooper's forehead, and concealing every feature above his placid mouth, on which, at times, they could perceive the glimmering of a melancholy smile. But that piece of crape, to their imagination, seemed to hang down before his heart, the symbol of a fearful secret between him and them. Were the veil but cast aside, they might speak freely of it, but not till then. Thus they sat a considerable time, speechless, confused, and shrinking uneasily from Mr. Hooper's eye, which they felt to be fixed upon them with an invisible glance. Finally, the deputies returned abashed to their constituents, pronouncing the matter too weighty to be handled, except by a council of the churches, if, indeed, it might not require a general synod.[6]

But there was one person in the village unappalled by the awe with which the black veil had impressed all beside herself. When the deputies returned without an explanation, or even venturing to demand one, she, with the calm energy of her character, determined to chase away the strange cloud that appeared to be settling round Mr. Hooper, every moment more darkly than before. As his plighted wife,[7] it should be her privilege to know what the black veil concealed. At the minister's first visit, therefore, she entered upon the subject with a direct simplicity, which made the task easier both for him and her. After he had seated himself, she fixed her eyes steadfastly upon the veil, but could discern nothing of the dreadful gloom that had so overawed the multitude: it was but a double fold of crape, hanging down from his forehead to his mouth, and slightly stirring with his breath.

"No," said she aloud, and smiling, "there is nothing terrible in this piece of crape, except that it hides a face which I am always glad to

impertinent (im purt´ 'n ənt) *adj.* not showing proper respect

Literary Analysis
Parable What might these details about Mr. Hooper's fiancée add to the parable's moral?

---

6. **synod** (sin´ əd) *n.* high governing body in certain Christian churches.
7. **plighted wife** fiancée.

look upon. Come, good sir, let the sun shine from behind the cloud. First lay aside your black veil; then tell me why you put it on."

Mr. Hooper's smile glimmered faintly.

"There is an hour to come," said he, "when all of us shall cast aside our veils. Take it not amiss, beloved friend, if I wear this piece of crape till then."

"Your words are a mystery, too," returned the young lady. "Take away the veil from them, at least."

"Elizabeth, I will," said he, "so far as my vow may suffer me. Know, then, this veil is a type and a symbol, and I am bound to wear it ever, both in light and darkness, in solitude and before the gaze of multitudes, and as with strangers, so with my familiar friends. No mortal eye will see it withdrawn. This dismal shade must separate me from the world: even you, Elizabeth, can never come behind it!"

"What grievous affliction hath befallen you," she earnestly inquired, "that you should thus darken your eyes forever?"

"If it be a sign of mourning," replied Mr. Hooper, "I, perhaps, like most other mortals, have sorrows dark enough to be typified by a black veil."

"But what if the world will not believe that it is the type of an innocent sorrow?" urged Elizabeth. "Beloved and respected as you are, there may be whispers that you hide your face under the consciousness of secret sin. For the sake of your holy office, do away this scandal!"

The color rose into her cheeks as she intimated the nature of the rumors that were already abroad in the village. But Mr. Hooper's mildness did not forsake him. He even smiled again—that same sad smile, which always appeared like a faint glimmering of light, proceeding from the obscurity beneath the veil.

"If I hide my face for sorrow, there is cause enough," he merely replied; "and if I cover it for secret sin, what mortal might not do the same?"

And with this gentle, but unconquerable obstinacy did he resist all her entreaties. At length Elizabeth sat silent. For a few moments she appeared lost in thought, considering, probably, what new methods might be tried to withdraw her lover from so dark a fantasy, which, if it had no other meaning, was perhaps a symptom of mental disease. Though of a firmer character than his own, the tears rolled down her cheeks. But in an instant, as it were, a new feeling took the place of sorrow: her eyes were fixed insensibly on the black veil, when, like a sudden twilight in the air, its terrors fell around her. She arose, and stood trembling before him.

"And do you feel it then, at last?" said he mournfully.

She made no reply, but covered her eyes with her hand, and turned to leave the room. He rushed forward and caught her arm.

"Have patience with me, Elizabeth!" cried he, passionately. "Do not desert me, though this veil must be between us here on earth. Be mine, and hereafter there shall be no veil over my face, no darkness

Reading Strategy
Drawing Inferences About Meaning In his reply to Elizabeth, what does Mr. Hooper suggest about the veil's meaning?

obstinacy (äb′ stə nə sē) *n.* stubbornness

Reading Check
Are the villagers able to confront Mr. Hooper directly about the veil? Why or why not?

Cemetery, Peter McIntyre, Courtesy of the artist

▲ **Critical Viewing** In what ways does the atmosphere in this painting reflect the mood of the story? **[Connect]**

between our souls! It is but a mortal veil—it is not for eternity! O! you know not how lonely I am, and how frightened, to be alone behind my black veil. Do not leave me in this miserable obscurity forever!"

"Lift the veil but once, and look me in the face," said she.

"Never! It cannot be!" replied Mr. Hooper.

"Then farewell!" said Elizabeth.

She withdrew her arm from his grasp, and slowly departed, pausing at the door, to give one long shuddering gaze, that seemed almost to penetrate the mystery of the black veil. But, even amid his grief, Mr. Hooper smiled to think that only a material emblem had separated him from happiness, though the horrors, which it shadowed forth,

Literary Analysis
Parable What message is conveyed by the passage beginning "But, even amid his grief"?

must be drawn darkly between the fondest of lovers. From that time no attempts were made to remove Mr. Hooper's black veil, or, by a direct appeal, to discover the secret which it was supposed to hide. By persons who claimed a superiority to popular prejudice, it was reckoned merely an eccentric whim, such as often mingles with the sober actions of men otherwise rational, and tinges them all with its own semblance of insanity. But with the multitude, good Mr. Hooper was irreparably a bugbear.[8] He could not walk the street with any peace of mind, so conscious was he that the gentle and timid would turn aside to avoid him, and that others would make it a point of hardihood to throw themselves in his way. The impertinence of the latter class compelled him to give up his customary walk at sunset to the burial ground; for when he leaned pensively over the gate, there would always be faces behind the gravestones, peeping at his black veil. A fable went the rounds that the stare of the dead people drove him thence. It grieved him, to the very depth of his kind heart, to observe how the children fled from his approach, breaking up their merriest sports, while his melancholy figure was yet afar off. Their instinctive dread caused him to feel more strongly than aught else, that a preternatural[9] horror was interwoven with the threads of the black crape. In truth, his own antipathy to the veil was known to be so great that he never willingly passed before a mirror, nor stooped to drink at a still fountain, lest, in its peaceful bosom, he should be affrighted by himself. This was what gave plausibility to the whispers, that Mr. Hooper's conscience tortured him for some great crime too horrible to be entirely concealed, or otherwise than so obscurely intimated. Thus, from beneath the black veil, there rolled a cloud into the sunshine, an ambiguity of sin or sorrow, which enveloped the poor minister, so that love or sympathy could never reach him. It was said that ghost and fiend consorted with him there. With self-shudderings and outward terrors, he walked continually in its shadow, groping darkly within his own soul or gazing through a medium that saddened the whole world. Even the lawless wind, it was believed, respected his dreadful secret, and never blew aside the veil. But still good Mr. Hooper sadly smiled at the pale visages of the worldly throng as he passed by.

Among all its bad influences, the black veil had the one desirable effect, of making its wearer a very efficient clergyman. By the aid of his mysterious emblem—for there was no other apparent cause—he became a man of awful power over souls that were in agony for sin. His converts always regarded him with a dread peculiar to themselves, affirming, though but figuratively, that, before he brought them to celestial light, they had been with him behind the black veil. Its gloom, indeed, enabled him to sympathize with all dark affections. Dying sinners cried aloud for Mr. Hooper, and would not yield their

---

8. **bugbear** *n.* something causing needless fear.
9. **preternatural** (prēt′ ər nāch′ ər əl) *adj.* supernatural.

Reading Strategy
Drawing Inferences About Meaning What can you infer about the people in the community based on their fear of Mr. Hooper's veil?

Literary Analysis
Parable Why is it significant that nature, as represented by the wind, respects the veil?

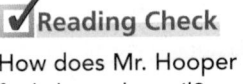
Reading Check
How does Mr. Hooper feel about the veil?

breath till he appeared; though ever, as he stooped to whisper conso-lation, they shuddered at the veiled face so near their own. Such were the terrors of the black veil, even when Death had bared his visage! Strangers came long distances to attend service at his church, with the mere idle purpose of gazing at his figure, because it was forbid-den them to behold his face. But many were made to quake ere they departed! Once, during Governor Belcher's[10] administration, Mr. Hooper was appointed to preach the election sermon. Covered with his black veil, he stood before the chief magistrate, the council, and the representatives, and wrought so deep an impression that the legis-lative measures of that year were characterized by all the gloom and piety of our earliest ancestral sway.

In this manner Mr. Hooper spent a long life, irreproachable in out-ward act, yet shrouded in dismal suspicions; kind and loving, though unloved, and dimly feared; a man apart from men, shunned in their health and joy, but ever summoned to their aid in mortal anguish. As years wore on, shedding their snows above his sable veil, he acquired a name throughout the New England churches, and they called him Father Hooper. Nearly all his parishioners, who were of mature age when he was settled, had been borne away by many a funeral: he had one congregation in the church, and a more crowded one in the churchyard; and having wrought so late into the evening, and done his work so well, it was now good Father Hooper's turn to rest.

Several persons were visible by the shaded candlelight, in the death chamber of the old clergyman. Natural connections[11] he had none. But there was the decorously grave, though unmoved physi-cian, seeking only to mitigate the last pangs of the patient whom he could not save. There were the deacons, and other eminently pious members of his church. There, also, was the Reverend Mr. Clark, of Westbury, a young and zealous divine, who had ridden in haste to pray by the bedside of the expiring minister. There was the nurse, no hired handmaiden of death, but one whose calm affection had endured thus long in secrecy, in solitude, amid the chill of age, and would not perish, even at the dying hour. Who, but Elizabeth! And there lay the hoary head of good Father Hooper upon the death pillow, with the black veil still swathed about his brow, and reaching down over his face, so that each more difficult gasp of his faint breath caused it to stir. All through life that piece of crape had hung between him and the world: it had separated him from cheerful brotherhood and woman's love, and kept him in that saddest of all prisons, his own heart; and still it lay upon his face, as if to deepen the gloom of his darksome chamber, and shade him from the sunshine of eternity.

---

10. **Governor Belcher** Jonathan Belcher (1682–1757), the royal governor of the Massachusetts Bay Colony, from 1730 to 1741.
11. **Natural connections** relatives.

Literary Analysis
Parable What message is Hawthorne conveying in his description of the veil as a partition, setting Mr. Hooper off from "cheerful brotherhood"?

For some time previous, his mind had been confused, wavering doubtfully between the past and the present, and hovering forward, as it were, at intervals, into the indistinctness of the world to come. There had been feverish turns, which tossed him from side to side, and wore away what little strength he had. But in his most convulsive struggles, and in the wildest vagaries of his intellect, when no other thought retained its sober influence, he still showed an awful solicitude lest the black veil should slip aside. Even if his bewildered soul could have forgotten, there was a faithful woman at his pillow, who, with averted eyes, would have covered that aged face, which she had last beheld in the comeliness of manhood. At length the death-stricken old man lay quietly in the torpor of mental and bodily exhaustion, with an imperceptible pulse, and breath that grew fainter and fainter, except when a long, deep, and irregular inspiration seemed to prelude the flight of his spirit.

The minister of Westbury approached the bedside.

"Venerable Father Hooper," said he, "the moment of your release is at hand. Are you ready for the lifting of the veil that shuts in time from eternity?"

Father Hooper at first replied merely by a feeble motion of his head; then, apprehensive, perhaps, that his meaning might be doubtful, he exerted himself to speak.

"Yea," said he, in faint accents, "my soul hath a patient weariness until that veil be lifted."

"And is it fitting," resumed the Reverend Mr. Clark, "that a man so given to prayer, of such a blameless example, holy in deed and thought, so far as mortal judgment may pronounce; is it fitting that a father in the church should leave a shadow on his memory, that may seem to blacken a life so pure? I pray you, my venerable brother, let not this thing be! Suffer us to be gladdened by your triumphant aspect as you go to your reward. Before the veil of eternity be lifted, let me cast aside this black veil from your face!"

And thus speaking, the Reverend Mr. Clark bent forward to reveal the mystery of so many years. But, exerting a sudden energy, that made all the beholders stand aghast, Father Hooper snatched both his hands from beneath the bedclothes, and pressed them strongly on the black veil, resolute to struggle, if the minister of Westbury would contend with a dying man.

"Never!" cried the veiled clergyman. "On earth, never!"

"Dark old man!" exclaimed the affrighted minister, "with what horrible crime upon your soul are you now passing to the judgment?"

Father Hooper's breath heaved; it rattled in his throat; but, with a mighty effort, grasping forward with his hands, he caught hold of life, and held it back till he should speak. He even raised himself in bed; and there he sat, shivering with the arms of death around him, while the black veil hung down, awful, at that last moment, in the gathered terrors of a lifetime. And yet the faint, sad smile, so often

Literary Analysis
Parable and Symbol
What does the minister of Westbury's question suggest about the veil's symbolic meaning?

☑Reading Check

On his deathbed, does Mr. Hooper wish the veil to be removed?

The Minister's Black Veil ◆ 347

there, now seemed to glimmer from its obscurity, and linger on Father Hooper's lips.

"Why do you tremble at me alone?" cried he, turning his veiled face round the circle of pale spectators. "Tremble also at each other! Have men avoided me, and women shown no pity, and children screamed and fled, only for my black veil? What, but the mystery which it obscurely typifies, has made this piece of crape so awful? When the friend shows his inmost heart to his friend; the lover to his best beloved; when man does not vainly shrink from the eye of his Creator, loathsomely treasuring up the secret of his sin; then deem me a monster, for the symbol beneath which I have lived, and die! I look around me, and, lo! on every visage a Black Veil!"

While his auditors shrank from one another, in mutual affright, Father Hooper fell back upon his pillow, a veiled corpse, with a faint smile lingering on the lips. Still veiled, they laid him in his coffin, and a veiled corpse they bore him to the grave. The grass of many years has sprung up and withered on that grave, the burial stone is moss-grown, and good Mr. Hooper's face is dust; but awful is still the thought that it moldered beneath the Black Veil!

Review and Assess

Thinking About the Selection

1. **Respond:** How would you have reacted to the veil if you had been (a) a member of Mr. Hooper's congregation or (b) another Puritan clergyman?

2. **(a) Recall:** How did his congregation regard Mr. Hooper before he began wearing the veil? **(b) Analyze:** In what ways does the veil affect Mr. Hooper's relationship with his congregation?

3. **(a) Recall:** What is the subject of Mr. Hooper's sermon on the day he first wears the veil? **(b) Compare and Contrast:** What emotions does Mr. Hooper evoke in his congregation that he never did before? **(c) Draw Conclusions:** To what do you attribute Mr. Hooper's new found ability to affect his listeners?

4. **(a) Recall:** According to the narrator, what is the veil's "one desirable effect"? **(b) Infer:** Why does the veil make Mr. Hooper a more effective minister?

5. **(a) Interpret:** Why does the veil have such a powerful effect on people? **(b) Synthesize:** Hawthorne suggests that all people carry secrets they choose not to reveal to anyone. Do you agree or disagree with this suggestion? Explain.

6. **Take a Position:** At some point in our lives, most human beings will feel guilty about something. Do you think that guilt is ever beneficial? Explain.

Review and Assess

Literary Analysis

Parable

1. In what ways does this **parable** convey the message that people possess the potential for both good and evil?

2. Why do you think Hawthorne does not reveal the reason Parson Hooper begins wearing the veil?

3. The Anti-Transcendentalists believed that the truths of existence are both elusive and disturbing. What disturbing truth does Hawthorne convey through Parson Hooper and his black veil?

Connecting Literary Elements

4. (a) With what emotions does Elizabeth regard the veil at first and later on? (b) What do her reactions suggest about the veil as a **symbol**?

5. (a) Use a chart like the one shown to analyze the emotional associations contained in three descriptions of the veil. (b) Is the veil symbolic of a single idea, or does it offer a range of possible interpretations?

Descriptive Detail	Emotional Associations	Symbolic Meaning

6. On his deathbed, Mr. Hooper says, "I look around me, and lo! on every visage a Black Veil!" What does this statement suggest about the veil's symbolic meaning?

Reading Strategy

Drawing Inferences About Meaning

7. Based on the villagers' reactions to Parson Hooper, **draw inferences** about human nature as Hawthorne sees it.

8. What can you infer about the author's attitude toward the Puritans from this story? Support your answer.

Extend Understanding

9. **Cultural Connection:** (a) Do you think a community's expectations that its leaders be without any guilt are realistic? (b) Are they fair? Explain.

Quick Review

A **parable** is a short, simple story with a moral message.

A **symbol** is something that has meaning in and of itself and also stands for something else.

To **draw inferences about meaning,** use details from the text as clues to an author's larger purpose.

 Take It to the Net
www.phschool.com
Take the interactive self-test online to check your understanding of the selection.

Integrate Language Skills

Vocabulary Development Lesson

Word Analysis: Latin Root -equi-

The Latin root -equi- means "equal." The spelling of the root changes slightly in the word **iniquity,** meaning "sin or gross injustice." Using your knowledge of this root, define the following words:

1. equidistant
2. equivalent
3. equate
4. equilibrium

Spelling Strategy

The prefix *in-*, meaning "not," as in *indecorous*, changes to *im-* before many words beginning with *p*, such as *impersonal*, or with *m*, such as *immature*. Complete the words below by adding the correct prefix.

1. __pertinent (impolite)
2. __iquity (evil)
3. __decorous (vulgar)
4. __passive (emotionless)

Concept Development: Synonyms

Review the vocabulary list on page 335. Then, select the letter of the best synonym for each numbered word.

1. venerable   **a.** wise
2. iniquity   **b.** rude
3. indecorous   **c.** honorable
4. ostentatious   **d.** whim
5. sagacious   **e.** timid
6. vagary   **f.** evil
7. tremulous   **g.** uncouth
8. waggery   **h.** stubbornness
9. impertinent   **i.** humor
10. obstinacy   **j.** showy

Grammar and Style Lesson

Varying Sentence Openers

By **varying sentence openers,** Hawthorne helps readers follow the story, from detail to detail and event to event. For example, some sentences begin with prepositional phrases; others begin with transitions. Look at these examples from the story:

Prepositional Phrase: *Among all its bad influences*, the black veil had the one desirable effect . . .

Transition: *Though reckoned a melancholy man*, Mr. Hooper had a placid cheerfulness for such occasions . . .

Looking at Style Review the story, and select two paragraphs that contain at least three different types of sentence openers. Identify the type of opener used in each sentence. Then, rewrite the two paragraphs so that all of the sentences have the same type of opener. Finally, explain why the rewritten paragraphs are less effective than the original ones.

Writing Application Write the opening paragraph to a short story. Engage readers, and lead them from detail to detail by using a variety of sentence openers.

W̶G Prentice Hall Writing and Grammar Connection: Chapter 20, Section 3

Writing Lesson

Response to a Short Story

Some aspects of this dark and powerful story probably made a distinct impression on you. Perhaps you were fascinated by the spectacle of the veil or upset by Parson Hooper's (or the villagers') behavior. Write a short paper in which you present your response to an element of the story. Support your response with specific details from the story.

Prewriting   Review the story, and note your thoughts and feelings about the characters, setting, plot, and symbols. Choose one element to address. Then, find details that you can use to help explain your reactions.

Drafting   In an introductory paragraph, identify the element on which you are focusing and explain your reaction to it. Then, explain the role of this element in the story, citing specific details for support.

Revising   Revise your response to make certain that you have included enough passages and details from the story to explain your reaction.

, which Hawthorne describes as a "gloomy shade,"

Model: Using Exact Quotations

Hawthorne never tells us why Parson Hooper decides to wear the veil. We know only that the veil conceals his entire face except for his chin and mouth.

The most effective way to cite details from a literary work is to use word-for-word quotations.

W͜G Prentice Hall Writing and Grammar Connection: Chapter 14, Section 2

Extension Activities

Listening and Speaking   As Elizabeth, plan and present a **monologue** in which you appeal to your fiancé to remove his black veil.

- Use a familiar tone of address.
- Maintain an appropriately Puritan air of restraint.
- Refer to Elizabeth's history with Mr. Hooper and her hopes for their future.

Give a dramatic presentation to the class.

Research and Technology   Read "The Wedding Knell"—another story in Hawthorne's *Twice-Told Tales*. Compare and contrast it with "The Minister's Black Veil." Then, prepare and deliver an **oral presentation** in which you discuss the two stories.

 **Take It to the Net**   www.phschool.com

Go online for an additional research activity using the Internet.

Prepare to Read

from Moby-Dick

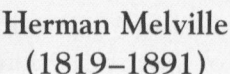

Herman Melville (1819–1891)

Herman Melville is one of America's greatest novelists. Unfortunately, his work was never fully appreciated during his lifetime, and he lived a life that was often filled with frustration and despair.

Melville was born in New York City, the son of a wealthy merchant. His family's comfortable financial situation changed drastically in 1830, however, when his father's import business failed. Two years later, Melville's father died, leaving the family in debt. Forced to leave school, Melville spent the rest of his childhood working as a clerk, a farmhand, and a teacher to help support his family.

Whaling in the South Pacific Melville became a sailor at the age of nineteen and spent several years working on whaling ships and exploring the South Pacific. He returned to the United States in 1844, after a brief period of service in the navy.

Soon thereafter, Melville began his career as a writer, using his adventures in the South Seas as material for his fiction. He quickly produced two popular and financially successful novels, *Typee* (1846) and *Omoo* (1847), both set in the Pacific islands. His third novel, *Mardi* (1849), was considerably more abstract and symbolic. When readers rejected the book and his fame began to fade, Melville grew increasingly melancholy. He continued writing, however, turning out two more novels, *Redburn* (1849) and *White-Jacket* (1850), over the next two years.

Writing in the Berkshires Using the profits from his popular novels, Melville bought a farm, known as Arrowhead, near Pittsfield, Massachusetts. There, he befriended the author Nathaniel Hawthorne, who lived in a neighboring village. Greatly encouraged by Hawthorne's interest and influenced by his reading of Shakespeare, Melville redoubled his own creative energies. He began producing deeper and more sophisticated works. In 1851, he published his masterpiece, *Moby-Dick*, under the title *The Whale*.

Moby-Dick is a complex novel with several layers of meaning. On the surface, it is the story of the fateful voyage of a whaling ship. On another level, it is the story of a bitter man's quest for vengeance and truth. On still another level, it is a philosophical examination of humanity's relationship to the natural world and the conflict between creativity and cruelty.

A Moment of Pride When he finished the book, Melville sensed the magnitude of his achievement. Unfortunately, his pleasure in his work was short-lived. Unable to appreciate the novel's depth, nineteenth-century readers responded unfavorably to *Moby-Dick*. It did not attract a wide audience.

Audiences also rejected his next two novels, *Pierre* (1852) and *The Confidence Man* (1857). Melville fell into debt and was forced to accept a job as an inspector at the New York customs house. Some of the short stories Melville published between 1852 and 1855—including "Bartleby the Scrivener," "The Encantadas," and "Benito Cereno"—reflect the author's circumstances at the time, including his contempt for hypocrisy and materialism.

Rediscovered Disillusioned and bitter, Melville turned away from writing fiction during the latter part of his life. He privately published several volumes of poetry. He also produced a handful of short stories and the moving novella *Billy Budd*. Melville died in 1891, unappreciated and unnoticed. In the 1920s, however, his novels and tales were rediscovered and hailed by scholars, and he finally received the recognition he deserved. Today, *Moby-Dick* is widely regarded as one of the finest novels in all of American literature.

Preview

Connecting to the Literature

Some situations demand fierce concentration. However, as this excerpt from one of literature's most famous works of fiction illustrates, when one focuses *too* intensely on a goal, attention can become obsession.

Literary Analysis

Symbol

A **symbol** is a person, place, or thing that has its own meaning and also represents something larger. The white whale of Melville's *Moby-Dick* is an extremely complex symbol. To understand its meaning, examine every aspect of the whale's behavior and appearance.

- Moby-Dick is massive, threatening, and awe-inspiring yet beautiful.
- Moby-Dick seems unpredictable but is controlled by natural laws.
- Moby-Dick seems immortal and indifferent to human suffering.

Analyzed in this way, Moby-Dick seems to symbolize all that is mysterious and uncontrollable in life.

Connecting Literary Elements

A **theme** is a central message revealed by a literary work, and is often expressed through the use of symbols, as well as characters' actions, descriptions, and imagery. In *Moby-Dick*, Melville explores the enormous theme of the mysteries of existence. As you read, look for points at which Melville addresses such ideas as good, evil, sacrifice, and revenge.

Reading Strategy

Recognizing Symbols

To **recognize symbols,** look for characters, places, or objects that are mentioned repeatedly or linked to larger concepts. For example, Ahab's description of Moby-Dick gives the whale symbolic meaning:

> I see in him outrageous strength, with an inscrutable malice sinewing it. That inscrutable malice is chiefly what I hate . . .

From this description, you might guess that Moby-Dick symbolizes nature's destructive power. Use a chart like the one shown to recognize and interpret symbols.

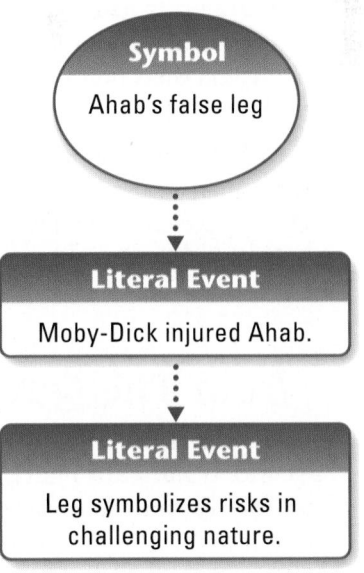

Vocabulary Development

inscrutable (in skrōōt′ ə bəl) *adj.* not able to be easily understood (p. 358)

maledictions (mal′ ə dik′ shənz) *n.* curses (p. 360)

prescient (presh′ ənt) *adj.* having foreknowledge (p. 364)

pertinaciously (pur′ tə na′ shəs lē) *adv.* holding firmly to some purpose (p. 366)

FROM MOBY-DICK

Herman Melville

Background

Moby-Dick is the story of a man's obsession with the dangerous and mysterious white whale that years before had taken off one of his legs. The man, Captain Ahab, guides the *Pequod*, a whaling ship, and its crew in relentless pursuit of this whale, Moby-Dick. Among the more important members of the crew are Starbuck, the first mate; Stubb, the second mate; Flask, the third mate; Queequeg, Tashtego, and Daggoo, the harpooners; and Ishmael, the young sailor who narrates the book.

When the crew signed aboard the *Pequod*, the voyage was to be nothing more than a business venture. However, in the following excerpt, Ahab makes clear to the crew that his purpose is to seek revenge against Moby-Dick.

from The Quarter-Deck

One morning shortly after breakfast, Ahab, as was his wont, ascended the cabin gangway to the deck. There most sea captains usually walk at that hour, as country gentlemen, after the same meal, take a few turns in the garden.

Soon his steady, ivory stride was heard, as to and fro he paced his old rounds, upon planks so familiar to his tread, that they were all over dented, like geological stones, with the peculiar mark of his walk. Did you fixedly gaze, too, upon that ribbed and dented brow;

there also, you would see still stranger footprints—the footprints of his one unsleeping, ever-pacing thought.

But on the occasion in question, those dents looked deeper, even as his nervous step that morning left a deeper mark. And, so full of his thought was Ahab, that at every uniform turn that he made, now at the mainmast and now at the binnacle,[1] you could almost see that thought turn in him as he turned, and pace in him as he paced; so completely possessing him, indeed, that it all but seemed the inward mold of every outer movement.

"D'ye mark him, Flask?" whispered Stubb; "the chick that's in him pecks the shell. 'Twill soon be out."

The hours wore on—Ahab now shut up within his cabin; anon, pacing the deck, with the same intense bigotry of purpose[2] in his aspect.

It drew near the close of day. Suddenly he came to a halt by the bulwarks, and inserting his bone leg into the auger hole there, and with one hand grasping a shroud, he ordered Starbuck to send everybody aft.

"Sir!" said the mate, astonished at an order seldom or never given on shipboard except in some extraordinary case.

"Send everybody aft," repeated Ahab. "Mastheads, there! come down!"

When the entire ship's company were assembled, and with curious and not wholly unapprehensive faces, were eyeing him, for he looked not unlike the weather horizon when a storm is coming up, Ahab, after rapidly glancing over the bulwarks, and then darting his eyes among the crew, started from his standpoint; and as though not a soul were nigh him resumed his heavy turns upon the deck. With bent head and half-slouched hat he continued to pace, unmindful of the wondering whispering among the men; till Stubb cautiously whispered to Flask, that Ahab must have summoned them there for the purpose of witnessing a pedestrian feat. But this did not last long. Vehemently pausing, he cried:

"What do ye do when ye see a whale, men?"

"Sing out for him!" was the impulsive rejoinder from a score of clubbed voices.

"Good!" cried Ahab, with a wild approval in his tones; observing the hearty animation into which his unexpected question had so magnetically thrown them.

"And what do ye next, men?"

"Lower away, and after him!"

"And what tune is it ye pull to, men?"

"A dead whale or a stove[3] boat!"

More and more strangely and fiercely glad and approving, grew the countenance of the old man at every shout; while the mariners began to

1. **binnacle** (bin´ ə kəl) *n.* case enclosing a ship's compass.
2. **bigotry of purpose** complete single-mindedness.
3. **stove** *v.* broken; smashed.

Literary Analysis
Symbol What might the "dents" on Ahab's furrowed brow symbolize?

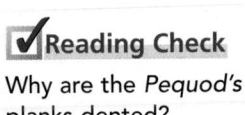

Reading Check
Why are the *Pequod's* planks dented?

gaze curiously at each other, as if marveling how it was that they themselves became so excited at such seemingly purposeless questions.

But, they were all eagerness again, as Ahab, now half-revolving in his pivot hole, with one hand reaching high up a shroud,[4] and tightly, almost convulsively grasping it, addressed them thus:

"All ye mastheaders have before now heard me give orders about a white whale. Look ye! d'ye see this Spanish ounce of gold?"—holding up a broad bright coin to the sun—"it is a sixteen-dollar piece, men. D'ye see it? Mr. Starbuck, hand me yon topmaul."

While the mate was getting the hammer, Ahab, without speaking, was slowly rubbing the gold piece against the skirts of his jacket, as if to heighten its luster, and without using any words was meanwhile lowly humming to himself, producing a sound so strangely muffled and inarticulate that it seemed the mechanical humming of the wheels of his vitality in him.

Receiving the topmaul from Starbuck, he advanced towards the mainmast with the hammer uplifted in one hand, exhibiting the gold with the other, and with a high raised voice exclaiming: "Whosoever of ye raises me a white-headed whale with a wrinkled brow and a crooked jaw; whosoever of ye raises me that white-headed whale, with three holes punctured in his starboard fluke[5]—look ye, whosoever of ye raises me that same white whale, he shall have this gold ounce, my boys!"

"Huzza! huzza!" cried the seamen, as with swinging tarpaulins they hailed the act of nailing the gold to the mast.

"It's a white whale, I say," resumed Ahab, as he threw down the topmaul: "a white whale. Skin your eyes for him, men; look sharp for white water; if ye see but a bubble, sing out."

All this while Tashtego, Daggoo, and Queequeg had looked on with even more intense interest and surprise than the rest, and at the mention of the wrinkled brow and crooked jaw they had started as if each was separately touched by some specific recollection.

"Captain Ahab," said Tashtego, "that white whale must be the same that some call Moby-Dick."

"Moby-Dick?" shouted Ahab. "Do ye know the white whale then, Tash?"

"Does he fantail[6] a little curious, sir, before he goes down?" said the Gay-Header deliberately.

Captain Ahab on the Deck of the Pequod, Rockwell Kent

▲ **Critical Viewing**
In what ways does this portrait of Ahab compare or contrast with your mental image of him? **[Compare and Contrast]**

Reading Strategy
Recognizing Symbols
What does Ahab's treatment of the gold coin suggest about its presence as a symbol?

---

4. **shroud** *n.* set of ropes from a ship's side to the masthead.
5. **starboard fluke** (flo͞ok) *n.* right half of a whale's tail.
6. **fantail** *v.* to spread the tail like a fan.

"And has he a curious spout, too," said Daggoo, "very bushy, even for a parmacetty,[7] and mighty quick, Captain Ahab?"

"And he have one, two, tree—oh! good many iron in him hide, too, Captain," cried Queequeg disjointedly, "all twiske-tee betwisk, like him—him—" faltering hard for a word, and screwing his hand round and round as though uncorking a bottle— "like him—him—"

"Corkscrew!" cried Ahab, "aye, Queequeg, the harpoons lie all twisted and wrenched in him; aye, Daggoo, his spout is a big one, like a whole shock of wheat, and white as a pile of our Nantucket wool after the great annual sheepshearing; aye, Tashtego, and he fantails like a split jib in a squall. Death and devils! men, it is Moby-Dick ye have seen—Moby-Dick— Moby-Dick!"

Literary Analysis
Symbol What image of Moby-Dick is created in this discussion?

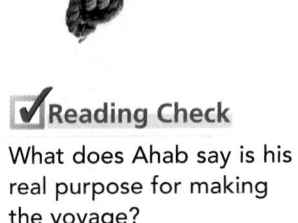

"Captain Ahab," said Starbuck, who, with Stubb and Flask, had thus far been eyeing his superior with increasing surprise, but at last seemed struck with a thought which somewhat explained all the wonder. "Captain Ahab, I have heard of Moby-Dick—but it was not Moby-Dick that took off thy leg?"

"Who told thee that?" cried Ahab; then pausing, "Aye, Starbuck; aye, my hearties all round; it was Moby-Dick that dismasted me; Moby-Dick that brought me to this dead stump I stand on now. Aye, aye," he shouted with a terrific, loud, animal sob, like that of a heart-stricken moose; "Aye, aye! it was that accursed white whale that razeed me; made a poor pegging lubber[8] for me forever and a day!" Then tossing both arms, with measureless imprecations he shouted out: "Aye, aye! and I'll chase him round Good Hope, and round the Horn, and round the Norway Maelstrom, and round perdition's flames before I give him up. And this is what ye have shipped for, men! to chase that white whale on both sides of land, and over all sides of earth, till he spouts black blood and rolls fin out. What say ye, men, will ye splice hands on it, now? I think ye do look brave."

"Aye, aye!" shouted the harpooneers and seamen, running closer to the excited old man: "A sharp eye for the white whale; a sharp lance for Moby-Dick!"

"God bless ye," he seemed to half sob and half shout. "God bless ye, men. Steward! go draw the great measure of grog. But what's this long face about, Mr. Starbuck; wilt thou not chase the white whale? art not game for Moby-Dick?"

"I am game for his crooked jaw, and for the jaws of Death too, Captain Ahab, if it fairly comes in the way of the business we follow; but I came here to hunt whales, not my commander's vengeance. How many barrels will thy vengeance yield thee even if thou gettest it, Captain Ahab? it will not fetch thee much in our Nantucket market."

---

7. **parmacetty** (pär´mə set´ ē) *n.* dialect for spermaceti, a waxy substance taken from a sperm whale's head and used to make candles.

8. **lubber** (lub´ ər) *n.* slow, clumsy person.

✓Reading Check

What does Ahab say is his real purpose for making the voyage?

"Nantucket market! Hoot! But come closer, Starbuck; thou requirest a little lower layer. If money's to be the measurer, man, and the accountants have computed their great countinghouse the globe, by girdling it with guineas, one to every three parts of an inch; then, let me tell thee, that my vengeance will fetch a great premium *here!*"

"He smites his chest," whispered Stubb, "what's that for? methinks it rings most vast, but hollow."

"Vengeance on a dumb brute!" cried Starbuck, "that simply smote thee from blindest instinct! Madness! To be enraged with a dumb thing, Captain Ahab, seems blasphemous."

"Hark ye yet again—the little lower layer. All visible objects, man, are but as pasteboard masks. But in each event—in the living act, the undoubted deed—there, some unknown but still reasoning thing puts forth the moldings of its features from behind the unreasoning mask. If man will strike, strike through the mask! How can the prisoner reach outside except by thrusting through the wall? To me, the white whale is that wall, shoved near to me. Sometimes I think there's naught beyond. But 'tis enough. He tasks me; he heaps me; I see in him outrageous strength, with an <u>inscrutable</u> malice sinewing it. That inscrutable thing is chiefly what I hate; and be the white whale agent, or be the white whale principal, I will wreak that hate upon him. Talk not to me of blasphemy, man; I'd strike the sun if it insulted me. For could the sun do that, then could I do the other; since there is ever a sort of fair play herein, jealousy presiding over all creations. But not my master, man, is even that fair play. Who's over me? Truth hath no confines. Take off thine eye! more intolerable than fiends' glarings is a doltish stare! So, so; thou reddenest and palest; my heat has melted thee to anger-glow. But look ye, Starbuck, what is said in heat, that thing unsays itself. There are men from whom warm words are small indignity. I meant not to incense thee. Let it go. Look! see yonder Turkish cheeks of spotted tawn—living, breathing pictures painted by the sun. The pagan leopards—the unrecking and unworshiping things, that live, and seek, and give no reasons for the torrid life they feel! The crew, man, the crew! Are they not one and all with Ahab, in this matter of the whale? See Stubb! he laughs! See yonder Chilean! he snorts to think of it. Stand up amid the general hurricane, thy one tossed sapling cannot, Starbuck! And what is it? Reckon it. 'Tis but to help strike a fin; no wondrous feat for Starbuck. What is it more? From this one poor hunt, then, the best lance out of all Nantucket, surely he will not hang back, when every foremasthand has clutched a whetstone. Ah! constrainings seize thee; I see! the billow lifts thee! Speak, but speak!—Aye, aye! thy silence, then, that voices thee. *(Aside)* Something shot from my dilated nostrils, he has inhaled it in his lungs. Starbuck now is mine; cannot oppose me now, without rebellion."

"God keep me!—keep us all!" murmured Starbuck, lowly.

But in his joy at the enchanted, tacit acquiescence of the mate, Ahab did not hear his foreboding invocation; nor yet the low laugh

Literary Analysis
Symbol and Theme What do Ahab's comments say about the value of money compared with great desire?

inscrutable (in skrōōt´ ə bəl) *adj.* not able to be easily understood

Literary Analysis
Symbol What insights into the whale's symbolic meaning can you gain from a close reading of this passage?

from the hold; nor yet the presaging vibrations of the winds in the cordage; nor yet the hollow flap of the sails against the masts, as for a moment their hearts sank in. For again Starbuck's downcast eyes lighted up with the stubbornness of life; the subterranean laugh died away; the winds blew on; the sails filled out; the ship heaved and rolled as before. Ah, ye admonitions and warnings! why stay ye not when ye come? But rather are ye predictions than warnings, ye shadows! Yet not so much predictions from without, as verifications of the fore-going things within. For with little external to constrain us, the innermost necessities in our being, these still drive us on.

"The measure! the measure!" cried Ahab.

Receiving the brimming pewter, and turning to the harpooneers, he ordered them to produce their weapons. Then ranging them before him near the capstan,[9] with their harpoons in their hands, while his three mates stood at his side with their lances, and the rest of the ship's company formed a circle round the group; he stood for an instant searchingly eyeing every man of his crew. But those wild eyes met his, as the bloodshot eyes of the prairie wolves meet the eye of their leader, ere he rushes on at their head in the trail of the bison; but, alas! only to fall into the hidden snare of the Indian.

Literature in context   History Connection

The Legend of the White Whale

Herman Melville's whaling experiences in the South Pacific provided him with rich material for his writing. While working aboard the whaling ship *Acushnet,* he often heard stories about an elusive, monstrous white whale. Melville expanded this legend—adding his knowledge of the day-to-day workings of a whaler—into his best-known work, *Moby-Dick.*

"Drink and pass!" he cried, handing the heavy charged flagon to the nearest seaman. "The crew alone now drink. Round with it, round! Short drafts—long swallows, men; 'tis hot as Satan's hoof. So, so; it goes round excellently. It spiralizes in ye; forks out at the serpent-snapping eye. Well done; almost drained. That way it went, this way it comes. Hand it me—here's a hollow! Men, ye seem the years; so brimming life is gulped and gone. Steward, refill!

"Attend now, my braves. I have mustered ye all round this capstan; and ye mates, flank me with your lances; and ye harpooneers, stand there with your irons; and ye, stout mariners, ring me in, that I may in some sort revive a noble custom of my fishermen fathers before

---

9. **capstan** (kap´ sten) *n.* large cylinder, turned by hand, around which cables are wound.

✓Reading Check

With whom does Ahab share a drink? For what purpose?

me. O men, you will yet see that—Ha! boy, come back? bad pennies come not sooner. Hand it me. Why, now, this pewter had run brimming again, wer't not thou St. Vitus' imp[10]—away, thou ague![11]

"Advance, ye mates! cross your lances full before me. Well done! Let me touch the axis." So saying, with extended arm, he grasped the three level, radiating lances at their crossed center; while so doing, suddenly and nervously twitched them; meanwhile glancing intently from Starbuck to Stubb; from Stubb to Flask. It seemed as though, by some nameless, interior volition, he would fain have shocked into them the same fiery emotion accumulated within the Leyden jar[12] of his own magnetic life. The three mates quailed before his strong, sustained, and mystic aspect. Stubb and Flask looked sideways from him; the honest eye of Starbuck fell downright.

"In vain!" cried Ahab; "but, maybe, 'tis well. For did ye three but once take the full-forced shock, then mine own electric thing, *that* had perhaps expired from out me. Perchance, too, it would have dropped ye dead. Perchance ye need it not. Down lances! And now, ye mates, I do appoint ye three cupbearers to my three pagan kinsmen there—yon three most honorable gentlemen and noblemen, my valiant harpooneers. Disdain the task? What, when the great Pope washes the feet of beggars, using his tiara for ewer? Oh, my sweet cardinals! your own condescension, that shall bend ye to it. I do not order ye; ye will it. Cut your seizings and draw the poles, ye harpooneers!"

Silently obeying the order, the three harpooneers now stood with the detached iron part of their harpoons, some three feet long, held, barbs up, before him.

"Stab me not with that keen steel! Cant them; cant them over! know ye not the goblet end? Turn up the socket! So, so; now, ye cupbearers, advance. The irons! take them; hold them while I fill!" Forthwith, slowly going from one officer to the other, he brimmed the harpoon sockets with the fiery waters from the pewter.

"Now, three to three, ye stand. Commend the murderous chalices! Bestow them, ye who are now made parties to this indissoluble league. Ha! Starbuck! but the deed is done! Yon ratifying sun now waits to sit upon it. Drink, ye harpooneers! drink and swear, ye men that man the deathful whaleboat's bow—Death to Moby-Dick! God hunt us all, if we do not hunt Moby-Dick to his death!" The long, barbed steel goblets were lifted; and to cries and <u>maledictions</u> against the white whale, the spirits were simultaneously quaffed down with a hiss. Starbuck paled, and turned, and shivered. Once more, and finally, the replenished pewter went the rounds among the frantic crew; when, waving his free hand to them, they all dispersed; and Ahab retired within his cabin.

---

10. **St. Vitus' imp** offspring of St. Vitus, the patron saint of people stricken with the nervous disorder chorea, which is characterized by irregular, jerking movements.
11. **ague** (ā′ gyōō) *n.* a chill or fit of shivering.
12. **Leyden** (līd′ ən) **jar** *n.* glass jar coated inside and out with tinfoil and having a metal rod connected to the inner lining; used to condense static electricity.

Literary Analysis
Symbol What is Ahab's symbolic purpose in having his harpooners drink from their weapons?

maledictions (mal′ ə dik′ shənz) *n.* curses

Moby-Dick, Rockwell Kent

After Moby-Dick has been sighted in the Pacific Ocean, the Pequod's boats pursue the whale for two days. One of the boats has been sunk, and Ahab's ivory leg has been broken off. However, as the next day dawns, the chase continues.

The Chase—Third Day

The morning of the third day dawned fair and fresh, and once more the solitary night man at the foremasthead was relieved by crowds of the daylight lookouts, who dotted every mast and almost every spar.

"D'ye see him?" cried Ahab; but the whale was not yet in sight.

"In his infallible wake, though; but follow that wake, that's all. Helm there; steady, as thou goest, and hast been going. What a lovely day again! were it a new-made world, and made for a summerhouse to the angels, and this morning the first of its throwing open to them, a fairer day could not dawn upon that world. Here's food for thought, had Ahab time to think; but Ahab never thinks; he only feels, feels, feels; that's tingling enough for mortal man! to think's audacity. God only has that right and privilege. Thinking is, or ought to be, a coolness and a calmness; and our poor hearts throb, and our poor brains beat too much for that. And yet, I've sometimes thought my brain was very calm—frozen calm, this old skull cracks so, like a glass in which the contents turned to ice, and shiver it. And still this hair is growing now; this moment growing, and heat must breed it; but no, it's like that sort of common grass that will grow anywhere, between the earthy clefts of Greenland ice or in Vesuvius lava. How the wild winds blow it; they whip it about me as the torn shreds of split sails lash the tossed ship they cling to. A vile wind that has no doubt blown ere this through prison corridors and cells, and wards of hospitals, and ventilated them, and now comes blowing hither as innocent as fleeces.[13] Out upon it!—it's tainted. Were I the wind, I'd blow no more on such a wicked, miserable world. I'd crawl somewhere to a cave, and slink there. And yet, 'tis a noble and heroic thing, the wind! who ever conquered it? In every fight it has the last and bitterest blow. Run tilting at it, and you but run through it. Ha! a coward wind that strikes stark-naked men, but will not stand to receive

---

13. **fleeces** (flēs´ əz) *n.* sheep.

▲ Critical Viewing
Draw an inference about the size of the whale pictured. On what details do you base your inference? **[Infer]**

Reading Strategy
Recognizing Symbols
What does the wind symbolize to Ahab?

✔ Reading Check
For how long has the *Pequod* pursued Moby-Dick?

a single blow. Even Ahab is a braver thing—a nobler thing than *that.* Would now the wind but had a body but all the things that most exasperate and outrage mortal man, all these things are bodiless, but only bodiless as objects, not as agents. There's a most special, a most cunning, oh, a most malicious difference! And yet, I say again, and swear it now, that there's something all glorious and gracious in the wind. These warm trade winds, at least, that in the clear heavens blow straight on, in strong and steadfast, vigorous mildness; and veer not from their mark, however the baser currents of the sea may turn and tack, and mightiest Mississippis of the land swift and swerve about, uncertain where to go at last. And by the eternal poles! these same trades that so directly blow my good ship on; these trades, or something like them—something so unchangeable, and full as strong, blow my keeled soul along! To it! Aloft there! What d'ye see?"

"Nothing, sir."

"Nothing! and noon at hand! The doubloon[14] goes a-begging! See the sun! Aye, aye, it must be so. I've oversailed him. How, got the start? Aye, he's chasing me now; not I, him—that's bad; I might have known it, too. Fool! the lines—the harpoons he's towing.

Aye, aye, I have run him by last night. About! about! Come down, all of ye, but the regular lookouts! Man the braces!"

Steering as she had done, the wind had been somewhat on the Pequod's quarter, so that now being pointed in the reverse direction, the braced ship sailed hard upon the breeze as she rechurned the cream in her own white wake.

"Against the wind he now steers for the open jaw," murmured Starbuck to himself, as he coiled the new-hauled main brace upon the rail. "God keep us, but already my bones feel damp within me, and from the inside wet my flesh. I misdoubt me that I disobey my God in obeying him!"

"Stand by to sway me up!" cried Ahab, advancing to the hempen basket.[15] "We should meet him soon."

"Aye, aye, sir," and straightway Starbuck did Ahab's bidding, and once more Ahab swung on high.

A whole hour now passed; gold-beaten out to ages. Time itself now held long breaths with keen suspense. But at last, some three points off the weather bow, Ahab descried the spout again, and instantly from the three mastheads three shrieks went up as if the tongues of fire had voiced it.

"Forehead to forehead I meet thee, this third time, Moby-Dick! On deck there!—brace sharper up; crowd her into the wind's eye. He's too far off to lower yet, Mr. Starbuck. The sails shake! Stand over that helmsman with

---

14. **doubloon** (du bloon´) *n.* old Spanish gold coin. (Ahab offered it as a reward to the first man to spot the whale.)

15. **hempen basket** rope basket. (The basket was constructed earlier by Ahab, so that he could be raised, by means of a pulley device, to the top of the mainmast.)

Literature in context Humanities Connec

The Whale as Archetype

An archetype is a basic or primordial image that recurs so consistently across cultures and time that it is considered universal. The term comes from the writings of Swiss psychologist Carl Jung (1875–1961), who believed that certain human experiences have been transferred through generations. According to Jung, it is this shared genetic memory, or "collective unconscious," that explains why archetypes evoke similar strong feelings in people of all cultures.

The whale had made many appearances in myth, folklore, literature, and art well before Melville used it as a central symbol in *Moby-Dick*. Perhaps the most famous is the biblical tale in which Jonah is swallowed by a whale and then cast ashore. Because the whale is the largest of all earthly creatures, its image evokes emotions of fear, awe, and respect, as well as a sense of the enormity of nature. In *Moby-Dick*, Melville understood and used these archetypal associations to create fiction of enduring power.

a topmaul! So, so; he travels fast, and I must down. But let me have one more good round look aloft here at the sea; there's time for that. An old, old sight, and yet somehow so young; aye, and not changed a wink since I first saw it, a boy, from the sand hills of Nantucket! The same!—the same!—the same to Noah as to me. There's a soft shower to leeward. Such lovely leewardings! They must lead somewhere—to something else than common land, more palmy than the palms. Leeward! the white whale goes that way; look to windward, then; the better if the bitterer quarter. But good-bye, good-bye, old masthead! What's this?—green? aye, tiny mosses in these warped cracks. No such green weather stains on Ahab's head! There's the difference now between man's old age and matter's. But aye, old mast, we both grow old together; sound in our hulls, though, are we not, my ship? Aye, minus a leg, that's all. By heaven this dead wood has the better of my live flesh every way. I can't compare with it; and I've known some ships made of dead trees outlast the lives of men made of the most vital stuff of vital fathers. What's that he said? he should still go before me, my pilot; and yet to be seen again? But where? Will I have eyes at the bottom of the sea, supposing I descend those endless stairs? and all night I've been sailing from him, wherever he did sink to. Aye, aye, like many more thou told'st direful truth as touching thyself, O Parsee; but, Ahab, there thy shot fell short. Good-bye, masthead—keep a good eye upon the whale, the while I'm gone. We'll talk tomorrow, nay, tonight, when the white whale lies down there, tied by head and tail."

He gave the word; and still gazing round him, was steadily lowered through the cloven blue air to the deck.

In due time the boats were lowered; but as standing in his shallop's stern, Ahab just hovered upon the point of the descent, he waved to the mate—who held one of the tackle ropes on deck—and bade him pause.

"Starbuck!"

"Sir?"

"For the third time my soul's ship starts upon this voyage, Starbuck."

"Aye, sir, thou wilt have it so."

"Some ships sail from their ports, and ever afterwards are missing, Starbuck!"

"Truth, sir: saddest truth."

"Some men die at ebb tide; some at low water; some at the full of the flood—and I feel now like a billow that's all one crested comb, Starbuck. I am old—shake hands with me, man."

Their hands met; their eyes fastened; Starbuck's tears the glue.

"Oh, my captain, my captain!—noble heart—go not—go not!—see, it's a brave man that weeps; how great the agony of the persuasion then!"

"Lower away!"—cried Ahab, tossing the mate's arm from him. "Stand by the crew!"

In an instant the boat was pulling round close under the stern.

"The sharks! the sharks!" cried a voice from the low cabin window there; "O master, my master, come back!"

Literary Analysis
Symbol What symbolic meaning do you find in the comparison between Ahab and the mast?

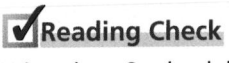Reading Check
What does Starbuck beg Ahab to do?

But Ahab heard nothing; for his own voice was high-lifted then; and the boat leaped on.

Yet the voice spake true; for scarce had he pushed from the ship, when numbers of sharks, seemingly rising from out the dark waters beneath the hull, maliciously snapped at the blades of the oars, every time they dipped in the water; and in this way accompanied the boat with their bites. It is a thing not uncommonly happening to the whaleboats in those swarming seas; the sharks at times apparently following them in the same prescient way that vultures hover over the banners of marching regiments in the east. But these were the first sharks that had been observed by the *Pequod* since the White Whale had been first descried; and whether it was that Ahab's crew were all such tiger-yellow barbarians, and therefore their flesh more musky to the senses of the sharks—a matter sometimes well known to affect them—however it was, they seemed to follow that one boat without molesting the others.

prescient (presh´ent) *adj.*
having foreknowledge

Moby-Dick, Rockwell Kent

"Heart of wrought steel!" murmured Starbuck gazing over the side, and following with his eyes the receding boat—"canst thou yet ring boldly to that sight?—lowering thy keel among ravening sharks, and followed by them, open-mouthed to the chase; and this the critical third day?—For when three days flow together in one continuous intense pursuit; be sure the first is the morning, the second the noon, and the third the evening and the end of that thing—be that end what it may. Oh! my God! what is this that shoots through me, and leaves me so deadly calm, yet expectant—fixed at the top of a shudder! Future things swim before me, as in empty outlines and skeletons; all the past is somehow grown dim. Mary, girl; thou fadest in pale glories behind me; boy! I seem to see but thy eyes grown wondrous blue.[16] Strangest problems of life seem clearing; but clouds sweep between—Is my journey's end coming? My legs feel faint; like his who has footed it all day. Feel thy heart—beats it yet? Stir thyself, Starbuck!—stave it off—move, move! speak aloud!—Masthead there! See ye my boy's hand on the hill?—Crazed—aloft there!—keep thy keenest eye upon the boats—mark well the whale!—Ho! again!—drive off that hawk! see! he pecks—he tears the vane"—pointing to the red flag flying at the maintruck—"Ha,

▲ Critical Viewing
What details from *Moby-Dick* did the artist probably use to create this illustration? **[Hypothesize]**

---

16. Mary . . . blue reference to Starbuck's wife and son.

he soars away with it!—Where's the old man now? see'st thou that sight, oh Ahab!—shudder, shudder!"

The boats had not gone very far, when by a signal from the mast-heads—a downward pointed arm, Ahab knew that the whale had sounded; but intending to be near him at the next rising, he held on his way a little sideways from the vessel; the becharmed crew maintaining the profoundest silence, as the head-beat waves hammered and hammered against the opposing bow.

"Drive, drive in your nails, oh ye waves! to their uttermost heads drive them in! ye but strike a thing without a lid; and no coffin and no hearse can be mine:—and hemp only can kill me! Ha! ha!"

Suddenly the waters around them slowly swelled in broad circles; then quickly upheaved, as if sideways sliding from a submerged berg of ice, swiftly rising to the surface. A low rumbling sound was heard; a subterraneous hum; and then all held their breaths; as bedraggled with trailing ropes, and harpoons, and lances, a vast form shot lengthwise, but obliquely from the sea. Shrouded in a thin drooping veil of mist, it hovered for a moment in the rainbowed air; and then fell swamping back into the deep. Crushed thirty feet upwards, the waters flashed for an instant like heaps of fountains, then brokenly sank in a shower of flakes, leaving the circling surface creamed like new milk round the marble trunk of the whale.

Literary Analysis
Symbol What symbolic meaning is suggested by the description of the whale's behavior as he breaks the water's surface?

"Give way!" cried Ahab to the oarsmen, and the boats darted forward to the attack; but maddened by yesterday's fresh irons that corroded in him, Moby-Dick seemed combinedly possessed by all the angels that fell from heaven. The wide tiers of welded tendons overspreading his broad white forehead, beneath the transparent skin, looked knitted together; as head on, he came churning his tail among the boats; and once more flailed them apart; spilling out the irons and lances from the two mates' boats, and dashing in one side of the upper part of their bows, but leaving Ahab's almost without a scar.

While Daggoo and Queequeg were stopping the strained planks; and as the whale swimming out from them, turned, and showed one entire flank as he shot by them again; at that moment a quick cry went up. Lashed round and round to the fish's back; pinioned in the turns upon turns in which, during the past night, the whale had reeled the involutions of the lines around him, the half-torn body of the Parsee was seen; his sable raiment frayed to shreds; his distended eyes turned full upon old Ahab.

The harpoon dropped from his hand.

"Befooled, befooled!"—drawing in a long lean breath—"Aye, Parsee! I see thee again—Aye, and thou goest before; and this, this then is the hearse that thou didst promise. But I hold thee to the last letter of thy word. Where is the second hearse? Away, mates, to the ship! those boats are useless now; repair them if ye can in time, and return to me; if not, Ahab is enough to die—Down, men! the first thing that but offers to jump from this boat I stand in, that thing I harpoon. Ye are not other men, but my arms and my legs; and so obey me—Where's the whale? gone down again?"

Reading Strategy
Recognizing Symbols
What does Ahab realize when he sees Parsee's body lashed to Moby-Dick?

**Reading Check**

What happens to Parsee?

But he looked too nigh the boat; for as if bent upon escaping with the corpse he bore, and as if the particular place of the last encounter had been but a stage in his leeward voyage, Moby-Dick was now again steadily swimming forward; and had almost passed the ship—which thus far had been sailing in the contrary direction to him, though for the present her headway had been stopped. He seemed swimming with his utmost velocity, and now only intent upon pursuing his own straight path in the sea.

"Oh! Ahab," cried Starbuck, "not too late is it, even now, the third day, to desist. See! Moby-Dick seeks thee not. It is thou, thou, that madly seekest him!"

Setting sail to the rising wind, the lonely boat was swiftly impelled to leeward, by both oars and canvas. And at last when Ahab was sliding by the vessel, so near as plainly to distinguish Starbuck's face as he leaned over the rail, he hailed him to turn the vessel about, and follow him, not too swiftly, at a judicious interval. Glancing upwards he saw Tashtego, Queequeg, and Daggoo, eagerly mounting to the three mast-heads; while the oarsmen were rocking in the two staved boats which had just been hoisted to the side, and were busily at work in repairing them, one after the other, through the portholes, as he sped, he also caught flying glimpses of Stubb and Flask, busying themselves on deck among bundles of new irons and lances. As he saw all this; as he heard the hammers in the broken boats; far other hammers seemed driving a nail into his heart. But he rallied. And now marking that the vane or flag was gone from the main masthead, he shouted to Tashtego, who had just gained that perch, to descend again for another flag, and a hammer and nails, and so nail it to the mast.

Whether fagged by the three days' running chase, and the resistance to his swimming in the knotted hamper he bore; or whether it was some latent deceitfulness and malice in him: whichever was true, the White Whale's way now began to abate, as it seemed, from the boat so rapidly nearing him once more; though indeed the whale's last start had not been so long a one as before. And still as Ahab glided over the waves the unpitying sharks accompanied him; and so pertinaciously stuck to the boat; and so continually bit at the plying oars, that the blades became jagged and crunched, and left small splinters in the sea, at almost every dip.

"Heed them not! those teeth but give new rowlocks to your oars. Pull on! 'tis the better rest, the sharks' jaw than the yielding water."

"But at every bite, sir, the thin blades grow smaller and smaller!"

"They will last long enough! pull on!—But who can tell"—he muttered—"whether these sharks swim to feast on the whale or on Ahab?—But pull on! Aye, all alive, now—we near him. The helm! take the helm! let me pass"—and so saying, two of the oarsmen helped him forward to the bows of the still flying boat.

At length as the craft was cast to one side, and ran ranging along with the White Whale's flank, he seemed strangely oblivious of its advance—as the whale sometimes will—and Ahab was fairly within

Literary Analysis
Symbol and Theme
What does Melville mean when he describes Ahab as being tormented by "far other hammers?"

pertinaciously (pʉr′ tə nā′ shəs lē) *adv.* holding firmly to some purpose

the smoky mountain mist, which, thrown off from the whale's spout, curled round his great Monadnock[17] hump; he was even thus close to him; when, with body arched back, and both arms lengthwise high-lifted to the poise, he darted his fierce iron, and his far fiercer curse into the hated whale. As both steel and curse sank to the socket, as if sucked into a morass, Moby-Dick sidewise writhed; spasmodically rolled his nigh flank against the bow, and, without staving a hole in it, so suddenly canted the boat over, that had it not been for the elevated part of the gunwale to which he then clung, Ahab would once more have been tossed into the sea. As it was, three of the oarsmen—who foreknew not the precise instant of the dart, and were therefore unprepared for its effects—these were flung out; but so fell, that, in an instant two of them clutched the gunwale again, and rising to its level on a combing wave, hurled themselves bodily inboard again; the third man helplessly dropping astern, but still afloat and swimming.

Almost simultaneously, with a mighty volition of ungraduated, instantaneous swiftness, the White Whale darted through the weltering sea. But when Ahab cried out to the steersman to take new turns with the line, and hold it so; and commanded the crew to turn round on their seats, and tow the boat up to the mark; the moment the treacherous line felt that double strain and tug, it snapped in the empty air!

"What breaks in me? Some sinew cracks!—'tis whole again; oars! oars! Burst in upon him!"

Hearing the tremendous rush of the sea-crashing boat, the whale wheeled round to present his blank forehead at bay; but in that evo-lution, catching sight of the nearing black hull of the ship; seemingly seeing in it the source of all his persecutions; bethinking it—it may be—a larger and nobler foe; of a sudden, he bore down upon its advancing prow, smiting his jaws amid fiery showers of foam.

Ahab staggered; his hand smote his forehead. "I grow blind; hands! stretch out before me that I may yet grope my way. Is't night?"

"The whale! The ship!" cried the cringing oarsmen.

"Oars! oars! Slope downwards to thy depths. O sea that ere it be forever too late, Ahab may slide this last, last time upon his mark! I see: the ship! the ship! Dash on, my men! will ye not save my ship?"

But as the oarsmen violently forced their boat through the sledge-hammering seas, the before whale-smitten bow-ends of two planks burst through, and in an instant almost, the temporarily disabled boat lay nearly level with the waves; its half-wading, splashing crew, trying hard to stop the gap and bale out the pouring water.

Meantime, for that one beholding instant, Tashtego's masthead hammer remained suspended in his hand; and the red flag, half wrapping him as with a plaid, then streamed itself straight out from him, as his own forward-flowing heart; while Starbuck and Stubb, standing upon the bowsprit beneath, caught sight of the down-coming monster just as soon as he.

---

17. **Monadnock** (mə nad´ näk) mountain in New Hampshire.

Literary Analysis
Symbol What symbolic connection between his own body and the boat does Ahab seem to feel?

Reading Strategy
Recognizing Symbols What is symbolized by the red flag streaming out from Tashtego?

Reading Check

What happens to the boat carrying Ahab when it nears Moby-Dick?

"The whale, the whale! Up helm, up helm! Oh, all ye sweet powers of air, now hug me close! Let not Starbuck die, if die he must, in a woman's fainting fit. Up helm I say—ye fools, the jaw! the jaw! Is this the end of all my bursting prayers? all my lifelong fidelities? Oh, Ahab, Ahab, lo, thy work. Steady! helmsman, steady. Nay, nay! Up helm again! He turns to meet us! Oh, his unappeasable brow drives on towards one, whose duty tells him he cannot depart. My God, stand by me now!"

"Stand not by me, but stand under me, whoever you are that will now help Stubb; for Stubb, too, sticks here. I grin at thee, thou grinning whale! Who ever helped Stubb, or kept Stubb awake, but Stubb's own unwinking eye? And now poor Stubb goes to bed upon a mattress that is all too soft; would it were stuffed with brushwood! I grin at thee, thou grinning whale! Look ye, sun, moon, and stars! I call ye assassins of as good a fellow as ever spouted up his ghost. For all that, I would yet ring glasses with thee, would ye but hand the cup! Oh, oh! oh, oh! thou grinning whale, but there'll be plenty of gulping soon! Why fly ye not, O Ahab! For me, off shoes and jacket to it; let Stubb die in his drawers! A most moldy and oversalted death, though—cherries! cherries! cherries! Oh, Flask, for one red cherry ere we die!"

"Cherries? I only wish that we were where they grow. Oh, Stubb, I hope my poor mother's drawn my part-pay ere this; if not, few coppers will now come to her, for the voyage is up."

From the ship's bows, nearly all the seamen now hung inactive; hammers, bits of plank, lances, and harpoons, mechanically retained in their hands, just as they had darted from their various employments; all their enchanted eyes intent upon the whale, which from side to side strangely vibrating his predestinating head, sent a broad band of overspreading semicircular foam before him as he rushed. Retribution, swift vengeance, eternal malice were in his whole aspect, and spite of all that mortal man could do, the solid white buttress of his forehead smote the ship's starboard bow, till men and timbers reeled. Some fell flat upon their faces. Like dislodged trucks, the heads of the harpooneers aloft shook on their bull-like necks. Through the breach, they heard the waters pour, as mountain torrents down a flume.

"The ship! The hearse!—the second hearse!" cried Ahab from the boat; "its wood could only be American!"

Diving beneath the settling ship, the whale ran quivering along its keel; but turning under water, swiftly shot to the surface again, far off the other bow, but within a few yards of Ahab's boat, where, for a time, he lay quiescent.

"I turn my body from the sun. What ho, Tashtego! let me hear thy hammer. Oh! ye three unsurrendered spires of mine; thou uncracked keel; and only god-bullied hull; thou firm deck, and haughty helm, and Polepointed prow—death-glorious ship! must ye then perish, and without me? Am I cut off from the last fond pride of meanest ship-wrecked captains? Oh, lonely death on lonely life! Oh, now I feel my

Literary Analysis
Symbol What details in this paragraph suggest that the whale has become a symbol of retribution?

Literary Analysis
Symbol and Theme What thematic elements come together in Ahab's climactic speech?

topmost greatness lies in my topmost grief. Ho, ho! from all your furthest bounds, pour ye now in, ye bold billows of my whole foregone life, and top this one piled comber of my death! Towards thee I roll, thou all-destroying but unconquering whale; to the last I grapple with thee; from hell's heart I stab at thee; for hate's sake I spit my last breath at thee. Sink all coffins and all hearses to one common pool! and since neither can be mine, let me then tow to pieces, while still chasing thee, though tied to thee, thou damned whale! *Thus*, I give up the spear!"

The harpoon was darted; the stricken whale flew forward; with igniting velocity the line ran through the groove;—ran foul. Ahab stooped to clear it; he did clear it; but the flying turn caught him round the neck, and voicelessly as Turkish mutes bowstring their victim, he was shot out of the boat, ere the crew knew he was gone. Next instant, the heavy eye splice in the rope's final end flew out of the stark-empty tub, knocked down an oarsman, and smiting the sea, disappeared in its depths.

For an instant, the tranced boat's crew stood still; then turned. "The ship? Great God, where is the ship?" Soon they through dim, bewildering mediums saw her sidelong fading phantom, as in the gaseous fata morgana,[18] only the uppermost masts out of water: while fixed by infatuation, or fidelity, or fate, to their once lofty perches, the pagan harpooneers still maintained their sinking lookouts on the sea. And now, concentric circles seized the lone boat itself, and all its crew, and each floating oar, and every lance pole, and spinning, animate and inanimate, all round and round in one vortex, carried the smallest chip of the *Pequod* out of sight.

But as the last whelmings intermixingly poured themselves over the sunken head of the Indian at the mainmast, leaving a few inches of the erect spar yet visible, together with long streaming yards of the flag, which calmly undulated, with ironical coincidings, over the destroying billows they almost touched—at that instant, a red arm and a hammer hovered backwardly uplifted in the open air, in the act of nailing the flag faster and yet faster to the subsiding spar. A sky hawk that tauntingly had followed the main-truck downwards from its natural home among the stars, pecking at the flag, and

---

18. fata morgana
(fät´ ə môr gän´ ə) *n.* mirage seen at sea.

✓**Reading Check**

What happens to the *Pequod*?

▼ **Critical Viewing**
In this image from a film version of Moby-Dick, how do the filmmakers use a sense of scale to suggest the whale's overwhelming power? **[Analyze]**

incommoding Tashtego there: this bird now chanced to intercept its broad fluttering wing between the hammer and the wood: and simultaneously feeling that ethereal thrill, the submerged savage beneath, in his deathgasp, kept his hammer frozen there: and so the bird of heaven, with archangelic shrieks, and his imperial beak thrust upwards, and his whole captive form folded in the flag of Ahab, went down with his ship, which, like Satan, would not sink to hell till she had dragged a living part of heaven along with her, and helmeted herself with it.

Now small fowls flew screaming over the yet yawning gulf; a sullen white surf beat against its steep sides; then all collapsed, and the great shroud of the sea rolled on as it rolled five thousand years ago.

Review and Assess

Thinking About the Selection

1. **Respond:** Do you admire, despise, or pity Captain Ahab? Explain.

2. **(a) Recall:** What does Ahab offer to the crew member who spots Moby-Dick? **(b) Infer:** Why does Ahab feel it necessary to offer this incentive to his crew?

3. **(a) Recall:** What happened to Ahab in his previous encounter with Moby-Dick? **(b) Interpret:** What does Ahab's obsession with Moby-Dick reveal about his character? **(c) Compare and Contrast:** In what ways is Starbuck different from Ahab?

4. **(a) Recall:** How does Starbuck interpret Ahab's obsession with Moby-Dick? **(b) Analyze:** Why does Starbuck obey Ahab even though he disagrees with him?

5. **(a) Recall:** What happens to Ahab, Moby-Dick, and the *Pequod* at the end? **(b) Analyze:** What does the final paragraph indicate about the relationship between humanity and nature?

6. **(a) Recall:** What is Moby-Dick's reaction when the *Pequod* first approaches his flank? **(b) Compare and Contrast:** How does Moby-Dick's reaction to the ship illuminate the differences between the whale in reality and in Ahab's imagination?

7. **(a) Interpret:** What does Ahab mean when he says, "Ahab never thinks; he only feels, feels, feels; that's tingling enough for mortal man! to think's audacity." **(b) Evaluate:** Do you think Ahab's beliefs about human nature are true? Explain.

8. **Take a Position:** This novel has been called a "voyage of the soul." Would you agree or disagree with that assessment? Explain.

Review and Assess

Literary Analysis

Symbol

1. What omens appear (a) as Ahab's whaleboat pulls away from the *Pequod* and (b) when Moby-Dick surfaces? (c) What is Ahab's reaction to these omens?

2. The color white is often used as a **symbol** for innocence, as well as for absence and death. What contradictory symbolic meanings does the whale's whiteness convey?

3. If the crew of the *Pequod* symbolizes humanity and Moby-Dick symbolizes nature, what do you think the ship's voyage symbolizes?

Connecting Literary Elements

4. (a) Use a chart like the one shown to compare and contrast the characters of Starbuck and Ahab. (b) What **theme** is Melville expressing through these contrasting characters?

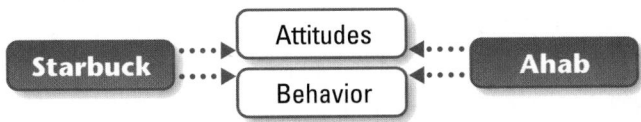

5. Considering the journey's symbolic meaning and its terrible outcome, speculate about the novel's overall theme, or central idea.

Reading Strategy

Recognizing Symbols

6. Identify events, dialogue, or descriptions that lead you to **recognize** Moby-Dick as a **symbol** of (a) nature's beauty, (b) nature's power, and (c) nature's immortality. Explain your reasoning.

7. How does this statement by Ishmael suggest a way to look at the symbolic nature of the events he describes:

    "Ah, ye admonitions and warnings! why stay ye not when ye come? But rather are ye predictions than warnings, ye shadows! Yet not so much predictions from without, as verifications of the foregoing things within."

Extend Understanding

8. **Psychology Connection:** (a) With what goals are people obsessed today? (b) In what cases, if any, are obsessions helpful?

Quick Review

A **symbol** is a person, place, or thing that has meaning in itself and also represents something larger.

A **theme** is a central message or insight revealed by a literary work.

To **recognize symbols,** look for characters, places, or objects that are stressed, mentioned repeatedly, or linked to larger ideas.

 Take It to the Net
www.phschool.com
Take the interactive self-test online to check your understanding of the selection.

Integrate Language Skills

Vocabulary Development Lesson

Word Analysis: Latin Prefix *mal-*

The Latin prefix *mal-* means "bad" or "badly." The word *malady* means illness and the word *maladjusted* means "badly adjusted." Select the letter of the definition that best matches each word below.

1. malcontent   a. active ill will
2. malevolent   b. likely to cause death
3. malign   c. wishing harm to others
4. malignant   d. dissatisfied
5. malice   e. to slander

Concept Development: Synonyms

Select the best synonym from the column on the right for each vocabulary word.

1. maledictions   a. tenaciously
2. prescient   b. curses; bad words
3. pertinaciously   c. mysterious
4. inscrutable   d. prophetic

Spelling Strategy

The letters *sc* usually make the sound of *sk*, as in *describe*. Sometimes, however, *sc* makes the sound of *sh*, as in *prescient*, or *s*, as in *science*. Indicate the sound *sc* makes in each of these words.

1. muscles   2. mascot   3. omniscient

Grammar and Style Lesson

Agreement With Collective Nouns

Collective nouns—such as *team* or *flock*—name a group of people or things. A collective noun may be either singular or plural, depending on whether the group it names is seen as a unit (singular) or as a collection of individuals (plural). The verb must always agree in number with the intended meaning of the collective noun.

> **Plural:** When the entire ship's company *were* assembled . . .
> **Singular:** The company *consists* of 150 sailors.

Practice Identify the collective noun in each sentence. Then, write the verb form that agrees with it.

1. The crew ___?___ up. (lines, line)

2. A team of horses ___?___ the hearse. (draws, draw)
3. The crew of the whaling ship ___?___ composed of fine, experienced sailors from all over the world. (is, are)
4. A flock of gulls ___?___ over the ship. (glides, glide)
5. A curious and horrified crowd ___?___ quickly near the site of the grisly accident. (gathers, gather)

Writing Application Use each of these collective nouns—*audience, herd, jury*—in two different sentences. In the first, construct a situation that calls for a singular verb; in the second, construct a sentence that requires a plural verb.

WG Prentice Hall Writing and Grammar Connection: Chapter 23, Section 1

Writing Lesson

Character Study

For some readers, Ahab's obsession with Moby-Dick borders on madness. For others, his persistence borders on greatness. Write an essay in which you make your own judgement of Ahab's character. To ensure that your readers understand your ideas, include a brief summary of the story.

Prewriting Gather and interpret details about Ahab. Organize your interpretations into a statement of opinion. This will serve as your working thesis.

Drafting Include information from the beginning, middle, and end of the story to create a brief summary. Then, state your thesis in your introduction. Use one body paragraph to develop each of your supporting ideas about Ahab's character.

Model: Writing a Summary

Beginning: The *Pequod* sets out.

Middle: Ahab tells the crew that he will kill Moby-Dick.

End: In a struggle with Moby-Dick, the ship is destroyed.

Summary: In Ahab's search for Moby-Dick, the *Pequod* is destroyed, and most of her crew killed.

> To write an effective summary, select key elements from the beginning, middle, and end of a text.

Revising Review your essay, making sure that your summary provides the necessary context, and that your opinion is supported by the text.

*W*G *Prentice Hall Writing and Grammar Connection: Chapter 14, Section 2*

Extension Activities

Listening and Speaking Present a **monologue** that Ishmael might have spoken to the whalers who rescued him. As you prepare, pay attention to the following elements:

- Use nautical terms like Melville's.
- Replicate Ishmael's tone.
- Describe the order of events clearly.
- Add descriptive details about the characters.

Write a monologue that is clear, dramatic, and forceful. Then, share it with the class.

Research and Technology Write a **report** concerning the species of whales that face possible extinction today and what efforts, if any, are being made to save them. Use a series of clear questions to direct your research. Locate answers using field studies, interviews, and news reports from written and electronic sources.

 **Take It to the Net** www.phschool.com

Go online for an additional research activity using the Internet.

CONNECTIONS
Literature Past and Present

Shadows of the Imagination

Edgar Allan Poe, Nathaniel Hawthorne, and Herman Melville are towering figures in American literature. They were fascinated by human behavior, especially that exhibited in extreme situations. Each portrays characters acting in disturbing or extraordinary ways because of an internal conflict or a crisis. Using their powerful imaginations, these writers transform realistic details of daily life into ambiguous, shadowy, and precarious worlds.

In Edgar Allan Poe's work, for instance, gloomy heroes like Roderick Usher languish as their mental equilibrium teeters and the outside world—which once seemed orderly and healthful—collapses. Likewise, many of Nathaniel Hawthorne's characters hold some secret, shadowy knowledge that leads them to behave in unsettling and unaccountable ways; often Hawthorne focuses on the odd ways human beings think and act when they are struggling with dark emotions such as guilt.

Modern Gothic In the twentieth century, only a few American writers have been inclined to embrace the dusky themes, characters, and atmospheres that stamped the work of their Gothic forebears. One of these writers is Joyce Carol Oates. Many of Oates's novels and stories concern individuals whose ordinary lives are suddenly upset by mysterious forces beyond their control. Much of the suspense and emotional power in Oates's fiction can be traced to her depiction of common people who seem powerless to save their identities from alteration or destruction by some shadowy force.

Where *Is* Here?

Joyce Carol Oates

For years they had lived without incident in their house in a quiet residential neighborhood when, one November evening at dusk, the doorbell rang, and the father went to answer it, and there on his doorstep stood a man he had never seen before. The stranger apologized for disturbing him at what was probably the dinner hour and explained that he'd once lived in the house— "I mean, I was a child in this house"—and since he was in the city on business he thought he would drop by. He had not seen the house since January 1949 when

▲ **Critical Viewing**
What details in this photograph lend an air of mystery—even menace—to an ordinary house? **[Analyze]**

he'd been eleven years old and his widowed mother had sold it and moved away but, he said, he thought of it often, dreamt of it often, and never more powerfully than in recent months. The father said, "Would you like to come inside for a few minutes and look around?" The stranger hesitated, then said firmly, "I think I'll just poke around outside for a while, if you don't mind. That might be sufficient." He was in his late forties, the father's approximate age. He wore a dark suit, conservatively cut; he was hatless, with thin silver-tipped neatly combed hair; a plain, sober, intelligent face and frowning eyes. The father, reserved by nature, but <u>genial</u> and even *gregarious* when taken unaware, said amiably, "Of course we don't mind. But I'm afraid many things have changed since 1949."

So, in the chill, damp, deepening dusk, the stranger wandered around the property while the mother set the dining room table and the father peered <u>covertly</u> out the window. The children were upstairs in their rooms. "Where is he now?" the mother asked. "He just went into the garage," the father said. "The garage! What does he want in there!" the mother said uneasily. "Maybe you'd better go out there with him." "He wouldn't want anyone with him," the father said. He moved stealthily to another window, peering through the curtains. A moment passed in silence. The mother, paused in the act of setting down plates, neatly folded paper napkins, and stainless-steel cutlery, said impatiently, "And where is he now? I don't like this." The father said, "Now he's coming out of the garage," and stepped back hastily from the window. "Is he going now?" the mother asked. "I wish I'd answered the door." The father watched for a moment in silence then said, "He's headed into the backyard." "Doing what?" the mother asked. "Not *doing* anything, just walking," the father said. "He seems to have a slight limp." "Is he an older man?" the mother asked. "I didn't notice," the father confessed. "Isn't that just like you!" the mother said.

She went on worriedly, "He could be anyone, after all. Any kind of thief, or mentally disturbed person, or even a murderer. Ringing our doorbell like that with no warning and you don't even know what he looks like!"

The father had moved to another window and stood quietly watching, his cheek pressed against the glass. "He's gone down to the old swings. I hope he won't sit in one of them, for memory's sake, and try to swing—the posts are rotted almost through." The mother drew breath to speak but sighed instead, as if a powerful current of feeling had surged through her. The father was saying, "Is it possible he remembers those swings from his childhood? I can't believe they're actually that old." The mother said vaguely, "They were old when we bought the house." The father said, "But we're talking about forty years or more, and that's a long time." The mother sighed again, involuntarily. "Poor man!" she murmured. She was standing before her table but no longer seeing it. In her hand were objects—forks, knives, spoons—she could not have named. She said, "We can't bar the door against him. That would be cruel." The father said, "What? No one has barred any door against anyone." "Put yourself in his place," the mother said. "He told me he didn't *want* to come inside," the father said. "Oh—isn't that just like you!" the mother said in exasperation.

Without a further word she went to the back door and called out for the stranger to come inside, if he wanted, when he had finished looking around outside.

genial (jēn´ yəl) *adj.* cheerful; friendly

gregarious (grə ger´ ē əs) *adj.* sociable

covertly (kō vərt´ lē) *adv.* secretly; surreptitiously

Thematic Connection
Both the villagers in "The Minister's Black Veil" and the couple in this story are unnerved by the sudden appearance of something mysterious. Compare the reactions each writer describes.

They introduced themselves rather shyly, giving names, and forgetting names, in the confusion of the moment. The stranger's handshake was cool and damp and tentative. He was smiling hard, blinking moisture from his eyes; it was clear that entering his childhood home was enormously exciting yet intimidating to him. Repeatedly he said, "It's so nice of you to invite me in—I truly hate to disturb you—I'm really so grateful, and so—" But the perfect word eluded him. As he spoke his eyes darted about the kitchen almost like eyes out of control. He stood in an odd stiff posture, hands gripping the lapels of his suit as if he meant to crush them. The mother, meaning to break the awkward silence, spoke warmly of their satisfaction with the house and with the neighborhood, and the father concurred, but the stranger listened only politely, and continued to stare, and stare hard. Finally he said that the kitchen had been so changed—"so modernized"— he almost didn't recognize it. The floor tile, the size of the windows, something about the position of the cupboards—all were different. But the sink was in the same place, of course; and the refrigerator and stove; and the door leading down to the basement—"That *is* the door leading down to the basement, isn't it?" He spoke strangely, staring at the door. For a moment it appeared he might ask to be shown the basement but the moment passed, fortunately—this was not a part of their house the father and mother would have been comfortable showing to a stranger.

Finally, making an effort to smile, the stranger said, "Your kitchen is so—pleasant." He paused. For a moment it seemed he had nothing further to say. Then, "A—controlled sort of place. My mother—When we lived here—" His words trailed off into a dreamy silence and the mother and father glanced at each other with carefully neutral expressions.

On the windowsill above the sink were several lushly blooming African violet plants in ceramic pots and these the stranger made a show of admiring. Impulsively he leaned over to sniff the flowers— "Lovely!"—though African violets have no smell. As if embarrassed he

▲ **Critical Viewing**
How does the writer create mystery and suspense from ordinary domestic items like these? **[Connect]**

✔**Reading Check**
What is the stranger doing in the house?

said, "Mother too had plants on this windowsill but I don't recall them ever blooming."

The mother said tactfully, "Oh they were probably the kind that don't bloom—like ivy."

In the next room, the dining room, the stranger appeared to be even more deeply moved. For some time he stood staring, wordless. With fastidious slowness he turned on his heel, blinking, and frowning, and tugging at his lower lip in a rough gesture that must have hurt. Finally, as if remembering the presence of his hosts, and the necessity for some display of civility, the stranger expressed his admiration for the attractiveness of the room, and its coziness. He'd remembered it as cavernous, with a ceiling twice as high. "And dark most of the time," he said wonderingly. "Dark by day, dark by night." The mother turned the lights of the little brass chandelier to their fullest: shadows were dispersed like ragged ghosts and the cut-glass fruit bowl at the center of the table glowed like an exquisite multifaceted jewel. The stranger exclaimed in surprise. He'd extracted a handkerchief from his pocket and was dabbing carefully at his face, where beads of perspiration shone. He said, as if thinking aloud, still wonderingly, "My father was a unique man. Everyone who knew him admired him. He sat *here*," he said, gingerly touching the chair that was in fact the father's chair, at one end of the table. "And Mother sat *there*," he said, merely pointing. "I don't recall my own place or my sister's but I suppose it doesn't matter. . . . I see you have four place settings, Mrs. . . .? Two children, I suppose?" "A boy eleven, and a girl thirteen," the mother said. The stranger stared not at her but at the table, smiling. "And so too *we* were—I mean, there were two of us: my sister and me."

The mother said, as if not knowing what else to say, "Are you—close?"

The stranger shrugged, distractedly rather than rudely, and moved on to the living room.

This room, cozily lit as well, was the most carefully furnished room in the house. Deep-piled wall-to-wall carpeting in hunter green, cheerful chintz drapes, a sofa and matching chairs in nubby heather green, framed reproductions of classic works of art, a gleaming gilt-framed mirror over the fireplace: wasn't the living room impressive as a display in a furniture store? But the stranger said nothing at first. Indeed, his eyes narrowed sharply as if he were confronted with a disagreeable spectacle. He whispered, "Here too! Here too!"

He went to the fireplace, walking, now, with a decided limp; he drew his fingers with excruciating slowness along the mantel as if testing its materiality. For some time he merely stood, and stared, and listened. He tapped a section of wall with his knuckles—"There used to be a large water stain here, like a shadow."

"Was there?" murmured the father out of politeness, and "Was there!" murmured the mother. Of course, neither had ever seen a water stain there.

Then, noticing the window seat, the stranger uttered a soft surprised cry, and went to sit in it. He appeared delighted: hugging his knees like

Thematic Connection
Compare the eerie quality of this scene with the darkness symbolized by the minister's black veil in Hawthorne's story.

a child trying to make himself smaller. "This was one of my happy places! At least when Father wasn't home. I'd hide away here for hours, reading, daydreaming, staring out the window! Sometimes Mother would join me, if she was in the mood, and we'd plot together—oh, all sorts of fantastical things!" The stranger remained sitting in the window seat for so long, tears shining in his eyes, that the father and mother almost feared he'd forgotten them. He was stroking the velvet fabric of the cushioned seat, gropingly touching the leaded windowpanes. Wordlessly, the father and mother exchanged a glance: who was this man, and how could they tactfully get rid of him? The father made a face signaling impatience and the mother shook her head without seeming to move it. For they couldn't be rude to a guest in their house.

The stranger was saying in a slow, dazed voice, "It all comes back to me now. How could I have forgotten! Mother used to read to me, and tell me stories, and ask me riddles I couldn't answer. 'What creature walks on four legs in the morning, two legs at midday, three legs in the evening?' 'What is round, and flat, measuring mere inches in one direction, and infinity in the other?' 'Out of what does our life arise? Out of what does our consciousness arise? Why are we here? Where *is* here?' "

The father and mother were perplexed by these strange words and hardly knew how to respond. The mother said uncertainly, "Our daughter used to like to sit here too, when she was younger. It *is* a lovely place." The father said with surprising passion, "I hate riddles—they're moronic some of the time and obscure the rest of the time." He spoke with such uncharacteristic rudeness, the mother looked at him in surprise.

Hurriedly she said, "Is your mother still living, Mr. . . .?" "Oh no. Not at all," the stranger said, rising abruptly from the window seat, and looking at the mother as if she had said something mildly preposterous. "I'm sorry," the mother said. "Please don't be," the stranger said. "We've all been dead—*they've* all been dead—a long time."

The stranger's cheeks were deeply flushed as if with anger and his breath was quickened and audible.

The visit might have ended at this point but so clearly did the stranger expect to continue on upstairs, so purposefully, indeed almost defiantly, did he limp his way to the stairs, neither the father nor the mother knew how to dissuade him. It was as if a force of nature, benign at the outset, now uncontrollable, had swept its way into their house! The mother followed after him saying nervously, "I'm not sure what condition the rooms are in, upstairs. The children's rooms especially—" The stranger muttered that he did not care in the slightest about the condition of the household and continued on up without a backward glance.

The father, his face burning with resentment and his heart accelerating as if in preparation for combat, had no choice but to follow the stranger and the mother up the stairs. He was flexing and unflexing his fingers as if to rid them of stiffness.

Reading Check

What does the stranger recall about the window seat?

On the landing, the stranger halted abruptly to examine a stained-glass fanlight—"My God, I haven't thought of this in years!" He spoke excitedly of how, on tiptoe, he used to stand and peek out through the diamonds of colored glass, red, blue, green, golden yellow: seeing with amazement the world outside so *altered.* "After such a lesson it's hard to take the world on its own terms, isn't it?" he asked. The father asked, annoyed, "On what terms should it be taken, then?" The stranger replied, regarding him levelly, with a just perceptible degree of disdain, "Why, none at all."

It was the son's room—by coincidence, the stranger's old room—the stranger most wanted to see. Other rooms on the second floor, the "master" bedroom in particular, he decidedly did not want to see. As he spoke of it, his mouth twisted as if he had been offered something repulsive to eat.

The mother hurried on ahead to warn the boy and to straighten up his room a bit. No one had expected a visitor this evening! "So you have two children," the stranger murmured, looking at the father with a small quizzical smile. "Why?" The father stared at him as if he hadn't heard correctly. "'Why'?" he asked. "Yes. *Why?*" the stranger repeated. They looked at each other for a long strained moment, then the stranger said quickly, "But you love them—of course." The father controlled his temper and said, biting off his words, "Of course."

"Of course, of course," the stranger murmured, tugging at his necktie and loosening his collar, "otherwise it would all come to an end." The two men were of approximately the same height but the father was heavier in the shoulders and torso; his hair had thinned more severely so that the scalp of the crown was exposed, flushed, damp with perspiration, sullenly alight.

With a stiff <u>avuncular</u> formality the stranger shook the son's hand. "So this is your room, now! So you live here, now!" he murmured, as if the fact were an astonishment. Not used to shaking hands, the boy was stricken with shyness and cast his eyes down. The stranger limped past him, staring. "The same!—the same!—walls, ceiling,

avuncular (ə vuŋ′ kyoo lər) *adj.* having traits considered typical of uncles: jolly, indulgent, stodgy

▼ **Critical Viewing**
What might the stranger say about a scene like the one shown here? **[Hypothesize]**

floor—window—" He drew his fingers slowly along the windowsill; around the frame; rapped the glass, as if, again, testing materiality; stooped to look outside—but it was night, and nothing but his reflection bobbed in the glass, ghostly and insubstantial. He groped against the walls, he opened the closet door before the mother could protest, he sat heavily on the boy's bed, the springs creaking beneath him. He was panting, red-faced, dazed. "And the ceiling overhead," he whispered. He nodded slowly and repeatedly, smiling. "And the floor beneath. That is what *is*."

He took out his handkerchief again and fastidiously wiped his face. He made a visible effort to compose himself.

The father, in the doorway, cleared his throat and said, "I'm afraid it's getting late—it's almost six."

The mother said, "Oh yes I'm afraid— I'm afraid it *is* getting late. There's dinner, and the children have their homework—"

The stranger got to his feet. At his full height he stood for a precarious moment swaying, as if the blood had drained from his head and he was in danger of fainting. But he steadied himself with a hand against the slanted dormer ceiling. He said, "Oh yes!—I know!—I've disturbed you terribly! —you've been so *kind*." It seemed, surely, as if the stranger *must* leave now, but, as chance had it, he happened to spy, on the boy's desk, an opened mathematics textbook and several smudged sheets of paper, and impulsively offered to show the boy a mathematical riddle—"You can take it to school tomorrow and surprise your teacher!"

So, out of dutiful politeness, the son sat down at his desk and the stranger leaned familiarly over him, demonstrating adroitly with a ruler and a pencil how "what we call 'infinity' " can be contained within a small geometrical figure on a sheet of paper. "First you draw a square; then you draw a triangle to fit inside the square; then you draw a second triangle, and a third, and a fourth, each to fit inside the square, but without their points coinciding, and as you continue— here, son, I'll show you—give me your hand, and I'll show you—the border of the triangles' common outline gets more complex and measures larger, and larger, and larger—and soon you'll need a magnifying glass to see the details, and then you'll need a microscope, and so on and so forth, forever, laying triangles neatly down to fit inside the original square *without their points coinciding—*!" The stranger spoke with increasing fervor; spittle gleamed in the corners of his mouth. The son stared at the geometrical shapes rapidly materializing on the sheet of paper before him with no seeming comprehension but with a rapt staring fascination as if he dared not look away.

After several minutes of this the father came abruptly forward and dropped his hand on the stranger's shoulder. "The visit is over," he said calmly. It was the first time since they'd shaken hands that the two men had touched, and the touch had a <u>galvanic</u> effect upon the stranger: he dropped ruler and pencil at once, froze in his stooped posture, burst into frightened tears.

galvanic (gal van´ ik) *adj.* startling; stimulating as if by electric current

**Reading Check**

What room in the house does the stranger most want to see? Why?

Now the visit truly was over; the stranger, at last, *was* leaving, having wiped away his tears and made a stoical effort to compose himself; but on the doorstep, to the father's astonishment, he made a final, preposterous appeal—he wanted to see the basement. "Just to sit on the stairs? In the dark? For a few quiet minutes? And you could close the door and forget me, you and your family could have your dinner and—"

The stranger was begging but the father was resolute. Without raising his voice he said, "No. *The visit is over.*"

He shut the door, and locked it.

Locked it! His hands were shaking and his heart beat angrily.

He watched the stranger walk away—out to the sidewalk, out to the street, disappearing in the darkness. Had the streetlights gone out?

Behind the father the mother stood apologetic and defensive, wringing her hands in a classic stance. "Wasn't that *sad!* Wasn't that—*sad!* But we had no choice but to let him in, it was the only decent thing to do." The father pushed past her without comment. In the living room he saw that the lights were flickering as if on the brink of going out; the patterned wallpaper seemed drained of color; a shadow lay upon it shaped like a bulbous cloud or growth. Even the robust green of the carpeting looked faded. Or was it an optical illusion? Everywhere the father looked, a pulse beat mute with rage. "*I* wasn't the one who opened the door to that man in the first place," the mother said, coming up behind the father and touching his arm. Without seeming to know what he did the father violently jerked his arm and thrust her away.

"Shut up. We'll forget it," he said.

"But—"

"*We'll forget it.*"

The mother entered the kitchen walking slowly as if she'd been struck a blow. In fact, a bruise the size of a pear would materialize on her forearm by morning. When she reached out to steady herself she misjudged the distance of the door frame—or did the door frame recede an inch or two—and nearly lost her balance.

In the kitchen the lights were dim and an odor of sourish smoke, subtle but unmistakable, made her nostrils pinch.

She slammed open the oven door. Grabbed a pair of pot holders with insulated linings. "*I* wasn't the one, . . ." she cried, panting, "and you know it."

Connecting Literature Past and Present

1. Mystery plays an important role in the works of Poe, Hawthorne, and Melville. What is the role of mystery in Oates's story?

2. Compare Parson Hooper in "The Minister's Black Veil" with the stranger in "Where *Is* Here?" (a) In what sense are they the most powerful figures in their respective stories? (b) What role does imagination play in their power?

Joyce Carol Oates

(b. 1938)

In her short stories, novels, poems, and plays, Joyce Carol Oates delves into the workings of the human mind. Her writtings often focuses on characters who are disturbed or who are searching anxiously for their identities. Oates grew up in a tiny town on the Erie Canal, and her earliest stories and first novel are accounts of life in Erie County. Oates's fictional Eden County is elaborately conceived and populated with inhabitants who turn up in various ways from story to story.

PART 3

The Human Spirit and the Natural World

Early Morning at Cold Spring, 1850,
Asher B. Durand, Montclair Art Museum,
Montclair, New Jersey

A Closer Look

Transcendentalism: The Seekers

Ralph Waldo Emerson Searched for the Nature of Truth and Revolutionized American Literature

For the Transcendentalists, the loose-knit group of writers, artists, and reformers who flourished in the 1830s and 1840s, the individual was at the center of the universe. For them, no institution, whether political or religious, was as powerful as the individual. So it is fitting that the most influential literary and philosophical movement in American history began with the struggles of one man.

A Crisis of Confidence In the early 1830s, a young Boston pastor found himself wrestling with his faith. His wife of less than two years had died of tuberculosis, and the grieving pastor began questioning his beliefs. At the time, many religious and scholarly institutions downplayed the importance of the individual. The Industrial Revolution, which introduced mass production, had shown that machines could actually replace people. Individuals, it seemed, did not matter.

The pastor was troubled by this notion. He did not believe that individuals were insignificant. On the contrary, he felt that the human mind was the most important force in the universe. The pastor was so passionate about his search for a new way of thinking that he resigned his position and traveled to Europe to visit with some of the great philosophers of the day.

That pastor was Ralph Waldo Emerson, and what seemed like one man's crisis of confidence became a revolution in American thought. When Emerson returned to the United States in 1833, he helped forge the Transcendentalist movement.

The Individual Is the World In practical terms, the Transcendentalist movement was a ripple in history, lasting a mere ten years and producing only two major books—Emerson's *Nature* (1836) and Thoreau's *Walden* (1854). Nevertheless, the influence of the Transcendentalists on American life and letters continues to this day.

According to Emerson, the human mind is so powerful it can unlock any mystery, from the intricacies of nature to the wonder of God. To Emerson, "the individual is the world." This was a radical thought in an age that gave all authority to the organized institutions of government, religion, and education.

Emerson first proposed his ideas in 1833 in a speech at Harvard University. His audience responded with great enthusiasm. Then, he took his ideas further, proposing that every soul and all of nature was part of an "Over-Soul," a universal spirit to which all beings returned after death. In other words, every being was part of the mind of God. In an 1842 lecture, Emerson noted that,

▼ **Critical Viewing** Judging from this image of a replica of Thoreau's cabin, what do you think life was like on Walden Pond? **[Speculate]**

"The Transcendentalist . . . believes in miracle, in the perpetual openness of the human mind to new influx of light and power; he believes in inspiration, and in ecstasy."

Meetings of Great Minds Many found Emerson's ideas blasphemous and denounced him as a heretic. Emerson's supporters, however, flocked to Concord, Massachusetts, to visit with him. During the height of Transcendentalist activities, Emerson's Concord house attracted so many great minds that it was dubbed the "Athens of America."

Amos Bronson Alcott Among Emerson's admirers were teacher and philosopher Amos Bronson Alcott, whose beliefs about education revolutionized American schools. Alcott insisted that students should not be taught through routine memorization, a practice common at that time. Instead, students should be challenged to think, to debate, and to discuss.

Margaret Fuller Feminist author and editor Margaret Fuller was another eminent Transcendentalist. Along with Emerson, Fuller was the driving force behind the Transcendentalist journal *The Dial*.

Henry David Thoreau Emerson's most famous protégé was Henry David Thoreau. As a twenty-year-old student, Thoreau heard Emerson speak at Harvard and was thrilled by his ideas. Not content to merely discuss Transcendentalist philosophy, Thoreau wanted to put it into action. In 1845, he built a rough cottage in the woods at Walden Pond and went there to live alone. He sought to experience life on a simpler level, in harmony with nature, untied to material things. Thoreau lived at Walden Pond for two years and wrote about his experiences. The result was his classic collection of essays, *Walden*.

▲ **Critical Viewing** What personality traits are conveyed in these images of Ralph Waldo Emerson and Margaret Fuller? Explain your responses. **[Interpret]**

A Lasting Legacy Like other Transcendentalists, Thoreau was a fierce abolitionist. In protest against slavery and the Mexican War, he refused to pay taxes and was imprisoned. Although Thoreau spent only a single night in jail, the experience gave him insights into the relationship of individuals to government. The theory of nonviolent civil disobedience that he developed as a result has had a profound effect on society, both in the United States and around the world. During India's struggle for independence in the 1940s, Mahatma Gandhi adopted Thoreau's ideas. Here in America, nonviolent civil protest served as the guiding principle for Dr. Martin Luther King, Jr., during the civil rights movement.

The influence of the Transcendentalists is so woven into the fabric of American culture that it is almost invisible, like the air—so bountiful we take it for granted. Yet, whenever writers celebrate the individual, whenever they look to the natural world as a mirror of human lives, whenever they state a belief in the power of intuition to grasp fundamental truths, they owe a debt to the great, brief meeting of minds in Concord.

Prepare to Read

from Nature ◆ *from* Self-Reliance ◆
Concord Hymn ◆ The Snowstorm

Ralph Waldo Emerson (1803–1882)

Individuality, independence, and an appreciation for the wonders of nature—these are just a few of the principles that Ralph Waldo Emerson helped to ingrain in our nation's identity. Although his ideas were sometimes considered controversial, he had a tremendous influence on the young people of his time, and his beliefs have continued to inspire people to this day.

Throughout his life, Emerson's mind was constantly in motion, generating new ideas and defining and redefining his view of the world. His natural eloquence in expressing these ideas—in essays, lectures, and poetry—makes him one of the most quoted writers in American literature.

A New England Childhood The son of a Unitarian minister, Emerson was born in Boston. When Emerson was eight, his father died. The boy turned to a brilliant and eccentric aunt, Mary Moody Emerson, who encouraged his independent thinking. At fourteen, Emerson entered Harvard, where he began the journal he was to keep all his life. After postgraduate studies at Harvard Divinity School, he became pastor of the Second Church of Boston.

Finding His Niche Emerson's career as a minister was short-lived. Grief-stricken at the death of his young wife, and dissatisfied with what he saw as the spiritual restrictions in Unitarianism, Emerson resigned after three years. He then went to Europe, where he met the English writers Thomas Carlyle, Samuel Taylor Coleridge, and William Wordsworth. On his return to the United States, Emerson settled in Concord, Massachusetts. He married again and began his lifelong career of writing.

Emerson's second wife, Lydia Jackson of Plymouth, provided a supportive and secure family life. Emerson was now receiving money from his first wife's legacy and, for the first time in his life, was not living in poverty. The Emerson household welcomed a slowly widening circle of friends and admirers that included many of the country's most important thinkers.

In time, Emerson became widely sought as a lecturer throughout the nation. In fact, many of his essays began as lectures. Emerson kept working on the ideas until he had honed them into essay form. His talks attracted people of many ages and social classes, but it was the young people of his time who were most receptive to the thoughts of this often controversial philosopher.

An Independent Thinker Emerson was a soft-spoken man, given to neither physical nor emotional excess. Beneath his calm, sober demeanor existed a restless, highly individualistic mind that resisted conformity. "Good men," he once wrote, "must not obey the laws too well."

Emerson first achieved national fame in 1841, when he published *Essays*, a collection based on material from his journals and lectures. He went on to publish several more volumes of nonfiction, including *Essays, Second Volume* (1844), *Representative Men* (1849), and *The Conduct of Life* (1860).

Though Emerson was known mostly for his essays and lectures, he considered himself primarily a poet. "I am born a poet," he once wrote, "of a low class without doubt, yet a poet. That is my nature and my vocation." He published two successful volumes of poetry, *Poems* (1847) and *May-Day and Other Pieces* (1867). Like his essays, Emerson's poems express his beliefs in individuality and in humanity's spiritual connection to nature.

Preview

Connecting to the Literature

"Be true to yourself." "Follow your dream." Most of us have faced the choices these sentiments address: whether to conform to the expectations of others, or follow our own inner voice. Emerson's writings address such choices. He comes down squarely in favor of nonconformity.

Literary Analysis

Transcendentalism

Transcendentalism was an intellectual movement founded by Emerson. These are the cornerstones of Transcendentalist beliefs:

- Human senses are limited; they convey knowledge of the physical world, but deeper truths can be grasped only through intuition.
- The observation of nature illuminates the nature of human beings.
- God, nature, and humanity are united in a shared universal soul, or Over-Soul.

These beliefs pervade all of Emerson's work.

Comparing Literary Works

The essays that appear here are concerned with the nature of the individual, but they explore two different arenas. In one, Emerson looks at the individual's relationship to nature, and in the other, he explores the individual's relationship to society. As you read, compare how Emerson depicts the individual in nature versus the way he describes the individual among his or her fellow human beings.

Reading Strategy

Challenging the Text

When you read a work that presents an argument, do not simply accept the ideas—challenge them. To **challenge a text**, question the author's assertions and reasoning. Compare the evidence the author offers with your personal experience or other reading. Then, decide whether you agree. Use a chart like the one shown here to record your thinking.

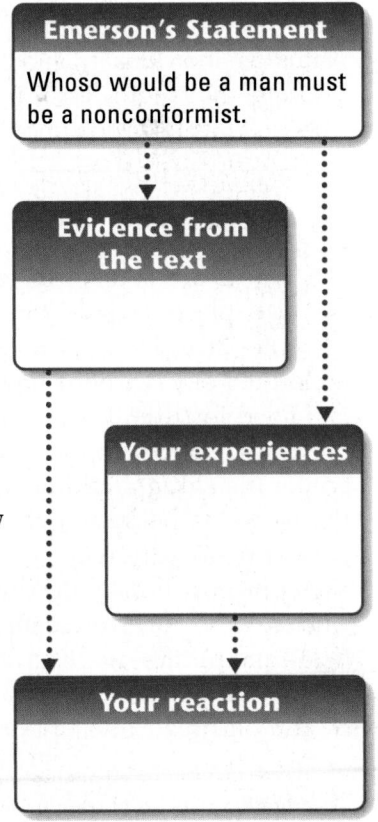

Vocabulary Development

blithe (blīth) *adj.* carefree (p. 388)

connate (kän' āt') *adj.* existing naturally; innate (p. 389)

chaos (kā' äs') *n.* disorder of matter and space, supposed to have existed before the ordered universe (p. 391)

aversion (ə vʉr' zhən) *n.* object arousing an intense dislike (p. 392)

suffrage (suf' rij) *n.* vote or voting (p. 392)

divines (də vīnz') *n.* clergy (p. 392)

radiant (rā' dē ənt) *adj.* shining brightly (p. 395)

tumultuous (too mul' choo əs) *adj.* rough; stormy (p. 395)

bastions (bas' chənz) *n.* fortifications (p. 396)

from Nature

Ralph Waldo Emerson

Background

During the 1830s and 1840s, Emerson and a small group of like-minded friends gathered regularly in his study to discuss philosophy, religion, and literature. Among them were Emerson's protégé, Henry David Thoreau, as well as educator Bronson Alcott, feminist writer Margaret Fuller, and ex-clergyman and author George Ripley. The intimate group, known as the Transcendental Club, developed a philosophical system that stressed intuition, individuality, and self-reliance. In 1836, Emerson published *Nature*, the lengthy essay (excerpted here) that became the Transcendental Club's unofficial statement of belief.

Nature is a setting that fits equally well a comic or a mourning piece. In good health, the air is a cordial of incredible virtue. Crossing a bare common,[1] in snow puddles, at twilight, under a clouded sky, without having in my thoughts any occurrence of special good fortune, I have enjoyed a perfect exhilaration. I am glad to the brink of fear. In the woods, too, a man casts off his years, as the snake his slough, and at what period soever of life is always a child. In the woods is perpetual youth. Within these plantations of God, a decorum and sanctity reign, a perennial festival is dressed, and the guest sees not how he should tire of them in a thousand years. In the woods, we return to reason and faith. There I feel that nothing can befall me in life—no disgrace, no calamity (leaving me my eyes), which nature cannot repair. Standing on the bare ground—my head bathed by the <u>blithe</u> air and uplifted into infinite space—all mean egotism

Literary Analysis
Transcendentalism
According to this passage, what is the relationship between Emerson and nature?

blithe (blīth) *adj.* carefree

---

1. **common** *n.* piece of open public land.

vanishes. I become a transparent eyeball; I am nothing; I see all; the currents of the Universal Being circulate through me; I am part or parcel of God. The name of the nearest friend sounds then foreign and accidental: to be brothers, to be acquaintances, master or servant, is then a trifle and a disturbance. I am the lover of uncontained and immortal beauty. In the wilderness, I find something more dear and <u>connate</u> than in the streets or villages. In the tranquil landscape, and especially in the distant line of the horizon, man beholds somewhat as beautiful as his own nature.

The greatest delight which the fields and woods minister is the suggestion of an occult relation between man and the vegetable. I am not alone and unacknowledged. They nod to me, and I to them. The

connate (kän′ āt′) *adj.* existing naturally; innate

☑ **Reading Check**

Which emotions does Emerson experience when in the woods?

Sunset, Frederick E. Church, Munson-Williams-Proctor Institute Museum of Art, Utica, New York

▲ **Critical Viewing** Emerson says that nature often allows us to become transparent eyeballs, seeing all, but remaining detached from the business of the world. In what ways does this image reinforce his statement? **[Support]**

waving of the boughs in the storm is new to me and old. It takes me by surprise, and yet is not unknown. Its effect is like that of a higher thought or a better emotion coming over me, when I deemed I was thinking justly or doing right.

Yet it is certain that the power to produce this delight does not reside in nature, but in man, or in a harmony of both. It is necessary to use these pleasures with great temperance. For nature is not always tricked[2] in holiday attire, but the same scene which yesterday breathed perfume and glittered as for the frolic of the nymphs is overspread with melancholy today. Nature always wears the colors of the spirit. To a man laboring under calamity, the heat of his own fire hath sadness in it. Then there is a kind of contempt of the landscape felt by him who has just lost by death a dear friend. The sky is less grand as it shuts down over less worth in the population.

---

2. **tricked** v. dressed.

Review and Assess
Thinking About the Selection

1. **Respond:** Which of your experiences have made you "glad to the brink of fear"? Explain.

2. **(a) Recall:** Under what circumstances, according to Emerson, does "mean egotism" vanish? **(b) Define:** How would you define Emerson's idea of "mean egotism"? **(c) Analyze Cause and Effect:** In nature, with what emotional state does Emerson suggest that "mean egotism" is replaced?

3. **(a) Recall:** When does Emerson become a "transparent eyeball"? **(b) Analyze:** What are the characteristics of this experience? **(c) Connect:** In what ways does this description reflect the Transcendentalist belief in an Over-Soul?

4. **(a) Recall:** Where does the power to produce nature's delight come from? **(b) Define:** In stating that there is a harmony between human beings and nature, do you think Emerson means the relationship is always serene, or not? Explain.

5. **(a) Infer:** According to Emerson, is our experience with nature the same every time we go to the woods? Explain. **(b) Interpret:** What does Emerson mean when he says that "Nature always wears the colors of the spirit"?

6. **(a) Evaluate:** What is Emerson's main point in this essay? **(b) Assess:** Do you find Emerson's message convincing? Explain why you do or do not accept his ideas about nature.

7. **Take a Position:** Do you find any evidence of Emerson's reverence for nature in American culture today? Explain.

from Self-Reliance

Ralph Waldo Emerson

There is a time in every man's education when he arrives at the conviction that envy is ignorance; that imitation is suicide; that he must take himself for better, for worse, as his portion; that though the wide universe is full of good, no kernel of nourishing corn can come to him but through his toil bestowed on that plot of ground which is given to him to till. The power which resides in him is new in nature, and none but he knows what that is which he can do, nor does he know until he has tried. Not for nothing one face, one character, one fact makes much impression on him, and another none. This sculpture in the memory is not without preestablished harmony. The eye was placed where one ray should fall, that it might testify of that particular ray. We but half express ourselves, and are ashamed of that divine idea which each of us represents. It may be safely trusted as proportionate and of good issues, so it be faithfully imparted, but God will not have his work made manifest by cowards. A man is relieved and gay when he has put his heart into his work and done his best; but what he has said or done otherwise, shall give him no peace. It is a deliverance which does not deliver. In the attempt his genius deserts him; no muse befriends; no invention, no hope.

Trust thyself: every heart vibrates to that iron string. Accept the place the divine providence has found for you; the society of your contemporaries, the connection of events. Great men have always done so and confided themselves childlike to the genius of their age, betraying their perception that the absolutely trustworthy was stirring at their heart, working through their hands, predominating in all their being. And we are now men, and must accept in the highest mind the same transcendent destiny; and not minors and invalids in a protected corner, but guides, redeemers, and benefactors. Obeying the Almighty effort and advancing on <u>Chaos</u> and the Dark. . . .

Society everywhere is in conspiracy against the manhood of every one of its members. Society is a joint-stock company in which the members agree for the better securing of his bread to each shareholder, to surrender the liberty and culture of the eater. The virtue

Literary Analysis
Transcendentalism
What does the passage beginning "Trust thyself" tell you about Emerson's belief in the importance of the individual?

chaos (kā´ äs´) *n.* disorder of matter and space, supposed to have existed before the ordered universe

✔**Reading Check**

What does Emerson believe about being true to oneself?

in most request is conformity. Self-reliance is its <u>aversion</u>. It loves not realities and creators, but names and customs.

Whoso would be a man must be a nonconformist. He who would gather immortal palms must not be hindered by the name of goodness, but must explore if it be goodness. Nothing is at last sacred but the integrity of your own mind. Absolve you to yourself, and you shall have the <u>suffrage</u> of the world. . . .

A foolish consistency is the hobgoblin of little minds, adored by little statesmen and philosophers and <u>divines</u>. With consistency a great soul has simply nothing to do. He may as well concern himself with his shadow on the wall. Speak what you think now in hard words and tomorrow speak what tomorrow thinks in hard words again, though it contradict everything you said today. "Ah, so you shall be sure to be misunderstood?"—is it so bad, then, to be misunderstood? Pythagoras was misunderstood, and Socrates, and Jesus, and Luther, and Copernicus, and Galileo, and Newton,[1] and every pure and wise spirit that ever took flesh. To be great is to be misunderstood. . . .

---

1. **Pythagoras . . . Newton** individuals who made major contributions to scientific, philosophical, or religious thinking.

aversion (ə vʉr′ zhən) *n.* object arousing an intense or definite dislike

suffrage (suf′ rij) *n.* vote or voting

divines (də vīnz′) *n.* clergy

Review and Assess

Thinking About the Selection

1. **Respond:** Which aspects, if any, of today's American culture reflect Emerson's belief in self-reliance?

2. **(a) Recall:** What terms does Emerson use to describe society? **(b) Interpret:** According to Emerson, what is society's main purpose? **(c) Draw Conclusions:** In what ways does Emerson believe people should be affected by the way others perceive them?

3. **(a) Recall:** According to Emerson, what do Pythagoras, Socrates, Jesus, Luther, Copernicus, Galileo, and Newton have in common? **(b) Support:** What evidence does Emerson use to support his claim that "to be great is to be misunderstood"?

4. **(a) Make a Judgment:** How important is Emerson's use of the adjective "foolish" in his discussion of consistency? **(b) Speculate:** Do you think there would be any circumstances in which Emerson would advocate the benefits of consistency? Explain.

5. **(a) Interpret:** According to Emerson, what role does the "divine" have in determining each person's circumstances? **(b) Generalize:** What would Emerson say is each person's reason for living? Explain.

6. **Apply:** Which of Emerson's statements, if any, would you choose as a guideline for personal conduct? Explain.

Concord Hymn

Sung at the Completion of the Battle Monument, April 19, 1836
Ralph Waldo Emerson

By the rude[1] bridge that arched the flood,
    Their flag to April's breeze unfurled,
Here once the embattled farmers stood,
    And fired the shot heard round the world.

5 The foe long since in silence slept;
    Alike the conqueror silent sleeps;
And Time the ruined bridge has swept
    Down the dark stream which seaward creeps.

On this green bank, by this soft stream,
10   We set today a votive[2] stone;
That memory may their deed redeem,
    When, like our sires, our sons are gone.

Spirit, that made those heroes dare
    To die, and leave their children free,
15 Bid Time and Nature gently spare
    The shaft we raise to them and thee.

---

1. **rude** (rōōd) *adj.* crude or rough in form or workmanship.
2. **votive** (vōt′ iv) *adj.* dedicated in fulfillment of a vow or pledge.

▲ Critical Viewing
"Concord Hymn" was written for the unveiling of this monument commemorating the minutemen, who fought the British at Lexington and Concord, Massachusetts, in April 1775. What aspect of the sculpture communicate the emotions of the poem? **[Connect]**

Review and Assess

Thinking About the Selection

1. **Respond:** What do you think of war monuments? Explain.
2. **(a) Recall:** What event took place by the "rude bridge"?
   (b) Interpret: What does the poet mean by the image of "the shot heard round the world"?
3. **(a) Recall:** What has happened to the bridge since the battle that took place there? **(b) Analyze:** How does the poem's organization reflect a sense of the passage of time?
4. **(a) Recall:** In the last stanza, whom does the poet address directly? **(b) Infer:** In what way does this direct address reflect Transcendentalist beliefs in an Over-Soul?
5. **Apply:** Which aspects of "Concord Hymn" would be appropriate for the dedication of other war monuments?

The Snowstorm

Ralph Waldo Emerson

Announced by all the trumpets of the sky,
Arrives the snow, and, driving o'er the fields,
Seems nowhere to alight: the whited air
Hides hills and woods, the river, and the heaven,
5   And veils the farmhouse at the garden's end.
The sled and traveler stopped, the courier's feet
Delayed, all friends shut out, the house mates sit
Around the <u>radiant</u> fireplace, enclosed
In a <u>tumultuous</u> privacy of storm.

radiant (rā′ dē ənt) *adj.*
shining brightly

tumultuous (tōō mul′ chōō
əs) *adj.* rough; stormy

✔**Reading Check**

What action of the wind
and snow does the poet
describe?

10 Come see the north wind's masonry.
    Out of an unseen quarry evermore
    Furnished with tile, the fierce artificer
    Curves his white <u>bastions</u> with projected roof
    Round every windward stake, or tree, or door.
15 Speeding, the myriad-handed, his wild work
    So fanciful, so savage, nought cares he
    For number or proportion. Mockingly,
    On coop or kennel he hangs Parian[1] wreaths;
    A swan-like form invests the hidden thorn;
20 Fills up the farmer's lane from wall to wall.

    Maugre[2] the farmer's sighs; and at the gate
    A tapering turret overtops the work.
    And when his hours are numbered, and the world
    Is all his own, retiring, as he were not,
25 Leaves, when the sun appears, astonished Art
    To mimic in slow structures, stone by stone,
    Built in an age, the mad wind's nightwork,
    The frolic architecture of the snow.

---

1. **Parian** (per´ ē ən) *adj.* referring to a fine, white marble of the Greek city Paros.
2. **Maugre** (mô´ gər) *prep.* in spite of.

Review and Assess

Thinking About the Selection

1. **Respond:** How does your attitude toward snow compare with Emerson's?

2. **(a) Recall:** In the first stanza, what effect does the storm have on the "sled and traveler," the "courier," and the "house mates"? **(b) Analyze:** Explain what Emerson means when he refers to the "tumultuous privacy of the storm" in line 9.

3. **(a) Recall:** In the second stanza, which words relate to the design and construction of buildings? **(b) Analyze:** What do these words suggest about the comparison the poet is making between the storm and an architect or artist?

4. **(a) Recall:** According to lines 25–28, what has the storm left behind "when the sun appears"? **(b) Synthesize:** Which aspects of Emerson's Transcendentalist beliefs does this image reflect?

5. **Speculate:** Emerson expresses a favorable attitude toward the snowstorm. Why might some people living in northern climates not share Emerson's attitude?

Review and Assess

Literary Analysis

Transcendentalism

1. What does "Nature" reveal about the **Transcendentalist** attitude toward nature? Support your answers with examples from the text.

2. Emerson writes: "Speak what you think now in hard words and tomorrow speak what tomorrow thinks in hard words, though it contradict everything you said today." In what ways does this statement reflect the Transcendentalist belief in intuition?

3. Does the image of a "transparent eyeball" effectively convey the Transcendentalist idea of a universal Over-Soul? Explain?

Comparing Literary Works

4. (a) Use a chart like the one shown to compare and contrast Emerson's descriptions of the bonds between people in society and those between people and nature. (b) Which bonds would Emerson say are more important? Explain.

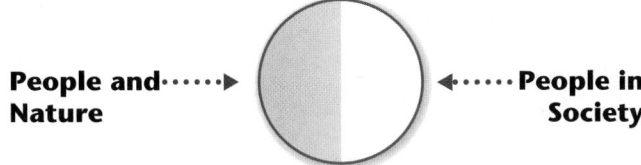

People and Nature ·····▶ ◀····· **People in Society**

5. In "Nature," Emerson says the woods are the "plantations of God," and in "Self-Reliance," he portrays individuals as "that divine idea which each of us represents." Do these passages express similar ideas about the relationship of God to people and the world? Explain.

Reading Strategy

Challenging the Text

6. Consider this assertion from "Self-Reliance": "A foolish consistency is the hobgoblin of little minds." **Challenge the text** by answering these questions: (a) What evidence does Emerson provide to support his position? (b) Offer two arguments against this statement. (c) Do you agree with this statement? Support your answer.

Extend Understanding

7. **Cultural Connection:** Some cultures view children as innocents, and others view them as inherently bad. How do you think the Transcendentalists viewed childhood? Support your answer.

Integrate Language Skills

Vocabulary Development Lesson

Word Analysis: Latin Root -radi-

The Latin root -radi- means "spoke" or "ray." This root contributes to the meaning of *radiant*—"shining brightly" or "giving off rays of light".

Knowing the meaning of the root -radi-, write a definition for each of these words.

1. radiator
2. radiate
3. radio
4. radius
5. radiation
6. radioactive

Spelling Strategy

A final silent *e* often helps create the sound of a long vowel followed by a voiced *th*—for example, as in *blithe*. Follow this principle to complete the spelling of each word.

1. brea__
2. clo__
3. li__
4. wri__
5. see__
6. la__

Concept Development: Antonyms or Synonyms?

Review the vocabulary list on page 387. Then, study each item below to identify which of the following word pairs are antonyms and which are synonyms.

1. chaos, order
2. aversion, repugnance
3. suffrage, vote
4. divines, ministers
5. blithe, anxious
6. connate, acquired
7. radiant, luminous
8. tumultuous, serene
9. bastions, bulwarks

Grammar and Style Lesson

Varying Sentence Length

In "Nature" and "Self-Reliance," Emerson often follows a very long sentence with one or more short ones. **Varying sentence length** enables Emerson to sustain the reader's interest and to establish rhythm. In addition, he often uses a short sentence to clarify or emphasize ideas he has expressed in the longer sentence preceding it. Notice this pattern in the example from "Nature":

> Crossing a bare common, in snow puddles, at twilight, under a clouded sky, without having in my thoughts any occurrence of special good fortune, I have enjoyed a perfect exhilaration. I am glad to the brink of fear.

Looking at Style Find three passages from Emerson's essays in which he varies the length of his sentences. Explain the effect of the sentence variations in each passage.

Writing Application Write one paragraph describing your walk home from school or some other short journey. Vary your sentence length to create rhythm and maintain reader interest.

After you draft, highlight your short sentences in one color and your long sentences in another color to see the pattern you have established. In what ways does varying your sentence length improve your writing?

W͟G Prentice Hall Writing and Grammar Connection: Chapter 20, Section 3

Writing Lesson

Critical Evaluation of a Philosophical Essay

Ever since they were first published, Emerson's essays have incited argument, and inspired imitation. Now, it is your turn to add your voice. Write a critical evaluation of "Self-Reliance." Include a summary of Emerson's points, a statement of opinion, and an assessment of the ways in which the argument is made.

Prewriting Reread "Self-Reliance," noting key ideas from the beginning, middle, and end. Observe how Emerson leads the reader from one thought to the next. Then, write one sentence that summarizes Emerson's argument. Phrase his ideas in your own words.

Drafting In your introduction, state the goals of your essay. Then, write out your summary of Emerson's essay. Follow the summary with a statement of your opinion of his ideas and how he presents them. Support your ideas with citations from the text.

Model: Using Relevant Citations

Emerson pays tribute to the value of being true to oneself. While most of us would agree with him in theory, how many of us withstand the pressures to conform? Emerson notes, "The virtue in most request is conformity."

> Citations specific to the argument keep the writing focused.

Revising Highlight any citations that do not effectively support your point. Replace weak citations with more relevant support.

Prentice Hall Writing and Grammar Connection: Chapter 14, Section 3

Extension Activities

Listening and Speaking Create a **public service announcement** urging people to resist conformity. Strengthen your position with two types of reasoning:

- inductive reasoning (use details to draw a general conclusion)
- deductive reasoning (build on a generally accepted principle)

Begin your announcement with a catchy phrase that will stick in listeners' minds. Then, record your announcement and share it with the class.

Research and Technology According to Emerson, the misunderstood individual joins the ranks of Pythagoras, Socrates, Jesus, Joan of Arc, and others. With a group, research and write a **profile** of one of these "great souls" to learn how or why the person was misunderstood. Share your profile with other groups. **[Group Activity]**

 **Take It to the Net** www.phschool.com

Go online for an additional research activity using the Internet.

Prepare to Read

from Walden ◆ *from* Civil Disobedience

Henry David Thoreau (1817–1862)

From the time he was a child, Henry David Thoreau was known by his Concord, Massachusetts, neighbors as an eccentric. He rarely followed rules. He was independent and strong-willed but casual about his studies. It was his mother's drive and encouragement that convinced him to pursue an education. Thoreau attended Concord Academy, a college preparatory school. Five years later, he enrolled at Harvard, where he pursued his studies in his own unique style. Although Harvard University's code called for students to wear black coats, Thoreau wore a green one.

Questioning Authority Thoreau always questioned the rules that were presented to him. When his objection to corporal punishment forced him to quit his first teaching job, Thoreau and his older brother John opened their own school in Concord. The school was quite successful, but they had to close it when John became ill.

In 1841, Thoreau moved into the house of another famous Concord resident, Ralph Waldo Emerson. He lived there for two years, performing odd jobs to pay for his room and board. While there, Thoreau became fascinated by Emerson's Transcendentalist beliefs. Soon, Thoreau became Emerson's close friend and devoted disciple. Deciding not to go back to teaching and refusing to pursue another career, Thoreau dedicated himself to testing the Transcendentalist philosophy through personal experience. By simplifying his needs, Thoreau was able to devote the rest of his life to exploring and writing about the spiritual relationship between humanity and nature and supporting his political and social beliefs.

On Walden Pond From 1845 to 1847, Thoreau lived alone in a cabin he built himself at Walden Pond outside of Concord. Thoreau's experiences during this period provided him with the material for his masterwork, *Walden* (1854). Condensing his experiences at Walden Pond into a single year, Thoreau used the four seasons as a structural framework for the book. A unique blend of natural observation, social criticism, and philosophical insight, *Walden* is now generally regarded as the supreme work of Transcendentalist literature.

Thoreau wrote throughout his life, but only *A Week on the Concord and Merrimack Rivers* and some poems were published—at Thoreau's own expense—during his lifetime. *The Maine Woods, Cape Cod,* and *A Yankee in Canada* were published posthumously. Carefully and deliberately crafted, Thoreau's work reflects the economy for which he strove throughout his life and about which he wrote in *Walden*.

A Noble Soul When Henry David Thoreau died of tuberculosis at the age of forty-four, his work had received little recognition. Yet he had achieved an inner success that few others have experienced. Speaking at Thoreau's funeral, Ralph Waldo Emerson commented, "The country knows not yet, or in the least part, how great a son it has lost. . . . But he, at least, is content. His soul was made for the noblest society; he had in a short life exhausted the capabilities of this world; wherever there is knowledge, wherever there is virtue, wherever there is beauty, he will find a home."

Thoreau's reputation has steadily grown since his death. His work has inspired writers, environmentalists, and social and political leaders. It has made generations of readers aware of the possibilities of the human spirit and the limitations of society.

Preview

Connecting to the Literature

In today's world, we use countless modern conveniences—cellular phones, computers, the Internet—often without stopping to think whether or not we truly need them. Thoreau took time to stop to think about what was truly essential in life.

Literary Analysis

Style

Style refers to the manner in which a writer puts his or her thoughts into words. Thoreau constructs paragraphs so that the sentences build to a climax. Thoreau also repeats his main ideas to reinforce his message. As you read his essays, watch for these signposts of Thoreau's style.

Comparing Literary Works

While both of these selections reveal Thoreau's style, each is written for a different purpose. One selection is lyrical, presenting ideas at a leisurely pace. The other, in contrast, is logical, advancing a focused argument. In both cases, Thoreau uses **metaphor**—a figure of speech that implies a comparison between two unlike things—to achieve his aims.

Lyrical: Time is but the stream I go a-fishing in . . .

Logical: [Government] is a sort of a wooden gun to the people themselves . . .

As you read, compare the metaphors Thoreau employs and notice how their use reveals the author's distinct reasons for writing.

Reading Strategy

Evaluating the Writer's Statement of Philosophy

As a reader, you are not bound to accept everything you see in print. In fact, when reading essays written about ideas, you should **evaluate the writer's philosophy**. To do this, pay special attention to the support the writer provides to back up his or her outlook. As you read Thoreau's works, compare his ideas and supporting details with your own experiences. Use a chart like the one shown here to organize your comparison.

Thoreau's ideas
People should simplify their lives
• supporting detail:
• supporting detail:

Your experiences

Your reaction

Vocabulary Development

dilapidated (də lap′ə dāt′ id) *adj.* in disrepair (p. 404)

sublime (sə blīm′) *adj.* noble; majestic (p. 406)

superfluous (sə pʉr′floo əs) *adj.* excessive; not necessary (p. 406)

evitable (ev′i tə bəl) *adj.* avoidable (p. 406)

magnanimity (mag′nə nim′ə tē) *n.* generosity (p. 409)

expedient (ek spē′ dē ənt) *n.* resource (p. 412)

posterity (päs ter′ə tē) *n.* all succeeding generations (p. 412)

alacrity (ə lak′rə tē) *n.* speed (p. 413)

from Walden

Henry David Thoreau

from Where I Lived, and What I Lived For

At a certain season of our life we are accustomed to consider every spot as the possible site of a house. I have thus surveyed the country on every side within a dozen miles of where I live. In imagination I have bought all the farms in succession, for all were to be bought, and I knew their price. I walked over each farmer's premises, tasted his wild apples, discoursed on husbandry[1] with him, took his farm at his price, at any price, mortgaging it to him in my mind; even put a higher price on it—took everything but a deed of it—took his word for his deed, for I dearly love to talk—cultivated it, and him too to some extent, I trust, and withdrew when I had enjoyed it long enough, leaving him to carry it on. This experience entitled me to be regarded as a sort of real-estate broker by my friends. Wherever I sat, there I might live, and the landscape radiated from me accordingly. What is a house but a sedes, a seat?—better if a country seat. I discovered many a site for a house not likely to be soon improved, which some might have thought too far from the village, but to my eyes the village was too far from it. Well, there might I live, I said; and there I did live, for an hour, a summer and a winter life; saw how I could let the years run off, buffet the winter through, and see the spring come in. The future inhabitants of this region, wherever they may place their houses, may be sure that they have been anticipated. An afternoon

---

1. husbandry (huz´ bən drē) *n.* farming.

From J. Lyndon Shanley, ed., Walden: The Writings of Henry D. Thoreau. Copyright © 1971 by Princeton University Press. Excerpts, pp. 81–98 and 320–333, reprinted with permission of Princeton University Press.

◀ **Critical Viewing** Based on this picture of Walden Pond, what do you think it would be like to live in such a place? **[Speculate]**

☑ **Reading Check**
Did Thoreau truly intend to purchase a farm?

suffed to lay out the land into orchard woodlot and pasture, and to decide what fine oaks or pines should be left to stand before the door, and whence each blasted tree could be seen to the best advantage; and then I let it lie, fallow[2] perchance, for a man is rich in proportion to the number of things which he can afford to let alone.

My imagination carried me so far that I even had the refusal of several farms—the refusal was all I wanted—but I never got my fingers burned by actual possession. The nearest that I came to actual possession was when I bought the Hollowell Place, and had begun to sort my seeds, and collected materials with which to make a wheelbarrow to carry it on or off with; but before the owner gave me a deed of it, his wife—every man has such a wife—changed her mind and wished to keep it, and he offered me ten dollars to release him. Now, to speak the truth, I had but ten cents in the world, and it surpassed my arithmetic to tell, if I was that man who had ten cents, or who had a farm, or ten dollars, or all together. However, I let him keep the ten dollars and the farm too, for I had carried it far enough; or rather, to be generous, I sold him the farm for just what I gave for it, and, as he was not a rich man, made him a present of ten dollars, and still had my ten cents, and seeds, and materials for a wheelbarrow left. I found thus that I had been a rich man without any damage to my poverty. But I retained the landscape, and I have since annually carried off what it yielded without a wheelbarrow. With respect to landscapes:

> "I am monarch of all I *survey,*
> My right there is none to dispute."[3]

I have frequently seen a poet withdraw, having enjoyed the most valuable part of a farm, while the crusty farmer supposed that he had got a few wild apples only. Why, the owner does not know it for many years when a poet has put his farm in rhyme, the most admirable kind of invisible fence, has fairly impounded it, milked it, skimmed it, and got all the cream, and left the farmer only the skimmed milk.

The real attractions of the Hollowell farm, to me, were: its complete retirement, being about two miles from the village, half a mile from the nearest neighbor, and separated from the highway by a broad field; its bounding on the river, which the owner said protected it by its fogs from frosts in the spring, though that was nothing to me; the gray color and ruinous state of the house and barn, and the dilapidated fences, which put such an interval between me and the last occupant; the hollow and lichen-covered apple trees, gnawed by rabbits, showing what kind of neighbors I should have; but above all, the recollection I had of it from my earliest voyages up the river, when the house was concealed behind a dense grove of red maples, through which I heard the house-dog bark. I was in haste to buy it, before the proprietor finished getting out some rocks, cutting down

Reading Strategy
Evaluating the Writer's Statement of Philosophy
Do you think this philosophical statement about a man's wealth applies in today's world? Can Thoreau support it?

Literary Analysis
Style What point does Thoreau make through his use of repetition in his description of the Hollowell farm?

dilapidated (də lap´ ə dāt´ id) *adj.* in disrepair

---

2. **fallow** (fal´ ō) *adj.* left uncultivated or unplanted.
3. **"I . . . dispute"** from William Cowper's *Verses Supposed to Be Written by Alexander Selkirk.*

the hollow apple trees, and grubbing up some young birches which had sprung up in the pasture, or, in short, had made any more of his improvements. To enjoy these advantages I was ready to carry it on; like Atlas,[4] to take the world on my shoulders—I never heard what compensation he received for that—and do all those things which had no other motive or excuse but that I might pay for it and be unmolested in my possession of it; for I knew all the while that it would yield the most abundant crop of the kind I wanted if I could only afford to let it alone. But it turned out as I have said.

All that I could say, then, with respect to farming on a large scale (I have always cultivated a garden) was that I had had my seeds ready. Many think that seeds improve with age. I have no doubt that time discriminates between the good and the bad; and when at last I shall plant, I shall be less likely to be disappointed. But I would say to my fellows, once for all, As long as possible live free and uncommitted. It makes but little difference whether you are committed to a farm or the county jail.

Old Cato,[5] whose "De Re Rustica" is my "Cultivator," says, and the only translation I have seen makes sheer nonsense of the passage, "When you think of getting a farm, turn it thus in your mind, not to buy greedily; nor spare your pains to look at it, and do not think it enough to go round it once. The oftener you go there the more it will please you, if it is good." I think I shall not buy greedily, but go round and round it as long as I live, and be buried in it first, that it may please me the more at last. . . .

I do not propose to write an ode to dejection, but to brag as lustily as chanticleer[6] in the morning, standing on his roost, if only to wake my neighbors up.

When first I took up my abode in the woods, that is, began to spend my nights as well as days there, which, by accident, was on Independence Day, or the fourth of July, 1845, my house was not finished for winter, but was merely a defense against the rain, without plastering or chimney, the walls being of rough weatherstained boards, with wide chinks, which made it cool at night. The upright white hewn studs and freshly planed door and window casings gave it a clean and airy look, especially in the morning, when its timbers were saturated with dew, so that I fancied that by noon some sweet gum would exude from them. To my imagination it retained throughout the day more or less of this auroral[7] character, reminding me of a certain house on a mountain which I had visited the year before. This was an airy and unplastered cabin, fit to entertain a traveling god, and where a goddess might trail her garments. The winds which passed over my dwelling were such as sweep over the ridges of mountains, bearing the broken strains, or celestial parts only,

---

4. **Atlas** (at´ ləs) from Greek mythology, a Titan who supported the heavens on his shoulders.
5. **Old Cato Roman statesman** (234–149 B.C.). "De Re Rustica" is Latin for "Of Things Rustic."
6. **chanticleer** (chan´ tə klir´) *n.* rooster.
7. **auroral** (ô rôr´ əl) *adj.* resembling the dawn.

Reading Strategy
Evaluating the Writer's Statement of Philosophy
What difference do you see between a person's commitment to a farm and to a jail?

**Reading Check**

What was the state of Thoreau's house in the woods when he first took up residence?

of terrestrial music. The morning wind forever blows, the poem of creation is uninterrupted; but few are the ears that hear it. Olympus♦ is but the outside of the earth everywhere. . . .

I went to the woods because I wished to live deliberately, to front only the essential facts of life, and see if I could not learn what it had to teach, and not, when I came to die, discover that I had not lived. I did not wish to live what was not life, living is so dear; nor did I wish to practice resignation, unless it was quite necessary. I wanted to live deep and suck out all the marrow of life, to live so sturdily and Spartanlike[8] as to put to rout all that was not life, to cut a broad swath and shave close, to drive life into a corner, and reduce it to its lowest terms, and, if it proved to be mean, why then to get the whole and genuine meanness of it, and publish its meanness to the world; or if it were <u>sublime</u>, to know it by experience, and be able to give a true account of it in my next excursion. For most men, it appears to me, are in a strange uncertainty about it, whether it is of the devil or of God, and have *somewhat hastily* concluded that it is the chief end of man here to "glorify God and enjoy him forever."[9]

Still we live meanly, like ants; though the fable tells us that we were long ago changed into men; like pygmies we fight with cranes:[10] it is error upon error, and clout upon clout, and our best virtue has for its occasion a <u>superfluous</u> and <u>evitable</u> wretchedness. Our life is frittered away by detail. An honest man has hardly need to count more than his ten fingers, or in extreme cases he may add his ten toes, and lump the rest. Simplicity, simplicity, simplicity! I say, let your affairs be as two or three, and not a hundred or a thousand; instead of a million count half a dozen, and keep your accounts on your thumbnail. In the midst of this chopping sea of civilized life, such are the clouds and storms and quicksands and thousand-and-one items to be allowed for, that a man has to live, if he would not founder and go to the bottom and not make his port at all, by dead reckoning,[11] and he must be a great calculator indeed who succeeds. Simplify, simplify. Instead of three meals a day, if it be necessary eat but one; instead of a hundred dishes, five; and reduce other things in proportion. Our life is like a German Confederacy,[12]

Literature in context History Connection

♦ *Olympus*

When he describes his home in the woods, Thoreau rhapsodizes about another mountain cabin he had seen, an airy place where a "goddess might trail her garments." Thoreau goes on to say, "Olympus is but the outside of the earth everywhere."

Mount Olympus, to which Thoreau is referring, is both a real mountain in northern Greece and an important setting in ancient Greek mythology. Described as the home of the gods, Olympus was off-limits to mortals. From it, Zeus ruled the twelve gods who governed the world. Ancient Greeks pictured their gods in human form with human flaws, so Olympus was far from perfect. But as a place of relative beauty, harmony, and enlightenment, it was better than Earth.

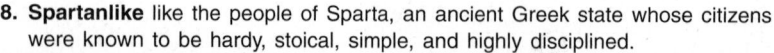

---

8. **Spartanlike** like the people of Sparta, an ancient Greek state whose citizens were known to be hardy, stoical, simple, and highly disciplined.
9. **"glorify . . . forever"** the answer to the question "What is the chief end of man?" in the Westminster catechism.
10. **like . . . cranes** In the *Iliad*, the Trojans are compared to cranes fighting against pygmies.
11. **dead reckoning** navigating without the assistance of stars.
12. **German Confederacy** At the time, Germany was a loose union of thirty-nine independent states, with no common government.

sublime (sə blīm´) *adj.* noble; majestic

superfluous (soo pʉr´ floo əs) *adj.* excessive; not necessary

evitable (ev´ i tə bəl) *adj.* avoidable

made up of petty states, with its boundary forever fluctuating, so that even a German cannot tell you how it is bounded at any moment. The nation itself, with all its so-called internal improvements, which, by the way, are all external and superficial, is just such an unwieldy and over-grown establishment, cluttered with furniture and tripped up by its own traps, ruined by luxury and heedless expense, by want of calculation and a worthy aim, as the million households in the land; and the only cure for it as for them is in a rigid economy, a stern and more than Spartan simplicity of life and elevation of purpose. It lives too fast. Men think that it is essential that the *Nation* have commerce, and export ice, and talk through a telegraph, and ride thirty miles an hour, without a doubt, whether *they* do or not; but whether we should live like baboons or like men, is a little uncertain. If we do not get out sleepers,[13] and forge rails, and devote days and nights to the work, but go to tinkering upon our *lives* to improve *them*, who will build railroads? And if rail-roads are not built, how shall we get to heaven in season? But if we stay at home and mind our business, who will want railroads? We do not ride on the railroad; it rides upon us. . . .

Time is but the stream I go a-fishing in. I drink at it; but while I drink I see the sandy bottom and detect how shallow it is. Its thin current slides away, but eternity remains. I would drink deeper; fish in the sky, whose bottom is pebbly with stars. I cannot count one. I know not the first letter of the alphabet. I have always been regretting that I was not as wise as the day I was born. The intellect is a cleaver; it discerns and rifts its way into the secret of things. I do not wish to be any more busy with my hands than is necessary. My head is hands and feet. I feel all my best faculties concentrated in it. My instinct tells me that my head is an organ for burrowing, as some creatures use their snout and forepaws, and with it I would mine and burrow my way through these hills. I think that the richest vein is somewhere hereabouts; so by the divining rod[14] and thin rising vapors I judge; and here I will begin to mine. . . .

from The Conclusion

I left the woods for as good a reason as I went there. Perhaps it seemed to me that I had several more lives to live, and could not spare any more time for that one. It is remarkable how easily and insensibly we fall into a particular route, and make a beaten track for ourselves. I had not lived there a week before my feet wore a path from my door to the pondside; and though it is five or six years since I trod it, it is still quite distinct. It is true, I fear that others may have fallen into it, and so helped to keep it open. The surface of the earth is soft and impress-ible by the feet of men; and so with the paths which the mind travels. How worn and dusty, then, must be the highways of the world, how

---

13. **sleepers** (slē′ pərz) *n.* ties supporting railroad tracks.
14. **divining rod** a forked branch or stick alleged to reveal underground water or minerals.

Reading Strategy
Evaluating the Writer's Statement of Philosophy
Evaluate this statement of philosophy about progress. Do you agree that railroads and other technology "ride upon us"?

Reading Check

Why did Thoreau go to the woods?

▲ **Critical Viewing**
What elements in this aerial photograph of Walden Pond reveal conventional notions of progress? What details suggest that the community has applied some of Thoreau's ideas? **[Analyze]**

deep the ruts of tradition and conformity! I did not wish to take a cabin passage, but rather to go before the mast and on the deck of the world, for there I could best see the moonlight amid the mountains. I do not wish to go below now.

I learned this, at least, by my experiment; that if one advances confidently in the direction of his dreams, and endeavors to live the life which he has imagined, he will meet with a success unexpected in common hours. He will put some things behind, will pass an invisible boundary; new, universal, and more liberal laws will begin to establish themselves around and within him; or the old laws be expanded, and interpreted in his favor in a more liberal sense, and he will live with the license of a higher order of beings. In proportion as he simplifies his life, the laws of the universe will appear less complex, and solitude will not be solitude, nor poverty poverty, nor weakness weakness. If you have built castles in the air, your work need not be lost; that is where they should be. Now put the foundations under them. . . .

Why should we be in such desperate haste to succeed, and in such desperate enterprises? If a man does not keep pace with his companions, perhaps it is because he hears a different drummer. Let him step to the music which he hears, however measured or far away. It is not important that he should mature as soon as an apple tree or an oak. Shall he turn his spring into summer? If the condition of things which we were made for is not yet, what were any reality which we can substitute? We will not be shipwrecked on a vain reality. Shall we with pains erect a heaven of blue glass over ourselves, though when it is done we shall be sure to gaze still at the true ethereal heaven far above, as if the former were not? . . .

Literary Analysis
Style and Metaphor
What metaphor does Thoreau use in the sentence beginning "If a man does not keep pace with his companions . . . "?

However mean your life is, meet it and live it; do not shun it and call it hard names. It is not so bad as you are. It looks poorest when you are richest. The faultfinder will find faults even in paradise. Love your life, poor as it is. You may perhaps have some pleasant, thrilling, glorious hours, even in a poorhouse. The setting sun is reflected from the windows of the almshouse[15] as brightly as from the rich man's abode; the snow melts before its door as early in the spring. I do not see but a quiet mind may live as contentedly there, and have as cheering thoughts, as in a palace. The town's poor seem to me often to live the most independent lives of any. Maybe they are simply great enough to receive without misgiving. Most think that they are above being supported by the town; but it oftener happens that they are not above supporting themselves by dishonest means, which should be more disreputable. Cultivate poverty like a garden herb, like sage. Do not trouble yourself much to get new things, whether clothes or friends. Turn the old; return to them. Things do not change; we change. Sell your clothes and keep your thoughts. God will see that you do not want society. If I were confined to a corner of a garret[16] all my days, like a spider, the world would be just as large to me while I had my thoughts about me. The philosopher said: "From an army of three divisions one can take away its general, and put it in disorder; from the man the most abject and vulgar one cannot take away his thought." Do not seek so anxiously to be developed, to subject yourself to many influences to be played on; it is all dissipation. Humility like darkness reveals the heavenly lights. The shadows of poverty and meanness gather around us, "and lo! creation widens to our view."[17] We are often reminded that if there were bestowed on us the wealth of Croesus,[18] our aims must still be the same, and our means essentially the same. Moreover, if you are restricted in your range by poverty, if you cannot buy books and newspapers, for instance, you are but confined to the most significant and vital experiences; you are compelled to deal with the material which yields the most sugar and the most starch. It is life near the bone where it is sweetest. You are defended from being a trifler. No man loses ever on a lower level by magnanimity on a higher. Superfluous wealth can buy superfluities only. Money is not required to buy one necessary of the soul. . . .

The life in us is like the water in the river. It may rise this year higher than man has ever known it, and flood the parched uplands; even this may be the eventful year, which will drown out all our muskrats. It was not always dry land where we dwell. I see far inland the banks which the stream anciently washed, before science began

---

15. **almshouse** *n.* home for people too poor to support themselves.
16. **garret** (gar´ it) *n.* attic.
17. **"and . . . view"** from the sonnet "To Night" by British poet Joseph Blanco White (1775–1841).
18. **Croesus** (krē´ səs) King of Lydia (d. 546 B.C.), believed to be the wealthiest person of his time.

Reading Strategy
Evaluating the Writer's Statement of Philosophy
Thoreau has strong opinions about how people should live, as shown in his advice to "cultivate poverty." Has he convinced you? Explain.

magnanimity (mag´ nə nim´ ə tē) *n.* generosity

✓**Reading Check**
What does Thoreau feel about superfluous wealth?

from *Walden* ◆ 409

to record its freshets. Everyone has heard the story which has gone the rounds of New England, of a strong and beautiful bug which came out of the dry leaf of an old table of apple-tree wood, which had stood in a farmer's kitchen for sixty years, first in Connecticut, and afterward in Massachusetts—from an egg deposited in the living tree many years earlier still, as appeared by counting the annual layers beyond it; which was heard gnawing out for several weeks, hatched

▼ **Critical Viewing**
In what ways does this replica of Thoreau's cabin reflect his desire to "front only the essential facts of life"? **[Interpret]**

perchance by the heat of an urn. Who does not feel his faith in a resurrection and immortality strengthened by hearing of this? Who knows what beautiful and winged life, whose egg has been buried for ages under many concentric layers of woodenness in the dead dry life of society, deposited at first in the alburnum[19] of the green and living tree, which has been gradually converted into the semblance of its well-seasoned tomb—heard perchance gnawing out now for years by the astonished family of man, as they sat round the festive board—may unexpectedly come forth from amidst society's most trivial and handselled furniture, to enjoy its perfect summer life at last!

I do not say that John or Jonathan[20] will realize all this; but such is the character of that morrow which mere lapse of time can never make to dawn. The light which puts out our eyes is darkness to us. Only that day dawns to which we are awake. There is more day to dawn. The sun is but a morning star.

---

19. **alburnum** (al bur´ nəm) *n.* soft wood between the bark and the heartwood, where water is conducted.
20. **John or Jonathan** average person.

Review and Assess

Thinking About the Selection

1. **Respond:** From your point of view, what would be the advantages and disadvantages of spending two solitary years in a natural setting?

2. **(a) Recall:** What advice does Thoreau offer to his "fellows" about ownership of land or property? **(b) Interpret:** What does Thoreau mean by his comment, "It makes but little difference whether you are committed to a farm or the county jail"?

3. **(a) Recall:** What advice does Thoreau offer to those who live in poverty? **(b) Analyze:** What does this advice suggest about Thoreau's definition of true wealth?

4. **(a) Recall:** According to Thoreau, by what is our life "frittered away"? **(b) Interpret:** What does Thoreau mean by his advice to "Simplify, simplify."?

5. **(a) Deduce:** What did Thoreau hope to achieve by living at Walden Pond? **(b) Make a Judgment:** Do you believe Thoreau felt his time at Walden was well spent? Explain.

6. **(a) Apply:** How would you define those things that are necessary to the soul? **(b) Take a Position:** Do you agree with Thoreau that "Money is not required to buy one necessary of the soul"? Explain.

from CIVIL DISOBEDIENCE

Henry David Thoreau

Background

The Mexican War was a conflict between Mexico and the United States that took place from 1846 to 1848. The war was caused by a dispute over the boundary between Texas and Mexico, as well as by Mexico's refusal to discuss selling California and New Mexico to the United States. Believing that President Polk had intentionally provoked the conflict before gaining congressional approval, Thoreau and many other Americans strongly objected to the war. In protest, Thoreau refused to pay his taxes and was forced to spend a night in jail. After that experience, Thoreau wrote "Civil Disobedience," urging people to resist governmental policies with which they disagree.

I heartily accept the motto, "That government is best which governs least";[1] and I should like to see it acted up to more rapidly and systematically. Carried out, it finally amounts to this, which also I believe: "That government is best which governs not at all"; and when men are prepared for it, that will be the kind of government which they will have. Government is at best but an expedient; but most governments are usually, and all governments are sometimes, inexpedient. The objections which have been brought against a standing army, and they are many and weighty, and deserve to prevail, may also at last be brought against a standing government. The standing army is only an arm of the standing government. The government itself, which is only the mode which the people have chosen to execute their will, is equally liable to be abused and perverted before the people can act through it. Witness the present Mexican war, the work of comparatively a few individuals using the standing government as their tool; for in the outset, the people would not have consented to this measure.

This American government—what is it but a tradition, though a recent one, endeavoring to transmit itself unimpaired to posterity, but each instant losing some of its integrity? It has not the vitality and force of a single living man; for a single man can bend it to his will. It is a sort of wooden gun to the people themselves; and, if ever they should use it in earnest as a real one against each other, it will surely split.

Reading Strategy
Evaluating the Writer's Statement of Philosophy
Before you read Thoreau's supporting arguments, do you think you will agree with his philosophy about government? Explain.

expedient (ik spē′ dē ənt) *n.* resource

posterity (päs ter′ ə tē) *n.* all succeeding generations

---

1. **"That . . . least"** the motto of the *United States Magazine and Democratic Review*, a literary-political journal.

But it is not the less necessary for this; for the people must have some complicated machinery or other, and hear its din, to satisfy that idea of government which they have. Governments show thus how successfully men can be imposed on, even impose on themselves, for their own advantage. It is excellent, we must all allow; yet this government never of itself furthered any enterprise, but by the alacrity with which it got out of its way. *It* does not keep the country free. *It* does not settle the West. *It* does not educate. The character inherent in the American people has done all that has been accomplished; and it would have done somewhat more, if the government had not sometimes got in its way. For government is an expedient by which men would fain succeed in letting one another alone; and, as has been said, when it is most expedient, the governed are most let alone by it. Trade and commerce, if they were not made of India rubber,[2] would never manage to bounce over the obstacles which legislators are continually putting in their way; and, if one were to judge these men wholly by the effects of their actions, and not partly by their intentions, they would deserve to be classed and punished with those mischievous persons who put obstructions on the railroads.

But, to speak practically and as a citizen, unlike those who call themselves no government men, I ask for, not at once no government, but *at once* a better government. Let every man make known what kind of government would command his respect, and that will be one step toward obtaining it. . . .

alacrity (ə lak´ rə tē) *n.* speed

---

2. **India rubber** a form of crude rubber.

Review and Assess

Thinking About the Selection

1. **Respond:** What kind of government commands your respect? Why?

2. **(a) Recall:** What motto does Thoreau accept? **(b) Analyze:** How would he like to see that motto implemented?

3. **(a) Recall:** How does Thoreau define the best possible kind of government? **(b) Draw Conclusions:** According to Thoreau, when will Americans get the best possible kind of government?

4. **(a) Summarize:** What is Thoreau asking his readers to do? **(b) Evaluate:** Does Thoreau present a convincing argument for acting on one's principles?

5. **(a) Criticize:** What arguments might you use to counter Thoreau's objections to the idea of a standing government? **(b) Support:** What examples might you provide to support an argument that government benefits individuals?

Review and Assess

Literary Analysis

Style

1. (a) Explain how the paragraph on simplicity in *Walden* demonstrates Thoreau's tendency to make sentences build to a climax. (b) Find another example in *Walden* of Thoreau's climactic **style.**

2. Thoreau often starts a paragraph with specific examples. He then applies them to a larger truth. (a) Find one such paragraph. (b) Do you think this approach is effective? Explain.

Comparing Literary Works

3. Use a chart like the one shown here to examine the meanings of Thoreau's **metaphors.**

Metaphor	Things compared	Meaning
I wanted to live deep and suck out all the marrow of life		

4. In *Civil Disobedience*, Thoreau describes government as "a wooden gun." In *Walden*, he describes "this chopping sea of civilized life." Does each of these metaphors function primarily as a logical or an artistic tool? Explain.

5. (a) In which essay does Thoreau make more elaborate use of metaphor? (b) How does this choice reflect the purpose of the essay?

Reading Strategy

Evaluating the Writer's Statement of Philosophy

6. Thoreau writes that people should simplify their lives. (a) What support for this belief does he provide? (b) How could you argue against this idea? (c) Is his argument convincing? Explain.

7. (a) What evidence does Thoreau use to support his contention that "That government is best which governs not at all"? (b) Do you agree with Thoreau? Explain.

Extend Understanding

8. **World Events Connection:** Would it be possible for Thoreau to conduct his "experiment" of living at Walden Pond in today's society? Why or why not?

Quick Review

Style is the manner in which a writer puts his or her thoughts into words.

Metaphors compare two unlike things, without the use of *like* or *as.*

To **evaluate the writer's statement of philosophy,** weigh the writer's supporting evidence and your own experience. Decide whether you agree or disagree.

 Take It to the Net
www.phschool.com
Take the interactive self-test online to check your understanding of these selections.

Integrate Language Skills

Vocabulary Development Lesson

Word Analysis: Latin Root -flu-

The Latin root -flu-, found in words like *fluid*, means "flow." The word *superfluous* means "overflowing" or "exceeding what is sufficient." Match each of the words with its definition. Check your answers in a dictionary.

    a. affluence   **b.** confluence   **c.** fluent

1. a flowing together, as in two streams
2. wealth; an abundant flow; prosperity
3. effortlessly smooth; flowing

Spelling Strategy

If a word ends in -ent, such as the word *expedient*, its parallel forms end in -ence (*expedience*) or -ency (*expediency*). For each of these words, correctly spell the parallel forms.

    1. resident   2. dependent   3. excellent

Concept Development: Synonyms

Select the word or phrase below whose meaning is closest to that of the first word.

1. dilapidated: (a) depressed, (b) in disrepair, (c) new
2. sublime: (a) tight, (b) filthy, (c) majestic
3. superfluous: (a) superb, (b) unnecessary, (c) wanted
4. evitable: (a) avoidable, (b) evident, (c) fair
5. magnanimity: (a) spontaneity, (b) horror, (c) kindness
6. expedient: (a) resource, (b) expense, (c) implosive
7. posterity: (a) future generations, (b) ancestors, (c) current generations
8. alacrity: (a) awareness, (b) readiness, (c) suspicion

Grammar and Style Lesson

Infinitives and Infinitive Phrases

Thoreau makes frequent use of infinitives and infinitive phrases. **Infinitive phrases** combine an **infinitive** (the basic form of the verb preceded by the word *to*) and its complements and modifiers. Infinitive phrases function as nouns, adjectives, or adverbs. In the examples below, the infinitive phrases are underlined.

> **Noun:** I dearly love *to talk*. (object of the verb *love*)
>
> **Adjective:** I had several more lives *to live*. (modifies the noun *lives*)
>
> **Adverb:** This was an airy . . . cabin, fit *to entertain a traveling god*. (modifies the participle *fit*)

Practice Find at least six infinitives or infinitive phrases in the paragraph of *Walden* (page 406) that begins "I went to the woods . . . " Identify the grammatical function of the infinitive in each phrase.

Writing Application Write two paragraphs describing how you plan to achieve a difficult goal. Use infinitive phrases such as *to shine* in persuasive statements: "Give my plan an opportunity *to shine*."

After you draft, highlight the infinitives and infinitive phrases in your paragraphs. For each, identify the function it serves in the sentence.

WG Prentice Hall Writing and Grammar Connection: Chapter 19, Section 2

Writing Lesson

Editorial

In the century-and-a-half-since Thoreau wrote *Walden*, life for most Americans has become increasingly complex rather than simpler. Write an editorial for a major newspaper either advocating or rejecting Thoreau's ideas of simplicity for today's world. Refer to the texts of *Walden* and *Civil Disobedience* to support your ideas.

Prewriting   Decide whether you think Thoreau was right or wrong, and brainstorm for a list of examples that support your point of view.

Drafting   Introduce Thoreau and outline his ideas. Use quotations from his work to illustrate your points. Make a strong statement either advocating or refuting his ideas, using your list of examples. Anticipate and answer the arguments of those who may disagree with you.

Model: Anticipating Opponents' Arguments

Today, Thoreau's ideas fall on deaf ears because everyone is glued to their cell phones. Instead of hearing his wisdom, people say, "But I can't live without my fax machine. It makes my life easier." Yet, people have less time with family, and less time for the simple pleasures of life than ever before.

> Anticipating and answering opponents' arguments creates a more persuasive piece of writing.

Revising   Reread your editorial, adding examples, anecdotes, or quotations as necessary to sharpen your argument.

Prentice Hall Writing and Grammar Connection: Chapter 7, Section 2

Extension Activities

Listening and Speaking With a group, stage a **debate** to argue the pros and cons of civil disobedience as a form of protest. Keep the following strategies in mind as you work:

- Develop several key arguments supporting your position.
- Use analogies to familiar situations to help listeners appreciate your points.

Incorporate formal debate strategies, such as the use of syllogisms (arguments that link a major and minor premise) to strengthen your arguments. **[Group Activity]**

Research and Technology Conduct research to find out what Walden Pond is like today and what efforts have been made to preserve it. Share your findings with the class in an **oral presentation**. Follow with a discussion of the way Walden Pond has changed since Thoreau's day.

 **Take It to the Net**   www.phschool.com

Go online for an additional research activity using the Internet.

PART 4

Looking at Literary Forms: Poetry

Walden Pond Revisited, 1942, N.C. Wyeth, Brandywine River Museum

As the nation's boundaries pushed west in the nineteenth century, writers were pioneering new styles of poetry. Walt Whitman abandoned traditional poetic forms in favor of free verse. Emily Dickinson combined striking languages and a highly imaginative view of the world. Together, these two influential poets set the stage for a new American poetry.

Prepare to Read

Emily Dickinson's Poetry

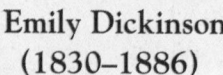

Emily Dickinson (1830–1886)

Of the 1,775 poems Emily Dickinson wrote during her lifetime, only seven were published before her death—and these few appeared anonymously. Dickinson was a private person who was extremely reluctant to reveal herself or her work to the world. As a result, few people outside her family and a small circle of friends knew of her poetic genius until after her death. Today, however, she is widely regarded as one of the greatest American poets.

A Life Apart Dickinson was born in Amherst, Massachusetts, the daughter of a prominent lawyer. As a child, she was energetic and enjoyed the tasks of daily life—cooking, sewing, playing with friends, winter sports, even studying at a boarding school. Her childhood was normal in many respects. However, as an adult she became increasingly isolated. Though she traveled as a young woman to Boston, Washington, D.C., and Philadelphia to visit friends, she rarely left her hometown as she grew older. In fact, after her father's death in 1874, she seldom left the house, and during the last ten years of her life, she remained entirely within her house and garden. Dickinson's circle of friends grew smaller and smaller, and she communicated with the few that remained mainly through notes and fragments of poems. She dressed only in white and would not allow her neighbors or any strangers to see her. When her health failed, she allowed her doctor to examine her only by observing her from a distance. Dickinson was fond of children, however, and sometimes lowered a basket of candy or fruit to them from her upstairs window.

Her Talent Is Recognized Though she chose to live most of her life in virtual isolation, Emily Dickinson was a deeply energetic, intense person. She possessed a clear sense of purpose—to write poetry—and devoted most of her time to doing so. Yet because she shared her work with few people, she sometimes doubted her abilities. In 1862, she sent four poems to Thomas Wentworth Higginson, an influential literary critic, and asked him to tell her whether her verse was "alive." Like the editors who first published her work after her death, Higginson sought to change her unconventional style—her eccentric use of punctuation and irregular meter and rhyme. He did not understand that she had crafted her poetry with great precision and that her unique style, marked by unconventional capitalization and the use of dashes, was an important element of her poetry. Still, he did recognize her talent and encouraged her to keep writing.

Dickinson's Legacy In 1886, after fighting illness for two years, Emily Dickinson died in the same house in which she had been born. After her death, her sister Lavinia discovered packets of poems in the drawers of Emily's dresser. Dickinson had given instructions that her poems were to be destroyed after her death. Nevertheless, the poems were organized and edited by various family members and were published in small installments. However, it was not until 1955, when *The Poems of Emily Dickinson* was published, that her work as a whole was revealed to the world and her genius fully recognized.

The Belle of Amherst In the years since the publication of her work, Dickinson has become the subject of numerous plays, novels, and poems that have romanticized her life and celebrated her genius with varying amounts of sentimentality and accuracy. But for the poets who came after her, Dickinson has no peer. She is a voice of intense delicacy and urgency, rising out of stillness.

Preview

Connecting to the Literature

Although you may not often share your private thoughts about life's "big topics," you probably have many ideas about them. In her poems, Dickinson shines light on her shadowy "private" thoughts as well as on ideas about such vast subjects as death, solitude, consciousness, and the soul.

Literary Analysis

Slant Rhyme

Poets use rhyme to create pleasant musical sounds and to unify groups of lines or stanzas. **Exact rhyme** occurs when two words have identical sounds in their final accented syllables. In **slant rhyme**, the final sounds are similar but not identical.

> Exact rhyme: *glove-above*
> Slant: *glove-prove*

Dickinson uses both exact and slant rhyme in her poetry. Her independence from strict rhyme is one of the reasons her poems are so surprising. As you read her poems, pay attention to her uses of both kinds of rhyme and consider the effects they create.

Comparing Literary Works

In all of her work, Emily Dickinson explored different aspects of human consciousness. In some poems, Dickinson saw human consciousness as an infinite universe. In others, she saw it as a small, isolated presence. In all of her poems, the conscious mind of the individual is "Where the meanings are." As you read these poems, compare the differing ways in which Dickinson defines human awareness.

Reading Strategy

Analyzing Images

Poets often link abstract concepts such as love, life, and death to concrete images, or word pictures. In reading poetry, it is helpful to **analyze images** to clarify the abstract meaning the author is conveying. As you read Emily Dickinson's poems, use a chart like the one shown here to help you understand her images.

Image	Abstract Idea
Carriage, slow journey	Death
School-children, grain, sunset	Life

Vocabulary Development

cornice (kôr′ nis) *n.* projecting decorative molding along the top of a building (p. 421)

surmised (sər mīzd′) *v.* guessed (p. 421)

oppresses (ə pres′ əz) *v.* weighs heavily on the mind (p. 424)

finite (fī′ nīt) *adj.* having measurable or definable limits (p. 427)

infinity (in fin′ i tē) *n.* endless or unlimited space, time, or distance (p. 427)

Because I could not stop for Death—

Emily Dickinson

Waiting Outside No. 12, Anonymous, Crane Kalman Gallery

Background

The extent of Emily Dickinson's gift was not generally recognized until 1955, when a new edition of her poems was published under the guidance of Thomas H. Johnson. Previous editors had changed Dickinson's poems to reflect conventional ideas about poetry, but Johnson's edition restored the poet's original versions. For the first time, Dickinson's poetry was printed as she had meant it to be read, and the world experienced the power of her complex mind captured in concrete imagery and simple but forceful language. Dickinson's work is often compared with that of the modern poets, and she is now acknowledged as a visionary who was far ahead of her time.

Because I could not stop for Death—
He kindly stopped for me—
The Carriage held but just Ourselves—
And Immortality.

▲ **Critical Viewing** In what ways do the details of this painting mirror Dickinson's poem? **[Analyze]**

5 We slowly drove—He knew no haste
And I had put away
My labor and my leisure too,
For his Civility—

We passed the School, where Children strove
10 At Recess—in the Ring—
We passed the Fields of Gazing Grain—
We passed the Setting Sun—

Or rather—He passed Us—
The Dews drew quivering and chill—
15 For only Gossamer,[1] my Gown—
My Tippet[2]—only Tulle[3]—

We paused before a House that seemed
A Swelling of the Ground—
The Roof was scarcely visible—
20 The Cornice—in the Ground—

Since then—'tis Centuries—and yet
Feels shorter than the Day
I first surmised the Horses Heads
Were toward Eternity—

Reading Strategy
Analyzing Images What idea do the images of Gossamer and Tulle suggest?

cornice (kôr´ nis) n. projecting decorative molding along the top of a building

surmised (sər mīzd´) v. guessed

---

1. **Gossamer** n. very thin, soft, filmy cloth.
2. **Tippet** n. scarflike garment worn over the shoulders and hanging down in front.
3. **Tulle** (tōōl) n. thin, fine netting used for scarves.

Review and Assess

Thinking About the Selection

1. **Respond:** Which images in this poem were the most vivid for you? Why?

2. **(a) Recall:** In the first two lines, what adverb defines Death's actions? **(b) Analyze:** In what sense is this depiction ironic?

3. **(a) Recall:** What three scenes does the carriage pass in stanza three? **(b) Interpret:** What is the significance of these images?

4. **(a) Recall:** How much time passes for the speaker in this poem? **(b) Speculate:** Why do you think the speaker notes that the time "feels shorter than the Day"? **(c) Compare and Contrast:** What does the speaker seem to feel about the experience of death in contrast with life?

5. **(a) Draw Conclusions:** What is the message of this poem? **(b) Take a Position:** Do you agree with the message? Explain.

I heard a Fly buzz – when I died

Emily Dickinson

Room With a Balcony, Adolph von Menzel, Staatliche Museen Preubischer Kulturbesitz Nationgalerie, Berlin

▲ **Critical Viewing** What details in this painting serve as an appropriate illustration for Dickinson's poem? **[Support]**

I heard a Fly buzz—when I died—
The Stillness in the Room
Was like the Stillness in the Air—
Between the Heaves of Storm—

5   The Eyes around—had wrung them dry—
And Breaths were gathering firm
For that last Onset—when the King
Be witnessed—in the Room—

I willed my Keepsakes—Signed away
10 What portion of me be
Assignable—and then it was
There interposed a Fly—

With Blue—uncertain stumbling Buzz—
Between the light—and me—
15 And then the Windows failed—and then
I could not see to see—

Literary Analysis
Slant Rhyme What two words form a slant rhyme in the third stanza?

Review and Assess

Thinking About the Selection

1. **Respond:** What was your first reaction to this poem? Explain.

2. **(a) Recall:** What do the speaker and those in attendance expect to experience when "the last Onset" occurs?
   (b) Recall: What happens instead? **(c) Analyze:** In what ways is this turn of events ironic?

3. **(a) Recall:** What actions has the speaker taken in preparation for death? **(b) Interpret:** Which "portion" of the speaker is "assignable," or able to be willed to others, and which is not?

4. **(a) Recall:** In the final stanza, what adjectives does the speaker use to describe the buzzing of the fly?
   (b) Draw Conclusions: What statement about dying is Dickinson making in this poem?

5. **Speculate:** If you were describing a deathbed scene from the perspective of the dying person, would you mention the buzzing of a fly? Why or why not?

There's a certain Slant of light,

Emily Dickinson

There's a certain Slant of light,
Winter Afternoons—
That <u>oppresses</u>, like the Heft
Of Cathedral Tunes—

5   Heavenly Hurt, it gives us—
We can find no scar,
But internal difference,
Where the Meanings, are—

None may teach it—Any—
10 'Tis the Seal Despair—
An imperial affliction
Sent us of the Air—

When it comes, the Landscape listens—
Shadows—hold their breath—
15 When it goes, 'tis like the Distance
On the look of Death—

oppresses (ə pres´ əz) v.
weighs heavily on the
mind

My life closed twice before its close

Emily Dickinson

My life closed twice before its close—
It yet remains to see
If Immortality unveil
A third event to me.

5   So huge, so hopeless to conceive
As these that twice befell.
Parting is all we know of heaven.
And all we need of hell.

The Soul selects her own Society

Emily Dickinson

The Soul selects her own Society—
Then—shuts the Door—
To her divine Majority—
Present no more—

5 Unmoved—she notes the Chariots—pausing—
At her low Gate—
Unmoved—an Emperor be kneeling
Upon her Mat—

I've known her—from an ample nation—
10 Choose One—
Then—close the Valves of her attention—
Like Stone—

Review and Assess

Thinking About the Selections

1. **Respond:** How does "My life closed twice before its close—" connect details of personal history to ideas about eternity?

2. **(a) Recall:** According to the speaker of "There's a certain Slant of light," in what ways does the winter light affect people? **(b) Analyze:** What does this light seem to represent to the speaker?

3. **(a) Interpret:** What is the third event to which the speaker of "My life closed before its close—" refers? **(b) Connect:** What is the relationship between the three events?

4. **(a) Recall:** In "The Soul selects her own Society—," what leaves the soul "unmoved"? **(b) Analyze:** How would you describe the soul's attitude toward the world's attractions?

5. **(a) Recall:** What happens after the soul makes her choice? **(b) Assess:** What adjectives would you use to characterize the speaker based on this choice?

6. **Relate:** Our culture places a premium on popularity for its own sake. What do Dickinson's poems suggest about other ways to view human relationships?

The Brain—is wider than the Sky—

Emily Dickinson

Twilight in the Wilderness, Frederick E. Church, The Cleveland Museum of Art

The Brain—is wider than the Sky—
For—put them side by side—
The one the other will contain
With ease—and You—beside—

5 The Brain is deeper than the sea—
For—hold them—Blue to Blue—
The one the other will absorb—
As Sponges—Buckets—do—

The Brain is just the weight of God—
10 For—Heft them—Pound for Pound—
And they will differ—if they do—
As Syllable from Sound—

▲ Critical Viewing
What feelings do the sweep of sky, mountains, and water in this painting evoke in you? [Respond]

There is a solitude of space

Emily Dickinson

There is a solitude of space
A solitude of sea
A solitude of death, but these
Society shall be
5   Compared with that profounder site
That polar privacy
A soul admitted to itself—
<u>Finite</u> <u>Infinity</u>.

finite (fī´ nīt´) *adj.* having measurable or definable limits

infinity (in fin´ i tē) *n.* endless or unlimited space, time, or distance

Review and Assess

Thinking About the Selections

1. **Respond:** Do you think it is a good idea for people to seek solitude? Why or why not?

2. **(a) Recall:** What comparisons does the speaker make in "The Brain is Wider Than the Sky"? **(b) Interpret:** What role does a surprising use of scale and size play in these comparisons?

3. **(a) Recall:** According to the poet, how is the brain wider than the sky? **(b) Recall:** How is the brain deeper than the sea? **(c) Interpret:** What do these images suggest about the power of the human mind and heart?

4. **(a) Compare and Contrast:** In what ways does the poet's comparison of the brain to God differ from the comparisons made in the earlier stanzas? **(b) Interpret:** What is the poet suggesting about the relationship between human consciousness and divinity?

5. **(a) Recall:** In "There is a solitude of space," what three things does the speaker compare to "polar privacy"? **(b) Contrast:** How does the solitude of "a soul admitted to itself" differ from the other solitudes described?

6. **Modify:** Dickinson did not give her poems titles, though her editors sometimes used a poem's first line. What titles would you give these two poems? Why?

Water, is taught by thirst.

Emily Dickinson

Water, is taught by thirst.
Land—by the Oceans passed.
Transport[1]—by throe[2]—
Peace—by its battles told—
5 Love, by Memorial Mold[3]—
Birds, by the Snow.

---

1. **Transport** ecstasy; rapture.
2. **throe** spasm or pang of pain.
3. **Memorial Mold** memorial grounds or cemetery.

Review and Assess

Thinking About the Selection

1. **Respond:** How many lines did you read before you understood the title of this poem?

2. **(a) Recall:** What is the relationship between each line's first word and the following words? **(b) Interpret:** What is the theme or message of this poem? **(c) Take a Position:** Do you agree or disagree with this message? Explain.

3. **(a) Relate:** What situations or experiences in your daily life demonstrate the theme of this poem? **(b) Extend:** Based on these situations, add two lines to this poem that are in keeping with the theme.

Review and Assess

Literary Analysis

Slant Rhyme

1. In "Because I could not stop for Death—," what three words create **slant rhymes** for *immortality*, *civility*, and *eternity*?

2. (a) Using a chart like the one here and the abc system it models for notating rhyme scheme, examine the pattern of rhyme in "There's a certain slant of light." (b) What is the effect of Dickinson's patterned use of both slant and full rhyme?

	Stanza One	Two	Three	Four
Line 1	*light* (a)			
Line 2	*noons* (b)			
Line 3	*Heft* (a-slant)			
Line 4	*Tunes* (b-full)			

Comparing Literary Works

3. Does *soul* have the same meaning in both "The Soul selects her own Society," and "There is a solitude of space"? Explain.

4. (a) Which poems present human consciousness as something boundless? (b) Which present consciousness as something limited? (c) How would you define Dickinson's view of the individual self?

Reading Strategy

Analyzing Images

5. What image does Dickinson use to describe a gravesite in "Because I could not stop for Death—"?

6. (a) Identify two images in "Water, is taught by thirst." (b) Identify two images in "The Brain—is wider than the Sky—." (c) How do these images help the speaker communicate a specific abstract idea?

Extend Understanding

7. **Humanities Connection:** In real life, people select a wide variety of different "societies." (a) What are some of the "societies" people enjoy in your community? (b) What do you think this tendency indicates about human beings?

Quick Review

Slant rhyme occurs when two words have similar, but not identical, vowel sounds.

To **analyze images,** determine whether—and how—they relate to larger ideas.

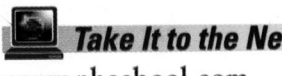 **Take It to the Net**

www.phschool.com

Take the interactive self-test online to check your understanding of these selections.

Integrate Language Skills

Vocabulary Development Lesson

Word Analysis: Latin Root *-finis-*

In "There is a solitude of space," Dickinson uses the words *finite* and *infinity*, both of which contain the Latin root *-finis-*, meaning "end" or "limit." A *finite* entity is limited in time or space; *infinity* is limitless. Explain the meaning of each of the following words, and then note how the root *-finis-* relates to the meaning of each one.

1. finish
2. confine
3. final
4. refinement

Spelling Strategy

When writing the noun forms of verbs ending in *-ess*, you will usually add the suffix *-or*, as in *oppress* + *-or* = *oppressor*. Write the noun form for each of the verbs listed below. Check your spelling in a dictionary.

1. confess
2. process
3. depress
4. profess

Concept Development: Synonyms

Review the vocabulary list on page 419. Then, identify the word or phrase whose meaning is most nearly the same as that of the first word in each item below.

1. cornice: (a) decorative ledge, (b) functional door, (c) elaborate spire
2. surmised: (a) explained, (b) inferred, (c) reduced
3. oppresses: (a) inhabits, (b) troubles, (c) judges
4. finite: (a) heavenly, (b) endless, (c) limited
5. infinity: (a) mystery, (b) multitude, (c) endlessness

Grammar and Style Lesson

Gerunds

A **gerund** is a verb form that ends in *-ing* and is used as a noun. Like nouns, gerunds function in sentences as subjects, direct objects, predicate nominatives, and objects of prepositions. The gerunds are italicized in the following examples.

Subject: *Writing* requires discipline.

Direct Object: Dickinson left her *writing* in her dresser.

Object of Preposition: She learned about *writing* by *practicing*.

Practice Identify each gerund below and tell how it is used in the sentence.

1. We paused before a House that seemed / A Swelling of the Ground—.
2. Writing was Dickinson's great passion.
3. Parting is all we know of heaven.
4. Her favorite activity was cooking.
5. Dickinson avoided traveling great distances.

Writing Application Write a paragraph of at least three sentences in which you describe a hobby—skiing or painting, for example. Include at least three gerunds.

W͞G Prentice Hall Writing and Grammar Connection: Chapter 19, Section 2

Writing Lesson

Letter to an Author

Dickinson's poetry may have stirred your emotions, challenged you to think about an idea or aspect of existence, or helped you to better understand yourself. Imagine that Dickinson is still alive. Write a letter to the poet in which you express your reactions to her verse. Be sure to use a clear organization in presenting your ideas.

Prewriting   Focus on one poem. Explore your thoughts and feelings about the poem and its effect on you. Edit your reactions down to three or four important points; then, consider how your notes support each idea.

Model: Creating Clear and Logical Organization

Salutation: Dear Emily Dickinson,

Intro: Explain that I admire her poetry.

First paragraph: Her poems explore complex ideas.

Second paragraph: Her imagery gives me new ways to think.

Conclusion: Thank her, and tell her to keep writing.

> An effective letter is organized clearly and logically.

Drafting   Open your letter with an explanation of why you are writing. Then, develop and support each important idea in a separate paragraph.

Revising   Check your tone and word choice. Confirm that you have conveyed your thoughts in a clear and logical way, with appropriate transitions from one paragraph to the next.

WG Prentice Hall Writing and Grammar Connection: Chapter 14, Section 3

Extension Activities

Listening and Speaking Choose three Dickinson poems to present in a **poetry reading.** Consider the meaning of each idea, image, and punctuation mark. Keep these tips in mind:

- Experiment with volume and tone until you achieve the desired effect.
- Speak clearly, letting the poem's meaning show in your emphasis.

Give a reading that you feel is as close as possible to the author's intention.

Research and Technology Dickinson was close to her brother Austin. Using a variety of sources, research him and their relationship. Then, select two of Dickinson's poems that seem to speak to her relationship with her brother. Combine your research and the poems in a **report.**

 **Take It to the Net**   www.phschool.com

Go online for an additional research activity using the Internet.

Prepare to Read

Walt Whitman's Poetry

Walt Whitman
(1819–1892)

In the preface to his first volume of poetry, the 1855 edition of *Leaves of Grass*, Walt Whitman wrote: "The proof of a poet is that his country absorbs him as affectionately as he absorbed it." Whitman's hopes for such proof of his own merit as a poet were deferred: He was harshly denounced for his first volume of poetry, but in the following decades, his poems gained popularity, and he became famous as "the Good Gray Poet" and "the Bard of Democracy." In his later years, Whitman was admired by writers and intellectuals on both sides of the Atlantic. Today, he is widely recognized as one of the greatest and most influential poets the United States has ever produced.

The Poet at Work Whitman was born on Long Island and raised in Brooklyn, New York. His education was not formal, but he read widely, including the works of Sir Walter Scott, Shakespeare, Homer, and Dante. Trained to be a printer, Whitman spent his early years alternating between printing jobs and newspaper writing. When he was twenty-seven, he became the editor of the Brooklyn *Eagle*, a respected newspaper, but the paper fired him in 1848 because of his opposition to slavery. After accepting a position on a paper in New Orleans, Whitman traveled across the country for the first time, observing the diversity of America's landscapes and people.

Whitman soon returned to New York City, however, and in 1850 quit journalism to devote his energy to writing poetry. Impressed by Ralph Waldo Emerson's prophetic description of a new kind of American poet, Whitman had been jotting down ideas and fragments of verse in a notebook for years. His work broke every poetic tradition of rhyme and meter as it celebrated America and the common man. When the first edition of *Leaves of Grass* was published in 1855, critics attacked Whitman's subject matter and abandonment of traditional poetic devices and forms. Noted poet John Greenleaf Whittier hated Whitman's poems so much that he hurled his copy of *Leaves of Grass* into the fireplace. Emerson, on the other hand, responded with great enthusiasm, remarking that the collection was "the most extraordinary piece of wit and wisdom that America has yet contributed."

The Bard of Democracy Though Whitman did publish other works in the course of his career, his life's work proved to be *Leaves of Grass*, which he continually revised, reshaped, and expanded until his death in 1892. The poems in later editions became less confusing, repetitious, and raucous, and more symbolic, expressive, and universal. He viewed the volume as a single long poem that expressed his evolving vision of the world. Using his poetry to convey his passionate belief in democracy, equality, and the spiritual unity of all forms of life, he celebrated the potential of the human spirit. Though Whitman's philosophy grew out of the ideas of the Transcendentalists, his poetry was mainly shaped by his ability to absorb and comprehend everything he observed. From its first appearance as twelve unsigned and untitled poems, *Leaves of Grass* grew to include 383 poems in its final, "death-bed" edition (1892). The collection captures the diversity of the American people and conveys the energy and intensity of all forms of life. In the century since Whitman's death, *Leaves of Grass* has become one of the most highly regarded collections of poetry ever written. There is little doubt that, according to his own definition, Whitman has proven himself as a poet.

Preview

Connecting to the Literature

You probably learn something new about yourself, your world, or life in general every day. As you will discover, Walt Whitman devoted his life and work to making new discoveries and reaching new understandings.

Literary Analysis

Free Verse

In contrast to verse written with a fixed meter or line pattern, **free verse** is poetry that has irregular meter and line length. Free verse is designed to re-create the cadences of natural speech. Thus, Whitman uses whatever rhythms and line lengths are appropriate to his message:

> Do I contradict myself?
> Very well then I contradict myself...

Though free verse is as old as the Psalms in the Bible, Whitman was the first American poet to use it. It proved to be the perfect form for this individualist, allowing him to express himself without formal restraints.

Comparing Literary Works

Along with his use of free verse, Whitman's **diction**—word choice and arrangement—also plays a key role in his voice. Whitman's diction is characterized by the use of two main techniques:

- The use of catalogs, or long lists
- The use of parallel forms—the repetition of phrases or sentences with similar structures or meanings.

In his poems, Whitman addresses a wide range of subjects, modifying his diction to complement each one. In some poems, his diction emphasizes important ideas. In others, it builds crescendos of emotion. As you read, compare the ways in which the poet's diction varies from poem to poem in order to serve the purpose and meaning of each work.

Reading Strategy

Inferring the Poet's Attitude

You can **infer a poet's attitude** toward a subject by examining his or her choice of words and details. Consider this passage from Whitman's "Song of Myself":

> I jump from the crossbeams and seize the clover and timothy,
> And roll head over heels . . .

Use a chart like the one shown to note key words and images in Whitman's poems and to clarify the attitudes each reveals.

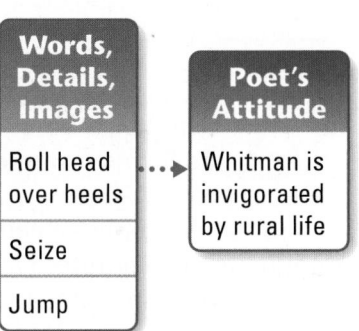

Vocabulary Development

abeyance (ə bāʹ əns) *n.* temporary suspension (p. 436)

effuse (e fyo͞ozʹ) *v.* pour out (p. 439)

from Preface to the 1855 Edition of
Leaves of Grass

Walt Whitman

Background

In his lifetime, Whitman's poetry, which broke traditional rules of rhythm and rhyme, provoked both glowing reviews and fiercely negative reactions. After receiving his complimentary copy of *Leaves of Grass,* Ralph Waldo Emerson had abundant praise for this poet. In a letter to Whitman, Emerson wrote:

> . . . I give you joy of your free and brave thought, I have great joy in it. I find incomparable things said incomparably well, as they must be. I find the courage of treatment, which so delights me, and which large perception only can inspire. I greet you at the beginning of a great career. . . .

More than a century after his death, Whitman's poetry is still regarded as some of the bravest, most generous, and most stirring in American literature.

America does not repel the past or what it has produced under its forms or amid other politics or the idea of castes or the old religions. . . . accepts the lesson with calmness . . . is not so impatient as has been supposed that the slough still sticks to opinions and manners and literature while the life which served its requirements has passed into the new life of the new forms . . . perceives that the corpse is slowly borne from the eating and sleeping rooms of the house . . . perceives that it waits a little while in the door . . . that it was fittest for its days . . . that its action has descended to the stalwart and well-shaped heir who approaches . . . and that he shall be fittest for his days.

Literary Analysis
Free Verse and Diction How does Whitman's use of parallel phrases beginning with "perceives" help establish an uplifting tone?

The Americans of all nations at any time upon the earth have probably the fullest poetical nature. The United States themselves are essentially the greatest poem. In the history of the earth hitherto the largest and most stirring appear tame and orderly to their ampler largeness and stir. Here at last is something in the doings of man that corresponds with the broadcast doings of the day and night. Here is not merely a nation but a teeming nation of nations. Here is action untied from strings necessarily blind to particulars and details magnificently moving in vast masses. Here is the hospitality which forever indicates heroes. . . . Here are the roughs and beards and space and ruggedness and nonchalance that the soul loves. Here the performance disdaining the trivial unapproached in the tremendous audacity of its crowds and groupings and the push of its perspective spreads with crampless and flowing breadth and showers its prolific and splendid extravagance. One sees it must indeed own the riches of the summer and winter, and need never be bankrupt while corn grows from the ground or the orchards drop apples or the bays contain fish or men beget children upon women. . . .

Reading Strategy
Inferring the Poet's Attitude What can you infer about Whitman's attitude toward America from his use of the images of "roughs and beards and space and ruggedness"? Explain.

Review and Assess

Thinking About the Selection

1. **Respond:** Do you think that Whitman's characterization of the United States is still accurate? Why or why not?

2. **(a) Recall:** What subject does Whitman address in the first paragraph? **(b) Interpret:** What does Whitman mean when he says "the corpse is slowly borne from the eating and sleeping rooms of the house"?

3. **(a) Recall:** According to Whitman, what makes America different from all other nations? **(b) Interpret:** What is the meaning of Whitman's notion that the United States "is not merely a nation but a teeming nation of nations"?

4. **(a) Recall:** What riches do the seasons offer? **(b) Interpret:** What does the poet's mention of these riches suggest about his vision of America's promise?

5. **(a) Recall:** According to Whitman, what is the greatest of all poems? **(b) Analyze:** Based on this statement, how is Whitman redefining the idea of a poem?

6. **Extend:** What parallels can you draw between Whitman's ideas about the United States and those expressed by Michel-Guillaume Jean de Crèvecoeur in *Letters From an American Farmer* on p. 208?

7. **Compare and Contrast:** How does Whitman's idea of the United States compare with your idea? Explain.

from Song *of* Myself

Walt Whitman

1

I celebrate myself, and sing myself,
And what I assume you shall assume,
For every atom belonging to me as good belongs to you.

I loaf and invite my soul,
5 I lean and loaf at my ease observing a spear of summer grass.

My tongue, every atom of my blood, formed from this soil, this air,
Born here of parents born here from parents the same, and their
    parents the same,
I, now thirty-seven years old in perfect health begin,
Hoping to cease not till death.

10 Creeds and schools in <u>abeyance</u>,
Retiring back a while sufficed at what they are, but never forgotten,
I harbor for good or bad, I permit to speak at every hazard,
Nature without check with original energy.

6

A child said *What is the grass?* fetching it to me with full hands,
How could I answer the child? I do not know what it is any
    more than he.

I guess it must be the flag of my disposition, out of hopeful
    green stuff woven.

Or I guess it is the handkerchief of the Lord,
5 A scented gift and remembrancer[1] designedly dropped,

---

1. **remembrancer** reminder.

Bearing the owner's name someway in the corners, that we
     may see and remark, and say *Whose?*

. . .

What do you think has become of the young and old men?
And what do you think has become of the women and children?

They are alive and well somewhere,
10 The smallest sprout shows there is really no death,
And if ever there was it led forward life, and does not wait at the
     end to arrest it,
And ceas'd the moment life appear'd.
All goes onward and outward, nothing collapses,
And to die is different from what anyone supposed, and luckier.

Reading Strategy
**Inferring the Poet's
Attitude** What attitude
toward the cycle of life is
suggested by Whitman's
use of the words
"onward," "outward,"
and "luckier"? Explain.

9

The big doors of the country barn stand open and ready,
The dried grass of the harvest-time loads the slow-drawn wagon.
The clear light plays on the brown gray and green intertinged,
The armfuls are pack'd to the sagging mow.

5 I am there, I help, I came stretch'd atop of the load,
I felt its soft jolts, one leg reclined on the other,
I jump from the crossbeams and seize the clover and timothy,
And roll head over heels and tangle my hair full of wisps.

14

The wild gander leads his flock through the cool night,
Ya-honk he says, and sounds it down to me like an invitation,
The pert may suppose it meaningless, but I listening close,
Find its purpose and place up there toward the wintry sky.

5 The sharp-hoof'd moose of the north, the cat on the house-sill,
     the chickadee, the prairie dog,
The litter of the grunting sow as they tug at her teats,
The brood of the turkey hen and she with her half-spread wings,
I see in them and myself the same old law.

The press of my foot to the earth springs a hundred affections,
10 They scorn the best I can do to relate them.

I am enamor'd of growing outdoors,
Of men that live among cattle or taste of the ocean or woods,
Of the builders and steerers of ships and the wielders of axes and
     mauls, and the drivers of horses,
I can eat and sleep with them week in and week out.

✓Reading Check

What aspects of life does
the poet celebrate in
this poem?

from *Song of Myself* ◆ 437

15 What is commonest, cheapest, nearest, easiest, is Me,
Me going in for my chances, spending for vast returns,
Adorning myself to bestow myself on the first that will take me,
Not asking the sky to come down to my good will,
Scattering it freely forever.

17

These are really the thoughts of all men in all ages and lands,
    they are not original with me,
If they are not yours as much as mine they are nothing, or next
    to nothing,
If they are not the riddle and the untying of the riddle they are
    nothing,
If they are not just as close as they are distant they are nothing.
5 This is the grass that grows wherever the land is and the water is,
This is the common air that bathes the globe.

51

The past and present wilt—I have fill'd them, emptied them,
And proceed to fill my next fold of the future.

Listener up there! what have you to confide to me?
Look in my face while I snuff the sidle of evening,[2]
5 (Talk honestly, no one else hears you, and I stay only a minute
    longer.)

Do I contradict myself?
Very well then I contradict myself,
(I am large, I contain multitudes.)
I concentrate toward them that are nigh,[3] I wait on the door-slab.

10 Who has done his day's work? who will soonest be through with
    his supper?
Who wishes to walk with me?

Will you speak before I am gone? will you prove already too late?

52

The spotted hawk swoops by and accuses me, he complains of
    my gab and my loitering.

I too am not a bit tamed, I too am untranslatable,
I sound my barbaric yawp over the roofs of the world.

---

2. **snuff . . . evening** put out the hesitant last light of day, which is moving sideways across the sky.
3. **nigh** near.

The last scud[4] of day holds back for me,
5 It flings my likeness after the rest and true as any on the
        shadow'd wilds,
   It coaxes me to the vapor and the dusk.

   I depart as air, I shake my white locks at the runaway sun,
   I effuse my flesh in eddies, and drift it in lacy jags.

   I bequeath myself to the dirt to grow from the grass I love,
10 If you want me again look for me under your boot soles.

   You will hardly know who I am or what I mean,
   But I shall be good health to you nevertheless,
   And filter and fiber your blood.

   Failing to fetch me at first keep encouraged,
15 Missing me one place search another,
   I stop somewhere waiting for you.

effuse (e fyo͞oz') v. pour out

_____

4. scud low, dark, wind-driven clouds.

Review and Assess

Thinking About the Selection

1. **Respond:** Which of the ideas expressed in "Song of Myself" do you find most—and least—appealing?

2. **(a) Recall:** From what does Whitman say his tongue and blood are formed? **(b) Analyze:** How does he view his relationship with nature? **(c) Analyze:** How does he view his relationship with other people?

3. **(a) Recall:** In Section 17, what natural images does Whitman use to communicate the idea that his thoughts belong to everyone? **(b) Generalize:** Which elements of these images convey a belief in the spiritual unity of all natural forms?

4. **(a) Recall:** In the second stanza of Section 51, where does the speaker use apostrophe—a direct address to an absent person? **(b) Infer:** Whom do you think the speaker is addressing in this stanza? Explain.

5. **(a) Recall:** In Section 52, where does the speaker say readers can find him? **(b) Infer:** What does he suggest will happen to his spirit and message after he is gone?

6. **Evaluate:** In Section 52, Whitman proudly characterizes his poetry as "barbaric yawp." What terms would you use to describe and evaluate his work?

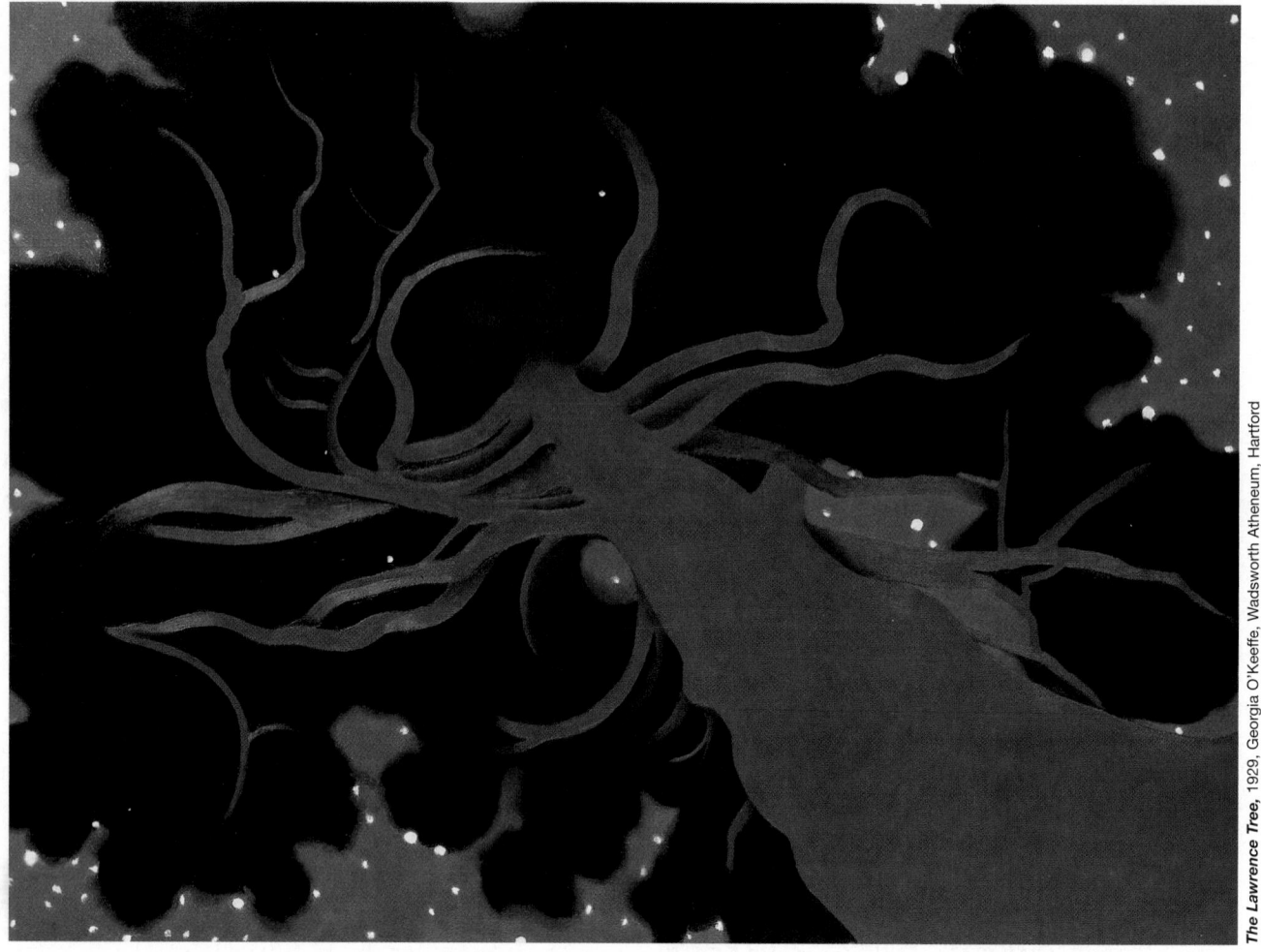

The Lawrence Tree, 1929, Georgia O'Keeffe, Wadsworth Atheneum, Hartford

When I Heard the Learn'd
Astronomer

Walt Whitman

When I heard the learn'd astronomer,
When the proofs, the figures, were ranged in columns before me,
When I was shown the charts and diagrams, to add, divide and
    measure them,
When I sitting heard the astronomer where he lectured with
    much applause in the lecture room,
5 How soon unaccountable I became tired and sick,
Till rising and gliding out I wander'd off by myself,
In the mystical moist night air, and from time to time,
Look'd up in perfect silence at the stars.

▲ **Critical Viewing**
In what ways does the artist's viewpoint in this painting compare with Whitman's in "When I Heard the Learn'd Astronomer"? **[Connect]**

By the Bivouac's Fitful Flame

Walt Whitman

By the bivouac's[1] fitful flame,
A procession winding around me, solemn and sweet and slow—
    but first I note,
The tents of the sleeping army, the fields' and woods' dim outline,
The darkness lit by spots of kindled fire, the silence,
5 Like a phantom far or near an occasional figure moving,
The shrubs and trees, (as I lift my eyes they seem to be stealthily
    watching me,)
While wind in procession thoughts, O tender and wondrous
    thoughts,
Of life and death, of home and the past and loved, and of those
    that are far away;
A solemn and slow procession there as I sit on the ground,
10 By the bivouac's fitful flame.

---

1. **bivouac** (biv′ wak′) *n.* night guard to prevent surprise attacks.

Review and Assess

Thinking About the Selections

1. **Respond:** To which of these poems do you relate most strongly? Why?

2. **(a) Recall:** In "When I Heard the Learn'd Astronomer," what does the speaker do in reaction to the lecture?
   (b) Connect: What do his actions reveal about his character?

3. **(a) Compare and Contrast:** In what ways does the "perfect silence" in the last line contrast with the lecture? **(b) Draw Conclusions:** What is the speaker saying about the value of science versus a personal experience with nature?

4. **(a) Recall:** In lines 3–4 of "By the Bivouac's Fitful Flame," what sights does the speaker look upon? **(b) Infer:** What is the procession to which he refers in line 2?

5. **(a) Recall:** Where does the speaker's mind go as he gazes upon the scene before him? **(b) Analyze:** Is the procession he refers to in line 9 the same one referred to earlier? Explain.

6. **Make a Judgment:** Whitman is known as a poet who celebrated life. Are these poems celebratory? If so, of what?

I Hear America Singing

Walt Whitman

I hear America singing, the varied carols I hear,
Those of mechanics, each one singing his as it should be blithe
    and strong,
The carpenter singing his as he measures his plank or beam,
The mason singing his as he makes ready for work, or leaves
    off work,
5 The boatman singing what belongs to him in his boat, the
    deckhand singing on the steamboat deck,
The shoemaker singing as he sits on his bench, the hatter[1]
    singing as he stands,
The wood-cutter's song, the ploughboy's on his way in the
    morning, or at noon intermission or at sundown,
The delicious singing of the mother, or of the young wife at work,
    or of the girl sewing or washing,
Each singing what belongs to him or her and to none else,
10 The day what belongs to the day—at night the party of young
    fellows, robust, friendly,
Singing with open mouths their strong melodious songs.

---

1. **hatter** person who makes, sells, or cleans hats.

Review and Assess

Thinking About the Selection

1. **Respond:** If Whitman were to write this poem today, do you think his message would be the same? Explain.

2. **(a) Recall:** What occupations does Whitman attribute to Americans? **(b) Draw Conclusions:** What does his catalog of occupations suggest about his vision of America?

3. **(a) Recall:** What word does Whitman use to describe all the workers' actions? **(b) Analyze:** In what ways does this word affect the poem's mood?

4. **(a) Recall:** What does Whitman describe the laborers doing at night? **(b) Analyze:** Why do you think the poem ends as it does?

5. **Evaluate:** Do you think Whitman romanticizes the life of a laborer? Explain your answer.

◀ **Critical Viewing**
What might Whitman say
about the work of this
farmer? **[Speculate]**

The Reaper, Louis C. Tiffany, National Academy of Design, New York City

A Noiseless Patient Spider

Walt Whitman

A noiseless patient spider,
I mark'd where on a little promontory it stood isolated,
Mark'd how to explore the vacant vast surrounding,
It launch'd forth filament, filament, filament, out of itself,
5 Ever unreeling them, ever tirelessly speeding them.

And you O my soul where you stand,
Surrounded, detached, in measureless oceans of space,
Ceaselessly musing, venturing, throwing, seeking the spheres
    to connect them,
Till the bridge you will need be form'd, till the ductile anchor hold,
10 Till the gossamer thread you fling catch somewhere, O my soul.

Review and Assess

Thinking About the Selection

1. **Respond:** Would your reaction to watching a spider spin a web be similar to Whitman's? Why or why not?

2. **(a) Recall:** In line three, what surrounds the spider?
   (b) Interpret: In line 6, what are the "measureless oceans of space" with which the speaker's soul is surrounded?

3. **(a) Recall:** Why does the spider "tirelessly" spin out filament?
   (b) Connect: How is the speaker's soul similar to the spider?

4. **(a) Recall:** What verbs does Whitman use to describe the spider's actions? **(b) Recall:** What verbs does he use to describe the activities of his soul? **(c) Compare and Contrast:** How are the two explorations the same, and how are they different?

5. **(a) Recall:** Who—or what—does the poet address directly?
   (b) Interpret: What is the speaker's attitude toward the recipient of this direct address?

6. **Synthesize:** Like the Transcendentalists, Whitman believed that the human spirit was mirrored in the world of nature. What aspects of "A Noiseless Patient Spider" reflect this belief?

7. **Evaluate:** Do you think the parallel Whitman draws between his soul and the spider is convincing? Explain.

Review and Assess

Literary Analysis

Free Verse

1. In what ways does the use of **free verse** allow the poet to express his ideas more freely in "Song of Myself"?

2. How would the impact of "When I Heard the Learn'd Astronomer" be different if it had regular meter and line length?

Comparing Literary Works

3. Use a chart like the one shown to analyze Whitman's use of lists in both "By the Bivouac's Fitful Flame" and "When I Heard the Learn'd Astronomer."

Poem	Cataloging	What the Details Share	Effect

4. In what ways does the **diction** in "When I Heard the Learn'd Astronomer," especially the use of parallel structures in the first four lines, reinforce Whitman's description of the astronomer?

5. What effect does the catalog, or list, of workers in "I Hear America Singing" have on the poem's message?

6. In your opinion, which poem represents the best match between subject and diction? Explain.

Reading Strategy

Inferring the Poet's Attitude

7. (a) In Section 14, lines 11–14, of "Song of Myself," what can you **infer** about Whitman's **attitude** toward people who work outdoors? (b) What language helps you draw this inference?

8. Note at least five descriptive words or phrases in "When I Heard the Learn'd Astronomer" that help you infer Whitman's attitude toward the science of astronomy and his feelings about the stars.

Extend Understanding

9. **Literature Connection:** It has been said that Whitman's entire body of work was a spiritual autobiography. Do you think this assessment is accurate? Explain.

Quick Review

Free verse is poetry that has irregular meter and line length.

Diction involves the writer's choice and arrangement of words, and includes the use of such devices as catalogs and parallel structures.

You can **infer the poet's attitude** by noting his or her choice of subjects, details, and words.

 Take It to the Net
www.phschool.com
Take the interactive self-test online to check your understanding of these selections.

Integrate Language Skills

Vocabulary Development Lesson

Word Analysis: Latin Root -fus-

In "Song of Myself" Whitman writes, "I effuse my flesh in eddies, and drift it in lacy jags." The word *effuse* means "pour" or "spread." It is based on the Latin root *-fus-*, meaning "pour," combined with the prefix *e-*, which means "out" or "away."

Each of the words in the left column is based on the root *-fus-*. Match each word with its definition in the right column.

1. profusion   a. rich or lavish supply

2. infuse   b. dispersed

3. effusive   c. gushing

4. diffuse   d. fill

Fluency: Denotations

Answer the following questions. Then, explain your answers.

1. If a judge hands down a ruling in *abeyance* of a particular law, is she enforcing that law?
2. Does light that *effuses* from a lamp spread softly or shine in a sharply focused beam?

Spelling Strategy

The sound of *y* followed by long *u* is often created by the letter *u* alone, as in *effuse*. Other spellings include *ew*, *ue*, *eu*, and *ou*. Complete each word below with the correct spelling.

1. p__ny (small)
2. f__d (major argument)
3. y__th (a child)
4. val__ (worth)

Grammar and Style Lesson

Pronoun and Antecedent Agreement

A **pronoun** must **agree** in number with its **antecedent**—the word to which it refers in the following ways:
- in number—singular or plural
- in gender—masculine or feminine

>   ANTECEDENT   PRONOUN
> **Singular:** The *shoemaker* singing as *he* sits on *his bench*. (masculine, singular)
>
>   ANTECEDENT
> **Plural:**   . . . The *past* and *present* wilt—
>   PRONOUN
>   I have fill'd *them* . . .

Two singular antecedents joined by *and* take a plural pronoun. Two singular antecedents joined by *or* take a singular pronoun.

Practice Choose the correct pronoun for each sentence below. Then, identify its antecedent.

1. The mare awoke, and then (she, it) stepped toward the door of the stall.
2. The woman and child opened (his, their) books and began to sing.
3. Life has (its, their) challenges and gratifications.
4. The shoemaker went on (their, his) lunch break.
5. All of the laborers received pay increases after (he, they) made requests.

Writing Application Write five sentences describing the work of various friends or family members. For each, use pronouns that correctly match their antecedents.

W/*G* *Prentice Hall Writing and Grammar Connection: Chapter 23, Section 2*

Writing Lesson

Imitation of an Author's Style

Write a poem in which you imitate Walt Whitman's unique style. Choose several elements of his style—word choice, tone, degree of formality, rhythm, use of lists, or organization—and use them throughout your poem.

Prewriting   Decide on a "Whitmanesque" topic, and review the characteristics of free verse. List or diagram sensory details and images related to your topic.

Model: Using a Cluster Diagram to Gather Details

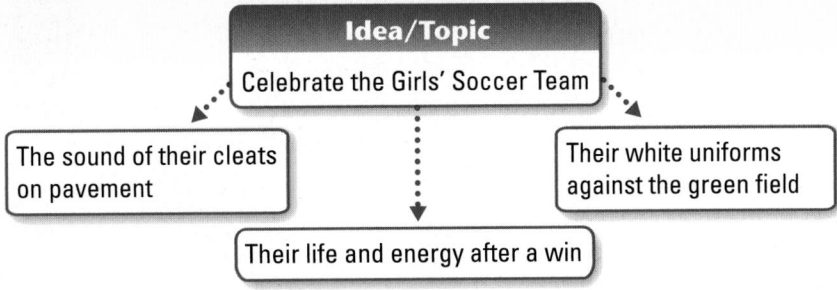

Idea/Topic
Celebrate the Girls' Soccer Team

The sound of their cleats on pavement

Their white uniforms against the green field

Their life and energy after a win

Drafting   Maintain a consistent style and tone, and let your meaning determine the lengths of lines and stanzas.

Revising   Read your poem aloud. Listen for natural rhythms of speech rather than formal rhythms or grammatical structures. Make any changes necessary to maintain the natural-sounding rhythms.

W̶G Prentice Hall Writing and Grammar Connection: Chapter 3, Section 3

Extension Activities

Listening and Speaking Whitman's poems capture America at the dawn of the Industrial Age. With a group, look through magazines for images that capture America's essence today. Make a **collage.** Then, present your findings to the class. Let the following tips guide your presentation:

- Explain why you included each image.
- Discuss how the themes of the collage compare to Whitman's vision of the country.

Include passages from Whitman's poetry that speak to the images you present. [**Group Activity**]

Research and Technology Compare the meter in Emily Dickinson's poetry with the free verse in Whitman's poetry. Use the Internet to locate and listen to oral readings of the two poets. Then, research the ways in which both poets have influenced American poetry. Deliver a **report** of your findings to the class.

 *Take It to the Net*   www.phschool.com

Go online for an additional research activity using the Internet.

CONNECTIONS
Literature Past and Present

The Emergence of an American Voice

Walt Whitman and Emily Dickinson were two of the poets most responsible for establishing a distinctly American poetic voice. The American poets who preceded them were all heavily influenced by the styles and themes of British poets of the time. Whitman and Dickinson, on the other hand, produced poetry that was fresh and original. Different in style and content from the work of any earlier poet, Whitman's poetry embodies the freedom that characterizes the American spirit and captures the immensity of the American landscape. Dickinson's poetry is filled with stylistic innovations and has a highly personal quality that parallels the American emphasis on individuality.

Whitman's Ideals, Today's World The America that Walt Whitman celebrates in his poetry has grown increasingly diverse. That increased diversity has once again expanded the boundaries of American literature, introducing readers to the traditions and issues of the many cultures represented in our population. Like Whitman and Dickinson, Langston Hughes helped establish a new American literature. He and a group of other African American poets associated with an artistic movement known as the Harlem Renaissance (see page 910) produced musical verse that captures the African American experience during the first half of the twentieth century. More recently, Angela de Hoyos and a growing number of Hispanic American poets brought the rhythms of the Spanish language to American literature, capturing the experiences of people descended from various Latin American cultures.

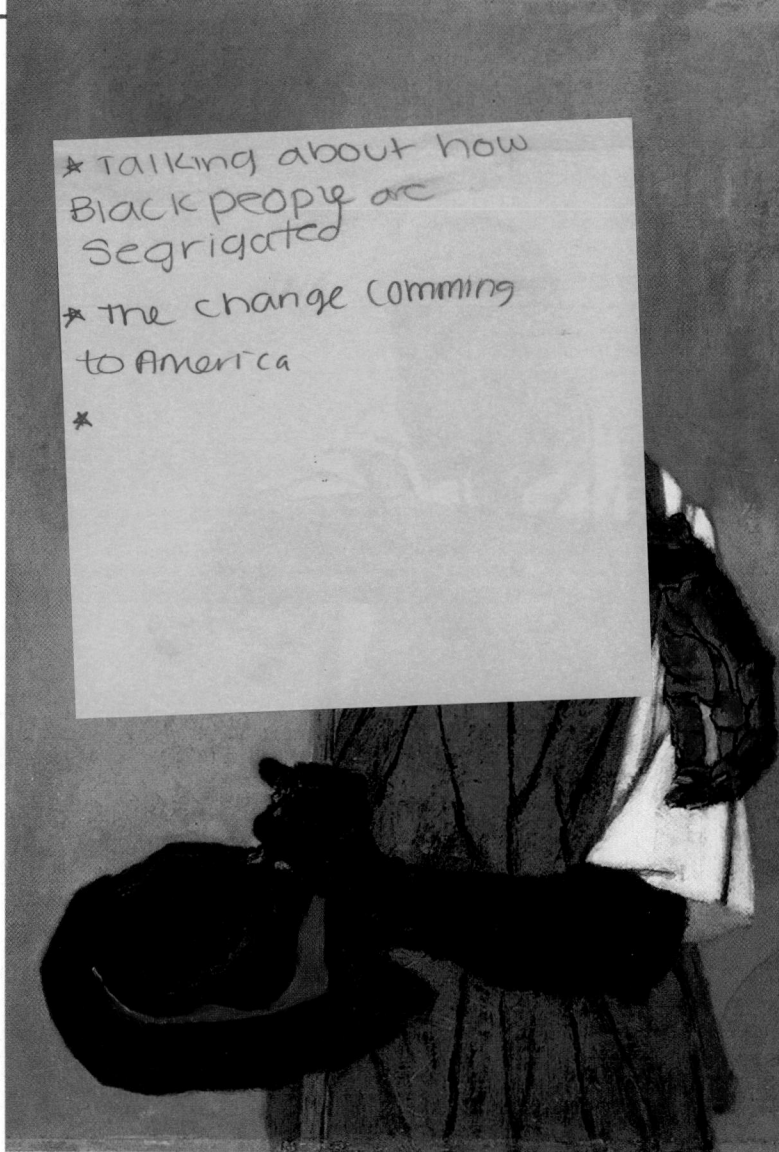

▲**Critical Viewing** Which image in this painting better illustrates the sentiments of this poem—the man or the lion? Explain. **[Make a Decision]**

Nobody Around Here Calls Me Citizen, 1943, Robert Gwathmey, University of Minnesota, © Estate Robert Gwathmey/Licensed by VAGA, New York, NY

I, Too

Langston Hughes

I, too, sing America.

present —
I am the darker brother.
They send me to eat in the kitchen
When company comes,
5 But I laugh,
And eat well,
And grow strong.

Future —
Tomorrow,
I'll be at the table
10 When company comes.
Nobody'll dare
Say to me,
"Eat in the kitchen,"
Then.

Besides —
15 Besides,
They'll see how beautiful I am
And be ashamed—

I, too, am America.

Langston Hughes

(1902–1967)

Langston Hughes emerged from the Harlem Renaissance as the most prolific and successful African American writer. Hughes published several volumes of poetry in which he experimented with a variety of forms and techniques and often tried to re-create the rhythms of contemporary jazz.

Mandolin, Rosa Ibarra

▲ **Critical Viewing** Compare the mood of this painting with the mood of the poem. **[Compare]**

To Walt Whitman

Angela de Hoyos

hey man, my brother
world-poet
prophet democratic
here's a guitar
5 for you
—a chicana guitar—
so you can spill out a song
for the open road
big enough for my people
10 —my Native Amerindian race
that I can't seem to find
in your poems

Angela de Hoyos

(b. 1940)
Angela de Hoyos has emerged as a voice of her times, celebrating her heritage and knowledge of what it means to live in a world of diversity.

De Hoyos first published poetry in high school. By her early twenties, her poetry was published in literary journals. Between 1969 and 1975, de Hoyos studied, wrote, and established her reputation through readings at Mexican American gatherings in the Southwest. She has published five collections of poetry.

Connecting Literature Past and Present

1. (a) Compare and contrast the message of American identity in Hughes's and de Hoyos's poems to Whitman's "I Hear America Singing." (b) What message do you think Hughes and de Hoyos are trying to convey?

2. In what ways do "To Walt Whitman" and "I, Too" reflect changes in the American literary voice since the time of Dickinson and Whitman?

Writing About Literature

Compare and Contrast Literary Trends

In its formative years, American literature comprised a fairly random assortment of individual efforts. There were no literary movements, and there was no strong sense of a distinctly American literature. By the early to mid 1800s, this had changed, and American writers began to produce a distinctive body of work. The stories, poems, and essays published during these decades explored a range of themes and set their ideas within a uniquely American landscape.

Using the assignment outlined in the yellow box, write an essay to address this period in American literary history.

Prewriting

Identify trends. Review each selection in this unit to see how it fits into a larger trend. These questions may help frame your review:

- Are the setting and theme explicitly American, or could the selection just as easily have been written by an English author?
- Does the work reflect American values such as independence and optimism, or does it reflect a traditional, European outlook on life?
- Is the author's voice personal and strongly individualistic? If so, in what ways is this expressed?
- What other literary works in the unit does the selection resemble? In what ways?

Use your review of each selection and your knowledge of history and literature to classify the pieces in this unit according to the trends they exemplify.

Select trends to compare or contrast. After classifying the selections that appear in this unit, determine which ones you want to explore in your essay. Decide whether you are more interested in comparing points of similarity between two emerging trends or in contrasting extreme differences between the old and the new.

Focus on similarities and differences. Once you have identified the selections you intend to analyze, use a chart like the one shown to closely analyze specific features.

Unique to Emerson	Similarities	Unique to Poe
Emerson's belief in the power of the individual expresses a core American value.	Both writers believed that some aspects of the truth were beyond the realm of physical reality.	Allusions to European art, music, and architecture in "The Fall of the House of Usher" show Poe's kinship with European traditions.

Assignment: Old vs. New in American Literature

Write an analytical essay that compares and contrasts one of the more distinctly American literary trends of this period with one of the more traditional schools of literature. Your essay will focus on two different trends and may require support from more than two authors.

Criteria:

- Include a thesis statement that identifies the trends and authors you will compare.
- Compare and contrast your subjects point by point, with references and quotations from the works.
- Approximate length: 1,500 words.

Read to Write
Reread the texts carefully, looking for ways in which they reveal—or do not reveal—distinctly American sensibilities.

Drafting

Outline. Use the information from your chart to create a working outline. In the major headings of the outline, indicate the most important points of similarity or difference between the two trends under discussion. Beneath each heading, list the supporting details from the literature.

Model: Devising a Working Outline

I.   Similarities between Poe and Emerson

    A.   belief in aspects of truth that are beyond physical reality

    B.   (other similarities)

II. Differences between Poe and Emerson

    A.   Emerson exhibits new American value of self-determination.

    B.   Poe's stories reflect the European belief in fate.

Refer to historical context. Writers are individuals, but they also reflect the times and places in which they live. As you draft, analyze the extent to which each writer's work expresses ideas that were either shared by their contemporaries or that were innovative—even radical—at the time.

Revising and Editing

Review content: Check the accuracy of details. All the opinions in your essay must be supported with accurate details from the selections. Verify the accuracy of details by going back and checking the source.

Review style: Vary sentence length and structure. Review your draft to evaluate your sentences. If you find too many long sentences in a row, break some of them down into shorter sentences. If you find a string of short, choppy sentences, combine some of them.

> **Repetitive sentence length and structure:** American writing flourished during the 1800s. Poe wrote disturbing horror stories. Emerson produced striking essays.

> **Improved sentence variety:** During the 1800s, American writing flourished. Poe wrote disturbing horror stories, while Emerson produced original and striking essays.

Publishing and Presenting

Create a comparison and contrast poster. To share your analysis with others, take the major points from your essay and distill them into brief statements. Place the statements on a poster, with comparisons in one section and contrasting points in another section. Use graphic elements to draw visual attention to your main points.

Prentice Hall Writing and Grammar Connection: Chapter 9

Write to Learn

If you have trouble finding details to support a conclusion, reconsider your ideas. Maybe you have jumped to a conclusion based on insufficient evidence. If so, rethink your argument.

Write to Explain

The reader cannot follow your thought process; he or she can only follow the arguments you note on the page. Make sure that you explain your reasons for drawing conclusions, and do not omit any steps in your thought process.

Writing WORKSHOP

Narration: Reflective Essay

A **reflective essay** is a work in which a writer explores a personal experience or event and reflects on its broader significance. In this workshop, you will write a reflective composition in which you describe a personal experience and examine its deeper meaning.

Assignment Criteria Your reflective composition should have the following characteristics:

- Writer as the main character
- The personal feelings, thoughts, or views of the writer
- Connections between specific incidents and broader themes
- An insight gained by the writer
- A balance between specific incidents and abstract ideas

To preview the criteria on which your reflective composition may be assessed, see the Rubric on page 457.

Prewriting

Choose a topic. To write a reflective essay, select a meaningful event from your life. To narrow down the possible subjects, **list and itemize.** First, list daily activities you engage in at home, at school, or in your community. Then, for each, itemize notable incidents that happened during these activities. Choose one event that has a wider meaning to explore in your reflective essay.

Draw comparisons. Once you have selected an experience to explore, use a diagram like the one shown to consider themes in the world at large that might compare to your own experience.

Exploring Back Roads

In My Life
- Be like my brothers
- Learn to navigate my world

In the World
- Connect to history
- Create sense of family continuity between generations

Find an insight. The experience you describe in your reflective essay caused you to learn something new about yourself or to see the world in a different light. Review your notes and write a sentence that connects your discovery to an event removed from your own experience. Consider including this insight in your draft.

> **Example:** When I saw how far I could travel by car, I admired the pioneers who plodded west on horseback.

Gather evidence. To connect your personal event with an incident in the outside world, you may need to do some research. Consult friends, family, the library, or the Internet and incorporate any relevant information into your draft.

Student Model

Before you begin writing, read this student model and review the characteristics of a successful reflective essay.

Graham Walker
Ruston, Louisiana

Back Roads to Tomorrow

They are small country roads—the ones that change color and ride when you cross a simple parish line. They have four-ton limits assigned to small bridges that hop over waters like Bear Creek and Black Lake Bayou. Their ragged shoulders are missing chunks of pavement and rise three inches above the packed red clay that supports the asphalt. Bright ribbons of tape hang from the lower limbs of pine trees to escort log trucks to jobs. Now and again a color will halt at a worn path entering a clean-bottomed plot of trees, but the others remain loyal to the country road.

These are the roads I grew up on.

It was usually just my oldest brother, Judd, and me. In a blue and gray Ford truck, we would branch out from our home in Taylor, Louisiana, with the windows down. Whether we went and looked at natural gas wells or whether we shot big turtles sunning themselves on logs in a bayou, it never took too much to keep us rolling along on those old Bienville back roads.

But it was not the pure riding experience that I enjoyed so much. It was the infinite knowledge of the roads that I believed I gained from those trips. I was in Back Roads 101: Knowing the Road. I made sure I asked my brother whether we would take a right here or keep straight at the inter-sections. I felt that I had to know three different ways to get to Minden, ten miles away, or which way the T below our house would take me in case I wanted to slip off for a spin in my pre-double digit years.

Looking back, I realize it was not my concern for my future driving years that led me to study those roads so intently and to map them in my memory. It was one of the lengths I went to so I could be like my three older brothers. All three of them knew the lay of the pavement throughout the Bienville Parish. They could tell me how to get wherever I wished by a back road route—even to Shreveport, I am sure. And more than I wanted to get to Shreveport, I wanted to be like them.

So I soon knew most of the roads they knew. I could tell anyone three different ways to get to Minden, or which way the T would take me. But I was mapping more than Bienville Parish.

Now I am driving. Those old Bienville roads have acquired new meaning. I know that if I hang a right at the T, I can get to the cemetery that holds my relations from 150 years back, the same people that first helped settle North Louisiana. None of my brothers ever knew about the cemetery, but I do. I even know three ways to get to Minden that my brother Judd did not teach me. On the roads that my family has traveled for over a century, I am just starting to find my way of traveling. That journey, I now understand, is what all my rides with my brothers were really about.

This descriptive language creates a strong sense of place and establishes a personal tone.

Graham is the main character in his essay.

Graham uses sensory details to convey a vivid picture of his experience.

Graham begins to draw connections between the specific experience and a deeper meaning.

Graham extends his personal experience into the abstract realm of family, identity, and history.

Drafting

Organize your reflection.
Develop a draft that follows a logical organization and places the incident you are describing in a broader context. The organizational format shown at right is an effective way to build a reflective essay.

Begin with a compelling lead.
Reflective writing gives you the opportunity to interest someone in your life. Simple opening sentences can provide just the right amount of information to grab a reader's attention.

> **Organize your essay**
>
> Identify an experience from your life.
> ▼
> Describe thoughts or feelings from the event.
> ▼
> Compare your experiences with other related events.
> ▼
> End with a lesson learned from reflecting on the event.

Examples: Whenever I hear the song "Memory," I burst into laughter.

My sister refuses to wear the color yellow.

Elaborate to make your writing personal. As you draft, include details, such as the thoughts and feelings you remember experiencing during the event. Note sensory images that will make those details more vivid. Refer back to the notes you took during prewriting, and add these thoughts, feelings, and images to your draft.

Revising

Revise to achieve balance. Review your draft to find the connections between your experience and events in the world at large. Use this strategy to create a balance between ideas in your draft:

1. Place a blue star next to sentences that develop your own experiences.

2. Place a red check next to sentences that allude to related outside experiences. If you have too few checks, add more examples.

3. Check that your draft effectively balances reflections on your own experience with thoughts on larger themes.

Model: Revising for Balance

☆Now I am driving. ☆Those old Bienville roads have acquired new meaning. ✓I know that if I hang a right at the T, I can get to the cemetery that holds my relations from 150 years back, the same people that first helped settle North Louisiana. ☆None of my brothers ever knew about the cemetery, but I do. ☆I even know three ways to get to Minden that my brother Judd did not teach me. ✓*On the roads that my family has traveled for over a century, I am just starting to find my way of traveling....*

> Graham added information that enlarges upon the specific experiences he describes.

Revise to vary sentences. Even though your reflective essay is about an event that happened to you, work to avoid beginning every sentence with *I*. Highlight the first word in every sentence in your draft, and vary sentence beginnings to make your writing more interesting.

Example: I remember the door. I remember it was locked. I remember being curious.

The door was locked, and I remember being curious.

Compare the model and nonmodel. What makes the model more effective?

Nonmodel	Model
They are small country roads. They change color and ride when you cross a parish line. They have four-ton limits. They have small bridges. The bridges hop over waters like Bear Creek and Black Lake Bayou.	They are small country roads— the ones that change color and ride when you cross a simple parish line. They have four-ton limits assigned to small bridges that hop over waters like Bear Creek and Black Lake Bayou.

Publishing and Presenting

Use the following technique to share your writing with a wider audience.

Deliver an oral presentation. Read your reflective composition aloud in front of your classmates. After you have finished reading, ask classmates to identify other outside events that would make good points of comparison with the personal event you explore in your composition.

 Prentice Hall Writing and Grammar Connection: Chapter 4

Read to Write

To see an example of a reflective essay, read "Suspended" by Joy Harjo, page 1049.

Rubric for Self-Assessment

Evaluate your reflective essay using the following criteria and rating scale:

Criteria	Rating Scale				
	Not very				Very
How clearly drawn is the writer as the main character?	1	2	3	4	5
How well are the personal feelings, thoughts, or views of the writer conveyed?	1	2	3	4	5
How effectively are comparisons between specific incidents and broader themes made?	1	2	3	4	5
How well are the insights gained by the writer described?	1	2	3	4	5
How well is the balance between specific incidents and abstract ideas set out?	1	2	3	4	5

Listening and Speaking WORKSHOP

Analyzing Media

Every day, most of us are bombarded with media messages, from advertisements to radio talk shows to television news broadcasts. All of these different forms of media are created for specific purposes. The following strategies will help you to analyze the purposes and identify the techniques media makers use to advance their aims.

Analyze Purpose

Most forms of media seek to persuade, inform, or entertain. To identify media purposes, use the following guidelines:

- **Define media types.** Persuasive media seeks to convince you to think or act in a particular way. Informative media explains or describes a topic. Entertainment media creates enjoyment for the audience.

- **Identify uses of language.** Word choice can provide signals about the purpose of a media presentation. For example, persuasive media may contain evaluative terms, informative media may include technical language, and entertainment media may contain emotional language.

- **Consider strategies.** Look for the reasoning behind the media maker's choices. For example, even in news broadcasts, set design and lighting create a specific environment.

Analyze Techniques

As you observe media, evaluate the use of these techniques.

- **Interviews.** Real people help viewers identify with the message of a presentation. Informative media such as newscasts might use interviews with people who have played a role in the story and who can share their personal reactions.

- **Format.** Performers may choose media to heighten dramatic or comedic effect. For example, radio disc jockeys might focus on amusing word plays, while comedians in a theater might use sight gags.

- **Music and sound effects.** The music used in a presentation should help to reinforce the tone. For example, advertisements directed at children may use high-spirited music, while those conveying public safety messages might use somber music.

> **Evaluation Form for Media Analysis**
>
> Name of Media _____
> Media Type and Purpose _____
> Intended Audience _____
>
> **Signal Characteristics:**
>   Word/content choice _____
>   Tone _____
>
> **Reasoning:**
> Why do you think the media maker made specific choices about structure, content, and style? _____
>
> **Techniques:**
>   Interviews _____
>   Format _____
>   Music/sound effects _____
>
> Were the techniques used in this presentation effective? Did they advance the purpose you identified above?

Activity: View and Analyze Watch television for a week as an active viewer. For each show you see, note the intended audience, the show's purpose, and the techniques used, and their intended effects. Use an evaluation form like the one shown to aid your analysis.

Assessment WORKSHOP

Inferences and Generalizations

The reading sections of some tests often require you to read a passage of fiction and draw inferences and generalizations about the plot, setting, characters, and mood. The following strategies will help you answer such test questions:

- As you read fiction, remember that to infer is to read between the lines, recognizing the implied message.
- Look in the passage for clues about the characters, setting, plot, and mood.
- Significant word choices, patterns of events, and other clues can help you understand the writer's implied message.

Test-Taking Strategies

- Before answering questions, review the passage and highlight the main points.
- Look for descriptive details to help you make inferences about character, setting, plot, and mood.

Sample Test Item

Directions: Read the passage, and then answer the question that follows.

A weak rain drizzled outside the cabin, and Dan sat at the kitchen table, trying to gather courage. The idea of quitting his new job filled him with fear. He thought returning home to Oregon would help. But as the thunder boomed outside, he tried in vain to overcome his worries. He was simply too afraid of failure to quit—even if he disliked his new boss and felt indifferent toward his co-workers.

1. In this passage, Dan's main conflict is with
   A the wilds of Oregon.
   B himself.
   C his new boss.
   D his co-workers.

Answer and Explanation

The correct answer is *B.* This answer describes Dan's internal struggle with fears of failure and future uncertainty if he quits his job. Answer *A* tells where Dan feels at home. *C* and *D* may be reasons to quit but are not his direct conflict.

▶ Practice

Directions: Read the passage, and then answer the questions that follow.

Ellen's plan to garden on the dusty plot of Oklahoma clay didn't surprise anyone. When the rain rotted her tomato sprouts, she simply planted more. When the deer nibbled her corn, she built a strong fence around the garden bed. When the summer skies withheld rain, she lugged bucketfuls of water from a nearby spring. And when the town amateur gardening contest gave out blue ribbons, Ellen won them all.

1. Which of the following most accurately describes Ellen?
   A talented
   B lucky
   C determined
   D strong

2. Which of the following inferences does the passage support?
   A Ellen lives with a large family.
   B Gardening is financially rewarding.
   C Oklahoma clay presents difficulties for gardening.
   D Tomatoes are easy to harvest.

The Fall of Richmond, Currier & Ives

> **" If we do not make common cause to save the good old ship of the Union on this voyage, nobody will have a chance to pilot her on another voyage. "**

—Abraham Lincoln, President of the United States of America, February 15, 1861

> **" I worked night and day for twelve years to prevent the war, but I could not. The North was mad and blind, would not let us govern ourselves, and so the war came. Now it must go on until the last man of this generation falls in his tracks and his children seize his musket and fight our battles. "**

—Jefferson Davis, President of the Confederate States of America, July 17, 1864

Timeline 1850–1914

American Events

- **1855** Walt Whitman publishes first edition of *Leaves of Grass*.
- **1855** *My Bondage and My Freedom*, Frederick Douglass's second autobiography, makes its appearance. ▼

- **1858** Lincoln-Douglas debates help make Abraham Lincoln a national figure.
- **1859** John Brown, an abolitionist, leads a raid on federal arsenal at Harpers Ferry, Virginia; he is hanged for treason.

- **1860** Republican Abraham Lincoln is elected United States president.
- **1860** South Carolina secedes from the Union.
- **1861** Civil War begins in April with firing on Fort Sumter.
- **1863** Lincoln issues the Emancipation Proclamation.
- **1865** General Robert E. Lee surrenders to General Ulysses S. Grant at Appomattox. ▼

KNOWN TO EVERYONE – LIKED BY ALL

- **1876** Mark Twain publishes *The Adventures of Tom Sawyer*. ▲
- **1876** Baseball's National League founded.
- **1877** The Compromise of 1877 ends military occupation of the South.
- **1877** Thomas Edison patents the phonograph.

World Events

- **1857** France: Gustave Flaubert completes *Madame Bovary*, a classic novel of realism.
- **1859** England: Charles Dickens adds to his fame with *A Tale of Two Cities*.
- **1859** England: Charles Darwin introduces theory of evolution in *The Origin of Species*.

- **1862** France: Louis Pasteur proposes modern germ theory of disease.
- **1865** England: Lewis Carroll completes *Alice's Adventures in Wonderland*.
- **1865** Germany: Karl Benz builds first automobile powered by the internal-combustion engine.

- **1869** Russia: Leo Tolstoy publishes *War and Peace*.
- **1874** France: Claude Monet gathers Impressionist painters for first exhibition.
- **1877** England: First tennis championship held at Wimbledon.

American and World Events

- **1883** Railroads adopt standard time zones.
- **1883** The Brooklyn Bridge is opened.
- **1884** Mark Twain publishes *The Adventures of Huckleberry Finn.*

- **1886** Statue of Liberty dedicated in New York Harbor. ▲
- **1888** Great mid-March blizzard in eastern United States piles 30-foot drifts in New York's Herald Square.

- **1890** Last major battle between U.S. troops and Native Americans fought at Wounded Knee, South Dakota.
- **1895** Stephen Crane publishes *The Red Badge of Courage.*
- **1895** First professional football game played in Latrobe, Pennsylvania.
- **1896** *The Country of the Pointed Firs,* Sarah Orne Jewett's masterpiece, appears.

- **1903** Jack London publishes *The Call of the Wild.*

- **1903** Wright Brothers stay aloft for 852 feet in their airplane at Kitty Hawk, North Carolina. ▲
- **1908** Henry Ford builds his first Model T. ▼

- **1885** French scientist Louis Pasteur administers the first successful rabies vaccination. ▶
- **1886** Russia: Leo Tolstoy completes *The Death of Ivan Ilyich.*

- **1891** England: Thomas Hardy publishes *Tess of the D'Urbervilles.*
- **1894** Sino-Japanese War breaks out; Japanese army easily defeats Chinese.
- **1895** Germany: Wilhelm Roentgen discovers X-rays.
- **1898** France: Pierre and Marie Curie discover radium and polonium.

- **1901** Italy: First transatlantic radio telegraphic message is achieved by Marconi.
- **1903** Spain: Pablo Picasso paints *The Old Guitarist.*
- **1904** Russo-Japanese War begins.
- **1905** Germany: Albert Einstein proposes his relativity theory.

Division, Reconciliation, and Expansion

(1850–1914)

The years between 1850 and 1914 witnessed a transformation of the United States. During those years, America changed from a decentralized, mostly agricultural nation to the modern industrial nation that we know today. This transformation began in the period leading up to the Civil War. In that war, Americans took up arms against one another to determine which should prevail: North or South? the federal Union or states' rights? freedom or slavery? The North won, the Union held, and slavery was abolished, but at a devastating cost to the nation.

Historical Background

Prelude to War By the mid-nineteenth century, it was evident that the North and the South had developed along very different lines. In the North, commerce, was king; in the South, cotton ruled. The Industrial Revolution and cheap transportation had helped turn northern towns and cities into centers of bustling activity. Education, banking, science, and reform movements—all were topics of interest and concern. Immigration, too, was changing the face of the North. A rising tide of Irish and German immigrants, among others, came seeking new lives in the United States. Most of these newcomers landed at seaports between Boston and Baltimore and settled in the northern states.

The South, in contrast, was a slower-paced region of plantations and small farms. There were cities, to be sure, but the area was defined by its cotton plantations, large and small. Sugar, rice, and tobacco were also important crops. The march of technological progress, with its hotly debated social issues and problems, had little impact on the prewar South. One issue, however, made an indelible impression: slavery. The South believed its lifeblood depended on the institution of slavery.

Disagreements between North and South over slavery were nothing new, but the controversy was rekindled in 1850 by the passage of the Fugitive Slave Act. It required all citizens—of free states as well as slave states—to help catch runaway slaves. Southerners saw the law as just; Northerners considered it an outrage.

The expansion of slavery into the West was hotly contested. In 1854, when the Kansas-Nebraska Act opened up a vast area of

▼ **Critical Viewing**
This picture shows a young Confederate soldier. Most of the soldiers in both armies were between the ages of 18 and 21. Some were even younger. What problems do you think a 16-year-old Union or Confederate soldier might have faced? **[Relate]**

previously free western land to slavery, the argument became a fight. "We will engage in competition for the virgin soil of Kansas," a senator from New York insisted. The "competition" turned Kansas into a bloody battleground.

Just as it dominated politics and preoccupied the nation, the controversy over slavery influenced the literature of the day, and in one classic case, literature fueled the controversy. Harriet Beecher Stowe's novel *Uncle Tom's Cabin*, published in 1852, vividly depicted the cruelty of slavery. The book became a powerful antislavery weapon, selling more than 300,000 copies within a year. Its impact was such that, within three years, no fewer than thirty southern novels came out attempting to counter its influence.

The deep national division intensified in 1859 when a group of antislavery extremists raided a federal arsenal at Harpers Ferry, West Virginia. Led by John Brown, the group had intended to provoke an armed slave revolt. The attempt failed and Brown was executed for treason, but his death only fed the controversy, which now threatened to escalate out of control.

The Union Is Dissolved The conflict between North and South came to a head when Abraham Lincoln was elected in 1860. Lincoln represented the newly formed Republican party, which had dedicated itself to halting the spread of slavery. South Carolina had threatened to secede if Lincoln was elected, and in December it did so. Five states followed South Carolina out of the Union. In February 1861, the secessionist states established the Confederate States of America.

Fighting began on April 12, 1861, when Confederate artillery fired on Union troops holding Fort Sumter, in Charleston Harbor. Many on both sides anticipated a short war ending in victory. No one could know what lay ahead: the carnage of Antietam, where more than 26,000 men fell in a single day; the deprivation of the siege of Vicksburg, where people survived by eating dogs and rats; the wholesale destruction of Georgia, when Union general William T. Sherman's troops marched to the sea. In fact, the devastating war would last four long years.

By the time Confederate general Robert E. Lee surrendered to Union general Ulysses S. Grant in the spring of 1865, nearly 620,000 soldiers on both sides had lost their lives. About 500,000 had been wounded. The South lay in ruins, its cities razed, its farms and plantations destroyed.

Lincoln guided the nation through the worst crisis in its history. He did not, however, have the chance to reconstruct the Union. Just days after Lee's surrender, Lincoln was assassinated. He died on April 15, 1865. The nation, war-torn and weary, would have to face the daunting tasks of reconciliation and reconstruction without him.

▲ **Critical Viewing** Robert E. Lee (left) and Ulysses S. Grant (right) were the leaders of the Confederate and Union armies, respectively. What can you infer about their different personalities and backgrounds by comparing and contrasting these photographs? Explain. **[Compare and Contrast]**

Abraham Lincoln—Legendary Hero or "Flawed and Complex Man"

Was Abraham Lincoln a legendary hero, someone to be compared with such historic figures as Lao-tse or Caesar, or was he a flawed human being? Two biographers disagree on the answer to this question.

Legendary Hero "Perhaps no human clay pot has held more laughter and tears.

"The facts and myths of his life are to be an American possession, shared widely over the world, for thousands of years, as the tradition of Knute or Alfred, Lao-tse or Diogenes, Pericles or Caesar, are kept. This because he was not only a genius in the science of neighborly human relationships and an artist in the personal handling of life from day to day, but a strange friend and a friendly stranger to all forms of life that he met."

—Carl Sandburg,
A Lincoln Preface

Flawed and Complex Man "The historical Lincoln, as I have tried to approximate him, was a flawed and complex man who had the gift of vision that let him see things few others ever see. When I say that he was flawed, I am not profaning his memory, as many of my correspondents have accused me of doing. On the contrary, the historical Lincoln comes out more heroic than the immortal Man of the People, because we see him overcoming his deficiencies and self-doubts, often against tremendous odds."

—Stephen B. Oates,
*Abraham Lincoln:
The Man Behind the Myths*

An Expanding America If conflict characterized the Civil War years, change—on an astonishing scale—characterized the period that followed. During the fifty-year period following the war, physical expansion and industrialization transformed the American landscape, economy, society, and identity.

The Homestead Act of 1862 promised 160 acres to anyone who would live on the land for a certain period and make minimal improvements to it. This shifted the westward movement into high gear. Half a million farmers, including tens of thousands of emancipated African Americans, staked claims on the Great Plains. Miners went west by the thousands, lured by the prospect of striking it rich in gold. Still others moved west to become cattle ranchers. Westward expansion was boosted by completion of the first transcontinental railroad in 1869. As the national railroad system grew, the covered wagon—symbol of the American pioneer—was replaced by the train as the principal means of transportation.

The Disappearing Frontier By 1890, the frontier as Americans had known it for centuries had ceased to exist. The steady influx of settlers, the burgeoning railroads, the growth of mining and cattle ranching—all had combined to transform the West. Gone were the great herds of buffalo. Gone was the expanse of open range. In its place was an enormous patchwork of plowed fields and grazing lands, separated by miles of barbed wire fencing.

Gone, too, were the Indian nations, many of which had depended on the buffalo for survival. By 1890, virtually all the Native Americans in the West had been forced from their land. Decades of fierce and bloody resistance had ultimately proved futile. "I am tired of fighting," Chief Joseph of the Nez Percé reportedly said after being hunted down by the United States Army in 1877. Like others before them, Chief Joseph and his people were sent to live in Indian Territory, in what is now Oklahoma.

However, even Indian Territory, which Congress had set aside in 1834, was not safe from white encroachment. In 1889, unassigned land in Indian Territory was opened up to settlers.

The frontier may have disappeared, but its legacy lived on in a rich western folk tradition. Larger-than-life folk heros like Pecos Bill were celebrated in tall tales and legends. The frontier survived, too, in the songs of sod busters, railroad workers, cowpokes, and miners.

A Changing American Society With the introduction of electricity in the 1880s, the second Industrial Revolution began in earnest. Electricity replaced steam power in many manufacturing industries. The now-familiar trappings of modern life began to make their appearance: electric lights, telephones, automobiles, motion pictures, and phonographs. The mass production of consumer goods sparked the rise of an important new medium: advertising. Skyscrapers, department stores, and mass transportation became part of city life—as did noise, traffic jams, air pollution, crime, and slums.

The country's industrial and urban growth was also fueled by immigration. In 1880, the population of the United States was just over 50 million. By the turn of the century, it was just under 76 million. A significant portion of this increase was due to the more than 9 million immigrants who came to the country during this twenty-year period. Most of the newcomers settled in cities. In the same period, millions of Americans left farms and small towns and moved to the cities to seek work. This influx swelled urban populations and provided an inexhaustible supply of cheap labor for industry.

The industrial boom of the late nineteenth century created new extremes of wealth and poverty. The wages of industrial workers were so low that a single worker, or even two, often could not support a family. Child labor became the norm among the poor working class. Immigrant families often lived in small, dark, unventilated apartments with no toilets. In these conditions, disease was rampant.

▲ **Critical Viewing** Some African Americans traveled to the West. In this picture, the Shores family poses in front of their Nebraska sod house. What opportunities might the West have offered African Americans that the East did not? **[Analyze a Situation]**

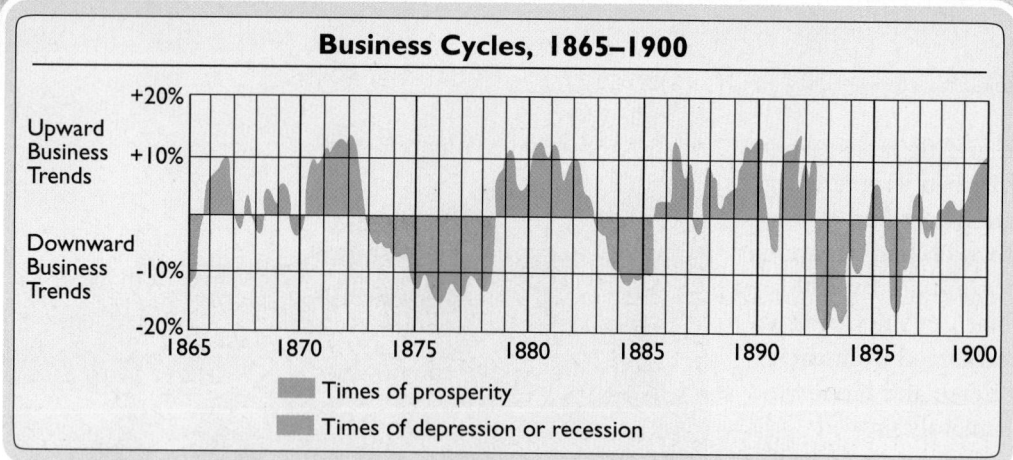

Business Cycles, 1865–1900

Times of prosperity

Times of depression or recession

Meanwhile, a relative handful of men—the owners of big industrial corporations—made fortunes and lived like royalty. Their ostentatious displays of wealth led Mark Twain to dub this period "The Gilded Age," implying a thin veneer of glitter over something of poor quality.

Indeed, just below the surface of the nation's prosperity, discontentment grew. Women, African Americans, and workers agitated for changes in their social, economic, and political status: Women still did not have the vote; most African Americans, despite emancipation, were hardly better off in 1914 than they had been in 1850; labor reform was desperately needed. Bitter struggles erupted between emerging workers' unions and management.

Literature of the Period

Oh, Freedom! Of the blacks who remained in slavery in the 1850s, a significant number worked on cotton plantations. On these plantations and elsewhere, the slaves developed a unique style of music, the black spiritual. Spirituals fused traditional African music with such sources as the Bible, Protestant hymns, and popular music of the day. To enslaved African Americans, spirituals were—in addition to moving expressions of faith—work songs, war songs, laments, lullabies, and funeral dirges.

Not all of the black voices of the period surfaced in spirituals. One of the great black abolitionist leaders was Frederick Douglass. Born into slavery in Maryland, Douglass escaped as a young man and settled in the North, where he became a persuasive orator against slavery. In 1845, he published the first version of *Narrative of the Life of Frederick Douglass*, his eloquent autobiography that was also an indictment of slavery.

Wartime Voices Thousands of diaries, letters, journals, and speeches were produced during the war, providing a richly detailed and moving record of what Americans—from the lowliest private to General Lee himself— experienced. The lengthy diary of Mary Chesnut, the wife of a high-ranking Confederate officer, is a notable example of the extraordinary literary output of the Civil War years.

One of the greatest masters of the language at mid-century was President Lincoln. His speeches and letters are models of clarity and eloquence. His

▲ **Critical Viewing**
The ups and downs of the economy, known as business cycles, were felt more sharply as the nation industrialized and more people worked for wages.
(a) Which years were the most prosperous? (b) In which years did severe depression strike?
[Read a Graph]

Gettysburg Address, a mere ten sentences in length, has become a classic expression of the meaning of American democracy.

Frontier Voices As America expanded westward, so, too, did America's literature. During this period, a number of writers represented the Midwest and the Far West for the first time. Some, like Bret Harte and Willa Cather, were born in the East or the South but later moved west. As a young man, Harte moved from New York to California. Cather moved from Virginia to Nebraska as a child. Mark Twain, one of the greatest writers in all of American literature, grew up in Hannibal, Missouri, but traveled widely, settling in a Nevada mining town during the Civil War. Twain drew on the colorful language and outsized sensibility of the West for his first short story, "The Notorious Jumping Frog of Calaveras County."

Not all the frontier voices were those of European settlers. Mexican Americans living in the Southwest had their own legends and tales. They also had songs, such as "The Legend of Gregorio Cortez," that can take their place beside such famous western ballads as "The Streets of Laredo." Also, few speeches in American history have been as eloquent as that given by Chief Joseph of the Nez Percé when accepting the terms of surrender from federal troops in 1877.

A Living Tradition

N. Scott Momaday and the Indian Oral Tradition

In an essay entitled "On Indian-White Relations: A Point of View," N. Scott Momaday, the Pulitzer Prize-winning author of Kiowa ancestry, responds to the beauty of the Indian oral tradition and of Indian oratory. The speech he cites was spoken by Satanta, a nineteenth-century Kiowa chief, but Momaday's observations might apply equally well to the famous speech by Chief Joseph on p. 602.

> The American Indian has a highly developed oral tradition. . . . One who has only an oral tradition thinks of language in this way: my words exist at the level of my voice. If I do not speak with care, my words are wasted. If I do not listen with care, my words are lost. If I do not remember carefully, the very purpose of words is frustrated. . . . [Momaday goes on to compare the elaborateness of a written executive order from the President, dated 1968, with the directness of the following speech by Satanta, who expresses his unwillingness to settle on a reservation.]

> I have heard that you intend to settle us on a reservation near the mountains. I don't want to settle. I love to roam over the prairies. There I feel free and happy, but when we settle down we grow pale and die. I have laid aside my lance, bow, and shield, and yet I feel safe in your presence. I have told the truth. I have no little lies hid about me, but I don't know how it is with the commissioners. Are they as clear as I am?

> [Satanta's speech] is in the plain style, a style that preserves, in its way, the power and beauty of language.

Realism and Naturalism The harsh reality of frontier life, coupled with artists' reactions to the Civil War—in fiction like Ambrose Bierce's "Incident at Owl Creek Bridge" and Stephen Crane's *The Red Badge of Courage*, for example—gave rise to a new movement in American literature called Realism. Realism in literature began after the Civil War. Although the outcome of the war had given the nation a hard-won sense of unity, the enormous cost in human life had shattered the nation's idealism. Young writers turned away from the Romanticism that was popular before the war. Instead, writers began to focus on portraying "real life" as ordinary people lived it and attempted to show characters and events in an honest, objective, almost factual way. Willa Cather, for example, was a Realist noted for her unflinching portrayal of the loneliness and cultural isolation of life on the prairie. In "A Wagner Matinée," she contrasts this isolation with the cultural richness of an eastern city.

Edith Wharton wrote fiction in the Realist vein, not about Western frontier life but about the Eastern high society into which she had been born. In *The House of Mirth* (1905), for example, she wrote about conflicts between the newly rich and the old aristocracy and about how social customs can prevent individuals from fulfilling themselves.

An important literary offshoot of Realism was Naturalism. Naturalist writers also depicted real people in real situations, but they believed that forces larger than the individual—nature, fate, heredity—shaped individual

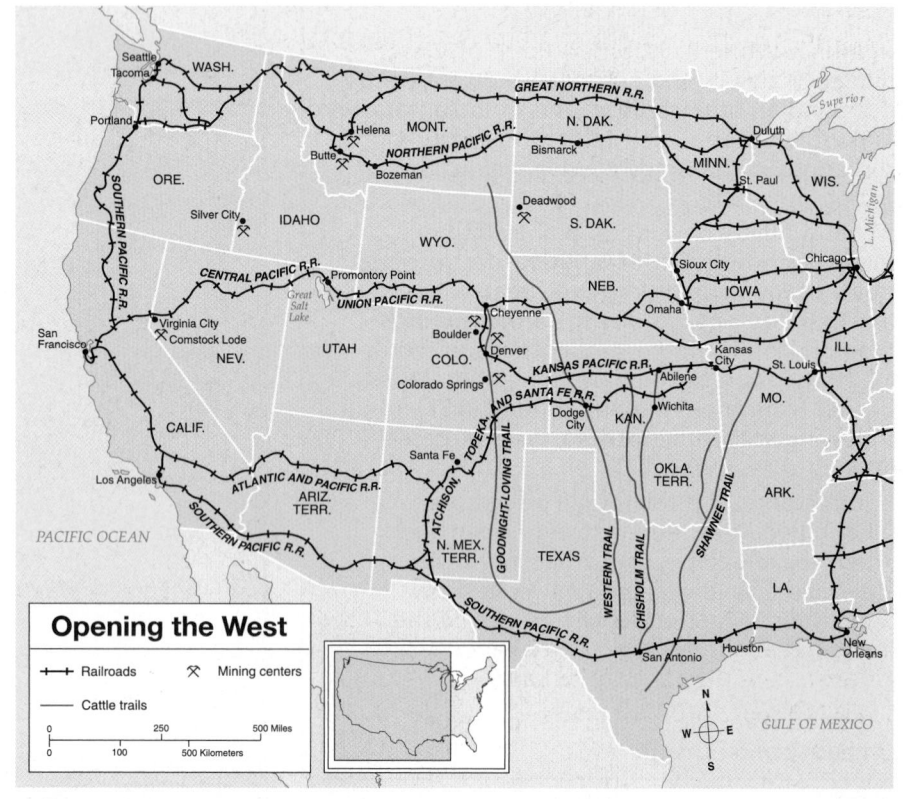

◀ **Critical Viewing** Transportation by rail, mining, and cattle grazing helped open the Great Plains for settlement, as shown on this map. (a) Which cattle trail ended in Abilene? In Cheyenne? (b) What relationship do you see between railroads and cattle trails? Between railroads and mining centers? **[Read a Map]**

Art in the Historical Context

The Ashcan School and Realism in Painting

At the beginning of the twentieth century, a group of artists working in Philadelphia and New York developed a Realist vision in their work. These painters realized that America was becoming increasingly urban, and they wanted to depict this new urban reality. Some critics insultingly called them the Ashcan School (*ashcan* means "garbage can"). This name has endured, but it is no longer considered an insult.

One prominent member of this movement was John Sloan (1871–1951). Sloan said that he saw a city as a "vast stage set where all sorts of lively business was in progress." His painting *Six O'Clock* (c. 1912) shows the "lively business" of a New York City rush hour.

▶ **Make an Inference** What qualities of urban life does Sloan capture?

Six O' Clock, John Sloan, Phillips Collection, Washington, D.C.

destiny. Jack London, for example, set much of his fiction in Alaska, where the environment was cruel and unforgiving. The theme of human endurance in the face of overwhelming natural forces pervades his fiction, including the short story "To Build a Fire."

If the reality these writers depicted seemed always to be a harsh one, it was because hardship influenced their artistic vision. It was a vision rooted in war, in the frontier, and, increasingly, in America's growing cities.

Literature of Discontent The social ills that grew out of industrialization came under the sharp eye and pen of many talented writers of the day. Kate Chopin's writing, for example, explored women's desire for equality and independence. The Naturalists saw industrialization as a force against which individuals were powerless.

In 1897, one of the finest of all volumes of American poems appeared, Edwin Arlington Robinson's *The Children of the Night*. This volume contains unsparing and unforgettable psychological portraits of a variety of small-town characters. Eighteen years later, *Spoon River Anthology* by Edgar Lee Masters presented a disturbingly candid portrait of small-town life in the form of epitaphs spoken by the dead themselves.

By 1914, America had grown up, and in a sense, American literature had, too. The Civil War, the closing of the frontier, and industrialization had brought about a loss of innocence, a shift from idealism to pragmatism in the American character. In their rejection of Romanticism and their embrace of Realism, American writers reflected this change.

THE DEVELOPMENT OF AMERICAN ENGLISH

Mark Twain and the American Language

BY RICHARD LEDERER

AMERICAN LITERATURE COMES OF AGE

On February 18, 1885, thirty thousand copies of Mark Twain's *The Adventures of Huckleberry Finn* were released in the United States. The novel turned out to be Twain's masterpiece, and it changed the direction of American letters. Twain captured the everyday speech of characters, instead of the more formal, standard English that writers before him used. In *The Adventures of Huckleberry Finn,* Twain used seven distinct dialects to reflect the speech patterns of various characters, and he also became the first important author to show the freshness and vitality of the new American idiom in narrative as well as in dialogue. Just as Geoffrey Chaucer's *The Canterbury Tales* is the first significant work written in English, *Huckleberry Finn* is the first novel of world rank to be written entirely in American.

READIN', WRITIN', AND TWAIN

Twain held strong opinions about a passel of subjects, and he possessed the gift of being able to state these views in memorable ways: "It's better to keep your mouth shut and appear stupid than to open it and remove all doubt"; "Be careful about reading health books. You may die of a misprint."

Twain also had a lot to say about style, literature, and the American language that he, more than any other writer, helped to shape.

- *On American English, compared with British English:* The property has gone into the hands of a joint stock company, and we own the bulk of the shares.
- *On dialects:* I have traveled more than anyone else, and I have noticed that even the angels speak English with an accent.
- *On choosing words:* The difference between the almost right word and the right word is really a large matter—'tis the difference between the lightning-bug and the lightning.
- *On style* (in a letter to a twelve-year-old boy): I notice that you use plain, simple language, short words, and brief sentences. That is the way to write English—it is the modern way and the best way. Stick to it; and don't let fluff and flowers and verbosity creep in.
- *On being concise:* A successful book is not made of what is in it, but what is left out of it.
- *On using short words:* I never write metropolis for seven cents when I can get the same for city. I never write policeman because I can get the same for cop.
- *On reading:* The man who does not read good books has no advantage over the man who can't read them.

ACTIVITIES

1. With a group, discuss Twain's statement on dialects, above. In your discussion, include some of the outstanding characteristics of the dialect that you speak.

2. Use one of Mark Twain's statements about writing or language, above, as the thesis for an essay or discussion on the subject.

3. In 1885, Twain wrote in his notebook, "My works are like water. The works of the great masters are like wine. But everyone drinks water." Choose a passage from one of Twain's stories or essays, and show how that passage exemplifies the author's philosophy of style.

A Nation Divided

Fight for the Standard, Wadsworth Atheneum, Hartford, Connecticut

Prepare to Read

An Episode of War ◆ Willie Has Gone to the War

Stephen Crane (1871–1900)

Stephen Crane had not even been born when the last battle of the American Civil War was fought, yet he is best remembered for his compelling depiction of the conflict. During his brief life, Crane worked to establish himself as both a leader of the Naturalist movement and one of the greatest writers of his time.

Early in his career, Crane worked as a newspaper writer in New York City. His experiences there inspired his first novel, *Maggie: A Girl of the Streets* (1893). Its grimly realistic portrayal of life in the city's slums was so frank and shocking that Crane was unable to find a publisher, so he printed the book at his own expense.

The Red Badge of Courage Crane's second novel, published in 1895, was *The Red Badge of Courage: An Episode of the American Civil War*. A psychological exploration of a young soldier's mental and emotional reactions under enemy fire, the wildly successful novel earned international acclaim for the twenty-four-year-old writer. Although Crane had never experienced military combat, he interviewed Civil War veterans and studied photographs, battle plans, and biographical accounts before writing the realistic battle scenes.

Crane later viewed war firsthand when he served as a newspaper correspondent during the Greco-Turkish War in 1897 and the Spanish-American War in 1898. His war experiences provided material for a collection of poetry, *War Is Kind* (1899), but they took their toll on his health. He died of tuberculosis at the age of twenty-eight.

An Untimely Death Knowing he was going to die, Crane worked intensely in the last years of his life. His novels, short stories, poems, and other writings fill twelve volumes. He is considered a literary prodigy who wrote as quickly and passionately as he lived. Like other Naturalists, Crane depicts characters who are manipulated by forces that are beyond their understanding or control. His most common themes include the harsh reality of war, the degradation of humanity, social rebellion, betrayal, and guilt. Crane also wrote of the physical, emotional, and intellectual responses of people under extreme pressure. For so young a writer with so little time, Crane accomplished much.

Stephen Foster (1826–1864)

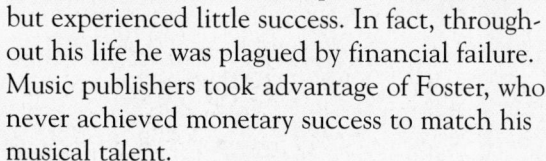

Stephen Foster was born in Pennsylvania on July 4, 1826—the fiftieth anniversary of American independence and the day that both Thomas Jefferson and John Adams died. As a young man, Foster worked as a bookkeeper but experienced little success. In fact, throughout his life he was plagued by financial failure. Music publishers took advantage of Foster, who never achieved monetary success to match his musical talent.

The popular minstrel songs and sentimental ballads that he wrote earned Foster an honored place in American music. Foster composed about 200 songs in his rather short lifetime, including such classics as "The Old Folks at Home" (popularly known as "Way Down Upon the Swanee River"), "Camptown Races," "Oh! Susanna," "My Old Kentucky Home," and "Jeanie With the Light Brown Hair." Foster collaborated with lyricist George Cooper on the Civil War ballad "Willie Has Gone to the War."

Preview

Connecting to the Literature

Being in control of a situation and making responsible decisions helps you take command of your life. This luxury was not granted to the Civil War soldiers who had very little control over their own destinies in battle.

Literary Analysis

Realism and Naturalism

In reaction to Romanticism—a movement which emphasized emotion, imagination, and nature—two literary movements emerged during the mid- to late-nineteenth century: **Realism and Naturalism.**

- Realism sought to portray life as faithfully and accurately as possible, focusing on ordinary people suffering the harsh realities of everyday life.
- Naturalism also sought to portray ordinary people's lives, but suggested that environment, heredity, and chance, or forces they could neither understand nor control, determined people's fate.

As you read, look for elements related to these two literary movements.

Comparing Literary Works

Both of these selections are set against a backdrop of the Civil War, but each presents a different perspective on the bloodiest conflict ever fought on American soil. As you read, determine which writer presents the more accurate description of events and which one presents a more idealized version of life during that bitter moment in history.

Reading Strategy

Recognizing Historical Details

The social and political climate surrounding these Civil War snapshots form part of their setting and context. When you **recognize historical details,** you determine how the attitudes of both writers and characters reflect the ideas of their day. As you read, use a chart like the one shown to record events that suggest historical context.

Event	Historical Context
Battles	
Medical Practices	
Political Situations	
Social Attitudes	

Vocabulary Development

precipitate (prē sip′ ə tāt′) v. cause to happen before expected or desired (p. 478)

aggregation (ag′ rə gā′ shən) n. group of distinct objects or individuals (p. 478)

inscrutable (in skroōt′ ə bəl) adj. impossible to see (p. 479)

disdainfully (dis dān′ fəl ē) adv. showing scorn or contempt (p. 480)

glade (glād) n. open space in a wood or forest (p. 482)

An
EPISODE
of War

Stephen Crane

Background

Both of these selections were inspired by the American Civil War, the bloodiest conflict in American history. The war claimed the lives of 600,000 soldiers—more American casualties than the combined total of all other wars in which the United States has fought. Hundreds of thousands more were left maimed by battle wounds and crude medical care.

When the war began, neither side was prepared to care for the wounded. The conditions were terrible, and twice as many Civil War soldiers died of infections as of combat wounds. As you read "An Episode of War," keep in mind that amputation was routine treatment for injured limbs. A wounded soldier knew that he faced the high probability of losing his arm or leg to a surgeon's saw.

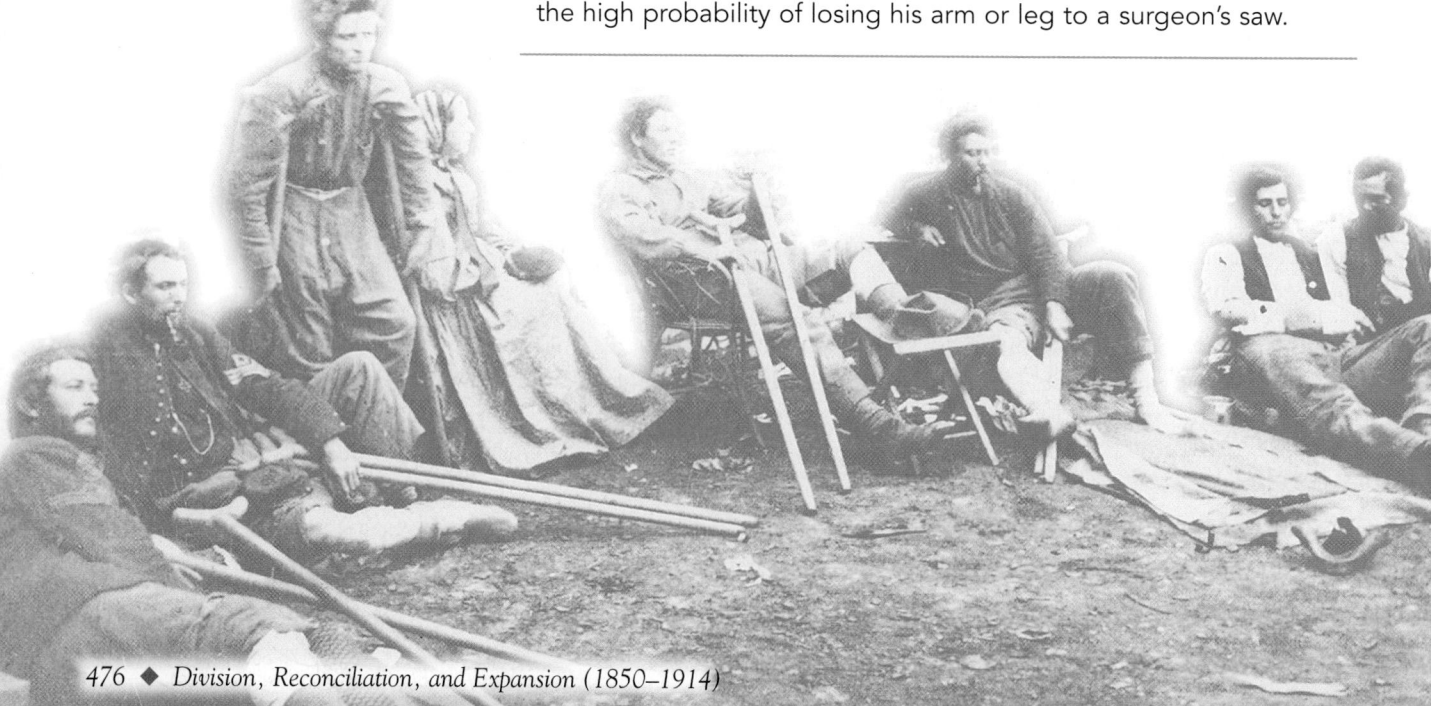

The lieutenant's rubber blanket lay on the ground, and upon it he had poured the company's supply of coffee. Corporals and other representatives of the grimy and hot-throated men who lined the breast-work[1] had come for each squad's portion.

The lieutenant was frowning and serious at this task of division. His lips pursed as he drew with his sword various crevices in the heap, until brown squares of coffee, astoundingly equal in size, appeared on the blanket. He was on the verge of a great triumph in mathematics, and the corporals were thronging forward, each to reap a little square, when suddenly the lieutenant cried out and looked quickly at a man near him as if he suspected it was a case of personal assault. The others cried out also when they saw blood upon the lieutenant's sleeve.

He had winced like a man stung, swayed dangerously, and then straightened. The sound of his hoarse breathing was plainly audible. He looked sadly, mystically, over the breast-work at the green face of a wood, where now were many little puffs of white smoke. During this moment the men about him gazed statuelike and silent, astonished and awed by this catastrophe which happened when catastrophes were not expected—when they had leisure to observe it.

As the lieutenant stared at the wood, they too swung their heads, so that for another instant all hands, still silent, contemplated the distant forest as if their minds were fixed upon the mystery of a bullet's journey.

The officer had, of course, been compelled to take his sword into his left hand. He did not hold it by the hilt. He gripped it at the middle of the blade, awkwardly. Turning his eyes from the hostile wood, he looked at the sword as he held it there, and seemed puzzled as to what to do with it, where to put it. In short, this weapon had of a sudden become a strange thing to him. He looked at it in a kind of stupefaction, as if he had been endowed with a trident, a sceptre,[2] or a spade.

Finally he tried to sheathe it. To sheathe a sword held by the left hand, at the middle of the blade, in a scabbard hung at the left hip, is a feat worthy of a sawdust ring.[3] This wounded officer engaged in a desperate struggle with the sword and the wobbling scabbard, and during the time of it breathed like a wrestler.

But at this instant the men, the spectators, awoke from their stone-like poses and crowded forward sympathetically. The orderly-sergeant

---

1. **breast-work** low wall put up quickly as a defense in battle.
2. **a trident, a sceptre** (trīd´ ent; sep´ tər) three-pronged spear; decorated ornamental rod or staff symbolizing royal authority.
3. **sawdust ring** ring in which circus acts are performed.

◀ **Critical Viewing** This is an actual photograph of a temporary Civil War hospital. Do you think that soldiers received quality treatment in this setting? On what details do you base your answer? **[Assess]**

Reading Strategy
Recognizing Historical Details What details in this passage set the story at the time of the Civil War?

✔**Reading Check**
What has just happened to the lieutenant?

took the sword and tenderly placed it in the scabbard. At the time, he leaned nervously backward, and did not allow even his finger to brush the body of the lieutenant. A wound gives strange dignity to him who bears it. Well men shy from his new and terrible majesty. It is as if the wounded man's hand is upon the curtain which hangs before the revelations of all existence—the meaning of ants, potentates,[4] wars, cities, sunshine, snow, a feather dropped from a bird's wing; and the power of it sheds radiance upon a bloody form, and makes the other men understand sometimes that they are little. His comrades look at him with large eyes thoughtfully. Moreover, they fear vaguely that the weight of a finger upon him might send him headlong, precipitate the tragedy, hurl him at once into the dim, grey unknown. And so the orderly-sergeant, while sheathing the sword, leaned nervously backward.

There were others who proffered assistance. One timidly presented his shoulder and asked the lieutenant if he cared to lean upon it, but the latter waved him away mournfully. He wore the look of one who knows he is the victim of a terrible disease and understands his helplessness. He again stared over the breast-work at the forest, and then, turning, went slowly rearward. He held his right wrist tenderly in his left hand as if the wounded arm was made of very brittle glass.

And the men in silence stared at the wood, then at the departing lieutenant; then at the wood, then at the lieutenant.

As the wounded officer passed from the line of battle, he was enabled to see many things which as a participant in the fight were unknown to him. He saw a general on a black horse gazing over the lines of blue infantry at the green woods which veiled his problems. An aide galloped furiously, dragged his horse suddenly to a halt, saluted, and presented a paper. It was, for a wonder, precisely like a historical painting.

To the rear of the general and his staff a group, composed of a bugler, two or three orderlies, and the bearer of the corps standard,[5] all upon maniacal horses, were working like slaves to hold their ground, preserve their respectful interval, while the shells boomed in the air about them, and caused their chargers to make furious quivering leaps.

A battery, a tumultuous and shining mass, was swirling toward the right. The wild thud of hoofs, the cries of the riders shouting blame and praise, menace and encouragement, and, last, the roar of the wheels, the slant of the glistening guns, brought the lieutenant to an intent pause. The battery swept in curves that stirred the heart; it made halts as dramatic as the crash of a wave on the rocks, and when it fled onward this aggregation of wheels, levers, motors had a beautiful unity, as if it were a missile. The sound of it was a war-chorus that reached into the depths of man's emotion.

precipitate (prē sip´ ə tāt´) *v.* cause to happen before expected or desired

Reading Strategy
Recognizing Historical Details Using your knowledge of the historical context, what do you think is the potential outcome of the lieutenant's injury?

aggregation (ag´ grə gā´ shən) *n.* group of distinct objects or individuals

---

4. potentates (pōt´ ən tāts) *n.* rulers; powerful people.
5. corps standard (kôr) flag or banner representing a military unit.

The lieutenant, still holding his arm as if it were of glass, stood watching this battery until all detail of it was lost, save the figures of the riders, which rose and fell and waved lashes over the black mass.

Later, he turned his eyes toward the battle, where the shooting sometimes crackled like bush-fires, sometimes sputtered with exasperating irregularity, and sometimes reverberated like the thunder. He saw the smoke rolling upward and saw crowds of men who ran and cheered, or stood and blazed away at the <u>inscrutable</u> distance.

He came upon some stragglers, and they told him how to find the field hospital. They described its exact location. In fact, these men, no longer having part in the battle, knew more of it than others. They told the performance of every corps, every division, the opinion of every general. The lieutenant, carrying his wounded arm rearward, looked upon them with wonder.

At the roadside a brigade was making coffee and buzzing with talk like a girls' boarding school. Several officers came out to him and

▲ **Critical Viewing**
What connections do you see between this photograph and Crane's description of the wounded lieutenant being helped by his men? **[Connect]**

inscrutable (in skrōōt′ ə bəl) *adj.* impossible to see

☑ **Reading Check**
Why does the lieutenant look upon the stragglers with wonder?

An Episode of War ◆ 479

inquired concerning things of which he knew nothing. One, seeing his arm, began to scold. "Why, man, that's no way to do. You want to fix that thing." He appropriated the lieutenant and the lieutenant's wound. He cut the sleeve and laid bare the arm, every nerve of which softly fluttered under his touch. He bound his handkerchief over the wound, scolding away in the meantime. His tone allowed one to think that he was in the habit of being wounded every day. The lieutenant hung his head, feeling, in this presence, that he did not know how to be correctly wounded.

The low white tents of the hospital were grouped around an old schoolhouse. There was here a singular commotion. In the foreground two ambulances interlocked wheels in the deep mud. The drivers were tossing the blame of it back and forth, gesticulating and berating, while from the ambulances, both crammed with wounded, there came an occasional groan. An interminable crowd of bandaged men were coming and going. Great numbers sat under the trees nursing heads or arms or legs. There was a dispute of some kind raging on the steps of the schoolhouse. Sitting with his back against a tree a man with a face as grey as a new army blanket was serenely smoking a corncob pipe. The lieutenant wished to rush forward and inform him that he was dying.

A busy surgeon was passing near the lieutenant. "Good-morning," he said, with a friendly smile. Then he caught sight of the lieutenant's arm, and his face at once changed. "Well, let's have a look at it." He seemed possessed suddenly of a great contempt for the lieutenant. This wound evidently placed the latter on a very low social plane. The doctor cried out impatiently, "What mutton-head had tied it up that way anyhow?" The lieutenant answered, "Oh, a man."

When the wound was disclosed the doctor fingered it <u>disdainfully</u>. "Humph," he said. "You come along with me and I'll 'tend to you." His voice contained the same scorn as if he were saying: "You will have to go to jail."

The lieutenant had been very meek, but now his face flushed, and he looked into the doctor's eyes. "I guess I won't have it amputated," he said.

"Nonsense, man! Nonsense! Nonsense!" cried the doctor. "Come along, now. I won't amputate it. Come along. Don't be a baby."

"Let go of me," said the lieutenant, holding back wrathfully, his glance fixed upon the door of the old schoolhouse, as sinister to him as the portals of death.

And this is the story of how the lieutenant lost his arm. When he reached home, his sisters, his mother, his wife, sobbed for a long time at the sight of the flat sleeve. "Oh, well," he said, standing shamefaced amid these tears, "I don't suppose it matters so much as all that."

Literary Analysis
Realism and Naturalism
What details of this description reflect the ideas of the Naturalists?

disdainfully (dis dān′ fəl ē) *adv.* showing scorn or contempt

▼ **Critical Viewing**
What do these Civil War surgical instruments suggest about the nature of the medical treatment the lieutenant faces? **[Interpret]**

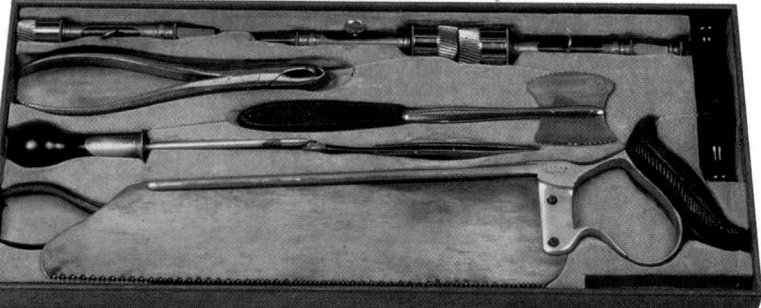

© Museum of the Confederacy, Richmond, Virginia

Willie Has Gone to the War

Words by George Cooper
Music by Stephen Foster

Young Soldier: Separate Study of a Soldier Giving Water to a Wounded Companion, 1861, Winslow Homer, Cooper-Hewitt, National Museum of Design, Smithsonian Institution

The blue bird is singing his lay,[1]
To all the sweet flow'rs of the dale,
The wild bee is roaming at play,
And soft is the sigh of the gale;
5   I stray by the brookside alone,
Where oft we have wander'd before,
And weep for my lov'd one, my own,
My Willie has gone to the war!

Willie has gone to the war, Willie,
10 Willie my lov'd one, my own;
Willie has gone to the war, Willie,
Willie my lov'd one is gone!

'Twas here, where the lily bells grow,
I last saw his noble young face,
15 And now while he's gone to the foe,
Oh! dearly I love the old place;
The whispering waters repeat
The name that I love o'er and o'er,
And daisies that nod at my feet,
20 Say Willie has gone to the war!

---

1. **lay** *n.* song or melody.

▲ **Critical Viewing** This teenaged Union soldier may have enlisted in the army hoping to find glory on the battlefield. In what way does "Willie Has Gone to the War" show another side to the experience of war? **[Contrast]**

✔**Reading Check**

Where does the speaker wait for Willie?

Willie has gone to the war, Willie,
Willie my lov'd one, my own;
Willie has gone to the war, Willie,
Willie my lov'd one is gone!

25 The leaves of the forest will fade,
The roses will wither and die,
But spring to our home in the <u>glade</u>,
On fairy like pinions[2] will fly;
And still I will hopefully wait
30 The day when these battles are o'er,
And pine like a bird for its mate,
Till Willie comes home from the war!

Willie has gone to the war, Willie,
Willie my lov'd one, my own;
35 Willie has gone to the war, Willie,
Willie my lov'd one is gone!

glade (glād) *n.* open space in a wood or forest

---

2. pinions (pin´ yənz) *n.* antiquated term meaning "wings."

Review and Assess
Thinking About the Selections

1. **Respond:** Which aspects of "An Episode of War" did you find particularly tragic or unsettling? Explain.

2. **(a) Recall:** What happens to cause the lieutenant's injury?
   (b) Analyze: How does the manner in which the lieutenant is wounded make him a sympathetic character?

3. **(a) Recall:** Describe the lieutenant's reaction when a soldier offers him a helpful shoulder. **(b) Infer:** What accounts for his mournful detachment?

4. **(a) Recall:** Note three examples of the lieutenant's distance from the uninjured people around him. **(b) Interpret:** What do these examples suggest about the way that he is seen by others, and the way in which he sees himself?

5. **Analyze:** In what ways does "Willie Has Gone to the War" romanticize the monotony and anguish of waiting for a soldier to return from war?

6. **Apply:** According to the Naturalists, humans are weak and ineffectual beings at the mercy of mysterious forces. In what way might this statement apply to "An Episode of War"?

7. **Take a Position:** In your view, is the story—in which no battle is described—more or less frightening than contemporary war movies? Explain.

Review and Assess

Literary Analysis

Realism and Naturalism

1. Explain how the lieutenant's rationing coffee at the time of his injury contributes to the quality of **Realism** in "An Episode of War."

2. In what way can the same situation be used to support the assertion that this story is distinctly **Naturalistic**?

3. Give two examples that show how the lieutenant exhibits the quiet, courageous endurance typical of characters in Naturalistic works.

4. Use a chart like the one shown to note two examples each of Realistic and Naturalistic characterization from the story.

Realism	Naturalism

5. Citing examples from the lyrics to support your argument, refute the statement that "Willie Has Gone to the War" reflects Realism.

Comparing Literary Works

6. (a) What details in the selections suggest that they were written about the same period of time? (b) What details make it seem as if the writers describe different historical events?

7. In your opinion, which selection would be more useful to historians? Explain.

Reading Strategy

Recognizing Historical Details

8. Using your knowledge of Civil War medical practices, why do you think the doctor promises the lieutenant that he will not amputate?

9. What does the lieutenant's struggle to resheath his sword tell you about battle practices of the Civil War?

10. How does the orderly-sergeant's sympathetic attitude to the lieutenant reflect the romantic notions Civil War officers had of their role in the war?

Extend Understanding

11. **Science Connection:** In what ways might a doctor describe the task of caring for the Civil War wounded?

Quick Review

Realism depicts ordinary people coping with everyday realities.

Naturalism focuses on people's helplessness in the face of chance.

To **recognize historical details,** look for elements that indicate the time period, and determine how the attitudes of both writers and characters reflect the ideas of their day.

 Take It to the Net
www.phschool.com
Take the interactive self-test online to check your understanding of these selections.

Integrate Language Skills

Vocabulary Development Lesson

Word Analysis: Latin Root -greg-

The word *aggregation* contains the root *-greg-*, meaning "herd" or "flock." An *aggregation* is a group of people or things considered as a whole, while a *congregation* is a group and a *gregarious* person enjoys being part of a crowd.

Copy the paragraph below, filling in each blank with the appropriate *-greg-* word from the following list.

  aggregate   gregarious   congregated

  The wounded soldiers ___?___ on the steps, waiting to see the doctor. They were silent, except for one ___?___ private who described his injury to everyone. In the ___?___, a nearby orderly reflected, wounded men are a quiet bunch, though there is always an exception.

Concept Development: Analogies

Copy the following analogies, completing each one with the appropriate vocabulary word.

1. *Quickly* is to *rapidly* as ___?___ is to *scornfully*.
2. *Hidden* is to *revealed* as ___?___ is to *obvious*.
3. *Brook* is to *stream* as ___?___ is to *meadow*.
4. *Laugh* is to *cry* as ___?___ is to *delay*.
5. *Sum* is to *parts* as ___?___ is to *individual*.

Spelling Strategy

The long *a* sound can be spelled *a*-consonant-*e*, as in *glade*, or it can be spelled *ai*, as in *disdain*. In your notebook, complete the spelling of these words.

1. precipit__   2. st__d   3. aggreg__

Grammar and Style Lesson

Usage: *Like* and *As*

Like and *as*, *as if*, and *as though* are often used interchangeably, but they actually serve different purposes. **Like** is a preposition; it takes a noun or pronoun as its object and introduces a prepositional phrase. **As, as if,** and **as though** are subordinating conjunctions that introduce subordinating—or less important—ideas.

> **Like:** He had winced *like a man stung. . . .* (preposition)
>
> **As if:** [The lieutenant] looked quickly at a man near him *as if he suspected it was a case of personal assault.* (introduces a clause)
>
> **As though:** The men regarded him *as though their hearts would break.* (introduces a clause)

Practice Rewrite the following sentences, correcting any errors in the use of *like, as, as if,* or *as though*. Write "correct" for sentences without errors.

1. The lieutenant divided the coffee evenly, just like he promised he would.
2. He staggered as though weak with fatigue.
3. The men stood as stones, frightened like they had never seen a man wounded.
4. The lieutenant stumbled toward the field hospital as if a man in a trance.
5. Like any wounded man, he dwelled on the possibility of amputation.

Writing Application Use *like, as, as if,* or *as though* at least three times in a description of a chance event you experienced.

W$_G$ *Prentice Hall Writing and Grammar Connection: Chapter 25, Section 2*

Writing Lesson

Field Report on Hospital Conditions

Imagine that a Civil War colonel wants to know why so many of his soldiers are dying from minor wounds. As the lieutenant, report to the colonel on the treatment you received and the problems you observed at the army hospital.

Prewriting Review the Background on page 476 and the photographs in the selection to develop a list of issues for your report. Jot down the precise details from the story you will use to support each issue. If necessary, consult a Civil War reference book for more facts.

Drafting State your report's purpose in an introduction. Then, present each issue and supporting details in a separate paragraph. Use precise details. Summarize your main points in the conclusion.

Model: Using Precise Details

We must have better conditions immediately or more men will die. The wounded are often neglected and forced to lie on filthy beds, or even the floor, for hours and even days at a time without being fed, bathed, or treated.

> Rather than simply stating that wounded soldiers are neglected, precise details like the ones highlighted provide a complete picture.

Revising Reread your report, checking for logical order and sufficiently precise supporting details. Take steps to improve your organization and strengthen or clarify your writing.

Prentice Hall Writing and Grammar Connection: Chapter 6, Section 3

Extension Activities

Listening and Speaking Among the most famous Civil War songs are "Battle Hymn of the Republic" and "Dixie." In a **musical presentation,** provide historic context and a discussion of a Civil War song of your choice.

- Evaluate several songs before choosing one.
- Consider the musical qualities of the song, such as the tempo and the mood.
- Provide background on the song's origins.

Play a recording of the song as part of your presentation.

Research and Technology In the library or on the Internet, research the definition of Naturalism and its presence in literature. Then, write a **definition essay,** defining Naturalism and giving examples of it from "An Episode of War." Be sure to include events in the story that reflect the belief that humankind is helpless in the face of events it cannot control.

 **Take It to the Net** www.phschool.com

Go online for an additional research activity using the Internet.

Prepare to Read

Swing Low, Sweet Chariot ◆ Go Down, Moses

Spirituals

Spirituals are folk songs that originated among enslaved and oppressed African Americans. They are one of the earliest and most widely known forms of American folk song to have survived to the twenty-first century. Spirituals took on the forms of anthems, ballads, shouts, and jubilees to reflect different moods and circumstances. Containing both social and religious content, spirituals helped to shape the conscious identity of an enslaved people; they also helped slaves persevere under the physical and psychological pressures of their daily life. These songs conveyed the singers' pain, their yearning for freedom, and their rage against slavery. In doing so, they brought to life the emotional impact of slavery, which divided our nation for decades and played a key role in causing the Civil War. Frederick Douglass, a slave who became one of the most important writers of his time, said of the spirituals, "Every tone was a testimony against slavery and a prayer to God for deliverance from chains." At the same time, the songs helped to replace lost African religious traditions and allowed men and women to maintain a connection to their musical heritage.

Song of the Fields

Plantation owners, fearing discontent among their slaves, encouraged field hands to sing while they picked cotton or sugar, reasoning that people who were busy singing could not plot escape or rebellion. They generally accepted spirituals because the songs had religious content. The slaves, however, found ways to benefit from singing. Their songs provided an outlet for the grief and frustration they often kept bottled up inside. Spirituals also fostered a sense of personal self-worth by portraying slaves as innocents of a mighty God, deserving of a heavenly reward for their earthly labors. By grafting their memories of traditional African music and rhythms onto religious hymns of early nineteenth-century Christian revivalists, enslaved Africans managed to hold on to part of their heritage. In addition, the language in some songs provided a means to communicate forbidden thoughts and feelings.

A Double Message

Many spirituals had a double meaning. Most included references to people, places, or events in the Bible. They frequently referred to Moses, who in the Old Testament led the Jews out of slavery in Egypt. Slaves identified with the ancient Israelites, who had once been the slaves of the Egyptians. Singing about the Israelites was a safe way to voice their own yearning for liberty. For example, in spirituals such as "Swing Low, Sweet Chariot" and "Go Down, Moses," slaves expressed their hope that they would someday escape to their own "promised land," just as the Israelites escaped to ancient Israel. References to figures and events in the Bible thus became a kind of code for the slaves' own experience. One work song did more than just express discontent; it gave directions for escape: In "Follow the Drinking Gourd," fugitive slaves were advised to follow the Big Dipper north to freedom.

Path to Popularity

Spirituals were almost unknown outside the South until after the Civil War. In 1867, a collection of African American music called *Slave Songs of the United States* was published. In 1871, a black choral group, the Jubilee Singers from Fisk University, traveled throughout the United States and to England and Germany singing spirituals to raise money for their school. The Jubilee Singers were extremely gifted, and became highly successful, even singing for Queen Victoria in England. Students from other schools followed their example and helped popularize the spiritual. Today, spirituals are performed by gospel singers, and their influence is apparent in contemporary music forms such as blues and jazz.

Preview

Connecting to the Literature

Songs have an amazing power to sway our emotions. They can soothe us when we are feeling sad or bring back special memories. As these two spirituals demonstrate, songs can even help people endure great hardships. As you read, think about a song that had a strong emotional impact on you.

Literary Analysis

Refrain

If you are searching for the meaning of a song or poem, you will often find it in the **refrain**—a word, phrase, line, or group of lines repeated at regular intervals throughout the work. Refrains serve these key functions:

- They emphasize the most important ideas.
- They help establish the rhythm of the song.

Most spirituals contain at least one refrain. For example, the line "Coming for to carry me home" is repeated throughout "Swing Low, Sweet Chariot." As you read these songs, think about the message each refrain conveys.

Comparing Literary Works

Most spirituals were not meant to be sung alone. Instead, the refrain facilitated a call-and-response format in which a leader sang the verses and the rest of the group acted like a chorus and sang the refrain. Each song produced a different mood or feeling within the group: some songs focused more on the pain or rage caused by the conditions of slavery, while other songs looked hopefully toward the future. Compare the mood of these two songs and imagine how you might feel as you sang or heard them.

Reading Strategy

Listening

Since songs are created for the ear and not the eye, **listening** is an especially important skill for appreciating lyrics.

- Read each spiritual aloud, listening to its rhythm.
- Pay attention to rhymes and other repeated sounds. For example, the opening line in "Go Down, Moses" contains three stressed syllables in a row.

Often, the rhythms and sounds of a song suggest a specific mood. As you read these spirituals, think about the different moods and effects that the sounds of the songs create. Record some of these effects in a chart like the one shown.

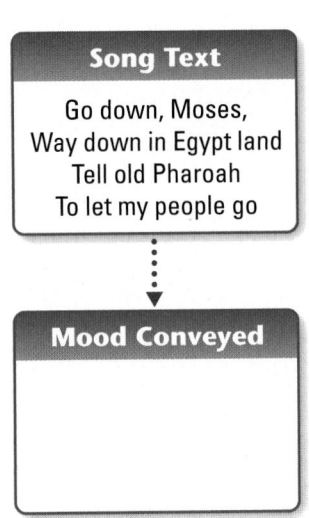

Song Text

Go down, Moses,
Way down in Egypt land
Tell old Pharoah
To let my people go

Mood Conveyed

Vocabulary Development

oppressed (ə prest´) *v.* kept down by cruel or unjust power (p. 490)

smite (smīt) *v.* to kill by a powerful blow (p. 490)

SWING LOW, SWEET CHARIOT

SPIRITUAL

▲ Critical Viewing
Looking at the clothing of the escaped slaves in this photograph, what can you infer about their lives as fugitives? **[Infer]**

Background

Africans first came to this country as slaves in 1619. Although the slave trade was banned in 1808, slavery remained legal. In response to slave rebellions of the 1820s and 1830s, many southern states enacted tough new laws that deprived slaves of nearly all their rights. In the years before the Civil War, many enslaved Africans fled captivity. They were hidden and transported by the Underground Railroad, a secret network of activists dedicated to helping fugitives reach freedom in the North and in Canada.

One of those activists was Harriet Tubman, who was born a slave around 1820. Tubman was called the Moses of her people. In the Bible, Moses led the Israelites out of captivity in Egypt. Following Moses' example, Tubman escaped along the Underground Railroad and then risked her life to return for her family. Driven by the desire to help others still oppressed, she returned to the South again and again to rescue other enslaved Africans, eventually leading more than 300 people to freedom.

Swing low, sweet chariot,
Coming for to carry me home,
Swing low, sweet chariot,
Coming for to carry me home.

5 I looked over Jordan[1] and what did I see
Coming for to carry me home,
A band of angels coming after me,
Coming for to carry me home.

If you get there before I do,
10 Coming for to carry me home,
Tell all my friends I'm coming too,
Coming for to carry me home.

Swing low, sweet chariot,
Coming for to carry me home,
15 Swing low, sweet chariot,
Coming for to carry me home.

Literary Analysis
Refrain In what ways does the song's refrain emphasize the speaker's yearning?

Review and Assess

Thinking About the Selection

1. **Respond:** What mood did this spiritual evoke in you? Explain.

2. **(a) Recall:** Where does the speaker want to go?
   (b) Infer: What do you think this place represents?

3. **(a) Recall:** In what vehicle will the speaker travel "home"?
   (b) Interpret: What do you think this vehicle represents?

4. **(a) Recall:** Who is coming over Jordan to carry the speaker home? **(b) Interpret:** If the song is an expression of the slaves' desire for escape, what do these figures represent?

5. **Interpret:** Knowing that spirituals were often "code" songs for escape, do you think there are any hidden messages in this song? Explain.

6. **Apply:** In what ways do you think such a song could offer comfort to the slaves?

GO DOWN, MOSES

SPIRITUAL

Go down, Moses,
Way down in Egypt land
Tell old Pharaoh
To let my people go.

5   When Israel was in Egypt land
Let my people go
<u>Oppressed</u> so hard they could not stand
Let my people go.

Go down, Moses,
10 Way down in Egypt land
Tell old Pharaoh
"Let my people go."

"Thus saith the Lord," bold Moses said,
"Let my people go;
15 If not I'll <u>smite</u> your first-born dead
Let my people go."

Go down, Moses,
Way down in Egypt land,
Tell old Pharaoh,
20 "Let my people go!"

oppressed (ə prest') *v.* kept down by cruel or unjust power

smite (smīt) *v.* to kill by a powerful blow

Review and Assess

Thinking About the Selection

1. **Respond:** What emotions does this song most strongly convey to you? Explain.

2. **(a) Recall:** Who is oppressed in this song? **(b) Connect:** What connection might these oppressed people have with the slaves?

3. **(a) Recall:** With what punishment does the Lord threaten the Egyptians if they refuse to free the Israelites? **(b) Interpret:** Whom do the Israelites represent?

4. **(a) Recall:** Whom does Moses tell to "let my people go"?
(b) **Interpret:** If this song is related to the slaves, whom might this figure represent?

5. **Evaluate:** Explain the effectiveness of the mix of formal and informal language in "Go Down, Moses."

Review and Assess

Literary Analysis

Refrain

1. What **refrains,** both lines and entire stanzas, are used in "Swing Low, Sweet Chariot"?
2. List the refrains, both lines and entire stanzas, used in "Go Down, Moses."
3. What idea or message is emphasized through the single-line refrain in "Go Down, Moses"?

Comparing Literary Works

4. In each **spiritual,** which lines might have been sung by a soloist and which by the chorus? Explain.
5. (a) What symbolic words do you note in each of the spirituals? (b) What do you think the symbols represent?
6. How might these spirituals soothe the feelings of longing, sadness, and injustice they express?
7. Compare the moods of these two spirituals.

Reading Strategy

Listening

8. Explain how each of the songs uses rhythm, rhyme, and repetition to reinforce meaning.
9. Using the sound elements you identified in both songs, compare the musical qualities of "Go Down, Moses" with those of "Swing Low, Sweet Chariot." Record your ideas in a chart like the one shown.

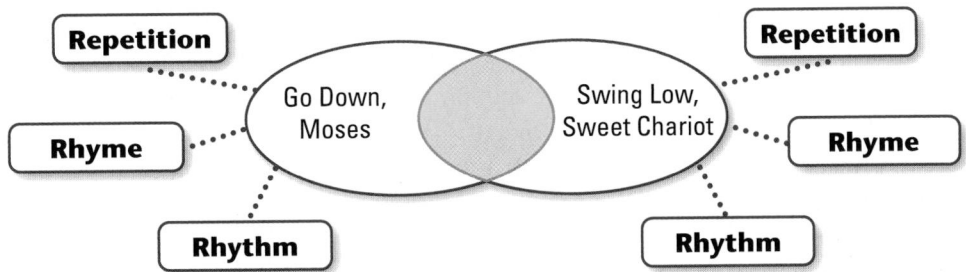

Extend Understanding

10. **Social Studies Connection:** Harriet Tubman once said, "We got to be free or die. And freedom's not bought with dust." What other American heroes would agree with her words? Explain your choices.

Quick Review

The **refrain** is a word, phrase, line, or group of lines repeated at regular intervals in a poem or song.

Spirituals are folk songs developed by enslaved Africans that often feature Biblical references and a call-and-response format.

Listening to a song's rhyme, rhythm, and repetition helps you appreciate its message and mood.

 Take It to the Net
www.phschool.com
Take the interactive self-test online to check your understanding of these selections.

Integrate Language Skills

Vocabulary Development Lesson

Word Analysis: Latin Root -press-

The root -press- means "push." People who are *oppressed* are pushed or kept down. Copy each sentence, completing each blank with an appropriate word formed with the root -press- and one of the prefixes defined below.

com- (together)   re- (back)
de- (down)   im- (into)

1. ____?____ the metal seal on the hot wax to make your mark.
2. Watch as I ____?____ the paper into a tight ball.
3. When you ____?____ the button, a buzzer sounds.
4. The enthusiastic fans weren't able to ____?____ their squeals.

Concept Development: Antonyms

Select the word that is the closest antonym, or opposite, of the first word.

1. oppressed: (a) crushed, (b) assisted, (c) punished
2. smite: (a) hit, (b) question, (c) caress

Spelling Strategy

When adding -ed to a word ending in a double consonant, keep both consonants, as in *oppress* + *ed* = *oppressed*. Match the correct word for each definition given below, adding -ed to each word to form a new word.

1. fixed in position   **a.** possess
2. ordered   **b.** boss
3. owned   **c.** install

Grammar and Style Lesson

Direct Address

In both these spirituals, the speaker uses **direct address** by speaking directly to someone or something by name.

When you use direct address, put a comma after the name if it comes first in the sentence, before the name if it comes last in the sentence, and on both sides of the name if it comes in the middle of the sentence.

> **Examples:** Swing low, *sweet chariot,*
> Coming for to carry me home.
>
> Go down, *Moses,*
> Way down in Egypt land.
> *Lord,* hear our prayer.

Practice Copy these sentences in your notebook. Underline the words of direct address and add punctuation where necessary.

1. Selena sing slowly and with great feeling.
2. The choir performed well Ms. Dodd.
3. Choir members please stand straight.
4. Everyone agrees Joe that you have a great voice.
5. Still Mr. Jones I'd rather play the guitar.

Writing Application Write three sentences or questions related to your interest in music. Include direct address, with correct punctuation, in each sentence.

WG Prentice Hall Writing and Grammar Connection: Chapter 27, Section 2

Writing Lesson

Reflective Essay

Imagine that you are a free person living in the South before the Civil War. You hear these spirituals, and for the first time, truly pay attention to the lyrics. In a reflective essay, analyze what the songs have taught you about the realities of slavery.

Prewriting   Freewrite about the songs by writing quickly and continuously for five minutes. Review your notes to choose a few ideas to explore.

> ### Model: Freewriting to Tap Personal Experiences
>
> I think "Go Down, Moses" expresses several emotions—pride, anger, sorrow, yearning. . . . That refrain, "Let my people go," really sums it up. Someone else is keeping me and my people from freedom. Let my people go. I can hardly imagine having to live my life like that . . .

> To capture ideas, freewriting relaxes the rules of grammar. Errors can be edited later.

Drafting   In your introduction, summarize the songs. Then, in the body of your essay, discuss the insights the songs have revealed to you.

Revising   A reflective essay should indicate the significance of an experience. Review your draft. If necessary, add more information to show what the songs mean to you, or how they might change your life.

W͟G *Prentice Hall Writing and Grammar Connection: Chapter 4, Section 2*

Extension Activities

Listening and Speaking With a small group, conduct a **choral reading** of a spiritual. Use a call-and-response format, with one student calling out the verses and the rest answering with the refrains. Each "soloist" should improvise to create at least one new verse. Use these tips to prepare:

- Determine who will say which lines.
- Learn your lines from memory.
- Emphasize the call-and-response format.

After you have practiced, perform the spiritual for your class. [**Group Activity**]

Research and Technology Using the Internet or other library resources, find several other spirituals to present in an **anthology.** For each song you include, write a brief introduction that provides background information or necessary context for readers.

 *Take It to the Net*   www.phschool.com

Go online for an additional research activity using the Internet.

Prepare to Read

from My Bondage and My Freedom

Frederick Douglass (1818–1895)

Frederick Douglass rose out of slavery to become one of the most gifted writers and orators of his time. Using these talents, he dedicated his life to fighting for the abolition of slavery and for civil rights. Douglass's life served as an inspiration and example for both blacks and whites throughout the country.

Early Years Douglass was born on a Maryland plantation. Historians believe that his name at birth was Frederick Augustus Bailey. At the age of eight, he was sent as a slave to the Baltimore home of the Auld family. While there, Douglass learned to read and write, at first with the strong encouragement of Mrs. Auld and later despite her objections. Learning soon became an unquenchable thirst for Douglass. He often traded biscuits for reading lessons from his playmates.

His reading fueled a quest for freedom. At age twenty, he escaped to Massachusetts, a free state, and took the surname Douglass to avoid arrest as a fugitive.

A Public Life Although he had never spoken in public before, Douglass delivered a tremendously powerful and moving debut speech at the 1841 convention of an abolitionist organization. Despite the constant fear of being arrested as a fugitive slave, he spent the next four years lecturing against slavery and arguing for the need for civil rights for all people.

Rumors spread that a man of such eloquence could not possibly have been a slave. In response, Douglass published his first autobiography, *Narrative of the Life of Frederick Douglass, an American Slave, Written By Himself* (1845). Fearing that the book would lead to his re-enslavement, Douglass then fled to England, where he spent years trying to gain British support for the abolitionist movement in the United States.

Freedom at Last After English friends raised money to buy his freedom, Douglass returned to the United States, established a newspaper for African Americans, and resumed lecturing. In 1855, he published *My Bondage and My Freedom*, an updated version of his autobiography.

During the Civil War, Douglass helped recruit African American soldiers for the Union army. After slavery was abolished, he fought vigorously for civil rights for African Americans. He became a consultant to President Lincoln and held several government positions, including United States minister to Haiti.

A Vision for the Future As an abolitionist, orator, and journalist, Douglass favored political methods for emancipating the slaves and bringing them into the mainstream of American life—a goal he was determined they should reach. In 1883, speaking as a vigorous fighter for civil rights, Douglass commented that the American people "must learn, or neglect to do so at their own peril. . . .The American people must stand each for all and all for each, without respect to color or race. . . . I expect to see the colored people of this country enjoying the same freedom, voting at the same ballot-box, using the same cartridge-box, going to the same schools, attending the same churches, . . . proud of the same country, fighting the same foe, and enjoying the same peace and all its advantages. . . ."

Douglass did not limit himself to fighting for the civil rights of African Americans. He also helped women in their battle to win the vote. Because he did not segregate his causes, Douglass is a model for all who struggle against injustice.

Preview

Connecting to the Literature

Imagine another person denying your right to read just as you were discovering the power of learning. If you were enslaved like Frederick Douglass, you would have no choice but to submit (or at least appear to submit) to your owner's wishes.

Literary Analysis

Autobiography

An **autobiography** is a person's written account of his or her own life, focusing on the events the author considers most significant. Because the writer's life is presented as he or she views it, the portrayal of people and events is colored by the author's feelings and beliefs. Usually, writers of autobiographies believe that their lives are interesting or important and can in some way help others. Frederick Douglass wrote his autobiography because he believed that his life proved that blacks were no less perceptive, intelligent, or capable than whites, as he states directly in these lines:

> I could talk and sing; I could laugh and weep; I could reason and remember . . .

As you read about the experiences that shaped Douglass's life, notice how they might serve as examples for others.

Connecting Literary Elements

When reading autobiographies, you can usually detect a clear **tone**—the writer's attitude toward the subject, characters, or audience. Tone is created through a choice of words and details. It may be formal or informal, friendly or distant. As you read, listen for Douglass's tone just as you would if he were speaking to you aloud.

Reading Strategy

Establishing a Purpose

Establishing a purpose for reading gives you an idea or concept on which to focus. For example, as you read from Douglass's autobiography, establish the purpose of learning about his special qualities and expanding your understanding of what it was like to be a slave. Record details that reflect this purpose in a chart like the one shown.

Vocabulary Development

congenial (kən jēn´ yəl) *adj.* agreeable (p. 497)

benevolent (bə nev´ ə lənt) *adj.* kindly; charitable (p. 497)

stringency (strin´ jən sē) *n.* strictness; severity (p. 497)

depravity (dē prav´ ə tē) *n.* corruption; wickedness (p. 497)

consternation (kän´ stər nā´ shən) *n.* great fear or shock that makes one feel helpless or bewildered (p. 499)

redolent (red´ əl ənt) *adj.* suggestive (p. 501)

The Chimney Corner, 1863, Eastman Johnson, Munson-Williams-Proctor Institute Museum of Art, Utica, New York

▲ **Critical Viewing** What might the light shining on the reader symbolize for Douglass? **[Interpret]**

from
My Bondage and My Freedom

Frederick Douglass

Background

Frederick Douglass was perhaps the most prominent African American leader of the nineteenth century, and his influence is still felt. As a crusader for human rights, Douglass served as a role model for African American leaders such as Booker T. Washington and W.E.B. DuBois. In our own era, the civil rights movement has drawn inspiration from Douglass, who opposed segregation decades before other voices were raised. As a young man, Douglass protested segregated seating on trains by sitting in cars reserved for whites until the authorities forcibly removed him. Later, he fought job discrimination against African Americans, protested segregation in school, and fought for civil rights for all Americans.

I lived in the family of Master Hugh, at Baltimore, seven years, during which time—as the almanac makers say of the weather—my condition was variable. The most interesting feature of my history here, was my learning to read and write, under somewhat marked disadvantages. In attaining this knowledge, I was compelled to resort to indirections by no means <u>congenial</u> to my nature, and which were really humiliating to me. My mistress—who had begun to teach me—was suddenly checked in her <u>benevolent</u> design, by the strong advice of her husband. In faithful compliance with this advice, the good lady had not only ceased to instruct me, herself, but had set her face as a flint against my learning to read by any means. It is due, however, to my mistress to say, that she did not adopt this course in all its <u>stringency</u> at the first. She either thought it unnecessary, or she lacked the <u>depravity</u> indispensable to shutting me up in mental darkness. It was, at least, necessary for her to have some training, and some hardening, in the exercise of the slaveholder's prerogative, to make her equal to forgetting my human nature and character, and to treating me as a thing destitute of a moral or an intellectual nature.

congenial (kən jēn′ yəl) *adj.* agreeable

benevolent (bə nev′ ə lənt) *adj.* kindly; charitable

stringency (strin′ jən sē) *n.* strictness; severity

depravity (di prav′ ə tē) *n.* corruption; wickedness

✔Reading Check

Why did Douglass's mistress stop teaching him to read and write?

Mrs. Auld—my mistress—was, as I have said, a most kind and tender-hearted woman; and, in the humanity of her heart, and the simplicity of her mind, she set out, when I first went to live with her, to treat me as she supposed one human being ought to treat another.

It is easy to see, that, in entering upon the duties of a slaveholder, some little experience is needed. Nature has done almost nothing to prepare men and women to be either slaves or slaveholders. Nothing but rigid training, long persisted in, can perfect the character of the one or the other. One cannot easily forget to love freedom; and it is as hard to cease to respect that natural love in our fellow creatures. On entering upon the career of a slaveholding mistress, Mrs. Auld was singularly deficient; nature, which fits nobody for such an office, had done less for her than any lady I had known. It was no easy matter to induce her to think and to feel that the curly-headed boy, who stood by her side, and even leaned on her lap; who was loved by little Tommy, and who loved little Tommy in turn; sustained to her only the relation of a chattel. I was *more* than that, and she felt me to be more than that. I could talk and sing; I could laugh and weep; I could reason and remember; I could love and hate. I was human, and she, dear lady, knew and felt me to be so. How could she, then, treat me as a brute, without a mighty struggle with all the noble powers of her own soul. That struggle came, and the will and power of the husband

▼ **Critical Viewing**
How does this idealized picture of plantation life contrast with Douglass's experiences as an enslaved African American? **[Contrast]**

A Home on the Mississippi, Currier & Ives, The Museum of the City of New York

was victorious. Her noble soul was overthrown; but, he that over-threw it did not, himself, escape the consequences. He, not less than the other parties, was injured in his domestic peace by the fall.

When I went into their family, it was the abode of happiness and contentment. The mistress of the house was a model of affection and tenderness. Her fervent piety and watchful uprightness made it impossible to see her without thinking and feeling—"that woman is a Christian." There was no sorrow nor suffering for which she had not a tear, and there was no innocent joy for which she did not [have] a smile. She had bread for the hungry, clothes for the naked, and comfort for every mourner that came within her reach. Slavery soon proved its ability to divest her of these excellent qualities, and her home of its early happiness. Conscience cannot stand much violence. Once thoroughly broken down, *who* is he that can repair the dam-age? It may be broken toward the slave, on Sunday, and toward the master on Monday. It cannot endure such shocks. It must stand entire, or it does not stand at all. If my condition waxed bad, that of the family waxed not better. The first step, in the wrong direction, was the violence done to nature and to conscience, in arresting the benevolence that would have enlightened my young mind. In ceasing to instruct me, she must begin to justify herself *to* herself; and, once consenting to take sides in such a debate, she was riveted to her position. One needs very little knowledge of moral philosophy, to see *where* my mistress now landed. She finally became even more violent in her opposition to my learning to read, than was her husband him-self. She was not satisfied with simply doing as *well* as her husband had commanded her, but seemed resolved to better his instruction. Nothing appeared to make my poor mistress—after her turning toward the downward path—more angry, than seeing me, seated in some nook or corner, quietly reading a book or a newspaper. I have had her rush at me, with the utmost fury, and snatch from my hand such newspaper or book, with something of the wrath and <u>consternation</u> which a traitor might be supposed to feel on being discovered in a plot by some dangerous spy.

Mrs. Auld was an apt woman, and the advice of her husband, and her own experience, soon demonstrated, to her entire satisfaction, that education and slavery are incompatible with each other. When this conviction was thoroughly established, I was most narrowly watched in all my movements. If I remained in a separate room from the family for any considerable length of time, I was sure to be suspected of having a book, and was at once called upon to give an account of myself. All this, however, was entirely *too late*. The first, and never to be retraced, step had been taken. In teaching me the alphabet, in the days of her simplicity and kindness, my mistress had given me the "inch," and now, no ordinary precaution could prevent me from taking the "ell."[1]

---

1. **ell** *n.* former English measure of length, equal to forty-five inches.

Literary Analysis
Autobiography Douglass blames the institution of slavery, rather than Mrs. Auld for the changes in the household. What does this tell you about him?

consternation (kän´ stər nā´ shən) *n.* great fear or shock that makes one feel helpless or bewildered

✔**Reading Check**
What extreme measure does Mrs. Auld take?

Seized with a determination to learn to read, at any cost, I hit upon many expedients to accomplish the desired end. The plea which I mainly adopted, and the one by which I was most successful, was that of using my young white playmates, with whom I met in the street, as teachers. I used to carry, almost constantly, a copy of Webster's spelling book in my pocket; and, when sent on errands, or when play time was allowed me, I would step, with my young friends, aside, and take a lesson in spelling. I generally paid my *tuition fee* to the boys, with bread, which I also carried in my pocket. For a single biscuit, any of my hungry little comrades would give me a lesson more valuable to me than bread. Not everyone, however, demanded this consideration, for there were those who took pleasure in teaching me, whenever I had a chance to be taught by them. I am strongly tempted to give the names of two or three of those little boys, as a slight testimonial of the gratitude and affection I bear them, but prudence forbids; not that it would injure me, but it might, possibly, embarrass them; for it is almost an unpardonable offense to do anything, directly or indirectly, to promote a slave's freedom, in a slave state. It is enough to say, of my warm-hearted little play fellows, that they lived on Philpot Street, very near Durgin & Bailey's shipyard.

Although slavery was a delicate subject, and very cautiously talked about among grownup people in Maryland, I frequently talked about it—and that very freely—with the white boys. I would, sometimes, say to them, while seated on a curbstone or a cellar door, "I wish I could be free, as you will be when you get to be men." "You will be free, you know, as soon as you are twenty-one, and can go where you like, but I am a slave for life. Have I not as good a right to be free as you have?" Words like these, I observed, always troubled them; and I had no small satisfaction in wringing from the boys, occasionally, that fresh and bitter condemnation of slavery, that springs from nature, unseared and unperverted.[2] Of all consciences let me have those to deal with which have not been bewildered by the cares of life. I do not remember ever to have met with a *boy*, while I was in slavery, who defended the slave system; but I have often had boys to console me, with the hope that something would yet occur, by which I might be made free. Over and over again, they have told me, that "they believed *I* had as good a right to be free as *they* had"; and that "they did not believe God ever made anyone to be a slave." The reader will easily see, that such little conversations with my play fellows, had no tendency to weaken my love of liberty, nor to render me contented with my condition as a slave.

The American Experience

Slave Narratives

From 1760 to the end of the Civil War, when slavery was officially abolished, the testimonies of hundreds of fugitive and former slaves appeared in the form of slave narratives. Like the precedent-setting *Interesting Narrative of the Life of Olaudah Equiano* (p. 44), these slave narratives exposed the inhumanities of the slave system. Former slaves recorded the oppressive conditions they suffered under their owners, not only to document their experiences but also to ensure that the reunified nation would not soon forget. These personal testimonies appeared in the form of narratives, reports, and interviews. The Federal Writers Project of the 1920s and 1930s gathered the narratives and documented them, creating an archive attesting to the terrible experience of American slavery.

---

2. **unperverted** (un´ pər vurt´ id) *adj.* uncorrupted; pure.

When I was about thirteen years old, and had succeeded in learning to read, every increase of knowledge, especially respecting the free states, added something to the almost intolerable burden of the thought—"I am a slave for life." To my bondage I saw no end. It was a terrible reality, and I shall never be able to tell how sadly that thought chafed my young spirit. Fortunately, or unfortunately, about this time in my life, I had made enough money to buy what was then a very popular schoolbook, the *Columbian Orator*. I bought this addition to my library, of Mr. Knight, on Thames street, Fell's Point, Baltimore, and paid him fifty cents for it. I was first led to buy this book, by hearing some little boys say they were going to learn some little pieces out of it for the exhibition. This volume was, indeed, a rich treasure, and every opportunity afforded me, for a time, was spent in diligently perusing it . . . The dialogue and the speeches were all <u>redolent</u> of the principles of liberty, and poured floods of light on the nature and character of slavery. As I read, behold! the very discontent so graphically predicted by Master Hugh, had already come upon me. I was no longer the light-hearted, gleesome boy, full of mirth and play, as when I landed first at Baltimore. Knowledge had come . . . This knowledge opened my eyes to the horrible pit, and revealed the teeth of the frightful dragon that was ready to pounce upon me, but it opened no way for my escape. I have often wished myself a beast, or a bird—anything, rather than a slave. I was wretched and gloomy, beyond my ability to describe. I was too thoughtful to be happy. It was this everlasting thinking which distressed and tormented me; and yet there was no getting rid of the subject of my thoughts. All nature was redolent of it. Once awakened by the silver trump[3] of knowledge, my spirit was roused to eternal wakefulness. Liberty! the inestimable birthright of every man, had, for me, converted every object into an asserter of this great right. It was heard in every sound, and beheld in every object. It was ever present, to torment me with a sense of my wretched condition. The more beautiful and charming were the smiles of nature, the more horrible and desolate was my condition. I saw nothing without seeing it, and I heard nothing without hearing it. I do not exaggerate, when I say, that it looked from every star, smiled in every calm, breathed in every wind, and moved in every storm.

I have no doubt that my state of mind had something to do with the change in the treatment adopted, by my once kind mistress toward me. I can easily believe, that my leaden, downcast, and discontented look, was very offensive to her. Poor lady! She did not know my trouble, and I dared not tell her. Could I have freely made her acquainted with the real state of my mind, and given her the reasons therefor, it might have been well for both of us. Her abuse of me fell upon me like the blows of the false prophet upon his ass;

---

3. trump trumpet.

redolent (red´ əl ənt) *adj.* suggestive

Literary Analysis
Autobiography and Tone
What does Douglass's tone here reveal about the importance of reading this book?

☑ Reading Check
What significant changes take place in Douglass after reading *Columbian Orator*?

she did not know that an *angel* stood in the way;[4] and—such is the relation of master and slave—I could not tell her. Nature had made us *friends*; slavery made us *enemies*. My interests were in a direction opposite to hers, and we both had our private thoughts and plans. She aimed to keep me ignorant; and I resolved to know, although knowledge only increased my discontent. My feelings were not the result of any marked cruelty in the treatment I received; they sprung from the consideration of my being a slave at all. It was *slavery*—not its mere *incidents*—that I hated. I had been cheated. I saw through the attempt to keep me in ignorance . . . The feeding and clothing me well, could not atone for taking my liberty from me. The smiles of my mistress could not remove the deep sorrow that dwelt in my young bosom. Indeed, these, in time, came only to deepen my sorrow. She had changed; and the reader will see that I had changed, too. We were both victims to the same overshadowing evil—*she,* as mistress, *I,* as slave. I will not censure her harshly; she cannot censure me, for she knows I speak but the truth, and have acted in my opposition to slavery, just as she herself would have acted, in a reverse of circumstances.

---

4. **blows . . . the way** allusion to a biblical tale (Numbers 22:21–35) about an ass that cannot move, though she is beaten by her master, because her path is blocked by an angel.

Review and Assess

Thinking About the Selection

1. **Respond:** Do you think it is possible to be a benevolent slaveholder? Why or why not?

2. **(a) Recall:** How does Douglass learn to read?
   (b) Recall: What does Mrs. Auld initially think about Douglass's reading? **(c) Draw Conclusions:** Why do you think she was later "violent in her opposition" to Douglass's reading?

3. **(a) Recall:** What is the attitude toward slavery of the white boys who help Douglass learn to read? **(b) Analyze:** Why do you think they have that attitude toward the slaves?

4. **(a) Recall:** What circumstance transforms Douglass from "light-hearted" to "wretched and gloomy"? **(b) Connect:** What does knowledge do for him?

5. **(a) Recall:** What consumed Douglass once he obtained knowledge? **(b) Support:** How does his experience prove his mistress's belief that education and slavery are incompatible?

6. **Apply:** Mahatma Gandhi wrote, "The moment the slave resolves that he will no longer be a slave, his fetters fall." Explain whether or not you feel Douglass was free even while in bondage.

Review and Assess

Literary Analysis

Autobiography

1. Douglass is relatively well cared for as a slave. In what way does he use his **autobiography** to make his case against slavery?

2. Find a passage in which Douglass conveys his opposition to slavery through his description of events.

3. In what ways would this account be different if it had been written by Mrs. Auld?

Connecting Literary Elements

4. (a) Describe Douglass's attitude toward Mrs. Auld. (b) Why do you think he feels as he does?

5. (a) What is the **tone** of the end of the selection? (b) Which specific words and phrases reveal Douglass's attitude toward slavery?

6. How does the tone—including word choice—of this selection support Douglass's desire to serve as a model?

Reading Strategy

Establishing a Purpose

7. Which of Douglass's special qualities are conveyed through this section of his autobiography? Explain.

8. Using a chart like the one shown, identify what you learned about the effects of slavery from Douglass's account.

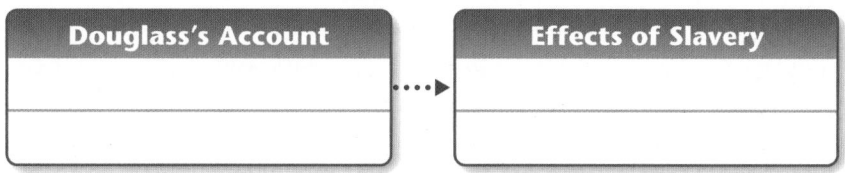

Douglass's Account		Effects of Slavery
	....▶	

9. In what ways did reading this selection add to your understanding of the effects of slavery? Expain.

Extend Understanding

10. **Social Studies Connection:** Many writers have paid tribute to Douglass's ideas. (a) Why do you think his messsage strikes such a chord with Americans? (b) In what ways does it reflect the core values on which America was founded?

Quick Review

An **autobiography** is the account of a person's life written in his or her own words.

The **tone** of a work reflects the author's attitude toward the subject, characters, or audience.

Establish a purpose for reading by choosing an idea or concept on which to focus.

 Take It to the Net
www.phschool.com
Take the interactive self-test online to check your understanding of the selection.

Integrate Language Skills

Vocabulary Development Lesson

Word Analysis: Latin Root -bene-

The Latin root -bene- means "well" or "good." The word *benevolent* literally means "with good wishes" or "kindly."

Define each of the following words, incorporating the meaning of the root -bene- into your definition.

1. benefit   **2.** benefactor   **3.** benediction

Spelling Strategy

When creating the noun form of an adjective that ends in -ent, replace the *t* with -ce or -cy: *benevolent* becomes *benevolence*. Add the -ce or -cy ending to each adjective below.

1. stringent   **3.** insistent

2. lenient   **4.** reverent

Fluency: Sentence Completion

Copy the following passage and fill in the blanks with the appropriate vocabulary words from the list on page 495.

I could see my otherwise ___?___ neighbor scowling with a look of ___?___, so I knew something was wrong. She spent hours in her well-manicured garden. It was usually ___?___ with the fragrance of roses, which she was ___?___ enough to share with me. The previously robust bushes were cut to the ground! I was stunned and silenced by the ___?___ of the deed. I could understand the ___?___ of her message as she sadly tacked up a KEEP OUT sign.

Grammar and Style Lesson

Correlative Conjunctions

Correlative conjunctions—pairs of connecting words—link similar kinds of words and word groups and connect ideas. In this example, the italicized words show the relationship between the two actions in the sentence.

> **Example:** . . . the good lady had *not only* ceased to instruct me, herself, *but* had set her face as a flint against my learning to read by any means.

Correlative conjunctions are usually used in these combinations:

- *either . . . or*
- *not only . . . but (also)*
- *whether . . . or*
- *neither . . . nor*
- *just as . . . so*

Practice For each item, create a logical sentence by adding a pair of correlative conjunctions from the italicized list.

1. ___?___ slave ___?___ mistress was truly free.

2. ___?___ Maryland ___?___ Mississippi and Tennessee were slave states.

3. ___?___ a slave ___?___ a slaveholder, all people are harmed by slavery.

4. ___?___ Douglass worked to abolish slavery, ___?___ did Sojourner Truth.

5. ___?___ Mrs. Auld ___?___ Mr. Auld would win the moral struggle.

Writing Application Write an original paragraph about slavery, using each of the five pairs of correlative conjunctions listed.

W͞G Prentice Hall Writing and Grammar Connection: Chapter 17, Section 4

Writing Lesson

College Admission Essay

A college application often requires you to write about an experience that helped shape you as a person. Just as Douglass described how knowledge freed him, you, too, can identify a key event or shaping force in your life, and write an essay explaining it.

Prewriting Outline the details of the event, and describe its effect on you. List the details in chronological order to establish organization.

Model: Planning a Clear and Logical Organization

A. Worked in local campaign office
1. Met the candidate; was inspired
2. Distributed flyers; polled voters
3. Phoned residents to encourage voting
B. Learned team work and the power of democracy

> Chronological order makes it easy for readers to follow an essay.

Drafting Introduce the experience and explain why you are writing about it. Then, write the body paragraphs to follow your outline. Conclude with a paragraph that insightfully sums up the impact of the experience on your life.

Revising Add time transition words like *first*, *next*, and *finally* to show chronological order and cause-effect words like *since* and *therefore* to reinforce the way this event helped shape you.

WG *Prentice Hall Writing and Grammar Connection: Chapter 4, Section 3*

Extension Activities

Listening and Speaking Select a passage from this selection to read to an audience of abolitionist sympathizers. Add statements of your own for emphasis that you believe would represent Douglass's intent and purpose. Consider the following:

- Add strong emotion to convey Douglass's tone.
- Use persuasive language to compel your audience.

Deliver the **oral presentation** to the class.

Research and Technology Using words, pictures, and sounds, work with a group to create a **multimedia presentation** that expresses the importance of literacy. Draw your materials from printed sources such as magazines, newspapers, and photographs. Consider recordings of speeches that will add vitality to your presentation. **[Group Activity]**

 **Take It to the Net** www.phschool.com

Go online for an additional research activity using the Internet.

Prepare to Read

An Occurrence at Owl Creek Bridge

Ambrose Bierce (1842–1914?)

Ambrose Bierce's writing and philosophy were shaped by his career as a Union officer in the Civil War. The extreme poverty in which he was raised helped to foster Bierce's unsentimental, pessimistic view of the world; the brutality he saw during the war only cemented his cynicism. Bierce explored themes of cruelty and death in his writing, earning himself the nickname "Bitter Bierce."

A Civil War Soldier Bierce was born in Ohio and raised on a farm in Indiana. Having educated himself by reading his father's books, he left the farm while in his teens to attend a military academy in Kentucky. When the Civil War broke out, he enlisted in the Union army. Bierce fought in several important battles, rose from private to lieutenant, and won many awards for bravery. Toward the end of the war he was seriously wounded, but he returned to battle a few months later.

Poisoned Pen After the war, Bierce settled in San Francisco as a journalist. His "Prattler" column, which appeared in *The Argonaut* (1877–1879), the *Wasp* (1881–1886), and the San Francisco *Sunday Examiner* (1887–1896), mixed political and social satire, literary reviews, and gossip. The broodingly handsome writer was dubbed "the wickedest man in San Francisco" for his cynical and often malicious commentary. Though his journalistic barbs angered many key political and business figures, Bierce's dark reputation only added to his personal popularity. He was a magnetic figure who charmed those around him despite the malice of his words.

Establishing His Legacy Although Bierce published many of his finest short stories in his column, he decided in the early 1890s to publish his collected short stories in two volumes entitled *Tales of Soldiers and Civilians* (1891) and *Can Such Things Be?* (1893). The concise, carefully plotted stories in these collections, set for the most part during the Civil War, capture the cruelty and futility of war and the indifference of death. Bierce's pessimism is also reflected in *The Devil's Dictionary* (1906), a book of humorous and cynical definitions, and in a book of quotations published after his death. Challenging, spiteful, or merely macabre, these comments more than justify Bierce's reputation as a hard-nosed, hard-boiled critic of nearly everything.

The Perfect Cynic Writer George Sterling wrote of Bierce, his longtime friend, that he "never troubled to conceal his justifiable contempt of humanity. . . . Bierce was a 'perfectionist,' a quality that in his case led to an intolerance involving merciless cruelty. He demanded in all others, men or women, the same ethical virtues that he found essential to his own manner of life. . . . To deviate from his point of view, indeed, to disagree with him even in slight particulars, was the unpardonable sin."

While he was successful professionally, Bierce found little happiness in a world where so few people met his expectations. His marriage ended in divorce, and both of his sons died at an early age. In 1913, at age 71, the lonely writer traveled to Mexico, a country in the midst of a bloody civil war. To this day, his fate is unknown, although a reasonable speculation is that he was killed during the siege of Ojinaga in 1914. "An Occurrence at Owl Creek Bridge" may foreshadow that death during wartime.

Preview

Connecting to the Literature

"All's fair in love and war." This phrase has been used to excuse everything from trivial lies to wide-scale atrocities. Do you think there are times when the rules of the game involve no rules at all?

Literary Analysis

Point of View

In this story, Bierce uses his main character's warped perception of time to distort the reader's sense of reality. The way that you perceive time in a story may depend on the **point of view** from which it is told.

- In stories told from an *objective point of view,* you follow the action without understanding any character's thoughts about the events.
- In stories told from a *third-person limited point of view,* the narrator relates the inner thoughts and feelings of a single character.

As the point of view in this story shifts from objective to third-person limited, the emotional tone and sense of time change as well.

Connecting Literary Elements

In order to convey the strange and stressful events of this story, Bierce uses a literary technique known as **stream-of-consciousness.** Using this style, Bierce reports thoughts and ideas the way the human mind experiences them—in short bursts, without full sentences, and often without clear or logical connections. As you read, try to fill in the missing pieces by considering which events spark the thoughts or feelings the narrator describes.

Reading Strategy

Identifying Chronological Order

In Bierce's story, the action jumps backward and forward in time. To see the true **chronological order,** reorder events to represent the sequence in which they occurred. To understand the order of events in this story, create a timeline like the one shown.

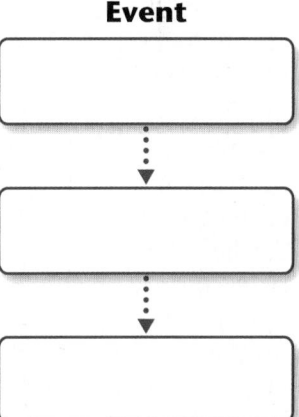

Event

Vocabulary Development

etiquette (et′ i kit) *n.* appropriate behavior and ceremonies (p. 509)

deference (def′ ər əns) *n.* respect; courtesy; regard (p. 509)

imperious (im pir′ ē əs) *adj.* urgent; imperative (p. 510)

dictum (dik′ təm) *n.* formal statement of fact or opinion (p. 511)

summarily (sə mer′ ə lē) *adv.* promptly and without formality (p. 511)

effaced (ə fāsd′) *adj.* erased; wiped out (p. 512)

oscillation (äs′ ə lā′ shən) *n.* act of swinging back and forth (p. 512)

apprised (ə prīzd′) *v.* informed; notified (p. 512)

malign (mə līn′) *adj.* malicious; very harmful (p. 515)

ineffable (in ef′ ə bəl) *adj.* too overwhelming to be spoken (p. 516)

An Occurrence at OWL CREEK BRIDGE

Ambrose Bierce

Background

The senseless violence, death, and destruction Ambrose Bierce witnessed during the American Civil War (1861–1865) convinced him that war was terrible and futile. He set much of his best fiction, including this story, against the backdrop of this divisive war in which the agricultural South, whose economy was based on slavery, battled the more industrialized North. Fought mostly in the South, the war caused hundreds of thousands of casualties on both sides.

I

A man stood upon a railroad bridge in northern Alabama, looking down into the swift water twenty feet below. The man's hands were behind his back, the wrists bound with a cord. A rope closely encircled his neck. It was attached to a stout cross timber above his head and the slack fell to the level of his knees. Some loose boards laid upon the sleepers supporting the metals of the railway supplied a footing for him and his executioners—two private soldiers of the Federal army, directed by a sergeant who in civil life may have been a deputy sheriff. At a short remove upon the same temporary platform was an officer in the uniform of his rank, armed. He was a captain. A sentinel at each end of the bridge stood with his rifle in the position known as "support," that is to say, vertical in front of the left shoulder, the hammer resting on the forearm thrown straight across the chest—a formal and unnatural position, enforcing an erect carriage of the body. It did not appear to be the duty of these two men to know what was occurring at the center of the bridge; they merely blockaded the two ends of the foot planking that traversed it.

Beyond one of the sentinels nobody was in sight; the railroad ran straight away into a forest for a hundred yards, then, curving, was lost to view. Doubtless there was an outpost farther along. The other bank of the stream was open ground—a gentle acclivity[1] topped with a stockade of vertical

---

1. **acclivity** (ə klivʹ ə tē) *n.* upward slope.

tree trunks, loopholed for rifles, with a single embrasure through which protruded the muzzle of a brass cannon commanding the bridge. Midway of the slope between bridge and fort were the spectators—a single company of infantry in line, at "parade rest," the butts of the rifles on the ground, the barrels inclining slightly backward against the right shoulder, the hands crossed upon the stock. A lieutenant stood at the right of the line, the point of his sword upon the ground, his left hand resting upon his right. Excepting the group of four at the center of the bridge, not a man moved. The company faced the bridge, staring stonily, motionless. The sentinels, facing the banks of the stream, might have been statues to adorn the bridge. The captain stood with folded arms, silent, observing the work of his subordinates, but making no sign. Death is a dignitary who when he comes announced is to be received with formal manifestations of respect, even by those most familiar with him. In the code of military etiquette silence and fixity are forms of deference.

The man who was engaged in being hanged was apparently about thirty-five years of age. He was a civilian, if one might judge from his habit, which was that of a planter. His features were good—a straight nose, firm mouth, broad forehead, from which his long, dark hair was combed straight back, falling behind his ears to the collar of his well-fitting frock coat. He wore a mustache and pointed beard, but no whiskers; his eyes were large and dark gray, and had a kindly expression which one would hardly have expected in one whose neck was in the hemp. Evidently this was no vulgar assassin. The liberal military code makes provision for hanging many kinds of persons, and gentlemen are not excluded.

The preparations being complete, the two private soldiers stepped aside and each drew away the plank upon which he had been standing. The sergeant turned to the captain, saluted and placed himself immediately behind that officer, who in turn moved apart one pace. These movements left the condemned man and the sergeant standing on the two ends of the same plank, which spanned three of the

etiquette (et´ i kit) *n.* appropriate behavior and ceremonies

deference (def´ ər əns) *n.* respect; courtesy; regard

▼ **Critical Viewing**
Which of the men in this photo seem to show an attitude of military etiquette? Explain. **[Interpret]**

✓**Reading Check**
What event is about to take place on the bridge?

crossties of the bridge. The end upon which the civilian stood almost, but not quite, reached a fourth. This plank had been held in place by the weight of the captain; it was now held by that of the sergeant. At a signal from the former the latter would step aside, the plank would tilt and the condemned man go down between two ties. The arrangement commended itself to his judgment as simple and effective. His face had not been covered nor his eyes bandaged. He looked a moment at his "unsteadfast footing," then let his gaze wander to the swirling water of the stream racing madly beneath his feet. A piece of dancing driftwood caught his attention and his eyes followed it down the current. How slowly it appeared to move! What a sluggish stream!

He closed his eyes in order to fix his last thoughts upon his wife and children. The water, touched to gold by the early sun, the brooding mists under the banks at some distance down the stream, the fort, the soldiers, the piece of drift—all had distracted him. And now he became conscious of a new disturbance. Striking through the thought of his dear ones was a sound which he could neither ignore nor understand, a sharp, distinct, metallic percussion like the stroke of a blacksmith's hammer upon the anvil; it had the same ringing quality. He wondered what it was, and whether immeasurably distant or near by—it seemed both. Its recurrence was regular, but as slow as the tolling of a death knell. He awaited each stroke with impatience and—he knew not why—apprehension. The intervals of silence grew progressively longer; the delays became maddening. With their greater infrequency the sounds increased in strength and sharpness. They hurt his ear like the thrust of a knife; he feared he would shriek. What he heard was the ticking of his watch.

He unclosed his eyes and saw again the water below him. "If I could free my hands," he thought, "I might throw off the noose and spring into the stream. By diving I could evade the bullets and, swimming vigorously, reach the bank, take to the woods and get away home. My home, thank God, is as yet outside their lines; my wife and little ones are still beyond the invader's farthest advance."

As these thoughts, which have here to be set down in words, were flashed into the doomed man's brain rather than evolved from it the captain nodded to the sergeant. The sergeant stepped aside.

II

Peyton Farquhar was a well-to-do planter, of an old and highly respected Alabama family. Being a slave owner and like other slave owners a politician he was naturally an original secessionist and ardently devoted to the Southern cause. Circumstances of an imperious nature, which it is unnecessary to relate here, had prevented him from taking service with the gallant army that had fought the disastrous campaigns ending with the fall of Corinth,[2] and he

---

2. **Corinth** Mississippi town that was the site of an 1862 Civil War battle.

Literary Analysis
Point of View What phrase indicates that the point of view has shifted from objective to third-person limited? Explain.

imperious (im pir′ ē əs) *adj.* urgent; imperative

chafed under the inglorious restraint, longing for the release of his energies, the larger life of the soldier, the opportunity for distinction. That opportunity, he felt, would come, as it comes to all in war time. Meanwhile he did what he could. No service was too humble for him to perform in aid of the South, no adventure too perilous for him to undertake if consistent with the character of a civilian who was at heart a soldier, and who in good faith and without too much qualification assented to at least a part of the frankly villainous <u>dictum</u> that all is fair in love and war.

One evening while Farquhar and his wife were sitting on a rustic bench near the entrance to his grounds, a gray-clad soldier rode up to the gate and asked for a drink of water. Mrs. Farquhar was only too happy to serve him with her own white hands. While she was fetching the water her husband approached the dusty horseman and inquired eagerly for news from the front.

"The Yanks are repairing the railroads," said the man, "and are getting ready for another advance. They have reached the Owl Creek bridge, put it in order and built a stockade on the north bank. The commandant has issued an order, which is posted everywhere, declaring that any civilian caught interfering with the railroad, its bridges, tunnels or trains will be <u>summarily</u> hanged. I saw the order."

"How far is it to the Owl Creek bridge?" Farquhar asked.

"About thirty miles."

"Is there no force on this side the creek?"

"Only a picket post[3] half a mile out, on the railroad, and a single sentinel at this end of the bridge."

"Suppose a man—a civilian and student of hanging—should elude the picket post and perhaps get the better of the sentinel," said Farquhar, smiling, "what could he accomplish?"

The soldier reflected. "I was there a month ago," he replied. "I observed that the flood of last winter had lodged a great quantity of driftwood against the wooden pier at this end of the bridge. It is now dry and would burn like tow."[4]

The lady had now brought the water, which the soldier drank. He thanked her ceremoniously, bowed to her husband and rode away. An hour later, after nightfall, he repassed the plantation, going northward in the direction from which he had come. He was a Federal scout.

III

As Peyton Farquhar fell straight downward through the bridge he lost consciousness and was as one already dead. From this state he

Literature in context — History Connection

The Battle of Shiloh

Owl Creek is the stream that runs through Tennessee at the sight of the Battle of Shiloh, one of the bloodiest battles of the Civil War where more than 20,000 soldiers died.

Railroad bridges like the Owl Creek Bridge were important during Civil War times because they enabled the armies access over bodies of water. It is the same Owl Creek which serves as the setting for Peyton Farquhar's "escape" into the torrent waters.

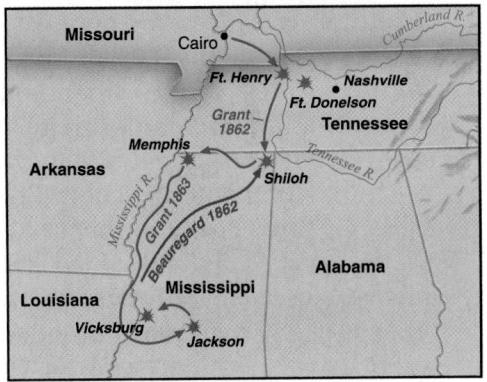

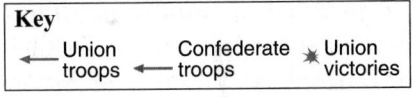

Key

Union troops → | Confederate troops ← | Union victories ✳

dictum (dik´ təm) *n.* formal statement of fact or opinion

summarily (sə mer´ ə lē) *adv.* promptly and without formality

✔ Reading Check

In the war that divides his nation, which side does Farquhar support?

---

3. **picket post** troops sent ahead with news of a surprise attack.
4. **tow** (tō) *n.* coarse, broken fibers of hemp or flax before spinning.

was awakened—ages later, it seemed to him—by the pain of a sharp pressure upon his throat, followed by a sense of suffocation. Keen, poignant agonies seemed to shoot from his neck downward through every fiber of his body and limbs. These pains appeared to flash along well-defined lines of ramification[5] and to beat with an inconceivably rapid periodicity. They seemed like streams of pulsating fire heating him to an intolerable temperature. As to his head, he was conscious of nothing but a feeling of fullness—of congestion. These sensations were unaccompanied by thought. The intellectual part of his nature was already <u>effaced</u>: he had power only to feel, and feeling was torment. He was conscious of motion. Encompassed in a luminous cloud, of which he was now merely the fiery heart, without material substance, he swung through unthinkable arcs of <u>oscillation</u>, like a vast pendulum. Then all at once, with terrible suddenness, the light about him shot upward with the noise of a loud plash; a frightful roaring was in his ears, and all was cold and dark. The power of thought was restored; he knew that the rope had broken and he had fallen into the stream. There was no additional strangulation; the noose about his neck was already suffocating him and kept the water from his lungs. To die of hanging at the bottom of a river!—the idea seemed to him ludicrous. He opened his eyes in the darkness and saw above him a gleam of light, but how distant, how inaccessible! He was still sinking, for the light became fainter and fainter until it was a mere glimmer. Then it began to grow and brighten, and he knew that he was rising toward the surface—knew it with reluctance, for he was now very comfortable. "To be hanged and drowned," he thought, "that is not so bad; but I do not wish to be shot. No; I will not be shot; that is not fair."

He was not conscious of an effort, but a sharp pain in his wrist <u>apprised</u> him that he was trying to free his hands. He gave the struggle his attention, as an idler might observe the feat of a juggler, without interest in the outcome. What splendid effort!—what magnificent, what superhuman strength! Ah, that was a fine endeavor! Bravo! The cord fell away; his arms parted and floated upward, the hands dimly seen on each side in the growing light. He watched them with a new interest as first one and then the other pounced upon the noose at his neck. They tore it away and thrust it fiercely aside, its undulations resembling those of a watersnake. "Put it back, put it back!" He thought he shouted these words to his hands, for the undoing of the noose had been succeeded by the direst pang that he had yet experienced. His neck ached horribly; his brain was on fire; his heart, which had been fluttering faintly, gave a great leap, trying to force itself out at his mouth. His whole body was racked and wrenched with an insupportable anguish! But his disobedient hands gave no heed to the command. They beat the water vigorously with quick, downward

Reading Strategy
Identifying Chronological Order Describe the shift in time that occurs between sections II and III.

effaced (ə fāsd´) *adj.* erased; wiped out

oscillation (äs´ ə lā´ shən) *n.* act of swinging back and forth

apprised (ə prīzd´) *v.* informed; notified

---

5. flash along well-defined lines of ramification spread out quickly along branches from a central point.

strokes, forcing him to the surface. He felt his head emerge; his eyes were blinded by the sunlight; his chest expanded convulsively, and with a supreme and crowning agony his lungs engulfed a great draft of air, which instantly he expelled in a shriek!

He was now in full possession of his physical senses. They were, indeed, preternaturally[6] keen and alert. Something in the awful disturbance of his organic system had so exalted and refined them that they made record of things never before perceived. He felt the ripples upon his face and heard their separate sounds as they struck. He looked at the forest on the bank of the stream, saw the individual trees, the leaves and the veining of each leaf—saw the very insects upon them: the locusts, the brilliant-bodied flies, the gray spiders stretching their webs from twig to twig. He noted the prismatic colors in all the dewdrops upon a million blades of grass. The humming of the gnats that danced above the eddies of the stream, the beating of the dragonflies' wings, the strokes of the water spiders' legs, like oars which had lifted their boat—all these made audible music. A fish slid along beneath his eyes and he heard the rush of its body parting the water.

He had come to the surface facing down the stream; in a moment the visible world seemed to wheel slowly round, himself the pivotal point, and he saw the bridge, the fort, the soldiers upon the bridge, the captain, the sergeant, the two privates, his executioners. They were in silhouette against the blue sky. They shouted and gesticulated, pointing at him. The captain had drawn his pistol, but did not fire; the others were unarmed. Their movements were grotesque and horrible, their forms gigantic.

Suddenly he heard a sharp report and something struck the water smartly within a few inches of his head, spattering his face with spray. He heard a second report, and saw one of the sentinels with his rifle at his shoulder, a light cloud of blue smoke rising from the muzzle. The man in the water saw the eye of the man on the bridge gazing into his own through the sights of the rifle. He observed that it was a gray eye and remembered having read that gray eyes were keenest, and that all famous marksmen had them. Nevertheless, this one had missed.

A counterswirl had caught Farquhar and turned him half round; he was again looking into the forest on the bank opposite the fort. The sound of a clear, high voice in a monotonous singsong now rang out behind him and came across the water with a distinctness that pierced and subdued all other sounds, even the beating of the ripples in his ears. Although no soldier, he had frequented camps enough to know the dread significance of that deliberate, drawling, aspirated

---

6. **preternaturally** (prēt′ ər nach′ ər əl ē) *adv.* abnormally; extraordinarily

▲ Critical Viewing
Based on this map, why is the bridge so important to the Union army? **[Interpret]**

☑ Reading Check

What unusual event happens upon Farquhar's hanging?

chant; the lieutenant on shore was taking a part in the morning's work. How coldly and pitilessly—with what an even, calm intonation, presaging,[7] and enforcing tranquillity in the men—with what accurately measured intervals fell those cruel words:

"Attention, company! . . . Shoulder arms! . . . Ready! . . . Aim! . . . Fire!"

Farquhar dived—dived as deeply as he could. The water roared in his ears like the voice of Niagara, yet he heard the dulled thunder of the volley and, rising again toward the surface, met shining bits of metal, singularly flattened, oscillating slowly downward. Some of them touched him on the face and hands, then fell away, continuing their descent. One lodged between his collar and neck; it was uncomfortably warm and he snatched it out.

As he rose to the surface, gasping for breath, he saw that he had been a long time under water; he was perceptibly farther down stream—nearer to safety. The soldiers had almost finished reloading; the metal ramrods flashed all at once in the sunshine as they were drawn from the barrels, turned in the air, and thrust into their sockets. The two sentinels fired again, independently and ineffectually.

The hunted man saw all this over his shoulder; he was now swimming vigorously with the current. His brain was as energetic as his arms and legs; he thought with the rapidity of lightning.

"The officer," he reasoned, "will not make that martinet's[8] error a second time. It is as easy to dodge a volley as a single shot. He has probably already given the command to fire at will. God help me, I cannot dodge them all!"

An appalling plash within two yards of him was followed by a loud, rushing sound, *diminuendo,*[9] which seemed to travel back through the air to the fort and died in an explosion which stirred the very river to its deeps! A rising sheet of water curved over him, fell down upon him, blinded him, strangled him! The cannon had taken a hand in the game. As he shook his head free from the commotion of the smitten water he heard the deflected shot humming through the air ahead, and in an instant it was cracking and smashing the branches in the forest beyond.

"They will not do that again," he thought; "the next time they will use a charge of grape.[10] I must keep my eye upon the gun; the smoke will apprise me—the report arrives too late; it lags behind the missile. That is a good gun."

Suddenly he felt himself whirled round and round—spinning like a top. The water, the banks, the forests, the now distant bridge, fort and men—all were commingled and blurred. Objects were represented

---

7. **presaging** (prē sāj´ iŋ) predicting; warning.
8. **martinet** (märt´ 'n et´) strict military disciplinarian.
9. *diminuendo* (də min´ yōō en´ dō) musical term used to describe a gradual reduction in volume.
10. **charge of grape** cluster of small iron balls—"grape shot"—that disperse once fired from a cannon.

Reading Strategy
Identifying Chronological Order What event might these words announce?

Literary Analysis
Point of View and Stream of Consciousness What clues does Bierce give you to suggest that the speaker may not be totally reliable as a witness?

by their colors only; circular horizontal streaks of color—that was all he saw. He had been caught in a vortex and was being whirled on with a velocity of advance and gyration that made him giddy and sick. In a few moments he was flung upon the gravel at the foot of the left bank of the stream—the southern bank—and behind a projecting point which concealed him from his enemies. The sudden arrest of his motion, the abrasion of one of his hands on the gravel, restored him, and he wept with delight. He dug his fingers into the sand, threw it over himself in handfuls and audibly blessed it. It looked like diamonds, rubies, emeralds; he could think of nothing beautiful which it did not resemble. The trees upon the bank were giant garden plants; he noted a definite order in their arrangement, inhaled the fragrance of their blooms. A strange, roseate[11] light shone through the spaces among their trunks and the wind made in their branches the music of aeolian harps.[12] He had no wish to perfect his escape—was content to remain in that enchanting spot until retaken.

A whiz and rattle of grapeshot among the branches high above his head roused him from his dream. The baffled cannoneer had fired him a random farewell. He sprang to his feet, rushed up the sloping bank, and plunged into the forest.

All that day he traveled, laying his course by the rounding sun. The forest seemed interminable; nowhere did he discover a break in it, not even a woodman's road. He had not known that he lived in so wild a region. There was something uncanny in the revelation.

By night fall he was fatigued, footsore, famishing. The thought of his wife and children urged him on. At last he found a road which led him in what he knew to be the right direction. It was as wide and straight as a city street, yet it seemed untraveled. No fields bordered it, no dwelling anywhere. Not so much as the barking of a dog suggested human habitation. The black bodies of the trees formed a straight wall on both sides, terminating on the horizon in a point, like a diagram in a lesson in perspective. Overhead, as he looked up through this rift in the wood, shone great golden stars looking unfamiliar and grouped in strange constellations. He was sure they were arranged in some order which had a secret and <u>malign</u> significance. The wood on either side was full of singular noises, among which—once, twice, and again, he distinctly heard whispers in an unknown tongue.

His neck was in pain and lifting his hand to it he found it horribly swollen. He knew that it had a circle of black where the rope had bruised it. His eyes felt congested: he could no longer close them. His tongue was swollen with thirst; he relieved its fever by thrusting it forward from between his teeth into the cold air. How softly the turf

malign (mə lin´) *adj.* malicious; very harmful

---

11. **roseate** (rō´ zē it) *adj.* rose-colored.
12. **aeolian** (ē ō´ lē ən) **harps** stringed instruments that produce music when played by the wind. In Greek mythology, Aeolus is the god of the winds.

**Reading Check**

What is Farquhar's state of mind after his dive?

had carpeted the untraveled avenue—he could no longer feel the roadway beneath his feet!

Doubtless, despite his suffering, he had fallen asleep while walking, for now he sees another scene—perhaps he has merely recovered from a delirium. He stands at the gate of his own home. All is as he left it, and all bright and beautiful in the morning sunshine. He must have traveled the entire night. As he pushes open the gate and passes up the wide white walk, he sees a flutter of female garments: his wife, looking fresh and cool and sweet, steps down from the veranda to meet him. At the bottom of the steps she stands waiting, with a smile of ineffable joy, an attitude of matchless grace and dignity. Ah, how beautiful she is! He springs forward with extended arms. As he is about to clasp her he feels a stunning blow upon the back of the neck; a blinding white light blazes all about him with a sound like the shock of a cannon—then all is darkness and silence!

Peyton Farquhar was dead; his body, with a broken neck, swung gently from side to side beneath the timbers of the Owl Creek bridge.

ineffable (in efʹ ə bəl) *adj.* too overwhelming to be spoken

Review and Assess

Thinking About the Selection

1. **Respond:** With what emotions did you respond to the story's ending? Explain your answer.

2. **(a) Recall:** In Part I, what do you learn about the condemned man? **(b) Analyze:** Bierce makes deliberate decisions about what information to reveal and when to reveal it. How do his choices create suspense?

3. **(a) Recall:** Identify one example of Farquhar's distorted perceptions. **(b) Interpret:** What causes this distortion?

4. **(a) Recall:** What does Farquhar visualize moments before he is hanged? **(b) Connect:** In what way is his journey connected with this earlier vision?

5. **(a) Recall:** What sensation does Farquhar experience "with terrible suddenness" after he has been hanged?
   (b) Distinguish: What details suggest that Farquhar's escape occurs in his mind?

6. **Evaluate:** Do you think the portrayal of Farquhar's final thoughts is realistic? Why or why not?

7. **(a) Extend:** What does this story suggest about the psychology of a person facing a life or death situation?
   (b) Speculate: Are such insights applicable in daily life, or merely in extreme circumstances, like those of war? Explain.

Review and Assess

Literary Analysis

Point of View

1. Analyze the story to find examples of the two different points of view Bierce uses. Complete the chart below to identify the effects of these choices.

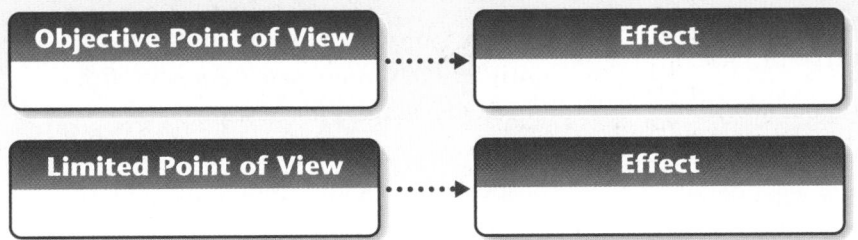

Objective Point of View ·····▶ **Effect**

Limited Point of View ·····▶ **Effect**

2. What is the effect of the shift in point of view in the last paragraph of the story?

Connecting Literary Elements

3. (a) What details in the second paragraph of section III are revealed through the use of **stream of consciousness**? (b) What "sharp pain" sparks Farquhar's thoughts? (c) In what ways does this passage mimic the natural, jumbled flow of thoughts?
4. Why is stream-of-consciousness technique particularly appropriate for this story?

Reading Strategy

Identifying Chronological Order

5. Which takes place first: Farquhar's encounter with the Federal scout or his preoccupation with the ticking of his watch?
6. How much real time do you estimate elapses from the opening to the closing scene of the story? Explain.
7. How did the story's ending change your initial perception of the sequence and duration of the events it describes?

Extend Understanding

8. **Social Studies Connection:** Farquhar was a civilian in the war—not a soldier. Do you think his death was justified? Why or why not?

Quick Review

Point of view is the vantage point from which a story is told.

In **objective point of view**, events are described without information about the thoughts or feelings of the characters.

Narration from a **third-person limited point of view** uses the pronouns *he, she,* or *it* and reveals the thoughts of a single character.

The **stream-of-consciousness** technique of narration captures the chaotic nature of the human thought process by jumping from one idea to another without transition.

To **identify chronological order,** reorder events into the proper time sequence.

 Take It to the Net
www.phschool.com
Take the interactive self-test online to check your understanding of the selection.

Integrate Language Skills

Vocabulary Development Lesson

Word Analysis: Latin Root -summa-

Summary suggests a brief, general idea. Likewise, *summarily* describes an action taken hastily or promptly. These words derive from the Latin word *summa*, meaning "sum, whole." Use your understanding of this root to decide whether each of the following statements is true or false.

1. *Consummate* professionals do poor work.
2. When you *summarize*, you elaborate.
3. A court *summation* covers every legal detail.

Spelling Strategy

When *gn* follows the vowel *i* at the end of a word, as in *sign*, you do not need a final *e* to make the vowel long. Complete the words below.

1. to speak evil of: mal__
2. to bring into line: al__
3. to give up one's position: res__

Fluency: Words in Context

Review the vocabulary words on page 507. Then, use them to answer these questions. Use each word from the list only once, and explain your answers.

1. Which four words best relate to a book entitled *Lady Windmere's Authoritative Guide to Manners for Servants*?
2. Which two words best relate to an unspeakably vicious comment?
3. Which three words best relate to a court clerk who hastily interrupts a judge to inform her that audiotaped evidence had been accidentally erased?
4. Which word relates to a table fan that revolves to cool an entire room?

Grammar and Style Lesson

Semicolons in Compound Sentences

Compound sentences are formed by linking independent clauses—clauses that can stand alone as sentences—with a **semicolon** rather than a conjunction. This style is used to connect two closely related ideas.

> **Example:** They hurt his ear like the thrust of a knife; he feared he would shriek.

Practice Choose from among the independent clauses below to create compound sentences. Use semicolons to join clauses that will form powerful sentences.

1. Plans of escape rushed through his mind.
2. Peyton Farquhar dropped from the bridge to the stream below.
3. The silent, interminable moment ended.
4. The shock of the cold water jolted him.
5. A thunderous roar shattered the calm.
6. Peyton Farquhar surveyed the landscape.

Writing Application Write a paragraph describing a scary experience. Mimic Bierce's style by using compound sentences joined by semicolons.

Looking at Style Bierce makes effective use of compound sentences in the objective parts of the story, where the pattern of short, linked clauses creates a rhythm like that of gunfire.

𝒲𝒢 *Prentice Hall Writing and Grammar Connection: Chapter 27, Section 3*

Writing Lesson

Critical Essay

Bierce was one of the first writers to use stream of consciousness—a style that imitates the natural flow of thoughts, images, and feelings. In an essay, explain how this style makes the story more dramatic. Use details from the story to support your ideas.

Prewriting   Reread the story and generate a list of passages where the use of stream of consciousness helps you to understand the speaker's thoughts. Then, select two or three passages to discuss.

Drafting   Focus on one passage at a time. Explain why the use of stream of consciousness reveals the character's thoughts with heightened realism and drama.

Revising   As you review your draft, note points where quotations from the story will help support your opinions and analysis. Make strong connections between your opinions and the passage you are quoting.

Model: Incorporating Quotations From the Story

> *In his own words, Farquhar thinks he "must have traveled the entire night."*

Through stream of consciousness, Bierce enables readers to empathize with Farquhar as he desperately imagines a struggle to save his life. The moment of full peace when he reunites with his wife is especially powerful.

> Appropriate quotations from the story create strong connections between the writer's opinions and the text.

W̶G̶ Prentice Hall Writing and Grammar Connection: Chapter 14, Section 3

Extension Activities

Listening and Speaking Locate scientific reports about the ways in which perceptions of time change when people are under duress. Write a **summary** of your findings and their connections to this story.

- Summarize the reports you have reviewed.
- Summarize the distortions of time that Farquhar experiences.
- Note the ways in which Bierce's use of time supports or contradicts the research.

Share your summary with the class.

Research and Technology Use the map on page 513 to estimate how long it would have taken Farquhar to reach the bridge, destroy it, and return. Include key information, such as Farquhar's mode of travel (on horse or foot) and rate of speed. Then, use slide show software or manual art materials to create a **visual model** of Farquhar's journey.

 Take It to the Net   www.phschool.com

Go online for an additional research activity using the Internet.

Prepare to Read

The Gettysburg Address ◆ Second Inaugural Address ◆ Letter to His Son

Abraham Lincoln (1809–1865)

Serving as president during one of the most tragic periods in American history, Abraham Lincoln fought to reunite a nation torn apart by war. His courage, strength, and dedication in the face of an overwhelming national crisis have made him one of the most admired and respected American presidents.

A man of humble origins, Lincoln developed an early interest in politics. He served in the Illinois state legislature and the United States Congress, where he earned a reputation as a champion of emancipation. In 1858, he ran for the United States Senate against Stephen Douglas. Lincoln lost the election, but his heated debates with Douglas brought him national recognition and helped him win the presidency in 1860.

Troubled Times Shortly after his election, the Civil War erupted. Throughout the war, Lincoln showed great strength and courage. He also demonstrated his gift for oratory. He was invited to make "a few appropriate remarks" in November 1863 for a dedication of the Gettysburg battlefield as a national cemetery. The world has long remembered what he said there.

Lincoln's great care as a writer shows in the Gettysburg Address, as it does in many of his other speeches. He worked diligently and thoughtfully to prepare messages that would have the effect he desired. Two important aspects of the Gettysburg speech are its brevity—just 272 words—and its reaffirmation of the democratic principles at the heart of American government. Lincoln was killed by an assassin's bullet in 1865 while attending the theater with his wife.

Robert E. Lee (1807–1870)

Robert E. Lee was born into a respected Virginia family and graduated with high honors from the United States Military Academy at West Point. During the Mexican War, Lee established a reputation as one of the finest military leaders in the United States Army.

Divided Loyalties Despite his military traditions, the job of commanding the Confederate army during the Civil War was not one that Robert E. Lee wanted. As the dispute over slavery grew, Lee was torn. A descendant of a number of distinguished patriots and statesmen, he believed in the Union and opposed both slavery and secession. Still, when President Lincoln offered him command of the Union forces, Lee refused to lead an army against his native state and resigned from the army, vowing to fight only in defense of Virginia.

A Difficult Task Unlike many Confederate leaders, Lee had no illusions about the South's power. Serving initially as commander of the army of northern Virginia and later of all the Confederate armies, he expected the widespread bloodshed and destruction caused by the war. He was an extraordinary military leader whose accomplishments and personal integrity in the face of overwhelming odds inspired great loyalty in both soldiers and civilians.

An avid letter writer, Lee wrote frequently to family members explaining his actions and expressing his feelings. On the eve of resigning his U.S. Army commission, Lee explored his divided loyalties in "Letter to His Son." After the war, Lee served as president of Washington College (now Washington and Lee) until his death.

Preview

Connecting to the Literature

Imagine being swept up in a conflict like the Civil War that pits friends and family members against each other. Divided loyalties, like those expressed by Robert E. Lee, were painfully common.

Literary Analysis

Diction

Diction, a writer's choice and arrangement of words, gives a piece of writing its unique quality. Whether formal or informal, concrete or abstract, the words a writer chooses help to convey feelings beyond the ideas presented. Look at these examples from the selections:

- **Lincoln:** To . . . extend this interest was the object for which the insurgents would rend the Union . . .
- **Lee:** I see that four states have declared themselves out of the Union . . .

As you read, contrast the ways in which Lincoln's and Lee's diction reflect the different audiences, purposes, and occasions of their writing.

Comparing Literary Works

Lee's diction in writing to his son was more informal than the public speech drafted by President Lincoln. Despite this contrast, both documents provide a window into the private and public conflicts of the Civil War. Compare and contrast the information and insights these selections provide about the nation's great war.

Reading Strategy

Using Background Knowledge

If you read a historical document without understanding the situations that inspired it, you may miss most of its underlying value and meaning. **Use prior background knowledge** of the Civil War to analyze ideas, actions, and decisions in historical context. Complete a chart like the one shown to organize your ideas.

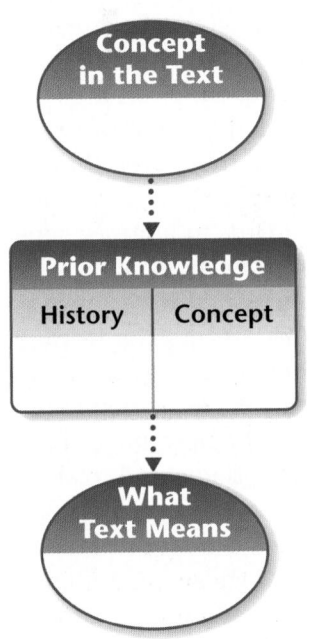

Vocabulary Development

consecrate (kän′ si krāt′) *v.* cause to be revered or honored (p. 522)

hallow (hal′ ō) *v.* honor as sacred (p. 522)

deprecated (dep′ rə kāt′ id) *v.* expressed disapproval of; (p. 524)

insurgents (in sʉr′ jənts) *n.* rebels; those who revolt against authority (p. 524)

discern (di sʉrn′) *v.* receive or recognize; make out clearly (p. 524)

scourge (skʉrj) *n.* cause of serious trouble or affliction (p. 524)

malice (mal′ is) *n.* ill will; spite (p. 524)

anarchy (an′ ər kē) *n.* absence of government (p. 525)

redress (ri dres′) *n.* atonement; rectification (p. 525)

The Gettysburg Address

Abraham Lincoln   November 19, 1863

Background

The battle of Gettysburg, Pennsylvania, fought in July 1863, was an important Union victory and marked a turning point in the war. More than 51,000 soldiers were injured in the battle. On November 19, 1863, while the war still raged, a military cemetery on the battlefield was dedicated. Unsure of President Lincoln's availability, the dedication organizers slated him as a secondary speaker, asking him to make only "a few appropriate remarks." In drafting that brief address, Lincoln wanted to lead the 15,000 American citizens attending the dedication through an emotional, final rite of passage. He also needed to gain continuing support for a bloody conflict that was far from over.

Four score and seven years ago our fathers brought forth on this continent a new nation, conceived in Liberty, and dedicated to the proposition that all men are created equal.

Now we are engaged in a great civil war, testing whether that nation, or any nation so conceived and so dedicated, can long endure. We are met on a great battle-field of that war. We have come to dedicate a portion of that field, as a final resting place for those who here gave their lives that that nation might live. It is altogether fitting and proper that we should do this.

But, in a larger sense, we can not dedicate—we can not consecrate—we can not hallow—this ground. The brave men, living and dead, who struggled here, have consecrated it, far above our poor power to add or detract. The world will little note, nor long remember what we say here, but it can never forget what they did here. It is for us the living, rather, to be dedicated here to the unfinished work which they who fought here have thus far so nobly advanced. It is rather for us to be here dedicated to the great task remaining before us—that from these honored dead we take increased devotion to that cause for which they gave the last full measure of devotion—that we here highly resolve that these dead shall not have died in vain—that this nation, under God, shall have a new birth of freedom—and that government of the people, by the people, for the people, shall not perish from the earth.

> **Literary Analysis**
> **Diction** What impression do you get of the speaker from the level of diction in "four score and seven years ago"?
>
> **consecrate** (kän′ si krāt′) v. cause to be revered or honored
>
> **hallow** (hal′ ō) v. honor as sacred

Second Inaugural Address

Abraham Lincoln
March 4, 1865

◀ **Critical Viewing**
What mood does the facial expression of this statue—the centerpiece of the Lincoln Memorial in Washington, D. C.—convey? [**Analyze**]

At this second appearing to take the oath of the presidential office, there is less occasion for an extended address than there was at the first. Then a statement, somewhat in detail, of a course to be pursued, seemed fitting and proper. Now, at the expiration of four years, during which public declarations have been constantly called forth on every point and phase of the great contest which still absorbs the attention, and engrosses the energies of the nation, little that is new could be presented. The progress of our arms, upon which all else chiefly depends, is as well known to the public as to myself; and it is, I trust, reasonably satisfactory and encouraging to all. With high hope for the future, no prediction in regard to it is ventured.

On the occasion corresponding to this four years ago, all thoughts were anxiously directed to an impending civil war. All dreaded it—all sought to avert it. While the inaugural address was being delivered from this place, devoted altogether to *saving* the Union without war,

✔**Reading Check**

Why does Lincoln say there is less call for an extended address than there was at his first inauguration?

insurgent agents were in the city seeking to *destroy* it without war—seeking to dissolve the Union, and divide effects, by negotiation. Both parties deprecated war; but one of them would *make* war rather than let the nation survive; and the other would *accept* war rather than let it perish. And the war came.

One eighth of the whole population were colored slaves, not distributed generally over the Union, but localized in the Southern part of it. These slaves constituted a peculiar and powerful interest. All knew that this interest was, somehow, the cause of the war. To strengthen, perpetuate, and extend this interest was the object for which the insurgents would rend the Union, even by war; while the government claimed no right to do more than to restrict the territorial enlargement of it. Neither party expected for the war, the magnitude, or the duration, which it has already attained. Neither anticipated that the *cause* of the conflict might cease with, or even before, the conflict itself should cease. Each looked for an easier triumph, and a result less fundamental and astounding. Both read the same Bible, and pray to the same God; and each invokes His aid against the other. It may seem strange that any men should dare to ask a just God's assistance in wringing their bread from the sweat of other men's faces; but let us judge not that we be not judged. The prayers of both could not be answered; that of neither has been answered fully. The Almighty has his own purposes. "Woe unto the world because of offences! for it must needs be that offences come; but woe to that man by whom the offence cometh!"[1] If we shall suppose that American Slavery is one of those offences which, in the providence of God,[2] must needs come, but which, having continued through His appointed time, He now wills to remove, and that He gives to both North and South, this terrible war, as the woe due to those by whom the offence came, shall we discern therein any departure from those divine attributes which the believers in a Living God always ascribe to Him? Fondly do we hope—fervently do we pray—that this mighty scourge of war may speedily pass away. Yet, if God wills that it continue, until all the wealth piled by the bond-man's two hundred and fifty years of unrequited toil shall be sunk, and until every drop of blood drawn with the lash, shall be paid by another drawn with the sword, as was said three thousand years ago, so still it must be said "the judgments of the Lord, are true and righteous altogether."[3]

With malice toward none; with charity for all; with firmness in the right, as God gives us to see the right, let us strive on to finish the work we are in; to bind up the nation's wounds; to care for him who shall have borne the battle, and for his widow, and his orphan—to do all which may achieve and cherish a just and lasting peace, among ourselves, and with all nations.

deprecated (dep´ rə kāt´ id) *v.* expressed disapproval of

insurgents (in sur´ jənts) *n.* rebels; those who revolt against authority

Literary Analysis
Diction What can you infer about Lincoln from his diction in the passage beginning "It may seem strange"?

discern (di surn´) *v.* receive or recognize; make out clearly

scourge (skurj) *n.* cause of serious trouble or affliction

malice (mal´ is) *n.* ill will; spite

---

1. **"Woe unto the world . . . offence cometh"** from Matthew 18:7 of the King James Version of the Bible.
2. **providence of God** benevolent care or wise guidance of God.
3. **"The judgments . . . altogether"** from Psalm 19:9.

Letter to His Son

Robert E. Lee January 23, 1861

I received Everett's[1] *Life of Washington* which you sent me, and enjoyed its perusal. How his spirit would be grieved could he see the wreck of his mighty labors! I will not, however, permit myself to believe, until all ground of hope is gone, that the fruit of his noble deeds will be destroyed, and that his precious advice and virtuous example will so soon be forgotten by his countrymen. As far as I can judge by the papers, we are between a state of <u>anarchy</u> and civil war. May God avert both of these evils from us! I fear that mankind will not for years be sufficiently Christianized to bear the absence of restraint and force. I see that four states[2] have declared themselves out of the Union; four more will apparently follow their example. Then, if the border states are brought into the gulf of revolution, one half of the country will be arrayed against the other. I must try and be patient and await the end, for I can do nothing to hasten or retard it.

The South, in my opinion, has been aggrieved by the acts of the North, as you say. I feel the aggression and am willing to take every proper step for <u>redress</u>. It is the principle I contend for, not individual or private benefit. As an American citizen, I take great pride in my

---

1. **Everett's** referring to Edward Everett (1794–1865), an American scholar and orator who made a long speech at Gettysburg before Lincoln delivered his famous address.
2. **four states** South Carolina, Mississippi, Florida, and Alabama.

▲ **Critical Viewing**
Why is this posture, on horseback, appropriate for a statue memorializing Robert E. Lee?
[Defend]

anarchy (an´ ər kē) *n.* absence of government

redress (ri dres´) *n.* atonement; rectification

✔ **Reading Check**

According to Lee, what is the political state of the country?

country, her prosperity and institutions, and would defend any state if her rights were invaded. But I can anticipate no greater calamity for the country than a dissolution of the Union. It would be an accumulation of all the evils we complain of, and I am willing to sacrifice everything but honor for its preservation. I hope, therefore, that all constitutional means will be exhausted before there is a resort to force. Secession is nothing but revolution. The framers of our Constitution never exhausted so much labor, wisdom, and forbearance in its formation, and surrounded it with so many guards and securities, if it was intended to be broken by every member of the Confederacy at will. It was intended for "perpetual union," so expressed in the preamble, and for the establishment of a government, not a compact, which can only be dissolved by revolution or the consent of all the people in convention assembled. It is idle to talk of secession. Anarchy would have been established, and not a government, by Washington, Hamilton, Jefferson, Madison, and the other patriots of the Revolution. . . . Still, a Union that can only be maintained by swords and bayonets, and in which strife and civil war are to take the place of brotherly love and kindness, has no charm for me. I shall mourn for my country and for the welfare and progress of mankind. If the Union is dissolved, and the government disrupted, I shall return to my native state and share the miseries of my people; and, save in defense, will draw my sword on none.

Reading Strategy
Using Background Knowledge Given what you know about Lee, why was he so committed to the Union and to Virginia?

Review and Assess

Thinking About the Selections

1. **Respond:** Which phrases in Lincoln's speeches do you find the most memorable? Explain your response.

2. **(a) Recall:** Briefly describe the occasion for each of Lincoln's speeches. **(b) Infer:** Beyond the stated reasons, what was Lincoln's underlying purpose in "The Gettysburg Address"? **(c) Infer:** What was his main purpose in the "Second Inaugural Address"?

3. **(a) Recall:** What vision of the nation does Lincoln describe at the close of both speeches? **(b) Connect:** In what way does an expression of this vision further his purpose?

4. **(a) Recall:** How does Lee define secession? **(b) Summarize:** In your own words, explain Lee's argument against secession.

5. **(a) Recall:** What gift has Lee's son given him? **(b) Connect:** Explain the line of reasoning that links Lee's acknowledgment of his son's gift to an argument against secession.

6. **Apply:** In what ways, if any, are Lincoln's speeches different from modern presidential addresses? Explain.

Review and Assess

Literary Analysis
Diction

1. Using a chart like the one shown here, analyze the **diction** of each writer.

	Examples of Diction	Audience	Purpose
Lincoln			
Lee			

2. In what ways does each writer's diction reflect and suit his audience and purpose?

Comparing Literary Works

3. (a) What words does Lincoln use to describe the war? (b) What words does Lee use to describe it?
4. (a) Based on the ideas and insights revealed in these selections, what personal qualities do you think Lee and Lincoln share? (b) In what ways do they differ?
5. Which voice do you find more engaging, Lincoln's or Lee's? Why?

Reading Strategy
Using Background Knowledge

6. Using **background knowledge,** explain why President Lincoln wrote such a short speech for his address at Gettysburg.
7. Why did Lincoln connect the honoring of the Gettysburg dead with the goal of continuing the war toward a Union victory?
8. In the "Second Inaugural Address," why did Lincoln suggest that both the war and an end to slavery were part of God's plan?
9. Why was Lee so opposed to secession?

Extend Understanding

10. **Social Studies Connection:** Lee describes the relationship between the states and the Union as "a government, not a compact." What are some of the ways in which people, organizations, and governments make compacts with one another?

Quick Review

Diction is a writer's choice and arrangement of words.

To **use background knowledge,** refer to information you already know about a subject to help you create meaning for current reading.

 Take It to the Net
www.phschool.com
Take the interactive self-test online to check your understanding of these selections.

Integrate Language Skills

Vocabulary Development Lesson

Word Analysis: Greek Word Part
-archy-

The word *anarchy* derives from the Greek word *archein*, meaning "to rule" or "to govern." With the prefix *an-*, meaning "without," *anarchy* means "without government." Use your knowledge of the root and the supplied information to write a definition for each word below.

1. monarchy (*mono* = single; one)
2. patriarchy (*patri* = father)
3. oligarchy (*olig* = few)

Spelling Strategy

Except when forming plurals, use *ss* to spell the *s* sound at the end of a word, as in *redress*. In your notebook, complete the spelling of the words below.

1. confe___   3. stre___

2. distre___   4. compre___

Grammar and Style Lesson

Parallel Structure

Parallel structure is the repeated expression of similar ideas in a similar grammatical form. Parallelism can involve the repeated use of similar words, phrases, clauses, or sentences. In the example, each phrase begins with the word *with*.

> *With* malice toward none; *with* charity for all; *with* firmness in the right . . .

Practice Identify the parallel structures in each of the following items.

1. Fondly do we hope—fervently do we pray—that this mighty scourge . . .

Concept Development: Synonyms

Review the vocabulary list on p. 521. Then, choose the word that is the best synonym, or word with similar meaning, for each first word.

1. consecrate: (a) destroy, (b) bless, (c) join
2. hallow: (a) honor, (b) greet, (c) enlarge
3. deprecated: (a) condemned, (b) proved, (c) enlarged
4. insurgents: (a) patriots, (b) loyalists, (c) rebels
5. discern: (a) hear, (b) understand, (c) ask
6. scourge: (a) punishment, (b) reward, (c) desire
7. malice: (a) grace, (b) scent, (c) spite
8. anarchy: (a) honor, (b) order, (c) chaos
9. redress: (a) atonement, (b) fear, (c) disturbance

2. . . . we cannot dedicate—we cannot consecrate—we cannot hallow—this ground . . .
3. . . . until all the wealth piled by the bondman's . . . and until every drop of blood . . .
4. All dreaded it—all sought to avert it.
5. . . . that government of the people, by the people, for the people . . .

Writing Application Rewrite a sentence from "Letter to His Son," using parallel structure to emphasize Lee's ideas.

Looking at Style Review Lincoln's speeches to find a particularly strong example of parallel structure. Explain your choice, noting the effect of the example you have chosen.

Writing Lesson

Diary Entry

It is the eve of the dedication of the cemetery at Gettysburg. As Lincoln, write a diary entry describing the message you will strive to deliver. Using the Gettysburg Address as your model, imagine Lincoln's feelings and note the main points he wanted to stress.

Prewriting Take notes on what you consider the three or four main points of the Gettysburg Address. Rank them in order of importance and summarize them in plain language. Spend a few minutes freewriting about each point. Use this as the basis of your draft.

Drafting From your notes, begin writing the diary entry. Use personal reflections and opinions as Lincoln would have in drafting the address. Emphasize your main points with persuasive language.

Revising Reread your draft to make sure it captures Lincoln's feelings with persuasive language. Add details to strengthen your argument.

Model: Revising to Add Persuasive Language

I know our country was born on the principle of
freedom because our forefathers believed all men to be
     we must fight to   *Slavery is wrong.*
equal. Now ~~I want to~~ stop a terrible evil. ~~We can't have~~
~~slavery.~~ We must ensure freedom and equality for all.

> Statements such as *we must fight* and *slavery is wrong* make the writing powerful and persuasive.

WG Prentice Hall Writing and Grammar Connection: Chapter 7, Section 3

Extension Activities

Speaking and Listening With a group, stage a **mock Supreme Court hearing** and argue for or against a state's rights to secede from the Union. After hearing arguments from "lawyers," each "judge" should render an opinion. As you plan, consider the following tips.

- Lawyers should present their strongest arguments.
- Judges should identify and rank the arguments before rendering a decision.

Stage the hearing in class. **[Group Activity]**

Research and Technology Develop a plan for an **Internet Web site** that provides information and images related to the Civil War. Create a flow chart that illustrates the links you plan to include in your site. If possible, use HTML software to develop an offline version of your site.

 **Take It to the Net**   www.phschool.com

Go online for an additional research activity using the Internet.

Public Documents

About Public Documents

What do the text of a law, the deed to a house, and minutes from a legislative meeting have in common? They are examples of public documents, official government papers that affect everyone living in a given part of a state or nation. These documents are referred to as public because they concern laws and issues that all citizens have a stake in. For this reason, these documents are made available for average citizens to read, analyze, and discuss.

The public document that you are about to read is one of the most important in United States history. It is the text of a formal announcement that President Abraham Lincoln signed on January 1, 1863, calling for the freeing of "all persons held as slaves" within the rebellious southern states. Many historians believe that this public document altered the nature of the Civil War.

Reading Strategy

Analyzing an Author's Beliefs

Some public documents, such as census reports, are almost completely objective; they merely record information without seeking to support a particular point of view. Sometimes, however, public documents contain opinions.

- Opinions may be hinted at through choice of words or the decision to emphasize certain details.

- In contrast, beliefs may be stated outright, making them explicit.

- Beliefs and opinions about a specific issue depend on assumptions—claims that must be true if the opinion or belief is true. Writers may state their assumptions, making them explicit. Often, though, writers' assumptions are simply implied in the argument they make. You can tell they are making these implicit assumptions by noting what general ideas must be true for their arguments to be true.

To identify an author's beliefs, follow the steps outlined in the chart shown.

As you read the Emancipation Proclamation, consider the implicit and explicit beliefs it represents.

Identifying an Author's Beliefs

Step one
Look for opinion words such as *I think, I believe,* or *in my opinion,* which signal explicit beliefs.

Step two
Look for other words that suggest opinion. These may be adjectives that have clear opposites. For example, a writer might say that a course of action is *just;* another might say it is *unfair.*

Step three
Look for details that suggest a specific point of view. Read the document sentence by sentence. Consider whether each detail is factual or whether someone could make an argument against it.

By the President of the United States of America:

A Proclamation.

The source and type of public document should always be clear.

Whereas, on the twenty-second day of September, in the year of our Lord one thousand eight hundred and sixty-two, a proclamation was issued by the President of the United States, containing, among other things, the following, to wit:

"That on the first day of January, in the year of our Lord one thousand eight hundred and sixty-three, all persons held as slaves within any State or designated part of a State, the people whereof shall then be in rebellion against the United States, shall be then, thenceforward, and forever free; and the Executive Government of the United States, including the military and naval authority thereof, will recognize and maintain the freedom of such persons, and will do no act or acts to repress such persons, or any of them, in any efforts they may make for their actual freedom"

Many public documents go into a great amount of detail. The details may slow down your reading of the document, but they are very important.

"That the Executive will, on the first day of January aforesaid, by proclamation, designate the States and parts of States, if any, in which the people thereof, respectively, shall then be in rebellion against the United States; and the fact that any State, or the people thereof, shall on that day be, in good faith, represented in the Congress of the United States by members chosen thereto at elections wherein a majority of the qualified voters of such State shall have participated, shall, in the absence of strong countervailing testimony, be deemed conclusive evidence that such State, and the people thereof, are not then in rebellion against the United States."

Now, therefore I, Abraham Lincoln, President of the United States, by virtue of the power in me vested as Commander-in-Chief, of the Army and Navy of the United States in time of actual armed rebellion against the authority and government of the United States, and as a fit and necessary war measure for suppressing said rebellion, do, on this first day of January, in the year of our Lord one thousand eight hundred and sixty-three, and in accordance with my purpose so to do publicly proclaimed for the full period of one hundred days, from the day first above mentioned, order and designate as the States and parts of States wherein the people thereof respectively, are this day in rebellion against the United States, the following, to wit:

Arkansas, Texas, Louisiana, (except the Parishes of St. Bernard, Plaquemines, Jefferson, St. John, St. Charles, St. James Ascension, Assumption, Terrebonne, Lafourche, St. Mary, St. Martin, and Orleans, including the City of New Orleans) Mississippi, Alabama, Florida, Georgia, South Carolina, North Carolina, and Virginia, (except the forty-eight counties designated as West Virginia, and also the counties of Berkley, Accomac, Northampton, Elizabeth City, York, Princess Ann, and Norfolk, including the cities of Norfolk and Portsmouth[)], and which excepted parts, are for the present, left precisely as if this proclamation were not issued.

And by virtue of the power, and for the purpose aforesaid, I do order and declare that all persons held as slaves within said designated States, and parts of States, are, and henceforward shall be free; and that the Executive government of the United States, including the military and naval authorities thereof, will recognize and maintain the freedom of said persons.

Legal and formal language *(for the purpose aforesaid; within said designated States)* is common in proclamations.

And I hereby enjoin upon the people so declared to be free to abstain from all violence, unless in necessary self-defence; and I recommend to them that, in all cases when allowed, they labor faithfully for reasonable wages.

And I further declare and make known, that such persons of suitable condition, will be received into the armed service of the United States to garrison forts, positions, stations, and other places, and to man vessels of all sorts in said service.

And upon this act, sincerely believed to be an act of justice, warranted by the Constitution, upon military necessity, I invoke the considerate judgment of mankind, and the gracious favor of Almighty God.

In witness whereof, I have hereunto set my hand and caused the seal of the United States to be affixed.

Done at the City of Washington, this first day of January, in the year of our Lord one thousand eight hundred and sixty three, and of the Independence of the United States of America the eighty-seventh.

> Considering their legal and, at times, historic effects, place and date are key elements of public documents.

By the President: *Abraham Lincoln*

Secretary of State. *William H. Seward*

Check Your Comprehension

1. According to Lincoln, why does he have the authority to make this proclamation?
2. Which parts of the United States that practiced slavery are not included in the proclamation?

Applying the Reading Strategy

Analyzing an Author's Beliefs

3. Identify Lincoln's explicit and implicit beliefs in the Emancipation Proclamation. Note beliefs about (a) the Constitution's authority, (b) the necessity of emancipation, (c) God's existence.

Activity

Writing a Proclamation

Consider creating a new national holiday or selecting a new national anthem. Then, write a proclamation of your own.

Comparing Informational Materials

Modern Proclamations

Find a contemporary government proclamation. Compare it to the Emancipation Proclamation in purpose and language.

PART 2

Focus on Literary Forms: Diaries, Journals, and Letters

Newspapers in the Trenches '64, William Sheppard,
Museum of the Confederacy, Richmond, Virginia

The Civil War was one of the most painful chapters of American history. The diaries, letters, and journals in this section tell the story of the tragic conflict between the states, allowing readers to experience the events through the eyes of people who experienced them firsthand.

Prepare to Read

Civil War Diaries, Journals, and Letters

Civil War Voices

The Civil War was one of the most painful chapters in American history, tearing families apart and scarring the lives of millions of soldiers and civilians. The following diaries, journals, and letters tell the story of the war through the eyes of just a few of those whose lives were affected by it.

A Daughter of the South No one was hurt when the opening shots of the war were fired on Fort Sumter on April 12, 1860, but **Mary Boykin Chesnut** (1823–1886) seems to have sensed the carnage to come. The daughter of a cotton plantation owner and United States senator, Mary Boykin was raised in an aristocratic family in Charleston, South Carolina. At the age of seventeen, she married James Chesnut, Jr., a wealthy lawyer and future senator. Her journal entries convey the Southern aristocracy's mingled optimism and dread that marked the opening days of the Civil War.

On the Front Lines Men hurried to enlist in what most believed would be a swift and glorious conflict. Some young men saw the military as an opportunity for respect and advancement as we learn from the account of Union soldier **Warren Lee Goss**. The harsh realities of the training camp and battlefield soon taught soldiers on both sides that lives and limbs were the price of glory. The cost was especially high at the Battle of Gettysburg—a stunning defeat for Confederate general Robert E. Lee. In his diary, Confederate soldier **Randolph McKim** recounts the bravery of his companions, many of whom were among the 51,000 killed or wounded at Gettysburg after Confederate troops advanced on Culp's Hill, led by McKim.

A Master Strategist Confederate general and military strategist **Thomas Jonathan "Stonewall" Jackson** (1824–1863) earned his nickname early in the war for his steadiness and determination during the Battle of Bull Run in 1861. Jackson, who recounted the battle in a letter to his wife, died two years after his great victory; he was accidentally shot by his own troops and died of complications.

Freedom's Cry The war raged on, but the Emancipation Proclamation, issued by President Lincoln on September 22, 1862, changed the purpose of the war. By declaring that all slaves would be freed on January 1, 1863, the Proclamation transformed the conflict into a war to end slavery, as well as a war to restore the Union. **Reverend Henry M. Turner,** a free-born African American who lived in Washington, D.C., recounts his community's joyous reaction to the news of Lincoln's proclamation.

The Enduring Battle When the war ended in 1865, abolitionist **Sojourner Truth** (1797–1883) had only begun to battle discrimination. A preacher and former slave, Truth also earned fame as an advocate of women's rights, temperance, and workplace and prison reform.

Born into slavery in Ulster County, New York, Truth was freed when the state emancipated slaves in 1827. In 1843, she began preaching along the east coast. During the Civil War, Truth gathered contributions of food and clothing for the African American regiments. She met with President Abraham Lincoln in the White House in 1864. Truth was a powerful speaker whose passion and charisma often drew large crowds to her informal lectures.

Preview

Connecting to the Literature

Today, you can learn about events almost immediately through instant access news sources. The Civil War took place before news networks were invented, however, so the best way to learn about the war and share the experiences of those involved is through their letters, journals, diaries, and photographs.

Literary Analysis

Diaries, Journals, and Letters

Diaries, journals, and letters are personal records of events, thoughts, feelings, and observations written on a day-to-day basis. These literary forms allow people to record immediate responses to their experiences.

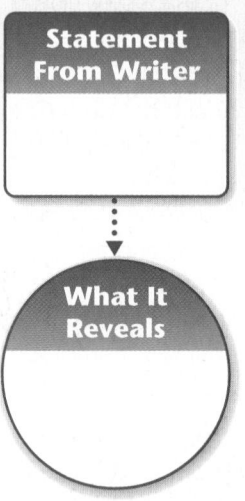

- Diaries and journals are generally for personal use. Usually written in an informal style, they capture the writers' ideas and emotions.
- Personal letters are not written for general publication, but because they are addressed to another person, the writing is not entirely private.

As you read these selections, use a chart like the one shown to analyze the information each selection provides and to determine what those details reveal about the writer.

Comparing Literary Works

The selections presented here reflect a wide spectrum of opinions and experiences related to the Civil War. As first-hand accounts of the period, these are valuable examples of **historical narratives.** In this kind of writing, people living through historic events describe their personal experiences and reactions, providing historians an intimate perspective on history. As you read, compare the different perspectives these selections offer of the Civil War.

Reading Strategy

Distinguishing Fact From Opinion

A *fact* is a statement that can be proved true; an *opinion* is a judgment that cannot be proved, though it can be supported by arguments. As you read, **distinguish facts from opinions** by determining whether a statement can be proved or whether it simply reflects the writer's opinions.

Vocabulary Development

capitulate (kə pich´ ə lāt´) *v.* surrender conditionally (p. 537)

audaciously (ô dā´ shəs lē) *adv.* boldly or daringly (p. 537)

foreboding (fôr bōd´ iŋ) *n.* presentiment (p. 537)

obstinate (äb´ stə nit) *adj.* stubborn (p. 538)

imprecations (im´ pri kā´ shənz) *n.* curses (p. 538)

serenity (sə ren´ ə tē) *n.* calmness (p. 539)

from *Mary Chesnut's* **Civil War**

Mary Chesnut

Background

In the early days of April 1861, the nation held its collective breath as the tension between North and South mounted. On April 12, the opening shots of the Civil War were fired on Fort Sumter, a Union military post in Charleston, South Carolina, as the city's citizens watched from their rooftops.

Filmmaker and historian Ken Burns, who produced the 1990 television documentary *The Civil War*, noted that during the war "Soldiers at the front and civilians at home left an astonishingly rich and moving record of what they saw and felt . . . hundreds of voices from across the spectrum of American experience, men and women whose lives were touched or destroyed or permanently changed by the war." Here, Mary Chesnut's journal is a memorable chapter in that record.

April 7, 1861. Today things seem to have settled down a little.

One can but hope still. Lincoln or Seward[1] have made such silly advances and then far sillier drawings back. There may be a chance for peace, after all.

Things are happening so fast.

My husband has been made an aide-de-camp[2] of General Beauregard.

Three hours ago we were quietly packing to go home. The convention has adjourned.

Now he tells me the attack upon Fort Sumter[3] may begin tonight. Depends upon Anderson and the fleet outside. The *Herald* says that this show of war outside of the bar is intended for Texas.

John Manning came in with his sword and red sash. Pleased as a boy to be on Beauregard's staff while the row goes on. He has gone with Wigfall to Captain Hartstene with instructions.

Mr. Chesnut is finishing a report he had to make to the convention.

Mrs. Hayne called. She had, she said, "but one feeling, pity for those who are not here."

---

1. **Seward** William Henry Seward (1801–1872), U.S. Secretary of State from 1861 through 1869.
2. **aide-de-camp** (ād´ də kamp´) *n.* officer serving as assistant and confidential secretary to a superior.
3. **Fort Sumter** fort in Charleston Harbor, South Carolina. At the time, the fort was occupied by Union troops commanded by Major Robert Anderson.

Literary Analysis
Diaries, Journals, and Letters What details of style and context tell you that you are reading a diary or journal entry?

Jack Preston, Willie Alston—"the take-life-easys," as they are called—with John Green, "the big brave," have gone down to the island—volunteered as privates.

Seven hundred men were sent over. Ammunition wagons rumbling along the streets all night. Anderson burning blue lights—signs and signals for the fleet outside, I suppose.

Today at dinner there was no allusion to things as they stand in Charleston Harbor. There was an undercurrent of intense excitement. There could not have been a more brilliant circle. In addition to our usual quartet (Judge Withers, Langdon Cheves, and Trescot) our two governors dined with us, Means and Manning.

These men all talked so delightfully. For once in my life I listened.

That over, business began. In earnest, Governor Means rummaged a sword and red sash from somewhere and brought it for Colonel Chesnut, who has gone to demand the surrender of Fort Sumter.

And now, patience—we must wait.

Why did that green goose Anderson go into Fort Sumter? Then everything began to go wrong.

Now they have intercepted a letter from him, urging them to let him surrender. He paints the horrors likely to ensue if they will not.

He ought to have thought of all that before he put his head in the hole.

April 12, 1861. Anderson will not capitulate.

Yesterday was the merriest, maddest dinner we have had yet. Men were more audaciously wise and witty. We had an unspoken foreboding it was to be our last pleasant meeting. Mr. Miles dined with us today. Mrs. Henry King rushed in: "The news, I come for the latest news—all of the men of the King family are on the island"—of which fact she seemed proud.

While she was here, our peace negotiator—or envoy—came in. That is, Mr. Chesnut returned—his interview with Colonel Anderson had been deeply interesting—but was not inclined to be communicative, wanted his dinner. Felt for Anderson. Had telegraphed to President Davis[4] for instructions.

What answer to give Anderson, etc., etc. He has gone back to Fort Sumter with additional instructions.

---

4. **President Davis** Jefferson Davis (1808–1889), president of the Confederacy (1861–1865).

Bombardment of Sumter, Harper's Weekly, 1861

▲ **Critical Viewing**
Describe the people's reaction to the bombing of Fort Sumter as depicted in this illustration.
[Analyze]

capitulate (kə pich´ ə lāt´) v. surrender conditionally

audaciously (ô dā´ shəs lē) adv. boldly or daringly

foreboding (fôr bōd´ iŋ) n. presentiment

☑ **Reading Check**

What does Colonel Chesnut demand?

When they were about to leave the wharf, A. H. Boykin sprang into the boat, in great excitement; thought himself ill-used. A likelihood of fighting—and he to be left behind!

I do not pretend to go to sleep. How can I? If Anderson does not accept terms—at four—the orders are—he shall be fired upon.

I count four—St. Michael chimes. I begin to hope. At half-past four, the heavy booming of a cannon.

I sprang out of bed. And on my knees—prostrate—I prayed as I never prayed before.

There was a sound of stir all over the house—pattering of feet in the corridor—all seemed hurrying one way. I put on my double gown and a shawl and went, too. It was to the housetop.

The shells were bursting. In the dark I heard a man say "waste of ammunition."

I knew my husband was rowing about in a boat somewhere in that dark bay. And that the shells were roofing it over—bursting toward the fort. If Anderson was <u>obstinate</u>—he was to order the forts on our side to open fire. Certainly fire had begun. The regular roar of the cannon—there it was. And who could tell what each volley accomplished of death and destruction.

The women were wild, there on the housetop. Prayers from the women and <u>imprecations</u> from the men, and then a shell would light up the scene. Tonight, they say, the forces are to attempt to land.

The *Harriet Lane*[5] had her wheelhouse[6] smashed and put back to sea.

We watched up there—everybody wondered. Fort Sumter did not fire a shot.

Today Miles and Manning, colonels now—aides to Beauregard—dined with us. The latter hoped I would keep the peace. I give him only good words, for he was to be under fire all day and night, in the bay carrying orders, etc.

Last night—or this morning truly—up on the housetop I was so weak and weary I sat down on something that looked like a black stool.

"Get up, you foolish woman—your dress is on fire," cried a man. And he put me out.

It was a chimney, and the sparks caught my clothes. Susan Preston and Mr. Venable then came up. But my fire had been extinguished before it broke out into a regular blaze.

Do you know, after all that noise and our tears and prayers, nobody has been hurt. Sound and fury, signifying nothing.[7] A delusion and a snare. . . .

Literary Analysis
Diaries, Journals, and Letters What characteristics of a diary or journal do these sentences have?

obstinate (äb´ stə nət) *adj.* stubborn

imprecations (im´ pri kā´ shənz) *n.* curses

Literary Analysis
Diaries, Journals, and Letters What do you learn about Mary Chesnut's life based on her dinner guests?

---

5. The *Harriet Lane* federal steamer that had brought provisions to Fort Sumter.
6. **wheelhouse** *n.* enclosed place on the upper deck of a ship, in which the helmsman stands while steering.
7. **Sound . . . nothing** from Shakespeare's *Macbeth,* Act V, Scene v, lines 27–28. Macbeth is contemplating the significance of life and death after learning of his wife's death.

Somebody came in just now and reported Colonel Chesnut asleep on the sofa in General Beauregard's room. After two such nights he must be so tired as to be able to sleep anywhere. . . .

April 13, 1861. Nobody hurt, after all. How gay we were last night.

Reaction after the dread of all the slaughter we thought those dreadful cannons were making such a noise in doing.

Not even a battery[8] the worse for wear.

Fort Sumter has been on fire. He has not yet silenced any of our guns. So the aides—still with swords and red sashes by way of uniform—tell us.

But the sound of those guns makes regular meals impossible. None of us go to table. But tea trays pervade the corridors, going everywhere.

Some of the anxious hearts lie on their beds and moan in solitary misery. Mrs. Wigfall and I solace ourselves with tea in my room.

These women have all a satisfying faith.

April 15, 1861. I did not know that one could live such days of excitement.

They called, "Come out—there is a crowd coming."

A mob indeed, but it was headed by Colonels Chesnut and Manning.

The crowd was shouting and showing these two as messengers of good news. They were escorted to Beauregard's headquarters. Fort Sumter had surrendered.

Those up on the housetop shouted to us, "The fort is on fire." That had been the story once or twice before.

When we had calmed down, Colonel Chesnut, who had taken it all quietly enough—if anything, more unruffled than usual in his serenity—told us how the surrender came about.

Wigfall was with them on Morris Island when he saw the fire in the fort, jumped in a little boat and, with his handkerchief as a white flag, rowed over to Fort Sumter. Wigfall went in through a porthole.

When Colonel Chesnut arrived shortly after and was received by the regular entrance, Colonel Anderson told him he had need to pick his way warily, for it was all mined.

As far as I can make out, the fort surrendered to Wigfall.

But it is all confusion. Our flag is flying there. Fire engines have been sent to put out the fire.

Everybody tells you half of something and then rushes off to tell something else or to hear the last news. . . .

---

8. **battery** *n.* artillery unit.

The American Experience

The Angel of the Battlefield

Like Mary Chesnut, many women were on the scene and also in action during the Civil War. Clara Barton is known for her brave assistance to wounded soldiers. Barton spent two years, from 1862–1864, at the front, delivering bandages, socks, and other goods to wounded soldiers. In so doing, she earned the name "Angel of the Battlefield." In 1864, Barton was given the position of superintendent of Union nurses. After the Civil War, she engaged in a search for missing soldiers and lectured about her war experiences.

In 1881, the American Red Cross organization was formed and Barton served as its first president. This organization still exists today and provides relief around the world during wartime and in times of disaster.

serenity (sə ren′ ə tē) *n.* calmness

Reading Check

What news do Colonels Chesnut and Manning bring back to camp?

Recollections of a Private

Warren Lee Goss

In the weeks that followed the attack on Fort Sumter, thousands of men on both sides volunteered to fight. Among the early enlistees was Warren Lee Goss of Massachusetts.

"Cold chills" ran up and down my back as I got out of bed after the sleepless night, and shaved preparatory to other desperate deeds of valor. I was twenty years of age, and when anything unusual was to be done, like fighting or courting, I shaved.

With a nervous tremor convulsing my system, and my heart thumping like muffled drumbeats, I stood before the door of the recruiting office, and before turning the knob to enter read and reread the advertisement for recruits posted thereon, until I knew all its peculiarities. The promised chances for "travel and promotion" seemed good, and I thought I might have made a mistake in considering war so serious after all. "Chances for travel!" I must confess now, after four years of soldiering, that the "chances for travel" were no myth; but "promotion" was a little uncertain and slow.

I was in no hurry to open the door. Though determined to enlist, I was half inclined to put it off awhile; I had a fluctuation of desires; I was fainthearted and brave; I wanted to enlist, and yet—Here I turned the knob, and was relieved. . . .

My first uniform was a bad fit: My trousers were too long by three or four inches; the flannel shirt was coarse and unpleasant, too large at the neck and too short elsewhere. The forage cap[1] was an ungainly bag with pasteboard top and leather visor; the blouse was the only part

---

1. **forage cap** cap worn by infantry soldiers.

> **Literary Analysis**
> **Diaries, Journals, and Letters** What details of Goss's writing style indicate that this is part of a diary or journal entry?

which seemed decent; while the overcoat made me feel like a little nubbin of corn in a large preponderance of husk. Nothing except "Virginia mud" ever took down my ideas of military pomp quite so low.

After enlisting I did not seem of so much consequence as I had expected. There was not so much excitement on account of my military appearance as I deemed justly my due. I was taught my facings, and at the time I thought the drillmaster needlessly fussy about shouldering, ordering, and presenting arms. At this time men were often drilled in company and regimental evolutions long before they learned the manual of arms, because of the difficulty of obtaining muskets. These we obtained at an early day, but we would willingly have resigned them after carrying them a few hours. The musket, after an hour's drill, seemed heavier and less ornamental than it had looked to be.

The first day I went out to drill, getting tired of doing the same things over and over, I said to the drill sergeant: "Let's stop this fooling and go over to the grocery." His only reply was addressed to a corporal: "Corporal, take this man out and drill him"; and the corporal did! I found that suggestions were not so well appreciated in the army as in private life, and that no wisdom was equal to a drillmaster's "Right face," "Left wheel," and "Right, oblique, march." It takes a raw recruit some time to learn that he is not to think or suggest, but obey. Some never do learn. I acquired it at last, in humility and mud, but it was tough. Yet I doubt if my patriotism, during my first three weeks' drill, was quite knee high. Drilling looks easy to a spectator, but it isn't. After a time I had cut down my uniform so that I could see out of it, and had conquered the drill sufficiently to see through it. Then the word came: on to Washington! . . .

Reading Strategy
Distinguishing Fact from Opinion Identify one opinion in this description of enlisting.

Review and Assess

Thinking About the Selections

1. **Respond:** Would you have volunteered to fight during the early days of the Civil War? Why or why not?

2. **(a) Recall:** What events does Mary Chesnut describe in her diary entries? **(b) Interpret:** What does her diary reveal about her attitude toward the war?

3. **(a) Summarize:** Describe Warren Lee Goss's feelings on the day he was to enlist in the army. **(b) Analyze:** How did Private Goss's attitudes and expectations change after he enlisted?

4. **(a) Recall:** According to Goss, what takes a long time for a recruit to learn? **(b) Infer:** What do you think happened to cause him to say, "I acquired it at last, in humility and mud, but it was tough"?

5. **Apply:** How might Chesnut's diary have been different if she had been from the North?

A *Confederate* Account of the Battle of Gettysburg

Randolph McKim

From July 1 to July 3, 1863, Union and Confederate troops fought near the small town of Gettysburg, Pennsylvania. After Union troops gained control of the hills surrounding the town, the Confederate troops commanded by Robert E. Lee launched a risky attack on the strongest Union position. When the attack failed, the Confederate troops were forced to retreat at a great cost of lives. The battle, the first in which troops commanded by Lee were defeated, marked a turning point in the war. In a diary entry, Confederate soldier Randolph McKim described the final day of the battle.

T hen came General Ewell's order to assume the offensive and assail the crest of Culp's Hill, on our right. . . . The works to be stormed ran almost at right angles to those we occupied. Moreover, there was a double line of entrenchments, one above the other, and each filled with troops. In moving to the attack we were exposed to enfilading fire[1] from the woods on our left flank, besides the double line of fire which we had to face in front, and a battery of artillery posted on a hill to our left rear opened upon us at short range. . . .

On swept the gallant little brigade, the Third North Carolina on the right of the line, next the Second Maryland, then the three Virginia regiments (10th, 23d, and 37th), with the First North Carolina on the extreme left. Its ranks had been sadly thinned, and its energies greatly depleted by those six fearful hours of battle that morning; but its nerve and spirit were undiminished. Soon, however, the left and center were checked and then repulsed, probably by the severe flank fire from the woods; and the small remnant of the Third North Carolina, with the stronger Second Maryland (I do not recall the banners of any other regiment), were far in advance of the rest of the line. On they pressed to within about twenty or thirty paces of the works—a small but gallant band of heroes daring to attempt what could not be done by flesh and blood.

The end soon came. We were beaten back to the line from which we had advanced with terrible loss, and in much confusion, but the enemy did not make a countercharge. By the strenuous efforts of the officers of the line and of the staff, order was restored, and we re-formed in the breastworks[2] from which we had emerged, there to be again exposed to an artillery fire exceeding in violence that of the early morning. It remains only to say that, like Pickett's men[3] later in the day, this single brigade was hurled unsupported against the enemy's works. Daniel's brigade remained in the breastworks during and after the charge, and neither from that command nor from any other had we any support. Of course it is to be presumed that General Daniel acted in obedience to orders. We remained in this breastwork after the charge about an hour before we finally abandoned the Federal entrenchments and retired to the foot of the hill.

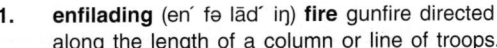

---

1. **enfilading** (en′ fə lād′ iŋ) **fire** gunfire directed along the length of a column or line of troops.
2. **breastworks** low walls put up quickly as a defense in battle.
3. **Pickett's men** General George Pickett was a Confederate officer who led the unsuccessful attack on the Union position.

Reading Strategy
Distinguishing Fact From Opinion What is Randolph McKim describing in the sentence beginning "On they pressed"? Is he stating the facts or giving his opinion?

◄ **Critical Viewing**
The battlefield of Gettysburg, shown here, draws visitors to this day. Which details of this picture memorialize the war? **[Interpret]**

✔ **Reading Check**
What happens at the end of the battle?

An Account of the Battle of Bull Run

Stonewall Jackson

Stonewall Jackson at Bull Run

In this letter to his wife, Confederate General Thomas "Stonewall" Jackson recounts the first southern victory of the war: a battle fought in July 1861, outside Washington, D.C., near a small stream named Bull Run.

My precious pet,

Yesterday we fought a great battle and gained a great victory, for which all the glory is due to God alone. Although under a heavy fire for several continuous hours, I received only one wound, the breaking of the longest finger of my left hand; but the doctor says the finger can be saved. It was broken about midway between the hand and knuckle, the ball passing on the side next [to] the forefinger. Had it struck the center, I should have lost the finger.

My horse was wounded, but not killed. Your coat got an ugly wound near the hip, but my servant, who is very handy, has so far repaired it that it doesn't show very much. My preservation was entirely due, as was the glorious victory, to our God, to whom be all the honor, praise and glory. The battle was the hardest that I have ever been in, but not near so hot in its fire. I commanded the center more particularly, though one of my regiments extended to the right for some distance. There were other commanders on my right and left. Whilst great credit is due to other parts of our gallant army, God made my brigade more instrumental than any other in repulsing the main attack. This is for your information only—say nothing about it. Let others speak praise, not myself.

▲ Critical Viewing

How does this depiction of Jackson enable the viewer to distinguish the general from his officers and soldiers? **[Analyze]**

Reading Strategy

Distinguishing Fact From Opinion Is the general being factual or stating his opinion in describing the nature of the victory and indicating to whom the glory belongs? Explain.

Reaction to the *Emancipation Proclamation*

Reverend Henry M. Turner

On September 22, 1862, President Lincoln issued the Emancipation Proclamation, declaring that all slaves in states still in rebellion would be free as of January 1, 1863. Because those states were not under Union control at the time, no slaves were actually set free that day. The Proclamation, however, was a powerful symbol of hope for those still in slavery and inspired a wave of Union support from free African Americans. In this account, Reverend Henry M. Turner, a free-born African American living in Washington, D.C., describes his people's reaction to the news of the Proclamation.

Seeing such a multitude of people in and around my church, I hurriedly sent up to the office of the first paper in which the proclamation of freedom could be printed, known as the *Evening Star,* and squeezed myself through the dense crowd that was waiting for the paper. The first sheet run off with the proclamation in it was grabbed for by three of us, but some active young man got possession of it and fled. The next sheet was grabbed for by several, and was torn into tatters. The third sheet from the press was grabbed for by several, but I succeeded in procuring so much of it as contained the proclamation, and off I went for life and death. Down Pennsylvania Avenue I ran as for my life, and when the people saw me coming with the paper in my hand they raised a shouting cheer that was almost deafening. As many as could get around me lifted me to a great platform, and I started to read the proclamation. I had run the best end of a mile,

Literary Analysis
Diaries, Journals, and Letters How would you describe the tone of Reverend Turner's description?

✓**Reading Check**

What do people do when they see the reverend running down the street?

I was out of breath, and could not read. Mr. Hinton, to whom I handed the paper, read it with great force and clearness. While he was reading every kind of demonstration and gesticulation was going on. Men squealed, women fainted, dogs barked, white and colored people shook hands, songs were sung, and by this time cannons began to fire at the navy yard, and follow in the wake of the roar that had for some time been going on behind the White House. . . . Great processions of colored and white men marched to and fro and passed in front of the White House and congratulated President Lincoln on his proclamation. The President came to the window and made responsive bows, and thousands told him, if he would come out of that palace, they would hug him to death. . . . It was indeed a time of times, and nothing like it will ever be seen again in this life.

Reading the Emancipation Proclamation, Artist unknown

▲ **Critical Viewing** In what way does this illustration relate to Reverend Turner's account? **[Connect]**

An Account of an *Experience* with *Discrimination*

Sojourner Truth

▲ Critical Viewing

In what ways does this image compare with your impression of Sojourner Truth based on her account? Explain.
[Compare and Contrast]

Although the Civil War brought an end to slavery, the struggle against racial discrimination was just beginning. Before the war, Sojourner Truth worked tirelessly to free slaves. After the war, she fought for a number of causes, including the woman's suffrage movement and the desegregation of public transportation. Once, when a driver of a street car refused her passage, she brought a local street to a standstill. With the support of a crowd behind her, the driver was forced to allow her on board. In the following letter, written on October 1, 1865, Sojourner Truth describes other encounters with racism.

A few weeks ago I was in company with my friend Josephine S. Griffing, when the conductor of a streetcar refused to stop his car for me, although [I was] closely following Josephine and holding on to the iron rail. They dragged me a number of yards before she succeeded in stopping them. She reported the conductor to the president of the City Railway, who dismissed him at once, and told me to take the number of the car whenever I was mistreated by a conductor or driver.

✔ Reading Check

What does Josephine S. Griffing do to help her friend?

On the 13th I had occasion to go for necessities for the patients in the Freedmen's Hospital where I have been doing and advising for a number of months. I thought now I would get a ride without trouble as I was in company with another friend, Laura S. Haviland of Michigan. As I ascended the platform of the car, the conductor pushed me, saying "Go back—get off here." I told him I was not going off, then "I'll put you off" said he furiously, clenching my right arm with both hands, using such violence that he seemed about to succeed, when Mrs. Haviland told him he was not going to put me off. "Does she belong to you?" said he in a hurried angry tone. She replied, "She does not belong to me, but she belongs to humanity." The number of the car was noted, and conductor dismissed at once upon the report to the president, who advised his arrest for assault and battery as my shoulder was sprained by his effort to put me off. Accordingly I had him arrested and the case tried before Justice Thompson. My shoulder was very lame and swollen, but is better. It is hard for the old slaveholding spirit to die. But die it must. . . .

Review and Assess

Thinking About the Selections

1. **Respond:** In what ways have these accounts added to your understanding of the Civil War? Explain.

2. **(a) Recall:** Explain the events described in the accounts of Randolph McKim and Stonewall Jackson. **(b) Compare:** How are they similar? **(c) Contrast:** How do they differ?

3. **(a) Recall:** What is the reaction to the Emancipation Proclamation among the members of Reverend Turner's audience? **(b) Speculate:** Why do you think the Emancipation Proclamation had such an emotional effect?

4. **(a) Recall:** What does the streetcar conductor say to Laura Haviland about Sojourner Truth? **(b) Infer:** What does his question reveal about the "old slaveholding spirit"?

5. **(a) Recall:** What happens to the conductor who wanted to refuse service to Truth? **(b) Connect:** What do details of these events of 1865 have in common with the Civil Rights Movement of the 1960s?

6. **(a) Compare and Contrast:** In what ways do the tones or attitudes of Sojourner Truth and Henry Turner differ? **(b) Speculate:** Why do you think their feelings are different?

7. **Take a Position:** If you were alive during the Civil War, which position might you have taken—the North's or South's? Explain.

Review and Assess

Literary Analysis

Diaries, Journals, and Letters

1. Note at least two examples from Mary Chesnut's **diaries** that indicate her dislike for the war.

2. Find three details or ideas that Jackson probably would have omitted from his **letter** if it were intended for publication.

3. What does Sojourner Truth's letter reveal about her personality?

Comparing Literary Works

4. What details about the Civil War can you learn from Mary Chesnut's diary that you might not learn from a history book?

5. What facts or details can you learn from two of the other selections?

6. (a) What makes these **historical narratives** valuable to students of the Civil War? (b) What might make them unreliable?

7. Which selection would you say is most valuable to historians? Why?

Reading Strategy

Distinguishing Fact From Opinion

8. **Distinguish the facts and opinions** in the following passage from Goss's account:

   The forage cap was an ungainly bag with pasteboard top and leather visor; the blouse was the only part which seemed decent; while the overcoat made me feel like a little nubbin of corn in a large preponderance of husk.

9. Identify two facts and two opinions from Jackson's account. Record them in a chart like the one shown.

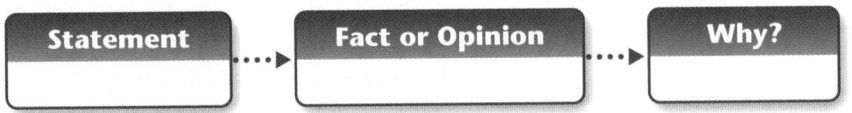

Statement		Fact or Opinion		Why?
	····▶		····▶	

10. In the accounts by Reverend Turner and Sojourner Truth, which contains more facts and which contains more opinions? Explain your answer.

Extend Understanding

11. **Social Studies Connection:** More than a century later, the Civil War continues to engage the interest of Americans. Why do you think this is so?

Quick Review

Diaries and journals are personal records of daily events, usually written in prose. A **personal letter** is one that is written without the intention of publication.

Historical narratives are personal accounts of significant historical events.

To **distinguish fact from opinion,** determine whether or not a statement can be proved conclusively true.

 Take It to the Net
www.phschool.com

Take the interactive self-test online to check your understanding of these selections.

Integrate Language Skills

Vocabulary Development Lesson

Word Analysis: Latin Prefix *ob-*

The word *obstinate* comes from a combination of the Latin prefix *ob-*, meaning "against," and a form of the Latin root *-stare-*, meaning "stand." Use your understanding of the meaning of *ob-* to match each word to the numbered item that most closely relates to it.

a. obstruction   **b.** obscure   **c.** object

1. voice opposition in the courtroom
2. a fallen tree blocking the road
3. cloud an issue with confusing arguments

Spelling Strategy

Verbs that end in *-ate* have noun forms ending in *-ion*. Drop the final *e* before adding the suffix, as in *imprecate/imprecation* and *capitulate/ capitulation*. Spell the noun forms of the following words:

1. celebrate   2. litigate   3. speculate

Grammar and Style Lesson

Capitalization of Proper Nouns

The name of a person, street, road, town, city, county, or state is considered a **proper noun** and should begin with a **capital letter.** Directional words (*east, west,* and so on) that are part of the name of a place should also begin with a capital, as in *West Virginia.*

> **Proper Nouns:** Why did that green goose *Anderson* go into *Fort Sumter?*

Practice Rewrite each of the following sentences in your notebook, correcting any errors in capitalization.

1. The *herald* says that this show of war outside of the bar is intended for texas.

Fluency: Sentence Completion

Complete these sentences with the correct word from the vocabulary list on page 535.

1. When the rifle jammed, the soldier muttered ___?___ at his bad luck.
2. There was no ___?___ to be found in the troubled hearts and minds of soldiers and civilians.
3. As enemy shells exploded in the distance, a sense of ___?___ hung over the camp like fog.
4. Despite the overwhelming odds facing his brigade, the general refused to ___?___.
5. What one person would call ___?___, another might call courageous.
6. After midnight, the spies crept ___?___ close to the enemy's encampment.

2. On swept the gallant little brigade, the third north Carolina on the right of the line, next the second maryland, and then the three virginia regiments.
3. Down Pennsylvania avenue I ran as for my life, and when the People saw me coming . . . they raised a shouting cheer.
4. Then came General Ewell's order to assume the offensive and assail the crest of culp's Hill.
5. They passed the White House and congratulated president Lincoln on his Proclamation.

Writing Application Write a paragraph about a recent trip you took. Be sure to name places and use capital letters when necessary.

𝒲𝒢 *Prentice Hall Writing and Grammar Connection: Chapter 26*

Writing Lesson

Problem-and-Solution Essay

Today, few take the time to write letters or keep a journal. In what way might this be a loss? In an essay, explore the personal benefits and historical value of engaging in this type of private writing. Use examples and insights from these selections to illustrate your point.

Prewriting Brainstorm for a list of the benefits of journal writing and the disadvantages that could occur when historical events are not documented in this way. Use a chart like the one shown to gather your ideas.

Model: Gathering Details

Personal Benefits	Historical Value	Loss From No Journal
Journals can be passed down through family.	History is documented for society at large.	Valuable information could be lost forever.

Drafting Begin with an introduction of the topic. Then, write one paragraph on three of your ideas, connecting them with personal experiences to provide insight. Tie your thoughts together in the conclusion.

Revising Compare your draft with your list to be sure you have included the essential points you want to make. Make sure that your personal reflections clearly connect with your main ideas.

W_G *Prentice Hall Writing and Grammar Connection: Chapter 4, Section 2*

Extension Activities

Listening and Speaking Rev. Turner recounts the emotional impact of the Emancipation Proclamation. Deliver a **dramatic reading** of the document, accompanied by music that conveys the tone of your interpretation. Consider the following:

- Read main points with emotion for emphasis.
- Make eye contact or use hand gestures that convey power or determination.

After practicing, present the reading to your class.

Research and Technology Research the Battle of Gettysburg, one of the turning points of the Civil War. Create a **model or map** of the battlefield, identify the locations of key events, and provide explanatory captions. Integrate Internet graphics and word-processed text. **[Group Activity]**

 **Take It to the Net**   www.phschool.com

Go online for an additional research activity using the Internet.

CONNECTIONS
Literature Past and Present

War Diaries, Journals, and Letters

The letters and diary and journal entries in Part 2 tell the story of the Civil War as seen through the eyes of people who experienced it firsthand. Each of these intimate literary forms presents personal views of the events of the time from eyewitnesses—none of whom was a professional writer. In her book *A Woman at War*, journalist Molly Moore records her impressions of a modern conflict, the Persian Gulf War between Iraq and a coalition of forces led by the United States. Although Moore, as a newspaper reporter, usually writes objective news stories, this personal account of her experiences as a witness to history makes exciting reading. In this excerpt, she relates her story behind the news story—what it was like to cover the Persian Gulf War from the military zone. Like the personal accounts you have already read, Moore's narrative reveals a human side to war.

Revealing the Hidden Faces of War The Civil War was a long, bloody conflict that tore the nation apart. Those living outside the war zone, however, never fully comprehended the horror and devastation wrought by the war. Communication was limited and slow. Newspapers, where available, were a key source of information, but the news they contained was often days old. The only way to really understand the impact of the war was to live through it.

In the late 1960s, Americans experienced their first "living-room war" as violent, disturbing footage of the Vietnam War flashed across television screens every evening. In 1991, the Persian Gulf War was a full-scale media event that unfolded in real time before the eyes of millions worldwide who watched round-the-clock coverage on satellite and cable news stations. Though viewers were able to "experience" war as never before, there is still something unique and compelling about a personal account by an eyewitness near the action. Molly Moore provides this account.

Gulf War Journal
from A Woman at War

Molly Moore

◆◇◆

In August 1990, Iraqi troops under the command of dictator Saddam Hussein invaded neighboring Kuwait, a tiny oil-rich nation on the Persian Gulf. Despite economic sanctions and repeated demands by the United Nations Security Council, Iraq refused to withdraw from Kuwait. In late November 1990, the council presented the invaders with an ultimatum: leave Kuwait by January 15, 1991, or a coalition of nations, including the United States, would use "all necessary means" to remove Iraqi troops from Kuwait. Iraq ignored the threat. Early on the morning of January 17, 1991, coalition forces began bombing Iraqi targets, marking the official launch of the Persian Gulf War, also known as Operation Desert Storm. Hundreds of reporters, Molly Moore among them, were gathered at the Dhahran International Hotel in Dhahran, Saudi Arabia, when the airstrike began.

◆◇◆

a thunderous roar jarred me out of a light sleep. The hotel windows rattled and the entire building shook. I recognized the sound almost instantly: The U.S. Air Force's 1st Tactical Fighter Wing was taking off outside my window. The fighter jets normally took off in pairs, seldom more than six at a time. But this was a massive, continuous wave of noise as a dozen or more of the F-15 Eagle fighters fired their afterburners and sped into the night sky. It could mean only one thing: The war had started. I glanced at my watch. It was 1:45 a.m.

Almost simultaneously I heard dozens of footsteps pounding down the hallways outside my door. The telephone rang. It was my *Washington Post* colleague in the room across the hall.

◀ **Critical Viewing** In what ways did computer-guided missiles such as the one in this photograph change the nature of combat? **[Speculate]**

✓**Reading Check**

What specific event awakens Moore from sleep?

"It's started," said Guy Gugliotta, a seasoned foreign correspondant who'd been sent to Saudi Arabia to relieve me when I'd returned to Washington in December.

"I just heard the planes take off," I replied, collecting notebooks and a pen from the small desk in my room.

"We just got the first pool report[1] from another air base up north," Gugliotta said. "I'm calling the foreign desk now."

"I'll be upstairs," I told him. "See you there."

I joined the mob surging up the steps to the military's Joint Information Bureau on the third floor of the hotel. Despite the months of waiting and speculation and the more than one hundred stories I'd written dissecting Operation Desert Shield, the enormity of the moment and the uncertainty of its consequences were almost overwhelming.

So much for "military disinformation." More than three hundred reporters now jammed the Dhahran International's opulent third-floor ballroom, which had been converted into large pressrooms. Reporters squeezed the public affairs officers for details and snatched copies of the media pool reports as soon as they were dictated by the pool of reporters assigned to an air base northwest of Dhahran.

Gugliotta joined me after giving the *Post* the meager information he had from the first pool report. "There's nothing coming out of Washington," he said. "Nobody has announced anything. Cheney[2] is supposed to make a statement later tonight."

An ABC *Nightline* reporter thrust a microphone into my face. "How do you feel about the information the military is providing about the war?"

I was tempted to say, "What information?" It's always a sure sign that there isn't any real information when reporters start interviewing each other.

"The only information we've gotten so far has been from the reporters on one of the pools," I replied. "At least that worked pretty well. Reporters were at the base where some of the first planes took off and they managed to get to a telephone to dictate a story before Washington even admitted the war had started."

Suddenly an ear-piercing siren wailed through the building.

"What is that?" I shouted to Gugliotta.

"Bomb shelter, get down to the bomb shelter," he yelled.

I followed the herd. As I sprinted down the stairs I noticed the signs that had been added since I'd left six weeks earlier: "To the shelters," with arrows pointing the way.

▼ **Critical Viewing**
These journalists are presenting their report from atop a tank. Why might the journalists have chosen this location for filming? **[Hypothesize]**

---

1. **pool report** During the Persian Gulf War, firsthand information was compiled, or pooled, in reports that then were released to all of the media organizations covering the war.
2. **Cheney** (chā′ nē) U.S. Secretary of Defense Richard Cheney. Cheney would become Vice President in 2001.

Almost six hundred hotel guests and staff spilled down the stair-wells in near panic. Had the Iraqis launched a counterattack? Were they roaring down the coastal highway toward Dhahran? Had Saddam Hussein fired Scud missiles at us? We'd known since August that the hotel was in a prime target zone. It sat beside the most active military airfield in Saudi Arabia.

In the basement, frantic hotel employees tried to guide the frenzied crowd into half a dozen rooms, including the kitchen. Above the din, Philip Congdon, a former officer of the British special forces, who had been hired as the hotel's defense consultant, threatened, "Sit down or you will be tried!"

I was in a group that was shoved into the kitchen and ordered to lie on the floor. We were surrounded by large plate-glass windows. An explosion would send shards ripping through the air. I crawled beneath a large steel table, thinking it might protect me from flying glass.

"Everyone please sit down and put on your gas masks," directed Congdon, a wiry man who looked to be in his early fifties. Even when

☑ **Reading Check**

From where did the reporters receive their information?

giving frightening directives, Congdon had one of those self-assured voices that could calm a hysterical mob.

The people around me were pulling gas masks over their faces. I panicked. I had no mask. *The Washington Post's* chemical protection suits had not yet arrived from British Aerospace in London even though we'd ordered them almost two months earlier.

"I don't have a mask," I called in a strained voice to Congdon. He looked at me with exasperation. "Just sit down, I'll get you something," he said impatiently.

Moments later he returned with a crude, spongy contraption that looked somewhat like a surgical mask and covered only my nose and mouth. I slipped it on, knowing it would merely postpone death a microsecond. I sat on the gritty kitchen floor, surrounded by slimy, rotting tomato halves and colleagues in full-face masks. If I could smell the stench of the tomatoes on the floor and the spoiled chicken parts on the counter above me, I figured chemical particles would have no trouble penetrating my pathetic mask.

The information vacuum was almost unbearable. We knew nothing about what was going on at the air base outside our windows or the world outside Saudi Arabia. The siren continued its annoying wail.

Someone pulled out a shortwave radio.

". . . In the event of an attack, there is likely to be a reprisal," the crackly voice said. "There is no reaction from the Iraqi side yet."

I breathed a little easier.

At 3:50 a.m., about thirty minutes after the siren sounded, the hotel security chief called an all clear, the signal that we could remove our gas masks and leave the basement shelter. The civil defense alert had been called because of uncertainty about how the Iraqi military would react to the first bombs dropped on Baghdad. As we pushed our way into the crowded corridors, Congdon warned, "You should be aware that the early stage of an offensive is the most likely time for an attack on Dhahran."

As soon as we were released from our temporary captivity, the JIB began activating emergency media pools in an effort to get reporters across the street to the air base, where pilots would soon be returning with tales of the first bombing runs. The reporters who would serve on these quick-reaction pools had been selected days earlier after acrimonious debates among feuding news organizations. Now, the public affairs officers couldn't find the *New York Times* reporter assigned to the pool. Guy Gugliotta volunteered to take his place. As he collected his sleeping bag and rucksack, Gugliotta rattled off the instructions for operating the satellite telephone the *Post* had leased for our war coverage. For a $53,000 leasing fee, we could have instant communications to Washington from anywhere on the battlefield, including the roof of the Dhahran International Hotel, where the high-tech contraption now sat.

Within the last hour, a convoy of humvees[3] with machine guns mounted on their roofs had formed a tight ring around the front of the hotel.

I began piecing together the details. At 1:30 a.m., the guided-missile cruiser USS *San Jacinto*, stationed in the Red Sea, had fired the opening shot of the war: a 1.6 ton, twenty-foot-long Tomahawk cruise missile aimed at downtown Baghdad. Minutes later fighter planes based across the street from our hotel, as well as warplanes from bases across the Arabian Peninsula, roared into the sky toward Iraq.

---

3. humvees large, rugged military vehicles known as High Mobility Multi-Purpose Wheeled Vehicles. The term *humvee* is derived from the acronym HMMWV.

Thematic Connection
Compare the description of this scene with the descriptions of fear and chaos expressed by Mary Chesnut and Randolph McKim.

Reading Check

In the early morning hours, what causes the reporters to put on gas masks and huddle on the kitchen floor?

Pool reports from reporters interviewing pilots began trickling into the JIB.

"Baghdad lit up like a Christmas tree," Air Force colonel George Walton told reporters as he climbed out of his F-4G Wild Weasel electronic warfare jet.

"It was the scariest thing I've ever done," Lieutenant Ian Long, a British Tornado pilot, recounted. "Some tracers came off the target[4] down our left-hand side. We tried to avoid that by going right. On our right-hand side was a mass of white explosions, and yellow explosions that looked like flak.[5] You're frightened of failure, you're frightened of dying. You're flying as low as you dare, but high enough to get the weapons off. As the bombs come off, you just run . . . "

I tried to telephone the new details to the *Post.* I dialed and redialed and redialed. The hotel's switchboard was jammed. I raced to the roof of the hotel. Since I had last been there six weeks earlier, it had become a jungle of satellite dishes, talk-show sets, and camera tripods. The hotel employees called it "Little Hollywood." Wires and electrical cords were coiled and stretched in every direction like a giant plate of spaghetti. It was dark and starting to mist.

I found the *Post* satellite telephone, a midget beside the monster network dishes. Its collapsible dish was about the size of a large umbrella. I pulled out my scribbled instructions and read them in the beam of my flashlight.

"Turn the generator on. The choke is on the back. Give pull one jerk. Adjust the choke." It operated like a lawn mower. Unlike a lawn mower, it started on the first try.

I switched on the telephone, encased in a metal box that looked like a large suitcase, and punched numbers on a keypad until "Indian"—as in Indian Ocean—appeared on a digital readout. I pressed the keypad again to find the designated satellite shore station at Perth, Australia. I dialed a code and *The Washington Post* foreign desk number. I heard three rings. "Foreign desk," said the perfectly clear voice on the other end of the telephone.

---

4. **"Some tracers . . . target** The Iraqi military bases targeted for bombing responded by firing tracers, ammunition that traces its own course with a visible trail of smoke or fire.
5. **flak** (flak) anti-aircraft gunfire.

Molly Moore

(b. 1956)

Molly Moore has worked for *The Washington Post* since 1981, covering local and state government; and the Pentagon for five years, including the Gulf War. She also served as a foreign correspondent in South Asia, covering India, Pakistan, Afghanistan, Bangladesh, Nepal, Bhutan and Sri Lanka. Moore says she wrote *A Woman at War* because she came away from the Gulf War believing that most of the world had seen only the television version that was portrayed as a quick and effortless victory by the American armed forces.

Connecting Literature Past and Present

1. Compare and contrast the way Mary Chesnut and Molly Moore get information about the wars.
2. Does Molly Moore's situation in the Dhahran International Hotel more closely resemble the situation of Mary Chesnut or of Randolph McKim? Explain your answer.

Forging New Frontiers

The Old Stage Coach of the Plains, Frederic Remington,
Amon Carter Museum, Fort Worth, Texas

Mark Twain: The American Bard

His humor captivated readers and created a new style of American writing.

In the late 1800s, readers might have known him as Thomas Jefferson Snodgrass, W. Epaminandos Adrastus Blab, or simply Josh. Today, we know Samuel Langhorne Clemens as Mark Twain, his most famous literary pseudonym. Whichever name he used, Twain pulled off a rare literary feat—he created stories, novels, and essays that were both wildly popular in his own day and models of wit and skill more than a century later. Twain was so influential that, fifty years after his death, Ernest Hemingway said "all American literature begins" with Twain's novel *The Adventures of Huckleberry Finn*.

Life on the River Born in 1835, Samuel Clemens grew up in the small town of Hannibal, Missouri. Hannibal was a river town, a stop on the Mississippi. Steamboat men, religious revivalists, circus performers, minstrel companies, showboat actors, and every other kind of traveler imaginable made appearances in Hannibal. As a boy, Clemens met many of the characters that he would later write about.

After his father's death in 1847, Clemens was forced to leave school and take a job as a printer's apprentice. During the 1850s, he wrote a few stories, some of which were published under the pseudonyms of Snodgrass, Blab, and Josh. Twain also traveled the country from St. Louis to New York to Iowa. When he returned home, he took a boat trip down the Mississippi. He had planned to go to South America to seek his fortune, but during the trip he recalled childhood memories of river life and decided to become a

▼ **Critical Viewing** What do you think it would have been like to captain a Mississippi riverboat like the one shown in this photograph? **[Speculate]**

MISSISSIPPI QUEEN

riverboat pilot. He served as a riverboat captain until 1861, when the Civil War closed the Mississippi River to boat traffic.

Mark Twain Is Born In 1862, Clemens took a job as a reporter on the Virginia City *Territorial Enterprise*. Working on the newspaper, he found his calling as a humorist. It was also the first time he used the name Mark Twain for his byline.

The new name, which is actually a signal yelled out by riverboat pilots, not only connected the writer to his youth, but also freed him to develop a new style. Before becoming "Twain," his work was typical of the low humor of the time, filled with bad puns and intentional misspellings. But in 1865, Twain published a short story entitled "The Notorious Jumping Frog of Calaveras County" (page 569). The story won the author fame and financial success, and it marked the first appearance of his distinctive comic style.

Ordinary American Speech The targets of Twain's jokes were not new. He distrusted technology and disliked machines. He railed against political figures, calling them swindlers and con men. What was new was Twain's feel for ordinary American people and their language. He wrote using the American English that people actually spoke. In that unlikely source, he found rich and comic poetry.

Twain's novels, like *Tom Sawyer* (1876) and *Huckleberry Finn* (1884), were unlike any other books the world had ever seen. At a time when most American writers were copying European novelists, Twain wrote about American themes. His heroes were dirt-poor and plain-spoken. In Twain's hands, the moral choices of his characters had as much drama and gravity as those of any tormented member of the nobility in a European novel.

Not everyone appreciated Twain's humor. The author fled Virginia City when a rival journalist, offended by a story, challenged him to a pistol duel. He was chased out of San Francisco by policemen angered by critical articles. Even as his fame grew, some critics dismissed him as little more than a jokester.

Despite the occasional disapproval of his work, the American public adopted Twain as one of their own. He made a fortune from his writings, settling with his wife and family into a Hartford, Connecticut, mansion that was elaborately decorated to look like the inside of a river steamboat. Though he squandered much of his money on bad investments, he remained comfortable throughout his life, garnering huge paychecks as a professional speaker.

The Old Man in a White Suit At the end of the 1800s, the deaths of Twain's wife and daughters left the writer bitter and cynical. Near the end of his life, Twain became so reclusive that a newspaper reported he was dead. Twain immediately wired the editors: "Reports of my death have been greatly exaggerated."

History has not exaggerated Twain's legacy. He was the first, and possibly the greatest, authentically American writer.

▲ **Critical Viewing**
In what ways does this illustration for an early edition of *The Adventures of Tom Sawyer* convey the wit that marks Twain's writing? **[Connect]**

Prepare to Read

The Boys' Ambition *from* Life on the Mississippi ◆
The Notorious Jumping Frog of Calaveras County

Mark Twain
(1835–1910)

Although Mark Twain is widely regarded as one of the greatest American writers, the world-renowned author once indicated that he would have preferred to spend his life as a Mississippi riverboat pilot. The comment was probably not entirely serious, but Twain so loved life on the river that as a young man, he did in fact work as a riverboat pilot for several years. His childhood on the banks of the Mississippi fostered more than a love of riverboats—it also became the basis for many of his most famous works, including *The Adventures of Tom Sawyer* (1876) and *The Adventures of Huckleberry Finn* (1884).

Life on the River Twain, whose given name was Samuel Langhorne Clemens, felt so closely tied to the Mississippi River that he even took his pen name, Mark Twain, from a river man's call meaning "two fathoms deep," indicating that the river is deep enough for a boat to pass safely. He grew up in the Mississippi River town of Hannibal, Missouri. His father died when he was eleven, and he left school to become a printer's apprentice. He worked as a printer in a number of different cities before deciding at age twenty-one to pursue a career as a riverboat pilot.

A Traveling Man When the Civil War closed traffic on the Mississippi, Twain went west to Nevada. There, he supported himself as a journalist and lecturer, developing the entertaining writing style that made him famous. In 1865, Twain published "The Notorious Jumping Frog of Calaveras County," his version of a tall tale he had heard in a mining camp in California while he was working as a gold prospector. The story made him an international celebrity.

Following the publication of *The Innocents Abroad* (1869), a successful book of humorous travel letters, Twain moved to Hartford, Connecticut, where he was to make his home for the rest of his life. There, Twain began using his past experiences as raw material for his books. He drew on his travels in the western mining region for *Roughing It* (1872). He turned to his childhood experiences on the Mississippi for *The Adventures of Tom Sawyer, Life on the Mississippi,* and his masterpiece, *The Adventures of Huckleberry Finn.*

A Restless Soul Twain traveled widely throughout his life, including residential stints in such major American cities as St. Louis, New York, Philadelphia, Cincinnati, and San Francisco. He made extended visits to England, Germany, Switzerland, Italy, and Palestine. His adventures, both at home and abroad, were fuel for a number of books. After living in Europe for several years, he returned home with his family. Following the death of his wife and three of their four children, Twain was unable to reproduce the balance between pessimism and humor that he had captured so brilliantly in *Huckleberry Finn.* In his later works, such as *A Connecticut Yankee in King Arthur's Court* (1889), *Pudd'nhead Wilson* (1894), and *The Man That Corrupted Hadleyburg* (1900), Twain's writing depicted an increasingly pessimistic view of society and human nature. However, he continued to display the same masterful command of language that had already established him as one of America's finest fiction writers.

Preview

Connecting to the Literature

Today's world is being transformed through almost daily advances in technology. During Twain's day, America was also changing quickly as new forms of transportation helped settlers venture across the expanding frontier.

Literary Analysis

Humor

Humor is writing intended to evoke laughter. Humorists use a variety of techniques to make their work amusing. Many western humorists of the 1800s perfected these comic techniques:

- Exaggerating and embellishing incidents to build comedy
- Using a narrator or story teller who takes a serious tone, adding humor by suggesting that the teller of the tale is unaware of its ridiculous qualities

As you read, take note of the details in these selections that make the stories humorous.

Comparing Literary Works

As these two selections demonstrate, Twain could find humor in any subject. However, instead of always writing just to get a laugh, he used humor for a variety of purposes. One of these stories is set in a California gold rush town and the story is deliberately funny. In the other, set on the Mississippi River, humor is secondary to the writer's goal of describing a place and a way of life. As you read, determine whether the ideas each story conveys are serious or not. Then consider the ways in which humor provides a vehicle for those ideas.

Reading Strategy

Understanding Regional Dialect

Much of the humor in Twain's writing comes from his colorful uses of language. Twain was a master at re-creating **regional dialect**—language specific to a particular area of the country. If you read unfamiliar words aloud, you will find that they are regional pronunciations of words you already know. Use a chart like the one shown to translate dialect into modern Standard English.

Vocabulary Development

transient (tran´ zē ənt) *adj.* not permanent (p. 565)

prodigious (prə dij´ əs) *adj.* of great power or size (p. 566)

eminence (em´ ə nəns) *n.* greatness; celebrity (p. 567)

garrulous (gar´ ə ləs) *adj.* talking too much (p. 569)

conjectured (kən jek´ chərd) *v.* guessed (p. 569)

monotonous (mə nät´ ən əs) *adj.* tiresome because unvarying (p. 569)

interminable (in tur´ mi nə bəl) *adj.* seeming to last forever (p. 569)

ornery (ôr´ nər ē) *adj.* having a mean disposition (p. 571)

Regional Dialect

. . . there couldn't be no solit'ry thing mentioned but that feller'd offer to bet on it, and take ary side you please. . . .

Standard English

Not one thing could be mentioned without him offering to bet on it, taking any side.

from Life on the MISSISSIPPI

Mark Twain

Paddle Steamboat Mississippi, Shelburne Museum, Shelburne, Vermont

▲ **Critical Viewing** How does the painting convey the excitement generated by the arrival of a steamboat? **[Analyze]**

Background

Mark Twain was an eyewitness to the nineteenth-century expansion of the western frontier. He was a young man when wagon trains left his home state of Missouri to cross the prairies, and he later saw the transcontinental railroad built. He traveled throughout the growing nation, working first on the Mississippi and then in the West, before settling in Connecticut. The rich variety of people and places he observed is reflected in the setting, characters, and dialogue of his uniquely American literature.

The Boys' Ambition

When I was a boy, there was but one permanent ambition among my comrades in our village[1] on the west bank of the Mississippi River. That was, to be a steamboatman. We had transient ambitions of other sorts, but they were only transient.

When a circus came and went, it left us all burning to become clowns; the first Negro minstrel show that came to our section left us all suffering to try that kind of life; now and then we had a hope that if we lived and were good, God would permit us to be pirates. These ambitions faded out, each in its turn; but the ambition to be a steamboatman always remained.

Once a day a cheap, gaudy packet[2] arrived upward from St. Louis, and another downward from Keokuk.[3] Before these events, the day was glorious with expectancy; after them, the day was a dead and empty thing. Not only the boys, but the whole village, felt this. After all these years I can picture that old time to myself now, just as it was then: the white town drowsing in the sunshine of a summer's morning; the streets empty, or pretty nearly so; one or two clerks sitting in front of the Water Street stores, with their splint-bottomed chairs tilted back against the wall, chins on breasts, hats slouched over their faces, asleep—with shingle shavings enough around to show what broke them down; a sow and a litter of pigs loafing along the sidewalk, doing a good business in watermelon rinds and seeds; two or three lonely little freight piles scattered about the levee;[4] a pile of skids[5] on the slope of the stone-paved wharf, and the fragrant town drunkard asleep in the shadow of them; two or three wood flats[6] at the head of the wharf, but nobody to listen to the peaceful lapping of the wavelets against them; the great Mississippi, the majestic, the magnificent Mississippi, rolling its mile-wide tide along, shining in

---

1. **our village** Hannibal, Missouri.
2. **packet** *n.* boat that travels a regular route, carrying passengers, freight, and mail.
3. **Keokuk** (kē´ ə kuk´) town in southeastern Iowa.
4. **levee** (lev´ ē) *n.* landing place along the bank of a river.
5. **skids** *n.* low, movable wooden platforms.
6. **flats** *n.* small, flat-bottomed boats.

transient (tran´ zē ənt) *adj.* not permanent

✔**Reading Check**

In what way did the boys' ambitions change with each new visitor to their town?

the sun; the dense forest away on the other side; the point above the town, and the point below, bounding the river-glimpse and turning it into a sort of sea, and withal a very still and brilliant and lonely one. Presently a film of dark smoke appears above one of those remote points; instantly a Negro drayman,[7] famous for his quick eye and <u>prodigious</u> voice, lifts up the cry, "S-t-e-a-m-boat a-comin'!" and the scene changes! The town drunkard stirs, the clerks wake up, a furious clatter of drays follows, every house and store pours out a human contribution, and all in a twinkling the dead town is alive and moving.

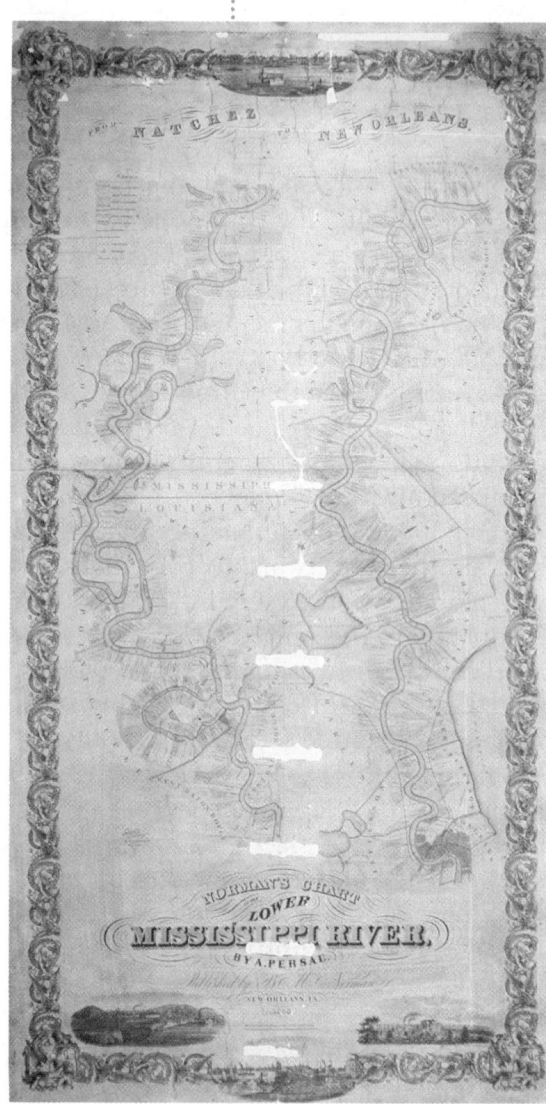

Drays, carts, men, boys, all go hurrying from many quarters to a common center, the wharf. Assembled there, the people fasten their eyes upon the coming boat as upon a wonder they are seeing for the first time. And the boat is rather a handsome sight, too. She is long and sharp and trim and pretty; she has two tall, fancy-topped chimneys, with a gilded device of some kind swung between them; a fanciful pilothouse, all glass and gingerbread, perched on top of the texas deck[8] behind them; the paddleboxes are gorgeous with a picture or with gilded rays above the boat's name; the boiler deck, the hurricane deck, and the texas deck are fenced and ornamented with clean white railings; there is a flag gallantly flying from the jackstaff;[9] the furnace doors are open and the fires glaring bravely; the upper decks are black with passengers; the captain stands by the big bell, calm, imposing, the envy of all; great volumes of the blackest smoke are rolling and tumbling out of the chimneys—a husbanded grandeur created with a bit of pitch pine just before arriving at a town; the crew are grouped on the forecastle;[10] the broad stage is run far out over the port bow, and an envied deckhand stands picturesquely on the end of it with a coil of rope in his hand; the pent steam is screaming through the gauge cocks; the captain lifts his hand, a bell rings, the wheels stop; then they turn back, churning the water to foam, and the steamer is at rest. Then such a scramble as there is to get aboard, and to get ashore, and to take in freight and to discharge freight, all at one and the same time; and such a yelling and cursing as the mates facilitate it all with! Ten minutes later the steamer is under way again, with no flag on the jackstaff and no black smoke issuing from the chimneys. After ten more minutes the town is dead again, and the town drunkard asleep by the skids once more.

prodigious (prə dij´ əs) *adj.* of great power or size

▲ **Critical Viewing** This map shows the location of plantation lands on the banks of the Mississippi. Why might the river have been a desirable location for plantations, as well as for towns? **[Infer]**

---

7. **drayman** (drā´ mən) *n.* driver of a dray, a low cart with detachable sides.
8. **texas deck** deck adjoining the officers' cabins, the largest cabins on the ship.
9. **jackstaff** (jak´ staf) *n.* small staff at the bow of a ship for flying flags.
10. **forecastle** (fōk´ səl) *n.* front part of the upper deck.

My father was a justice of the peace, and I supposed he possessed the power of life and death over all men and could hang anybody that offended him. This was distinction enough for me as a general thing; but the desire to be a steamboatman kept intruding, nevertheless. I first wanted to be a cabin boy, so that I could come out with a white apron on and shake a tablecloth over the side, where all my old comrades could see me; later I thought I would rather be the deckhand who stood on the end of the stage plank with the coil of rope in his hand, because he was particularly conspicuous. But these were only daydreams—they were too heavenly to be contemplated as real possibilities. By and by one of our boys went away. He was not heard of for a long time. At last he turned up as apprentice engineer or striker on a steamboat. This thing shook the bottom out of all my Sunday-school teachings. That boy had been notoriously worldly, and I just the reverse; yet he was exalted to this <u>eminence</u>, and I left in obscurity and misery. There was nothing generous about this fellow in his greatness. He would always manage to have a rusty bolt to scrub while his boat tarried at our town, and he would sit on the inside guard and scrub it, where we could all see him and envy him and loathe him. And whenever his boat was laid up he would come home and swell around the town in his blackest and greasiest clothes, so that nobody could help remembering that he was a steamboatman; and he used all sorts of steamboat technicalities in his talk, as if he were so used to them that he forgot common people could not understand them. He would speak of the labboard[11] side of a horse in an easy, natural way that would make one wish he was dead. And he was always talking about "St. Looey" like an old citizen; he would refer casually to occasions when he "was coming down Fourth Street," or when he was "passing by the Planter's House," or when there was a fire and he took a turn on the brakes of "the old Big Missouri"; and then he would go on and lie about how many towns the size of ours were burned down there that day. Two or three of the boys had long been persons of consideration among us because they had been to St. Louis once and had a vague general knowledge of its wonders, but the day of their glory was over now. They lapsed into a humble silence, and learned to disappear when the ruthless cub engineer approached. This fellow had money, too, and hair oil. Also an ignorant silver watch and a showy brass watch chain. He wore a leather belt and used no suspenders. If ever a youth was cordially admired and hated by his comrades, this one was. No girl could withstand his charms. He cut out every boy in the village. When his boat blew up at last, it diffused a tranquil contentment among us such as we had not known for months. But when he came home the next week, alive, renowned, and appeared in church all battered up and bandaged, a shining hero, stared at and wondered over by everybody, it seemed to us that the partiality of Providence for an undeserving reptile had reached a point where it was open to criticism.

eminence (em′ i nəns) *n.* greatness; celebrity

Reading Strategy
Understanding Regional Dialect What does the apprentice engineer's use of riverboat jargon reveal about him?

 **Reading Check**

What activities and actions of the boy who worked on a steamship inspired envy?

---

11. **labboard** (lab′ ərd) larboard, the left-hand side of a ship.

This creature's career could produce but one result, and it speedily followed. Boy after boy managed to get on the river. The minister's son became an engineer. The doctor's and the postmaster's sons became mud clerks; the wholesale liquor dealer's son became a barkeeper on a boat; four sons of the chief merchant, and two sons of the county judge, became pilots. Pilot was the grandest position of all. The pilot, even in those days of trivial wages, had a princely salary—from a hundred and fifty to two hundred and fifty dollars a month, and no board to pay. Two months of his wages would pay a preacher's salary for a year. Now some of us were left disconsolate. We could not get on the river—at least our parents would not let us.

So by and by I ran away. I said I never would come home again till I was a pilot and could come in glory. But somehow I could not manage it. I went meekly aboard a few of the boats that lay packed together like sardines at the long St. Louis wharf, and very humbly inquired for the pilots, but got only a cold shoulder and short words from mates and clerks. I had to make the best of this sort of treatment for the time being, but I had comforting daydreams of a future when I should be a great and honored pilot, with plenty of money, and could kill some of these mates and clerks and pay for them.

Review and Assess

Thinking About the Selection

1. **Respond:** Would working on a riverboat appeal to you? Explain why or why not.

2. **(a) Recall:** What is the one permanent ambition of the narrator and his boyhood friends? **(b) Connect:** How does this childhood ambition reflect the American spirit that gave rise to the settlement of new frontiers?

3. **(a) Recall:** How do the people of Hannibal respond to the arrival of the steamboat? **(b) Interpret:** What impression does Twain convey of this town by this response?

4. **(a) Recall:** What happens to the young apprentice engineer? **(b) Infer:** How would you describe the attitude of the other boys toward the apprentice engineer?

5. **(a) Hypothesize:** Do you think Twain could have written so well about riverboat life had he not become a pilot himself? Explain. **(b) Apply:** In what ways do you think Twain's love for the Mississippi River contributed to his success as a writer?

6. **Evaluate:** The last paragraph suggests that the narrator was driven by a desire for glory. Is a desire for glory a reasonable motivation in life? Explain.

The Notorious Jumping Frog of Calaveras County

Mark Twain

Mark Twain (Samuel L. Clemens) Riding the Celebrated Jumping Frog—an English caricature, 1872, Frederic Waddy

In compliance with the request of a friend of mine, who wrote me from the East, I called on good-natured, <u>garrulous</u> old Simon Wheeler, and inquired after my friend's friend, Leonidas W. Smiley, as requested to do, and I hereunto append the result. I have a lurking suspicion that *Leonidas W.* Smiley is a myth; that my friend never knew such a personage: and that he only <u>conjectured</u> that if I asked old Wheeler about him, it would remind him of his infamous *Jim* Smiley, and he would go to work and bore me to death with some exasperating reminiscence of him as long and as tedious as it should be useless to me. If that was the design, it succeeded.

I found Simon Wheeler dozing comfortably by the barroom stove of the dilapidated tavern in the decayed mining camp of Angel's, and I noticed that he was fat and baldheaded, and had an expression of winning gentleness and simplicity upon his tranquil countenance. He roused up, and gave me good day. I told him a friend of mine had commissioned me to make some inquiries about a cherished companion of his boyhood named *Leonidas W.* Smiley—*Rev. Leonidas W.* Smiley, a young minister of the Gospel, who he had heard was at one time a resident of Angel's Camp. I added that if Mr. Wheeler could tell me anything about this Rev. Leonidas W. Smiley, I would feel under many obligations to him.

Simon Wheeler backed me into a corner and blockaded me there with his chair, and then sat down and reeled off the <u>monotonous</u> narrative which follows this paragraph. He never smiled, he never frowned, he never changed his voice from the gentle-flowing key to which he tuned his initial sentence, he never betrayed the slightest suspicion of enthusiasm; but all through the <u>interminable</u> narrative there ran a vein of impressive earnestness and sincerity, which showed me plainly that, so far from his imagining that there was anything ridiculous or funny about his story, he regarded it as a really

▲ **Critical Viewing**
Would Twain have been amused or offended by this caricature of himself? Explain. **[Make a Judgment]**

garrulous (gar´ ə ləs) *adj.* talking too much

conjectured (kən jek´ chərd) *v.* guessed

monotonous (mə nät´ ən əs) *adj.* tiresome because unvarying

interminable (in tur´ mi nə bəl) *adj.* seeming to last forever

✓ **Reading Check**
What does the narrator suspect about Leonidas W. Smiley?

important matter, and admired its two heroes as men of transcendent genius in *finesse*. I let him go on in his own way, and never interrupted him once.

"Rev. Leonidas W. H'm, Reverend Le—well, there was a feller here once by the name of *Jim* Smiley, in the winter of '49—or maybe it was the spring of '50—I don't recollect exactly, somehow, though what makes me think it was one or the other is because I remember the big flume[1] warn't finished when he first come to the camp; but anyway, he was the curiousest man about always betting on anything that turned up you ever see, if he could get anybody to bet on the other side; and if he couldn't he'd change sides. Any way that suited the other man would suit *him*—any way just so's he got a bet, *he* was satisfied. But still he was lucky, uncommon lucky; he most always come out winner. He was always ready and laying for a chance; there couldn't be no solit'ry thing mentioned but that feller'd offer to bet on it, and take ary side you please, as I was just telling you. If there was a horse race, you'd find him flush or you'd find him busted at the end of it; if there was a dogfight, he'd bet on it; if there was a cat fight, he'd bet on it; if there was a chicken fight, he'd bet on it; why, if there was two birds setting on a fence, he would bet you which one would fly first; or if there was a camp meeting,[2] he would be there reg'lar to bet on Parson Walker, which he judged to be the best exhorter about here and so he was too, and a good man. If he even see a straddle bug[3] start to go anywheres, he would bet you how long it would take him to get to—to wherever he was going to, and if you took him up, he would foller that straddle bug to Mexico but what he would find out where he was bound for and how long he was on the road. Lots of the boys here has seen that Smiley, and can tell you about him. Why, it never made no difference to *him*—he'd bet on *any* thing—the dangdest feller. Parson Walker's wife laid very sick once, for a good while, and it seemed as if they warn't going to save her; but one morning he come in, and Smiley up and asked him how she was, and he said she was considable better—thank the Lord for his inf'nite mercy—and coming on so smart that with the blessing of Prov'dence she'd get well yet; and Smiley, before he thought, says, 'Well, I'll resk two-and-a-half she don't anyway.'

Thish-yer Smiley had a mare—the boys called her the fifteen-minute nag, but that was only in fun, you know, because of course she was faster than that—and he used to win money on that horse, for all she was so slow and always had the asthma, or the distemper, or the consumption, or something of that kind. They used to give her two or three hundred yards start, and then pass her under way; but always at the fag end[4] of the race she'd get excited and desperate like,

Reading Stategy
Understanding Regional Dialect What examples of dialect do you notice as Wheeler's tale begins?

Literary Analysis
Humor What is humorous about this description of the mare?

---

1. **flume** (floom) *n.* artificial channel for carrying water to provide power and transport objects.
2. **camp meeting** religious gathering at the mining camp.
3. **straddle bug** insect with long legs.
4. **fag end** last part.

and come cavorting and straddling up, and scattering her legs around limber, sometimes in the air, and sometimes out to one side among the fences, and kicking up m-o-r-e dust and raising m-o-r-e racket with her coughing and sneezing and blowing her nose—and *always* fetch up at the stand just about a neck ahead, as near as you could cipher it down.

And he had a little small bull-pup, that to look at him you'd think he warn't worth a cent but to set around and look <u>ornery</u> and lay for a chance to steal something. But as soon as money was up on him he was a different dog; his under-jaw'd begin to stick out like the fo' castle[5] of a steamboat, and his teeth would uncover and shine like the furnaces. And a dog might tackle him and bullyrag him, and bite him, and throw him over his shoulder two or three times, and Andrew Jackson—which was the name of the pup—Andrew Jackson would never let on but what *he* was satisfied, and hadn't expected nothing else—and the bets being doubled and doubled on the other side all the time, till the money was all up; and then all of a sudden he would grab that other dog jest by the j'int of his hind leg and freeze to it—not chaw, you understand, but only just grip and hang on till they threwed up the sponge, if it was a year. Smiley always come out winner on that pup, till

---

5. **fo'castle** (fōkʹ səl) *n.* forecastle; the forward part of the upper deck.

▲ **Critical Viewing**
Which moment of the story is depicted in this illustration? **[Connect]**

Reading Strategy
Understanding Regional Dialect How would you rephrase the sentence beginning "And he had . . ." in Standard English?

ornery (ôrʹ nər ē) *adj.* having a mean disposition

☑ **Reading Check**

What was most unusual about Smiley and his betting habits?

he harnessed a dog once that didn't have no hind legs, because they'd been sawed off in a circular saw, and when the thing had gone along far enough, and the money was all up, and he come to make a snatch for his pet holt,[6] he see in a minute how he'd been imposed on, and how the other dog had him in the door, so to speak, and he 'peared surprised, and then he looked sorter discouraged-like, and didn't try no more to win the fight, and so he got shucked out bad. He give Smiley a look, as much as to say his heart was broke, and it was his fault, for putting up a dog that hadn't no hind legs for him to take holt of, which was his main dependence in a fight, and then he limped off a piece and laid down and died. It was a good pup, was that Andrew Jackson, and would have made a name for hisself if he'd lived, for the stuff was in him and he had genius—I know it, because he hadn't no opportunities to speak of, and it don't stand to reason that a dog could make such a fight as he could under them circumstances if he hadn't no talent. It always makes me feel sorry when I think of that last fight of his'n, and the way it turned out.

Well, thish-yer Smiley had rat terriers,[7] and chicken cocks,[8] and tomcats and all them kind of things, till you couldn't rest, and you couldn't fetch nothing for him to bet on but he'd match you. He ketched a frog one day, and took him home, and said he cal'lated to educate him; and so he never done nothing for three months but set in his back yard and learn that frog to jump. And you bet you he *did* learn him, too. He'd give him a little punch behind, and the next minute you'd see that frog whirling in the air like a doughnut—see him turn one summerset, or maybe a couple, if he got a good start, and come down flatfooted and all right, like a cat. He got him up so in the matter of ketching flies, and kep' him in practice so constant, that he'd nail a fly every time as fur as he could see him. Smiley said all a frog wanted was education, and he could do 'most anything—and I believe him. Why, I've seen him set Dan'l Webster down here on this floor—Dan'l Webster was the name of the frog—and sing out, "Flies, Dan'l, flies!" and quicker'n you could wink he'd spring straight up and snake a fly off'n the counter there, and flop down on the floor ag'in as solid as a gob of mud, and fall to scratching the side of his head with his hind foot as indifferent as if he hadn't no idea he'd been doin' any more'n any frog might do. You never see a frog so modest and straightfor'ard as he was, for all he was so gifted. And when it come to fair and square jumping on a dead level, he could get over more ground at one straddle than any animal of his breed you ever see. Jumping on a dead level was his strong suit, you understand; and when it come to that, Smiley would ante up money on him as long as he had a red.[9] Smiley was monstrous proud of his frog, and well he

Literary Analysis
Humor What embellishments in this passage make the description humorous?

---

6. **holt** hold.
7. **rat terriers** dogs skilled in catching rats.
8. **chicken cocks** roosters trained to fight.
9. **a red** red cent; colloquial expression for "any money at all."

might be, for fellers that had traveled and been everywheres all said he laid over any frog that ever *they* see.

Well, Smiley kep' the beast in a little lattice box, and he used to fetch him downtown sometimes and lay for a bet. One day a feller—a stranger in the camp, he was—come acrost him with his box, and says:

'What might it be that you've got in the box?'

And Smiley says, sorter indifferent-like, 'It might be a parrot, or it might be a canary, maybe, but it ain't—it's only just a frog.'

And the feller took it, and looked at it careful, and turned it round this way and that, and says, 'H'm—so 'tis. Well, what's *he* good for?'

'Well,' Smiley says, easy and careless, 'he's good enough for *one* thing, I should judge—he can outjump any frog in Calaveras county.'

The feller took the box again, and took another long, particular look, and give it back to Smiley, and says, very deliberate, 'Well,' he says, 'I don't see no p'ints about that frog that's any better'n any other frog.'

'Maybe you don't,' Smiley says. 'Maybe you understand frogs and maybe you don't understand 'em; maybe you've had experience, and maybe you ain't only a amature, as it were. Anyways, I've got *my* opinion, and I'll resk forty dollars that he can outjump any frog in Calaveras county.'

And the feller studied a minute, and then says, kinder sad like, 'Well, I'm only a stranger here, and I ain't got no frog; but if I had a frog, I'd bet you.'

And then Smiley says, 'That's all right—that's all right—if you'll hold my box a minute, I'll go and get you a frog.' And so the feller took the box, and put up his forty dollars along with Smiley's, and set down to wait.

So he set there a good while thinking and thinking to hisself, and then he got the frog out and prized his mouth open and took a teaspoon and filled him full of quailshot[10]—filled him pretty near up to his chin—and set him on the floor. Smiley he went to the swamp and slopped around in the mud for a long time, and finally he ketched a frog, and fetched him in, and give him to this feller, and says:

'Now, if you're ready, set him alongside of Dan'l, with his forepaws just even with Dan'l's, and I'll give the word.' Then he says, 'One— two—three—*git*!' and him and the feller touched up the frogs from behind, and the new frog hopped off lively, but Dan'l give a heave, and hysted up his shoulders—so—like a Frenchman, but it warn't no use—he couldn't budge; he was planted as solid as a church, and he couldn't no more stir than if he was anchored out. Smiley was a good deal surprised, and he was disgusted too, but he didn't have no idea what the matter was, of course.

The feller took the money and started away; and when he was going out at the door, he sorter jerked his thumb over his shoulder— so—at Dan'l, and says again, very deliberate, 'Well,' he says, 'I don't see no p'ints about that frog that's any better'n any other frog.'

---

10. **quailshot** small lead pellets used for shooting quail.

Literary Analysis
Humor How does the use of dialect add to the humor of this passage?

✔**Reading Check**

What bet does Smiley make concerning Dan'l Webster?

Smiley he stood scratching his head and looking down at Dan'l a long time, and at last he says, 'I do wonder what in the nation that frog throw'd off for—I wonder if there ain't something the matter with him—he 'pears to look mighty baggy, somehow.' And he ketched Dan'l by the nap of the neck, and hefted him, and says, 'Why blame my cats if he don't weigh five pound!' and turned him upside down and he belched out a double handful of shot. And then he see how it was, and he was the maddest man—he set the frog down and took out after that feller, but he never ketched him. And—"

Here Simon Wheeler heard his name called from the front yard, and got up to see what was wanted. And turning to me as he moved away, he said: "Just set where you are, stranger, and rest easy—I ain't going to be gone a second."

But, by your leave, I did not think that a continuation of the history of the enterprising vagabond *Jim* Smiley would be likely to afford me much information concerning the Rev. *Leonidas W.* Smiley, and so I started away.

At the door I met the sociable Wheeler returning, and he button-holed me and recommenced:

"Well, thish-yer Smiley had a yaller one-eyed cow that didn't have no tail, only just a short stump like a bannanner, and—"

However, lacking both time and inclination, I did not wait to hear about the afflicted cow, but took my leave.

Review and Assess

Thinking About the Selection

1. **Respond:** If Mark Twain were a stand-up comic today, would you want to see him perform? Explain why or why not.

2. **(a) Recall:** What prompts Simon Wheeler to tell the story of Jim Smiley? **(b) Infer:** Why had the narrator's friend suggested that he ask Wheeler about Leonidas Smiley?

3. **(a) Recall:** What was Jim Smiley's response to any event? **(b) Infer:** Based on this behavior, what can you infer about his character?

4. **(a) Recall:** Why was Smiley so proud of his frog? **(b) Draw Conclusions:** Why is the frog important to Smiley?

5. **(a) Evaluate:** Does this story convey the character of Simon Wheeler as effectively as it does the character of Jim Smiley, the subject of the tale? **(b) Hypothesize:** Why might Twain have chosen to develop the story this way?

6. **Apply:** Telling tall tales like this one was a common form of entertainment on the western frontier. What does such a tale suggest about the characters of the developing West?

Review and Assess

Literary Analysis

Humor

1. In "The Boys' Ambition," what does Twain's use of the word "heavenly" to describe ordinary steamboat activities, such as shaking out a tablecloth or holding a rope, add to the **humor** of his narrative?

2. Find two examples of exaggeration in "The Notorious Jumping Frog of Calaveras County," and explain why each is amusing.

3. (a) How does the use of **dialect** in "The Notorious Jumping Frog" add to the story's humor? (b) Why would the story be less effective if Wheeler spoke in Standard English?

Comparing Literary Works

4. (a) What is Twain's main purpose in "The Boys' Ambition"? (b) In what ways does humor help him achieve this purpose?

5. (a) What is Twain's main purpose in telling the story of the notorious jumping frog? (b) How does humor help him achieve this purpose?

6. In which selection does Twain seem to view the characters with more respect? Explain your choice.

Reading Strategy

Understanding Regional Dialect

7. Interpret the following passage in your own words:

> . . . he 'peared surprised, and then he looked sorter discouraged-like, and didn't try no more to win the fight, and so he got shucked out bad.

8. Interpret the given examples of dialect in Standard English by completing a chart like the one shown.

Regional Dialect	St. Looey	chaw	yaller	bannanner	thish-yer
Standard English					

Extend Understanding

9. **Career Connection:** Why do you think young people dream of romantic or adventurous careers, like Twain's riverboat pilot or its modern equivalent, the astronaut?

Quick Review

Humor is writing meant to evoke laughter.

To **understand regional dialect,** sound out words so that you may recognize their Standard English counterparts.

 Take It to the Net
www.phschool.com
Take the interactive self-test online to check your understanding of these selections.

Integrate Language Skills

Vocabulary Development Lesson

Word Analysis: Greek Prefix *mono-*

The Greek prefix *mono-* means "alone," "one," or "single." A monotonous storyteller uses a single tone, without varying voice quality or pace.

Use your understanding of the prefix *mono-* and the definition of the roots given below to tell the meaning of the new word formed by adding the prefix *mono-*.

1. *theism* = belief in god   3. *lith* = stone
2. *logue* = speaking   4. *chrome* = color

Spelling Strategy

The vowels *a*, *o*, and *u* after the letter *g* indicate the "hard" sound of *g*, as in *garrulous*, *gob*, and *guide*. The vowels *i* and *e* after *g* often indicate the "soft" *g* sound, as in *prodigious* and *generous*. Identify whether the *g* sound in each of these words is hard or soft:

1. vagabond   2. managed   3. obligation

Concept Development: Antonyms

Antonyms are words with opposite meanings. Review the words in the vocabulary list on page 563. Then, select the letter of the word in the right column that is the best antonym for each vocabulary word in the left column.

1. transient   a. varied
2. prodigious   b. meager
3. eminence   c. quiet
4. garrulous   d. permanent
5. conjectured   e. kind
6. monotonous   f. verified
7. interminable   g. obscurity
8. ornery   h. brief

Grammar and Style Lesson

Double Negatives

Double negatives are created by using two negative words in a sentence where only one is needed. In effect, two negatives cancel each other out, thereby changing the intended meaning of a sentence. Double negatives are not accepted in Standard English, but they do appear in some regional dialects. Here, Simon Wheeler speaks with a double negative:

Examples: "... he had*n't no* opportunities to speak of ..."

"there could*n't* be *no* solit'ry thing mentioned but that feller'd offer to bet on it ..."

Practice Rewrite the following sentences from the story, revising them to eliminate double negatives.

1. Why, it never made no difference to him. ...
2. ... you couldn't fetch nothing for him to bet on but he'd match you.
3. ... maybe you've had experience and maybe you ain't only a amature.
4. ... it warn't no use—he couldn't budge.
5. ... a yaller one-eyed cow that didn't have no tail ...

Looking at Style Explain how Simon Wheeler's frequent use of double negatives fits his character and contributes to the story's humor.

W͞G Prentice Hall Writing and Grammar Connection: Chapter 25, Section 1

Writing Lesson

Analytic Essay

Mark Twain wrote, "The humorous story may be spun out to great length, and may wander around as much as it pleases, and arrive nowhere in particular . . . [It] is told gravely; the teller does his best to conceal the fact that he even dimly suspects there is anything funny about it." Write an essay discussing Twain's use of these techniques in "Jumping Frog."

Prewriting   Select several humorous passages to assess according to the main ideas in Twain's comment. Create a chart like the one shown to organize your thoughts.

Model: Organizing to Show Comparison

spins out at length	arrives nowhere	is told gravely	conceals humor

Drafting   Organize your essay point by point, connecting Twain's comment to passages from the story. Make sure you clearly explain the connection in each case.

Revising   Review your essay to find places where you could elaborate by providing examples, details, or quotations to support your ideas. Return to your notes or to the story to find needed support.

W̶G Prentice Hall Writing and Grammar Connection: Chapter 14, Section 3

Extension Activities

Listening and Speaking In "The Boys' Ambition," Twain wrote about one of his career dreams. Prepare a list of questions about a career that interests you. Then, conduct an **interview** with someone in that field. Be sure to include the following questions:

- Why did you choose this career?
- How did you prepare for it?
- What are its responsibilities and rewards?
- What advice would you give about this career?

Share your findings with the class.

Research and Technology With a group, create a **multimedia report** on Mississippi riverboats. Draw information from a variety of sources, such as audio and video clips, newspapers, magazines, CD-ROMs, and the Internet to convey the sights and sounds of nineteenth-century riverboat life. **[Group Activity]**

 **Take It to the Net**   www.phschool.com

Go online for an additional research activity using the Internet.

Prepare to Read

The Outcasts of Poker Flat

Bret Harte
(1836–1902)

A literary pioneer, Bret Harte played a key role in creating a vivid, lasting portrait of the Old West. His stories, filled with picturesque, intriguing characters and colorful dialogue, provided much of post-Civil War America with its first glimpse of western life and established the Old West as a popular literary setting. In their locations, plots, characters, and uses of both humor and violence, the roots of the Hollywood western can be traced back to Harte's tales.

Heading West Harte was born and raised in Albany, New York. In 1854, when he was eighteen, he traveled across the country to California, a land undergoing a turbulent period of rapid growth due to the discovery of gold in 1848. During his first few years in California, Harte worked as a schoolteacher, tutor, messenger, clerk, and prospector. While Harte's life seemed to have little direction at the time, his observations of the rugged, often violent, life in the mining camps and the towns and cities of the new frontier provided him with the inspiration for his most successful short stories.

A Career of Ups and Downs After working as a typesetter and writer for two California periodicals and publishing two books of verse, *Outcroppings* (1865) and *The Lost Galleon* (1867), Harte became the editor in 1868 of the *Overland Monthly*, a new literary magazine. At that time, the country's population and geographical area were both expanding at a rapid pace. Yet, there were few ways for people to learn about life in regions other than their own.

The American public was eager to learn about life in the new frontier. Harte's writing addressed this need. When he published his story "The Luck of Roaring Camp," in *Overland Monthly's* second issue, he immediately became famous. Over the next two years, he published "The Outcasts of Poker Flat" and several other stories for the magazine about life on the frontier. His popularity continued to climb.

Following the publication of *The Luck of Roaring Camp and Other Sketches* in 1870, Harte's popularity reached its peak. In 1871, *The Atlantic Monthly*, a distinguished literary magazine, contracted to pay Harte the large sum of $10,000 for any twelve sketches or stories he contributed over the next year. Harte returned to the East to fulfill his contract, but the stories he wrote were flat and disappointing compared with his earlier work. His celebrity waned almost as quickly as it had grown.

A Political Appointment Harte continued to publish stories, short novels, and plays during the next twenty years, but most of his later work was unsuccessful. Some friends helped him land a diplomatic post, however, and from 1878 to 1885 Harte served as a United States consul in Germany and Scotland. He retired to London for the remainder of his life.

Recognition by His Peers Richard O'Conner, a biographer of Harte, summarized Harte's legacy this way:

> "Kipling said he owed 'many things' to the storyteller's art he learned from reading Harte . . . [and] H. L. Mencken believed he was entitled to a 'sort of immortality' . . . and the even tougher critic Ambrose Bierce granted Harte a place 'very close to the head' of all American writers."

Preview

Connecting to the Literature

The "outcasts" in Bret Harte's story are tested by circumstances. Think about a situation in which you, or someone that you know, described an event as, "a real test of character." What qualities did the situation bring out in the people involved?

Literary Analysis

Regionalism

Regionalism is a literary movement in which writers attempt to depict and analyze the distinctive and unique qualities of a geographical area and its people. Stories like "The Outcasts of Poker Flat" paint vivid and engaging portraits of what life was like in the far reaches of the country. As you read, notice how Harte captures the characteristics of the region and its inhabitants.

Connecting Literary Elements

The unique characters in this story are an essential part of the **local color** of a rough mining town in the Sierras. An aspect of regionalism, local color highlights characteristics and details unique to a specific area. Local color captures the physical environment, as well as the mood of a time and a place, and includes the ways in which people talk and how they think. Use a chart like the one shown to record the elements of local color in the story.

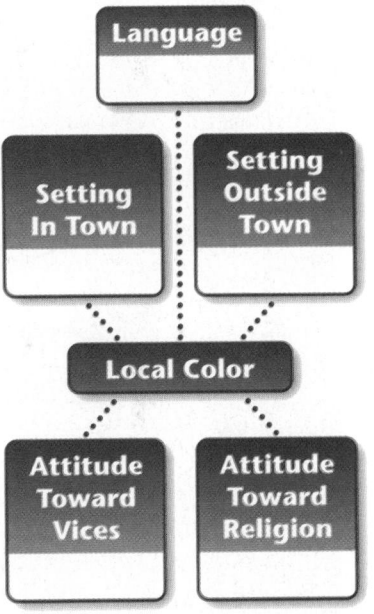

Reading Strategy

Questioning the Text

When you read any literature, **question the text** to improve your involvement and understanding. Ask yourself questions like these:

- What is happening?
- What is the author's purpose?
- What are the motives for the characters' actions?

Look for answers to questions like these as you read.

Vocabulary Development

expatriated (eks pā′ trē āt id) *adj.* deported; driven from one's native land (p. 582)

anathema (ə nath′ ə mə) *n.* curse (p. 582)

bellicose (bel ə kōs) *adj.* quarrelsome (p. 583)

recumbent (ri kum′ bənt) *adj.* resting (p. 583)

equanimity (ek′ wə nim ə tē) *n.* composure (p. 583)

vociferation (vō sif ər ā shən) *n.* loud or vehement shouting (p. 587)

vituperative (vī t′ōō′ pər ə tiv) *adj.* spoken abusively (p. 588)

querulous (kwer′ ə ləs) *adj.* inclined to find fault (p. 588)

THE OUTCASTS OF POKER FLAT

BRET HARTE

Edge of Town, Charles Burchfield, The Nelson-Atkins Museum of Art, Kansas City, Missouri

▲ **Critical Viewing** Does the mood of this painting echo the mood of the story's opening paragraphs? Explain. **[Compare]**

Background

Mr. Oakhurst, a gambler and the main character of "The Outcasts of Poker Flat," is a generous, genial man who is seemingly nonchalant in the face of danger. As you read the story, you may find yourself wondering how true-to-life Mr. Oakhurst is. Harte's biographer, Henry Childs Merwin, described a real-life character named Lucky Bill, a gambler who demonstrated traits similar to Mr. Oakhurst's. According to Merwin, Lucky Bill was known for his generosity, and, although he was hanged by a vigilance committee, he was also known to have advised his own son to avoid bad company, keep out of saloons, and lead an industrious and honest life.

As Mr. John Oakhurst, gambler, stepped into the main street of Poker Flat on the morning of the twenty-third of November, 1850, he was conscious of a change in its moral atmosphere since the preceding night. Two or three men, conversing earnestly together, ceased as he approached, and exchanged significant glances. There was a Sabbath lull in the air which, in a settlement unused to Sabbath influences, looked ominous.

Mr. Oakhurst's calm, handsome face betrayed small concern in these indications. Whether he was conscious of any predisposing cause was another question. "I reckon they're after somebody," he reflected; "likely it's me." He returned to his pocket the handkerchief with which he had been whipping away the red dust of Poker Flat from his neat boots, and quietly discharged his mind of any further conjecture.

In point of fact, Poker Flat was "after somebody." It had lately suffered the loss of several thousand dollars, two valuable horses, and a prominent citizen. It was experiencing a spasm of virtuous reaction, quite as lawless and ungovernable as any of the acts that had provoked it. A secret committee had determined to rid the town of all improper persons. This was done permanently in regard of two men who were then hanging from the boughs of a sycamore in the gulch, and temporarily in the banishment of certain other objectionable characters. I regret to say that some of these were ladies. It is but due to the sex, however, to state that their impropriety was professional, and it was only in such easily established standards of evil that Poker Flat ventured to sit in judgment.

Mr. Oakhurst was right in supposing that he was included in this category. A few of the committee had urged hanging him as a possible example, and a sure method of reimbursing themselves from his pockets of the sums he had won from them. "It's agin justice," said Jim Wheeler, "to let this yer young man from Roaring Camp—an entire stranger—carry away our money." But a crude sentiment of equity residing in the breasts of those who had been fortunate enough to win from Mr. Oakhurst overruled this narrower local prejudice.

Mr. Oakhurst received his sentence with philosophic calmness, none the less coolly that he was aware of the hesitation of his judges. He was

Literary Analysis
Regionalism What does this passage reveal about some of the inhabitants of Poker Flat?

**Reading Check**

Why are the residents of Poker Flat "after somebody"?

too much of a gambler not to accept Fate. With him life was at best an uncertain game, and he recognized the usual percentage in favor of the dealer.

A body of armed men accompanied the deported wickedness of Poker Flat to the outskirts of the settlement. Besides Mr. Oakhurst, who was known to be a coolly desperate man, and for whose intimidation the armed escort was intended, the <u>expatriated</u> party consisted of a young woman familiarly known as the "Duchess"; another, who had won the title of "Mother Shipton";[1] and "Uncle Billy," a suspected sluice robber[2] and confirmed drunkard. The cavalcade provoked no comments from the spectators, nor was any word uttered by the escort. Only, when the gulch which marked the uttermost limit of Poker Flat was reached, the leader spoke briefly and to the point. The exiles were forbidden to return at the peril of their lives.

As the escort disappeared, their pent-up feelings found vent in a few hysterical tears from the Duchess, some bad language from Mother Shipton, and a Parthian volley of expletives[3] from Uncle Billy. The philosophic Oakhurst alone remained silent. He listened calmly to Mother Shipton's desire to cut somebody's heart out, to the repeated statements of the Duchess that she would die in the road, and to the alarming oaths that seemed to be bumped out of Uncle Billy as he rode forward. With the easy good humor characteristic of his class, he insisted upon exchanging his own riding horse, "Five Spot," for the sorry mule which the Duchess rode. But even this act did not draw the party into any closer sympathy. The young woman readjusted her somewhat draggled plumes with a feeble, faded coquetry; Mother Shipton eyed the possessor of "Five Spot" with malevolence, and Uncle Billy included the whole party in one sweeping <u>anathema</u>.

The road to Sandy Bar—a camp that, not having as yet experienced the regenerating influences of Poker Flat, consequently seemed to offer some invitation to the emigrants—lay over a steep mountain range. It was distant a day's severe travel. In that advanced season, the party soon passed out of the moist, temperate regions of the foothills into the dry, cold, bracing air of the Sierras.♦ The trail was narrow and difficult. At noon the Duchess, rolling out of her saddle upon the ground, declared her intention of going no farther, and the party halted.

---

1. **"Mother Shipton"** English woman who lived in the sixteenth century and was suspected of being a witch.
2. **sluice robber** person who steals gold from sluices—long troughs used for sifting gold.
3. **Parthian . . . expletives** hostile remarks made while leaving. The Parthians were an ancient society whose cavalrymen usually shot at the enemy while retreating or pretending to retreat.

The spot was singularly wild and impressive. A wooded amphitheater, surrounded on three sides by precipitous cliffs of naked granite, sloped gently toward the crest of another precipice that overlooked the valley. It was, undoubtedly, the most suitable spot for a camp, had camping been advisable. But Mr. Oakhurst knew that scarcely half the journey to Sandy Bar was accomplished, and the party were not equipped or provisioned for delay. This fact he pointed out to his companions curtly, with a philosophic commentary on the folly of "throwing up their hand before the game was played out." But they were furnished with liquor, which in this emergency stood them in place of food, fuel, rest, and prescience. In spite of his remonstrances, it was not long before they were more or less under its influence. Uncle Billy passed rapidly from a bellicose state into one of stupor, the Duchess became maudlin, and Mother Shipton snored. Mr. Oakhurst alone remained erect, leaning against a rock calmly surveying them.

Mr. Oakhurst did not drink. It interfered with a profession which required coolness, impassiveness, and presence of mind, and, in his own language, he "couldn't afford it." As he gazed at his recumbent fellow exiles, the loneliness begotten of his pariah trade, his habits of life, his very vices, for the first time seriously oppressed him. He bestirred himself in dusting his black clothes, washing his hands and face, and other acts characteristic of his studiously neat habits, and for a moment forgot his annoyance. The thought of deserting his weaker and more pitiable companions never perhaps occurred to him. Yet he could not help feeling the want of that excitement which singularly enough, was most conducive to that calm equanimity for which he was notorious. He looked at the gloomy walls that rose a thousand feet sheer above the circling pines around him; at the sky, ominously clouded; at the valley below, already deepening into shadow. And, doing so, suddenly he heard his own name called.

A horseman slowly ascended the trail. In the fresh, open face of the newcomer Mr. Oakhurst recognized Tom Simson, otherwise known as the "Innocent" of Sandy Bar. He had met him some months before over a "little game," and had, with perfect equanimity, won the entire fortune—amounting to some forty dollars—of that guileless youth. After the game was finished, Mr. Oakhurst drew the youthful speculator behind the door and thus addressed him: "Tommy, you're a good little man, but you can't gamble worth a cent. Don't try it over again." He then handed him his money back, pushed him gently from the room, and so made a devoted slave of Tom Simson.

There was a remembrance of this in his boyish and enthusiastic greeting of Mr. Oakhurst. He had started, he said, to go to Poker Flat to seek his fortune. "Alone?" No, not exactly alone; in fact (a giggle), he had run away with Piney Woods. Didn't Mr. Oakhurst remember Piney? She that used to wait on the table at the Temperance House? They had been engaged a long time, but old Jake Woods had objected, and so they had run away, and were going to Poker Flat to be married, and here they were. And they were tired out, and how lucky it

bellicose (bel´ ə kōs) *adj.* quarrelsome

recumbent (ri kum´ bənt) *adj.* resting

equanimity (ek´ wə nim ə tē) *n.* composure

 **Reading Check**

What occurred between Oakhurst and Simson the last time they met?

was they had found a place to camp and company. All this the Innocent delivered rapidly, while Piney, a stout, comely damsel of fifteen, emerged from behind the pine tree, where she had been blushing unseen, and rode to the side of her lover.

Mr. Oakhurst seldom troubled himself with sentiment, still less with propriety; but he had a vague idea that the situation was not fortunate. He retained, however, his presence of mind sufficiently to kick Uncle Billy, who was about to say something, and Uncle Billy was sober enough to recognize in Mr. Oakhurst's kick a superior power that would not bear trifling. He then endeavored to dissuade Tom Simson from delaying further, but in vain. He even pointed out the fact that there was no provision, nor means of making a camp. But, unluckily, the Innocent met this objection by assuring the party that he was provided with an extra mule loaded with provisions and by the discovery of a rude attempt at a log house near the trail. "Piney can stay with Mrs. Oakhurst," said the Innocent, pointing to the Duchess, "and I can shift for myself."

Nothing but Mr. Oakhurst's admonishing foot saved Uncle Billy from bursting into a roar of laughter. As it was, he felt compelled to retire up the canyon until he could recover his gravity. There he confided the joke to the tall pine trees, with many slaps of his leg, contortions of his face, and the usual profanity. But when he returned to the party, he found them seated by a fire—for the air had grown strangely chill and the sky overcast—in apparently amicable conversation. Piney was actually talking in an impulsive, girlish fashion to the Duchess, who was listening with an interest and animation she had not shown for many days. The Innocent was holding forth, apparently with equal effect, to Mr. Oakhurst and Mother Shipton, who was actually relaxing into amiability. "Is this yer a d——d picnic?" said Uncle Billy with inward scorn as he surveyed the sylvan[4] group, the glancing firelight, and the tethered animals in the foreground. Suddenly an idea mingled with the alcoholic fumes that disturbed his brain. It was apparently of a jocular nature, for he felt impelled to slap his leg again and cram his fist into his mouth.

As the shadows crept slowly up the mountain, a slight breeze rocked the tops of the pine trees, and moaned through their long and gloomy aisles. The ruined cabin, patched and covered with pine boughs, was set apart for the ladies. As the lovers parted, they unaffectedly exchanged a kiss, so honest and sincere that it might have been heard above the swaying pines. The frail Duchess and the malevolent Mother Shipton were probably too stunned to remark upon this last evidence of simplicity, and so turned without a word to the hut. The fire was replenished, the men lay down before the door, and in a few minutes were asleep.

---

4. **sylvan** (sil´ vən) *adj.* characteristic of the forest.

The American Experience

America's Love for the Western

The American West was settled from the middle to late 1800s. As settlers moved west on the Santa Fe and Oregon trails, they developed thriving businesses in livestock. Cow towns grew up around railroad stations, and immense cattle drives moved across the plains. This period in American life provided the material for the American western—a literary and film genre that has been a staple of popular culture ever since.

Both legendary and real-life characters, such as Jesse James, Wild Bill Hickok, Kit Carson, and Buffalo Bill Cody, were featured in stagecoach dramas and books. Soon, filmmakers produced minute-long "Cowboys and Indians" flicks. By 1939, the film industry was booming and Hollywood churned out westerns. The biggest box office returns went to villains such as Jesse James and Billy the Kid—outlaws whose brawling and gun fighting, often aboard burning or runaway trains, provided hours of diversion for American filmgoers.

Literary Analysis

Regionalism and Local Color In what ways does this description of both the physical environment and the characters reflect qualities unique to the region?

Mr. Oakhurst was a light sleeper. Toward morning he awoke benumbed and cold. As he stirred the dying fire, the wind, which was now blowing strongly, brought to his cheek that which caused the blood to leave it—snow!

He started to his feet with the intention of awakening the sleepers, for there was no time to lose. But turning to where Uncle Billy had been lying, he found him gone. A suspicion leaped to his brain and a curse to his lips. He ran to the spot where the mules had been tethered; they were no longer there. The tracks were already rapidly disappearing in the snow.

The momentary excitement brought Mr. Oakhurst back to the fire with his usual calm. He did not waken the sleepers. The Innocent slumbered peacefully, with a smile on his good-humored, freckled face; the virgin Piney slept beside her frailer sisters as sweetly as though attended by celestial guardians; and Mr. Oakhurst, drawing his blanket over his shoulders, stroked his mustaches and waited for the dawn. It came slowly in a whirling mist of snowflakes that dazzled and confused the eye. What could be seen of the landscape appeared magically changed. He looked over the valley, and summed up the present and future in two words—"snowed in!"

A careful inventory of the provisions, which, fortunately for the party, had been stored within the hut and so escaped the felonious fingers of Uncle Billy, disclosed the fact that with care and prudence they might last ten days longer. "That is," said Mr. Oakhurst, sotto voce[5] to the Innocent, "if you're willing to board us. If you ain't—and perhaps you'd better not—you can wait till Uncle Billy gets back with provisions." For some occult reason, Mr. Oakhurst could not bring himself to disclose Uncle Billy's rascality, and so offered the hypothesis that he had wandered from the camp and had accidentally stampeded the animals. He dropped a warning to the Duchess and Mother Shipton, who of course knew the facts of their associate's defection. "They'll find out the truth about us *all* when they find out anything," he added, significantly, "and there's no good frightening them now."

Tom Simson not only put all his worldly store at the disposal of Mr. Oakhurst, but seemed to enjoy the prospect of their enforced seclusion. "We'll have a good camp for a week, and then the snow'll melt, and we'll all go back together." The cheerful gaiety of the young man, and Mr. Oakhurst's calm, infected the others. The Innocent with the aid of pine boughs extemporized a thatch for the roofless cabin, and the Duchess directed Piney in the rearrangement of the interior with a taste and tact that opened the blue eyes of that provincial maiden to their fullest extent. "I reckon now you're used to fine things at Poker Flat," said Piney. The Duchess turned away sharply to conceal something that reddened her cheek through its professional tint, and Mother Shipton requested Piney not to "chatter." But when Mr. Oakhurst returned from a weary search for the trail, he heard

---

5. **sotto voce** (sät′ ō vō′ chē) in an undertone.

Reading Strategy
Questioning the Text
What question can you ask about Oakhurst's discovery that Uncle Billy is missing?

✔**Reading Check**

What explanation does Oakhurst give for Uncle Billy's disappearance?

the sound of happy laughter echoed from the rocks. He stopped in some alarm, and his thoughts first naturally reverted to the whisky, which he had prudently cached.[6] "And yet it don't somehow sound like whisky," said the gambler. It was not until he caught sight of the blazing fire through the still-blinding storm and the group around it that he settled to the conviction that it was "square fun."

Whether Mr. Oakhurst had cached his cards with the whisky as something debarred the free access of the community, I cannot say.

---

6. **cached** (kasht) *v.* hidden.

▼ **Critical Viewing**
Compare and contrast this photograph of the Sierras with the group's wintry surroundings.
[Compare and Contrast]

It was certain that, in Mother Shipton's words, he "didn't say cards once" during that evening. Haply the time was beguiled by an accordion, produced somewhat ostentatiously by Tom Simson from his pack. Notwithstanding some difficulties attending the manipulation of this instrument, Piney Woods managed to pluck several reluctant melodies from its keys, to an accompaniment by the Innocent on a pair of bone castanets. But the crowning festivity of the evening was reached in a rude camp-meeting hymn, which the lovers, joining hands, sang with great earnestness and <u>vociferation</u>. I fear that a certain defiant tone and Covenanter's[7] swing to its chorus, rather than any devotional quality, caused it speedily to infect the others, who at last joined in the refrain:

> "I'm proud to live in the service of the Lord,
> And I'm bound to die in His army."[8]

The pines rocked, the storm eddied and whirled above the miserable group, and the flames of their altar leaped heavenward as if in token of the vow.

At midnight the storm abated, the rolling clouds parted, and the stars glittered keenly above the sleeping camp. Mr. Oakhurst, whose professional habits had enabled him to live on the smallest possible amount of sleep, in dividing the watch with Tom Simson somehow managed to take upon himself the greater part of that duty. He excused himself to the Innocent by saying that he had "often been a week without sleep." "Doing what?" asked Tom. "Poker!" replied Oakhurst, sententiously; "when a man gets a streak of luck, he don't get tired. The luck gives in first. Luck," continued the gambler, reflectively, "is a mighty queer thing. All you know about it for certain is that it's bound to change. And it's finding out when it's going to change that makes you. We've had a streak of bad luck since we left Poker Flat—you come along, and slap you get into it, too. If you can hold your cards right along you're all right. For," added the gambler, with cheerful irrelevance,

> " 'I'm proud to live in the service of the Lord,
> And I'm bound to die in His army.' "

The third day came, and the sun, looking through the white-curtained valley, saw the outcasts divide their slowly decreasing store of provisions for the morning meal. It was one of the peculiarities of that mountain climate that its rays diffused a kindly warmth over the wintry landscape, as if in regretful commiseration of the past. But it revealed drift on drift of snow piled high around the hut—a hopeless,

---

7. **Covenanter's** (kuv´ ə nan´ tərz) seventeenth-century Scottish Presbyterians who resisted the rule of the Church of England.
8. **"I'm . . . army"** lines from the early American spiritual "Service of the Lord."

Literary Analysis
Regionalism and Local Color What aspects of local color does this description of the evening's music convey?

vociferation (vō sif ər ā´ shən) *n.* loud or vehement shouting

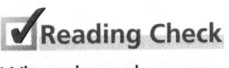

Reading Check
What does the group do in the evening before going to sleep?

uncharted, trackless sea of white lying below the rocky shores to which the castaways still clung. Through the marvelously clear air the smoke of the pastoral village of Poker Flat rose miles away. Mother Shipton saw it, and from a remote pinnacle of her rocky fastness hurled in that direction a final malediction. It was her last vituperative attempt, and perhaps for that reason was invested with a certain degree of sublimity. It did her good, she privately informed the Duchess. "Just you go out there and cuss, and see." She then set herself to the task of amusing "the child," as she and the Duchess were pleased to call Piney. Piney was no chicken, but it was a soothing and original theory of the pair thus to account for the fact that she didn't swear and wasn't improper.

When night crept up again through the gorges, the reedy notes of the accordion rose and fell in fitful spasms and long-drawn gasps by the flickering campfire. But music failed to fill entirely the aching void left by insufficient food, and a new diversion was proposed by Piney— storytelling. Neither Mr. Oakhurst nor his female companions caring to relate their personal experiences, this plan would have failed too but for the Innocent. Some months before he had chanced upon a stray copy of Mr. Pope's[9] ingenious translation of the *Iliad*.[10] He now proposed to narrate the principal incidents of that poem—having thoroughly mastered the argument and fairly forgotten the words—in the current vernacular of Sandy Bar. And so for the rest of that night the Homeric demigods again walked the earth. Trojan bully and wily Greek wrestled in the winds, and the great pines in the canyon seemed to bow to the wrath of the son of Peleus.[11] Mr. Oakhurst listened with quiet satisfaction. Most especially was he interested in the fate of "Ash-heels," as the Innocent persisted in denominating the "swift-footed Achilles."

So with small food and much of Homer and the accordion, a week passed over the heads of the outcasts. The sun again forsook them, and again from leaden skies the snowflakes were sifted over the land. Day by day closer around them drew the snowy circle, until at last they looked from their prison over drifted walls of dazzling white that towered twenty feet above their heads. It became more and more difficult to replenish their fires, even from the fallen trees beside them, now half-hidden in the drifts. And yet no one complained. The lovers turned from the dreary prospect and looked into each other's eyes, and were happy. Mr. Oakhurst settled himself coolly to the losing game before him. The Duchess, more cheerful than she had been, assumed the care of Piney. Only Mother Shipton—once the strongest of the party—seemed to sicken and fade. At midnight on the tenth day she called Oakhurst to her side. "I'm going," she said, in a voice of querulous weakness, "but don't say anything about it. Don't waken the kids. Take the bundle from under my head and open it."

vituperative (vī too͞ō′ pər ə tiv) *adj.* spoken abusively

querulous (kwer′ ə ləs) *adj.* inclined to find fault

---

9. Mr. Pope English poet Alexander Pope (1688–1744).
10. *Iliad* (il′ ē əd) Greek epic poem written by Homer that tells the story of the Trojan War.
11. son of Peleus (pē′ lē əs) Achilles (ə kil′ ēz), the Greek warrior hero in the *Iliad*.

Mr. Oakhurst did so. It contained Mother Shipton's rations for the last week, untouched. "Give 'em to the child," she said, pointing to the sleeping Piney. "You've starved yourself," said the gambler. "That's what they call it," said the woman, querulously, as she lay down again and, turning her face to the wall, passed quietly away.

The accordion and the bones were put aside that day, and Homer was forgotten. When the body of Mother Shipton had been committed to the snow, Mr. Oakhurst took the Innocent aside, and showed him a pair of snowshoes, which he had fashioned from the old pack saddle. "There's one chance in a hundred to save her yet," he said, pointing to Piney; "but it's there," he added, pointing toward Poker Flat. "If you can reach there in two days she's safe." "And you?" asked Tom Simson. "I'll stay here," was the curt reply.

The lovers parted with a long embrace. "You are not going, too?" said the Duchess as she saw Mr. Oakhurst apparently waiting to accompany him. "As far as the canyon," he replied. He turned suddenly, and kissed the Duchess, leaving her pallid face aflame and her trembling limbs rigid with amazement.

Night came, but not Mr. Oakhurst. It brought the storm again and the whirling snow. Then the Duchess, feeding the fire, found that some-one had quietly piled beside the hut enough fuel to last a few days longer. The tears rose to her eyes, but she hid them from Piney.

The women slept but little. In the morning, looking into each other's faces, they read their fate. Neither spoke; but Piney, accepting the position of the stronger, drew near and placed her arm around the Duchess's waist. They kept this attitude for the rest of the day. That night the storm reached its greatest fury, and, rending asunder the protecting pines, invaded the very hut.

Toward morning they found themselves unable to feed the fire, which gradually died away. As the embers slowly blackened, the Duchess crept closer to Piney, and broke the silence of many hours: "Piney, can you pray?" "No, dear," said Piney, simply. The Duchess, without knowing exactly why, felt relieved, and, putting her head upon Piney's shoulder, spoke no more. And so reclining, the younger and purer pillowing the head of her soiled sister upon her virgin breast, they fell asleep.

The wind lulled as if it feared to waken them. Feathery drifts of snow, shaken from the long pine boughs, flew like white-winged birds, and settled about them as they slept. The moon through the rifted clouds looked down upon what had been the camp. But all human stain, all trace of earthly travail, was hidden beneath the spotless mantle mercifully flung from above.

They slept all that day and the next, nor did they waken when voices and footsteps broke the silence of the camp. And when pitying fingers brushed the snow from their wan faces, you could scarcely have told from the equal peace that dwelt upon them which was she that had sinned. Even the law of Poker Flat recognized this, and turned away, leaving them still locked in each other's arms.

Reading Strategy
Questioning the Text
Why did the gambler make only one pair of shoes?

Reading Strategy
Questioning the Text
What question might you ask about Mr. Oakhurst's decision to stay?

✔ Reading Check
What happens to Mother Shipton?

But at the head of the gulch, on one of the largest pine trees, they found the deuce of clubs pinned to the bark with a bowie knife. It bore the following, written in pencil, in a firm hand:

BENEATH THIS TREE
LIES THE BODY
OF
JOHN OAKHURST,
WHO STRUCK A STREAK OF BAD LUCK
ON THE 23D OF NOVEMBER, 1850
AND
HANDED IN HIS CHECKS
ON THE 7TH DECEMBER, 1850.

And pulseless and cold, with a Derringer[12] by his side and a bullet in his heart, though still calm as in life, beneath the snow lay he who was at once the strongest and yet the weakest of the outcasts of Poker Flat.

---

12. Derringer small pistol.

Review and Assess

Thinking About the Selection

1. **Respond:** Which character did you admire the most? Why?

2. **(a) Recall:** At the opening of the story, what has the secret committee of Poker Flat decided? **(b) Infer:** What motivates the committee to take action against Mr. Oakhurst?

3. **(a) Recall:** Who joins the outcasts at their camp?
   (b) Analyze: What effect do the newcomers have on the outcasts?

4. **(a) Recall:** What does Mr. Oakhurst discover when he awakens after his first night at the camp? **(b) Draw Conclusions:** What do you think happened to Uncle Billy?

5. **(a) Recall:** What does Mother Shipton do with her rations?
   (b) Analyze: Why do you think she does this?

6. **(a) Recall:** What explanation does Oakhurst give for his ability to go without sleep? **(b) Infer:** Do you think Oakhurst knew their "luck" was about to run out? Explain.

7. **(a) Recall:** What does the rescue party discover?
   (b) Interpret: What theme or message might their discovery—and this story—convey?

8. **Apply:** Although the characters in the story have little in common, they band together. For what reasons do people tend to draw together in life? Explain.

Review and Assess

Literary Analysis

Regionalism

1. Find three details that establish the **regionalism** of the story.
2. (a) Find a passage in which Harte describes the physical environment. (b) What details help you picture the California landscape?
3. What point about the culture of the West does Harte convey? Explain.

Connecting Literary Elements

4. What inferences about the **local color** of Poker Flat can you make from the following passage?

   > A few of the committee had urged hanging him as a possible example, and a sure method of reimbursing themselves from his pocket of the sums he had won from them.

5. Explain why the story would not be as effective if the setting were changed—for example—to New England.

Reading Strategy

Questioning the Text

6. What is meant by the following passage?

   > There was a Sabbath lull in the air which, in a settlement unused to Sabbath influences, looked ominous.

7. What does Harte mean when he writes that Oakhurst "was at once the strongest and yet the weakest of the outcasts of Poker Flat"?
8. Find three complex passages in the text. Use a chart like the one shown to record your questions and answers.

Passage From Text	Question	Answer

Extend Understanding

9. **Social Studies Connection:** What conclusions can you draw about law in the settlements that emerged during the Gold Rush?

Integrate Language Skills

Vocabulary Development Lesson

Word Analysis: Latin Word Part -bel-

The word *bellicose*, like *belligerent*, uses the Latin word part *-bel-* from the word *bellum*, meaning "war." Both *bellicose* and *belligerent* mean "warlike" or "ready to fight or quarrel."

Choose the letter of the item that best defines the italicized word in each sentence.

   a. quarrelsome   **b.** act of resistance

1. The *rebellion* was the result of opposition to the government.
2. He must control his rage and not be so *bellicose*.

Spelling Strategy

In English words, the letter *q* is almost always followed by the letter *u*, as in *querulous*. Find a synonym that begins with *qu* for each of the following words.

1. argued   2. nauseated   3. mission

Concept Development: Synonyms

Select the letter of the word that is closest in meaning to the first word.

1. expatriated: (a) honored, (b) ignored, (c) expelled
2. anathema: (a) curse, (b) riddle, (c) chant
3. bellicose: (a) strong, (b) quarrelsome, (c) beautiful
4. recumbent: (a) full, (b) reclining, (c) unnecessary
5. equanimity: (a) fairness, (b) precision, (c) serenity
6. vociferation: (a) uncertainty, (b) loudness, (c) cleverness
7. vituperative: (a) scolding, (b) healthful, (c) complex
8. querulous: (a) trustworthy, (b) mysterious, (c) disagreeable

Grammar and Style Lesson

Coordinating Conjunctions in Compound Sentences

Coordinating conjunctions connect words or groups of words. These conjunctions include *and*, *but*, *for*, *nor*, *or*, *so*, and *yet*. Place a comma before a coordinating conjunction that joins the independent clauses in a compound sentence.

> They slept all day, *and* they did not awaken . . .

Practice Use the coordinating conjunction provided to form compound sentences.

1. He wasn't joking. She continued. (*yet*)
2. He raced to the gate. The plane was about to depart. (*for*)
3. Vitamins can be good supplements. They are no substitute for a healthy diet. (*but*)
4. The cat jumped up onto the table. It spilled the milk. (*and*)
5. I am very tired. I will take a nap. (*so*)

Writing Application As a newspaper editor serving mining towns, write a brief editorial about the outcasts and their fate. Use at least two compound sentences.

Writing Lesson

Critical Review

Write a critical review of "The Outcasts of Poker Flat" to appear in a magazine targeted at fans of westerns. Support your opinion of the story while analyzing its plot, main ideas, and effect on the reader.

Prewriting   Select passages describing the characters, conflicts, main ideas, or setting that move you to respond. Jot down your thoughts on each of these passages.

Drafting   Begin with an introduction that summarizes your opinions about the story. Then, analyze each passage you have selected, and explain what it reveals about the story.

Revising   The evaluative words you use to convey praise or judgment about the story should be precise. Review your conclusion to be sure it incorporates language that conveys a strong evaluation.

Model: Revising to Include Evaluative Modifiers

These examples reinforce my belief that this story is

well-crafted and entertaining

~~interesting and good.~~ People who like westerns will find

engaging and

Harte's setting and the characters realistic.

> Specific modifiers such as *well-crafted, entertaining,* and *engaging* convey the writer's attitude toward the work.

 Prentice Hall Writing and Grammar Connection: Chapter 14, Section 4

Extension Activities

Listening and Speaking   As Tom Simson, the only survivor of the stranded group, prepare and deliver a **eulogy**—a speech in honor of someone who has died—for Mr. Oakhurst. Speaking candidly but respectfully, be sure to include these details:

- Colorful, informal "western" language
- Personal experiences you have had with Mr. Oakhurst.

After rehearsing, deliver the eulogy to classmates.

Research and Technology   Use library databases or the Internet to learn about the activities at the center of the gold rush. Then, develop a **prospecting and mining report,** identifying the main steps in each of these processes. Include photographs, flow-charts, or other visuals to communicate your findings.

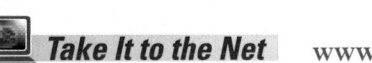 **Take It to the Net**   www.phschool.com

Go online for an additional research activity using the Internet.

Prepare to Read

Heading West ◆ I Will Fight No More Forever

Miriam Davis Colt (1815–c.1900)

Miriam Davis Colt was one of a quarter of a million Americans who traveled across the United States in the mid-1800s to forge a new frontier. These pioneers knew they were making history, and hundreds of them kept diaries to send to relatives back east or to pass down to their children.

The Women's Perspective Usually, the pioneer men, filled with a sense of destiny and excitement, made the decision to sell their homes and move their families west. The women's diaries, however, reveal a different point of view. Many women describe their anguish at leaving home, their struggle to maintain some domestic comforts in harsh conditions, and their fear of the dangers ahead.

A Vision of the Future The women, nevertheless, did share their husbands' belief that they were building a better future for their children. The path to that future might be hard, but it was also filled with moments of sudden beauty, like the "crab-apple trees . . . blooming in sheets of whiteness" that Colt saw by the side of a Kansas road as she and her family traveled to a new life in a "city" established by a group of vegetarians. Her family was one of many that invested money to create this new settlement, where they hoped to live with people "whose tastes and habits" would coincide with their own.

The Extending Frontier In 1856, when Colt and her family set out on their journey, they were heading for Kansas. At the time, Kansas was considered to be in the far "West," the destination for many emigrants from the country's Eastern regions. It was not until later in the 19th century that settlers sought the even further reaches of California and Oregon, journeys which required the treacherous crossings of the plains and mountains, and presented even more spectacular hardships than those suffered by the Colts.

Chief Joseph (1840–1904)

Chief Joseph was born in the Wallowa Valley in what is now Oregon. In 1871, he succeeded his father as leader of the Nez Percé (nez′ pʉrs′ or pər sā′) tribe. At that time, the United States government was trying to force the tribe to relocate to Idaho. The Nez Percé had signed a treaty in 1863 giving the government control of the tribe's land, but Chief Joseph felt that the treaty was illegal and refused to recognize it.

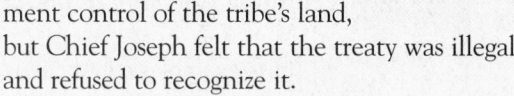

A Reluctant Warrior In 1877, the dispute between the Nez Percé and the United States government erupted into war. Chief Joseph, hoping to join forces with the Sioux, led his people on a long march through Idaho and Montana, during which the outnumbered Nez Percé frequently clashed with federal troops. Under Chief Joseph's astute and able military leadership, they won several battles.

The Bitter End By the fall, however, the Nez Percé were cold, starving, and scattered. On October 5, after defeat in a battle in the Bear Paw Mountains of Montana, Chief Joseph finally surrendered. The Nez Percé were sent to live in a barren Oklahoma territory. There, many of them became ill and died.

The speech in which Chief Joseph finally accepted defeat contains some of the most achingly sad and beautiful words ever spoken. Because of the attention his words received, Chief Joseph became for many a symbol of the Nez Percé and their tragic plight.

Preview

Connecting to the Literature

Both Chief Joseph and Miriam Davis Colt had to say goodbye to the places they called home. Think about how you would feel if you suddenly had to leave everything that you loved, with no possibility of ever returning.

Literary Analysis

Tone

Tone is a quality of language you encounter every day in speech. Two people might say the exact same words, but differences in tone reveal their distinct emotions. In much the same way, a writer's attitude emerges in his or her tone. Consider the optimistic tone in this passage from Colt's diary:

> Full of hope, as we leave the smoking embers of our camp-fire this morning. Expect tonight to arrive at our new home.

The tone of a literary work is established by the writer's choice of descriptions and details. Use a chart like the one shown to interpret the tone of these selections.

> ### Excerpt
> No escort is seen! No salute is heard! We move slowly and drippingly into town . . . .
>
> ### Tone
> Angry, even sarcastic

Comparing Literary Works

These selections put a human face on two different aspects of the western expansion of the United States. Fueled by hope, Colt journeyed in search of a new life. In contrast, Chief Joseph lost the battle to save his people and their ancient way of life. These opposing circumstances are reflected in each piece's **mood**—the feeling created in the reader. As you read, compare the conflicts that motivated each writer. Note the circumstances and emotions each experienced, and identify the mood that each evokes.

Reading Strategy

Responding

The selections you are about to read describe life-changing events, the kind that are sure to evoke responses that will affect your appreciation of the works. As you read, take time to **respond** to the literature. Note the emotions you feel, and the images each work prompts in your imagination.

Vocabulary Development

genial (jēn´ yəl) *adj.* promoting life and growth (p. 597)

pervading (pər vād´ iŋ) *adj.* spreading throughout (p. 597)

terra firma (ter´ ə fur´ mə) (Latin) *n.* firm earth; solid ground (p. 597)

emigrants (em´ i grənts) *n.* people who leave one area to move to another (p. 598)

profusion (prō fyo͞o´ zhən) *n.* abundance; rich supply (p. 598)

depredations (dep´ rə dā´ shənz) *n.* acts of robbing (p. 598)

nonplused (nän´ plüsd´) *adj.* bewildered; perplexed (p. 600)

HEADING WEST

Miriam Davis Colt

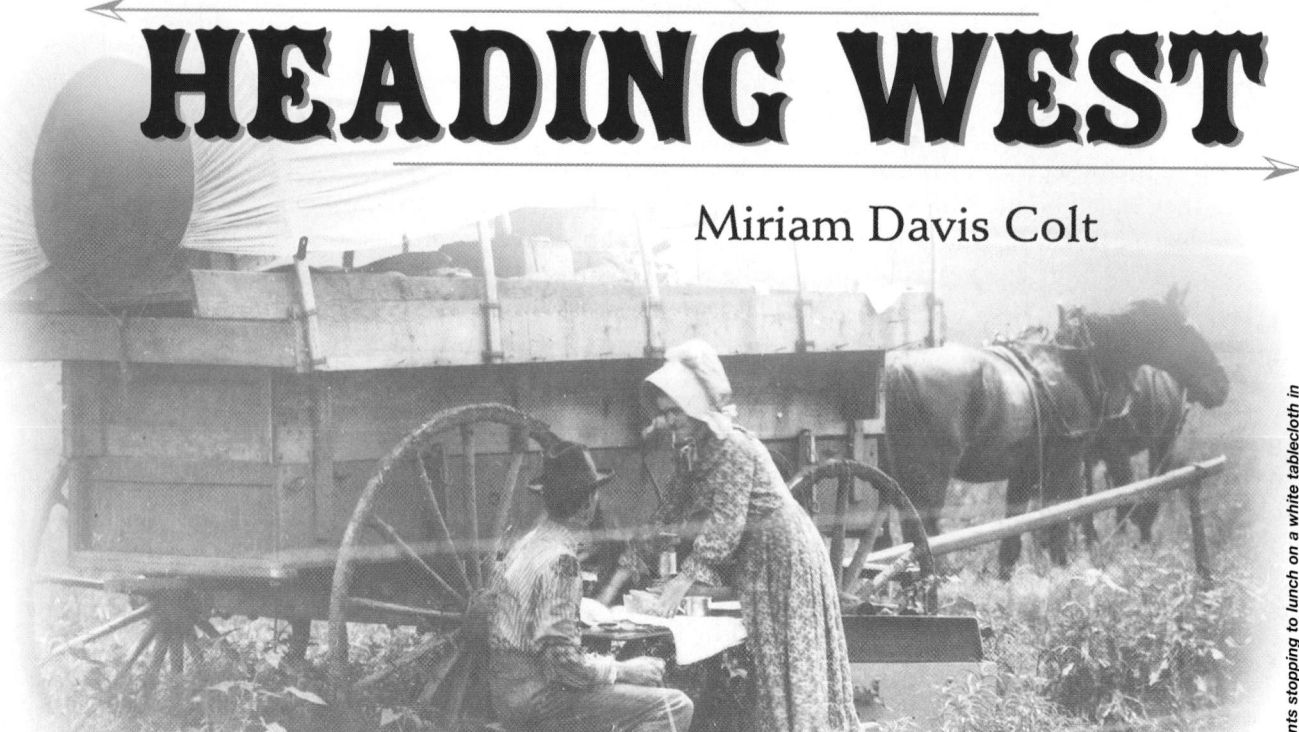

Background

Most of the settlers of the American West, like Miriam Davis Colt and her family, were farmers who sought a better life for themselves and their children. A better life meant fertile land that they could own, cultivate, and pass on to their children. For Native Americans, however, the land was a gift that belonged to no one individual. "The earth is the mother of all people, and all people should have equal rights upon it," Chief Joseph once said. These opposing views were a source of ongoing strife in frontier America.

▲ Critical Viewing
Which details of this photograph of pioneers stopping for lunch seem surprising or out of place? **[Analyze]**

JANUARY 5TH, 1856. We are going to Kansas. The Vegetarian Company that has been forming for many months, has finally organized, formed its constitution, elected its directors, and is making all necessary preparations for the spring settlement . . . . We can have, I think, good faith to believe, that our directors will fulfill on their part; and we, as settlers of a new country, by going in a company will escape the hardships attendant on families going in singly, and at once find ourselves surrounded by improving society in a young and flourishing city. It will be better for ourselves pecuniarily,[1] and better in the future for our children.

Literary Analysis
Tone What is the tone of this description of Colt's experiences on January 5?

---

1. **pecuniarily** (pi kyōō′ nē er′ i lē) *adv.* financially.

My husband has long been a practical vegetarian, and we expect much from living in such a <u>genial</u> clime, where fruit is so quickly grown, and with people whose tastes and habits will coincide with our own.

JANUARY 15TH. We are making every necessary preparation for our journey, and our home in Kansas. My husband has sold his farm, purchased shares in the company, sent his money as directed by H.S. Clubb . . . . I am very busy in repairing all of our clothing, looking over bags of pieces, tearing off and reducing down, bringing everything into as small a compass as possible, so that we shall have no unnecessary baggage.

APRIL 15TH. Have been here in West Stockholm, at my brother's, since Friday last. Have visited Mother very hard, for, in all probability, it is the last visit we shall have until we meet where parting never comes—believe we have said everything we can think of to say.

APRIL 16TH. Antwerp, N.Y. Bade our friends good bye, in Potsdam, this morning, at the early hour of two o'clock.

APRIL 22ND. Have been on the cars[2] again since yesterday morning. Last night was a lovely moonlit night, a night of thought, as we sped almost with lightning speed, along in the moonlight, past the rail fences.
Found ourselves in this miserable hotel before we knew it. Miserable fare—herring boiled with cabbage—miserable, dirty beds, and an odor <u>pervading</u> the house that is not at all agreeable. Mistress gone.

APRIL 23RD. On board steamer "Cataract," bound for Kansas City.

APRIL 24TH. A hot summer day. The men in our company are out in the city, purchasing wagons and farming implements, to take along on the steamer up to Kansas City.

APRIL 28TH. The steamer struck a "snag" last night; gave us a terrible jar; tore off a part of the kitchen; ladies much frightened. Willie is not very well; the water is bad; it affects all strangers.

APRIL 30TH. Here we are, at Kansas City, all safely again on <u>terra firma</u>. Hasten to the hotel—find it very much crowded. Go up, up, up, and upstairs to our lodging rooms.

MAY 1ST. Take a walk out onto the levee—view the city, and see that it takes but a few buildings in this western world to make a city. The houses and shops stand along on the levee, extending back into the hillsides. The narrow street is literally filled with huge merchandise wagons bound for Santa Fe. The power attached to these wagons

---

2. **cars** train cars.

genial (jēn´ yəl) *adj.* promoting life and growth

Reading Strategy
Responding How would you feel if you were allowed to keep only a few items out of all the things you own?

pervading (pər vād´ iŋ) *adj.* spreading throughout

terra firma (ter´ ə fur´ mə) *n.* firm earth; solid ground (Latin)

✔**Reading Check**
Why do the Colts decide to travel to Kansas?

is seven or eight and sometimes nine pair of long-eared mules, or as many pair of oxen, with a Mexican driver who wields a whip long enough to reach the foremost pair, and who does not hesitate to use it with severity, and a noise, too.

Large droves of cattle are driven into town to be sold to <u>emigrants</u>, who like us, are going into the Territory. Our husbands are all out today buying oxen, provisions and cooking utensils for our ox-wagon journey into the Territory.

This is the anniversary of my wedding-day, and as I review the past pleasant years as they have passed, one after another, until they now number eleven, a shadow comes over me, as I try to look away into the future and ask, "What is my destiny?"

Ah! away with all these shadowings. We shall be very busy this year in making our home comfortable, so that no time can be spared for that dreaded disease, "home-sickness," to take hold of us, and we mean to obey physical laws,[3] thereby securing to ourselves strength of body and vigor of mind.

MAY 2ND. A lovely day. Our husbands are loading the ox-wagons. . . . Women and children walk along up the hill out of this "Great City," wait under a tree—what a beautiful country is spread out before us! Will our Kansas scenery equal this . . . ?

One mile from the city, and Dr. Thorn has broke his wagon tongue;[4] it must be sent back to Kansas City to be mended. Fires kindled—women cooking—supper eaten sitting round on logs, stones and wagon tongues. This I am sure is a "pic-nic." We expect "pic-nic" now all the time. We are shaded by the horse-chestnut, sweet walnut, and spreading oak; flowers blooming at our feet, and grasshoppers in <u>profusion</u> hopping in every direction. This is summer time.

MAY 3RD. The women and children, who slept in their wagons last night, got a good drenching from the heavy shower. It was fortunate for mother, sister, myself and children, that lodgings were found for us in a house. My husband said not a rain drop found him; he had the whole wagon to himself, besides all of our Indian blankets. Father, it seems, fell back a little and found a place to camp in a tavern (not a hotel), where he fell in with the scores of Georgians who loaded a steamer and came up the river the same time that we did. He said he had to be very shrewd indeed not to have them find out that he was a "Free States"[5] man. These Bandits have been sent in here, and will commit all sorts of <u>depredations</u> on the Free State settlers, and no doubt commit many a bloody murder.

Have passed Westport, the foothold for Border-Ruffianism. The town looks new, but the hue is dingy. Our drivers used their goads

emigrants (em´ i grənts) *n.* people who leave one area to move to another

Literary Analysis
Tone What is Colt's tone as she looks back on her life?

profusion (prō fyo͞o´ zhən) *n.* abundance; rich supply

depredations (dep´ rə dā´ shənz) *n.* acts of robbing

---

3. **physical laws** community's by-laws that dictated members abstain from alcohol and meat.
4. **wagon tongue** harnessing pole attached to the front axle of a horse-drawn vehicle.
5. **"Free States"** Free Soil movement; a group whose goal was to keep slavery out of the western territories.

to hurry up the oxen's heavy tread, for we felt somewhat afraid, for we learned the Georgians had centered here. Here, too, came in the Santa Fe and Indian trade—so here may be seen the huge Mexican wagon, stubborn mule, swarthy driver with his goad-like whip, and the red man of the prairie on his fleet Indian pony, laden with dried meat, furs, and buffalo robes.

"What! fast in the mud, and with our wagon tongue broke?" "Why yes, to be sure." So a long time is spent before my husband and Dr. House can put our vehicle in moving order again. Meanwhile, we women folks and children must sit quietly in the wagon to keep out of the rain—lunch on soda biscuit, look at the deep, black mud in which our wagon is set, and inhale the sweet odor that comes from the blossoms of the crab-apple trees that are blooming in sheets of whiteness along the roadside. . . .

MAY 6TH. Dined on the prairie, and gathered flowers, while our tired beasts filled themselves with the fresh, green grass. . . . Have driven 18 miles to-day . . . so here we are, all huddled into this little house 12 by 16—cook supper over the fire . . . fill the one bed lengthwise and crosswise; the family of the house take to the trundle-bed,[6] while the floor is covered . . . with men, women and children, rolled in Indian blankets like silk worms in cocoons.

MAY 11TH. "Made" but a few miles yesterday. Forded the Little Osage; the last river, they say, we have to ford . . . our "noble lords" complained of the great weight of the wagons. . . . That our wagon is heavily loaded, have only to make a minute of what we have stowed away in it—eight trunks, one valise, three carpet bags, a box of soda crackers, 200 lbs. flour, 100 lbs. corn meal, a few lbs. of sugar, rice, dried apple, one washtub of little trees, utensils for cooking, and two provision boxes—say nothing of mother, a good fat sister, self, and two children, who ride through the rivers. . . .

At nightfall came to a log-cabin at the edge of the wood, and inquired of the "Lord of the Castle" if some of the women and children could take shelter under his roof for the night; the masculine number and whichever of the women that chose, couching in the wagons and under them. He said we could. His lady, who was away, presently came, with bare feet, and a white sack twisted up and thrown over her shoulder, with a few quarts of corn meal in the end that hung down her back. I said to myself—"Is that what I have got to come to?" She seemed pleased to have company—allowed us the first chance of the broad, Dutch-backed fireplace with its earthy hearth, and without pot hooks or trammels,[7] to make ready our simple evening repast. . . .

---

6. **trundle-bed** low, portable bed that can be stored beneath a larger bed.
7. **trammels** (tram´ əlz) *n.* devices for hanging several pothooks in a fireplace.

The American Experience

Moving West

The search for "greener pastures" has been a constant factor in our nation's history. The phrase "The Great Migration" describes a steady westward shift of the American population. It includes the westward movement of the Puritans from Europe to the New World in the 1630s, of the coastal colonists to inland farms and towns, and of pioneer families headed west over the plains and prairies throughout the nineteenth century. Transience was fundamental to pioneer life, as "movers" continually searched for the next open space. Of course, some pioneers—the "stickers"— had strong urges to put down roots and develop communities. The Great American Migration blends tales of how both the movers and the stickers endured physical, financial, political, and spiritual challenges in hopes of establishing better lives for themselves and for their families.

✔Reading Check

What methods of travel do the Colts use in their journey?

Are now [May 11th] crossing the 20 mile prairie, no roads—Think Mrs. Voorhees will get walking enough crossing this prairie. She is quite a pedestrian, surely, for she has walked every bit of the way in, so far, from Kansas City, almost 100 miles.

Arrive at Elm Creek—no house to lodge in tonight—campfire kindled—supper cooked, and partaken of with a keen relish, sitting in family groups around the "great big" fire. Some will sleep in wagons, others under the canopy of the blue vault of Heaven. The young men have built some shady little bowers of the green boughs; they are looking very cosily under them, wrapped in their white Indian blankets.

We ladies, or rather, "emigrant women," are having a chat around the camp-fire—the bright stars are looking down upon us—we wonder if we shall be neighbors to each other in the great "Octagon City. . . ."

MAY 12TH. Full of hope, as we leave the smoking embers of our camp-fire this morning. Expect tonight to arrive at our new home.

It begins to rain, rain, rain, like a shower; we move slowly on, from high prairie, around the deep ravine—are in sight of the timber that skirts the Neosho river. Have sent three men in advance to announce our coming; are looking for our Secretary, (Henry S. Clubb) with an escort to welcome us into the embryo city. If the booming of cannon is not heard at our approach, shall expect a salute from the firing of Sharp's rifles, certainly.

No escort is seen! no salute is heard! We move slowly and drippingly into town just at nightfall—feeling not a little <u>nonplused</u> on learning that our worthy, or unworthy Secretary was out walking in the rain with his *dear* wife. We leave our wagons and make our way to the large camp-fire. It is surrounded by men and women cooking their suppers—while others are busy close by, grinding their hominy[8] in hand mills.

---

8. **hominy** (häm´ ə nē) *n.* dry corn, usually ground and boiled for food.

Literary Analysis
Tone and Mood What contrasting moods does Colt seem to feel as the settlers near their new home?

nonplused (nän´ plüsd´) *adj.* bewildered; perplexed

▼ **Critical Viewing**
This 1866 photograph shows covered wagons on Main Street in Ottawa, Kansas. What does Colt's diary suggest about the importance of towns like this one to the wagon trains of settlers traveling westward? **[Draw Conclusions]**

Covered wagons on Main Street in Ottawa, Kansas, 1866, Kansas State Historical Society

Look around, and see the grounds all around the camp-fire are covered with tents, in which the families are staying. Not a house is to be seen. In the large tent here is a cook stove—they have supper prepared for us; it consists of hominy, soft Johnny cake (or corn bread, as it is called here), stewed apple, and tea. We eat what is set before us, "asking no questions for conscience' sake."

The ladies tell us they are sorry to see us come to this place; which shows us that all is not right. Are too weary to question, but with hope depressed go to our lodgings, which we find around in the tents, and in our wagons.

MAY 13TH. Can anyone imagine our disappointment this morning, on learning from this and that member, that no mills have been built; that the directors, after receiving our money to build mills, have not fulfilled the trust reposed in them, and that in consequence, some families have already left the settlement . . . ?

As it is, we find the families, some living in tents of cloth, some of cloth and green bark just peeled from the trees, and some wholly of green barn, stuck up on the damp ground, without floors or fires. Only two stoves in the company. . . .

We see that the city grounds, which have been surveyed . . . contain only one log cabin, 16 by 16, muddled between the logs on the inside, instead of on the outside; neither door nor window; the roof covered with "shakes" (western shingles), split out of oak I should think, 3½ feet in length, and about as wide as a sheet of fools cap paper.[9]

---

9. **fools cap paper** writing paper usually measuring 13 by 16 inches.

Review and Assess

Thinking About the Selection

1. **Respond:** Would you have had the courage and determination to leave your home and family to become a pioneer? Explain.

2. **(a) Recall:** What financial arrangements did the Colts make as part of their preparations for heading west? **(b) Evaluate:** Do you think they were too naive and trusting? Explain.

3. **(a) Recall:** What is the appearance of the settler woman whom Colt describes meeting in her entry of May 11? **(b) Analyze:** What does this settler woman suggest to Colt about her own future?

4. **Compare and Contrast:** How do Colt's expectations about life at Octagon City compare with reality?

5. **Synthesize:** Based on Colt's experiences, explain which character traits you feel were necessary to being a successful pioneer.

I Will Fight No More Forever
Chief Joseph

Tell General Howard I know his heart. What he told me before, I have in my heart. I am tired of fighting. Our chiefs are killed. Looking Glass is dead. Toohoolhoolzote is dead. The old men are all dead. It is the young men who say yes and no. He who led on the young men is dead. It is cold and we have no blankets. The little children are freezing to death. My people, some of them, have run away to the hills and have no blankets, no food; no one knows where they are—perhaps freezing to death. I want to have time to look for my children and see how many I can find. Maybe I shall find them among the dead. Hear me, my chiefs. I am tired; my heart is sick and sad. From where the sun now stands I will fight no more forever.

Review and Assess

Thinking About the Selection

1. **Respond:** Chief Joseph says that he knows his enemy's heart. Have you ever felt that you knew something with your heart rather than with your head? What is the difference?

2. **(a) Recall:** What has happened to the other Nez Percé chiefs? **(b) Infer:** Who has been left to carry on the fight? **(c) Speculate:** Why do you think Chief Joseph directs part of his speech to his chiefs?

3. **(a) Recall:** What reasons does Chief Joseph give for his surrender? **(b) Evaluate:** Would Chief Joseph's speech have been more or less effective had it contained more detailed explanations of his reasons for surrender? Explain.

4. **(a) Recall:** What does Chief Joseph want to do now that the battle is lost? **(b) Infer:** Based on this speech, how would you describe Chief Joseph's relationship to his people? Explain.

5. **Synthesize:** Although Chief Joseph delivered his speech to confirm his tribe's surrender, the speech had another, equally important purpose. What was that purpose?

6. **Take a Position:** Do you think surrender was the right choice? Why or why not?

Review and Assess

Literary Analysis

Tone

1. Find two examples of an upbeat, positive **tone** in Miriam Davis Colt's diary.

2. Find two examples of a negative, downcast tone in Colt's diary.

3. A military leader might adopt many tones when admitting defeat. (a) What is the overall tone of Chief Joseph's surrender? (b) What details contribute to this tone?

Comparing Literary Works

4. Chief Joseph's speech generates a single **mood,** while Colt's journal entries inspire varying moods. Identify a passage in Colt's work that most closely echoes the mood of Chief Joseph's speech.

5. Both Colt and Chief Joseph face struggles and disappointments as they work for what they feel is right, yet their conflicts differ greatly. Identify the conflict each writer faces. Then, compare and contrast these conflicts.

6. Using a Venn diagram like the one shown, compare the future Chief Joseph faces with the one Colt faces. (a) How are their hopes for the future different? (b) How are their hopes similar?

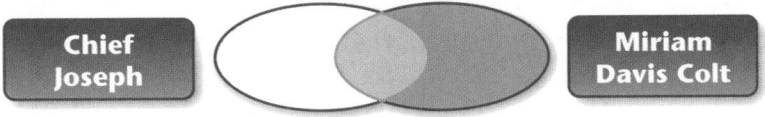

Reading Strategy

Responding

7. (a) Cite a passage from Colt's journal that affected you strongly, and describe your response. (b) Cite a passage from Chief's Joseph's speech that affected you deeply, and describe your response.

8. Did the way in which you responded to each of these selections affect your appreciation of it? Explain.

Extend Understanding

9. **Social Studies Connection:** Moving west was a risky and difficult endeavor for pioneers. Why were so many of them willing to emigrate west despite the dangers?

Quick Review

Tone is a writer's attitude toward his or her subject.

Mood, or atmosphere, is the feeling created in the reader by a literary work or passage.

To **respond** to literature, regonize your personal reactions to the work and notice how the writing affected you.

 Take It to the Net
www.phschool.com

Take the interactive self-test online to check your understanding of these selections.

Integrate Language Skills

Vocabulary Development Lesson

Word Analysis: Latin Term *terra firma*

Miriam Davis Colt uses the Latin term *terra firma*, which means "firm earth" or "solid ground." If you encounter an unfamiliar Latin word or phrase when reading, you can often find its meaning in a dictionary.

Follow the directions for each item below by writing sentences including the term *terra firma*.

1. Describe the Pilgrims landing on Plymouth Rock after months at sea in a tiny boat.
2. Describe a hot-air balloon safely touching down after a rough flight.

Spelling Strategy

When adding *-ed* to a one-syllable word that ends in a single consonant preceded by a vowel, double the final consonant. For example, *rub* becomes *rubbed*. Add *-ed* to each of the following words.

1. brag   2. stop   3. flit

Fluency: Word Choice

Select the word from the vocabulary list on page 595 that best describes or relates to each description below.

1. People who left America to live in another country
2. Acts committed by hostile invading troops against civilians
3. The personality of a pleasant host
4. The scents in a perfume shop
5. A buffet of more than fifty sumptuous and inviting desserts
6. An auto mechanic perplexed by a car he cannot fix despite six days of problem solving
7. A phrase said when stepping off a roller coaster

Grammar and Style Lesson

Sentence Fragments

Sentence fragments are incomplete sentences that may lack either a subject or a verb.

Although they may lend a sense of urgency to a piece of writing, sentence fragments are not acceptable in formal English.

Fragment:	Expect tonight to arrive at our new home. (*no subject*)
Fragment:	Even if we traveled for five more days. (*not a complete thought*)

Practice Identify which of the following sentences is incomplete. Then, rewrite each sentence fragment as a complete sentence.

1. A hot summer day.
2. Have been here in West Stockholm, at my brother's, since Friday last.
3. Hasten to the hotel—find it very much crowded.
4. We are going to Kansas.
5. Dined on the prairie and gathered flowers.

Looking at Style Write an evaluation in which you explain how Colt's use of sentence fragments affects your understanding of her experiences.

WG *Prentice Hall Writing and Grammar Connection: Chapter 20, Section 4*

Writing Lesson

Position Paper on Development

The vast stretches of land where both Chief Joseph and Miriam Davis Colt lived have almost disappeared. Imagine that you live in a town where the last open piece of land is about to be turned into a mall. Support or oppose the development in a position paper—a formal piece of writing that argues one side of a controversial issue.

Prewriting   List the reasons you support or oppose the project, along with facts to back up your reasons.

Drafting   Start with a clear statement of your position. Provide reasons and specific details to support your case. End with a persuasive conclusion.

Revising   Make sure your argument flows smoothly from one paragraph to the next. Check this coherence by highlighting and evaluating the transitions you have used.

Model: Revising for Coherence

The mall will not create jobs, as some believe. Instead of new

In addition,

jobs, we will get traffic and pollution. The mall will steal

business from locally owned shops.

> Using transition words and phrases builds coherence in a piece of writing.

WG Prentice Hall Writing and Grammar Connection: Chapter 7, Section 4

Extension Activities

Listening and Speaking Chief Joseph's speech so moved the officers who heard it that they were unable to speak. Recite the speech for the class in an **oral interpretation**. Use these tips to prepare:

- Identify the tone of Chief Joseph's voice as he gave his speech.
- Think about his bearing—how he held his body.

Picture Chief Joseph in your imagination as you re-create his speech. Then, ask classmates to evaluate your presentation.

Research and Technology The history of the West is full of stories like that of the Colts, who sought an ideal—or utopian—way of life. Using a variety of research tools, research these communities and their effect on the development of the American frontier. Identify how these communities attracted new members. Then, produce a **marketing brochure** to draw new settlers to such a community.

 Take It to the Net   www.phschool.com

Go online for an additional research activity using the Internet.

Prepare to Read

To Build a Fire

Jack London (1876–1916)

Jack London had endured more hardships by the age of twenty-one than most people experience in a lifetime. His struggles gave him a sympathy for the working class and a lasting dislike of drudgery. They also provided inspiration for novels and short stories, and became the foundation of his success as a writer.

Difficult Beginnings London grew up in San Francisco in extreme poverty. At the age of eleven, he left school and supported himself through a succession of unskilled jobs—working as a paper boy, in bowling alleys, on ice wagons, and in canneries and mills. Despite the long hours spent toiling at these jobs, London was able to read constantly, borrowing travel and adventure books from the library.

The books London read inspired him to travel, and his job experiences led him to become active in fighting for the rights of workers. He sailed to Japan on a sealing expedition and joined a cross-country protest march with a group of unemployed workers. After being arrested for vagrancy near Buffalo, New York, London decided to educate himself and reshape his life. He completed high school in a single year and then enrolled at the University of California.

After only one semester, however, the lure of fortune and adventure proved irresistible. In 1897, London abandoned his studies and traveled to the Alaskan Yukon in search of gold. Although he was unsuccessful as a miner, London's experiences in Alaska taught him about the human desire for wealth and power and about humankind's inability to control the forces of nature. While in Alaska, London also absorbed memories and stories that would make him a household name.

A Writing Life Once back in California, London became determined to earn a living as a writer. He rented a typewriter and worked up to fifteen hours a day, spinning his Alaskan adventures into short stories and novels.

According to legend, London's stack of rejection slips from publishers grew to five feet in height. Even so, London persevered. He wrote diligently every morning, setting himself a 1,000-word minimum.

In 1903, he earned national fame when he published the popular novel *The Call of the Wild*. He soon became the highest-paid and most-industrious writer in the country. During his career, London produced more than fifty books, including both fiction and nonfiction, and earned more than a million dollars—the first American writer to earn such a staggering sum. Several of his novels, including *The Call of the Wild* (1903), *The Sea-Wolf* (1904), and *White Fang* (1906), have become American classics. His best works depict an individual's struggle for survival against the powerful forces of nature. "To Build a Fire," for example, tells the story of an unnamed man's fight to survive the bitter cold of the Alaskan wilderness.

Recognition by His Peers The well-known writer Upton Sinclair wrote that Jack London "was the true king of our storytellers." London's friend Oliver Madox Hueffer agreed. He recalled that London "was the ideal yarnster—his spoken stories were even better than his written—and one reason why I think him likely to be numbered as among the writers of real mark was that he was perfectly unconscious of it. Like Peter Pan, he never grew up, and he lived in his own stories with such intensity that he ended by believing them himself."

Preview

Connecting to the Literature

Some people enjoy pushing themselves to their limits through sports such as rock climbing and sky diving. In some cases, as in this story, people push themselves to such extremes that they place their lives in jeopardy.

Literary Analysis

Conflict

Conflict, the struggle between two opposing forces, can take two forms:

- **internal,** occurring within the mind of a character
- **external,** occurring between a character and society, nature, another person, God, or fate.

A character's efforts to resolve conflict form the basis for the plot of a literary work. In "To Build a Fire," a man is in the throes of a deadly external conflict, struggling to survive in the bitter cold of the Alaskan wilderness.

Connecting Literary Elements

Irony involves a contrast between what is stated and what is meant, or between what is expected to happen and what actually happens. In **dramatic irony,** there is a contradiction between what a character thinks and what the reader knows to be true. Dramatic irony often serves to heighten the sense of conflict. For example, in "To Build a Fire," the reader knows that the temperature is far lower than the man realizes:

> He pulled the mitten on hurriedly and stood up. He was a bit frightened. He stamped up and down until the stinging returned into the feet. It certainly was cold, was his thought.

As you read, notice those passages where it is clear that the reader understands more than the man does.

Reading Strategy

Predicting

The main character in this story fails to recognize the depth of the conflict he faces until it is too late. A more alert person might have interpreted the signs of danger, anticipated their outcome, and taken action. As a reader, you too can anticipate, or **predict,** what will happen by noting clues that hint at later events. Use a chart like the one shown to identify clues and record your predictions.

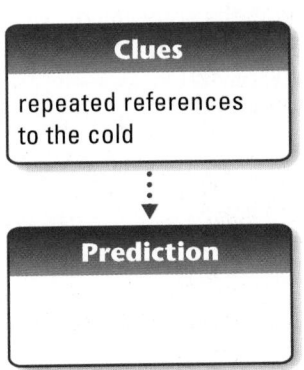

Clues

repeated references to the cold

Prediction

Vocabulary Development

conjectural (kən jek′ chər əl) *adj.* based on guesswork (p. 609)

unwonted (un wän′ tid) *adj.* unusual; unfamiliar (p. 610)

conflagration (kän′ flə grā′ shən) *n.* big, destructive fire (p. 615)

peremptorily (pər emp′ tə rə lē) *adj.* decisively; commandingly (p. 619)

To Build a Fire
Jack London

▲ **Critical Viewing**
Which words or passages from the story could be used to describe this scene?
[Analyze]

Background

The United States Secretary of State William Seward purchased Alaska from Russia in 1867 for two cents an acre. Many Americans, believing it to be nothing but a frozen, barren wasteland, called the purchase "Seward's Folly." In 1896, the discovery of a rich lode of gold in the Yukon, part of the Arctic wilderness, led to the Klondike stampede of 1897–1898. Thousands of prospectors headed for the frozen north, lured by the promise of quick riches. Jack London was among the first of these prospectors. He may have searched for more than gold, however. London once commented, "True, the new territory was mostly barren; but its several hundred thousand square miles of frigidity at least gave breathing space to those who else would have suffocated at home."

Day had broken cold and gray, exceedingly cold and gray, when the man turned aside from the main Yukon[1] trail and climbed the high earth-bank, where a dim and little-traveled trail led eastward through the fat spruce timberland. It was a steep bank, and he paused for breath at the top, excusing the act to himself by looking at his watch. It was nine o'clock. There was no sun nor hint of sun, though there was not a cloud in the sky. It was a clear day, and yet there seemed an intangible pall over the face of things, a subtle gloom that made the day dark, and that was due to the absence of sun. This fact did not worry the man. He was used to the lack of sun. It had been days since he had seen the sun, and he knew that a few more days must pass before that cheerful orb, due south, would just peep above the skyline and dip immediately from view.

The man flung a look back along the way he had come. The Yukon lay a mile wide and hidden under three feet of ice. On top of this ice were as many feet of snow. It was all pure white, rolling in gentle undulations where the ice jams of the freeze-up had formed. North and south, as far as his eye could see, it was unbroken white, save for a dark hairline that curved and twisted from around the spruce-covered island to the south, and that curved and twisted away into the north, where it disappeared behind another spruce-covered island. This dark hairline was the trail—the main trail—that led south five hundred miles to the Chilcoot Pass, Dyea,[2] and salt water; and that led north seventy miles to Dawson, and still on to the north a thousand miles to Nulato,[3] and finally to St. Michael on Bering Sea, a thousand miles and half a thousand more.

But all this—the mysterious, far-reaching hairline trail, the absence of sun from the sky, the tremendous cold, and the strangeness and weirdness of it all—no impression on the man. It was not because he was long used to it. He was a newcomer in the land, a *chechaquo*,[4] and this was his first winter. The trouble with him was that he was without imagination. He was quick and alert in the things of life, but only in the things, and not in the significances. Fifty degrees below zero meant eighty-odd degrees of frost. Such fact impressed him as being cold and uncomfortable, and that was all. It did not lead him to meditate upon his frailty as a creature of temperature, and upon man's frailty in general, able only to live within certain narrow limits of heat and cold; and from there on it did not lead him to the <u>conjectural</u> field of immortality and man's place in the universe. Fifty degrees below zero stood for a bite of frost that hurt and that must be guarded against by the use of mittens, earflaps, warm moccasins, and thick socks. Fifty degrees below zero was to him just precisely fifty degrees below zero. That there should be anything more to it than that was a thought that never entered his head.

---

1. **Yukon** (yōō′ kän) territory in northwestern Canada, east of Alaska; also, a river.
2. **Dyea** (dī′ ā) former town in Alaska at the start of the Yukon trail.
3. **Dawson . . . Nulato** former gold-mining villages in the Yukon.
4. *chechaquo* (chē chä′ kwō) slang for newcomer.

Reading Strategy
Predicting What do you predict will happen to the "newcomer" in the "tremendous cold and the strangeness and weirdness"? Why?

conjectural (kən jek′ chər əl) *adj.* based on guesswork

**Reading Check**
Where is the man, and what weather conditions is he experiencing?

As he turned to go on, he spat speculatively. There was a sharp, explosive crackle that startled him. He spat again. And again, in the air, before it could fall to the snow, the spittle crackled. He knew that at fifty below spittle crackled on the snow, but this spittle had crackled in the air. Undoubtedly it was colder than fifty below—how much colder he did not know. But the temperature did not matter. He was bound for the old claim on the left fork of Henderson Creek, where the boys were already. They had come over across the divide from the Indian Creek country, while he had come the roundabout way to take a look at the possibilities of getting out logs in the spring from the islands in the Yukon. He would be in to camp by six o'clock; a bit after dark, it was true, but the boys would be there, a fire would be going, and a hot supper would be ready. As for lunch, he pressed his hand against the protruding bundle under his jacket. It was also under his shirt, wrapped up in a handkerchief and lying against the naked skin. It was the only way to keep the biscuits from freezing. He smiled agreeably to himself as he thought of those biscuits, each cut open and sopped in bacon grease, and each enclosing a generous slice of fried bacon.

He plunged in among the big spruce trees. The trail was faint. A foot of snow had fallen since the last sled had passed over, and he was glad he was without a sled, traveling light. In fact, he carried nothing but the lunch wrapped in the handkerchief. He was surprised, however, at the cold. It certainly was cold, he concluded, as he rubbed his numb nose and cheekbones with his mittened hand. He was a warm-whiskered man, but the hair on his face did not protect the high cheekbones and the eager nose that thrust itself aggressively into the frosty air.

At the man's heels trotted a dog, a big native husky, the proper wolf dog, gray-coated and without any visible or temperamental difference from its brother, the wild wolf. The animal was depressed by the tremendous cold. It knew that it was no time for traveling. Its instinct told it a truer tale than was told to the man by the man's judgment. In reality, it was not merely colder than fifty below zero; it was colder than sixty below, than seventy below. It was seventy-five below zero. Since the freezing point is thirty-two above zero, it meant that one hundred and seven degrees of frost obtained. The dog did not know anything about thermometers. Possibly in its brain there was no sharp consciousness of a condition of very cold such as was in the man's brain. But the brute had its instinct. It experienced a vague but menacing apprehension that subdued it and made it slink along at the man's heels, and that made it question eagerly every unwonted movement of the man as if expecting him to go into camp or to seek shelter somewhere and build a fire. The dog had learned fire, and it wanted fire, or else to burrow under the snow and cuddle its warmth away from the air.

The frozen moisture of its breathing had settled on its fur in a fine powder of frost, and especially were its jowls, muzzle, and eyelashes

---

Literary Analysis
Conflict The great elaboration on the cold in this description points out the central conflict in this story. With what or whom is the man in conflict?

Literary Analysis
Conflict and Irony In what ways does the description of the dog's instinct create a sense of dramatic irony?

unwonted (un wän´ tid) *adj.* unusual; unfamiliar

whitened by its crystalled breath. The man's red beard and mustache were likewise frosted, but more solidly, the deposit taking the form of ice and increasing with every warm, moist breath he exhaled. Also, the man was chewing tobacco, and the muzzle of ice held his lips so rigidly that he was unable to clear his chin when he expelled the juice. The result was that a crystal beard of the color and solidity of amber was increasing its length on his chin. If he fell down it would shatter itself, like glass, into brittle fragments. But he did not mind the appendage. It was the penalty all tobacco-chewers paid in that country, and he had been out before in two cold snaps. They had not been so cold as this, he knew, but by the spirit thermometer[5] at Sixty Mile he knew they had been registered at fifty below and at fifty-five.

He held on through the level stretch of woods for several miles, crossed a wide flat, and dropped down a bank to the frozen bed of a small stream. This was Henderson Creek, and he knew he was ten miles from the forks. He looked at his watch. It was ten o'clock. He was making four miles an hour, and he calculated that he would arrive at the forks at half past twelve. He decided to celebrate that event by eating his lunch there.

The dog dropped in again at his heels, with a tail drooping discouragement, as the man swung along the creek bed. The furrow of the old sled trail was plainly visible, but a dozen inches of snow covered the marks of the last runners. In a month no man had come up or down that silent creek. The man held steadily on. He was not much given to thinking, and just then particularly he had nothing to think about save that he would eat lunch at the forks and that at six o'clock he would be in camp with the boys. There was nobody to talk to; and, had there been, speech would have been impossible because of the ice-muzzle on his mouth. So he continued monotonously to chew tobacco and to increase the length of his amber beard.

Once in a while the thought reiterated itself that it was very cold and that he had never experienced such cold. As he walked along he rubbed his cheekbones and nose with the back of his mittened hand. He did this automatically, now and again changing hands. But rub as he would, the instant he stopped his cheekbones went numb, and the following instant the end of his nose went numb. He was sure to frost his cheeks; he knew that, and experienced a pang of regret that he had not devised a nose strap of the sort Bud wore in cold snaps. Such a strap passed across the cheeks, as well, and saved them. But it didn't

---

5. **spirit thermometer** thermometer containing alcohol; used in extreme cold.

Literature in context   History Connection

Dogs and the Yukon

Dogs, like the one that accompanies the man in London's "To Build a Fire," have long played a key role in the life of the Alaskan Yukon. For centuries, native people in Alaska have bred dogs to serve a variety of purposes, including transportation. When the Yukon gold rush that began in the 1890s brought thousands of miners to the northern wilderness, the problem of transportation became acute. In 1910, the federal government constructed a trail more than 1,000 miles long for use by dog sled teams. That trail became known as the Iditarod.

Sled dogs were—and are— some of the most powerful draft animals on Earth. A team of twenty dogs is capable of pulling a ton or more. Though the man in London's story does not treat his dog with affection, for many dog sled drivers these valiant dogs provided warmth and companionship on the long, cold trail.

✔ Reading Check

Is the man aware of how cold it truly is? How do you know?

matter much, after all. What were frosted cheeks? A bit painful, that was all; they were never serious.

Empty as the man's mind was of thoughts, he was keenly observant, and he noticed the changes in the creek, the curves and bends and timber jams, and always he sharply noted where he placed his feet. Once, coming around a bend, he shied abruptly, like a startled horse, curved away from the place where he had been walking, and retreated several paces back along the trail. The creek he knew was frozen clear to the bottom—no creek could contain water in that arctic winter—but he knew also that there were springs that bubbled out from the hillsides and ran along under the snow and on top the ice of the creek. He knew that the coldest snaps never froze these springs, and he knew likewise their danger. They were traps. They hid pools of water under the snow that might be three inches deep, or three feet. Sometimes a skin of ice half an inch thick covered them, and in turn was covered by the snow. Sometimes there were alternate layers of water and ice skin, so that when one broke through he kept on breaking through for a while, sometimes wetting himself to the waist.

That was why he had shied in such panic. He had felt the give under his feet and heard the crackle of a snow-hidden ice skin. And to get his feet wet in such a temperature meant trouble and danger. At the very least it meant delay, for he would be forced to stop and build a fire, and under its protection to bare his feet while he dried his socks and moccasins. He stood and studied the creek bed and its banks, and decided that the flow of water came from the right. He reflected awhile, rubbing his nose and cheeks, then skirted to the left, stepping gingerly and testing the footing for each step. Once clear of the danger, he took a fresh chew of tobacco and swung along at his four-mile gait.

In the course of the next two hours he came upon several similar traps. Usually the snow above the hidden pools had a sunken, candied appearance that advertised the danger. Once again, however, he had a close call; and once, suspecting danger, he compelled the dog to go on in front. The dog did not want to go. It hung back until the man shoved it forward, and then it went quickly across the white, unbroken surface. Suddenly it broke through, floundered to one side, and got away to firmer footing. It had wet its forefeet and legs, and almost immediately the water that clung to it turned to ice. It made quick efforts to lick the ice off its legs, then dropped down in the snow and began to bite out the ice that had formed between the toes. This was a matter of instinct. To permit the ice to remain would mean sore feet. It did not know this. It merely obeyed the mysterious prompting that arose from the deep crypts of its being. But the man knew, having achieved a judgment on the subject, and he removed the mitten from his right hand and helped tear out the ice particles. He did not expose his fingers more than a minute, and was astonished at the swift numbness that smote them. It certainly was cold. He pulled on the mitten hastily, and beat the hand savagely across his chest.

Reading Strategy
Predicting Based on this passage describing the hidden creek, what do you predict might happen?

Literary Analysis
Conflict Until now, the man has struggled with the cold. What other element of conflict is introduced in the passages describing the creek?

At twelve o'clock the day was at its brightest. Yet the sun was too far south on its winter journey to clear the horizon. The bulge of the earth intervened between it and Henderson Creek, where the man walked under a clear sky at noon and cast no shadow. At half-past twelve, to the minute, he arrived at the forks of the creek. He was pleased at the speed he had made. If he kept it up, he would certainly be with the boys by six. He unbuttoned his jacket and shirt and drew forth his lunch. The action consumed no more than a quarter of a minute, yet in that brief moment the numbness laid hold of the exposed fingers. He did not put the mitten on, but, instead, struck the fingers a dozen sharp smashes against his leg. Then he sat down on a snow-covered log to eat. The sting that followed upon the striking of his fingers against his leg ceased so quickly that he was startled. He had had no chance to take a bite of biscuit. He struck the fingers repeatedly and returned them to the mitten, baring the other hand for the purpose of eating. He tried to take a mouthful, but the ice muzzle prevented. He had forgotten to build a fire and thaw out. He chuckled at his foolishness, and as he chuckled he noted the numbness creeping into the exposed fingers. Also, he noted that the stinging which had first come to his toes when he sat down was already passing away. He wondered whether the toes were warm or numb. He moved them inside the moccasins and decided that they were numb.

He pulled the mitten on hurriedly and stood up. He was a bit frightened. He stamped up and down until the stinging returned into the feet. It certainly was cold, was his thought. That man from Sulphur Creek had spoken the truth when telling how cold it sometimes got in the country. And he had laughed at him at the time! That showed one must not be too sure of things. There was no mistake about it, it was cold. He strode up and down, stamping his feet and threshing his arms, until reassured by the returning warmth. Then he got out matches and proceeded to make a fire. From the undergrowth, where high water of the previous spring had lodged a supply of seasoned twigs, he got his firewood. Working carefully from a small beginning, he soon had a roaring fire, over which he thawed the ice from his face and in the protection of which he ate his biscuits. For the moment the cold of space was outwitted. The dog took satisfaction in the fire, stretching out close enough for warmth and far enough away to escape being singed.

When the man had finished, he filled his pipe and took his comfortable time over a smoke. Then he pulled on his mittens, settled the earflaps of his cap firmly about his ears, and took the creek trail up the left fork. The dog was disappointed and yearned back toward the fire. This man did not know cold. Possibly all the generations of his ancestry had been ignorant of cold, of real cold, of cold one hundred and seven degrees below freezing point. But the dog knew; all its ancestry knew, and it had inherited the knowledge. And it knew that it was not good to walk abroad in such fearful cold. It was the time to lie snug in a hole in the snow and wait for a curtain of cloud to be

Literary Analysis
Conflict and Irony In what ways is the man's thought that "one must not be too sure of things" ironic?

✔**Reading Check**

Why do the hidden creeks present such peril?

drawn across the face of outer space whence this cold came. On the other hand, there was no keen intimacy between the dog and the man. The one was the toil slave of the other, and the only caresses it had ever received were the caresses of the whiplash and of harsh and menacing throat sounds that threatened the whiplash. So the dog made no effort to communicate its apprehension to the man. It was not concerned in the welfare of the man; it was for its own sake that it yearned back toward the fire. But the man whistled, and spoke to it with the sound of whiplashes, and the dog swung in at the man's heels and followed after.

The man took a chew of tobacco and proceeded to start a new amber beard. Also, his moist breath quickly powdered with white his mustache, eyebrows, and lashes. There did not seem to be so many springs on the left fork of the Henderson, and for half an hour the man saw no signs of any. And then it happened. At a place where there were no signs, where the soft, unbroken snow seemed to advertise solidity beneath, the man broke through. It was not deep. He wet himself halfway to the knees before he floundered out to the firm crust.

He was angry, and cursed his luck aloud. He had hoped to get into camp with the boys at six o'clock, and this would delay him an hour, for he would have to build a fire and dry out his footgear. This was imperative at that low temperature—he knew that much; and he turned aside to the bank, which he climbed. On top, tangled in the underbrush about the trunks of several small spruce trees, was a high-water deposit of dry firewood—sticks and twigs, principally, but also larger portions of seasoned branches and fine, dry, last year's grasses. He threw down several large pieces on top of the snow. This served for a foundation and prevented the young flame from drowning itself in the snow it otherwise would melt. The flame he got by touching a match to a small shred of birch bark that he took from his pocket. This burned even more readily than paper. Placing it on the foundation, he fed the young flame with wisps of dry grass and with the tiniest dry twigs.

He worked slowly and carefully, keenly aware of his danger. Gradually, as the flame grew stronger, he increased the size of the twigs with which he fed it. He squatted in the snow, pulling the twigs out from their entanglement in the brush and feeding directly to the flame. He knew there must be no failure. When it is seventy-five below zero, a man must not fail in his first attempt to build a fire—that is, if his feet are wet. If his feet are dry, and he fails, he can run along the trail for half a mile and restore his circulation. But the circulation of wet and freezing feet cannot be restored by running when it is seventy-five below. No matter how fast he runs, the wet feet will freeze the harder.

▲ Critical Viewing
In what ways does this image convey both the starkness of the Yukon wilderness and the dog's comfort in that landscape? **[Assess]**

Reading Strategy
Predicting Now that he is wet, what do you predict will happen to the man?

All this the man knew. The old-timer on Sulphur Creek had told him about it the previous fall, and now he was appreciating the advice. Already all sensation had gone out of his feet. To build the fire he had been forced to remove his mittens, and the fingers had quickly gone numb. His pace of four miles an hour had kept his heart pumping blood to the surface of his body and to all the extremities. But the instant he stopped, the action of the pump eased down. The cold of space smote the unprotected tip of the planet, and he, being on that unprotected tip, received the full force of the blow. The blood of his body recoiled before it. The blood was alive, like the dog, and like the dog it wanted to hide away and cover itself up from the fearful cold. So long as he walked four miles an hour, he pumped that blood, willy-nilly, to the surface; but now it ebbed away and sank down into the recesses of his body. The extremities were the first to feel its absence. His wet feet froze the faster, and his exposed fingers numbed the faster, though they had not yet begun to freeze. Nose and cheeks were already freezing, while the skin of all his body chilled as it lost its blood.

But he was safe. Toes and nose and cheeks would be only touched by the frost, for the fire was beginning to burn with strength. He was feeding it with twigs the size of his finger. In another minute he would be able to feed it with branches the size of his wrist, and then he could remove his wet foot-gear, and, while it dried, he could keep his naked feet warm by the fire, rubbing them at first, of course, with snow. The fire was a success. He was safe. He remembered the advice of the old-timer on Sulphur Creek, and smiled. The old-timer had been very serious in laying down the law that no man must travel alone in the Klondike after fifty below. Well, here he was; he had had the accident; he was alone; and he had saved himself. Those old-timers were rather womanish, some of them, he thought. All a man had to do was to keep his head, and he was all right. Any man who was a man could travel alone. But it was surprising, the rapidity with which his cheeks and nose were freezing. And he had not thought his fingers could go lifeless in so short a time. Lifeless they were, for he could scarcely make them move together to grip a twig, and they seemed remote from his body and from him. When he touched a twig, he had to look and see whether or not he had hold of it. The wires were pretty well down between him and his finger ends.

All of which counted for little. There was the fire, snapping and crackling and promising life with every dancing flame. He started to untie his moccasins. They were coated with ice; the thick German socks were like sheaths of iron halfway to the knees; and the moccasin strings were like rods of steel all twisted and knotted as by some conflagration. For a moment he tugged with his numb fingers, then, realizing the folly of it, he drew his sheath-knife.

But before he could cut the strings, it happened. It was his own fault or, rather, his mistake. He should not have built the fire under the spruce tree. He should have built it in the open. But it had been

Literary Analysis
Conflict and Irony Has the man saved himself, as he believes? What does the reader understand about the old-timer's advice that the man does not?

conflagration (kän´ flə grā´ shən) n. big, destructive fire

✔**Reading Check**
What does the man do after he falls into the creek?

easier to pull the twigs from the brush and drop them directly on the fire. Now the tree under which he had done this carried a weight of snow on its boughs. No wind had blown for weeks, and each bough was fully freighted. Each time he had pulled a twig he had communicated a slight agitation to the tree—an imperceptible agitation, so far as he was concerned, but an agitation sufficient to bring about the disaster. High up in the tree one bough capsized its load of snow. This fell on the boughs beneath, capsizing them. This process continued, spreading out and involving the whole tree. It grew like an avalanche, and it descended without warning upon the man and the fire, and the fire was blotted out! Where it had burned was a mantle of fresh and disordered snow.

The man was shocked. It was as though he had just heard his own sentence of death. For a moment he sat and stared at the spot where the fire had been. Then he grew very calm. Perhaps the old-timer on Sulphur Creek was right. If he had only had a trail mate he would have been in no danger now. The trail mate could have built the fire. Well, it was up to him to build the fire over again, and this second time there must be no failure. Even if he succeeded, he would most likely lose some toes. His feet must be badly frozen by now, and there would be some time before the second fire was ready.

Such were his thoughts, but he did not sit and think them. He was busy all the time they were passing through his mind. He made a new foundation for a fire, this time in the open, where no treacherous tree could blot it out. Next, he gathered dry grasses and tiny twigs from the high-water flotsam. He could not bring his fingers together to pull them out, but he was able to gather them by the handful. In this way he got many rotten twigs and bits of green moss that were undesirable, but it was the best he could do. He worked methodically, even collecting an armful of the larger branches to be used later when the fire gathered strength. And all the while the dog sat and watched him, a certain yearning wistfulness in its eyes, for it looked upon him as the fire provider, and the fire was slow in coming.

When all was ready, the man reached in his pocket for a second piece of birch bark. He knew the bark was there, and, though he could not feel it with his fingers, he could hear its crisp rustling as he fumbled for it. Try as he would, he could not clutch hold of it. And all the time, in his consciousness, was the knowledge that each instant his feet were freezing. This thought tended to put him in a panic, but he fought against it and kept calm. He pulled on his mittens with his teeth, and threshed his arms back and forth, beating his hands with all his might against his sides. He did this sitting down, and he stood up to do it; and all the while the dog sat in the snow, its wolf brush of a tail curled around warmly over its forefeet, its sharp wolf ears pricked forward intently as it watched the man. And the man, as he beat and threshed with his arms and hands, felt a great surge of envy as he regarded the creature that was warm and secure in its natural covering.

After a time he was aware of the first faraway signals of sensation in his beaten fingers. The faint tingling grew stronger till it evolved into a stinging ache that was excruciating, but which the man hailed with satisfaction. He stripped the mitten from his right hand and fetched forth the birch bark. The exposed fingers were quickly going numb again. Next he brought out his bunch of sulphur matches. But the tremendous cold had already driven the life out of his fingers. In his effort to separate one match from the others, the whole bunch fell in the snow. He tried to pick it out of the snow, but failed. The dead fingers could neither touch nor clutch. He was very careful. He drove the thought of his freezing feet, and nose, and cheeks, out of his mind, devoting his whole soul to the matches. He watched, using the sense of vision in place of that of touch, and when he saw his fingers on each side the bunch, he closed them—that is, he willed to close them, for the wires were down, and the fingers did not obey. He pulled the mitten on the right hand, and beat it fiercely against his knee. Then, with both mittened hands, he scooped the bunch of matches, along with much snow, into his lap. Yet he was no better off.

After some manipulation he managed to get the bunch between the heels of his mittened hands. In this fashion he carried it to his mouth. The ice crackled and snapped when by a violent effort he opened his mouth. He drew the lower jaw in, curled the upper lip out of the way, and scraped the bunch with his upper teeth in order to separate a match. He succeeded in getting one, which he dropped on his lap. He was no better off. He could not pick it up. Then he

▲ **Critical Viewing**
Study the eyes of this husky. What human characteristics would you attribute to its eyes? Which, if any, of those characteristics apply to the dog in the story? **[Infer; Relate]**

Reading Strategy
Predicting As the man struggles to light the matches, what do you predict about his success? Why?

✔**Reading Check**
What happens to ruin the man's fire?

devised a way. He picked it up in his teeth and scratched it on his leg. Twenty times he scratched before he succeeded in lighting it. As it flamed he held it with his teeth to the birch bark. But the burning brimstone went up his nostrils and into his lungs, causing him to cough spasmodically. The match fell into the snow and went out.

The old-timer on Sulphur Creek was right, he thought in the moment of controlled despair that ensued: after fifty below, a man should travel with a partner. He beat his hands, but failed in exciting any sensation. Suddenly he bared both hands, removing the mittens with his teeth. He caught the whole bunch between the heels of his hands. His arm muscles not being frozen enabled him to press the hand heels tightly against the matches. Then he scratched the bunch along his leg. It flared into flame, seventy sulphur matches at once! There was no wind to blow them out. He kept his head to one side to escape the strangling fumes, and held the blazing bunch to the birch bark. As he so held it, he became aware of sensation in his hand. His flesh was burning. He could smell it. Deep down below the surface he could feel it. The sensation developed into pain that grew acute. And still he endured it, holding the flame of the matches clumsily to the bark that would not light readily because his own burning hands were in the way, absorbing most of the flame.

At last, when he could endure no more, he jerked his hands apart. The blazing matches fell sizzling into the snow, but the birch bark was alight. He began laying dry grasses and the tiniest twigs on the flame. He could not pick and choose, for he had to lift the fuel between the heels of his hands. Small pieces of rotten wood and green moss clung to the twigs, and he bit them off as well as he could with his teeth. He cherished the flame carefully and awkwardly. It meant life, and it must not perish. The withdrawal of blood from the surface of his body now made him begin to shiver, and he grew more awkward. A large piece of green moss fell squarely on the little fire. He tried to poke it out with his fingers, but his shivering frame made him poke too far, and he disrupted the nucleus of the little fire, the burning grasses and tiny twigs separating and scattering. He tried to poke them together again, but in spite

Literary Analysis
Conflict The man is now fully aware of how cold it actually is. What is the conflict with which he now struggles desperately?

▼ **Critical Viewing**
Compare and contrast this landscape with the one in London's story. **[Compare and Contrast]**

of the tenseness of the effort, his shivering got away with him, and the twigs were hopelessly scattered. Each twig gushed a puff of smoke and went out. The fire provider had failed. As he looked apathetically about him, his eyes chanced on the dog, sitting across the ruins of the fire from him, in the snow, making restless, hunching movements, slightly lifting one forefoot and then the other, shifting its weight back and forth on them with wistful eagerness.

The sight of the dog put a wild idea into his head. He remembered the tale of the man, caught in a blizzard, who killed a steer and crawled inside the carcass, and so was saved. He would kill the dog and bury his hands in the warm body until the numbness went out of them. Then he could build another fire. He spoke to the dog, calling it to him; but in his voice was a strange note of fear that frightened the animal, who had never known the man to speak in such way before. Something was the matter, and its suspicious nature sensed danger—it knew not what danger, but somewhere, somehow, in its brain arose an apprehension of the man. It flattened its ears down at the sound of the man's voice, and its restless, hunching movements and the liftings and shiftings of its forefeet became more pronounced; but it would not come to the man. He got on his hands and knees and crawled toward the dog. This unusual posture again excited suspicion, and the animal sidled mincingly away.

The man sat up in the snow for a moment and struggled for calmness. Then he pulled on his mittens, by means of his teeth, and got upon his feet. He glanced down at first in order to assure himself that he was really standing up, for the absence of sensation in his feet left him unrelated to the earth. His erect position in itself started to drive the webs of suspicion from the dog's mind; and when he spoke peremptorily, with the sound of whiplashes in his voice, the dog rendered its customary allegiance and came to him. As it came within reaching distance, the man lost his control. His arms flashed out to the dog, and he experienced genuine surprise when he discovered that his hands could not clutch, that there was neither bend nor feeling in the fingers. He had forgotten for the moment that they were

Literary Analysis
Conflict What conflict is intensified in the passage beginning "the sight of the dog . . ."?

peremptorily (pər emp´ tər ə lē) *adj.* decisively; commandingly

✓ **Reading Check**

What happens to the man's second attempt to build a fire?

frozen and that they were freezing more and more. All this happened quickly, and before the animal could get away, he encircled its body with his arms. He sat down in the snow, and in this fashion held the dog, while it snarled and whined and struggled.

But it was all he could do, hold its body encircled in his arms and sit there. He realized that he could not kill the dog. There was no way to do it. With his helpless hands he could neither draw nor hold his sheath-knife nor throttle the animal. He released it, and it plunged wildly away, with tail between its legs, and still snarling. It halted forty feet away and surveyed him curiously, with ears sharply pricked forward. The man looked down at his hands in order to locate them, and found them hanging on the ends of his arms. It struck him as curious that one should have to use his eyes in order to find out where his hands were. He began threshing his arms back and forth, beating the mittened hands against his sides. He did this for five minutes, violently, and his heart pumped enough blood up to the surface to put a stop to his shivering. But no sensation was aroused in the hands. He had an impression that they hung like weights on the ends of his arms, but when he tried to run the impression down, he could not find it.

A certain fear of death, dull and oppressive, came to him. This fear quickly became poignant as he realized that it was no longer a mere matter of freezing his fingers and toes, or of losing his hands and feet, but that it was a matter of life and death with the chances against him. This threw him into a panic, and he turned and ran up the creek-bed along the old, dim trail. The dog joined in behind and kept up with him. He ran blindly, without intention, in fear such as he had never known in his life. Slowly, as he plowed and floundered through the snow, he began to see things again—the banks of the creek, the old timber jams, the leafless aspens, and the sky. The running made him feel better. He did not shiver. Maybe, if he ran on, his feet would thaw out; and, anyway, if he ran far enough, he would reach camp and the boys. Without doubt he would lose some fingers and toes and some of his face; but the boys would take care of him, and save the rest of him when he got there. And at the same time there was another thought in his mind that said he would never get to the camp and the boys; that it was too many miles away, that the freezing had too great a start on him, and that he would soon be stiff and dead. This thought he kept in the background and refused to consider. Sometimes it pushed itself forward and demanded to be heard, but he thrust it back and strove to think of other things.

It struck him as curious that he could run at all on feet so frozen that he could not feel them when they struck the earth and took the weight of his body. He seemed to himself to skim along above the surface, and to have no connection with the earth. Somewhere he had once seen a winged Mercury,[6] and he wondered if Mercury felt as he felt when skimming over the earth.

Reading Strategy
Predicting Does the man still have a chance for survival? Explain why or why not.

---

6. **Mercury** from Roman mythology, the wing-footed messenger of the gods.

His theory of running until he reached camp and the boys had one flaw in it: he lacked the endurance. Several times he stumbled, and finally he tottered, crumpled up, and fell. When he tried to rise, he failed. He must sit and rest, he decided, and next time he would merely walk and keep on going. As he sat and regained his breath, he noted that he was feeling quite warm and comfortable. He was not shivering, and it even seemed that a warm glow had come to his chest and trunk. And yet, when he touched his nose or cheeks, there was no sensation. Running would not thaw them out. Nor would it thaw out his hands and feet. Then the thought came to him that the frozen portions of his body must be extending. He tried to keep this thought down, to forget it, to think of something else; he was aware of the panicky feeling that it caused, and he was afraid of the panic. But the thought asserted itself, and persisted, until it produced a vision of his body totally frozen. This was too much, and he made another wild run along the trail. Once he slowed down to a walk, but the thought of the freezing extending itself made him run again.

And all the time the dog ran with him, at his heels. When he fell down a second time, it curled its tail over its forefeet and sat in front of him, facing him, curiously eager and intent. The warmth and security of the animal angered him, and he cursed it till it flattened down its ears appeasingly. This time the shivering came more quickly upon the man. He was losing in his battle with the frost. It was creeping into his body from all sides. The thought of it drove him on, but he ran no more than a hundred feet, when he staggered and pitched headlong. It was his last panic. When he had recovered his breath and control, he sat up and entertained in his mind the conception of meeting death with dignity. However, the conception did not come to him in such terms. His idea of it was that he had been making a fool of himself, running around like a chicken with its head cut off—such was the simile that occurred to him. Well, he was bound to freeze anyway, and he might as well take it decently. With this new-found peace of mind came the first glimmerings of drowsiness. A good idea, he thought, to sleep off to death. It was like taking an anaesthetic. Freezing was not so bad as people thought. There were lots worse ways to die.

He pictured the boys finding his body next day. Suddenly he found himself with them, coming along the trail and looking for himself. And, still with them, he came around a turn in the trail and found himself lying in the snow. He did not belong with himself any more, for even then he was out of himself; standing with the boys and looking at himself in the snow. It certainly was cold, was his thought. When he got back to the States he could tell the folks what real cold was. He drifted on from this to a vision of the old-timer on Sulphur Creek. He could see him quite clearly, warm and comfortable, and smoking a pipe.

"You were right, old hoss; you were right," the man mumbled to the old-timer of Sulphur Creek.

Literary Analysis
Conflict and Irony As the man begins to feel "quite warm and comfortable" what does the reader know that the man does not?

Reading Check

What does the man try to do when he realizes he is freezing to death?

Then the man drowsed off into what seemed to him the most comfortable and satisfying sleep he had ever known. The dog sat facing him and waiting. The brief day drew to a close in a long, slow twilight. There were no signs of a fire to be made, and, besides, never in the dog's experience had it known a man to sit like that in the snow and make no fire. As the twilight drew on, its eager yearning for the fire mastered it, and with a great lifting and shifting of forefeet, it whined softly, then flattened its ears down in anticipation of being chidden[7] by the man. But the man remained silent. Later, the dog whined loudly. And still later it crept close to the man and caught the scent of death. This made the animal bristle and back away. A little longer it delayed, howling under the stars that leaped and danced and shone brightly in the cold sky. Then it turned and trotted up the trail in the direction of the camp it knew, where were the other food providers and fire providers.

---

7. chidden scolded.

Review and Assess

Thinking About the Selection

1. **Respond:** Could you imagine yourself falling into the same circumstances as the man? How could you avoid them?

2. **(a) Recall:** What advice from an old-timer does the man choose to ignore? **(b) Infer:** What does this decision suggest about the man's character?

3. **(a) Recall:** What do the dog's instincts tell it about the cold? **(b) Compare and Contrast:** By contrast, why does the extreme cold "make no impression" on the man? **(c) Make a Judgment:** Which is better equipped to survive in the cold, the dog or the man? Explain.

4. **(a) Recall:** What trap does the man try—unsuccessfully—to avoid? **(b) Analyze Cause and Effect:** What deadly chain of events is started by his inability to avoid the trap?

5. **(a) Recall:** When the man breaks through the snow into the icy water, he becomes angry and curses. What is it that he curses? **(b) Evaluate:** Is the outcome of the story due to fate, to the man's character, or to some other cause? Explain.

6. **(a) Assess:** Why do you think London did not give the man a name? **(b) Speculate:** How might the effect of this story be different if the man had a name?

7. **(a) Draw Conclusions:** What does the story suggest about human strength in the face of nature's power? **(b) Take a Position:** Is London's message true? Explain.

Review and Assess

Literary Analysis

Conflict

1. (a) What external **conflict** is central to the plot of "To Build a Fire"? (b) Use a chart like the one shown to examine the details London uses to portray the central conflict.

The Man versus ?	Details
	1. _____
	2. _____
	3. _____

2. Does the man's awareness of the conflict intensify as the story unfolds? Explain.
3. What events finally resolve the conflict?
4. What is the **internal conflict** that develops as the story progresses?

Connecting Literary Elements

5. What is ironic about the fact that the man breaks through the snow and steps in the spring?
6. What is ironic about the location in which he builds his fire?
7. In what way do London's descriptions of the dog's feelings and its instincts about survival increase the story's dramatic **irony**?

Reading Strategy

Predicting

8. (a) What information do the man's recollections of his conversation with the old-timer provide? (b) In what ways does this information help you **predict** the end of the story?
9. (a) At what point did you first predict that the man would not survive his journey? (b) On what clues did you base your prediction?

Extend Understanding

10. **Social Studies Connection:** Suppose that you were the editor of a newspaper in Alaska during the time of the Klondike Gold Rush. If you learned of this man's sad tale, what might you have written in an editorial about the event?

Integrate Language Skills

Vocabulary Development Lesson

Word Analysis: Latin Root -ject-

The Latin root -ject- means "to throw." If you *reject* an idea, you throw it back. Each word below contains the root -ject-. Use the clues to match each word with the situation to which it applies.

1. object
   (*ob* = toward; over; against)

2. conjecture
   (*con* = with; *ure* = noun of action)

3. abject
   (*ab* = away from)

4. eject
   (*e* = out; away)

a. you throw your thoughts in with others

b. you speak out against something

c. you remove someone from the premises

d. you feel this way when your friends shun you

Fluency: Sentence Completions

Fill in the blanks with the appropriate words from the vocabulary list on page 607.

A lightning storm in the parched woodland sparked a ___?___. The shy fire chief acted with ___?___ authority, ___?___ ordering all firefighters to work round the clock, though his estimates of how long it would take to overcome the fire were ___?___ at best.

Spelling Strategy

To add a suffix to a word ending in a *y* preceded by a consonant, change the *y* to *i* (*peremptory* + *ly* = *peremptorily*). For each of the following sentences, write the correct form of the word in italics.

1. Last year, my parents *accompany* me on my trip to Alaska.
2. We *happy* watched as the winning run scored.

Grammar and Style Lesson

Adverb Clauses

An **adverb clause** is a group of words with a subject and a verb that cannot stand by itself as a sentence. Adverb clauses modify verbs, adjectives, or other adverbs, explaining *how, where, when, why, to what extent,* or *under what circumstances.*

> Day had broken cold and gray, exceedingly cold and gray, *when the man turned aside from the main Yukon trail* . . . . (tells *when*)

Practice Identify the adverb clause and the word it modifies in each item below.

1. North and south, as far as the eye could see, it was unbroken white . . . .

2. A foot of snow had fallen since the last sled had passed over.
3. He made a new foundation for a fire, where no treacherous tree could blot it out.
4. If he kept it up, he would certainly be with the boys by six.
5. At last, when he could endure no more, he jerked his hands apart.

Writing Application Write four sentences describing a frightening encounter with nature. Use at least one adverb clause in each sentence. Identify the function of each adverb clause in your draft.

W͟G Prentice Hall Writing and Grammar Connection: Chapter 19, Section 3

Writing Lesson

Literary Analysis

A literary analysis explores how the elements of a piece of literature, such as plot, setting, characters, and point of view, work together to convey a message. Write a literary analysis in which you explain the message of "To Build a Fire," and discuss how the various elements of the story contribute to its meaning.

Prewriting   Review the story to identify London's message about the relationship between humanity and nature. Gather details that support your interpretation.

Drafting   In your introduction, state your thesis and outline your main points. Focus each body paragraph on one main point. Cite supporting details from the story.

Model: Elaborating to Support an Argument

<u>The dog, equipped by centuries of evolution for life in the bitter cold, serves as a symbolic foil to the man.</u> Unlike the man, who disregards plain evidence, ". . . the dog knew; all its ancestry knew, and it had inherited the knowledge. And it knew that it was not good to walk abroad in such fearful cold."

> Providing details from the work helps to elaborate on the main point, underlined here.

Revising   Review your draft, making sure your thesis is clear and your support is convincing. Look for opportunities to elaborate on your key points.

Prentice Hall Writing and Grammar Connection: Chapter 14, Section 4

Extension Activities

Listening and Speaking If the dog could voice its thoughts about the man, what would it say? Write and present an **enactment** of the dog's thoughts and feelings as a scene of this story unfolds. Keep these tips in mind as you work:

- Refer to the text of the story for accuracy.
- Include details that reflect the dog's highly developed senses of smell and hearing.

Work to create a specific sense of character, so that your dog has an individual voice.

Research and Technology The man in the story dies of hypothermia, or subnormal body temperature. Research this condition using a variety of sources, including the Internet. Then, create a word-processed **booklet** of guidelines for avoiding hypothermia.

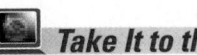 **Take It to the Net**   www.phschool.com

Go online for an additional research activity using the Internet.

CONNECTIONS
Literature Past and Present
Forging New Frontiers

Among the greatest legends of the American West were the cowboys, who drove longhorn cattle from the open ranges of Texas up to the railroad yards in Kansas. As they made the journey, cowboys faced loneliness and danger—yet they seemed glamourous to those who lived more settled lives. The cowboy came to symbolize a side of the American dream that was being lost to development. Toward the end of the nineteenth century, the spread of the railroads and the fencing of the once open range spelled the end for most working cowboys. However, the national obsession with the cowboy myth refused to die.

The Western For most of the twentieth century, fictional cowboys pursued their lonely quests in thousands of books and movies. The first western movie, *The Great Train Robbery*, was made in 1903, and hundreds more were filmed in the decades that followed. In all of them, the cowboy was a solitary hero forced to prove himself in the wilderness. Beginning in 1903, an Ohio dentist named Zane Grey published more than eighty westerns, many of which are still popular today.

Contemporary writers like Larry McMurtry and Cormac McCarthy have tapped into this American passion. Their novels set in the West have captured the public's imagination and enjoy both popular and critical success.

from

Lonesome Dove

Larry McMurtry

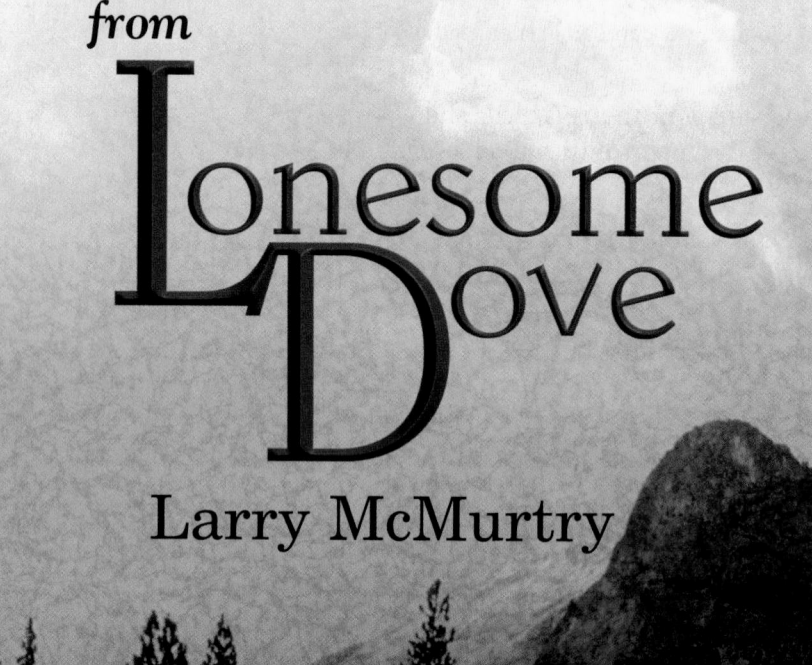

Captain Woodrow Call and Augustus McCrae are two former Texas Rangers who helped bring peace to the Texas frontier. Call now feels a yearning for adventure. With his friend Augustus, he gathers together a ragtag bunch of cowboys and embarks on a cattle drive from Lonesome Dove, Texas, on the Rio Grande, to the wilderness of Montana.

In the late afternoon they strung a rope corral around the remuda,[1] so each hand could pick himself a set of mounts, each being allowed four picks. It was slow work, for Jasper Fant and Needle Nelson could not make up their minds. The Irishmen and the boys had to take what was left after the more experienced hands had chosen.

Augustus did not deign to make a choice at all. "I intend to ride old Malaria all the way," he said, "or if not I'll ride Greasy."

Once the horses were assigned, the positions had to be assigned as well.

"Dish, you take the right point," Call said. "Soupy can take the left and Bert and Needle will back you up."

Dish had assumed that, as a top hand, he would have a point, and no one disputed his right, but both Bert and Needle were unhappy that Soupy had the other point. They had been with the outfit longer, and felt <u>aggrieved</u>.

The Spettle boys were told to help Lippy with the horse herd, and Newt, the Raineys and the Irishmen were left with the drags. Call saw that each of them had bandanas, for the dust at the rear of the herd would be bad.

They spent an hour patching on the wagon, a vehicle Augustus regarded with scorn. "That dern wagon won't get us to the Brazos,"[2] he said.

"Well, it's the only wagon we got," Call said.

"You didn't assign me no duties, nor yourself either," Augustus pointed out.

"That simple," Call said. "I'll scare off bandits and you can talk to Indian chiefs."

"You boys let these cattle string out," he said to the men. "We ain't in no big hurry."

Augustus had ridden through the cattle and had come back with a count of slightly over twenty-six hundred.

"Make it twenty-six hundred cattle and two pigs," he said. "I guess we've seen the last of the dern Rio Grande. One of us ought to make a speech, Call. Think of how long we've rode this river."

Call was not willing to indulge him in any dramatics. He mounted the mare and went over to help the boys get the cattle started. It was

---

1. **remuda** (rə mōō′ də) *n.* group of extra saddle horses kept as a supply of remounts.
2. **the Brazos** (brä′ zəs) river in central and southeastern Texas.

aggrieved (ə grēvd′) *v.* offended; wronged

Thematic Connection
What does this group have in common with the characters in "The Outcasts of Poker Flat"?

✔**Reading Check**
Why are Bert and Needle unhappy?

not a hard task. Most of the cattle were still wild as antelope and instinctively moved away from the horsemen. In a few minutes they were on the trail, strung out for more than a mile. The point riders soon disappeared in the low brush.

Lippy and the Spettle boys were with the wagon. With the dust so bad, they intended to keep the horses a fair distance behind.

Bolivar sat on the wagon seat, his ten-gauge across his lap. In his experience trouble usually came quick, when it came, and he meant to keep the ten-gauge handy to discourage it.

Newt had heard much talk of dust, but had paid little attention to it until they actually started the cattle. Then he couldn't help noticing it, for there was nothing else to notice. The grass was sparse, and every hoof sent up its little spurt of dust. Before they had gone a mile he himself was white with it, and for moments actually felt lost, it was so thick. He had to tie the bandana around his nose to get a good breath. He understood why Dish and the other boys were so anxious to draw assignments near the front of the herd. If the dust was going to be that bad all the way, he might as well be riding to Montana with his eyes shut. He would see noth-

▲ Critical Viewing
Based on the descriptions in the selection, would you characterize this image of a cattle drive as realistic or romanticized? Explain. [Distinguish]

ing but his own horse and the few cattle that happened to be within ten yards of him. A grizzly bear could walk in and eat him and his horse both, and they wouldn't be missed until breakfast the next day.

But he had no intention of complaining. They were on their way, and he was part of the outfit. After waiting for the moment so long, what was a little dust?

Once in a while, though, he dropped back a little. His bandana got sweaty, and the dust caked on it so that he felt he was inhaling mud. He had to take it off and beat it against his leg once in a while. He was riding Mouse, who looked like he could use a bandana of his own. The dust seemed to make the heat worse, or else the heat made the dust worse.

The second time he stopped to beat his bandana, he happened to notice Sean leaning off his horse as if he were trying to vomit. The horse and Sean were both white, as if they had been rolled in powder, though the horse Sean rode was a dark bay.

"Are you hurt?" he asked anxiously.

"No, I was trying to spit," Sean said. "I've got some mud in my mouth. I didn't know it would be like this."

"I didn't either," Newt said.

"Well, we better keep up," he added nervously—he didn't want to neglect his responsibilities. Then to his dismay, he looked back and saw twenty or thirty cattle standing behind them. He had ridden right past them in the dust. He immediately loped back to get them, hoping the Captain hadn't noticed. When he turned back, two of the wild heifers spooked. Mouse, a good cow horse, twisted and jumped a medium-sized chaparral[3] bush in an effort to gain a step on the cows. Newt had not expected the jump and lost both stirrups, but fortunately diverted the heifers so that they turned back into the main herd. He found his heart was beating fast, partly because he had almost been thrown and partly because he had nearly left thirty cattle behind. With such a start, it seemed to him he would be lucky to get to Montana without disgracing himself.

Call and Augustus rode along together, some distance from the herd. They were moving through fairly open country, flats of chaparral with only here and there a strand of mesquite.[4] That would soon change: the first challenge would be the brush country, an almost impenetrable band of thick mesquite between them and San Antonio. Only a few of the hands were experienced in the brush, and a bad run of some kind might cost them hundreds of cattle.

"What do you think, Gus?" Call asked. "Think we can get through the brush, or had we better go around?"

Augustus looked amused. "Why, these cattle are like deer, only faster." he said. "They'll get through the brush fine. The problem will be with the hands. Half of them will probably get their eyes poked out."

"I still don't know what you think," Call said.

"The problem is, I ain't used to being consulted," Augustus said. "I'm usually sitting on the porch drinking whiskey at this hour. As for the brush, my choice would be to go through. It's that or go down to the coast and get et by the mosquitoes."

"Where do you reckon Jake will end up?" Call asked.

"In a hole in the ground, like you and me," Augustus said.

"I don't know why I ever ask you a question," Call said.

"Well, last time I seen Jake he had a thorn in his hand," Augustus said. "He was wishing he'd stayed in Arkansas and taken to his hanging."

They rode up on a little knobby hill and stopped for a moment to watch the cattle. The late sun shone through the dust cloud, making the white dust rosy. The riders to each side of the herd were spread wide, giving the cattle lots of room. Most of them were horned stock, thin and light, their hides a mixture of colors. The riders at the rear were all but hidden in the rosy dust.

"Them boys on the drags won't even be able to get down from their horses unless we take a spade and spade 'em off a little," Augustus said.

"It won't hurt 'em," Call said. "They're young."

Open Range, 1942, Maynard Dixon, Museum of Western Art, Denver, Colorado

---

3. **chaparral** (chap´ ə ral´) *n.* thicket of shrubs or thorny bushes.
4. **mesquite** (mes kēt´) *n.* type of small, thorny tree.

Thematic Connection
Which other selections in Part 3 make use of the exaggeration and dry wit that fill this exchange between Call and McCrae? Explain.

**Reading Check**
Why is Call concerned about the stretch of trail that the cowboys are about to go through?

In the clear late afternoon light they could see all the way back to Lonesome Dove and the river and Mexico. Augustus regretted not tying a jug to his saddle—he would have liked to sit on the little hill and drink for an hour. Although Lonesome Dove had not been much of a town, he felt sure that a little whiskey would have made him feel sentimental about it. Call merely sat on the hill, studying the cattle. It was clear to Augustus that he was not troubled in any way by leaving the border or the town.

"It's odd I partnered with a man like you, Call," Augustus said. "If we was to meet now instead of when we did, I doubt we'd have two words to say to one another."

"I wish it could happen, then, if it would hold you to two words," Call said. Though everything seemed peaceful, he had an odd, confused feeling at the thought of what they had undertaken. He had quickly convinced himself it was necessary, this drive. Fighting the Indians had been necessary, if Texas was to be settled. Protecting the border was necessary, else the Mexicans would have taken south Texas back.

A cattle drive, for all its difficulty, wasn't so imperative. He didn't feel the old sense of adventure, though perhaps it would come once they got beyond the settled country. Augustus, who could almost read his mind, almost read it as they were stopped on the little knob of a hill.

"I hope this is hard enough for you, Call," he said. "I hope it makes you happy. If it don't, I give up. Driving all these skinny cattle all that way is a funny way to maintain an interest in life, if you ask me."

"Well, I didn't," Call said.

"No, but then you seldom ask," Augustus said. "You should have died in the line of duty, Woodrow. You'd know how to do that fine. The problem is you don't know how to live."

"Whereas you do?" Call asked.

"Most certainly," Augustus said. "I've lived about a hundred to your one. I'll be a little riled if I end up being the one to die in the line of duty, because this ain't my duty and it ain't yours, either. This is just fortune hunting."

"Well, we wasn't finding one in Lonesome Dove," Call said. He saw Deets returning from the northwest, ready to lead them to the bedground. Call was glad to see him—he was tired of Gus and his talk. He spurred the mare on off the hill. It was only when he met Deets that he realized Augustus hadn't followed. He was still sitting on old Malaria, back on the little hill, watching the sunset and the cattle herd.

Connecting Literature Past and Present

1. Do you think the cattle drive on which Woodrow Call embarks fails to live up to his romantic expectations?

2. How does this fictional story compare with Miriam Davis Colt's account, "Heading West"?

3. Not all historical periods capture the modern imagination. Why do you think stories about the American West are still popular today?

Larry McMurtry

(b. 1936)

Larry McMurtry, a descendant of Texas cattle ranchers, published his first western when he was only twenty-six. In his many novels, McMurtry has trained a humorous, critical eye on the culture of the American West. Labeled by some critics as the creator of the "urban western," McMurtry first attracted attention as a new kind of writer of western novels who mixed the traditional elements of the genre with sharp social observation and a strong dose of dark humor.

PART 4 Living in a Changing World

Channel to the Mills, 1913, Edwin M. Dawes,
Minneapolis Institute of Arts

Living in a Changing World ◆ 631

Prepare to Read

The Story of an Hour

Kate Chopin (1850–1904)

Despite her conservative, aristocratic upbringing, Kate O'Flaherty Chopin (shō´ pan) became one of the most powerful and controversial writers of her time. In her stories, sketches, and novels, she not only captured the local color of Louisiana but also boldly explored the role of women in society.

Family Life Kate O'Flaherty was born in St. Louis, Missouri, the daughter of a wealthy businessman. When Kate was five years old, her father died in a railroad accident. The young Kate was taken out of school and educated at home for the next two years by her mother, grandmother, and great-grandmother. When she was twenty, Kate married Oscar Chopin, a Louisiana cotton trader. The couple settled in New Orleans, where they lived for ten years before moving to a plantation in rural northwestern Louisiana.

Tragedy Strikes In 1882, Chopin's husband died, leaving her to raise their six children on her own. Chopin carried on the work of the plantation alone for more than a year, using her knowledge of finance and developing skills as a business-woman. However, in 1884 she yielded to her mother's urgings, sold most of her holdings, and returned to St. Louis with her children. Her mother's sudden death in 1885 left Chopin in deep sorrow. It was at the suggestion of her family doctor, who was concerned about her emotional health, that she began to write fiction. Chopin kept St. Louis as her home for the rest of her life and devoted much of her energy to writing.

Chopin the Writer and Rebel Influenced by American Regionalists such as Sarah Orne Jewett, and fascinated by the mixture of cultures in Louisiana, Chopin focused on capturing the essence of life in Louisiana in her writing. Like most of her other works, Chopin's first novel, *At Fault* (1890), was set in a small Louisiana town inhabited by Creoles, descendants of the original French and Spanish settlers, and Cajuns, descendants of French Canadian settlers who arrived later. Through her vivid descriptions and use of dialect, Chopin captured the local color of the region. In her stories, published in *Bayou Folk* (1894) and *A Night In Acadie* (1897), she exhibited her deep understanding of the different attitudes and concerns of the Louisiana natives.

Her charming portraits of Louisiana life often obscured the fact that she explored themes considered radical at the time: the nature of marriage, racial prejudice, and women's desire for social, economic, and political equality. Chopin understood the risk she took in challenging social boundaries, but felt that true art required bravery. She once wrote, "The artist must possess the courageous soul that dares and defies."

The Awakening Chopin's finest novel, *The Awakening* (1899), is a psychological account of a woman's search for independence and fulfillment. Because the novel explored the issue of infidelity, it aroused a storm of protest. The book was severely attacked by critics and eventually banned. As a result, Chopin's reputation was badly damaged. Then, in the 1950s, *The Awakening* was resurrected. Today, the book is among the five most-read American novels in colleges and universities. Chopin is now considered an early practitioner of American Realism—a literary style that seeks to avoid sentimental depictions of life. She is widely respected for her portrayal of the psychology of women and her ability to capture local color.

Preview

Connecting to the Literature

Often, life-changing events—a chance encounter with someone who becomes important in our lives, the loss of a loved one, a sudden move to a new place—sneak up on us unexpectedly. The story you are about to read focuses on a woman's surprising reaction to a shocking piece of news.

Literary Analysis

Irony

Irony involves a contrast between what is stated and what is meant, or between what is expected and what actually happens. In literature, readers frequently encounter three types of irony:

- **Verbal irony** is the use of words to suggest the opposite of their usual meaning.
- **Dramatic irony** occurs when readers are aware of something that a character in a literary work does not know.
- **Situational irony** occurs when the outcome of an action or situation is very different from what one expects.

As you read, decide which type of irony best describes the events in this story.

Connecting Literary Elements

The **climax** is the high point of interest or suspense in a story. It also marks the moment at which the conflict is resolved. As in many other works of fiction or drama, the climax of "The Story of an Hour" involves a keen sense of irony.

Reading Strategy

Recognizing Ironic Details

The details of a story often lead readers to have certain expectations. When events are not resolved as details have led us to expect, we recognize a sense of irony. While reading "The Story of an Hour," use a chart like the one shown to note how specific details imply certain feelings, circumstances, or events that may not, in fact, be what they appear. After reading the story, note whether or not your expectations were met.

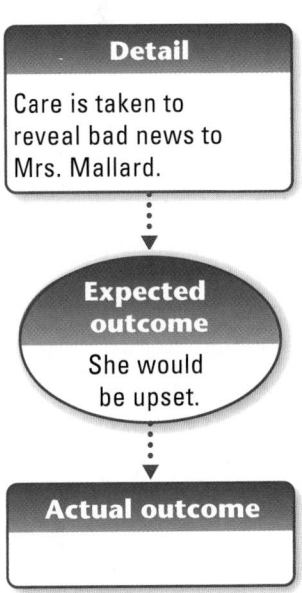

Detail

Care is taken to reveal bad news to Mrs. Mallard.

Expected outcome

She would be upset.

Actual outcome

Vocabulary Development

forestall (fôr stôl′) v. prevent by acting ahead of time (p. 636)

repression (ri presh′ ən) n. restraint (p. 637)

elusive (ē lōō′ siv) adj. hard to grasp (p. 637)

tumultuously (tōō mul′ chōō wəs lē) adv. in an agitated way (p. 637)

importunities (im′ pôr tōōn′ ə tēz) n. persistent requests or demands (p. 638)

The Story of an Hour

Kate Chopin

Afternoon in Piedmont, Xavier Martinez, Courtesy of the Oakland Museum

Background

"The Story of an Hour" was considered daring in the nineteenth century. The editors of at least two magazines refused the story because they thought it was immoral. They wanted Chopin to soften her female character, to make her less independent and unhappy in her marriage. Undaunted, Chopin continued to deal with issues of women's growth and emancipation in her writing, advancing ideas that are widely accepted today.

▶ **Critical Viewing** This story presents a "subtle and elusive" revelation. What connection do you see between the light shining through the uncovered portion of the window and such a discovery? **[Connect]**

*K*nowing that Mrs. Mallard was afflicted with a heart trouble, great care was taken to break to her as gently as possible the news of her husband's death.

It was her sister Josephine who told her, in broken sentences; veiled hints that revealed in half concealing. Her husband's friend Richards was there, too, near her. It was he who had been in the newspaper office when intelligence of the railroad disaster was received, with Brently Mallard's name leading the list of "killed." He had only taken the time to assure himself of its truth by a second telegram, and had hastened to <u>forestall</u> any less careful, less tender friend in bearing the sad message.

She did not hear the story as many women have heard the same, with a paralyzed inability to accept its significance. She wept at once, with sudden, wild abandonment, in her sister's arms. When the storm of grief had spent itself she went away to her room alone. She would have no one follow her.

There stood, facing the open window, a comfortable, roomy armchair. Into this she sank, pressed down by a physical exhaustion that haunted her body and seemed to reach into her soul.

She could see in the open square before her house the tops of trees that were all aquiver with the new spring life. The delicious breath of rain was in the air. In the street below a peddler was crying his wares. The notes of a distant song which someone was singing reached her faintly, and countless sparrows were twittering in the eaves.

There were patches of blue sky showing here and there through the clouds that had met and piled one above the other in the west facing her window.

She sat with her head thrown back upon the cushion of the chair, quite motionless, except when a sob came up into her throat and shook her, as a child who has cried itself to sleep continues to sob in its dreams.

forestall (fôr stôl´) *v.* prevent by acting ahead of time

Reading Strategy
Recognizing Ironic Details Considering the news she has just received, what is ironic about the details Mrs. Mallard notices through her window?

She was young, with a fair, calm face, whose lines bespoke <u>repression</u> and even a certain strength. But now there was a dull stare in her eyes, whose gaze was fixed away off yonder on one of those patches of blue sky. It was not a glance of reflection, but rather indicated a suspension of intelligent thought.

There was something coming to her and she was waiting for it, fearfully. What was it? She did not know; it was too subtle and <u>elusive</u> to name. But she felt it, creeping out of the sky, reaching toward her through the sounds, the scents, the color that filled the air.

Now her bosom rose and fell <u>tumultuously</u>. She was beginning to recognize this thing that was approaching to possess her, and she was striving to beat it back with her will—as powerless as her two white slender hands would have been.

When she abandoned herself, a little whispered word escaped her slightly parted lips. She said it over and over under her breath: "free, free, free!" The vacant stare and the look of terror that had followed it went from her eyes. They stayed keen and bright. Her pulses beat fast, and the coursing blood warmed and relaxed every inch of her body.

She did not stop to ask if it were or were not a monstrous joy that held her. A clear and exalted perception enabled her to dismiss the suggestion as trivial.

She knew that she would weep again when she saw the kind, tender hands folded in death; the face that had never looked save with love upon her, fixed and gray and dead. But she saw beyond that bitter moment a long procession of years to come that would belong to her absolutely. And she opened and spread her arms out to them in welcome.

There would be no one to live for her during those coming years; she would live for herself. There would be no powerful will bending hers in that blind persistence with which men and women believe they have a right to impose a private will upon a fellow creature. A kind intention or a cruel intention made the act seem no less a crime as she looked upon it in that brief moment of illumination.

And yet she had loved him—sometimes. Often she had not. What did it matter! What could love, the unsolved mystery, count for in face of this possession of self-assertion which she suddenly recognized as the strongest impulse of her being!

"Free! Body and soul free!" she kept whispering.

Josephine was kneeling before the closed door with her lips to the keyhole, imploring for admission. "Louise, open the door! I beg; open the door—you will make yourself ill. What are you doing, Louise? For heaven's sake open the door."

"Go away. I am not making myself ill." No; she was drinking in a very elixir of life[1] through that open window.

---

1. **elixir of life** (i liks´ ər) imaginary substance believed in medieval times to prolong life indefinitely.

repression (ri presh´ ən) *n.* restraint

elusive (ē loo´ siv) *adj.* hard to grasp

tumultuously (too mul´ choo əs lē) *adv.* in an agitated way

Reading Strategy
Recognizing Ironic Details What does the passage describing "a long procession of years" lead you to expect?

 **Reading Check**
What is the general state of Mrs. Mallard's health?

Her fancy was running riot along those days ahead of her. Spring days, and summer days, and all sorts of days that would be her own. She breathed a quick prayer that life might be long. It was only yesterday she had thought with a shudder that life might be long.

She arose at length and opened the door to her sister's <u>importunities</u>. There was a feverish triumph in her eyes, and she carried herself unwittingly like a goddess of Victory. She clasped her sister's waist, and together they descended the stairs. Richards stood waiting for them at the bottom.

Someone was opening the front door with a latchkey. It was Brently Mallard who entered, a little travel-stained, composedly carrying his gripsack[2] and umbrella. He had been far from the scene of accident, and did not know there had been one. He stood amazed at Josephine's piercing cry; at Richards's quick motion to screen him from the view of his wife.

But Richards was too late.

When the doctors came they said she had died of heart disease— of joy that kills.

importunities (im´ pôr tōōn´ i tēz) *n.* persistent requests or demands

---

2. **gripsack** (grip´ sak) *n.* small bag for holding clothes.

Review and Assess

Thinking About the Selection

1. **Respond:** Were you surprised by the end of the story? Explain why or why not.

2. **(a) Recall:** At the beginning of the story, what does the narrator call the ailment that afflicts Mrs. Mallard? **(b) Interpret:** What, in addition to a medical condition, might the narrator mean by this phrase?

3. **(a) Recall:** What does Mrs. Mallard see as she gazes out the window of her room? **(b) Connect:** In what ways does the scene outside Mrs. Mallard's window foreshadow the feelings that sweep over her as she sits in her chair?

4. **(a) Recall:** What word does Mrs. Mallard whisper to herself repeatedly? **(b) Infer:** What has Mrs. Mallard apparently resented about her marriage?

5. **(a) Recall:** According to the doctors, what is the cause of Mrs. Mallard's sudden death? **(b) Draw Conclusions:** What do you believe is the actual reason for Mrs. Mallard's death?

6. **(a) Speculate:** Why do you think Chopin does not elaborate more about Mrs. Mallard's death? **(b) Evaluate:** Is this choice effective? Explain.

7. **Evaluate:** Would "The Story of an Hour" seem believable as a modern tale? Explain.

Review and Assess

Literary Analysis

Irony

1. (a) In what ways is Mrs. Mallard's reaction to her husband's death an example of **situational irony?** (b) Do you think Mrs. Mallard is as surprised by her reaction as the reader is? Explain.

2. (a) In what ways is Mrs. Mallard's death an example of situational irony? (b) Note two details from earlier in the story that add to the poignancy of this ironic ending.

3. In what way is the diagnosis of Mrs. Mallard's cause of death an example of **dramatic irony?**

4. Use a chart like the one shown to examine elements of irony evident in the story's descriptive passages.

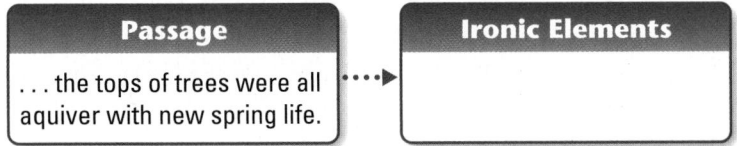

Passage	Ironic Elements
. . . the tops of trees were all aquiver with new spring life.	

Connecting Literary Elements

5. Review the story to identify the moment of **climax**.

6. What is ironic about the story's climax?

Reading Strategy

Recognizing Ironic Details

7. What **ironic details** lead you to believe that Mrs. Mallard will be truly grieved by her husband's death?

8. Which detail in the second paragraph makes Mr. Mallard's arrival at the end all the more ironic?

Extend Understanding

9. **Sociology Connection:** With her husband dead, Mrs. Mallard notes:

   "There would be no powerful will bending hers in that blind persistence with which men and women believe they have a right to impose a private will upon a fellow creature."

   Do you think this statement accurately reflects interactions between people in close relationships? Explain.

Integrate Language Skills

Vocabulary Development Lesson

Word Analysis: Anglo-Saxon Prefix *fore-*

The Anglo-Saxon prefix *fore-* means "before," in the sense of time, place, or condition. Using this knowledge, write a definition for each of the following words.

1. foretell
3. forestall
2. foreman
4. forefathers

Spelling Strategy

To form the plural of a word that ends in a consonant plus *y*, change the *y* to *i* and add *es*—for example, *importunity* becomes *importunities*. For words that end in a vowel plus *y*, add *s* to form the plural, as in *days* or *monkeys*. Write the plurals of the following words.

1. agency
2. attorney
3. penalty

Fluency: Word Choice

Replace the italicized words or phrases in the following sentences with the appropriate vocabulary word from the list on page 633.

1. Chopin gave in to her mother's *insistent pleas* and returned to St. Louis.
2. A doctor thought that writing would *head off* a slide into depression.
3. Chopin exposed the conventions of her time that kept women in a state of near constant *restraint*.
4. Her characters often lived *in a state of agitation*.
5. Outrage over one of her novels taught Chopin that acclaim can be *difficult to hold on to*.

Grammar and Style Lesson

Appositives and Appositive Phrases

An **appositive** is a noun or pronoun placed near another noun or pronoun to provide more information about it. When an appositive is accompanied by its own modifiers, it forms an **appositive phrase.**

If an appositive can be omitted from a sentence without altering its basic meaning, it must be set off by commas. If the appositive is essential to the sentence's meaning, commas are not used. Appositive phrases are always set off by commas or dashes.

Nonessential: Richards, the attorney, was also present.

Essential: The long novel *Moby-Dick* has a tragic ending.

Practice Rewrite each sentence below, incorporating the information given as an appositive.

1. Mrs. Mallard was not grieved by her husband's death. (*unconventional woman*)
2. She sank gratefully into the chair. (*comfortable, roomy armchair*)
3. She felt like a new woman as she left her room. (*the goddess of Victory*)
4. Her friend tried to shield the visitor from Mrs. Mallard's sight. (Richards)
5. Though "travel-stained," the person at the door was very much alive. (*Brently Mallard*)

Writing Application Write a paragraph in which you use at least three appositives or appositive phrases to describe three people.

W/G *Prentice Hall Writing and Grammar Connection: Chapter 19, Section 1*

Writing Lesson

Reflective Essay

In a reflective essay, a writer describes personal experiences and conveys his or her feelings about them. Draw upon your memory and observations to write your own "Story of an Hour" about a moment when your life dramatically changed. As you write your essay, strive for a personal tone.

Prewriting   To gather details for your essay, use a diagram like the one shown. Write your topic in the center circle and then write your observations and feelings about the topic on spokes radiating from the circle.

Model: Gathering Details

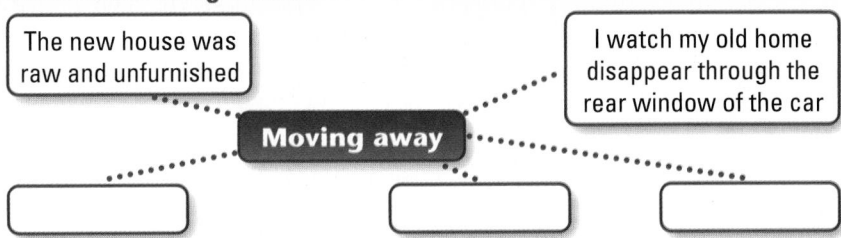

Drafting   Organize the details in either chronological order or order of importance. Use words and phrases that come naturally, and write honestly about your subject.

Revising   Read your essay, focusing on sections that could be made clearer. Add or eliminate details to strengthen the overall impression.

Prentice Hall Writing and Grammar Connection: Chapter 4, Section 2

Extension Activities

Listening and Speaking   What might Mrs. Mallard have made of her life if her husband had not returned? Present a **soliloquy** in which she reflects on her life ten years later. As you work, address these questions:

- Has Mrs. Mallard's heart trouble improved, or not?
- What has it meant to "live for herself"?

Create an authentic voice for Mrs. Mallard, so that she is a believable extension of Chopin's character.

Research and Technology   Research the status of women in another culture, and present an **oral report** comparing women's lives in the United States with those in the culture you have researched. Use a variety of research tools, including the Internet. After your report, lead your class in a discussion of the issues you have raised.

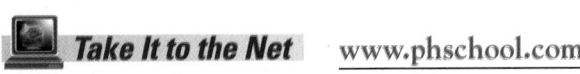 **Take It to the Net**   www.phschool.com

Go online for an additional research activity using the Internet.

Prepare to Read

April Showers

Edith Wharton (1862–1937)

Colorful Old New York, the high society of London and Paris, the French Riviera—these settings, from the late nineteenth century through the 1930s, were all part of Edith Wharton's world. They also played an important role in the creation of her remarkable literary career and the more than fifty volumes she published.

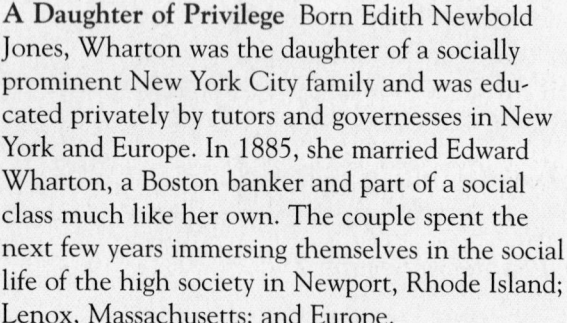

A Daughter of Privilege Born Edith Newbold Jones, Wharton was the daughter of a socially prominent New York City family and was educated privately by tutors and governesses in New York and Europe. In 1885, she married Edward Wharton, a Boston banker and part of a social class much like her own. The couple spent the next few years immersing themselves in the social life of the high society in Newport, Rhode Island; Lenox, Massachusetts; and Europe.

Surprisingly, it was on the advice of a doctor that Wharton began to write fiction. Wharton was caring for her husband, known as Teddy, who had become chronically ill, and the doctor advised Wharton to take up writing as a way to relieve stress. Her first stories appeared in *Scribner's* magazine. Several volumes of her fiction were published around the turn of the century. However, it was her best-selling novel *The House of Mirth* (1905)—a devastating portrait of a young woman who tries and fails to survive in New York high society—that established her as an important writer. It was well received by critics and reached a wide audience.

Watching the Shift in Power Wharton was a master at re-creating the staid, rule-bound atmosphere of the upper-class society of her time. As a member of that elite, Wharton witnessed the transfer of wealth and power from the families of her friends to the new masters of the Industrial Revolution. She observed the lack of energy and purpose among the members of her own class. Even though her group maintained a strict code of honor and morality, it was not enough to stop the rise of what she considered the amoral and vulgar robber barons. This disruption of the older class system is the background for much of her fiction.

An Expatriate Writer In 1913, Wharton moved to Paris. She began a friendship with the novelist Henry James, who became her literary mentor, as well as with other writers who helped her refine her work. As World War I loomed, she produced some of her finest novels: *Ethan Frome* (1911), *The Reef* (1912), and *The Custom of the Country* (1913). During the war, Wharton remained in France and wrote little. Instead, she organized aid for Belgian refugees. Wharton also collected American money for the cause well before America entered the war. She received honors from the French government for her efforts.

Age of Innocence In 1920, her novel *The Age of Innocence*, which more than seventy years later was made into a popular movie, won the Pulitzer Prize. Wharton also published *Old New York* (1924), *The Mother's Recompense* (1925), and 85 short stories. In addition, she published an autobiography, *A Backward Glance*, in 1934. In her fiction, which continues to attract readers and earn critical acclaim, Wharton explores the conflict between money and morality and exposes the cruelty of the social "game," with its rivalries, rules, and punishments.

Wharton continued to write until her death in 1937. She is buried in the American cemetery at Versailles in France.

Preview

Connecting to the Literature

It takes courage to risk having your work criticized or rejected. In this story, a young writer braves the world of publishing—and gets not one surprise, but two.

Literary Analysis

Elements of Plot

Like most short story writers, Wharton brings together the **elements of plot** to lead readers through the events of a story.

- The **exposition** introduces characters, setting, and situation.
- An event sets up the **conflict,** or struggle.
- During the **rising action,** the conflict is developed.
- The conflict increases until it reaches a **climax,** or high point of suspense.
- The events that follow the climax are the **falling action**.
- The story ends with the **resolution** of the central conflict.

As you read, use a chart like the one shown to record the events as they develop in Wharton's story.

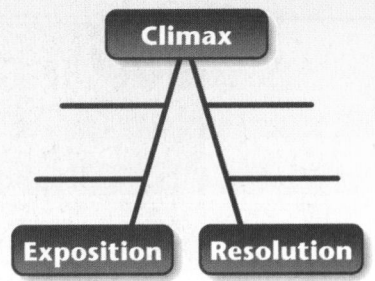

Connecting Literary Elements

In his literary criticism, Edgar Allan Poe, the great horror writer, wrote that a short story should create "a certain unique or **single effect.**" His ideas, which have influenced writers ever since, state that each character, incident, and detail in a story should contribute to the single effect. As you read "April Showers," note the details Wharton includes and consider what single effect the story creates.

Reading Strategy

Anticipating Events

As you read this story, you will probably find yourself **anticipating events**—looking forward to what happens next. Anticipating events is more emotional than the logical process of predicting. When you anticipate events, you connect to characters as you watch their lives unfold.

Vocabulary Development

admonitory (ad män′ i tôr′ ē) *adj.* warning (p. 645)

manuscript (man′ yoo skript′) *n.* document submitted to a publisher (p. 645)

retrospective (re′ trə spek′ tiv) *adj.* looking back on or directed to the past (p. 646)

antagonism (an tag′ ə niz′ əm) *n.* hostility (p. 647)

contrition (kən trish′ ən) *n.* remorse for having done wrong (p. 647)

commiseration (kə miz′ ər ā′ shən) *n.* sympathy (p. 652)

April Showers

Edith Wharton

Memories, 1885–86, William Merritt Chase, Munson–Williams–Proctor Institute Museum of Art, Utica, New York

Background

The publishing world of the late nineteenth and early twentieth centuries was far different from today's book world. If Wharton's novels were published today, they would stand on bookstore shelves crowded with many other novels. Wharton's publisher would probably send her on a whirlwind book tour; you might even hear her books read on audiotape by a famous actor. Around the turn of the century, however, things were different. Novels were customarily serialized in magazines and newspapers. *The House of Mirth,* one of Wharton's most famous novels, appeared in *Scribner's* magazine before it was published as a book in 1905. Readers of the time would eagerly await the next monthly installment of the latest novel by their favorite author. Some great writers, including England's Charles Dickens earlier in the century, established their reputations this way.

"But Guy's heart slept under the violets on Muriel's grave."

It was a beautiful ending; Theodora had seen girls cry over last chapters that weren't half as pathetic. She laid her pen aside and read the words over, letting her voice linger on the fall of the sentence; then, drawing a deep breath, she wrote across the foot of the page the name by which she had decided to become known in literature—Gladys Glyn.

Downstairs the library clock struck two. Its muffled thump sounded like an <u>admonitory</u> knock against her bedroom floor. Two o'clock! and she had promised her mother to be up early enough to see that the buttons were sewn on Johnny's reefer, and that Kate had her cod-liver oil before starting for school!

Lingeringly, tenderly she gathered up the pages of her novel—there were five hundred of them—and tied them with the blue satin ribbon that her Aunt Julia had given her. She had meant to wear the ribbon with her new dotted muslin on Sundays, but this was putting it to a nobler use. She bound it round her <u>manuscript</u>, tying the ends in a pretty bow. Theodora was clever at making bows, and could have trimmed hats beautifully, had not all her spare moments been given to literature. Then, with a last look at the precious pages, she sealed and addressed the package. She meant to send it off next morning to the Home Circle. She knew it would be hard to obtain access to a paper which numbered so many popular authors among its contributors, but she had been encouraged to make the venture by something her Uncle James had said the last time he had come down from Boston.

He had been telling his brother, Doctor Dace, about his new house out at Brookline. Uncle James was prosperous, and was always moving into new houses with more "modern improvements." Hygiene was his passion, and he migrated in the wake of sanitary plumbing.

◀ **Critical Viewing** What emotions does this portrait evoke? In what ways do they relate to Theodora's literary hopes and dreams? **[Connect]**

admonitory (ad män´ i tôr´ ē) *adj.* warning

manuscript (man´ yōō skript´) *n.* document submitted to a publisher

 **Reading Check**

What prevents Theodora from helping her mother?

"The bathrooms alone are worth the money," he was saying, cheerfully, "although it is a big rent. But then, when a man's got no children to save up for—" he glanced compassionately round Doctor Dace's crowded table "—and it is something to be in a neighborhood where the drainage is A-one. That's what I was telling our neighbor. Who do you suppose she is, by the way?" He smiled at Theodora. "I rather think that young lady knows all about her. Ever heard of Kathleen Kyd?"

Kathleen Kyd! The famous "society novelist," the creator of more "favorite heroines" than all her predecessors put together had ever turned out, the author of *Fashion and Passion, An American Duchess, Rhona's Revolt.* Was there any intelligent girl from Maine to California whose heart would not have beat faster at the mention of that name?

"Why, yes," Uncle James was saying, "Kathleen Kyd lives next door. Frances G. Wollop is her real name, and her husband's a dentist. She's a very pleasant, sociable kind of woman; you'd never think she was a writer. Ever hear how she began to write? She told me the whole story. It seems she was a saleswoman in a store, working on starvation wages, with a mother and a consumptive sister to support. Well, she wrote a story one day, just for fun, and sent it to the *Home Circle.* They'd never heard of her, of course, and she never expected to hear from them. She did, though. They took the story and passed their plate for more. She became a regular contributor and eventually was known all over the country. Now she tells me her books bring her in about ten thousand a year. Rather more than you and I can boast of, eh, John? Well, I hope *this* household doesn't contribute to her support." He glanced sharply at Theodora. "I don't believe in feeding youngsters on sentimental trash; it's like sewer gas—doesn't smell bad, and infects the system without your knowing it."

Theodora listened breathlessly. Kathleen Kyd's first story had been accepted by the *Home Circle,* and they had asked for more! Why should Gladys Glyn be less fortunate? Theodora had done a great deal of novel reading—far more than her parents were aware of—and felt herself competent to pronounce upon the quality of her own work. She was almost sure that "April Showers" was a remarkable book. If it lacked Kathleen Kyd's lightness of touch, it had an emotional intensity never achieved by that brilliant writer. Theodora did not care to amuse her readers; she left that to more frivolous talents. Her aim was to stir the depths of human nature, and she felt she had succeeded. It was a great thing for a girl to be able to feel that about her first novel. Theodora was only seventeen; and she remembered, with a touch of <u>retrospective</u> compassion, that George Eliot[1] had not become famous till she was nearly forty.

No, there was no doubt about the merit of "April Showers." But would not an inferior work have had a better chance of success? Theodora recalled the early struggles of famous authors, the notorious

---

1. **George Eliot** pseudonym of Mary Ann Evans (1819–1880), a celebrated English novelist.

<u>antagonism</u> of publishers and editors to any new writer of exceptional promise. Would it not be wiser to write the book down to the average reader's level, reserving for some later work the great "effects" into which she had thrown all the fever of her imagination? The thought was sacrilege! Never would she lay hands on the sacred structure she had reared; never would she resort to the inartistic expedient of modifying her work to suit the popular taste. Better obscure failure than a vulgar triumph. The great authors never stooped to such concessions, and Theodora felt herself included in their ranks by the firmness with which she rejected all thought of conciliating an unappreciative public. The manuscript should be sent as it was.

She woke with a start and a heavy sense of apprehension. The *Home Circle* had refused "April Showers!" No, that couldn't be it; there lay the precious manuscript, waiting to be posted. What was it, then? Ah, that ominous thump below stairs—nine o'clock striking! It was Johnny's buttons!

She sprang out of bed in dismay. She had been so determined not to disappoint her mother about Johnny's buttons! Mrs. Dace, helpless from chronic rheumatism, had to entrust the care of the household to her eldest daughter; and Theodora honestly meant to see that Johnny had his full complement of buttons, and that Kate and Bertha went to school tidy. Unfortunately, the writing of a great novel leaves little time or memory for the lesser obligations of life, and Theodora usually found that her good intentions matured too late for practical results.

Her <u>contrition</u> was softened by the thought that literary success would enable her to make up for all the little negligences of which she was guilty. She meant to spend all her money on her family; and already she had visions of a wheeled chair for her mother, a fresh wallpaper for the doctor's shabby office, bicycles for the girls, and Johnny's establishment at a boarding school where sewing on his buttons would be included in the curriculum. If her parents could have guessed her intentions, they would not have found fault with her as they did; and Doctor Dace, on this particular morning, would not have looked up to say, with his fagged, ironical air:

"I suppose you didn't get home from the ball till morning?"

Theodora's sense of being in the right enabled her to take the thrust with a dignity that would have awed the unfeeling parent of fiction.

"I'm sorry to be late, father," she said.

Doctor Dace, who could never be counted on to behave like a father in a book, shrugged his shoulders impatiently.

"Your sentiments do you credit, but they haven't kept your mother's breakfast warm."

"Hasn't mother's tray gone up yet?"

"Who was to take it, I should like to know? The girls came down so late that I had to hustle them off before they'd finished breakfast, and Johnny's hands were so dirty that I sent him back to his room to make himself decent. It's a pretty thing for the doctor's children to be the dirtiest little savages in Norton!"

antagonism (an tag′ ə niz′ əm) *n.* hostility

Literary Analysis
Elements of Plot Where does the exposition end and the rising action begin?

contrition (kən trish′ ən) *n.* remorse for having done wrong

Literary Analysis
Elements of Plot and Single Effect What single effect has the story developed up to this point? Which details help you decide?

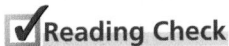
Reading Check

What are some of Theodora's family responsibilities?

Theodora had hastily prepared her mother's tray, leaving her own breakfast untouched. As she entered the room upstairs, Mrs. Dace's patient face turned to her with a smile much harder to bear than her father's reproaches.

"Mother, I'm so sorry—"

"No matter, dear. I suppose Johnny's buttons kept you. I can't think what that boy does to his clothes!"

Theodora sat the tray down without speaking. It was impossible to own to having forgotten Johnny's buttons without revealing the cause of her forgetfulness. For a few weeks longer she must bear to be misunderstood; then—ah, then if her novel were accepted, how gladly would she forget and forgive! But what if it were refused? She turned aside to hide the dismay that flushed her face. Well, then she would admit the truth—she would ask her parents' pardon, and settle down without a murmur to an obscure existence of mending and combing.

She had said to herself that after the manuscript had been sent, she would have time to look after the children and catch up with the mending; but she had reckoned without the postman. He came three times a day; for an hour before each ring she was too excited to do anything but wonder if he would bring an answer this time, and for an hour afterward she moved about in a leaden stupor of disappointment. The children had never been so trying. They seemed to be always coming to pieces, like cheap furniture; one would have supposed they had been put together with bad glue. Mrs. Dace worried herself ill over Johnny's tatters, Bertha's bad marks at school, and Kate's open abstention from cod-liver oil; and Doctor Dace, coming back late from a long round of visits to a fireless office with a smoky lamp, called out furiously to know if Theodora would kindly come down and remove the "East, West, home's best" that hung above the empty grate.

In the midst of it all, Miss Sophy Brill called. It was very kind of her to come, for she was the busiest woman in Norton. She made it her duty to look after other people's affairs, and there was not a house in town but had the benefit of her personal supervision. She generally came when things were going wrong, and the sight of her bonnet on the doorstep was a surer sign of calamity than a crepe bow on the bell. After she left, Mrs. Dace looked very sad, and the doctor punished Johnny for warbling down the entry:

> "Miss Sophy Brill
> Is a bitter pill!"

while Theodora, locking herself in her room, resolved with tears that she would never write another novel.

The week was a long nightmare. Theodora could neither eat nor sleep. She was up early enough, but instead of looking after the children and seeing that breakfast was ready, she wandered down the road to meet the postman, and came back wan and empty-handed, oblivious of her morning duties. She had no idea how long the suspense would last; but she didn't see how authors could live if they were kept waiting more than a week.

Then, suddenly, one afternoon—she never quite knew how or when it happened—she found herself with a *Home Circle* envelope in her hands, and her dazzled eyes flashing over a wild dance of words that wouldn't settle down and make sense.

"Dear Madam:" [They called her *Madam!* And then; yes, the words were beginning to fall into line now.] "Your novel, 'April Showers,' has been received, and we are glad to accept it on the usual terms. A serial on which we were counting for immediate publication has been delayed by the author's illness, and the first chapters of 'April Showers' will therefore appear in our midsummer number. Thanking you for favoring us with your manuscript, we remain," and so forth.

Theodora found herself in the wood beyond the schoolhouse. She was kneeling on the ground, brushing aside the dead leaves and pressing her lips to the little bursting green things that pushed up eager tips through last year's decay. It was spring—spring! Everything was crowding toward the light and in her own heart hundreds of germinating hopes had burst into sudden leaf. She wondered if the thrust of those little green fingers hurt the surface of the earth as her springing raptures hurt—yes, actually hurt!—her hot, constricted breast! She looked up through interlacing boughs at a tender, opaque blue sky full of the coming of a milky moon. She seemed enveloped in an atmosphere of loving comprehension. The brown earth throbbed with her joy, the treetops trembled with it, and a sudden star broke through the branches with an audible "I know!"

Theodora, on the whole, behaved very well. Her mother cried, her father whistled and said he supposed he must put up with grounds in his coffee now, and be thankful if he ever got a hot meal again; while the children took the most deafening and harassing advantage of what seemed a sudden suspension of the laws of nature.

Within a week everybody in Norton knew that Theodora had written a novel, and that it was coming out in the *Home Circle.* On Sundays, when she walked up the aisle, her friends dropped their prayer books and the soprano sang false in her excitement. Girls with more pin money than Theodora had ever dreamed of copied her hats and imitated her way of speaking. The local paper asked her for a poem; her old school teachers stopped to shake hands and grew shy over their congratulations; and Miss Sophy Brill came to call. She had put on her Sunday bonnet and her manner was almost abject. She ventured, very timidly, to ask her young friend how she wrote, whether it "just came to her," and if she had found that the kind of pen she used made any difference; and wound up by begging Theodora to write a sentiment in her album.

Even Uncle James came down from Boston to talk the wonder over. He called Theodora a "sly baggage," and proposed that she should give him her earnings to invest in a new patent grease-trap company. From what Kathleen Kyd had told him, he thought Theodora would

Reading Strategy
Anticipating Events
What event do you and Theodora anticipate as she opens the envelope?

✓ **Reading Check**

What exciting news does Theodora receive?

probably get a thousand dollars for her story. He concluded by suggesting that she should base her next romance on the subject of sanitation, making the heroine nearly die of sewer gas poisoning because her parents won't listen to the handsome young doctor next door, when he warns them that their plumbing is out of order. That was a subject that would interest everybody, and do a lot more good than the sentimental trash most women wrote.

At last the great day came. Theodora had left an order with the bookseller for the midsummer number of the *Home Circle* and before the shop was open she was waiting on the sidewalk. She clutched the precious paper and ran home without opening it. Her excitement was almost more than she could bear. Not heeding her father's call to breakfast, she rushed upstairs and locked herself in her room. Her hands trembled so that she could hardly turn the pages. At last—yes, there it was: "April Showers."

The paper dropped from her hands. What name had she read beneath the title? Had her emotion blinded her?

"April Showers, by Kathleen Kyd."

Kathleen Kyd! Oh, cruel misprint! Oh, dastardly typographer! Through tears of rage and disappointment Theodora looked again; yes, there was no mistaking the hateful name. Her glance ran on. She found herself reading a first paragraph that she had never seen before. She read farther. All was strange. The horrible truth burst upon her: *It was not her story!*

She never knew how she got back to the station. She struggled through the crowd on the platform, and a gold-banded arm pushed her into the train just starting for Norton. It would be dark when she reached home; but that didn't matter—nothing mattered now. She sank into her seat, closing her eyes in the vain attempt to shut out the vision of the last few hours; but minute by minute memory forced her to relive it; she felt like a rebellious school child dragged forth to repeat the same detested "piece."

Although she did not know Boston well, she had made her way easily enough to the *Home Circle* building; at least, she supposed she had, since she remembered nothing till she found herself ascending the editorial stairs as easily as one does incredible things in dreams. She must have walked very fast, for her heart was beating furiously, and she had barely breath to whisper the editor's name to a young man who looked out at her from a glass case, like a zoological specimen. The young man led her past other glass cases containing similar specimens to an inner enclosure which seemed filled by an enormous presence. Theodora felt herself enveloped in the presence, submerged by it, gasping for air as she sank under its rising surges.

Women and Publishing

Theodora had dreams of seeing her name and her work in print. However, there was little opportunity for women in the 1800s who harbored such dreams—they were merely expected to tend to the home.

Magazines such as *Women's Home Companion, The Ladies World,* and *Ladies' Home Journal* emerged in the 1800s as prospective forums for women's literary works. Although these publications were popular, they focused largely on housekeeping issues, fashion, and etiquette instead of literature. For example, a March 1894 article in *Ladies' Home Journal* gave instruction on "Wedding Etiquette" and "The Art of Dressing the Bride."

Gradually fragments of speech floated to the surface. "'April Showers?' Mrs. Kyd's new serial? Your manuscript, you say? You have a letter from me? The name, please? Evidently some unfortunate misunderstanding. One moment." And then a bell ringing, a zoological specimen ordered to unlock a safe, her name asked for again, the manuscript, her own precious manuscript, tied with Aunt Julia's ribbon, laid on the table before her, and her outcries, her protests, her interrogations, drowned in a flood of bland apology: "An unfortunate accident—Mrs. Kyd's manuscript received the same day—extraordinary coincidence in the choice of a title—duplicate answers sent by mistake—Miss Dace's novel hardly suited to their purpose—should of course have been returned—regrettable oversight—accidents would happen—sure she understood."

The voice went on, like the steady pressure of a surgeon's hand on a shrieking nerve. When it stopped she was in the street. A cab nearly ran her down, and a car bell jangled furiously in her ears. She clutched her manuscript, carrying it tenderly through the crowd, like a live thing that had been hurt. She could not bear to look at its soiled edges and the ink stain on Aunt Julia's ribbon.

The train stopped with a jerk and she opened her eyes. It was dark, and by the windy flare of gas on the platform she saw the Norton passengers getting out. She stood up stiffly and followed them. A warm wind blew into her face the fragrance of the summer woods, and she remembered how, two months earlier, she had knelt among the dead leaves, pressing her lips to the first shoots of green. Then for the first time she thought of home. She had fled away in the morning without a word, and her heart sank at the thought of her mother's fears. And her father—how angry he would be! She bent her head under the coming storm of his derision.

The night was cloudy, and as she stepped into the darkness beyond the station a hand was slipped in hers. She stood still, too weary to feel frightened, and a voice said, quietly:

"Don't walk so fast, child. You look tired."

"Father!" Her hand dropped from his, but he recaptured it and drew it through his arm. When she found voice, it was to whisper, "You were at the station?"

"It's such a good night I thought I'd stroll down and meet you."

Her arm trembled against his. She could not see his face in the dimness, but the light of his cigar looked down on her like a friendly eye, and she took courage to falter out: "Then you knew—"

"That you'd gone to Boston? Well, I rather thought you had."

They walked on slowly, and presently he added, "You see, you left the *Home Circle* lying in your room."

How she blessed the darkness and the muffled sky! She could not have borne the scrutiny of the tiniest star.

"Then mother wasn't very much frightened?"

"Why, no, she didn't appear to be. She's been busy all day over some toggery of Bertha's."

Literary Analysis
Elements of Plot
What details indicate that Theodora's mood is different when she returns from Boston?

Reading Strategy
Anticipating Events What event are you anticipating during Theodora's conversation with her father?

✔**Reading Check**

What happens in Boston?

Theodora choked. "Father, I'll—" She groped for words, but they eluded her. "I'll do things—differently; I haven't meant—" Suddenly she heard herself bursting out: "It was all a mistake, you know—about my story. They didn't want it; they won't have it!" and she shrank back involuntarily from his impending mirth.

She felt the pressure of his arm, but he didn't speak, and she figured his mute hilarity. They moved on in silence. Presently he said:

"It hurts a bit just at first, doesn't it?"

"O father!"

He stood still, and the gleam of his cigar showed a face of unexpected participation.

"You see I've been through it myself."

"You, father? You?"

"Why, yes. Didn't I ever tell you? I wrote a novel once. I was just out of college, and didn't want to be a doctor. No; I wanted to be a genius, so I wrote a novel."

The doctor paused, and Theodora clung to him in a mute passion of <u>commiseration</u>. It was as if a drowning creature caught a live hand through the murderous fury of the waves.

"Father—O father!"

"It took me a year—a whole year's hard work; and when I'd finished it the public wouldn't have it, either; not at any price and that's why I came down to meet you, because I remembered my walk home."

Reading Strategy
Anticipating Events
Do you find Dr. Dace's reaction surprising in any way? Explain.

commiseration (kə miz´ ər ā´ shən) *n.* sympathy

Review and Assess

Thinking About the Selection

1. **Respond:** Did this story surprise you? Explain.

2. **(a) Recall:** What is Theodora's job in the family?
   (b) Evaluate: Does she do her job well? Why or why not?

3. **(a) Recall:** As the story begins, what does Theodora hope to accomplish? **(b) Analyze:** Does Theodora feel confident about her ability and her hopes? Support your answer.

4. **(a) Recall:** In what way does the acceptance of Theodora's story change the way others behave toward her?
   (b) Interpret: Do you think it changes Theodora? Explain.

5. **(a) Recall:** What does Theodora do when she sees that the story in the magazine is not her story? **(b) Relate:** Would you have acted differently? Explain.

6. **(a) Recall:** What is Theodora's father's reaction to her experience? **(b) Assess:** What do you think is the importance of Doctor Dace in the story?

7. **Take a Position:** Do you think Theodora was treated fairly by the publishing company? Explain.

Review and Assess

Literary Analysis

Elements of Plot

1. Describe the central **conflict** of this story.
2. What incident introduces the conflict?
3. What is the **climax** of the story? Explain.
4. What events make up the story's **falling action**?

Connecting Literary Elements

5. (a) Review the following details to state the single effect the story creates.

   - Theodora has a blue satin ribbon around her novel.
   - Kathleen Kyd's first story is accepted by *Home Circle*.
   - Theodora does not do her chores.
   - *Home Circle's* offices are in Boston, a sophisticated city.

   (b) Explain the ways in which each detail contributes to the effect you have identified.

Reading Strategy

Anticipating Events

6. What was your emotional response to the letter Theodora received from *Home Circle* magazine? Explain.
7. What did you think would happen next?
8. How did the news that *Home Circle* had published the wrong story affect your sense of anticipation?
9. Using a chart like the one shown, find three passages in the story in which you **anticipated** what would happen based on what you had previously read.

Event	What You Thought Would Happen
1.	
2.	
3.	

Extend Understanding

10. **Career Connection:** If Theodora were trying to get published today, what options besides magazines might she explore?

Quick Review

The **elements of plot** follow these stages: The **exposition** introduces a story's characters, setting, and situation. The **conflict** is the internal or external struggle in a story. The events of the **rising action** lead to a **climax**, or high point, in a story. The events that occur after the climax are called the **falling action**. The **resolution** is the end of the central conflict.

In writing constructed to achieve a **single effect**, every character, event, and detail contributes to an overall mood or idea.

When you **anticipate events**, you connect to characters' lives and look forward to what might happen next.

 Take It to the Net
www.phschool.com
Take the interactive self-test online to check your understanding of the selection.

Integrate Language Skills

Vocabulary Development Lesson

Word Analysis: Latin Root -man-/-manu-

The Latin root -man-/-manu- means "hand," so *manuscript* literally means "a handwritten document." Using your knowledge of this root, define the following words.

1. manufacture
2. manual
3. manipulate
4. emancipate

Spelling Strategy

The suffix *-ory* is preceded by the letter *t* in many adjectives formed from verbs: *admonish* becomes *admonitory* and *accuse* becomes *accusatory*. Write the adjective that is formed from each verb:

1. anticipate
2. manipulate
3. contribute
4. reform

Concept Development: Synonyms

Write the letter of the word closest in meaning to each of the following words from the vocabulary list on page 643.

1. admonitory: (a) sorry (b) warning (c) financial
2. retrospective: (a) futuristic (b) under (c) back
3. antagonism: (a) hostility (b) fright (c) arrogance
4. contrition: (a) regret (b) jocularity (c) passivity
5. manuscript: (a) draft (b) map (c) autograph
6. commiseration: (a) wrath (b) sympathy (c) angst

Grammar and Style Lesson

Gerund Phrases

A **gerund phrase** is a group of words serving as a noun and consisting of a gerund (the *-ing* verb form) and its modifiers or complements. Like nouns, gerund phrases function as subjects, direct objects, subject complements, and objects of prepositions.

Subject: *Writing short stories* is my hobby.

Direct Object: They exchanged their *writing about characters.*

Indirect Object: She gives her *writing about challenges* full attention.

Object of Preposition: She'd do anything for better *writing about themes.*

Practice In each numbered item below, underline at least one gerund phrase and identify its function in the sentence.

1. Unfortunately, the writing of a great novel leaves little time or memory for the lesser obligations of life . . .
2. . . . instead of looking after the children and seeing that breakfast was ready . . .
3. Theodora's sense of being in the right enabled her . . .
4. . . . there was no mistaking the hateful name.
5. . . . there is no forgetting the terrible thing that was done.

Writing Application Write a paragraph about a favorite sport, using at least three gerund phrases to explain how it is played.

W/G *Prentice Hall Writing and Grammar Connection: Chapter 19, Section 2*

Writing Lesson

Personal Narrative

Most writers experience rejection many times before publishing. Dr. Dace is sympathetic to Theodora because he had faced such rejection himself. As Dr. Dace, write a personal narrative explaining your experience as a struggling writer, and applying it to your relationship with your daughter.

Prewriting Reread the last three lines of the story. Then, as Dr. Dace, list details of the events that led to the rejection of your manuscript. Jot down some of the feelings associated with that rejection.

Drafting Writing in the first-person, refer to your notes and describe the experience and its effect on you. Use carefully chosen language to describe the feelings associated with it.

Revising Reread your narrative, making sure you have included sensory descriptions to make your experience more vivid. End on a positive note, with pointers about working toward a dream.

Model: Elaborating to Add Emotional Depth

I know well the heartache of seeing your hard work treated as if it were worthless. I will never forget the day my own manuscript was rejected. I thought my whole world had ended. I could hardly speak for days.

> Sensory descriptions such as *heartache* and *I could hardly speak* add emotional depth.

 Prentice Hall Writing and Grammar Connection: Chapter 5, Section 2

Extension Activities

Speaking and Listening Imagine that Theodora's neighbors throw a surprise party to celebrate her story. As Theodora, write a brief **speech** explaining to your neighbors what happened in Boston. Be sure to include the following details:

- The reason for going to Boston
- Your discussion with the publisher
- The lessons you learned from your ordeal

After rehearsing, deliver the speech to your class.

Research and Technology Research the ways in which publishing has expanded since Wharton's time. Modern publishing encompasses print media, such as newspapers, books, and magazines, as well as multimedia produced for CD-ROM and the Internet. Create a **flowchart** to highlight the new facets of publishing.

 Take It to the Net www.phschool.com

Go online for an additional research activity using the Internet.

Prepare to Read

Douglass ◆ We Wear the Mask

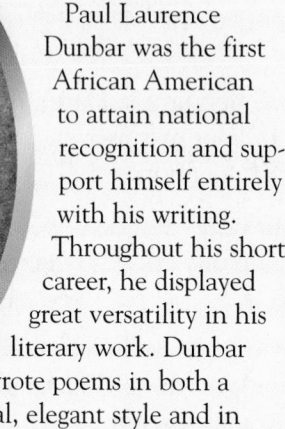

Paul Laurence Dunbar (1872–1906)

Paul Laurence Dunbar was the first African American to attain national recognition and support himself entirely with his writing. Throughout his short career, he displayed great versatility in his literary work. Dunbar wrote poems in both a formal, elegant style and in regional dialect. He also wrote four novels and four volumes of short stories.

A Literary Child Dunbar was born in Dayton, Ohio, the son of former slaves. Encouraged by his mother, he began writing poetry at an early age. During high school, Dunbar, who was the only African American student in his class, frequently recited his poetry during school assemblies. He also served as president of the literary society, class poet, and editor of the school newspaper.

Dunbar Attains Recognition Following his graduation, Dunbar sought work in a legal office or a newspaper, but he found it difficult because of his race. He finally took a job as an elevator operator, earning four dollars a week and supporting himself while continuing to write. He first earned recognition among writers and critics in 1892, when he gave a poetry reading during a meeting of the Western Association of Writers. A year later, he took out a loan and published his first collection of poetry, *Oak and Ivy*. In 1895, he published a second collection, *Majors and Minors*, which was received with great enthusiasm by critics. In fact, William Dean Howells, the leading critic of the day, was so impressed with the book that he wrote an introduction for Dunbar's next collection, *Lyrics of a Lowly Life* (1896). That book sold over twelve thousand copies and established Dunbar's reputation and audience.

Characters, Themes, and Forms Dunbar's fiction often focuses on daily life in the vanished world of the southern plantation. Sometimes, however, his writing revolves around social problems facing African Americans in Midwestern towns and urban ghettoes at the turn of the century. His characters include farmers, politicians, preachers, traders, entertainers, and professional people.

Popularity at a Price Dunbar composed poems in two styles—one formal and elegant, the other informal, using a rural dialect, which he called "jingles in a broken tongue." His gift for re-creating dialect and using it to create believable characters was profound. However, it also drew criticism. Called the "Poet Laureate of the Negro Race" by Booker T. Washington, Dunbar was criticized by other African Americans who believed that his dialect poems pandered to white readers' desire for sentimental stereotypes of prewar African Americans. In poems such as "Douglass" and "We Wear the Mask," however, Dunbar demonstrates a command of the English language that was often overlooked, capturing the struggles of African Americans in a dignified, graceful manner.

Despite his success as a poet, Dunbar was disillusioned by the critics' tendency to focus on the poetry he wrote in dialect, while virtually ignoring the poetry he wrote in more formal verse.

An Untimely Death By his late twenties, Dunbar was a nationally prominent poet. Unfortunately, his life was cut short by tuberculosis in 1906. By the end of his life, his poetry was so popular that he was able to write from Florida, "Down here one finds my poems recited everywhere."

Preview

Connecting to the Literature

The rules of courtesy often dictate that people smile even when they feel sad or disappointed. Paul Laurence Dunbar describes such a reaction in his poems as he explores the struggle for identity and truth.

Literary Analysis

Rhyme

Rhyme, which along with rhythm gives poetry its musical quality, is the repetition of sounds in the accented syllables of two or more words appearing close together. Poets use rhyme in different ways:

- **True rhyme** occurs when the vowel sounds and any consonants appearing after them are exactly the same, as in *days* and *ways*.
- **Slant rhymes** link two similar (but not exact) vowel sounds, as in *prove* and *love*.
- **End rhymes** occur at the ends of two or more poetic lines.
- **Internal rhymes** appear within a single line.

As you read the following poems, take note of Dunbar's use of rhyme.

Comparing Literary Works

Each of the following poems addresses African American struggles for racial identity, but they express different emotions. While "Douglass" expresses indignation for the injustices suffered by African Americans, "We Wear the Mask" conveys a profound sorrow. As you read these two poems, compare Dunbar's varying attitudes and identify the emotions each one evokes in you.

Reading Strategy

Interpreting

Poets often mean much more than the surface of their poems might initially convey. For example, to **interpret** "We Wear the Mask," consider who "we" refers to and the time and historical context in which the poem was written. Then, consider what the image of a mask suggests—what it reveals and what it hides. Use a chart like the one shown to help interpret and understand these poems.

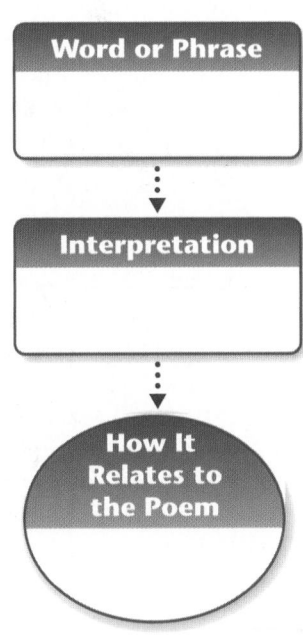

Vocabulary Development

salient (sāl′ yənt) *adj.* standing out from the rest (p. 659)

tempest (tem′ pist) *n.* violent storm (p. 659)

stark (stärk) *adj.* stiff; rigid (p. 659)

guile (gīl) *n.* craftiness (p. 660)

myriad (mir′ ē əd) *adj.* countless (p. 660)

▲ **Critical Viewing** Why is a civil rights activist like Frederick Douglass an appropriate inspiration for Dunbar? **[Speculate]**

Douglass

Paul Laurence Dunbar

Background

Paul Laurence Dunbar was among the last generation to have an ongoing contact with former African American slaves. As a child, Dunbar heard many stories from his father, who had escaped captivity and joined the Civil War cause. In these poems, Dunbar speaks of the social issues faced by those struggling to rebuild the country after the Civil War. He expresses the pain of racial injustice and conveys the ongoing struggles of African Americans to achieve equality.

Ah, Douglass,[1] we have fall'n on evil days,
    Such days as thou, not even thou didst know,
    When thee, the eyes of that harsh long ago
Saw, <u>salient</u>, at the cross of devious ways,
5 And all the country heard thee with amaze.
    Not ended then, the passionate ebb and flow.
    The awful tide that battled to and fro;
We ride amid a <u>tempest</u> of dispraise.

Now, when the waves of swift dissension swarm,
10   And Honor, the strong pilot, lieth[2] <u>stark</u>,
Oh, for thy voice high-sounding o'er the storm,
    For thy strong arm to guide the shivering bark,[3]
The blast-defying power of thy form,
    To give us comfort through the lonely dark.

---

1. **Douglass** Frederick Douglass, an American abolitionist (1818–1895).
2. **lieth** (līʹ eth) v. lies.
3. **bark** boat.

salient (sālʹ yənt) *adj.* standing out from the rest

tempest (temʹ pist) *n.* violent storm

stark (stärk) *adj.* stiff; rigid

✔Reading Check

What does the speaker say is the difference between the current time and the time in which Douglass lived?

We Wear the Mask

Paul Laurence Dunbar

We wear the mask that grins and lies,
It hides our cheeks and shades our eyes—
This debt we pay to human guile;
With torn and bleeding hearts we smile,
5 And mouth with myriad subtleties.

Why should the world be overwise,
In counting all our tears and sighs?
Nay, let them only see us, while
    We wear the mask.

10 We smile, but, O great Christ, our cries
To thee from tortured souls arise.
We sing, but oh the clay is vile
Beneath our feet, and long the mile;
But let the world dream otherwise,
15   We wear the mask!

guile (gīl) *n.* craftiness

myriad (mir´ ē əd) *adj.* countless

Literary Analysis
Rhyme What is the effect of the lack of rhyme in lines 9 and 15, where the poet repeats the title?

Review and Assess

Thinking About the Selections

1. **Respond:** How do you feel when you must appear or behave as others expect?

2. **(a) Recall:** Who is the Douglass to whom Dunbar refers?
   (b) Draw Conclusions: Why do you think the speaker addresses Douglass?

3. **(a) Infer:** When was Douglass's voice heard by the nation?
   (b) Compare: How does Douglass's message relate to what the speaker of "Douglass" describes?

4. **(a) Infer:** Who is the "we" in this poem? **(b) Analyze:** What struggles do they face? **(c) Interpret:** What is the "lonely dark"?

5. **(a) Recall:** In "We Wear the Mask," what emotions does the mask hide? **(b) Draw Conclusions:** Why do you think they wear the mask?

6. **(a) Extend:** How might Dunbar like to see the world change?
   (b) Apply: If Dunbar were alive today, do you think he would still have the views he expresses in this poem? Why or why not?

Review and Assess

Literary Analysis

Rhyme

1. List all the words in "We Wear the Mask" that are **true rhymes** with the word *lies*.
2. What **slant rhyme** does Dunbar use in this poem?
3. The **rhyme scheme,** or pattern, in the first stanza of "Douglass" can be expressed as *abbaabba*. (The letter *a* stands for words rhyming with *days* and the letter *b* stands for words rhyming with *know.*) What is the rhyme scheme for the second stanza?
4. In your opinion, what is the effect of rhyme in these poems?

Comparing Literary Works

5. (a) Note three emotions Dunbar addresses in "Douglass."
   (b) Note three emotions he expresses in "We Wear the Mask."
   (c) In what ways is the emotional content of these poems similar?
   (d) In what ways is it different?
6. (a) In what ways are the tones or attitudes of these poems similar?
   (b) In what ways do they differ?
7. Which poem do you think is more personal—related most directly to Dunbar's daily experience? Explain.

Reading Strategy

Interpreting

8. What situation might Dunbar's speaker be describing for African Americans in general in "We Wear the Mask"?
9. Poets use symbolic language—words and images that represent larger ideas. In a chart like the one shown, list and **interpret** the symbolic language you find in both poems.

	Symbolic Language	Interpretation
"Douglass"		
"We Wear the Mask"		

Extend Understanding

10. **Social Studies Connection:** How might Dunbar have characterized the situation of African Americans in the past decade? Explain.

Quick Review

Rhyme occurs when two or more words have similar or identical vowel and final consonant sounds in their accented syllables.

To **interpret** a poem, consider the poet's word choice, symbolism, and historical context to discover the poet's deeper meaning.

 Take It to the Net
www.phschool.com
Take the interactive self-test online to check your understanding of these selections.

Integrate Language Skills

Vocabulary Development Lesson

Word Analysis: Forms of *guile*

The word *guile* is a noun meaning "craftiness." By adding prefixes or suffixes to *guile*, you can form related words such as the adjective *guileless* ("innocent" or "naïve") and the verb *beguile* ("mislead" or "trick").

Combine *guile* with the suffixes below to create six words. Label each word's part of speech.

1. *-ful*
2. *-fully*
3. *-fulness*
4. *-less*
5. *-lessly*
6. *-lessness*

Concept Development: Antonyms

An antonym is a word meaning the opposite of another. Match each word in the left column with its antonym in the right column.

1. guile   a. tranquility; stillness
2. tempest   b. not many
3. salient   c. elastic; flexible
4. stark   d. inconspicuous
5. myriad   e. honesty

Spelling Strategy

There is no spelling rule governing the use of y as a vowel; you will need to memorize the spelling of such words. For each of these pairs of words, choose the correct spelling.

1. pyre/pire   2. tipe/type   3. myriad/miriad

Grammar and Style Lesson

Punctuation of Interjections

An **interjection,** a word used to express emotion, has no grammatical relation to other words in a sentence. An interjection can express a variety of sentiments, such as happiness, fear, anger, pain, surprise, sorrow, exhaustion, or hesitation. Use a comma to punctuate an interjection that expresses mild emotion. Use an exclamation point to punctuate an interjection that expresses strong emotion. Consider the following examples:

> **Mild Emotion:** *Ah*, Douglass, we have fall'n on evil days, . . .

> **Strong Emotion:** *Oh!* If you could only help!

Practice Add a comma or an exclamation point to correct the punctuation of the interjections in each of the following sentences. Capitalize the resulting sentences as necessary.

1. Hey we need you to guide us!
2. Ah we long to be comforted by your wisdom!
3. No I'm afraid I can't reveal my authentic feelings.
4. Oh is that what you think?
5. Yes one must remain as strong as possible in the face of a great challenge.

Writing Application Write a paragraph on a topic that has special meaning for you. Use at least three examples of interjections.

 Prentice Hall Writing and Grammar Connection: Chapter 17, Section 4

Writing Lesson

Poem to Honor a Hero

Think of another historical figure who, if alive today, might help inspire people to solve some of society's problems. Compose a poem in which you address this hero as Dunbar addresses Douglass.

Prewriting   First, list the accomplishments and character traits that contribute to your subject's heroism. Then, brainstorm for sensory details and descriptions of behavior that illustrate this person's ability to tackle challenging aspects of today's world.

Drafting   Choose a form for your poem, such as a regular rhythm and rhyme scheme or free verse. Use images and sound devices that convey a vivid main impression of your subject.

Model: Creating a Main Impression

Oh, Martin Luther King, like an oak in a storm,

Your life was not in vain.

Through all the blustering wind and rain,

Your strength was our gain.

> The images comparing the subject to an oak convey the sense of the subject as a powerful figure.

Revising   Reread your poem. Consider adding or eliminating details to sharpen the main impression of your subject. If necessary, use images and descriptive language to convey your ideas more effectively.

 Prentice Hall Writing and Grammar Connection: Chapter 7, Section 3

Extension Activities

Listening and Speaking   Prepare an **oral interpretation** of one of the two Dunbar poems. Begin by analyzing the meaning and form of each line. The following tips will help you:

- Look for interjections and imagery that emphasize tone and cadence.
- Read the poem aloud several times to evoke emotion.

Present your oral interpretation to the class, inviting classmates to comment.

Research and Technology   Dunbar's work received mixed reviews from critics. Using library and Internet resources, conduct research to find examples of both positive and negative responses. In a **report,** summarize your findings and then take a position about Dunbar's legacy as a poet.

 **Take It to the Net**   www.phschool.com

Go online for an additional research activity using the Internet.

Prepare to Read

Luke Havergal ◆ Richard Cory ◆ Lucinda Matlock ◆ Richard Bone

Edwin Arlington Robinson (1869–1935)

In his mid-thirties, Edwin Arlington Robinson earned twenty cents per hour as a New York City subway inspector. Yet, friends helped him arrange the private printing of three books of his poetry during these lean times, allowing Robinson to become the most successful American poet of the 1920s.

Robinson grew up in Gardiner, Maine, a small town that was the model for Tilbury Town, the fictional setting of many of his poems. He attended college for two years, but he was forced to return to Gardiner after his father's death. Upon his return, Robinson began writing poetry, depending on friends and patrons for financial support. Four years later, he returned to New York City, hoping to improve his financial situation. When President Theodore Roosevelt appointed him to a post at the New York Customhouse, Robinson was set free from his financial worries.

The Inner Struggle Robinson continued to write poems and established his poetic voice. His best poems focus on people's inner struggles. They paint portraits of desperate characters who view their lives as trivial and meaningless or who long to live in another place or time. Despite his characters' pessimistic outlook, Robinson's poems possess a certain dignity that results from his traditional style, command of language, and imagination and wit.

Robinson found success when his fourth volume of verse, *The Town Down the River* (1910), sold well and received much critical acclaim. He went on to publish many acclaimed books and receive three Pulitzer Prizes.

Edgar Lee Masters (1868–1950)

For years, Edgar Lee Masters practiced criminal law by day in a successful Chicago firm and wrote poems, plays, and essays by night. In 1914, however, Masters' direction as a writer changed dramatically when a friend gave him a copy of *Selected Epitaphs from the Greek Anthology*. This collection included many concise, interconnected epitaphs that captured the essence of people's personal lives.

Spoon River Anthology Using the structure suggested by that anthology, and abandoning conventional rhyme and meter, Masters wrote a series of poems about the lives of people in rural southern Illinois. Published as *Spoon River Anthology* in 1915, the book provoked strong reactions among critics and became a bestseller. The volume was so successful that Masters quit his law career and moved to New York to earn a living as a writer.

The anthology consists of 244 epitaphs for characters buried in the mythical Spoon River cemetery. The dead themselves serve as the speakers of the poems, often revealing secrets they kept hidden during their lifetimes. Many types of people are represented, including storekeepers, housewives, and murderers. Some had happy lives, but many more had lives filled with frustration and despair. Presented together, the epitaphs paint a vivid portrait of the loneliness and isolation confronting people in small Midwestern towns around the turn of the century.

Masters went on to produce other volumes of poetry, novels, biographies, and his autobiography, *Across Spoon River*. However, he is still remembered almost exclusively for *Spoon River Anthology*.

Preview

Connecting to the Literature

Have you ever wondered how you will be remembered a century from now? The following poems create a memorable impression of four characters from small-town America one hundred years ago. Compare them with the impression you would like to leave behind.

Literary Analysis

Speaker

The **speaker** is the voice of a poem. Although the speaker is often the poet, it can also be a fictional character or a non-human entity. For example, the speakers of the poems in Masters' *Spoon River Anthology* are characters buried in a cemetery in the fictional town of Spoon River, as these lines from "Lucinda Matlock" demonstrate:

> At ninety-six I had lived enough, that is all,
> And passed to a sweet repose.

Instead of using a neutral speaker, Masters allows characters to speak candidly for themselves. In this way, the poet can delve deeply into the minds and hearts of Spoon River's former citizens.

Comparing Literary Works

All of these poems share the common themes of life and death. The speakers—some of whose voices come from the grave—examine the quality of the lives they have lived. Lucinda Matlock, whose life was long and satisfying, says "It takes life to love Life." By contrast, Richard Cory appears to have lived with terrible secrets. As you read these poems, compare the speakers and the message each expresses about how we spend our days.

Reading Strategy

Recognizing Attitudes

The **attitudes** and beliefs of a poem's speaker color the depiction of the characters, settings, and events. As you read a poem, determine who the speaker is, and look for clues to the speaker's attitudes or outlook on life. For example, in "Lucinda Matlock," the speaker believes that the younger generation is not as tough and hard-working as her generation was. Use a chart like the one shown to help you recognize the speaker's attitudes in these poems.

Speaker's Attitude	Evidence

Vocabulary Development

imperially (im pir´ ē əl ē) *adv.* majestically (p. 668)

repose (ri pōz´) *n.* state of being at rest (p. 669)

degenerate (dē jen´ ər it) *adj.* morally corrupt (p. 669)

epitaph (ep´ ə taf´) *n.* inscription on a tombstone or grave marker (p. 670)

Luke Havergal

Edwin Arlington Robinson

Background

Two years into Edwin Arlington Robinson's college career at Harvard, he was forced to leave school to support his family, which had suffered devastating financial losses. Both of Robinson's brothers died young after lives marred by failure. Robinson himself endured years of poverty. When success finally arrived it was abundant, but the years of struggle had shaped Robinson's worldview. He filled his poems with the voices of the lost and the sorrowful, exploring the themes of personal defeat and unfulfilled longing. Luke Havergal, who suffers the loss of a loved one, and Richard Cory, who suffers with hidden pain, are typical of his work.

Go to the western gate, Luke Havergal,
There where the vines cling crimson on the wall,
And in the twilight wait for what will come.
The leaves will whisper there of her, and some,
5 Like flying words, will strike you as they fall;
But go, and if you listen she will call.
Go to the western gate, Luke Havergal—
Luke Havergal.

No, there is not a dawn in eastern skies
10 To rift the fiery night that's in your eyes;
But there, where western glooms are gathering,
The dark will end the dark, if anything:
God slays Himself with every leaf that flies,
And hell is more than half of paradise.
15 No, there is not a dawn in eastern skies—
In eastern skies.

Out of a grave I come to tell you this,
Out of a grave I come to quench the kiss
That flames upon your forehead with a glow
20 That blinds you to the way that you must go.
Yes, there is yet one way to where she is,
Bitter, but one that faith may never miss.
Out of a grave I come to tell you this—
To tell you this.

25 There is the western gate, Luke Havergal,
There are the crimson leaves upon the wall.
Go, for the winds are tearing them away,—
Nor think to riddle the dead words they say,
Nor any more to feel them as they fall;
30 But go, and if you trust her she will call.
There is the western gate, Luke Havergal—
Luke Havergal.

Literary Analysis
Speaker Who is the "I" who speaks in this poem?

✔**Reading Check**

What will happen at the Western gate if Luke Havergal goes there?

RICHARD CORY

Edwin Arlington Robinson

Whenever Richard Cory went down town,
We people on the pavement looked at him:
He was a gentleman from sole to crown,
Clean favored, and <u>imperially</u> slim.

5 And he was always quietly arrayed,
And he was always human when he talked;
But still he fluttered pulses when he said,
"Good-morning," and he glittered when he walked.

And he was rich—yes, richer than a king—
10 And admirably schooled in every grace:
In fine, we thought that he was everything
To make us wish that we were in his place.

So on we worked, and waited for the light,
And went without the meat, and cursed the bread;
15 And Richard Cory, one calm summer night,
Went home and put a bullet through his head.

The Thinker (Portrait of Louis N. Kenton, 1900), Thomas Eakins, The Metropolitan Museum of Art

▲ **Critical Viewing**
Do you think this painting more accurately suggests Richard Cory or the poem's speaker? Explain.
[Connect]

imperially (im pir′ ē əl ē) *adv.* majestically

Review and Assess

Thinking About the Selections

1. **Respond:** Were you surprised by the last line of "Richard Cory"? Explain.

2. **(a) Recall:** Why should Luke Havergal go to the gate?
   (b) Speculate: What might the gate symbolize?

3. **(a) Recall:** In "Luke Havergal," from where has the speaker come? **(b) Interpret:** What is the speaker's message?

4. **(a) Recall:** Why was Richard Cory envied? **(b) Contrast:** In what ways does Richard Cory differ from the other townspeople?

5. **(a) Recall:** What does Cory do one night? **(b) Infer:** Do you think the town was surprised by his action? Explain.

6. **(a) Apply:** Why might Richard Cory have been miserable?
   (b) Relate: What do you think are the keys to individual happiness?

Lucinda Matlock

Edgar Lee Masters

I went to the dances at Chandlerville,
And played snap-out[1] at Winchester.
One time we changed partners,
Driving home in the moonlight of middle June,
5 And then I found Davis.
We were married and lived together for seventy years,
Enjoying, working, raising the twelve children,
Eight of whom we lost
Ere I had reached the age of sixty.
10 I spun, I wove, I kept the house, I nursed the sick,
I made the garden, and for holiday
Rambled over the fields where sang the larks,
And by Spoon River gathering many a shell,
And many a flower and medicinal weed—
15 Shouting to the wooded hills, singing to the green valleys.
At ninety-six I had lived enough, that is all,
And passed to a sweet <u>repose</u>.
What is this I hear of sorrow and weariness,
Anger, discontent and drooping hopes?
20 <u>Degenerate</u> sons and daughters,
Life is too strong for you—
It takes life to love Life.

repose (ri pōz´) *n.* state of being at rest

degenerate (dē jen´ ər it) *adj.* morally corrupt

---

1. **snap-out** game in which a long line of players who are holding hands spin around in a circle, causing the players on the ends to be flung off by centrifugal force.

Review and Assess

Thinking About the Selection

1. **Respond:** What is your opinion of Lucinda Matlock? Is she someone you would strive to emulate? Why or why not?

2. **(a) Recall:** Summarize Lucinda Matlock's domestic life.
   (b) Analyze: What is her attitude about her life?

3. **(a) Recall:** How old was Lucinda Matlock when she died?
   (b) Infer: Why might she have thought she "lived enough"?

4. **(a) Recall:** Whom does she address at the end of the poem?
   (b) Interpret: What is the meaning of Matlock's message to those she addresses?

5. **(a) Apply:** How might Matlock respond to the complaint that life today is too complex? **(b) Connect:** Do you agree? Explain.

Richard Bone

Edgar Lee Masters

When I first came to Spoon River
I did not know whether what they told me
Was true or false.
They would bring me the <u>epitaph</u>
5 And stand around the shop while I worked
And say "He was so kind," "He was wonderful,"
"She was the sweetest woman," "He was a consistent Christian."
And I chiseled for them whatever they wished,
All in ignorance of its truth.
10 But later, as I lived among the people here,
I knew how near to the life
Were the epitaphs that were ordered for them as they died.

But still I chiseled whatever they paid me to chisel
and made myself party to the false chronicles
15 Of the stones,
Even as the historian does who writes
Without knowing the truth,
Or because he is influenced to hide it.

epitaph (ep′ ə taf′) *n.*
inscription on a tomb-
stone or grave marker

Review and Assess

Thinking About the Selection

1. **Respond:** What is your opinion of Richard Bone after reading this poem? Explain.

2. **(a) Recall:** What is Richard Bone's occupation?
   (b) Infer: What does he learn after years in Spoon River?
   (c) Speculate: Does his attitude change? If so, how?

3. **(a) Interpret:** Why does Bone think the epitaphs are "false chronicles"? **(b) Speculate:** Why do you think the townspeople compose such epitaphs for their loved ones?

4. **Analyze:** Explain why Bone might compare a tombstone carver to a historian.

5. **Apply:** Do you think Bone played an important role in Spoon River? Support your answer.

Review and Assess

Literary Analysis

Speaker

1. What details suggest that the **speaker** of "Richard Cory" is speaking for the entire town?
2. In what ways does the speaker's admiration for Richard Cory add to the power of the poem?
3. (a) In what ways might "Lucinda Matlock" be different if Masters had used a different speaker? (b) If "Richard Cory" spoke for himself, how might the poem be different?
4. The speakers in Master's *Spoon River Anthology* are dead. Why might this allow them to discuss their lives more openly?

Comparing Literary Works

5. In both "Luke Havergal" and "Lucinda Matlock," voices speak from the grave. Compare and contrast the messages they deliver.
6. If Richard Bone were asked to carve epitaphs for Luke Havergal, Richard Cory, and Lucinda Matlock, what would he write? Explain each response.

Reading Strategy

Recognizing Attitudes

7. In what way does the speaker's **attitude** toward Richard Cory differ from Cory's attitude toward himself? Support your answer.
8. Identify and explain the attitude of the speaker in "Richard Bone."
9. Use a chart like this to describe Lucinda Matlock's outlook on life.

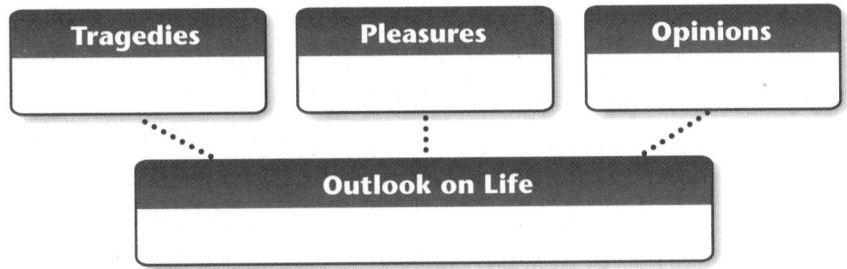

Extend Understanding

10. **Psychology Connection:** Consider the ways in which these characters deal with change and explain other, healthier options.

Quick Review

The **speaker** is the voice of a poem.

To **recognize the attitudes** of a poem's speaker, look for details that suggest how a speaker feels about a subject.

 Take It to the Net
www.phschool.com
Take the interactive self-test online to check your understanding of these selections.

Integrate Language Skills

Vocabulary Development Lesson

Word Analysis: Latin Root -pose-

The word *repose* combines the Latin root *-pose-* ("place" or "rest") with the prefix *re-* ("back"). Using this word analysis, *repose* can be defined as "the state of being at rest."

Use each of the words below to complete the sentences.

a. depose **b.** impose **c.** interpose

1. He hated to ____?____ on his friends, but he was unable to find a hotel room.
2. Each time audience members ____?____ comments, the speaker loses his train of thought.
3. When we ____?____ the prime minister, we will set this nation on a course toward true freedom.

Concept Development: Synonyms

Write the letter of the best synonym for the first word.

1. imperially: (a) grandly, (b) scornfully, (c) strongly
2. repose: (a) model, (b) silence, (c) ease
3. degenerate: (a) evil, (b) degraded, (c) slow
4. epitaph: (a) inscription, (b) homily, (c) graph

Spelling Strategy

In many English words of Greek origin, *ph* is used to spell the *f* sound, as in *epitaph*, *trophy*, and *physique*. For each of the following pairs, choose the correct spelling.

1. symfonic/symphonic 3. decifer/decipher
2. sinful/sinphul   4. catastrofe/catastrophe

Grammar and Style Lesson

Noun Clauses

A **noun clause** is a subordinate clause used as a noun. It can be used as a subject, a predicate nominative, a direct object, an indirect object, or the object of a preposition. Noun clauses are commonly introduced by words such as *that*, *which*, *where*, *what*, *who*, *whatever*, *whoever*, and *why*.

Subject: *Whoever knows about life* will tell you.

Direct Object: We thought *that he was everything*.

Predicate Nominative: He is *whatever we admire*.

Object of a Preposition: He tells his story to *whomever will listen*.

Practice Copy the following sentences and underline the noun clause in each. Explain the function of each noun clause.

1. There is yet one way to where she is.
2. I chiseled for them whatever they wished.
3. I did not know whether what they told me was true or false.
4. I knew how near to the life were the epitaphs that were ordered.
5. I chiseled whatever they paid me to chisel.

Writing Application Write three or four sentences to describe different aspects of a familiar person or place. In your writing, include at least three noun clauses.

W͚G *Prentice Hall Writing and Grammar Connection: Chapter 19, Section 3*

Writing Lesson

Firsthand Biography

Poems like Robinson's and Masters's are one way to create vivid portraits of people. Another way to present a portrait of a person is through a firsthand biography—a story about events in the life of a person with whom the writer has a personal relationship. Write a firsthand biography in which you share your impressions of a person.

Prewriting After you have selected your subject, list his or her key personality traits and the events that reveal them. Then, arrange these details in their order of importance.

Drafting Focus your draft on a single event or a series of events that illustrate the person's most important personality traits. Use transitional words like the ones shown.

Model: Choosing Transitions

Sequence	Superiority	Inferiority
first	good	few
second	better	last
primarily	best	less importantly
last	above all	least effective
finally	more importantly	worst of all

Revising Review your biography and add more details to make sure that it conveys the impression of your subject that you intended.

W̶G̶ Prentice Hall Writing and Grammar Connection: Chapter 4, Connected Assignment

Extension Activities

Speaking and Listening Find a copy of folk duo Simon and Garfunkel's adaptation of "Richard Cory" and compare it with the poem, addressing the following issues:

- Is the song effective?
- Does it capture the message of the poem?
- In what ways, if any, does the song alter Robinson's meaning?

Lead a **class discussion** in which you compare the poem to the song. **[Group Activity]**

Research and Technology Review *Spoon River Anthology* to find several poems that convey a similar theme, such as jealousy, honesty, or love. Prepare an **illustrated booklet** of these poems. In addition to providing images that enhance the meaning of the poems, write an introduction explaining the connection among the poems.

 **Take It to the Net**   www.phschool.com

Go online for an additional research activity using the Internet.

Prepare to Read

A Wagner Matinée

Willa Cather (1873–1947)

Although Willa Cather lived more than half her life in New York City, she turned again and again to the Nebraska prairie of her youth—at the time, a recently settled area of the American frontier—for inspiration and material for her writing. Cather captured with unflinching honesty the difficulties of life on the expanding frontier.

A Prairie Childhood Born in a small town in western Virginia, Cather moved to the Nebraska frontier when she was nine. Many of her new neighbors were immigrants struggling to build new lives while preserving their native cultures. Commenting on the diversity that surrounded her during her childhood, Cather once wrote, "On Sundays we could drive to a Norwegian church and listen to a sermon in that language, or to a Danish or Swedish church. We could go to a French Catholic settlement or into a Bohemian township and hear one in Czech, or we could go to the church with the German Lutherans."

In addition to all that she learned from observing the diverse group of people who surrounded her, Cather received a rich formal education, studying foreign languages, history, classical music, and opera. In 1891, Cather left home to study at the University of Nebraska, becoming one of the first women to receive a college education.

The Making of a Literary Giant After graduating from the University of Nebraska in 1895, Cather worked as an editor at a Pittsburgh newspaper while she wrote poems and short stories in her spare time. Her first collection of stories, *The Troll Garden*, was published in 1905. In 1906, she moved to New York and joined the editorial staff of *McClure's Magazine*. After her first novel, *Alexander's Bridge*, was published in 1912, Cather left *McClure's* to devote herself to writing. She remained in New York for the rest of her life, but her memories of the prairie inspired her greatest work.

Over the next 35 years, Cather produced ten novels, two short-story collections, and two collections of essays. Among her outstanding works are *O Pioneers!* (1913), *My Ántonia* (1918), and *One of Ours* (1922), all of which capture the flavor of life on the Midwestern prairie. *One of Ours* won Cather the Pulitzer Prize in 1923. Cather then shifted her attention from the Midwest to New Mexico in *Death Comes for the Archbishop* (1927) and to seventeenth-century Canada in *Shadows on the Rock* (1931).

Portraits of Prairie Life Although Cather's fiction was by no means limited to "prairie stories"—her fictional settings ranged from contemporary New York City to the American Southwest to Quebec—it was her stories about Nebraskan immigrants that most appealed to readers and critics. In these stories, she displayed her admiration for the courage and spirit of the immigrants and other settlers of the frontier. At the same time, she conveyed an intense awareness of the loss felt by the pioneers and the loneliness and isolation from which they suffered. In "A Wagner Matinée," for example, Cather captures this sense of loneliness and isolation by contrasting the stark realities of frontier life with the possibilities of life in a more cultured world.

Preview

Connecting to the Literature

Music can exert a powerful tug on our feelings, memories, and fantasies. In this story, a woman experiences a flood of long-buried emotions when she attends a special concert.

Literary Analysis

Characterization

A writer uses **characterization** to reveal a character's personality. Characterization is generally developed through one of the following methods:

- Direct statements about the character
- Physical descriptions
- The character's actions, thoughts, or comments
- Comments about the character made by other characters.

As you read, note how these methods of characterization are used to develop the personality of Aunt Georgiana.

Connecting Literary Elements

When a story is told by a character involved in the action, the writer is using **first-person point of view**. In such a story, all impressions of events, places, and characters are filtered through the narrator. In "A Wagner Matinée," Aunt Georgiana is presented to the reader exactly as she is perceived by the narrator—her nephew, Clark.

Reading Strategy

Clarifying

Cather's story is packed with details about its main character. To fully understand the character's actions, **clarify** the details that are provided. This may involve reading a footnote or looking up a word in a dictionary. You may also need to reread a passage to refresh your memory about previous details or even read ahead to find details that clarify meaning. Use a chart like the one shown to clarify difficult passages from the text.

Detail	Clarifying Strategy
"Howard followed her."	Reread to find out who Howard is.
inexplicable	Look the word up in the dictionary.
"took a homestead in Red Willow County"	Find out where Red Willow County is.

Vocabulary Development

reverential (rev′ə ren′ shəl) *adj.* caused by a feeling of deep respect and love (p. 679)

tremulously (trem′ yoo ləs lē) *adv.* fearfully; timidly (p. 679)

semi-somnambulant (sem′ i säm nam′ byoo lənt) *adj.* half-sleepwalking (p. 679)

inert (in urt′) *adj.* motionless (p. 680)

prelude (prel′ yood′) *n.* introductory section or movement of a work of music (p. 682)

jocularity (jäk′ yoo lar′ ə tē) *n.* joking good humor (p. 683)

From Arkansas, George Schreiber, Sheldon Swope Art Museum, Terre Haute, Indiana

▲ **Critical Viewing** In what ways does the woman in the painting seem like Aunt Georgiana? **[Connect; Interpret]**

A Wagner Matinée

Willa Cather

Background

When "A Wagner Matinée" first appeared in 1904, Cather's readers would have been as familiar with Richard Wagner (Väg nər) as people are today with the Beatles. Wagner, who was German, was one of the nineteenth century's greatest composers. His operas are characterized by their adventurous harmonic language and their innovative intermarriage of music and drama. Although many critics judged Wagner's music unfavorably during his lifetime, his operas became enormously popular after his death in 1883.

I received one morning a letter written in pale ink, on glassy, blue-lined notepaper, and bearing the postmark of a little Nebraska village. This communication, worn and rubbed, looking as though it had been carried for some days in a coat pocket that was none too clean, was from my Uncle Howard. It informed me that his wife had been left a small legacy by a bachelor relative who had recently died, and that it had become necessary for her to come to Boston to attend to the settling of the estate. He requested me to meet her at the station, and render her whatever services might prove necessary. On examining the date indicated as that of her arrival, I found it no later than tomorrow. He had characteristically delayed writing until, had I been away from home for a day, I must have missed the good woman altogether.

The name of my Aunt Georgiana called up not alone her own figure, at once pathetic and grotesque, but opened before my feet a gulf of recollections so wide and deep that, as the letter dropped from my hand, I felt suddenly a stranger to all the present conditions of my existence, wholly ill at ease and out of place amid the surroundings

✔**Reading Check**

Why is Aunt Georgiana going to Boston?

of my study. I became, in short, the gangling farmer boy my aunt had known, scourged with chilblains and bashfulness, my hands cracked and raw from the corn husking. I felt the knuckles of my thumb tentatively, as though they were raw again. I sat again before her parlor organ, thumbing the scales with my stiff, red hands, while she beside me made canvas mittens for the huskers.

The next morning, after preparing my landlady somewhat, I set out for the station. When the train arrived I had some difficulty in finding my aunt. She was the last of the passengers to alight, and when I got her into the carriage she looked not unlike one of those charred, smoked bodies that firemen lift from the *débris* of a burned building. She had come all the way in a day coach; her linen duster[1] had become black with soot and her black bonnet gray with dust during the journey. When we arrived at my boardinghouse the landlady put her to bed at once, and I did not see her again until the next morning.

Whatever shock Mrs. Springer experienced at my aunt's appearance she considerately concealed. Myself, I saw my aunt's misshapen figure with that feeling of awe and respect with which we behold explorers who have left their ears and fingers north of Franz Josef Land,[2] or their health somewhere along the upper Congo.[3] My Aunt Georgiana had been a music teacher at the Boston Conservatory, somewhere back in the latter sixties. One summer, which she had spent in the little village in the Green Mountains[4] where her ancestors had dwelt for generations, she had kindled the callow[5] fancy of the most idle and shiftless of all the village lads, and had conceived for this Howard Carpenter one of those absurd and extravagant passions which a handsome country boy of twenty-one sometimes inspires in a plain, angular, spectacled woman of thirty. When she returned to her duties in Boston, Howard followed her; and the upshot of this inexplicable infatuation was that she eloped with him, eluding the reproaches of her family and the criticism of her friends by going with him to the Nebraska frontier. Carpenter, who of course had no money, took a homestead in Red Willow County,[6] fifty miles from the railroad. There they measured off their eighty acres by driving across the prairie in a wagon, to the wheel of which they had tied a red cotton handkerchief, and counting its revolutions. They built a dugout in the red hillside, one of those cave dwellings whose inmates usually reverted to the conditions of primitive savagery. Their water they got from the lagoons where the buffalo drank, and their slender stock of provisions was always at the mercy of bands of roving Indians. For thirty years my aunt had not been farther than fifty miles from the homestead.

Literary Analysis
Characterization What do the contrasting details of Aunt Georgiana's life in Boston and Nebraska reveal about her character?

---

1. **duster** *n.* short, loose smock worn to protect clothing from dust.
2. **Franz Josef Land** group of islands in the Arctic Ocean.
3. **Congo** river in central Africa.
4. **Green Mountains** mountains in Vermont.
5. **callow** (kal′ ō) *adj.* immature; inexperienced.
6. **Red Willow County** county in southwestern Nebraska that borders on Kansas.

But Mrs. Springer knew nothing of all this, and must have been considerably shocked at what was left of my kinswoman. Beneath the soiled linen duster, which on her arrival was the most conspicuous feature of her costume, she wore a black stuff dress whose ornamentation showed that she had surrendered herself unquestioningly into the hands of a country dressmaker. My poor aunt's figure, however, would have presented astonishing difficulties to any dressmaker. Her skin was yellow from constant exposure to a pitiless wind, and to the alkaline water which transforms the most transparent cuticle into a sort of flexible leather. She wore ill-fitting false teeth. The most striking thing about her physiognomy, however, was an incessant twitching of the mouth and eyebrows, a form of nervous disorder resulting from isolation and monotony, and from frequent physical suffering.

In my boyhood this affliction had possessed a sort of horrible fascination for me, of which I was secretly very much ashamed, for in those days I owed to this woman most of the good that ever came my way, and had a <u>reverential</u> affection for her. During the three winters when I was riding herd for my uncle, my aunt, after cooking three meals for half a dozen farmhands, and putting the six children to bed, would often stand until midnight at her ironing board, hearing me at the kitchen table beside her recite Latin declensions and conjugations, and gently shaking me when my drowsy head sank down over a page of irregular verbs. It was to her, at her ironing or mending, that I read my first Shakespeare; and her old textbook of mythology was the first that ever came into my empty hands. She taught me my scales and exercises, too, on the little parlor organ which her husband had bought her after fifteen years, during which she had not so much as seen any instrument except an accordion, that belonged to one of the Norwegian farmhands. She would sit beside me by the hour, darning and counting, while I struggled with the "Harmonious Blacksmith"; but she seldom talked to me about music, and I understood why. She was a pious woman; she had the consolation of religion; and to her at least her martyrdom was not wholly sordid. Once when I had been doggedly beating out some passages from an old score of "Euryanthe" I had found among her music books, she came up to me and, putting her hands over my eyes, gently drew my head back upon her shoulder, saying <u>tremulously</u>, "Don't love it so well, Clark, or it may be taken from you. Oh! dear boy, pray that whatever your sacrifice be it is not that."

When my aunt appeared on the morning after her arrival, she was still in a <u>semi-somnambulant</u> state. She seemed not to realize that she was in the city where she had spent her youth, the place longed for hungrily for half a lifetime. She had been so wretchedly trainsick throughout the journey that she had no recollection of anything but her discomfort, and, to all intents and purposes, there were but a few hours of nightmare between the farm in Red Willow County and my study on Newbury Street. I had planned a little pleasure for her that afternoon, to repay her for some of the glorious moments she had given me when

Literary Analysis
Characterization and First-Person Narrator
Which details of this paragraph show who is narrating this story?

reverential (rev´ ə ren´ shəl) *adj.* caused by a feeling of deep respect and love

tremulously (trem´ yoo ləs lē) *adv.* fearfully; timidly

semi-somnambulant (sem´ i säm nam´ byoo lənt) *adj.* half-sleepwalking

✔**Reading Check**

When Clark was a boy, what subjects did he learn from his aunt?

we used to milk together in the straw-thatched cowshed, and she, because I was more than usually tired, or because her husband had spoken sharply to me, would tell me of the splendid performance of Meyerbeer's *Les Huguenots*[7] she had seen in Paris in her youth. At two o'clock the Boston Symphony Orchestra was to give a Wagner◆ program, and I intended to take my aunt, though as I conversed with her I grew doubtful about her enjoyment of it. Indeed, for her own sake, I could only wish her taste for such things quite dead, and the long struggle mercifully ended at last. I suggested our visiting the Conservatory and the Common[8] before lunch, but she seemed altogether too timid to wish to venture out. She questioned me absently about various changes in the city, but she was chiefly concerned that she had forgotten to leave instructions about feeding half-skimmed milk to a certain weakling calf, "Old Maggie's calf, you know, Clark," she explained, evidently having forgotten how long I had been away. She was further troubled because she had neglected to tell her daughter about the freshly opened kit of mackerel in the cellar, that would spoil if it were not used directly.

I asked her whether she had ever heard any of the Wagnerian operas, and found that she had not, though she was perfectly familiar with their respective situations and had once possessed the piano score of *The Flying Dutchman*. I began to think it would have been best to get her back to Red Willow County without waking her, and regretted having suggested the concert.

From the time we entered the concert hall, however, she was a trifle less passive and <u>inert</u>, and seemed to begin to perceive her surroundings. I had felt some trepidation[9] lest one might become aware of the absurdities of her attire, or might experience some painful embarrassment at stepping suddenly into the world to which she had been dead for a quarter of a century. But again I found how superficially I had judged her. She sat looking about her with eyes as impersonal, almost as stony, as those with which the granite Ramses[10] in a museum watches the froth and fret that ebbs and flows about his pedestal, separated from it by the lonely stretch of centuries. I have seen this same aloofness in old miners who drift into the Brown Hotel at Denver, their pockets full of bullion, their linen soiled, their haggard faces unshorn, and who

◆ **Wagner Operas**

Aunt Georgiana has a strong reaction to the music of Richard Wagner, the composer of *The Flying Dutchman* (1843). Wagner rejected some of the traditions of opera. To that end, he usually avoided lengthy musical speeches and instead originated the *leit-motif*, a dominant recurring musical theme used to symbolize an important emotion or event. Wagner also wrote what he called "music dramas." An entire series of these works, which would later be called *The Ring of the Nibelung*, consumed twenty-six years of his life. In "A Wagner Matinée," the audience hears excerpts from the *Ring* and from *Siegfried*, an opera based on the adventures of a legendary hero in medieval German literature.

inert (in ʉrt´) *adj.* motionless

---

7. **Les Huguenots** (lāz hyōō´ gə nät´) opera written in 1836 by Giacomo Meyerbeer (1791–1864).
8. **Common** Boston Common, a small park in Boston.
9. **trepidation** (trep´ ə dā´ shən) *n.* fearful anxiety; apprehension.
10. **Ramses** (ram´ sēz) one of the eleven Egyptian kings by that name who ruled from c. 1292 to c. 1075 B.C.

stand in the thronged corridors as solitary as though they were still in a frozen camp on the Yukon, or in the yellow blaze of the Arizona desert, conscious that certain experiences have isolated them from their fellows by a gulf no haberdasher could conceal.

The audience was made up chiefly of women. One lost the contour of faces and figures, indeed any effect of line whatever, and there was only the color contrast of bodices past counting, the shimmer and shading of fabrics soft and firm, silky and sheer, resisting and yielding: red, mauve, pink, blue, lilac, purple, ecru, rose, yellow, cream, and white, all the colors that an impressionist finds in a sunlit landscape, with here and there the dead black shadow of a frock coat. My Aunt Georgiana regarded them as though they had been so many daubs of tube paint on a palette.

When the musicians came out and took their places, she gave a little stir of anticipation, and looked with quickening interest down over the rail at that invariable grouping; perhaps the first wholly familiar thing that had greeted her eye since she had left old Maggie and her weakling calf. I could feel how all those details sank into her soul, for I had not forgotten how they had sunk into mine when I came fresh from plowing forever and forever between green aisles of corn, where, as in a treadmill, one might walk from daybreak to dusk without perceiving a shadow of change in one's environment. I reminded myself of the impression made on me by the clean profiles of the musicians, the gloss of their linen; the dull black of their coats, the beloved shapes of the instruments, the patches of yellow light thrown by the green-shaded stand-lamps on the smooth, varnished bellies of the cellos and the bass viols in the rear, the restless, wind-tossed forest of fiddle necks and bows; I recalled how, in the first orchestra I had ever heard, those long bow strokes seemed to draw the soul out of me, as a conjuror's stick reels out paper ribbon from a hat.

The first number was the Tannhäuser overture. When the violins drew out the first strain of the Pilgrims' chorus, my Aunt Georgiana clutched my coat sleeve. Then it was that I first realized that for her this singing of basses and stinging frenzy of lighter strings broke a silence of thirty years, the inconceivable silence of the plains. With the battle between the two motifs, with the bitter frenzy of the Venusberg[11] theme and its ripping of strings, came to me an overwhelming sense of the waste and wear we are so powerless to combat. I saw again the tall, naked house on the prairie, black and grim as a wooden fortress; the black pond where I had learned to swim, the rain-gullied clay about the naked house; the four dwarf ash seedlings on which the dishcloths were always hung to dry before the kitchen door. The world there is the flat world of the ancients; to the east, a cornfield that stretched to daybreak; to the west, a corral that stretched to sunset; between, the sordid conquests of peace, more merciless than those of war.

---

11. **Venusberg** (vē′ nəs bʉrg′) legendary mountain in Germany where Venus, the Roman goddess of love, held court.

Literary Analysis
Characterization What does Aunt Georgiana's excitement about the upcoming performance reveal about her?

**Reading Check**
What is Clark's initial feeling about being in public with Aunt Georgiana? How does that attitude change?

The overture closed. My aunt released my coat sleeve, but she said nothing. She sat staring at the orchestra through a dullness of thirty years, through the films made, little by little, by each of the three hundred and sixty-five days in every one of them. What, I wondered, did she get from it? She had been a good pianist in her day, I knew, and her musical education had been broader than that of most music teachers of a quarter of a century ago. She had often told me of Mozart's operas and Meyerbeer's, and I could remember hearing her sing, years ago, certain melodies of Verdi. When I had fallen ill with a fever she used to sit by my cot in the evening, while the cool night wind blew in through the faded mosquito netting tacked over the window, and I lay watching a bright star that burned red above the cornfield, and sing "Home to our mountains, oh, let us return!" in a way fit to break the heart of a Vermont boy near dead of homesickness already.

I watched her closely through the <u>prelude</u> to *Tristan and Isolde*, trying vainly to conjecture what that warfare of motifs, that seething turmoil of strings and winds, might mean to her. Had this music any message for her? Did or did not a new planet swim into her ken? Wagner had been a sealed book to Americans before the sixties. Had she anything left with which to comprehend this glory that had flashed around the world since she had gone from it? I was in a fever of curiosity, but Aunt Georgiana sat silent upon her peak in Darien.[12] She preserved this utter immobility throughout the numbers from the *Flying Dutchman*, though her fingers worked mechanically upon her black dress, as though of themselves they were recalling the piano score they had once played. Poor old hands! They were stretched and pulled and twisted into

prelude (prel′ yo͞od) *n.* introductory section of a work of music

---

12. peak in Darien (der′ ē ən′) mountain on the Isthmus of Panama; from "On First Looking at Chapman's Homer" by English poet John Keats (1795–1821).

mere tentacles to hold, and lift, and knead with; the palms unduly swollen, the fingers bent and knotted, on one of them a thin worn band that had once been a wedding ring. As I pressed and gently quieted one of those groping hands, I remembered, with quivering eyelids, their services for me in other days.

Soon after the tenor began the "Prize Song," I heard a quick-drawn breath, and turned to my aunt. Her eyes were closed, but the tears were glistening on her cheeks, and I think in a moment more they were in my eyes as well. It never really dies, then, the soul? It withers to the outward eye only, like that strange moss which can lie on a dusty shelf half a century and yet, if placed in water, grows green again. My aunt wept gently throughout the development and elaboration of the melody.

During the intermission before the second half of the concert, I questioned my aunt and found that the "Prize Song" was not new to her. Some years before there had drifted to the farm in Red Willow County a young German, a tramp cow puncher who had sung in the chorus at Bayreuth,[13] when he was a boy, along with the other peasant boys and girls. Of a Sunday morning he used to sit on his blue gingham-sheeted bed in the hands' bedroom, which opened off the kitchen, cleaning the leather of his boots and saddle, and singing the "Prize Song," while my aunt went about her work in the kitchen. She had hovered about him until she had prevailed upon him to join the country church, though his sole fitness for this step, so far as I could gather, lay in his boyish face and his possession of this divine melody. Shortly afterward he had gone to town on the Fourth of July, lost his money at a faro[14] table, ridden a saddled Texas steer on a bet, and disappeared with a fractured collarbone.

"Well, we have come to better things than the old *Trovatore* at any rate, Aunt Georgie?" I queried, with well-meant <u>jocularity</u>.

jocularity (jăk´ yŏŏ lar´ ə tē) *n.* joking good humor

Her lip quivered and she hastily put her handkerchief up to her mouth. From behind it she murmured, "And you've been hearing this ever since you left me, Clark?" Her question was the gentlest and saddest of reproaches.

"But do you get it, Aunt Georgiana, the astonishing structure of it all?" I persisted.

"Who could?" she said, absently; "why should one?"

The second half of the program consisted of four numbers from the *Ring.* This was followed by the forest music from *Siegfried*[15] and the program closed with Siegfried's funeral march. My aunt wept quietly, but almost continuously. I was perplexed as to what measure of musical comprehension was left to her, to her who had heard nothing for so many years but the singing of gospel hymns in Methodist

---

13. **Bayreuth** (bī roit´) city in Germany known for its annual Wagnerian music festivals.
14. **faro** (fer´ ō) gambling game in which players bet on the cards to be turned up from the top of the dealer's deck.
15. **Siegfried** (sēg´ frēd) opera based on the adventures of Siegfried, a legendary hero in medieval German literature.

Reading Check

Describe Aunt Georgiana's reaction during the "Prize Song."

services at the square frame schoolhouse on Section Thirteen. I was unable to gauge how much of it had been dissolved in soapsuds, or worked into bread, or milked into the bottom of a pail.

The deluge of sound poured on and on; I never knew what she found in the shining current of it; I never knew how far it bore her, or past what happy islands, or under what skies. From the trembling of her face I could well believe that the *Siegfried* march, at least, carried her out where the myriad graves are, out into the gray, burying grounds of the sea; or into some world of death vaster yet, where, from the beginning of the world, hope has lain down with hope, and dream with dream and, renouncing, slept.

The concert was over; the people filed out of the hall chattering and laughing, glad to relax and find the living level again, but my kinswoman made no effort to rise. I spoke gently to her. She burst into tears and sobbed pleadingly, "I don't want to go, Clark, I don't want to go!"

I understood. For her, just outside the door of the concert hall, lay the black pond with the cattle-tracked bluffs, the tall, unpainted house, naked as a tower, with weather-curled boards; the crook-backed ash seedlings where the dishcloths hung to dry, the gaunt, moulting turkeys picking up refuse about the kitchen door.

Review and Assess

Thinking About the Selection

1. **Respond:** Do you feel sorry for Aunt Georgiana? Why or why not?

2. **(a) Recall:** What part did Boston play in Aunt Georgiana's earlier life? **(b) Compare and Contrast:** In what ways would you compare and contrast life in Boston and life in Red Willow County?

3. **(a) Recall:** As a boy, what did the narrator practice on the "parlor organ" in the Nebraska farmhouse? **(b) Interpret:** What does Aunt Georgiana mean when she says, "Don't love it so well, Clark, or it may be taken from you"? **(c) Connect:** Do the events of the story reinforce her statement? Explain.

4. **(a) Recall:** What physical reactions indicate that Aunt Georgiana is affected powerfully by the concert?
   (b) Analyze: Why does the music have this effect on her?

5. **(a) Recall:** What memories do the "Prize Song" evoke in Aunt Georgiana? **(b) Connect:** How does Aunt Georgiana react at the end of the concert?

6. **Take a Position:** Would it have been better for Aunt Georgiana if she had not come to Boston? Explain.

Review and Assess

Literary Analysis

Characterization

1. What is revealed about Aunt Georgiana's character through descriptions of her appearance or comments by her and other characters? Record your findings in a chart like the one shown.

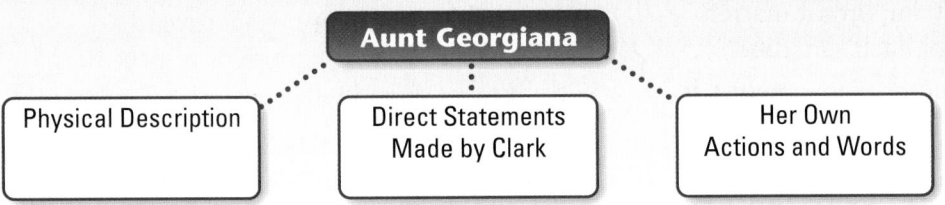

2. What does Aunt Georgiana's reaction to the opera reveal about her personality?
3. What do his thoughts and feelings about his aunt reveal about Clark's personality?

Connecting Literary Elements

4. What effect does Clark's **first-person point of view** have on your perception of Aunt Georgiana?
5. (a) Find two examples of events Clark recalls from living with Aunt Georgiana. (b) How do these events help to shape your impression of her?
6. (a) How do Clark's feelings toward his aunt change during the course of the story? (b) How do his feelings affect your response to her?
7. If the story were told by Aunt Georgiana, how would it change?

Reading Strategy

Clarifying

8. Which details about the harshness of life in Nebraska help to **clarify** your understanding of Aunt Georgiana's background?
9. Which details about Aunt Georgiana's life in Nebraska help you understand her timid behavior upon arriving in Boston?
10. Explain the significance of the fact that Aunt Georgiana's husband bought her "a little parlor organ" after fifteen years in Nebraska.

Extend Understanding

11. **Cultural Connection:** How are people's personalities shaped by the environment in which they live? Support your answer.

Quick Review

Characterization is the variety of techniques a writer uses to reveal a character's personality.

When a story is told in the **first-person point-of-view,** a character involved in the action relates the events.

To **clarify meaning** about something you do not understand, reread a passage, read a footnote, look up a word, or read ahead.

 Take It to the Net
www.phschool.com
Take the interactive self-test online to check your understanding of the selection.

Integrate Language Skills

Vocabulary Development Lesson

Concept Development:
Words From Music

Musical vocabulary can have two meanings. A *prelude* is a musical introduction, but it also refers to preparation for any important matter. Select the best definition for each sentence.

overture: (a) an introductory movement to an extended musical work, (b) any first movement

concert: (a) a performance of several short compositions, (b) working together

1. We put a *concerted* effort into the game.
2. He made an *overture* to pay my bill.

Spelling Strategy

When adding the suffix -*ial* to words ending in two consonants, keep the spelling of the base word. For example, *reverent* becomes *reverential*. Fill in the blanks with -*ial* words.

1. A talented person has great *p__ial*.
2. Our speed grew at an *ex__ial* rate.

Fluency: Word Meanings

Review the words in the vocabulary list on p. 675. Then, answer the following questions. Explain your responses.

1. If students are *reverential* toward a teacher, do they ignore or respect her?
2. Who is most likely to speak *tremulously*— a musician, a truck driver, or a child?
3. Does *semi-somnambulant* describe someone who is angry, dazed, or busy?
4. Is an *inert* substance motionless or weightless?
5. As a *prelude* to bad news, would you expect sarcasm or seriousness?
6. Is *jocularity* likely to be the trademark of a funeral director or a talk-show host?

Grammar and Style Lesson

Reflexive and Intensive Pronouns

Both reflexive and intensive pronouns end in -*self* or -*selves*, but they function differently. **Reflexive pronouns** refer to the subject and are necessary to the meaning of a sentence. **Intensive pronouns** emphasize a word in a sentence, but can be omitted without changing the meaning of a sentence. Consider the following examples:

Reflexive: He took *himself* to the box office.

Intensive: *Myself*, I saw her approaching.

Practice Identify the reflexive and intensive pronouns in these sentences.

1. Cather devoted herself to writing.
2. She quit her job to give herself time.
3. For Cather, writing itself was a full-time job.
4. Books don't write themselves.
5. Cather herself said writing was challenging.

Writing Application Write a description of a conversation among three or more people. Use reflexive and intensive pronouns.

WG Prentice Hall Writing and Grammar Connection: Chapter 17, Section 1

Writing Lesson

Editorial

"A Wagner Matinée" provoked an outcry among Nebraskans who felt Cather had portrayed the state unfairly. Cather responded that the story was a tribute to pioneer strength and endurance. As the editor of a Nebraska newspaper, take a position and write an editorial stating and defending your view.

Prewriting   Reread the story. Analyze the details Cather gives to portray both Nebraska and Boston, and decide whether or not you agree with her views. Jot down your thoughts that support or rebut Cather.

Drafting   Arrange your views in order of priority. Provide both factual evidence and emotional appeals to support your statements.

Revising   Reread your editorial to make sure that your language is specific and persuasive and that you have defended your views. Replace vague words to make your writing stronger and add more support as needed.

Model: Using Specific Language

Cather implies that Boston offers more than Nebraska.

While it may be true that Boston is a center for art,

      cultural resources   *pollution and congestion*

Nebraska offers many ~~things~~ without the ~~trouble~~ of a

major city.

> Specific references such as *cultural resources* and *pollution and congestion* make the editorial clear and persuasive.

 Prentice Hall Writing and Grammar Connection: Chapter 15, Section 2

Extension Activities

Listening and Speaking   With a classmate, take on the roles of Aunt Georgiana and Clark. Create **monologues** that give contrasting interpretations of the effect of the opera on Aunt Georgiana. Consider the following details:

- What memories were drawn out?
- What were the physical reactions?

Present both monologues to the class.
[Group Activity]

Research and Technology   Listen to a recording of one of Wagner's operas, and research the opera's story. Give a **musical presentation** of one of the passages from the opera to your classmates, explaining the piece's significance in the opera.

 Take It to the Net   www.phschool.com

Go online for an additional research activity using the Internet

CONNECTIONS
Literature Past and Present

Living in a Changing World

Writer Joyce Carol Oates once described Willa Cather as "a passionate chronicler of her time and place." The same can be said of Anna Quindlen. Although separated by nearly a century, both writers explore similar emotional terrain, charting the inner struggles and conflicts of the individual in a changing society.

A New Literary Sensibility The America of Willa Cather's youth was a nation in the midst of rapid and massive change. Industry and technology were booming. Confronted by these changes in society and its values, many writers struggled to find meaning in lives that were isolated from others. Out of this struggle, a new literary movement emerged. Known as Realism, this body of literature was often colored by loneliness and alienation.

A Loss of Community With the dawning of the Information Age, America is again undergoing a transformation. While some find the changes exciting, for others the loneliness and alienation of a century ago are still a reality. The symptoms are not hard to spot. People log anonymously onto chat rooms or spend hours watching television instead of chatting with flesh-and-blood neighbors. They move every few years in pursuit of better jobs, often losing family and community ties.

In her column "Life in the '30s," Anna Quindlen took the school, the neighborhood, and the office as her territory. In her work, Quindlen reveals a profound underside of loneliness and isolation.

Cats

Anna Quindlen

The cats came with the house. They lived in the backyards, tiger gray, orange marmalade, calico, black. They slithered through the evergreens at the back perimeter, and during mating season their screams were terrible. Sometimes I shook black pepper along the property line, and for a night or two all was still. Then the rain came and they were back.

The cats came because of the woman next door. She and her husband, said to be bedridden, had lived on the third floor for many years. Every evening after dinner she went into the alley with a foil pie plate heaped with cat food and scraps: cabbage, rice, the noodles from chicken noodle soup, whatever they had had for dinner. Before she would even get to the bottom of the stairs the cats would begin to assemble, narrowing their eyes. She would talk to them roughly in a voice like sandpaper, coarse from years of cigarette smoke. ". . . Cats," she grumbled as she bent to put the food down.

She had only two interests besides the cats: my son and her own. She and her husband had one grown child. I never heard her say a bad word about him. He had reportedly walked and talked early, been as beautiful as a child star, never given a bit of trouble. He always

✔**Reading Check**

What are the neighbor's main interests?

▲ **Critical Viewing**
In what ways are these cats like the ones Quindlen describes? How are they different? **[Compare and Contrast]**

sent a large card on Mother's Day, and each Christmas a poinsettia came, wrapped in green foil with a red bow. He was in the military, stationed here and there. During the time we lived next door to her, he came home once. She said it broke his heart not to see his father more. She said they had always been close when he lived at home, that he played baseball for the high school team and that his father never missed a game. He was a crack shortstop, she said, and a superior hitter.

She called my son "Bop Bop" because of the way he bounced in my arms. It was one of the first things he learned to say, and when he was in the backyard on summer evenings he would call "Bop Bop" plaintively until she came to her apartment window. As she raised the screen the cats would begin to mass in a great Pavlovian[1] gesture at the head of the alley. "Are you being a good boy?" she would call down. Bop Bop would smile up, his eyes shining. "Cat," he said, pointing, and the cats looked, too. Some summer nights she and my little boy would sit together companionably on the front stoop, watching the cars go by. She did not talk to him very much, and she wasn't tender, but when he was very good and not terribly dirty she sometimes

---

1. **Pavlovian** (pav lō′ vē ən) *adj.* referring to Russian physiologist Ivan Pavlov (1849–1936), who showed that acquired habits depend on chains of conditioned reflexes.

said he looked just like her own little boy, only his hair wasn't quite as thick.

Last year she fell on the street and broke her hip, but while she was in the hospital, they found that she had fallen because she had had a stroke, and she had had a stroke because of brain cancer. I went to see her in the hospital, and brought a picture of my son. She propped it against the water pitcher. She asked me to take care of her parakeet until she came home, to look in on her husband and to feed the cats. At night, when I came back from work, they would be prowling the yards, crying pitifully. My dogs lunged at the back windows.

When the ambulance brought her home, she looked like a scarecrow, her arms broomsticks in the armholes of her housecoat, her white hair wild. A home health-care aide came and cared for her and her husband. The woman across the street told me she was not well enough to take the bird back. The cats climbed the fire escape and banged against the screens with their bullet heads, but the aide shooed them away. My son would stand in the backyard and call "Bop Bop" at the window. One evening she threw it open and leaned out, a death's head, and shouted at him, and he cried. "Bop Bop is very sick," I said, and gave him a Popsicle.

She died this winter, a month after her husband. Her son came home for the funerals with his wife, and together they cleaned out the apartment. We sent roses to the funeral home, and the son's wife sent a nice thank-you note. The bird died the next month. Slowly the cats began to disperse. The two biggest, a tom and a female, seem to have stayed. I don't really feed them, but sometimes my son will eat lunch out back; if he doesn't finish his food, I will leave it on the table. When I look out again it is gone, and the dogs are a little wild.

My son likes to look through photo albums. In one there is a picture of her leaning out the window, and a picture of him looking up with a self-conscious smile. He calls them both "Bop Bop." I wonder for how long he will remember, and what it will mean to him, years from now, when he looks at the picture and sees her at her window, what reverberations will begin, what lasting lessons will she have subliminally taught him, what lasting lessons will she not so subliminally have taught me.

Thematic Connection
Setting Compare and contrast the alienated and disconnected life of Quindlen's neighbor with that of Aunt Georgiana in "A Wagner Matinée."

Anna Quindlen

(b. 1953)

Anna Quindlen was a *New York Times* reporter and editor and an aspiring novelist when the *Times* asked her to write a weekly column. She accepted the offer, never dreaming of where it might lead. Quindlen's column, "Life in the '30s," was a well-loved *Times* feature for more than two years, beginning in 1986. Quindlen's approach to the column—honest, personal, empathetic, astute—helps explain its immense popularity. She won a Pulitzer Prize for a commentary in 1992.

Connecting Literature Past and Present

1. With which characters from the selections in this section does Quindlen's neighbor have the most in common?

2. In what ways do Quindlen's neighbor and the character from another selection try to give meaning to their lonely lives?

3. Could "Cats" have been written one hundred years ago? Why or why not?

Writing About Literature

Compare and Contrast Literary Themes

Many of the selections in this unit address the American experience in the years just before and during the Civil War. Unlike other wars, in which the enemy was a separate and distant power, the Civil War pitted neighbor against neighbor, friend against friend, son against father. The enemy, as both an idea and a reality, had never before posed so painful or complex a problem.

Explore this issue in greater depth by completing the assignment given in the yellow box at right.

Prewriting

Review the material. After reading the selections in this unit, make notes exploring your impressions about each writer's attitude toward the enemy. Use the following questions to organize your thinking:

- Did each writer seem sure of the rightness of his or her cause?
- Did each writer seem eager for armed conflict?
- Did any writer express fear that the enemy might be victorious?
- Did any writer express sympathy for or understanding of the enemy?
- Did any writer seem to lack strong feeling toward the enemy?

As you address these and other questions, write brief statements identifying the selections that show the strongest connections or present the starkest contrasts.

Select works to compare and contrast. To create an engaging essay, the writers whose work you select should present marked differences or surprising similarities. Use a chart like the one shown to develop your analysis of the selections.

Model: Charting to Analyze Similarities and Differences

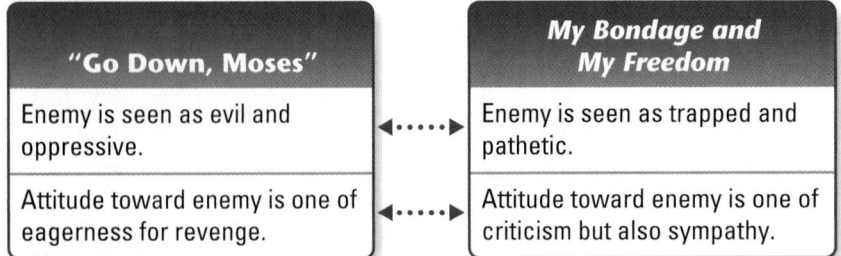

"Go Down, Moses"		*My Bondage and My Freedom*
Enemy is seen as evil and oppressive.	◀·····▶	Enemy is seen as trapped and pathetic.
Attitude toward enemy is one of eagerness for revenge.	◀·····▶	Attitude toward enemy is one of criticism but also sympathy.

After completing your analysis, identify the points of comparison and contrast that you find most interesting and important. Determine an initial approach to organizing your essay. You may either compare three selections in depth, or discuss a larger number of selections more briefly.

Assignment: Attitudes Toward the Enemy

Write an analytical essay that compares and contrasts the way three or more writers viewed the enemy during or directly preceding the American Civil War.

Criteria:

- Include a clear thesis statement that sums up the similarities or differences among the writers' attitudes toward the enemy.
- Support your thesis with details from at least three selections.
- Approximate length: 1,500 words

Read to Write

Reread the selections, paying careful attention to the attitudes behind the words.

Drafting

Organize examples. Make some organizational decisions before you begin to write. For example, consider using either one of the following strategies:

- **Grouping Ideas:** With this type of organization you discuss all the similarities between selections, and then discuss all of the differences.
- **Grouping Selections:** With this type of organization, you break your discussion down selection by selection, analyzing both similarities and differences for each one.

Draw conclusions. As you draft, draw conclusions about writers' attitudes toward the enemy based on the specific selections you have chosen to analyze. Make sure that you offer clear supporting evidence for every point you make.

Revising and Editing

Review content: Check for completeness and accuracy. Once you have decided to discuss a particular selection, you have a responsibility to analyze it thoroughly and accurately. You may not merely skim it for the details that support your thesis. Instead, you must account for each aspect of the selection that is relevant to your subject.

> ### Model: Revising for Thoroughness
>
> In "Go Down, Moses," the attitude of the slave toward the slaveowner is one of moral condemnation and rage. In *My Bondage and My Freedom*, however, Frederick Douglass ~~expresses sympathy for his master's wife.~~ ∧ *condemns his owner's wife, arguing that she is morally corrupt because she is a slaveowner. Surprisingly, he also expresses some sympathy for her position.*

Review style: Correctly punctuate and capitalize titles. Make sure you have correctly formatted and capitalized titles. The titles of full-length books are generally capitalized and italicized or underlined, while those of shorter works usually appear capitalized in quotation marks.

Publishing and Presenting

Generate a poster. Use the ideas developed in your essay to create a poster about attitudes toward the enemy during the Civil War. Emphasize main ideas with headlines. Then, note your primary supporting evidence.

*W*G *Prentice Hall Writing and Grammar Connection: Chapter 9*

Write to Learn

The writers whose works you are exploring cared deeply about their subjects. By writing about them, you, too, can develop your own ideas about moral and political conflict.

Write to Explain

Because you will be making subtle distinctions about attitudes and emotions, make sure that your language is especially precise. Your reader must always know exactly what you are talking about.

Writing WORKSHOP

Research: Research Paper

A **research paper** is a formal, written presentation of research on a single topic, based on information gathered from a variety of sources. In this workshop, you will write a research paper that presents your findings on a subject of interest to you.

Assignment Criteria Your research paper should demonstrate the following characteristics of research writing:

- A clear thesis statement
- Factual support from a variety of sources
- An explanation of how sources vary in their representation of events
- Consideration of the reliability of sources
- A clear organizational strategy
- A complete bibliography or works-cited list

To preview the criteria on which your research paper may be assessed, see the Rubric on page 699.

Prewriting

Choose a topic. Identify an area of interest, and brainstorm for a list of focused categories. For example, you might choose the categories of American presidents or wars. Within these categories, narrow your list further. Review your final list for a topic you would like to research.

Identify your purpose. Consider a question you would like to answer. Make sure the question is general enough to allow you to find sufficient material but narrow enough to be meaningful and manageable.

Sample Question: Is Phillis Wheatley a significant American poet?

Gather information. As you do research, create an index card recording each relevant fact or scholarly opinion that you find. Record the author, title, publisher, city, and date of publication of each source you consult.

Determine your audience. Use a chart like the one shown to determine the appropriate level of information to include in your paper.

Model: Charting to Analyze Audience

Audience	Specialized References Requiring Definition
Novices	Neoclassical, Milton, Pope, heroic couplet, panegyric, Homer, Virgil, Ovid, Aeschylus, Sophocles
General Audiences	Neoclassical, Milton, Pope, heroic couplet, panegyric
Experts	panegyric

Student Model

Before you begin writing, review this student model and note the characteristics of an effective research paper.

Lauren Shepherd
Tupelo, Mississippi

The Writing Style of Phillis Wheatley

In an era when African Americans were struggling to carve an identity for themselves, Phillis Wheatley emerged as the first truly significant black poet in American literature. Although many do not consider her to be an important writer judged by today's values of originality, she persevered through the challenges of her social status to become not only a celebrated poet but the starting point for the study of African-American literature. In this paper, I will discuss her work as a whole, and present a detailed analysis of one of her most famous poems, "To His Excellency General Washington."

Religious Message Wheatley was highly educated for her time, and had read the classics as well as the best English poets (Miller, de Dwyer, Wood 48). She was deeply influenced by the work of the great English poet John Milton (1608–1674), who saw himself as a writer in the service of God. Like Milton, Wheatley expressed a constant awareness of "God, His Son, His beneficence and His power." Almost every one of Wheatley's poems develops around a central theme of religious morality, and sometimes has an "air of message from the pulpit" (Mason 15–17). One theme, Christian salvation, underlies nearly everything she wrote (Redding 10).

Wheatley's religious messages are often conveyed through embellished Bible stories. In fact, a tradition within African American literature of augmenting biblical accounts with creative license and poetic flair can be traced directly to Wheatley. Both her poems "Goliath and Gath" and "Isaiah LXIII" add creative information to a foundation of biblical narrative.

African Influences In addition to the key role of Christian religious messages in Wheatley's work, many of her writings also exhibit a subtle presence of African traditions. For example, Wheatley uses solar imagery throughout her body of poems. Her frequent use of sun imagery in such poems as "A Hymn to the Morning," and "A Hymn to Evening," suggest that her early religious training in Africa may have consisted of some kind of hierophantic—or sun—worship (Smith, Baechler, Litz 474). Wheatley usually uses such sun imagery as a metaphor for Christian revelation, thus connecting the two essential elements of her religious life.

Also reminiscent of Wheatley's childhood in Africa is her constant interest in panegyric—or praise—poetry. In many of the cultures of Africa, poets were instructed that political praise constituted the very core of their responsibility as writers (Smith, Baechler, Litz 476). In keeping with that tradition, the majority of Wheatley's works are directed toward politically and socially prominent individuals, such as George Whitehead, a famous English clergyman, and George Washington (Johnson 29).

> Lauren clearly states her thesis in the opening paragraph.

> Lauren provides thorough support for all the opinions expressed in this passage.

> Subheads add to the orderliness of her essay.

> Lauren provides factual support for an interesting literary analysis.

Racial Consciousness Although many have ventured to say that Wheatley's "unquestioning embrace of New England and white cultures" prompted her to neglect the issue of slavery (Smith, Baechler, Litz 476), a closer examination of her poetry reveals that she was quite "race conscious" (Davis 192). She refers to herself on several occasions as "Africa's muse," and even uses her skin color and presumed low social status as a reference point for her religious message of salvation (Davis 192–193).

Neoclassical Style The majority of Wheatley's poems adhere to the established patterns of the neoclassical style. Neoclassicism was a widespread movement in the visual and literary arts that began in the 1760s and lasted until the 1840s and 1850s. Classical history and mythology provided much of the subject matter of Neoclassical works. The poetry of Homer, Virgil, and Ovid, and the plays of Aeschylus, Sophocles, and Euripides provided the bulk of classical sources. Neoclassical writers, such as Alexander Pope (1688–1744) stressed order, harmony, and restraint.

Like the Neoclassicists she admired, Wheatley's work was noted for an unfaltering preoccupation with regular rhyme and rhythm (Mason 14). Breaking out of her usual form on only six occasions Wheatley most frequently wrote using the heroic couplet—two-line stanzas written in iambic pentameter—that Alexander Pope made so effective (Mason 20). Considering that she is labeled as a spontaneous poet who would write during bouts of inspiration, the general regularity of her meter is remarkable. The influence of the Neoclassical writers also shows in Wheatley's use of elevated language (Mason 16), and in her numerous classical and mythological allusions.

"To His Excellency General Washington" The poem "To His Excellency General Washington" serves as a good example of Wheatley's style. Troubled by poor health since her arrival in America in 1761, when she was only eight years old (Perkins et al. 272), Wheatley traveled from Boston to London in 1773 in hope that the sea air would improve her well-being. Upon her return to the rebellious colonies in 1774, she found the fighting in the Boston vicinity had escalated. Wheatley composed her poem to George Washington and crossed the battle lines to deliver it in person. Two years later, Wheatley received a letter from the General himself thanking her for her adulation but insisting that she had placed him on too high a pedestal. In April 1776, Thomas Paine published her poem, its accompanying note, and Washington's reply in *Pennsylvania Magazine or American Monthly Museum* (Sheeler 8–10).

Although Washington's response to Wheatley's poem was modest, Wheatley gives the reader clear insight as to her opinions of the man. The entire poem is devoted to the veneration of the Continental Army and the leadership of General Washington. Wheatley adheres to her favorite poetic form of heroic couplets. She does not merely revere Washington, she portrays him as a royal figure, referring to him as "Your Excellency," and ascribing to him "a crown, a mansion and a throne that shine."

> The essay provides a variety of interpretations of the material.

> Necessary background information is essential to the readers' understanding.

> Lauren refers to other points of view regarding Wheatley's work.

> The essay makes use of a variety of historical documents, including this primary source.

Wheatley resorts to a striking use of personification in the poem. In the opening lines, she mentions the sorrow of "mother earth" at the bloodshed ravaging the land. In line 15, she personifies heaven as a maiden with a "fair face." Her use of alliteration in that image adds to its effect. Wheatley also gives life to the "nations" in line 33, and describes Brittania as a defeated being who "droops the pensive head" (line 35).

Perhaps Wheatley's most notable use of personification lies in her image of the American colonies as the Goddess Columbia (line 9) who is a "native of the skies" (line 11). Wheatley created this new goddess in honor of Christopher Columbus. Later popularized by Revolutionary War poets such as Philip Freneau, the image of Columbia had its first appearance in Wheatley's poem (Jensen).

Wheatley also weaves various allusions into her poem, For example, the European countries in conflict with America are said to be "Gallic powers" (line 30). This allusion refers to the Gallic Wars at the time of Julius Caesar when France was called Gaul. Further evidence of her classical knowledge appears in the reference to "Aeolus," the God of the wind (line 15). Aeolus appeared in Homer's *Odyssey* (Tripp 24), which Wheatley read in Alexander Pope's famous translation. Wheatley scholars generally agree that Pope's translation of Homer greatly affected her poetry (Mason 16).

Although Phillis Wheatley never achieved a truly original poetic style, she is undoubtedly an important figure in American literature. She transcended racial and language barriers to occupy a significant position in the social and intellectual scene of both Boston and London. If one judges her work based on the impact of her poetry on her contemporaries, she is an important pioneer in the development of American literature.

> Lauren concludes by reiterating her thesis.

Works Cited

Davis, Arthur P. "Personal Elements in the Poetry of Phillis Wheatley." Phylon: The Atlanta University Review of Race and Culture. 13 vols. June 1953, pp. 191–198.

Johnson, James Weldon., ed. The Book of American Negro Poetry. New York: Harcourt Bruce Jovanovich Inc., 1922.

Mason, Julian D., Jr., ed. The Poems of Phillis Wheatley. North Carolina: The University of North Carolina Press, 1989.

Miller, James E., Jr., Carlota Cárdenas de Dwyer, and Kerry M. Wood. The United States in Literature. Illinois: Scott, Foresman, and Company, 1985.

Perkins, George, et al., eds. The American Tradition in Literature. 1 vol. New York: McGraw-Hill Publishing Company, 1990.

Redding, J. Saunders. To Make a Poet Black. New York: Cornell University Press, 1988.

Sheeler, Karissa L. Phillis Wheatley. 11 February 2000. http://www.kutztown.edu/faculty/reagan/wheat1.html.

Smith, Valerie., Lea Baechler, and A. Walton Litz., eds. African American Writers. New York: Charles Scribner's Sons, 1991.

Tripp, Edward. Cromwell's Handbook of Classical Mythology. New York: Thomas Y. Cromwell Company, 1970.

> A complete Works-Cited list provides information on the sources Lauren references in the essay.

Drafting

Propose a thesis statement. An effective thesis statement expresses a position that can be supported by research. Review your notes and develop a statement that reflects a general tendency in the data you collected. Incorporate this statement into your draft.

Choose a type of organization. There are numerous effective methods for organizing your information and ideas. Depending on the main purpose of your paper, you may want to present events in the order in which they occurred, in order of importance, by comparing and contrasting events or trends, or by relating elements of a single event or topic to the whole. Use a chart like the one shown to select an organizational strategy that is best suited to your topic, audience, and purpose.

Write a formal outline. After you have selected an organizational strategy, prepare a formal outline.

Prepare to credit sources. When you include a direct quotation, present an original idea that is not your own, or report a fact that is available in only one source, you must include documentation. As you draft, circle ideas or words that are not your own. Use parentheses to note the author's last name and the page numbers of the materials used. Later, you can use this record to create formal citations.

Organizational Approaches

Purpose of Paper: Examine Wheatley's style and argue her importance in American literature	
Approach	**Benefit/Drawback**
Chronological	Does not establish her significance
Order of importance	Possible
Comparison and contrast	Not as useful
Parts to whole	Since I am exploring elements of her life and work, this makes best sense.

Revising

Revise to confirm your facts. When presenting material as fact, confirm that the information is accurate.

- Review your draft and mark points at which you state facts without providing documentation.
- If the fact is essential to your thesis, you must provide a reliable source.
- If the fact is not essential, or cannot be supported with data, remove it from your draft.

Model: Revising for Accuracy

~~Wheatley was~~ troubled by poor health since her arrival in America.

in 1761, when she was only eight years old, Wheatley traveled from Boston to London in 1773 in hope that the sea air would improve her well-being (Perkins et al. 272).

Lauren added additional information with reliable citation to clearly document the validity of her claim.

Revise for variety. Avoid using the same word repeatedly. Add variety with pronouns, synonyms, and proper nouns. In the following example, note how proper nouns spice up the language.

> **General names and places:** The poetry of Latin and Greek writers provided the bulk of classical sources.

> **Specific names and places:** The poetry of Homer, Virgil, and Ovid and the plays of Aeschylus, Sophocles, and Euripides provided the bulk of classical sources.

Publishing and Presenting

Create a reference list. Your research paper should document all your sources of information. A works-cited page provides readers with full bibliographic information on each source you cite. Standards for documentation are set by several organizations.

Identify the format your teacher prefers. Following that format, check that each entry is complete and properly punctuated. (For more information, see Writing Criticism and Citing sources, page R30.)

Deliver an oral presentation. Present the findings of your research paper in an oral report. Provide classmates with a handout outlining key points and indicating the sources you used in your research.

Submit your paper to an appropriate journal. Research the scholarly journals and magazines that publish essays in the field covered by your paper. Select a journal, and submit your essay for possible publication.

$\mathcal{W}_{G}$ *Prentice Hall Writing and Grammar Connection: Chapter 13*

Rubric for Self-Assessment

Evaluate your research paper using the following criteria and rating scale:

Criteria	Rating Scale				
	Not very				Very
How clearly worded is the thesis statement?	1	2	3	4	5
Is the thesis supported with a variety of sources?	1	2	3	4	5
Are differences between sources clearly explained?	1	2	3	4	5
Is the reliability of sources adequately addressed?	1	2	3	4	5
How effective is the organizational strategy?	1	2	3	4	5
How complete is the bibliography or works-cited list?	1	2	3	4	5

Speakers employ many kinds of arguments to convince listeners of the soundness of their positions. These arguments sometimes contain logical fallacies that can influence listeners' responses. The listening strategies outlined below will help you critically review persuasive speeches and recognize logical fallacies. Use the form on this page to record your reactions.

Critique Reasoning

In order to be persuasive, arguments must be logical and rational. Consider the following in critiquing persuasive arguments.

- **Challenge generalizations.** Make sure the speaker supports general claims with facts or verifiable experiences. Listen for generalizations drawn from samples that may be too small to represent broad truths.

- **Identify circular reasoning.** Listen for arguments in which the support merely restates the claim—for example, "Teenagers should not be hired because they lack experience." To check for circular reasoning, study the proof and make sure it offers new information.

- **Spot bandwagon effect.** Speakers may urge listeners' agreement by appealing to the desire for acceptance in a group. Likewise, a speaker may cite a celebrity's support. Analyze arguments on their merits, and avoid accepting a bandwagon appeal.

Critique Information

Speakers may also build arguments on faulty or misleading information. Listen for the following kinds of misleading structures.

- **Attack *ad hominem*** In this type of argument, named for the Latin phrase meaning "to the man," a speaker attacks an opponent personally, rather than responding to his or her arguments.

- **Red Herring** Named for the odorous fish once used to distract hunting dogs, the red herring argument presents dramatic but irrelevant information designed to confuse and distract listeners.

- **False Causality** When speakers suggest that events or facts have a cause-and-effect relationship, determine whether the events are actually causally linked or merely sequential or coincidental.

Activity:
Oral Address and Feedback Choose a topic about which you feel strongly and deliver a persuasive oral address stating your position and urging listeners' agreement. Take turns with classmates delivering addresses and critiquing arguments.

Feedback Form for Persuasive Arguments

Rating System: Logical Fallacies
+ = Not Present
✔ = Sometimes Present
− = Present Often

Reasoning
Weak generalizations _____
Circular reasoning _____
Bandwagon effect _____

Information
Attack *ad hominum* _____
Red herring _____
False causality _____

Answer the following questions:
Was the speaker's argument built on any faulty reasoning or information?

Without that faulty reasoning or information, does the speaker's argument remain convincing?

Assessment WORKSHOP

Context Clues

The reading sections of some tests often require you to use context to determine the meaning of unfamiliar or uncommon words and figurative expressions. The following strategies will help you answer such test questions:

- Remember that context is defined as the words and phrases that surround a word or figurative expression and provide clues to its meaning.
- Try to determine the meaning of certain words and figurative expressions by restating the passage in your own words.
- Read the passage, leaving out the unfamiliar word, and then substitute your possible meaning to see if it makes sense.

Test-Taking Strategies

- Restate the passage in your own words to clarify the author's message.
- Familiar words sometimes have unfamiliar meanings. Use phrases and sentences surrounding the word to help determine its meaning in the passage.

Sample Test Item

Directions: Read the passage, and then answer the question that follows.

The practice of celebrating Thanksgiving dates back to the year 1621, when the Pilgrims of Plymouth, Massachusetts, joined with local Wampanoag Indians to give thanks for the bountiful harvest. The feast included ducks, geese, corn, potatoes, lobsters, bass, clams, and dried fruit. For the Pilgrims, the food was like manna to the Israelites.

1. Judging from the context of the passage, what might you determine the meaning of the word *bountiful* to be?

    A lacking

    B spoiled

    C abundant

    D tasty

Answer and Explanation

The correct answer is **C**, because the context of *bountiful* includes a lengthy list of food and "giving thanks." Answers *A* and *B* describe a harvest that would not be worth celebrating. *D* could be correct, but no information in the text supports the idea that the food tasted good.

Practice

Directions: Read the passage, and then answer the questions that follow.

Amy and Jane listened closely to the weather forecast as they packed their bags. For nearly a year, they had eagerly anticipated taking a ski trip to Colorado. As they listened to the ominous predictions of freezing rain, sleet, and snow, their hearts sank like lead. Such dangerous weather conditions would surely ground their plane and force them to cancel their plans.

1. Judging from the context of the passage in which it is used, which of these words best defines the word *ominous*?

    A optimistic

    B troubling

    C incorrect

    D long-range

2. Judging from context, which of these phrases best defines the idiom *their hearts sank like lead*?

    A their spirits rose

    B they changed their minds

    C they experienced sudden despair

    D they felt balanced

Nighthawks, 1942, Edward Hopper, The Art Institute of Chicago

> **We asked the cyclone to go around our barn but it didn't hear us.**
>
> — Carl Sandburg
> from *The People, Yes*

Timeline 1914–1946

American Events

- **1915** Olympic track and field champion Jim Thorpe begins his professional football career. ◄

- **1916** *Chicago Poems* by Carl Sandburg appears.

- **1917** United States enters World War I.

- **1918** President Wilson announces his 14 Points in peace plan.

- **1919** Prohibition becomes law; repealed in 1933.

- **1919** Sherwood Anderson publishes *Winesburg, Ohio.*

- **1920** Nineteenth Amendment to Constitution gives U.S. women the right to vote. ▲

- **1922** T. S. Eliot publishes *The Waste Land.*

- **1923** Wallace Stevens publishes *Harmonium.*

- **1925** F. Scott Fitzgerald publishes *The Great Gatsby.*

- **1926** Langston Hughes publishes *The Weary Blues.*

- **1926** Ernest Hemingway publishes *The Sun Also Rises.*

- **1927** Charles Lindbergh flies solo and nonstop from New York to Paris.

- **1929** Stock market crashes in October, followed by Great Depression of the 1930s. ►

World Events

- **1915** England: Because of the war in Europe, travelers are cautioned against transatlantic voyages. The *Lusitania* would be sunk despite these warnings.

- **1917** Russia: Bolsheviks seize control of Russia in October Revolution.

- **1918** Worldwide influenza epidemic kills as many as 20 million people.

- **1919** France: Treaty of Versailles ends World War I. ►

- **1921** England: D. H. Lawrence publishes *Women in Love.*

- **1922** Ireland: James Joyce publishes *Ulysses.*

- **1924** Germany: Thomas Mann publishes *The Magic Mountain.*

- **1925** England: Virginia Woolf publishes *Mrs. Dalloway.*

- **1925** France: French sign Pact of Locarno with Germany, committing both parties to avoid using force to change the boundary line between them.

- **1928** China: Chiang Kai-shek becomes head of Nationalist government.

- **1928** Germany: Kurt Weill and Bertolt Brecht write and produce *The Threepenny Opera.*

- **1929** Japan: Collapse of American silk market hurts workers and farmers.

American and World Events

- **1933** President Roosevelt closes banks; Congress passes New Deal laws.
- **1939** John Steinbeck publishes *The Grapes of Wrath.*
- **1939** *The Wizard of Oz* and *Gone With the Wind* appear in movie theaters. ▼

- **1940** Richard Wright publishes *Native Son.*
- **1940** Civil Aeronautics Board is created to regulate U.S. commercial air traffic.
- **1941** Japanese bomb American naval base at Pearl Harbor, bringing U.S. into World War II. ▲
- **1944** Roosevelt is reelected president for an unprecedented fourth term.

- **1945** Atom bombs dropped on Hiroshima and Nagasaki.
- **1945** Truman declares September 2 V-J Day, or Victory Over Japan Day. World War II ends. ▼

- **1930** India: Mahatma Gandhi leads famous march to the sea to protest British tax on salt.
- **1931** Spain: Salvador Dali paints *Persistence of Memory.* ▶
- **1933** Germany: Adolf Hitler becomes German chancellor.
- **1936** Spain: Spanish Civil War begins.
- **1939** Poland: German blitzkrieg invasion of Poland sets off World War II.

- **1940** France: French government signs armistice with Germany.
- **1942** France: Albert Camus completes *The Stranger.*

- **1945** Germany: Dresden is hit by Allied firebombing raid. Firestorm virtually destroys city.
- **1945** United Nations Charter signed at end of World War II.

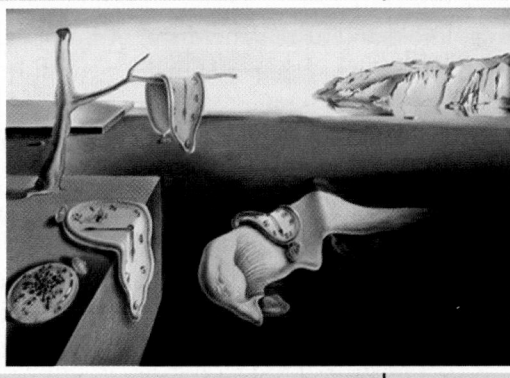

Disillusion, Defiance, and Discontent
(1914–1946)

The America that entered the twentieth century was a nation achieving world dominance while simultaneously losing some of its youthful innocence and brash confidence. Two world wars, a dizzying decade of prosperity, and a devastating worldwide depression marked this era. With these events came a new age in American literature. The upheavals of the early twentieth century ushered in a period of artistic experimentation and lasting literary achievement.

Historical Background

The years immediately preceding World War I were characterized by an overwhelming sense of optimism. Numerous technological advances occurred, dramatically affecting people's lives and creating a sense of promise for the future. While a number of serious social problems still existed, politicians began to initiate reforms aimed at solving those problems. When World War I broke out in 1914, however, President Woodrow Wilson was forced to turn his attention away from the troubles at home and focus on the events in Europe.

War in Europe World War I was one of the bloodiest and most tragic conflicts ever to occur. It involved a struggle between the Allies (Britain, France, Belgium, Italy, Serbia, Montenegro, Japan, and Russia; later, Russia would drop out of the conflict and the United States would join) and the Central Powers (Germany, Austria-Hungary, and Turkey). When the initial advances of the German forces were halted, the conflict in Europe was transformed into a trench war. The introduction of the machine gun made it virtually impossible for one side to launch a successful attack on its opponents' trenches, however, and the war dragged on for several years, claiming almost an entire generation of European men.

President Wilson wanted the United States to remain neutral in the war, but that proved impossible. In 1915, a German submarine sank the *Lusitania*, pride of the British merchant fleet. More than 1,200 people on board lost their lives, including 128 Americans. After the sinking, American public opinion favored the Allies. When Germany resumed unrestricted submarine warfare two years later, the United States joined the Allied cause.

At first, the reality of war did not sink in. Americans were confident and carefree as the troops set off overseas. That cheerful mood soon passed. A number of famous American writers saw the war firsthand and learned of its horror. E. E. Cummings, Ernest Hemingway, and John Dos Passos served as

THE NAVY NEEDS YOU! DON'T **READ** AMERICAN HISTORY— **MAKE IT!**

U·S·NAVY RECRUITING STATION

▲ **Critical Viewing**
Recruiting posters like this one urged Americans to help the war effort during World War I. Why do you think this poster would or would not have been effective in persuading people to enlist? **[Evaluate an Advertisement]**

ambulance drivers. Hemingway later served in the Italian infantry and was seriously wounded. Other, less famous writers fought and died in France. Among them were the poets Joyce Kilmer, who wrote "Trees," and Alan Seeger, who wrote "I Have a Rendezvous with Death."

Prosperity and Depression The era following the end of the Great War in November 1918 was not a peaceful one for America: President Wilson's dream of seeing the United States join the League of Nations failed, and in the big cities of America, from 1920 to 1933, Prohibition made the sale of liquor illegal, leading to bootlegging, speakeasies, widespread law breaking, and sporadic warfare among competing gangs.

Throughout the 1920s, the nation seemed to be on a binge. After a brief recession in 1920 and 1921, the economy boomed. New buildings rose everywhere, creating new downtown sections in many cities—Omaha, Des Moines, and Minneapolis among them. Radio arrived, and so did jazz. Movies became big business, and spectacular movie palaces sprang up across the country. Fads

Close-up on History

Women Get the Vote

One of the most important events of the immediate postwar period was the passage of the Nineteenth Amendment to the Constitution, giving women the right to vote.

The struggle to grant women the vote, or suffrage, went back many years, but it gathered significant momentum in the early 1900s. Carrie Chapman Catt, a former school principal and reporter, spoke out forcefully for women's suffrage. Catt was also a brilliant organizer, and she devised a state-by-state campaign to win the vote for women. Her campaign succeeded as year by year more states in the West and Midwest gave women the vote, although in most cases, they could exercise this right only in state elections. Gradually, more women called for an amendment to the Constitution to give them a voice in national elections, too.

The suffragist leader Alice Paul and others met with President Wilson soon after he took office in 1913. Although Wilson was not opposed to women's suffrage, he did not support a constitutional amendment. Suffragists became disillusioned after numerous meetings with Wilson and, in January 1917, began to picket at the White House. After several months, police began arresting the protesters. Paul and other arrested women went on a hunger strike, but prison officials force-fed them. Upon their release from prison, Paul and the other women resumed their picketing. They were a determined group.

By early 1918, not long before the end of World War I, the tide began to turn in favor of the suffrage cause. The tireless work of Catt, Paul, and others began to pay off. President Wilson agreed to support the suffrage amendment.

Finally, in 1919, Congress passed the Nineteenth Amendment, and by August 1920, three fourths of the states had ratified it. The amendment doubled the number of eligible voters in the United States and eliminated a long-standing injustice.

abounded: raccoon coats, flagpole sitting, and a dance called the Charleston. The great literary interpreter of the Roaring Twenties was F. Scott Fitzgerald. In *This Side of Paradise* and *The Great Gatsby*, Fitzgerald vividly captured the essence of life during this frenzied decade.

Writers flocked to Greenwich Village, in New York City. In 1923, playwright Eugene O'Neill founded the Greenwich Village Theatre, where experimental dramas were performed. Thomas Wolfe taught English at New York University in the Village while writing his novel *Look Homeward Angel.*

In late October 1929, the stock market crashed, marking the beginning of the Great Depression. By mid-1932, about 12 million people—one quarter of the work force—were out of work. Even as bread lines formed and the numbers of unemployed grew, most business leaders remained optimistic. However, the situation continued to worsen. In the presidential election of 1932, New York's governor Franklin D. Roosevelt defeated incumbent president Herbert Hoover. Roosevelt initiated the New Deal, a package of major economic reforms, to strengthen the economy. Roosevelt's policies helped bring an end to the Depression, and these policies, together with his leadership in World War II, earned him reelection in 1936, 1940, and again in 1944.

World War II Only twenty years after the Treaty of Versailles had ended World War I, the German invasion of Poland touched off World War II. As in the earlier war, most Americans wanted to remain neutral. Even after the fall of France in 1940, the dominant mood in the United States was one of isolationism. However, when the Japanese attacked Pearl Harbor, Hawaii, on December 7, 1941, America could stay neutral no longer. The United States declared war on the Axis powers—Japan, Germany, and Italy.

After years of bitter fighting on two fronts, the Allies—the United States, Great Britain, the Soviet Union, and France—defeated Nazi Germany. Japan surrendered three months later, after the United States had dropped atomic bombs on two Japanese cities. Peace, and the atomic age, had arrived.

Literature of the Period

The Birth of Modernism The devastation of World War I brought about an end to the sense of optimism that had characterized the years immediately preceding the war. Many people were left with a feeling of uncertainty and disillusionment. No longer trusting the ideas and values of the world out of which the war had developed, people sought to find new ideas that better suited twentieth-century life. The quest for new ideas occurred in the world of literature as well, and a major literary movement known as Modernism was born.

Modernists experimented with a wide variety of new approaches and techniques, producing a remarkably diverse body of literature. Yet the Modernists shared a common purpose: They sought to capture the essence of modern life

▲ **Critical Viewing** The Charleston was a popular dance during the Roaring Twenties. Why do nightclubs featuring music and dance flourish during periods of prosperity? **[Make an Inference]**

in both the form and content of their work. To reflect the fragmentation of the modern world, the Modernists constructed their works out of fragments, omitting the expositions, transitions, resolutions, and explanations used in traditional literature. In poetry, they abandoned traditional forms and meters in favor of free verse, whose rhythms they improvised to suit individual poems. The themes of their works were usually implied, rather than directly stated, creating a sense of uncertainty and forcing readers to draw their own conclusions. In general, Modernist works demanded more from readers than the works of earlier American writers. At the same time, the Modernists helped to earn American literature a place in the world's esteem.

Imagism The Modernist movement was ushered in by a poetic movement known as Imagism. This movement, which lasted from 1909 to 1917, attracted followers in both the United States and England. The Imagists rebelled against the sentimentality of nineteenth-century poetry. They demanded

Point /Counterpoint

Women, Followers—or Cofounders—of Modernism?

Were the female writers and editors who worked alongside men like Pound and Eliot useful followers and helpers of these men, or were they fully contributing cofounders of Modernism? Two scholars disagree about where the credit for founding Imagism should be given.

Women, Followers of Modernism "With energy and dispatch, Pound began collecting poetry. . . . He then asked Hilda Doolittle to show him some poems in the tearoom of the British Museum, in the 'rather prissy milieu of some infernal bun shop full of English spinsters,' as Aldington put it. Pound read Hilda's new poems with admiration. According to Aldington, Pound popped his pince-nez, an affectation he had learned from Yeats, when he read her 'Hermes of the Ways,' a poem he immediately cut and changed to make its pristine clarity even more penetrating, and signed the poem 'H.D., Imagiste.' In the space of a few moments Pound had created a literary movement and its first acolytes."

—John Tytell,
Ezra Pound: The Solitary Volcano

Women, Cofounders of Modernism "It is also apparent that a number of women's achievements have been credited to Pound in whole or in part. H.D. made the first real critical comments about the poetry of Marianne Moore, and Moore credited H.D. with suggesting that Moore write prose for the *Dial*—both activities that have been attributed to Pound. Cyrena Pondrom has demonstrated that H.D. also created the poetic style that became known as Imagism. . . . H.D., and especially Amy Lowell, played central roles in disseminating Imagism. . . . Literary histories, however, often give Pound full credit for the development and promotion of Imagism."

—Jayne E. Marek,
Women Editing Modernism

instead hard, clear expression, concrete images, and the language of everyday speech. Their models came from Greek and Roman classics, Chinese and Japanese poetry, and the free verse of the French poets of their day. Among the writers associated with the earliest phase of Imagism were H.D. (Hilda Doolittle) and Ezra Pound. When Pound moved on from Imagism, other leaders took over, among them H.D. Amy Lowell, a Massachusetts poet, led the Imagist movement in the United States in its final years.

The Expatriates Postwar disenchantment led a number of American writers to become expatriates, or exiles. Many of these writers settled in Paris, where they were influenced by Gertrude Stein, the writer who coined the phrase "lost generation" to describe those who were disillusioned by World War I. Stein lived in Paris from 1902 until her death in 1946, and her home attracted many major authors, including Sherwood Anderson, F. Scott Fitzgerald, and Ernest Hemingway.

Fitzgerald and Hemingway are the best known of the expatriates, but they are by no means the only ones. Ezra Pound spent most of his adult life in England, France, and Italy. T. S. Eliot, born in St. Louis, went to Europe in 1914, soon settled in England, and lived there until his death in 1965. Some critics have called Eliot's long, despairing poem *The Waste Land* the most important poem of the century.

Most of the "lost generation" saw very little in their civilization to praise or even accept. Archibald MacLeish, an expatriate from 1923 to 1928, wrote several volumes of verse expressing the chaos and hopelessness of those years. MacLeish eventually broke with the expatriates, however. He returned to the United States in the 1930s and became increasingly concerned about the rise of dictatorships. A supporter of President Roosevelt's New Deal, he served as Librarian of Congress during World War II.

New Approaches During the years between the two world wars, writers in both the United States and Europe explored new literary territories. Influenced by developments in modern psychology, writers began using the stream-of-consciousness technique, attempting to re-create the natural flow of a character's thoughts. Drawing its name from the work of psychologist William James, this technique involves the presentation of a series of thoughts, memories, and insights, connected only by a character's natural associations.

The landmark stream-of-consciousness novel is *Ulysses*, published in 1922 by the Irish writer James Joyce. A number of American novelists soon adopted the technique, most notably William Faulkner in

▼ Critical Viewing Dorothea Lange took this photograph, which has become a symbol of the Great Depression. What does it "say" about this period? **[Draw a Conclusion]**

The Sound and the Fury. Katherine Anne Porter's short stories and the three novels in John Dos Passos's *U.S.A.* also use stream-of-consciousness narration. The trilogy by Dos Passos includes other devices unusual in a fictional work, such as brief biographies of well-known Americans and quotations from newspapers and magazines.

Poets also sought to stretch the old boundaries. E. E. Cummings's poems attracted special attention because of their wordplay, unique typography, and special punctuation. These devices are more than mere oddities in Cummings's poetry. They are vital to its intent and its meaning.

William Carlos Williams, a New Jersey physician and poet, began by writing poetry like that of John Keats, radically changed his style under the influence of Imagism, and turned an attentive eye on his local world. Unlike the writers who traveled to Europe, Williams sought meaning in American sights and sounds and used informal, conversational speech. His epic poem, *Paterson*, is named for a New Jersey city. He had a great influence on two important poets of the next generation, Allen Ginsberg and A.R. Ammons.

Wallace Stevens, an insurance executive, wrote a more intellectual and self-consciously elegant poetry than that of Williams. Throughout his work, Stevens explored the shifting relationship between reality and the fictions that the imagination creates. His poetry was inspirational for such later poets as James Merrill and John Ashbery.

Marianne Moore is famous for her lines measured by syllable counts, her use of quotations from such real-world texts as "business documents and school books," and her quirky, unforgettable images—in "Poetry," she compares an "immovable critic twitching his skin" to "a horse."

Writers of International Renown The Modernists dramatically altered the complexion of American literature. At the same time, many of these writers earned international acclaim that equaled that of their European literary contemporaries.

Proof of this acclaim is the number of Americans who won the Nobel Prize for Literature. This international award was established in 1901 with funds bequeathed by Alfred Nobel, the Swedish inventor of dynamite. The first American to win the Nobel Prize for Literature was Sinclair Lewis. A native of Sauk Center, Minnesota, Lewis fictionalized his hometown as Gopher Prairie in his first important novel, *Main Street.* Lewis, one of the great satirists of the era, wrote two more classics within the next few years. *Babbitt* was about an American businessman, while *Arrowsmith* dealt with the medical profession.

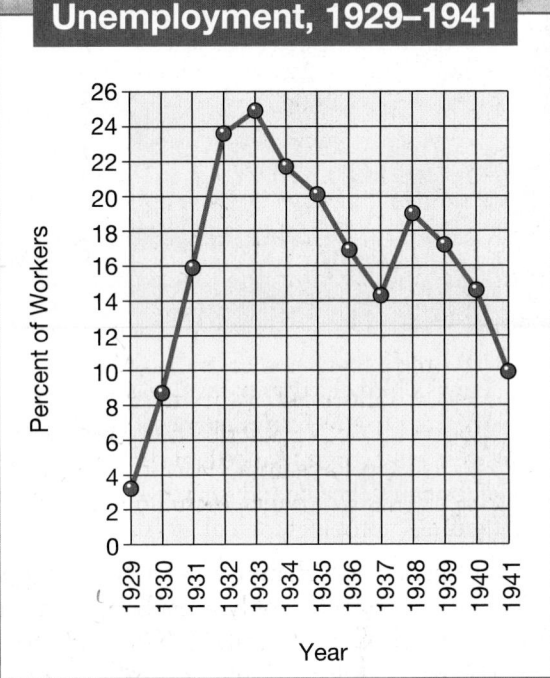

Unemployment, 1929–1941

▲ **Critical Viewing** During the Depression, millions of Americans were out of work. According to the graph, what happened to unemployment between 1936 and 1941? **[Interpret a Pattern]**

Lewis's Nobel Prize in 1930 was the first of many for American writers. In 1936, the prize went to Eugene O'Neill, ranked by most critics as America's greatest playwright. Among his best-known plays are *Desire Under the Elms*, *The Iceman Cometh*, and *Long Day's Journey Into Night*. O'Neill's plays are sometimes autobiographical, generally tragic, and often experimental. His *Strange Interlude*, produced in 1928, uses stream-of-consciousness asides to reveal the inner feelings of characters. These feelings often contrast with their actual spoken words.

Then, in 1938, the Nobel Prize for Literature went to Pearl S. Buck, an American who spent her early years in China. Buck wrote about that country with understanding and compassion. *The Good Earth* is considered her finest work.

After T. S. Eliot, who had become a British subject, won the award in 1948, William Faulkner won it the following year. Most of Faulkner's novels and short stories are set in mythical Yoknapatawpha County, Mississippi, which closely resembled the region of Mississippi where Faulkner lived. In addition to *The Sound and the Fury*, Faulkner wrote such enduring works as *Light in August* and *The Hamlet*.

Later, Ernest Hemingway and John Steinbeck also won Nobel Prizes for Literature. Hemingway's simple, direct, journalistic style of writing, evident in such novels as *The Sun Also Rises* and *A Farewell to Arms*, influenced a generation of young writers. Much of his best writing focuses on World War I and its aftermath. Many of Steinbeck's works depict the Depression, especially as it affected migrant workers and dust-bowl farmers. Two of Steinbeck's most memorable novels are *Of Mice and Men* and *The Grapes of Wrath*.

The Harlem Renaissance A new literary age was dawning, not only in Greenwich Village and among expatriates in Paris, but also in northern Manhattan, in Harlem. African American writers, mostly newcomers from the South, were creating their own renaissance there. It began in 1921 with the publication of Countee Cullen's "I Have a Rendezvous With Life (with apologies to Alan Seeger)." Another poem by a promising young African American writer—"The Negro Speaks of Rivers," by Langston Hughes— followed six months later.

What occurred thereafter was a burst of creative activity by African American writers, few of whom, other than Cullen, had been born in New York City. Most of them moved to Harlem during the renaissance. Claude

McKay, for example, was from Jamaica. His most famous book was *Harlem Shadows*, a collection of poems published in 1922. A year later came Jean Toomer's *Cane*, a collection of stories, verses, and a play.

The Harlem Renaissance was publicly recognized in March 1924, when young African American writers met the literary editors of the city. Carl Van Doren, editor of the *Century*, noted that black writers, long "oppressed and handicapped . . . have gathered stores of emotion and are ready to burst forth with a new eloquence."

The Harlem phenomenon continued throughout the 1920s and into the 1930s. Arna Bontemps, born in Louisiana, published his first novel, *God Sends Sunday*, in 1931. The writers of this renaissance belonged to no single school of literature, but they did form a coherent group. They saw themselves as part of a new and exciting movement. In addition to producing their own exceptional works, they opened the door for the African American writers who would follow them.

A Continuing Tradition World War II did not end the literary revival that had begun after World War I. Many of the older writers continued to produce novels, short stories, plays, and poems. Meanwhile, a new generation of writers arose after World War II to keep American literature at the leading edge of the world's artistic achievement.

A Writer's Voice

Anne Spencer, Poet of the Harlem Renaissance

Women who participated in the Harlem Renaissance tend to get less attention than the men. That is why it is worth mentioning Anne Spencer (1882–1975), a poet whose work compares favorably with that of her more famous contemporaries: James Weldon Johnson, Langston Hughes, Jean Toomer, and Claude McKay.

Spencer grew up and was educated in Virginia. Her poetry became well known when Johnson selected some of her work to appear in *The Book of American Negro Poetry* (1922). During the Harlem Renaissance, she received visits from such distinguished writers as Johnson, McKay, and W.E.B. Du Bois, author of *The Souls of Black Folk* (1903).

In the following brief poem, Spencer writes in the voice of Paul Laurence Dunbar (1872–1906), an African American poet of the previous generation. Dunbar had written powerful poems like "Douglass" and "We Wear the Mask" (see pages 658 and 660). Here, Spencer indicates the value of his work by having him rank himself with three famous British Romantic poets, all of whom, like Dunbar himself, died young.

Dunbar (1920)

Ah, how poets sing and die!
Make one song and Heaven takes it;
Have one heart and Beauty breaks it;
Chatterton, Shelley, Keats, and I—
Ah, how poets sing and die!

THE DEVELOPMENT OF AMERICAN ENGLISH

Slang As It Is Slung

BY RICHARD LEDERER

Slang is hot and slang is cool. Slang is nifty and slang is wicked. Slang is the bee's knees and the cat's whiskers. Slang is far out, groovy, and outa sight. Slang is fresh, fly, and phat. Slang is bodacious and fantabulous. Slang is ace, awesome, copacetic, the max, and totally tubular.

Those are many ways of saying that, if variety is the spice of life, slang is the spice of language. Slang adds gusto to the feast of words, as long as speakers and writers remember that too much spice can kill the feast of any dish.

Slang has added spice to the feast of American literature as American writers have increasingly written in an American voice, with the words and rhythms of everyday American discourse. Listen to the Harlem Renaissance poet Langston Hughes:

Good morning, daddy!
Ain't you heard
The boogie-woogie rumble
Of a dream deferred?

DEFINING THE "LINGO"

What is slang? In the preface to their *Dictionary of American Slang,* Harold Wentworth and Stuart Berg Flexner define slang as "the body of words and expressions frequently used by or intelligible to a rather large portion of the general American public, but not accepted as good, formal usage by the majority." Slang, then, is seen as a kind of vagabond language that prowls the

outskirts of respectable speech, yet few of us can get along without it. Even our statespersons have a hard time getting by without such colloquial or slang expressions as "hit the nail on the head," "team effort," or "pass the buck."

WHAT'S IN THIS NAME?

Nobody is quite sure where the word *slang* comes from. According to H. L. Mencken, the word slang developed in the eighteenth century (it was first recorded in 1756) either from an erroneous past tense of *sling* (*sling-slang-slung*) or from language itself, as in *(thieve)s'lang(uage)* and *(beggar)s'lang(uage).* The second theory makes the point that jargon and slang originate and are used by a particular trade or class group, but slang words come to be slung around to some extent by a whole population.

Slang is a prominent part of our American wordscape. In fact, *The Dictionary of American Slang* estimates that slang makes up perhaps a fifth of the words we use. Many of our most valuable and pungent words have begun their lives keeping company with thieves, vagrants, and hipsters. As Mr. Dooley, a fictional Irish saloon keeper, once observed, "When we Americans get through with the English language, it will look as if it has been run over by a musical comedy."

ACTIVITY

Student slang is a rich vein of metaphor and word formation. With your classmates, compile a dictionary of the slang used in your school. Provide a sentence or two illustrating the use of each slang term you define.

PART 1

Facing Troubled Times

No Place to Go, 1935, Maynard Dixon, The Herald Clark Memorial Collection, Courtesy of Brigham Young University Museum of Fine Arts

Prepare to Read

The Love Song of J. Alfred Prufrock

T. S. Eliot (1888–1965)

Always well-spoken and somberly attired, Thomas Stearns Eliot was outwardly the model of convention. His work, in contrast, was revolutionary in both form and content.

Beginnings Born into a wealthy family in St. Louis, Missouri, Eliot grew up in an environment that promoted his intellectual development. He attended Harvard University, where he published a number of poems in *The Harvard Advocate*, the school's literary magazine. In 1910, the year Eliot received his master's degree in philosophy, he completed "The Love Song of J. Alfred Prufrock."

A Literary Sensation Just before the outbreak of World War I, Eliot moved to England. In 1915, he married Vivien Haigh-Wood, a deeply troubled young woman with whom he had a tumultuous relationship. During this period, he also became acquainted with Ezra Pound, another young American poet. Pound urged Harriet Monroe, the editor of *Poetry* magazine, to publish "Prufrock," thus making Eliot's work available to the public for the first time. Shortly thereafter, Eliot published a collection titled *Prufrock and Other Observations* (1917), which caused a sensation in the literary world. Eliot had used techniques, such as an intentionally fragmented structure, that were utterly new. Focusing on the frustration and despair of modern urban life, the poems in Eliot's first book also set the tone for the other poems he would write during the early stages of his career. These early poems alone earned Eliot a lasting place among the finest writers of the twentieth century.

Facing a New World Eliot made his literary mark against the backdrop of a rapidly changing society. Telephones, radios, automobiles—all were transforming life at an unprecedented pace in the early decades of the twentieth century. Uncertain and disillusioned with the values and ideologies that had produced the devastation of World War I, many people were searching for new ideas and values. Eliot was among a group of such writers and visual artists who called themselves Modernists. Modernist poets sought a break with the literary traditions of the past. They believed that poetry had to reflect the genuine, fractured experience of life in the twentieth century, not a romanticized idea of what life was once like. Eliot's exploration of the uncertainty of modern life struck a chord among readers, who were stunned by his revolutionary poetic imagery.

In 1922, Eliot published *The Waste Land*, his most celebrated work. Although Eliot himself once dismissed *The Waste Land* as "a piece of rhythmical grumbling," most readers saw it as a profound critique of the spiritual barrenness of the modern world. The poem is filled with allusions to classical and world literature and to Eastern culture and religion. It was widely read and had an enormous impact on writers and critics. *The Waste Land* is still considered one of the finest works ever written.

A Return to Tradition In his search for something beyond the "waste land" of modern society, Eliot became a member of the Church of England in 1927. He began to explore religious themes in poems such as "Ash Wednesday" (1930) and *Four Quartets* (1943)—works that suggest that he believed religion could heal the wounds inflicted by society. In later years, he wrote several plays, including *Murder in the Cathedral* (1935) and *The Cocktail Party* (1949), as well as a sizable body of literary criticism. In 1948, Eliot received the Nobel Prize for Literature.

Preview

Connecting to the Literature

You may be able to remember occasions when you have wished you had a different personality. Maybe you would have preferred to be more outgoing or more assertive—the type of person who makes things happen. The character of J. Alfred Prufrock speaks to this feeling in all of us.

Literary Analysis

Dramatic Monologue

A troubled J. Alfred Prufrock invites an unidentified companion—perhaps a part of his own personality—to walk with him as he reflects aloud about his bitter realization that life and love are passing him by. Prufrock's so-called love song is a **dramatic monologue**—a poem or speech in which a character addresses a silent listener. As you read this dramatic monologue, use a chart like the one shown to record Prufrock's observations about life, details of his personality, and internal conflicts.

Connecting Literary Elements

Just as you might refer to a movie you once saw or a book you once read, Prufrock refers to people and historical or literary events that hold meaning for him. For example, in this passage, he alludes to Shakespeare:

> No! I am not Prince Hamlet, nor was meant to be;
> Am an attendant lord, one that will do
> To swell a progress, start a scene or two . . .

These references, or **allusions,** form a literary shorthand that paints a picture of Prufrock and his culture. As you read, use footnotes and guided reading questions to help you understand these allusions.

> **Prufrock's Observations**
>
> _____
>
> **Personality Traits**
>
> _____
>
> **Internal Conflicts**
>
> _____

Reading Strategy

Listening

This poem contains some of the most famous and haunting passages in literature. One of the reasons the poem affects readers so intensely is its musicality—the sweep and fall of the lines, the repetition and rhyme, and the sounds of the words. To fully appreciate the poem, you must **listen** to it. Try reading the poem aloud, paying attention to the rhythms and repetitions. Consider how the musicality of the poem contributes to its mood and meaning.

Vocabulary Development

insidious (in sid′ ē əs) *adj.* secretly treacherous (p. 718)

digress (dī gres′) *v.* depart temporarily from the main subject (p. 720)

malingers (mə liŋ′ gerz) *v.* pretends to be ill (p. 720)

meticulous (mə tik′ yōō ləs) *adj.* extremely careful about details (p. 721)

obtuse (äb tōōs′) *adj.* slow to understand or perceive (p. 721)

The Love Song of
J. Alfred Prufrock
T. S. Eliot

Background

In this poem, surely one of the strangest "love songs" ever written, J. Alfred Prufrock, a stuffy and inhibited man who is pained by his own passivity, invites the reader, or some unnamed visitor, to join him in a journey. Where Prufrock is and where he is going—to a party, a museum, a tea party, or some other gathering—is open to debate. The most important part of this journey, however, takes place within the inner landscape of Prufrock's emotions, memory, and intellect as he meditates on his life.

S'io credessi che mia risposta fosse
a persona che mai tornasse al mondo,
questa fiamma staria senza più scosse.
Ma per ciò che giammai di questo fondo
non tornò vivo alcun, s'i'odo il vero,
senza tema d'infamia ti rispondo.[1]

Let us go then, you and I,
When the evening is spread out against the sky
Like a patient etherized[2] upon a table;
Let us go, through certain half-deserted streets,
5 The muttering retreats
Of restless nights in one-night cheap hotels
And sawdust restaurants with oyster-shells:
Streets that follow like a tedious argument
Of <u>insidious</u> intent
10 To lead you to an overwhelming question . . .
Oh, do not ask, "What is it?"
Let us go and make our visit.

1. **S'io credessi . . . ti rispondo** The epigraph is a passage from Dante's *Inferno*, in which one of the damned, upon being requested to tell his story, says: "If I believed my answer were being given to someone who could ever return to the world, this flame (his voice) would shake no more. But since no one has ever returned alive from this depth, if what I hear is true, I will answer you without fear of disgrace."
2. **etherized** (ē´ thə rīzd) *v.* anesthetized with ether.

In the room the women come and go
Talking of Michelangelo.[3]
15 The yellow fog that rubs its back upon the window-panes,
The yellow smoke that rubs its muzzle on the window-panes,
Licked its tongue into the corners of the evening,
Lingered upon the pools that stand in drains,
Let fall upon its back the soot that falls from chimneys,
20 Slipped by the terrace, made a sudden leap,
And seeing that it was a soft October night,
Curled once about the house, and fell asleep.

And indeed there will be time[4]
For the yellow smoke that slides along the street
25 Rubbing its back upon the window-panes;
There will be time, there will be time
To prepare a face to meet the faces that you meet;
There will be time to murder and create,
And time for all the works and days[5] of hands
30 That lift and drop a question on your plate;
Time for you and time for me,
And time yet for a hundred indecisions,
And for a hundred visions and revisions.
Before the taking of a toast and tea.

35 In the room the women come and go
Talking of Michelangelo.
And indeed there will be time
To wonder, "Do I dare?" and, "Do I dare?"
Time to turn back and descend the stair,
40 With a bald spot in the middle of my hair—
(They will say: "How his hair is growing thin!")
My morning coat, my collar mounting firmly to the chin,
My necktie rich and modest, but asserted by a simple pin–
(They will say: "But how his arms and legs are thin!")
45 Do I dare
Disturb the universe?
In a minute there is time
For decisions and revisions which a minute will reverse.

For I have known them all already, known them all—
50 Have known the evenings, mornings, afternoons,
I have measured out my life with coffee spoons;
I know the voices dying with a dying fall

Literary Analysis

Dramatic Monologue and Allusion What might Prufrock's allusion to Michelangelo suggest about the women at the party?

Literary Analysis

Dramatic Monologue What emotions does the speaker express in the description of his physical appearance?

---

3. **Michelangelo** (mī´ kəl an´ jə lō) a famous Italian artist and sculptor (1475–1564).
4. **there will be time** These words echo the narrator's plea in English poet Andrew Marvell's "To His Coy Mistress": "Had we but world enough and time . . . "
5. **works and days** Ancient Greek poet Hesiod wrote a poem about farming called "Works and Days."

✔ **Reading Check**

At what time of day is the poem set?

Beneath the music from a farther room.
So how should I presume?

55 And I have known the eyes already, known them all—
The eyes that fix you in a formulated phrase,
And when I am formulated, sprawling on a pin,
When I am pinned and wriggling on the wall,
Then how should I begin
60 To spit out all the butt-ends of my days and ways?
And how should I presume?

And I have known the arms already, known them all—
Arms that are braceleted and white and bare
(But in the lamplight, downed with light brown hair!)
65 Is it perfume from a dress
That makes me so <u>digress</u>?
Arms that lie along a table, or wrap about a shawl.
And should I then presume?
And how should I begin?

. . . .

70 Shall I say, I have gone at dusk through narrow streets
And watched the smoke that rises from the pipes
Of lonely men in shirt-sleeves, leaning out of windows? . . .

I should have been a pair of ragged claws
Scuttling across the floors of silent seas.[6]

. . . .

75 And the afternoon, the evening, sleeps so peacefully!
Smoothed by long fingers,
Asleep . . . tired . . . or it <u>malingers</u>,
Stretched on the floor, here beside you and me.
Should I, after tea and cakes and ices,
80 Have the strength to force the moment to its crisis?
But though I have wept and fasted, wept and prayed,
Though I have seen my head (grown slightly bald) brought in
upon a platter,[7]
I am no prophet—and here's no great matter;
I have seen the moment of my greatness flicker,
85 And I have seen the eternal Footman[8] hold my coat, and snicker.
And in short, I was afraid.

digress (di gres´) v. depart
temporarily from the
main subject

malingers (mə liŋ´ gərz) v.
pretends to be ill

Literary Analysis
Dramatic Monologue
When he says "I have
seen the moment of my
greatness flicker," what
observation does Prufrock
make about himself?

---

6. **I should . . . seas** In Shakespeare's *Hamlet,* the hero, Hamlet, mocks the aging Lord
Chamberlain, Polonius, saying, "You yourself, sir, should be old as I am, if like a crab
you could go backward" (II.ii. 205–206).
7. **head . . . platter** a reference to the prophet John the Baptist, whose head was
delivered on a platter to Salome as a reward for her dancing (Matthew 14:1–11).
8. **eternal Footman** death.

And would it have been worth it, after all,
After the cups, the marmalade, the tea,
Among the porcelain, among some talk of you and me,
90 Would it have been worth while,
To have bitten off the matter with a smile,
To have squeezed the universe into a ball
To roll it towards some overwhelming question.
To say: "I am Lazarus,[9] come from the dead,
95 Come back to tell you all. I shall tell you all"—
If one, settling a pillow by her head,
        Should say: "That is not what I meant at all.
        That is not it, at all."

And would it have been worth it, after all,
100 Would it have been worth while,
After the sunsets and the dooryards and the sprinkled streets,
After the novels, after the teacups, after the skirts that trail
        along the floor—
And this, and so much more?—
It is impossible to say just what I mean!
105 But as if a magic lantern[10] threw the nerves in patterns on a
        screen:
Would it have been worth while
If one, settling a pillow or throwing off a shawl,
And turning toward the window, should say:
        "That is not it at all,
110   That is not what I meant, at all."

        . . . . . .

No! I am not Prince Hamlet, nor was meant to be;
Am an attendant lord, one that will do
To swell a progress,[11] start a scene or two,
Advise the prince; no doubt, an easy tool,
115 Deferential, glad to be of use,
Politic, cautious, and <u>meticulous;</u>
Full of high sentence,[12] but a bit <u>obtuse;</u>
At times, indeed, almost ridiculous—
Almost, at times, the Fool.

120 I grow old . . . I grow old . . .
I shall wear the bottoms of my trousers rolled.

Shall I part my hair behind? Do I dare to eat a peach?
I shall wear white flannel trousers, and walk upon the beach.
I have heard the mermaids singing, each to each.

---

9. **Lazarus** (laz´ ə rəs) Lazarus is resurrected from the dead by Jesus in John 11:1–44.
10. **magic lantern** an early device used to project images on a screen.
11. **To swell a progress** to add to the number of people in a parade or scene from a play.
12. **Full of high sentence** speaking in a very ornate manner, often offering advice.

Reading Strategy
Listening How does the use of rhyme contribute to the effect of this stanza?

meticulous (mə tik´ yoo ləs) *adj.* extremely careful about details

obtuse (äb toos´) *adj.* slow to understand or perceive

**Reading Check**

What question does Prufrock repeatedly ask himself?

125 I do not think that they will sing to me.

I have seen them riding seaward on the waves
Combing the white hair of the waves blown back
When the wind blows the water white and black.

We have lingered in the chambers of the sea
130 By sea-girls wreathed with seaweed red and brown
Till human voices wake us, and we drown.

Review and Assess

Thinking About the Selection

1. **(a) Respond:** What is your primary feeling for Prufrock—pity or irritation? Why? **(b) Respond:** What advice would you give him if he were your friend?

2. **(a) Recall:** What does the speaker say in the opening quotation from Dante's *Inferno*? **(b) Interpret:** What does this quotation suggest about the content of the poem that follows?

3. **(a) Recall:** What details does Prufrock use in lines 36–45 to describe his appearance? **(b) Infer:** At what stage of life is Prufrock?

4. **(a) Recall:** In lines 69–71, what kind of streets does Prufrock describe? **(b) Interpret:** In what ways do these streets differ from those that Prufrock would more customarily visit?

5. **(a) Recall:** In lines 48–53, what image does Prufrock use to describe how he has "measured out" his life?
(b) Analyze: Judging from this metaphor, how has Prufrock lived?

6. **(a) Recall:** In lines 96–97, what is the woman's reaction to Prufrock? **(b) Recall:** In line 124, how does Prufrock describe the mermaids' reaction to him? **(c) Connect:** How does Prufrock seem to feel about women's interest in him?

7. **(a) Recall:** In line 85, who or what does Prufrock see?
(b) Make a Judgment: Do you think Prufrock is simply afraid of death, or are his fears more complicated? Explain.

8. **(a) Interpret:** Describe the scenes outlined in the poem's opening and closing stanzas. **(b) Compare and Contrast:** How do the moods of these scenes differ?

9. **(a) Generalize:** Do you think that Prufrock accurately represents many people today? **(b) Relate:** Do we live in a time when it is difficult, even impossible, to be the heroes of our own lives? Explain.

Review and Assess

Literary Analysis

Dramatic Monologue

1. What do his descriptions of the sky and the city in lines 1–12 suggest about Prufrock's outlook on life?

2. (a) How can the first line of this **dramatic monologue** be interpreted to suggest that Prufrock sees himself as divided, both seeking and fearing action? (b) At what other points does he express a deeply conflicted sense of self?

Connecting Literary Elements

3. Some of Prufrock's **allusions** paint imaginary portraits that reveal his sense of self. Use a chart like the one shown to examine these allusions and what they suggest about Prufrock's self-image.

Allusion	Prufrock's Meaning	His Self-Image
No! I am not Prince Hamlet . . .		

4. (a) What is suggested by the repeated reference to Michelangelo? (b) In what ways would the portrayal of Prufrock's world be quite different if that reference were to something less refined?

Reading Strategy

Listening

5. In the lines referring to Michelangelo, what is the impact of the use of rhyme?

6. What is the effect of the repetition of "there will be time" in lines 23–34 and again in lines 37–48?

7. What effect do the ellipsis points (three dots used to indicate an elongated pause or an omission) have on the way you hear lines 120–121?

Extend Understanding

8. **Humanities Connection:** Prufrock says there will be time "To prepare a face to meet the faces that you meet." Does this statement accurately describe how people relate to each other? All the time? Sometimes? Explain.

Integrate Language Skills

Vocabulary Development Lesson

Word Analysis: Greek Prefix *di-*

The Greek prefix *di-* (or *dis-*) means "apart" or "away." The word digress means "to move away from a subject." Each of the following sentences includes a word containing the prefix *di-*. Indicate whether each sentence is true or false.

1. A path *diverges* if it branches off.
2. If you are *diverted*, your focus is sharp.
3. A *diverse* menu features many similar foods.

Spelling Strategy

When you form adjectives by adding the *-ious* suffix to stems ending in *d*, use the spelling *-ious*, as in *studious*. An exception to this rule is the word *hideous*. Add the correctly spelled *-ious* suffix to each stem below.

1. insid_____ 2. perfid_____ 3. invid_____

Concept Development: Synonyms

Review the words from the vocabulary list on page 717. Then, choose the letter of the word that is the best synonym, or word with a similar meaning, for the first word.

1. insidious: (a) innocent, (b) wealthy, (c) dangerous, (d) certified
2. digress: (a) wander, (b) contain, (c) hesitate, (d) elaborate
3. malingers: (a) fakes, (b) studies, (c) boasts, (d) anticipates
4. meticulous: (a) messy, (b) absurd, (c) careful, (d) tart
5. obtuse: (a) intense, (b) stupid, (c) friendly, (d) prompt

Grammar and Style Lesson

Adjectival Modifiers

Adjectival modifiers, phrases or clauses which modify nouns or pronouns, can have many different grammatical structures. In the examples below, the adjectival modifiers are italicized.

Prepositional Phrase: sawdust restaurants *with oyster shells* (modifies *restaurants*)

Participial Phrase: a patient *etherized upon a table* (modifies *patient*)

Adjective Clause: Streets *that follow like a tedious argument* (modifies *streets*)

Infinitive Phrase: prepare a face *to meet the faces* . . . (modifies *face*)

Practice Copy these sentences. Underline the adjectival modifier, and then circle the noun it modifies in each of the sentences below.

1. The cups of tea sat on the tray.
2. The guests talking in the next room were gossiping about J. Alfred Prufrock.
3. People who secretly disliked each other chatted politely.
4. The hostess said it was time to serve tea.
5. Prufrock entered a drawing room crowded with indifferent faces.

Writing Application Write a brief paragraph describing J. Alfred Prufrock. Include at least two adjectival modifiers in your description.

Prentice Hall Writing and Grammar Connection: Chapter 19, Sections 1–3

Writing Lesson

Character Analysis

Ever since Eliot's "Love Song" was published in 1915, J. Alfred Prufrock has fascinated readers. For some, Prufrock is merely a man who fails to achieve his dreams. For others, Prufrock embodies larger failings of the modern age—an absence of heroism, or a general weariness. Write an essay analyzing Prufrock's character, and make your own judgment about this famous literary creation.

Prewriting   Reread the poem, taking notes about Prufrock's character. Pay attention to details that suggest reasons for Prufrock's passivity and fears, and cite passages to use as support for your point of view.

Drafting   Begin by noting the title and author of the work, and stating what you believe about Prufrock's character. Use quotes from the poem and precise language to develop your ideas in each body paragraph.

Revising   Review your essay. Highlight any words that seem vague or inappropriate, and replace them with better, more specific word choices.

Model: Revising for Accuracy

         sweeping   *pines for*

Prufrock's lament is ~~big~~. He ~~talks about~~ all that he has lost

or that he never had—youth and love. He is keenly aware

      even tormented by

of, ~~and really upset about~~ the passage of time.

> Replacing vague words with specific ones makes a piece of writing more accurate and powerful.

WG Prentice Hall Writing and Grammar Connection: Chapter 14, Section 2

Extension Activities

Listening and Speaking With a classmate, **role-play** a talk-show host's interview with Prufrock. Explore the reasons for Prufrock's poor self-esteem, and try to build his self-image. Consider the following tips as you plan:

- Create a list of appropriate interview questions that require in-depth responses.
- Develop Prufrock's responses within the context of his character.

Present your role play. [**Group Activity**]

Research and Technology Modernism has had a lasting effect on art, literature, and popular culture. Use printed and online sources to research the movement and its impact. If possible, download some appropriate examples of Modernist literature or artwork to illustrate your conclusions. Present your findings in a **report.**

 **Take It to the Net**   www.phschool.com

Go online for an additional research activity using the Internet.

Prepare to Read

The Imagist Poets

Ezra Pound (1885–1972)

As both an editor and a poet, Ezra Pound inspired the dramatic changes in American poetry that characterized the Modern Age. Pound's insistence that writers "make it new" led many poets to discard the forms, techniques, and ideas of the past and to experiment with new approaches to poetry.

Pound influenced the work of the Irish poet William Butler Yeats, as well as that of T. S. Eliot, William Carlos Williams, H. D., Marianne Moore, and Ernest Hemingway—a "who's who" of the literary voices of the age. He is best remembered, however, for his role in the development of Imagism.

Despite his preoccupation with originality and inventiveness, Pound's work often drew upon the poetry of ancient cultures. Many of his poems are filled with literary and historical allusions, which can make the poems difficult to interpret without having the appropriate background information.

Fall From Grace In 1925, Pound settled in Italy. Motivated by the mistaken belief that a country governed by a powerful dictator was the most conducive environment for the creation of art, Pound became an outspoken supporter of Italian dictator Benito Mussolini during World War II. In 1943, the American government indicted Pound for treason; in 1945, he was arrested by American troops and imprisoned. After being flown back to the United States in 1945, he was judged psychologically unfit to stand trial and was confined to a hospital for the criminally insane. There he remained until 1958, when he was released due largely to the efforts of the literary community he had so doggedly supported over the years. He returned to Italy, where he lived until his death.

William Carlos Williams (1883–1963)

Unlike his fellow Imagists, William Carlos Williams spent most of his life in the United States, where he pursued a double career as a poet and a pediatrician in New Jersey. He felt that his experiences as a doctor helped provide him with inspiration as a poet, crediting medicine for his ability to "gain entrance to . . . the secret gardens of the self."

The child of immigrants, Williams grew up speaking Spanish, French, and British English. Nevertheless, he was enamored of American language and life. He rejected the views of his college friend, Ezra Pound, who believed in using allusions to history, religion, and ancient literature. Williams focused instead on capturing the essence of modern American life by depicting ordinary people, objects, and experiences using current, everyday language.

The Poetry of Daily Life In volumes such as *Spring and All* (1923) and *In the American Grain* (1925), Williams captured the essence of American life and landscape. He avoided offering explanations, remarking that a poet should deal in "No ideas but in things"—concrete images that speak for themselves, evoking emotions and ideas.

In his later work, Williams departed from pure Imagism in order to write more expansively. His five-volume poem *Paterson* (1946–58) explores the idea of a city as a symbol for a man. The poem is based on the real city of Paterson, New Jersey.

Williams continued to write even after his failing health forced him to give up his medical practice. In 1963, he received a Pulitzer Prize for *Pictures from Breughel and Other Poems*, his final volume of poetry.

H. D. (Hilda Doolittle) (1886–1961)

In 1913, when Ezra Pound reshaped three of Hilda Doolittle's poems and submitted them to *Poetry* magazine under the name "H. D., Imagiste," the Imagist movement was born. The publication of the poems also served to launch the successful career of the young poet, who continued to publish under the name H. D. throughout her life.

Born in Pennsylvania, Doolittle was only fifteen when she first met Ezra Pound, who was studying at the University of Pennsylvania. In 1911, Doolittle moved to London and renewed her acquaintance with Pound. She married a close friend of his, the English poet Richard Aldington, but the marriage struggled and failed during World War I when Aldington left to fight in France. Doolittle remained a short while in London, where she became a leader of the Imagist group. She returned to the United States and settled in California, where she remained for a year before going back to England. In 1921, she moved to Switzerland, and lived there until her death.

Classically Inspired Like the Greek lyrics that she so greatly admired, H. D.'s early poems were brief, precise, and direct. Often emphasizing light, color, and physical textures, she created vivid, emotive images. Like other Imagist poets, H. D. used everyday speech, carefully and sparingly chosen to evoke an emotional response, to freeze a single moment in time. She also abandoned traditional rhythmical patterns, instead creating innovative musical lines in her poetry. With these unusual techniques, H. D. focused much of her poetry and prose on the issues of her day—World Wars I and II, the growing interest in the human psyche created by Sigmund Freud's work, and the blossoming film medium.

In 1925, almost all of H. D.'s early poems were gathered in *Collected Poems*, a volume that also contained her translations from the *Odyssey* and from the Greek poet Sappho. She also wrote a play—*Hippolytus Temporizes*, which appeared in 1927—and two prose works—*Palimpsest* (1926) and *Hedylus* (1928). During the later stages of her career, she focused on writing longer works, including an epic poem. H. D. is best remembered, however, for her early Imagist poetry.

Background on Imagism

Imagism was a literary movement established in the early 1900s by Ezra Pound and other poets. As the name suggests, the Imagists concentrated on the direct presentation of images, or word pictures. An Imagist poem expressed the essence of an object, person, or incident, without providing explanations. Through the spare, clean presentation of an image, the Imagists hoped to freeze a single moment in time and to capture the emotions of that moment. To accomplish this purpose, the Imagists used the language of everyday speech, carefully choosing each word. They also shied away from traditional poetic patterns, focusing instead on creating new, musical rhythms.

The Imagists were strongly influenced by traditional Chinese and Japanese poetry. Many Imagist poems bear a close resemblance to the Japanese verse forms of haiku and tanka, which generally evoke an emotional response through the presentation of a single image or a pair of contrasting images.

The Imagist movement was short-lived, lasting only until about 1918. However, for many years that followed, the poems of Pound, Williams, H.D. and other Imagists continued to influence the work of other poets, including Wallace Stevens, T.S. Eliot, and Hart Crane.

Preview

Connecting to the Literature

You may know what it is like to have a song stick in your mind, but have you ever had an image lodge there? The poems you are about to read capture in words some of the striking images that lodged in the minds and emotions of the Imagists.

Literary Analysis

Imagist Poetry

Imagist poems focus on evoking emotion and sparking the imagination through the vivid presentation of a limited number of images. "In a Station of the Metro," for example, presents just two images and consists of only two lines and fourteen well-chosen words. Few poems have been written that convey so much meaning with such brevity.

Comparing Literary Works

In his essay "A Few Don'ts by an Imagiste," Ezra Pound describes the image as something more than a simple word-picture. Instead, he says it is "that which presents an intellectual and emotional complex in an instant of time."

For Pound, the image brings the reader a new way of seeing—on the physical level through the senses, and on higher levels through the emotions and intellect. As you read these poems, think about which ones best achieve the effect of "that sense of sudden growth" that Pound believed was the highest achievement of art.

Reading Strategy

Engaging Your Senses

These poems are filled with vivid imagery—words or phrases that appeal to the senses. As you encounter each image, **engage your senses** by re-creating in your mind the sights, sounds, smells, tastes, and physical sensations associated with the image. Also note that some images appeal to more than one sense. For example, you can almost see and feel the thickness in the air as H. D. calls on the wind in "Heat":

Cut the heat— / plow through it, / Turning it on either side

Use a chart like the one shown to record the ways in which you engage your senses as you read these poems.

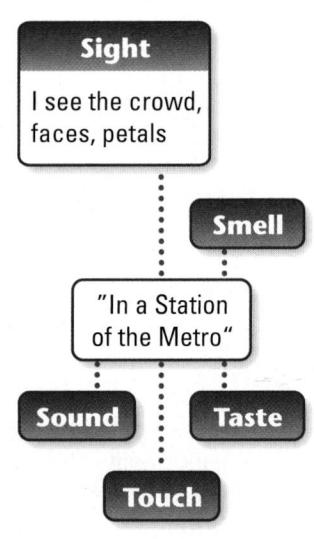

Vocabulary Development

voluminous (və lōōm′ ə nəs) *adj.* of enough material to fill volumes (p. 729)

dogma (dôg′ mə) *n.* authoritative doctrines or beliefs (p. 729)

apparition (ap′ ə rish′ ən) *n.* act of appearing or becoming visible (p. 734)

A Few Don'ts by an
IMAGISTE[1]

Ezra Pound

Background

Ezra Pound was one of the leading figures in the Imagist movement. As the name suggests, Imagists concentrated on the focused presentation of images, or word-pictures. For example, Pound's original draft of "In a Station of the Metro" consisted of 30 lines. Pound whittled away at the poem until he arrived at a work of only 14 words of great precision and power. In this essay, Pound discusses his beliefs about what poetry should and should not be.

An "Image" is that which presents an intellectual and emotional complex in an instant of time. I use the term "complex" rather in the technical sense employed by the newer psychologists, such as Hart, though we might not agree absolutely in our application.

It is the presentation of such a "complex" instantaneously which gives that sense of sudden liberation; that sense of freedom from time limits and space limits; that sense of sudden growth, which we experience in the presence of the greatest works of art.

It is better to present one Image in a lifetime than to produce <u>voluminous</u> works.

All this, however, some may consider open to debate. The immediate necessity is to tabulate A LIST OF DON'TS for those beginning to write verses. But I can not put all of them into Mosaic negative.[2]

To begin with, consider the three rules recorded by Mr. Flint,[3] . . . not as <u>dogma</u>—never consider anything as dogma—but as the result of long contemplation, which, even if it is some one else's contemplation, may be worth consideration. . . .

LANGUAGE

Use no superfluous word, no adjective, which does not reveal something.

voluminous (və lōōm´ ə nəs) *adj.* of enough material to fill volumes

dogma (dôg´ mə) *n.* authoritative doctrines or beliefs

1. **Imagiste** French for *Imagist.*
2. **Mosaic negative** refers to the ten commandments presented by Moses to the Israelites in the Old Testament of the Bible. Many of the commandments are in the negative and begin with the words "Thou shalt not . . ."
3. **the three rules recorded by Mr. Flint** English Imagist poet Frank Stuart Flint noted that Imagist poets adhered to the following three rules or guidelines.
    1. Direct treatment of the "thing," whether subjective or objective.
    2. To use absolutely no word that did not contribute to the presentation.
    3. As regarding rhythm to compose in sequence of the musical phrase, not in sequence of a metronome.

Reading Check

According to Pound, what is an image?

Don't use such an expression as "dim lands *of peace*." It dulls the image. It mixes an abstraction with the concrete. It comes from the writer's not realizing that the natural object is always the *adequate* symbol.

Go in fear of abstractions. Don't retell in mediocre verse what has already been done in good prose. Don't think any intelligent person is going to be deceived when you try to shirk all the difficulties of the unspeakably difficult art of good prose by chopping your composition into line lengths. . . .

Don't imagine that the art of poetry is any simpler than the art of music, or that you can please the expert before you have spent at least as much effort on the art of verse as the average piano teacher spends on the art of music. . . .

RHYTHM AND RHYME

. . . Don't imagine that a thing will "go" in verse just because it's too dull to go in prose.

Don't be "viewy"—leave that to the writers of pretty little philosophic essays. Don't be descriptive; remember that the painter can describe a landscape much better than you can, and that he has to know a deal more about it.

Literary Analysis
Imagist Poetry Why is this rule of avoiding abstractions consistent with the goals of Imagist poetry?

▲ **Critical Viewing** What key details might be emphasized in an Imagist poem about this portrait of Ezra Pound? **[Synthesize]**

When Shakespeare talks of the "Dawn in russet mantle clad" he presents something which the painter does not present. There is in this line of his nothing that one can call description; he presents. . . .

Don't chop your stuff into separate *iambs*.[4] Don't make each line stop dead at the end, and then begin every next line with a heave. Let the beginning of the next line catch the rise of the rhythm wave, unless you want a definite longish pause.

In short, behave as a musician, a good musician, when dealing with that phase of your art which has exact parallels in music. The same laws govern, and you are bound by no others. . . .

A rhyme must have in it some slight element of surprise if it is to give pleasure; it need not be bizarre or curious, but it must be well used if used at all. . . .

Don't mess up the perception of one sense by trying to define it in terms of another. This is usually only the result of being too lazy to find the exact word. To this clause there are possibly exceptions.

The first three simple proscriptions[5] will throw out nine-tenths of all the bad poetry now accepted as standard and classic; and will prevent you from many a crime of production. . . .

---

4. **iambs** (ī´ ambz´) *n.* metrical feet consisting of two syllables, the first unaccented, the other accented.
5. **The first three simple proscriptions** reference to Flint's three rules outlined in footnote #3.

Review and Assess

Thinking About the Selection

1. **Respond:** What is your reaction to Pound's ideas about poetry?
2. **(a) Recall:** What three rules does Pound invite readers to consider? **(b) Define:** What is the difference between dogma and the results of "long contemplation"?
   (c) Speculate: Why did Pound prefer a list of "don'ts" to a list of "do's"?
3. **(a) Recall:** What does Pound consider preferable to abstractions? **(b) Analyze:** Why would the use of abstractions be offensive to an Imagist poet?
4. **(a) Recall:** Does Pound consider Shakespeare's image an example of description or presentation? **(b) Distinguish:** How does presentation differ from description?
5. **(a) Recall:** What rule does Pound suggest should govern the rhythm of a poem? **(b) Interpret:** What does a good musician do that a poet should emulate?
6. **Evaluate:** Do you think following Pound's "don'ts" would make it easier or more difficult to write poetry?

The River-Merchant's Wife:

A Letter

Ezra Pound

While my hair was still cut straight across my forehead
I played about the front gate, pulling flowers.
You came by on bamboo stilts, playing horse,
You walked about my seat, playing with blue plums.
5 And we went on living in the village of Chokan:[1]
Two small people, without dislike or suspicion.

At fourteen I married My Lord you.
I never laughed, being bashful.
Lowering my head, I looked at the wall.
10 Called to, a thousand times, I never looked back.

At fifteen I stopped scowling,
I desired my dust to be mingled with yours
Forever and forever and forever.
Why should I climb the lookout?

15 At sixteen you departed,
You went into far Ku-to-yen,[2] by the river of swirling eddies,
And you have been gone five months.
The monkeys make sorrowful noise overhead.

Literary Analysis
Imagist Poetry What details in this stanza are most effective in conveying an image?

---

1. **Chokan** (chō´ kän´) a suburb of Nanking, a city in the People's Republic of China.
2. **Ku-to-yen** (ko͞o´ tō´ yen´) an island in the Yangtze (yaŋk´ sē) River.

You dragged your feet when you went out.
20 By the gate now, the moss is grown, the different mosses,
Too deep to clear them away!
The leaves fall early this autumn, in wind.
The paired butterflies are already yellow with August
Over the grass in the West garden;
25 They hurt me. I grow older.
If you are coming down through the narrows of the river Kiang,

Please let me know beforehand,
And I will come out to meet you
        As far as Cho-fu-Sa.[3]

By Rihaku

---

3. **Cho-fu-Sa** (chō´ foo´ sä´) a beach along the Yangtze River, several hundred miles from Nanking.

Literary Analysis
Imagist Poetry What details make this stanza appeal to both the senses and the emotions?

✔**Reading Check**
Who is the speaker in this poem? Whom does she address?

Landscape Album in Various Styles, Ch'a Shih-piao, The Cleveland Museum of Art

▲ **Critical Viewing** In what ways does the mood of this drawing mirror the mood of "The River-Merchant's Wife: A Letter"? **[Analyze]**

In a Station of the Metro[1]

Ezra Pound

The <u>apparition</u> of these faces in the crowd;
Petals on a wet, black bough.

apparition (ap´ ə rish´ ən)
n. act of appearing
or becoming visible

---

1. **Metro** the Paris subway.

Review and Assess

Thinking About the Selections

1. **Respond:** Of all the images contained in the two poems by Ezra Pound, which did you find the most striking? Why?

2. **(a) Recall:** In "The River-Merchant's Wife," how old is the speaker when she marries? **(b) Compare and Contrast:** In what ways are her feelings for her husband at age fifteen different from those when she first marries?

3. **(a) Recall:** What happens when the river-merchant's wife is sixteen? **(b) Analyze:** How does she feel about this change?

4. **(a) Recall:** In "In a Station of the Metro," what two things does Pound compare? **(b) Interpret:** In what ways does this poem capture the essence of a single moment?
   (c) Analyze: Given the poem's setting, why is the image of "Petals on a wet, black bough" surprising?

5. **Take a Position:** What do you like about Pound's poetry? What do you dislike? Explain.

The Red Wheelbarrow

William Carlos Williams

so much depends
upon

a red wheel
barrow

5   glazed with rain
water

beside the white
chickens.

The Great Figure

William Carlos Williams

Among the rain
and lights
I saw the figure 5
in gold
5   on a red
fire truck
moving
tense
unheeded
10   to gong clangs
siren howls
and wheels rumbling
through the dark city.

The Figure 5 in Gold, Charles Demuth, Metropolitan Museum of Art

▶ **Critical Viewing** Artist Charles Demuth created this work of art to accompany his friend Williams's poem. What elements of his illustration convey the energy and clamor of the poem? **[Connect]**

THIS IS JUST TO SAY

William Carlos Williams

I have eaten
the plums
that were in
the icebox
5 and which
you were probably
saving
for breakfast

Forgive me
10 they were delicious
so sweet
and so cold

Review and Assess

Thinking About the Selections

1. **Respond:** Which of the three poems by Williams evokes the strongest emotional response in you? Why?

2. **(a) Classify:** In "The Red Wheelbarrow," to what sense does the image appeal most? **(b) Analyze:** In what way does this poem reflect the Imagist emphasis on the concrete?

3. **(a) Recall:** Which words has Williams divided to run on two separate lines? **(b) Analyze:** What is the effect of this arrangement of words?

4. **(a) Recall:** In "The Great Figure," what detail is the focus of the speaker's experience of the fire truck? **(b) Interpret:** In focusing on this detail, what might Williams be saying about beauty and modern life?

5. **(a) Recall:** What is the intention of the speaker in "This Is Just to Say"? **(b) Connect:** Which details in the second stanza challenge the speaker's sincerity?

6. **Evaluate:** Which elements of these poems reflect Williams's interest in portraying—and celebrating—everyday American life?

PEAR TREE H.D.

Silver dust
lifted from the earth,
higher than my arms reach,
you have mounted,
5 O silver,
higher than my arms reach
you front us with great mass;

no flower ever opened
so staunch a white leaf,
10 no flower ever parted silver
from such rare silver;

O white pear,
your flower-tufts
thick on the branch
15 bring summer and ripe fruits
in their purple hearts.

▼ **Critical Viewing**
Which phrases from the poem best describe this image of a pear tree in full flower? **[Evaluate]**

✔**Reading Check**

What image does the poet use to describe the pear tree flowers?

HEAT
H. D.

O wind, rend open the heat,
cut apart the heat,
rend it to tatters.

Fruit cannot drop
5 through this thick air—
fruit cannot fall into heat
that presses up and blunts
the points of pears
and rounds the grapes.

10 Cut the heat—
plow through it,
turning it on either side
of your path.

Overhanging Cloud in July, (1947/1959), Charles Burchfield, Watercolor on paper, 39 1/2″ x 35 1/2″, Collection of Whitney Museum of American Art, Purchase, with funds from the Friends of the Whitney Museum of American Art

▲ **Critical Viewing**
Does this painting capture the oppressive heat of a humid summer day as effectively as the poem does? Explain. **[Evaluate]**

Review and Assess

Thinking About the Selections

1. **Respond:** How do these two poems by H. D. make you feel?

2. **(a) Recall:** What is the "silver dust" referred to in the first stanza of "Pear Tree"? **(b) Interpret:** In what sense is the silver dust "lifted from the earth"?

3. **(a) Recall:** What does the pear tree's blossom anticipate? **(b) Infer:** What time of year is the speaker describing?

4. **(a) Recall:** In "Heat," what is the reaction of the fruit to the air? **(b) Interpret:** What specific type of heat is the speaker describing?

5. **(a) Recall:** Which verbs does the speaker use to describe lessening the heat? **(b) Analyze:** What impression of the heat do these verbs create?

6. **Generalize:** Based on these two poems, how would you define the poet's relationship to nature?

Review and Assess

Literary Analysis

Imagist Poetry

1. Does "The River-Merchant's Wife: A Letter" qualify as a purely **Imagist poem**? Why or why not?

2. What effect does Pound's choice of the word *apparition*—commonly used to describe a ghostly figure—to mean "appearance" contribute to "In a Station of the Metro"?

Comparing Literary Works

3. In what ways is Pound's advice to (a) avoid abstractions and (b) avoid superfluous words evident in all of these poems?

4. (a) Use a chart like the one shown to compare and contrast the use of color in the poems by H. D. and Williams. (b) What emotions do these uses of color evoke?

Poem	Color(s)	Emotional Effect

5. Although Pound wrote "the painter can describe a landscape much better than you can," in what ways are these poems like paintings?

6. Which of these poems best exemplifies Pound's idea of the image as "that which presents an intellectual and emotional complex in an instant of time"? Explain your choice.

Reading Strategy

Engaging Your Senses

7. What other **senses**, besides sight, can you engage to re-create the images of "Petals on a wet, black bough"? Explain.

8. Identify two examples of passages in "The River-Merchant's Wife" in which you were able to engage the sense of smell.

Extend Understanding

9. **Literature Connection:** "The River-Merchant's Wife: A Letter" is an adaptation of a poem by the Chinese poet Li T'ai Po. What challenges and opportunities face a poet in translating a work of literature from one language and culture to another?

Quick Review

Imagist poetry focuses on evoking emotion and vivid mental associations through the presentation of concise, unadorned images.

By **engaging your senses,** you can fully experience the images in poetry.

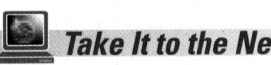 **Take It to the Net**
www.phschool.com
Take the interactive self-test online to check your understanding of these selections.

Integrate Language Skills

Vocabulary Development Lesson

Word Analysis: Forms of *appear*

Several common English words are forms of the verb *appear*, meaning "to come into sight or into being" or "to become understood."

apparent   appearance   apparition

Complete each of the following sentences with the correct word from the list above.

1. He made a brief ___?___ at the awards dinner—just long enough to pick up his trophy and say a few words.
2. When midnight found the toddlers still running around the house, it became ___?___ that the babysitter was no longer in control.
3. The ___?___ of a face at the window nearly stopped her heart with fear.

Concept Development: Synonyms

Select the letter of the best synonym, or word of similar meaning, for the numbered word.

1. dogma: (a) doctrine, (b) legality, (c) statement
2. voluminous: (a) loud, (b) arrogant, (c) comprehensive
3. apparition: (a) suspicious, (b) vision, (c) face

Spelling Strategy

You may need to drop the *d* when adding the prefix *ad-* to a word or word stem beginning with the consonants *p, g, s,* or *c.* If so, you must also double the consonant, as in *appear.* Use this principle to correctly spell the words below.

1. *ad-* + gressor   2. *ad-* + sign   3. *ad-* + prove

Grammar and Style Lesson

Concrete and Abstract Nouns

Nouns can be classified according to the item they name. A **concrete noun** names something that can be perceived with one or more of the five senses. Concrete nouns have a physical, tangible reality. An **abstract noun** names something that cannot be seen, heard, smelled, tasted, or touched. These may be qualities, characteristics, emotions, or ideas that are not perceived mainly through the senses.

> **Concrete:** *I played about the front gate, pulling flowers.*
>
> **Abstract:** *Two small people, without dislike or suspicion.*

Practice Label the italicized nouns in these sentences as either *concrete* or *abstract.*

1. Don't use such an *expression* as "dim lands of *peace*."
2. The *leaves* fell early this autumn, in *wind.*
3. I saw the figure 5 in gold on a red firetruck moving tense unheeded to gong *clangs* siren howls and wheels rumbling through the dark *city.*
4. Cut the *heat*—plow through it . . .
5. I have eaten the *plums* that were in the icebox and which you were probably saving for *breakfast.*

Looking at Style Explain why you would expect to find mainly concrete nouns in an Imagist poem.

WG Prentice Hall Writing and Grammar Connection: Chapter 17, Section 1

Writing Lesson

An Editor's Review of Manuscript

Imagine that you are a magazine editor who has just received a manuscript from an Imagist poet. Write a letter to the poet explaining why you will or will not publish his or her poems. Be simple, honest, and kind, and include constructive criticism.

Prewriting   Choose a poet and reread the poems. Take notes on the strengths and weaknesses of each poem, citing relevant passages.

Drafting   Write a letter that explains why you will or will not publish the poems. Discuss strengths, and identify flaws. Select specific words that best convey your meaning.

Revising   Review your draft, highlighting any words that are inaccurate or vague. Then, replace those words with better, more specific choices.

Model: Revising for Brevity and Clarity

deceptively simple

Your poems are small and ~~not complex~~, but are rich in imagery

wry

and ideas. I especially enjoyed the ~~incredible~~ tone of "This Is

Just to Say."

> Replacing vague words with specific words helps to express ideas exactly.

W͟G Prentice Hall Writing and Grammar Connection: Chapter 16, Section 1

Extension Activities

Listening and Speaking Of "The Red Wheelbarrow," Roy Harvey Pearce writes: "At its worst this is togetherness in a chickenyard. At its best it is an exercise in the creation of the poetic out of the anti-poetic." Which view do you hold? Defend your view in an **informal debate** with classmates. To prepare, keep these tips in mind:

- Find examples to support both positions, and then decide which you will argue.
- Use examples for the opposing side to develop arguments against that position.

As you debate, be as clear and as eloquent as possible. **[Group Activity]**

Research and Technology Select one of the Imagist poems and **illustrate** it, either with artworks of your own or with clippings or printouts from magazines, the Internet, and other sources. If possible, create your illustration using graphic arts software and integrate them in a file with the text of the poem. Then, post your work in the classroom with a brief explanation of its imagery, and use it as the basis for an oral interpretation or reading of the poem.

 **Take It to the Net**   www.phschool.com

Go online for an additional research activity using the Internet.

Prepare to Read

Winter Dreams

F. Scott Fitzgerald (1896–1940)

When you open the pages of one of F. Scott Fitzgerald's books, you are transported back in time to the Roaring Twenties, a decade unlike any other in American history. Many Americans lived with reckless abandon, attending wild parties, wearing glamorous clothing, and striving for fulfillment through material wealth. Yet, this quest for pleasure was often accompanied by a sense of inner despair. Fitzgerald was able to successfully capture the paradox of this glittering, materialistic, and often self-destructive lifestyle because he actually lived it. Like many of his characters, he led a fast-paced life and longed to attain the wealth and social status of the upper class. He also experienced the emptiness conveyed in his stories.

A Quick Rise to Fame Francis Scott Key Fitzgerald was born in St. Paul, Minnesota, into a family with high social aspirations but little wealth. The family had a small claim on history: One of their distant relatives was Francis Scott Key, the writer of "The Star Spangled Banner," after whom Fitzgerald was named. As a young man, Fitzgerald was eager to improve his social standing. He entered Princeton University in 1913, where he pursued the type of high-profile social life for which he would later become famous. Fitzgerald failed to graduate, perhaps as a result of his self-indulgent lifestyle, and soon enlisted in the army.

His first novel, *This Side of Paradise* (1920), published shortly after his discharge from the service, was an instant success. With the fame and wealth the novel brought him, Fitzgerald was able to court Zelda Sayre, a southern belle with whom he had fallen in love while in the army. They married in 1920. Together, they blazed an extravagant trail across the societies of both New York and Europe, mingling with rich and famous artists and aristocrats and spending money recklessly.

An American Masterpiece Despite the couple's pleasure-seeking lifestyle, Fitzgerald remained a productive writer, publishing dozens of short stories. In 1925, he published his most successful novel, *The Great Gatsby*, the story of a self-made man whose dreams of love and social acceptance lead to scandal and corruption and ultimately end in tragedy. The novel displayed Fitzgerald's fascination with—and growing distrust of—the wealthy society he had embraced. The book is widely considered to be Fitzgerald's masterpiece, one of the greatest novels in American literature.

Fortunes Turn After the 1929 stock market crash, Fitzgerald's world began to crumble. His wife suffered a series of nervous breakdowns, his reputation as a writer declined, and financial setbacks forced him to seek work as a Hollywood screenwriter. Despite these setbacks, however, he managed to produce many more short stories and a fine second novel, *Tender Is the Night* (1934). Though well-regarded by critics, the book was not a financial success. In the last year of his life, Fitzgerald, who had once been the highest-paid author in the country, earned just $13.13 from his writing.

Fitzgerald was in the midst of writing *The Last Tycoon*, a novel about a Hollywood film mogul, when he died of a heart attack in 1940. His editor approached the novelist John O'Hara about finishing the book, but O'Hara declined. In a letter O'Hara wrote to author John Steinbeck, he explained his refusal, saying that "Fitzgerald was a better just plain writer than all of us put together. Just words writing."

Preview

Connecting to the Literature

Even when you know, deep down, that someone is not right for you, you may continue to long for that person. Such a struggle between reason and emotion forms the heart of this story.

Literary Analysis

Characterization

Fitzgerald creates intimate portraits of Dexter and Judy through **characterization**—the revelation of characters' personalities.

- In **direct characterization,** the writer tells the reader what the character is like.
- In **indirect characterization,** characters' traits are revealed through their thoughts, actions, and words, and by what other characters say to or about them.

Fitzgerald brings characters into sharp focus through both methods.

Connecting Literary Elements

Characters' motivations—their reasons for acting as they do—may come from internal sources, such as feelings of loneliness, or external sources, such as danger. As you read, identify characters' motivations for their actions.

Reading Strategy

Drawing Conclusions About Characters

Fitzgerald often leaves it up to the reader to draw conclusions about his characters. To **draw conclusions,** combine information from the story with your own experience. Consider this example:

> Dexter stood perfectly still . . . if he moved forward a step his stare would be in her line of vision—if he moved backward he would lose his full view of her face.

If you have ever wanted to hide your interest in someone but could not stop looking, you can conclude that Dexter is enthralled by Judy. Use a chart like the one shown to draw conclusions.

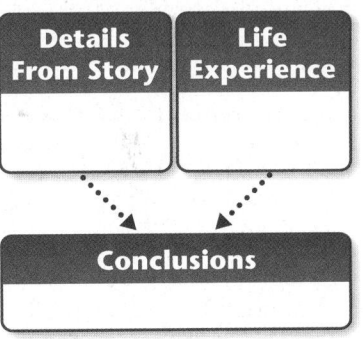

Vocabulary Development

fallowness (fal´ ō nis) *n.* inactivity (p. 745)

preposterous (prē päs´ tər əs) *adj.* ridiculous (p. 746)

fortuitous (fôr tōō´ ə təs) *adj.* fortunate (p. 747)

sinuous (sin´ yōō əs) *adj.* moving in and out; wavy (p. 751)

mundane (mun´ dān´) *adj.* commonplace; ordinary (p. 752)

poignant (poin´ yənt) *adj.* sharply painful to the feelings (p. 756)

pugilistic (pyōō´ jəl is´ tik) *adj.* looking for a fight (p. 758)

somnolent (säm´ nə lənt) *adj.* sleepy; drowsy (p. 759)

WINTER DREAMS

F. Scott Fitzgerald

Background

Written in 1922, this story unfolds against the background of the Jazz Age. Focusing on Dexter Green's obsession with Judy Jones, a beautiful young woman from a prominent wealthy family, Fitzgerald explores the connections between love, money, and social status. Through Dexter, he shows what life was like in the 1920s for an ambitious young man driven by the desire for "glittering things."

I

Some of the caddies were poor as sin and lived in one-room houses with a neurasthenic[1] cow in the front yard, but Dexter Green's father owned the second best grocery store in Black Bear—the best one was "The Hub," patronized by the wealthy people from Sherry Island—and Dexter caddied only for pocket money.

---

1. **neurasthenic** (nๅๅr´ əs thēn´ ik) *adj.* here, weak, tired.

In the fall when the days became crisp and gray, and the long Minnesota winter shut down like the white lid of a box, Dexter's skis moved over the snow that hid the fairways of the golf course. At these times the country gave him a feeling of profound melancholy—it offended him that the links should lie in enforced <u>fallowness</u>, haunted by ragged sparrows for the long season. It was dreary, too, that on the tees where the gay colors fluttered in summer there were now only the desolate sandboxes knee deep in crusted ice. When he crossed the hills the wind blew cold as misery, and if the sun was out he tramped with his eyes squinted up against the hard dimensionless glare.

In April the winter ceased abruptly. The snow ran down into Black Bear Lake scarcely tarrying for the early golfers to brave the season with red and black balls. Without elation, without an interval of moist glory, the cold was gone. Dexter knew that there was something dismal about this Northern spring, just as he knew there was something gorgeous about the fall. Fall made him clinch his hands and tremble and repeat idiotic sentences to himself, and make brisk abrupt gestures of command to imaginary audiences and armies. October filled him with hope which November raised to a sort of ecstatic triumph, and in this mood the fleeting brilliant impressions of the summer at Sherry Island were ready grist to his mill. He became a golf champion and defeated Mr. T. A. Hedrick in a marvelous match played a hundred times over the fairways of his imagination, a match each detail of which he changed about untiringly—sometimes he won with almost laughable ease, sometimes he came up magnificently from behind. Again, stepping from a Pierce-Arrow automobile, like Mr. Mortimer Jones, he strolled frigidly into the lounge of the Sherry Island Golf Club—or perhaps, surrounded by an admiring crowd, he gave an exhibition of fancy diving from the springboard of the club raft. . . . Among those who watched him in open-mouthed wonder was Mr. Mortimer Jones.

And one day it came to pass that Mr. Jones—himself and not his ghost—came up to Dexter with tears in his eyes and said that Dexter was the——best caddy in the club, and wouldn't he decide not to quit if Mr. Jones made it worth his while, because every other——caddy in the club lost one ball a hole for him—regularly——

"No, sir," said Dexter decisively, "I don't want to caddy any more." Then, after a pause: "I'm too old."

"You're not more than fourteen. Why the devil did you decide just this morning that you wanted to quit? You promised that next week you'd go over to the state tournament with me."

"I decided I was too old."

Dexter handed in his "A Class" badge, collected what money was due him from the caddy master, and walked home to Black Bear Village.

"The best——caddy I ever saw," shouted Mr. Mortimer Jones over a drink that afternoon. "Never lost a ball! Willing! Intelligent! Quiet! Honest! Grateful!"

fallowness (fal′ ō nis) *n.* inactivity

Reading Strategy
Drawing Conclusions About Characters What conclusions do you draw about Dexter's circumstances and desires based on this description of his "winter dreams"?

✓**Reading Check**

What does Dexter do for pocket money?

The little girl who had done this was eleven—beautifully ugly as little girls are apt to be who are destined after a few years to be inexpressibly lovely and bring no end of misery to a great number of men. The spark, however, was perceptible. There was a general ungodliness in the way her lips twisted down at the corners when she smiled, and in the—Heaven help us!—in the almost passionate quality of her eyes. Vitality is born early in such women. It was utterly in evidence now, shining through her thin frame in a sort of glow.

She had come eagerly out on to the course at nine o'clock with a white linen nurse and five small new golf clubs in a white canvas bag which the nurse was carrying. When Dexter first saw her she was standing by the caddy house, rather ill at ease and trying to conceal the fact by engaging her nurse in an obviously unnatural conversation graced by startling and irrelevant grimaces from herself.

"Well, it's certainly a nice day, Hilda," Dexter heard her say. She drew down the corners of her mouth, smiled, and glanced furtively around, her eyes in transit falling for an instant on Dexter.

Then to the nurse:

"Well, I guess there aren't very many people out here this morning, are there?"

The smile again—radiant, blatantly artificial—convincing.

"I don't know what we're supposed to do now," said the nurse looking nowhere in particular.

"Oh, that's all right. I'll fix it up."

Dexter stood perfectly still, his mouth slightly ajar. He knew that if he moved forward a step his stare would be in her line of vision—if he moved backward he would lose his full view of her face. For a moment he had not realized how young she was. Now he remembered having seen her several times the year before—in bloomers.

Suddenly, involuntarily, he laughed, a short abrupt laugh—then, startled by himself, he turned and began to walk quickly away.

"Boy!"

Dexter stopped.

"Boy——"

Beyond question he was addressed. Not only that, but he was treated to that absurd smile, that preposterous smile—the memory of which at least a dozen men were to carry into middle age.

"Boy, do you know where the golf teacher is?"

"He's giving a lesson."

"Well, do you know where the caddy master is?"

"He isn't here yet this morning."

"Oh." For a moment this baffled her. She stood alternately on her right and left foot.

"We'd like to get a caddy," said the nurse. "Mrs. Mortimer Jones sent us out to play golf, and we don't know how without we get a caddy."

Here she was stopped by an ominous glance from Miss Jones, followed immediately by the smile.

preposterous (prē päs′ tər əs) *adj.* ridiculous

"There aren't any caddies here except me," said Dexter to the nurse, "and I got to stay here in charge until the caddy master gets here."

"Oh."

Miss Jones and her retinue now withdrew, and at a proper distance from Dexter became involved in a heated conversation, which was concluded by Miss Jones taking one of the clubs and hitting it on the ground with violence. For further emphasis she raised it again and was about to bring it down smartly upon the nurse's bosom, when the nurse seized the club and twisted it from her hands.

"You little mean old *thing*!" cried Miss Jones wildly.

Another argument ensued. Realizing that the elements of the comedy were implied in the scene, Dexter several times began to laugh, but each time restrained the laugh before it reached audibility. He could not resist the monstrous conviction that the little girl was justified in beating the nurse.

The situation was resolved by the <u>fortuitous</u> appearance of the caddy master, who was appealed to immediately by the nurse.

"Miss Jones is to have a little caddy, and this one says he can't go."

"Mr. McKenna said I was to wait here till you came," said Dexter quickly.

"Well, he's here now." Miss Jones smiled cheerfully at the caddy master. Then she dropped her bag and set off at a haughty mince toward the first tee.

"Well?" The caddy master turned to Dexter.

"What you standing there like a dummy for? Go pick up the young lady's clubs."

"I don't think I'll go out today," said Dexter.

"You don't——"

"I think I'll quit."

The enormity of his decision frightened him. He was a favorite caddy, and the thirty dollars a month he earned through the summer were not to be made elsewhere around the lake. But he had received a strong emotional shock, and his perturbation required a violent and immediate outlet.

It is not so simple as that, either. As so frequently would be the case in the future, Dexter was unconsciously dictated to by his winter dreams.

II

Now, of course, the quality and the seasonability of these winter dreams varied, but the stuff of them remained. They persuaded Dexter several years later to pass up a business course at the State university—his father, prospering now, would have paid his way—for the precarious advantage of attending an older and more famous university in the East, where he was bothered by his scanty funds. But do not get the impression, because his winter dreams happened to be concerned at first with musings on the rich, that there was anything

Literary Analysis
Characterization and Character's Motivation
What motivates Judy Jones's behavior in fighting with her nurse?

fortuitous (fôr tōō′ ə təs) *adj.* fortunate

✔**Reading Check**
What does Dexter do when told to go out and caddy for Miss Jones?

merely snobbish in the boy. He wanted not association with glittering things and glittering people—he wanted the glittering things themselves. Often he reached out for the best without knowing why he wanted it—and sometimes he ran up against the mysterious denials and prohibitions in which life indulges. It is with one of those denials and not with his career as a whole that this story deals.

He made money. It was rather amazing. After college he went to the city from which Black Bear Lake draws its wealthy patrons. When he was only twenty-three and had been there not quite two years, there were already people who liked to say: "Now *there's* a boy—" All about him rich men's sons were peddling bonds precariously, or investing patrimonies precariously, or plodding through the two dozen volumes of the "George Washington Commercial Course," but Dexter borrowed a thousand dollars on his college degree and his confident mouth, and bought a partnership in a laundry.

▲ **Critical Viewing**
Golf was once a game reserved for the wealthy. It is on a golf course like the one in this painting that Dexter meets Judy for the first time. How might this setting have affected Dexter's perception of Judy? **[Analyze]**

It was a small laundry when he went into it, but Dexter made a specialty of learning how the English washed fine woolen golf stockings without shrinking them, and within a year he was catering to the trade that wore knickerbockers. Men were insisting that their Shetland hose and sweaters go to his laundry, just as they had insisted on a caddy who could find golf balls. A little later he was doing their wives' lingerie as well—and running five branches in different parts of the city. Before he was twenty-seven he owned the largest string of laundries in his section of the country. It was then that he sold out and went to New York. But the part of his story that concerns us goes back to the days when he was making his first big success.

When he was twenty-three Mr. Hart—one of the gray-haired men who like to say "Now there's a boy"—gave him a guest card to the Sherry Island Golf Club for a weekend. So he signed his name one day on the register, and that afternoon played golf in a foursome with Mr. Hart and Mr. Sandwood and Mr. T. A. Hedrick. He did not consider it necessary to remark that he had once carried Mr. Hart's bag over this same links, and that he knew every trap and gully with his eyes shut—but he found himself glancing at the four caddies who trailed them, trying to catch a gleam or gesture that would remind him of himself, that would lessen the gap which lay between his present and his past.

It was a curious day, slashed abruptly with fleeting, familiar impressions. One minute he had the sense of being a trespasser—in the next he was impressed by the tremendous superiority he felt toward Mr. T. A. Hedrick, who was a bore and not even a good golfer any more.

Golf Course–California, 1917, George Wesley Bellows, Cincinnati Art Museum

Then, because of a ball Mr. Hart lost near the fifteenth green, an enormous thing happened. While they were searching the stiff grasses of the rough there was a clear call of "Fore!" from behind a hill in their rear. And as they all turned abruptly from their search a bright new ball sliced abruptly over the hill and caught Mr. T. A. Hedrick in the abdomen.

"By Gad!" cried Mr. T. A. Hedrick, "they ought to put some of these crazy women off the course. It's getting to be outrageous."

A head and a voice came up together over the hill:

"Do you mind if we go through?"

"You hit me in the stomach!" declared Mr. Hedrick wildly.

"Did I?" The girl approached the group of men. "I'm sorry. I yelled 'Fore!' "

Her glance fell casually on each of the men—then scanned the fairway for her ball.

"Did I bounce into the rough?"

It was impossible to determine whether this question was ingenuous or malicious. In a moment, however, she left no doubt, for as her partner came up over the hill she called cheerfully:

"Here I am! I'd have gone on the green except that I hit something."

As she took her stance for a short mashie shot, Dexter looked at her closely. She wore a blue gingham dress, rimmed at throat and shoulders with a white edging that accentuated her tan. The quality of exaggeration, of thinness, which had made her passionate eyes and down-turning mouth absurd at eleven, was gone now. She was arrestingly beautiful. The color in her cheeks was centered like the color in a picture—it was not a "high" color, but a sort of fluctuating and feverish warmth, so shaded that it seemed at any moment it would recede and disappear. This color and the mobility of her mouth gave a continual impression of flux, of intense life, of passionate vitality—balanced only partially by the sad luxury of her eyes.

She swung her mashie impatiently and without interest, pitching the ball into a sand pit on the other side of the green. With a quick, insincere smile and a careless "Thank you!" she went on after it.

"That Judy Jones!" remarked Mr. Hedrick on the next tee, as they waited—some moments—for her to play on ahead. "All she needs is to be turned up and spanked for six months and then to be married off to an old-fashioned cavalry captain."

"My God, she's good looking!" said Mr. Sandwood, who was just over thirty.

Reading Strategy
Drawing Conclusions About Characters What does Judy's behavior toward the men on the golf course suggest about her character?

Reading Check

What "enormous thing" happens near the fifteenth green?

"Good looking!" cried Mr. Hedrick contemptuously, "she always looks as if she wanted to be kissed! Turning those big coweyes on every calf in town!"

It was doubtful if Mr. Hedrick intended a reference to the maternal instinct.

"She'd play pretty good golf if she'd try," said Mr. Sandwood.

"She has no form," said Mr. Hedrick solemnly.

"She has a nice figure," said Mr. Sandwood.

"Better thank the Lord she doesn't drive a swifter ball," said Mr. Hart, winking at Dexter.

Later in the afternoon the sun went down with a riotous swirl of gold and varying blues and scarlets, and left the dry, rustling night of Western summer. Dexter watched from the veranda of the golf club, watched the even overlap of the waters in the little wind, silver molasses under the harvest moon. Then the moon held a finger to her lips and the lake became a clear pool, pale and quiet. Dexter put on his bathing suit and swam out to the farthest raft, where he stretched dripping on the wet canvas of the springboard.

There was a fish jumping and a star shining and the lights around the lake were gleaming. Over on a dark peninsula a piano was playing the songs of last summer and of summers before that—songs from *Chin-Chin* and *The Count of Luxemburg* and *The Chocolate Soldier*[2]— and because the sound of a piano over a stretch of water had always seemed beautiful to Dexter he lay perfectly quiet and listened.

The tune the piano was playing at that moment had been gay and new five years before when Dexter was a sophomore at college. They had played it at a prom once when he could not afford the luxury of proms, and he had stood outside the gymnasium and listened. The sound of the tune precipitated in him a sort of ecstasy and it was with that ecstasy he viewed what happened to him now. It was a mood of intense appreciation, a sense that, for once, he was magnificently attuned to life and that everything about him was radiating a brightness and a glamor he might never know again.

A low, pale oblong detached itself suddenly from the darkness of the Island, spitting forth the reverberate sound of a racing motorboat. Two white streamers of cleft water rolled themselves out behind it and almost immediately the boat was beside him, drowning out the hot tinkle of the piano in the drone of its spray. Dexter raising himself on his arms was aware of a figure standing at the wheel, of two dark eyes regarding him over the lengthening space of water—then the boat had gone by and was sweeping in an immense and purposeless circle of spray round and round in the middle of the lake. With equal eccentricity one of the circles flattened out and headed back toward the raft.

"Who's that?" she called, shutting off her motor. She was so near now that Dexter could see her bathing suit, which consisted apparently of pink rompers.

---

2. *Chin-Chin . . . The Chocolate Soldier* popular operettas of the time.

Literary Analysis
Characterization What information about Judy Jones does Fitzgerald provide in this discussion among the golfers?

The nose of the boat bumped the raft, and as the latter tilted rakishly he was precipitated toward her. With different degrees of interest they recognized each other.

"Aren't you one of those men we played through this afternoon?" she demanded.

He was.

"Well, do you know how to drive a motorboat? Because if you do I wish you'd drive this one so I can ride on the surfboard behind. My name is Judy Jones"—she favored him with an absurd smirk—rather, what tried to be a smirk, for, twist her mouth as she might, it was not grotesque, it was merely beautiful—"and I live in a house over there on the Island, and in that house there is a man waiting for me. When he drove up at the door I drove out of the dock because he says I'm his ideal."

There was a fish jumping and a star shining and the lights around the lake were gleaming. Dexter sat beside Judy Jones and she explained how her boat was driven. Then she was in the water, swimming to the floating surfboard with a <u>sinuous</u> crawl. Watching her was without effort to the eye, watching a branch waving or a sea gull flying. Her arms, burned to butternut, moved sinuously among the dull platinum ripples, elbow appearing first, casting the forearm back with a cadence of falling water, then reaching out and down, stabbing a path ahead.

They moved out into the lake; turning, Dexter saw that she was kneeling on the low rear of the now uptilted surfboard.

"Go faster," she called, "fast as it'll go."

Obediently he jammed the lever forward and the white spray mounted at the bow. When he looked around again the girl was standing up on the rushing board, her arms spread wide, her eyes lifted toward the moon.

"It's awful cold," she shouted. "What's your name?"

He told her.

"Well, why don't you come to dinner tomorrow night?"

His heart turned over like the flywheel of the boat, and, for the second time, her casual whim gave a new direction to his life.

III

Next evening while he waited for her to come downstairs, Dexter peopled the soft deep summer room and the sun porch that opened from it with the men who had already loved Judy Jones. He knew the sort of men they were—the men who when he first went to college had entered from the great prep schools with graceful clothes and the deep tan of healthy summers. He had seen that, in one sense, he was better than these men. He was newer and stronger. Yet in acknowledging to himself that he wished his children to be like them he was admitting that he was but the rough, strong stuff from which they eternally sprang.

Literary Analysis
Characterization and Characters' Motivations
What motivates Judy Jones to get in her boat and approach Dexter?

sinuous (sin´ yo͞o əs) *adj.* moving in and out; wavy

✓**Reading Check**

Where is Dexter when he meets Judy Jones for the third time?

When the time had come for him to wear good clothes, he had known who were the best tailors in America, and the best tailors in America had made him the suit he wore this evening. He had acquired that particular reserve peculiar to his university, that set it off from other universities. He recognized the value to him of such a mannerism and he had adopted it; he knew that to be careless in dress and manner required more confidence than to be careful. But carelessness was for his children. His mother's name had been Krimelich. She was a Bohemian of the peasant class and she had talked broken English to the end of her days. Her son must keep to the set patterns.

At a little after seven Judy Jones came downstairs. She wore a blue silk afternoon dress, and he was disappointed at first that she had not put on something more elaborate. This feeling was accentuated when, after a brief greeting, she went to the door of a butler's pantry and pushing it open called: "You can serve dinner, Martha." He had rather expected that a butler would announce dinner, that there would be a cocktail. Then he put these thoughts behind him as they sat down side by side on a lounge and looked at each other.

"Father and mother won't be here," she said thoughtfully.

He remembered the last time he had seen her father, and he was glad the parents were not to be here tonight—they might wonder who he was. He had been born in Keeble, a Minnesota village fifty miles farther north, and he always gave Keeble as his home instead of Black Bear Village. Country towns were well enough to come from if they weren't inconveniently in sight and used as footstools by fashionable lakes.

They talked of his university, which she had visited frequently during the past two years, and of the nearby city which supplied Sherry Island with its patrons, and whither Dexter would return next day to his prospering laundries.

During dinner she slipped into a moody depression which gave Dexter a feeling of uneasiness. Whatever petulance she uttered in her throaty voice worried him. Whatever she smiled at—at him, at a chicken liver, at nothing—it disturbed him that her smile could have no root in mirth, or even in amusement. When the scarlet corners of her lips curved down, it was less a smile than an invitation to a kiss.

Then, after dinner, she led him out on the dark sun porch and deliberately changed the atmosphere.

"Do you mind if I weep a little?" she said.

"I'm afraid I'm boring you," he responded quickly.

"You're not. I like you. But I've just had a terrible afternoon. There was a man I cared about, and this afternoon he told me out of a clear sky that he was poor as a church mouse. He'd never even hinted it before. Does this sound horribly mundane?"

"Perhaps he was afraid to tell you."

"Suppose he was," she answered. "He didn't start right. You see, if I'd thought of him as poor—well, I've been mad about loads of poor men, and fully intended to marry them all. But in this case, I hadn't thought of him that way, and my interest in him wasn't strong

Literary Analysis
Characterization What does this description reveal about Dexter's and Judy's relationship?

mundane (mun dān´) *adj.* commonplace; ordinary

enough to survive the shock. As if a girl calmly informed her fiancè that she was a widow. He might not object to widows, but——

"Let's start right," she interrupted herself suddenly. "Who are you, anyhow?"

For a moment Dexter hesitated. Then:

"I'm nobody," he announced. "My career is largely a matter of futures."

"Are you poor?"

"No," he said frankly, "I'm probably making more money than any man my age in the Northwest. I know that's an obnoxious remark, but you advised me to start right."

There was a pause. Then she smiled and the corners of her mouth drooped and an almost imperceptible sway brought her closer to him, looking up into his eyes. A lump rose in Dexter's throat, and he waited breathless for the experiment, facing the unpredictable compound that would form mysteriously from the elements of their lips. Then he saw—she communicated her excitement to him, lavishly, deeply, with kisses that were not a promise but a fulfillment. They aroused in him not hunger demanding renewal but surfeit that would demand more surfeit . . . kisses that were like charity, creating want by holding back nothing at all.

It did not take him many hours to decide that he had wanted Judy Jones ever since he was a proud, desirous little boy.

IV

It began like that—and continued, with varying shades of intensity, on such a note right up to the denouement. Dexter surrendered a part of himself to the most direct and unprincipled personality with which he had ever come in contact. Whatever Judy wanted, she went after with the full pressure of her charm. There was no divergence of method, no jockeying for position or premeditation of effects—there was a very little mental side to any of her affairs. She simply made men conscious to the highest degree of her physical loveliness. Dexter had no desire to change her. Her deficiencies were knit up with a passionate energy that transcended and justified them.

When, as Judy's head lay against his shoulder that first night, she whispered, "I don't know what's the matter with me. Last night I thought I was in love with a man and tonight I think I'm in love with you——" it seemed to him a beautiful and romantic thing to say. It was the exquisite excitability that for the moment he controlled and owned. But a week later he was compelled to view this same quality in a different light. She took him in her roadster to a picnic supper, and after supper she disappeared, likewise in her roadster, with another man. Dexter became enormously upset and was scarcely able to be decently civil to the other people present. When she assured him that she had not kissed the other man, he knew she was lying—yet he was glad that she had taken the trouble to lie to him.

Literary Analysis
Characterization What does this conversation reveal about the characters of Dexter and Judy?

Literary Analysis
Characterization and Character's Motivation Why is Dexter so willing to accept Judy's lies?

✔**Reading Check**

Where do Dexter and Judy have dinner?

He was, as he found before the summer ended, one of a varying dozen who circulated about her. Each of them had at one time been favored above all others—about half of them still basked in the solace of occasional sentimental revivals. Whenever one showed signs of dropping out through long neglect, she granted him a brief honeyed hour, which encouraged him to tag along for a year or so longer. Judy made these forays upon the helpless and defeated without malice, indeed half unconscious that there was anything mischievous in what she did.

When a new man came to town everyone dropped out—dates were automatically canceled.

The helpless part of trying to do anything about it was that she did it all herself. She was not a girl who could be "won" in the kinetic sense—she was proof against cleverness, she was proof against charm; if any of these assailed her too strongly she would immediately resolve the affair to a physical basis, and under the magic of her physical splendor the strong as well as the brilliant played her game and not their own. She was entertained only by the gratification of her desires and by the direct exercise of her own charm. Perhaps from so much youthful love, so many youthful lovers, she had come, in self-defense, to nourish herself wholly from within.

Succeeding Dexter's first exhilaration came restlessness and dissatisfaction. The helpless ecstasy of losing himself in her was opiate rather than tonic. It was fortunate for his work during the winter that those moments of ecstasy came infrequently. Early in their acquaint-ance it had seemed for a while that there was a deep and spontaneous mutual attraction—that first August, for example— three days of long evenings on her dusky veranda, of strange wan kisses through the late afternoon, in shadowy alcoves or behind the protecting trellises of the garden arbors, of mornings when she was fresh as a dream and almost shy at meeting him in the clarity of the rising day. There was all the ecstasy of an engagement about it, sharpened by his realization that there was no engagement. It was during those three days that, for the first time, he had asked her to marry him. She said "maybe some day," she said "kiss me," she said, "I'd like to marry you," she said "I love you"—she said—nothing.

The three days were interrupted by the arrival of a New York man who visited at her house for half September. To Dexter's agony, rumor engaged them. The man was the son of the president of a great trust company. But at

▼ Critical Viewing
The mood of this painting is serene. How might this portrait be different if the artist were striving to communicate Judy Jones's energy and magnetic beauty? [Modify]

The Morning Sun, © 1920, Pauline Palmer, Rockford Art Museum

the end of a month it was reported that Judy was yawning. At a dance one night she sat all evening in a motorboat with a local beau, while the New Yorker searched the club for her frantically. She told the local beau that she was bored with her visitor, and two days later he left. She was seen with him at the station, and it was reported that he looked very mournful indeed.

On this note the summer ended. Dexter was twenty-four, and he found himself increasingly in a position to do as he wished. He joined two clubs in the city and lived at one of them. Though he was by no means an integral part of the stag lines at these clubs, he managed to be on hand at dances where Judy Jones was likely to appear. He could have gone out socially as much as he liked—he was an eligible young man, now, and popular with downtown fathers. His confessed devotion to Judy Jones had rather solidified his position. But he had no social aspirations and rather despised the dancing men who were always on tap for the Thursday or Saturday parties and who filled in at dinners with the younger married set. Already he was playing with the idea of going East to New York. He wanted to take Judy Jones with him. No disillusion as to the world in which she had grown up could cure his illusion as to her desirability.

Remember that—for only in the light of it can what he did for her be understood.

Eighteen months after he first met Judy Jones he became engaged to another girl. Her name was Irene Scheerer, and her father was one of the men who had always believed in Dexter. Irene was light-haired and sweet and honorable, and a little stout, and she had two suitors whom she pleasantly relinquished when Dexter formally asked her to marry him.

Summer, fall, winter, spring, another summer, another fall—so much he had given of his active life to the incorrigible lips of Judy Jones. She had treated him with interest, with encouragement, with malice, with indifference, with contempt. She had inflicted on him the innumerable little slights and indignities possible in such a case—as if in revenge for having ever cared for him at all. She had beckoned him and yawned at him and beckoned him again and he had responded often with bitterness and narrowed eyes. She had brought him ecstatic happiness and intolerable agony of spirit. She had caused him untold inconvenience and not a little trouble. She had insulted him, and she had ridden over him, and she had played his interest in her against his interest in his work—for fun. She had done everything to him except to criticize him—this she had not done—it seemed to him only because it might have sullied the utter indifference she manifested and sincerely felt toward him.

When autumn had come and gone again it occurred to him that he could not have Judy Jones. He had to beat this into his mind but he convinced himself at last. He lay awake at night for a while and argued it over. He told himself the trouble and the pain she had caused him, he enumerated her glaring deficiencies as a wife. Then he said to himself that he loved her, and after a while he fell asleep. For a week,

Literary Analysis

Characterization What do Judy Jones's varying responses to Dexter's marriage proposals reveal about her feelings for him?

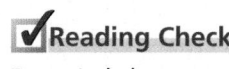

Reading Check

Does Judy have more than one suitor? Explain.

lest he imagined her husky voice over the telephone or her eyes opposite him at lunch, he worked hard and late, and at night he went to his office and plotted out his years.

At the end of a week he went to a dance and cut in on her once. For almost the first time since they had met he did not ask her to sit out with him or tell her that she was lovely. It hurt him that she did not miss these things—that was all. He was not jealous when he saw that there was a new man tonight. He had been hardened against jealousy long before.

He stayed late at the dance. He sat for an hour with Irene Scheerer and talked about books and about music. He knew very little about either. But he was beginning to be master of his own time now, and he had a rather priggish[3] notion that he—the young and already fabulously successful Dexter Green—should know more about such things.

That was in October, when he was twenty-five. In January, Dexter and Irene became engaged. It was to be announced in June, and they were to be married three months later.

The Minnesota winter prolonged itself interminably, and it was almost May when the winds came soft and the snow ran down into Black Bear Lake at last. For the first time in over a year Dexter was enjoying a certain tranquility of spirit. Judy Jones had been in Florida, and afterward in Hot Springs, and somewhere she had been engaged, and somewhere she had broken it off. At first, when Dexter had definitely given her up, it had made him sad that people still linked them together and asked for news of her, but when he began to be placed at dinner next to Irene Scheerer people didn't ask him about her any more—they told him about her. He ceased to be an authority on her.

May at last. Dexter walked the streets at night when the darkness was damp as rain, wondering that so soon, with so little done, so much of ecstasy had gone from him. May one year back had been marked by Judy's <u>poignant</u>, unforgivable, yet forgiven turbulence—it had been one of those rare times when he fancied she had grown to care for him. That old penny's worth of happiness he had spent for this bushel of content. He knew that Irene would be no more than a curtain spread behind him, a hand moving among gleaming teacups, a voice calling to children . . . fire and loveliness were gone, the magic of nights and the wonder of the varying hours and seasons . . . slender lips, down-turning, dropping to his lips and bearing him up into a heaven of eyes . . . The thing was deep in him. He was too strong and alive for it to die lightly.

In the middle of May when the weather balanced for a few days on the thin bridge that led to deep summer he turned in one night

poignant (poin´ yənt) *adj.* sharply painful to the feelings

---

3. priggish (prig´ gish) *adj.* excessively proper and smug.

at Irene's house. Their engagement was to be announced in a week now—no one would be surprised at it. And tonight they would sit together on the lounge at the University Club and look on for an hour at the dancers. It gave him a sense of solidity to go with her— she was so sturdily popular, so intensely "great."

He mounted the steps of the brownstone house and stepped inside.

"Irene," he called.

Mrs. Scheerer came out of the living room to meet him.

"Dexter," she said, "Irene's gone upstairs with a splitting headache. She wanted to go with you but I made her go to bed."

"Nothing serious, I——"

"Oh, no. She's going to play golf with you in the morning. You can spare her for just one night, can't you, Dexter?"

Her smile was kind. She and Dexter liked each other. In the living room he talked for a moment before he said good night.

Returning to the University Club, where he had rooms, he stood in the doorway for a moment and watched the dancers. He leaned against the doorpost, nodded at a man or two—yawned.

"Hello, darling."

The familiar voice at his elbow startled him. Judy Jones had left a man and crossed the room to him—Judy Jones, a slender enameled doll in cloth of gold: gold in a band at her head, gold in two slipper points at her dress's hem. The fragile glow of her face seemed to blossom as she smiled at him. A breeze of warmth and light blew through the room. His hands in the pockets of his dinner jacket tightened spasmodically. He was filled with a sudden excitement.

"When did you get back?" he asked casually.

"Come here and I'll tell you about it."

She turned and he followed her. She had been away—he could have wept at the wonder of her return. She had passed through enchanted streets, doing things that were like provocative music. All mysterious happenings, all fresh and quickening hopes, had gone away with her, come back with her now.

She turned in the doorway.

"Have you a car here? If you haven't, I have."

"I have a coupé."

In then, with a rustle of golden cloth. He slammed the door. Into so many cars she had stepped—like this—like that—her back against the leather, so—her elbow resting on the door—waiting. She would have been soiled long since had there been anything to soil her— except herself—but this was her own self outpouring.

With an effort he forced himself to start the car and back into the street. This was nothing, he must remember. She had done this before, and he had put her behind him, as he would have crossed a bad account from his books.

He drove slowly downtown and, affecting abstraction, traversed the deserted streets of the business section, peopled here and there where a movie was giving out its crowd or where consumptive or

Reading Strategy
Drawing Conclusions About Characters What conclusions about Dexter's feelings for Irene do you draw from this description of "a sense of solidity"?

**Reading Check**

What is Dexter's relationship to Irene Scheerer?

<u>pugilistic</u> youth lounged in front of pool halls. The clink of glasses and the slap of hands on the bars issued from saloons, cloisters of glazed glass and dirty yellow light.

She was watching him closely and the silence was embarrassing, yet in this crisis he could find no casual word with which to profane the hour. At a convenient turning he began to zigzag back toward the University Club.

"Have you missed me?" she asked suddenly.

"Everybody missed you."

He wondered if she knew of Irene Scheerer. She had been back only a day—her absence had been almost contemporaneous with his engagement.

"What a remark!" Judy laughed sadly—without sadness. She looked at him searchingly. He became absorbed in the dashboard.

"You're handsomer than you used to be," she said thoughtfully. "Dexter, you have the most rememberable eyes."

He could have laughed at this, but he did not laugh. It was the sort of thing that was said to sophomores. Yet it stabbed at him.

"I'm awfully tired of everything, darling." She called everyone darling, endowing the endearment with careless, individual camaraderie.[4] "I wish you'd marry me."

The directness of this confused him. He should have told her now that he was going to marry another girl, but he could not tell her. He could as easily have sworn that he had never loved her.

"I think we'd get along," she continued, on the same note, "unless probably you've forgotten me and fallen in love with another girl."

Her confidence was obviously enormous. She had said, in effect, that she found such a thing impossible to believe, that if it were true he had merely committed a childish indiscretion—and probably to show off. She would forgive him, because it was not a matter of any moment but rather something to be brushed aside lightly.

"Of course you could never love anybody but me," she continued, "I like the way you love me. Oh, Dexter, have you forgotten last year?"

"No, I haven't forgotten."

"Neither have I!"

Was she sincerely moved—or was she carried along by the wave of her own acting?

"I wish we could be like that again," she said, and he forced himself to answer:

"I don't think we can."

"I suppose not. . . . I hear you're giving Irene Scheerer a violent rush."

There was not the faintest emphasis on the name, yet Dexter was suddenly ashamed.

"Oh, take me home," cried Judy suddenly; "I don't want to go back to that idiotic dance—with those children."

---

4. **camaraderie** (käm´ ə räd´ ə rē) *n.* warm, friendly feelings.

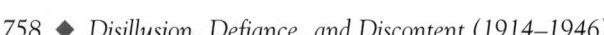

Reading Strategy
Drawing Conclusions About Characters Given the information Fitzgerald provides in this conversation, what can you conclude about Judy's experiences during her absence?

Then, as he turned up the street that led to the residence district, Judy began to cry quietly to herself. He had never seen her cry before.

The dark street lightened, the dwellings of the rich loomed up around them, he stopped his coupé in front of the great white bulk of the Mortimer Joneses' house, <u>somnolent</u>, gorgeous, drenched with the splendor of the damp moonlight. Its solidity startled him. The strong walls, the steel of the girders, the breadth and beam and pomp of it were there only to bring out the contrast with the young beauty beside him. It was sturdy to accentuate her slightness—as if to show what a breeze could be generated by a butterfly's wing.

He sat perfectly quiet, his nerves in wild clamor, afraid that if he moved he would find her irresistibly in his arms. Two tears had rolled down her wet face and trembled on her upper lip.

"I'm more beautiful than anybody else," she said brokenly, "why can't I be happy?" Her moist eyes tore at his stability—her mouth turned slowly downward with an exquisite sadness: "I'd like to marry you if you'll have me, Dexter. I suppose you think I'm not worth having, but I'll be so beautiful for you, Dexter."

A million phrases of anger, pride, passion, hatred, tenderness fought on his lips. Then a perfect wave of emotion washed over him, carrying off with it a sediment of wisdom, of convention, of doubt, of honor. This was his girl who was speaking, his own, his beautiful, his pride.

"Won't you come in?" He heard her draw in her breath sharply. Waiting.

"All right," his voice was trembling, "I'll come in."

V

It was strange that neither when it was over nor a long time afterward did he regret that night. Looking at it from the perspective of ten years, the fact that Judy's flare for him endured just one month seemed of little importance. Nor did it matter that by his yielding he subjected himself to a deeper agony in the end and gave serious hurt to Irene Scheerer and to Irene's parents, who had befriended him. There was nothing sufficiently pictorial about Irene's grief to stamp itself on his mind.

Dexter was at bottom hard-minded. The attitude of the city on his action was of no importance to him, not because he was going to leave the city, but because any outside attitude on the situation seemed superficial. He was completely indifferent to popular opinion. Nor, when he had seen that it was no use, that he did not possess in himself the power to move fundamentally or to hold Judy Jones, did he bear any malice toward her. He loved her, and he would love her until the day he was too old for loving—but he could not have her. So he tasted the deep pain that is reserved only for the strong, just as he had tasted for a little while the deep happiness.

Even the ultimate falsity of the grounds upon which Judy terminated the engagement that she did not want to "take him away" from

Literary Analysis
Characterization
What does this wistful remark about her lack of happiness add to Fitzgerald's portrait of Judy's character?

✓**Reading Check**
How long does Dexter's romance with Judy Jones last?

Irene—Judy who had wanted nothing else—did not revolt him. He was beyond any revulsion or any amusement.

He went East in February with the intention of selling out his laundries and settling in New York—but the war came to America in March and changed his plans. He returned to the West, handed over the management of the business to his partner, and went into the first officers' training camp in late April. He was one of those young thousands who greeted the war with a certain amount of relief, welcoming the liberation from webs of tangled emotion.

VI

This story is not his biography, remember, although things creep into it which have nothing to do with those dreams he had when he was young. We are almost done with them and with him now. There is only one more incident to be related here, and it happens seven years farther on.

It took place in New York, where he had done well—so well that there were no barriers too high for him. He was thirty-two years old, and, except for one flying trip immediately after the war, he had not been West in seven years. A man named Devlin from Detroit came into his office to see him in a business way, and then and there this incident occurred, and closed out, so to speak, this particular side of his life.

"So you're from the Middle West," said the man Devlin with careless curiosity. "That's funny—I thought men like you were probably born and raised on Wall Street. You know—wife of one of my best friends in Detroit came from your city. I was an usher at the wedding."

Dexter waited with no apprehension of what was coming.

"Judy Simms," said Devlin with no particular interest; "Judy Jones she was once."

"Yes, I knew her." A dull impatience spread over him. He had heard, of course, that she was married—perhaps deliberately he had heard no more.

"Awfully nice girl," brooded Devlin meaninglessly, "I'm sort of sorry for her."

"Why?" Something in Dexter was alert, receptive, at once.

"Oh, Lud Simms has gone to pieces in a way. I don't mean he ill-uses her, but he drinks and runs around——"

"Doesn't she run around?"

"No. Stays at home with her kids."

"Oh."

"She's a little too old for him," said Devlin.

"Too old!" cried Dexter. "Why, man, she's only twenty-seven."

He was possessed with a wild notion of rushing out into the streets and taking a train to Detroit. He rose to his feet spasmodically.

"I guess you're busy," Devlin apologized quickly. "I didn't realize——"

"No, I'm not busy," said Dexter, steadying his voice. "I'm not busy at all. Not busy at all. Did you say she was—twenty-seven? No, I said she was twenty-seven."

"Yes, you did," agreed Devlin dryly.

"Go on, then. Go on."

"What do you mean?"

"About Judy Jones."

Devlin looked at him helplessly.

"Well, that's—I told you all there is to it. He treats her like the devil. Oh, they're not going to get divorced or anything. When he's particularly outrageous she forgives him. In fact, I'm inclined to think she loves him. She was a pretty girl when she first came to Detroit."

A pretty girl! The phrase struck Dexter as ludicrous.

"Isn't she—a pretty girl, anymore?"

"Oh, she's all right."

"Look here," said Dexter, sitting down suddenly. "I don't understand. You say she was a 'pretty girl' and now you say she's 'all right.' I don't understand what you mean—Judy Jones wasn't a pretty girl, at all. She was a great beauty. Why, I knew her. I knew her. She was ——"

Devlin laughed pleasantly.

"I'm not trying to start a row," he said. "I think Judy's a nice girl and I like her. I can't understand how a man like Lud Simms could fall madly in love with her, but he did." Then he added: "Most of the women like her."

Dexter looked closely at Devlin, thinking wildly that there must be a reason for this, some insensitivity in the man or some private malice.

"Lots of women fade just like *that*," Devlin snapped his fingers. "You must have seen it happen. Perhaps I've forgotten how pretty she was at her wedding. I've seen her so much since then, you see. She has nice eyes."

A sort of dullness settled down upon Dexter. For the first time in his life he felt like getting very drunk. He knew that he was laughing loudly at something Devlin had said, but he did not know what it was or why it was funny. When, in a few minutes, Devlin went he lay down on his lounge and looked out the window at the New York skyline into which the sun was sinking in dull lovely shades of pink and gold.

He had thought that having nothing else to lose he was invulnerable at last—but he knew that he had just lost something more, as surely as if he had married Judy Jones and seen her fade away before his eyes.

The dream was gone. Something had been taken from him. In a sort of panic he pushed the palms of his hands into his eyes and tried to bring up a picture of the waters lapping on Sherry Island and the moonlit veranda, and gingham on the golf links and the dry sun and the gold color of her neck's soft down. And her mouth damp to his kisses and her eyes plaintive with melancholy and her freshness

Literary Analysis
Characterization and Character's Motivation
Why do you think Dexter is "obsessed by a wild notion"? What need drives his behavior?

**Reading Check**

According to Devlin, in what ways has Judy changed since Dexter last saw her?

like new fine linen in the morning. Why, these things were no longer in the world! They had existed and they existed no longer.

For the first time in years the tears were streaming down his face. But they were for himself now. He did not care about mouth and eyes and moving hands. He wanted to care, and he could not care. For he had gone away and he could never go back any more. The gates were closed, the sun was gone down, and there was no beauty but the gray beauty of steel that withstands all time. Even the grief he could have borne was left behind in the country of illusion, of youth, of the richness of life, where his winter dreams had flourished.

"Long ago," he said, "long ago, there was something in me, but now that thing is gone. Now that thing is gone, that thing is gone. I cannot cry. I cannot care. That thing will come back no more."

Review and Assess

Thinking About the Selection

1. **Respond:** Do you feel sorry for Judy? For Dexter? Explain.

2. **(a) Recall:** What emotions does Dexter feel during the different seasons of the year? **(b) Interpret:** During the winter, how does Dexter reflect upon his summer activities? **(c) Make a Judgment:** Would you say Dexter's memories of the summer are accurate or idealized? Explain.

3. **(a) Recall:** At the beginning of Section II, what does the narrator say Dexter wants? **(b) Interpret:** In what ways does Judy embody Dexter's ambitions?

4. **(a) Recall:** What actions does Dexter take as a result of his first two meetings with Judy? **(b) Connect:** Find two examples in the story that demonstrate the effects of Judy's casual decisions or behavior on Dexter's life.

5. **(a) Interpret:** What is Irene like? Briefly describe her. **(b) Draw Conclusions:** What does the decision to become engaged to Irene symbolize for Dexter?

6. **(a) Interpret:** What is Dexter's response to Judy whenever she reappears in his life? **(b) Analyze:** Why do Dexter's feelings for Judy remain unchanged even after he finally loses her?

7. **Evaluate:** Are Dexter's values and ideals influenced by the times in which he lived, or would his feelings for Judy Jones have been the same in any era? Explain.

Review and Assess

Literary Analysis

Characterization

1. (a) Use a chart like the one shown to analyze Fitzgerald's use of **characterization** to portray Judy and Dexter. (b) What do you learn about the characters in each example?

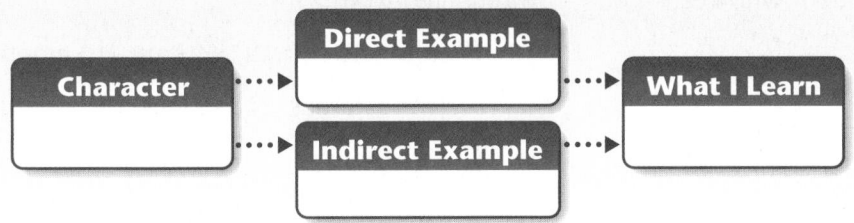

2. Note ways in which both types of characterization work together to create consistent portraits.

3. (a) What traits do Dexter and Judy share? (b) In what ways are they different? (c) Which details of characterization lead you to your answers?

Connecting Literary Elements

4. What details in the story reveal Dexter's **motivation** to be successful?

5. (a) What need drives Judy? (b) For what does she yearn?

6. Judy tells Dexter that she cannot be happy. In what ways does her behavior throughout the story contribute to her unhappiness?

Reading Strategy

Drawing Conclusions About Characters

7. Demonstrate what you have learned about the characters of Dexter and Judy by writing an account of their last meeting. What did they say and how did they act as their relationship ended?

8. In what ways do the characters of Dexter and Judy reflect Fitzgerald's complex views of material wealth and social status?

Extend Understanding

9. **Social Studies Connection:** (a) How do you think Fitzgerald defines the American Dream? (b) Do you agree with critics who have said that Fitzgerald's vision of that dream is conflicted, or divided? Explain.

Quick Review

Writers use both **direct** and **indirect** methods of **characterization** to reveal the personalities of their characters.

A **character's motivations** are the needs and desires that drive his or her behavior, thoughts, feelings, and speech.

To **draw conclusions about characters,** connect clues from the text with your own life experiences.

 Take It to the Net

www.phschool.com

Take the interactive self-test online to check your understanding of the selection.

Integrate Language Skills

Vocabulary Development Lesson

Word Analysis: Latin Root -somn-

The word *somnolent* meaning "sleepy," is built on the Latin root *-somn-*, which means "sleep." Using each of the words defined below, write a brief paragraph about a student who keeps nodding off in class.

1. insomnia: *n.* inability to sleep
2. somnolent: *adj.* sleepy; drowsy
3. somniloquist: *n.* one who talks while asleep

Spelling Strategy

Usually, when forming adjectives by adding the suffix *-ic*, do not change the spelling of the base word: *pugilist* becomes *pugilistic*. Add *-ic* to the words below. Then, use each adjective in a sentence.

1. antagonist   2. futurist   3. angel

Concept Development: Antonyms

Review the vocabulary list on page 743. Then, choose the letter of the word that is the better antonym, or word of opposite meaning, for each numbered word.

1. fallowness   (a) activity, (b) emptiness
2. preposterous   (a) serious, (b) sarcastic
3. fortuitous   (a) wealthy, (b) cursed
4. sinuous   (a) straight, (b) slippery
5. mundane   (a) legal, (b) amazing
6. poignant   (a) dull, (b) moving
7. pugilistic   (a) tough, (b) peace-loving
8. somnolent   (a) alert, (b) hard

Grammar and Style Lesson

Dashes

Dashes (—) are a form of punctuation which create a longer, more emphatic pause than commas. They signal information that interrupts the flow of text. Dashes can indicate an abrupt change of thought, a dramatic interrupting idea, or a summary statement.

In Fitzgerald's story, dashes draw readers' attention to the information they set off. Look at this example:

> **Example:** When he was twenty-three, Mr. Hart—one of the gray-haired men who liked to say "Now *there's* a boy"—gave him a guest card to the Sherry Island Golf Club for a weekend.

Practice Insert dashes where necessary in the following sentences.

1. Mr. Hart one of those golfers who like to yell *Fore!* at the top of their lungs gave him a guest card to a prestigious local golf club.
2. He was glad her parents were not there they might wonder who he was.
3. Whatever she smiled at him, at a chicken liver, at nothing it disturbed him . . .
4. He had the notion that she and this was the strange part actually had feelings for him.
5. "I'd like to marry you," she said "I love you" she said nothing.

Writing Application Write a brief description of someone you admire. Use dashes to set off a few pieces of information you want readers to notice.

 Prentice Hall Writing and Grammar Connection: Chapter 27, Section 5

Writing Lesson

Character Analysis

Fitzgerald portrays Dexter Green as a fully rounded character with believable thoughts, feelings, strengths, and weaknesses. Explore Dexter's behavior and motivations in a character analysis. Support your ideas with examples from the story.

Prewriting Scan the story for examples of Dexter's appearance, words, actions, and motivations. Note how he changes during the story, and then decide whether Dexter's actions are heroic or simply foolish.

Drafting In your introduction, name the author, title, and featured character, and then state your most important idea. Describe Dexter's behavior with specific examples, and quote from the text to support your judgment.

Model: Elaborating for Information

Dexter was an outsider looking in on an elegant world. He was so close to it, he could almost touch it, and that combination of proximity and distance drove him. As Fitzgerald tells us, "He wanted not association with glittering things and glittering people—he wanted the glittering things themselves."

> Direct quotations from the text provide support for the analysis.

Revising Make sure your essay clearly communicates your opinion. Where needed, add quotations or other details to support your points.

*W*G *Prentice Hall Writing and Grammar Connection: Chapter 14, Section 3*

Extension Activities

Listening and Speaking Select a song that might remind Dexter of Judy. Play the song for the class and give a **presentation** about why it is appropriate. Use these tips to guide your work:

- Consider both current music and music from the Jazz Age.
- Alternate between discussion and musical passages, using the song to emphasize your points.

Conclude by addressing the relationship between music and emotions, and speculate about why songs are so powerful.

Research and Technology Using a variety of sources, research the lives of F. Scott and Zelda Fitzgerald. Then, write a **report** on their relationship and lifestyle. Incorporate various critical views of the connections between F. Scott's relationship with Zelda and his fiction and take a position to explain which one seems most accurate to you.

 **Take It to the Net** www.phschool.com

Go online for an additional research activity using the Internet.

Prepare to Read

The Turtle *from* The Grapes of Wrath

John Steinbeck
(1902–1968)

No writer captures more vividly than John Steinbeck what it was like to live through the Great Depression of the 1930s.

His stories and novels, many of which are set in the agricultural region of northern California where he grew up, capture the poverty, desperation, and social injustice experienced by many working-class Americans during this bleak period in our nation's history. As in the works of Naturalist writers like Stephen Crane and Jack London, Steinbeck's characters struggle desperately against forces beyond their understanding or control. Many of those characters suffer tragic fates, yet they almost always manage to exhibit bravery and retain a sense of dignity throughout their struggles. Steinbeck's ability to combine harsh critiques of the political and social systems of his times with genuine artistry in his characterization, plot, and language is unique in American literature.

Modest Beginnings Steinbeck was born in Salinas, California, the son of a county official and a schoolteacher. By his late teens, he was already supporting himself by working as a laborer. After graduating from high school, he enrolled at Stanford University. He left before graduating, however, and spent the next five years drifting across the country, working in a variety of odd jobs, including that of fish hatcher, fruit picker, laboratory assistant, surveyor, apprentice painter, and journalist. Through these experiences, Steinbeck discovered firsthand what it means to survive by manual labor. He also gathered material that he would later use in his books to create authentic portraits of working-class life.

First Success Steinbeck's first three books received little—or negative—attention from critics. However, this changed in 1935 when he published *Tortilla Flat*, his fourth book. The book received the California Commonwealth Club's Gold Medal for best novel by a California author. Two years later, the author earned even greater recognition and acclaim with *Of Mice and Men* (1937). This novel, which portrays two migrant workers whose dream of owning a farm ends in tragedy, became a bestseller and was made into a Broadway play and a movie.

The Great American Novel Steinbeck went on to write what is generally regarded as his finest novel. *The Grapes of Wrath* (1939) is the historically authentic story of the Joad family, Oklahoma farmers dispossessed of their land and forced to become migrant farmers in California. "The Turtle" is an excerpt from the opening pages of this novel, which won the National Book Award and the Pulitzer Prize. The book aroused public sympathy for the plight of migratory farm workers and established Steinbeck as one of the most highly regarded writers of his day.

Steinbeck produced several more successful works during his later years, including *Cannery Row* (1945), *The Pearl* (1947), *East of Eden* (1952), and *The Winter of Our Discontent* (1961). In 1962, he received the Nobel Prize for Literature. In accepting that award, Steinbeck noted his belief that literature can sustain people through hard times. He added that it is the writer's responsibility to celebrate the human "capacity for greatness of heart and spirit—for gallantry in defeat, for courage, compassion and love. In the endless war against weakness and despair, these are the bright rally flags of hope and of emulation." Steinbeck's belief in social justice, and in the human ability to learn from and rise above suffering, infused all his work.

Preview

Connecting to the Literature

Sometimes, a single event can seem to mirror all of life. For example, one long and complicated journey with many detours and wrong turns might be seen as representing the experience of growing up. As you read this selection, think about how the small events it describes could represent something much bigger.

Literary Analysis

Theme

John Steinbeck's narrative about a brief episode in a turtle's life conveys an important **theme,** or insight into life. An author's theme is rarely directly stated. Instead, it is revealed indirectly through these means:

- Characters' comments and actions
- Events in the plot
- The use of literary devices, such as symbols

Sometimes, even small details can serve an important role in conveying a theme, and deserve attention as you read.

Connecting Literary Elements

At first glance, this is just a simple story about a turtle. However, when looked at symbolically, the story grows in power and meaning. Steinbeck's use of **symbols**—people, places, or things that represent something larger than their literal meanings—helps to communicate his theme. To understand the story's symbolism, think about the qualities Steinbeck attributes to each person, place, animal, or object, and how each one might represent some aspect of life.

Reading Strategy

Finding Clues to Theme

To interpret the theme of a story, become a literary detective. Look carefully for **clues to the theme** in the writer's use of symbols, his choice of details, and the ways characters react to one another. For example, Steinbeck includes only slight descriptions of how two motorists react when they spot the turtle. As brief as they are, these descriptions provide important clues to the theme. When you encounter such clues, consider the broader or underlying meanings they suggest. Gather clues in a chart like the one shown.

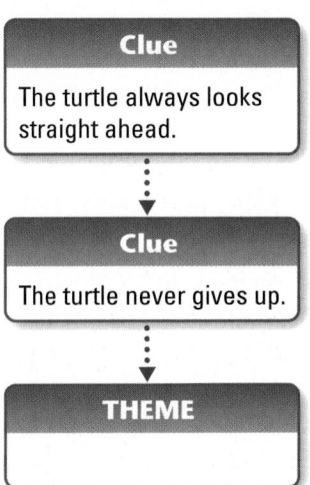

Clue

The turtle always looks straight ahead.

Clue

The turtle never gives up.

THEME

Vocabulary Development

embankment (em baŋk´ mənt) *n.* mound of earth or stone built to hold back water or support a roadway (p. 769)

protruded (prō trōōd´ id) *v.* pushed or thrust outward (p. 769)

The Turtle

from **The Grapes of Wrath**

John Steinbeck

▲ **Critical Viewing**
What elements of this turtle's anatomy make it especially suited for the landscape Steinbeck describes? **[Connect]**

Background

The Great Depression of the 1930s was a time of unequaled economic distress. In 1932, a quarter of Americans—at least 12 million—were out of work. One of many factors contributing to the Depression was a widespread drought in Oklahoma. The drought was so severe that farmland literally blew away in massive dust storms. Hoping to find relief and work, many farmers fled to the city. This is the situation faced by the Joad family, whose story is told by Steinbeck in his novel *The Grapes of Wrath*. This tale of the turtle serves as the introduction to that epic book, and provides a point of reference for the story of human struggle that follows.

The concrete highway was edged with a mat of tangled, broken, dry grass, and the grass heads were heavy with oat beards to catch on a dog's coat, and foxtails to tangle in a horse's fetlocks, and clover burrs to fasten in sheep's wool; sleeping life waiting to be spread and dispersed, every seed armed with an appliance of dispersal, twisting darts and parachutes for the wind, little spears and balls of tiny thorns, and all waiting for animals and for the wind, for a man's trouser cuff or the hem of a woman's skirt, all passive but armed with appliances of activity, still, but each possessed of the anlage[1] of movement.

The sun lay on the grass and warmed it, and in the shade under the grass the insects moved, ants and ant lions to set traps for them, grasshoppers to jump into the air and flick their yellow wings for a second, sow bugs like little armadillos, plodding restlessly on many tender feet. And over the grass at the roadside a land turtle crawled, turning aside for nothing, dragging his high-domed shell over the grass. His hard legs and yellow-nailed feet threshed slowly through the grass, not really walking, but boosting and dragging his shell along. The barley beards slid off his shell, and the clover burrs fell on him and rolled to the ground. His horny beak was partly opened, and his fierce, humorous eyes, under brows like fingernails, stared straight ahead. He came over the grass leaving a beaten trail behind him, and the hill, which was the highway <u>embankment</u>, reared up ahead of him. For a moment he stopped, his head held high. He blinked and looked up and down. At last he started to climb the embankment. Front clawed feet reached forward but did not touch. The hind feet kicked his shell along, and it scraped on the grass, and on the gravel. As the embankment grew steeper and steeper, the more frantic were the efforts of the land turtle. Pushing hind legs strained and slipped, boosting the shell along, and the horny head <u>protruded</u> as far as the neck could stretch. Little by little the shell slid up the embankment until at last a parapet[2] cut straight across its line of march, the shoulder of the road, a concrete wall four inches high. As though they worked independently the hind legs pushed the shell against the wall. The head upraised and peered over the wall to the broad smooth plain of cement. Now the hands, braced on top of the wall, strained and lifted, and the shell came slowly up and rested its front end on the wall. For a moment the turtle rested. A red ant ran into the shell, into the soft skin inside the shell, and suddenly head and legs snapped in, and the armored tail clamped in sideways. The red ant was crushed between body and legs. And one head of wild oats was clamped into the shell by a front leg. For a long moment the turtle lay still, and then the neck crept out and the old humorous frowning eyes looked about and the legs and tail came out. The back legs went to work, straining like elephant legs, and the shell tipped

---

1. **anlage** (än′ lä′ gə) *n.* foundation; basis; the initial cell structure from which an embryonic part develops.
2. **parapet** (par′ ə pet′) *n.* a low wall or edge of a roof, balcony, or similar structure.

Reading Strategy
Finding Clues to Theme
What does this description of "sleeping life" suggest about the story's theme?

embankment (em baŋk′ mənt) *n.* mound of earth or stone built to hold back water or support a roadway

protruded (prō trood′ id) *v.* pushed or thrust outward

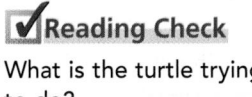

Reading Check
What is the turtle trying to do?

to an angle so that the front legs could not reach the level cement plain. But higher and higher the hind legs boosted it, until at last the center of balance was reached, the front tipped down, the front legs scratched at the pavement, and it was up. But the head of wild oats was held by its stem around the front legs.

Now the going was easy, and all the legs worked, and the shell boosted along, waggling from side to side. A sedan driven by a forty-year-old woman approached. She saw the turtle and swung to the right, off the highway, the wheels screamed and a cloud of dust boiled up. Two wheels lifted for a moment and then settled. The car skidded back onto the road, and went on, but more slowly. The turtle had jerked into its shell, but now it hurried on, for the highway was burning hot.

And now a light truck approached, and as it came near, the driver saw the turtle and swerved to hit it. His front wheel struck the edge of the shell, flipped the turtle like a tiddly-wink, spun it like a coin, and rolled it off the highway. The truck went back to its course along the right side. Lying on its back, the turtle was tight in its shell for a long time. But at last its legs waved in the air, reaching for something to pull it over. Its front foot caught a piece of quartz and little by little the shell pulled over and flopped upright. The wild oat head fell out and three of the spearhead seeds stuck in the ground. And as the turtle crawled on down the embankment, its shell dragged dirt over the seeds. The turtle entered a dust road and jerked itself along, drawing a wavy shallow trench in the dust with its shell. The old humorous eyes looked ahead, and the horny beak opened a little. His yellow toe nails slipped a fraction in the dust.

Literary Analysis
Theme and Symbol
What symbolic meaning might be given to turtle's actions after it is hit by the truck?

Review and Assess

Thinking About the Selection

1. **Respond:** How did you feel as you watched the turtle proceed?

2. **(a) Recall:** What obstacles does the turtle encounter?
   (b) Make a Judgment: Which of these is most dangerous?

3. **(a) Recall:** What happens to the turtle in his encounter with the two drivers? **(b) Compare and Contrast:** Based on their actions, what kinds of people do the two drivers seem to be?

4. **(a) Recall:** What happens to the red ant that slips inside the turtle's shell? **(b) Distinguish:** What does this event suggest about the turtle's capacity to defend itself?

5. **(a) Recall:** What happens to the wild oat head at the end of the story? **(b) Analyze:** What is the author suggesting about the relationships between different forms of life?

6. **Evaluate:** Do you think the turtle makes an effective symbol of the struggles of ordinary people? Explain.

Review and Assess

Literary Analysis

Theme

1. What parallels do you see between the experiences of the turtle and human experiences?
2. In what way are the wild oat seeds related to the story's **theme**?
3. What connection do the images from the beginning of the story of "sleeping life waiting to be spread" have to the story's theme?
4. Using your answers to questions 1–3, state the story's theme.

Connecting Literary Elements

5. Knowing that this story served as the introduction to *The Grapes of Wrath*, a novel about a displaced Depression-era farming family seeking a better life, what do you think the turtle symbolizes?
6. (a) Use a chart like the one shown to examine the turtle's actions at each stage of its journey. (b) What does the turtle's journey symbolize?

	Obstacles	Turtle's Reactions	Symbolic Meaning
Climbs Embankment			
Crosses Road			

Reading Strategy

Finding Clues to Theme

7. Steinbeck uses the words *dragging, turning aside for nothing,* and *thrashed slowly* to describe the turtle. (a) What effect do these words have on your perception of the turtle? (b) How do you think Steinbeck wants readers to respond to the turtle?
8. (a) Which characters can be seen as representing nature—or the simple life—and which represent the modern world? Explain. (b) Which does Steinbeck likely feel is more important? Explain.

Extend Understanding

9. **Career Connection:** Which of the turtle's personal qualities would be advantageous or disadvantageous in today's business world? Explain.

Quick Review

A story's **theme** is its central message.

Symbols are people, places, or things that represent ideas or qualities larger than their literal meanings.

To **find clues to theme,** consider the details a writer provides and identify their underlying meaning.

 Take It to the Net
www.phschool.com
Take the interactive self-test online to check your understanding of the selection.

Integrate Language Skills

Vocabulary Development Lesson

Word Analysis: Latin Prefix *pro-*

In this story, John Steinbeck uses the word *protruded*, which begins with the Latin prefix *pro-*, meaning "forward." Knowing this meaning helps you to define the whole word *protruded*, which means "thrust forward," and other words beginning with the prefix *pro-*.

Add the prefix *pro-* to the word roots below. Then, write a brief definition of each word and use it in a sentence.

1. *-ject*   4. *-hibit*
2. *-ceed*   5. *-duce*
3. *-gress*   6. *-pose*

Fluency: True or False?

Use your knowledge of the words from the vocabulary list on page 767 to decide whether these statements are true or false.

1. An *embankment* is at the bottom of a lake.
2. When the cat's paw *protruded*, it stuck out.

Spelling Strategy

In some words, the prefix or suffix is embedded, and removing the prefix or suffix leaves only a word part. For each of the following words, note whether or not the underlined prefix or suffix can be removed to make a base word.

1. terri<u>fy</u>   2. <u>ag</u>gressor   3. <u>im</u>possible

Grammar and Style Lesson

Parallel Structure

Parallel structure is the expression of similar ideas using similar grammatical form. Parallel structures can involve the use of adjectives, verbs, phrases, or entire sentences.

The use of parallel structures helps to emphasize key ideas and link similar concepts. In "The Turtle," John Steinbeck uses numerous parallel structures to add sophistication to his writing and to indicate the connection between actions and ideas. Look at these examples.

> **Adjectives:** The concrete highway was edged with a mat of *tangled, broken, dry* grass . . .
>
> **Infinitive Phrases:** . . . the grass heads were heavy with oat beards *to catch* on a dog's coat, and foxtails *to tangle* in a horse's fetlocks, and clover burrs *to fasten* in sheep's wool . . .

Practice Identify the parallel grammatical elements in each sentence.

1. . . . all waiting for animals and for the wind, for a man's trouser cuff . . .
2. . . . a land turtle crawled, turning aside for nothing, dragging his high-domed shell over the grass.
3. His front wheel struck the edge of the shell, flipped the turtle like a tiddly-wink, spun it like a coin, and rolled it off the highway.
4. . . . ants and ant lions to set traps for them, grasshoppers to jump into the air . . .
5. A red ant ran into the shell, into the soft skin . . .

Writing Application Write a short description of a natural event, like a storm or a flight of geese. Use parallel structure to call attention to the key details in your description.

WG Prentice Hall Writing and Grammar Connection: Chapter 20, Section 6

Writing Lesson

Essay About Historical Context

John Steinbeck wrote "The Turtle" as a prelude for his novel *The Grapes of Wrath*, which portrays the struggles of a Depression-era farm family. Steinbeck intended that readers draw parallels between the prelude and the novel. Write an essay connecting the events described in "The Turtle" to the lives of ordinary people during the Great Depression.

Prewriting Research the Great Depression to learn how people reacted to adverse economic circumstances. Then, review "The Turtle" and draw parallels.

Drafting First, provide information about the Depression. In your body paragraphs, note facts and data and explain parallels you found to "The Turtle." Cite the sources of these facts as you draft.

Model: Providing Internal Documentation

The Great Depression of the 1930s was a time of economic disaster. Stock prices fell 40 percent, 9,000 banks failed, and 9 million savings accounts were wiped out. (*http://www.britannica.com,* Great Depression)

> When citing sources without providing a full reference list at the end of the essay, include all source information parenthetically.

Revising Review your essay. Make sure that you have provided enough historical context to support your observations. Add information as needed, and provide correct citations about where you found the material.

Prentice Hall Writing and Grammar Connection: Chapter 12, Section 5

Extension Activities

Listening and Speaking After preparing a list of questions, conduct an **interview** with someone who lived through the Great Depression. Share your findings with the class. Use the following tips:

- Come to the interview with a tape recorder and writing materials.
- Request your subject's permission to record the conversation.

Frame your post-interview presentation with an engaging introduction and conclusion.

Research and Technology With a partner, pare "The Turtle" down to its essential thematic message. Write and illustrate a **cartoon strip** conveying that message. If possible, use graphic arts software to lay out and generate your cartoon. **[Group Activity]**

Take It to the Net www.phschool.com

Go online for an additional research activity using the Internet.

Prepare to Read

old age sticks ◆ anyone lived in a pretty how town ◆ The Unknown Citizen

E. E. Cummings (1894–1962)

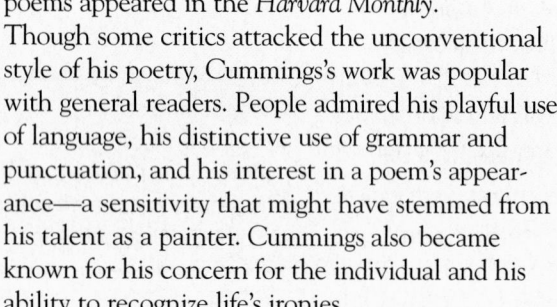

After working in the French ambulance corps and spending three months behind bars as a political prisoner during World War I, Edward Estlin Cummings studied painting in Paris and subsequently began writing poetry in New York City. A graduate of Harvard University, his first published poems appeared in the *Harvard Monthly*. Though some critics attacked the unconventional style of his poetry, Cummings's work was popular with general readers. People admired his playful use of language, his distinctive use of grammar and punctuation, and his interest in a poem's appearance—a sensitivity that might have stemmed from his talent as a painter. Cummings also became known for his concern for the individual and his ability to recognize life's ironies.

Form vs. Content Although Cummings's poems tend to be unconventional in form and style, they generally express traditional ideas. In his finest poems, Cummings explores the customary poetic terrain of love and nature but makes innovative use of grammar and punctuation to reinforce meaning. Many of his poems also contain comic touches as Cummings addresses the confusing aspects of modern life. Cummings was also a skillful satirist who used his poems to challenge accepted notions and fixed beliefs.

Cummings received a number of awards for his work, including the Boston Fine Arts Poetry Festival Award and the Bollingen Prize in Poetry. In 1968, six years after his death, a volume of his poetry, *The Complete Poems, 1913–1968*, was published. At the time of his death, he was the second most widely read poet in the United States, after Robert Frost.

W. H. Auden (1907–1973)

Although he was influenced by the Modernist poets, Wystan Hugh Auden adopted only those aspects of Modernism with which he felt comfortable. At the same time, he maintained many elements of traditional poetry. Throughout his career, he wrote with insight about people struggling to preserve their individuality in an increasingly conformist society.

Auden was born in England and attended Oxford University. At age twenty-three, he both published his first volume of poetry and developed a passionate interest in politics. He spoke out against poverty in England and the rise of Nazism in Germany.

A New Country In 1939, just before World War II, Auden moved from England to the United States. That move was coincident with his rediscovery of his Christian beliefs. His works *The Double Man* (1941) and *For the Time Being* (1944) depict religion as a way of coping with a disjointed modern society. Despite the comfort he found in religion, Auden became disillusioned with modern life in his later years. He used his poetry to explore the responsibilities of the artist in what he saw as a faithless modern age.

Auden earned the Pulitzer Prize in 1948 for his long narrative poem *The Age of Anxiety* (1947), which explores the confusion associated with post-World War II life. He later produced several more volumes of poetry and a large body of literary criticism. He also anthologized others' works and coauthored at least one musical composition—a libretto for the opera *The Rake's Progress*. From 1954 to 1973, Auden served as Chancellor of the Academy of American Poets.

Preview

Connecting to the Literature

Do you ever wonder how you can express your individuality and distinguish yourself from the rest of humanity—or even from your immediate circle of friends? The following poems address this human desire.

Literary Analysis

Satire

Satire is writing in which an author uses humor to ridicule or criticize certain individuals, institutions, types of behavior, or even humanity in general. The purpose of satire is to promote changes in society or in the world. By poking fun at problems, satirists use the force of laughter to persuade readers to accept their point of view. As you read, think about the serious point each poet makes through satire.

Comparing Literary Works

Satirical writings vary in **tone**—a quality that reveals a writer's attitude toward his or her subject, characters, or audience. The tone of a satirical work may be tolerant, humorous, bitter, or biting, and is revealed through the writer's choices of words and details. For example, in naming his characters "anyone" and "noone," Cummings suggests the lack of distinction that comes with excessive conformity. His satire is biting, though it is softened by other elements of the poem:

> one day anyone died i guess
> (and noone stooped to kiss his face)

As you read these poems, compare each poet's tone, and identify the varying kinds of satire that result.

Reading Strategy

Relating Structure to Meaning

You can often connect the ideas of poetry with the form the words take:

- **Structure** is the way a poem is put together in words, lines, and stanzas.
- **Meaning** is the central idea the poet wants to convey.

In his poems, Cummings plays typographical games and breaks rules of grammar and syntax. His structure suits his theme: individual challenges to convention. Use a chart like the one shown to link structure to meaning.

Vocabulary Development

statistics (stə tis′ tiks) *n.* science of collecting and arranging facts about a particular subject in the form of numbers (p. 779)

psychology (sī käl′ ə jē) *n.* science dealing with the mind and with mental and emotional processes (p. 780)

"anyone lived in a pretty how town"

Structure	Meaning
Nine stanzas of four lines apiece	The regularity of the stanzas emphasizes the routine of town life.

old age sticks

E. E. Cummings

old age sticks
up Keep
Off
signs)&

5   youth yanks them
down(old
age
cries No

Tres)&(pas)
10 youth laughs
(sing
old age

scolds Forbid
den Stop
15 Must
n't Don't

&)youth goes
right on
gr
20 owing old

Remember Now the Days of Thy Youth, 1950, Paul Starrett Sample, Hood Museum of Art, Dartmouth College, Hanover, NH

▲ **Critical Viewing** Do you think that the elderly men in this painting could belong to the group that Cummings describes, or are they a different sort? On what details did you base your conclusion? **[Speculate]**

anyone lived in a pretty how town

E. E. Cummings

Background

E. E. Cummings's style is among the most distinctive of any American poet. He molded his poems into unconventional shapes by varying line lengths and inserting unusual spaces between letters and lines. Many of his poems contain little punctuation; the few marks that do appear often highlight important ideas. In addition, Cummings rarely uses capital letters, except for emphasis. Another distinguishing mark of his style is his use of the lower-case *i* when his speakers refer to themselves. This small *i* is meant to convey the idea of a self as a small part of mass society and Cummings's belief in the need for modesty.

anyone lived in a pretty how town
(with up so floating many bells down)
spring summer autumn winter
he sang his didn't he danced his did.

5   Women and men(both little and small)
cared for anyone not at all
they sowed their isn't they reaped their same
sun moon stars rain

children guessed(but only a few
10 and down they forgot as up they grew
autumn winter spring summer)
that noone loved him more by more

when by now and tree by leaf
she laughed his joy she cried his grief
15 bird by snow and stir by still
anyone's any was all to her

 **Reading Check**

Which words are repeated in these stanzas?

someones married their everyones
laughed their cryings and did their dance
(sleep wake hope and then)they
20 said their nevers they slept their dream

stars rain sun moon
(and only the snow can begin to explain
how children are apt to forget to remember
with up so floating many bells down)

25 one day anyone died i guess
(and noone stooped to kiss his face)
busy folk buried them side by side
little by little and was by was

all by all and deep by deep
30 and more by more they dream their sleep
noone and anyone earth by april
wish by spirit and if by yes.

Women and men(both dong and ding)
summer autumn winter spring
35 reaped their sowing and went their came
sun moon stars rain

Reading Strategy
Relating Structure to Meaning How do the regular stanzas of four lines each reinforce the ideas of the poem?

Review and Assess

Thinking About the Selections

1. **Respond:** What parts of your life do you see in these poems? Explain.

2. **(a) Recall:** In "old age sticks," what actions do old age and youth take? **(b) Compare and Contrast:** Explain the differences Cummings points out between youth and old age.

3. **(a) Recall:** In the final stanza of "old age sticks," what does the poem say is happening to youth? **(b) Interpret:** Explain the irony in this final stanza.

4. **(a) Recall:** What does Cummings name the main male and female characters in "anyone lived in a pretty how town"? **(b) Speculate:** What is the poet suggesting in this choice?

5. **(a) Recall:** What does Cummings say the people do with their cryings and their dreams? **(b) Interpret:** What message is the poet conveying about the ideas of individuality and conformity?

6. **Evaluate:** Which poem presents a more positive view of life? Explain.

The Unknown Citizen

W. H. Auden

(To JS/07/M/378 This Marble Monument Is Erected by the State)

Turret Lathe Operator, Grant Wood, Cedar Rapids Museum of Art, Cedar Rapids, Iowa. Courtesy Associated American Artists, © Estate of Grant Wood/Licensed by VAGA, New York, NY

▲ **Critical Viewing** In what ways does the man in this painting appear to fit Auden's description of "the unknown citizen"? **[Analyze]**

He was found by the Bureau of <u>Statistics</u> to be
One against whom there was no official complaint,
And all the reports on his conduct agree
That, in the modern sense of an old-fashioned word, he was a saint,
5　For in everything he did he served the Greater Community.
Except for the War till the day he retired
He worked in a factory and never got fired,
But satisfied his employers, Fudge Motors Inc.
Yet he wasn't a scab or odd in his views,
10　For his Union reports that he paid his dues,
(Our report on his Union shows it was sound)

statistics (stə tis´ tiks) *n.* science of collecting and arranging facts about a particular subject in the form of numbers

✓**Reading Check**

What makes the subject of the poem "a saint"?

And our Social <u>Psychology</u> workers found
That he was popular with his mates and liked a drink.
The Press are convinced that he bought a paper every day
15 And that his reactions to advertisements were normal in every way.
Policies taken out in his name prove that he was fully insured,
And his Health-card shows he was once in hospital but left it cured.
Both Producers Research and High-Grade Living declare
He was fully sensible to the advantages of the Installment Plan
20 And had everything necessary to the Modern Man,
A phonograph, a radio, a car and a frigidaire.
Our researchers into Public Opinion are content
That he held the proper opinions for the time of year;
When there was peace, he was for peace; when there was war,
  he went.
25 He was married and added five children to the population.
Which our Eugenist[1] says was the right number for a parent of
  his generation,
And our teachers report that he never interfered with their
  education.
Was he free? Was he happy? The question is absurd:
Had anything been wrong, we should certainly have heard.

psychology (sī kälˊ ə jē) *n.*
science dealing with the
mind and with mental
and emotional processes

Reading Strategy
**Relating Structure to
Meaning** Why do you
think Auden capitalizes
words in line 18?

---

1. **Eugenist** (yōō jenˊ ist) *n.* a specialist in eugenics, the movement devoted to improving
the human species through genetic control.

Review and Assess

Thinking About the Selection

1. **Respond:** Have you ever felt as though you have been
   reduced to a number? Explain your answer.

2. **(a) Recall:** How does the state identify the unknown citizen
   in the poem's subtitle? **(b) Interpret:** What do these numbers
   and letters suggest?

3. **(a) Recall:** Identify at least three facts the state knows about
   the citizen's life. **(b) Interpret:** In what ways is the citizen
   "unknown" to the state? **(c) Deduce:** Why might the state
   have heard nothing about these aspects of the citizen's life?

4. **(a) Recall:** What questions does the speaker refer to as "absurd"?
   (b) Make a Judgment: Are these questions actually absurd?
   Explain. **(c) Analyze:** In what ways do the final two lines clarify
   the poet's attitude or beliefs?

5. **Apply:** Which aspects of the society in the poem are like
   contemporary America? Which are different? Explain.

6. **Evaluate:** What types of information about the man do you
   feel are missing from the poem? Explain.

Review and Assess

Literary Analysis

Satire

1. What changes might E.E. Cummings like to see in the world of "old age sticks"?

2. Based on "anyone lived in a pretty how town," what small-town qualities and behaviors does Cummings **satirize**?

3. (a) Using a chart like the one shown here, name four groups that report on the unknown citizen's activities. (b) What do the concerns of the state and these groups reveal about society as a whole?

JS/07/M/378

4. (a) Based on "The Unknown Citizen," what values do you think Auden holds dear? (b) What type of society do you think he supports?

Comparing Literary Works

5. In what way does each of the poems explore the conflict between individuality and conformity to a group?

6. (a) Identify the tone, or attitude, of each poem. (b) Note two details from each poem that reveal the tone. (c) Which tone do you find most effective for the purpose of satire? Explain.

Reading Strategy

Relating Structure to Meaning

7. How does the **structure** of "old age sticks" relate to the idea of rules and rule-breaking as it is presented in the poem?

8. Discuss how Auden's style of capitalization affects the meaning and tone of his poem.

Extend Understanding

9. **Cultural Connection:** In what way have bureaucracies such as government agencies or corporations affected our sense of individuality and identity? Explain.

Quick Review

Satire is writing in which an author uses humor to ridicule or criticize a topic.

Tone is the author's attitude toward his or her subject, characters, or audience.

To **relate structure to meaning,** consider how the arrangement of words, lines, and stanzas might reflect the poem's central ideas.

 Take It to the Net
www.phschool.com
Take the interactive self-test online to check your understanding of these selections.

Integrate Language Skills

Vocabulary Development Lesson

Word Analysis: Greek Root -psych-

The name Psyche—a heroine in a Greek myth—comes from a Greek word meaning "breath" or "soul." The Greek root -psych- means "soul" or "mind," and it forms the basis for a number of English words, including *psychology*. Write definitions for the following -psych- words. Then, write a sentence using each word.

1. psychiatry
2. psychosomatic
3. psychotic
4. psychiatrist

Spelling Strategy

Some words begin with the *s* sound but are actually spelled *ps*: *psychology, psalm*. These words derive from the Greek letter *psi*, pronounced *si*. Complete the spelling of the words below. Then, write a sentence for each.

1. __ychopath
2. __ychic
3. __oriasis

Fluency: Context

The word *psychology* refers to the science dealing with mental and emotional processes. The word *statistics* refers to the science of tabulation or counting. Decide whether each of the following situations relates more closely to psychology or statistics.

1. Teacher assigns class lesson on grieving process.
2. Teacher keeps records of completed assignments.
3. You explain your dream to a friend.
4. Scientist publishes paper on blood diseases in New York State.
5. A star athlete's endorsement boosts product sales in the first two weeks following an advertisement's release.

Grammar and Style Lesson

Parentheses

Parentheses are used to enclose extra information that is interruptive or loosely related to the rest of the sentence but that does not deserve special attention. Use parentheses instead of dashes and commas to set off such information.

> **Example:** My father's new truck (the one he bought last month) has a lot of power.

Practice Rewrite each of the following sentences, adding parentheses to improve the clarity.

1. No person at least no sensible person could accuse Cummings of being a conformist.
2. Cummings's unconventional poetry except for the love poems can be silly, serious, and witty.
3. Auden's poetry especially when read by an actor always affects listeners.
4. Auden's political viewpoints I'd guess were formed over time.
5. The works of two poets except for their different punctuation styles have much in common.

Writing Application Write a paragraph about one of your hobbies, using parentheses at least twice to set off information.

$\mathcal{W}_G$ *Prentice Hall Writing and Grammar Connection: Chapter 27, Section 5*

Writing Lesson

Introduction to a Poetry Reading

Poetry readings—in coffee shops, bookstores, libraries, or community centers—often feature the work of more than one writer. Imagine that you have been asked to organize a reading of Auden's and Cummings's poetry. Write an introduction that welcomes your audience, provides some background information on the poets, and briefly compares their work.

Prewriting   Reread the poems. Develop a central idea about similarities and differences in the work of Cummings and Auden. Jot down details or examples from the poems that support this main idea.

Model: Gathering Details of Support

Theme: Cummings uses a highly ordered stanza structure in "anyone lived in a pretty how town."

Structure: In "The Unknown Citizen," Auden explores the effect of a highly organized society on individuals.

> Specific references to poetry will strengthen an introduction to the works.

Drafting   Keep your remarks brief but informative and well supported with details. Use a conversational writing style suitable to oral delivery.

Revising   Make sure you provide enough information to prepare the audience for the poetry they will hear. Revise to ensure that your details are relevant and support your main points.

W︠G Prentice Hall Writing and Grammar Connection: Chapter 14, Section 2

Extension Activities

Listening and Speaking The poem "anyone lived in a pretty how town" is set in the country. How might the poem be different if it were set in a city? In a **group discussion,** brainstorm the topic. Consider the following:

- What kinds of lives would people live?
- How would the setting change the activities?
- In what ways might it affect relationships?

After discussing the differences, write a revision based on an urban setting, and share it with the class. **[Group Activity]**

Research and Technology Auden speaks out against totalitarianism—a system in which the government takes control of civil life. Use the Internet to investigate totalitarian governments in Europe after World War I. Compile your findings in a **written report.** Incorporate spreadsheets on the topic in your word-processor document.

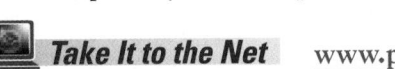 **Take It to the Net**   www.phschool.com

Go online for an additional research activity using the Internet.

Prepare to Read

The Far and the Near

Thomas Wolfe (1900–1938)

A man of tremendous energy, appetites, and size, Thomas Wolfe poured out thousands of pages of fiction during his brief career. Driven by the desire to experience all life had to offer, he pursued variety. He lived in the city and in the country, in America and in Europe, in the North and in the South. He reflected this passion for life in his work—in its sheer volume, in the expanses of time and territory it covers, and in his characters who were symbols of greater humanity.

An Instant Success Born in Asheville, North Carolina, Wolfe grew up in a large, eccentric family whose members later served as models for his fiction. His mother speculated in real estate. His father made tombstones. Shortly before the age of sixteen, Wolfe entered the University of North Carolina. There, he became interested in playwriting, a focus he pursued during and after his postgraduate studies at Harvard. Wolfe eventually moved to New York City, where he taught composition at New York University and wrote plays in his spare time.

Unable to find success as a playwright, Wolfe turned to writing fiction. With the assistance of Maxwell Perkins, the leading editor of the time, Wolfe published his first novel in 1929, the loosely autobiographical *Look Homeward, Angel*. The novel was a critical and financial success and earned Wolfe widespread recognition. In 1930, Wolfe was awarded a Guggenheim fellowship that allowed him to travel extensively in Europe.

A New Direction Inspired by the success of his first novel, Wolfe began working on a sequel. Once again, Perkins helped him shorten and shape the novel, which was published in 1935 as *Of Time and the River*. The novel sold well, yet Wolfe was criticized for basing his work too closely on his own life and for his reliance on Perkins.

A New Direction Stung by the criticism, Wolfe switched publishers and struck out on a new course. He became obsessed with the idea that his duty as a writer was to act as a social historian, to interpret his time and place. Unfortunately, he died of a brain infection before he could finish another novel.

Wolfe did, however, leave several thousand pages of manuscript in the hands of another editor, Edward Aswell. Aswell shaped Wolfe's drafts into two more books, *The Web and the Rock* (1939) and *You Can't Go Home Again* (1940).

Sharp Contrasts The contrasts between Wolfe's early, highly personal writings and his later, more socially focused work can perhaps be traced to the differences between his brooding, ambitious mother and his outgoing but self-indulgent father. Certainly, contrast plays a key role in much of Wolfe's writing.

As if to nurture To develop these differences in his work, Wolfe pursued life with an enormous appetite. He said, "I will go everywhere and see everything. I will meet all the people I can. I will think all the thoughts, feel all the emotions I am able, and I will write, write, write."

Final Assessment Had he not died so young, there is little doubt that Wolfe's literary output would have been great. Despite the criticism that he lacked discipline, his talent was profound. In his novels and short stories he displayed a strong sense of time and place, an ability to create vivid and realistic descriptions, and a deep understanding of the human condition. All of these abilities find expression in Wolfe's story "The Far and the Near," which explores the often painful disparity between imagination and real life.

Preview

Connecting to the Literature

At some time in your life, you have probably looked forward to an experience, only to find that it was not what you had dreamed of. In this story, a man learns the difference between hopes, dreams, and sober reality.

Literary Analysis

Climax and Anticlimax

The **climax** in a story is the high point of interest, the moment at which the conflict is resolved. When that resolution is unexpectedly disappointing, ridiculous, or trivial, it is called an **anticlimax.** Like a climax, an anticlimax is the biggest moment in the story, but it is more a low point than a high point in the action. The reader, who has been led to expect that something important or serious is about to occur, is suddenly confronted with the letdown of a seemingly inappropriate resolution. When used effectively, anticlimax can create a variety of effects, from pathos— sorrow or sympathy—to humor.

Connecting Literary Elements

To keep readers engaged, writers must grab their interest early. Once a story's central conflict is introduced, the events leading up to the climax help build readers' anticipation. These events constitute a story's **rising action.** As you read, identify the elements of the rising action to see how they add to your expectations of the climax.

Reading Strategy

Predicting

This story about a train engineer's life is a bit like a real train ride: Signposts guide the way to the final destination. These clues enable you to **predict** upcoming events and outcomes. Watch for signals in the story's details that can help you predict where the action is headed. Consider this passage from the story:

> Every day, a few minutes after two o'clock in the afternoon, the limited express . . . passed this spot.

Because the writer tells you the place is important, you might predict that the story will involve "this spot" in some way. As you read, predict what is to come. Record the information in a chart like the one shown here.

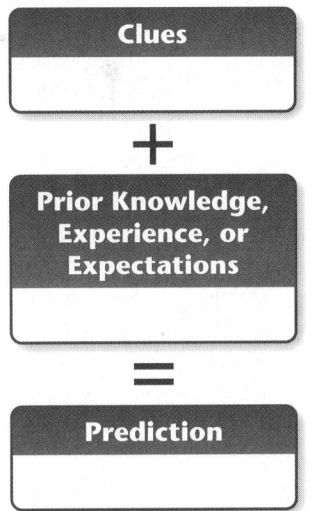

Clues

+

Prior Knowledge, Experience, or Expectations

=

Prediction

Vocabulary Development

tempo (tem´ pō) *n.* rate of activity of a sound or motion; pace (p. 788)

sallow (sal´ ō) *adj.* sickly; pale yellow (p. 789)

sullen (sul´ ən) *adj.* sulky; glum (p. 790)

timorous (tim´ ər əs) *adj.* full of fear (p. 790)

visage (viz´ ij) *n.* appearance (p. 790)

The Far and the Near

Thomas Wolfe

Background

With the driving of the "golden spike" on May 10, 1869, at Promontory, Utah, the first transcontinental rail link was completed. Finishing the western half had taken more than six years, the work of thousands, and the lives of many. With its completion, America's love affair with the railways had officially begun. Now, people could travel the width of the young nation in relative comfort; they could strike out for the inexpensive land available to homesteaders; they could return East to visit relatives. In many ways, the nation grew more united. Cities grew at railroad hubs such as Chicago and St. Louis. As the railroad crisscrossed the nation, untamed land and lifestyles, like those of cowboys, disappeared. America became a nation of towns like the one the engineer in "The Far and the Near" observes from his perch in the train engine.

O n the outskirts of a little town upon a rise of land that swept back from the railway there was a tidy little cottage of white boards, trimmed vividly with green blinds. To one side of the house there was a garden neatly patterned with plots of growing vegetables, and an arbor for the grapes which ripened late in August. Before the house there were three mighty oaks which sheltered it in their clean and massive shade in summer, and to the other side there was a border of gay flowers. The whole place had an air of tidiness, thrift, and modest comfort.

Every day, a few minutes after two o'clock in the afternoon, the limited express between two cities passed this spot. At that moment the great train, having halted for a breathing

Literary Analysis
Climax, Anticlimax, and Rising Action What effect does the routine of "every day" have on your expectations of the story?

**Reading Check**

What happens everyday a few minutes after two o'clock?

◀ **Critical Viewing** In what ways might this painting reflect the engineer's perspective on the farms and villages he sees along his train route? **[Analyze]**

space at the town nearby, was beginning to lengthen evenly into its stroke, but it had not yet reached the full drive of its terrific speed. It swung into view deliberately, swept past with a powerful swaying motion of the engine, a low smooth rumble of its heavy cars upon pressed steel, and then it vanished in the cut. For a moment the progress of the engine could be marked by heavy bellowing puffs of smoke that burst at spaced intervals above the edges of the meadow grass, and finally nothing could be heard but the solid clacking tempo of the wheels receding into the drowsy stillness of the afternoon.

Every day for more than twenty years, as the train had approached this house, the engineer had blown on the whistle, and every day, as soon as she heard this signal, a woman had appeared on the back porch of the little house and waved to him. At first she had a small child clinging to her skirts, and now this child had grown to full womanhood, and every day she, too, came with her mother to the porch and waved.

The engineer had grown old and gray in service. He had driven his great train, loaded with its weight of lives, across the land ten thousand times. His own children had grown up and married, and four times he had seen before him on the tracks the ghastly dot of tragedy converging like a cannon ball to its eclipse of horror at the boiler head[1]—a light spring wagon filled with children, with its clustered row of small stunned faces; a cheap automobile stalled upon the tracks, set with the wooden figures of people paralyzed with fear; a battered hobo walking by the rail, too deaf and old to hear the whistle's warning; and a form flung past his window with a scream—all this the man had seen and known. He had known all the grief, the joy, the peril and the labor such a man could know; he had grown seamed and weathered in his loyal service, and now, schooled by the qualities of faith and courage and humbleness that attended his labor, he had grown old, and had the grandeur and the wisdom these men have.

But no matter what peril or tragedy he had known, the vision of the little house and the women waving to him with a brave free motion of the arm had become fixed in the mind of the engineer as something beautiful and enduring, something beyond all change and ruin, and something that would always be the same, no matter what mishap, grief or error might break the iron schedule of his days.

The sight of the little house and of these two women gave him the most extraordinary happiness he had ever known. He had seen them in a thousand lights, a hundred weathers. He had seen them through the harsh bare light of wintry gray across the brown and frosted stubble of the earth, and he had seen them again in the green luring sorcery of April.

He felt for them and for the little house in which they lived such tenderness as a man might feel for his own children, and at length the picture of their lives was carved so sharply in his heart that he

---

tempo (tem´ pō) *n.* rate of activity of a sound or motion; pace

Literary Analysis
Climax, Anticlimax, and Rising Action In what ways does this detailed description of the old man's experiences with "grief and joy" add to your expections of the story?

felt that he knew their lives completely, to every hour and moment of the day, and he resolved that one day, when his years of service should be ended, he would go and find these people and speak at last with them whose lives had been so wrought into his own.

That day came. At last the engineer stepped from a train onto the station platform of the town where these two women lived. His years upon the rail had ended. He was a pensioned servant of his company, with no more work to do. The engineer walked slowly through the station and out into the streets of the town. Everything was as strange to him as if he had never seen this town before. As he walked on, his sense of bewilderment and confusion grew. Could this be the town he had passed ten thousand times? Were these the same houses he had seen so often from the high windows of his cab? It was all as unfamiliar, as disquieting as a city in a dream, and the perplexity of his spirit increased as he went on.

Presently the houses thinned into the straggling outposts of the town, and the street faded into a country road—the one on which the women lived. And the man plodded on slowly in the heat and dust. At length he stood before the house he sought. He knew at once that he had found the proper place. He saw the lordly oaks before the house, the flower beds, the garden and the arbor, and farther off, the glint of rails.

Yes, this was the house he sought, the place he had passed so many times, the destination he had longed for with such happiness. But now that he had found it, now that he was here, why did his hand falter on the gate; why had the town, the road, the earth, the very entrance to this place he loved turned unfamiliar as the landscape of some ugly dream? Why did he now feel this sense of confusion, doubt and hopelessness?

At length he entered by the gate, walked slowly up the path and in a moment more had mounted three short steps that led up to the porch, and was knocking at the door. Presently he heard steps in the hall, the door was opened, and a woman stood facing him.

And instantly, with a sense of bitter loss and grief, he was sorry he had come. He knew at once that the woman who stood there looking at him with a mistrustful eye was the same woman who had waved to him so many thousand times. But her face was harsh and pinched and meager; the flesh sagged wearily in <u>sallow</u> folds, and the small eyes peered at him with timid suspicion and uneasy doubt. All the brave freedom, the warmth and the affection that he had read into her gesture, vanished in the moment that he saw her and heard her unfriendly tongue.

And now his own voice sounded unreal and ghastly to him as he tried to explain his presence, to tell her who he was and the reason he had come. But he faltered on, fighting stubbornly against the

The American Railroad
The first railroad in America was built in 1826; it ran three miles—from Quincy, Massachusetts, to the Neponset River. Fourteen years later, the first steam locomotive was built in New York, running seventeen miles from Albany to Schenectady. By the late 1800s, a complete network of rail lines linked the entire nation, opening every corner of the country to settlement and growth. Businesses and towns developed where rail lines crossed. As the railroads expanded, the economy of the country also grew. Freight cars carried coal and other products while passenger rails made it easy for people to resettle or visit relatives in other parts of the country. Thousands of new jobs were created, and the United States soon became the greatest industrial nation in the world. Thus began America's love for the railroad.

Literary Analysis
Climax and Anticlimax
Explain why the woman's appearance is anticlimactic.

sallow (sal′ ō) *adj.* sickly; pale yellow

**Reading Check**

What does the engineer do after retiring from the railroad?

horror of regret, confusion, disbelief that surged up in his spirit, drowning all his former joy and making his act of hope and tenderness seem shameful to him.

At length the woman invited him almost unwillingly into the house, and called her daughter in a harsh shrill voice. Then, for a brief agony of time, the man sat in an ugly little parlor, and he tried to talk while the two women stared at him with a dull, bewildered hostility, a <u>sullen</u>, <u>timorous</u> restraint.

And finally, stammering a crude farewell, he departed. He walked away down the path and then along the road toward town, and suddenly he knew that he was an old man. His heart, which had been brave and confident when it looked along the familiar vista of the rails, was now sick with doubt and horror as it saw the strange and unsuspected <u>visage</u> of an earth which had always been within a stone's throw of him, and which he had never seen or known. And he knew that all the magic of that bright lost way, the vista of that shining line, the imagined corner of that small good universe of hope's desire, was gone forever, could never be got back again.

sullen (sul´ ən) *adj.* sulky; glum

timorous (tim´ ər əs) *adj.* full of fear

visage (viz´ ij) *n.* appearance

Review and Assess

Thinking About the Selection

1. **Respond:** As you read about the engineer's approaching visit to the little town, what did you hope he would find?

2. **(a) Recall:** What has been the engineer's daily experience for the last twenty years? **(b) Interpret:** What does this tell you about the engineer's life?

3. **(a) Recall:** How does the engineer feel about the little house and the two women? **(b) Infer:** What do the house and the women represent to him?

4. **(a) Recall:** What event makes the engineer's visit to the town possible? **(b) Recall:** What is the engineer's first impression of the town when he comes to visit? **(c) Connect:** When does he first sense that his experience is unlikely to match his expectations?

5. **(a) Recall:** What realization does the engineer come to at the end of the story? **(b) Contrast:** In what ways do the engineer's observations in the final scene contrast with his expectations?

6. **Analyze:** Considering the title of the story, what do you think Wolfe is saying about human longing?

7. **Apply:** The engineer is crushed when he discovers his optimism was not based on reality. Is it possible to confront reality and remain hopeful about life at the same time? Explain.

Review and Assess

Literary Analysis
Climax and Anticlimax

1. (a) What is the story's **anticlimax**? Support your answer. (b) In what way does the anticlimax resolve the story's central conflict?

2. What effect does the anticlimax have on both the engineer and the reader?

3. Why do you suppose Wolfe chose to give this story an anticlimax rather than a **climax**? Explain.

4. If you were to rewrite this story with a climax rather than an anticlimax: (a) What details would change? (b) How would such a revised story end?

Connecting Literary Elements

5. (a) When in the story does the rising action begin? (b) Using a chart like the one shown, list three events in the rising action that led to the moment of greatest tension.

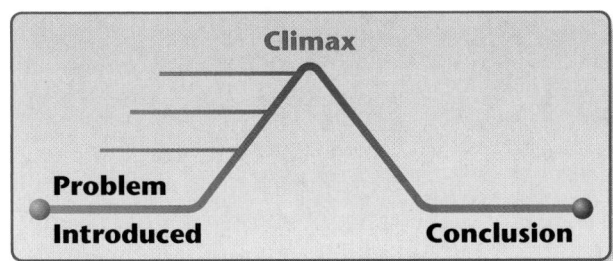

6. How does the repetition of the engineer's attachment to the woman and her house contribute to the tension created in the story's **rising action**?

Reading Strategy
Predicting

7. When you read about the engineer's decision to visit the two women after retiring, what did you **predict** would happen?

8. Based on your own experience, did you predict that the engineer's view of the world would change when he stepped down from the "high windows of his cab"? Explain.

Extend Understanding

9. **Cultural Connection:** In what way does the romantic notion of train travel add to the distortion between the engineer's view of the world from far away and his view up close?

Quick Review

The **climax** is the high point of interest or suspense in a story. An **anticlimax** is an unexpectedly disappointing or trivial resolution.

The **rising action** in a story begins when the conflict is introduced and includes the events that create the tension and lead to the climax.

To **predict,** use clues in the story to make educated guesses about upcoming events and outcomes.

 Take It to the Net
www.phschool.com
Take the interactive self-test online to check your understanding of the selection.

Integrate Language Skills

Vocabulary Development Lesson

Word Analysis: Latin Root -temp-

Built on the Latin root -temp-, meaning "time," *tempo* means "pace" or "the rate of activity of a sound or motion." Using this knowledge define the following words:

1. temporary
2. contemporary
3. extemporaneous
4. tempo

Spelling Strategy

The *j* sound can be spelled in a few ways, including *ge* as in *visage*, or *j* as in *juice*. In your notebook, complete each of the following words using either *j* or *g*.

1. ed__e
2. __enerous
3. re__ect

Fluency: Words in Context

For each item, follow the directions by writing a sentence using a word from the vocabulary list on page 785.

1. Describe a man who has been ill for many weeks.
2. Describe how a child might feel before visiting the dentist.
3. Describe a student giving an outrageous excuse for failing a test.
4. Write the first sentence of a story about a girl who is unhappy and angry about her life.
5. Describe an activity in a busy office.

Grammar and Style Lesson

Restrictive and Nonrestrictive Participial Phrases

A **participial phrase** consists of a participle (a form of a verb that acts as an adjective) and its modifiers or complements. The entire phrase acts as an adjective. If the phrase is essential to the sentence's meaning, it is **restrictive** and not set off by commas. If it is not essential, it is **nonrestrictive** and should be set off by commas.

> **Restrictive:** . . . a light spring wagon *filled with children*. (essential)
>
> **Nonrestrictive:** And finally, *stammering a crude farewell*, he departed. (not essential)

Practice Copy these passages, identifying participial phrases and adding commas as necessary.

1. . . . and now schooled by the humbleness that attended his labor he had grown old . . .
2. . . . four times he had seen before him on the tracks a ghastly dot of tragedy converging like a cannon ball to its eclipse of horror at the boiler head . . .
3. . . . He had driven his great train loaded with its weight of lives across the land ten thousand times.
4. . . . nothing could be heard but the solid clacking tempo of the wheels receding into the drowsy stillness of the afternoon.
5. On the outskirts of a little town was a tidy little cottage trimmed with green blinds.

Looking at Style Explain how each of the participial phrases in the Practice enables Wolfe to insert action into a description.

Writing Application Describe a let down you have experienced, using two participial phrases.

W̶G̶ Prentice Hall Writing and Grammar Connection: Chapter 19, Section 2

Writing Lesson

Comparison-and-Contrast Essay

Write an essay in which you compare the two viewpoints suggested by the title "The Far and the Near." Explain how the engineer's view of things depends on distance from or proximity to them. Consider what the story suggests about the dreams we dream from afar.

Prewriting   Reread the story and note passages that reflect the engineer's thoughts and feelings about the world from a distance.

Drafting   Address each of the passages you have selected, comparing the engineer's thoughts and reflections while riding the train to the realities he later experiences.

Revising   Reread your essay to make sure you have drawn a strong comparison between the engineer's experiences of life from both vantage points. Strengthen your word choices to emphasize contrasts.

Model: Revising to Build Contrast

green and lush

From a distance, the backyards appear ~~pretty~~ and the

tidy little cottages

~~houses~~ look like havens of hospitality and warmth. Up close,

overgrown weeds,   *peeling clapboard*

however, the ~~grass~~, scattered trash, and ~~siding~~ tell another story

cold and neglected

of a community.

> The additional descriptive details make a contrast more striking.

WG Prentice Hall Writing and Grammar Connection: Chapter 9, Section 2

Extension Activities

Speaking and Listening Some people feel that train travel is truly magical. Conduct an **interview** with someone who has traveled by rail. Start by asking questions like these:

- How did the landscape appear from the train?
- What was romantic or exciting about the journey?
- In what way is rail travel different from auto trips?

Share your findings with the class.

Research and Technology In a group, research the evolution of the railroad and the nation's love affair with it. Devise a research outline. Then, contribute sections to a **written report** explaining the history of the railroad and the changes that have taken place in recent decades. **[Group Activity]**

 **Take It to the Net**   www.phschool.com

Go online for an additional research activity using the Internet.

Prepare to Read

Of Modern Poetry ◆ Anecdote of the Jar ◆ Ars Poetica ◆ Poetry

Wallace Stevens (1879–1955)

Wallace Stevens believed that the goal of poetry was to capture the interaction between fantasy and reality. He spent his career writing poems that delve into the imagination and the ways in which it shapes our perception of the physical world. He uses elaborate imagery and precise words to express his philosophical themes. Stevens depended largely on the natural world for his inspiration because nature, he said, is the only certainty.

Insurance Executive by Day Stevens was born and raised in Reading, Pennsylvania. After completing his education at Harvard University, he took a job at the Hartford Accident and Indemnity Company, an insurance company in Hartford, Connecticut, and eventually became the company's vice president. He did not publish his first collection of poetry, *Harmonium* (1923), until he was forty-three years old. In *Harmonium* and much of his other work, Stevens uses dazzling imagery to capture the beauty of the physical world while expressing the dependence of that beauty on the perceptions of the observer. Although the book received little public attention, it was praised by critics and launched Stevens's literary career.

Stevens published many volumes of poetry, including *Ideas of Order* (1935), *Parts of a World* (1942), *Transport to Summer* (1947), and *The Auroras of Autumn* (1950). His *Collected Poems* earned him the Pulitzer Prize in 1955. Despite his success as a poet, however, Stevens continued his career in insurance until the end of his life. "It gives a man character as a poet to have this daily contact with a job," he once said. A brilliant and unusual figure, he is now regarded as one of the most important poets of the twentieth century.

Archibald MacLeish (1892–1982)

Archibald MacLeish was born in Glencoe, Illinois. MacLeish was trained as a lawyer but, unlike Stevens, he turned his back on his first career to devote himself completely to poetry. His early poems, such as "Ars Poetica," are experimental in form, reflecting the influence of the Modernists. By contrast, his later poems are more traditional and accessible. As unrest spread throughout the world in the 1930s, MacLeish used poetry to explore political and social issues. Over the course of his career, MacLeish produced more than thirty books and won three Pulitzer Prizes.

Marianne Moore (1887–1972)

Born in Kirkwood, Missouri, Marianne Moore first gained a footing in the literary world as the editor of *The Dial*, a highly regarded literary journal. In that role, she encouraged many new writers by publishing their work. However, she was hesitant to publish her own work, although it had been admired by many noted poets. In fact, her first book, *Poems* (1921), was published without her knowledge.

As a Modernist, Moore wrote poems that were unconventional, precise, inventive, and witty. Unlike most other Modernists, however, she chose not to write about the state of modern civilization. Instead, she explored subjects such as animals and nature. "Poetry," one of her best-known poems, delves into the subject of poetry itself.

Preview

Connecting to the Literature

You probably have your own special way of looking at the subjects you care about most deeply. In these selections, three major poets present their views on a subject about which they are deeply passionate: poetry.

Literary Analysis

Simile

A **simile** is a comparison between two seemingly different things. Signal words such as *like* or *as* indicate the comparison. For example, the word *like* signals the comparison in the following simile:

> The sound of the explosion echoed through the air like thunder.

By comparing the sound of an explosion to thunder, the simile stresses its loud, jarring power. Like poetry itself, similes show us the world in startling new ways. As you read, compare the similes used by each poet.

Comparing Literary Works

The poets whose works appear in these selections devote their attention to the genre of poetry itself. Although the art of writing poetry defies definition, each writer attempts an explanation. The poets use imagery to give body to their ideas. Like similes, **imagery** creates word pictures for readers. Most often, imagery works by appealing to the five senses—sight, smell, touch, sound, or taste. Compare the types of images each poet presents and determine the ways in which these images advance each poet's explanation of poetry.

Reading Strategy

Paraphrasing

Because poetry is written in verse and is likely to contain unexpected words and images, it can be difficult to understand. One way to make sure that you grasp what you are reading is to **paraphrase**—to identify key ideas and restate them in your own words. Paraphrasing can remove barriers that make some poems seem too difficult to understand. In a chart like the one shown, list the difficult passages and paraphrase them.

> **Difficult Passage**
>
> "I, too, dislike it: there are things that are more important beyond/all this fiddle."
>
> **Paraphrased**
>
> I also dislike poetry. It's nonsense, and a lot of other things are more important.

Vocabulary Development

suffice (sə fīs´) *v.* be adequate; meet the needs of (p. 796)

insatiable (in sā´ shə bəl) *adj.* constantly wanting more (p. 796)

slovenly (sluv´ ən lē) *adj.* untidy (p. 797)

dominion (də min´ yən) *n.* power to rule (p. 797)

palpable (pal´ pə bəl) *adj.* able to be touched, felt, or handled (p. 798)

derivative (də riv´ ə tiv) *adj.* not original; based on something else (p. 800)

literalists (lit´ ər əl ists) *n.* those who take words at their exact meaning (p. 801)

Of Modern Poetry

Wallace Stevens

Background

Wallace Stevens's poetry reflects the influence of the Symbolist literary movement. Originating in the last half of the nineteenth century, Symbolist poets believed that ideas and emotions are difficult to communicate because people perceive the world in such personal ways. These poets tried to convey meaning through symbols—people, places, and objects that represent ideas beyond their concrete meaning. As a result, the work of Symbolist poets like Stevens can often be interpreted in many different ways.

The poem of the mind in the act of finding
What will <u>suffice</u>. It has not always had
To find: the scene was set; it repeated what
Was in the script.
            Then the theatre was changed
5 To something else. Its past was a souvenir.

It has to be living, to learn the speech of the place.
It has to face the men of the time and to meet
The women of the time. It has to think about war
And it has to find what will suffice. It has
10 To construct a new stage. It has to be on that stage
And, like an <u>insatiable</u> actor, slowly and
With meditation, speak words that in the ear,
In the delicatest ear of the mind, repeat,
Exactly, that which it wants to hear, at the sound
15 Of which, an invisible audience listens,
Not to the play, but to itself, expressed
In an emotion as of two people, as of two
Emotions becoming one. The actor is
A metaphysician[1] in the dark, twanging
20 An instrument, twanging a wiry string that gives
Sounds passing through sudden rightnesses, wholly
Containing the mind, below which it cannot descend,
Beyond which it has no will to rise.
                  It must
Be the finding of a satisfaction, and may
25 Be of a man skating, a woman dancing, a woman
Combing. The poem of the act of the mind.

suffice (sə fīs´) *v.* be adequate; meet the needs of

insatiable (in sā´ shə bəl) *adj.* constantly wanting more

Reading Strategy
Paraphrasing Restate the sentence in lines 18–24 in your own words.

---

1. **metaphysician** (met´ ə fə zish´ ən) *n.* a person versed in philosophy, especially those branches that seek to explain the nature of being or of the universe.

Anecdote of the Jar

Wallace Stevens

I placed a jar in Tennessee,
And round it was, upon a hill.
It made the <u>slovenly</u> wilderness
Surround that hill.

5   The wilderness rose up to it,
And sprawled around, no longer wild.
The jar was round upon the ground
And tall and of a port in air.

It took <u>dominion</u> everywhere.
10 The jar was gray and bare.
It did not give of bird or bush,
Like nothing else in Tennessee.

slovenly (sluv′ ən lē) *adj.*
untidy

dominion (də min′ yən) *n.*
power to rule

Review and Assess

Thinking About the Selections

1. **(a) Recall:** In the first stanza of "Of Modern Poetry," what does the poet say happened to the theater?
   (b) Interpret: What does "the theatre" represent?

2. **(a) Recall:** What does the poem suggest about the relationship poetry must have with the people of its time?
   (b) Analyze: Does the poet believe the work of poetry to be difficult? Explain.

3. **(a) Recall:** In "Anecdote of the Jar," how does the wilderness receive the jar? **(b) Analyze:** How does the jar affect the wilderness?

4. **(a) Recall:** What words describe the jar in the first and third stanzas? **(b) Compare and Contrast:** How does the image of the jar in the third stanza differ from its depiction in the first?

5. **Evaluate:** Does the jar effectively symbolize the human imagination? Support your answer.

Ars Poetica[1]

Archibald MacLeish

A poem should be <u>palpable</u> and mute
As a globed fruit.

Dumb
As old medallions to the thumb,

5   Silent as the sleeve-worn stone
Of casement ledges where the moss has grown—

A poem should be wordless
As the flight of birds.

A poem should be motionless in time
10 As the moon climbs,

---

1. **Ars Poetica** The title is an allusion to Horace's "Ars Poetica," or "The Art of Poetry," which was composed about 20 B.C.

palpable (pal´ pə bəl) *adj.* able to be touched, felt, or handled

Literary Analysis
Simile Identify the simile in line 5 and explain what two things MacLeish compares.

◀ **Critical Viewing** Which of the poem's images can be found in this photograph? **[Interpret]**

Leaving, as the moon releases
Twig by twig the night-entangled trees,

Leaving, as the moon behind the winter leaves.
Memory by memory the mind—

15 A poem should be motionless in time
As the moon climbs.

A poem should be equal to:
Not true.

For all the history of grief
20 An empty doorway and a maple leaf.

For love
The leaning grasses and two lights above the sea—

A poem should not mean
But be.

Review and Assess

Thinking About the Selection

1. **Respond:** Do you like the way poetry is described in this poem? Why or why not?

2. **(a) Recall:** Identify at least three items the speaker compares to poetry. **(b) Analyze:** What do you think the speaker means by saying that a poem should be "palpable and mute," "wordless," and "motionless in time"?

3. **(a) Recall:** With what images can a poem show the history of grief, as the speaker states? **(b) Recall:** With what images should it show love? **(c) Speculate:** Why do you think MacLeish chose to focus on these emotions?

4. **(a) Interpret:** What contradiction do you see in lines 7–8? **(b) Analyze:** What do you think this contradiction suggests about the subject, poetry?

5. **(a) Interpret:** What contrast does the poet make in the final two lines? **(b) Define:** How would you define the difference between *meaning* and *being*?

6. **Extend:** In what ways do you think poetry can touch the human spirit? Explain.

Poetry

Marianne Moore

Untitled, 1984, Alexander Calder, Solomon R. Guggenheim Museum, New York

I, too, dislike it: there are things that are important beyond all this
    fiddle.
    Reading it, however, with a perfect contempt for it, one discovers in
  it after all, a place for the genuine.
        Hands that can grasp, eyes
5   that can dilate, hair that can rise
           if it must, these things are important not because a

high-sounding interpretation can be put upon them but because they
    are
    useful. When they become so <u>derivative</u> as to become unintelligible,
  the same thing may be said for all of us, that we
        do not admire what
10   we cannot understand: the bat
           holding on upside down or in quest of something to

eat, elephants pushing, a wild horse taking a roll, a tireless wolf under
    a tree, the immovable critic twitching his skin like a horse that feels
      a flea, the base-
    ball fan, the statistician—
15   nor is it valid
           to discriminate against "business documents and

▲ Critical Viewing
Write a sentence describing this painting "with a perfect contempt for it." Explain what the result shows you about Moore's point in lines 2–3. **[Connect]**

derivative (də riv´ ə tiv) *adj.* not original; based on something else

Literary Analysis
Simile What does the simile comparing a critic to a horse suggest about the speaker's attitude toward critics?

school-books"; all these phenomena are important. One must make a
    distinction
        however: when dragged into prominence by half poets, the result is
            not poetry,
        nor till the poets among us can be
20   "literalists of
                the imagination"—above
                    insolence and triviality and can present

        for inspection, "imaginary gardens with real toads in them," shall we
            have
        it. In the meantime, if you demand on the one hand,
25   the raw material of poetry in
                all its rawness and
            that which is on the other hand
                genuine, you are interested in poetry.

literalists (lit′ ər əl ists)
n. those who take
words at their exact
meaning

Review and Assess

Thinking About the Selection

1. **Respond:** In your opinion, which word or phrase best describes Moore's poem—"fiddle," "derivative," or "genuine"? Explain.

2. **(a) Recall:** What does the speaker say a person discovers when reading poetry "with a perfect contempt for it"?
   (b) Interpret: What type of poetry does the speaker dislike?

3. **(a) Recall:** What does the speaker say happens when poems become derivative? **(b) Synthesize:** What qualities does the speaker believe good poetry should possess?

4. **(a) Interpret:** What apparent contradiction exists in the phrase "literalists of the imagination"? **(b) Analyze:** In what way is the meaning of this phrase furthered by Moore's image of "imaginary gardens with real toads"? **(c) Generalize:** From where is Moore suggesting good poetry derives its power?

5. **Extend:** Do you think that the lyrics of today's popular music meet Moores' criteria for good poetry? Why or why not?

Review and Assess

Literary Analysis

Simile

1. In "Ars Poetica," what does the word "globed" suggest about a poem?
2. Find four **similes** in "Ars Poetica" and interpret their meaning. Analyze them in a chart like the one shown.

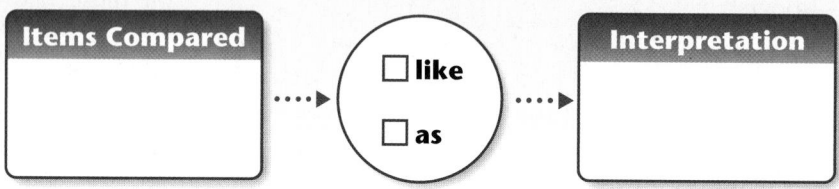

Items Compared ····▶ ☐ **like** ☐ **as** ····▶ **Interpretation**

3. How do all the similes work together in this poem to create a vision of poetry as something that "should not mean / But be"?

Comparing Literary Works

4. Based on "Of Modern Poetry," how would you summarize Steven's definition of poetry?
5. (a) Identify the **image** in lines 9–14 in "Ars Poetica." (b) How does this image help you understand MacLeish's definition of poetry?
6. (a) To what senses do Marianne Moore's images of animal behavior appeal? (b) What unites the images in defining poetry for Moore?
7. (a) Select one key image from each poem that captures the poet's beliefs about poetry. Explain your choice. (b) How do the poets' ideas about poetry compare? (c) How do they contrast?

Reading Strategy

Paraphrasing

8. Paraphrase the following passages from the poems, giving them straightforward and direct meanings:
   (a) from "Anecdote of the Jar," lines 5–8
   (b) from "Poetry," lines 6–8 ("these things . . . useful.")

Extend Understanding

9. **Career Connection:** These poems express distinct ideas about the characteristics good poems possess. Select another field of artistic endeavor and identify various elements that make for quality work.

Integrate Language Skills

Vocabulary Development Lesson

Word Analysis: Latin Root -satis-

The word *insatiable* contains the Latin root *-satis-*, which means "enough." Combined with the prefix *in-*, meaning "not," you can determine that *insatiable* will suggest "not enough." Use your knowledge of *-satis-* to define each word below.

1. satisfy
2. satisfactory
3. satiate
4. satiety

Spelling Strategy

When choosing between the suffixes *-able* and *-ible* to form adjectives, opt for *-able* if you are unsure of the spelling. Like *insatiable*, many more adjectives are formed with *-able* than with *-ible*. Add *-able* or *-ible* to each word part below. Then, check your choice in a dictionary.

1. avail__
2. reli__
3. palp__
4. illeg__
5. fall__
6. pli__

Fluency: Context

Follow the instructions below to write a sentence for each item, using a word from the vocabulary list on page 795. Use each word once.

1. Describe someone who never exercises imagination.
2. Define the territory governed by a king.
3. Describe the quality of a peach in a beautiful painting.
4. Explain why a friend's room is always such a terrible mess.
5. Criticize a musician whose work lacks originality.
6. Explain why a minimum amount of nutritional food is not enough to maintain one's health.
7. Criticize a sibling who always wants more possessions.

Grammar and Style Lesson

Subject Complements

Subject complements are nouns, pronouns, and adjectives that follow linking verbs (often forms of the word "to be") and identify or describe the subjects.

Sentences containing subject complements are effective when defining something.

>   S   LV   SC
> **Noun:** The actor is a *metaphysician* . . .
>
>   S   LV SC
> **Pronoun:** The poet is *she* who is a literalist of the imagination.
>
>   S   LV   SC
> **Adjective:** A poem should be *wordless* . . .

Practice Copy each of the following sentences. Underline the subject complement in each one and label it a noun, a pronoun, or an adjective.

1. The winner of this year's poetry prize is you!
2. The subject of the poem was a waterfall.
3. Good poetry should be thrilling.
4. Poets are deep thinkers.
5. The oldest book in the library is a volume of poetry.

Writing Application Write a brief descriptive poem about a familiar person or object. Begin each line with the name of the person or object. Follow it with a linking verb and a subject complement.

W͞G *Prentice Hall Writing and Grammar Connection: Chapter 18, Section 3*

Writing Lesson

Definition

Stevens, Moore, and MacLeish were not only three of the most important American poets of the twentieth century, they were three of the deepest thinkers about the art of poetry. Write an essay in which you compare and contrast the ideas expressed in two of these poems about poetry. Note the distinct ways in which each poet explains, above all, why poetry is important.

Prewriting   Reread each poem and paraphrase the ideas it presents. Compare and contrast the ideas and determine an organizing principle or main idea to develop in your essay.

Drafting   Begin by introducing each poet and providing a general statement about his or her beliefs about poetry. Then, write a brief statement of your main point. Develop your ideas, with quotes from the poems in the body paragraphs.

Model: Providing Necessary Background

Wallace Stevens believed that human beings perceive the world in an entirely subjective way. For Stevens, reality itself was an expression of the imagination. These views come through in his ideas about poetry.

> The inclusion of general information about a subject's point of view clarifies the ideas that will follow.

Revising   Review your draft, making sure that you have supported your ideas with appropriate quotations from the poem. Replace any less effective quotations with better choices.

Prentice Hall Writing and Grammar Connection: Chapter 9, Section 3

Extension Activities

Speaking and Listening In a small group, analyze different poets' views of poetry. Then, stage a **round-table discussion** on the issue "What Is Poetry?" Each group member should take a poet's position. Use the following tips as a guide:

- Develop a central argument of your view.
- Include logical appeals based on examples.
- Incorporate emotional appeals, such as a poem's impact on you or others.

Share the results of your discussion.
[Group Activity]

Research and Technology Create a **collection of poems** on another topic, such as sports or nature, that focus on a guiding question. Use print and online poetry reference sources to locate appropriate poems. Include an introduction that explains how the poems relate to one another.

 **Take It to the Net**   www.phschool.com

Go online for an additional research activity using the Internet.

Focus on Literary Forms: The Short Story

PART 2

Do It Yourself Landscape, Andy Warhol.
Museum Ludwig, Cologne, photo courtesy
of Rheinisches Bildarchiv Köln

T he short story has been a part of American literature since Edgar Allan Poe defined the genre in the 1800s. Every generation of writers brings a new energy to the form, revitalizing it by reflecting the changing values, attitudes, and issues of the times. The Modern Age was a critical period in the growth of the American short story, as writers such as Hemingway and Fitzgerald carried the form to new heights.

Prepare to Read

In Another Country ◆ The Corn Planting ◆ A Worn Path

Ernest Hemingway (1899–1961)

Ernest Hemingway's fiction expressed the sentiments of many members of the post-World War I generation. He wrote about people's struggles to maintain a sense of dignity while living in a sometimes hostile world.

The Red Cross Hemingway, the son of a physician, was born and raised in Oak Park, Illinois, a suburb of Chicago. In high school, he played football and wrote newspaper columns. Eager to serve in World War I, he tried to join the army but was repeatedly turned away due to an eye defect. He joined the Red Cross ambulance corps instead and, in 1918, was sent to the Italian front. Just before his nineteenth birthday, he was severely wounded and spent several months recovering in a hospital in Milan, Italy. His experiences during the war helped shape his view of the world and provide material for his writing.

Expatriates After the war, Hemingway had a difficult time readjusting to life in the United States. To establish himself as a writer, he went to Paris as a foreign correspondent for the *Toronto Star*. In Paris, he befriended Ezra Pound, Gertrude Stein, F. Scott Fitzgerald, and other American writers and artists living overseas. The literary advice of these friends and his work as a journalist helped him develop his concise, concrete, and highly charged writing style.

In 1925, Hemingway published his first major work, *In Our Time*, a series of loosely connected short stories. A year later he published *The Sun Also Rises*, a novel about a group of British and American expatriates trying to overcome the pain and disillusionment of life in the modern world.

Hemingway became as famous for his lifestyle as he was for his writing. Constantly pursuing adventure, he hunted big game in Africa, attended bullfights in Spain, held records for deep-sea fishing in the Caribbean, and participated in amateur boxing.

The full body of Hemingway's work—including *A Farewell to Arms* (1929), *For Whom the Bell Tolls* (1940), and *The Old Man and the Sea* (1952)—earned him the Nobel Prize for Literature in 1954.

Sherwood Anderson (1876–1941)

Sherwood Anderson was one of the most influential American writers of the first half of the twentieth century. The third of seven children, Anderson was raised in a small town in Ohio. His father was a harness maker and house painter who was not always able to earn enough money to support the family. At fourteen, Anderson dropped out of high school to work, taking a variety of unskilled jobs. He eventually joined the army to serve in the Spanish-American War, which ended just before he arrived in Cuba. At the age of twenty-three, after a year of military service, Anderson returned to his hometown and finished high school.

His Best-known Work After, completing high-school, Anderson moved to Chicago to pursue a writing career. He worked as an advertising copy-writer and met poets Carl Sandburg and Edgar Lee Masters and novelist Theodore Dreiser. After witnessing the success of Masters's *Spoon River Anthology*, Anderson began his own fictional explorations of life in rural America. Using his boyhood observations and experiences as material, he created his best-known work, *Winesburg, Ohio* (1919), a unified collection of short stories. In this work, Anderson presents small-town life in a strikingly different manner from earlier works of literature. He looks beneath the surface of the characters' lives to construct psychological portraits. He also uses everyday speech to capture the essence of characters, a technique he borrowed from Mark Twain.

In addition to writing, Anderson became a successful businessman heading the Anderson Manufacturing Company, which made paint and roof-pitch. He did not enjoy business, and in his mid-thirties, he abandoned the company to devote himself to writing. Although Anderson's literary reputation rests mainly on *Winesburg, Ohio*, he also published other successful books, including *Windy McPherson's Son* (1916), *The Triumph of the Egg* (1921), *Horses and Men* (1923), and *Death in the Woods and Other Stories* (1933).

Eudora Welty (1909–2001)

Eudora Welty's stories and novels capture life in the deep South, creating images of the landscape and conveying the shared attitudes and values of the people. She often confronts the hardships of life in poor rural areas. Despite her awareness of people's suffering, her writing remains optimistic.

Welty was born in Jackson, Mississippi, where she spent most of her life. She attended Mississippi State College for Women before transferring to the University of Wisconsin, from which she graduated in 1929. Hoping to pursue a career in advertising, she moved to New York and enrolled at Columbia University School of Business. However, because of the worsening economic depression, she was unable to find steady employment and returned to Jackson in 1931.

Writing Fiction After accepting a job as a publicist for a government agency, Welty spent several years traveling throughout Mississippi, taking photographs and interviewing people. Her experiences and observations inspired her to write, and in 1936 her first short story, "Death of a Traveling Salesman," was published.

In her fiction, Welty displays an acute sense of detail and a deep sense of compassion toward her characters. For example, in "A Worn Path," she paints a sympathetic portrait of an old woman whose feelings of love and sense of duty motivate her to make a long, painful journey through the woods.

One of the leading American writers of the twentieth century, Welty published numerous collections of short stories and novels. In 1973, her novel *The Optimist's Daughter* won the Pulitzer Prize.

Background

World War I was the first truly global war, involving nations on every continent but Antarctica. The Great War, as it was also called, began in Europe in 1914, sparked by nationalist pride and systems of alliances among nations. The Central Powers (Germany, Austria, Turkey) fought the Allies (England, France, Russia) with other nations joining one side or the other. Italy, where Hemingway's "In Another Country" takes place, was not strategically important, but it helped the Allies by drawing Central Power troops away from other battle areas.

The war lasted four brutal years. Throughout most of the conflict, a stalemate existed. Both sides were dug into trenches, and took turns rushing one another. Each rush was greeted by a barrage of machine-gun fire, with thousands falling dead. Other soldiers fell to new weapons of killing—inventions such as airplanes, long-range artillery, and poison gas—that many people had hoped would deter aggressors and prevent war. Many of the wounded were saved, however, by advances in medical treatment, such as surgical disinfectants and rehabilitative techniques to strengthen injured limbs.

Preview

Connecting to the Literature

In each of these stories, characters undertake journeys that dramatically affect their lives. As you read, notice the ways in which their journeys compare to ones that you have made.

Literary Analysis

Point of View

The **point of view** of a story is the perspective from which it is told.

- In stories told from the **first-person point of view,** the person telling the story participates in the action, uses the pronoun *I,* and shares his or her own thoughts and feeling about events.

- Stories told from a **limited third-person point of view** are told by an anonymous speaker who stands outside the action and does not use the pronoun *I.* The speaker both relates the events of the story and conveys the thoughts of one of the characters.

As you read, use a chart like the one shown to analyze the type of narration each story demonstrates.

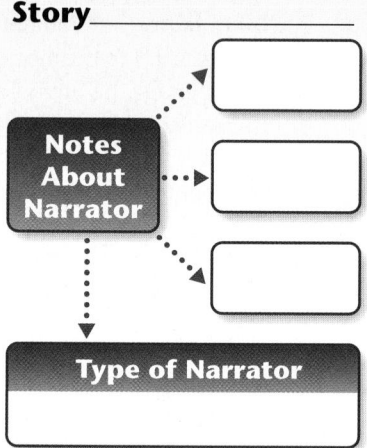

Comparing Literary Works

Each of these stories is told from a different point of view. In each case, the **narrator,** or person telling the story, controls information and directly influences the reader's perceptions. Examine the effects of different points of view by comparing the information each narrator shares. Notice the biases each displays and the level of sympathy or interest each generates. Finally, determine the reasons you think each author chose the narrative point of view he or she did and how that choice gives a specific shape to the story.

Reading Strategy

Identifying With Characters

Even if your journeys differ from the ones taken by these characters, you might feel as though you know them. When you **identify with characters,** you relate to their thoughts and feelings and connect them with your own experiences. As you read, identify with characters by comparing your life experiences with theirs.

Vocabulary Development

invalided (in´ və lid´ id) *v.* released because of illness or disability (p. 814)

grave (grāv) *adj.* serious; solemn (p. 821)

limber (lim´ bər) *adj.* flexible (p. 821)

obstinate (äb´ stə nit) *adj.* stubborn (p. 827)

IN ANOTHER COUNTRY

ERNEST HEMINGWAY

I n the fall the war[1] was always there, but we did not go to it any more. It was cold in the fall in Milan[2] and the dark came very early. Then the electric lights came on, and it was pleasant along the streets looking in the windows. There was much game hanging outside the shops, and the snow powdered in the fur of the foxes and the wind blew their tails. The deer hung stiff and heavy and empty, and small birds blew in the wind and the wind turned their feathers. It was a cold fall and the wind came down from the mountains.

---

1. **the war** World War I (1914–1918).
2. **Milan** (mi lan´) a city in northern Italy.

▲ **Critical Viewing** What mood is conveyed in this image of a hospital serving soldiers during World War I? Which details contribute to the mood? **[Interpret]**

We were all at the hospital every afternoon, and there were different ways of walking across the town through the dusk to the hospital. Two of the ways were alongside canals, but they were long. Always, though, you crossed a bridge across a canal to enter the hospital. There was a choice of three bridges. On one of them a woman sold roasted chestnuts. It was warm, standing in front of her charcoal fire, and the chestnuts were warm afterward in your pocket. The hospital was very old and very beautiful, and you entered through a gate and walked across a courtyard and out a gate on the other side. There were usually funerals starting from the courtyard. Beyond the old hospital were the new brick pavilions, and there we met every afternoon and were all very polite and interested in what was the matter, and sat in the machines that were to make so much difference.

The doctor came up to the machine where I was sitting and said: "What did you like best to do before the war? Did you practice a sport?"

I said: "Yes, football."

"Good," he said. "You will be able to play football again better than ever."

My knee did not bend and the leg dropped straight from the knee to the ankle without a calf, and the machine was to bend the knee and make it move as in riding a tricycle. But it did not bend yet, and instead the machine lurched when it came to the bending part. The doctor said: "That will all pass. You are a fortunate young man. You will play football again like a champion."

In the next machine was a major who had a little hand like a baby's. He winked at me when the doctor examined his hand, which was between two leather straps that bounced up and down and flapped the stiff fingers, and said: "And will I too play football, captain-doctor?" He had been a very great fencer, and before the war the greatest fencer in Italy.

The doctor went to his office in a back room and brought a photograph which showed a hand that had been withered almost as small as the major's, before it had taken a machine course, and after was a little larger. The major held the photograph with his good hand and looked at it very carefully. "A wound?" he asked.

"An industrial accident," the doctor said.

"Very interesting, very interesting," the major said, and handed it back to the doctor.

"You have confidence?"

"No," said the major.

There were three boys who came each day who were about the same age I was. They were all three from Milan, and one of them was to be a lawyer, and one was to be a painter, and one had intended to be a soldier, and after we were finished with the machines, sometimes we walked back together to the Café Cova, which was next door to the Scala.[3] We walked the short way through the communist quarter

---

3. the Scala (ska´ la) an opera house in Milan.

because we were four together. The people hated us because we were officers, and from a wine-shop someone called out, "A basso gli ufficiali!"[4] as we passed. Another boy who walked with us sometimes and made us five wore a black silk handkerchief across his face because he had no nose then and his face was to be rebuilt. He had gone out to the front from the military academy and been wounded within an hour after he had gone into the front line for the first time. They rebuilt his face, but he came from a very old family and they could never get the nose exactly right. He went to South America and worked in a bank. But this was a long time ago, and then we did not any of us know how it was going to be afterward. We only knew then that there was always the war, but that we were not going to it any more.

We all had the same medals, except the boy with the black silk bandage across his face, and he had not been at the front long enough to get any medals. The tall boy with a very pale face who was to be a lawyer had been a lieutenant of Arditi[5] and had three medals of the sort we each had only one of. He had lived a very long time with death and was a little detached. We were all a little detached, and there was nothing that held us together except that we met every afternoon at the hospital. Although, as we walked to the Cova through the tough part of town, walking in the dark, with light and singing coming out of the wine-shops, and sometimes having to walk into the street when the men and women would crowd together on the sidewalk so that we would have had to jostle them to get by, we felt held together by there being something that had happened that they, the people who disliked us, did not understand.

We ourselves all understood the Cova, where it was rich and warm and not too brightly lighted, and noisy and smoky at certain hours, and there were always girls at the tables and the illustrated papers on a rack on the wall. The girls at the Cova were very patriotic, and I found that the most patriotic people in Italy were the café girls— and I believe they are still patriotic.

The boys at first were very polite about my medals and asked me what I had done to get them. I showed them the papers, which were written in very beautiful language and full of *fratellanza* and *abnegazione*,[6] but which really said, with the adjectives removed,

"The War to End All Wars"

In this story, the characters struggle courageously against their disillusionment with war and technology. World War I resulted in astonishing destruction and massive death as a result of new technologies such as airplanes, poison gas, and long-range artillery. Many who enlisted did so expecting a swift victory, but the war lasted four grueling years. Up to ten million soldiers died, as well as many civilians. Some people believed that the widespread destruction and loss of life would make World War I "The War to End All Wars," but subsequent conflicts have proved them wrong.

---

4. **"A basso gli ufficiali!"** (a ba´ so lye oo fe cha´ le) "Down with officers!" (Italian).
5. **Arditi** (är dē´ tē) a select group of soldiers chosen specifically for dangerous campaigns.
6. *fratellanza* (frä tāl än´ tsä) **and** *abnegazione* (äb´ nā gä tzyō´ nā) "brotherhood" and "self-denial" (Italian).

✔ Reading Check

What do the narrator and the "three boys" have in common?

that I had been given the medals because I was an American. After that their manner changed a little toward me, although I was their friend against outsiders. I was a friend, but I was never really one of them after they had read the citations, because it had been different with them and they had done very different things to get their medals. I had been wounded, it was true; but we all knew that being wounded, after all, was really an accident. I was never ashamed of the ribbons, though, and sometimes, after the cocktail hour, I would imagine myself having done all the things they had done to get their medals; but walking home at night through the empty streets with the cold wind and all the shops closed, trying to keep near the street lights, I knew that I would never have done such things, and I was very much afraid to die, and often lay in bed at night by myself, afraid to die and wondering how I would be when I went back to the front again.

The three with the medals were like hunting-hawks; and I was not a hawk, although I might seem a hawk to those who had never hunted; they, the three, knew better and so we drifted apart. But I stayed good friends with the boy who had been wounded his first day at the front, because he would never know now how he would have turned out; so he could never be accepted either, and I liked him because I thought perhaps he would not have turned out to be a hawk either.

The major, who had been the great fencer, did not believe in bravery, and spent much time while we sat in the machines correcting my grammar. He had complimented me on how I spoke Italian, and we talked together very easily. One day I had said that Italian seemed such an easy language to me that I could not take a great interest in it; every-thing was so easy to say. "Ah yes," the major said. "Why, then, do you not take up the use of grammar?" So we took up the use of gram-mar, and soon Italian was such a difficult language that I was afraid to talk to him until I had the grammar straight in my mind.

The major came very regularly to the hos-pital. I do not think he ever missed a day, although I am sure he did not believe in the machines. There was a time when none of us believed in the machines, and one day the major said it was all nonsense. The machines were new then and it was we who were to prove them. It was an idiotic idea, he said, "a theory, like another." I had not learned my grammar, and he said I was a stupid impossible disgrace, and he was a

Reading Analysis
Identifying With Characters Have you ever been in a situation like the narrator's where you did not feel fully accepted or part of a group? How did it make you feel?

▼ **Critical Viewing**
How might you have reacted to this World War I operating room if you had been a wounded soldier? Explain. **[Relate]**

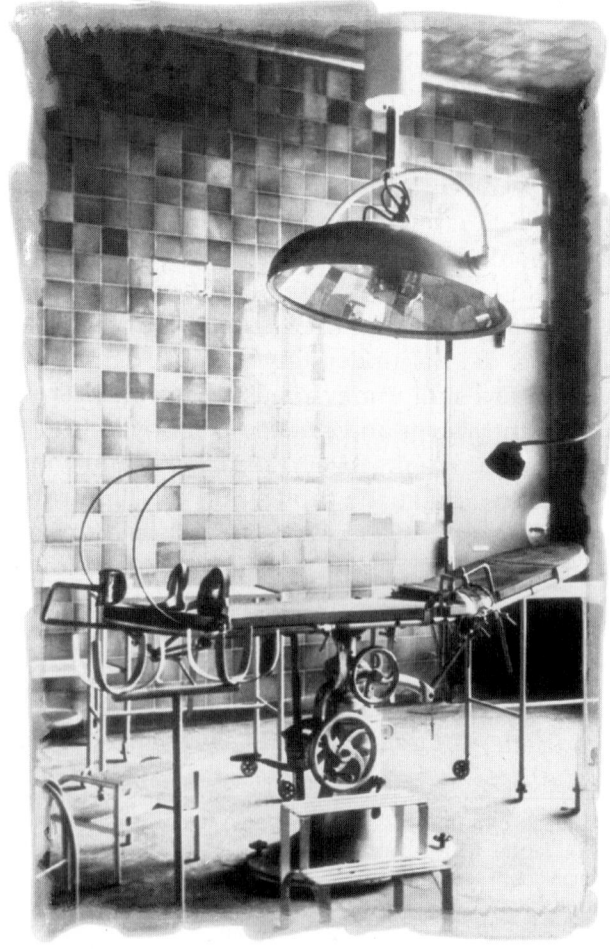

fool to have bothered with me. He was a small man and he sat straight up in his chair with his right hand thrust into the machine and looked straight ahead at the wall while the straps thumped up and down with his fingers in them.

"What will you do when the war is over if it is over?" he asked me. "Speak grammatically!"

"I will go to the States."

"Are you married?"

"No, but I hope to be."

"The more of a fool you are," he said. He seemed very angry. "A man must not marry."

"Why, Signor Maggiore?"[7]

"Don't call me 'Signor Maggiore.'"

"Why must not a man marry?"

"He cannot marry. He cannot marry," he said angrily. "If he is to lose everything, he should not place himself in a position to lose

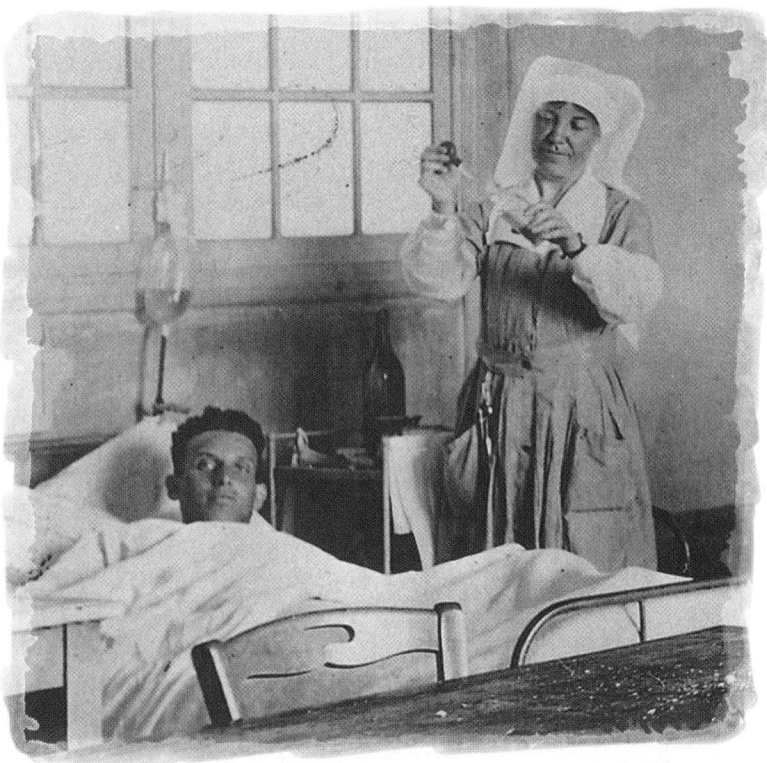

▲ **Critical Viewing**
Does this World War I military hospital compare with the hospital Hemingway describes? Explain. **[Compare and Contrast]**

that. He should not place himself in a position to lose. He should find things he cannot lose."

He spoke very angrily and bitterly, and looked straight ahead while he talked.

"But why should he necessarily lose it?"

"He'll lose it," the major said. He was looking at the wall. Then he looked down at the machine and jerked his little hand out from between the straps and slapped it hard against his thigh. "He'll lose it," he almost shouted. "Don't argue with me!" Then he called to the attendant who ran the machines. "Come and turn this damned thing off."

He went back into the other room for the light treatment and the massage. Then I heard him ask the doctor if he might use his telephone and he shut the door. When he came back into the room, I was sitting in another machine. He was wearing his cape and had his cap on, and he came directly toward my machine and put his arm on my shoulder.

"I am so sorry," he said, and patted me on the shoulder with his good hand. "I would not be rude. My wife has just died. You must forgive me."

"Oh—" I said, feeling sick for him. "I am so sorry."

He stood there biting his lower lip. "It is very difficult," he said. "I cannot resign myself."

---

7. **Signor Maggiore** (sēn yōr′ mäj jō′ rā) "Mr. Major" (Italian); a respectful way of addressing an officer.

**Reading Check**

Why does the mayor believe "a man must not marry"?

He looked straight past me and out through the window. Then he began to cry. "I am utterly unable to resign myself," he said and choked. And then crying, his head up looking at nothing, carrying himself straight and soldierly, with tears on both his cheeks and biting his lips, he walked past the machines and out the door.

The doctor told me that the major's wife, who was very young and whom he had not married until he was definitely <u>invalided</u> out of the war, had died of pneumonia. She had been sick only a few days. No one expected her to die. The major did not come to the hospital for three days. Then he came at the usual hour, wearing a black band on the sleeve of his uniform. When he came back, there were large framed photographs around the wall of all sorts of wounds before and after they had been cured by the machines. In front of the machine the major used were three photographs of hands like his that were completely restored. I do not know where the doctor got them. I always understood we were the first to use the machines. The photographs did not make much difference to the major because he only looked out of the window.

invalided (in´ və lid id) *v.* released because of illness or disability

Review and Assess

Thinking About the Selection

1. **Respond:** What emotion did this story arouse most strongly in you? Explain.

2. **(a) Recall:** Why does the narrator go to the hospital every day? **(b) Infer:** What type of attitudes would you say he encounters from other patients at the hospital in the same situation? Explain.

3. **(a) Recall:** What does the narrator say about the machines at the hospital? **(b) Interpret:** Why do you think he has developed this attitude toward the machines?

4. **(a) Recall:** How do the people in the communist quarter of the city react to the officers? **(b) Relate:** How do you think these reactions make the officers feel?

5. **(a) Recall:** What happens to the major's wife? **(b) Recall:** How does the major react? **(c) Analyze:** Do you find what happened ironic or surprising? Explain.

6. **Interpret:** Given the setting of the story, a hospital during wartime, what might be the significance of the major's interest in grammar?

7. **Apply:** Do you think this story reflects the sense of disillusionment that arose among writers and artists during World War I? Explain.

The Corn PLANTING

SHERWOOD ANDERSON

The farmers who come to our town to trade are a part of the town life. Saturday is the big day. Often the children come to the high school in town.

It is so with Hatch Hutchenson. Although his farm, some three miles from town, is small, it is known to be one of the best-kept and best-worked places in all our section. Hatch is a little gnarled old figure of a man. His place is on the Scratch Gravel Road and there are plenty of poorly kept places out that way.

Hatch's place stands out. The little frame house is always kept painted, the trees in his orchard are whitened with lime halfway up the trunks, and the barn and sheds are in repair, and his fields are always clean-looking.

Hatch is nearly seventy. He got a rather late start in life. His father, who owned the same farm, was a Civil War man and came home badly wounded, so that, although he lived a long time after the war, he couldn't work much. Hatch was the only son and stayed at home, working the place until his father died. Then, when he was nearing fifty, he married a schoolteacher of forty, and they had a son. The schoolteacher was a small one like Hatch. After they married, they both stuck close to the land. They seemed to fit into their farm life as certain people fit into the clothes they wear. I have noticed something about people who make a go of marriage. They grow more and more alike. Then even grow to look alike.

Their one son, Will Hutchenson, was a small but remarkably strong boy. He came to our high school in town and pitched on our town baseball team. He was a fellow always cheerful, bright and alert, and a great favorite with all of us.

For one thing, he began as a young boy to make amusing little drawings. It was a talent. He made drawings of fish and pigs and cows, and they looked like people you knew. I never did know, before, that people could look so much like cows and horses and pigs and fish.

Literary Analysis
Point of View From whose point of view is this story being told? Support your answer.

✔**Reading Check**

What is the overall condition of the Hutchenson farm?

When he had finished in the town high school, Will went to Chicago, where his mother had a cousin living, and he became a student in the Art Institute out there. Another young fellow from our town was also in Chicago. He really went two years before Will did. His name was Hal Weyman, and he was a student at the University of Chicago. After he graduated, he came home and got a job as principal of our high school.

Hal and Will Hutchenson hadn't been close friends before, Hal being several years older than Will, but in Chicago they got together, went together to see plays, and, as Hal later told me, they had a good many long talks.

I got it from Hal that, in Chicago, as at home here when he was a young boy, Will was immediately popular. He was good-looking, so the girls in the art school liked him, and he had a straightforwardness that made him popular with all the young fellows.

Hal told me that Will was out to some party nearly every night, and right away he began to sell some of his amusing little drawings and to make money. The drawings were used in advertisements, and he was well paid.

He even began to send some money home. You see, after Hal came back

▼ **Critical Viewing**
In what way does corn play an important part of this story? **[Connect]**

here, he used to go quite often out to the Hutchenson place to see Will's father and mother. He would walk or drive out there in the afternoon or on summer evenings and sit with them. The talk was always of Will.

Hal said it was touching how much the father and mother depended on their one son, how much they talked about him and dreamed of his future. They had never been people who went about much with the town folks or even with their neighbors. They were of the sort who work all the time, from early morning till late in the evenings, and on moonlight nights, Hal said, and after the little old wife had got the supper, they often went out into the fields and worked again.

You see, by this time old Hatch was nearing seventy and his wife would have been ten years younger. Hal said that whenever he went out to the farm they quit work and came to sit with him. They might be in one of the fields, working together, but when they saw him in the road, they came running. They had got a letter from Will. He wrote every week.

The little old mother would come running following the father. "We got another letter, Mr. Weyman," Hatch would cry, and then his wife, quite breathless, would say the same thing, "Mr. Weyman, we got a letter."

The letter would be brought out at once and read aloud. Hal said the letters were always delicious. Will larded them with little sketches. There were humorous drawings of people he had seen or been with, rivers of automobiles on Michigan Avenue in Chicago, a policeman at a street crossing, young stenographers hurrying into office buildings. Neither of the old people had ever been to the city and they were curious and eager. They wanted the drawings explained, and Hal said they were like two children wanting to know every little detail Hal could remember about their son's life in the big city. He was always at them to come there on a visit and they would spend hours talking of that.

"Of course," Hatch said, "we couldn't go."

"How could we?" he said. He had been on that one little farm since he was a boy. When he was a young fellow, his father was an invalid and so Hatch had to run things. A farm, if you run it right, is very exacting. You have to fight weeds all the time. There are the farm animals to take care of. "Who would milk our cows?" Hatch said. The idea of anyone but him or his wife touching one of the Hutchenson cows seemed to hurt him. While he was alive, he didn't want anyone else plowing one of his fields, tending his corn, looking after things about the barn. He felt that way about his farm. It was a thing you couldn't explain, Hal said. He seemed to understand the two old people.

It was a spring night, past midnight, when Hal came to my house and told me the news. In our town we have a night telegraph operator at the railroad station and Hal got a wire. It was really addressed to Hatch Hutchenson, but the operator brought it to Hal. Will Hutchenson was dead, had been killed. It turned out later that he

Literary Analysis
Point of View and Narrator How does the narrator interact with other characters?

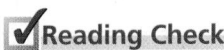

Reading Check

How does the narrator describe Hal's relationship to Will?

was at a party with some other young fellows and there might have been some drinking. Anyway, the car was wrecked, and Will Hutchenson was killed. The operator wanted Hal to go out and take the message to Hatch and his wife, and Hal wanted me to go along.

I offered to take my car, but Hal said no, "Let's walk out," he said. He wanted to put off the moment, I could see that. So we did walk. It was early spring, and I remember every moment of the silent walk we took, the little leaves just coming on the trees, the little streams we crossed, how the moonlight made the water seem alive. We loitered and loitered, not talking, hating to go on.

Then we got out there, and Hal went to the front door of the farmhouse while I stayed in the road. I heard a dog bark, away off somewhere. I heard a child crying in some distant house. I think that Hal, after he got to the front door of the house, must have stood there for ten minutes, hating to knock.

Then he did knock, and the sound his fist made on the door seemed terrible. It seemed like guns going off. Old Hatch came to the door, and I heard Hal tell him. I know what happened. Hal had been trying, all the way out from town, to think up words to tell the old couple in some gentle way, but when it came to the scratch, he couldn't. He blurted everything right out, right into old Hatch's face.

That was all. Old Hatch didn't say a word. The door was opened, he stood there in the moonlight, wearing a funny long white night-gown, Hal told him, and the door went shut again with a bang, and Hal was left standing there.

He stood for a time, and then came back out into the road to me. "Well," he said, and "Well," I said. We stood in the road looking and listening. There wasn't a sound from the house.

And then—it might have been ten minutes or it might have been a half-hour—we stood silently, listening and watching, not knowing what to do—we couldn't go away——"I guess they are trying to get so they can believe it," Hal whispered to me. I got his notion all right. The two old people must have thought of their son Will always only in terms of life, never of death.

We stood watching and listening, and then, suddenly, after a long time, Hal touched me on the arm. "Look," he whispered. There were two white-clad figures going from the house to the barn. It turned out, you see, that old Hatch had been plowing that day. He had finished plowing and harrowing a field near the barn.

The two figures went into the barn and presently came out. They went into the field, and Hal and I crept across the farmyard to the barn and got to where we could see what was going on without being seen.

It was an incredible thing. The old man had got a hand corn-planter out of the barn and his wife had got a bag of seed corn, and there, in the moonlight, that night, after they got that news, they were planting corn.

It was a thing to curl your hair—it was so ghostly. They were both in their nightgowns. They would do a row across the field, coming

**Reading Strategy
Identifying With Characters** Putting yourself in Hal's place, how do you think he felt telling the Hutchensons about Will's death?

quite close to us as we stood in the shadow of the barn, and then, at the end of each row, they would kneel side by side by the fence and stay silent for a time. The whole thing went on in silence. It was the first time in my life I ever understood something, and I am far from sure now that I can put down what I understood and felt that night—I mean something about the connection between certain people and the earth—a kind of silent cry, down into the earth, of these two old people, putting corn down into the earth. It was as though they were putting death down into the ground that life might grow again—something like that.

They must have been asking something of the earth, too. But what's the use? What they were up to in connection with the life in their field and the lost life in their son is something you can't very well make clear in words. All I know is that Hal and I stood the sight as long as we could, and then we crept away and went back to town, but Hatch Hutchenson and his wife must have got what they were after that night, because Hal told me that when he went out in the morning to see them and to make the arrangements for bringing their dead son home, they were both curiously quiet and Hal thought in command of themselves. Hal said he thought they had got something. "They have their farm and they have still got Will's letters to read," Hal said.

Review and Assess

Thinking About the Selection

1. **Respond:** With which character did you identify the most in this story? Why?

2. **(a) Recall:** Why does Hatch Hutchenson choose not to go off to make his own way in the world? **(b) Interpret:** What does the narrator mean by the statement that Hatch "got a rather late start in life"?

3. **(a) Recall:** What did the Hutchensons always do when Hal came to visit? **(b) Analyze:** Why do you think they did this? **(c) Infer:** Why do you think the Hutchensons spend so much time working in their fields?

4. **(a) Recall:** Why is Hal given the task of taking the bad news to the Hutchensons? **(b) Evaluate:** Do you think Hal does a good job of telling them about Will's death? Why or why not?

5. **(a) Recall:** What do the Hutchensons do after learning their son has died? **(b) Interpret:** How does the narrator explain their reaction? **(c) Evaluate:** Do you agree with his assessment? Explain.

6. **Apply:** What message about life do you think this story conveys? Support your answer.

A Worn Path

Eudora Welty

It was December—a bright frozen day in the early morning. Far out in the country there was an old Negro woman with her head tied in a red rag, coming along a path through the pinewoods. Her name was Phoenix Jackson. She was very old and small and she walked slowly in the dark pine shadows, moving a little from side to side in her steps, with the balanced heaviness and lightness of a pendulum in a grandfather clock. She carried a thin, small cane made from an umbrella, and with this she kept tapping the frozen earth in front of her. This made a <u>grave</u> and persistent noise in the still air, that seemed meditative like the chirping of a solitary little bird.

She wore a dark striped dress reaching down to her shoe tops, and an equally long apron of bleached sugar sacks, with a full pocket all neat and tidy, but every time she took a step she might have fallen over her shoelaces, which dragged from her unlaced shoes. She looked straight ahead. Her eyes were blue with age. Her skin had a pattern all its own of numberless branching wrinkles and as though a whole little tree stood in the middle of her forehead, but a golden color ran underneath, and the two knobs of her cheeks were illumined by a yellow burning under the dark. Under the red rag her hair came down on her neck in the frailest of ringlets, still black, and with an odor like copper.

Now and then there was a quivering in the thicket. Old Phoenix said, "Out of my way, all you foxes, owls, beetles, jack rabbits, coons and wild animals! . . . Keep out from under these feet, little bobwhites[1]. . . . Keep the big wild hogs out of my path. Don't let none of those come running my direction. I got a long way." Under her small black-freckled hand her cane, <u>limber</u> as a buggy whip, would switch at the brush as if to rouse up any hiding things.

On she went. The woods were deep and still. The sun made the pine needles almost too bright to look at, up where the wind rocked. The cones dropped as light as feathers. Down in the hollow was the mourning dove—it was not too late for him.

The path ran up a hill. "Seem like there is chains about my feet, time I get this far," she said, in the voice of argument old people keep to use with themselves. "Something always take a hold of me on this hill—pleads I should stay."

---

1. **bobwhites** *n.* partridges.

◀ **Critical Viewing** What details in this image suggest Phoenix's strong character? **[Connect]**

grave (grāv) *adj.* serious; solemn

limber (lim′ bər) *adj.* flexible

✔ Reading Check

What are some of Phoenix Jackson's distinguishing features?

After she got to the top she turned and gave a full, severe look behind her where she had come. "Up through pines," she said at length. "Now down through oaks."

Her eyes opened their widest, and she started down gently. But before she got to the bottom of the hill a bush caught her dress.

Her fingers were busy and intent, but her skirts were full and long, so that before she could pull them free in one place they were caught in another. It was not possible to allow the dress to tear. "I in the thorny bush," she said. "Thorns, you doing your appointed work. Never want to let folks pass, no sir. Old eyes thought you was a pretty little *green* bush."

Finally, trembling all over, she stood free, and after a moment dared to stoop for her cane.

"Sun so high!" she cried, leaning back and looking, while the thick tears went over her eyes. "The time getting all gone here."

At the foot of this hill was a place where a log was laid across the creek.

"Now comes the trial," said Phoenix.

Putting her right foot out, she mounted the log and shut her eyes. Lifting her skirt, leveling her cane fiercely before her, like a festival figure in some parade, she began to march across. Then she opened her eyes and she was safe on the other side.

"I wasn't as old as I thought," she said.

But she sat down to rest. She spread her skirts on the bank around her and folded her hands over her knees. Up above her was a tree in a pearly cloud of mistletoe. She did not dare to close her eyes, and when a little boy brought her a plate with a slice of marble cake on it she spoke to him. "That would be acceptable," she said. But when she went to take it there was just her own hand in the air.

So she left that tree, and had to go through a barbed-wire fence. There she had to creep and crawl, spreading her knees and stretching her fingers like a baby trying to climb the steps. But she talked loudly to herself: she could not let her dress be torn now, so late in the day, and she could not pay for having her arm or her leg sawed off if she got caught fast where she was.

At last she was safe through the fence and risen up out in the clearing. Big dead trees, like black men with one arm, were standing in the purple stalks of the withered cotton field. There sat a buzzard.

"Who you watching?"

In the furrow she made her way along.

"Glad this not the season for bulls," she said, looking sideways, "and the good Lord made his snakes to curl up and sleep in the winter. A pleasure I don't see no two-headed snake coming around that tree, where it come once. It took a while to get by him, back in the summer."

She passed through the old cotton and went into a field of dead corn. It whispered and shook and was taller than her head. "Through the maze now," she said, for there was no path.

Then there was something tall, black, and skinny there, moving before her.

Reading Strategy
Identifying With Characters Why do you suppose Phoenix is talking her way through the woods?

Literary Analysis
Point of View and Narrator What private information does the narrator share in the paragraph beginning "But she sat down to rest." What is the effect?

At first she took it for a man. It could have been a man dancing in the field. But she stood still and listened, and it did not make a sound. It was as silent as a ghost.

"Ghost," she said sharply, "who be you the ghost of? For I have heard of nary death close by."

But there was no answer—only the ragged dancing in the wind.

She shut her eyes, reached out her hand, and touched a sleeve. She found a coat and inside that an emptiness, cold as ice.

"You scarecrow," she said. Her face lighted. "I ought to be shut up for good," she said with laughter. "My senses is gone. I too old. I the oldest people I ever know. Dance, old scarecrow," she said, "while I dancing with you."

She kicked her foot over the furrow, and with mouth drawn down, shook her head once or twice in a little strutting way. Some husks blew down and whirled in streamers about her skirts.

Then she went on, parting her way from side to side with the cane, through the whispering field. At last she came to the end, to a wagon track where the silver grass blew between the red ruts. The quail were walking around like pullets, seeming all dainty and unseen.

"Walk pretty," she said. "This the easy place. This the easy going."

She followed the track, swaying through the quiet bare fields, through the little strings of trees silver in their dead leaves, past cabins silver from weather, with the doors and windows boarded shut, all like old women under a spell sitting there. "I walking in their sleep," she said, nodding her head vigorously.

In a ravine she went where a spring was silently flowing through a hollow log. Old Phoenix bent and drank. "Sweet gum[2] makes the water sweet," she said, and drank more. "Nobody know who made this well, for it was here when I was born."

The track crossed a swampy part where the moss hung as white as lace from every limb. "Sleep on, alligators, and blow your bubbles." Then the track went into the road.

Deep, deep the road went down between the high green-colored banks. Overhead the live-oaks met, and it was as dark as a cave.

A black dog with a lolling tongue came up out of the weeds by the ditch. She was meditating, and not ready, and when he came at her she only hit him a little with her cane. Over she went in the ditch, like a little puff of milkweed.[3]

Down there, her senses drifted away. A dream visited her, and she reached her hand up, but nothing reached down and gave her a pull. So she lay there and presently went to talking. "Old woman," she said to herself, "that black dog come up out of the weeds to stall you off, and now there he sitting on his fine tail, smiling at you."

A white man finally came along and found her—a hunter, a young man, with his dog on a chain.

---

2. **sweet gum** *n.* a tree that produces a fragrant juice.
3. **milkweed** *n.* a plant with pods that, when ripe, release feathery seeds.

Literary Analysis
Point of View From what point of view is the story being told? How do you know?

**Reading Check**
What is Phoenix Jackson's attitude as she walks?

A Worn Path ◆ 823

"Well, Granny!" he laughed. "What are you doing there?"

"Lying on my back like a June bug waiting to be turned over, mister," she said, reaching up her hand.

He lifted her up, gave her a swing in the air, and set her down. "Anything broken, Granny?"

"No sir, them old dead weeds is springy enough," said Phoenix, when she had got her breath. "I thank you for your trouble."

▼ Critical Viewing
Does this image accurately represent the path Phoenix travels? Why or why not?
[Evaluate]

"Where do you live, Granny?" he asked, while the two dogs were growling at each other.

"Away back yonder, sir, behind the ridge. You can't even see it from here."

"On your way home?"

"No sir, I going to town."

"Why, that's too far! That's as far as I walk when I come out myself, and I get something for my trouble." He patted the stuffed bag he carried, and there hung down a little closed claw. It was one of the bobwhites, with its beak hooked bitterly to show it was dead. "Now you go on home, Granny!"

"I bound to go to town, mister," said Phoenix. "The time come around."

He gave another laugh, filling the whole landscape. "I know you old colored people! Wouldn't miss going to town to see Santa Claus!"

But something held old Phoenix very still. The deep lines in her face went into a fierce and different radiation. Without warning, she had seen with her own eyes a flashing nickel fall out of the man's pocket onto the ground.

"How old are you, Granny?" he was saying.

"There is no telling, mister," she said, "no telling."

Then she gave a little cry and clapped her hands and said, "Git on away from here, dog! Look! Look at that dog!" She laughed as if in admiration. "He ain't scared of nobody. He a big black dog." She whispered, "Sic him!"

"Watch me get rid of that cur," said the man. "Sic him, Pete! Sic him!"

Phoenix heard the dogs fighting, and heard the man running and throwing sticks. She even heard a gunshot. But she was slowly bending forward by that time, further and further forward, the lids stretched down over her eyes, as if she were doing this in her sleep. Her chin was lowered almost to her knees. The yellow palm of her hand came out from the fold of her apron. Her fingers slid down and along the ground under the piece of money with the grace and care they would have in lifting an egg from under a setting hen. Then she slowly straightened up, she stood erect, and the nickel was in her apron pocket. A bird flew by. Her lips moved. "God watching me the whole time. I come to stealing."

The man came back, and his own dog panted about them. "Well, I scared him off that time," he said, and then he laughed and lifted his gun and pointed it at Phoenix.

She stood straight and faced him.

"Doesn't the gun scare you?" he said, still pointing it.

"No, sir, I seen plenty go off closer by, in my day, and for less than what I done," she said, holding utterly still.

He smiled, and shouldered the gun. "Well, Granny," he said, "you must be a hundred years old, and scared of nothing. I'd

Literary Analysis
Point of View What detail in this paragraph reveals the point of view from which the story is told? Explain.

Reading Check

Whom and what does Phoenix encounter on her journey?

give you a dime if I had any money with me. But you take my advice and stay home, and nothing will happen to you."

"I bound to go on my way, mister," said Phoenix. She inclined her head in the red rag. Then they went in different directions, but she could hear the gun shooting again and again over the hill.

She walked on. The shadows hung from the oak trees to the road like curtains. Then she smelled woodsmoke, and smelled the river, and she saw a steeple and the cabins on their steep steps. Dozens of little black children whirled around her. There ahead was Natchez[4] shining. Bells were ringing. She walked on.

In the paved city it was Christmas time. There were red and green electric lights strung and criss-crossed everywhere, and all turned on in the daytime. Old Phoenix would have been lost if she had not distrusted her eyesight and depended on her feet to know where to take her.

She paused quietly on the sidewalk where people were passing by. A lady came along in the crowd, carrying an armful of red-, green- and silver-wrapped presents; she gave off perfume like the red roses in hot summer, and Phoenix stopped her.

"Please, missy, will you lace up my shoe?" She held up her foot.

"What do you want, Grandma?"

"See my shoe," said Phoenix. "Do all right for out in the country, but wouldn't look right to go in a big building."

"Stand still then, Grandma," said the lady. She put her packages down on the sidewalk beside her and laced and tied both shoes tightly.

"Can't lace em with a cane," said Phoenix. "Thank you, missy. I doesn't mind asking a nice lady to tie up my shoe, when I gets out on the street."

Moving slowly and from side to side, she went into the big building, and into a tower of steps, where she walked up and around and around until her feet knew to stop.

She entered a door, and there she saw nailed up on the wall the document that had been stamped with the gold seal and framed in the gold frame, which matched the dream that was hung up in her head.

"Here I be," she said. There was a fixed and ceremonial stiffness over her body.

"A charity case, I suppose," said an attendant who sat at the desk before her.

But Phoenix only looked above her head. There was sweat on her face, the wrinkles in her skin shone like a bright net.

"Speak up, Grandma," the woman said. "What's your name? We must have your history, you know. Have you been here before? What seems to be the trouble with you?"

Old Phoenix only gave a twitch to her face as if a fly were bothering her.

"Are you deaf?" cried the attendant.

But then the nurse came in.

---

4. **Natchez** (nach´ iz) a town in southern Mississippi.

Literary Analysis
Point of View What response does this dialogue describing the way others see Phoenix evoke in you? Why?

"Oh, that's just old Aunt Phoenix," she said. "She doesn't come for herself—she has a little grandson. She makes these trips just as regular as clockwork. She lives away back off the Old Natchez Trace." She bent down. "Well, Aunt Phoenix, why don't you just take a seat? We won't keep you standing after your long trip." She pointed.

The old woman sat down, bolt upright in the chair.

"Now, how is the boy?" asked the nurse.

Old Phoenix did not speak.

"I said, how is the boy?"

But Phoenix only waited and stared straight ahead, her face very solemn and withdrawn into rigidity.

"Is his throat any better?" asked the nurse. "Aunt Phoenix, don't you hear me? Is your grandson's throat any better since the last time you came for the medicine?"

With her hands on her knees, the old woman waited, silent, erect and motionless, just as if she were in armor.

"You mustn't take up our time this way, Aunt Phoenix," the nurse said. "Tell us quickly about your grandson, and get it over. He isn't dead, is he?"

At last there came a flicker and then a flame of comprehension across her face, and she spoke.

"My grandson. It was my memory had left me. There I sat and forgot why I made my long trip."

"Forgot?" The nurse frowned. "After you came so far?"

Then Phoenix was like an old woman begging a dignified forgiveness for waking up frightened in the night. "I never did go to school. I was too old at the Surrender,"[5] she said in a soft voice. "I'm an old woman without an education. It was my memory fail me. My little grandson, he is just the same, and I forgot it in the coming."

"Throat never heals, does it?" said the nurse, speaking in a loud, sure voice to old Phoenix. By now she had a card with something written on it, a little list. "Yes. Swallowed lye. When was it?— January—two-three years ago—"

Phoenix spoke unasked now. "No, missy, he not dead, he just the same. Every little while his throat begin to close up again, and he not able to swallow. He not get his breath. He not able to help himself. So the time come around, and I go on another trip for the soothing medicine."

"All right. The doctor said as long as you came to get it, you could have it," said the nurse. "But it's an obstinate case."

"My little grandson, he sit up there in the house all wrapped up, waiting by himself," Phoenix went on. "We is the only two left in the world. He suffer and it don't seem to put him back at all. He got a sweet look. He going to last. He wear a little patch quilt and peep out holding his mouth open like a little bird. I remembers so plain now. I not going to forget him again, no, the whole enduring time. I could tell him from all the others in creation."

---

5. **the Surrender** the surrender of the Confederate army, which ended the Civil War.

Literary Analysis
Point of View and Narrator Here, the narrator does not share Phoenix's thoughts. How does this affect you as a reader? Explain.

obstinate (äb′ stə nət) *adj.* stubborn

**Reading Check**

Why is Phoenix at the doctor's office?

"All right." The nurse was trying to hush her now. She brought her a bottle of medicine. "Charity," she said, making a check mark in a book.

Old Phoenix held the bottle close to her eyes, and then carefully put it into her pocket.

"I thank you," she said.

"It's Christmas time, Grandma," said the attendant. "Could I give you a few pennies out of my purse?"

"Five pennies is a nickel," said Phoenix stiffly.

"Here's a nickel," said the attendant.

Phoenix rose carefully and held out her hand. She received the nickel and then fished the other nickel out of her pocket and laid it beside the new one. She stared at her palm closely, with her head on one side.

Then she gave a tap with her cane on the floor.

"This is what come to me to do," she said. "I going to the store and buy my child a little windmill they sells, made out of paper. He going to find it hard to believe there such a thing in the world. I'll march myself back where he is waiting, holding it straight up in this hand."

She lifted her free hand, gave a little nod, turned around, and walked out of the doctor's office. Then her slow step began on the stairs, going down.

Review and Assess

Thinking About the Selection

1. **Respond:** Do you think Welty's use of language suits her story, or would you have used language differently? Explain.

2. **(a) Recall:** At what time of year does the story take place?
   (b) Interpret: What is significant about the story taking place at this time?

3. **(a) Recall:** What obstacles does Phoenix encounter on her journey? **(b) Analyze:** How does she deal with each of those obstacles?

4. **(a) Recall:** For what reason does Phoenix make her journey?
   (b) Interpret: What emotions does her journey express?

5. **(a) Recall:** In what way does Phoenix initially respond to the questions asked by the attendant and the nurse? **(b) Infer:** What does their reaction reveal about their attitudes toward her?
   (c) Assess: Do you think Phoenix sees herself as others see her?

6. **Synthesize:** In mythology, the Phoenix is a bird that rises from the ashes. Why do you think the author named the main character of this story Phoenix?

7. **Assess:** In what specific ways do you think Phoenix Jackson's character has been shaped by hardship? Explain.

Review and Assess

Literary Analysis

Point of View

1. (a) Identify three details that show Hemingway's story was written using a **first-person point of view**. (b) How would the story be different if Hemingway had used a **third-person point of view**?

2. (a) What point of view does Anderson use in "The Corn Planting"? (b) Is the narrator of "The Corn Planting" the best character to tell the story? Why or why not?

3. How would "A Worn Path" be different if Welty had told the story from Phoenix Jackson's first-person point of view?

4. Using a different point of view from the original, rewrite a paragraph from one of the stories. Then, compare the two versions. (a) What is gained in your version? (b) What is lost?

Comparing Literary Works

5. (a) For each selection, identify the type of **narrator** being used. (b) Note specific ways in which each narrator allows some information to be revealed and some to be hidden.

6. (a) Compare the emotions the narrator evokes in you in each story. (b) In what way does the author's choice of a narrator create a different level of emotional involvement in each story?

Reading Strategy

Identifying With Characters

7. Among the three stories, choose the characters with whom you **identify** most and least. Provide reasons for your choices.

8. Did you find yourself sympathizing with Phoenix Jackson? Why or why not?

9. Using a diagram like the one shown, list one personality trait, interest, or value you might share with a character in each story.

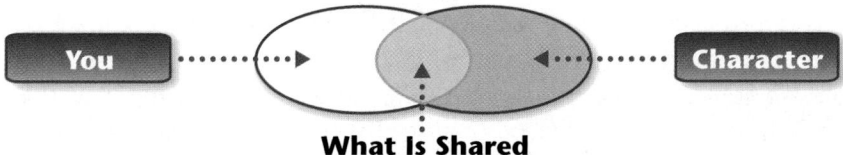

What Is Shared

Extend Understanding

10. **Social Studies Connection:** What does Hemingway's story tell you about war that a history textbook might not?

Quick Review

Point of view is the perspective from which a story is told. The **first-person point of view** features a narrator who participates in the action. In a story using **limited third-person point of view**, the story is told by a narrator who stands outside the action and conveys the thoughts and feelings of a single character.

The **narrator** is the speaker who tells the story.

To **identify with characters**, connect their thoughts and feelings with your own experiences.

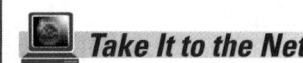 **Take It to the Net**
www.phschool.com
Take the interactive self-test online to check your understanding of these selections.

Integrate Language Skills

Vocabulary Development Lesson

Word Analysis: Latin Root -val-

The Latin root -val- means "strength" or "value." Use a dictionary to define each of the words below. Then, write a sentence explaining how each word's definition might relate to the meaning of -val-.

1. valid
2. equivalent
3. valor
4. prevail

Spelling Strategy

When words begin with the letters *gn* or *kn*, as in *gnarled, gnaw, knee,* and *knock,* the *g* or *k* is silent. In your notebook, complete the spelling of the following words.

1. __nu
2. __nife
3. __nit
4. __nat

Fluency: Clarify Word Meaning

Review the words from the vocabulary list on page 808 and notice the way each word is used in the selections. Then, answer yes or no to each question. Explain each of your answers.

1. If a soldier is *invalided*, has he or she been transferred to combat duty?

2. Would someone bringing *grave* news be smiling?

3. Would a gymnast need to be *limber* before performing?

4. Would you want to pair up for a project with someone described as *obstinate*?

Grammar and Style Lesson

Punctuating Dialogue

Dialogue is one of the most effective tools in a writer's toolkit. Dialogue brings characters to life by letting readers "hear" the characters' own words. Because each writer carefully punctuates the dialogue, you can easily tell who is speaking each line.

To correctly punctuate dialogue, always put quotation marks around the speaker's exact words. Place periods and commas inside the quotation marks.

> **Example:** "Ghost," she said sharply, "who be you the ghost of? For I have heard of nary death close by."

Practice The punctuation marks in the following pieces of dialogue have been misplaced or omitted. Rewrite each item, using correct punctuation.

1. "No" said the major.
2. "Well, he said, and Well," I said.
3. "Don't argue with me"!
4. I offered to take my car, but Hal said No, Let's walk out.
5. "How old are you, Granny"? he was asking.

Looking at Style When you compare the amount of dialogue in these three stories, you'll notice that "The Corn Planting" has the least. How does this difference affect the way you relate to the characters? Explain.

W͞G Prentice Hall Writing and Grammar Connection: Chapter 5, Section 4

Writing Lesson

Memorial Speech

As Hal Weyman in "The Corn Planting," write the speech you might give at Will's memorial service. In your remarks, acknowledge both Will's family and his dreams. Also include personal traits revealed from the story.

Prewriting   Reread the story and note personal details about Will. Look for Hal's opinions about Will's strength, talents, and personality.

Drafting   To begin, identify Will Hutchenson, and explain the sad occasion for the speech. Organize your main points in order of importance, noting the memories of greatest significance. Retell anecdotes in a style reflecting Hal's character.

Revising   Reread your speech to make sure it reveals Will's personality and expresses his dreams. Highlight and revise vague words and add details that evoke emotion.

Model: Revising to Add Emotional Appeal

person whom I'll never forget because
he had endless enthusiasm for life.

Will Hutchenson was a ~~great guy.~~ An only child, he was the source of pride for his parents. ~~He was talented.~~ He dreamed of becoming a successful artist, and he had talent that was too young to die.

> Phrases such as *endless enthusiasm for life* and *a talent that was too young to die* add emotional appeal.

WG Prentice Hall Writing and Grammar Connection: Chapter 28, Section 1

Extension Activities

Speaking and Listening Write and narrate **a sequel** to Welty's "A Worn Path" that describes what happens when Phoenix Jackson gets home. Use these questions to help you plan:

- Is Phoenix's grandson alive?
- Is anyone else present?
- What does Phoenix feel and do?
- How will your story end?

In an oral presentation, share your story with your class.

Research and Technology Hemingway's story drew upon his service in the Italian army. Conduct research on the Internet and in the library to find information on the role Italy played in World War I, as well as on Hemingway's participation. Prepare a **research report** on your findings, including maps and charts as visual aids.

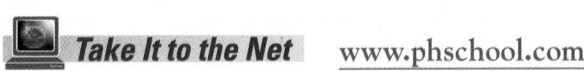 **Take It to the Net**   www.phschool.com

Go online for an additional research activity using the Internet.

CONNECTIONS
Literature Past and Present
Facing Troubled Times

The Modernist writers had a deep sense of uncertainty. The war that had cost the world so much seemed to have accomplished little. Searching for values suited to a new era, Modernists focused on themes of confusion and the apparent meaninglessness of life. For contemporary Americans today, the world is even more fragmented. Grace Paley's story "Anxiety," with its implied theme of world doom, reflects the uncertainty brought about by changes in technology and politics.

Twentieth Century Short Stories The stories by Ernest Hemingway, Sherwood Anderson, Eudora Welty, and Paley were all written during the twentieth century, and share themes of uncertainty, ambiguity, and disillusionment. Paley's contemporary short story reflects the pace of our increasingly urban culture. Her story also raises new issues of concern—nuclear warfare, for example—and, consisting almost entirely of unpunctuated dialogue, blurs structural form more than do the other stories.

ANXIETY
Grace Paley

The young fathers are waiting outside the school. What curly heads! Such graceful brown mustaches. They're sitting on their haunches eating pizza and exchanging information. They're waiting for the 3 P.M. bell. It's springtime, the season of first looking out the window. I have a window box of greenhouse marigolds. The young fathers can be seen through the ferny leaves.

The bell rings. The children fall out of school, tumbling through the open door. One of the fathers sees his child. A small child. Is she Chinese? A little. Up u-u-p, he says and hoists her to his shoulders. U-u-p, says the second father, and hoists his little boy. The little boy sits on top of his father's head for a couple of seconds before sliding to his shoulders. Very funny, says the father.

They start off down the street, right under and past my window. The two children are still laughing. They try to whisper a secret. The fathers haven't finished their conversation. The frailer father is uncomfortable; his little girl wiggles too much.

Stop it this minute, he says.

Oink oink, says the little girl.

What'd you say?

Oink oink, she says.

The young father says What! three times. Then he seizes the child, raises her high above his head, and sets her hard on her feet.

What'd I do so bad, she says, rubbing her ankle. Just hold my hand, screams the frail and angry father.

I lean far out the window. Stop! Stop! I cry.

The young father turns, shading his eyes, but sees. What? he says. His friend says, Hey? Who's that? He probably thinks I'm a family friend, a teacher maybe.

Who're you? he says.

I move the pots of marigold aside. Then I'm able to lean my elbow way out into unshadowed visibility. Once, not too long ago, the tenements were speckled with women like me in every third window up to the fifth story, calling the children from play to receive orders and instruction. This memory enables me to say strictly, Young man, I am an older person who feels free because of that to ask questions and give advice.

Oh? he says, laughs with a little embarrassment, says to his friend, Shoot if you will that old gray head.[1] But he's joking, I know, because he has established himself, legs apart, hands behind his back, his neck arched to see and hear me out.

How old are you? I call. About thirty or so?

Thirty-three.

First I want to say you're about a generation ahead of your father in your attitude and behavior toward your child.

Really? Well? Anything else, ma'am.

Son, I said, leaning another two, three dangerous inches toward him. Son, I must tell you that madmen intend to destroy this beautifully made planet. That the murder of our children by these men has got to become a terror and a sorrow to you, and starting now, it had better interfere with any daily pleasure.

Speech, speech, he called.

I waited a minute, but he continued to look up. So, I said, I can tell by your general appearance and loping walk that you agree with me.

I do, he said, winking at his friend; but turning a serious face to mine, he said again, Yes, yes, I do.

Well then, why do you become so angry at that little girl whose future is like a film which suddenly cuts to white. Why did you nearly slam this little doomed person to the ground in your uncontrollable anger.

Let's not go too far, said the young father. She *was* jumping around on my poor back and hollering oink oink.

---

1. **Shoot . . . head** a reference to John Greenleaf Whittier's 1864 Civil War poem, "Barbara Frietchie," which contains the line, "'Shoot, if you must, this old gray head, / But spare your country's flag,' she said."

✔ Reading Check

What do the young fathers do while they wait outside the school?

When were you angriest—when she wiggled and jumped or when she said oink?

He scratched his wonderful head of dark well-cut hair. I guess when she said oink.

Have you ever said oink oink? Think carefully. Years ago, perhaps?

No. Well maybe. Maybe.

Whom did you refer to in this way?

He laughed. He called to his friend, Hey Ken, this old person's got something. The cops. In a demonstration. Oink oink, he said, remembering, laughing.

The little girl smiled and said, Oink oink.

Shut up, he said.

What do you deduce from this?

That I was angry at Rosie because she was dealing with me as though I was a figure of authority, and it's not my thing, never has been, never will be.

I could see his happiness, his nice grin, as he remembered this.

So, I continued, since those children are such lovely examples of what may well be the last generation of humankind, why don't you start all over again, right from the school door, as though none of this had ever happened.

Thank you, said the young father. Thank you. It would be nice to be a horse, he said, grabbing little Rosie's hand. Come on Rosie, let's go. I don't have all day.

U-up, says the first father. U-up, says the second.

Giddap, shout the children, and the fathers yell neigh neigh, as horses do. The children kick their fathers' horsechests, screaming giddap giddap, and they gallop wildly westward.

I lean way out to cry once more, Be careful! Stop! But they've gone too far. Oh, anyone would love to be a fierce fast horse carrying a beloved beautiful rider, but they are galloping toward one of the most dangerous street corners in the world. And they live beyond that trisection across other dangerous avenues.

So I must shut the window after patting the April-cooled marigolds with their rusty smell of summer. Then I sit in the nice light and wonder how to make sure that they gallop safely home through the airy scary dreams of scientists and the bulky dreams of automakers. I wish I could see just how they sit down at their kitchen tables for a healthy snack (orange juice or milk and cookies) before going out into the new spring afternoon to play.

Connecting Literature Past and Present

1. Explain how the title "Anxiety" might fit the stories by Hemingway, Anderson and Welty.

2. Which time period do you find more uncertain—post World War I or Grace Paley's nuclear age? Explain.

Grace Paley

(b. 1922)

Grace Paley, a native New Yorker, has a strong concern for urban community life. This concern, along with her interest in social issues, is reflected in her highly praised short story collections, such as *Enormous Changes at the Last Minute* (1974) and *Later the Same Day* (1985). Sometimes referred to as a writer's writer, Paley's work is often studied in writing workshops. Her style is crisp and deceptively simple. Nonetheless, "Anxiety" embodies an implicit theme of moral concern worth consideration in our age.

From Every Corner of the Land

The Tower, Charles Demuth, Columbus Museum of Art, Ohio

Prepare to Read

Chicago ◆ Grass

Carl Sandburg (1878–1967)

You may enjoy the work of a contemporary poet or songwriter who seems to speak right to you. The poetry of Carl Sandburg seemed to speak directly to many of the people of his time. It celebrated the lives and the vitality of ordinary Americans, and made Sandburg one of the most popular poets of his day.

No writer better captured the spirit of industrial America than did Carl Sandburg, whose poems paint vivid portraits of the working class, capturing its energy and enthusiasm. In his poems about mills and factories, meatpacking houses, and railroads, he paid tribute to the struggles and hopes of the poor.

Modest Beginnings The son of Swedish immigrants, Sandburg was born and raised in Galesburg, Illinois. He was forced to leave school after eighth grade in order to help support his family. As an adolescent, he worked as a laborer, and when he was nineteen, he set out to see the country. He did so by hitching rides on freight trains. In 1898, after spending six years working at a variety of odd jobs, Sandburg enlisted in the army. Though the Spanish-American War was being fought at the time, Sandburg did not see combat. After the war, he attended Lombard College, but dropped out before graduating. He then spent several years traveling around the country, again working at a variety of jobs.

The Bard of Chicago In 1912, Sandburg settled in Chicago, one of the nation's great industrial cities. He made his living as a newspaper reporter and began to publish poetry in *Poetry* magazine, a highly regarded literary journal based in Chicago. His first book, *Chicago Poems*, published in 1916, sold well and was praised for its passion and vigor. Sandburg soon earned widespread recognition and helped establish Chicago as one of the nation's leading literary centers. During the next ten years, he published three more successful collections of poetry: *Cornhuskers* (1918), *Smoke and Steel* (1920), and *Slabs of the Sunburnt West* (1922).

Writing Lincoln's Life While continuing to write poetry, Sandburg began touring the country, delivering lectures on Walt Whitman and Abraham Lincoln—two men whom he greatly admired—and starting a career as a folk singer. He also spent a great deal of time collecting material for a biography of Lincoln, and he prepared an anthology of American folk songs he had heard during his travels. He collected these songs from cowboys, lumberjacks, factory workers, and hobos. *The American Songbag* appeared in 1927. In 1940, Carl Sandburg received a Pulitzer Prize for his multi-volume biography of Lincoln, and in 1951 he received a second Pulitzer Prize for his *Complete Poems*. Sandburg was also awarded the United States Presidential Medal in 1964, and he was asked to address a joint session of Congress on the 150th anniversary of Lincoln's birth.

Power of Positive Thinking Sandburg was an optimist who believed in the power of ordinary Americans to fulfill their dreams. He was not interested in experimenting with complicated syntax or images, as were some other poets of his generation. Instead, he reached out to his readers with poems that were concrete and direct. Sandburg offered a variety of definitions of poetry, among them these two: "Poetry is a search for syllables to shoot at the barriers of the unknown and the unknowable," and "Poetry is the opening and closing of a door, leaving those who look through to guess about what is seen during a moment."

Preview

Connecting to the Literature

If you have ever celebrated the comeback of someone who seemed to have been defeated, then you understand the spirit in which Carl Sandburg wrote. In reading these poems, you will see that Sandburg recognized people's and cities' failures, but he cheered the invincibility of their souls.

Literary Analysis

Apostrophe

Apostrophe is a literary device in which the speaker or narrator directly addresses a person or thing. For example, in "Chicago," Sandburg addresses the city as if it were a person:

> They tell me you are wicked and I believe them . . .

> And they tell me you are crooked and I answer: Yes . . .

As you read "Chicago," think about the effect of this technique, and identify the reasons that Sandburg chose to speak directly to the city of Chicago.

Comparing Literary Works

These poems concern two very different subjects and evoke distinct emotions. "Chicago" is a celebration of life in an industrial city, while "Grass" is a lament for loss of life in war. In "Chicago," the speaker addresses the city directly; in "Grass," it is the grass itself that speaks. Despite these differences, the poet uses similar techniques to achieve his aims. For example, both poems use **personification,** figurative language in which a non-human subject is given human qualities. As you read, use a chart like the one shown to examine the ways in which Sandburg uses personification, but to different effect in each poem.

Reading Strategy

Responding

When you **respond** to a poem, you think about the message that the poet has conveyed and reflect on how you feel personally about the topic. You take the time to consider how the poet's message relates to your own life and to the world in which you live, and to think about how you can use or apply what you have learned from the poem. As you read these poems, connect your own experiences to the images and ideas Sandburg presents.

Vocabulary Development

brutal (brōōt′ əl) *adj.* cruel and without feeling; savage; violent (p. 839)

wanton (wän′ tən) *adj.* senseless; unjustified (p. 839)

cunning (kun′ iŋ) *adj.* skillful in deception; crafty; sly (p. 839)

Chicago

Carl Sandburg

Background

The 1920s was a time of excitement in America. The economy was booming, and jazz was the rage. Sandburg's poems of industrial America celebrate the energy of the times.

Hog Butcher for the World,
Tool Maker, Stacker of Wheat,
Player with Railroads and the Nation's Freight Handler;
Stormy, husky, brawling,
5   City of the Big Shoulders:

They tell me you are wicked and I believe them, for I have seen
    your painted women under the gas lamps luring the farm
    boys.
And they tell me you are crooked and I answer: Yes, it is true I
    have seen the gunman kill and go free to kill again.
And they tell me you are brutal and my reply is: On the faces of
    women and children I have seen the marks of wanton hunger.
And having answered so I turn once more to those who sneer at
    this my city, and I give them back the sneer and say to them:
10 Come and show me another city with lifted head singing so proud
    to be alive and coarse and strong and cunning.
Flinging magnetic curses amid the toil of piling job on job, here is
    a tall bold slugger set vivid against the little soft cities;
Fierce as a dog with tongue lapping for action, cunning as a
    savage pitted against the wilderness,
        Bareheaded,
        Shoveling,
15   Wrecking,
        Planning,
        Building, breaking, rebuilding,
Under the smoke, dust all over his mouth, laughing with
    white teeth,
Under the terrible burden of destiny laughing as a young man
    laughs,
20 Laughing even as an ignorant fighter laughs who has never lost
    a battle,
Bragging and laughing that under his wrist is the pulse, and
    under his ribs the heart of the people,
            Laughing!
Laughing the stormy, husky, brawling laughter of Youth, half-
    naked, sweating, proud to be a Hog Butcher, Tool Maker,
    Stacker of Wheat, Player with Railroads and Freight Handler
    to the Nation.

◄ **Critical Viewing** In what ways does this bustling street scene of Chicago reflect Sandburg's poem **[Connect]**

brutal (brōōt´ əl) *adj.* cruel and without feeling; savage; violent

wanton (wän´ tən) *adj.* senseless; unjustified

cunning (kun´ iŋ) *adj.* skillful in deception; crafty; sly

✔ **Reading Check**
Who is the "you" the speaker addresses?

Grass
Carl Sandburg

Pile the bodies high at Austerlitz and Waterloo.[1]
Shovel them under and let me work—
    I am the grass; I cover all.

And pile them high at Gettysburg
5 And pile them high at Ypres and Verdun.[2]
Shovel them under and let me work.
Two years, ten years, and passengers ask the conductor:
    What place is this?
    Where are we now?

10   I am grass.
      Let me work.

---

1. **Austerlitz** (ôs´ tər lits´) **and Waterloo** sites of battles of the Napoleonic Wars.
2. **Ypres** (ē´ pr) **and Verdun** (vər dun´) sites of battles of World War I.

Review and Assess
Thinking About the Selections

1. **Respond:** Unlike some poets, Sandburg tells you what to feel and think. How do you react to his directness? Why?

2. **(a) Recall:** In "Chicago," what names does the speaker use to address the city in the first stanza? **(b) Interpret:** What do these names tell you about the city's economy and atmosphere?

3. **(a) Recall:** What three specific faults concerning his city does the speaker acknowledge? **(b) Interpret:** In what ways do these faults affect the speaker's attitude toward the city?

4. **(a) Recall:** In the first stanza of "Grass," what does the grass claim to be able to do? **(b) Draw Conclusions:** Is Sandburg suggesting that the death and destruction of war can be covered over and easily forgotten? Support your answer.

5. **(a) Distinguish:** In what ways is the city described in "Chicago" similar to and different from other cities with which you are familiar? **(b) Apply:** What do the differences among American cities reveal about the nation's character?

Review and Assess

Literary Analysis

Apostrophe

1. (a) In which lines of "Chicago" does Sandburg address the city directly? (b) What effect does this use of **apostrophe** create?
2. (a) Using a chart like the one shown, contrast the lines in the poem that directly address the city with those that address others. (b) Which section contains more positive images?

Imagery		Chicago	Others		Imagery
	◀┈┈			┈┈▶	

Comparing Literary Works

3. (a) Compare and contrast the use of specific details in "Chicago" and "Grass." (b) In what ways does the choice and amount of detail suit each poem's subject? (c) What distinct moods do these details evoke?
4. (a) Identify at least one feeling Sandburg has for Chicago that he might feel toward a friend. Support your answer with examples. (b) In "Grass," with what two words does the poet **personify** the grass?
5. In what ways do the uses of personification serve the distinct goals of each of these poems? Explain

Reading Strategy

Responding

6. Which words or images in "Chicago" were most striking to you? Explain.
7. (a) In what tone of voice do you imagine the grass speaks? (b) What is your **response** to the grass's message?

Extend Understanding

8. **Literature Connection:** Some critics have said that Sandburg opened poetry to new subjects by writing about industry and laborers. Other poets of his day, like T.S. Eliot, wrote about more intellectual subjects. What benefits or harm do you see—for poetry or popular culture—in Sandburg's appeal to the common person?

Integrate Language Skills

Vocabulary Development Lesson

Related Words: *brutal*

The word *brutal* means "cruel, crude, or harsh." Use this information and your knowledge about parts of speech to complete each sentence using a related word from the list below.

brute   brutality   brutalize   brutish

1. Sam was so rough with my brother that I told him he was behaving like a ___?___ and asked him to leave.

2. Many who participated in World War I were stunned by the ___?___ on the front lines.

3. Use your knife and fork, and stop that ___?___ behavior at once!

4. Those who ___?___ innocent animals should receive the harshest punishment.

Concept Development: Synonyms

Select the letter of the word that is closest in meaning to each of the numbered vocabulary words.

1. brutal: (a) unwise, (b) violent, (c) heavy
2. cunning: (a) suspicious, (b) diligent, (c) crafty
3. wanton: (a) rapid, (b) kind, (c) rash

Spelling Strategy

In the word *brute*, the final *e* marks the long sound of the vowel that precedes it. When a suffix beginning with a vowel is added to such a word, the final *e* is usually dropped: *brute* becomes *brutish*. For each of the following words, create a new word containing the given suffix.

1. bare (add *-est*)   3. smoke (add *-ily*)
2. pile (add *-ing*)   4. care (add *-ing*)

Grammar and Style Lesson

Sentence Types

There are four sentence types. A **declarative** sentence makes a statement and ends with a period. An **interrogative** sentence asks a question and ends with a question mark. An **imperative** sentence is a statement and gives a command or makes a request; it ends with a period. An **exclamatory** sentence expresses a strong emotion and ends with an exclamation point.

Declarative: I am grass.

Interrogative: What place is this?

Imperative: Pile the bodies high.

Exclamatory: Look at that man!

Practice Add the correct end punctuation, and label the sentence type for each of the following examples.

1. Shovel me under and let me work
2. I have seen hunger on children's faces
3. Where are we now
4. Show me another city
5. I am overjoyed by this response

Writing Application Write a paragraph in which you praise and/or criticize your city or town. Use all four types of sentences in your essay.

W͞G Prentice Hall Writing and Grammar Connection: Chapter 20, Section 1

Writing Lesson

Essay Analyzing the Use of Repetition

Using either "Chicago," or "Grass," write an essay analyzing Sandburg's use of repetition. Explain the ways in which the poet's use of repetition emphasizes particular ideas and heightens specific emotions.

Prewriting   Select a poem to analyze, and examine it for examples of repetition. Note which elements—words, phrases, sentence structures, or grammatical forms—are repeated, and consider their effect.

Drafting   In your introduction, briefly summarize the poem, and state your main point about its use of repetition. Develop your ideas, with quotes from the poem, in the body paragraphs.

Revising   Review your draft, and make sure that you have explained your ideas in a consistent way. Use contrasting colors to underline any contradictory information. If you cannot connect the contradictions to your main idea, delete them.

Model: Revising to Connect Contradictory Information

Reading "Chicago" is like riding the rapids on a river; you are

swept along in a stream of words, and <u>do not stop to examine the</u>

However,

<u>validity of the ideas.</u> The ideas in a Sandburg poem are important.

> Transitional words, such as "however" connect contradictory information to a main idea.

WG Prentice Hall Writing and Grammar Connection: Chapter 8, Section 2

Extension Activities

Listening and Speaking Acting as the city of Chicago, deliver a **stand-up comedy routine.** First, research Chicago's history for events you can turn into anecdotes. Then, use these tips to prepare:

- Decide what your attitude will be—tough or sensitive.
- Find body language to fit your attitude.

When presenting your routine, appeal to your audience's experiences, and create a bond that will result in laughter.

Research and Technology Using the Internet and other sources, research the population of Chicago. Collect statistics related to that population, including totals of men, women, and children, and so on. Create a **report** that demonstrates how the population of Chicago today reflects its history.

 **Take It to the Net**   www.phschool.com

Go online for an additional research activity using the Internet.

Prepare to Read

The Jilting of Granny Weatherall

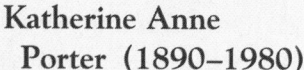

Katherine Anne Porter (1890–1980)

Katherine Anne Porter's life spanned World War I, the Great Depression, World War II, and the rise of the nuclear age, making her deeply aware of what she called "the heavy threat of world catastrophe." For Porter, her exceptionally well-crafted fiction was an "effort to grasp the meaning of those threats, to trace them to their sources, and to understand the logic of this majestic and terrible failure of the life of man in the Western world." Her stories were often set in the South and featured characters at pivotal moments in their lives, faced with dramatic change, the constricting bonds of family, and the weight of the past.

A descendant of legendary pioneer Daniel Boone, Porter was born in Indian Creek, Texas. She was raised in poverty and haphazardly educated in convent schools. Commenting on her schooling, Porter said that she received a "fragmentary, but strangely useless and ornamental education." Instead, she added, her true education came by reading five writers—American authors Henry James, T.S. Eliot, and Ezra Pound, Irish writer James Joyce, and Irish poet W.B. Yeats.

Beginnings as a Writer Porter began writing at an early age, though she did not publish her first book until she was forty years old. As a young adult, she worked as a journalist. Her work took her to many places, including Mexico City, where she lived for eight years. She became deeply involved in Mexican politics and culture, even writing a study of Mexican crafts. While in Mexico, Porter also developed an interest in writing fiction, and in 1922 she published her first story, "María Concepción," in *Century*, a highly regarded literary magazine. Eight years later, she published her first book, *Flowering Judas* (1930). The book, a collection of six short stories, was praised by critics and earned Porter widespread recognition. *Flowering Judas and Other Stories*, an expanded edition of the book containing ten stories, was published in 1935.

Literary Achievements Katherine Anne Porter went on to produce several other major works, including *Noon Wine* (1937); *Pale Horse, Pale Rider* (1939); *The Leaning Tower and Other Stories* (1944); and *Ship of Fools* (1962)—Porter's only novel. Her last major work, *The Never-Ending Wrong*, a nonfiction account of the trial of Sacco and Vanzetti during the 1920s, was published in 1977. Although her body of work was relatively small in comparison to those of other major writers of her time, her work consistently received high praise from critics and earned her a place among the finest writers of the twentieth century. Her *Collected Stories* (1965) was awarded the Pulitzer Prize and the National Book Award. In addition, her novel, *Ship of Fools*, was made into a popular film.

A First-Rate Artist In his review of *The Leaning Tower and Other Stories*, critic Edmund Wilson tried to account for the "elusive" quality that made Porter an "absolutely first-rate artist." He said, "These stories are not illustrations of anything that is reducible to a moral law or a political or social analysis or even a principle of human behavior. What they show us are human relationships in their constantly shifting phases and in the moments of which their existence is made. There is no place for general reflections; you are to live through the experiences as the characters do." You will discover that Wilson's observations can be applied to "The Jilting of Granny Weatherall," which takes readers on a journey through the various phases of an elderly woman's life in the moments leading up to her death.

Preview

Connecting to the Literature

Think about the drifting thoughts and images that greet you as you fall asleep. If you can remember these semi-conscious thoughts of yours, you may be able to understand Granny Weatherall a little better. The old woman in this story is visited by a host of such images from her past. As you read, try to uncover the meaning of her memories.

Literary Analysis

Stream of Consciousness

People's thoughts do not flow in neat patterns; they proceed in streams of insight, memory, and reflection. During the early 1900s, some writers began using a literary device called **stream of consciousness**, in which they tried to capture the natural flow of thought. These narratives usually

- present sequences of thought as if they were issuing directly from a character's mind.
- omit transitional words and phrases found in ordinary prose.
- connect details only through a character's associations.

Note the way Granny Weatherall's thoughts wander among memories, dream-like images, and accurate perceptions of the present moment.

Connecting Literary Elements

Stream-of-consciousness narratives often involve the use of **flashback**, or interruptions in which an earlier event is described. A flashback may take the form of a character's memory, a story told by a character, a dream or daydream, or a switch by the narrator to a time in the past.

As you read, pay attention to the details that trigger Granny's flashbacks, determine the form of the flashback, and decide how each relates to events in the present. Use a chart like the one shown to link past to present in the story.

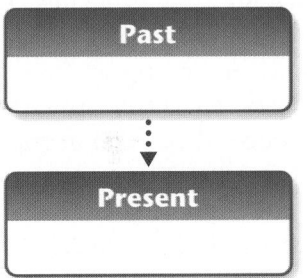

Reading Strategy

Clarifying Sequence of Events

This story evokes an array of different moments spanning eighty years as Granny Weatherall drifts in and out of reality. To stay oriented, **clarify the sequence of events**. Watch for jumps in Granny's thinking, often signaled by a shift from present-moment dialogue to Granny's inner thoughts.

Build Vocabulary

piety (pī´ ə tē) *n.* devotion to religious duties (p. 852)

frippery (frip´ ər ē) *n.* showy display of elegance (p. 853)

dyspepsia (dis pep´ shə) *n.* indigestion (p. 854)

The Jilting of Granny Weatherall

Katherine Anne Porter

Background

Katherine Anne Porter's view of life and the literature she created were shaped by the universal sense of disillusionment resulting from World War I, the despair of the Great Depression, and the World War II horrors of Nazism and nuclear warfare. Sometimes, as in the novel *Ship of Fools*, Porter focused on social and political issues such as Nazism. In contrast, works like "The Jilting of Granny Weatherall" pinpointed the dissolving families and communities of the modern age.

She flicked her wrist neatly out of Doctor Harry's pudgy careful fingers and pulled the sheet up to her chin. The brat ought to be in knee breeches. Doctoring around the country with spectacles on his nose! "Get along now, take your schoolbooks and go. There's nothing wrong with me."

Doctor Harry spread a warm paw like a cushion on her forehead where the forked green vein danced and made her eyelids twitch. "Now, now, be a good girl, and we'll have you up in no time."

"That's no way to speak to a woman nearly eighty years old just because she's down. I'd have you respect your elders, young man."

"Well, Missy, excuse me," Doctor Harry patted her cheek. "But I've got to warn you, haven't I? You're a marvel, but you must be careful or you're going to be good and sorry."

"Don't tell me what I'm going to be. I'm on my feet now, morally speaking. It's Cornelia. I had to go to bed to get rid of her."

Her bones felt loose, and floated around in her skin, and Doctor Harry floated like a balloon around the foot of the bed. He floated and pulled down his waistcoat and swung his glasses on a cord. "Well, stay where you are, it certainly can't hurt you."

"Get along and doctor your sick," said Granny Weatherall. "Leave a well woman alone. I'll call for you when I want you. . . . Where were you forty years ago when I pulled through milk leg[1] and double pneumonia? You weren't even born. Don't let Cornelia lead you on,"

Literary Analysis
Stream of Consciousness
While Granny is engaged in a dialogue with the doctor, what is really happening in the room?

---

1. **milk leg** painful swelling of the leg.

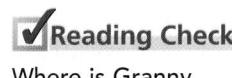

Garden of Memories, Charles Burchfield, The Museum of Modern Art

▲ **Critical Viewing** What elements of this surreal illustration of an old woman in her "garden of memories" might represent Granny Weatherall? **[Connect]**

she shouted, because Doctor Harry appeared to float up to the ceiling and out. "I pay my own bills, and I don't throw my money away on nonsense!"

She meant to wave good-bye, but it was too much trouble. Her eyes closed of themselves, it was like a dark curtain drawn around the bed. The pillow rose and floated under her, pleasant as a hammock in a light wind. She listened to the leaves rustling outside the window.

☑ **Reading Check**

Where is Granny Weatherall as she speaks to the doctor?

The Jilting of Granny Weatherall ◆ 847

No, somebody was swishing newspapers: no, Cornelia and Doctor Harry were whispering together. She leaped broad awake, thinking they whispered in her ear.

"She was never like this, never like this!" "Well, what can we expect?" "Yes, eighty years old. . . ."

Well, and what if she was? She still had ears. It was like Cornelia to whisper around doors. She always kept things secret in such a public way. She was always being tactful and kind. Cornelia was dutiful; that was the trouble with her. Dutiful and good: "So good and dutiful," said Granny, "that I'd like to spank her." She saw herself spanking Cornelia and making a fine job of it.

"What'd you say, Mother?"

Granny felt her face tying up in hard knots.

"Can't a body think, I'd like to know?"

"I thought you might want something."

"I do. I want a lot of things. First off, go away and don't whisper."

She lay and drowsed, hoping in her sleep that the children would keep out and let her rest a minute. It had been a long day. Not that she was tired. It was always pleasant to snatch a minute now and then. There was always so much to be done, let me see: tomorrow.

Tomorrow was far away and there was nothing to trouble about. Things were finished somehow when the time came; thank God there was always a little margin over for peace: then a person could spread out the plan of life and tuck in the edges orderly. It was good to have everything clean and folded away, with the hair brushes and tonic bottles sitting straight on the white embroidered linen: the day started without fuss and the pantry shelves laid out with rows of jelly glasses and brown jugs and white stone-china jars with blue whirligigs and words painted on them: coffee, tea, sugar, ginger, cinnamon, allspice: and the bronze clock with the lion on top nicely dusted off. The dust that lion could collect in twenty-four hours! The box in the attic with all those letters tied up, well, she'd have to go through that tomorrow. All those letters—George's letters and John's letters and her letters to them both—lying around for the children to find afterwards made her uneasy. Yes, that would be tomorrow's business. No use to let them know how silly she had been once.

While she was rummaging around she found death in her mind and it felt clammy and unfamiliar. She had spent so much time preparing for death there was no need for bringing it up again. Let it take care of itself now. When she was sixty she had felt very old, finished, and went around making farewell trips to see her children and grandchildren, with a secret in her mind: This is the very last of your mother, children! Then she made her will and came down with

House Calls

In this story, eighty-year-old Ellen Weatherall dies at home, having been attended by the family doctor. Up until the 1930s, it was a common practice for doctors to deliver most of their services in the home. At that time, medical technology was simple enough that home treatment was as good as—or better than—treatment given in the hospital. However, after World War II, the field of medicine changed dramatically. New techniques for diagnosing and treating illness required special facilities. For example, doctors making house calls could not use X-rays or blood tests to diagnose patients, nor could they perform surgery. People went to the hospital where the resources were available, and the doctor's house call faded into memory.

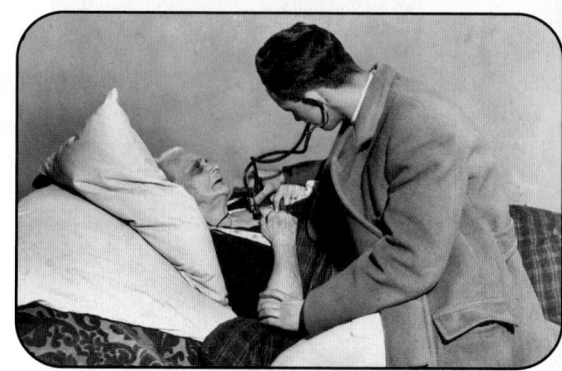

a long fever. That was all just a notion like a lot of other things, but it was lucky too, for she had once for all got over the idea of dying for a long time. Now she couldn't be worried. She hoped she had better sense now. Her father had lived to be one hundred and two years old and had drunk a noggin of strong hot toddy on his last birthday. He told the reporters it was his daily habit, and he owed his long life to that. He had made quite a scandal and was very pleased about it. She believed she'd just plague Cornelia a little.

"Cornelia! Cornelia!" No footsteps, but a sudden hand on her cheek. "Bless you, where have you been?"

"Here, mother."

"Well, Cornelia, I want a noggin of hot toddy."

"Are you cold, darling?"

"I'm chilly, Cornelia. Lying in bed stops the circulation. I must have told you that a thousand times."

Well, she could just hear Cornelia telling her husband that Mother was getting a little childish and they'd have to humor her. The thing that most annoyed her was that Cornelia thought she was deaf, dumb, and blind. Little hasty glances and tiny gestures tossed around her and over her head saying, "Don't cross her, let her have her way, she's eighty years old," and she sitting there as if she lived in a thin glass cage. Sometimes Granny almost made up her mind to pack up and move back to her own house where nobody could remind her every minute that she was old. Wait, wait, Cornelia, till your own children whisper behind your back!

In her day she had kept a better house and had got more work done. She wasn't too old yet for Lydia to be driving eighty miles for advice when one of the children jumped the track, and Jimmy still dropped in and talked things over: "Now, Mammy, you've a good business head, I want to know what you think of this?. . ." Old. Cornelia couldn't change the furniture around without asking. Little things, little things! They had been so sweet when they were little. Granny wished the old days were back again with the children young and everything to be done over. It had been a hard pull, but not too much for her. When she thought of all the food she had cooked, and all the clothes she had cut and sewed, and all the gardens she had made—well, the children showed it. There they were, made out of her, and they couldn't get away from that. Sometimes she wanted to see John again and point to them and say, Well, I didn't do so badly, did I? But that would have to wait. That was for tomorrow. She used to think of him as a man, but now all the children were older than their father, and he would be a child beside her if she saw him now. It seemed strange and there was something wrong in the idea. Why, he couldn't possibly recognize her. She had fenced in a hundred acres once, digging the post holes herself and clamping the wires with just a negro boy to help. That changed a woman. John would be looking for a young woman with the peaked Spanish comb in her hair and the painted fan. Digging post holes changed a woman. Riding country roads in the winter when women had

Literary Analysis
Stream of Consciousness
Notice the path of Granny's thoughts. What are some topics she touches on, and how are they linked in her mind?

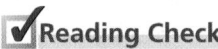

Reading Check

What journey did Granny Weatherall take when she was sixty years old? Why?

their babies was another thing: sitting up nights with sick horses and sick children and hardly ever losing one. John, I hardly ever lost one of them! John would see that in a minute, that would be something he could understand, she wouldn't have to explain anything!

It made her feel like rolling up her sleeves and putting the whole place to rights again. No matter if Cornelia was determined to be everywhere at once, there were a great many things left undone on this place. She would start tomorrow and do them. It was good to be strong enough for everything, even if all you made melted and changed and slipped under your hands, so that by the time you finished you almost forgot what you were working for. What was it I set out to do? she asked herself intently, but she could not remember. A fog rose over the valley, she saw it marching across the creek swallowing the trees and moving up the hill like an army of ghosts. Soon it would be at the near edge of the orchard, and then it was time to go in and light the lamps. Come in, children, don't stay out in the night air.

Lighting the lamps had been beautiful. The children huddled up to her and breathed like little calves waiting at the bars in the twilight. Their eyes followed the match and watched the flame rise and settle in a blue curve, then they moved away from her. The lamp was lit, they didn't have to be scared and hang on to mother any more. Never, never, never more. God, for all my life I thank Thee. Without Thee, my God, I could never have done it. Hail Mary, full of grace.

I want you to pick all the fruit this year and see that nothing is wasted. There's always someone who can use it. Don't let good things rot for want of using. You waste life when you waste good food. Don't let things get lost. It's bitter to lose things. Now, don't let me get to thinking, not when I am tired and taking a little nap before supper. . . .

The pillow rose about her shoulders and pressed against her heart and the memory was being squeezed out of it: oh, push down the pillow, somebody: it would smother her if she tried to hold it. Such a fresh breeze blowing and such a green day with no threats in it. But he had not come, just the same. What does a woman do when she has put on the white veil and set out the white cake for a man and he doesn't come? She tried to remember. No, I swear he never harmed me but in that. He never harmed me but in that . . . and what if he did? There was the day, the day, but a whirl of dark smoke rose and covered it, crept up and over into the bright field where everything was planted so carefully in orderly rows. That was hell, she knew hell when she saw it. For sixty years she had prayed against remembering him and against losing her soul in the deep pit of hell, and now the two things were mingled in one and the thought of him was a smoky cloud from hell that moved and crept in her head when she had just got rid of Doctor Harry and was trying to rest a minute. Wounded vanity, Ellen, said a sharp voice in the top of her mind. Don't let your wounded vanity get the upper hand of you. Plenty of girls get jilted. You were jilted, weren't you? Then stand up to it. Her eyelids wavered and let in streamers of

Literary Analysis
Stream of Consciousness and Flashback What do you learn about Granny from this flashback to a time when her children were small?

Literary Analysis
Stream of Consciousness What memory does Granny try to keep from surfacing? Why?

blue-gray light like tissue paper over her eyes. She must get up and pull the shades down or she'd never sleep. She was in bed again and the shades were not down. How could that happen? Better turn over, hide from the light, sleeping in the light gave you nightmares. "Mother, how do you feel now?" and a stinging wetness on her forehead. But I don't like having my face washed in cold water!

Hapsy? George? Lydia? Jimmy? No, Cornelia, and her features were swollen and full of little puddles. "They're coming, darling, they'll all be here soon." Go wash your face, child, you look funny.

Instead of obeying, Cornelia knelt down and put her head on the pillow. She seemed to be talking but there was no sound. "Well, are you tongue-tied? Whose birthday is it? Are you going to give a party?"

Cornelia's mouth moved urgently in strange shapes. "Don't do that, you bother me, daughter."

"Oh, no, Mother. Oh, no. . . ."

Nonsense. It was strange about children. They disputed your every word. "No what, Cornelia?"

"Here's Doctor Harry."

"I won't see that boy again. He just left five minutes ago."

"That was this morning, Mother. It's night now. Here's the nurse."

"This is Doctor Harry, Mrs. Weatherall. I never saw you look so young and happy!"

"Ah, I'll never be young again—but I'd be happy if they'd let me lie in peace and get rested."

She thought she spoke up loudly, but no one answered. A warm weight on her forehead, a warm bracelet on her wrist, and a breeze went on whispering, trying to tell her something. A shuffle of leaves in the everlasting hand of God, He blew on them and they danced and rattled. "Mother, don't mind, we're going to give you a little hypodermic." "Look here, daughter, how do ants get in this bed? I saw sugar ants yesterday." Did you send for Hapsy too?

It was Hapsy she really wanted. She had to go a long way back through a great many rooms to find Hapsy standing with a baby on her arm. She seemed to herself to be Hapsy also, and the baby on Hapsy's arm was Hapsy and himself and herself, all at once, and there was no surprise in the meeting. Then Hapsy melted from within and turned flimsy as gray gauze and the baby was a gauzy shadow, and Hapsy came up close and said, "I thought you'd never come," and looked at her very searchingly and said, "You haven't changed a bit!" They leaned forward to kiss, when Cornelia began whispering from a long way off, "Oh, is there anything you want to tell me? Is there anything I can do for you?"

Yes, she had changed her mind after sixty years and she would like to see George. I want you to find George. Find him and be sure to tell him I forgot him. I want him to know I had my husband just the same and my children and my house like any other woman. A good house too and a good husband that I loved and fine children out of him. Better than I hoped for even. Tell him I was given back everything he took

Literary Analysis
Stream of Consciousness
What actual events are taking place in the room, and in what ways do they affect Granny's thoughts?

**Reading Check**
What happened to Granny sixty years ago?

away and more. Oh, no, oh, God, no, there was something else besides the house and the man and the children. Oh, surely they were not all? What was it? Something not given back. . . . Her breath crowded down under her ribs and grew into a monstrous frightening shape with cutting edges; it bored up into her head, and the agony was unbelievable: Yes, John, get the Doctor now, no more talk, my time has come.

When this one was born it should be the last. The last. It should have been born first, for it was the one she had truly wanted. Everything came in good time. Nothing left out, left over. She was strong, in three days she would be as well as ever. Better. A woman needed milk in her to have her full health.

"Mother, do you hear me?"

"I've been telling you—"

"Mother, Father Connolly's here."

"I went to Holy Communion only last week. Tell him I'm not so sinful as all that."

"Father just wants to speak to you."

He could speak as much as he pleased. It was like him to drop in and inquire about her soul as if it were a teething baby, and then stay on for a cup of tea and a round of cards and gossip. He always had a funny story of some sort, usually about an Irishman who made his little mistakes and confessed them, and the point lay in some absurd thing he would blurt out in the confessional showing his struggles between native <u>piety</u> and original sin. Granny felt easy about her soul. Cornelia, where are your manners? Give Father Connolly a chair. She had her secret comfortable understanding with a few favorite saints who cleared a straight road to God for her. All as surely signed and sealed as the papers for the new Forty Acres. Forever . . . heirs and assigns[2] forever. Since the day the wedding cake was not cut, but thrown out and wasted. The whole bottom dropped out of the world, and there she was blind and sweating with nothing under <u>her</u> feet and the walls falling away. His hand had caught her under the breast, she had not fallen, there was the freshly polished floor with the green rug on it, just as before. He had cursed like a sailor's parrot and said, "I'll kill him for you." Don't lay a hand on him, for my sake leave something to God. "Now, Ellen, you must believe what I tell you. . . ."

So there was nothing, nothing to worry about any more, except sometimes in the night one of the children screamed in a nightmare, and they both hustled out shaking and hunting for the matches and calling, "There, wait a minute, here we are!" John, get the doctor now, Hapsy's time has come. But there was Hapsy standing by the bed in a white cap. "Cornelia, tell Hapsy to take off her cap. I can't see her plain."

Her eyes opened very wide and the room stood out like a picture she had seen somewhere. Dark colors with the shadows rising towards the ceiling in long angles. The tall black dresser gleamed with nothing

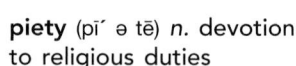

piety (pī´ ə tē) *n.* devotion to religious duties

Literary Analysis
Stream of Consciousness and Flashback What event central to Granny's life do you learn more about in this flashback?

---

2. **assigns** persons to whom property is transferred.

on it but John's picture, enlarged from a little one, with John's eyes
very black when they should have been blue. You never saw him, so
how do you know how he looked? But the man insisted the copy was
perfect, it was very rich and handsome. For a picture, yes, but it's not
my husband. The table by the bed had a linen cover and a candle and
a crucifix. The light was blue from Cornelia's silk lampshades. No sort
of light at all, just <u>frippery</u>. You had to live forty years with kerosene
lamps to appreciate honest electricity. She felt very strong and she
saw Doctor Harry with a rosy nimbus around him.

"You look like a saint, Doctor Harry, and I vow that's as near as
you'll ever come to it."

"She's saying something."

"I heard you, Cornelia. What's all this carrying on?"

"Father Connolly's saying—"

Cornelia's voice staggered and bumped like a cart in a bad road. It
rounded corners and turned back again and arrived nowhere. Granny
stepped up in the cart very lightly and reached for the reins, but a
man sat beside her and she knew him by his hands, driving the cart.
She did not look in his face, for she knew without seeing, but looked
instead down the road where the trees leaned over and bowed to each
other and a thousand birds were singing a Mass. She felt like singing
too, but she put her hand in the bosom of her dress and pulled out a
rosary, and Father Connolly murmured Latin in a very solemn voice
and tickled her feet.[3] My God, will you stop that nonsense? I'm a
married woman. What if he did run away and leave me to face the
priest by myself? I found another a whole world better. I wouldn't
have exchanged my husband for anybody except St. Michael[4] himself,
and you may tell him that for me with a thank you in the bargain.

Light flashed on her closed eyelids, and a deep roaring shook her.
Cornelia, is that lightning? I hear thunder. There's going to be a storm.
Close all the windows. Call the children in. . . . "Mother, here we are,
all of us." "Is that you, Hapsy?" "Oh, no, I'm Lydia. We drove as fast
as we could." Their faces drifted above her, drifted away. The rosary
fell out of her hands and Lydia put it back. Jimmy tried to help, their
hands fumbled together, and Granny closed two fingers around
Jimmy's thumb. Beads wouldn't do, it must be something alive. She
was so amazed her thoughts ran round and round. So, my dear Lord,
this is my death and I wasn't even thinking about it. My children have
come to see me die. But I can't, it's not time. Oh, I always hated surprises. I wanted to give Cornelia the amethyst set—Cornelia, you're to
have the amethyst set, but Hapsy's to wear it when she wants, and,
Doctor Harry, do shut up. Nobody sent for you. Oh, my dear Lord, do
wait a minute. I meant to do something about the Forty Acres, Jimmy
doesn't need it and Lydia will later on, with that worthless husband of
hers. I meant to finish the altar cloth and send six bottles of wine to

---

3. **murmured . . . feet** administered the last rites of the Catholic Church.
4. **St. Michael** one of the archangels.

frippery (frip´ ər ē) *n.*
showy display of
elegance

Literary Analysis
Stream of Consciousness
What is the connecting
link between Granny's
thoughts about her
amethyst set, the Forty
acres, and the altar cloth?

 **Reading Check**

What does Granny finally
realize is happening to her?

Sister Borgia for her dyspepsia. I want to send six bottles of wine to Sister Borgia, Father Connolly, now don't let me forget.

Cornelia's voice made short turns and tilted over and crashed. "Oh, Mother, oh, Mother, oh Mother. . . ."

"I'm not going, Cornelia. I'm taken by surprise. I can't go."

You'll see Hapsy again. What about her? "I thought you'd never come." Granny made a long journey outward, looking for Hapsy. What if I don't find her? What then? Her heart sank down and down, there was no bottom to death, she couldn't come to the end of it. The blue light from Cornelia's lampshade drew into a tiny point in the center of her brain, it flickered and winked like an eye, quietly it fluttered and dwindled. Granny lay curled down within herself, amazed and watchful, staring at the point of light that was herself; her body was now only a deeper mass of shadow in an endless darkness and this darkness would curl around the light and swallow it up. God, give a sign!

For the second time there was no sign. Again no bridegroom and the priest in the house. She could not remember any other sorrow because this grief wiped them all away. Oh, no, there's nothing more cruel than this—I'll never forgive it. She stretched herself with a deep breath and blew out the light.

dyspepsia (dis pep´ shə) *n.* indigestion

Review and Assess

Thinking About the Selection

1. **Respond:** If you were at Granny Weatherall's deathbed, what would you say to help comfort her?

2. **(a) Recall:** Who sits with Granny during her final hours?
   (b) Analyze: What is Granny's attitude toward this person?

3. **(a) Recall:** What are the names of Granny's children?
   (b) Interpret: Which of her children does Granny long to see?
   (c) Deduce: Why is she unable to see this child?

4. **(a) Recall:** As she drifts in and out of consciousness, what memory is "squeezed out" of Granny's heart? **(b) Interpret:** How does Granny try to talk herself out of the pain of this memory?

5. **(a) Interpret:** What memories and details suggest Granny's physical and emotional strength? **(b) Analyze:** Why might the author have chosen "Weatherall" as an appropriate surname for Granny?

6. **(a) Infer:** As she nears death, why does Granny say she "can't go"? **(b) Connect:** What is the connection between her experience of having been jilted sixty years ago and her experiences in the final paragraph?

7. **Speculate:** In what ways might this story have been different if Granny had confronted George after he jilted her?

Review and Assess

Literary Analysis

Stream of Consciousness

1. What effect does the use of **stream of consciousness** have on the reader's perceptions of Granny's children and of Doctor Harry?

2. (a) Find two points at which Granny's thoughts drift from one subject to another that is seemingly unrelated. (b) What natural associations connect her thoughts in each of these examples?

3. In what ways does the stream-of-consciousness technique allow for ambiguity—the presence of different and even conflicting meanings—for specific events or for the story as a whole?

4. Is stream of consciousness an effective technique for this story? Explain.

Connecting Literary Elements

5. (a) What details trigger Granny's **flashback** to lighting the lamps when her children were young? (b) What is the connection between this flashback and her experiences in the present?

6. Use a chart like the one shown to analyze three flashbacks in the story. Identify the form each flashback takes (dream, memory, and so on) and note what you learn about Granny's life from each one.

Form	Trigger		What we learn
		...▶	

Reading Strategy

Clarifying Sequence of Events

7. **Clarify the sequence of events** presented in this story by rearranging them in chronological order.

8. Does the jumbled sequence of events as they appear in the story create a complete picture of Granny's life? Explain.

Extend Understanding

9. **Psychology Connection:** This story was written around 1930. Do you think a young person's experience of being left at the altar would have a less profound impact on his or her life if it happened today? Explain your answer.

Integrate Language Skills

Vocabulary Development Lesson

Word Analysis: Greek Prefix *dys-*

The Greek prefix *dys-*, which means "difficult" or "bad," can help you unlock the meanings of many challenging words.

Write a definition of each word below by combining the meaning of the prefix *dys-* with the clues in parentheses. After you have finished, check your definitions in a dictionary and revise if necessary.

1. dysentery (*entery* = intestine)
2. dysfunctional (*functional* = working properly)
3. dyslexia (*lexis* = word or speech)
4. dyspepsia (*pepsis* = digestion)
5. dystopia (*topos* = place)

Fluency: Sentence Completions

Select the word from the vocabulary list on p. 845 that best completes each sentence.

1. Kelly showed her ___?___ by attending religious services daily.
2. "Pizza aggravates my ___?___," said Mr. Otis.
3. The skaters strutted by, displaying their ___?___ for all to admire.

Spelling Strategy

The suffixes *-ety* and *-ity* change an adjective into a noun. The suffix may be accompanied by other spelling changes as well. For example, *pious* becomes *piety*. For each word below, create a new word using the suffix *-ety* or *-ity*.

1. anxious   2. illegal   3. creative

Grammar and Style Lesson

Imperative Sentences

An **imperative sentence** states a request or gives an order. The subject, *you*, is implied and thus is usually not stated. In this example, notice that the sentence contains three verbs and an implied subject:

> **Example:** "Get along now, take your schoolbooks and go." (*The subject* you *is implied*.)

Practice Review each of the following pairs of sentences. In each pair, identify which example is imperative.

1. (a) Will you get along and doctor your sick?
   (b) Get along and doctor your sick.
2. (a) I want you to stay where you are.
   (b) Stay where you are.
3. (a) They shouldn't be whispering.
   (b) Go away and don't whisper.
4. (a) Be a good girl, and you'll get well.
   (b) If you are good, you'll get well.
5. (a) Don't worry about it.
   (b) You need not worry about it.

Writing Application Rewrite these sentences to make them imperative:

1. Won't you please leave a well woman alone?
2. You shouldn't let Cornelia lead you on.
3. Can't a body think?

W͟G Prentice Hall Writing and Grammar Connection: Chapter 20, Section 1

Writing Lesson

Stream-of-Consciousness Monologue

A monologue is a dramatic form in which only a single character speaks. Create a character, and write a monologue. Like Katherine Anne Porter, incorporate the character's thoughts and memories in a stream-of-consciousness presentation.

Prewriting   List descriptive words and phrases you associate with your character. Group these under the headings "Actions," "Feelings," "Comments," and "Attitudes."

Drafting   Select several memories around which to organize the monologue. To heighten the stream-of-consciousness effect, write without transitions.

> ### Model: Using Details to Create a Vivid Character
>
> Here's the jetway, a chute, really, can't go back. *Tickets out, please!*
> Flying alone that night—was I nine, eleven?—daring myself to
> peer at the tiny lights outside the scratched plastic oval, and the
> awesome blackness of the lake beyond.

The use of specific images emphasizes the character's feelings.

Revising   Read your monologue aloud to hear whether or not it sounds like a genuine and private voice. Add clues to help your audience follow the thought stream and clarify the purpose of the monologue.

 Prentice Hall Writing and Grammar Connection: Chapter 5, Section 4

Extension Activities

Listening and Speaking Suppose that Ellen Weatherall (Granny) and George meet ten years after the jilting. With a partner, role-play the **conversation** they have. To prepare, keep these tips in mind:

- Note details about Ellen's life and how it has changed since the jilting.
- Create a story to explain George's behavior and his life since the jilting.

As you role-play, use language to express the characters' feelings and thoughts and to reflect the time and place in which they live. **[Group Activity]**

Research and Technology Hospice care—benevolent care of terminally ill people—is a growing area of medical specialization. Using a variety of sources, including the Internet and community resources, research the growing hospice field. Use your findings to prepare an **oral report** detailing how Granny might have been cared for in a modern hospice.

 Take It to the Net   www.phschool.com

Go online for an additional research activity using the Internet.

Prepare to Read

Race at Morning ◆ Nobel Prize Acceptance Speech

William Faulkner
(1897–1962)

For some writers, the place of their roots is a wellspring of story material. Oxford, Mississippi, was such a place for William Faulkner. It became the basis for the imaginary world of Yoknapatawpha County—the setting of many of his novels and stories.

A Writer's Roots Although Faulkner never finished high school, he read a great deal and developed an interest in writing from an early age. In 1918, he enlisted in the British Royal Flying Corps and was sent to Canada for training. However, World War I ended before he had a chance to see combat, and he returned to Mississippi. A few years later, longing for a change of scene, Faulkner moved to New Orleans. There, he became friends with author Sherwood Anderson, who offered encouragement and helped get Faulkner's first novel, *Soldier's Pay,* published. In 1926, Faulkner returned home to Oxford, Mississippi, to devote himself to his writing.

A Gold Mine of Inspiration In what he called his "own little postage stamp of native soil," Faulkner uncovered a "gold mine" of inspiration. So compelling and complex was this source of inspiration that Faulkner decided to create a "cosmos of my own"—the fictional county of Yoknapatawpha. From Oxford, Faulkner wrote a series of novels about the decay of traditional values as small communities became swept up in the changes of the modern age. He saw immense dramas acted out in his small, rural town, and he used jumbled time sequences, stream-of-consciousness narration, dialect, page-long sentences, and other difficult techniques to show what he called "the human heart in conflict with itself."

A Slow Spread of Recognition For many years, Faulkner was dismissed as an eccentric—an unimportant regional writer. Gradually, however, critics began to take him seriously. Today, Faulkner is generally considered the most innovative American writer of his time.

Experimenting With Narration The novel that first earned him critical acclaim was *The Sound and the Fury* (1929), a complex book exploring the downfall of an old southern family as seen through the eyes of three brothers, one of whom suffers from severe mental retardation. A year later, Faulkner published *As I Lay Dying,* the story of a poor family's six-day journey to bury their mother. Told from fifteen different points of view and exploring people's varying perspectives of death, the novel was a masterpiece of narrative experimentation. Other innovative works followed, including *Absalom, Absalom!* (1936), which is told by four speakers offering different interpretations of events.

Hollywood Years To earn money during the 1930s and 1940s, Faulkner wrote screenplays in Hollywood. Many of the films he worked on—including *Gunga Din* (1939), *To Have and Have Not* (1945), and *The Big Sleep* (1946)— have become classics of the American cinema.

In some of Faulkner's later works, such as *The Unvanquished* (1938) and *The Hamlet* (1940), he returned to a more traditional style. Yet in these novels, Faulkner continued developing the history of Yoknapatawpha County and its people.

Despite the critical success of his fiction, Faulkner did not earn widespread public recognition until 1946, when *The Portable Faulkner* was published. Four years later, he was awarded the Nobel Prize following the publication of *Intruder in the Dust* (1948), a novel in which he confronted the issue of racism. The narrative techniques he pioneered continue to challenge and inspire writers today.

Preview
Connecting to the Literature

You may have experienced moments when you felt a bond with another person, even though few words passed between you. In this story, a boy confirms his bond to a father figure, not in words, but in an activity the two share—a hunting expedition in the bayous of rural Mississippi.

Literary Analysis
Dialect

Faulkner is a master of **dialect,** a manner of speaking that is common to a particular region or group. Dialect affects pronunciation, word choice, and grammatical structure. Look at the italicized words in this example:

> It was *jest dust-dark*; I had *jest* fed the horses and *clumb* back down . . .

Jest is the way the narrator pronounces *just*. *Dust-dark* is his word for *dusk*, and *clumb* is the way he forms the past participle of *climb*. Faulkner's brilliant use of dialect helps to paint portraits of the characters and lets the reader know more about the fictional world he explores.

Comparing Literary Works

In his famous Nobel Prize acceptance speech, Faulkner voiced some of his beliefs about the importance of literature. He noted that the urgency of a story—its reason for existing—must reflect "the old universal truths . . . —love and honor and pity and pride and compassion and sacrifice." As you read "Race at Morning," think about how it mirrors the beliefs about literature Faulkner expresses in his speech.

Reading Strategy
Breaking Down Long Sentences

Faulkner is famous for writing in long sentences. To meet the challenge, **break down each long sentence** into smaller units of meaning. Using the punctuation as a guide, divide the sentence into sections. Determine the meaning of each section. Then, look for transitions that show how the sections fit together. Use a chart like the one shown to help you.

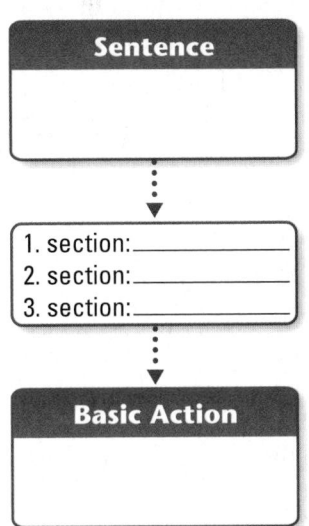

Vocabulary Development

bayou (bī´ ōō´) *n.* marshy inlet (p. 860)

distillery (di stil´ ər ē) *n.* place where alcoholic liquors are distilled (p. 861)

buck (buk) *n.* male animal, especially a male deer (p. 862)

moiling (moi´ liŋ) *v.* churning; swirling (p. 862)

switch (swich) *n.* slender, flexible twig or whip (p. 862)

scrabbling (skrab´ liŋ) *v.* scrambling (p. 866)

swag (swag) *n.* suspended cluster of branches (p. 868)

glade (glād) *n.* open space surrounded by woods (p. 868)

Race at Morning

William Faulkner

Buck and Doe Alerted, Arthur Fitzwilliam Tait, Superstock

I was in the boat when I seen him. It was jest dust-dark; I had jest
fed the horses and clumb back down the bank to the boat and
shoved off to cross back to camp when I seen him, about half a
quarter up the river, swimming; just his head above the water, and
it no more than a dot in that light. But I could see that rocking chair
he toted on it and I knowed it was him, going right back to that
canebrake[1] in the fork of the <u>bayou</u> where he lived all year until the
day before the season opened, like the game wardens had give him a
calendar, when he would clear out and disappear, nobody knowed
where, until the day after the season closed. But here he was, coming

---

1. canebrake *n.* area overgrown with the tall, woody reeds of cane plants.

▲ **Critical Viewing**
Compare the mood of
this painting with the
narrator's description of
the bayou on page 862.
[Compare]

bayou (bī´ o͞o´) *n.* marshy
inlet

back a day ahead of time, like maybe he had got mixed up and was using last year's calendar by mistake. Which was jest too bad for him, because me and Mister Ernest would be setting on the horse right over him when the sun rose tomorrow morning.

So I told Mister Ernest and we et supper and fed the dogs, and then I holp Mister Ernest in the poker game, standing behind his chair until about ten o'clock, when Roth Edmonds said, "Why don't you go to bed, boy?"

"Or if you're going to set up," Willy Legate said, "why don't you take a spelling book to set up over? He knows every cuss word in the dictionary, every poker hand in the deck and every whisky label in the distillery, but he can't even write his name. Can you?" he says to me.

"I don't need to write my name down," I said. "I can remember in my mind who I am."

"You're twelve years old," Walter Ewell said. "Man to man now, how many days in your life did you ever spend in school?"

"He ain't got time to go to school," Willy Legate said. "What's the use in going to school from September to middle of November, when he'll have to quit then to come in here and do Ernest's hearing for him? And what's the use in going back to school in January, when in jest eleven months it will be November fifteenth again and he'll have to start all over telling Ernest which way the dogs went?"

"Well, stop looking into my hand, anyway," Roth Edmonds said.

"What's that? What's that?" Mister Ernest said. He wore his listening button in his ear all the time, but he never brought the battery to camp with him because the cord would bound to get snagged ever time we run through a thicket.

"Willy says for me to go to bed!" I hollered.

"Don't you never call nobody 'mister'?" Willy said.

"I call Mister Ernest 'mister.'" I said.

"All right," Mister Ernest said. "Go to bed then. I don't need you."

"That ain't no lie," Willy said. "Deaf or no deaf, he can hear a fifty-dollar raise if you don't even move your lips."

So I went to bed, and after a while Mister Ernest come in and I wanted to tell him again how big them horns looked even half a quarter away in the river. Only I would 'a' had to holler, and the only time Mister Ernest agreed he couldn't hear was when we would be setting on Dan, waiting for me to point which way the dogs was going. So we jest laid down, and it wasn't no time Simon was beating the bottom of the dishpan with the spoon, hollering, "Raise up and get your four o'clock coffee!" and I crossed the river in the dark this time, with the lantern, and fed Dan and Roth Edmondziz horse. It was going to be a fine day, cold and bright; even in the dark I could see the white frost on the leaves and bushes—jest exactly the kind of day that big old son of a gun laying up there in that brake would like to run.

Then we et, and set the stand-holder across for Uncle Ike McCaslin to put them on the stands where he thought they ought to be, because he was the oldest one in camp. He had been hunting deer in these

Literary Analysis
Dialect What can you infer are the meanings of *jest* and *setting on*?

distillery (di stil´ ə rē) *n.* place where alcoholic liquors are distilled

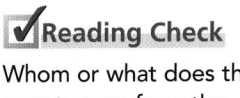
Reading Check
Whom or what does the narrator see from the boat?

woods for about a hundred years, I reckon, and if anybody would know where a <u>buck</u> would pass, it would be him. Maybe with a big old buck like this one, that had been running the woods for what would amount to a hundred years in a deer's life, too, him and Uncle Ike would sholy manage to be at the same place at the same time this morning—provided, of course, he managed to git away from me and Mister Ernest on the jump. Because me and Mister Ernest was going to git him.

Then me and Mister Ernest and Roth Edmonds sent the dogs over, with Simon holding Eagle and the other old dogs on leash because the young ones, the puppies, wasn't going nowhere until Eagle let him, nohow. Then me and Mister Ernest and Roth saddled up, and Mr. Ernest got up and I handed him up his pump gun and let Dan's bridle[2] go for him to git rid of the spell of bucking he had to git shut of ever morning until Mister Ernest hit him between the ears with a gun barrel. Then Mister Ernest loaded the gun and give me the stirrup,[3] and I got up behind him and we taken the fire road up toward the bayou, the four big dogs dragging Simon along in front with his single-barrel britch-loader slung on a piece of plow line across his back, and the puppies <u>moiling</u> along in ever'body's way. It was light now and it was going to be jest fine; the east already yellow for the sun and our breaths smoking in the cold still bright air until the sun would come up and warm it, and a little skim of ice in the ruts, and ever leaf and twig and <u>switch</u> and even the frozen clods frosted over, waiting to sparkle like a rainbow when the sun finally come up and hit them. Until all my insides felt light and strong as a balloon, full of that light cold strong air, so that it seemed to me like I couldn't even feel the horse's back I was straddle of—jest the hot strong muscles moving under the hot strong skin, setting up there without no wait atall, so that when old Eagle struck and jumped, me and Dan and Mister Ernest would go jest like a bird, not even touching the ground. It was jest fine. When that big old buck got killed today, I knowed that even if he had put it off another ten years, he couldn't 'a' picked a better one.

And sho enough, as soon as we come to the bayou we seen his foot in the mud where he had come up out of the river last night, spread in the soft mud like a cow's foot, big as a cow's, big as a mule's, with Eagle and the other dogs laying into the leash rope now until Mister Ernest told me to jump down and help Simon hold them. Because me and Mister Ernest knowed exactly where he would be—a little cane-brake island in the middle of the bayou, where he could lay up until whatever doe or little deer the dogs had happened to jump could go up or down the bayou in either direction and take the dogs on away, so he could steal out and creep back down the bayou to the river and swim it, and leave the country like he always done the day the season opened.

Which is jest what we never aimed for him to do this time. So we left Roth on his horse to cut him off and turn him over Uncle Ike's

---

buck (buk) *n.* male animal, especially a male deer

moiling (moil′ in) *v.* churning; swirling

switch (swich) *n.* slender, flexible twig or whip

Reading Strategy
Breaking Down Long Sentences Break down the long sentence beginning "Because me and Mister Ernest," into sections to clarify the action.

---

2. **bridle** *n.* headgear with which a horse is guided.
3. **stirrup** *n.* rings or other devices attached to the saddle of a horse and used to support the rider's feet.

standers if he tried to slip back down the bayou, and me and Simon, with the leashed dogs, walked on up the bayou until Mister Ernest on the horse said it was fur enough; then turned up into the woods about half a quarter above the brake because the wind was going to be south this morning when it riz, and turned down toward the brake, and Mister Ernest give the word to cast them,[4] and we slipped the leash and Mr. Ernest give me the stirrup again and I got up.

Old Eagle had done already took off because he knowed where that old son of a gun would be laying as good as we did, not making no racket atall yet, but jest boring on through the buck vines with the other dogs trailing along behind him, and even Dan seemed to know about that buck, too, beginning to souple up and jump a little through the vines, so that I taken my holt in Mister Ernest's belt already before the time had come for Mister Ernest to touch him. Because when we got strung out, going fast behind a deer, I wasn't on Dan's back much of the time nohow, but mostly jest strung out from my holt on Mister Ernest's belt, so that Willy Legate said that when we was going through the woods fast, it looked like Mister Ernest had a boy-size pair of empty overalls blowing out of his hind pocket.

So it wasn't even a strike, it was a jump. Eagle must 'a' walked right up behind him or maybe even stepped on him while he was laying there still thinking it was day after tomorrow. Eagle jest threw his head back and up and said, "There he goes," and we even heard the buck crashing through the first of the cane. Then all the other dogs was hollering behind him, and Dan give a squat to jump, but it was against the curb[5] this time, not jest the snaffle,[6] and Mister Ernest let him down into the bayou and swung him around the brake and up the other bank. Only he never had to say, "Which way?" because I was already pointing past his shoulder, freshening my holt on the belt jest as Mister Ernest touched Dan with that big old rusty spur on his nigh heel, because when Dan felt it he would go off jest like a stick of dynamite, straight through whatever he could bust and over and under what he couldn't, over it like a bird or under it crawling on his knees like a mole or a big coon, with Mister Ernest still on him because he had the saddle to hold on to, and me still there because I had Mister Ernest to hold on to; me and Mister Ernest not riding him, but jest going along with him, provided we held on. Because when the jump come, Dan never cared who else was there neither; I believe to my soul he could 'a' cast and run them dogs by hisself, without me or Mister Ernest or Simon or nobody.

That's what he done. He had to; the dogs was already almost out of hearing. Eagle must 'a' been looking right up that big son of a gun's

Literary Analysis
Dialect In the phrase "beginning to souple up," which word shows the speaker is using dialect? What does the word mean in Standard English?

✔ **Reading Check**

What do the hunters notice in the mud of the bayou?

---

4. **cast them** send them ranging overland in search of a trail.
5. **curb** *n.* chain or strap used to restrain a horse.
6. **snaffle** *n.* the part of a bridle that is inserted into the mouth of a horse.

tail until he finally decided he better git on out of there. And now they must 'a' been getting pretty close to Uncle Ike's standers, and Mister Ernest reined Dan back and held him, squatting and bouncing and trembling like a mule having his tail roached,[7] while we listened for the shots. But never none come, and I hollered to Mister Ernest we better go on while I could still hear the dogs, and he let Dan off, but still there wasn't no shots, and now we knowed the race had done already passed the standers, like that old son of a gun actually was a hant,[8] like Simon and the other field hands said he was, and we busted out of a thicket, and sho enough there was Uncle Ike and Willy standing beside his foot in a soft patch.

"He got through us all," Uncle Ike said. "I don't know how he done it. I just had a glimpse of him. He looked big as a elephant, with a rack on his head you could cradle a yellin' calf in. He went right on down the ridge. You better get on, too; that Hog Bayou camp might not miss him."

So I freshened my holt and Mister Ernest touched Dan

Winter in Southern Louisiana, Ellsworth Woodward, Mississippi Museum of Art

again. The ridge run due south; it was clear of vines and bushes so we could go fast, into the wind, too, because it had riz now, and now the sun was up, too; though I hadn't had time to notice it, bright and strong and level through the woods, shining and sparkling like a rainbow on the frosted leaves. So we would hear the dogs again any time now as the wind got up; we could make time now, but still holding Dan back to a canter,[9] because it was either going to be quick, when he got down to the standers from that Hog Bayou camp eight

▲ **Critical Viewing**
In what ways does this painting add to your appreciation of the story's bayou setting? **[Connect]**

---

7. roached *v.* cut so that the remainder stands upright, as with an animal's mane.
8. hant *n.* ghost.
9. canter *n.* three-beat gait resembling, but smoother and slower than, a gallop.

miles below ourn, or a long time, in case he got by them, too. And sho enough, after a while we heard the dogs; we was walking Dan now to let him blow a while, and we heard them, the sound coming faint up the wind, not running now, but trailing because the big son of a gun had decided a good piece back, probably, to put a end to this foolishness, and picked hisself up and soupled out and put about a mile between hisself and the dogs—until he run up on them other standers from that camp below. I could almost see him stopped behind a bush, peeping out and saying, "What's this? What's this? Is this whole durn country full of folks this morning?" Then looking back over his shoulder at where old Eagle and others was hollering along after him while he decided how much time he had to decide what to do next.

Except he almost shaved it too fine. We heard the shots; it sounded like a war. Old Eagle must 'a' been looking right up his tail again and he had to bust on through the best way he could. "Pow, pow, pow, pow" and then "Pow, pow, pow, pow," like it must 'a' been three or four ganged right up on him before he had time even to swerve, and me hollering, "No! No! No! No!" because he was ourn. It was our beans and oats he et and our brake he laid in; we had been watching him every year, and it was like we had raised him, to be killed at last on our jump, in front of our dogs, by some strangers that would probably try to beat the dogs off and drag him away before we could even git a piece of the meat.

"Shut up and listen," Mister Ernest said. So I done it and we could hear the dogs; not just the others, but Eagle, too, not trailing no scent now and not baying[10] no downed meat neither, but running hot on sight long after the shooting was over. I jest had time to freshen my holt. Yes, sir, they was running on sight. Like Willy Legate would say, if Eagle jest had a drink of whisky he would ketch that deer; going on, done already gone when we broke out of the thicket and seen the fellers that had done the shooting, five or six of them, squatting and crawling around, looking at the ground and the bushes, like maybe if they looked hard enough, spots of blood would bloom out on the stalks and leaves like frogstools or hawberries, with old Eagle still in hearing and still telling them that what blood they found wasn't coming out of nothing in front of him.

"Have any luck, boys?" Mister Ernest said.

"I think I hit him," one of them said. "I know I did. We're hunting blood now."

"Well, when you find him, blow your horn and I'll come back and tote him in to camp for you," Mister Ernest said.

So we went on, going fast now because the race was almost out of hearing again, going fast, too, like not jest the buck, but the dogs, too, had took a new leash on life from all the excitement and shooting.

---

10. baying v. barking with long, deep tones.

We was in strange country now because we never had to run this fur before, we had always killed before now; now we had come to Hog Bayou that runs into the river a good fifteen miles below our camp. It had water in it, not to mention a mess of down trees and logs and such, and Mister Ernest checked Dan again, saying, "Which way?" I could just barely hear them, off to the east a little, like the old son of a gun had give up the idea of Vicksburg or New Orleans, like he first seemed to have, and had decided to have a look at Alabama, maybe, since he was already up and moving; so I pointed and we turned up the bayou hunting for a crossing, and maybe we could 'a' found one, except that I reckon Mister Ernest decided we never had time to wait.

We come to a place where the bayou had narrowed down to about twelve or fifteen feet, and Mister Ernest said, "Look out, I'm going to touch him," and done it; I didn't even have time to freshen my holt when we was already in the air, and then I seen the vine—it was a loop of grapevine nigh as big as my wrist, looping down right across the middle of the bayou—and I thought he seen it, too, and was jest waiting to grab it and fling it over our heads to go under it, and I know Dan seen it because he even ducked his head to jump under it. But Mister Ernest never seen it atall until it skun back along Dan's neck and hooked under the head of the saddle horn,[11] us flying on through the air, the loop of the vine gitting tighter and tighter until something somewhere was going to have to give. It was the saddle girth. It broke, and Dan going on and scrabbling up the other bank bare nekkid except for the bridle, and me and Mister Ernest and the saddle, Mister Ernest still setting in the saddle holding the gun, and me still holding onto Mister Ernest's belt, hanging in the air over the bayou in the tightened loop of that vine like in the drawed-back loop of a big rubber-banded slingshot, until it snapped back and shot across the bayou and flang us clear, me still holding onto Mister Ernest's belt and on the bottom now, so that when we lit I would 'a' had Mister Ernest and the saddle both on top of me if I hadn't clumb fast around the saddle and up Mister Ernest's side, so that when we landed, it was the saddle first, then Mister Ernest, and me on top, until I jumped up, and Mister Ernest still laying there with jest the white rim of his eyes showing.

"Mister Ernest!" I hollered, and then clumb down to the bayou and scooped my cap full of water and clumb back and throwed it in his face, and he opened his eyes and laid there on the saddle cussing me.

"God dawg it," he said, "why didn't you stay behind where you started out?"

---

11. **saddle horn** n. knob at the front and top of a saddle.

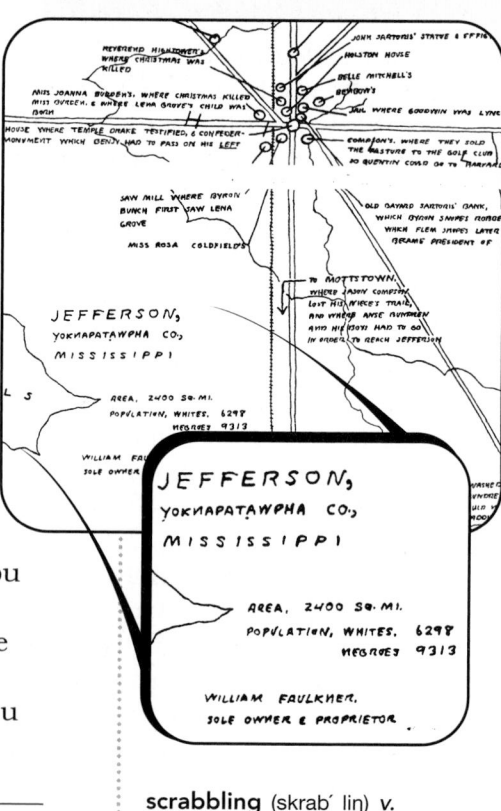

Literature in context Literature Connection

A Guide to Yoknapatawpha County

This story, like most of William Faulkner's work, is set in or near the fictional county of Yoknapatawpha (Yok´ nuh puh TAW´ fuh). Using his real home of Lafayette County as a pattern, Faulkner created an amazingly detailed world—one that was as precise in its geography, history, characters, and language as any real place. In his 1936 novel *Absalom, Absalom!*, Faulkner included a map of Yoknapatawpha county (detail shown below) that he had drawn and annotated. In the map's key, he included information about the county's geographical size (2,400 square miles) and its population (Total: 15,611; Whites, 6298; Negroes, 9313). He also signed the map "William Faulkner, Sole Owner & Proprietor." According to Faulkner, the name Yoknapatawpha is derived from two Chickasaw words, yocona and petopha, and means "water flowing slow through the flatland."

scrabbling (skrab´ lin) v. scrambling

"You was the biggest!" I said. "You would 'a' mashed me flat!"

"What do you think you done to me?" Mister Ernest said. "Next time, if you can't stay where you start out, jump clear. Don't climb on top of me no more. You hear?"

"Yes, sir," I said.

So he got up then, still cussing and holding his back, and clumb down to the water and dipped some in his hand onto his face and neck and dipped some more up and drunk it, and I drunk some, too, and clumb back and got the saddle and the gun, and we crossed the bayou on the down logs. If we could jest ketch Dan; not that he would have went them fifteen miles back to camp, because, if anything, he would have went on by hisself to try to help Eagle ketch that buck. But he was about fifty yards away, eating buck vines, so I brought him back, and we taken Mister Ernest's galluses[12] and my belt and tied the saddle back on Dan. It didn't look like much, but maybe it would hold.

"Provided you don't let me jump him through no more grapevines without hollering first," Mister Ernest said.

"Yes, sir," I said. "I'll holler first next time—provided you'll holler a little quicker when you touch him next time, too." But it was all right; we jest had to be a little easy getting up. "Now which-a-way?" I said. Because we couldn't hear nothing now, after wasting all this time. And this was new country, sho enough. It had been cut over and growed up in thickets we couldn't 'a' seen over even standing up on Dan.

But Mister Ernest never even answered. He jest turned Dan along the bank of the bayou where it was a little more open and we could move faster again, soon as Dan and us got used to that homemade cinch strop[13] and got a little confidence in it. Which jest happened to be east, or so I thought then, because I never paid no particular attention to east then because the sun—I don't know where the morning had went, but it was gone, the morning and the frost, too—was up high now, even if my insides had told me it was past dinnertime.

And then we heard him. No, that's wrong; what we heard was shots. And that was when we realized how fur he had come, because the only camp we knowed about in that direction was the Hollyknowe camp, and Hollyknowe was exactly twenty-eight miles from Van Dorn, where me and Mister Ernest lived—jest the shots, no dogs nor nothing. If old Eagle was still behind him and the buck was still alive, he was too wore out now to even say, "Here he comes."

"Don't touch him!" I hollered. But Mister Ernest remembered that cinch strop, too, and he jest let Dan off the snaffle. And Dan heard them shots, too; picking his way through the thickets, hopping the vines and logs when he could and going under them when he couldn't. And sho enough, it was jest like before—two or three men squatting

Literary Analysis
Dialect How would you restate the passage beginning "If we could jest ketch Dan" in Standard English?

---

12. **galluses** n. suspenders.
13. **cinch strop** n. strap that encircles the body of an animal and is used to fasten something on its back.

**Reading Check**

What happens to Mister Ernest when Dan hits the grapevine?

and creeping among the bushes, looking for blood that Eagle had done already told them wasn't there. But we never stopped this time, jest trotting on by with Dan hopping and dodging among the brush and vines dainty as a dancer. Then Mister Ernest swung Dan until we was going due north.

"Wait!" I hollered. "Not this way."

But Mister Ernest jest turned his face back over his shoulder. It looked tired, too, and there was a smear of mud on it where that ere grapevine had snatched him off the horse.

"Don't you know where he's heading?" he said. "He's done done his part, give everybody a fair open shot at him, and now he's going home, back to that brake in our bayou. He ought to make it exactly at dark."

And that's what he was doing. We went on. It didn't matter to hurry now. There wasn't no sound nowhere; it was that time in the early afternoon in November when don't nothing move or cry, not even birds, the peckerwoods and yellowhammers and jays, and it seemed to me like I could see all three of us—me and Mister Ernest and Dan—and Eagle, and the other dogs, and that big old buck, moving through the quiet woods in the same direction, headed for the same place, not running now but walking, that had all run the fine race the best we knowed how, and all three of us now turned like on a agreement to walk back home, not together in a bunch because we didn't want to worry or tempt one another, because what we had all three spent this morning doing was no playacting jest for fun, but was serious, and all three of us was still what we was—that old buck that had to run, not because he was skeered, but because running was what he done the best and was proudest at; and Eagle and the dogs that chased him, not because they hated or feared him, but because that was the thing they done the best and was proudest at; and me and Mister Ernest and Dan, that run him not because we wanted his meat, which would be too tough to eat anyhow, or his head to hang on a wall, but because now we could go back and work hard for eleven months making a crop, so we would have the right to come back here next November—all three of us going back home now, peaceful and separate, but still side by side, until next year, next time.

Then we seen him for the first time. We was out of the cut-over now; we could even 'a' cantered, except that all three of us was long past that, and now you could tell where west was because the sun was already half-way down it. So we was walking, too, when we come on the dogs—the puppies and one of the old ones—played out, laying in a little wet <u>swag</u>, panting, jest looking up at us when we passed, but not moving when we went on. Then we come to a long open <u>glade</u>, you could see about half a quarter, and we seen the three other old dogs and about a hundred yards ahead of them Eagle, all walking, not making no sound; and then suddenly, at the fur end of the glade, the buck hisself getting up from where he had been resting for the dogs to come up, getting up without no hurry, big, big as a mule, tall as a

Reading Strategy
Breaking Down Long Sentences Why do you think Faulkner chose to combine all of this information into one long sentence beginning "There wasn't no sound"?

swag (swag) *n.* suspended cluster of branches

glade (glād) *n.* open space surrounded by woods

Old Man and the Boy, John Head, Russell A. Fink Gallery

mule, and turned without no hurry still, and the white underside of his tail for a second or two more before the thicket taken him.

It might 'a' been a signal, a good-bye, a farewell. Still walking, we passed the other three old dogs in the middle of the glade, laying down, too, now jest where they was when the buck vanished, and not trying to get up neither when we passed; and still that hundred yards ahead of them, Eagle, too, not laying down, because he was still on his feet, but his legs was spraddled and his head was down; maybe jest waiting until we was out of sight of his shame, his eyes saying plain as talk when we passed, "I'm sorry, boys, but this here is all."

Mister Ernest stopped Dan. "Jump down and look at his feet," he said.

"Ain't nothing wrong with his feet," I said. "It's his wind has done give out."

"Jump down and look at his feet," Mister Ernest said.

So I done it, and while I was stooping over Eagle I could hear the pump gun go, "Snick-cluck, Snick-cluck. Snick-cluck" three times, except that I never thought nothing then. Maybe he was jest running the shells through to be sho it would work when we seen him again or maybe to make sho they was all buckshot.[14] Then I got up again, and

---

14. **buckshot** *n.* large lead shot used for shooting deer and other big game.

▲ **Critical Viewing** Do you think this painting effectively illustrates the story? Explain. **[Evaluate]**

✓ **Reading Check**

What does Mister Ernest do with the pump gun as the boy checks Dan's feet?

Race at Morning ◆ 869

we went on, still walking; a little west of north now, because when we seen his white flag that second or two before the thicket hid it, it was on a beeline for that notch in the bayou. And it was evening, too, now. The wind had done dropped and there was a edge to the air and the sun jest touched the tops of the trees now, except jest now and then, when it found a hole to come almost level through onto the ground. And he was taking the easiest way, too, now, going straight as he could. When we seen his foot in the soft places he was running for a while at first after his rest. But soon he was walking, too, like he knowed, too, where Eagle and the dogs was.

And then we seen him again. It was the last time—a thicket, with the sun coming through a hole onto it like a searchlight. He crashed jest once; then he was standing there broadside to us, not twenty yards away, big as a statue and red as gold in the sun, and the sun sparking on the tips of his horns—they was twelve of them—so that he looked like he had twelve lighted candles branched around his head, standing there looking at us while Mister Ernest raised the gun and aimed at his neck, and the gun went, "Click. Snick-cluck. Click, Snick-cluck. Click. Snick-cluck" three times, and Mister Ernest still holding the gun aimed while the buck turned and give one long bound, the white underside of his tail like a blaze of fire, too, until the thicket and the shadows put it out; and Mister Ernest laid the gun slow and gentle back across the saddle in front of him, saying quiet and peaceful, and not much louder than jest breathing, "God dawg. God dawg."

Then he jogged me with his elbow and we got down, easy and careful because of that ere cinch strop and he reached into his vest and taken out one of the cigars. It was busted where I had fell on it, I reckon, when we hit the ground. He throwed it away and taken out the other one. It was busted, too, so he bit off a hunk of it to chew and throwed the rest away. And now the sun was gone even from the tops of the trees and there wasn't nothing left but a big red glare in the west.

"Don't worry," I said. "I ain't going to tell them you forgot to load your gun. For that matter, they don't need to know we ever seed him."

"Much oblige," Mister Ernest said. There wasn't going to be no moon tonight neither, so he taken the compass off the whang leather loop in his buttonhole and handed me the gun and set the compass on a stump and stepped back and looked at it. "Just about the way we're headed now," he said, and taken the gun from me and opened it and put one shell in the britch and taken up the compass, and I taken Dan's reins and we started, with him in front with the compass in his hand.

And after a while it was full dark; Mister Ernest would have to strike a match ever now and then to read the compass, until the stars come out good and we could pick out one to follow, because I said, "How fur do you reckon it is?" A little more than one box of matches." So we used a star when we could, only we couldn't see it

Reading Strategy
Breaking Down Long Sentences What information is conveyed in the long sentence beginning "He crashed just once"? Why do you think Faulkner chose to provide this information in such a long sentence?

all the time because the woods was too dense and we would git a little off until he would have to spend another match. And now it was good and late, and he stopped and said, "Get on the horse."

"I ain't tired," I said.

"Get on the horse," he said. "We don't want to spoil him."

Because he had been a good feller ever since I had knowed him, which was even before that day two years ago when maw went off with the Vicksburg roadhouse feller and the next day pap didn't come home neither, and on the third one Mister Ernest rid Dan up to the door of the cabin on the river he let us live in, so pap could work his piece of land and run his fish line, too, and said, "Put that gun down and come on here and climb up behind."

So I got in the saddle even if I couldn't reach the stirrups, and Mister Ernest taken the reins and I must 'a' went to sleep, because the next thing I knowed a button hole of my lumberjack was tied to the saddle horn with that ere whang cord off the compass, and it was good and late now and we wasn't fur, because Dan was already smelling water, the river. Or maybe it was the feed lot itself he smelled, because we struck the fire road not a quarter below it, and soon I could see the river, too, with the white mist laying on it soft and still as cotton. Then the lot, home; and up yonder in the dark, not no piece akchully, close enough to hear us unsaddling and shucking corn prob'ly, and sholy close enough to hear Mister Ernest blowing his horn at the dark camp for Simon to come in the boat and git us, that old buck in his brake in the bayou; home, too, resting, too, after the hard run, waking hisself now and then, dreaming of dogs behind him or maybe it was the racket we was making would wake him, but not neither of them for more than jest a little while before sleeping again.

Then Mister Ernest stood on the bank blowing until Simon's lantern went bobbing down into the mist; then we clumb down to the landing and Mister Ernest blowed again now and then to guide Simon, until we seen the lantern in the mist, and then Simon and the boat; only it looked like ever time I set down and got still, I went back to sleep, because Mister Ernest was shaking me again to git out and climb the bank into the dark camp, until I felt a bed against my knees and tumbled into it.

Then it was morning, tomorrow; it was all over now until next November, next year, and we could come back. Uncle Ike and Willy and Walter and Roth and the rest of them had come in yestiddy, soon as Eagle taken the buck out of hearing and they knowed that deer was gone, to pack up and be ready to leave this morning for Yoknapatawpha, where they lived, until it would be November again and they could come back again.

So, as soon as we et breakfast, Simon run them back up the river in the big boat to where they left their cars and pickups, and now it wasn't nobody but jest me and Mister Ernest setting on the back against the kitchen wall in the sun; Mister Ernest smoking a cigar—a whole one this time that Dan hadn't had no chance to jump

✔ **Reading Check**

What does Mister Ernest do when he sees the buck for the last time?

through a grapevine and bust. He hadn't washed his face neither where that vine had throwed him into the mud. But that was all right, too; his face usually did have a smudge of mud or tractor grease or beard stubble on it, because he wasn't jest a planter; he was a farmer, he worked as hard as ara one of his hands and tenants—which is why I knowed from the very first that we would git along, that I wouldn't have no trouble with him and he wouldn't have no trouble with me, from that very first day when I woke up and maw had done gone off with that Vicksburg roadhouse feller without even waiting to cook breakfast, and the next morning pap was gone, too, and it was almost night the next day when I heard a horse coming up and I taken the gun that I had already throwed a shell into the britch when pap never came home last night, and stood in the door while Mister Ernest rid up and said, "Come on. Your paw ain't coming back neither."

"You mean he give me to you?" I said.

"Who cares?" He said. "Come on. I brought a lock for the door. We'll send the pickup back tomorrow for whatever you want."

So I come home with him and it was all right, it was jest fine—his wife had died about three years ago—without no women to worry us or take off in the middle of the night with a durn Vicksburg roadhouse jake without even wanting to cook breakfast. And we would go home this afternoon, too, but not jest yet; we always stayed one more day after the others left because Uncle Ike always left what grub they hadn't et, and the rest of the homemade corn whisky he drunk and that town whisky of Roth Edmondziz he called Scotch that smelled like it come out of a old bucket of roof paint; setting in the sun for one more day before we went back home to get ready to put in next year's crop of cotton and oats and beans and hay; and across the river yonder, behind the wall of trees where the big woods started, that old buck laying up today in the sun, too—resting today, too, without nobody to bother him until next November.

So at least one of us was glad it would be eleven months and two weeks before he would have to run that fur that fast again. So he was glad of the very same thing we was sorry of, and so all of a sudden I thought about how maybe planting and working and then harvesting oats and cotton and beans and hay wasn't jest something me and Mister Ernest done three hundred and fifty-one days to fill in the time until we could come back hunting again, but it was something we had to do, and do honest and good during the three hundred and fifty-one days, to have the right to come back into the big woods and hunt for the other fourteen; and the fourteen days that old buck run in front of dogs wasn't jest something to fill his time until the three hundred and fifty-one when he didn't have to, but the running and the risking in front of guns and dogs was something he had to do for fourteen days to have the right not to be bothered for the other three hundred and fifty-one. And so the hunting and the farming wasn't two different things atall—they was jest the other side of each other.

"Yes," I said. "All we got to do now is put in that next year's crop. Then November won't be no time away at all."

"You ain't going to put in the crop next year," Mister Ernest said. "You're going to school."

So at first I didn't even believe I had heard him. "What?" I said. "Me? Go to school?"

"Yes," Mister Ernest said.

"You must make something out of yourself."

"I am," I said. "I'm doing it now. I'm going to be a hunter and a farmer like you."

"No," Mister Ernest said. "That ain't enough any more. Time was when all a man had to do was just farm eleven and a half months, and hunt the other half. But not now. Now just to belong to the farming business and the hunting business ain't enough. You got to belong to the business of mankind."

"Mankind?" I said.

"Yes," Mister Ernest said. "So you're going to school. Because you got to know why. You can belong to the farming and hunting business and you can learn the difference between what's right and what's wrong, and do right. And that used to be enough—just to do right. But not now. You got to know why it's right and why it's wrong, and be able to tell the folks that never had no chance to learn it; teach them how to do what's right, not just because they know it's right, but because they know now why it's right because you just showed them, told them, taught them why. So you're going to school."

"It's because you been listening to that durn Will Legate and Walter Ewell!" I said.

"No," Mister Ernest said.

"Yes!" I said. "No wonder you missed that buck yestiddy, taking ideas from the very fellers that let him get away, after me and you had run Dan and the dogs durn nigh clean to death! Because you never even missed him! You never forgot to load that gun! You had done already unloaded it a purpose! I heard you!"

"All right, all right," Mister Ernest said. "Which would you rather have? His bloody head and hide on the kitchen floor yonder and half his meat in a pickup truck on the way to Yoknapatawpha County,

✔Reading Check

What is the reason the boy will not plant the crop next year?

or him with his head and hide and meat still together over yonder in that brake, waiting for next November for us to run him again?"

"And git him, too," I said. "We won't even fool with no Willy Legate and Walter Ewell next time."

"Maybe," Mister Ernest said.

"Yes," I said.

"Maybe," Mister Ernest said. "The best word in our language, the best of all. That's what mankind keeps going on: Maybe. The best days of his life ain't the ones when he said 'Yes' beforehand: they're the ones when all he knew to say was 'Maybe.' He can't say 'Yes' until afterward because he not only don't know it until then, he don't want to know 'Yes' until then . . . Step in the kitchen and make me a toddy. Then we'll see about dinner."

"All right," I said. I got up. "You want some of Uncle Ike's corn or that town whisky of Roth Edmondziz?"

"Can't you say Mister Roth or Mister Edmonds?" Mister Ernest said.

"Yes, sir," I said. "Well, which do you want? Uncle Ike's corn or that ere stuff of Roth Edmondziz?"

Review and Assess

Thinking About the Selection

1. **Respond:** If you had the opportunity, would you join the hunters on their yearly trip to the bayou? Explain.

2. **(a) Recall:** During the card game, what do the men reveal about the narrator's school career? **(b) Speculate:** Why might Faulkner include a discussion about school early in the story?

3. **(a) Recall:** What happened to the boy's parents?
   (b) Recall: Under what circumstances did the boy go to live with Mister Ernest? **(c) Support:** Find two examples from the story that support the conclusion that the boy trusts and feels relaxed with Mister Ernest.

4. **(a) Infer:** When Mister Ernest fires at the deer, it does not die. Why not? **(b) Analyze:** According to Mister Ernest, why is it better to have let the deer live than to have killed it?

5. **(a) Recall:** Why does Mister Ernest say the boy will not be planting next year's crop? **(b) Interpret:** What are Mr. Ernest's hopes for the boy?

6. **Evaluate:** Evaluate Faulkner's success in connecting the significance of the hunt to the significance of Mister Ernest's plans for the boy.

7. **(a) Generalize:** What values or moral code do you think Mister Ernest lives by? **(b) Take a Position:** Are Mister Ernest's values universal, or are they particular to a time and place? Explain.

Nobel Prize Acceptance Speech

WILLIAM FAULKNER

Background

The Swedish chemist Alfred Nobel earned fame as the inventor of dynamite. Nobel had intended dynamite to be used safely in mining and construction, but disasters often occurred, and his name became associated with tragedy. Nobel eventually succeeded in making dynamite safer. Later, he sought to make the world a better place by establishing a foundation to encourage achievement and diplomacy. The Nobel Prizes, given for achievement in the fields of physics, chemistry, medicine, literature, and world peace, are the result of his efforts. They are the world's most prestigious awards. When William Faulkner received the Nobel Prize for literature in 1950, he gave an acceptance speech that is among the simplest and most moving examples of oratory in our literature.

Stockholm, Sweden
December 10, 1950

I feel that this award was not made to me as a man, but to my work—a life's work in the agony and sweat of the human spirit, not for glory and least of all for profit, but to create out of the materials of the human spirit something which did not exist before. So this award is only mine in trust. It will not be difficult to find a dedication for the money part of it commensurate with the purpose and significance of its origin. But I would like to do the same with the acclaim too, by using this moment as a pinnacle from which I might be listened to by the young men and women already dedicated to the same anguish and travail, among whom is already that one who will some day stand here where I am standing.

Our tragedy today is a general and universal physical fear so long sustained by now that we can even bear it. There are no longer problems of the spirit. There is only the question: When will I be blown up? Because of this, the young man or woman writing today has forgotten the problems of the human heart in conflict with itself which alone can make good writing because only that is worth writing about, worth the agony and the sweat.

He must learn them again. He must teach himself that the basest of all things is to be afraid; and, teaching himself that, forget it forever, leaving no room in his workshop for anything but the old verities and

Reading Check

What does Faulkner believe is the only subject that can yield good writing?

truths of the heart, the old universal truths lacking which any story is ephemeral and doomed—love and honor and pity and pride and compassion and sacrifice. Until he does so, he labors under a curse. He writes not of love but of lust, of defeats in which nobody loses anything of value, of victories without hope and, worst of all, without pity or compassion. His griefs grieve on no universal bones, leaving no scars. He writes not of the heart but of the glands.

Until he relearns these things, he will write as though he stood among and watched the end of man. I decline to accept the end of man. It is easy enough to say that man is immortal simply because he will endure: that when the last ding-dong of doom has clanged and faded from the last worthless rock hanging tideless in the last red and dying evening, that even then there will still be one more sound: that of his puny inexhaustible voice, still talking. I refuse to accept this. I believe that man will not merely endure: he will prevail. He is immortal, not because he alone among creatures has an inexhaustible voice, but because he has a soul, a spirit capable of compassion and sacrifice and endurance. The poet's, the writer's, duty is to write about these things. It is his privilege to help man endure by lifting his heart, by reminding him of the courage and honor and hope and pride and compassion and pity and sacrifice which have been the glory of his past. The poet's voice need not merely be the record of man, it can be one of the props, the pillars to help him endure and prevail.

Review and Assess

Thinking About the Selection

1. **Respond:** Do you agree with Faulkner's definition of good literature? If not, how would you revise it?

2. **(a) Recall:** According to Faulkner, why are there no longer problems of the spirit? **(b) Deduce:** What is the physical fear to which he refers?

3. **(a) Recall:** According to Faulkner, what alone is the subject matter of good writing? **(b) Interpret:** Why does he view most modern literature as ephemeral?

4. **(a) Recall:** According to Faulkner, will humanity endure or prevail? **(b) Define:** In what way does Faulkner define the difference between enduring and prevailing?

5. **(a) Recall:** According to Faulkner, what is a writer's "duty"? **(b) Interpret:** What distinction does he draw about "the poet's voice" in his explanation of how humanity can prevail?

6. **(a) Extend:** What events not long before 1950 gave rise to the fear of which Faulkner speaks? **(b) Hypothesize:** If he were alive today, would he say we have lost or retained that fear? Explain.

Review and Assess

Literary Analysis

Dialect

1. Use a chart like the one shown to analyze the following passage of **dialect** in "Race at Morning."

   > So I come home with him and it was all right, it was jest fine—his wife had died about three years ago—without no women to worry us or take off in the middle of the night with a durn Vicksburg roadhouse jake . . .

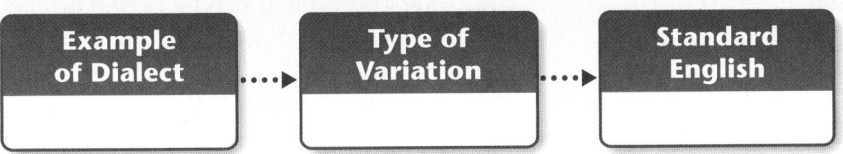

Example of Dialect	....▶	Type of Variation	....▶	Standard English

2. If you were to rewrite "Race at Morning" in Standard English, (a) What would be lost? (b) What would be gained?

Comparing Literary Works

3. (a) In what ways does Mister Ernest's insistence on the boy's attending to the "business of mankind" reflect the message of Faulkner's speech? (b) What is the "business of mankind"?

4. (a) According to Mister Ernest, why is "maybe" the best word in the language? (b) In what ways does Mr. Ernest's explanation relate to the message of human potential in Faulkner's speech?

Reading Strategy

Breaking Down Long Sentences

5. Select a long sentence from "Race at Morning." (a) Using the punctuation as a guide, divide the sentence into sections. (b) Identify the section of the sentence that contains its subject. (c) Rewrite each section as a separate sentence, connected by transitions.

6. In **breaking down** his **long sentences,** what insights do you gain into Faulkner's style?

Extend Understanding

7. **Media Connection:** Identify several popular films you have seen. Then, decide whether Faulkner would have approved of each one. Explain your responses.

Quick Review

Dialect is a manner of speaking that is common to a particular region or group. Dialect affects pronunciation, word choice, and grammatical structure.

Break down long sentences into smaller units of meaning in order to better understand them.

 Take It to the Net
www.phschool.com
Take the interactive self-test online to check your understanding of these selections.

Integrate Language Skills

Vocabulary Development Lesson

Word Analysis: Latin Suffix -ery

The Latin suffix -ery (or -ry), meaning "state or quality of," "place of," or "a kind of behavior," is used to form nouns from verbs or other nouns. For example, the verb *distill* means "to refine" or "to extract." The noun *distillery* means a place where something is distilled. Use this information to define each of the following words.

    1. creamery   **2.** finery   **3.** snobbery

Spelling Strategy

Nouns meaning "state or quality of" or "place of" often end in -ery, as in the words *slavery* and *refinery*. The ending -ary is usually reserved for nouns designating a person or thing related to or connected with something (such as *functionary*) or for adjectives meaning "related to" or "connected with" (such as *budgetary*). Create new nouns for the words below using one of these two suffixes.

    1. trick   **2.** diet   **3.** diction

Concept Development: Definitions

Review the vocabulary list on p. 859. Then, answer each of the following questions, basing your answers on the meaning of the italicized words.

1. Can you plow a *bayou*?

2. Are the typical products of a *distillery* suitable for children to consume?

3. Is a *buck* a male animal?

4. Would a *moiling* puppy be standing still?

5. Might you find a *switch* in the woods?

6. Is *scrabbling* a quick movement?

7. Is a *swag* something you would find in the forest?

8. If you wanted to get some sun, would you head for a *glade*?

Grammar and Style Lesson

Correct Use of Irregular Verb Forms

The narrator of "Race at Morning" often mistakenly conjugates **irregular verbs**—verbs whose past tenses and past participles are not formed by adding -ed or -d to the present form—as regular verbs. While the boy's speech captures his dialect, helping Faulkner place the story in a specific setting, these kinds of conjugations are considered incorrect in Standard English.

> **Incorrect:** I *knowed* it was him.
>
> **Correct:** I *knew* it was him.

Practice Rewrite each incorrect verb that follows in its correct irregular form. Then, write a sentence that uses each verb correctly.

    1. eated   **4.** gived
    2. rised   **5.** throwed
    3. goed

Writing Application Select three sentences from "Race at Morning" in which the characters conjugate irregular verbs incorrectly. Then, rewrite the sentences using Standard English. Consult a grammar book, if necessary.

WG *Prentice Hall Writing and Grammar Connection: Chapter 21, Section 1*

Writing Lesson

Critical Review

In his Nobel Prize acceptance speech, Faulkner notes that the writer's duty is to help people "endure by lifting their hearts, by reminding them of the courage and honor and hope and pride and compassion and pity and sacrifice which have been the glory of their past." Choose a short story and evaluate it in terms of how well the author fulfills Faulkner's ideal.

Prewriting Choose a story for analysis, and read it closely. Make notes about whether the author has succeeded or failed, according to Faulkner's standards.

Drafting Start your review with a statement of your position. Then, elaborate by providing details and passages from the story.

Model: Drafting to Elaborate on an Idea

In "The Story of an Hour," Kate Chopin fulfills Faulkner's criteria for writing about "truths of the heart." The core of the tale rests in Mrs. Mallard's thoughts and feelings as she greets the prospect of personal freedom: "Free! Body and soul free!" she exults.

> Including specific information elaborates on a basic idea.

Revising Reread your review to confirm you have provided solid supporting evidence for your ideas.

Prentice Hall Writing and Grammar Connection: Chapter 14, Section 3

Extension Activities

Listening and Speaking As a radio announcer, create a **broadcast** of the hunt in "Race at Morning." Prepare your broadcast by reviewing the story closely and making an outline of events. To the basic outline, add details about

- the weather.
- the activities.
- the apparent feelings of the men, horses, dogs, and deer.

Allow your voice to reveal tension or excitement as your reading of the hunt progresses. Close with an insight into the story's events.

Research and Technology With a classmate, stage a **debate** about the pros and cons of hunting. Prepare for the debate by gathering information, opinions, and facts that represent the wide range of opinions on this subject. Then, argue the subject from the point of view of farmers, animals rights supporters, hunting enthusiasts, and others. **[Group Activity]**

 **Take It to the Net** www.phschool.com

Go online for an additional research activity using the Internet.

Prepare to Read

Robert Frost's Poetry

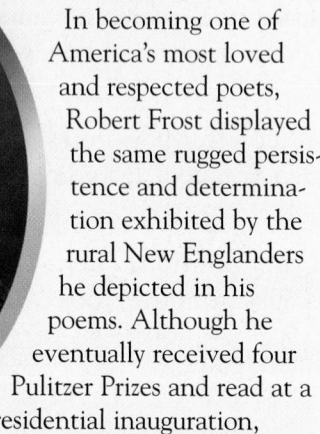

**Robert Frost
(1874–1963)**
In becoming one of America's most loved and respected poets, Robert Frost displayed the same rugged persistence and determination exhibited by the rural New Englanders he depicted in his poems. Although he eventually received four Pulitzer Prizes and read at a presidential inauguration, Frost's success as a poet did not come overnight or easily. Only after years of rejection by book and magazine publishers did he finally achieve the acceptance for which he had worked so hard.

Early Struggles Frost was born in San Francisco, California. His father died when Frost was eleven, and his mother moved the family to the textile city of Lawrence, Massachusetts. After graduating from high school, Frost briefly attended Dartmouth College. Disliking college life, he left school and spent time working as a farmer, mill hand, journalist, and schoolteacher. During his spare time, he wrote poetry and dreamed of someday being able to support himself solely by writing.

The English Years Frost married and spent ten years farming in New Hampshire. In 1912, unable to get his poems published, he sold the farm and moved his family to England. Once there, he hoped to establish himself as a poet. While living in England, Frost befriended a number of well-known poets, including Ezra Pound, and succeeded in publishing two collections of poetry, *A Boy's Will* (1913) and *North of Boston* (1914). When Frost returned to the United States in

1915, he discovered that his success in England had spread across the Atlantic, and he was on the road to fame.

Critical Acclaim Frost went on to publish several more volumes of poetry, for which he received many awards. He also taught at Amherst College, the University of Michigan, Harvard University, and Dartmouth College and lectured and read at dozens of other schools. Recognition of his poetry did not stop him from farming in Vermont and New Hampshire. In 1960, at John F. Kennedy's invitation, Frost became the first poet to read his work at a presidential inauguration.

New England Life Frost's poetry was popular not only with critics and intellectuals, but also among the general public. He used traditional verse forms and conversational language to paint vivid portraits of the New England landscape and lifestyle. Despite their apparent simplicity, however, his poems are filled with profound meanings, compelling readers to delve beneath the surface to fully appreciate his work.

"Ice on a hot stove" Frost was emphatic about his belief that a poem should reveal its meaning in a continuous process. He wrote: "Like a piece of ice on a hot stove the poem must ride on its own melting. A poem may be worked over since it is in being, but may not be worried into being. Its most precious quality will remain its having run itself and carried away the poet with it. Read it a hundred times: it will forever keep its freshness as a petal keeps its fragrance. It can never lose its sense of a meaning that once unfolded by surprise as it went."

Like his poetry, Frost's personality also had multiple levels. In his public appearances, Frost presented himself as a jovial, folksy farmer who just happened to write poetry. In reality, however, Frost was a deep thinker whose darker, complicated personality sometimes mystified those who knew him.

Preview

Connecting to the Literature

Popular psychology holds that we are, at least in part, products of our environments, suggesting that the way we feel and act on a busy city street will be different from our emotions and behavior when surrounded by nature. In these poems, the setting plays an integral role in creating mood and meaning.

Literary Analysis

Blank Verse

Many of Frost's poems do not contain rhyme, but their lines have a regular pattern of stressed and unstressed syllables, or *meter*.

- The basic unit of meter is a *foot*—usually one stressed syllable and one or more unstressed syllables.
- The most common foot is the *iamb*—one unstressed syllable followed by a stressed syllable.
- A line containing five iambs is written in *iambic pentameter*.
- Verse consisting of unrhymed lines of iambic pentameter is called **blank verse.**

As you read Frost's poems, use a chart like the one shown to identify those that have been written in blank verse and those that are in rhyming iambic pentameter.

Comparing Literary Works

Five of these poems by Frost can be categorized as **pastorals**—poems that deal with rural settings. Traditionally, pastoral poems have presented idealized views of rural life. In Frost's hands, however, rural life is sometimes fraught with ethical lapses, accidents, and even violence. As you read these poems, look closely at how the poet portrays rural life, and examine the differing ways in which the setting contributes to each poem's larger meaning.

Reading Strategy

Reading Blank Verse

One way to appreciate **blank verse** is to read it aloud in sentences rather than in poetic lines. Avoid pausing at the end of each line. Instead, follow the punctuation as if you were reading prose: pause briefly after commas, and pause longer after periods. Notice how the flow of blank verse recreates the natural cadences of speech.

Vocabulary Development

poise (poiz) *n.* balance; stability (p. 883)

rueful (rōō′ fəl) *adj.* feeling or showing someone sorrow or pity (p. 889)

luminary (lōō′ mə ner′ ē) *adj.* giving off light (p. 892)

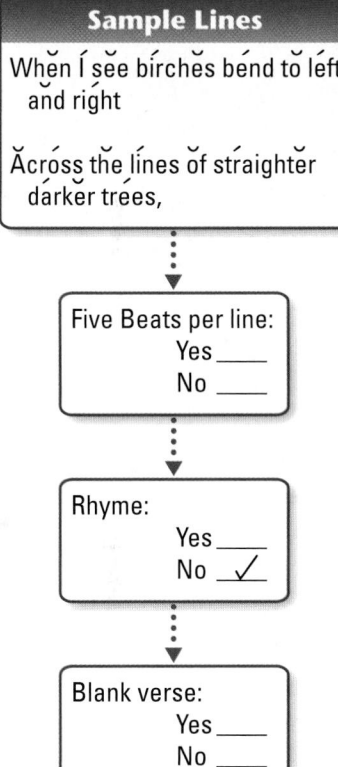

Sample Lines

When I see birches bend to left and right

Across the lines of straighter darker trees,

Five Beats per line:
Yes ____
No ____

Rhyme:
Yes ____
No ✓

Blank verse:
Yes ____
No ____

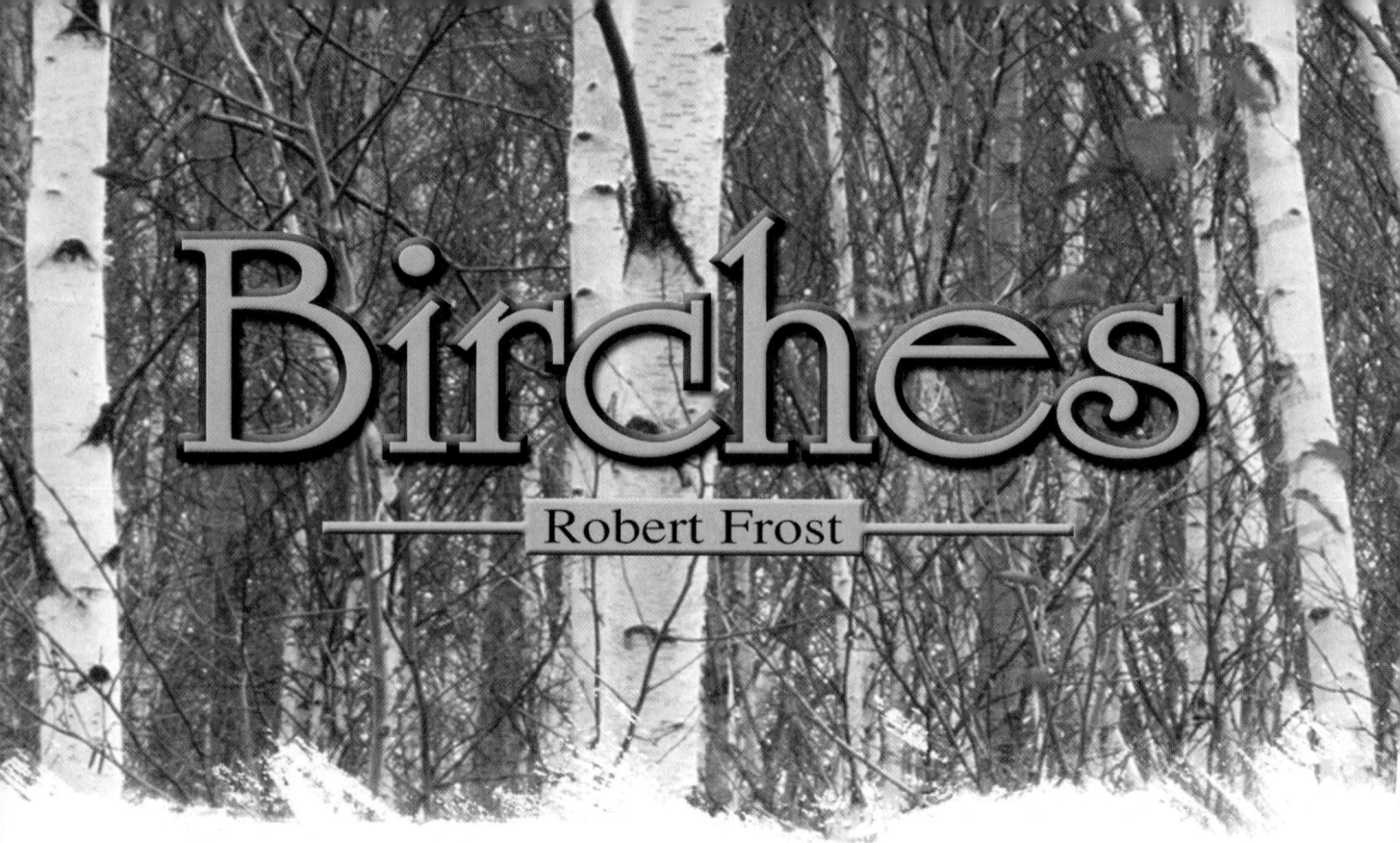

Birches

Robert Frost

Background

Robert Frost spent most of his life in New Hampshire, Vermont, and
Massachusetts. Much of his poetry reflects not only the New England
landscape, but also its distinctive personalities. Despite Frost's city roots,
he was able to gain the acceptance of his country neighbors and to enter
their world—a place that was usually closed to outsiders. In so doing,
Frost gathered a wealth of material for his poetry.

When I see birches bend to left and right
Across the lines of straighter darker trees,
I like to think some boy's been swinging them.
But swinging doesn't bend them down to stay
5   As ice storms do. Often you must have seen them
Loaded with ice a sunny winter morning
After a rain. They click upon themselves
As the breeze rises, and turn many-colored
As the stir cracks and crazes their enamel.
10   Soon the sun's warmth makes them shed crystal shells
Shattering and avalanching on the snow crust—
Such heaps of broken glass to sweep away
You'd think the inner dome of heaven had fallen.
They are dragged to the withered bracken by the load,
15   And they seem not to break; though once they are bowed

▲ **Critical Viewing**
Frost's poem is based on
his reaction to birch trees.
What response does this
photograph of birches
evoke in you? **[Connect]**

So low for long, they never right themselves:
You may see their trunks arching in the woods
Years afterwards, trailing their leaves on the ground
Like girls on hands and knees that throw their hair
20 Before them over their heads to dry in the sun.
But I was going to say when Truth broke in
With all her matter of fact about the ice storm,
I should prefer to have some boy bend them
As he went out and in to fetch the cows—
25 Some boy too far from town to learn baseball,
Whose only play was what he found himself,
Summer or winter, and could play alone.
One by one he subdued his father's trees
By riding them down over and over again
30 Until he took the stiffness out of them,
And not one but hung limp, not one was left
For him to conquer. He learned all there was
To learn about not launching out too soon
And so not carrying the tree away
35 Clear to the ground. He always kept his <u>poise</u>
To the top branches, climbing carefully

Literary Analysis
Blank Verse and Pastorals
What picture of rural life is conveyed in this description of the boy's summer activities?

poise (poiz) *n.* balance; stability

☑**Reading Check**
What does the speaker think of when he sees birches bend to left and right?

With the same pains you use to fill a cup
Up to the brim, and even above the brim.
Then he flung outward, feet first, with a swish,
40 Kicking his way down through the air to the ground.
So was I once myself a swinger of birches.
And so I dream of going back to be.
It's when I'm weary of considerations,
And life is too much like a pathless wood
45 Where your face burns and tickles with the cobwebs
Broken across it, and one eye is weeping
From a twig's having lashed across it open.
I'd like to get away from earth awhile
And then come back to it and begin over.
50 May no fate willfully misunderstand me
And half grant what I wish and snatch me away
Not to return. Earth's the right place for love:
I don't know where it's likely to go better.
I'd like to go by climbing a birch tree,
55 And climb black branches up a snow-white trunk
Toward heaven, till the tree could bear no more,
But dipped its top and set me down again.
That would be good both going and coming back.
One could do worse than be a swinger of birches.

Reading Strategy
Reading Blank Verse
Does reading lines 43–47
as a sentence help to
clarify its meaning?
Explain.

Review and Assess

Thinking About the Selection

1. **Respond:** Do you ever yearn to escape from reality for a while? Why or why not?

2. **(a) Recall:** What is the connection between the ice storm and the bent birches? **(b) Recall:** What does the speaker prefer to think when he sees birches "bend to left and right"? **(c) Interpret:** What does the speaker feel about the facts concerning the real causes of the bowed trees?

3. **(a) Recall:** What is the connection between the "swinger of birches" and the speaker? **(b) Interpret:** What does the activity of swinging on birches come to symbolize for the speaker in the poem?

4. **(a) Interpret:** What does the speaker say he'd like to "begin over"? **(b) Analyze:** What aspects of this poem reflect the speaker's conflicting attitudes about life?

5. **Speculate:** What kinds of events, experiences, and feelings in his life might have caused the speaker to make the admission contained in lines 48–49?

Stopping by Woods on a Snowy Evening

Robert Frost

Whose woods these are I think I know.
His house is in the village though;
He will not see me stopping here
To watch his woods fill up with snow.

5   My little horse must think it queer
To stop without a farmhouse near
Between the woods and frozen lake
The darkest evening of the year.

He gives his harness bells a shake
10   To ask if there is some mistake.
The only other sound's the sweep
Of easy wind and downy flake.

The woods are lovely, dark and deep,
But I have promises to keep,
15   And miles to go before I sleep,
And miles to go before I sleep.

▲ **Critical Viewing**
What elements of this scene differ from the scene the speaker describes? What do the two scenes have in common? **[Compare and Contrast]**

Literary Analysis
Blank Verse Is this poem an example of blank verse? Explain.

✔ **Reading Check**
At what exact time of year is this poem set?

Mending Wall

Robert Frost

= nature

[Something there is that doesn't love a wall,
That sends the frozen-ground-swell under it
And spills the upper boulders in the sun,
And makes gaps even two can pass <u>abreast</u>.

5 The work of hunters is another thing:
I have come after them and made repair
Where they have left not one stone on a stone,
But they would have the rabbit out of hiding,
To please the yelping dogs. The gaps I mean,

10 No one has seen them made or heard them made,
But at spring mending-time we find them there.
I let my neighbor know beyond the hill;
And on a day we meet to walk the line
And set the wall between us once again.

15 We keep the wall between us as we go.
To each the boulders that have fallen to each.
And some are <u>loaves</u> and some so nearly balls
We have to use a spell to make them balance:
"Stay where you are until our backs are turned!"

20 We wear our fingers rough with handling them.
Oh, just another kind of outdoor game,
One on a side. It comes to little more:
There where it is we do not need the wall:

Literary Analysis
Blank Verse and Pastorals
What activities do lines
5–9 suggest are part of
rural life?

▼ **Critical Viewing**
What elements of this
picture suggest that walls
do not belong in the
natural world? **[Analyze]**

He is all pine and I am apple orchard.
25 My apple trees will never get across
And eat the cones under his pines, I tell him.
He only says, "Good fences make good neighbors."
Spring is the mischief in me, and I wonder
If I could put a notion in his head:
30 "*Why* do they make good neighbors? Isn't it
Where there are cows? But here there are no cows.
Before I built a wall I'd ask to know
What I was walling in or walling out,
And to whom I was like to give offense.
35 Something there is that doesn't love a wall,
That wants it down." I could say "Elves" to him,
But it's not elves exactly, and I'd rather
He said it for himself. I see him there,
Bringing a stone grasped firmly by the top
40 In each hand, like an old-stone savage armed.
He moves in darkness as it seems to me,
Not of woods only and the shade of trees.
He will not go behind his father's saying,
And he likes having thought of it so well
45 He says again, "Good fences make good neighbors."

Reading Strategy
Reading Blank Verse
Read lines 28–31 as sentences. In what ways are their meanings clarified?

Review and Assess

Thinking About the Selections

1. **Respond:** Which of the poems on pages 885–887 made the strongest impression on you? Explain.

2. **(a) Recall:** In the first stanza of "Stopping by Woods on a Snowy Evening," what two actions does the speaker engage in? **(b) Infer:** What internal conflict do the actions create?

3. **(a) Recall:** What phrase is repeated in the poem's last two lines? **(b) Analyze:** How does this repetition reinforce the theme?

4. **(a) Recall:** In "Mending Wall," what two causes of gaps in walls does the speaker identify? **(b) Speculate:** In what ways are these two causes expressions of a general force the speaker struggles to name? **(c) Interpret:** Why does this force not love a wall?

5. **(a) Recall:** What saying does the neighbor repeat? **(b) Interpret:** What does this saying mean?

6. **(a) Recall:** What image does the speaker use to characterize his neighbor as he repairs the wall? **(b) Interpret:** What is the meaning of the "darkness" in which the man walks?

7. **Make a Judgment:** Are both the neighbor's and the speaker's ideas about the value of walls valid? Explain.

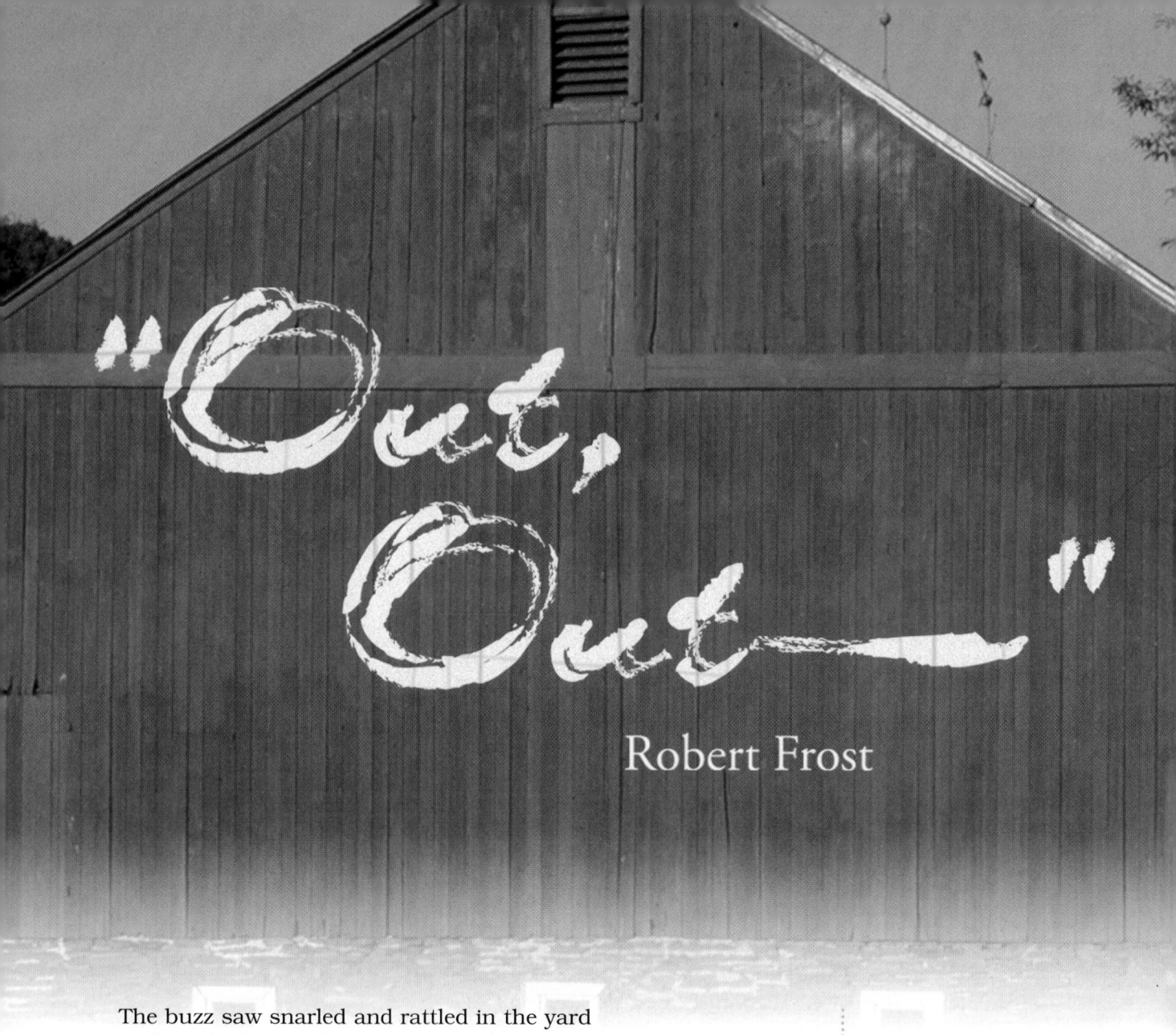

"Out, Out—"

Robert Frost

The buzz saw snarled and rattled in the yard
And made dust and dropped stove-length sticks of wood,
Sweet-scented stuff when the breeze drew across it.
And from there those that lifted eyes could count
5   Five mountain ranges one behind the other
Under the sunset far into Vermont.
And the saw snarled and rattled, snarled and rattled,
As it ran light, or had to bear a load.
And nothing happened: day was all but done.
10 Call it a day, I wish they might have said
To please the boy by giving him the half hour
That a boy counts so much when saved from work.
His sister stood beside them in her apron
To tell them "Supper." At the word, the saw,
15 As if to prove saws knew what supper meant,

Literary Analysis
Blank Verse Which words or phrases in lines 10–12 capture the rhythms of everyday speech?

Leaped out at the boy's hand, or seemed to leap—
He must have given the hand. However it was,
Neither refused the meeting. But the hand!
The boy's first outcry was a <u>rueful</u> laugh,
20 As he swung toward them holding up the hand,
Half in appeal, but half as if to keep
The life from spilling. Then the boy saw all—
Since he was old enough to know, big boy
Doing a man's work, though a child at heart—
25 He saw all spoiled. "Don't let him cut my hand off—
The doctor, when he comes. Don't let him, sister!"
So. But the hand was gone already.
The doctor put him in the dark of ether.[1]
He lay and puffed his lips out with his breath.
30 And then—the watcher at his pulse took fright.
No one believed. They listened at his heart.
Little—less—nothing!—and that ended it.
No more to build on there. And they, since they
Were not the one dead, turned to their affairs.

---

1. **ether** (ē′ thər) *n.* chemical compound used as an anesthetic.

Review and Assess

Thinking About the Selection

1. **Respond:** What do you find more disturbing—the boy's death or the onlookers' reaction to it? Explain.

2. **(a) Recall:** Where is the poem set? **(b) Connect:** In what ways does the description of the setting contrast with the events of the poem?

3. **(a) Recall:** At what time of day does the accident occur? **(b) Support:** What is ironic about the fact that the boy is cut at precisely that moment?

4. **(a) Recall:** What are the boy's first and second responses to the accident? **(b) Interpret:** What does the speaker mean by the expression "the boy saw all" in line 22?

5. **(a) Recall:** In the last line, what is the family's response to the boy's death? **(b) Speculate:** How do you explain this response?

6. **Connect:** The poem's title comes from a scene in William Shakespeare's *Macbeth* in which Macbeth laments the death of his wife with these words: "Out, out, brief candle! / Life's but a walking shadow, a poor player, / That struts and frets his hour upon the stage, / And then is heard no more." What does this quotation reveal about the poem's theme?

rueful (rōō′ fəl) *adj.* feeling or showing someone sorrow or pity

Literary Analysis
Blank Verse and Pastorals
In what ways do lines 19–34 portray a harsh view of rural life?

The Gift OUTRIGHT

Robert Frost

Background

During the planning stages of John F. Kennedy's presidential inauguration, his staff approached Robert Frost with a request: Would the poet write and recite a poem for the inauguration? Frost declined to write something new but agreed to recite "The Gift Outright." President Kennedy had a second request: Would Frost change the word "would" to "will" in the last line of the poem? The poet agreed. Shortly before the inauguration date, Frost was struck by inspiration and, despite his earlier refusal, drafted a forty-two-line poem, "Dedication," especially for the ceremony. The weather on inauguration day was windy, clear, and sunny. As Frost stood at the podium reading his new poem, the glare of the sun and the whipping wind made it almost impossible for him to see the words on the page. After struggling through the first half of "Dedication," he gave up the effort, and recited "The Gift Outright" from memory.

The land was ours before we were the land's.
She was our land more than a hundred years
Before we were her people. She was ours
In Massachusetts, in Virginia,
5   But we were England's, still colonials,
Possessing what we still were unpossessed by,
Possessed by what we now no more possessed.
Something we were withholding made us weak
Until we found out that it was ourselves
10   We were withholding from our land of living,
And forthwith found salvation in surrender.
Such as we were we gave ourselves outright
(The deed of gift was many deeds of war)
To the land vaguely realizing westward,
15   But still unstoried, artless, unenhanced,
Such as she was, such as she would become.

Reading Strategy
Reading Blank Verse In what ways does reading this poem aloud as sentences help clarify the poet's meaning?

Review and Assess

Thinking About the Selection

1. **Respond:** What does this poem make you feel about America's past and future? Explain.

2. **(a) Recall:** According to the speaker, what was the relationship between the land and the people in colonial America? **(b) Interpret:** What do you think the poet means by the phrase "the land was ours"?

3. **(a) Recall:** According to the speaker, where did the national allegiance of most Americans in colonial America lie? **(b) Interpret:** To where does the speaker say this sense of allegiance shifted?

4. **(a) Recall:** According to the speaker, what were we "withholding" in early America? **(b) Infer:** To what does the speaker suggest earlier generations surrendered in order to become true Americans? **(c) Synthesize:** What does this poem suggest about the meaning of citizenship?

5. **(a) Recall:** In what action did the early Americans find salvation? **(b) Connect:** What is the meaning of the poem's title?

6. **(a) Interpret:** Does the poet suggest there was a price to pay for the "gift outright"? **(b) Analyze:** According to the poet, what was that price, and who paid it?

7. **Generalize:** What picture of American history does this poem create? **(b) Evaluate:** Do you think this poem suggests that American history is a story of continuous progress? Explain.

ACQUAINTED WITH THE NIGHT

Robert Frost

I have been one acquainted with the night.
I have walked out in rain—and back in rain.
I have outwalked the furthest city light.

I have looked down the saddest city lane.
5 I have passed by the watchman on his beat
And dropped my eyes, unwilling to explain.

I have stood still and stopped the sound of feet
When far away an interrupted cry
Came over houses from another street,

10 But not to call me back or say good-by;
And further still at an unearthly height
One luminary clock against the sky

Proclaimed the time was neither wrong nor right.
I have been one acquainted with the night.

Literary Analysis
Blank Verse How do you know that this poem is not an example of blank verse?

luminary (lōō′ mə ner′ ē) *adj.* giving off light

Review and Assess

Thinking About the Selection

1. **Respond:** How did this poem make you feel? Explain.
2. **(a) Recall:** What is the speaker's reaction when he sees the night watchman? **(b) Interpret:** What is the speaker "unwilling to explain"?
3. **(a) Recall:** What does the speaker hear in the third stanza? **(b) Infer:** From line 10, what does it seem the speaker hoped for?
4. **(a) Recall:** What is proclaimed in the final stanza? **(b) Analyze:** What emotional state is suggested by this proclamation?
5. **(a) Generalize:** What does night symbolize in this poem? **(b) Analyze:** In what ways does Frost's use of repetition heighten the symbolism of the poem?
6. **Evaluate:** How does this poem demonstrate Frost's ability to write poems that seem simple but present deeper meaning?

Review and Assess

Literary Analysis

Blank Verse

1. (a) Find two instances in "Out, Out—" where Frost deviates from **blank verse.** (b) In what ways do these metrical variations emphasize a specific idea or image?

2. (a) Identify the two poems presented here that are not written in blank verse. (b) What poetic device distinguishes them from the other poems? (c) How is the sound of these poems different from those that are written in blank verse?

Comparing Literary Works

3. (a) What details of "Out, Out—" and "Mending Wall" present a dark view of rural life? (b) What human failings do these poems depict?

4. What ideas about land ownership and boundaries do "Stopping by Woods on a Snowy Evening" and "Mending Wall" express?

5. In "Birches," the speaker expresses ambivalence about life, though he adds "Earth's the right place for love." (a) Use a chart like the one shown to determine the nature of his ambivalence. (b) Do Frost's other poems express similar ambivalence? Explain.

Reading Strategy

Reading Blank Verse

6. (a) Rewrite "The Gift Outright" as five sentences. (b) What is the effect of this approach?

7. Read "Out, Out—", pausing at the end of each of the poetic lines. Then, read the poem as a series of sentences. How does each reading affect your understanding of the poem?

Extend Understanding

8. **Psychology Connection:** Pausing to observe nature provides the speaker with a temporary escape from reality in "Stopping by Woods on a Snowy Evening." Why do you think people sometimes need to find this type of temporary escape?

Quick Review

Blank verse is poetry written in unrhymed iambic pentameter.

A **pastoral** is a poem that features people in rural settings.

Reading blank verse as sentences (rather than as poetic lines) helps you appreciate how blank verse captures the rhythms of everyday speech.

 Take It to the Net
www.phschool.com
Take the interactive self-test online to check your understanding of these selections.

Integrate Language Skills

Vocabulary Development Lesson

Word Analysis: Latin Root -lum-

Along with several related English words, including *luminous* and *illuminate*, the word *luminary* (which means "giving off light") is based on the Latin root *-lum-*, meaning "light."

Complete these sentences using the appropriate word from the list below.

a. luminous   **b.** illuminate   **c.** illumination

1. Is that single bulb enough to ___?___ the entire room?

2. The leaves of the linden tree were bathed in ___?___ sunlight.

3. The students found ___?___ in the wise words of the philosopher.

Concept Development: Analogies

Complete the following analogies using the words from the vocabulary list on page 881.

1. *Scorching* is to *fire* as ___?___ is to *moon*.
2. *Swiftness* is to *runner* as ___?___ is to *dancer*.
3. *Joyful* is to *celebrant* as ___?___ is to *mourner*.

Spelling Strategy

The one-syllable word *full* is spelled with two *l*'s. However, in words of more than one syllable, such as *rueful* and *stressful*, the suffix *-ful* is spelled with only one *l*. Turn each of the following phrases into a word using a form of the key word and the suffix *-ful*.

1. full of bliss   2. full of mourning

Grammar and Style Lesson

Uses of Infinitives

An **infinitive** is a verb form consisting of the base form of a verb, usually with the word *to*. An **infinitive phrase** consists of an infinitive plus any modifiers or complements, all acting together as a single part of speech. Infinitives and infinitive phrases can be used as adjectives, adverbs, or nouns.

> **Adverb:** But swinging doesn't bend them down *to stay*. (The infinitive acts as an adverb that modifies *bend*.)
>
> **Noun:** Before I built a wall I'd ask *to know* . . . (The infinitive acts as a noun serving as the direct object of the verb *ask*.)

Practice For each of the following items, identify the infinitive or infinitive phrase and determine whether it functions as a noun, an adjective, or an adverb.

1. As he went out . . . to fetch the cows— . . .
2. And on a day we meet to walk the line . . .
3. But I have promises to keep, / And miles to go before I sleep . . .
4. Not one was left . . . to conquer.
5. Such heaps of broken glass to sweep away . . .

Writing Application Using at least three infinitives or infinitive phrases, describe an outdoor activity in which you recently participated.

W͟G Prentice Hall Writing and Grammar Connection: Chapter 19, Section 2

Writing Lesson

Introduction to an Anthology

An anthology is a collection of literature often focused on a specific theme or time period. Anthologies frequently include an introduction that provides an overview of the content and comments on the works. Write an introduction to an anthology that includes poems by Robert Frost.

Prewriting   Reread Frost's poems, and make notes about his style and themes. Select the characteristics you will address, and identify poems to cite. Then, sketch out a table of contents.

Drafting   Start with a general statement about the poems you chose. Follow by touching on a few key points related to this statement. Focus each paragraph on one key point, supported with passages from the poems.

Revising   As you review your work, make sure that you have clearly linked your ideas. Add transitions to introduce examples where necessary.

Model: Revising to Smooth Transitions

For example,

Frost's appreciation of beauty is never simple. In "Stopping

by Woods on a Snowy Evening," he reminds us that

someone else owns the lovely scene.

> Phrases like *for example* provide transitions that improve clarity.

WG *Prentice Hall Writing and Grammar Connection: Chapter 3, Section 2*

Extension Activities

Listening and Speaking   Present a **eulogy** for the boy whose death is described in "Out, Out—." Use these tips to prepare:

- Use clues in the poem to create a sense of the boy's personality.
- Pay tribute to the boy "who did a man's work."
- Address the boy's family in an appropriate manner.

Deliver the eulogy at a "memorial service" in the classroom. **[Group Activity]**

Research and Technology   Using a variety of sources, locate recordings of Frost reciting his poems. Select two poems that appeal to you and play the recordings for the class as part of an **interpretive presentation.** Deliver a brief analysis of each poem in which you consider the impressions created by Frost's delivery.

 **Take It to the Net**   www.phschool.com

Go online for an additional research activity using the Internet.

Prepare to Read

The Night the Ghost Got In ◆ *from* Here Is New York

James Thurber (1894–1961)

James Thurber's essays, plays, sketches, cartoons, and short stories, such as the well-known "The Secret Life of Walter Mitty," generally evolved from his own experiences. In his humorous autobiographical sketches, Thurber embellishes facts and describes events in an amusing manner. In his short stories, Thurber's characters typically struggle against the unpleasant realities of modern life, often with comical consequences. In his cartoons, Thurber portrays men, women, and a profusion of animals—especially dogs—facing the trials of everyday life.

The New Yorker Thurber was born in Columbus, Ohio. After attending Ohio State University, he joined *The New Yorker* magazine staff in 1927 as managing editor. From there, or so he claimed, he quickly worked his way down to writer. Until the end of his life, Thurber regularly contributed stories, essays, and cartoons to the magazine's pages. He also worked closely with the celebrated writer E. B. White.

Thurber is one of the few humorists whose work is part of the American literary canon. About his comic genius, Thurber was quite modest: "I write humor the way a surgeon operates, because it is a livelihood, because I have a great urge to do it, because many interesting challenges are set up, and because I have the hope it may do some good."

In much of his work, Thurber's humor reveals an edge of unhappiness, especially in his later years when his failing vision caused him much pain and bitterness. Yet he continued to write and draw as well as he could.

Thurber's many published works include *The Owl in the Attic and Other Perplexities* (1931), *The Seal in the Bedroom and Other Predicaments* (1932), *Fables for Our Time* (1940), and the bestselling *My World and Welcome to It* (1942).

E. B. White (1899–1985)

Capturing the interest of adults as well as children, E(lwyn) B(rooks) White established himself as one of the best-loved writers of the twentieth century. His precisely worded essays set a standard against which today's essays can still be judged.

White grew up in Mount Vernon, New York, and studied literature at Cornell University. As an undergraduate, White served as the editor of the *Cornell Daily Sun*. Later, he began a long association with *The New Yorker* magazine. His humorous, topical essays helped to establish *The New Yorker* as one of the nation's most successful general-interest magazines. White produced essays for *The New Yorker* on a weekly basis until 1938. In these essays, many of which are collected in his books *Every Day Is Saturday* (1934) and *Quo Vadimus?* (1939), White used his talents as a humorist to explore numerous social and political themes.

Transcendentalist Influence Influenced by the writings and philosophies of Henry David Thoreau, White believed in simplicity and individualism. These values emerge in nearly everything he wrote. A brilliant observer, he often satirized the complexities of modern life. In fact, in an effort to simplify his own life, White bought a farmhouse in Brooklin, Maine, in 1939; thereafter, he and his family spent most of their time there. White said that the animals in the barn gave him ideas. Some of these ideas took shape in White's work for children.

Two of his children's books—*Stuart Little* (1945) and *Charlotte's Web* (1952)—are among the most beloved children's books of all time. In addition, White's revision of William Strunk, Jr.'s classic style manual, *The Elements of Style*, has become a classic in its own right.

Preview

Connecting to the Literature

Different people are amused by different things. You can discover something about yourself by noting which parts of these essays make you laugh.

Literary Analysis

Informal Essay

"The Night the Ghost Got In" and "Here Is New York" are both **informal essays,** brief nonfiction pieces characterized by a relaxed, conversational style and structure. Informal essays usually address a narrow subject, are loosely organized, and include digressions from the main point. Consider this example from "The Night the Ghost Got In":

> Glass tinkled into the bedroom occupied by a retired engraver named Bodwell and his wife. Bodwell had been for some years in rather a bad way and was subject to mild "attacks."

Informal essays give you a glimpse into a writer's personality. As you read these selections, consider what each suggests about its author. Record your findings in a chart like the one shown.

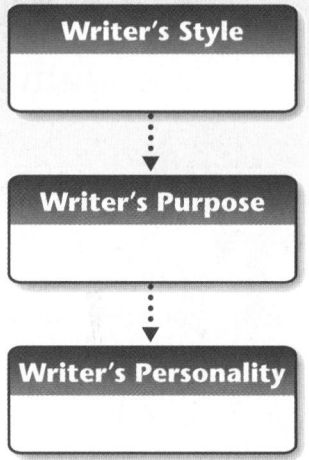

Comparing Literary Works

Although the topics are entirely different, both of these selections are humorous and intended to provoke laughter. Thurber's **humor** revolves around an exaggerated account of a childhood experience, while White's humor satirizes—pokes fun at—New York City. Humor writers must have the ability to perceive the ridiculous, comical, or ludicrous aspects of a personality or situation. Humorists often exaggerate details and embellish facts for comic effect. As you read, compare the elements that make these essays humorous.

Reading Strategy

Recognizing Hyperbole

These informal essays draw humor from **hyperbole,** or exaggerations and outrageous overstatements. Examples include bizarre events in Thurber's essay and White's litany of probable disasters. To recognize hyperbole, look for details that seem too absurd to be true.

Vocabulary Development

intuitively (in tōō´ i tiv lē) *adv.* instinctively (p. 899)

blaspheming (blas fēm´ iŋ) *v.* cursing (p. 902)

aspiration (as´ pə rā´ shən) *n.* strong ambition (p. 904)

subterranean (sub´ tə rā´ nē ən) *adj.* underground (p. 904)

claustrophobia (klôs´ trə fō´ bē ə) *n.* fear of being in a confined space (p. 904)

cosmopolitan (käz´ mə päl´ ə tən) *adj.* at ease in all countries or places (p. 904)

The Night the Ghost Got In

James Thurber

The Night the Ghost Got In, Copyright 1933, 1961, James Thurber, From *My Life and Hard Times,* published by Harper & Row.

The ghost that got into our house on the night of November 17, 1915, raised such a hullabaloo of misunderstandings that I am sorry I didn't just let it keep on walking, and go to bed. Its advent caused my mother to throw a shoe through a window of the house next door and ended up with my grandfather shooting a patrolman. I am sorry, therefore, as I have said, that I ever paid any attention to the footsteps.

They began about a quarter past one o'clock in the morning, a rhythmic, quick-cadenced walking around the dining-room table. My mother was asleep in one room upstairs, my brother Herman in another; grandfather was in the attic, in the old walnut bed which, as you will remember, once fell on my father. I had just stepped out of the bathtub and was busily rubbing myself with a towel when I heard the steps. They were the steps of a man walking rapidly around the dining-room table downstairs. The light from the bathroom shone down the back steps, which dropped directly into the dining-room; I could see the faint shine of plates on the plate-rail; I couldn't see the table. The steps kept going round and round the table; at regular intervals a board creaked, when it was trod upon. I supposed at first that it was my father or my brother Roy, who had gone to Indianapolis but were expected home at any time. I suspected next that it was a burglar. It did not enter my mind until later that it was a ghost.

After the walking had gone on for perhaps three minutes, I tiptoed to Herman's room. "Psst!" I hissed, in the dark, shaking him. "Awp," he said, in the low, hopeless tone of a despondent beagle—he always half suspected that something would "get him" in the night. I told him who I was. "There's something downstairs!" I said. He got up and followed me to the head of the back staircase. We listened together. There was no sound. The steps had ceased. Herman looked at me in some alarm: I had only the bath towel around my waist. He wanted to go back to bed, but I gripped his arm. "There's something down

▲ **Critical Viewing**
The humor in Thurber's drawing echoes the humor in his story. What makes this sketch funny? **[Analyze]**

Literary Analysis
Informal Essay What characteristics of the informal essay does this passage include?

there!" I said. Instantly the steps began again, circled the dining-room table like a man running, and started up the stairs toward us, heavily, two at a time. The light still shone palely down the stairs; we saw nothing coming; we only heard the steps. Herman rushed to his room and slammed the door. I slammed shut the door at the stairs top and held my knee against it. After a long minute, I slowly opened it again. There was nothing there. There was no sound. None of us ever heard the ghost again.

The slamming of the doors had aroused mother: she peered out of her room. "What on earth are you boys doing?" she demanded. Herman ventured out of his room. "Nothing," he said, gruffly, but he was, in color, a light green. "What was all that running around downstairs?" said mother. So she had heard the steps, too! We just looked at her. "Burglars!" she shouted <u>intuitively</u>. I tried to quiet her by starting lightly downstairs.

"Come on, Herman," I said.

"I'll stay with Mother," he said. "She's all excited."

I stepped back onto the landing.

"Don't either of you go a step," said mother. "We'll call the police." Since the phone was downstairs, I didn't see how we were going to call the police—nor did I want the police—but mother made one of her quick, incomparable decisions. She flung up a window of her bedroom which faced the bedroom windows of the house of a neighbor, picked up a shoe, and whammed it through a pane of glass across the narrow space that separated the two houses. Glass tinkled into the bedroom occupied by a retired engraver named Bodwell and his wife. Bodwell had been for some years in rather a bad way and was subject to mild "attacks." Most everybody we knew or lived near had *some* kind of attacks.

It was now about two o'clock of a moonless night; clouds hung black and low. Bodwell was at the window in a minute, shouting, frothing a little, shaking his fist. "We'll sell the house and go back to Peoria," we could hear Mrs. Bodwell saying. It was some time before mother "got through" to Bodwell. "Burglars!" she shouted. "Burglars in the house!" Herman and I hadn't dared to tell her that it was not burglars but ghosts, for she was even more afraid of ghosts than of burglars. Bodwell at first thought that she meant there were burglars in his house, but finally he quieted down and called the police for us over an extension phone by his bed. After he had disappeared from the window, mother suddenly made as if to throw another shoe, not because there was further need of it, but, as she later explained, because the thrill of heaving a shoe through a window glass had enormously taken her fancy. I prevented her.

The police were on hand in a commendably short time: a Ford sedan full of them, two on motorcycles, and a patrol wagon with about eight in it and a few reporters. They began banging at our front door. Flashlights shot streaks of gleam up and down the walls, across the yard, down the walk between our house and Bodwell's. "Open up!"

intuitively (in tōō´ i tiv lē) *adv.* instinctively

Literary Analysis
Informal Essay and Humor What does the humorous digression about the thrill of heaving a shoe reveal about the mother?

✔**Reading Check**

Who does Mother think the intruders are?

The Night the Ghost Got In ◆ 899

cried a hoarse voice. "We're men from Headquarters!" I wanted to go down and let them in, since there they were, but mother wouldn't hear of it. "You haven't a stitch on," she pointed out. "You'd catch your death." I wound the towel around me again. Finally the cops put their shoulders to our big heavy front door with its thick beveled glass and broke it in: I could hear a rending of wood and a splash of glass on the floor of the hall. Their lights played all over the living-room and crisscrossed nervously in the dining-room, stabbed into hallways, shot up the front stairs and finally up the back. They caught me standing in my towel at the top. A heavy policeman bounded up the steps. "Who are you?" he demanded. "I live here," I said. "Well, whattsa matta, ya hot?" he asked. I was, as a matter of fact, cold; I went to my room and pulled on some trousers. On my way out, a cop stuck a gun into my ribs. "Whatta you doin' here?" he demanded. "I live here," I said.

▲ **Critical Viewing**
Thurber created this cartoon to accompany "The Night the Ghost Got In." Describe the way in which the illustration adds to the humorous effect of the essay. **[Assess]**

The officer in charge reported to mother. "No sign of nobody, lady," he said. "Musta got away—whatt'd he look like?" "There were two or three of them," mother said, "whooping and carrying on and slamming doors." "Funny," said the cop. "All ya windows and doors was locked on the inside tight as a tick."

Downstairs, we could hear the tromping of the other police. Police were all over the place; doors were yanked open, drawers were yanked open, windows were shot up and pulled down, furniture fell with dull thumps. A half-dozen policemen emerged out of the darkness of the front hallway upstairs. They began to ransack the floor: pulled beds away from walls, tore clothes off hooks in the closets, pulled suitcases and boxes off shelves. One of them found an old zither[1] that Roy had won in a pool tournament. "Looky here, Joe," he said, strumming it with a big paw. The cop named Joe took it and turned it over. "What is it?" he asked me. "It's an old zither our guinea pig used to sleep on," I said. It was true that a pet guinea pig we once had would never sleep anywhere except on the zither, but I should never have said so. Joe and the other cop looked at me a long time. They put the zither back on a shelf.

"No sign o' nuthin'," said the cop who had first spoken to mother. "This guy," he explained to the others, jerking a thumb at me, "was nekked. The lady seems historical." They all nodded, but said nothing;

---

1. zither (zith´ ər) *n.* musical instrument with thirty to forty strings stretched across a flat soundboard and played with the fingers.

just looked at me. In the small silence we all heard a creaking in the attic. Grandfather was turning over in bed. "What's 'at?" snapped Joe. Five or six cops sprang for the attic door before I could intervene or explain. I realized that it would be bad if they burst in on grandfather unannounced, or even announced. He was going through a phase in which he believed that General Meade's men, under steady hammering by Stonewall Jackson, were beginning to retreat and even desert.

When I got to the attic, things were pretty confused. Grandfather had evidently jumped to the conclusion that the police were deserters from Meade's army, trying to hide away in his attic. He bounded out of bed wearing a long flannel nightgown over long woolen underwear, a nightcap, and a leather jacket around his chest. The cops must have realized at once that the indignant white-haired old man belonged in the house, but they had no chance to say so. "Back, ye cowardly dogs!" roared grandfather. "Back t' the lines, ye yellow, lily-livered cattle!" With that, he fetched the officer who found the zither a flat-handed smack alongside his head that sent him sprawling. The others beat a retreat, but not fast enough; grandfather grabbed Zither's gun from its holster and let fly. The report seemed to crack the rafters; smoke filled the attic. A cop cursed and shot his hand to his shoulder. Somehow, we all finally got downstairs again and locked the door against the old gentleman. He fired once or twice more in the darkness and then went back to bed. "That was grandfather," I explained to Joe, out of breath. "He thinks you're deserters." "I'll say he does," said Joe.

Literary Analysis
Informal Essay Which words in this paragraph reflect a relaxed, conversational style?

✓**Reading Check**
What does grandfather think is happening?

The Night the Ghost Got In, Copyright 1933, 1961, James Thurber, From *My Life and Hard Times,* published by Harper & Row.

◀**Critical Viewing**
Compare this illustration with Thurber's description of the police investigation. What makes each funny? **[Evaluate]**

The cops were reluctant to leave without getting their hands on somebody besides grandfather; the night had been distinctly a defeat for them. Furthermore, they obviously didn't like the "layout"; something looked—and I can see their viewpoint—phony. They began to poke into things again. A reporter, a thin-faced, wispy man, came up to me. I had put on one of mother's blouses, not being able to find anything else. The reporter looked at me with mingled suspicion and interest. "Just what the heck is the real lowdown here, Bud?" he asked. I decided to be frank with him. "We had ghosts," I said. He gazed at me a long time as if I were a slot machine into which he had, without results, dropped a nickel. Then he walked away. The cops followed him, the one grandfather shot holding his now-bandaged arm, cursing and blaspheming. "I'm gonna get my gun back from that old bird," said the zither-cop. "Yeh," said Joe. "You—and who else?" I told them I would bring it to the station house the next day.

"What was the matter with that one policeman?" mother asked, after they had gone. "Grandfather shot him," I said. "What for?" she demanded. I told her he was a deserter. "Of all things!" said mother. "He was such a nice-looking young man."

Grandfather was fresh as a daisy and full of jokes at breakfast next morning. We thought at first he had forgotten all about what had happened, but he hadn't. Over his third cup of coffee, he glared at Herman and me. "What was the idee of all them cops tarry-hootin' round the house last night?" he demanded. He had us there.

blaspheming (blas fēm´ iŋ) v. cursing

Review and Assess

Thinking About the Selection

1. **Respond:** What do you consider the most humorous point in the essay? Why?

2. **(a) Recall:** What event sets off the family's reactions?
   (b) Classify: Describe how each member of the family reacts.
   (c) Distinguish: In what way does Thurber's portrayal of himself in the situation differ from his portrayal of the other characters?

3. **(a) Recall:** Why are the police summoned?
   (b) Support: How does this lack of communication contribute to the humor of the essay?

4. **(a) Recall:** What does grandfather do when the police burst into his room? **(b) Infer:** Why do you think he does this?

5. **Speculate:** In what way might the narrator's family and the police have reacted if they thought it was a ghost in the house?

6. **Take a Position:** This essay describes an event that took place in 1915. Do you think modern readers can still enjoy it? Why or why not?

from HERE IS NEW YORK

E. B. White

Background

America has a strong tradition of humor writing. Much of that humor builds on self-ridicule, with people poking fun at their own missteps and failures. Americans seem especially willing to laugh at themselves when they fail to achieve all that they attempt. Although he loves New York City and its energy and excitement, E. B. White still finds plenty to satirize in "Here Is New York."

New York is nothing like Paris; it is nothing like London; and it is not Spokane multiplied by sixty, or Detroit multiplied by four. It is by all odds the loftiest of cities. It even managed to reach the highest point in the sky at the lowest moment of the Depression. The Empire State Building shot 1250 feet into the air when it was madness to put out as much as six inches of new growth. (The building has a mooring mast that no dirigible[1] has ever tied to; it employs a man to flush toilets in slack times; it has been hit by an airplane in a fog, struck countless times by lightning, and been jumped off of by so many unhappy people that pedestrians instinctively quicken step when passing Fifth Avenue and Thirty-fourth Street.)

Manhattan has been compelled to expand skyward because of the absence of any other direction in which to grow. This,

---

1. **dirigible** (dir′ə jə bəl) n. large, long airship.

▶ Critical Viewing
What objects in this photograph confirm White's attitude about New York? Explain. [Connect]

more than any other thing, is responsible for its physical majesty. It is to the nation what the white church spire is to the village—the visible symbol of aspiration and faith, the white plume saying that the way is up. The summer traveler swings in over Hell Gate Bridge and from the window of his sleeping car as it glides above the pigeon lofts and back yards of Queens looks southwest to where the morning light first strikes the steel peaks of midtown, and he sees its upward thrust unmistakable: the great walls and towers rising, the smoke rising, the heat not yet rising, the hopes and ferments of so many awakening millions rising—this vigorous spear that presses heaven hard.

It is a miracle that New York works at all. The whole thing is implausible. Every time the residents brush their teeth, millions of gallons of water must be drawn from the Catskills and the hills of Westchester. When a young man in Manhattan writes a letter to his girl in Brooklyn, the love message gets blown to her through a pneumatic[2] tube—*pfft*—just like that. The subterranean system of telephone cables, power lines, steam pipes, gas mains, and sewer pipes is reason enough to abandon the island to the gods and the weevils. Every time an incision is made in the pavement, the noisy surgeons expose ganglia[3] that are tangled beyond belief. By rights New York should have destroyed itself long ago, from panic or fire or rioting or failure of some vital supply line in its circulatory system or from some deep labyrinthine short circuit. Long ago the city should have experienced an insoluble traffic snarl at some impossible bottleneck. It should have perished of hunger when food lines filed for a few days. It should have been wiped out by a plague starting in its slums or carried in by ships' rats. It should have been overwhelmed by the sea that licks at it on every side. The workers in its myriad cells should have succumbed to nerves, from the fearful pall of smoke-fog that drifts over every few days from Jersey, blotting out all light at noon and leaving the high offices suspended, men groping and depressed, and the sense of world's end. It should have been touched in the head by the August heat and gone off its rocker.

Mass hysteria is a terrible force, yet New Yorkers seem always to escape it by some tiny margin: they sit in stalled subways without claustrophobia, they extricate themselves from panic situations by some lucky wisecrack, they meet confusion and congestion with patience and grit—a sort of perpetual muddling through. Every facility is inadequate—the hospitals and schools and the playgrounds are over-crowded, the express highways are feverish, the unimproved highways and bridges are bottlenecks, there is not enough air and not enough light, and there is usually either too much heat or too little. But the city makes up for its hazards and its deficiencies by supplying its citizens with massive doses of a supplementary vitamin: the sense of belonging to something unique, cosmopolitan, mighty, and unparalleled.

---

2. **pneumatic** (no͞o mat´ ik) *adj.* filled with compressed air.
3. **ganglia** (gaŋ´ glē ə) *n.* mass of nerve cells serving as center of force, energy, activity.

aspiration (as´ pə rā´ shən) *n.* strong ambition

subterranean (sub´ tə rā´ nē ən) *adj.* underground

Reading Strategy
Recognizing Hyperbole
Which details in the passage beginning "Long ago" are examples of hyperbole?

claustrophobia (klôs´ trə fō´ bē ə) *n.* fear of being in a confined space

cosmopolitan (käz´ mə päl´ ə tən) *adj.* at ease in all countries or places

To an outlander a stay in New York can be and often is a series of small embarrassments and discomforts and disappointments: not understanding the waiter, not being able to distinguish between a sucker joint and a friendly saloon, riding the wrong subway, being slapped down by a bus driver for asking an innocent question, enduring sleepless nights when the street noises fill the bedroom. Tourists make for New York, particularly in summertime—they swarm all over the Statue of Liberty (where many a resident of the town has never set foot), they invade the Automat,[4] visit radio studios, St. Patrick's Cathedral, and they window shop. Mostly they have a pretty good time. But sometimes in New York you run across the disillusioned—a young couple who are obviously visitors, newlyweds perhaps, for whom the bright dream has vanished. The place has been too much for them; they sit languishing in a cheap restaurant over a speechless meal.

The oft-quoted thumbnail sketch of New York is, of course: "It's a wonderful place, but I'd hate to live there." I have an idea that people from villages and small towns, people accustomed to the convenience and the friendliness of neighborhood over-the-fence living, are unaware that life in New York follows the neighborhood pattern. The city is literally a composite of tens of thousands of tiny neighborhood units. There are, of course, the big districts and big units: Chelsea and Murray Hill and Gramercy (which are residential units), . . . Greenwich Village (a unit dedicated to the arts and other matters), and there is Radio City (a commercial development), Peter Cooper Village (a housing unit), the Medical Center (a sickness unit) and many other sections each of which has some distinguishing characteristic. But the curious thing about New York is that each large geographical unit is composed of countless small neighborhoods. Each neighborhood is virtually self-sufficient. Usually it is no more than two or three blocks long and a couple of blocks wide. Each area is a city within a city within a city. Thus, no matter where you live in New York, you will find within a block or two a grocery store, a barbershop, a newsstand and shoeshine shack, an ice-coal-and-wood cellar (where you write your order on a pad outside as you walk by), a dry cleaner, a laundry, a delicatessen (beer and sandwiches delivered at any hour to your door), a flower shop, an undertaker's parlor, a movie house, a radio-repair shop, a stationer, a haberdasher,[5] a tailor, a drugstore, a garage, a tearoom, a saloon, a hardware store, a liquor store, a shoe-repair shop. Every block or two, in most residential sections of New York, is a little main street. A man starts for work in the morning and before he has gone two hundred yards he has completed half a dozen missions: bought a paper, left a pair of shoes to be soled, picked up a pack of cigarettes, . . . written a message to the unseen forces of the wood cellar, and notified the dry cleaner that a pair of trousers awaits call. Homeward-bound

---

4. **Automat** *n.* restaurant in which patrons get food from small compartments with doors opened by putting coins into slots.
5. **haberdasher** *n.* person whose work is selling men's clothing, such as hats, shirts, neckties, and gloves.

Literary Analysis
Informal Essay What does the relaxed, conversational style of this passage reveal about White's attitude toward New York?

✔ **Reading Check**
According to the writer, what difficulties might a visitor to New York encounter?

eight hours later, he buys a bunch of pussy willows, a Mazda bulb, a drink, a shine—all between the corner where he steps off the bus and his apartment. So complete is each neighborhood, and so strong the sense of neighborhood, that many a New Yorker spends a lifetime within the confines of an area smaller than a country village. Let him walk two blocks from his corner and he is in a strange land and will feel uneasy till he gets back.

Storekeepers are particularly conscious of neighborhood boundary lines. A woman friend of mine moved recently from one apartment to another, a distance of three blocks. When she turned up, the day after the move, at the same grocer's that she had patronized for years, the proprietor was in ecstasy—almost in tears—at seeing her. "I was afraid," he said, "now that you've moved away I wouldn't be seeing you anymore." To him, *away* was three blocks, or about 750 feet.

I am, at the moment of writing this, living not as a neighborhood man in New York but as a transient, or vagrant, in from the country for a few days. Summertime is a good time to reexamine New York and to receive again the gift of privacy, the jewel of loneliness. In summer the city contains (except for tourists) only die-hards and authentic characters. No casual, spotty dwellers are around, only the real article. And the town has a somewhat relaxed air, and one can lie in a loincloth, gasping and remembering things.

Review and Assess

Thinking About the Selection

1. **Respond:** Would you like to visit the New York City of E. B. White's description? Why or why not?

2. **(a) Recall:** According to this essay, what are three ways in which New Yorkers escape mass hysteria? **(b) Connect:** What does New York City offer its citizens in return to help them cope with the city's deficiencies?

3. **(a) Recall:** According to White, what is New York City like for tourists? **(b) Hypothesize:** Describe the way in which someone working in New York City's tourist industry might respond to E. B. White's representation of the city for "outlanders"?

4. **(a) Recall:** What terms does White use to describe New York's neighborhoods? **(b) Compare and Contrast:** In what ways do these neighborhoods compare to small towns?

5. **(a) Draw Conclusions:** What qualities of New York City enable it to function against all odds? **(b) Summarize:** What general conclusions does White's essay reach about the city?

6. **Extend:** How might the city's mayor or a New York State Senator respond to White's description?

Review and Assess

Literary Analysis

Informal Essay

1. Cite an especially strong example of language that reflects the conversational style of Thurber's **informal essay.** Explain your choice.
2. What does "Here Is New York" suggest about White's attitude toward New York and the modern world it symbolizes? Support your answer.
3. What does their calm detachment in the midst of describing chaotic events reveal about the writers' views of the world around them?

Comparing Literary Works

4. (a) How would you describe the dominant type of **humor** Thurber uses in his informal essay? (b) In what ways does it compare to the humor used by E.B. White?
5. Although White uses humor to make fun of New York, his writing actually reveals some of the city's unique qualities. Using a chart like the one shown, cite three examples of hidden praise.

Humorous Passage	What It Reveals

6. (a) What does each author's use of humor add to his exploration of social or political issues? (b) Does the presence of humor allow the writer to convey ideas that would otherwise be difficult for readers to accept? Explain.

Reading Strategy

Recognizing Hyperbole

7. Cite an example of **hyperbole** from each essay and explain in what ways it represents an exaggeration.
8. For what purpose does Thurber exaggerate the behavior of his grandfather in his essay?
9. How is White's use of hyperbole appropriate for his subject?

Extend Understanding

10. **Career Connection:** Name three careers in today's world that might provide work for humorists. Explain how humor is used in each case.

Quick Review

An **informal essay** is a brief nonfiction work that has been written to entertain. It is characterized by a relaxed, conversational style and structure.

In literature, **humor** is writing that attempts to amuse by evoking laughter.

To **recognize hyperbole,** look for the deliberate exaggeration of facts and overstatements that create a comic effect.

 Take It to the Net
www.phschool.com
Take the interactive self-test online to check your understanding of these selections.

Integrate Language Skills

Vocabulary Development Lesson

Word Analysis: Latin Root *-terr-*

The prefix *sub-* means "under" and the Latin root *-terr-* means "earth" or "land." Therefore, the word *subterranean* means "under Earth's surface." Use the meaning of *-terr-* and context clues to choose the best word for each sentence.

   a. terrain   b. extraterrestrial   c. terrarium

1. The ____?____ visited from another planet.
2. Put some earth in a glass jar and plant some seeds to make a ____?____.

Spelling Strategy

Words such as *blaspheme* and *telephone* spell the *f* sound with *ph*. These words derive from Greek and are spelled with the Greek letter *phi* (fi). Write a *ph* word that fits each definition.

1. a portrait taken with a camera
2. a piece of music for an orchestra

Fluency: Words in Context

Review the vocabulary list on page 897. Then, answer *yes* or *no* to each question below. Explain your responses.

1. If Susan has an *aspiration* to sail around the world, does she have a vague notion?
2. Must you dig to reach *subterranean* pipes in a city?
3. Would you get in trouble for *blaspheming* in class?
4. Would a *cosmopolitan* person enjoy the streets of Paris?
5. If you heard a very loud bang, would you *intuitively* wince?
6. Would a person suffering from *claustrophobia* enjoy riding in an elevator?

Grammar and Style Lesson

Commas in Series

Commas in series are placed between three or more parallel items to link them. Sometimes, coordinating conjunctions such as "and," "or," or "but" precede the final item. Separate the items in a list with commas.

> **Example:** Bodwell was at the window in a minute, shouting, frothing a little, shaking his fist.

Practice Rewrite these sentences, inserting commas in their appropriate places.

1. The subterranean system of telephone cables power lines steam pipes gas mains and sewer pipes is the reason to . . .
2. Instantly the steps began again circled the dining room table like a man running and started up the stairs toward us . . .
3. Their lights . . . crisscrossed nervously in the dining-room stabbed into hallways shot up the front stairs and finally up the back.
4. You will find within a block or two a grocery store a barbershop a newsstand and shoeshine rack . . .
5. Doors were yanked open drawers were yanked open windows were shot up and pulled down furniture fell with dull thumps.

Writing Application Write a paragraph, using two sets of commas in series.

W̶G̶ Prentice Hall Writing and Grammar Connection: Chapter 27, Section 2

Writing Lesson

Critical Response

E. B. White once said, "The most widely appreciated humorists are those who create characters and tell tales . . ." Write an essay responding to this statement. Cite passages from these humorous essays for support.

Prewriting Review the selections and identify the most humorous characters. Jot down notes about what makes each of them funny. Select the ones you will write about to support your opinions.

Drafting Begin by presenting your response to White's statement. Then, use the examples of humorous characters and passages from the selections to support your position.

Revising Strengthen your essay by incorporating direct quotations that clearly support your opinions.

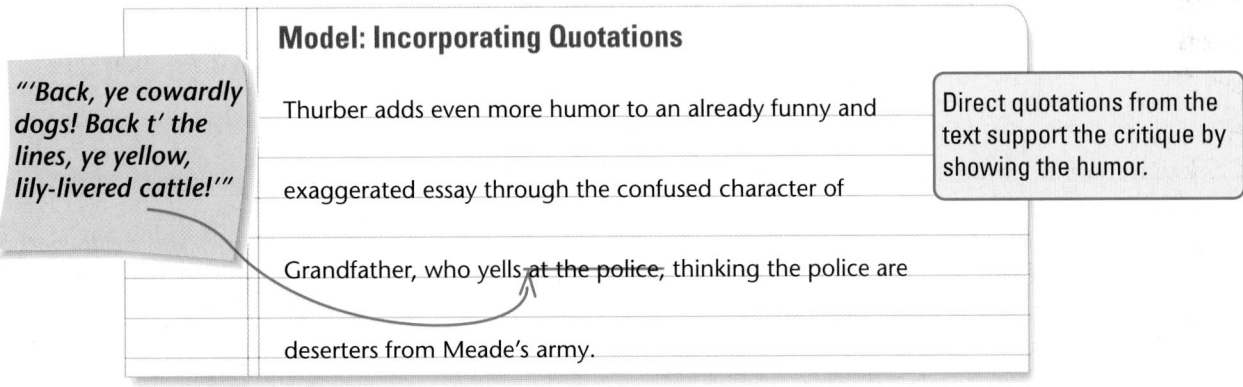

"'Back, ye cowardly dogs! Back t' the lines, ye yellow, lily-livered cattle!'"

Model: Incorporating Quotations

Thurber adds even more humor to an already funny and

exaggerated essay through the confused character of

Grandfather, who yells at the police, thinking the police are

deserters from Meade's army.

Direct quotations from the text support the critique by showing the humor.

W̶G̶ Prentice Hall Writing and Grammar Connection: Chapter 14, Section 3

Extension Activities

Listening and Speaking With a partner, conduct a **role play** of Thurber and White discussing their essays in the offices of *The New Yorker*. Constructively criticize each other's work, considering the following:

- What makes the essays funny?
- In what ways are they similar?
- In what ways do they differ?
- What would you add or change?

Present your role play to the class.

Research and Technology Thurber and White both worked for *The New Yorker*. Using the Internet and other sources, research "The Algonquin Roundtable," a group of wits associated with *The New Yorker* who met on a regular basis. With classmates, deliver your findings in a **written report. [Group Activity]**

 **Take It to the Net** www.phschool.com

Go online for an additional research activity using the Internet.

A Closer Look

The Harlem Renaissance: A Cultural Revolution

In the 1920s, the New York City neighborhood of Harlem became the artistic home of black America.

Harlem in the 1920s: For some it conjures images of wild times, of jazz sessions at hot spots like the Cotton Club, of seedy speakeasies with names like the Clam Bake and the Hot Feet.

For others, it brings to mind the artistic genius of writers like Langston Hughes and Zora Neale Hurston, and painters like Aaron Douglas. Harlem in the 1920s was home to an event that America had never seen before—a flowering of African American talent that left an astonishing cultural legacy.

A Celebration of African American Life Known as the Harlem Renaissance, this remarkable period in America's cultural life marked the first time that African American artists were taken seriously by the culture at large. The artists of the Harlem Renaissance celebrated their culture and exalted their heritage. "Negro life is seizing its first chances for group expression and self determination," wrote sociologist Alain Locke in 1926. Harlem became what Locke termed "the center of a spiritual coming of age."

The artists and writers of the Renaissance did not share a style. Langston Hughes's realistic poems of downtrodden but determined people bear little resemblance to Countee Cullen's elegant sonnets. Instead, these artists shared the urgent need to document the experiences of their people.

The Center of the World Life for African Americans after World War I was filled with grave disappointment. Although many had served side-by-side with white soldiers in Europe, they returned home to find continued racism barring their paths to the American Dream. In the early 1900s, hundreds of thousands of African Americans embarked on what has come to be called the Great Migration, moving from the rural South to the industrial cities of the North. As more and more African Americans settled in Harlem, the neighborhood became a meeting ground for writers, musicians, performers, and thinkers.

The work they produced was unique. Before the Renaissance, many African American writers sought to emulate whites. By contrast, the

▼ **Critical Viewing** In this image of jazz great Duke Ellington leading his band, how do the positioning of the musicians and the use of light and shadow echo the rhythms and energy of jazz music? **[Analyze]**

Renaissance writers celebrated their racial identity. The goal was to create, as Hughes put it, "an expression of our individual dark-skinned selves."

An Outpouring of Expression Their output was impressive. From the 1920s through the mid-1930s, sixteen African American writers published more than fifty volumes of poetry and fiction—an astounding amount of work at the time. Other African American artists made their marks in painting, music, and theater. Blues singer Bessie Smith performed to packed houses. Musicians Jelly Roll Morton, Louis Armstrong, and Duke Ellington laid the foundations of jazz, a form of music scholars argue is the only truly American art form. In the visual arts, Aaron Douglas incorporated African images into his paintings and illustrations.

Zora and Langston, Phoebe Beasley

Although he was one of the youngest in the movement, Langston Hughes may have been its most influential advocate. His poems combined the rhythms of jazz and blues with stories of Harlem life and captured the struggles of "workers, roustabouts, and singers and job hunters."

Other writers, such as Countee Cullen and Claude McKay, a Jamaican immigrant, wrote in more classical forms. Novelist Zora Neale Hurston combined African folklore with realistic narratives. Today, her novel *Their Eyes Were Watching God* is considered a major work.

A Powerful Legacy In the decades since it ended, the impact of the Harlem Renaissance has been a subject of debate. Most scholars agree that it opened doors for the acceptance of art and writing by African Americans. However, some say that the Renaissance artists were too interested in seeking the approval of the white establishment. Even Langston Hughes admitted that few African Americans had read his work.

Still, the Harlem Renaissance gave Americans a language with which to begin to discuss the problems of racism. It also broke ground for writers who came later. Mid-century writers such as Richard Wright, Ralph Ellison, and James Baldwin stand in a direct line of descent from the writers of the Renaissance.

Today, Nobel Prize–winner Toni Morrison, novelist and poet Alice Walker, popular mystery writer Walter Mosley, and hundreds of other writers, painters, and musicians owe a debt to the artists of the Harlem Renaissance. In its own time, it raised America's consciousness about racism. For thousands of aspiring writers and artists, the Harlem Renaissance was proof that art excludes no one. On the contrary, music, art, and literature provide all human beings the tools with which we can express and celebrate ourselves.

▲ **Critical Viewing** What elements of the lives and works of Langston Hughes and Zora Neale Hurston are expressed in this image of the two writers? **[Interpret]**

Prepare to Read

from Dust Tracks on a Road

Zora Neale Hurston (1891–1960)

Throughout her career as a writer, Zora Neale Hurston was recognized as an influential author and a pioneering force in the documentation of African American culture. Still, she died penniless and was buried in an unmarked grave in a segregated cemetery in Fort Pierce, Florida. Hurston was almost entirely forgotten until author Alice Walker set out on a mission to locate and mark her grave, recording the experience in a 1975 *Ms.* magazine article. Walker's effort restored Hurston to her rightful place in American literature as "the dominant black woman writer" of her time.

Early Influences Hurston was one of the first American writers to recognize that a cultural heritage was valuable in its own right. Her unshakable self-confidence and strong sense of personal worth were fostered by a childhood in Eatonville, Florida, America's first fully incorporated African American township. One of eight children, Hurston was, by her own account, a spirited, curious child who "always wanted to go." Her mother explained this urge to wander by claiming that travel dust had been sprinkled at the door the day Zora was born.

Hurston's childhood abruptly ended when her mother died. Hurston went to live with a series of friends and relatives. By age fourteen, she was supporting herself.

Two Careers Hurston developed an interest in writing while studying at Howard University. In 1925, she moved to New York City, where her gift for storytelling and her outgoing personality helped her to make friends quickly. She soon published a story and a play, firmly establishing herself as one of the bright new talents of the Harlem Renaissance, the blossoming of literature and painting among African Americans in the 1920s, centered in New York. She began attending Barnard College, where her work came to the attention of prominent anthropologist Franz Boas, who convinced Hurston to begin graduate studies in anthropology at Columbia University. With an academic grant, she began a second career as a folklorist.

Preserving a Culture During the Great Migration, when African Americans from the South migrated by the hundreds of thousands to the north—where jobs awaited them in industrial cities like Detroit and Chicago—Hurston moved against the tide. She returned to the South for six years to document the art of "the Negro farthest down." She collected African American folk tales and, in 1935, published *Mules and Men*, the first volume of black American folklore compiled by an African American. Hurston's work helped to document the roots of African American tales in the stories, songs, and myths of Africa. Her second folklore collection, *Tell My Horse* (1938), also provided descriptions of African American cultural beliefs and ritual practices transported from Africa.

The Road to Obscurity Hurston achieved strong critical and popular success during the 1930s and 1940s after publishing the novels *Jonah's Gourd Vine* (1934), *Their Eyes Were Watching God* (1937), and *Moses, Man of the Mountain* (1939). She also wrote numerous short stories, plays, and her prize-winning autobiography, *Dust Tracks on a Road* (1942), which was the most commercially successful of her works.

Unfortunately, controversy and personal scandal led Hurston's career into obscurity. At the time of her death, none of her books were in print. It was not until the 1970s that, with the assistance of Alice Walker, there was a resurgence of interest in Hurston's work. Rescued from the shadows of literary history, she is now generally regarded as one of the important literary figures of the twentieth century.

Preview

Connecting to the Literature

As a child, Zora Neale Hurston was passionate about literature, and that passion led to her success as a writer. As you read, think about an interest of your own that may not only shape your character but also change your life.

Literary Analysis

Social Context in Autobiography

Autobiography is a nonfiction account of a writer's life told in his or her own words. Autobiographical writing documents the writer's feelings about key events and experiences. In addition to personal insights, autobiographies also reveal **social context**—the attitudes and customs of the culture in which the writer lived. The excerpt from Hurston's autobiography recalls an event from her childhood and provides a glimpse of life in her African American community in the South.

Connecting Literary Elements

In this selection, Hurston helps the scenery and settings of her memories come to life through the use of **dialogue**. The words the people speak reflect their culture and reveal their personalities. By showcasing human interaction, dialogue makes literature more conversational, readable, and enjoyable. As you read, notice the ways in which the dialogue adds nuance and color to your understanding of Hurston's experience.

Reading Strategy

Analyzing How a Writer Achieves Purpose

Hurston's **purpose**—to share her personal experience and show the vitality of the African American community—determines her choice of words, details, characters, and events. By linking her choices to her goals, you can analyze her success in achieving her purpose.

As you read, note key words, details, characters, and events in a chart like the one shown. Then review your notes to evaluate how Hurston achieves her purpose.

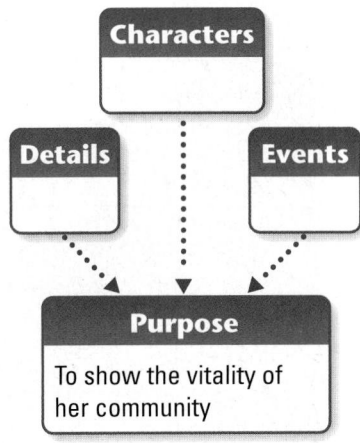

Vocabulary Development

foreknowledge (fôr′ näl ij) *n.* awareness of something before it happens or exists (p. 915)

brazenness (brā′ zən nis) *n.* shamelessness; boldness; impudence (p. 915)

caper (kā′ pər) *n.* prank (p. 915)

exalted (eg zôlt′ id) *adj.* filled with joy or pride; elated (p. 916)

geography (jē äg′ rə fē) *n.* study of Earth's surface (p. 917)

avarice (av′ ə ris) *n.* extreme desire for wealth; greed (p. 918)

from
Dust Tracks on a Road

Zora Neale Hurston

▲ **Critical Viewing** What elements of this photograph document the economic realities many of these children probably faced? **[Analyze]**

Background

In this excerpt from Zora Neale Hurston's autobiography, the young Zora experiences an event that opens her eyes to the world of literature and sets the stage for her career as a writer. Hurston would go on to compile African American folklore—traditional stories—and to write her own critically acclaimed fiction.

I used to take a seat on top of the gatepost and watch the world go by. One way to Orlando[1] ran past my house, so the carriages and cars would pass before me. The movement made me glad to see it. Often the white travelers would hail me, but more often I hailed them, and asked, "Don't you want me to go a piece of the way with you?"

They always did. I know now that I must have caused a great deal of amusement among them, but my self-assurance must have carried the point, for I was always invited to come along. I'd ride up the road for perhaps a half-mile, then walk back. I did not do this with the permission of my parents, nor with their <u>foreknowledge</u>. When they found out about it later, I usually got a whipping. My grandmother worried about my forward ways a great deal. She had known slavery and to her my <u>brazenness</u> was unthinkable.

"Git down offa dat gate-post! You li'l sow, you! Git down! Setting up dere looking dem white folks right in de face! They's gowine[2] to lynch you, yet. And don't stand in dat doorway gazing out at 'em neither. Youse too brazen to live long."[3]

Nevertheless, I kept right on gazing at them, and "going a piece of the way" whenever I could make it. The village seemed dull to me most of the time. If the village was singing a chorus, I must have missed the tune.

Perhaps a year before the old man[4] died, I came to know two other white people for myself. They were women.

It came about this way. The whites who came down from the North were often brought by their friends to visit the village school. A Negro school was something strange to them, and while they were always sympathetic and kind, curiosity must have been present, also. They came and went, came and went. Always, the room was hurriedly put in order, and we were threatened with a prompt and bloody death if we cut one <u>caper</u> while the visitors were present. We always sang a spiritual, led by Mr. Calhoun himself. Mrs. Calhoun always stood

---

1. **Orlando** (ôr lan´ dō) city in central Florida, about five miles from Eatonville, Hurston's hometown.
2. **gowine** "going."
3. **"Git down . . . live long"** Hurston's grandmother's fears reflect the belief of many people at the time that it was inappropriate for African Americans to be assertive toward whites.
4. **the old man** white farmer who had developed a friendship with Hurston.

Literary Analysis
Social Context in Autobiography What do you learn about the social context from Zora's parents' stern warning about talking with white folk?

foreknowledge (fôr´ näl´ ij) *n.* awareness of something before it happens or exists

brazenness (brā´ zən nis) *n.* shamelessness; boldness; impudence

caper (kā´ pər) *n.* prank

✓**Reading Check**

Why does her grandmother worry about Zora's sitting on the gatepost and accepting rides from strangers?

in the back, with a palmetto switch[5] in her hand as a squelcher. We were all little angels for the duration, because we'd better be. She would cut her eyes and give us a glare that meant trouble, then turn her face towards the visitors and beam as much as to say it was a great privilege and pleasure to teach lovely children like us. They couldn't see that palmetto hickory in her hand behind all those benches, but we knew where our angelic behavior was coming from.

Usually, the visitors gave warning a day ahead and we would be cautioned to put on shoes, comb our heads, and see to ears and fingernails. There was a close inspection of every one of us before we marched in that morning. Knotty heads, dirty ears and fingernails got hauled out of line, strapped and sent home to lick the calf over again.

This particular afternoon, the two young ladies just popped in. Mr. Calhoun was flustered, but he put on the best show he could. He dismissed the class that he was teaching up at the front of the room, then called the fifth grade in reading. That was my class.

So we took our readers and went up front. We stood up in the usual line, and opened to the lesson. It was the story of Pluto and Persephone. It was new and hard to the class in general, and Mr. Calhoun was very uncomfortable as the readers stumbled along, spelling out words with their lips, and in mumbling undertones before they exposed them experimentally to the teacher's ears.

Then it came to me. I was fifth or sixth down the line. The story was not new to me, because I had read my reader through from lid to lid, the first week that Papa had bought it for me.

That is how it was that my eyes were not in the book, working out the paragraph which I knew would be mine by counting the children ahead of me. I was observing our visitors, who held a book between them, following the lesson. They had shiny hair, mostly brownish. One had a looping gold chain around her neck. The other one was dressed all over in black and white with a pretty finger ring on her left hand. But the thing that held my eyes were their fingers. They were long and thin, and very white, except up near the tips. There they were baby pink. I had never seen such hands. It was a fascinating discovery for me. I wondered how they felt. I would have given those hands more attention, but the child before me was almost through. My turn next, so I got on my mark, bringing my eyes back to the book and made sure of my place. Some of the stories I had reread several times, and this Greco-Roman myth was one of my favorites. I was <u>exalted</u> by it, and that is the way I read my paragraph.

"Yes, Jupiter had seen her (Persephone). He had seen the maiden picking flowers in the field. He had seen the chariot of the dark monarch pause by the maiden's side. He had seen him when he seized Persephone. He had seen the black horses leap down Mount Aetna's fiery throat. Persephone was now in Pluto's dark realm and he had made her his wife."

---

5. **palmetto** (pal met′ ō) **switch** whip made from the fan-shaped leaves of the palmetto, a type of palm tree.

exalted (eg zôlt′ id) *adj.* filled with joy or pride; elated

The two women looked at each other and then back to me. Mr. Calhoun broke out with a proud smile beneath his bristly moustache, and instead of the next child taking up where I had ended, he nodded to me to go on. So I read the story to the end, where flying Mercury, the messenger of the Gods, brought Persephone back to the sunlit earth and restored her to the arms of Dame Ceres, her mother, that the world might have springtime and summer flowers, autumn and harvest. But because she had bitten the pomegranate[6] while in Pluto's kingdom, she must return to him for three months of each year, and be his queen. Then the world had winter, until she returned to earth.

School Bell Time, 1978 From the Profile/Part 1: The Twenties series (Mecklenburg County), Romare Bearden, Collection: Kingsborough Community College, The City University of New York; © Romare Bearden Foundation/ Licensed by VAGA, New York, NY

The class was dismissed, and the visitors smiled us away and went into a low-voiced conversation with Mr. Calhoun for a few minutes. They glanced my way once or twice and I began to worry. Not only was I barefooted, but my feet and legs were dusty. My hair was more uncombed than usual, and my nails were not shiny clean. Oh, I'm going to catch it now. Those ladies saw me, too. Mr. Calhoun is promising to 'tend to me. So I thought.

Then Mr. Calhoun called me. I went up thinking how awful it was to get a whipping before company. Furthermore, I heard a snicker run over the room. Hennie Clark and Stell Brazzle did it out loud, so I would be sure to hear them. The smart-aleck was going to get it. I slipped one hand behind me and switched my dress tail at them, indicating scorn.

"Come here, Zora Neale," Mr. Calhoun cooed as I reached the desk. He put his hand on my shoulder and gave me little pats. The ladies smiled and held out those flower-looking fingers towards me. I seized the opportunity for a good look.

"Shake hands with the ladies, Zora Neale," Mr. Calhoun prompted and they took my hand one after the other and smiled. They asked if I loved school, and I lied that I did. There was *some* truth in it, because I liked geography and reading, and I liked to play at recess time. Who ever it was invented writing and arithmetic got no thanks from me. Neither did I like the arrangement where the teacher could sit up there with a palmetto stem and lick me whenever he saw fit. I hated things I couldn't do anything about. But I knew better than to bring that up right there, so I said yes, I *loved* school.

---

6. **pomegranate** (päm´ gran´ it) *n.* round, red-skinned fruit with many seeds.

▲ **Critical Viewing**
How does the mood of this image compare or contrast with the mood of Hurston's writing? Explain. **[Compare and Contrast]**

Reading Strategy
Analyzing How a Writer Achieves Purpose Why do you think Hurston includes this description of her response to taunting classmates? How does it help you to understand young Zora's experience?

geography (jē äg´ rə fē) *n.* study of Earth's surface

✔**Reading Check**
Why is Zora afraid to approach her teacher after reading so well?

"I can tell you do," Brown Taffeta gleamed. She patted my head, and was lucky enough not to get sandspurs in her hand. Children who roll and tumble in the grass in Florida are apt to get sandspurs in their hair. They shook hands with me again and I went back to my seat.

When school let out at three o'clock, Mr. Calhoun told me to wait. When everybody had gone, he told me I was to go to the Park House, that was the hotel in Maitland,[7] the next afternoon to call upon Mrs. Johnstone and Miss Hurd. I must tell Mama to see that I was clean and brushed from head to feet, and I must wear shoes and stockings. The ladies liked me, he said, and I must be on my best behavior.

The next day I was let out of school an hour early, and went home to be stood up in a tub full of suds and be scrubbed and have my ears dug into. My sandy hair sported a red ribbon to match my red and white checked gingham dress, starched until it could stand alone. Mama saw to it that my shoes were on the right feet, since I was careless about left and right. Last thing, I was given a handkerchief to carry, warned again about my behavior, and sent off, with my big brother John to go as far as the hotel gate with me.

First thing, the ladies gave me strange things, like stuffed dates and preserved ginger, and encouraged me to eat all that I wanted. Then they showed me their Japanese dolls and just talked. I was then handed a copy of *Scribner's Magazine*,[8] and asked to read a place that was pointed out to me. After a paragraph or two, I was told with smiles, that that would do.

I was led out on the grounds and they took my picture under a palm tree. They handed me what was to me then a heavy cylinder done up in fancy paper, tied with a ribbon, and they told me goodbye, asking me not to open it until I got home.

My brother was waiting for me down by the lake, and we hurried home, eager to see what was in the thing. It was too heavy to be candy or anything like that. John insisted on toting it for me.

My mother made John give it back to me and let me open it. Perhaps, I shall never experience such joy again. The nearest thing to that moment was the telegram accepting my first book. One hundred goldy-new pennies rolled out of the cylinder. Their gleam lit up the world. It was not <u>avarice</u> that moved me. It was the beauty of the thing. I stood on the mountain. Mama let me play with my pennies for a while, then put them away for me to keep.

That was only the beginning. The next day I received an Episcopal hymn-book bound in white leather with a golden cross stamped into the front cover, a copy of *The Swiss Family Robinson*, and a book of fairy tales.

I set about to commit the song words to memory. There was no music written there, just the words. But there was to my consciousness music in between them just the same. "When I Survey the Wondrous Cross"

---

7. **Maitland** (māt′ lənd) city in Florida, close to Eatonville.
8. *Scribner's Magazine* literary magazine no longer published.

Reading Strategy
Analyzing How a Writer Achieves Purpose Why do you think Hurston includes this incident in which her mother prepares her for her meeting with the women at the hotel?

avarice (av′ ər is) *n.* extreme desire for wealth; greed

seemed the most beautiful to me, so I committed that to memory first of all. Some of them seemed dull and without life, and I pretended they were not there. If white people liked trashy singing like that, there must be something funny about them that I had not noticed before. I stuck to the pretty ones where the words marched to a throb I could feel.

A month or so after the young ladies returned to Minnesota, they sent me a huge box packed with clothes and books. The red coat with a wide circular collar and the red tam[9] pleased me more than any of the other things. My chums pretended not to like anything that I had, but even then I knew that they were jealous. Old Smarty had gotten by them again. The clothes were not new, but they were very good. I shone like the morning sun.

But the books gave me more pleasure than the clothes. I had never been too keen on dressing up. It called for hard scrubbings with Octagon soap suds getting in my eyes, and none too gentle fingers scrubbing my neck and gouging in my ears.

In that box were *Gulliver's Travels, Grimm's Fairy Tales, Dick Whittington, Greek and Roman Myths,* and best of all, *Norse Tales.* Why did the Norse tales strike so deeply into my soul? I do not know, but they did. I seemed to remember seeing Thor swing his mighty short-handled hammer as he sped across the sky in rumbling thunder, lightning flashing from the tread of his steeds and the wheels of his chariot. The great and good Odin, who went down to the well of knowledge to drink, and was told that the price of a drink from that fountain was an eye. Odin drank deeply, then plucked out one eye without a murmur and handed it to the grizzly keeper, and walked away. That held majesty for me.

Of the Greeks, Hercules moved me most. I followed him eagerly on his tasks. The story of the choice of Hercules as a boy when he met Pleasure and Duty, and put his hand in that of Duty and followed her steep way to the blue hills of fame and glory, which she pointed out at the end, moved me profoundly. I resolved to be like him. The tricks and turns of the other Gods and Goddesses left me cold. There were other thin books about this and that sweet and gentle little girl who gave up her heart to Christ and good works. Almost always they died from it, preaching as they passed. I was utterly indifferent to their deaths. In the first place I could not conceive of death, and in the next place they never had any funerals that amounted to a hill of beans, so I didn't care how soon they rolled up their big, soulful, blue eyes and kicked the bucket. They had no meat on their bones.

But I also met Hans Andersen and Robert Louis Stevenson. They seemed to know what I wanted to hear and said it in a way that

---

9. **tam** (tam) *n.* cap with a wide, round, flat top and sometimes a center pompom.

✔ **Reading Check**

Of all the gifts she receives, what gives Zora the most pleasure? Explain.

tingled me. Just a little below these friends was Rudyard Kipling in his *Jungle Books.* I loved his talking snakes as much as I did the hero.

I came to start reading the Bible through my mother. She gave me a licking one afternoon for repeating something I had overheard a neighbor telling her. She locked me in her room after the whipping, and the Bible was the only thing in there for me to read. I happened to open to the place where David[10] was doing some mighty smiting, and I got interested. David went here and he went there, and no matter where he went, he smote 'em hip and thigh. Then he sung songs to his harp awhile, and went out and smote some more. Not one time did David stop and preach about sins and other things. All David wanted to know from God was who to kill and when. He took care of the other details himself. Never a quiet moment. I liked him a lot. So I read a great deal more in the Bible, hunting for some more active people like David. Except for the beautiful language of Luke and Paul,[11] the New Testament still plays a poor second to the Old Testament for me. The Jews had a God who laid about Him when they needed Him. I could see no use waiting until Judgment Day to see a man who was just crying for a good killing, to be told to go and roast. My idea was to give him a good killing first, and then if he got roasted later on, so much the better.

---

10. **David** in the Bible, the second king of Israel, the land of the Hebrews.
11. **Luke and Paul** two Christian Apostles who wrote parts of the New Testament.

Review and Assess

Thinking About the Selection

1. **Respond:** What do you think about young Zora's preferences in reading? Which of the stories would you like to read?

2. **(a) Recall:** What does Zora do when white travelers pass by her house? **(b) Infer:** What does this activity tell you about her?

3. **(a) Recall:** Who are the two white women Zora meets, and why are they at her school? **(b) Support:** How can you tell that these two women made an impression on Hurston?

4. **(a) Recall:** What does Zora find fascinating about the two visitors? **(b) Infer:** What does her fascination suggest about her life experiences so far?

5. **(a) Recall:** Describe Zora's response to the gifts she receives. **(b) Infer:** What does her preference reveal about her?

6. **Evaluate:** Do you think it is important to have self-confidence, as Zora did, in order to succeed in life? Why or why not?

Review and Assess

Literary Analysis

Social Context in Autobiography

1. (a) Why might Zora's grandmother be worried about her granddaughter's brazenness? (b) What can you infer about the **social context** and cultural attitudes, based on her grandmother's statements?

2. What do you learn about the social context through the following details of Hurston's **autobiography:** (a) the schoolroom being cleaned for visitors, (b) students reading mythology, and (c) Zora going to school barefoot?

3. Find three more details that reveal the attitudes of Hurston's culture. Record them in a chart like the one shown.

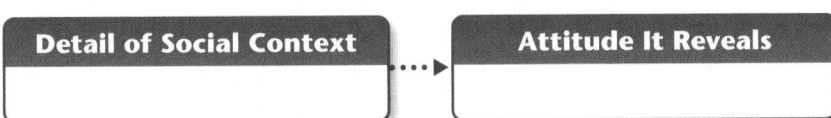

Detail of Social Context		Attitude It Reveals

Connecting Literary Elements

4. What important information about Hurston is revealed in the opening **dialogue** she has with her grandmother?

5. Identify an example of dialogue that reveals a distinct trait of Hurston's personality. Explain how it does so.

6. What general impression do you get of the school and of education in the community based on the dialogue between Hurston, her teacher, and the two visitors?

Reading Strategy

Analyzing How a Writer Achieves Purpose

7. Why does Hurston include the actual words of her grandmother in dialect?

8. What small incidents and details does Hurston use to reveal her reputation as a smart-aleck in school?

9. For what purpose do you think Hurston included her meeting with the Minnesotans in her autobiography?

Extend Understanding

10. **Cultural Connection:** In what ways can relationships with mentors such as Hurston's improve a young person's life?

Quick Review

In **autobiography,** a writer tells his or her own life story.

Autobiographies often reveal **social context—** the attitudes or customs of a culture or specific time period.

The use of **dialogue,** or conversation between characters, makes a scene come alive and helps to define such things as the characters' personalities, social class, and education.

To **analyze how a writer achieves purpose,** consider the way details and events that are described work toward a specific goal.

 **Take It to the Net**
www.phschool.com
Take the interactive self-test online to check your understanding of the selection.

Integrate Language Skills

Vocabulary Development Lesson

Word Analysis: Greek Root -graph-

The Greek root -graph- means "write." For example, *geography* means "the study of, or writing about, Earth." Define the following words, incorporating the meaning of -graph- into your definitions.

1. autograph
2. telegraph
3. biography
4. graphic

Spelling Strategy

In many words, the *j* sound is spelled -*dg*-, as in *knowledge* or *pudgy*. Complete each sentence with a word in which the *j* sound is spelled -*dg*-.

1. A ___?___ rules in a court.
2. I ordered a hot ___?___ sundae.
3. The heavy table would not ___?___.

Concept Development: Analogies

Review the vocabulary list on page 913 and note how each word is used in the context of the selection. Then, select the correct word to complete each of the following analogies.

1. *Hindsight* is to *past* as ___?___ is to *future*.
2. *Trick* is to *magician* as ___?___ is to *prankster*.
3. *Indifference* is to *concern* as ___?___ is to *shyness*.
4. *Dejected* is to *loser* as ___?___ is to *winner*.
5. *Zoology* is to *animals* as ___?___ is to *Earth's surface*.
6. *Cruelty* is to *kindness* as ___?___ is to *selflessness*.

Grammar and Style Lesson

Parallelism in Coordinate Elements

Parallel coordinate elements—those linked by coordinating conjunctions such as *and, but, or, nor,* or *so*—may be nouns, adjectives, adverbs, clauses, or phrases. To make elements that are linked with coordinating conjunctions parallel, put them in the same grammatical form.

> **Example:** She *cut* her eyes <u>and</u> *gave* us a glare that meant trouble. (past tense verb)

Practice Copy the following sentences. Circle the coordinating conjunction(s) and underline the parallel coordinate elements.

1. Nevertheless, I kept right on gazing at them, and "going a piece of the way" . . .

2. I did not do this with the permission of my parents, nor with their foreknowledge.
3. Then [David] sung songs to his harp awhile, and went out and smote some more.
4. I must tell Mama to see that I was clean and brushed from head to feet, and I must wear shoes and stockings.
5. I was given a handkerchief to carry, warned again about my behavior, and sent off . . .

Writing Application Write a paragraph about the importance of self-confidence. Include at least two parallel coordinate elements linked by coordinating conjunctions.

𝒲𝒢 *Prentice Hall Writing and Grammar Connection: Chapter 20, Section 6*

Writing Lesson

Moment of Inspiration

Hurston's encounter with the Minnesotans was a turning point in her life, leading to a greater love of reading and learning. Write a personal narrative about a moment in your life that inspired you to act or think differently.

Prewriting   Jot down some of your interests, such as sports, hobbies, movies, or travel, and consider their origins. Think of incidents that were "moments of inspiration." Select one as the focus of your narrative, and explore its impact in a cause-and-effect diagram like the one shown.

Model: Analyzing Cause and Effect

Cause	Effects
My ninth-grade teacher introduced me to writing poetry in a creative way.	As a result, I feel confident in my ability and want to pursue a career as a poet.

Drafting   Start your essay by showing the effects of your moment of inspiration and then flashing back to reconstruct the moment itself. Use the details in your cause-and-effect diagram to help you.

Revising   Reread your narrative to make sure the connection between inspiration and reaction is clear. Make sure you have demonstrated, rather than explained, its impact on your life.

*W*G *Prentice Hall Writing and Grammar Connection: Chapter 4, Section 2*

Extension Activities

Listening and Speaking Develop and deliver a **campaign speech** in which young Zora hopes to persuade her classmates to elect her class president. Include details that reveal Zora's self-image and portray her character. The following tips will help you:

- Review the selection to identify Zora's qualities.
- Outline her accomplishments.
- Discuss goals that will benefit the class.

Practice the speech with a partner before presenting it to your class.

Research and Technology With a group, select three folk tales from Hurston's *Mules and Men* or from another book of folk tales collected in the United States. Compile them in a booklet, creating a **folk tale collection**. In the booklet, write an introduction, prepare a table of contents, choose art or illustrations and include brief reviews of each tale. [**Group Activity**]

 **Take It to the Net**   www.phschool.com

Go online for an additional research activity using the Internet.

Prepare to Read

The Negro Speaks of Rivers ◆ Ardella ◆ Dream Variations ◆ Refugee in America ◆ The Tropics in New York

Langston Hughes (1902–1967)

Langston Hughes emerged from the Harlem Renaissance, a cultural movement of the 1920s, as the most prolific and successful African American writer in the country. In his poetry, he expressed pride in his heritage and voiced displeasure with the oppression he witnessed. Although Hughes is best known for his powerful poetry, he also wrote plays, fiction, autobiographical sketches, and screenplays.

Born in Missouri and raised in Kansas, Illinois, and Ohio, Hughes attended high school in Cleveland, where he contributed poetry to the school literary magazine. In 1921, he moved to New York City to attend Columbia University, but a year later he left school to travel to Europe and to Africa as a merchant seaman.

First Success On his return to New York, Hughes published his first volume of poetry, *The Weary Blues* (1926). The book attracted attention and earned him wide recognition. Hughes published several other volumes of poetry, including *The Dream Keeper* (1932), *Fields of Wonder* (1947), and *Montage of a Dream Deferred* (1951). He experimented with a variety of forms and techniques in his poetry and often tried to re-create the rhythms of contemporary jazz.

Like many of the Harlem Renaissance writers, Hughes was not born in Harlem and lived a large part of his life elsewhere. Nevertheless, he identified Harlem as a source of inspiration for black artists. Harlem was where he felt most welcome and nourished. Today, Hughes is recognized as one of the most popular and enduring African American writers of the twentieth century.

Claude McKay (1890–1948)

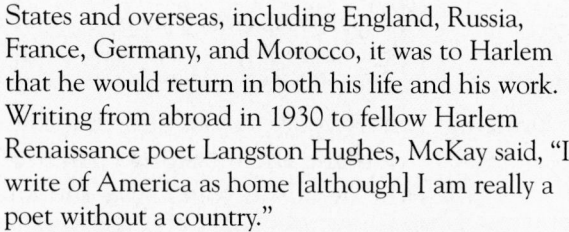

In much of his work, Claude McKay—poet, novelist, journalist, and activist—evokes the colors and rhythms of life on his native island of Jamaica. While McKay retained a lifelong attachment to Jamaica, he regarded Harlem as a spiritual home. Although he frequently lived elsewhere in the United States and overseas, including England, Russia, France, Germany, and Morocco, it was to Harlem that he would return in both his life and his work. Writing from abroad in 1930 to fellow Harlem Renaissance poet Langston Hughes, McKay said, "I write of America as home [although] I am really a poet without a country."

Jamaican Roots The son of farm workers, Festus Claudius McKay received his early education from his brother, Uriah Theophilus, who was a schoolteacher. When he was fourteen, McKay moved to Kingston, Jamaica's capital. While living in Kingston, McKay met a British folklorist who encouraged him to begin writing poetry that reflected Jamaica's indigenous culture. When his collection *Songs of Jamaica* (1912) won an award from the Institute of Arts and Letters, McKay was able to emigrate to the United States. He claimed he was coming to America to study agriculture, but he really came to advance his literary career.

After spending time at Tuskegee Institute and Kansas State College, McKay moved to Harlem in 1914. There, he held down various jobs and opened a restaurant with a friend. McKay's poem "The Tropics in New York" is marked by nostalgia for his homeland—a feeling echoed in the title of his autobiography, *A Long Way From Home* (1937).

Preview

Connecting to the Literature

Many factors shape our identities—the places we come from, the people who nurture us or cause us pain, and the experiences that touch our lives. In these poems, two eloquent writers examine the factors that helped to shape their identities.

Literary Analysis

Speaker

The **speaker** is the voice of a poem. Often, the speaker is the poet. However, a speaker may also be an imaginary person, a group of people, an animal, or an inanimate object. In "The Tropics in New York," Claude McKay's speaker is a homesick adult who is probably the poet himself:

> A wave of longing through my body swept,
> And, hungry for the old, familiar ways
> I turned aside and bowed my head and wept.

As you read these poems, look for clues that reveal the identity of the speaker. Use a chart like the one shown to record your observations.

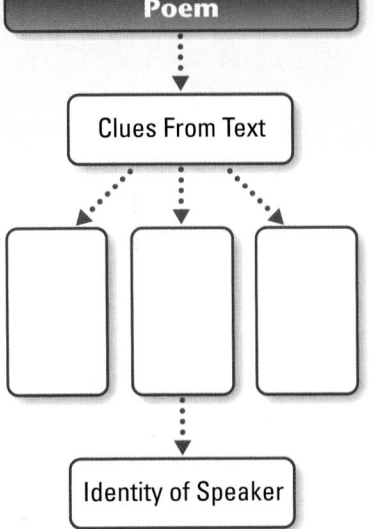

Comparing Literary Works

Through imagery and vivid memories, each of these poems expresses a sense of African American culture, identity, or homeland. For example, both "The Negro Speaks of Rivers" and "The Tropics in New York" describe homelands through references to ancient rivers, to the Mississippi, and to the tropics. As you read these poems, compare the images of African American culture and identity the poets describe.

Reading Strategy

Drawing Inferences About the Speaker

Most often, a poem's speaker is not revealed directly. Instead, the reader must **draw inferences,** or come to conclusions, based on the speaker's choice of words and the details included in the poem. Once you have determined the speaker's identity, you can draw inferences about the speaker's attitudes, feelings, and experiences.

As you read these poems, look for clues about the speakers, and draw inferences about both their personal qualities and the attitude toward life each expresses.

Vocabulary Development

lulled (luld) *v.* calmed or soothed by a gentle sound or motion (p. 926)

dusky (dus´ kē) *adj.* dim; shadowy (p. 926)

liberty (lib´ ər tē) *n.* condition of being free from control by others (p. 929)

The Negro Speaks of Rivers

LANGSTON HUGHES

Background

"The Negro Speaks of Rivers" was Langston Hughes's first great poem. Hughes is said to have written it when he was a senior in high school, although it was published several years later. Hughes's poetry was influenced by Carl Sandburg and by Walt Whitman, whom he considered to be the greatest American poets. Like Whitman's "Song of Myself," "The Negro Speaks of Rivers" uses the first-person point of view to express the experience and identity of an entire community.

I've known rivers:
I've known rivers ancient as the world and older than the flow
    of human blood in human veins.

My soul has grown deep like the rivers.

I bathed in the Euphrates when dawns were young.
5 I built my hut near the Congo and it <u>lulled</u> me to sleep.
I looked upon the Nile and raised the pyramids above it.
I heard the singing of the Mississippi when Abe Lincoln went
    down to New Orleans, and I've seen its muddy bosom turn
    all golden in the sunset.

I've known rivers:
Ancient, <u>dusky</u> rivers.

10 My soul has grown deep like the rivers.

lulled (luld) *v.* calmed or soothed by a gentle sound or motion

dusky (dus´ kē) *adj.* dim; shadowy

Ardella

LANGSTON HUGHES

I would liken you
To a night without stars
Were it not for your eyes.
I would liken you
5   To a sleep without dreams
Were it not for your songs.

Review and Assess

Thinking About the Selections

1. **(a) Respond:** What do you associate with the places Hughes describes in "The Negro Speaks of Rivers"? **(b) Respond:** What places do you associate with your culture or your ancestry?

2. **(a) Recall:** In "The Negro Speaks of Rivers," what has happened to the speaker's soul? **(b) Interpret:** Based on lines 3 and 10, what do you think is the theme of this poem?

3. **(a) Recall:** Identify four rivers the speaker names in "The Negro Speaks of Rivers." **(b) Interpret:** What does the age of rivers imply about people of African ancestry?

4. **Apply:** In what respects can the human race as a whole be compared with rivers?

5. **(a) Recall:** To what two images does the speaker compare Ardella? **(b) Interpret:** What is unusual about these comparisons? **(c) Infer:** What is the speaker's feeling toward Ardella?

6. **Evaluate:** Is Hughes's comparison in "Ardella" effective? Why or why not?

7. **(a) Speculate:** Why do love poems often compare people to nature? **(b) Evaluate:** What is the effect of such comparisons?

Dream Variations

LANGSTON HUGHES

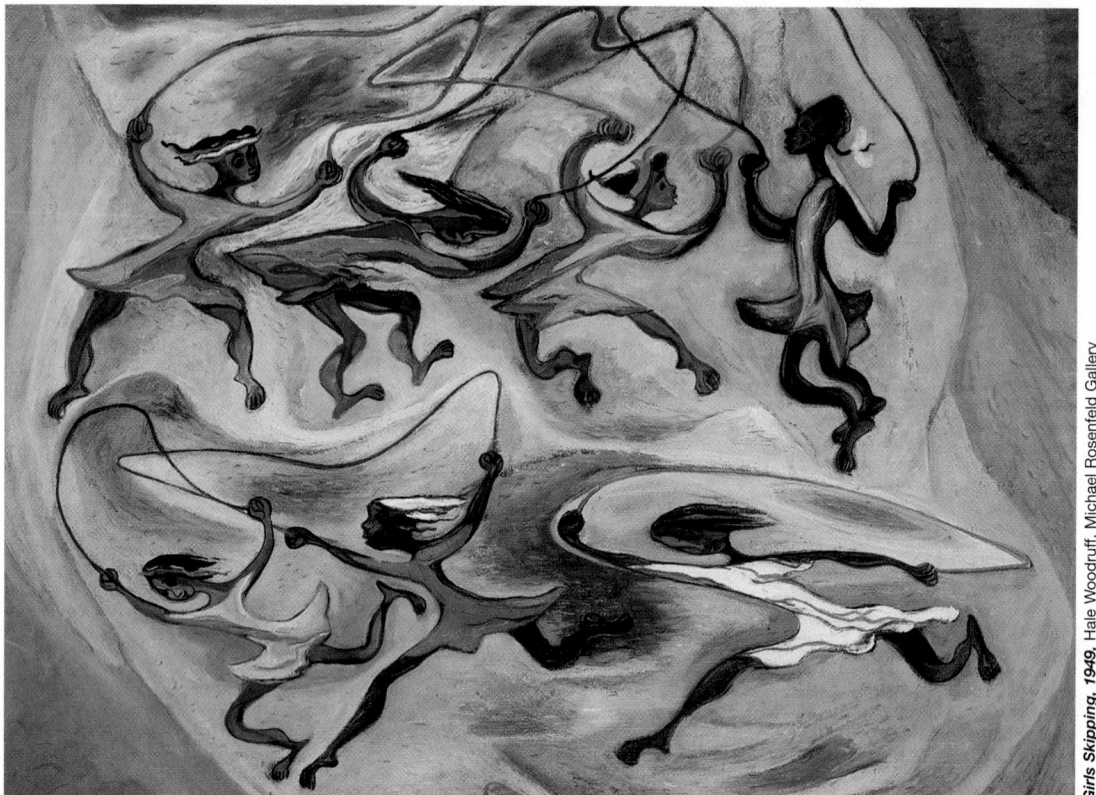

Girls Skipping, 1949, Hale Woodruff, Michael Rosenfeld Gallery

To fling my arms wide
In some place of the sun,
To whirl and to dance
Till the white day is done.
5   Then rest at cool evening
Beneath a tall tree
While night comes on gently,
    Dark like me—
That is my dream!

10   To fling my arms wide
In the face of the sun,
Dance! Whirl! Whirl!
Till the quick day is done.
Rest at pale evening . . .
15   A tall, slim tree . . .
Night coming tenderly
    Black like me.

▲ **Critical Viewing**
How does the motion of the figures in this drawing reflect the mood of the poem? **[Connect]**

Reading Strategy
Drawing Inferences About the Speaker
Based on lines 10–12, decribe the speaker's personality.

Refugee in America

LANGSTON HUGHES

There are words like *Freedom*
Sweet and wonderful to say.
On my heart-strings freedom sings
All day everyday.

5   There are words like *Liberty*
That almost make me cry.
If you had known what I knew
You would know why.

liberty (lib´ ər tē) *n.* condition of being free from control by others

Review and Assess

Thinking About the Selections

1. **Respond:** What mood or emotions did you feel in reading "Dream Variations"? Explain.

2. **(a) Recall:** In "Dream Variations," what does the speaker want to do till the "white" day is done? **(b) Analyze:** What double meaning can you identify in the phrase "white day"?

3. **(a) Recall:** What words does Hughes use to describe color or images of darkness? **(b) Analyze:** In what ways are color and images of darkness used to express meaning?

4. **(a) Recall:** In "Refugee in America," what is the speaker's reaction to words like "freedom" and "liberty"? **(b) Interpret:** In what way does the title of the poem connect these words to the poem itself?

5. **(a) Recall:** What words of emotion are expressed in "Refugee in America"? **(b) Evaluate:** In what way do these emotions contribute to the mood conveyed by the poem? Explain.

6. **Apply:** What common goal do the speakers in these poems share? Explain.

The Tropics in New York

Claude McKay

Bananas ripe and green, and ginger-root,
    Cocoa in pods and alligator pears,
And tangerines and mangoes and grape fruit,
    Fit for the highest prize at parish fairs,

5 Set in the window, bringing memories
    Of fruit-trees laden by low-singing rills,
And dewy dawns, and mystical blue skies
    In benediction over nun-like hills.

My eyes grew dim, and I could no more gaze;
10   A wave of longing through my body swept,
And, hungry for the old, familiar ways
    I turned aside and bowed my head and wept.

Review and Assess

Thinking About the Selection

1. **Respond:** The fruit in the window evokes memories of the speaker's birthplace. What objects could evoke memories of your own past?

2. **(a) Recall:** What fruits are set in the window? **(b) Assess:** In what regions are such fruits generally grown?

3. **(a) Recall:** What specific memories does the fruit stir in the speaker? **(b) Infer:** Why do you think the speaker weeps?

4. **(a) Interpret:** How does the title "The Tropics in New York" contribute to the poem's meaning? **(b) Interpret:** What is ironic about the title and the actual meaning of the poem?

5. **Analyze:** What impressions of his homeland does the speaker convey in this poem?

6. **Take a Position:** Do you think people can find happiness after they have made drastic changes? Why or why not?

Review and Assess

Literary Analysis

Speaker

1. (a) Who is the **speaker** of "The Negro Speaks of Rivers"?
   (b) What effect does the title have on your ability to identify the speaker? Explain.
2. What can you infer about the identity and circumstances of the speaker in "Ardella"?
3. Describe the speaker of "Refugee in America."
4. What might the effect of "Tropics in New York" be if it were delivered by an adolescent son or daughter of the speaker?

Comparing Literary Works

5. (a) Compare the references to homeland in "The Negro Speaks of Rivers" and "The Tropics in New York." (b) Which derive from personal experience? (c) Which are almost mythic? Explain.
6. Compare the messages about freedom in "Refugee in America" and "Dream Variations," citing specific lines.
7. Explain the importance of place to the speakers in each poem.
8. What do these poems reveal about the shared experiences of African Americans with different backgrounds?

Reading Strategy

Drawing Inferences About the Speaker

9. In the third stanza of "The Negro Speaks of Rivers," what can you infer about the identity of a speaker who has raised the ancient pyramids and was also in New Orleans thousands of years later?
10. In each poem, find one line that reveals a characteristic of the speaker. Record your findings in a chart like the one shown.

Passage	What It Reveals About Speaker

Extend Understanding

11. **Cultural Connection:** What kinds of community and commercial services would you suggest to help immigrants stay in touch with their culture?

Quick Review

The **speaker** is the voice of a poem.

To **draw inferences about the speaker,** look closely at the speaker's choice of words and details included in a work.

 Take It to the Net
www.phschool.com

Take the interactive self-test online to check your understanding of these selections.

Integrate Language Skills

Vocabulary Development Lesson

Word Analysis: Latin Root -lib-

The root -lib- derives from *liber*, the Latin word for "free." Match the following words with their definitions.

1. liberty
2. ad-lib
3. liberate
4. liberal

a. improvise
b. generous
c. freedom
d. release from slavery

Fluency: Completing Sentences

Use words from the vocabulary list on page 925 to complete the following sentence.

The fading light, ___?___ and soft, ___?___ the prisoner to sleep, and soon he was dreaming again of his lost ___?___ .

Spelling Strategy

One-syllable words, such as *lull* and *roll*, end in double *l* because the words have only one vowel. By contrast, one-syllable words such as *seal* and *peal* end with only one *l* because the words have two vowels. Considering this rule, choose a word that ends with a single or double *l* for each definition.

1. not shiny or bright (d_____)
2. to take something that does not belong to you (st_____)
3. to write the letters of a word correctly (sp_____)
4. to praise someone (ext_____)

Grammar and Style Lesson

Verb Tenses: Past and Present Perfect

The tenses of verbs allow you to express time within one of three main catergories; the present, the past, and the future. The **past tense** shows an action or condition that began and ended at a given time in the past. By contrast, the **present perfect tense** shows an action or condition that occurred at an indefinite time in the past—or one that begins in the past and continues into the present. This tense is formed with the helping verb *have* or *has* used before the past participle of the main verb.

Past: I *built* my hut near the Congo and it *lulled* me to sleep. (action ended)

Present Perfect: I've *known* rivers . . . (action continues into present)

Practice Copy these sentences in your notebook. Circle the verbs in each sentence, and label each verb as *past tense* or *present perfect tense*.

1. My soul has grown deep like the rivers.
2. I turned aside and bowed my head and wept.
3. I've known rivers ancient as the world and older than the flow of human blood in human veins.
4. If you had known what I knew . . .
5. I bathed in the Euphrates when dawns were young.

Writing Application Write a paragraph about a memory you have of your past. Include verbs in both the past tense and the present perfect tense.

W̶G̶ Prentice Hall Writing and Grammar Connection: Chapter 21, Section 2

Writing Lesson

Poetry Comparison

Langston Hughes committed himself to writing about the African American experience. His poetry focuses on themes of racial identity, pride, and perseverance. To add to your knowledge of Hughes's work, read "I, Too" on page 449. Write an essay addressing the themes you find in the Hughes poems you have read.

Prewriting   As you read the poems, list the images and messages you find in each one. Compare your notes and identify common themes that you can address.

Drafting   Begin your draft by introducing the common themes. In the body of your essay, include direct quotations to support your ideas. End with a conclusion that ties your ideas together.

Model: Using Quotations to Connect Themes

In "Refugee in America," Hughes refers to past suffering, saying, "If you had known what I knew." This message of perseverance parallels Hughes's message in "I, Too," in which he says, "But I laugh,/And eat well,/And grow strong."

> Using quotations from the poems helps to make clear connections to the themes.

Revising   Reread your essay to make sure you have made strong connections between the poems. Review your introduction and conclusion to be sure they support your main points and provide insight to readers.

 Prentice Hall Writing and Grammar Connection: Chapter 9, Section 2

Extension Activities

Listening and Speaking Examine pictures, library books, and historic records of Jamaican life, and list the characteristics you find most intriguing. Consider the following in your research:

- What are the unique aspects of Jamaican culture?
- Compare these ideas, beliefs, or customs with their parallels in American culture.

Give a **presentation** to classmates comparing American and Jamaican cultures.

Research and Technology Using text and graphics, design a series of **posters** that depict the variety of cultural contributions made by African Americans during the 1920s. Include a range of mediums, such as literature, art, and drama. Display the work for your classmates.

 **Take It to the Net**   www.phschool.com

Go online for an additional research activity using the Internet.

Prepare to Read

From the Dark Tower ◆ A Black Man Talks of Reaping ◆ Storm Ending

Countee Cullen (1903–1946)

Unlike most other poets of his day, Countee Cullen used traditional forms and methods. Yet, no other poet expressed the sentiments of African Americans during the early 1900s more eloquently than did Cullen.

A Literary Life Cullen was born in Louisville, Kentucky, and raised by foster parents in New York. An outstanding student, Cullen worked on his high-school newspaper and literary magazine and began to write poetry seriously. He graduated from New York University and later earned a master's degree in English and French from Harvard University. His first collection of poetry, *Color*, was published in 1925. This was followed by *Copper Sun* (1927), *The Ballad of the Brown Girl* (1927), and *The Black Christ* (1929). In 1932, Cullen published *One Way to Heaven*, a satirical novel. In his later years, he published two children's books, *The Lost Zoo* (1940) and *My Lives and How I Lost Them* (1942).

Arna Bontemps (1902–1973)

Arna Bontemps was one of the most scholarly figures of the Harlem Renaissance. Throughout his career as an editor, a novelist, a dramatist, and a poet, his work for social justice made him "the conscience of an era."

Born in Louisiana and raised in California, Bontemps came to New York during the height of the Harlem Renaissance. After teaching at several religious academies, he wrote *Black Thunder* (1936), a highly acclaimed novel about a Virginia slave revolt. In subsequent years, he published poems, biographies, dramas, and books for young readers. He also ran the library at Fisk University in Nashville, making it a major center for African American studies. In 1967, after the death of his friend Langston Hughes, Bontemps compiled *Hold Fast to Dreams* (1969), a poetry anthology. The bulk of the extensive correspondence between Hughes and Bontemps was donated to Yale University, where scholars can study this vivid chronicle of African American literary life.

Jean Toomer (1894–1967)

Like other Harlem Renaissance writers, Jean Toomer was interested in the cultural roots of his people. In his work, he expressed the cultural belief that black heritage and pride were vital to the happiness and freedom of African Americans.

A Major Work Born in Washington, D.C., Nathan Pinchback Toomer attended New York University. He then taught for a few years in Georgia. In 1920, Toomer changed his first name to Jean, to honor the hero of a novel that inspired him. Following the appearance of *Cane* (1923), an unusual book of prose sketches, poems, stories, and a one-act play, Toomer was widely viewed as one of the most talented writers of the Harlem Renaissance. When Toomer's publishing output dwindled, *Cane* fell into obscurity. In recent years, however, *Cane* has been recognized and celebrated as a significant work of the Harlem Renaissance.

Preview

Connecting to the Literature

If you see trouble ahead, you might say that a storm is brewing. In the same way, these poems capture the experiences of the African American people through striking images of nature or familiar activities and events.

Literary Analysis

Metaphor

A **metaphor** is an implied comparison between two seemingly dissimilar things used to make writing more vivid, and meaningful. In these lines, Countee Cullen compares African American life to the toil of planting.

> We shall not always plant while others reap
> The golden increment of bursting fruit . . .

Although metaphors are usually brief, they may also be elaborate, lengthy comparisons. An **extended metaphor** is a comparison that is developed throughout the course of a poem. As you read "Storm Ending," look for the extended metaphor Toomer develops.

Comparing Literary Works

Metaphors are often conveyed through the use of **imagery**—descriptive language that appeals to the senses. These three poets use imagery to express their feelings about the African American experience. Two of these poems offer images of planting, while the third presents images of a huge storm. Usually, readers associate agricultural imagery with growth, and storm imagery with destruction. However, these poems challenge readers' expectations. As you read, use a chart like the one shown to analyze each poem's imagery, and to assess the emotions and attitudes it conveys.

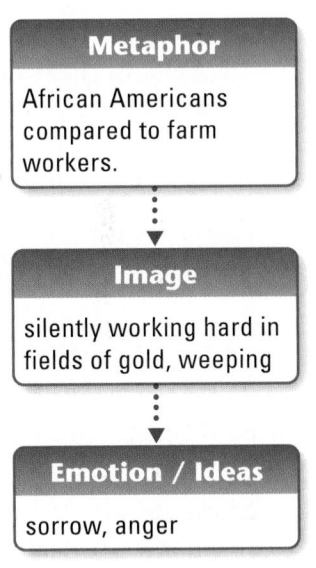

Reading Strategy

Connecting to Historical Context

Many works of literature bear a direct relation to the time and place in which they were written. A reader must **connect** such works to their **historical contexts** in order to understand and appreciate them. To fully grasp the following poems—born in the cultural movement known as the Harlem Renaissance in the 1920s—review the information on page 910.

Vocabulary Development

increment (in´krə mənt) *n.* increase, as in a series (p. 936)

countenance (koun´ tə nəns) *v.* approve; tolerate (p. 936)

beguile (bē gīl´) *v.* charm or delight (p. 936)

stark (stärk) *adj.* severe (p. 937)

reaping (rēp´ iŋ) *v.* cutting or harvesting grain from a field (p. 937)

glean (glēn) *v.* collect the remaining grain after reaping (p. 937)

From The Dark Tower
Countee Cullen (To Charles S. Johnson)

Background

Countee Cullen dedicated this poem to Charles S. Johnson, an African American sociologist, editor, and author of a landmark study of race relations in the 1920s. Johnson was the editor of the publication *Opportunity: Journal of Negro Life* and helped to nurture the writers and artists of the Harlem Renaissance. Cullen served as assistant editor of the publication.

We shall not always plant while others reap
The golden <u>increment</u> of bursting fruit,
Not always <u>countenance</u>, abject and mute,
That lesser men should hold their brothers cheap;
5 Not everlastingly while others sleep
Shall we <u>beguile</u> their limbs with mellow flute,
Not always bend to some more subtle brute;
We were not made eternally to weep.

The night whose sable breast relieves the stark,
10 White stars is no less lovely being dark,
And there are buds that cannot bloom at all
In light, but crumple, piteous, and fall;
So in the dark we hide the heart that bleeds,
And wait, and tend our agonizing seeds.

increment (in´ krə mənt) *n.* increase, as in a series

countenance (koun´ tə nəns) *v.* approve; tolerate

beguile (bē gīl´) *v.* charm or delight

Review and Assess

Thinking About the Selection

1. **Respond:** Can you identify or empathize with the speaker of this poem? Why or why not?

2. **(a) Recall:** Which word is repeated five times in the first stanza? **(b) Analyze:** What is the effect of this repetition?

3. **(a) Recall:** What contrast or opposition does the speaker set up in lines 9–10? **(b) Interpret:** What does Cullen mean by "no less lovely being dark"?

4. **(a) Infer:** Who is the "we" in the poem? **(b) Interpret:** What distinction does the speaker draw between the circumstances of "we" and those of "others"?

5. **Evaluate:** Do you think that waiting is an appropriate response to the conflicts described in the poem? Explain.

Hoeing, Robert Gwathmey, Carnegie Institute Museum of Art, Pittsburgh, Pennsylvania, © Estate of Robert Gwathmey/Licensed by VAGA, New York, NY

◀ **Critical Viewing**
What emotion does this image convey? In what way does it compare with the mood of the poem? **[Compare and Contrast]**

A Black Man Talks of Reaping
Arna Bontemps

I have sown beside all waters in my day.
I planted deep, within my heart the fear
that wind or fowl would take the grain away.
I planted safe against this <u>stark</u>, lean year.

5   I scattered seed enough to plant the land
in rows from Canada to Mexico
but for my <u>reaping</u> only what the hand
can hold at once is all that I can show.

Yet what I sowed and what the orchard yields
10 my brother's sons are gathering stalk and root;
small wonder then my children <u>glean</u> in fields
they have not sown, and feed on bitter fruit.

stark (stärk) *adj.* severe

reaping (rēp´ iŋ) *v.* cutting or harvesting grain from a field

glean (glēn) *v.* collect the remaining grain after reaping

✔**Reading Check**

What does the speaker have to show for all his labor?

Storm Ending

Jean Toomer

Thunder blossoms gorgeously above our heads,
Great, hollow, bell-like flowers,
Rumbling in the wind,
Stretching clappers to strike our ears . . .
5   Full-lipped flowers
Bitten by the sun
Bleeding rain
Dripping rain like golden honey—
And the sweet earth flying from the thunder.

Reading Strategy
Connecting to Historical Context How might the imagery of thunder relate to the ending of slavery?

Review and Assess

Thinking About the Selections

1. **Respond:** What did you see as you read these poems? What did you hear?

2. **(a) Recall:** In "A Black Man Talks of Reaping," why does the speaker plant "deep"? **(b) Draw Conclusions:** What do you think is meant by the "stark, lean year"?

3. **(a) Recall:** In "A Black Man Talks of Reaping," how much seed does the speaker scatter? **(b) Recall:** How much grain is he allowed to harvest? **(c) Infer:** Who reaps what the speaker has sown?

4. **(a) Recall:** In "Storm Ending," what natural event does the poem describe? **(b) Analyze:** What is the speaker's attitude toward the event described? **(c) Support:** Which words best convey this attitude?

5. **(a) Infer:** What does Bontemps suggest about what African Americans have received in exchange for their hard work? **(b) Apply:** In what way does Bontemps's poem comment on the idea that "Whatsoever a man soweth, that shall he also reap"?

Review and Assess

Literary Analysis

Metaphor

1. (a) Identify the **metaphors** Countee Cullen uses in "From the Dark Tower." (b) What details does he use to extend them?

2. (a) What metaphor appears in Bontemps's poem? (b) How does he express and develop the metaphor in each stanza?

3. (a) What two things are compared in the extended metaphor presented in "Storm Ending"? (b) Describe the way in which Toomer establishes this comparison in the first four lines. (c) Describe how he develops it in the lines that follow.

Comparing Literary Works

4. Using a chart like the one shown, identify and analyze the dominant **image** conveyed by each poem.

Poem	Image	Interpretation	Emotion

5. (a) What theme or central message do these poems share? (b) In what ways do their uses of imagery serve to convey those messages?

6. Rank the three poems from most optimistic to most pessimistic. Explain your decisions.

Reading Strategy

Connecting to Historical Context

7. How can you deepen your appreciation of "From the Dark Tower" by reflecting on the northern migration of nearly one million African Americans in the late 1800s and early 1900s?

8. Identify a fact of **historical context** that enriches your reading of "A Black Man Talks of Reaping." Explain.

9. Does your interpretation of "Storm Ending" change when you connect to historical context? Explain.

Extend Understanding

10. **Historical Connection:** What historical factors may have contributed to the decline of the Harlem Renaissance around 1935?

Quick Review

A **metaphor** is an implied comparison between two seemingly dissimilar things.

An **extended metaphor** is a comparison that is developed throughout the length of a literary work.

Imagery is the descriptive language writers use to create word pictures or images for readers.

To **connect to historical context,** interpret a work by linking it with the time and place in which it was written.

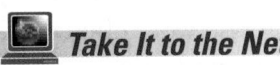 **Take It to the Net**
www.phschool.com

Take the interactive self-test online to check your understanding of these selections.

Integrate Language Skills

Vocabulary Development Lesson

Word Analysis: Latin Root -cre-

Like *increase*, and *create*, the word *increment* contains the Latin root *-cre-*, which means "to grow." Use your knowledge of the root *-cre-* to define these words:

1. crescendo
2. creation
3. increment

Spelling Strategy

The letter *g* usually makes a "hard" sound when it is followed by *a, h, o,* or *u,* as in *gather, ghost,* and *beguile*. For a "soft" sound, *g* is usually followed by *e, i,* or *y*. Indicate whether the *g* sounds in these words are hard or soft.

1. gorgeously   2. garbage   3. gyromagnetic

Concept Development: Synonyms

Review the vobcaulary list on page 935. Then, write the letter of the best synonym for each numbered word.

1. reap: (a) harvest, (b) sow, (c) plow

2. countenance: (a) cheer, (b) tolerate, (c) disregard

3. increment: (a) increase, (b) stability, (c) decrease

4. stark: (a) gentle, (b) steep, (c) severe

5. glean: (a) distribute, (b) weigh, (c) collect

Grammar and Style Lesson

Placement of Adjectives

An **adjective** is a word used to describe a noun or a pronoun. Adjectives can be placed *before* or *after* the nouns or pronouns they modify.

> **Before:** this *stark, lean* <u>year</u> (modifies *year*)
>
> **After:** I've scattered <u>seed</u> *enough* to plant the land (modifies *seed*)

When adjectives follow the noun they modify, they may have more emphasis in a sentence.

In poetry, a literary form characterized by precise word choice and deliberately sculpted lines and stanzas, adjectives can effectively add meaning and build imagery. While poets choose adjectives with care, they also select nouns and verbs to achieve poetic effects.

Practice Rewrite the following sentences, altering the position of the italicized adjectives. Be sure that the adjectives modify the same noun in your sentence as in the original. Make any necessary changes in wording and punctuation.

1. The *cold, merciless* wind chilled us.
2. We saw the ocean, *vast and cobalt*.
3. The *penniless but determined* refugees came to America to start anew.
4. The bird, *cold and hungry*, pecked the ground for worms.
5. *Tired*, we workers fell to exhaustion.

Writing Application Write a paragraph about a poem in this grouping. Include three adjectives and vary the placement of these modifiers.

W̶G̶ Prentice Hall Writing and Grammar Connection: Chapter 27, Section 2

Writing Lesson

Comparison-and-Contrast Essay

Although Countee Cullen and Jean Toomer were associated with the same literary movement, each had a distinct style. In an essay, compare and contrast the qualities of Cullen's structured sonnet and Toomer's open lyric.

Prewriting In a chart, identify the points of comparison between the two poets, such as their uses of metaphors and imagery. Then, consider each poem's message and its sound—the musical quality, which may be lilting and gentle or harsh and driving.

Model: Identifying Points of Comparison

Drafting In your introduction, briefly describe the poems. Then, using your chart, draft a point-by-point comparison, addressing each element of comparison with examples from the poems.

Revising Reread your essay to be sure you have addressed both similarities and differences between the two poems. Add vivid and descriptive language to strengthen comparisons, quoting sufficiently from the poems to support them.

W̵G Prentice Hall Writing and Grammar Connection: Chapter 9, Section 2

Extension Activities

Listening and Speaking Select and compare two other poems by Countee Cullen, and give a **dramatic reading** to the class. As you practice, consider these tips:

- Select the poems based on connections between theme and image.
- As you read, enhance meaning by emphasizing key words.

After reading the poems, invite questions and comments from the class.

Research and Technology With a group, choose an artist or musician from the Harlem Renaissance period and research his or her life and accomplishments. Present your findings to your class in an organized **research report.** [Group Activity]

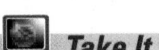 **Take It to the Net** www.phschool.com

Go online for an additional research activity using the Internet.

READING INFORMATIONAL MATERIALS

Public Relations Documents

About Public Relations Documents

Businesses and organizations create many documents to convey messages to the public. These documents include brochures, advertisements, and flyers. They also include press releases and public service announcements. All of these documents are important; however, the heart of an organization lies in its mission, or purpose. For that reason, an organization's mission statement is one of its most important documents. Most mission statements contain three kinds of information:

- **Who We Are**—This is a set of basic facts about the business or organization that has issued the statement.
- **What We Do**—These details show what the business or organization offers.
- **Why We Do It**—This information expresses the philosophy and goals of the business or organization.

The mission statement at right outlines the *Who, What,* and *Why* for a museum in Boston, Massachusetts. As you read it, think about the information that it provides, why this information is offered, who is the intended audience, and why such a document would be useful.

Reading Strategy

Making Inferences

As you read, you gather information. Some information is stated in the text itself. Other information may take the form of assumptions that are based on what you know. Such assumptions, which combine a reading of the text with your own experience, are called inferences.

Making an inference requires you to combine two kinds of knowledge and then to determine whether unstated information is likely to be supported by that knowledge.

Look for Details		**Relate Your Experience**		**Make and Check an Inference**
In an article about a fire, notice details about the intensity of the blaze.	**+**	Recall fires that you have seen.	**=**	Both skill and courage played a part in putting out the fire. Check against firefighters' actions. Verify.

Mission Statement

Most businesses and organizations create informational documents that communicate to potential partners, customers, or contributors their overall purpose and the scope of their activities. The examples shown here include a mission statement on this page that briefly expresses the organization's purpose and a calendar of events on page 944 that shows how that purpose is carried out and invites people to come and participate.

MUSEUM OF AFRO-AMERICAN HISTORY

Boston and Nantucket

Mission Statement

A Foundation for the Future

In one well-crafted sentence, the museum says, "This is *who we are*." More details follow, but this is the single most important statement about the museum.

The mission of the Museum of Afro-American History is to preserve, conserve and interpret the contributions of people of African descent and those who have found common cause with them in the struggle for liberty, dignity, and justice for all Americans. Therefore, we:

As part of a list of museum features, this explains *what we do* information. Similar information appears at the end of the statement, but its purpose is more general.

- collect and exhibit artifacts of distinction in this field and acquire and maintain physical structures and sites through the end of the 19th century;

- educate the public about the importance of the Afro-American historical legacy in general, its Boston and New England heritages, in particular;

- celebrate the enduring vitality of African American culture;

Here is *why we do it* information—an expression of the museum's philosophy and goals.

- and advance on our own and in collaboration with others an appreciation of the past for the benefit of the custodians of the future.

MUSEUM OF AFRO-AMERICAN HISTORY BOSTON

Calendar of Events

Events take place at 8 Smith Court, Beacon Hill, unless otherwise noted.

A calender of events provides basic information, such as where and when activities take place.

SATURDAY, FEB. 3, 7:30 P.M.

READING AND BOOK SIGNING

On Her Own Ground: The Life and Times of Madam C.J. Walker

A'Lelia Bundles, former deputy bureau chief of ABC News in Washington and great-great granddaughter of Madam C.J. Walker, will discuss the writing of *On Her Own Ground*, the first historically accurate account of this legendary entrepreneur and social activist.

Sponsored by the Collection of African American Literature, a partnership between the Museum of Afro-American History, Suffolk University, and Boston African American Historic Site.

REFRESHMENTS AND BOOK SALES FOLLOWING. FREE

Information about sponsoring organizations is usually included.

TUESDAYS, 10:30-11:30 A.M.

Stories from African American Literature and Lore

Vibrant stories and activities presenting history for preschool aged children and parents. FREE

FRIDAY, FEB. 16, 6 P.M.-9 A.M.

Museum Overnight: Underground Railroad

Descriptions of events are brief but inviting.

Spend the night at the Museum exploring the Underground Railroad through the escape routes on Beacon Hill. Design and build your own safe house. Includes dinner, storytelling, activities, breakfast and a special "bundle" to take home.

GRADE 5-6. $30 NON-MEMBER $25 MEMBERS.

SUNDAY, MARCH 18, 3 P.M.

Marian Anderson/Roland Hayes Concert Series: A New Beginning
Makanda Ken McIntyre Jazz Quartet. Original jazz selections and standard favorites from this world-class composer and improviser. McIntyre, a Boston native and NY resident, is a master of the alto sax, bass clarinet, oboe, flute, and bassoon. Reception immediately following.

Sponsored in part by the Office of Community Collaborations and Program Development at the New England Conservatory.

Any fees must be indicated.

$10 NON-MEMBER; FREE MEMBER; GROUP RATES AVAILABLE.

Check Your Comprehension

1. Summarize the museum's mission, and name two goals that result from that mission.
2. Review the calendar of events to determine (a) in what ways the museum collaborates with others and (b) in what ways the museum educates the public.

Applying the Reading Strategy

Making Inferences

3. Copy and complete this chart of inferences about the Museum of Afro-American History. Verify each inference by noting a supporting detail from the mission statement or calendar of events.

Inference	Verification
Some African American artists found a creative outlet in New England.	
The museum founders thought that African American history had been misrepresented.	
The museum has little information about the civil rights movement of the 1960s.	

Activity

Writing a Mission Statement

Write a mission statement for one of the following organizations:
- a museum devoted to a scientific or artistic topic
- a magazine devoted to a sport or hobby
- a Web site devoted to a historical person

Before you write, think about the philosophy—a system of values—that you believe merits public attention. Then, identify the goals related to your topic that would arise from that philosophy.

Comparing Informational Materials

Comparative Mission Statements

Prepare a list of questions that you could use to evaluate the effectiveness of mission statements. Then, using either print sources or the Internet, find mission statements from two similar businesses or organizations. You might compare restaurants, hospitals, libraries, or charities. Apply your questions. Then, prepare a presentation in which you explain which mission statement you find more effective.

In the past, historians described the United States as a "melting pot" to suggest that people of different ethnic backgrounds came to the country and blended into a single American culture. Today, many Americans argue that the "melting pot" metaphor is not accurate. They say that the United States is a multicultural society in which many distinct cultures exist side by side, retaining their individual identities. New phrases that describe the country's diversity call the United States a quilt, a rainbow, a salad bowl, or a mosaic.

In today's United States, ethnic communities nurture their own cultures and traditions while they still hold many distinctly American beliefs such as freedom and equality. Just a few examples of such communities are the Chinatowns in New York and San Francisco, Arab communities in Michigan, and Scandinavian communities in the Midwest.

Writers Celebrate Differences Today's writers explore the many ways of being an American. Hispanic Americans are growing in number and becoming increasingly vocal. Hispanic novelists, playwrights, and poets such as Ricardo Sánchez reflect on the ways in which their Hispanic roots intersect with American culture to create new influences and identities.

i yearn

Ricardo Sánchez

i yearn this morning
what i've yearned
since i left

    almost a year ago . . .

5   it is hollow
this
being away
from everyday life

in the barrios[1]
10 of my homeland . . .
all those cities
like el paso, los angeles,
albuquerque,
denver, san antonio
15   (off into chicano
        infinitum![2]);

i yearn
to hear spanish
spoken in caló[3]—
20 that special way
chicanos[4] roll their
    tongues
to form
words
25 which dart or glide;

i yearn
for foods
that have character
and strength—the kind
30 that assail yet caress
you with the zest of life;

more than anything,
i yearn, my people,
for the warmth of you
35 greeting me with "¿qué tal,
hermano?"[5]
and the knowing that you
    mean it
when you tell me that you love
40 the fact that we exist . . .

---

1. **barrios** (bär´ ē ōs) *n.* Spanish-speaking neighborhood.
2. **infinitum** (in´ fə nīt´ əm) *n.* Latin for "that which is endless."
3. **caló** (kä lō´) *n.* slang.
4. **chicanos** (chē kä´ nōs) *n.* Mexican Americans, usually capitalized.
5. **¿qué tal, hermano?** (kā täl´ er mä´ nō) Spanish for "How are things, brother?"

Connecting Literature Past and Present

1. Compare Ricardo Sánchez's homesickness in "i yearn" to that of Claude McKay in "The Tropics in New York."

2. (a) According to this poem, what are the difficulties of a multicultural society? (b) What are the benefits?

Ricardo Sanchez

(1941–1995)

Born in El Paso, Texas, and raised in a Hispanic neighborhood, Ricardo Sánchez believed that his mission was to bring Mexican culture and traditions into the lives of his fellow Mexican Americans. He often wrote about the challenge faced by those who try to create a coherent identity from a mix of two cultures: Mexican and American. Sánchez was an activist as well as a writer and an academic. As a lecturer, consultant, developer of television programs, and poet, Sánchez worked to educate all Americans about Mexican American culture.

Writing About Literature

Evaluate Literary Trends

The Imagist poets wrote with clear ideas about poetry and provided specific criteria with which to judge the success or failure of a poem. Ezra Pound expressed these ideas in his essay "A Few Don'ts by an Imagiste." To a great extent, poems by such Imagists as Pound, William Carlos Williams, and H.D. can be measured according to the criteria Pound defined.

Using the assignment outlined in the yellow box, write an essay evaluating this literary trend.

Prewriting

Summarize Pound's main points. Reread Pound's essay, and take careful notes about each of his main points. Avoid using Pound's own language in your notes. Instead, paraphrase—or restate in your own words—his ideas. Translating his advice into your own words will allow you to be sure you understand his often complex concepts. It will also help you to determine which of his ideas will require additional explanation or definition for your readers.

Evaluate line by line. In all works of literature, every word plays an important part within the whole. In Imagist poetry, which, by its very nature, is compressed and focused, a single word carries even greater weight than in most other genres. Judge the success of each poem you have selected by weighing each word according to Pound's criteria. You may want to make a photocopy of the poems and write notes directly on the pages.

Create a scorecard. Use your notes to create an Imagist scorecard, like the one shown below. In the first column, list the criteria you will use to judge each poem. Across the top, list the titles of the poems you have chosen to analyze. In each box, place a *P* (for *Pass*) for each criterion that a given poem fulfills. Place an *F* (for *Fail*) for each criterion that a poem fails to meet.

Model: Analyzing According to Criteria

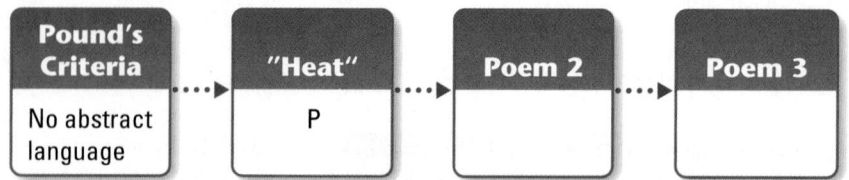

Pound's Criteria	"Heat"	Poem 2	Poem 3
No abstract language	P		

For each of the poems you are discussing, use the results of your scorecard to write a one-sentence statement about whether or not it fulfills Pound's criteria. These statements will serve as the foundation for the concepts you will develop more completely as you draft. Your statement should note the most prominent ways in which the poem succeeds or fails.

Assignment:
Following the Rules

Write an analytical essay that evaluates the success with which at least three Imagist poems fulfill the goals set out in Pound's essay "A Few Don'ts by an Imagiste."

Criteria:
- Clearly restate Pound's main ideas.
- Evaluate the effectiveness of specific words, lines, and images in at least three poems according to Pound's ideas.
- Approximate length: 1,500 words.

Read to Write

As you read each poem, ask yourself whether it meets Pound's criteria. The point is not whether or not you like the poem, but whether it fulfills specific artistic objectives.

Drafting

Transform your notes into sentences. Notes written in preparation for writing an essay are abbreviated ideas—kernels of the points you will develop more completely in a draft. Using the notes you made as part of your prewriting activities, construct one or more complete sentences that fully express the idea each note represents.

Combine sentences into paragraphs. Write at least one paragraph on Pound's essay and at least one on each poem you have analyzed. In each paragraph about a poem, evaluate the author's success in meeting Pound's criteria. Refer to your scorecard for details. Make sure each sentence supports or explains your "grade."

🖊 **Write to Learn**

As you work on your essay, you may discover new ideas about the poems. Allow for this, and incorporate your discoveries into your work.

Revising and Editing

Review content: Check the soundness of your thinking. Check your evaluation of each poem to make sure it is based on the criteria you have compiled from Pound's essay. Remember: The point is not whether you personally like a poem but whether it fulfills the stated requirements.

🖊 **Write to Explain**

The foundation of your essay is your examination of Pound's essay. Make sure that your explanation of Pound's ideas is simple and clear.

> **Model: Revising to Focus on Criteria**
>
> "In a Station of the Metro" almost perfectly obeys Pound's dictate that a poem should "go in fear of abstractions." This brief description of faces in a crowd is intensely visual and concrete. ~~I love this poem because I know exactly what he means.~~ *One possible weakness is the word* apparition. *Because the word refers to something that is not really there, it can be interpreted as an abstraction.*

Review style: Vary sentence length and word choice. Poets select and arrange words not only for their meanings but also for their sounds and rhythms. Learn from their example. When revising your essay, work to avoid using the same words repeatedly, and make changes to avoid using sentences of the same length and structure.

Publishing and Presenting

Give an oral presentation. Share your ideas with the class. If possible, use an overhead projector or a slideshow program to project the poems you are discussing. Alternatively, you can simply copy the poems on the board. Then, as you read your essay aloud for the class, use a pointer to indicate words or phrases that are especially relevant to your discussion. Invite questions and comments from the class.

𝒲𝒢 *Prentice Hall Writing and Grammar Connection: Chapter 14*

Writing WORKSHOP

Research: Multimedia Presentation

A **multimedia presentation** is a technique for sharing information with an audience by enhancing narration and explanation with media, including video images, slides, audiotape recordings, music, and fine art. In this workshop, you will plan, draft, and revise a multimedia presentation.

Assignment Criteria Your multimedia presentation should have the following characteristics:

- Integrated audio and visual components
- Reinforcement of each element by the appropriate medium
- A clear and logical organization
- Innovative use of media to convey concepts

To preview the criteria on which your multimedia presentation may be assessed, see the Rubric on page 953.

Prewriting

Choose a topic. Select a subject for which multimedia material will be readily available. To narrow the field of possible topics, **list** musicians or artists whose work you enjoy, films you know well, or professional sports teams you watch regularly. Make sure you can imagine the audio or visual material that would support your ideas. Then, choose a topic.

Create a media checklist. In a chart, list the various kinds of media that would be available for the topic you have chosen. Use the right-hand column of the chart to note specific media that would be most useful for your topic.

Media Checklist	
☑ Music	*Mysterious music*
☑ Videos	*Historic roller coaster*
☑ Art	*Sketches of design*
☑ Photographs	*Dragon memorabilia*
☐ Computer Presentation	
☑ Interviews	*People waiting in line*

Research your topic. As you gather materials, note creative ways to involve viewers. Consult your library for audio or video clips of interviews, documentaries, music, and art resources. Search the Internet for a wide range of resources. Remember: almost any medium can be used with your presentation, provided it helps to explain your topic.

Identify a thesis. Review your notes and the materials you have gathered. Develop a main idea—one clear statement that will express the focus of your multimedia presentation. You may include this statement in whatever portion of your presentation will best convey the idea, whether audiotape, videotape, art, or text.

Student Model

Before you begin writing, read this student model and review the characteristics of effective multimedia presentations.

Afton Kapala
Ventura, California

The Dragon's Lair

Text	Video and Audio	
(cue video and audio) For thousands of years, dragons have played a major role in the human imagination. They represent the awesome power of nature, and the extremes of human emotion.	**Video:** dragons from ancient China, Babylonia, Rome, to Wales, and Anglo-Saxon England, to today (film and TV shows) **Audio:** music from ancient past to today	Afton's subject is rich and well-suited to a multimedia format.
Today, Bombshell Roller Coasters harnesses the power of dragon lore in our latest roller coaster design. **(pause for emphasis; cue video)** . . . the Dragon's Lair. **(pause as video plays)**	**Video:** computer animation of Dragon's Lair in motion with zooms in and out to show detail	
(cue slide) Our design represents the latest and best in roller coaster technology. **(use pointer to highlight features)** The coaster will begin with a 95-meter peak, followed by a drop, followed by a 76-meter peak and drop. The rest of the ride includes banked turns, loops, and a smaller hill.	**Slide:** coaster route schematic design	Afton does not attempt to be flashy if it is not appropriate. This slide of a schematic design is appropriate for the text.
(cue audio and first slide) After they buy tickets, customers will enter our air-conditioned concourse, **(cue second slide)** where they can buy snacks and dragon memorabilia. **(cue third slide)** Our Ground Dragons—customer service agents in costume—will provide customers with great photo opportunities.	**Slide:** dragon memorabilia (hats, flashlights, stuffed animals, etc.) **Slide:** costumed ground dragon	The text, audio, and visual elements convey an increasing level of detail in a clear, logical way.
(cue slide) Why would Magic Mountain want to buy this ride? For nearly two centuries roller coasters have been a huge public attraction. **(cue video)**	**Slide:** question mark **Video with voiceover:** historic roller coasters—Russian Mountains (1800s), the Cyclone (1900s), the Fireball (1920s), and the Skyliner (1960s)	
All of those great coasters represent the past, but the Dragon's Lair is the future. It will keep crowds coming, generating great revenues for years to come.	**Video morphs to:** computer-animated image of the Dragon's Lair	This use of video transforming into computer animation is an innovative and effective use of media.

Drafting

Sketch an outline. Before you begin to draft actual text, create a working outline to shape your sequence of ideas. The chart shown here details an effective sequence for a presentation.

Organize your presentation. Once you have gathered sufficient information, elaborate on your outline sketch by planning the media elements to include under each main heading. Jot down any additional ideas for incorporating other media to convey your ideas.

Plan your delivery. Draft a script based on the outline sketch. Use stage direction format to indicate posture, body language, and voice inflection during your presentation. Note points at which you may wish to use a pointer or other tool.

Strike a balance. As you draft, strive to strike a balance between the narrative, audio, and visual elements you will use. As in all research writing, weave your ideas into those of others using transitions and appropriate recognition of sources.

Organize Your Presentation

Introduction: Address the topic and introduce the thesis statement in an innovative, attention-getting way.

Body: Offer in-depth coverage of the topic and provide at least two examples—at least one of which should be conveyed in a medium other than text—to reinforce the thesis.

Conclusion: Sum up research and restate the thesis.

Revising

Revise to clarify sequence. A seamless presentation is the goal of any multimedia demonstration. Because your presentation may involve apparatus that requires time for setup, hold a test-run with a partner.

1. Run through your presentation, incorporating all audiovisual elements.
2. Ask your partner to comment on parts that lacked clarity or seemed unpolished.

If necessary, revise the sequence to clarify connections between ideas or eliminate awkward transitions.

Model: Revising to Smooth Transitions

(cue slide)

~~(cue video)~~ Our design represents the latest and best in roller coaster technology. ~~(cue slide and audio)~~ **(pointer to highlight features)** The coaster will begin with a 95-meter peak, followed by a drop, followed by a 76-meter peak and drop. The rest of the ride includes banked turns, loops, and a smaller hill.

~~Video: computer animation of Dragon's Lair~~
Slide: coaster route schematic design
~~Audio: People screaming~~

Afton deleted the video and audio elements of this section because the transitions were too complicated to handle smoothly.

Revise to vary media. Review your script for overuse of one form of media. By using a variety of media to enhance your narration, you can spice up your presentation, and hold your viewers' interest.

Without Variety: Play audio interview of quarterback
Play audio interview of ballerina

With Variety: Show video footage of quarterback
Voiceover interview of ballerina

The plans below show the multimedia element of a presentation. Compare the model and the nonmodel. Why is the model more effective than the nonmodel?

Nonmodel	Model
Slide: computer schematic	**Video:** computer animation of Dragon's Lair
Slide: station schematics	**Slide:** station schematics
Slide: train schematics	**Hand-outs:** circulate design specifications
Slide: people standing on line	**Video:** interviews with customers waiting on line

Publishing and Presenting

Consider this activity to share your writing with a wider audience.

Deliver an oral presentation. Deliver your multimedia presentation for your classmates. Invite questions. Afterwards, write a brief analysis of your experience.

- Get to know your material so you can speak without a script, and familiarize yourself with the equipment you will be using.
- Give a practice performance to friends or family members.
- Give equipment a final check for problems before delivering your presentation.

 Prentice Hall Writing and Grammar Connection: Chapter 13

Rubric for Self-Assessment

Evaluate your multimedia presentation using the following criteria and rating scale:

Criteria	Rating Scale				
	Not very				Very
How well does the presentation integrate audio and visual components?	1	2	3	4	5
How effectively is each element reinforced by the appropriate medium?	1	2	3	4	5
Is the presentation clear and logically organized?	1	2	3	4	5
How innovatively does the presentation make use of media to convey concepts?	1	2	3	4	5

Listening and Speaking WORKSHOP

Evaluating Communication Methods

Many of the communication methods we are most affected by, such as television broadcasts or films, appear in a visual medium. Listening skills can be useful in analyzing such materials and identifying the techniques used to present information and opinions. The strategies described below will help you interpret arguments and understand information presented through such media. Use the form on this page to record your responses.

Evaluate Presentations

Use the following strategies to evaluate presentations.

- **Recognize purpose.** Distinct forms of media have specific goals. Some seek to entertain, some seek to persuade, and others seek to inform. Some seek to do all three.

- **Analyze structure.** Note the ways in which each form of media structures information. For example, the evening news might build on short oral summaries supported by photographs or film footage. An advertisement might present a short persuasive message accompanied by a series of quick images. Learn to notice the ways in which the structure affects your perception.

- **Weigh objectivity and subjectivity.** News reports, for example, are meant to present current events in an objective manner, without bias or opinion. Often, such shows also include editorials that convey subjective opinions. Consider how the objectivity or subjectivity of a presentation affects your understanding of events.

Evaluate Communication Techniques

Media makers use various techniques to communicate information. Look for the following in evaluating audiovisual media:

- **Music or slogans:** Audiovisual media makers may use music to set a mood or emphasize visual imagery. Slogans, which you will often hear repeated, grab your attention and stick in your mind.

- **Charged sounds and images:** Powerful images, such as videos of gurgling babies or of starving children, evoke strong emotional reactions. Used responsibly, they give substance to reported facts.

Activity:
Listen, View, and Evaluate Watch the television news, a film documentary, or a news magazine/interview program. Use the evaluation form shown here to interpret media techniques.

Feedback Form for Audiovisual Media

Presentation
Topic: entertainment _____ information _____
Structure: length _____
    balance between visual and audio _____
Point of view: objective _____ subjective _____

Techniques
Note your responses to media makers' use of the techniques listed below. Use this ranking system:
+ = effective, ✔ = acceptable, – = inappropriate.
Music/slogans: _____
Loaded sounds/images: _____

Your Evaluation
Do you feel the events addressed by this medium were presented objectively and thoroughly?

How did the techniques you identified affect your response to the media? Explain.

Assessment WORKSHOP

Sentence-Completion Questions

The reading sections of some tests require you to correctly answer sentence-completion questions. Use the following strategies to help you understand and answer these types of questions.

- Use the context and your own knowledge to predict which word would best complete the sentence.
- If the word you anticipated is not among the answers presented, look for a synonym of the word or other related words.
- Analyze the sentence meaning, deciding if it is positive or negative, and eliminate choices that have the opposite sense.

Test-Taking Strategy

Try each word choice in the sentence to see whether it makes sense. Often, you can eliminate some of the choices because they are illogical, the wrong part of speech, or inconsistent with the sentence's meaning.

Sample Test Item

Directions: Read the following sentences and select the answers that best complete their meanings.

1. When Julie skipped three classes and two band practices after months of perfect attendance, her friends wondered about her ____?____ behavior.

   A erratic

   B reasonable

   C slow

   D arrogant

2. Olivia's mastery of formal etiquette was just one example of her ____?____ behavior.

   A crude

   B suspicious

   C refined

   D temporary

Answer and Explanation

1. The correct answer is **A**, because it is closest to the meaning of the sentence. Julie's behavior is erratic, or inconsistent. The other choices are not supported by the information in the paragraph.

2. The correct answer is **C**. Formal etiquette suggests refined behavior.

▷ Practice

Directions: Read the following sentences and select the answer that best completes each sentence.

1. Those who believe it is barbaric and cruel to keep large animals in captivity think that to visit a zoo is ____?____.

   A unfortunate

   B advisable

   C immoral

   D courageous

2. Although my good friend had ____?____ the movie, I was ____?____ by the weak plot.

   A recommended; disappointed

   B enjoyed; impressed

   C criticized; convinced

   D proposed; frightened

3. Surprisingly, Umberto loved peanuts but found peanut butter ____?____.

   A creamy

   B exquisite

   C old-fashioned

   D repugnant

> **❝** *Sometimes I can see the future stretched out in front of me—just as plain as day. The future hanging over there at the edge of my days. Just waiting for me.* **❞**
>
> — Lorraine Hansberry

Timeline 1946–Present

American Events

- **1945** United States grants independence to the Philippines.
- **1949** *Death of a Salesman* by Arthur Miller is first produced.
- **1952** Ralph Ellison publishes *Invisible Man.* ▼
- **1954** Supreme Court rules public school segregation to be unconstitutional.

- **1955** Flannery O'Connor publishes *A Good Man Is Hard to Find.* ▼

- **1959** Alaska and Hawaii admitted to the Union as the 49th and 50th states.
- **1961** Joseph Heller publishes *Catch-22.*
- **1962** Environmental protection movement spurred by Rachel Carson's book *Silent Spring.*
- **1963** President John F. Kennedy assassinated in Dallas.

- **1966** *Ariel,* Sylvia Plath's last collection of poems, appears.
- **1968** Martin Luther King, Jr., civil rights leader, murdered in Memphis.
- **1969** Astronaut Neil Armstrong becomes the first person to set foot on the moon. ▲
- **1972** Last U.S. combat troops leave Vietnam; peace pact signed in 1973. ▶

World Events

- **1947** India-Pakistan: India and Pakistan granted independence from Great Britain.
- **1948** Israel: United Nations establishes state of Israel.
- **1948** Germany: Soviet Union blockades Allied sectors of Berlin.
- **1950** England: Doris Lessing publishes *The Grass Is Singing.*
- **1954** England: *Lord of the Flies* by William Golding appears.

- **1956** Argentina: Jorge Luis Borges publishes *Extraordinary Tales.*
- **1957** Ghana: Ghana emerges as independent nation.
- **1957** USSR: *Doctor Zhivago* by Boris Pasternak appears.
- **1959** Germany: East Germany builds Berlin Wall.
- **1961** Cuba: Fidel Castro comes to power.
- **1962** USSR: *One Day in the Life of Ivan Denisovich* by Alexander Solzhenitsyn appears.

- **1967** Israel: Israel gains territory from Arab states in Six-Day War.
- **1969** Northern Ireland: Long period of violence begins between Catholics and Protestants.
- **1972** China: Nixon makes historic visit to China. ▼

American and World Events

- **1980** Ronald Reagan elected president.
- **1982** Vietnam Veterans Memorial dedicated in Washington, D.C. ▼

- **1987** President Reagan and Soviet leader Mikhail Gorbachev sign the INF treaty, agreeing to ban short-range and medium-range nuclear missiles. ▲
- **1988** George Bush elected president.
- **1990** Congress passes the Americans With Disabilities Act, prohibiting discrimination against people with disabilities.
- **1992** Bill Clinton elected president.
- **1993** Toni Morrison wins Nobel Prize for Literature.

- **1995** Amy Tan publishes her third novel, *The Hundred Secret Senses.*
- **1996** Summer Olympic Games held in Atlanta, Georgia.
- **1997** Frank McCourt's autobiography *Angela's Ashes* wins Pulitzer Prize.
- **2000** George W. Bush defeats Al Gore in an extremely close and controversial presidential election.
- **2001** Novelist and short story writer Eudora Welty dies.
- **2001** Hijacked planes crash into the World Trade Center in New York and the Pentagon in Washington, D.C., on the same day. Thousands of lives are lost.

- **1979** India: Mother Teresa wins Nobel Prize for Peace.
- **1979** Vietnam: Hundreds of thousands of "boat people" flee Vietnam.
- **1979** Trinidad: V. S. Naipaul publishes *A Bend in the River.*
- **1979** England: Margaret Thatcher becomes British prime minister.
- **1981** Poland: Polish trade union movement, Solidarity, suppressed.

- **1986** USSR: Chernobyl nuclear disaster spreads radioactive cloud across Eastern Europe.
- **1989** Eastern Europe: Berlin Wall comes down.
- **1989** China: Pro-democracy demonstrations violently suppressed at Tiananmen Square.
- **1991** Middle East: Unified forces led by U.S. defeat Iraq in Persian Gulf War.
- **1994** South Africa: Nelson Mandela becomes the first democratically elected president.

- **1997** China: Hong Kong returns to Chinese rule, ending British rule. ▼

- **1999** Conflict between Albanians and Serbs in Kosovo leads to a war between Serbia and NATO forces. Then, a peace agreement is signed.
- **2001** Serbia: Serbian leader Slobodan Milosevic is arrested.

Prosperity and Protest
(1946–PRESENT)

Looking to the future is a natural part of the human experience. Much of the technology that has become widespread since 1945—television and computers in particular—shows us a brighter future. The new technology often makes life easier. Paradoxically, it also introduces complexities that were unknown in earlier days.

The years from the end of World War II to the present day have been a time of change. Great strides have been made in civil rights and women's rights. Popular entertainment has changed dramatically, not just in presentation (for example, from radio to television, from phonograph records to CDs) but also in style (for example, from big bands to rock music and hip-hop). These changes and others have had an effect on American literature.

JACKIE ROBINSON 3b-of *BROOKLYN DODGERS*

Historical Background

The United States emerged from World War II as the most powerful nation on Earth. Proud of their role in the Allied victory, Americans now wanted life to return to normal. Soldiers came home, the rationing of scarce goods ended, and the nation prospered. Despite postwar jubilation, however, the dawn of the nuclear age and the dominance of the Soviet Union throughout Eastern Europe meant that nothing would be the same again.

In 1945, the United Nations was created amid high hopes that it would prevent future wars. Nonetheless, the Cold War between the Soviet Union and the West began as soon as World War II ended. It was in Asia, however, that the first armed conflict came. In 1950, President Harry S. Truman sent American troops to help anticommunist South Korean forces turn back a North Korean invasion.

From Quiet Pride to Activism Americans of the 1950s are sometimes referred to as "the Silent Generation." Many of them had lived through both the Great Depression and World War II. When peace finally arrived, they were glad to adopt a quiet, somewhat complacent attitude. They greatly admired President Dwight D. Eisenhower, one of America's wartime heroes.

In October 1957, the Soviet Union launched *Sputnik*, the first artificial satellite to orbit Earth. This Soviet space triumph spurred many people to call

▲ **Critical Viewing** African Americans could not play baseball in the major leagues until Jackie Robinson broke the color barrier in 1947. What effects— both in sports and in society—did Robinson's breakthrough have? **[Analyze Cause and Effect]**

for changes in American science and education. President John F. Kennedy, elected in 1960, promised to "get the nation moving again." He had little time to do so, however, before his assassination in 1963.

After Kennedy's assassination came an escalating and increasingly unpopular war in Vietnam. A wave of protest followed. Gone were the calm of the Eisenhower years and the high hopes of Kennedy's brief administration. In their place came idealistic but strident demands for rapid change: greater "relevance" in education, more progress on civil rights, an immediate end to the Vietnam War. It was a time of crisis and confrontations, but it brought a great deal of genuine progress.

Real and lasting gains were made in civil rights after World War II. Segregation in the public schools was outlawed by the Supreme Court in 1954. Tragedy struck in 1968, however, when civil rights leader Martin Luther King, Jr., was assassinated in Memphis, Tennessee. Riots broke out in many cities across the nation.

Point/Counterpoint

The Dropping of the Atomic Bomb on Japan— Inevitable or Unjustifiable?

Was the dropping of the atomic bomb on Japan, an act that introduced the nuclear age, an inevitable event or an unjustifiable decision? Two equally distinguished historians disagree on this important question.

Inevitable Event

"Conceivably, as many would later argue, the Japanese might have surrendered before November and the scheduled invasion. Conceivably, they could have been strangled by naval blockade, forced to surrender by continued fire bombing, with its dreadful toll. . . . But no one close to Truman was telling him not to use the new weapon. General Marshall fully expected the Japanese to fight on even if the bomb were dropped. . . . That it might make the invasion unnecessary was too much to expect. . . . 'Truman made no decision because there was no decision to be made,' recalled George Elsey. . . . 'He could no more have stopped it than a train moving down a track. . . .'"

—*Truman*, David McCullough

Unjustifiable Decision

"The use of the atomic bomb was not really needed to produce this result [the surrender of Japan and the long-awaited end of the war]. With nine-tenths of Japan's shipping sunk or disabled, her air and sea forces crippled, her industries wrecked, and her people's food supplies shrinking fast, her collapse was already certain— as Churchill said.

"The U.S. Strategic Bombing Survey report emphasized this point, while adding: '. . . it seems clear that, even without the atomic bombing attacks, air supremacy could have exerted sufficient pressure to bring about unconditional surrender and obviate the need for invasion.'"

—*History of the Second World War*, B. H. Liddell Hart

Literature of the Period

Variety and Promise The turbulence of contemporary times has contributed to the development of a looseknit variety of approaches known as Postmodernism. Listed here are some of the general ways in which Postmodernism tends to differ from its precursor, Modernism.

Modernism
- Viewed the massive casualties of World War I as undercutting pretensions to rationality and civilization
- Influenced by Freud's studies of the unconscious and a new interest in the art of primitive peoples
- Loss of trust in rationality, balanced by a newfound trust in the artist's ability to glean meaning from the irrational
- Confidence that the work of art is a unique and powerful creation with its own individual aura or atmosphere
- Tendency to view the work of art as a perfected product rather than as an incomplete and ongoing process
- Some confidence in the truth of the Renaissance notion that a great work of art is immortal and ensures immortality for its author
- Belief that "high" culture and "low" culture are separated by a meaningful dividing line and that a work of fine art is inherently superior to a cartoon

Postmodernism
- Viewed World War II, with the Holocaust and the dropping of the A-bomb, as undercutting assumptions of life's meaning
- Influenced by studies of media and language and by the explosive growth of information technology
- Some loss of trust in the artist's ability to access the irrational and return with a sense of renewal and greater meaning
- Less confidence that the work of art is unique, coupled with a sense that culture endlessly duplicates and copies itself
- Greater interest in the work of art as a process that reflects on its own making as it evolves
- Loss of confidence in the Renaissance notion that a great work of art is immortal and ensures immortality for its author
- Loss of belief in the meaningful dividing line between "high" culture and "low" culture, so that in Pop Art, the subject matter of fine art can be a cartoon

In the spirit of Postmodernism, some writers have explored new literary forms and techniques, composing works from dialogue alone, creating works that blend fiction and nonfiction, and experimenting with the physical appearance of their work. Still other writers, using more traditional forms, have focused on capturing the essence of contemporary life in the content of their works, addressing the impersonal and commercial nature of today's world.

A Quest for Stability The upheavals of the 1960s brought a conservative reaction. Many Americans longed for a return to "the good old days." President Richard M. Nixon, elected in 1968, promised to end the Vietnam War and to restore order in the nation. Nixon's achievements were soon overshadowed by the Watergate affair—the burglarizing of Democratic Party headquarters under the direction of Nixon government officials. This scandal forced his resignation from the presidency in 1974.

Civil rights activism continued during the 1970s, and another movement attracted growing attention—the women's liberation movement. Although women had earned the right to vote in 1920, discrimination still existed. Women received lower pay than men did for the same jobs, and promotion was more difficult. Betty Friedan's *The Feminine Mystique*, published in 1963, called for change. The women's movement grew steadily throughout the 1970s.

After Jimmy Carter's one-term presidency in the late 1970s, the nation sent Ronald Reagan to the White House. A former film star and governor of California, Reagan proved a popular and persuasive president. His reelection in 1984 was one of the biggest landslide victories in American history. In 1988, George Bush, Reagan's vice president, was elected to the presidency. Seeking reelection in 1992, Bush faced a tough fight against high unemployment, a recession, growing dissatisfaction with government, and his youthful opponent. Democrat Bill Clinton and his running mate, Al Gore—the youngest ticket in American history—won the election. Despite the 1994 elections that voted many Democratic Congress members out of office, Clinton won reelection in 1996. However, in 2000, Al Gore lost to George Bush's son, George W. Bush, in an election that was extremely controversial.

The Changing Scene Commercial television was still in its infancy at the end of World War II, but it was on the verge of spectacular growth. Over the next few years, television changed the leisure habits of Americans.

The postwar period was a time of explosive suburban growth, made possible by the automobile. At first, most suburban homeowners worked in a city and commuted to their jobs by train, bus, or car. Then, major corporations began establishing suburban headquarters, and workers could live nearby or commute short distances from one suburb to another. Even more recently, advanced technology has allowed people to "telecommute," or work in home offices and stay connected by Internet, phone, and fax.

The world has changed dramatically since 1945, and it is still changing. One of the most dramatic examples is the development of the Internet in a few short years from a military and scientific communication system to a global information network. The changes have had an impact on the literature of the time, although this impact has not always been obvious.

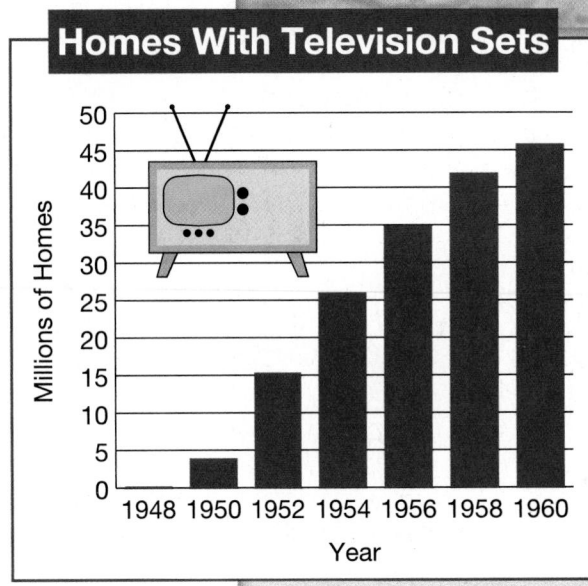

Homes With Television Sets

Year (horizontal axis): 1948, 1950, 1952, 1954, 1956, 1958, 1960
Millions of Homes (vertical axis): 0 to 50

▲ **Critical Viewing** Before 1950, television was a novelty. By the end of the decade, however, television sets were a common feature in American homes. What factors might have influenced the steady rise in television ownership? **[Draw Conclusions]**

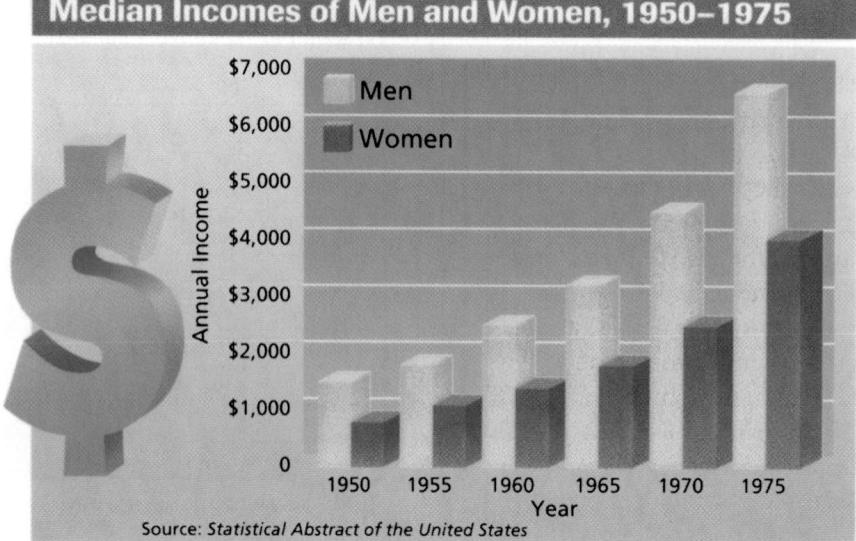

Median Incomes of Men and Women, 1950–1975

Men
Women

Annual Income

$7,000
$6,000
$5,000
$4,000
$3,000
$2,000
$1,000
0

1950   1955   1960   1965   1970   1975

Year

Source: Statistical Abstract of the United States

◀ **Critical Viewing**
Between 1950 and 1975, women's incomes continued to lag behind men's earnings, partly because many low-paying fields such as nursing and teaching were traditionally considered "women's work." Did the income gap increase or decrease between 1950 and 1975? **[Analyze]**

Authors for a New Era Although contemporary writers have produced a wide variety of impressive works, it is all but impossible to predict which writers will achieve lasting fame and which will not. Time is needed to certify greatness. Modern readers and critics have their favorites, of course. Some of them will undoubtedly become part of America's enduring literary legacy.

Every writer owes a debt to those writers who have gone before. In that sense, literature is cumulative. The earliest American literature, except for that of the Native Americans, was based on European models. Writers in the United States today can look to a rich heritage of their own. Contemporary novelists are well aware of Nathaniel Hawthorne, Mark Twain, Ernest Hemingway, and William Faulkner. Short-story writers know Edgar Allan Poe, Willa Cather, and Eudora Welty. Poets study Emily Dickinson, Walt Whitman, and Langston Hughes. Playwrights are familiar with Eugene O'Neill and Thornton Wilder.

Renowned contemporary novelists include Carson McCullers, Norman Mailer, Bernard Malamud, John Updike, Flannery O'Connor, Joyce Carol Oates, Anne Tyler, and Alice Walker. Many of these novelists have written short stories as well. Flannery O'Connor and John Updike are modern masters of the short-story form. Other writers, such as Donald Barthelme and Ann Beattie, have written novels but are better known for their short stories. Isaac Bashevis Singer, a Polish-born New Yorker who wrote in Yiddish, was famous for both his novels and his short stories. He won the Nobel Prize for Literature in 1978. John Cheever, a respected novelist, won the Pulitzer Prize for Fiction in 1979 for his collected short stories, many of which concern suburban life.

Just as Realism and Romanticism have tended to merge in recent literature, so, curiously, have fiction and nonfiction. Truman Capote's *In Cold Blood*, published in 1966, was billed as a "nonfiction novel." Capote, primarily a novelist and short-story writer, used fictional techniques to analyze a real and seemingly senseless crime. Later authors, such as E. L. Doctorow in his novel *Ragtime*, combined historical figures with purely fictional characters. This technique has aroused some controversy.

Increasing attention has been paid recently to the place of nonfiction in the literary hierarchy. The essay has always been considered an important literary form, and some outstanding essays are published every year. James Baldwin and John McPhee are accomplished essayists. Among the many notable longer works of nonfiction are Paul Theroux's *The Great Railway Bazaar*, N. Scott Momaday's *The Names*, and Barry Lopez's *Arctic Dreams*.

Poetry Within the Tradition A number of the famed prewar poets continued to publish extensively after the war. Robert Frost, Marianne Moore, Wallace Stevens, E. E. Cummings, William Carlos Williams, and Ezra Pound all produced major collections of their works.

During the late 1940s and the 1950s, many poets starting out in the shadow of these great names were content to work within the technical boundaries established in the earlier part of the century. Nevertheless, poets like Theodore Roethke and Elizabeth Bishop created important and memorable work. Roethke, a master of poetic rhythm, was deeply influenced by his father, a strong-willed greenhouse owner in Saginaw, Michigan. The best of Roethke's poems recall his childhood life in and around the greenhouse. Bishop's poems are beautifully crafted, with precise and memorable descriptions that sometimes suggest realities beyond the physical.

Art in the Historical Context

California Artist Wayne Thiebaud

After World War II, Abstract Expressionists like Jackson Pollock inaugurated Postmodernist painting with works that seemed to be "about" their own making and whose swirls and shapes represented an inner rather than an outer reality. In California, however, a group of painters admired the energy of abstract work but wanted to use it in depicting what critic Donald Goddard called "California scenes filled with California light."

One of these artists was Wayne Thiebaud, a former cartoonist and designer. In his earlier work, Thiebaud demonstrated a fascination with such objects as shoes, ties, and ice cream cones. These paintings influenced the movement known as Pop Art. In later works, Thiebaud depicted landscapes. His San Francisco landscapes, like this one, render cityscapes in abstract terms but also capture "California light" and, in the roller-coaster swoop of a hill, convey a sense of surprise.

▶ **Critical Viewing** Which specific features in this painting suggest that Thiebaud was influenced by painters who use only abstract forms? Explain. **[Analyze]**

Art is Corner Apartments (Down 18th Street). 1980, Wayne Thiebaud, at Hirshorn Museum, Smithsonian Institution

A Living Tradition

A. R. Ammons, Emersonian Postmodernist

A. R. Ammons, a North Carolinian, brought the verve of Southern speech to poetry. In a long, outrageous poem humorously entitled *Garbage* (1993), Ammons takes trash—or the reprocessing of it—as a symbol of our times. Unlike Modernists who strove to create poems as perfect, well-constructed artifacts, Ammons, in good Postmodernist style, creates a talky, sprawling, shifting poem that is itself like a trash heap and that considers, among so many other things, its own making.

Emerson might have blinked and rubbed his eyes hard if he could have read this poem. However, he also might have recognized in it his own, distinctly American belief in renewal. He wrote in his essay "Compensation": "And such should be the outward biography of man in time, a putting off of dead circumstances day by day, as he renews his raiment day by day. . . ."

from *Garbage* by A. R. Ammons

garbage has to be the poem of our time because
garbage is spiritual, believable enough

to get our attention, getting in the way, piling
up, stinking, turning brooks brownish and

creamy white: what else deflects us from the
errors of our illusionary ways . . .

       *   *   *

. . . here the driver knows,

where the consummations gather, where the disposal
flows out of form, where the last translations

cast away their immutable bits and scraps,
flits of steel, shivers of bottle and tumbler,

here is the gateway to beginning, here the portal
of renewing change . . .

New Directions in Poetry However, some poets challenged the boundaries of the art. Allen Ginsberg and A.R. Ammons, inspired by the work of William Carlos Williams, wrote bolder, more sprawling poems. In a Postmodernist spirit, Ginsberg's *Howl* and Ammons's *Tape for the Turn of the Year* and *Garbage* engaged powerfully with contemporary realities, dramatic and mundane alike. They dared to take in more confusion and chaos, even at the expense of their own apparent "perfection" as works of art.

The Literature of Personal and Group Identity Robert Lowell, a great-nephew of the poet James Russell Lowell, began his career in the postwar years as a creator of powerful, though traditional, poems. However, in the late 1950s, he began to reread William Carlos Williams. The result was *Life Studies*, a breakthrough book in which Lowell abandoned tight, traditional forms and opened his work to the frustrations and confusions of his own personal and family history. Lowell was followed by others who revealed personal secrets, like Anne Sexton and Sylvia Plath. Rightly or wrongly, they were dubbed "confessional poets."

The tumultuous 1960s brought great changes in behavior and awareness—the civil rights movement, the protests against the Vietnam War, and the women's movement are three examples—that affected the subject matter of all literature. In poetry, as in fiction, these changes inspired a movement that encouraged the proud assertion and passionate exploration of personal, ethnic, and racial identity. It is important to realize, however, that this flowering of work that began in the 1960s, and still continues, had its roots in earlier decades. For example, African American poet Rita Dove, who won a Pulitzer Prize for *Thomas and Beulah* in 1986, could certainly acknowledge a debt to Robert Hayden and to Gwendolyn Brooks, who in 1950, became the first African American writer to win a Pulitzer Prize for her book *Annie Allen*.

Other writers in this rainbow movement are Native Americans N. Scott Momaday, also a Pulitzer Prize winner, and Joy Harjo; Asian Americans Maxine Hong Kingston, Amy Tan, and Garret Hongo; and Latino and Latina writers Martín Espada, Sandra Cisneros, and Julia Alvarez. Adrienne Rich, strongly influenced by the women's movement, began changing her poetry in mid-career, loosening her formal structures and dealing with previously unexpressed conflicts and aspirations of women.

These and other writers are proving that, in literature as in society, America's strength lies in its diversity. Although it is too early to assess their achievements, it seems likely that some of the works they are producing today will become the classics of tomorrow.

Beyond the Horizon

One of the features of literary evolution is its unpredictability: No one knows in which direction it will develop next. Of this, however, we can be reasonably sure: The novel is not dead, as some were proclaiming in the 1950s and 1960s. Poetry is not dead, nor is the short story. Literature has great resilience. While it may be profoundly influenced by other media—radio, television, film—it has not been replaced by them. Indeed, for sheer technical virtuosity, there has probably never been a more impressive group of American writers at work than at the present time.

▼ **Critical Viewing**
In a few short years, the Internet has become an accepted part of American life. What benefits does it offer and what problems, if any, does it pose?
[Make a Judgment]

THE DEVELOPMENT OF AMERICAN ENGLISH

Brave New Words

BY RICHARD LEDERER

The history of a living language like English is a history of constant change. Language is like a tree that sheds its leaves and grows new ones so that it may live on. New words, like new leaves, are essential to a living, healthy vocabulary.

A language draws its nutrients from the environment in which its speakers live. This growth is not new to English. Throughout history, as English speakers and writers have met with new objects, experiences, and ideas, they have needed new words to describe them. Nowadays, an average of 5,000 new words enter our language each year!

In almost every case, we cobble these new words from already existing word-making materials called morphemes. Morphemes are prefabricated bits of meaning from which words are made.

The Anglo-Saxons, who were the earliest speakers of our language, used a vivid term to describe the great wealth of English. They called it *word-hoard*. This stock of words grows considerably with each new development in science, medicine, and technology.

One of the major technologies of our lives is the computer. As the wonders of the computer have unfolded, we have acquired a new *user-friendly* (a compound composed of Latin and Anglo-Saxon word parts) vocabulary by piecing together morphemes from Latin, Greek, and early English.

We English speakers needed a name for the system of networks that connects computers around the world. So we combined the Latin prefix *inter*, "together," with the Anglo-Saxon word for a mesh fabric, and — presto! — we came up with the *Internet*. Then, we required a name for the complete set of documents on all Internet servers. So we mixed three Anglo-Saxon words into — ta da! — the World Wide Web.

The growing study of life on other worlds we have labeled astrobiology or exobiology, from the Greek word parts *astro* ("star") and *exo* ("outer") + *bio* ("life") + *logy* ("study of").

We have been aware of genes for more than a century, but only recently have scientists studied whole sets of genes and their interactions. The entire chomosomal makeup of an organism we now call the *genome* — a blend of two Greek words, *gen(e)* and *(chromos)ome*. The same blend names the field — *genomics*.

Over the past few decades, we have acquired countless new words for the brave new worlds of science, technology, and medicine. Scientific and medical breakthroughs seem to make the headlines almost every day, but our English "word-hoard" will never run out of prefixes, suffixes, and roots to identify these new concepts.

ACTIVITIES

1. Identify the word parts and original languages of these computer terms: *home page, inkjet,* and *laptop.*
2. Identify the word parts and original languages of these scientific terms: *black hole, camcorder,* and *supercluster.*

PART 1

Literature Confronts the Everyday

Television Moon, 1978–79, Alfred Leslie, Wichita Art Museum, Wichita, Kansas

Prepare to Read

The Life You Save May Be Your Own

Flannery O'Connor (1925–1964)

Flannery O'Connor's work reflects her intense commitment to her personal beliefs. In her exaggerated, tragic, and at times shockingly violent tales, she forces readers to confront such human faults as hypocrisy, insensitivity, self-centeredness, and prejudice. Many of her stories revolve around death and exhibit a dark sense of humor. Some critics have objected to the presence of such comic doom in her fiction, but O'Connor felt that she was portraying the world accurately. She once said, "People are always complaining that the modern novelist has no hope and that the picture he paints of the world is unbearable. The only answer to this is that people without hope do not write novels."

The Habit of Art Born in Savannah, Georgia, Flannery O'Connor was raised in the small Georgia town of Milledgeville. She earned her undergraduate degree from Georgia State College for Women and then left her home state to attend the celebrated University of Iowa Writers' Workshop. While still in graduate school, she published her first short story, "Geranium."

In 1950, O'Connor became ill with lupus, a serious disease that restricted her independence. She moved back to the family farm outside Milledgeville, where she lived with her mother. "I have never been anywhere but sick," she wrote. "In a sense, sickness is a place more instructive than a trip to Europe." Despite her illness, O'Connor committed herself not only to her writing but also to "the habit of art," an enlivened way of thinking and seeing. In 1952, at the age of twenty-seven, she published her first novel, *Wise Blood*, the story of a violent rivalry among members of a fictional religious sect in the South. In 1955, she published her first collection of stories, *A Good Man Is Hard to Find*. It was followed by a second novel, *The Violent Bear It Away* (1960), and *Everything That Rises Must Converge* (1965), another collection of short stories.

A Triumphant Spirit Throughout most of her adult life, O'Connor lived with physical pain and the awareness that she would probably die young. Despite her condition, she often seemed joyous, entertaining friends at home and painting watercolors of the peacocks that she and her mother raised on the farm. Still, her disease set her apart from other people, and O'Connor felt a deep sense of kinship with eccentrics and outsiders. In her fiction, she often portrays those who are outcast or suffering. Many of her characters are social misfits or people who are physically or mentally challenged. Although she paints these characters in an unsentimental way, O'Connor brings to their stories an underlying sense of sympathy, which reflects both her own physical problems and her strong Catholic faith.

Religious Faith Flannery O'Connor was raised as a devout Catholic in a region of the American South that was predominantly Protestant. She considered herself a religious writer in a world that had abandoned true religious values. In an effort to point out the spiritual failings of the modern world, O'Connor often highlights characters with powerfully stated convictions but dubious moral and intellectual capabilities. "The Life You Save May Be Your Own" is a typical O'Connor work. In its grim depiction of a group of outcasts with sharply exaggerated physical characteristics and personality traits, the story conveys shrewd insights, a powerful moral message, and an urgent sense of the tragic realities of life in the modern world.

Preview

Connecting to the Literature

In this story, a stranger appears at a remote farm where an elderly widow lives alone with her unmarried daughter. The woman must decide whether or not to trust the drifter. Similar decisions confront all of us as strangers enter our lives as potential friends or enemies.

Literary Analysis

Grotesque Characters

The word *grotesque* in literature does not mean ugly or disgusting, as it sometimes does in popular speech. In literature, the **grotesque character** is one who has become bizarre or twisted, usually through some kind of obsession. Grotesque traits may be expressed in a character's physical appearance. Or, they may be hidden, visible only in a character's actions and emotions. In this story, all of the characters can be classified as grotesques. As you read, look for examples of absurd or extreme behavior, distortions, and striking incongruities that combine to create images of the grotesque.

Connecting Literary Elements

Writers create portraits of characters through **characterization**—the revelation of personality. There are two methods of characterization. With **direct characterization,** the writer simply tells the reader what a character is like. With **indirect characterization,** characters' traits are revealed

- through the character's words, thoughts, and actions.
- through descriptions of the character's appearance or background.
- through what other characters say about him or her.
- through the ways in which other characters react or respond.

Use a chart like the one shown to examine O'Connor's use of indirect characterization in portraying the cast of grotesque characters in this story.

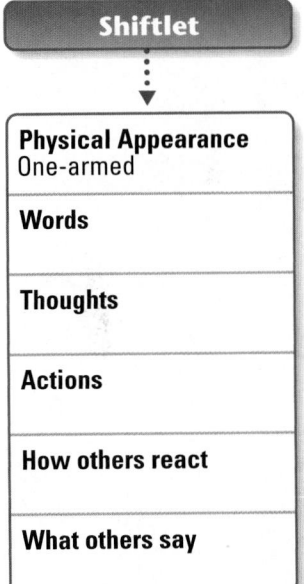

Shiftlet

| Physical Appearance
One-armed |
| Words |
| Thoughts |
| Actions |
| How others react |
| What others say |

Reading Strategy

Making Predictions

When you find yourself wondering how a series of events will unfold, pause and **predict** what will happen. Predict outcomes by looking back and weighing what you have read. Pay heed to hints the author has dropped, and measure these against your own understanding of human behavior.

Vocabulary

desolate (des´ ə lit) *adj.* forlorn; wretched (p. 973)

listed (list´ id) *v.* tilted; inclined (p. 973)

ominous (äm´ ə nəs) *adj.* threatening; sinister (p. 975)

ravenous (rav´ ə nəs) *adj.* extremely eager (p. 977)

morose (mə rōs´) *adj.* gloomy; sullen (p. 980)

guffawing (gə fô´ iŋ) *adj.* laughing in a loud, coarse manner (p. 982)

Deep Fork Overlook, Joan Marron-LaRue

▲ **Critical Viewing** Why might an automobile be so valuable in a rural area like the one in this story? **[Draw Conclusions]**

The Life You Save May Be Your Own

Flannery O'Connor

Background

Gothic literature, a genre of fiction that developed in Britain in the late 1700s, features horror and violence. Traditional gothic tales are often set against dramatic, gloomy backdrops—remote castles, deserted fortresses, and the like. Such literature acknowledges evil as a real force and ascribes to some characters a dark side that lures them to violent or wicked acts. Flannery O'Connor borrowed some devices from Gothic fiction, such as a foreboding atmosphere and grotesque characters, but she set her stories in an unremarkable American landscape. The story you are about to read is a perfect example of her exploration of the gothic under the familiar sunlight of the American South.

The old woman and her daughter were sitting on their porch when Mr. Shiftlet came up their road for the first time. The old woman slid to the edge of her chair and leaned forward, shading her eyes from the piercing sunset with her hand. The daughter could not see far in front of her and continued to play with her fingers. Although the old woman lived in this <u>desolate</u> spot with only her daughter and she had never seen Mr. Shiftlet before, she could tell, even from a distance, that he was a tramp and no one to be afraid of. His left coat sleeve was folded up to show there was only half an arm in it and his gaunt figure <u>listed</u> slightly to the side as if the breeze were pushing him. He had on a black town suit and a brown felt hat that was turned up in the front and down in the back and he carried a tin tool box by a handle. He came on, at an amble, up her road, his face turned toward the sun which appeared to be balancing itself on the peak of a small mountain.

The old woman didn't change her position until he was almost into her yard; then she rose with one hand fisted on her hip. The daughter, a large girl in a short blue organdy dress, saw him all at once and jumped up and began to stamp and point and make excited speechless sounds.

Mr. Shiftlet stopped just inside the yard and set his box on the ground and tipped his hat at her as if she were not in the least afflicted; then he turned toward the old woman and swung the hat all the way off. He had long black slick hair that hung flat from a part in the middle to beyond the tips of his ears on either side. His face descended in forehead for more than half its length and ended suddenly with his features just balanced over a jutting steel-trap jaw.

desolate (des´ ə lit) *adj.* forlorn; wretched

listed (list´ id) *v.* tilted; inclined

✔**Reading Check**

In this opening scene, who does the old woman notice coming up her road?

He seemed to be a young man but he had a look of composed dissatisfaction as if he understood life thoroughly.

"Good evening," the old woman said. She was about the size of a cedar fence post and she had a man's gray hat pulled down low over her head.

The tramp stood looking at her and didn't answer. He turned his back and faced the sunset. He swung both his whole and his short arm up slowly so that they indicated an expanse of sky and his figure formed a crooked cross. The old woman watched him with her arms folded across her chest as if she were the owner of the sun, and the daughter watched, her head thrust forward and her fat helpless hands hanging at the wrists. She had long pink-gold hair and eyes as blue as a peacock's neck.

He held the pose for almost fifty seconds and then he picked up his box and came on to the porch and dropped down on the bottom step. "Lady," he said in a firm nasal voice, "I'd give a fortune to live where I could see me a sun do that every evening."

"Does it every evening," the old woman said and sat back down. The daughter sat down too and watched him with a cautious sly look as if he were a bird that had come up very close. He leaned to one side, rooting in his pants pocket, and in a second he brought out a package of chewing gum and offered her a piece. She took it and unpeeled it and began to chew without taking her eyes off him. He offered the old woman a piece but she only raised her upper lip to indicate she had no teeth.

Mr. Shiftlet's pale sharp glance had already passed over everything in the yard—the pump near the corner of the house and the big fig tree that three or four chickens were preparing to roost in—and had moved to a shed where he saw the square rusted back of an automobile. "You ladies drive?" he asked.

"That car ain't run in fifteen year," the old woman said. "The day my husband died, it quit running."

"Nothing is like it used to be, lady," he said. "The world is almost rotten."

"That's right," the old woman said. "You from around here?"

"Name Tom T. Shiftlet," he murmured, looking at the tires.

"I'm pleased to meet you," the old woman said. "Name Lucynell Crater and daughter Lucynell Crater. What you doing around here, Mr. Shiftlet?"

He judged the car to be about a 1928 or '29 Ford. "Lady," he said, and turned and gave her his full attention, "lemme tell you something. There's one of these doctors in Atlanta that's taken a knife and cut the human heart—the human heart," he repeated, leaning forward, "out of a man's chest and held it in his hand," and he held his hand out, palm up, as if it were slightly weighted with the human heart, "and studied it like it was a day-old chicken, and lady," he said, allowing a long significant pause in which his head slid forward and his clay-colored eyes brightened, "he don't know no more about it than you or me."

Literary Analysis
Grotesque Characters
What exaggerated traits do you perceive in this description of the three characters?

Literary Analysis
Grotesque Characters and Characterization
What personality traits are suggested by this description of Mr. Shiftlet's "pale sharp glance"?

"That's right," the old woman said.

"Why, if he was to take that knife and cut into every corner of it, he still wouldn't know no more than you or me. What you want to bet?"

"Nothing," the old woman said wisely. "Where you come from, Mr. Shiftlet?"

He didn't answer. He reached into his pocket and brought out a sack of tobacco and a package of cigarette papers and rolled himself a cigarette, expertly with one hand, and attached it in a hanging position to his upper lip. Then he took a box of wooden matches from his pocket and struck one on his shoe. He held the burning match as if he were studying the mystery of flame while it traveled dangerously toward his skin. The daughter began to make loud noises and to point to his hand and shake her finger at him, but when the flame was just before touching him, he leaned down with his hand cupped over it as if he were going to set fire to his nose and lit the cigarette.

He flipped away the dead match and blew a stream of gray into the evening. A sly look came over his face. "Lady," he said, "nowadays, people'll do anything anyways. I can tell you my name is Tom T. Shiftlet and I come from Tarwater, Tennessee, but you never have seen me before: how you know I ain't lying? How you know my name ain't Aaron Sparks, lady, and I come from Singleberry, Georgia, or how you know it's not George Speeds and I come from Lucy, Alabama, or how you know I ain't Thompson Bright from Toolafalls, Mississippi?"

Reading Strategy
Making Predictions
In what ways might Mr. Shiftlet's speech about lying be a clue to later events?

"I don't know nothing about you," the old woman muttered, irked.

"Lady," he said, "people don't care how they lie. Maybe the best I can tell you is, I'm a man; but listen lady," he said and paused and made his tone more <u>ominous</u> still, "what is a man?"

The old woman began to gum a seed. "What you carry in that tin box, Mr. Shiftlet?" she asked.

"Tools," he said, put back. "I'm a carpenter."

"Well, if you come out here to work, I'll be able to feed you and give you a place to sleep but I can't pay. I'll tell you that before you begin," she said.

ominous (äm′ ə nəs) *adj.* threatening; sinister

There was no answer at once and no particular expression on his face. He leaned back against the two-by-four that helped support the porch roof. "Lady," he said slowly, "there's some men that some things mean more to them than money." The old woman rocked without comment and the daughter watched the trigger that moved up and down in his neck. He told the old woman then that all most people were interested in was money, but he asked what a man was made for. He asked her if a man was made for money, or what. He asked her what she thought she was made for but she didn't answer, she only sat rocking and wondered if a one-armed man could put a new roof on her garden house. He asked a lot of questions that she didn't answer. He told her that he was twenty-eight years old and had lived a varied life. He had been a gospel singer, a foreman on the railroad, an assistant in an undertaking parlor, and he come over the radio for three months with Uncle Roy and his Red Creek Wranglers. He said he had

**Reading Check**

In what ways does young Lucynell try to communicate? Can she speak?

fought and bled in the Arm Service of his country and visited every foreign land and that everywhere he had seen people that didn't care if they did a thing one way or another. He said he hadn't been raised thataway.

A fat yellow moon appeared in the branches of the fig tree as if it were going to roost there with the chickens. He said that a man had to escape to the country to see the world whole and that he wished he lived in a desolate place like this where he could see the sun go down every evening like God made it to do.

"Are you married or are you single?" the old woman asked.

There was a long silence. "Lady," he asked finally, "where would you find you an innocent woman today? I wouldn't have any of this trash I could just pick up."

The daughter was leaning very far down, hanging her head almost between her knees watching him through a triangular door she had made in her overturned hair; and she suddenly fell in a heap on the floor and began to whimper. Mr. Shiftlet straightened her out and helped her get back in the chair.

"Is she your baby girl?" he asked.

"My only," the old woman said "and she's the sweetest girl in the world. I would give her up for nothing on earth. She's smart too. She can sweep the floor, cook, wash, feed the chickens, and hoe. I wouldn't give her up for a casket of jewels."

"No," he said kindly, "don't ever let any man take her away from you."

"Any man come after her," the old woman said, "'ll have to stay around the place."

Mr. Shiftlet's eye in the darkness was focused on a part of the automobile bumper that glittered in the distance. "Lady," he said, jerking his short arm up as if he could point with it to her house and yard and pump, "there ain't a broken thing on this plantation that I couldn't fix for you, one-arm jackleg or not. I'm a man," he said with a sullen dignity, "even if I ain't a whole one. I got," he said, tapping his knuckles on the floor to emphasize the immensity of what he was going to say, "a moral intelligence!" and his face pierced out of the darkness into a shaft of doorlight and he stared at her as if he were astonished himself at this impossible truth.

The old woman was not impressed with the phrase. "I told you you could hang around and work for food," she said, "if you don't mind sleeping in that car yonder."

"Why listen, lady, " he said with a grin of delight, "the monks of old slept in their coffins!"

"They wasn't as advanced as we are," the old woman said.

The next morning he began on the roof of the garden house while Lucynell, the daughter, sat on a rock and watched him work. He had not been around a week before the change he had made in the place was apparent. He had patched the front and back steps, built a new hog pen, restored a fence, and taught Lucynell, who was completely

Literary Analysis
Grotesque Characters and Characterization
What does this dialogue about her daughter reveal about the old woman?

Reading Strategy
Making Predictions
What prediction can you make about Mr. Shiftlet based on his capable performance in his work?

deaf and had never said a word in her life, to say the word "bird." The big rosy-faced girl followed him everywhere, saying "Burrttddt ddbirrrttdt," and clapping her hands. The old woman watched from a distance, secretly pleased. She was <u>ravenous</u> for a son-in-law.

Mr. Shiftlet slept on the hard narrow back seat of the car with his feet out the side window. He had his razor and a can of water on a crate that served him as a bedside table and he put up a piece of mirror against the back glass and kept his coat neatly on a hanger that he hung over one of the windows.

In the evenings he sat on the steps and talked while the old woman and Lucynell rocked violently in their chairs on either side of him. The old woman's three mountains were black against the dark blue sky and were visited off and on by various planets and by the moon after it had left the chickens. Mr. Shiftlet pointed out that the reason he had improved this plantation was because he had taken a personal interest in it. He said he was even going to make the automobile run.

He had raised the hood and studied the mechanism and he said he could tell that the car had been built in the days when cars were really built. You take now, he said, one man puts in one bolt and another man puts in another bolt and another man puts in another bolt so that it's a man for a bolt. That's why you have to pay so much for a car: you're paying all those men. Now if you didn't have to pay

▲ **Critical Viewing**
Which aspects of the story are reflected in this painting? **[Connect]**

ravenous (rav′ ə nəs) *adj.* extremely eager

✔**Reading Check**

For what is the old woman "ravenous"?

but one man, you could get you a cheaper car and one that had had a personal interest taken in it, and it would be a better car. The old woman agreed with him that this was so.

Mr. Shiftlet said that the trouble with the world was that nobody cared, or stopped and took any trouble. He said he never would have been able to teach Lucynell to say a word if he hadn't cared and stopped long enough.

"Teach her to say something else," the old woman said.

"What you want her to say next?" Mr. Shiftlet asked.

The old woman's smile was broad and toothless and suggestive. "Teach her to say 'sugarpie,'" she said.

Mr. Shiftlet already knew what was on her mind.

The next day he began to tinker with the automobile and that evening he told her that if she would buy a fan belt, he would be able to make the car run.

The old woman said she would give him the money. "You see that girl yonder?" she asked, pointing to Lucynell who was sitting on the floor a foot away, watching him, her eyes blue even in the dark. "If it was ever a man wanted to take her away, I would say, 'No man on earth is going to take that sweet girl of mine away from me!' but if he was to say, 'Lady, I don't want to take her away, I want her right here,' I would say, 'Mister, I don't blame you none. I wouldn't pass up a chance to live in a permanent place and get the sweetest girl in the world myself. You ain't no fool,' I would say."

"How old is she?" Mr. Shiftlet asked casually.

"Fifteen, sixteen," the old woman said. The girl was nearly thirty but because of her innocence it was impossible to guess.

"It would be a good idea to paint it too," Mr. Shiftlet remarked. "You don't want it to rust out."

"We'll see about that later," the old woman said.

The next day he walked into town and returned with the parts he needed and a can of gasoline. Late in the afternoon, terrible noises issued from the shed and the old woman rushed out of the house, thinking Lucynell was somewhere having a fit. Lucynell was sitting on a chicken crate, stamping her feet and screaming, "Burrddtt! bddurrddttt!" but her fuss was drowned out by the car. With a volley of blasts it emerged from the shed, moving in a fierce and stately way. Mr. Shiftlet was in the driver's seat, sitting very erect. He had an expression of serious modesty on his face as if he had just raised the dead.

That night, rocking on the porch, the old woman began her business, at once. "You want you an innocent woman, don't you?" she asked sympathetically. "You don't want none of this trash."

"No'm, I don't," Mr. Shiftlet said.

"One that can't talk," she continued, "can't sass you back or use foul language. That's the kind for you to have. Right there," and she pointed to Lucynell sitting crosslegged in her chair, holding both feet in her hands.

"That's right," he admitted. "She wouldn't give me any trouble."

"Saturday," the old woman said, "you and her and me can drive into town and get married."

Mr. Shiftlet eased his position on the steps.

"I can't get married right now," he said. "Everything you want to do takes money and I ain't got any."

"What you need with money?" she asked.

"It takes money," he said. "Some people'll do anything anyhow these days, but the way I think, I wouldn't marry no woman that I couldn't take on a trip like she was somebody. I mean take her to a hotel and treat her. I wouldn't marry the Duchesser Windsor," he said firmly, "unless I could take her to a hotel and giver something good to eat.

"I was raised thataway and there ain't a thing I can do about it. My old mother taught me how to do."

"Lucynell don't even know what a hotel is," the old woman muttered. "Listen here, Mr. Shiftlet," she said, sliding forward in her chair, "you'd be getting a permanent house and a deep well and the most innocent girl in the world. You don't need no money. Lemme tell you something: there ain't any place in the world for a poor disabled friendless drifting man."

The ugly words settled in Mr. Shiftlet's head like a group of buzzards in the top of a tree.

He didn't answer at once. He rolled himself a cigarette and lit it and then he said in an even voice, "Lady, a man is divided into two parts, body and spirit."

The old woman clamped her gums together.

"A body and a spirit," he repeated. "The body, lady, is like a house: it don't go anywhere; but the spirit, lady, is like a automobile: always on the move, always . . ."

"Listen, Mr. Shiftlet," she said, "my well never goes dry and my house is always warm in the winter and there's no mortgage on a thing about this place. You can go to the courthouse and see for yourself. And yonder under that shed is a fine automobile." She laid the bait carefully. "You can have it painted by Saturday. I'll pay for the paint."

In the darkness, Mr. Shiftlet's smile stretched like a weary snake waking up by a fire. After a second he recalled himself and said, "I'm only saying a man's spirit means more to him than anything else. I would have to take my wife off for the weekend without no regards at all for cost. I got to follow where my spirit says to go."

"I'll give you fifteen dollars for a weekend trip," the old woman said in a crabbed voice. "That's the best I can do."

"That wouldn't hardly pay for more than the gas and the hotel," he said. "It wouldn't feed her."

"Seventeen-fifty," the old woman said. "That's all I got so it isn't any use you trying to milk me. You can take a lunch."

Mr. Shiftlet was deeply hurt by the word "milk." He didn't doubt that she had more money sewed up in her mattress but he had already told her he was not interested in her money. "I'll make that

Literary Analysis
Grotesque Characters and Characterization
What is revealed about Mr. Shiftlet and the old woman in this exchange about marriage and money?

Reading Strategy
Making Predictions
What predictions about Mr. Shiftlet can you make based on his discussion of body and spirit?

☑**Reading Check**
What does Mr. Shiftlet do with the old car?

do," he said and rose and walked off without treating with her further.

On Saturday the three of them drove into town in the car that the paint had barely dried on and Mr. Shiftlet and Lucynell were married in the Ordinary's office while the old woman witnessed. As they came out of the courthouse, Mr. Shiftlet began twisting his neck in his collar. He looked <u>morose</u> and bitter as if he had been insulted while someone held him. "That didn't satisfy me none," he said. "That was just something a woman in an office did, nothing but paper work and blood tests. What do they know about my blood? If they was to take my heart and cut it out," he said, "they wouldn't know a thing about me. It didn't satisfy me at all."

"It satisfied the law," the old woman said sharply.

"The law," Mr. Shiftlet said and spit. "It's the law that don't satisfy me."

He had painted the car dark green with a yellow band around it just under the windows. The three of them climbed in the front seat and the old woman said, "Don't Lucynell look pretty? Looks like a baby doll." Lucynell was dressed up in a white dress that her mother had uprooted from a trunk and there was a Panama hat on her head with a bunch of red wooden cherries on the brim. Every now and then her placid expression was changed by a sly isolated little thought like a shoot of green in the desert.

"You got a prize!" the old woman said.

Mr. Shiftlet didn't even look at her. They drove back to the house to let the old woman off and pick up the lunch. When they were ready to leave, she stood staring in the window of the car, with her fingers clenched around the glass. Tears began to seep sideways out of her eyes and run along the dirty creases in her face. "I ain't ever been parted with her for two days before," she said.

Mr. Shiftlet started the motor.

"And I wouldn't let no man have her but you because I seen you would do right. Goodbye, Sugarbaby," she said, clutching at the sleeve of the white dress. Lucynell looked straight at her and didn't seem to see her there at all. Mr. Shiftlet eased the car forward so that she had to move her hands.

The early afternoon was clear and open and surrounded by pale blue sky. Although the car would go only thirty miles an hour, Mr. Shiftlet imagined a terrific climb and dip and swerve that went entirely to his head so that he forgot his morning bitterness. He had always wanted an automobile but he had never been able to afford one before. He drove very fast because he wanted to make Mobile by nightfall.

Occasionally he stopped his thoughts long enough to look at Lucynell in the seat beside him. She had eaten the lunch as soon as they were out of the yard and now she was pulling the cherries off the hat one by one and throwing them out the window. He became depressed in spite of the car. He had driven about a hundred miles when he decided that she must be hungry again and at the next small town they came to, he stopped in front of an aluminum-painted

morose (mə rōs′) *adj.* gloomy; sullen

Reading Strategy
Making Predictions
Based on this speech about his dissatisfaction, what do you predict will happen to the newlyweds?

Literary Analysis
Grotesque Characters
Why is the old woman upset as she parts from her daughter?

eating place called The Hot Spot and took her in and ordered her a plate of ham and grits. The ride had made her sleepy and as soon as she got up on the stool, she rested her head on the counter and shut her eyes. There was no one in The Hot Spot but Mr. Shiftlet and the boy behind the counter, a pale youth with a greasy rag hung over his shoulder. Before he could dish up the food, she was snoring gently.

"Give it to her when she wakes up," Mr. Shiftlet said. "I'll pay for it now." The boy bent over her and stared at the long pink-gold hair and the half-shut sleeping eyes. Then he looked up and stared at Mr. Shiftlet. "She looks like an angel of Gawd," he murmured.

"Hitchhiker," Mr. Shiftlet explained. "I can't wait. I got to make Tuscaloosa."

The boy bent over again and very carefully touched his finger to a strand of the golden hair and Mr. Shiftlet left.

He was more depressed than ever as he drove on by himself. The late afternoon had grown hot and sultry and the country had flattened out. Deep in the sky a storm was preparing very slowly and without thunder as if it meant to drain every drop of air from the earth before it broke. There were times when Mr. Shiftlet preferred not to be alone. He felt too that a man with a car had a responsibility to others and he kept his eye out for a hitchhiker. Occasionally he saw a sign that warned: "Drive carefully. The life you save may be your own."

The narrow road dropped off on either side into dry fields and here and there a shack or a filling station stood in a clearing. The sun began to set directly in front of the automobile. It was a reddening ball that through his windshield was slightly flat on the bottom and top. He saw a boy in overalls and a gray hat standing on the edge of the road and he slowed the car down and stopped in front of him. The boy didn't have his hand raised to thumb the ride, he was only standing there, but he had a small cardboard suitcase and his hat was set on his head in a way to indicate that he had left somewhere for good. "Son," Mr. Shiftlet said, "I see you want a ride."

The boy didn't say he did or he didn't but he opened the door of the car and got in, and Mr. Shiftlet started driving again. The child held the suitcase on his lap and folded his arms on top of it. He turned his head and looked out the window away from Shiftlet. Mr. Shiftlet felt oppressed. "Son," he said after a minute, "I got the best old mother in the world so I reckon you only got the second best."

The boy gave him a quick dark glance and then turned his face back out the window.

"It's nothing so sweet," Mr. Shiftlet continued, "as a boy's mother. She taught him his first prayers at her knee, she give him love when no other would, she told him what was right and what wasn't, and she seen that he done the right thing. Son," he said, "I never rued a

Southern Regionalism

While writers have the capacity to invent whole new worlds, they are human beings who are influenced by their environments. Regional writers are those who use specific geographical areas—usually their home turf—as settings. Yet regionalists do more than simply set their fiction in familiar locales; they incorporate the distinct culture of an area, including characteristic speech patterns, customs, beliefs, history, and folklore into the very fabric of their stories. This marriage of place, sensibility, and style goes beyond mere reporting to present a sophisticated treatment of the culture of a region. With the best regional writers, local detail helps to create stories of universal impact. You need not be from the American South to appreciate the work of such great Southern regional writers as Flannery O'Connor, Truman Capote, Carson McCullers, Tennessee Williams, William Faulkner, Eudora Welty, or Robert Penn Warren.

✔**Reading Check**

What does Mr. Shiftlet do when Lucynell falls asleep at The Hot Spot?

day in my life like the one I rued when I left that old mother of mine."

The boy shifted in his seat but he didn't look at Mr. Shiftlet. He unfolded his arms and put one hand on the door handle.

"My mother was a angel of Gawd," Mr. Shiftlet said in a very strained voice. "He took her from heaven and giver to me and I left her." His eyes were instantly clouded over with a mist of tears. The car was barely moving.

The boy turned angrily in the seat. "You go to the devil!" he cried. "My old woman is a flea bag and yours is a stinking pole cat!" and with that he flung the door open and jumped out with his suitcase into the ditch.

Mr. Shiftlet was so shocked that for about a hundred feet he drove along slowly with the door still open. A cloud, the exact color of the boy's hat and shaped like a turnip, had descended over the sun, and another, worse looking, crouched behind the car. Mr. Shiftlet felt that the rottenness of the world was about to engulf him. He raised his arm and let it fall again to his breast. "Oh Lord!" he prayed. "Break forth and wash the slime from this earth!"

The turnip continued slowly to descend. After a few minutes there was a guffawing peal of thunder from behind and fantastic raindrops, like tin-can tops, crashed over the rear of Mr. Shiftlet's car. Very quickly he stepped on the gas and with his stump sticking out the window he raced the galloping shower into Mobile.

guffawing (gə fô´ iŋ) *adj.* laughing in a loud, coarse manner

Review and Assess

Thinking About the Selection

1. **Respond:** How did you react to the people in this story? In what way, if any, do they remind you of people you have met?

2. **(a) Recall:** What is Mrs. Crater's first reaction to Shiftlet when she sees him from a distance as the story begins? **(b) Infer:** What object on the Crater farm does Mr. Shiftlet want? **(c) Analyze:** What clues about Mr. Shiftlet's true character does Mrs. Crater seem to not notice?

3. **(a) Recall:** What arguments does Mrs. Crater use to persuade Shiftlet to marry Lucynell? **(b) Interpret:** What factors cause Shiftlet to agree to the marriage?

4. **(a) Recall:** What prayer does Shiftlet offer at the end of the story? **(b) Analyze:** What is ironic about the way in which his prayer is answered? **(c) Generalize:** What does this event suggest about those whose behavior contradicts their professed beliefs?

5. **Make a Judgment:** When Mrs. Crater decides to marry Lucynell to Shiftlet, the girl seems to have no control over her fate. Do Mrs. Crater's actions have any moral justification? Explain.

Review and Assess

Literary Analysis

Grotesque Characters

1. Note two uses of physical description that create an exaggerated or **grotesque** effect for (a) Mrs. Crater, (b) Mr. Shiftlet, and (c) Lucynell.

2. Use a chart like the one shown to examine Mrs. Crater and Mr. Shiftlet. (a) What primary goal or obsession controls each character? (b) What actions does each undertake as a result of the obsession?

Character	Controlling Goal	Actions Undertaken

3. (a) In what ways are these characters exaggerated? (b) In what ways are they realistic?

Connecting Literary Elements

4. How does the narrator's observation that Mr. Shiftlet's figure "formed a crooked cross" contribute to his **characterization**?

5. What does Mr. Shiftlet's name suggest about his character?

6. (a) What is the cause of Lucynell's innocence? (b) What does the story suggest about the fate of such innocence?

Reading Strategy

Making Predictions

7. (a) What **predictions** did you make about Mr. Shiftlet's actions concerning Mrs. Crater and Lucynell when he first appeared? (b) What actually happened?

8. (a) What predictions did you make when Mr. Shiftlet departed with Lucynell after their wedding? (b) What actually happened?

9. In what ways do the story's actual events surprise the reader?

Extend Understanding

10. **Social Studies Connection:** In today's world, what educational opportunities or living situations might be available to a mentally challenged woman like Lucynell?

Quick Review

Grotesque characters become ludicrous or bizarre through their obsession with an idea, an assumption, or a value.

Characterization is the art of revealing character. With **direct characterization,** the writer simply states what a character is like. With **indirect characterization,** the writer reveals characters through their words, thoughts, actions, physical appearance, and by what other characters say and how they react.

To **make predictions,** use information from the text to anticipate how events will unfold later in the story.

 Take It to the Net
www.phschool.com
Take the interactive self-test online to check your understanding of the selection.

Integrate Language Skills

Vocabulary Development Lesson

Word Analysis: Latin Root -sol-

The Latin word root *-sol-*, meaning "alone," builds the meaning of these words:

   a. *desolate*: isolated, uninhabited
   b. *solitary*: alone, without company
   c. *soloist*: one who performs by him- or herself

Use your knowledge of the Latin root *-sol-* to answer the following questions.

1. Is *solitaire* a game played by a single person or by a group of players?
2. In a *soliloquy*, do two actors have an exchange or does one actor address the audience?
3. Would a pilot have a co-pilot on a *solo* flight?
4. Would a person who usually loves to take long walks alone enjoy the state of *solitude*?

Concept Development: Context

For each sentence, indicate whether the word in italics is used correctly. If it is used incorrectly, write a new correct sentence.

1. With fresh paint and flower boxes, the cottage had a *desolate* appearance.
2. The rickety fence *listed* in the strong winds.
3. In an *ominous* voice, the jury foreperson read the guilty verdict.
4. After a huge dinner, we were *ravenous*.
5. Your *morose* reaction shows your happiness.
6. He was *guffawing* at the comic's antics.

Spelling Strategy

When you add a suffix to a word that ends in *w*, never double the *w*. For each word below, create a new word by adding the given suffix.

1. *-er* to shallow   3. *-al* to withdraw
2. *-ing* to glow   4. *-ed* to hallow

Grammar and Style Lesson

Subjunctive Mood

The **subjunctive mood** is any verb form indicating possibility, supposition, or desire.

- If a verb expresses a condition contrary to fact, use the past-tense form *were*.
- If a verb demands, recommends, or suggests, use the third-person singular verb form without the usual *-s*, *-es*, or *-ies* ending.

Look at these examples:

Contrary to fact: Mr. Shiftlet talked as if he *were* an ethical person.

Demands/suggests: Mrs. Crater suggested that Shiftlet *marry* her daughter.

Practice Determine whether the subjunctive mood is needed in each example. Then, write the correct form of the verb in parentheses to complete each sentence.

1. I wouldn't trust that broker, if I (be) you.
2. He requires that customers (pay) in cash.
3. Every summer, she (rent) a cottage.
4. He asks that each one (try) a sample.
5. The sample usually (taste) good.

Writing Application Write two different sentences using the subjunctive mood. For the first, express a condition contrary to fact. For the second, suggest a preferred course of action.

Prentice Hall Writing and Grammar Connection: Chapter 21, Section 3

Writing Lesson

Deposition

A deposition is a witness's formal, written testimony—a legal first-person recounting of events. Imagine that Mr. Shiftlet has been accused of stealing Mrs. Crater's car and of abandoning Lucynell. As a witness, write a deposition that may be used against him.

Prewriting List Mr. Shiftlet's statements and actions and the effects you know or imagine they had. Locate quotations from the story that support your testimony.

Drafting Begin by explaining, in objective detail, what Mr. Shiftlet did. Establish clear transitions that show cause and effect. Include relevant quotations to back up your statements. Finally, end by explaining why you believe that Mr. Shiftlet's actions were criminal.

Revising Be sure that you have described events in a clear and logical way. Add any transition words necessary to clarify causes and effects.

Model: Revising to Show Cause and Effect

At The Hot Spot, Mr. Shiftlet paid in advance for Lucynell's

, so that

meal he could leave her without arousing suspicion. He said

thus

that she was just a hitchhiker, justifying his leaving without her.

> Transition words like *thus* and *so that* clarify cause and effect.

WG Prentice Hall Writing and Grammar Connection: Chapter 10, Section 4

Extension Activities

Listening and Speaking In a small group, conduct a **Readers Theatre** of the story.

- Name three students to be the narrator, Mrs. Crater, and Mr. Shiftlet.

- Have a fourth student act out Lucynell as the narrator describes her.

Follow your presentation with a discussion in which audience members comment on the author's use of stylistic devices to advance character and motive. **[Group Activity]**

Research and Technology People's posture or gestures may "speak" louder than their words. Conduct library and Internet research to prepare a **body language presentation.** Describe how body language reveals character. Link your findings to the selection and provide simple demonstrations to illustrate your main points.

 **Take It to the Net** www.phschool.com

Go online for an additional research activity using the Internet.

Prepare to Read

The First Seven Years

Bernard Malamud (1914–1986)

"I write . . . to explain life to myself and to keep me related to men," Bernard Malamud once commented when describing his life's work. He was a writer who possessed a strong social and political conscience, though he often insisted publicly that he was only interested in "the story." He explored the power of art to liberate people, always believing that "the purpose of freedom is to create it for others."

Childhood of Two Cultures Bernard Malamud was born in Brooklyn, New York, the son of Russian immigrants. His father was a grocer who, like so many immigrants, worked diligently to forge a better life for his family. According to his own account, Malamud's boyhood was "comparatively happy." He grew up hearing the constant mingling of Yiddish and English—an experience that contributed to his fine ear for the rhythms of spoken dialogue. Through his family's attention to Jewish culture, he developed a taste for Manhattan's Second Avenue Yiddish Theater, where two of his mother's relatives sometimes performed. A favored boyhood pastime was listening to his father recount tales of Jewish life in pre-Revolutionary Russia. Young Bernard began to display his father's gift for telling stories when, recovering from pneumonia at age nine, he spent hours in the back room of the family store writing down the stories he had composed to tell his friends.

A Literary Range Malamud attended City College of New York and Columbia University and began publishing stories in a number of well-known magazines. Despite his strong connection to Yiddish folk tales—many of Malamud's stories are drawn from this oral tradition—his work depicts a broad range of settings and characters. From the gifted baseball player in *The Natural* (1952), Malamud's first novel, to the handyman living in czarist Russia in the Pulitzer Prize-winning *The Fixer* (1966), all of his characters come across as real and accessible, with universal hopes and concerns.

Malamud's other novels include *The Assistant* (1957), *A New Life* (1961), *The Tenants* (1971), and *Dubin's Lives* (1979). He also wrote numerous short stories, many of which were published in *The Magic Barrel* (1958), which won the National Book Award.

Capturing Life's Lessons In much of his writing, Malamud uses Jewish characters to represent all of humanity, capturing their attempts to maintain a link to their cultural heritage while trying to cope with modern realities. While some of his characters achieve success, others experience disappointment. By portraying failure as well as triumph, Malamud reveals the essence of the human experience and creates a delicate balance between tragedy and comedy. Some of his stories amuse readers as the characters try to negotiate between fulfilling their ideals and meeting the practical demands of their lives.

A Touch of Magic Malamud often tells his stories in spare, compressed prose, sprinkled with flashes of highly charged metaphorical language. He allows magical events to happen in gloomy city neighborhoods, and gives his hard-working characters unexpected flashes of passion. Other Malamud stories move readers to sadness as characters struggle courageously within tragic circumstances. "The First Seven Years" depicts a Polish immigrant's desire to see his daughter achieve a better life. His notion of that life, however, is not the same as hers.

Preview

Connecting to the Literature

When parents or teachers push you to study hard, learn a skill, or practice an instrument, they hope to help you achieve a better life. Similarly, the father in this story pushes his daughter in a certain direction in the hope that she will find happiness. However, her idea of happiness does not match his.

Literary Analysis

Epiphany

In a traditional short story, the plot moves toward resolution, a point at which the conflict is untangled and the outcome of the action becomes clear. However, many twentieth-century writers turned away from such traditional plot structures. These writers constructed plots that move toward an **epiphany,** a moment when a character has a flash of insight that may alter the nature of the conflict without resolving it. In this story, the main character experiences an epiphany that requires him to reexamine long-held assumptions.

Connecting Literary Elements

Conflict, a struggle between opposing forces, is a key element of narrative literature because most plots develop from conflict. There are two main types of conflict:

- **Internal conflict** takes place within a character and involves a person's struggle with ideas, beliefs, or attitudes.
- **External conflict** takes place between a character and an outside force, such as society, nature, or an enemy.

As you read this story, think about the conflicts each character experiences. Use a chart like the one shown to examine the conflicts, and categorize them as either internal or external.

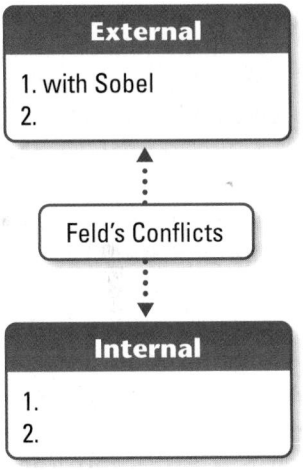

Reading Strategy

Identifying With Characters

When you **identify with characters,** you connect their thoughts, feelings, circumstances and actions to your own experience. Identifying with characters allows you to get more emotionally involved in your reading.

Vocabulary

diligence (dil´ ə jəns) *n.* constant, careful effort; perseverance (p. 988)

connivance (kə nī´ vəns) *n.* secret cooperation (p. 989)

illiterate (i lit´ ər it) *adj.* unable to read or write (p. 989)

unscrupulous (un skrōō´ pyə ləs) *adj.* unethical; unprincipled (p. 991)

repugnant (ri pug´ nənt) *adj.* offensive; disagreeable (p. 991)

discern (di surn´) *v.* to perceive or recognize; make out clearly (p. 994)

The First Seven Years

Bernard Malamud

Background

This story takes place in the 1950s, a prosperous decade in the United States. Both the Great Depression and World War II had ended and the baby boom was in full swing. People were upwardly mobile; if they worked hard, they were virtually assured that their status in society would improve. Parents labored for wealth so that their children would have easier lives, yet some children took material comfort for granted. They became more interested in matters of the spirit. Malamud's story explores the gap in values that sometimes occurred between children of the 1950s and their parents.

Feld, the shoemaker, was annoyed that his helper, Sobel, was so insensitive to his reverie that he wouldn't for a minute cease his fanatic pounding at the other bench. He gave him a look, but Sobel's bald head was bent over the last[1] as he worked and he didn't notice. The shoemaker shrugged and continued to peer through the partly frosted window at the nearsighted haze of falling February snow. Neither the shifting white blur outside, nor the sudden deep remembrance of the snowy Polish village where he had wasted his youth could turn his thoughts from Max the college boy, (a constant visitor in the mind since early that morning when Feld saw him trudging through the snowdrifts on his way to school) whom he so much respected because of the sacrifices he had made throughout the years—in winter or direst heat—to further his education. An old wish returned to haunt the shoemaker: that he had had a son instead of a daughter, but this blew away in the snow for Feld, if anything, was a practical man. Yet he could not help but contrast the <u>diligence</u> of the boy, who was a peddler's son, with Miriam's unconcern for an education. True, she was always with a book in her hand, yet when the opportunity arose for a college education, she had said no she would rather find a job. He had begged her to go, pointing out how many fathers could not afford to send their children to college, but she said she wanted to be independent. As for education, what was it, she asked, but books,

▲ **Critical Viewing**
What does this image reveal about the setting of the story? **[Predict]**

diligence (dil´ ə jəns) *n.* constant, careful effort; perseverance

---

1. **last** *n.* block shaped like a person's foot, on which shoes are made or repaired.

which Sobel, who diligently read the classics, would as usual advise her on. Her answer greatly grieved her father.

A figure emerged from the snow and the door opened. At the counter the man withdrew from a wet paper bag a pair of battered shoes for repair. Who he was the shoemaker for a moment had no idea, then his heart trembled as he realized, before he had thoroughly discerned the face, that Max himself was standing there, embarrassedly explaining what he wanted done to his old shoes. Though Feld listened eagerly, he couldn't hear a word, for the opportunity that had burst upon him was deafening.

He couldn't exactly recall when the thought had occurred to him, because it was clear he had more than once considered suggesting to the boy that he go out with Miriam. But he had not dared speak, for if Max said no, how would he face him again? Or suppose Miriam, who harped so often on independence, blew up in anger and shouted at him for his meddling? Still, the chance was too good to let by: all it meant was an introduction. They might long ago have become friends had they happened to meet somewhere, therefore was it not his duty—an obligation—to bring them together, nothing more, a harmless <u>connivance</u> to replace an accidental encounter in the subway, let's say, or a mutual friend's introduction in the street? Just let him once see and talk to her and he would for sure be interested. As for Miriam, what possible harm for a working girl in an office, who met only loud-mouthed salesmen and <u>illiterate</u> shipping clerks, to make the acquaintance of a fine scholarly boy? Maybe he would awaken in her a desire to go to college; if not—the shoemaker's mind at last came to grips with the truth—let her marry an educated man and live a better life.

When Max finished describing what he wanted done to his shoes, Feld marked them, both with enormous holes in the soles which he pretended not to notice, with large white-chalk x's, and the rubber heels, thinned to the nails, he marked with o's, though it troubled him he might have mixed up the letters. Max inquired the price, and the shoemaker cleared his throat and asked the boy, above Sobel's insistent hammering, would he please step through the side door there into the hall. Though surprised, Max did as the shoemaker requested, and Feld went in after him. For a minute they were both silent, because Sobel had stopped banging, and it seemed they understood neither was to say anything until the noise began again. When it did, loudly, the shoemaker quickly told Max why he had asked to talk to him.

"Ever since you went to high school," he said, in the dimly-lit hallway, "I watched you in the morning go to the subway to school, and I said always to myself, this is a fine boy that he wants so much an education."

"Thanks," Max said, nervously alert. He was tall and grotesquely thin, with sharply cut features, particularly a beak-like nose. He was wearing a loose, long slushy overcoat that hung down to his ankles,

Literary Analysis
Epiphany and Conflict Is Feld's conflict in speaking to Max primarily internal or external? Explain.

connivance (kə nī′ vəns) *n.* secret cooperation

illiterate (i lit′ ər it) *adj.* unable to read or write

✔**Reading Check**
What hope does Feld hold for his daughter Miriam and the college boy Max?

looking like a rug draped over his bony shoulders, and a soggy, old brown hat, as battered as the shoes he had brought in.

"I am a business man," the shoemaker abruptly said to conceal his embarrassment, "so I will explain you right away why I talk to you. I have a girl, my daughter Miriam—she is nineteen—a very nice girl and also so pretty that everybody looks on her when she passes by in the street. She is smart, always with a book, and I thought to myself that a boy like you, an educated boy—I thought maybe you will be interested sometime to meet a girl like this." He laughed a bit when he had finished and was tempted to say more but had the good sense not to.

Reading Strategy
Identifying With Characters How do you think Feld feels during this exchange with Max? Why?

Max stared down like a hawk. For an uncomfortable second he was silent, then he asked, "Did you say nineteen?"

"Yes."

"Would it be all right to inquire if you have a picture of her?"

"Just a minute." The shoemaker went into the store and hastily returned with a snapshot that Max held up to the light.

"She's all right," he said.

Feld waited.

"And is she sensible—not the flighty kind?"

"She is very sensible."

After another short pause, Max said it was okay with him if he met her.

"Here is my telephone," said the shoemaker, hurriedly handing him a slip of paper. "Call her up. She comes home from work six o'clock."

Max folded the paper and tucked it away into his worn leather wallet.

"About the shoes," he said. "How much did you say they will cost me?"

"Don't worry about the price."

"I just like to have an idea."

"A dollar—dollar fifty. A dollar fifty," the shoemaker said.

At once he felt bad, for he usually charged two twenty-five for this kind of job. Either he should have asked the regular price or done the work for nothing.

Later, as he entered the store, he was startled by a violent clanging and looked up to see Sobel pounding with all his might upon the naked last. It broke, the iron striking the floor and jumping with a thump against the wall, but before the enraged shoemaker could cry out, the assistant had torn his hat and coat from the hook and rushed out into the snow.

Literary Analysis
Epiphany and Conflict What do Sobel's actions and Feld's reactions suggest about a conflict between the two men?

So Feld, who had looked forward to anticipating how it would go with his daughter and Max, instead had a great worry on his mind. Without his temperamental helper he was a lost man, especially since it was years now that he had carried the store alone. The shoemaker had for an age suffered from a heart condition that threatened collapse if he dared exert himself. Five years ago, after an attack, it had appeared as though he would have either to sacrifice his business upon the auction block and live on a pittance thereafter, or put himself at the mercy of some unscrupulous employee who would in the end probably ruin him. But just at the moment of his darkest despair, this Polish refugee, Sobel, appeared one night from the street and begged for work. He was a stocky man, poorly dressed, with a bald head that had once been blond, a severely plain face and soft blue eyes prone to tears over the sad books he read, a young man but old—no one would have guessed thirty. Though he confessed he knew nothing of shoemaking, he said he was apt and would work for a very little if Feld taught him the trade. Thinking that with, after all, a landsman,[2] he would have less to fear than from a complete stranger, Feld took him on and within six weeks the refugee rebuilt as good a shoe as he, and not long thereafter expertly ran the business for the thoroughly relieved shoemaker.

Feld could trust him with anything and did, frequently going home after an hour or two at the store, leaving all the money in the till, knowing Sobel would guard every cent of it. The amazing thing was that he demanded so little. His wants were few; in money he wasn't interested—in nothing but books, it seemed—which he one by one lent to Miriam, together with his profuse, queer written comments, manufactured during his lonely rooming house evenings, thick pads of commentary which the shoemaker peered at and twitched his shoulders over as his daughter, from her fourteenth year, read page by sanctified page, as if the word of God were inscribed on them. To protect Sobel, Feld himself had to see that he received more than he asked for. Yet his conscience bothered him for not insisting that the assistant accept a better wage than he was getting, though Feld had honestly told him he could earn a handsome salary if he worked elsewhere, or maybe opened a place of his own. But the assistant answered, somewhat ungraciously, that he was not interested in going elsewhere, and though Feld frequently asked himself what keeps him here? why does he stay? he finally answered it that the man, no doubt because of his terrible experiences as a refugee, was afraid of the world.

After the incident with the broken last, angered by Sobel's behavior, the shoemaker decided to let him stew for a week in the rooming house, although his own strength was taxed dangerously and the business suffered. However, after several sharp nagging warnings from both his wife and daughter, he went finally in search of Sobel, as he had once before, quite recently, when over some fancied slight— Feld had merely asked him not to give Miriam so many books to read because her eyes were strained and red—the assistant had left the place in a huff, an incident which, as usual, came to nothing for he had returned after the shoemaker had talked to him, and taken his seat at the bench. But this time, after Feld had plodded through the snow to Sobel's house—he had thought of sending Miriam but the idea became repugnant to him—the burly landlady at the door

---

2. **landsman** *n.* fellow countryman.

unscrupulous (un skrŌŌp′ yə ləs) *adj.* unethical; unprincipled

Literary Analysis
Epiphany and Conflict
What are some of the conflicts Feld experiences in regard to Sobel?

repugnant (ri pug′ nənt) *adj.* offensive; disagreeable

**Reading Check**

Under what circumstances did Sobel begin working for Feld?

informed him in a nasal voice that Sobel was not at home, and though Feld knew this was a nasty lie, for where had the refugee to go? still for some reason he was not completely sure of—it may have been the cold and his fatigue—he decided not to insist on seeing him. Instead he went home and hired a new helper.

Having settled the matter, though not entirely to his satisfaction, for he had much more to do than before, and so, for example, could no longer lie late in bed mornings because he had to get up to open the store for the new assistant, a speechless, dark man with an irritating rasp as he worked, whom he would not trust with the key as he had Sobel. Furthermore, this one, though able to do a fair repair job, knew nothing of grades of leather or prices, so Feld had to make his own purchases: and every night at closing time it was necessary to count the money in the till and lock up. However, he was not dissatisfied, for he lived much in his thoughts of Max and Miriam. The college boy had called her, and they had arranged a meeting for this coming Friday night. The shoemaker would personally have preferred Saturday, which he felt would make it a date of the first magnitude, but he learned Friday was Miriam's choice, so he said nothing. The day of the week did not matter. What mattered was the aftermath. Would they like each other and want to be friends? He sighed at all the time that would have to go by before he knew for sure. Often he was tempted to talk to Miriam about the boy, to ask whether she thought she would like his type—he had told her only that he considered Max a nice boy and had suggested he call her—but the one time he tried she snapped at him—justly—how should she know?

At last Friday came. Feld was not feeling particularly well so he stayed in bed, and Mrs. Feld thought it better to remain in the bedroom with him when Max called. Miriam received the boy, and her parents could hear their voices, his throaty one, as they talked. Just before leaving, Miriam brought Max to the bedroom door and he stood there a minute, a tall, slightly hunched figure wearing a thick, droopy suit, and apparently at ease as he greeted the shoemaker and his wife, which was surely a good sign. And Miriam, although she had worked all day, looked fresh and pretty. She was a large-framed girl with a well-shaped body, and she had a fine open face and soft hair. They made, Feld thought, a first-class couple.

Miriam returned after 11:30. Her mother was already asleep, but the shoemaker got out of bed and after locating his bathrobe went into the kitchen, where Miriam, to his surprise, sat at the table, reading.

"So where did you go?" Feld asked pleasantly.

"For a walk," she said, not looking up.

"I advised him," Feld said, clearing his throat, "he shouldn't spend so much money."

"I didn't care."

The shoemaker boiled up some water for tea and sat down at the table with a cupful and a thick slice of lemon.

"So how," he sighed after a sip, "did you enjoy?"

"It was all right."

He was silent. She must have sensed his disappointment, for she added, "You can't really tell much the first time."

"You will see him again?"

Turning a page, she said that Max had asked for another date.

"For when?"

"Saturday."

"So what did you say?"

"What did I say?" she asked, delaying for a moment—"I said yes."

Afterwards she inquired about Sobel, and Feld, without exactly knowing why, said the assistant had got another job. Miriam said nothing more and began to read. The shoemaker's conscience did not trouble him; he was satisfied with the Saturday date.

During the week, by placing here and there a deft question, he managed to get from Miriam some information about Max. It surprised him to learn that the boy was not studying to be either a doctor or lawyer but was taking a business course leading to a degree in accountancy. Feld was a little disappointed because he thought of accountants as bookkeepers and would have preferred "a higher profession." However, it was not long before he had investigated the subject and discovered that Certified Public Accountants were highly respected people, so he was thoroughly content as Saturday approached. But because Saturday was a busy day, he was much in the store and therefore did not see Max when he came to call for Miriam. From his wife he learned there had been nothing especially revealing about their meeting. Max had rung the bell and Miriam had got her coat and left with him—nothing more. Feld did not probe, for his wife was not particularly observant. Instead, he waited up for Miriam with a newspaper on his lap, which he scarcely looked at so lost was he in thinking of the future. He awoke to find her in the room with him, tiredly removing her hat. Greeting her, he was suddenly inexplicably afraid to ask anything about the evening. But since she volunteered nothing he was at last forced to inquire how she had enjoyed herself. Miriam began something noncommittal but apparently changed her mind, for she said after a minute, "I was bored."

When Feld had sufficiently recovered from his anguished disappointment to ask why, she answered without hesitation, "Because he's nothing more than a materialist."

"What means this word?"

"He has no soul. He's only interested in things."

He considered her statement for a long time but then asked, "Will you see him again?"

"He didn't ask."

"Suppose he will ask you?"

"I won't see him."

Literary Analysis
Epiphany and Conflict
What does this conversation suggest are some of Miriam's conflicts with her father?

Literary Analysis
Epiphany and Conflict
Why do you think Feld was "suddenly inexplicably afraid to ask anything about the evening"?

Reading Check
What is Miriam's reaction to her first date with Max?

He did not argue: however, as the days went by he hoped increasingly she would change her mind. He wished the boy would telephone, because he was sure there was more to him than Miriam, with her inexperienced eye, could <u>discern</u>. But Max didn't call. As a matter of fact he took a different route to school, no longer passing the shoemaker's store, and Feld was deeply hurt.

Then one afternoon Max came in and asked for his shoes. The shoemaker took them down from the shelf where he had placed them, apart from the other pairs. He had done the work himself and the soles and heels were well built and firm. The shoes had been highly polished and somehow looked better than new. Max's Adam's apple went up once when he saw them, and his eyes had little lights in them.

"How much?" he asked, without directly looking at the shoemaker.

"Like I told you before," Feld answered sadly. "One dollar fifty cents."

Max handed him two crumpled bills and received in return a newly-minted silver half dollar.

He left. Miriam had not been mentioned. That night the shoemaker discovered that his new assistant had been all the while stealing from him, and he suffered a heart attack.

Though the attack was very mild, he lay in bed for three weeks. Miriam spoke of going for Sobel, but sick as he was Feld rose in wrath against the idea. Yet in his heart he knew there was no other way, and the first weary day back in the shop thoroughly convinced him, so that night after supper he dragged himself to Sobel's rooming house.

He toiled up the stairs, though he knew it was bad for him, and at the top knocked at the door. Sobel opened it and the shoemaker entered. The room was a small, poor one, with a single window facing the street. It contained a narrow cot, a low table and several stacks of books piled haphazardly around on the floor along the wall, which made him think how queer Sobel was, to be uneducated and read so much. He had once asked him, Sobel, why you read so much? and the assistant could not answer him. Did you ever study in a college someplace? he had asked but Sobel shook his head. He read, he said, to know. But to know what, the shoemaker demanded, and to know, why? Sobel never explained, which proved he read much because he was queer.

Feld sat down to recover his breath. The assistant was resting on his bed with his heavy back to the wall. His shirt and trousers were clean, and his stubby fingers, away from the shoemaker's bench, were strangely pallid. His face was thin and pale, as if he had been shut in this room since the day he had bolted from the store.

"So when you will come back to work?" Feld asked him.

To his surprise, Sobel burst out, "Never."

discern (di surn´) v. to perceive or recognize; make out clearly

Literary Analysis
Epiphany and Conflict
What conflicts does Feld experience in this passage? Which are internal, and which external?

▼ **Critical Viewing**
Which item mentioned in the story is shown in this photograph? **[Connect]**

Jumping up, he strode over to the window that looked out upon the miserable street. "Why should I come back?" he cried.

"I will raise your wages."

"Who cares for your wages!"

The shoemaker, knowing he didn't care, was at a loss what else to say.

"What do you want from me, Sobel?"

"Nothing."

"I always treated you like you was my son."

Sobel vehemently denied it. "So why you look for strange boys in the street they should go out with Miriam? Why you don't think of me?"

The shoemaker's hands and feet turned freezing cold. His voice became so hoarse he couldn't speak. At last he cleared his throat and croaked, "So what has my daughter got to do with a shoemaker thirty-five years old who works for me?"

"Why do you think I worked so long for you?" Sobel cried out. "For the stingy wages I sacrificed five years of my life so you could have to eat and drink and where to sleep?"

"Then for what?" shouted the shoemaker.

"For Miriam," he blurted—"for her."

The shoemaker, after a time, managed to say, "I pay wages in cash, Sobel," and lapsed into silence. Though he was seething with excitement, his mind was coldly clear, and he had to admit to himself he had sensed all along that Sobel felt this way. He had never so much as thought it consciously, but he had felt it and was afraid.

"Miriam knows?" he muttered hoarsely.

"She knows."

"You told her?"

"No."

"Then how does she know?"

"How does she know?" Sobel said, "because she knows. She knows who I am and what is in my heart."

Feld had a sudden insight. In some devious way, with his books and commentary, Sobel had given Miriam to understand that he loved her. The shoemaker felt a terrible anger at him for his deceit.

"Sobel, you are crazy," he said bitterly. "She will never marry a man so old and ugly like you."

Sobel turned black with rage. He cursed the shoemaker, but then, though he trembled to hold it in, his eyes filled with tears and he broke into deep sobs. With his back to Feld, he stood at the window, fists clenched, and his shoulders shook with his choked sobbing.

Watching him, the shoemaker's anger diminished. His teeth were on edge with pity for the man, and his eyes grew moist. How strange and sad that a refugee, a grown man, bald and old with his miseries, who had by the skin of his teeth escaped Hitler's incinerators,[3] should fall in

---

3. **Hitler's incinerators** During World War II, millions of Jews were murdered by the Nazis under the direction of German dictator Adolf Hitler (1889–1945).

Reading Strategy
Identifying With Characters Put yourself in Sobel's position. Why is he so angry with Feld?

Literary Analysis
Epiphany How can you tell that Feld is having an epiphany?

**Reading Check**

How does Sobel feel about Miriam? In what way has he expressed his feelings?

love, when he had got to America, with a girl less than half his age. Day after day, for five years he had sat at his bench, cutting and hammering away, waiting for the girl to become a woman, unable to ease his heart with speech, knowing no protest but desperation.

"Ugly I didn't mean," he said half aloud.

Then he realized that what he had called ugly was not Sobel but Miriam's life if she married him. He felt for his daughter a strange and gripping sorrow, as if she were already Sobel's bride, the wife, after all, of a shoemaker, and had in her life no more than her mother had had. And all his dreams for her—why he had slaved and destroyed his heart with anxiety and labor—all these dreams of a better life were dead.

The room was quiet. Sobel was standing by the window reading, and it was curious that when he read he looked young.

"She is only nineteen," Feld said brokenly. "This is too young yet to get married. Don't ask her for two years more, till she is twenty-one, then you can talk to her."

Sobel didn't answer. Feld rose and left. He went slowly down the stairs but once outside, though it was an icy night and the crisp falling snow whitened the street, he walked with a stronger stride.

But the next morning, when the shoemaker arrived, heavy-hearted, to open the store, he saw he needn't have come, for his assistant was already seated at the last, pounding leather for his love.

Literary Analysis
Epiphany and Conflict
What realization brings Feld such a strong feeling of sorrow?

Review and Assess

Thinking About the Selection

1. **Respond:** Which ambitions for Miriam's future seem more worthy to you—Feld's or Miriam's? Explain.

2. **(a) Recall:** Under what circumstances does Feld first notice Max? **(b) Interpret:** Why is Max so appealing to Feld?

3. **(a) Recall:** To Feld, what values does Max seem to embody? **(b) Interpret:** Does Max really share Feld's values? Explain.

4. **(a) Recall:** How does Miriam react to her second date with Max? **(b) Compare and Contrast:** Explain the differences between Miriam's feelings for Max and her feelings for Sobel.

5. **(a) Recall:** What is Sobel's background? **(b) Speculate:** In what ways do the events of history that Sobel experienced add to his characterization?

6. **(a) Interpret:** What does education represent to Feld and Max? **(b) Compare and Contrast:** How does Sobel's love of reading compare with both Feld's and Max's feelings about education?

7. **Make a Judgment:** Do you think Feld was right to interfere in Miriam's life? Explain.

Review and Assess

Literary Analysis

Epiphany

1. Use a chart like the one shown to examine the **epiphanies** the characters experience in this story.

Character	Epiphany

⋯▶ When it Occurs / What it Reveals

2. What new ideas does Feld's epiphany introduce that challenge the values he has always held?

3. In what ways might Feld's epiphany (a) change his thinking in the future? (b) affect his attitude toward Miriam? (c) affect his attitude toward Sobel?

Connecting Literary Elements

4. (a) With what external **conflicts** does Feld struggle? (b) What internal conflicts trouble him? (c) Which conflicts affect Feld the most?

5. (a) What external conflicts does Sobel face? (b) What internal conflicts trouble him?

6. (a) What image of Sobel begins the story? (b) What image of Sobel ends it? (c) What meaning do you find in the relationship of the beginning of the story to its ending?

7. (a) At the end of this story, have the characters' situations changed? (b) If so, in what ways? If not, how might they change in the future?

Reading Strategy

Identifying With Characters

8. (a) Choose a character from "The First Seven Years" and list as many connections as possible to your own experience. (b) Imagine yourself in the character's situation. How would you feel? What actions might you take?

Extend Understanding

9. **Social Studies Connection:** For generations, many skilled trades in the United States, such as shoemaking, baking, stone cutting, or woodworking, have attracted immigrant workers. Why do you think this has so often been the case?

Quick Review

An **epiphany** is a sudden revelation or flash of insight.

A **conflict** is a struggle between opposing forces. **Internal conflict** takes place within the character and is characterized by the person's struggle with ideas. **External conflict** takes place between a character and an outside force, such as society, nature, or an enemy.

To **identify with characters,** connect their thoughts, feelings, circumstances, and actions to your own experience.

 Take It to the Net
www.phschool.com
Take the interactive self-test online to check your understanding of the selection.

Integrate Language Skills

Vocabulary Development Lesson

Word Analysis: Latin Root -litera-

The root -litera- comes from the Latin word *littera*, which means "letter." Write a definition for each of the following words containing the root -litera-. Then, check your definitions against those in a dictionary.

1. literary
2. literal
3. alliteration
4. literacy

Spelling Strategy

When you hear the *j* sound in the middle of a word, that sound is often produced by the letter *g*, as in *diligence*. In your notebook, spell each word below by adding the letter that forms the *j* sound.

1. intelli__ent
2. ori__inality
3. in_ustice
4. ad_udicate

Concept Development: Context

Review the vocabulary list on p. 987. Then, select the word you might find in each of these newspaper articles.

1. "Reading Rate Declines Among Adults"
2. "Residents Complain of Dump's Disagreeable Smell"
3. "Hard-Working Teens Turn Vacant Lot Into Garden"
4. "Dishonorable Band of Thieves Gets Nabbed"
5. "Girl of Ten Recognizes Error in Mayor's Speech"
6. "Five Executives Caught Plotting a Takeover"

Grammar and Style Lesson

Usage: *who* and *whom*

The correct use of *who* and *whom* helps an author clarify which character is being described. **Who,** like *he* or *she*, is used as a subject or subject complement. **Whom,** like *him* or *her*, is used as a direct object or as an object of the preposition. Study these examples:

> **Subject:** The diligence of the boy, *who* was a poor man's son, was inspiring. (*Who* serves as the subject of the adjective clause *who was . . . son.*)
>
> **Object:** Max, the college boy, *whom* he so much respected, was not a deep thinker. (*Whom* serves as the direct object of *respected*.)

Practice Identify which word—*who* or *whom*—correctly completes each sentence. Then, identify the word's function in the sentence.

1. She knows ___?___ I am . . .
2. Feld, ___?___ had looked forward to hearing about Max, was too nervous to ask.
3. There was little hope for a girl ___?___ met only loud-mouthed salesmen.
4. He had to open the store for the assistant, ___?___ he would not trust with the key.
5. He called Sobel, ___?___ he expected would be eagerly waiting.

Writing Application Write two sentences using *who* and *whom* correctly. In the first sentence, use the word that functions as a subject. In the second, use the word that functions as an object.

 Prentice Hall Writing and Grammar Connection: Chapter 22, Section 2

Writing Lesson

Personality Profile

Malamud creates a believable and engaging character in Feld, the shoemaker. Suppose you are developing a television show based on "The First Seven Years." Write a personality profile of Feld to be used by your producers.

Prewriting Before Feld's television character can be fully crafted, actors and producers need to know what he looks like and how he behaves. Use a cluster diagram like the one shown to jot down physical characteristics and personal qualities you observe in Feld.

Model: Clustering to Generate Details

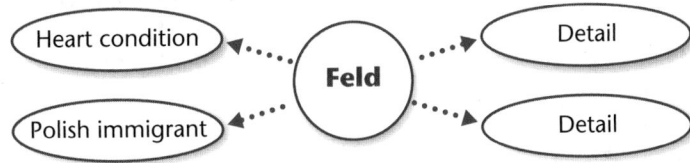

Drafting Begin with an informative detail or image of Feld. Expand your profile in layers, referring to your cluster diagram as needed.

Revising Have a classmate create a new cluster diagram based on your profile. Compare it to your prewriting diagram to discover key information you may have omitted.

W͜G Prentice Hall Writing and Grammar Connection: Chapter 6, Section 2

Extension Activities

Listening and Speaking Review the story to find details about Sobel's past, and create a **presentation** explaining how his past affected his personality, values, and decisions. Use these tips to prepare:

- Estimate Sobel's date of birth and possible birthplace.
- Conduct historical research to identify events Sobel experienced and include information from nonfiction accounts of those events.

Following your presentation, lead a class discussion about the issues raised by Sobel's life.

Research and Technology Using a variety of sources, including the Internet, conduct **cultural research** on a present-day society that adheres to the tradition of arranged marriages. Prepare a multimedia report, including text, quotations, images, and sound. In your report, balance the positive and negative aspects of such a tradition.

 **Take It to the Net** www.phschool.com

Go online for an additional research activity using the Internet.

Prepare to Read

The Brown Chest

John Updike (b. 1932)

John Updike's fiction spins the gold of insight from the straw of everyday experience. Through his depictions of ordinary situations and everyday events, Updike explores some of the most important issues of our time and offers glimpses of the underlying significance of everyday life in contemporary America. Updike transfigures outwardly ordinary people, places, objects, and events with flashes of insight, grief, and love. His short stories, novels, plays, and poems have given shape to the lives of many Americans—children and adults, rich and poor, ordinary and gifted.

An Only Child John Updike was born and raised in Shillington, Pennsylvania. His father was a high-school teacher and his mother a writer who published a novel, *Enchanted,* in 1971. Updike thinks his experience as an only child helped to nurture his artistic temperament: "I'm sure that my capacities to fantasize and to make coherent fantasies, to have patience to sit down day after day and to whittle a fantasy out of paper, all that relates to being an only child." The young Updike coped with numerous personal drawbacks. For one thing, he suffered from intense bouts of hay fever and psoriasis, a painful skin disease. For another, he stammered.

A Fine Artist Updike excelled in drawing as well as writing. In his early years, he focused his hopes on a career as a cartoonist, following in the path of James Thurber. As he matured, his interest shifted toward writing, and by age eighteen, he had decided to pursue a career as a writer. After graduating from Harvard, where he edited the *Harvard Lampoon,* Updike studied for a year in England at the Ruskin School of Drawing and Fine Art. When he returned to the United States, he became a staff writer for *The New Yorker* magazine, where James Thurber and E. B. White had made names for themselves earlier. *The New Yorker* published many of his short stories as well as his poems and literary criticism.

The Personal and the Global Updike has received wide acclaim for his many novels, as well as for volumes of poetry, criticism, and short stories. His thematic concerns are broad: Four novels featuring a character called Harry "Rabbit" Angstrom magnify the meaning of everyday moments. Novels such as *The Coup* (1978), *Brazil* (1994), and *In the Beauty of the Lilies* (1996) use a wider lens to examine how historical and political issues have affected people across the globe. Updike is also a master of the short story form, which is ideal for capturing flashes of insight into ordinary existence. Many of his stories, like his novels, are set in suburban America, which he often uses as a symbol of detachment from worldly concerns.

Updike's many honors include the National Book Award, and two Pulitzer Prizes for fiction. Of Updike, literary critic David Thorburn has written, "His steady productiveness has brought him a substantial and international audience, whose loyalty has nourished his faith in the traditional literary genres, and especially his belief in the power of realistic fiction to illuminate contemporary life." Updike has had a great influence on the generation of writers who were born after him. Some follow his tradition, while others rebel against his studied naturalism.

In the story "The Brown Chest," a man sifts through his family's accumulated belongings, focusing again and again on a chest filled with objects that call up memories. Set in rural and suburban locales, written with impeccable style, and expressing the extraordinary within the ordinary, it is vintage Updike.

Preview

Connecting to the Literature

Whether it is a drawer stuffed with old Scout badges or a box holding valentines from the third grade, most of us have a place to keep things we cannot bear to throw away. In this story, a chest full of family mementos becomes an emotional touchstone for a man's entire life.

Literary Analysis

Atmosphere

In literature, **atmosphere** refers to the emotional quality of the world the author creates. Atmosphere arises from descriptions, especially those of the setting, and mirrors the emotions of the characters. In this story, descriptions of the brown storage chest create an atmosphere that varies as the main character's life develops. As you read, note how the story's atmosphere changes to reflect the main character's thoughts and feelings.

Connecting Literary Elements

Updike's ability to choose the best possible word to convey his meaning contributes to the power and beauty of his prose. For example, note the clarity of the image he creates with the words in italics:

> She spoke only to Gordon, as if a *pane of shyness* protected her from his *hoary* father . . .

As you read, notice other examples of Updike's **precise word choices,** and analyze how each one helps create atmosphere and meaning.

Reading Strategy

Breaking Down Long Sentences

Updike tends to use long sentences that might be difficult to follow. To help your understanding, **break down long sentences** into their component parts. Use the punctuation—dashes, commas, parentheses, colons, and semi-colons—to divide the sentence into manageable sections, as in the example shown. Then, summarize the meaning of the sentence.

Vocabulary

mottled (mät´ 'ld) *adj.* blotched or streaked (p. 1004)

assimilate (ə sim´ ə lāt´) *v.* to absorb or incorporate (p. 1005)

unfathomable (un fath´ əm ə bəl) *adj.* unable to be understood (p. 1006)

egregious (ē grē´ jəs) *adj.* outstanding for undesirable qualities; remarkably bad (p. 1006)

proprietorial (prō prī´ ə tôr´ ē əl) *adj.* like someone who owns something (p. 1007)

evanescent (ev´ ə nes´ ənt) *adj.* short-lived; tending to fade or disappear (p. 1008)

Sentence in Sections

- These pieces that his infant eyes had grazed,
- and that had framed his parents' lives,
- seemed sadly shabby now, . . .
- useless used furniture he had lacked the courage to discard.

↓

Summary

The Brown Chest

John Updike

Background

The chest in Updike's story is a kind of time capsule of the early twentieth century. It contains auburn curls from a haircut in 1919, recalling the bobbed styles that were popular after World War I. The 1925 wedding dress probably had a short hem in front and a long one in back. The photograph of the main character's father as a college football player in the early 1920s probably shows him wearing a leather helmet that provided much less protection than synthetic helmets do today. During the period profiled by the items in the chest, there was no videotape to help future generations grasp what life was like. As a result, these family mementos provide one of the few means of gaining insight into the past.

In the first house he lived in, it sat up on the second floor, a big wooden chest, out of the way and yet not. For in this house, the house that he inhabited as if he would never live in any other, there were popular cheerful places, where the radio played and the legs of grown-ups went back and forth, and there were haunted bad places, like the coal bin behind the furnace, and the attic with its spiders and smell of old carpet, where he would never go without a grown-up close with him, and there were places in between, that were out of the main current but were not menacing, either, just neutral, and neglected. The entire front of the house had this neglected quality, with its guest bedroom where guests hardly ever stayed; it held a gray-painted bed with silver moons on the headboard and corner posts shaped at the top like mushrooms, and a little desk by the window where his mother sometimes, but not often, wrote letters and confided sentences to her diary in her tiny backslanting hand. If she had never done this, the room would have become haunted, even though it looked out on the busy street with its telephone wires and daytime swish of cars; but the occasional scratch of her pen

Literary Analysis
Atmosphere and Precise Word Choices What does the word "swish" add to this description of the street?

▲ Critical Viewing
What qualities does this chest share with the one depicted in the story? [Connect]

exerted just enough pressure to keep away the frightening shadows, the sad spirits from long ago, locked into events that couldn't change.

Outside the guest-bedroom door, the upstairs hall, having narrowly sneaked past his grandparent's bedroom's door, broadened to be almost a room, with a window all its own, and a geranium on the sill shedding brown leaves when the women of the house forgot to water it, and curtains of dotted swiss[1] he could see the telephone wires through, and a rug of braided rags shaped like the oval tracks his Lionel train[2] went around and around the Christmas tree on, and, to one side, its front feet planted on the rag rug, with just enough space left for the attic door to swing open, the chest.

It was big enough for him to lie in, but he had never dared try. It was painted brown, but in such a way that the wood grain showed through, as if paint very thinned with turpentine had been used. On the side, wavy stripes of paint had been allowed to run, making dribbles like the teeth of a big wobbly comb. The lid on its brown had patches of yellow freckles. The hinges were small and black, and there was a keyhole that had no key. All this made the chest, simple in shape as it was, strange, and ancient, and almost frightening. And when he, or the grown-up with him, lifted the lid of the chest, an amazing smell rushed out—deeply sweet and musty, of mothballs and cedar, but that wasn't all of it. The smell seemed also to belong to the

---

1. **dotted swiss** sheer fabric covered in woven dots.
2. **Lionel train** The Lionel Company is a famous manufacturer of model trains, which were a very popular hobby during Updike's youth.

✔ Reading Check
What object in the upstairs hallway seems "strange and ancient" to the boy?

contents—lace tablecloths and wool blankets on top, but much more underneath. The full contents of the chest never came quite clear, perhaps because he didn't want to know. His parents' college diplomas seemed to be under the blankets, and other documents going back still farther, having to do with his grandparents, their marriage, or the marriage of someone beyond even them. There was a folded old piece of paper with drawn-on hearts and designs and words in German. His mother had once tried to explain the paper to him, but he hadn't wanted to listen. A thing so old disgusted him. And there were giant Bibles, and squat books with plush covers and a little square <u>mottled</u> mirror buried in the plush of one. These books had fat pages edged in gold, thick enough to hold, on both sides, stiff brown pictures, often oval, of dead people. He didn't like looking into these albums, even when his mother was explaining them to him. The chest went down and down, into the past, and he hated the feeling of that well of time, with its sweet deep smell of things unstirring, waiting, taking on the moldy flavor of time, not moving unless somebody touched them.

Then everything moved: the moving men came one day and everything in the house that had always been in a certain place was swiftly and casually uplifted and carried out the door. In the general upheaval the week before, he had been shocked to discover, glancing in, that at some point the chest had come to contain drawings he had done as a child, and his elementary-school report cards, and photographs—studio photographs lovingly mounted in folders of dove-gray cardboard with deckle edges[3]—of him when he was five. He was now thirteen.

The new house was smaller, with more outdoors around it. He liked it less on both accounts. Country space frightened him, much as the coal bin and the dark triangles under the attic eaves had—spaces that didn't have enough to do with people. Fields that were plowed one day in the spring and harvested one day in the fall, woods where dead trees were allowed to topple and slowly rot without anyone noticing, brambled-around spaces where he felt nobody had ever been before he himself came upon them. Heaps and rows of overgrown stones and dumps of rusty cans and tinted bottles indicated that other people in fact had been here, people like those who had posed in their Sunday clothes in the gilded albums, but the traces they left weren't usable, the way city sidewalks and trolley-car tracks were usable. His instinct was to stay in the little thick-walled country house, and read, and eat sandwiches he made for himself of raisins and peanut butter, and wait for this phase of his life to pass. Moving from the first house, leaving it behind, had taught him that a life had phases.

The chest, on that day of moving, had been set in the new attic, which was smaller than the other, and less frightening, perhaps

---

3. **deckle edges** rough edges of paper, often regarded as decorative.

mottled (mät´ ld) *adj.* blotched or streaked

Literary Analysis
Atmosphere and Precise Word Choices What specific word choices help to paint a clear picture of the boy's discomfort in the country?

because gaps in the cedar-shingled roof let dabs of daylight in. When the roof was being repaired, the whole space was thrown open to the weather, and it rained in, on all the furniture there was no longer room for, except up here or in the barn. The chest was too important for the barn; it perched on the edge of the attic steps, so an unpainted back he had never seen before, of two very wide pale boards, became visible. At the ends of each board were careless splashes of the thin brown paint—stain, really—left by the chestmaker when he had covered the sides.

The chest's contents, unseen, darkened in his mind. Once in a great while his mother had to search in there for something, or to confide a treasure to its depths, and in those moments, peeking in, he was surprised at how full the chest seemed, fuller than he remembered, of dotted-swiss curtains and crocheted lap rugs and photographs in folders of soft cardboard, all smelling of camphor and cedar. There the chest perched, an inch from the attic stairwell, and there it stayed, for over forty years.

Then it moved again. His children, adults all, came from afar and joined him in the house, where their grandmother had at last died, and divided up the furniture—some for them to carry away, some for the local auctioneer to sell, and some for him, the only survivor of that first house, with its long halls and haunted places, to keep and to <u>assimilate</u> to his own house, hundreds of miles away.

Two of the three children, the two that were married, had many responsibilities and soon left; he and his younger son, without a wife and without a job, remained to empty the house and pack the U-Haul van they rented. For days they lived together, eating takeout food, poisoning mice and trapping cats, moving from crowded cellar to jammed attic like sick men changing position in bed, overwhelmed by decisions, by accumulated possessions, now and then fleeing the house to escape the oppression of the past. He found the iron scales, quite rusted by the cellar damp, whereon his grandmother used to weigh out bundles of asparagus against a set of cylindrical weights. The weights were still heavy in his hand, and left rust stains on his palm. He studied a tin basin, painted in a white-on-gray spatter-pattern that had puzzled him as a child with its apparent sloppiness, and he could see again his grandfather's paper-white feet soaking in suds that rustled as the bubbles popped one by one.

The chest, up there in the attic along with old rolled carpets and rocking chairs with broken cane seats, stacked hatboxes from the Thirties and paperback mysteries from the Forties, was too heavy to lift, loaded as it was. He and his younger son took out layers of blankets and plush-covered albums, lace tablecloths and linen napkins; they uncovered a long cardboard box labelled in his mother's handwriting "Wedding Dress 1925," and, underneath that, rumpled silk dresses that a small girl might have worn when the century was young, and patent-leather baby shoes, and a gold-plated horseshoe, and faithful notations of the last century's weather kept by his grandfather's

assimilate (ə sim′ ə lāt′) *v.* to absorb or incorporate

Literary Analysis
Atmosphere What adjectives might you use to describe the atmosphere in this paragraph about emptying the house? Which words contribute to that atmosphere?

Reading Check
Where does the chest go when the family moves?

father in limp diaries bound in red leather, and a buggy-whip. A little box labelled in his mother's handwriting "Haircut July 1919" held, wrapped in tissue paper, coils of auburn hair startlingly silky to the touch. There were stiff brown photographs of his father's college football team, his father crouching at right tackle in an unpadded helmet, and of a stageful of posing young people among whom he finally found his mother, wearing a flimsy fairy dress and looking as if she had been crying. And so on and on, until he couldn't bear it and asked his son to help him carry the chest, half unemptied, down the narrow attic stairs whose bare wooden treads had been troughed[4] by generations of use, and then down the slightly broader stairs carpeted decades ago, and out the back door to the van. It didn't fit; they had to go back to the city ten miles away to rent a bigger van. Even so, packing everything in was a struggle. At one point, exasperated and anxious to be gone, his broad-backed son, hunched in the body of the U-Haul van, picked up the chest single-handed, and inverted it, lid open, over some smaller items to save space. The old thin-painted wood gave off a sharp *crack*, a piercing quick cry of injury.

The chest came to rest in his barn. He now owned a barn, not a Pennsylvania barn with stone sides and pegged oak beams but a skimpier, New England barn, with a flat tarred roof and a long-abandoned horse stall. He found the place in the chest lid, near one of the little dark hinges, where a split had occurred, and with a few carefully driven nails repaired the damage well enough. He could not blame the boy, who was named Gordon, after his paternal grandfather, the one-time football player crouching for his picture in some sunny autumn when Harding[5] was President. On the drive north in a downpour, Gordon had driven the truck, and his father tried to read the map, and in the dim light of the cab failed, and headed him the wrong way out of Westchester County, so they wound up across the Hudson River, amid blinding headlights, on an <u>unfathomable</u>, exitless highway. After that <u>egregious</u> piece of guidance, he could not blame the boy for anything, even for failing to get a job while concentrating instead on perfecting his dart game in the fake pubs of Boston. In a way not then immediately realized, the map-reading blunder righted the balance between them, himself and his son, as when under his grandmother's gnarled hands another stalk of asparagus would cause the tray holding the rusty cylindrical weights to rise with a soft *clunk*.

They arrived an hour late, after midnight. The unloading, including the reloading of the righted chest, all took place by flashlight, hurriedly, under the drumming sound of rain on the flat roof.

Now his barn felt haunted. He could scarcely bear to examine his inherited treasure, the chairs and cabinets and chinaware and faded best-sellers and old-fashioned bridge lamps clustered in a corner

---

4. **troughed** (trôf´ d) *v.* worn into troughs or grooves.
5. **Harding** Warren G. Harding (1865–1923), twenty-ninth president of the United States, from 1921 to 1923.

unfathomable (un fath´ əm ə bəl) *adj.* unable to be understood

egregious (ē grē´ jəs) *adj.* outstanding for undesirable qualities; remarkably bad

beyond the leaf-mulcher and the snow-blower and the rack of motorcycle tires left by the youngest son of the previous owner of the barn. He was the present owner. He had never imagined, as a child, owning so much. His wife saw no place in their house for even the curly-maple[6] kitchen table and the walnut corner cupboard, his mother's pride. This section of the barn became, if not as frightening as the old coal bin, a place he avoided. These pieces that his infant eyes had grazed, and that had framed his parents' lives, seemed sadly shabby now, cheap in their time, most of them, and yet devoid of antique value: useless used furniture he had lacked the courage to discard.

So he was pleased, one winter day, two years after their wayward drive north, to have Gordon call and ask if he could come look at the furniture in the barn. He had a job, he said, or almost, and was moving into a bigger place, out from the city. He would be bringing a friend, he vaguely added. A male friend, presumably, to help him lift and load what he chose to take away.

But the friend was a female, small and exquisite, with fascinating large eyes, the whites white as china, and a way of darting back and forth like a hummingbird, her wings invisible. "Oh," she exclaimed, over this and that, explaining to Gordon in a breathy small voice how this would be useful, and that would fit right in. "Lamps!" she said. "I love lamps."

"You see, Dad," the boy explained, the words pronounced softly yet in a manner so momentous that it seemed to take all the air in the barn to give them utterance, "Morna and I are planning to get married."

"Morna"—a Celtic name, fittingly elfin. The girl was magical, there in the cold barn, emitting puffs of visible breath, moving through the clutter with quick twists of her denim-clad hips and graceful stabs of her narrow white hands. She spoke only to Gordon, as if a pane of shyness protected her from his hoary[7] father—at this late phase of his life a kind of ogre, an ancestral, <u>proprietorial</u> figure full of potency and ugliness. "Gordon, what's this?" she asked.

The boy was embarrassed, perhaps by her innocent avidity.[8] "Tell her, Dad."

---

6. **curly-maple** maple wood with a pronounced wavy grain.
7. **hoary** (hôr´ ē) *adj.* ancient; old.
8. **avidity** (ə vid´ ə tē) *n.* eagerness.

▲ **Critical Viewing** How do the items in the chest tell the story of the family that owns it? **[Analyze]**

proprietorial (prō prī´ ə tôr´ ē əl) *adj.* like someone who owns something

✓**Reading Check**

What part of the man's property feels "haunted"? Why?

"Our old guest bed." Which he used to lie diagonally across, listening to his mother's pen scratch as her diary tried to hold fast her days. Even then he knew it couldn't be done.

"We could strip off the ghastly gray, I guess," the boy conceded, frowning in the attempt to envision it and the work involved. "We *have* a bed," he reminded her.

"And this?" she went on, leaving the bed hanging in a realm of future possibility. Her headscarf had slipped back, exposing auburn hair glinting above the vapor of her breath, in <u>evanescent</u> present time.

She had paused at the chest. Her glance darted at Gordon, and then, receiving no response, at the present owner, looking him in the eyes for the first time. The ogre smiled. "Open it."

"What's in it?" she asked.

He said, "I forget, actually."

Delicately but fearlessly, she lifted the lid, and out swooped, with the same vividness that had astonished and alarmed his nostrils as a child, the sweetish deep cedary smell, undiminished, cedar and camphor and paper and cloth, the smell of family, family without end.

evanescent (ev′ ə nes′ ənt) *adj.* short-lived; tending to fade or disappear

Review and Assess

Thinking About the Selection

1. **Respond:** The brown chest clearly has had a profound effect upon the man in the story. What object or objects in your life have emotional power over you, and why?

2. **(a) Recall:** What are the boy's earliest impressions of the chest? **(b) Interpret:** In what ways does his attitude toward the chest change over time?

3. **(a) Recall:** What mementos does the chest hold early in the man's life? **(b) Infer:** What happens to some mementos of the man's childhood? **(c) Draw Conclusions:** What vision of life does the chest embody?

4. **(a) Recall:** What event "righted the balance" between the man and his son? **(b) Analyze:** Why does that event cause the man to reevaluate his feelings toward his son?

5. **(a) Recall:** What does the man notice about Morna's hair toward the story's end? **(b) Connect:** What connection does this detail establish between Morna and the chest?
   (c) Generalize: What is suggested by Morna's presence about the enduring nature of family?

6. **(a) Recall:** How much time passes in the story?
   (b) Evaluate: How well does Updike succeed in showing the passage of time within the confines of the short-story format?

Review and Assess

Literary Analysis

Atmosphere

1. What **atmosphere** is created by the description of the chest in the upstairs hallway when the boy is young?

2. (a) What atmosphere is suggested by the phrase "the oppression of the past"? (b) What details does Updike use to illustrate that phrase?

3. (a) Describe the changes in the atmosphere that occur when Morna enters the story. (b) To what do you attribute these changes? (c) What might Morna represent to the main character?

Connecting Literary Elements

4. In the opening paragraphs, what **precise word choices** heighten the sense of neglect in the unused rooms of the house?

5. Use a chart like the one shown to analyze specific details that appeal to the senses in Updike's first description of the chest.

6. (a) On page 1007, what references to fairy tale creatures does Updike use to contrast the main character and Morna? (b) In what ways are Updike's word choices particularly apt?

Reading Strategy

Breaking Down Long Sentences

7. Select a long sentence from the story. (a) Use the punctuation marks to break the sentence into meaningful sections. (b) What action or actions are being performed in the sentence?

8. (a) Rewrite the sentence as a series of short sentences. (b) Compare the benefits of long sentences with those of short sentences.

Extend Understanding

9. **Humanities Connection:** (a) In what ways has technology affected people's ability to hold onto the past? (b) What are the benefits and drawbacks of these technological advances?

Quick Review

Atmosphere is the emotional quality of the world the author creates in a piece of writing.

Precise word choices involve the selection of the most appropriate, vivid, and specific words to create a desired effect.

To **break down long sentences,** use punctuation marks to separate sentences into component parts.

 Take It to the Net
www.phschool.com
Take the interactive self-test online to check your understanding of the selection.

Integrate Language Skills

Vocabulary Development Lesson

Word Analysis: Latin Root -sim-

The Latin word root -sim- means "the same." Match the word containing the root -sim- in the left column with its definition in the right column.

1. simultaneous   a. alike or comparable
2. simulation   b. occuring at nearly the same moment
3. similar   c. a close copy or replica

Spelling Strategy

When adding a prefix to a word, do not change the spelling—for example, un- + fathomable forms unfathomable. Complete the words in the sentences below by affixing the prefix that makes sense. Use anti- or kilo-.

1. The chest weighs fifty __grams.
2. The __war candidate won the election.

Fluency: Word Choice

Replace the italicized word or phrase in each sentence with the appropriate word from the vocabulary list on page 1001.

1. The boy found the adults' attachment to the chest *impossible to figure out*.

2. The covers of the old books were *spotted*.

3. The man had an *ownerlike* interest in the chest.

4. His joy in the chest was *likely to disappear soon*.

5. He couldn't *incorporate* the old chest into his modern life.

6. If he had made any *outstandingly bad* errors, there was no evidence of them.

Grammar and Style Lesson

Adverb Clauses

Adverb clauses are subordinate clauses that modify verbs, adjectives, or adverbs by telling where, when, in what way, to what extent, under what condition, or why. Adverb clauses begin with conjunctions like *when, where, as if, if, because, in,* and *so*.

> **Modifying Verb:** The Louisiana territory <u>entered</u> the Union *after Jefferson negotiated the purchase*.
>
> **Modifying Adjective:** *Whenever the soldier told stories of battle*, the children were <u>amazed</u>.
>
> **Modifying Adverb:** The story was <u>longer</u> *than the one yesterday was*.

Adverb clauses allow writers to quickly link events in a single sentence.

Practice Identify the adverb clause in each sentence and tell whether it modifies a verb, adjective, or adverb.

1. Because Updike is beloved by readers, he receives much fan mail.
2. Although years have passed since he lived in Pennsylvania, he still has vivid memories.
3. The boy in the story felt the weight of the past whenever he opened the chest.
4. After the chest was moved, it seemed less frightening.
5. The audience applauded madly as Updike entered the lecture hall.

Writing Application Write a paragraph describing a vivid memory. Use three sentences containing adverb clauses.

W̶G *Prentice Hall Writing and Grammar Connection: Chapter 19, Section 3*

Writing Lesson

Analysis of a Symbol

John Updike's story "The Brown Chest" uses a single symbol—the storage chest—as a lens through which to view a man's life. The chest means different things to the main character as he grows from boyhood to maturity. Write an essay analyzing the symbolic meaning of the chest at different points in the main character's life.

Prewriting   Review the story, and take notes about the main character's feelings about the chest as his life progresses. Identify quotes you can use to support each part of your analysis.

Drafting   Introduce the story and author, and give a brief summary of the plot. Then, state the main idea you will develop. Determine an organizational strategy to give order to your ideas.

Revising   Review your essay, and highlight any sections that seem out of order. Reorder those sections for logic and clarity.

> **Model: Revising for Clear Organization**
>
> *To his young mind, the chest holds ghosts—all those who are dead and gone.*
>
> As a child, the man in John Updike's story is frightened by the brown chest. As a man, he values the past.
>
> Exploring ideas in chronological order creates a clear organization.

𝒲𝒢 Prentice Hall Writing and Grammar Connection: Chapter 14, Section 3

Extension Activities

Listening and Speaking With another student, role-play a **conversation** between Gordon and Morna on their way home from visiting the barn. Use these tips to prepare:

- Note each character's response both to the items in the barn and to Gordon's father.

- Create a voice for each character that reflects his or her portrayal in the story.

Make sure that each character has equal time to exchange distinct impressions of the visit. **[Group Activity]**

Research and Technology Using a variety of sources, including the Internet, conduct research and create a **feature article on fashions** of the 1920s. Illustrate the article with photos, drawings, images of magazine covers, or other graphics. Identify major fashion trend-setters of the period, and note connections between fashion and the social atmosphere of the time.

 *Take It to the Net*   www.phschool.com

Go online for an additional research activity using the Internet.

Prepare to Read

Hawthorne ◆ Gold Glade ◆ Traveling Through the Dark ◆ The Light Comes Brighter ◆ The Adamant

Robert Lowell (1917–1977)

Robert Lowell was born into one of America's oldest, most prominent families, which included the poets James Russell Lowell and Amy Lowell; Josiah Winslow, a governor of the Plymouth colony; and John Stark, a Revolutionary War general. Lowell found his ancestry to be embarrassing at best, and some critics believe that he often wrote about history because he was so tormented by his own.

Lowell first used traditional poetic forms and techniques, but in the late 1950s he began writing freer, more direct poems in what came to be called the "confessional" mode. His volume *Life Studies* (1959) launched a school of confessional poetry that included Sylvia Plath, John Berryman, and Anne Sexton.

Robert Penn Warren (1905–1989)

Among the most versatile, prolific, and distinguished writers of our time, Robert Penn Warren won the first of his three Pulitzer Prizes for *All the King's Men* (1946), a fictional study of a Southern politician (based on Louisiana Governor Huey Long). Warren's poetry collections include *Promises* (1957) and *Now and Then: Poems* (1978). Although Warren consistently used Southern settings and characters in his writing, he treated universal themes, such as the love of the land that fills the poem "Gold Glade."

Theodore Roethke (1908–1963)

Theodore Roethke (ret´ kē) was born in Saginaw, Michigan, where his family owned several large commercial greenhouses. As a boy, Roethke was a passionate observer of the plants that grew in the greenhouses. These observations later provided him with ideas for many of his poems.

Throughout his life, Roethke found it difficult to relate to other people. He found a refuge, though, in nature and poetry. At age thirty-three, Roethke published his first volume of poetry, launching a career as one of the most acclaimed poets of his day. He won the Pulitzer Prize for *The Waking* (1953) and the National Book Award for *The Far Field* (1964).

William Stafford (1914–1993)

William Stafford spent key parts of his life in Kansas, Iowa, and Oregon. These regions influenced his poetry, both in its content and in its serene, unadorned language. A believer in the sanctity of life, Stafford served in World War II as a conscientious objector. Focusing on such subjects as the threat of nuclear war and the beauty of nature, Stafford wrote of his fear that modern technology would someday destroy the wilderness. He did not publish his first volume of verse, *West of Your City* (1960), until he was forty-six, after years of working in the U.S. Forest Service.

Preview

Connecting to the Literature

Sometimes, when you least expect it, you make the most surprising discoveries about yourself and the world around you. In a similar way, the four poets whose work follows make discoveries in unexpected places.

Literary Analysis

Style and Diction

A writer's **style** is the manner in which he or she puts ideas into words. Style generally concerns *form* rather than *content.* In poetry, style is determined by a poet's use of these elements:

- Tone
- Sound devices
- Symbolism
- Rhythm
- The length and arrangement of lines
- Figurative language
- Punctuation and capitalization

Another important aspect of style is **diction,** or word choice. As you read these poems, note the ways in which each poet's style and diction not only reflect varying degrees of formality but also help establish a unique voice.

Comparing Literary Works

In his poem "Hawthorne," Robert Lowell describes a young Nathaniel Hawthorne as "meditating" about the "true/and insignificant." For Lowell, part of Hawthorne's greatness lies in his search for truth within the ordinary—the insignificant, rather than the grand. With this idea in mind, examine how Lowell might have felt about the other poems that appear here. Explore whether or not they begin in meditations upon the "true and insignificant," or in ideas that are more lofty and abstract.

Reading Strategy

Paraphrasing

Some poems contain passages that are especially difficult to understand because of unusual vocabulary, complex sentences, or the ambiguities of poetic language. To improve your comprehension, **paraphrase,** or restate in your own words, any difficult passages you encounter. As you read these poems, use a chart like the one shown to aid your understanding.

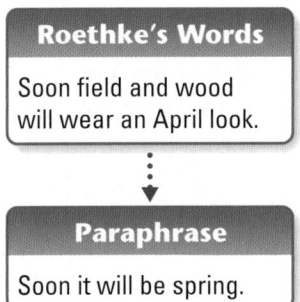

Roethke's Words

Soon field and wood will wear an April look.

↓

Paraphrase

Soon it will be spring.

Vocabulary

brooding (bro͞od´ iŋ) *v.* pondering in a troubled or mournful way (p. 1016)

furtive (fu̇r´ tiv) *adj.* sneaky; stealthy (p. 1016)

meditation (med´ ə tā´ shən) *n.* deep thought or solemn reflection (p. 1016)

declivity (dē kliv´ ə tē) *n.* downward slope (p. 1017)

exhaust (eg zôst´) *n.* discharge of used steam or gas from an engine (p. 1020)

vestiges (ves´ tij iz) *n.* traces (p. 1021)

Hawthorne

Robert Lowell

Follow its lazy main street lounging
from the alms house to Gallows Hill[1]
along a flat, unvaried surface
covered with wooden houses
5   aged by yellow drain
like the unhealthy hair of an old dog.
You'll walk to no purpose
in Hawthorne's Salem.

---

1. **Gallows Hill** hill in Salem, Massachusetts, where nineteen people who were accused
   of practicing witchcraft were hanged.

Crowninshield's Wharf, George Ropes, Peabody Museum of Salem

◀ **Critical Viewing**
What does this scene suggest about the port of Salem? In what ways is the painting similar to Lowell's description of the town? In what ways is it different? **[Compare and Contrast]**

I cannot resilver the smudged plate.[2]

10 I drop to Hawthorne, the customs officer,[3]
measuring coal and mostly trying to keep warm—
to the stunted black schooner,
the dismal South-end dock,
the wharf-piles with their fungus of ice.
15 On State Street[4]
a steeple with a glowing dial-clock
measures the weary hours,
the merciless march of professional feet.

Even this shy distrustful ego
20 sometimes walked on top of the blazing roof,
and felt those flashes
that char the discharged cells of the brain.

Look at the faces—
Longfellow, Lowell, Holmes and Whittier!

---

2. **resilver . . . plate** Early photographs were taken on a metal plate coated with silver.
3. **customs officer** Nathaniel Hawthorne worked as a customs officer in Salem.
4. **State Street** street in the business district of Boston.

**Reading Check**

Why does the town of Salem remind the speaker of Nathaniel Hawthorne?

Hawthorne ◆ 1015

25 Study the grizzled silver of their beards.
Hawthorne's picture,
however, has a blond mustache
and golden General Custer[5] scalp.
He looks like a Civil War officer.
30 He shines in the firelight. His hard
survivor's smile is touched with fire.

Leave him alone for a moment or two,
and you'll see him with his head
bent down, <u>brooding</u>, brooding,
35 eyes fixed on some chip,
some stone, some common plant,
the commonest thing,
as if it were the clue.
The disturbed eyes rise,
40 <u>furtive</u>, foiled, dissatisfied
from <u>meditation</u> on the true
and insignificant.

---

5. **General Custer** George Armstrong Custer (1839–1876), Civil War general

brooding (broo͞od´ iŋ) v.
pondering in a troubled
or mournful way

furtive (fʉr´ tiv) adj.
sneaky; stealthy

meditation (med´ ə tā´
shən) n. deep thought
or solemn reflection

Review and Assess

Thinking About the Selection

1. **Respond:** What is your opinion of Nathaniel Hawthorne, based on the way he is portrayed in this poem?

2. **(a) Recall:** What action is described in the first stanza? **(b) Interpret:** Which images in the first stanza contribute to the impression of Salem as a stagnant, decaying town?

3. **(a) Recall:** What does the speaker imagine Hawthorne doing in the third stanza? **(b) Interpret:** What image of professional people is created by the images in that stanza?

4. **(a) Recall:** Which words in lines 15–17 convey an image of the passage of time? **(b) Interpret:** What impression of time is suggested by this image?

5. **(a) Infer:** Who is the "shy, distrustful ego"? **(b) Analyze:** What is the significance of the image of this person walking "on top of the blazing roof"? **(c) Compare and Contrast:** Based on lines 23–31, how does the speaker view Hawthorne in comparison to his literary contemporaries?

6. **(a) Speculate:** In what ways has Hawthorne served as a literary landmark for Lowell? **(b) Extend:** Think of your own field of interest. Who would serve as a landmark for you? Explain.

Gold Glade

Robert Penn Warren

Background

Following an English tradition dating back to 1616, the Library of Congress named Robert Penn Warren as the first Poet Laureate of the United States in 1985. Since then, some of America's best and brightest literary talents have held the title of Poet Laureate. Unlike their British counterparts, American poets laureate are under no obligation to write poems to commemorate special occasions. Though they receive a sizable stipend and an office in the Library of Congress for the duration of the one-year term, poets laureate are free to continue writing (or not writing) as they choose.

Wandering, in autumn, the woods of boyhood,
Where cedar, black, thick, rode the ridge,
Heart aimless as rifle, boy-blankness of mood,
I came where ridge broke, and the great ledge,
5 Limestone, set the toe high as treetop by dark edge

Of a gorge, and water hid, grudging and grumbling,
And I saw, in mind's eye, foam white on
Wet stone, stone wet-black, white water tumbling,
And so went down, and with some fright on
10 Slick boulders, crossed over. The gorge-depth drew night on,
But high over high rock and leaf-lacing, sky
Showed yet bright, and <u>declivity</u> wooed
My foot by the quietening stream, and so I
Went on, in quiet, through the beech wood:
15 There, in gold light, where the glade gave, it stood.

Literary Analysis

Style and Diction In the very first stanza, what do you notice about the poet's innovative diction?

declivity (dē kliv′ ə tē) *n.* downward slope

✔ Reading Check

Where is the speaker wandering?

The glade was geometric, circular, gold,
No brush or weed breaking that bright gold of leaf-fall.
In the center it stood, absolute and bold
Beyond any heart-hurt, or eye's grief-fall.
20 Gold-massy in air, it stood in gold light-fall,

No breathing of air, no leaf now gold-falling,
No tooth-stitch of squirrel, or any far fox bark,
No woodpecker coding, or late jay calling.
Silence: gray-shagged, the great shagbark[1]
25 Gave forth gold light. There could be no dark.

But of course dark came, and I can't recall
What county it was, for the life of me.
Montgomery, Todd, Christian—I know them all.
Was it even Kentucky or Tennessee?
30 Perhaps just an image that keeps haunting me.

No, no! in no mansion under earth,
Nor imagination's domain of bright air,
But solid in soil that gave it its birth,
It stands, wherever it is, but somewhere.
35 I shall set my foot, and go there.

---

1. **shagbark** hickory tree.

Literary Analysis
Style and Diction
Which words in this stanza are repeated? What is the effect?

Review and Assess

Thinking About the Selection

1. **Respond:** What are some of your memories of autumn? In what ways do they compare to the speaker's memories?

2. **(a) Recall:** What majestic thing does the speaker find in the center of the glade? **(b) Define:** What are "heart-hurt" and "grief-fall"? **(c) Analyze:** Why is the glade "beyond" those things?

3. **(a) Recall:** Where does the action of the poem shift from past to present? **(b) Interpret:** Describe the change in tone that occurs at that point.

4. **(a) Interpret:** In lines 21–25, what are the dominant sensory impressions? **(b) Deduce:** What emotions does the speaker seem to feel in that stanza? **(c) Analyze:** What does the speaker mean by saying, "There could be no dark"?

5. **(a) Interpret:** What does the gold glade represent to the speaker? **(b) Speculate:** Is the glade a real place to which the speaker could actually return? Explain. **(c) Evaluate:** Is this poem an accurate portrayal of memory? Explain.

1018 ◆ *Prosperity and Protest (1946–Present)*

Traveling Through the Dark

William Stafford

Traveling through the dark I found a deer
dead on the edge of the Wilson River road.
It is usually best to roll them into the canyon:
that road is narrow; to swerve might make more dead.

5 By glow of the tail-light I stumbled back of the car
   and stood by the heap, a doe, a recent killing;
   she had stiffened already, almost cold.
   I dragged her off; she was large in the belly.

   My fingers touching her side brought me the reason—
10 her side was warm; her fawn lay there waiting,
   alive, still, never to be born.
   Beside that mountain road I hesitated.

   The car aimed ahead its lowered parking lights;
   under the hood purred the steady engine.
15 I stood in the glare of the warm <u>exhaust</u> turning red;
   around our group I could hear the wilderness listen.

   I thought hard for us all—my only swerving—,
   then pushed her over the edge into the river.

exhaust (eg zôst´) *n.*
discharge of used steam
or gas from an engine

Review and Assess

Thinking About the Selection

1. **Respond:** If you could meet him, what would you say to
   William Stafford about this poem?

2. **(a) Recall:** Where does the speaker find the dead deer?
   (b) Speculate: How do you think the deer met her fate?

3. **(a) Recall:** What discovery does the speaker make when
   he examines the deer more closely? **(b) Infer:** Why does
   the speaker hesitate upon making this discovery?

4. **(a) Interpret:** With what details does the speaker personify his
   car in the fourth stanza? **(b) Connect:** In what ways does the
   speaker's description of the car echo his discovery about the deer?

5. **(a) Deduce:** What factors does the speaker weigh in his
   decision about what to do with the deer? **(b) Analyze:** In
   what ways does the title reflect the speaker's moral dilemma?

6. **(a) Make a Judgment:** Do you think the speaker makes
   the proper decision? Explain. **(b) Interpret:** What details
   in the poem suggest the speaker's emotion or attitude about
   what he has done? Explain.

7. **Generalize:** What does this poem reveal about the relationship
   between humanity and nature in the modern world?

The Light Comes Brighter

Theodore Roethke

The light comes brighter from the east; the caw
Of restive crows is sharper on the ear.
A walker at the river's edge may hear
A cannon crack announce an early thaw.

5 The sun cuts deep into the heavy drift,
Though still the guarded snow is winter-sealed,
At bridgeheads buckled ice begins to shift,
The river overflows the level field.

Once more the trees assume familiar shapes,
10 As branches loose last <u>vestiges</u> of snow.
The water stored in narrow pools escapes
In rivulets; the cold roots stir below.

Soon field and wood will wear an April look,
The frost be gone, for green is breaking now;
15 The ovenbird[1] will match the vocal brook,
The young fruit swell upon the pear-tree bough.

And soon a branch, part of a hidden scene,
The leafy mind, that long was tightly furled,
Will turn its private substance into green,
20 And young shoots spread upon our inner world.

---

1. **ovenbird** common name for any of the many birds that build a domelike nest on the ground.

Literary Analysis
Style and Diction What do you notice about the rhythm, length, and arrangements of lines in this poem?

vestiges (ves´ tij iz) *n.* traces

✔ **Reading Check**
What seasonal process does this poem describe?

The Adamant

Theodore Roethke

Thought does not crush to stone.
The great sledge drops in vain.
Truth never is undone;
Its shafts remain.

5 The teeth of knitted gears
Turn slowly through the night,
But the true substance bears
The hammer's weight.

Compression cannot break
10 A center so congealed;
The tool can chip no flake:
The core lies sealed.

Reading Strategy
Paraphrasing How might you paraphrase the opening two lines of this poem?

Review and Assess

Thinking About the Selections

1. **Respond:** Which of these poems made a stronger impression on you? Why?

2. **(a) Recall:** In "The Light Comes Brighter," what change of seasons is described? **(b) Distinguish:** Identify two images that suggest that change involves action and even violence.

3. **(a) Recall:** In the final line, what adjective does the poet use to describe the "world"? **(b) Analyze:** What do you think the poet is saying about the creative process?

4. **(a) Interpret:** In "The Adamant," which words and phrases suggest industrial machinery? **(b) Analyze:** In what ways does this imagery emphasize the indestructibility of truth? **(c) Speculate:** Why might truth be indestructible?

5. **Make a Judgment:** Does Roethke demonstrate an optimistic or a pessimistic outlook in "The Adamant"? Explain.

Review and Assess

Literary Analysis
Style and Diction

1. Do the **style** and organization of Lowell's poem "Hawthorne" adhere to a traditional poetic form? Explain.

2. (a) What formal structure does Roethke use in his poem "The Light Comes Brighter"? (b) Why would such an orderly structure make sense for this poem?

3. (a) In "Gold Glade," which letter sounds does Warren use most to create alliteration—the repetition of initial consonants? (b) What is the effect?

4. (a) Use a chart like the one shown to analyze each poet's **diction.** (b) How does diction help to create a distinct voice in each poem?

Poet	Formal or Informal	Plain or Ornate	Abstract or Concrete	Effect
Stafford	informal	plain	concrete	casual, familiar

Comparing Literary Works

5. (a) Which of these poems describe everyday life? Explain. (b) What grand or important ideas, if any, do the poets discover through the lens of ordinary experience?

6. (a) Which of these poems attempts to define an abstract idea? Explain. (b) What details do the poets use to give form to their ideas?

7. Which of these poems best expresses Lowell's idea that the "true and insignificant" is the subject of great poetry? Explain your choice.

Reading Strategy
Paraphrasing

8. Paraphrase each of the following passages: (a) "Gold Glade," lines 16–20; (b) "The Adamant," lines 5–8.

9. For each, explain whether the paraphrase helped you to see something that was previously unclear.

Extend Understanding

10. **Social Studies Connection:** (a) What aspects of a city like Salem stay constant over time? (b) What aspects change?

Quick Review

Style is the manner in which a writer puts ideas into words. **Diction** is a writer's word choice.

To clarify the meaning of a difficult passage, **paraphrase** it—restate it in your own words.

 Take It to the Net
www.phschool.com
Take the interactive self-test online to check your understanding of these selections.

Integrate Language Skills

Vocabulary Development Lesson

Related Words: *exhaust*

As a noun, the word *exhaust* means "the discharge of used steam or gas from an engine." *Exhaust* may also function as a verb meaning "to empty completely" or "to tire out." Other words related to *exhaust* include the following:

inexhaustible   exhausted   exhaustion

Complete each of the following sentences with one of the related words listed above.

1. The ___?___ I felt was due to lack of sleep.

2. The marathon runner had become completely ___?___.

3. A fit athlete, her energy level was usually ___?___.

Grammar and Style Lesson

Subject and Verb Agreement

Subjects and verbs must agree in number, even if the verb is separated from its subject by intervening words. Study this example from "The Light Comes Brighter:"

> **Example:** . . . the <u>caw</u> / Of restive crows <u>is</u> sharper on the ear.

The singular verb *is* agrees with the singular subject *caw*, not with the plural noun *crows*, which is not the subject of its clause.

Practice Identify the subject in each of the following sentences. Then, choose the correct form of the verb in parentheses.

1. The water (escapes, escape) in rivulets.

Concept Development: Synonyms

Select the word in the second column that is the best synonym for each word in the first column.

1. brooding		a. slope	
2. furtive		b. fumes	
3. meditation		c. traces	
4. declivity		d. worrying	
5. vestiges		e. pensiveness	
6. exhaust		f. sneaky	

Spelling Strategy

When adding a suffix to a word that ends in one consonant preceded by two vowels, do not double the final consonant: *brood* becomes *brooding*. Add the given suffix to each of these words.

1. *-ing* to foot 2. *-en* to wood 3. *-less* to root

2. Walkers at the river's edge (hears, hear) a cannon crack.
3. The teeth of knitted gears (turns, turn) slowly through the night.
4. My fingers touching her side (reveals, reveal) the reason.
5. The leafy mind, that was tightly furled, (turns, turn) its private substance into green.

Writing Application For each of the following fragments add a verb that agrees in number with the subject, and complete the sentence.

1. The many leaves beyond the rake . . .
2. His troubled heart, churning in pain . . .
3. My fingers touching her side . . .
4. The water stored in narrow pools . . .

𝒲G *Prentice Hall Writing and Grammar Connection: Chapter 23, Section 1*

Writing Lesson

Critical Response

On the art of writing poetry, Robert Lowell once said, "In life we speak with many false voices; occasionally, if we are lucky, we find a true one in our poems." Choose one of these poems and write an essay in which you discuss whether or not it achieves a "true" voice.

Prewriting   Select the poem that you like the most. Reread it, taking notes about its message, imagery, and style. Assess why the poem speaks to you. Based on your assessment, create a list of criteria for a poem that has a "true" voice.

> **Model: Identifying Criteria**
>
> Judging from my reading of "Traveling Through the Dark,"
> a true voice
> - deals with a moral question
> - uses plain words, but in a beautiful way
> - is not heroic

A list of criteria lays the foundation for the development of ideas in an essay.

Drafting   Begin by identifying the poem you have selected, and briefly describe its subject. Then, introduce your criteria. Use body paragraphs to explain how each of your criteria apply to the poem.

Revising   Review your essay, and make sure that each body paragraph clearly speaks to one item on your list of criteria.

WG Prentice Hall Writing and Grammar Connection: Chapter 14, Section 3

Extension Activities

Listening and Speaking Watch the film based on Robert Penn Warren's novel "All the King's Men." Then, prepare an **evaluation** of the film. To prepare, keep these tips in mind:

- Offer a brief summary of the story.
- Evaluate how effectively the film expresses ideas visually.

As you work, pay close attention to strategies the filmmakers use to shape viewers' perceptions of events and characters. [**Group Activity**]

Research and Technology Conduct library and Internet research to learn more about Robert Lowell and confessional poetry. Prepare and give an **oral presentation** in which you share your findings on the confessional poets and their work. Recite two or three of the poems you like best.

 **Take It to the Net**   www.phschool.com

Go online for an additional research activity using the Internet.

Prepare to Read

Average Waves in Unprotected Waters

Anne Tyler (b. 1941)

As the wife of a child psychiatrist and the mother of two daughters, Anne Tyler has for years successfully juggled the demands of family life while maintaining her commitment to writing. She works at home in her starkly plain study, seated on a daybed. She pens her fiction in longhand so that, as she explains it, she can hear her characters speak. During occasional bouts of insomnia, she records her ideas in boxes of index cards.

Everyday People Tyler, who has remained a private person despite her fame, lives in Baltimore, Maryland, a city that provides a strong setting for her work. Many of her stories focus on the loneliness and isolation of ordinary middle-class people.

Young Talent Born in Minneapolis, Tyler spent most of her early childhood in Quaker communes in the Midwest and South. This experience, she recalls, was helpful to her as a writer because it enabled her to look "at the normal world with a certain amount of distance and surprise." After attending high school in Raleigh, North Carolina, she enrolled at Duke University to study Russian when she was sixteen. After graduating from college, she worked as a bibliographer at Duke and then moved to Montreal, Canada, where she held a job as a librarian at McGill University.

Tyler began her writing career with a series of short stories, few of which were published. Then, at age twenty-four, she published her first work, the novel *If Morning Ever Comes*. The book depicts a young man who returns home and attempts to find his identity amid overpowering family expectations. Since then Tyler has produced a string of novels to ever-increasing acclaim. Among them are *Dinner at the Homesick Restaurant* (1982); *The Accidental Tourist* (1985), which was made into a film in 1988; *Breathing Lessons* (1988), winner of the 1989 Pulitzer Prize for Fiction; *A Patchwork Planet* (1998); and *Back When We Were Grown Ups* (2000). Tyler has also published numerous short stories in literary magazines like *The New Yorker*.

Serious Fiction When Tyler works on a novel, she follows a pattern. First, she writes out a draft in longhand. She then reads the draft to "find out what it means." She revises the draft to enhance "the subconscious intentions" she has discovered in the work. Tyler keeps the goal of writing "serious fiction" firmly in sight. Her characters are not fictionalized versions of people from her own life; instead, they are products of a fertile imagination that are drawn with her gift for fine, realistic detail.

Eccentrics Tyler has a flair for creating eccentric people in improbable yet touching plots. Her compassion, wit, and use of the precise details of domestic life flavor her tales of relationships and family dynamics. Her overall theme may be seen as the persistent endurance of the human spirit in the face of the inevitable struggles and strains of daily life.

"Average Waves in Unprotected Waters," which was first published in *The New Yorker* in 1977, displays Tyler's ability to create well-developed, realistic characters and to evoke an emotional response through an unsentimental portrayal of the characters' tragic lives.

Preview

Connecting to the Literature

A family move, a transfer to a new school—these events can present both problems and challenges. In this story, the main character faces the reality that a painful change in her life just may be for the better.

Literary Analysis

Foreshadowing

Foreshadowing is the use of details or clues that hint at what will occur later in a plot or suggest a certain outcome. Foreshadowing builds suspense because it makes the reader wonder what will happen next or how the story will end, as this passage demonstrates:

> Maybe she felt to blame that he was going. But she'd done the best she could: babysat him all these years and only given up when he'd grown too strong and wild to manage.

As you read, notice how Tyler's use of foreshadowing keeps you guessing about the story's outcome.

Connecting Literary Elements

An effective use of foreshadowing can heighten the suspense for readers and pique their interest to read further. **Suspense** is a feeling of growing uncertainty about the outcome of events in a literary work. Writers create suspense by raising questions in readers' minds. Because most people are curious or concerned, they keep reading to find out what will happen next. As you read, notice how the suspense makes you anxious to learn the outcome.

Reading Strategy

Putting Events in Order

Most stories are written in chronological order—the order in which events happen in real time. Sometimes, however, the writer interrupts the sequence to present a flashback—a scene or an event from an earlier time. As you read Tyler's story, **put the events in order** by noting the sequence in which they actually occurred. Create a chain-of-events diagram like the one shown to record the events in order, from the earliest to the latest.

Order of Events

Vocabulary Development

orthopedic (ôr´ thō pē´ dik) *adj.* correcting posture or other disorders of the skeletal system (p. 1030)

transparent (trans per´ ənt) *adj.* capable of being seen through (p. 1031)

stocky (stäk´ ē) *adj.* solidly built; sturdy (p. 1031)

staunch (stônch) *adj.* strong; unyielding (p. 1032)

viper (vī´pər) *n.* type of snake; a malicious person (p. 1032)

Average Waves in Unprotected Waters

Anne Tyler

Background

The decision to institutionalize a child is an extremely difficult one. In this story, Anne Tyler explores a single mother's attempts to care for a severely mentally challenged child. When this story was written in the mid-1970s, a single parent may have felt she had few other options available to her. Then, as now, the cost of private care was so high that many patients were placed in state-run or charitable hospitals where lack of funding sometimes resulted in grim conditions, outdated equipment, and an inadequate staff. Fortunately, an array of educational, medical, and counseling programs for children with special needs today makes it possible for many of them who might once have been institutionalized to remain at home.

As soon as it got light, Bet woke him and dressed him, and then she walked him over to the table and tried to make him eat a little cereal. He wouldn't, though. He could tell something was up. She pressed the edge of the spoon against his lips till she heard it click on his teeth, but he just looked off at a corner of the ceiling—a knobby child with great glassy eyes and her own fair hair. Like any other nine-year-old, he wore a striped shirt and jeans, but the shirt was too neat and the jeans too blue, unpatched and unfaded, and would stay that way till he outgrew them. And his face was elderly—pinched, strained, tired—though it should have looked as unused as his jeans. He hardly ever changed his expression.

She left him in his chair and went to make the beds. Then she raised the yellowed shade, rinsed a few spoons in the bathroom sink, picked up some bits of magazines he'd torn the night before. This was a rented room in an ancient, crumbling house, and nothing you could do to it would lighten its cluttered look. There was always that feeling of too many lives layered over other lives, like the layers of brownish wallpaper her child had peeled away in the corner by his bed.

She slipped her feet into flat-heeled loafers and absently patted the front of her dress, a worn beige knit she usually saved for Sundays. Maybe she should take it in a little; it hung from her shoulders like a sack. She felt too slight and frail, too wispy for all she had to do today. But she reached for her coat anyhow, and put it on and tied a blue kerchief under her chin. Then she went over to the table and slowly spun, modeling the coat. "See, Arnold?" she said. "We're going out."

Arnold went on looking at the ceiling, but his gaze turned wild and she knew he'd heard.

◀ **Critical Viewing** How might this busy scene at a train station represent the isolation or alienation Bet feels in this story? **[Connect]**

Literary Analysis
Foreshadowing What details in this paragraph hint that something unusual, or even unpleasant, may lie ahead?

✔**Reading Check**
What is Arnold's reaction as his mother busily prepares to leave the house?

She fetched his jacket from the closet—brown corduroy, with a hood. It had set her back half a week's salary. But Arnold didn't like it; he always wanted his old one, a little red duffel coat he'd long ago outgrown. When she came toward him, he started moaning and rocking and shaking his head. She had to struggle to stuff his arms in the sleeves. Small though he was, he was strong, wiry; he was getting to be too much for her. He shook free of her hands and ran over to his bed. The jacket was on, though. It wasn't buttoned, the collar was askew, but never mind; that just made him look more real. She always felt bad at how he stood inside his clothes, separate from them, passive, unaware of all the buttons and snaps she'd fastened as carefully as she would a doll's.

She gave a last look around the room, checked to make sure the hot plate was off, and then picked up her purse and Arnold's suitcase. "Come along, Arnold," she said.

He came, dragging out every step. He looked at the suitcase suspiciously, but only because it was new. It didn't have any meaning for him. "See?" she said. "It's yours. It's Arnold's. It's going on the train with us."

But her voice was all wrong. He would pick it up, for sure. She paused in the middle of locking the door and glanced over at him fearfully. Anything could set him off nowadays. He hadn't noticed, though. He was too busy staring around the hallway, goggling at a freckled, walnut-framed mirror as if he'd never seen it before. She touched his shoulder. "Come, Arnold," she said.

They went down the stairs slowly, both of them clinging to the sticky mahogany railing. The suitcase banged against her shins. In the entrance hall, old Mrs. Puckett stood waiting outside her door— a huge, soft lady in a black crepe dress and <u>orthopedic</u> shoes. She was holding a plastic bag of peanutbutter cookies, Arnold's favorites. There were tears in her eyes. "Here, Arnold," she said, quavering. Maybe she felt to blame that he was going. But she'd done the best she could: babysat him all these years and only given up when he'd grown too strong and wild to manage. Bet wished Arnold would give the old lady some sign—hug her, make his little crowing noise, just take the cookies, even. But he was too excited. He raced on out the front door, and it was Bet who had to take them. "Well, thank you, Mrs. Puckett," she said. "I know he'll enjoy them later."

"Oh, no . . ." said Mrs. Puckett, and she flapped her large hands and gave up, sobbing.

They were lucky and caught a bus first thing. Arnold sat by the window. He must have thought he was going to work with her; when they passed the red-and-gold Kresge's sign, he jabbered and tried to stand up. "No, honey," she said, and took hold of his arm. He settled down then and let his hand stay curled in hers awhile. He had very small, cool fingers, and nails as smooth as thumbtack heads.

At the train station, she bought the tickets and then a pack of Wrigley's spearmint gum. Arnold stood gaping at the vaulted ceiling,

orthopedic (ôr´ thō pē´ dik) adj. correcting posture or other disorders of the skeletal system

Literary Analysis
Foreshadowing What does Mrs. Puckett's behavior hint about the events to come?

with his head flopped back and his arms hanging limp at his sides. People stared at him. She would have liked to push their faces in. "Over here, honey," she said, and she nudged him toward the gate, straightening his collar as they walked.

He hadn't been on a train before and acted a little nervous, bouncing up and down in his seat and flipping the lid of his ashtray and craning forward to see the man ahead of them. When the train started moving, he crowed and pulled at her sleeve. "That's right, Arnold. Train. We're taking a trip," Bet said. She unwrapped a stick of chewing gum and gave it to him. He loved gum. If she didn't watch him closely, he sometimes swallowed it—which worried her a little because she'd heard it clogged your kidneys; but at least it would keep him busy. She looked down at the top of his head. Through the blond prickles of his hair, cut short for practical reasons, she could see his skull bones moving as he chewed. He was so thin-skinned, almost <u>transparent</u>; sometimes she imagined she could see the blood traveling in his veins.

When the train reached a steady speed, he grew calmer, and after a while he nodded over against her and let his hands sag on his knees. She watched his eyelashes slowly drooping—two colorless, fringed crescents, heavier and heavier, every now and then flying up as he tried to fight off sleep. He had never slept well, not ever, not even as a baby. Even before they'd noticed anything wrong, they'd wondered at his jittery, jerky catnaps, his tiny hands clutching tight and springing open, his strange single wail sailing out while he went right on sleeping. Avery said it gave him the chills. And after the doctor talked to them Avery wouldn't have anything to do with Arnold anymore—just walked in wide circles around the crib, looking stunned and sick. A few weeks later, he left. She wasn't surprised. She even knew how he felt, more or less. Halfway, he blamed her; halfway, he blamed himself. You can't believe a thing like this will just fall on you out of nowhere.

She'd had moments herself of picturing some kind of evil gene in her husband's ordinary, <u>stocky</u> body—a dark little egg like a black jelly bean, she imagined it. All his fault. But other times she was sure the gene was hers. It seemed so natural; she never could do anything as well as most people. And then other times she blamed their marriage. They'd married too young, against her parents' wishes. All she'd wanted was to get away from home. Now she couldn't remember why. What was wrong with home? She thought of her parents' humped green trailer, perched on cinder blocks near a forest of masts in Salt Spray, Maryland. At this distance (parents dead, trailer rusted to bits, even Salt Spray changed past recognition), it seemed to her that her old life had been beautifully free and spacious. She closed her eyes and saw wide gray skies. Everything had been ruled by the sea. Her father (who'd run a fishing boat for tourists) couldn't arrange his day till he'd heard the marine forecast—the wind, the tides, the small-craft warnings, the height of average waves in unprotected waters. He loved to fish, offshore and on, and he swam every chance he could get. He'd tried to teach her to bodysurf, but it hadn't worked out.

transparent (trans per´ ənt) *adj.* capable of being seen through

stocky (stäk´ ē) *adj.* solidly built; sturdy

Reading Strategy
Putting Events in Order
What clues tell you that Bet is recalling the past?

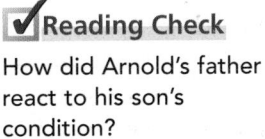**Reading Check**

How did Arnold's father react to his son's condition?

There was something about the breakers: she just gritted her teeth and stood <u>staunch</u> and let them slam into her. As if standing staunch were a virtue, really. She couldn't explain it. Her father thought she was scared, but it wasn't that at all.

She'd married Avery against their wishes and been sorry ever since—sorry to move so far from home, sorrier when her parents died within a year of each other, sorriest of all when the marriage turned grim and cranky. But she never would have thought of leaving him. It was Avery who left; she would have stayed forever. In fact, she did stay on in their apartment for months after he'd gone, though the rent was far too high. It wasn't that she expected him back. She just took some comfort from enduring.

Arnold's head snapped up. He looked around him and made a gurgling sound. His chewing gum fell onto the front of his jacket. "Here, honey," she told him. She put the gum in her ashtray. "Look out the window. See the cows?"

He wouldn't look. He began bouncing in his seat, rubbing his hands together rapidly.

"Arnold? Want a cookie?"

If only she'd brought a picture book. She'd meant to and then forgot. She wondered if the train people sold magazines. If she let him get too bored, he'd go into one of his tantrums, and then she wouldn't be able to handle him. The doctor had given her pills just in case, but she was always afraid that while he was screaming he would choke on them. She looked around the car. "Arnold," she said, "see the . . . see the hat with feathers on? Isn't it pretty? See the red suitcase? See the, um . . ."

The car door opened with a rush of clattering wheels and the conductor burst in, singing "Girl of my dreams, I love you." He lurched down the aisle, plucking pink tickets from the back of each seat. Just across from Bet and Arnold, he stopped. He was looking down at a tiny black lady in a purple coat, with a fox fur piece biting its own tail around her neck. "You!" he said.

The lady stared straight ahead.

"You, I saw you. You're the one in the washroom."

A little muscle twitched in her cheek.

"You got on this train in Beulah, didn't you. Snuck in the washroom. Darted back like you thought you could put something over on me. I saw that bit of purple! Where's your ticket gone to?"

She started fumbling in a blue cloth purse. The fumbling went on and on. The conductor shifted his weight.

"Why!" she said finally. "I must've left it back in my other seat."

"What other seat?"

"Oh, the one back . . ." She waved a spidery hand.

The conductor sighed. "Lady," he said, "you owe me money."

"I do no such thing!" she said. "Viper! Monger! Hitler!"[1] Her voice screeched up all at once; she sounded like a parrot. Bet winced and

---

1. **Hitler** German dictator Adolf Hitler (1889–1945).

felt herself flushing, as if *she* were the one. But then at her shoulder she heard a sudden, rusty clang, and she turned and saw that Arnold was laughing. He had his mouth wide open and his tongue curled, the way he did when he watched "Sesame Street." Even after the scene had worn itself out, and the lady had paid and the conductor had moved on, Arnold went on chortling and la-la-ing, and Bet looked gratefully at the little black lady, who was settling her fur piece fussily and muttering under her breath.

From the Parkinsville Railroad Station, which they seemed to be tearing down or else remodeling—she couldn't tell which—they took a taxicab to Parkins State Hospital. "Oh, I been out there many and many a time," said the driver. "Went out there just the other—"

But she couldn't stop herself; she had to tell him before she forgot. "Listen," she said, "I want you to wait for me right in the driveway. I don't want you to go on away."

"Well, fine," he said.

"Can you do that? I want you to be sitting right by the porch or the steps or whatever, right where I come out of, ready to take me back to the station. Don't just go off, and—"

"I *got* you, I got you," he said.

She sank back. She hoped he understood.

Arnold wanted a peanut-butter cookie. He was reaching and whimpering. She didn't know what to do. She wanted to give him anything he asked for, anything; but he'd get it all over his face and arrive not looking his best. She couldn't stand it if they thought he was just ordinary and unattractive. She wanted them to see how small and neat he was, how somebody cherished him. But it would be awful if he went into one of his rages. She broke off a little piece of cookie from the bag. "Here," she told him. "Don't mess, now."

He flung himself back in the corner and ate it, keeping one hand flattened across his mouth while he chewed.

The hospital looked like someone's great, pillared mansion, with square brick buildings all around it. "Here we are," the driver said.

"Thank you," she said. "Now you wait here, please. Just wait till I get—"

"*Lady,*" he said. "I'll wait."

She opened the door and nudged Arnold out ahead of her. Lugging the suitcase, she started toward the steps. "Come on, Arnold," she said.

He hung back.

"Arnold?"

Maybe he wouldn't allow it, and they would go on home and never think of this again.

But he came, finally, climbing the steps in his little hobbled way. His face was clean, but there were a few cookie crumbs on his jacket. She set down the suitcase to brush them off. Then she buttoned all his buttons and smoothed his shirt collar over his jacket collar before she pushed open the door.

Literary Analysis
Foreshadowing and Suspense What questions does Bet's request raise in your mind?

**Reading Check**

What instruction does Bet give the taxicab driver?

In the admitting office, a lady behind a wooden counter showed her what papers to sign. Secretaries were clacketing typewriters all around. Bet thought Arnold might like that, but instead he got lost in the lights—chilly, hanging ice-cube-tray lights with a little flicker to them. He gazed upward, looking astonished. Finally a flat-fronted nurse came in and touched his elbow. "Come along, Arnold. Come, Mommy. We'll show you where Arnold is staying," she said.

They walked back across the entrance hall, then up wide marble steps with hollows worn in them. Arnold clung to the banister. There was a smell Bet hated, pine-oil disinfectant, but Arnold didn't seem to notice. You never knew; sometimes smells could just put him in a state.

Literary Analysis
Foreshadowing and Suspense Why does the mundane smell of disinfectant create suspense?

The nurse unlocked a double door that had chicken-wired windows. They walked through a corridor, passing several fat, ugly women in shapeless gray dresses and ankle socks. "Ha!" one of the women said, and fell giggling into the arms of a friend. The nurse said, "*Here* we are." She led them into an enormous hallway lined with little white cots. Nobody else was in it; there wasn't a sign that children lived here except for a tiny cardboard clown picture hanging on one vacant wall. "This one is your bed, Arnold," said the nurse. Bet laid the suitcase on it. It was made up so neatly, the sheets might have been painted on. A steely-gray blanket was folded across the foot. She looked over at Arnold, but he was pivoting back and forth to hear how his new sneakers squeaked on the linoleum.

"Usually," said the nurse, "we like to give new residents six months before the family visits. That way they settle in quicker, don't you see." She turned away and adjusted the clown picture, though as far as Bet could tell it was fine the way it was. Over her shoulder, the nurse said, "You can tell him goodbye now, if you like."

"Oh," Bet said. "All right." She set her hands on Arnold's shoulders. Then she laid her face against his hair, which felt warm and fuzzy. "Honey," she said. But he went on pivoting. She straightened and told the nurse, "I brought his special blanket."

"Oh, fine," said the nurse, turning toward her again. "We'll see that he gets it."

"He always likes to sleep with it; he has ever since he was little."

"All right."

"Don't wash it. He hates if you wash it."

"Yes. Say goodbye to Mommy now, Arnold."

"A lot of times he'll surprise you. I mean there's a whole lot to him. He's not just—"

"We'll take very good care of him, Mrs. Blevins, don't worry."

"Well," she said. " 'Bye, Arnold."

She left the ward with the nurse and went down the corridor. As the nurse was unlocking the doors for her, she heard a single, terrible scream, but the nurse only patted her shoulder and pushed her gently on through.

In the taxi, Bet said, "Now, I've just got fifteen minutes to get to the station. I wonder if you could hurry?"

Literary Analysis
Foreshadowing and Suspense What actions do you anticipate after Arnold's scream?

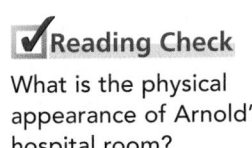

Girl Looking at Landscape, 1957, Richard Diebenkorn, oil on canvas, 59 x 60 3/8 inches, (149.9 x 153.4 cm), Gift of Mr. and Mrs. Alan H. Temple, 61.49, Collection of Whitney Museum of American Art, photograph by Geoffrey Clements, N.Y., Photograph copyright © 1997: Whitney Museum of American Art

▲ **Critical Viewing** Bet probably experienced a range of emotions after leaving the hospital. Which of her possible emotions are reflected in this painting? **[Interpret]**

"Sure thing," the driver said.

She folded her hands and looked straight ahead. Tears seemed to be coming down her face in sheets.

Once she'd reached the station, she went to the ticket window. "Am I in time for the twelve-thirty-two?" she asked.

"Easily," said the man. "It's twenty minutes late."

"What?"

"Got held up in Norton somehow."

"But you can't!" she said. The man looked startled. She must be a sight, all swollen-eyed and wet-cheeked. "Look," she said, in a lower voice. "I figured this on purpose. I chose the one train from Beulah that would let me catch another one back without waiting. I do not want to sit and wait in this station."

☑Reading Check

What is the physical appearance of Arnold's hospital room?

"Twenty *minutes,* lady. That's all it is."

"What am I going to do?" she asked him.

He turned back to his ledgers.

She went over to a bench and sat down. Ladders and scaffolding towered above her, and only ten or twelve passengers were dotted through the rest of the station. The place looked bombed out—nothing but a shell. "Twenty minutes!" she said aloud. "What am I going to do?"

Through the double glass doors at the far end of the station, a procession of gray-suited men arrived with briefcases. More men came behind them, dressed in work clothes, carrying folding chairs, black trunklike boxes with silver hinges, microphones, a wooden lectern, and an armload of bunting. They set the lectern down in the center of the floor, not six feet from Bet. They draped the bunting across it—an arc of red, white, and blue. Wires were connected, floodlights were lit. A microphone screeched. One of the workmen said, "Try her, Mayor." He held the microphone out to a fat man in a suit, who cleared his throat and said, "Ladies and gentlemen, on the occasion of the expansion of this fine old railway station—"

"Sure do get an echo here," the workman said. "Keep on going."

The Mayor cleared his throat again. "If I may," he said, "I'd like to take about twenty minutes of your time, friends."

He straightened his tie. Bet blew her nose, and then she wiped her eyes and smiled. They had come just for her sake, you might think. They were putting on a sort of private play. From now on, all the world was going to be like that—just something on a stage, for her to sit back and watch.

Review and Assess

Thinking About the Selection

1. **Respond:** What do you think of Bet's new outlook? Explain.

2. **(a) Recall:** Where is Bet taking Arnold? **(b) Recall:** Why is she taking him there? **(c) Interpret:** Does Arnold seem to suspect anything different? Support your answer.

3. **(a) Summarize:** Summarize what you learn about Bet's childhood and marriage. **(b) Connect:** How does Bet's behavior while her father teaches her to bodysurf relate to her behavior later in life?

4. **(a) Infer:** Why does Bet insist that the cab driver wait for her outside the hospital? **(b) Draw Conclusions:** What does this action reveal about Bet's needs and fears?

5. **(a) Analyze:** What is the meaning of the story's final sentence? **(b) Connect:** How does the story's title relate to its meaning?

6. **Take a Position:** Do you think that most people today would act as Bet did if they were in her place? Why or why not?

Review and Assess

Literary Analysis

Foreshadowing

1. How does Arnold's reluctance to cooperate with his mother at the beginning of the story **foreshadow** the story's main event?
2. Using a chart like the one shown, find three other examples of foreshadowing from the story, and analyze their effect on the reader.

3. Would the story be less effective if Tyler did not use foreshadowing? Explain.

Connecting Literary Elements

4. How does Tyler's use of foreshadowing help to build **suspense**?
5. In what ways does Bet's concern that the cab driver may not wait for her create suspense?
6. (a) What is suspenseful about the train being delayed twenty minutes? (b) Did you anticipate a different ending? Explain.
7. (a) Note three points in the story where you felt the greatest suspense. (b) List the questions each of these moments raised in your mind. (c) In what ways were those questions answered?
8. At what point in the story does the suspense end? Why?

Reading Strategy

Putting Events in Order

9. State the main events and details of the story in chronological order.
10. (a) What flashback does Bet have? (b) What prompts this flashback, and what causes it to end?
11. (a) What does this flashback add to your understanding of the story? (b) Do you think the story would suffer without it? Why or why not?

Extend Understanding

12. **Career Connection:** Bet entrusts the life of her son to others. What qualities would you look for in a caregiver for children like Arnold who are mentally challenged?

Quick Review

Foreshadowing is the placement of hints or clues in a narrative to suggest later events.

Suspense is a feeling of growing uncertainty about the outcome of events in a literary work.

A **flashback** is a scene or an event from an earlier time that interrupts the chronological presentation of events.

To **put events in order,** note the sequence in which they occur in real time.

 Take It to the Net
www.phschool.com

Take the interactive self-test online to check your understanding of the selection.

Integrate Language Skills

Vocabulary Development Lesson

Word Analysis: Latin Prefix *trans-*

The Latin prefix *trans-* means "across," "over," or "through." Something *transparent* is clear enough to be seen through. Explain how the meaning of the prefix relates to the meaning of each word.

1. transcribe
2. transcontinental
3. transportation
4. transplant

Spelling Strategy

To add a suffix to a word ending in two consonants, retain both consonants. For example, *bunt + ing = bunting* and *thank + ful = thankful*. Using this rule, add a suffix to each word.

1. Bet thought back on her child_____.
2. Treat everyone with kind_____.
3. Arnold offered resist_____ to his mother.

Fluency: Sentence Completion

Review the words in the vocabulary list on page 1027. Then, choose the letter of the word or phrase that best completes each of the following statements.

1. Something *transparent* might be made of (a) glass, (b) wool, (c) stainless steel.
2. A *stocky* person looks (a) bored, (b) rich, (c) sturdy.
3. A *staunch* ally (a) betrays you, (b) always stands by you, (c) abandons you.
4. *Orthopedic* shoes (a) make you look taller, (b) correct your posture, (c) cost less than most other shoes.
5. A *viper* might (a) bite you, (b) sing to you, (c) shake your hand.

Grammar and Style Lesson

Correct Use of Adjectives and Adverbs

Adjectives modify nouns or pronouns; **adverbs** modify verbs, adjectives, or other adverbs.

Always use an adjective, not an adverb, after linking verbs such as *be, am, is,* or *seem* if the modifier describes the subject.

Always use an adverb, never an adjective, to modify an action verb.

In the following examples, the verbs are underlined and the modifiers are in italics.

Adverb: She could never do anything as *well* as most people. (modifies the verb *could do*)

Adjective: The collar was *askew*. (modifies the noun *collar*)

Practice For each item, choose the correct modifier and identify the word it modifies.

1. Arnold stared (suspicious, suspiciously).
2. Sometimes Arnold looked (pathetic, pathetically) in his neatly buttoned clothes.
3. Arnold usually behaved (good, well).
4. Arnold chewed his gum (careful, carefully).
5. The hospital smelled (awful, awfully).
6. After Bet left Arnold there, she felt very (bad, badly).

Writing Application Write two sentences for each modifier given. Construct one sentence so that the modifier serves as an adjective, and the other so that the modifier serves as an adverb.

1. early
2. lone / lonely

*W*G *Prentice Hall Writing and Grammar Connection: Chapter 17, Section 3*

Writing Lesson

Social Worker's Report

Imagine that you are the social worker assigned to Bet and Arnold's case. Write a report explaining Arnold's condition and summarizing the events that led to Bet's decision to have her son institutionalized.

Prewriting Scan the story for details that indicate that Bet can no longer care for Arnold. Categorize the information into causes and effects to show how each detail contributes to Bet's decision.

Model: Listing Causes and Effects

Causes	Effects
1. Arnold cannot dress or feed himself. 2. He is getting bigger and stronger.	1. He requires a lot of care. 2. "He was getting to be too much for her."

Drafting Build your report on the information you gathered. Use clear transitions to show cause-and-effect and other relationships. Work to maintain the objective tone of an effective social worker.

Revising Read your report as though you were a supervisor reviewing the case for the first time. Make sure the draft includes sufficient details to support the conclusion. Check that your facts are accurate, your word choice is precise, and that you establish clear cause-and-effect relationships.

 Prentice Hall Writing and Grammar Connection: Chapter 10, Section 4

Extension Activities

Listening and Speaking Imagine that the subject of the mayor's speech was the need for more funding and improved care at state-run institutions. Prepare and present a **political speech** he might give using Arnold's case to support his points. Consider these ideas in your speech:

- The benefits for the needy children
- The expertise of health care professionals
- The humanitarian effort

Present the speech to the class.

Research and Technology With a group, research autism, Down's syndrome, or another childhood condition that causes severe mental or emotional challenges. Check the Internet or the library for information. Present your findings in a medical **research report.** [Group Activity]

 **Take It to the Net** www.phschool.com

Go online for an additional research activity using the Internet.

Prepare to Read

from The Names ◆ Mint Snowball ◆ Suspended

N. Scott Momaday (b. 1934)

A member of the Kiowa nation, N. Scott Momaday was born in Lawton, Oklahoma. As a child, he often visited his grand-parents, whose home was a meeting place for elderly Kiowas. Momaday describes these people as being "made of lean leather."

Inspired by his boyhood experi-ences, Momaday devoted himself to preserving his Kiowa heritage. After receiving his doctorate from Stanford University, Momaday wrote his first book, *House Made of Dawn* (1969), a novel about a young Native American torn between his roots and white society. The book earned Momaday a Pulitzer Prize. In the mid-1960s, the author made a pilgrimage to his grandmother's grave in western Oklahoma. He wrote about that experience in his best-known work, *The Way to Rainy Mountain* (1969), a collection of personal anecdotes and retellings of Kiowa myths and legends.

Momaday has since published poetry, essays, anecdotes, and retellings of Kiowa legends. His work provides the reader with a deeper under-standing of Native American culture, both past and present.

Naomi Shihab Nye (b. 1952)

Arab American poet Naomi Shihab Nye spent her teenage years in Jerusalem, far from the cities of St. Louis, Missouri, and San Antonio, Texas, where she had been a child. Her father had emigrated from Palestine and settled in St. Louis, Missouri, where he and his wife operated stores specializing in imported goods. When Naomi was fourteen, the family moved back to Jerusalem to be near her father's Arab relatives. Nye says the family's years in Jerusalem enabled her to discover her heritage.

In addition to publishing award-winning volumes of poetry, Nye has also created picture books for children. This versatile writer, whose work is built on the sturdy foundation of everyday experiences, believes that "the primary source of poetry has always been local life, random characters met on the streets, our own ancestry sifting down to us through small essential daily tasks."

Joy Harjo (b. 1951)

The influence of Joy Harjo's Native American Creek (or Muscogee) and Cherokee heritage is evident in many aspects of her life, including her writing. Born in Tulsa, Oklahoma, Harjo became interested in dance and joined a troupe of Native American dancers when she was a teenager. Her essay "Suspended" demonstrates music's ability to become a transport, a vehicle through which Harjo can connect her cultural heritage to her creative and everyday world.

Harjo attended the Institute of American Indian Arts, the University of New Mexico, and the Writers' Workshop of the University of Iowa. In addition to publishing books of poetry and prose, Harjo has also written film scripts and taught at the state universities of California, New Mexico, and Montana.

Preview

Connecting to the Literature

Watching home videos or flipping through family photos may bring back special memories of a treasured toy, a long-forgotten friend, or a special occasion. As you read these selections, think about childhood experiences that helped form your sense of self.

Literary Analysis

Anecdote

An **anecdote** is a short account of an amusing or interesting event. People tell anecdotes all the time, mostly for entertainment. Essayists recount anecdotes to make a point, make generalizations, or illustrate conclusions, as in this example from "Mint Snowball":

> Perhaps the clue to my entire personality connects to the lost Mint Snowball. I have always felt out-of-step with my environment, disjointed in the modern world.

Identify the anecdotes in these essays and the generalizations or conclusions they inspire. Use a chart like the one shown to help you.

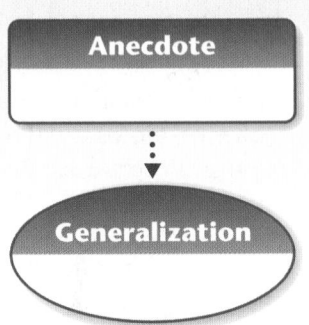

Comparing Literary Works

These essays describe **rites of passage**—events that mark personal transitions that have cultural significance. Momaday and Harjo write about unique experiences while Nye describes a lost recipe that was a link to her cultural heritage. As you read, compare how the experiences of the writers created in them a new awareness of self and the world around them.

Reading Strategy

Relating to Your Own Experiences

Many common experiences know no cultural boundaries. If you have ever taken a journey, yearned for the past, or experienced an inner awakening, you can find a connection between your experiences and the ones expressed in these selections. **Relating to your own experiences** will increase your understanding and enjoyment of the essays.

Vocabulary Development

supple (sup´ əl) *adj.* able to bend and move easily and nimbly (p. 1043)

concocted (kən käkt´ əd) *v.* made by combining various ingredients (p. 1047)

flamboyant (flam boi´ ənt) *adj.* too extravagant (p. 1047)

elixir (i liks´ ər) *n.* supposed remedy for all ailments (p. 1047)

permeated (pur´ mē āt´ id) *adj.* penetrated and spread through (p. 1047)

replicate (rep´ li kāt´) *v.* duplicate (p. 1048)

revelatory (rev´ ə lə tôr´ ē) *adj.* revealing; disclosing (p. 1049)

confluence (kän´ floo əns) *n.* a flowing together (p. 1050)

from
The Names

N. Scott Momaday

Background

If you were asked to name a literary form associated with personal, creative expression, the essay might not be your immediate response. However, the essay's flexibility provides an excellent arena for personal expression. Although they are a form of nonfiction, essays can be as moving, entertaining, and enriching as your favorite piece of fiction. In each of the three essays that follow, the writer uses a vivid memory as the springboard to an analysis of her or his identity.

I sometimes think of what it means that in their heyday—in 1830, say—the Kiowas owned more horses *per capita* than any other tribe on the Great Plains, that the Plains Indian culture, the last culture to evolve in North America, is also known as "the horse culture" and "the centaur[1] culture," that the Kiowas tell the story of a horse that died of shame after its owner committed an act of cowardice, that I am a Kiowa, that therefore there is in me, as there is in the Tartars,[2] an old, sacred notion of the horse. I believe that at some point in my racial life, this notion must needs be expressed in order that I may be true to my nature.

It happened so: I was thirteen years old, and my parents gave me a horse. It was a small nine-year-old gelding of that rare, soft color that is called strawberry roan. This my horse and I came to be, in the course of our life together, in good understanding, of one mind, a true story and history of that large landscape in which we made the one entity of whole motion, one and the same center of an intricate, pastoral composition, evanescent,[3] ever changing. And to this my horse I gave the name Pecos.

On the back of my horse I had a different view of the world. I could see more of it, how it reached away beyond all the horizons I had ever

Reading Strategy
Relating to Your Own Experiences Have you ever had great affection for a pet that can help you to relate to this experience? Explain.

---

1. **centaur** (sen′ tôr) *adj.* pertaining to a mythical creature with the head and upper body of a man and the lower body of a horse.
2. **Tartars** (tär′ tərz) *n.* nomadic Turkish peoples who took part in the invasions of Eastern Europe during the Middle Ages.
3. **evanescent** (ev′ ə nes′ ənt) *adj.* transient; tending to fade from sight.

Passion of Paints, Bob Peters

seen; and yet it was more concentrated in its appearance, too, and more accessible to my mind, my imagination. My mind loomed upon the farthest edges of the earth, where I could feel the full force of the planet whirling into space. There was nothing of the air and light that was not pure exhilaration, and nothing of time and eternity. Oh, Pecos, *un poquito mas!* Oh, my hunting horse! Bear me away, bear me away!

It was appropriate that I should make a long journey. Accordingly I set out one early morning, traveling light. Such a journey must begin in the nick of time, on the spur of the moment, and one must say to himself at the outset: Let there be wonderful things along the way; let me hold to the way and be thoughtful in my going; let this journey be made in beauty and belief.

I sang in the sunshine and heard the birds call out on either side. Bits of down from the cottonwoods drifted across the air, and butterflies fluttered in the sage. I could feel my horse under me, rocking at my legs, the bobbing of the reins to my hand; I could feel the sun on my face and the stirring of a little wind at my hair. And through the hard hooves, the slender limbs, the supple shoulders, the fluent back of my horse I felt the earth under me. Everything was under me, buoying me up; I rode across the top of the world. My mind soared; time and again I saw the fleeting shadow of my mind moving about me as it went winding upon the sun.

When the song, which was a song of riding, was finished, I had Pecos pick up the pace. Far down on the road to San Ysidro

▲ **Critical Viewing**
Using the third paragraph of the essay as a guide, how do you think Momaday would describe this painting?
[Hypothesize]

supple (sup′ əl) *adj.* able to bend and move easily and nimbly

✔**Reading Check**
What is Momaday's idea of a great journey?

from *The Names* ◆ 1043

I overtook my friend Pasqual Fragua. He was riding a rangy, stiff-legged black and white stallion, half wild, which horse he was breaking for the rancher Cass Goodner. The horse skittered and blew as I drew up beside him. Pecos began to prance, as he did always in the company of another horse. "Where are you going?" I asked in the Jemez language. And he replied, "I am going down the road." The stallion was hard to manage, and Pasqual had to keep his mind upon it; I saw that I had taken him by surprise. "You know," he said after a moment, "when you rode up just now I did not know who you were." We rode on for a time in silence, and our horses got used to each other, but still they wanted their heads.[4] The longer I looked at the stallion the more I admired it, and I suppose that Pasqual knew this, for he began to say good things about it: that it was a thing of good blood, that it was very strong and fast, that it felt very good to ride it. The thing was this: that the stallion was half wild, and I came to wonder about the wild half of it; I wanted to know what its wildness was worth in the riding. "Let us trade horses for a while," I said, and, well, all right, he agreed. At first it was exciting to ride the stallion, for every once in a while it pitched and bucked and wanted to run. But it was heavy and raw-boned and full of resistance, and every step was a jolt that I could feel deep down in my bones. I saw soon enough that I had made a bad bargain, and I wanted my horse back, but I was ashamed to admit it. There came a time in the late afternoon, in the vast plain far south of San Ysidro, after thirty miles, perhaps, when I no longer knew whether it was I who was riding the stallion or the stallion who was riding me. "Well, let us go back now," said Pasqual at last. "No. I am going on; and I will have my horse back, please," I said, and he was surprised and sorry to hear it, and we said goodbye. "If you are going south or east," he said, "look out for the sun, and keep your face in the shadow of your hat. *Vaya con Dios.*"[5] And I went on my way alone then, wiser and better mounted, and thereafter I held on to my horse. I saw no one for a long time, but I saw four falling stars and any number of jackrabbits, roadrunners, and coyotes, and once, across a distance, I saw a bear, small and black, lumbering in the ravine. The mountains drew close and withdrew and drew close again, and after several days I swung east.

Now and then I came upon settlements. For the most part they were dry, burnt places with Spanish names: Arroyo Seco, Las Piedras, Tres Casas. In one of these I found myself in a narrow street between high adobe walls. Just ahead, on my left, was a door in the wall. As I approached the door was flung open, and a small boy came running out, rolling a hoop. This happened so suddenly that Pecos shied very sharply, and I fell to the ground, jamming the thumb of my left hand. The little boy looked very worried and said that he was sorry to have caused such an accident. I waved the matter off, as if it were nothing;

Literary Analysis
Anecdote What do you think Momaday means by the phrase "wiser and better mounted"?

---

4. **. . . they wanted their heads** The horses wanted to be free of the control of the reins.
5. **Vaya con Dios** (vī yə kən dē′ ōs) "Go with God" (Spanish).

but as a matter of fact my hand hurt so much that tears welled up in my eyes. And the pain lasted for many days. I have fallen many times from a horse, both before and after that, and a few times I fell from a running horse on dangerous ground, but that was the most painful of them all.

In another settlement there were some boys who were interested in racing. They had good horses, some of them, but their horses were not so good as mine, and I won easily. After that, I began to think of ways in which I might even the odds a little, might give some advantage to my competitors. Once or twice I gave them a head start, a reasonable head start of, say, five or ten yards to the hundred, but that was too simple, and I won anyway. Then it came to me that I might try this: we should all line up in the usual way, side by side, but my competitors should be mounted and I should not. When the signal was given I should then have to get up on my horse while the others were breaking away; I should have to mount my horse during the race. This idea appealed to me greatly, for it was both imaginative and difficult, not to mention dangerous; Pecos and I should have to work very closely together. The first few times we tried this I had little success, and over a course of a hundred yards I lost four races out of five. The principal problem was that Pecos simply could not hold still among the other horses. Even before they broke away he was hard to manage, and when they were set running nothing could hold him back, even for an instant. I could not get my foot in the stirrup, but I had to throw myself up across the saddle on my stomach, hold on as best I could, and twist myself into position, and all this while racing at full speed. I could ride well enough to accomplish this feat, but it was a very awkward and inefficient business. I had to find some way to use the whole energy of my horse, to get it all into the race. Thus far I had managed only to break his motion, to divert him from his purpose and mine. To correct this I took Pecos away and worked with him through the better part of a long afternoon on a broad reach of level ground beside an irrigation ditch. And it was hot, hard work. I began by teaching him to run straight away while I ran beside him a few steps, holding on to the saddle horn, with no pressure on the reins. Then, when we had mastered this trick, we proceeded to the next one, which was this: I placed my weight on my arms, hanging from the saddle horn, threw my feet out in front of me, struck them to the ground, and sprang up against the saddle. This I did again and again, until Pecos came to expect it and did not flinch or lose his stride. I sprang a little higher each time. It was in all a slow process of trial and error, and after two or three hours both Pecos and I were covered with bruises and soaked through with perspiration. But we had much to show for our efforts, and at last the moment came

Literature
in context Mythology Connection

The Centaur

In the first paragraph of this essay, N. Scott Momaday refers to the Plains Indian culture as "the centaur culture." In alluding to that mythical creature with the upper body of a man and the lower body of a horse, Momaday indirectly places his discussion within the larger context of legend and cultural history. According to Greek legend, centaurs like the one shown here were a race of wild, lawless, inhospitable beings who dwelled in the mountains of Thessaly, in northern Greece. However, one centaur, Chiron, taught many Greek heroes and was well known for his wisdom and for his knowledge of medicine.

✓ **Reading Check**

Why were Momaday and Pecos training together?

when we must put the whole performance together. I had not yet leaped into the saddle, but I was quite confident that I could now do so; only I must be sure to get high enough. We began this dress rehearsal then from a standing position. At my signal Pecos lurched and was running at once, straight away and smoothly. And at the same time I sprinted forward two steps and gathered myself up, placing my weight precisely at my wrists, throwing my feet out and together, perfectly. I brought my feet down sharply to the ground and sprang up hard, as hard as I could, bringing my legs astraddle of my horse—and everything was just right, except that I sprang too high. I vaulted all the way over my horse, clearing the saddle by a considerable margin, and came down into the irrigation ditch. It was a good trick, but it was not the one I had in mind, and I wonder what Pecos thought of it after all. Anyway, after a while I could mount my horse in this way and so well that there was no challenge in it, and I went on winning race after race.

I went on, farther and farther into the wide world. Many things happened. And in all this I knew one thing: I knew where the journey was begun, that it was itself a learning of the beginning, that the beginning was infinitely worth the learning. The journey was well undertaken, and somewhere in it I sold my horse to an old Spanish man of Vallecitos. I do not know how long Pecos lived. I had used him hard and well, and it may be that in his last days an image of me like thought shimmered in his brain.

Review and Assess

Thinking About the Selection

1. **Respond:** What kind of animal seems "sacred" or special in some way to you? Why?

2. **(a) Recall:** What inspires Momaday's decision to take a journey? **(b) Draw Conclusions:** What do you think such a journey meant to him, and how did it make him feel?

3. **(a) Recall:** What does Momaday trade with Pasqual? **(b) Analyze:** What motivates him to make this trade?

4. **(a) Recall:** What does Momaday see and do on his journey? **(b) Draw Conclusions:** Why is it significant that his first long journey was on horseback?

5. **(a) Support:** Provide one detail that shows that Pecos was an extremely good horse. **(b) Infer:** What does the writer mean when he says that he "had used him hard and well"? **(c) Draw Conclusions:** Why do you suppose Momaday sold the horse?

6. **Apply:** What life lesson have you learned that was "infinitely worth the learning"?

Mint Snowball

Naomi Shihab Nye

My great-grandfather on my mother's side ran a drugstore in a small town in central Illinois. He sold pills and rubbing alcohol from behind the big cash register and creamy ice cream from the soda fountain. My mother remembers the counter's long polished sweep, its shining face. She twirled on the stools. Dreamy fans. Wide summer afternoons. Clink of nickels in anybody's hand. He sold milkshakes, cherry cokes, old fashioned sandwiches. What did an old fashioned sandwich look like? Dark wooden shelves. Silver spigots on chocolate dispensers.

My great-grandfather had one specialty: a Mint Snowball which he invented. Some people drove all the way in from Decatur just to taste it. First he stirred fresh mint leaves with sugar and secret ingredients in a small pot on the stove for a very long time. He <u>concocted</u> a <u>flamboyant</u> <u>elixir</u> of mint. Its scent clung to his fingers even after he washed his hands. Then he shaved ice into tiny particles and served it mounted in a glass dish. <u>Permeated</u> with mint syrup. Scoops of rich vanilla ice cream to each side. My mother took a bite of minty ice and ice cream mixed together. The Mint Snowball tasted like winter. She closed her eyes to see the Swiss village my great-grandfather's parents came from. Snow frosting the roofs. Glistening, dangling spokes of ice.

Before my great-grandfather died, he sold the recipe for the mint syrup to someone in town for one hundred dollars. This hurt my

concocted (kən käkt´ əd) v. made by combining various ingredients

flamboyant (flam boi´ ənt) adj. too extravagant

elixir (il iks´ ər) n. supposed remedy for all ailments

permeated (pʉr´ mē āt´ id) adj. penetrated and spread through

✔**Reading Check**
Describe Nye's great-grandfather's specialty.

grandfather's feelings. My grandfather thought he should have inherited it to carry on the tradition. As far as the family knew, the person who bought the recipe never used it. At least not in public. My mother had watched my grandfather make the syrup so often she thought she could <u>replicate</u> it. But what did he have in those little unmarked bottles? She experimented. Once she came close. She wrote down what she did. Now she has lost the paper.

replicate (rep´ li kāt) *v.* duplicate

Perhaps the clue to my entire personality connects to the lost Mint Snowball. I have always felt out-of-step with my environment, disjointed in the modern world. The crisp flush of cities makes me weep. Strip centers, Poodle grooming and Take-out Thai. I am angry over lost department stores, wistful for something I have never tasted or seen.

Although I know how to do everything one needs to know—change airplanes, find my exit off the interstate, charge gas, send a fax—there is something missing. Perhaps the stoop of my great-grandfather over the pan, the slow patient swish of his spoon. The spin of my mother on the high stool with her whole life in front of her, something fine and fragrant still to happen. When I breathe a handful of mint, even pathetic sprigs from my sunbaked Texas earth, I close my eyes. Little chips of ice on the tongue, their cool slide down. Can we follow the long river of the word "refreshment" back to its spring? Is there another land for me? Can I find any lasting solace in the color green?

Review and Assess

Thinking About the Selection

1. **Respond:** Do you feel out of step with the modern world or in tune with it? Explain your feelings.

2. **(a) Recall:** Whose memory provides the description of the drugstore and of the Mint Snowball? **(b) Connect:** Why does this memory evoke the country from which her ancestors came?

3. **(a) Recall:** What happened to the original Mint Snowball recipe? **(b) Recall:** Which family member comes close to duplicating the recipe? **(c) Infer:** Why do you think it was impossible to replicate?

4. **(a) Interpret:** What connection is made between the Mint Snowball and the author's life? **(b) Infer:** What does Nye consider lost as a result of the vanished recipe?

5. **(a) Analyze:** What is the mood of the final paragraph of the essay? **(b) Analyze:** Which details create that mood?

6. **Evaluate:** Does the image of this family dessert successfully capture a time long passed? Explain.

SUSPENDED

Joy Harjo

Getting Down, Joseph Holston

◀ **Critical Viewing**
Does this illustration of a jazz musician effectively convey Harjo's belief that jazz is "a way to speak beyond the confines of ordinary language"? Explain. **[Evaluate]**

Once I was so small that I could barely peer over the top of the backseat of the black Cadillac my father polished and tuned daily; I wanted to see everything. It was around the time I acquired language, or even before that time, when something happened that changed my relationship to the spin of the world. My concept of language, of what was possible with music was changed by this <u>revelatory</u> moment. It changed even the way I looked at the sun. This suspended integer of time probably escaped ordinary notice in my parents' universe, which informed most of my vision in the ordinary world. They were still omnipresent gods. We were driving somewhere in Tulsa, the northern border of the Creek Nation.[1] I don't know where we were going or

revelatory (rev´ ə lə tôr´ ē) *adj.* revealing; disclosing

✔ Reading Check

At what stage of Harjo's life does this narrative take place?

---

1. **Creek Nation** nation of Native American peoples, mainly Muscogean, formerly of Georgia and Alabama. Most now live in Oklahoma and Florida.

where we had been, but I know the sun was boiling the asphalt, the car windows open for any breeze as I stood on tiptoes on the floorboard behind my father, a handsome god who smelled of Old Spice, whose slick black hair was always impeccably groomed, his clothes perfectly creased and ironed. The radio was on. I loved the radio, jukeboxes or any magic thing containing music even then.

I wonder now what signaled this moment, a loop of time that on first glance could be any place in time. I became acutely aware of the line the jazz trumpeter was playing (a sound I later associated with Miles Davis). I didn't know the word jazz or trumpet, or the concepts. I don't know how to say it, with what sounds or words, but in that confluence of hot southern afternoon, in the breeze of aftershave and humidity, I followed that sound to the beginning, to the place of the birth of sound. I was suspended in whirling stars, a moon to which I'd traveled often by then. I grieved my parents' failings, my own life which I saw stretched the length of that rhapsody.

My rite of passage into the world of humanity occurred then, via jazz. The music made a startling bridge between familiar and strange lands, an appropriate vehicle, for though the music is predominantly west African in concept, with European associations, jazz was influenced by the Creek (or Muscogee) people, for we were there when jazz was born. I recognized it, that humid afternoon in my formative years, as a way to speak beyond the confines of ordinary language. I still hear it.

confluence (kän′ flo͞o əns) *n.* a flowing together

Review and Assess

Thinking About the Selection

1. **Respond:** Can you recall a personal experience that was important in your life but is difficult for you to analyze or describe?

2. **(a) Recall:** During what season did Harjo's experience take place? **(b) Support:** How do you know?

3. **(a) Recall:** Describe the appearance of Harjo's father. **(b) Analyze:** Which details of her description reveal the way she feels about her father?

4. **(a) Recall:** What kind of music was playing on the car radio? **(b) Draw Conclusions:** What did the music teach Harjo about communication?

5. **Deduce:** How does Harjo suggest that growing up involves sadness and disillusion?

6. **Apply:** What does this essay suggest about the mysterious workings of every person's inner world?

Review and Assess

Literary Analysis

Anecdote

1. (a) Identify two **anecdotes** in Momaday's essay. (b) What connects these anecdotes to the theme introduced in the opening paragraph?
2. In what ways is the lost recipe significant in Nye's life and in the development of her personality?
3. (a) Describe the way in which Harjo's experience of jazz affected her in a single moment. (b) How did the experience change her life?

Comparing Literary Works

4. What **rite of passage** did Momaday experience through his journey and the later selling of his horse?
5. Explain the significance of Harjo's statement, "My rite of passage into the world of humanity occurred then . . ."
6. Nye feels a great loss over her inability to recreate the Mint Snowball. If she still had the recipe, how might it have served as a rite of passage for her?
7. When a person experiences a rite of passage, he or she learns an adult truth about life and leaves childhood behind. What truths about life do each of these authors learn? Support your answer.

Reading Strategy

Relating to Your Own Experiences

8. Use a chart like the one shown to note the relationships you can find between these selections and your own experiences.

Writer's Experience	My Experience	How They Relate

9. Which writer's experiences or reflections were most accessible to you? Why?

Extend Understanding

10. **Literature Connection:** Relate "The Mint Snowball" to another literary work that expresses the theme of yearning for a way of life that is long gone. How are they similar? How do they differ?

Integrate Language Skills

Vocabulary Development Lesson

Word Analysis: Latin Prefix con-

The Latin prefix con- means "with" or "together." Combined with *fluence*, it produces *confluence*, meaning "flowing together." Define each of the following words, using "with" or "together."

1. conference
2. congregated
3. concocted
4. conform

Spelling Strategy

Many words end in -*ent* or -*ence*, such as *dependent* and *dependence*. However, there are exceptions, such as *flamboyant* and *flamboyance*, which end in -*ant* or -*ance*. In your notebook, complete the spelling of words in each sentence.

1. He was reluct____ to ride on the horse.
2. She showed defer____ to her grandfather.
3. She was a descend____ of the pilgrims.

Concept Development: Analogies

Select the word that best completes the analogy.

1. comfortable : chair :: supple : ____?____
   (a) dancer (b) flexible
2. stitched : clothing :: concocted : ____?____
   (a) potion (b) scientist
3. shy : timid :: flamboyant : ____?____
   (a) showy (b) nervous
4. treatment : disease :: elixir : ____?____
   (a) ailment (b) doctor
5. spread : rumor :: permeated : ____?____
   (a) filled (b) odor
6. design : create :: replicate : ____?____
   (a) count (b) copy
7. illuminating : lamp :: revelatory : ____?____
   (a) celebration (b) news
8. join : split :: confluence : ____?____
   (a) divergence (b) river

Grammar and Style Lesson

Elliptical Clauses

The term *elliptical* comes from the word *ellipsis*, meaning "omission." In an **elliptical clause,** one or more words are omitted because they are understood. An elliptical clause is only understood if the context makes clear what the missing elements are—for example, in many cases, the word *that* is omitted.

Examples: Her mother enjoyed the dessert *more than* [. . .] *any other.*
(*she enjoyed* is understood)

I hoped [. . .] *she would like it.*
(*that* is understood)

Practice Copy each sentence, underline the elliptical clause, and write the understood word(s).

1. Pecos ran faster than the other horses.
2. Momaday thought the stallion was better than his own horse.
3. Nye's great-grandfather sold the recipe he invented.
4. Harjo recalls hearing the music in the car more vividly than she does any other early experience.
5. She noticed more than she had before.

Writing Application Write two sentences containing elliptical clauses.

W̶G̶ Prentice Hall Writing and Grammar Connection: Chapter 22, Section 2

Writing Lesson

Reflective Essay

Each of these writers shares a moment from the past and reflects on its importance. Choose a significant event and write a reflective essay exploring its meaning.

Prewriting Brainstorm for a list of events that affected you earlier. For each, write two or three reasons why the event was significant. Decide which one you will write about.

Drafting After describing the event or experience, provide the insight to explain its effect on you. Include details that build the emotional impact of your insight.

Model: Elaborating to Add Emotional Depth

It was during my aunt's visit in the summer of 1996 that I discovered my pride in my Native American heritage. Through her stories about my grandparents and their struggles, I finally learned to celebrate what makes my life different instead of trying to hide it.

> Words like *proud, finally*, and *celebrate* relate the symbolic meaning of the event.

Revising Ask a classmate to read your draft to see if he or she can identify with your experience. Then, revise your draft, adding elaboration to ensure that readers will understand the importance of the event and the feelings it inspired in you.

W̶G̶ Prentice Hall Writing and Grammar Connection: Chapter 4, Section 3

Extension Activities

Listening and Speaking A line of jazz gave Joy Harjo a new vision of the world. Listen to a piece of music that does the same for you. Then, using these tips, conduct a **musical analysis,** explaining the music's effect on you:

- Describe the images that are evoked by the melody.
- If there are any lyrics, connect them with your own experiences.

Play the music for your class and discuss your feelings about it.

Research and Technology Like music, photography also has the power to evoke memory. With a group, create a word-processed **class anthology** of photographs and memories. Include personal photographs with anecdotal notes. Provide an introduction to the anthology, and illustrations or art to enhance your booklet. **[Group Activity]**

 **Take It to the Net** www.phschool.com

Go online for an additional research activity using the Internet.

Prepare to Read

Everyday Use

Alice Walker (b. 1944)

Born in Eatonton, Georgia, Alice Walker was the eighth and youngest child in a family of sharecroppers. Of her childhood, Walker writes, "It was great fun being cute. But then, one day, it ended."

The self-confidence of her childhood was challenged by an accident with a BB gun that scarred and nearly blinded her. Eight years old when the accident happened, Walker reports that she did not lift her head for six years. It was during this time of self-imposed isolation that she indulged her passion for reading. It was not until the family could afford surgery that Walker finally had the scar tissue on her eye removed. With that surgery, her self-confidence returned.

Civil Rights Walker became one of the most popular students in her high school and graduated as both class valedictorian and prom queen. She attended Spelman College, an elite college for African American women in Atlanta. While at Spelman, Walker became deeply involved in the civil rights movement. In August 1963, she traveled to Washington, D.C., to take part in the March on Washington for Jobs and Freedom. The guest speaker that day was Dr. Martin Luther King. Unable to see him through the crowd, Walker perched in a tree to get a better view. From there, she heard Dr. King deliver his famous "I Have a Dream" address.

After two years at Spelman, Walker learned that she had won a scholarship for full tuition to Sarah Lawrence College in Bronxville, New York. Although she was reluctant to leave Spelman and her civil rights activities, Walker's teachers persuaded her to accept the offer.

From Prom Queen to Poet At Sarah Lawrence, Walker studied under famed poets Muriel Rukeyser and Jane Cooper, who encouraged her and nurtured her talent. Walker's first collection of poetry, *Once* (1968), was written while she was a student at Sarah Lawrence.

After graduating from Sarah Lawrence, Walker moved to Mississippi to continue her work in the civil rights movement. During this period, she also taught African American studies at Jackson State University, where she was a writer-in-residence.

Cultural Pride Much of Alice Walker's fiction—novels including *The Third Life of Grange Copeland* (1970) and story collections including *In Love and Trouble* (1973) and *You Can't Keep a Good Woman Down* (1981)—delves into the lives of African American women and their experiences throughout history and in the modern world.

Walker's fiction and essays reflect a pride in her personal heritage and the culture of her people. She draws inspiration from the creative efforts of countless African American artists who, long ago, survived the oppression of slavery. In looking at today's world, Walker explores the connections between sexism and racism and the effects of both on individuals and their relationships.

The Color Purple With the publication of *The Color Purple* in 1982, Walker shot to international fame. The novel portrays women who are oppressed by the abusive men in their lives, but go on to find inner strength and personal dignity. Awarded both a Pulitzer Prize and a National Book Award, the book was later adapted into a successful motion picture. Walker took an active role in the making of the film, and received a hero's welcome at its premier in her home town of Eatonton.

"Everyday Use" explores Walker's maternal heritage, describing the creative legacy of "ordinary" black southern women. The title essay of Walker's *In Search of Our Mothers' Gardens* can be considered the nonfiction counterpart of "Everyday Use."

Preview

Connecting to the Literature

Time and new experiences can create divisions between people—even close relatives. In this story, distance and the passage of time lead a mother and her daughter to two very different views of the world.

Literary Analysis

Character's Motivation

To truly know a character, you have to understand that **character's motivation,** the reasons behind his or her thoughts, actions, and speech. Characters may be motivated by their values, experiences, needs, or dreams. These lines of "Everyday Use" are clues to the narrator's motivation.

> Maggie will be nervous until her sister goes . . . She thinks her sister has held life always in the palm of one hand, that "no" is a word the world never learned to say to her.

This quotation suggests that the narrator is motivated, at least in part, by feelings of love and protectiveness for Maggie. As you read, ask yourself:

- Why is this character doing or saying this?
- What need or goal does she hope to satisfy?

Connecting Literary Elements

"Everyday Use" is written in the **first-person point of view,** featuring a narrator who is a character in the story. When a story is told from the first-person point of view, the narrator's motivations may be easily understood. As you read, examine the thoughts and feelings of the narrator to understand her actions in the story.

Reading Strategy

Contrasting Characters

As this story opens, you learn that two sisters and their life experiences are quite different. By **contrasting characters,** or identifying the ways in which they differ, you can uncover the major conflict in the story. Use a Venn diagram like the one shown to note the personalities and details in behavior and speech that separate Dee from Maggie. Consider the ways their experiences have shaped their differences.

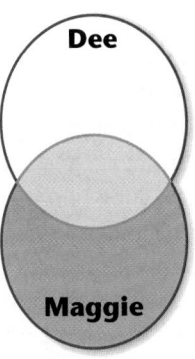

Vocabulary Development

furtive (fur′ tiv) *adj.* sneaky (p. 1059)

lye (lī) *n.* strong alkaline solution used in cleaning and making soap (p. 1059)

oppress (ə pres′) *v.* keep down by cruel or unjust use of power or authority (p. 1060)

doctrines (däk′ trinz) *n.* religious beliefs or principles (p. 1061)

Everyday Use

Alice Walker

Background

In this story, the character Dee, the narrator's daughter, is interested in a butter churn and a quilt—two homely artifacts that reveal her family's history. Today, such home-crafted pieces are celebrated for their beauty, but most folk art was originally created for utilitarian purposes. People took pride in creating items that were attractive as well as useful. The quilt in this story is an especially important symbol. Like most folk art, quilts served many purposes: keeping people warm, recycling worn-out clothing, providing a focal point for social gatherings of women, and preserving precious bits of family history for future generations. The differing ways in which each character regards the quilt become a critical point of division in this story.

▲ **Critical Viewing**
In what ways can quilts like these and the ones described in "Everyday Use" represent people's lives? **[Connect]**

I will wait for her in the yard that Maggie and I made so clean and wavy yesterday afternoon. A yard like this is more comfortable than most people know. It is not just a yard. It is like an extended living room. When the hard clay is swept clean as a floor and the fine sand around the edges lined with tiny, irregular grooves, anyone can come and sit and look up into the elm tree and wait for the breezes that never come inside the house.

Maggie will be nervous until after her sister goes: she will stand hopelessly in corners, homely and ashamed of the burn scars down her arms and legs, eyeing her sister with a mixture of envy and awe. She thinks her sister has held life always in the palm of one hand, that "no" is a word the world never learned to say to her.

Reading Strategy
Contrasting Characters
What contrasts do you learn about Maggie and her sister from the narrator's comments in this passage?

You've no doubt seen those TV shows where the child who has "made it" is confronted, as a surprise, by her own mother and father, tottering in weakly from backstage. (A pleasant surprise, of course: What would they do if parent and child came on the show only to curse out and insult each other?) On TV mother and child embrace and smile into each other's faces. Sometimes the mother and father weep, the child wraps them in her arms and leans across the table to tell how she would not have made it without their help. I have seen these programs.

Sometimes I dream a dream in which Dee and I are suddenly brought together on a TV program of this sort. Out of a dark and soft-seated limousine I am ushered into a bright room filled with many people. There I meet a smiling, gray, sporty man like Johnny Carson who shakes my hand and tells me what a fine girl I have. Then we are on the stage and Dee is embracing me with tears in her eyes. She pins on my dress a large orchid, even though she has told me once that she thinks orchids are tacky flowers.

In real life I am a large, big-boned woman with rough, man-working hands. In the winter I wear flannel nightgowns to bed and overalls during the day. I can kill and clean a hog as mercilessly as a man. My fat keeps me hot in zero weather. I can work outside all day, breaking ice to get water for washing; I can eat pork liver cooked over the open fire minutes after it comes steaming from the hog. One winter I knocked a bull calf straight in the brain between the eyes with a sledge hammer and had the meat hung up to chill before nightfall. But of course all of this does not show on television. I am the way my daughter would want me to be: a hundred pounds lighter, my skin like an uncooked barley pancake. My hair glistens in the hot bright lights. Johnny Carson has much to do to keep up with my quick and witty tongue.

Literary Analysis
Character's Motivation
What do you think motivates the narrator to feel this way about herself in her dream?

✔**Reading Check**
Who are Maggie and her mother waiting to welcome?

But that is a mistake. I know even before I wake up. Who ever knew a Johnson with a quick tongue? Who can even imagine me looking a strange white man in the eye? It seems to me I have talked to them always with one foot raised in flight, with my head turned in whichever way is farthest from them. Dee, though. She would always look anyone in the eye. Hesitation was no part of her nature.

"How do I look, Mama?" Maggie says, showing just enough of her thin body enveloped in pink skirt and red blouse for me to know she's there, almost hidden by the door.

"Come out into the yard," I say.

Have you ever seen a lame animal, perhaps a dog run over by some careless person rich enough to own a car, sidle up to someone who is ignorant enough to be kind to him? That is the way my Maggie walks. She has been like this, chin on chest, eyes on ground, feet in shuffle, ever since the fire that burned the other house to the ground.

Dee is lighter than Maggie, with nicer hair and a fuller figure. She's a woman now, though sometimes I forget. How long ago was it that the other house burned? Ten, twelve years? Sometimes I can still hear the flames and feel Maggie's arms sticking to me, her hair smoking and her dress falling off her in little black papery flakes. Her eyes seemed stretched open, blazed open by the flames reflected in them. And Dee. I see her standing off under the sweet gum tree she used to dig gum out of; a look of concentration on her face as she watched the last dingy gray board of the house fall in toward the red-hot brick chimney. Why don't you do a dance around the ashes? I'd want to ask her. She had hated the house that much.

I used to think she hated Maggie, too. But that was before we raised the money, the church and me, to send her to Augusta to school. She used to read to us without pity; forcing words, lies, other folks' habits, whole lives upon us two, sitting trapped and ignorant underneath her voice. She washed us in a river of make-believe, burned us with a lot of knowledge we didn't necessarily need to know. Pressed us to her with the serious way she read, to shove us away at just the moment, like dimwits, we seemed about to understand.

Dee wanted nice things. A yellow organdy dress to wear to her graduation from high school; black pumps to match a green suit she'd made from an old suit somebody gave me. She was determined to stare down any disaster in her efforts. Her eyelids would not flicker for minutes at a time. Often I fought off the temptation to shake her. At sixteen she had a style of her own, and knew what style was.

I never had an education myself. After second grade the school was closed down. Don't ask me why: in 1927 colored asked fewer questions than they do now. Sometimes Maggie reads to me. She stumbles along good-naturedly but can't see well. She knows she is not bright. Like good looks and money, quickness passed her by. She will marry John

Literary Analysis
Character's Motivation and First-Person Point of View What does the narrator's memory of the fire reveal about her point of view toward her two daughters?

Reading Strategy
Contrasting Characters What contrasts between herself and Dee does the narrator describe?

Thomas (who has mossy teeth in an earnest face) and then I'll be free to sit here and I guess just sing church songs to myself. Although I never was a good singer. Never could carry a tune. I was always better at a man's job. I used to love to milk till I was hooved in the side in '49. Cows are soothing and slow and don't bother you, unless you try to milk them the wrong way.

I have deliberately turned my back on the house. It is three rooms, just like the one that burned, except the roof is tin; they don't make shingle roofs any more. There are no real windows, just some holes cut in the sides, like the portholes in a ship, but not round and not square, with rawhide holding the shutters up on the outside. This house is in a pasture, too, like the other one. No doubt when Dee sees it she will want to tear it down. She wrote me once that no matter where we "choose" to live, she will manage to come see us. But she will never bring her friends. Maggie and I thought about this and Maggie asked me, "Mama, when did Dee ever *have* any friends?"

She had a few. <u>Furtive</u> boys in pink shirts hanging about on wash-day after school. Nervous girls who never laughed. Impressed with her they worshiped the well-turned phrase, the cute shape, the scalding humor that erupted like bubbles in <u>lye</u>. She read to them.

When she was courting Jimmy T she didn't have much time to pay to us, but turned all her faultfinding power on him. He *flew* to marry a cheap city girl from a family of ignorant flashy people. She hardly had time to recompose herself.

When she comes I will meet—but there they are!

Maggie attempts to make a dash for the house, in her shuffling way, but I stay her with my hand. "Come back here," I say. And she stops and tries to dig a well in the sand with her toe.

It is hard to see them clearly through the strong sun. But even the first glimpse of leg out of the car tells me it is Dee. Her feet were always neat-looking, as if God himself had shaped them with a certain style. From the other side of the car comes a short, stocky man. Hair is all over his head a foot long and hanging from his chin like a kinky mule tail. I hear Maggie suck in her breath. "Uhnnnh," is what it sounds like. Like when you see the wriggling end of a snake just in front of your foot on the road. "Uhnnnh."

Dee next. A dress down to the ground, in this hot weather. A dress so loud it hurts my eyes. There are yellows and oranges enough to throw back the light of the sun. I feel my whole face warming from the heat waves it throws out. Earrings gold, too, and hanging down to her shoulders. Bracelets dangling and making noises when she moves her arm up to shake the folds of the dress out of her armpits. The dress is loose and flows, and as she walks closer, I like it. I hear Maggie go "Uhnnnh" again. It is her sister's hair. It stands straight up like the wool on a sheep. It is black as night and around the edges are two long pigtails that rope about like small lizards disappearing behind her ears.

furtive (fur´ tiv) *adj.* sneaky

lye (lī) *n.* strong alkaline solution used in cleaning and making soap

Literary Analysis
Character's Motivation
What motivates Maggie to try to run for the house?

 **Reading Check**

What traumatic event occurred in the lives of the mother and her daughters?

"Wa-su-zo-Tean-o!"[1] she says, coming on in that gliding way the dress makes her move. The short stocky fellow with the hair to his navel is all grinning and he follows up with "Asalamalakim,[2] my mother and sister!" He moves to hug Maggie but she falls back, right up against the back of my chair. I feel her trembling there and when I look up I see the perspiration falling off her chin.

"Don't get up," says Dee. Since I am stout it takes something of a push. You can see me trying to move a second or two before I make it. She turns, showing white heels through her sandals, and goes back to the car. Out she peeks next with a Polaroid. She stoops down quickly and lines up picture after picture of me sitting there in front of the house with Maggie cowering behind me. She never takes a shot without making sure the house is included. When a cow comes nibbling around the edge of the yard she snaps it and me and Maggie and the house. Then she puts the Polaroid in the back seat of the car, and comes up and kisses me on the forehead.

Meanwhile Asalamalakim is going through motions with Maggie's hand. Maggie's hand is as limp as a fish, and probably as cold, despite the sweat, and she keeps trying to pull it back. It looks like Asalamalakim wants to shake hands but wants to do it fancy. Or maybe he don't know how people shake hands. Anyhow, he soon gives up on Maggie.

"Well," I say. "Dee."

"No, Mama," she says. "Not 'Dee,' Wangero Leewanika Kemanjo!"

"What happened to 'Dee'?" I wanted to know.

"She's dead," Wangero said. "I couldn't bear it any longer, being named after the people who <u>oppress</u> me."

"You know as well as me you was named after your aunt Dicie," I said. Dicie is my sister. She named Dee. We called her "Big Dee" after Dee was born.

"But who was *she* named after?" asked Wangero.

"I guess after Grandma Dee," I said.

"And who was she named after?" asked Wangero.

"Her mother," I said, and saw Wangero was getting tired. "That's about as far back as I can trace it," I said. Though, in fact, I probably could have carried it back beyond the Civil War through the branches.

"Well," said Asalamalakim, "there you are."

"Uhnnnh," I heard Maggie say.

"There I was not," I said, "before 'Dicie' cropped up in our family, so why should I try to trace it that far back?"

He just stood there grinning, looking down on me like somebody inspecting a Model A car. Every once in a while he and Wangero sent eye signals over my head.

"How do you pronounce this name?" I asked.

Literary Analysis
Character's Motivation
Why does Dee take so many photographs?

oppress (ə pres´) v. keep down by cruel or unjust use of power or authority

---

1. **Wa-su-zo-Tean-o** (wä sōō zō tēn´ ō) African greeting.
2. **Asalamalakim** *Salaam aleikhim* (sə läm´ ä lĭ´ kēm´) Islamic greeting meaning "Peace be with you."

"You don't have to call me by it if you don't want to," said Wangero.

"Why shouldn't I?" I asked. "If that's what you want us to call you, we'll call you."

"I know it might sound awkward at first," said Wangero.

"I'll get used to it," I said. "Ream it out again."

Well, soon we got the name out of the way. Asalamalakim had a name twice as long and three times as hard. After I tripped over it two or three times he told me to just call him Hakim-a-barber. I wanted to ask him was he a barber, but I didn't really think he was, so I didn't ask.

"You must belong to those beef-cattle people down the road," I said. They said "Asalamalakim" when they met you, too, but they didn't shake hands. Always too busy: feeding the cattle, fixing the fences, putting up salt-lick shelters, throwing down hay. When the white folks poisoned some of the herd the men stayed up all night with rifles in their hands. I walked a mile and a half just to see the sight.

Hakim-a-barber said, "I accept some of their <u>doctrines</u>, but farming and raising cattle is not my style." (They didn't tell me, and I didn't ask, whether Wangero (Dee) had really gone and married him.)

doctrines (däk´ trinz) n. religious beliefs or principles

We sat down to eat and right away he said he didn't eat collards[3] and pork was unclean. Wangero, though, went on through the chitlins[4] and corn bread, the greens and everything else. She talked a blue streak over the sweet potatoes. Everything delighted her. Even the fact that we still used the benches her daddy made for the table when we couldn't afford to buy chairs.

"Oh, Mama!" she cried. Then turned to Hakim-a-barber. "I never knew how lovely these benches are. You can feel the rump prints," she said, running her hands underneath her and along the bench. Then she gave a sigh and her hand closed over Grandma Dee's butter dish. "That's it!" she said. "I knew there was something I wanted to ask you if I could have." She jumped up from the table and went over in the corner where the churn stood, the milk in it clabber by now. She looked at the churn and looked at it.

"This churn top is what I need," she said. "Didn't Uncle Buddy whittle it out of a tree you all used to have?"

"Yes," I said.

"Uh huh," she said happily. "And I want the dasher, too."

"Uncle Buddy whittle that, too?" asked the barber.

---

3. **collards** (käl´ ərdz) n. leaves of the collard plant, often referred to as "collard greens."

4. **chitlins** (chit´ lənz) n. chitterlings, a pork dish popular among southern African Americans.

☑Reading Check

Why has Dee changed her name?

Dee (Wangero) looked up at me.

"Aunt Dee's first husband whittled the dash," said Maggie so low you almost couldn't hear her. "His name was Henry, but they called him Stash."

"Maggie's brain is like an elephant's," Wangero said, laughing. "I can use the churn top as a centerpiece for the alcove table," she said, sliding a plate over the churn, "and I'll think of something artistic to do with the dasher."

When she finished wrapping the dasher the handle stuck out. I took it for a moment in my hands. You didn't even have to look close to see where hands pushing the dasher up and down to make butter had left a kind of sink in the wood. In fact, there were a lot of small sinks; you could see where thumbs and fingers had sunk into the wood. It was beautiful light yellow wood, from a tree that grew in the yard where Big Dee and Stash had lived.

After dinner Dee (Wangero) went to the trunk at the foot of my bed and started rifling through it. Maggie hung back in the kitchen over the dishpan. Out came Wangero with two quilts. They had been pieced by Grandma Dee and then Big Dee and me had hung them on the quilt frames on the front porch and quilted them. One was in the Lone Star pattern. The other was Walk Around the Mountain. In both of them were scraps of dresses Grandma Dee had worn fifty and more years ago. Bits and pieces of Grandpa Jarrell's Paisley shirts. And one teeny faded blue piece, about the size of a penny matchbox, that was from Great Grandpa Ezra's uniform that he wore in the Civil War.

"Mama," Wangero said sweet as a bird. "Can I have these old quilts?"

I heard something fall in the kitchen, and a minute later the kitchen door slammed.

"Why don't you take one or two of the others?" I asked. "These old things was just done by me and Big Dee from some tops your grandma pieced before she died."

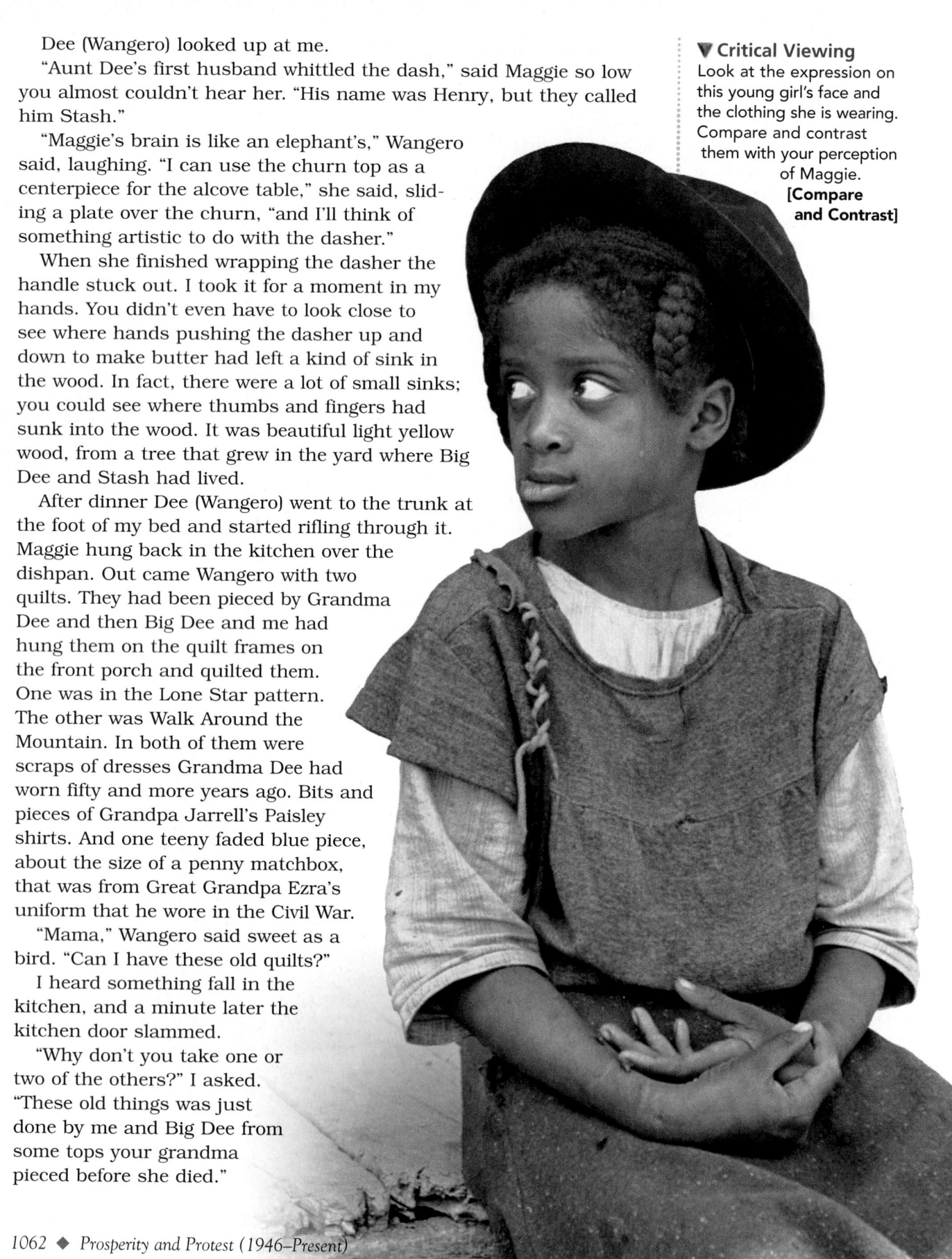

▼ Critical Viewing
Look at the expression on this young girl's face and the clothing she is wearing. Compare and contrast them with your perception of Maggie.
[Compare and Contrast]

"No," said Wangero. "I don't want those. They are stitched around the borders by machine."

"That'll make them last better," I said.

"That's not the point," said Wangero. "These are all pieces of dresses Grandma used to wear. She did all this stitching by hand. Imagine!" She held the quilts securely in her arms, stroking them.

"Some of the pieces, like those lavender ones, come from old clothes her mother handed down to her," I said, moving up to touch the quilts. Dee (Wangero) moved back just enough so that I couldn't reach the quilts. They already belonged to her.

"Imagine!" she breathed again, clutching them closely to her bosom.

"The truth is," I said, "I promised to give them quilts to Maggie, for when she marries John Thomas."

She gasped like a bee had stung her.

"Maggie can't appreciate these quilts!" she said. "She'd probably be backward enough to put them to everyday use."

"I reckon she would," I said. "God knows I been saving 'em for long enough with nobody using 'em. I hope she will!" I didn't want to bring up how I had offered Dee (Wangero) a quilt when she went away to college. Then she had told me they were old-fashioned, out of style.

"But they're *priceless*!" she was saying now, furiously; for she has a temper. "Maggie would put them on the bed and in five years they'd be in rags. Less than that!"

"She can always make some more," I said. "Maggie knows how to quilt."

Dee (Wangero) looked at me with hatred. "You just will not understand. The point is these quilts, *these quilts*!"

"Well," I said, stumped. "What would *you* do with them?"

"Hang them," she said. As if that was the only thing you *could* do with quilts.

Maggie by now was standing in the door. I could almost hear the sound her feet made as they scraped over each other.

"She can have them, Mama," she said, like somebody used to never winning anything, or having anything reserved for her.

"I can 'member Grandma Dee without the quilts."

I looked at her hard. She had filled her bottom lip with checker-berry snuff and it gave her face a kind of dopey, hangdog look. It was Grandma Dee and Big Dee who taught her how to quilt herself. She stood there with her scarred hands hidden in the folds of her skirt.

Reading Strategy
Contrasting Characters
In what way does the dispute over the quilts reveal differences between the two sisters?

✔**Reading Check**

Why does Dee think Maggie should not have the quilts?

She looked at her sister with something like fear but she wasn't mad at her. This was Maggie's portion. This was the way she knew God to work.

When I looked at her like that something hit me in the top of my head and ran down to the soles of my feet. Just like when I'm in church and the spirit of God touches me and I get happy and shout. I did something I never had done before: hugged Maggie to me, then dragged her on into the room, snatched the quilts out of Miss Wangero's hands and dumped them into Maggie's lap. Maggie just sat there on my bed with her mouth open.

"Take one or two of the others," I said to Dee.

But she turned without a word and went out to Hakim-a-barber.

"You just don't understand," she said, as Maggie and I came out to the car.

"What don't I understand?" I wanted to know.

"Your heritage," she said. And then she turned to Maggie, kissed her, and said, "You ought to try to make something of yourself, too, Maggie. It's really a new day for us. But from the way you and Mama still live you'd never know it."

She put on some sunglasses that hid everything above the tip of her nose and her chin.

Maggie smiled; maybe at the sunglasses. But a real smile, not scared. After we watched the car dust settle I asked Maggie to bring me a dip of snuff. And then the two of us sat there just enjoying, until it was time to go in the house and go to bed.

Review and Assess

Thinking About the Selection

1. **Respond:** How did you feel about Dee's behavior on her visit home? Explain.

2. **(a) Recall:** How was Maggie injured? **(b) Compare and Contrast:** How did Maggie and Dee each react to that dramatic experience?

3. **(a) Recall:** What objects does Dee ask to have?
   (b) Recall: What does Dee intend to do with the items she requests? **(c) Interpret:** What is ironic about her request for these objects and her professed interest in her heritage?

4. **(a) Interpret:** What do the quilts symbolize?
   (b) Compare and Contrast: In what ways do the quilts hold different meanings for Dee and for Maggie?

5. **Infer:** What seems to have been Dee's main purpose in visiting her home?

6. **Take a Position:** Should Dee's mother have given some of the family heirlooms to Dee? Why or why not?

Review and Assess

Literary Analysis

Character's Motivation

1. What appears to **motivate** Dee's interest in her heritage?
2. (a) List three personality traits that enable Dee to return home after a long absence and assume she may take things from the house. (b) Give three examples that reveal Maggie's character.
3. What does the narrator's act of snatching the quilts from Dee reveal about her personal values?
4. Explain Dee's complex motivations when she uses the word "heritage" and describes Maggie as "backward."

Connecting Literary Elements

5. Using a chart like the one shown, analyze the narrator's feelings toward Dee and Maggie.

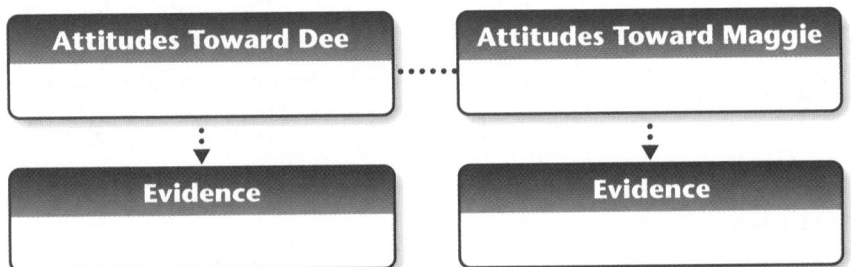

6. (a) What is your attitude toward each sister? (b) How does Walker's choice of narrator influence your response?
7. In what ways might the story change if it were told by Dee? Explain.

Reading Strategy

Contrasting Characters

8. How do Maggie and Dee differ (a) physically, (b) intellectually, and (c) emotionally?
9. (a) What does each sister know about her heritage? (b) To what extent does each sister think it is important to incorporate knowledge of her African heritage into her daily life?

Extend Understanding

10. **Cultural Connection:** What message does the story convey about family relationships and the meaning of heritage?

Quick Review

A **character's motivations** are the reasons for his or her thoughts, feelings, actions, and speech.

A story using the **first-person point of view** is told from the vantage point of a narrator who is involved in the action and who uses the first-person pronoun "I."

To **contrast characters,** identify the ways in which they differ.

 Take It to the Net
www.phschool.com
Take the interactive self-test online to check your understanding of the selection.

Integrate Language Skills

Vocabulary Development Lesson

Word Analysis: Latin Root -doc- / -doct-

The word *doctrines*, meaning "teachings, ideas, or beliefs," includes the Latin root *-doc- / -doct-*, meaning "teach." By combining this information with context clues, choose the best word to complete each sentence.

documents   indoctrinate   docile   documentary

1. We watched a ___?___ on the history of quilt-making in America.
2. A ___?___ learner is one who accepts without question anything he or she is taught.
3. The political leader worked to ___?___ his followers by repeating his ideology every day.
4. Immigrants were asked to show ___?___ to prove their citizenship in their original country.

Concept Development: Analogies

Complete each analogy using a word from the vocabulary list on page 1055.

1. *Flour* is to *pie crust* as ___?___ is to *soap.*
2. *Encourage* is to *coach* as ___?___ is to *dictator.*
3. *Competitive* is to *athlete* as ___?___ is to *prowler.*
4. *Moral* is to *lesson* as ___?___ is to *belief.*

Spelling Strategy

To add a suffix to a word ending in two consonants, retain both consonants and add the suffix: *oppress* + *-ive* = *oppressive.* Add a suffix to each of the words below and write a sentence for each.

1. distress   2. will   3. obsess

Grammar and Style Lesson

Sentence Fragments

A sentence expresses a complete thought with a subject and a verb. **Sentence fragments** are parts of sentences incorrectly punctuated as though they were complete. The fragment in this example lacks a subject:

Example: Never could carry a tune. (missing a subject: *Who?*)

Although it was a quilt made by my mother. (does not express a complete thought)

While fragments are not acceptable in formal writing, writers do use them to imitate the way people speak.

Practice Explain why each example is a sentence fragment, and identify the missing sentence part. Rewrite each fragment as a complete sentence.

1. Furtive boys in pink shirts hanging about on washday after school.
2. Nervous girls who never laughed.
3. Earrings gold, too, and hanging down to her shoulder.
4. Always too busy: feeding the cattle, fixing the fences, putting up salt-lick shelters.
5. Your heritage.

Writing Application Write a dialogue between characters from "Everyday Use." Incorporate fragments to capture speech patterns.

𝒲𝒢 *Prentice Hall Writing and Grammar Connection: Chapter 20, Section 4*

Writing Lesson

Review of a Short Story

Write a critical review of "Everyday Use," explaining whether you think the story is effective. Note your reactions to the story and explain whether the characters are believable and interesting. Consider the story's message, and express your opinion about its importance.

Prewriting   Review the story and list your responses, both positive and negative. Beside each item, note the page numbers of appropriate examples. Review your chart, and summarize your opinion in a sentence or two.

Drafting   Begin by stating your overall opinion of the story. Then, present a series of paragraphs in which you support your ideas with details.

Revising   Evaluate your draft to replace weak modifiers with precise adjectives and adverbs that capture your reactions. Be sure your writing is accurate by checking that you have copied all quotations exactly.

Model: Revising to Add Precise Details

genuine

Dee, as Wangero, appeared ~~nice~~, but she was ~~really~~

~~quite~~ insincere. She was not at all interested in ~~the~~

her heritage

~~things~~, but rather in appearances.

> Replacing weak modifiers with specific words makes writing more precise and interesting. Words like *really* do not add meaning to the work.

WG   *Prentice Hall Writing and Grammar Connection: Chapter 14, Section 3*

Extension Activities

Listening and Speaking   With a partner, dramatize the narrator's dream of a **television talk show** reunion with Dee. Consider these techniques:

- Use appropriate dialogue for the scene.
- Create skillful and artistic staging.
- Make your characters interesting and believable.

After rehearsing to achieve command of your text, present the dramatization to your class. **[Group Activity]**

Research and Technology   The names *Wangero* and *Hakim-a-barber* come from one of the more than 800 languages spoken in Africa today. Conduct research on one of the four major language families. Create an **African languages presentation,** including audio and videotapes and maps of the region, to your class.

 **Take It to the Net**   www.phschool.com

Go online for an additional research activity using the Internet.

Prepare to Read

from The Woman Warrior

Maxine Hong Kingston (b. 1940)

"I was born to be a writer," Maxine Hong Kingston once told an interviewer. "In the midst of any adventure, a born writer has a desire to hurry home and put it into words."

Crossing Cultures Although Kingston was born in America, she did not begin describing her adventures in English until she was nearly ten because the language spoken at home was Say Yup, a Chinese dialect spoken around Canton, now known as Guangzhou, China. Kingston's parents came from a village near Canton. Her father left first for "the Golden Mountain" of America and settled in New York City. His training as a poet and calligrapher was unmarketable in the United States, so he earned a living working in the laundry business. Kingston's mother, who was trained as a midwife, used the money her husband sent home to run a clinic in their native village. She did so until 1939, when she escaped war-torn China and joined her husband. Not long afterward, the couple resettled in Stockton, California, where Maxine Hong was born.

Building a Love for Story Young Maxine, whose Chinese name is Ting Ting, was a shy and quiet girl who repeated kindergarten because she spoke very little English. While at home, however, she listened intently to the stories told by family members and friends; this love of storytelling later influenced her writing style as Kingston developed her "talk stories." By the time she was nine years old, she mastered English and began writing poetry. Soon, she began to earn straight A's in school.

Kingston won a scholarship to the University of California at Berkeley, which she attended in the 1960s during its heyday as a center of intellectual activity and political activism. There, she met Earll Kingston and married him in 1962. After graduation, the Kingstons supported themselves as teachers while pursuing success in their chosen fields—Earll in acting, Maxine in writing. They lived in Hawaii for many years but returned to the mainland with their son, settling in Oakland, California.

A Bestseller Kingston shot to success with her first and best-known book, *The Woman Warrior: Memoirs of a Girlhood Among Ghosts*. The subtitle refers to the pale "ghosts" of white America as well as the "ghosts" of the narrator's ancestors in China. *The Woman Warrior*, a unique blend of folklore, myth, feminism, and autobiography, won the National Book Critics' Circle Award in 1976. The major focus of the book is on Brave Orchid—Kingston's mother. Brave Orchid tells her daughter about China and the female members of their family through her talk stories—a blend of truth and fiction, tales of ancient heroes, family secrets, and important cultural traditions and values passed from generation to generation.

Kingston earned the National Book Critics' Circle Award a second time in 1980 for *China Men*. In 1989, she published the novel *Tripmaster Monkey*. A slow, methodical writer, Kingston labors over numerous revisions to her books. For at least eight years, she has been working on her next book, tentatively titled *The Fifth Book of Peace*.

Preview

Connecting to the Literature

At some point in your life, you have probably felt that your older relatives view the world quite differently than you do. In families whose adults and children were born in different countries, these differences can be especially pronounced, as they are in this selection.

Literary Analysis

Memoirs

Most **memoirs** are first-person nonfiction narratives that recount historically or personally significant events in which the writer was a participant or an eyewitness. The following excerpt from Kingston's memoir blends the historical and the personal:

> To while away time, she and her niece talked about the Chinese passengers. These new immigrants had it easy. On Ellis Island the people were thin after forty days at sea and had no fancy luggage.

Kingston skillfully incorporates details of culture and time period into an account of a memorable day in her life.

Connecting Literary Elements

Memoirs are, by definition, acts of memory—accounts of individual experience told in the first person point of view. In most memoirs, the writer uses "I" to narrate events. Kingston, however, defies convention by using the **limited third-person point of view**—the story is related by a narrator who uses the pronoun "she" to describe herself. This unusual use of point of view helps to blur the line between fact and fiction. As you read, think about why Kingston made this choice.

Reading Strategy

Applying Background Information

Background information given in a book jacket, an introduction, or footnote can help you fully appreciate a literary work. In this textbook, you can gain such information from the author biography, the Prepare to Read pages, and the Background. As you read, record the information you learn from these features in a chart like the one shown.

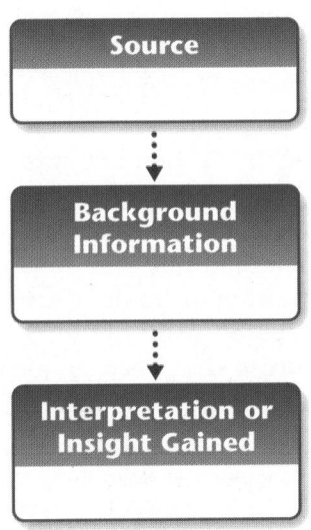

Vocabulary Development

hysterically (hi ster´ i klē) *adv.* in a highly emotional manner (p. 1071)

encampment (en kamp´ mənt) *n.* place where a person has set up camp (p. 1072)

inaudibly (in ôd´ ə blē) *adv.* in a manner that cannot be heard (p. 1074)

gravity (grav´ i tē) *n.* seriousness (p. 1075)

oblivious (ə bliv´ ē əs) *adj.* lacking all awareness (p. 1075)

from The Woman Warrior

Maxine Hong Kingston

Background

The *Woman Warrior* is an innovative memoir that attempts to capture the experience of growing up in a bicultural world—part Chinese, part American. To accomplish her purpose, Kingston mingles the narrative with "talk stories," tales full of magical events that she heard as a girl from her mother, Brave Orchid. The subtitle of the book, *Memoir of a Girlhood Among Ghosts*, refers both to white America, whose pale inhabitants remind Brave Orchid of ghosts, and to the family's ancestors in China. In this excerpt, Brave Orchid reunites with her sister, one of the ghosts of her past.

W hen she was about sixty-eight years old, Brave Orchid took a day off to wait at San Francisco International Airport for the plane that was bringing her sister to the United States. She had not seen Moon Orchid for thirty years. She had begun this waiting at home, getting up a half-hour before Moon Orchid's plane took off in Hong Kong.[1] Brave Orchid would add her will power to the forces that keep an airplane up. Her head hurt with the concentration. The plane had to be light, so no matter how tired she felt, she

---

1. **took off in Hong Kong** After mainland China fell to the Communists in the late 1940's, many native Chinese fled first to Hong Kong (a British colony until 1997) before emigrating to the United States.

dared not rest her spirit on a wing but continuously and gently pushed up on the plane's belly. She had already been waiting at the airport for nine hours. She was wakeful.

Next to Brave Orchid sat Moon Orchid's only daughter, who was helping her aunt wait. Brave Orchid had made two of her own children come too because they could drive, but they had been lured away by the magazine racks and the gift shops and coffee shops. Her American children could not sit for very long. They did not understand sitting; they had wandering feet. She hoped they would get back from the pay TV's or the pay toilets or wherever they were spending their money before the plane arrived. If they did not come back soon, she would go look for them. If her son thought he could hide in the men's room, he was wrong.

"Are you all right, Aunt?" asked her niece.

"No, this chair hurts me. Help me pull some chairs together so I can put my feet up."

She unbundled a blanket and spread it out to make a bed for herself. On the floor she had two shopping bags full of canned peaches, real peaches, beans wrapped in taro leaves,[2] cookies, Thermos bottles,[3] enough food for everybody, though only her niece would eat with her. Her bad boy and bad girl were probably sneaking hamburgers, wasting their money. She would scold them.

Many soldiers and sailors sat about, oddly calm, like little boys in cowboy uniforms. (She thought "cowboy" was what you would call a Boy Scout.) They should have been crying <u>hysterically</u> on their way to Vietnam.[4] "If I see one that looks Chinese," she thought, "I'll go over and give him some advice." She sat up suddenly; she had forgotten about her own son, who was even now in Vietnam. Carefully she split her attention, beaming half of it to the ocean, into the water to keep him afloat. He was on a ship. He was in Vietnamese waters. She was sure of it. He and the other children were lying to her. They had said he was in Japan, and then they said he was in the Philippines. But when she sent him her help, she could feel that he was on a ship in Da Nang.[5] Also she had seen the children hide the envelopes that his letters came in.

"Do you think my son is in Vietnam?" she asked her niece, who was dutifully eating.

"No. Didn't your children say he was in the Philippines?"

"Have you ever seen any of his letters with Philippine stamps on them?"

"Oh, yes. Your children showed me one."

Literary Analysis
Memoirs Whose impressions are described in this passage about "her American children"?

hysterically (hi ster´ i klē) adv. in a highly emotional manner

Reading Strategy
Applying Background Information How do footnotes 4 and 5 help to clarify this passage?

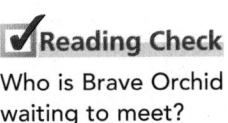
Reading Check
Who is Brave Orchid waiting to meet?

---

2. **taro** (te´ rō) **leaves** leaves of an edible tuberous plant widely eaten in Asia.
3. **Thermos** (thʉr´ məs) **bottles** insulated containers for holding liquids and keeping them warm or cold.
4. **Vietnam** southeast Asian nation where, in the late 1960s when this selection takes place, the U.S. had joined the conflict known as the Vietnam War (1954–1975).
5. **Da Nang** (da naŋ) city in central Vietnam that was the site of an important U.S. military base during the Vietnam War; also spelled Danang.

"I wouldn't put it past them to send the letters to some Filipino they know. He puts Manila[6] postmarks on them to fool me."

"Yes, I can imagine them doing that. But don't worry. Your son can take care of himself. All your children can take care of themselves."

"Not him. He's not like other people. Not normal at all. He sticks erasers in his ears, and the erasers are still attached to the pencil stubs. The captain will say, 'Abandon ship,' or 'Watch out for bombs,' and he won't hear. He doesn't listen to orders. I told him to flee to Canada,[7] but he wouldn't go."

She closed her eyes. After a short while, plane and ship under control, she looked again at the children in uniforms. Some of the blond ones looked like baby chicks, their crew cuts like the downy yellow on baby chicks. You had to feel sorry for them even though they were Army and Navy Ghosts.

Suddenly her son and daughter came running. "Come, Mother. The plane's landed early. She's here already." They hurried, folding up their mother's <u>encampment</u>. She was glad her children were not useless. They must have known what this trip to San Francisco was about then. "It's a good thing I made you come early," she said.

Brave Orchid pushed to the front of the crowd. She had to be in front. The passengers were separated from the people waiting for them by glass doors and walls. Immigration Ghosts were stamping papers. The travellers crowded along some conveyor belts to have their luggage searched. Brave Orchid did not see her sister anywhere. She stood watching for four hours. Her children left and came back. "Why don't you sit down?" they asked.

"The chairs are too far away," she said.

"Why don't you sit on the floor then?"

No, she would stand, as her sister was probably standing in a line she could not see from here. Her American children had no feelings and no memory.

To while away time, she and her niece talked about the Chinese passengers. These new immigrants had it easy. On Ellis Island[8] the people were thin after forty days at sea and had no fancy luggage.

"That one looks like her," Brave Orchid would say.

"No, that's not her."

Ellis Island had been made out of wood and iron. Here everything was new plastic, a ghost trick to lure immigrants into feeling safe and spilling their secrets. Then the Alien Office could send them right back. Otherwise, why did they lock her out, not letting her help her sister answer questions and spell her name? At Ellis Island when the ghost asked Brave Orchid what year her husband had cut off his

encampment (en kamp´ mənt) *n.* place where a person has set up camp

Reading Strategy
Applying Background Information What information in footnote 8 helps to clarify this passage?

---

6. **Manila** (mə nil´ ə) capital of the Philippines.
7. **flee to Canada** During the Vietnam War era, thousands of Americans fled to Canada to escape the military draft, even though such draft dodgers were subject to prosecution upon returning to the U.S.
8. **Ellis Island** island in the harbor off New York City that was the chief U.S. immigration station from 1892 to 1943.

pigtail, a Chinese who was crouching on the floor motioned her not to talk. "I don't know," she had said. If it weren't for that Chinese man, she might not be here today, or her husband either. She hoped some Chinese, a janitor or a clerk, would look out for Moon Orchid. Luggage conveyors fooled immigrants into thinking the Gold Mountain was going to be easy.

Brave Orchid felt her heart jump—Moon Orchid. "There she is," she shouted. But her niece saw it was not her mother at all. And it shocked her to discover the woman her aunt was pointing out. This was a young woman, younger than herself, no older than Moon Orchid the day the sisters parted. "Moon Orchid will have changed a little, of course," Brave Orchid was saying. "She will have learned to wear western clothes." The woman wore a navy blue suit with a bunch of dark cherries at the shoulder.

"No, Aunt," said the niece. "That's not my mother."

"Perhaps not. It's been so many years.

Yes, it is your mother. It must be. Let her come closer, and we can tell. Do you think she's too far away for me to tell, or is it my eyes getting bad?"

"It's too many years gone by," said the niece.

Brave Orchid turned suddenly—another Moon Orchid, this one a neat little woman with a bun. She was laughing at something the person ahead of her in line said. Moon Orchid was just like that, laughing at nothing. "I would be able to tell the difference if one of them would only come closer," Brave Orchid said with tears, which she did not wipe. Two children met the woman with the cherries, and she shook their hands. The other woman was met by a young man. They looked at each other gladly, then walked away side by side.

Up close neither one of those women looked like Moon Orchid at all. "Don't worry, Aunt," said the niece. "I'll know her."

"I'll know her too. I knew her before you did."

The niece said nothing, although she had seen her mother only five years ago. Her aunt liked having the last word.

Finally Brave Orchid's children quit wandering and drooped on a railing. Who knew what they were thinking? At last the niece called out, "I see her! I see her! Mother! Mother!" Whenever the doors parted, she shouted, probably embarrassing the American cousins, but she didn't care. She called out, "Mama! Mama!" until the crack in the sliding doors became too small to let in her voice. "Mama!" What a strange word in an adult voice. Many people turned to see what adult was calling, "Mama!" like a child. Brave Orchid saw an old, old woman jerk her head up, her little eyes blinking confusedly, a woman whose nerves leapt toward the sound anytime she heard "Mama!" Then she relaxed to her own business again. She was a tiny, tiny lady, very thin, with little fluttering hands, and her hair was in a gray knot. She was dressed in a gray wool suit; she wore pearls around

New American Voices

During the 1970s, two vigorous social movements—feminism and multiculturalism—had a major impact on American literature. For the first time, the writings of minority women began to appear in the mainstream press. In 1970, African American author Toni Cade Bambara published an influential anthology of fiction, nonfiction, and poetry entitled *The Black Woman*. In that same year, Toni Morrison, who would later win the 1993 Nobel Prize for literature, published her first novel, *The Bluest Eye*. When Maxine Hong Kingston's *The Woman Warrior* appeared in 1976, it represented yet another utterly new voice. In the decades to follow, these writings influenced the work of younger minority women, including Julia Alvarez, Sandra Cisneros, Amy Tan, and Gish Jen. Thus, a new sub-genre emerged, giving voice to women of all backgrounds and enriching the landscape of American literature.

✓ **Reading Check**

How does Moon Orchid's physical appearence compare with those of the women Brave Orchid mistakes for her sister?

her neck and in her earlobes. Moon Orchid *would* travel with her jewels showing. Brave Orchid momentarily saw, like a larger, younger outline around this old woman, the sister she had been waiting for. The familiar dim halo faded, leaving the woman so old, so gray. So old. Brave Orchid pressed against the glass. *That* old lady? Yes, that old lady facing the ghost who stamped her papers without questioning her was her sister. Then, without noticing her family, Moon Orchid walked smiling over to the Suitcase Inspector Ghost, who took her boxes apart, pulling out puffs of tissue. From where she was, Brave Orchid could not see what her sister had chosen to carry across the ocean. She wished her sister would look her way. Brave Orchid thought that if she were entering a new country, she would be at the windows. Instead Moon Orchid hovered over the unwrapping, surprised at each reappearance as if she were opening presents after a birthday party.

"Mama!" Moon Orchid's daughter kept calling. Brave Orchid said to her children, "Why don't you call your aunt too? Maybe she'll hear us if all of you call out together." But her children slunk away. Maybe that shame-face they so often wore was American politeness.

"Mama!" Moon Orchid's daughter called again, and this time her mother looked right at her. She left her bundles in a heap and came running. "Hey!" the Customs Ghost yelled at her. She went back to clear up her mess, talking <u>inaudibly</u> to her daughter all the while. Her daughter pointed toward Brave Orchid. And at last Moon Orchid looked at her—two old women with faces like mirrors.

inaudibly (in ôd′ə blē) *adv.* in a manner that cannot be heard

▼ **Critical Viewing**
How might life in the city of San Francisco, shown in this image, compare or contrast with life in Hong Kong from where Moon Orchid has just arrived? **[Compare and Contrast]**

Their hands reached out as if to touch the other's face, then returned to their own, the fingers checking the grooves in the forehead and along the sides of the mouth. Moon Orchid, who never understood the <u>gravity</u> of things, started smiling and laughing, pointing at Brave Orchid. Finally Moon Orchid gathered up her stuff, strings hanging and papers loose, and met her sister at the door, where they shook hands, <u>oblivious</u> to blocking the way.

"You're an old woman," said Brave Orchid.

"Aiaa. *You're* an old woman."

"But *you* are really old. Surely, you can't say that about me. I'm not old the way you're old."

"But you really are old. You're one year older than I am."

"Your hair is white and your face all wrinkled."

"You're so skinny."

"You're so fat."

"Fat women are more beautiful than skinny women."

The children pulled them out of the door-way. One of Brave Orchid's children brought the car from the parking lot, and

gravity (grav′ i tē) *n.* seriousness

oblivious (ə bliv′ ē əs) *adj.* lacking all awareness

☑**Reading Check**

Why is the reunion between Brave Orchid and her sister delayed?

the other heaved the luggage into the trunk. They put the two old ladies and the niece in the back seat. All the way home—across the Bay Bridge,[9] over the Diablo hills,[10] across the San Joaquin River[11] to the valley, the valley moon so white at dusk—all the way home, the two sisters exclaimed every time they turned to look at each other, "Aiaa! How old!"

Brave Orchid forgot that she got sick in cars, that all vehicles but palanquins[12] made her dizzy. "You're so old," she kept saying. "How did you get so old?"

Brave Orchid had tears in her eyes. But Moon Orchid said, "You look older than I. You *are* older than I," and again she'd laugh. "You're wearing an old mask to tease me." It surprised Brave Orchid that after thirty years she could still get annoyed at her sister's silliness.

---

9. **Bay Bridge** one of the bridges across San Francisco Bay.
10. **Diablo** (dē äb′ lō) **hills** hills outside San Francisco.
11. **San Joaquin** (wô kēn′) **River** river of central California; its valley is one of the state's richest agricultural areas.
12. **palanquins** (pal′ ən kēnz′) hand-carried covered litters once widely used to transport people in China and elsewhere in eastern Asia.

Review and Assess

Thinking About the Selection

1. **Respond:** With which character do you identify the most? Why?

2. **(a) Recall:** Identify the family members waiting for Moon Orchid at the airport, and briefly describe each one's behavior. **(b) Interpret:** What do Brave Orchid's thoughts about her children's behavior reveal about her?

3. **(a) Recall:** What two things does Brave Orchid try to keep safe by applying her willpower? **(b) Connect:** What does this behavior reveal about Brave Orchid's worldview?

4. **(a) Interpret:** What is Brave Orchid's main impression when she finally sees Moon Orchid? **(b) Draw Conclusions:** When the two sisters finally meet, why do they speak to each other as they do?

5. **(a) Infer:** What seems to be Brave Orchid's attitude toward America and American culture? **(b) Apply:** What does this selection suggest about the conflicts that face immigrants and the children of immigrants in America?

6. **Evaluate:** Do you think Kingston succeeds in evoking the lives of people from very different cultures? Explain your answer.

Review and Assess

Literary Analysis

Memoirs

1. Using a chart like the one shown, list details to show how this **memoir** incorporates historical details with personal ones.

Historical Details	Personal Details

2. (a) Cite two memories Brave Orchid has while waiting at the airport. (b) Are these memories typical features of a memoir? Why or why not?

3. Explain how a memoir such as Kingston's could be meaningful to many women growing up in a bicultural world.

Connecting Literary Elements

4. Whose impressions provide the **third-person limited narration** of this excerpt?

5. Brave Orchid is Kingston's mother. (a) What role does Kingston herself play in this excerpt? (b) What techniques more commonly found in fiction does Kingston use to create her mother as a literary character?

6. How might Brave Orchid's story have been different if the narrative had been written with her voice, using *I* instead of *she*? Explain.

Reading Strategy

Applying Background Information

7. (a) From what province in China might Moon Orchid be coming? (b) What evidence did you use to draw your conclusion?

8. What does the narrator mean by (a) Army and Navy Ghosts? (b) Customs Ghosts?

9. (a) Where might the family be headed in the last paragraphs? (b) How do you know?

Extend Understanding

10. **Social Studies Connection:** Immigration brings with it the time-less struggle between tradition and change. Choose a culture—your own or another—and discuss the conflicts that people of this culture are likely to face when they come to live in America.

Integrate Language Skills

Vocabulary Development Lesson

Word Analysis: Latin Root -aud-

The Latin word root -aud- indicates "hearing" or "sound." The adverb *inaudibly* means "in a tone too low to be heard." Explain how the meaning of the root is connected to each of these words.

1. audiocassette
2. auditory
3. auditorium
4. audition

Spelling Strategy

When adding the suffix *-ly* or *-less* to a word ending in *l*, or when adding *-ness* to a word ending in *n*, keep all the letters of the base word. For example, *tail* becomes *tailless*.

Add *-ly*, *-less*, or *-ness* to each word in italics to create a new word that fits the clue.

1. happening all of a *sudden*
2. with *hysterical* feelings

Fluency: Sentence Completion

Review the vocabulary list on page 1069. Then, copy each sentence, replacing the blank with the appropriate word.

1. We left our homey ___?___ and hiked up the mountain.

2. ___?___ to the clock, she worked on into the night.

3. When she replied ___?___, I asked her to speak up.

4. The boy yelled ___?___ when he thought he was lost.

5. The ___?___ of the situation silenced all bickering.

Grammar Lesson

Punctuating a Quotation Within a Quotation

For clarity, use single quotation marks to enclose a quotation within a quotation.

> **Example:** "The captain will say, 'Abandon ship,' or 'Watch out for bombs,' and he won't hear."

Remember to also place commas and periods inside closing quotation marks, but keep colons, and semicolons outside. Question marks and exclamation points can be placed either inside or outside the quotation marks, depending on the words to which they apply.

Practice Copy this paragraph about the characters in *The Woman Warrior*, adding all the missing single quotation marks.

> "My sister wrote, I am coming to America," Brave Orchid told her family. "She asked, Will you be able to pick me up? I told her, Yes, I will leave my house before your plane takes off from Hong Kong. Do you think she knows I am excited?"

Writing Application Write a second paragraph in which Brave Orchid quotes her sister. Use single quotation marks to indicate quotations within quotations. Punctuate according to the rules that apply.

WG Prentice Hall Writing and Grammar Connection: Chapter 27, Section 4

Writing Lesson

Character Analysis

In an essay, analyze Brave Orchid's character. Identify three or four of her personality traits, and connect them to her background and behavior. Cite appropriate supporting examples from the selection.

Prewriting List Brave Orchid's character traits, using such words as *bossy* or *nervous*. Next to each trait, note the background, attitudes, and behaviors connected with them. Then, select the traits you will write about.

Drafting In the first paragraph of your essay, introduce Brave Orchid and *The Woman Warrior*. Include information about where she was born, her culture, her emigration to America, and her character. In the body paragraphs of your essay, address each one of those elements.

Revising Highlight Brave Orchid's character traits and be sure you have connected them with her behaviors. To do so, cite examples from the selection.

Model: Revising to Provide Support

Because of her hard life, Brave Orchid was skeptical about American conveniences. *For example, she felt that the luggage conveyors at American airports fooled immigrants into thinking life would be much easier here.*

> Added information from the selection supports a specific idea.

Prentice Hall Writing and Grammar Connection: Chapter 28, Section 3

Extension Activities

Listening and Speaking When *The Woman Warrior* won a 1976 award for nonfiction, many debated whether or not it fit that category. Hold a **panel discussion** to address the issue. Use the following tips:

- Identify criteria to determine whether the work fits the definition of nonfiction.
- Quote Kingston's own comments on the topic.

Present the discussion, inviting questions from classmates. **[Group Activity]**

Research and Technology Conduct research to prepare a written **immigration report** about the arrival of Chinese immigrants in the United States. Find at least two historical records to analyze. Supplement your report with a chart of statistical information. Present your findings to your class.

 Take It to the Net www.phschool.com

Go online for an additional research activity using the Internet.

Prepare to Read

Antojos

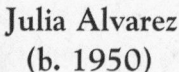

Julia Alvarez
(b. 1950)

Julia Alvarez was born in New York City but raised in the Dominican Republic. When her father's involvement in a plot to overthrow that country's dictator, Rafael Trujillo, was uncovered, the family was forced to flee to the United States. It was 1960. When Alvarez arrived in the United States, she spoke only Spanish and had few friends. "I came into English as a ten-year-old from the Dominican Republic, and I consider this radical uprooting from my culture, my native language, my country, the reason I began writing," Alvarez once explained.

Writing to Ease the Pain While moving to a new country changed her life forever, Alvarez quickly found her voice as a writer. She said, "I landed, not in the United States, but in the English language. That became my new home . . . which you never had to lose, because it was a portable homeland." As a young adult, Alvarez found that writing helped her deal with the pain of adjustment to a new culture and language. "In high school, I fell in love with how words can make you feel complete in a way that I hadn't felt complete since leaving the island," she said. Alvarez found herself turning more and more to writing "as the one place where I felt I belonged and could make sense of myself, my life, all that was happening to me."

After graduating from college, where she was awarded several poetry prizes, Alvarez earned a masters degree in creative writing at Syracuse University. She went on to join the Kentucky Arts Commission's poetry-in-the-schools program. For two years, she traveled around Kentucky teaching poetry. She then held a variety of teaching jobs before settling in Vermont as a Professor of English at Middlebury College.

Writing to Understand For Alvarez, writing "is happening all the time. When you go outside and you see the way a blade of grass bends in the breeze—when you're a writer, you're thinking about how that's happening." She also says that writing "is a way to understand yourself. You learn how you feel about things, but you're also making your little statement about things, and that makes you feel a little bit more powerful."

Alvarez's poetry often focuses on her personal experiences and on details of daily life as well as her Caribbean heritage. She has published two volumes of poetry, *Homecoming* (1984) and *The Other Side* (1995).

A Storytelling Tradition After *Homecoming* was published, Alvarez began to focus on a new area of writing: fiction. "My own island background was steeped in a tradition of storytelling that I wanted to explore in prose," Alvarez explained. The move to prose proved fruitful, for Alvarez has won fame for three novels rooted in Hispanic American tradition: *How the García Girls Lost Their Accents* (1991), *In the Time of the Butterflies* (1994), and *¡Yo!* (1997). Her fiction, like her poetry, can be viewed as semi-autobiographical, dealing with both the immigrant experience and her own bicultural identity.

As the story "Antojos" illustrates, Alvarez has also shown that she is a talented short-story writer. Like her novels, "Antojos" relates the story of a Dominican woman who has settled in the United States. The story captures what happens when she revisits her homeland and confronts the culture she had left behind.

Preview

Connecting to the Literature

If you have ever felt vulnerable in the presence of strangers whose motives might be questionable, you will understand how the main character in this story feels. Read to discover if her fears are justified.

Literary Analysis

Plot

Plot is the sequence of events in a literary work. In most narrative literature, the plot involves characters and a central conflict. Most plots follow a specific sequence, often referred to as the dramatic arc:

- **Exposition:** The basic situation is introduced.
- **Inciting incident:** The central conflict or struggle is revealed.
- **Development:** The conflict increases in intensity.
- **Climax:** The conflict reaches its most intense point.
- **Denouement:** Information is given about events that occur after the climax.
- **Resolution:** The story ends with details that reveal insight.

Plot events that lead up to the climax comprise the rising action. The events that follow the climax comprise the falling action.

Connecting Literary Elements

A **flashback** is an interruption in the chronological presentation of events in a story. Writers use flashbacks to highlight a scene or event from an earlier time, thus providing valuable information about the characters' backgrounds, personalities, and motives. When you come to a flashback in "Antojos," consider what it reveals about the character and her situation.

Reading Strategy

Identifying With a Character

You can often understand literature better if you **identify with a character** who appears in the work. Think about what you and the character have in common. For example, as you read "Antojos," note qualities you share with the main character, Yolanda. List similarities in a chart like the one shown.

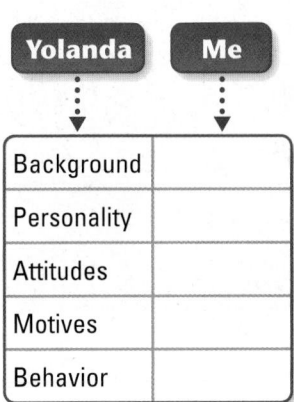

Vocabulary Development

dissuade (di swād´) *v.* convince someone not to do something (p. 1084)

loath (lōth) *adj.* reluctant (p. 1086)

appease (ə pēz´) *v.* satisfy (p. 1087)

machetes (mə shet´ ēz) *n.* large heavy knives with broad blades (p. 1088)

collusion (kə lōō´ zhən) *n.* secret agreement; conspiracy (p. 1089)

docile (däs´ əl) *adj.* easy to direct or manage; obedient (p. 1089)

enunciated (ē nun´ sē āt´ əd) *v.* pronounced; stated precisely (p. 1091)

Antojos[1]

JULIA ALVAREZ

Fruit Vendor, 1951, Olga Costa, Museo de Arte Moderno, Mexico

▲ **Critical Viewing** What elements of this artist's portrayal of fruit mirror Yolanda's feelings about guavas? **[Compare]**

---

1. **Antojos** (än tō´ hōs) Spanish for "cravings." The story explores the additional connotations of the word.

Background

Alvarez's homeland, the Dominican Republic, won independence in 1844 after a successful rebellion against Haitian rule. Since then, however, the country has suffered through several dictatorships and frequent foreign domination. One of the most ruthless dictators was Rafael Trujillo, who ruled the country from 1930 until he was assassinated in 1961. Julia Alvarez's father was part of the underground movement against Trujillo, and it was this involvement that forced the Alvarez family to flee the country. Three months after the family left, three of her father's co-conspirators were killed. Alvarez's emigration experience and her feelings of displacement and exile have influenced much of her writing, including the story that appears here.

For the first time since Yolanda had reached the hills, there was a shoulder on the left side of the narrow road. She pulled the car over out of a sense of homecoming: every other visit she had stayed with her family in the capital.

Once her own engine was off, she heard the sound of another motor, approaching, a pained roar as if the engine were falling apart. She made out an undertow of men's voices. Quickly, she got back into the car, locked the door, and pulled off the shoulder, hugging her right side of the road.

—Just in time too. A bus came lurching around the curve, obscuring her view with a belching of exhaust, the driver saluting or warning with a series of blasts on his horn. It was an old army bus, the official name brushed over with paint that didn't quite match the regulation gray. The passengers saw her only at the last moment, and all up and down her side of the bus, men poked out of the windows, hooting and yelling, waving purple party flags, holding out bottles and beckoning to her. She speeded up and left them behind, the small compact climbing easily up the snakey highway, its well-oiled hum a gratifying sound after the hullabaloo of the bus.

She tried the radio again, but all she could tune to was static even here on the summit hills. She would have to wait until she got to the coast to hear news of the hunger march in the capital. Her family had been worried that trouble would break out, for the march had been scheduled on the anniversary of the failed revolution nineteen years ago today. A huge turnout was expected. She bet that bus she had just passed had been delayed by breakdowns on its way to the capital. In fact, earlier on the road when she had first set out, Yolanda had passed buses and truckloads of men, drinking and shouting slogans. It crossed her mind that her family had finally agreed to loan her a car because they knew she'd be far safer on the north coast than in the capital city where revolutions always broke out.

The hills began to plane out into a high plateau, the road widening. Left and right, roadside stands began appearing. Yolanda slowed

Literary Analysis

Plot In this opening paragraph, what do you learn about the story's basic situation, including the character and setting?

✔**Reading Check**

What political event is occurring in the city as Yolanda drives into the hills?

down and kept an eye out for guavas, supposedly in season this far north. Piled high on wooden stands were fruits she hadn't seen in so many years: pinkish-yellow mangoes, and tamarind pods oozing their rich sap, and small cashew fruits strung on a rope to keep them from bruising each other. There were little brown packets of roasted cashews and bars of milk fudge wrapped in waxed paper and tied with a string, the color of which told what filling was inside the bar. Strips of meat, buzzing with flies, hung from the windows of butcher stalls. An occasional display of straw hats and baskets and hammocks told that tourists sometimes did pass by here. Looking at the stores spread before her, it was hard to believe the poverty the organizers of the march kept discussing on the radio. There seemed to be plenty here to eat—except for guavas.

In the capital, her aunts had plied her with what she most craved after so many years away. "Any little *antojo,* you must tell us!" They wanted to spoil her, so she'd stay on in her nativeland before she forgot where she had come from. "What exactly does it mean, *antojo?*" Yolanda asked. Her aunts were proven right: After so many years away, their niece was losing her Spanish.

"An *antojo*—" The aunts exchanged quizzical looks. "How to put it? An *antojo* is like a craving for something you have to eat."

A cousin blew out her cheeks. "Calories."

An *antojo,* one of the older aunts continued, was a very old Spanish word from before "your United States was thought of," she added tartly. In the countryside some *campesinos*[2] still used the word to mean possession by an island spirit demanding its due.

Her island spirit certainly was a patient soul, Yolanda joked. She hadn't had her favorite *antojo,* guavas, since her last trip seven years ago. Well, on this trip, her aunts promised, Yoyo could eat guavas to her heart's content. But when the gardener was summoned, he wasn't so sure. Guavas were no longer in season, at least not in the hotter lowlands of the south. Maybe up north, the chauffeur could pick her up some on his way back from some errand. Yolanda took this opportunity to inform her aunts of her plans: she could pick the guavas herself when she went up north in a few days.

—She was going up north? By herself? A woman alone on the road! "This is not the States." Her old aunts had tried to <u>dissuade</u> her. "Anything can happen." When Yolanda challenged them, "What?" they came up with boogeymen stories that made her feel as if she were talking to china dolls.[3] Haitian hougans[4] and Communist kidnappers. "And Martians?" Yolanda wanted to tease them. They had led such sheltered lives, riding from one safe place to another in their air-conditioned cars.

<hr/>

2. *campesinos* (käm´ pe sē´ nōs) "poor farmers; simple rural dwellers" (Spanish).
3. **china dolls** old-fashioned, delicate dolls made of fragile high-quality porcelain or ceramic ware.
4. **Haitian hougans** (ŌŌ gänz´) voodoo priests or cult leaders.

Literary Analysis
Plot and Flashback What information about Yolanda and her family is conveyed in this flashback?

dissuade (di swād´) *v.* convince someone not to do something

She had left the fruit stands behind her and was approaching a compound very much like her family's in the capital. The underbrush stopped abruptly at a high concrete wall, topped with broken bottle glass. Parked at the door was a chocolate brown Mercedes. Perhaps the owners had come up to their country home for the weekend to avoid the troubles in the capital?

Just beyond the estate, Yolanda came upon a small village— ALTAMIRA in rippling letters on the corrugated tin roof of the first little house. It was a little cluster of houses on either side of the road, a good place to stretch her legs before what she'd heard was a steep and slightly (her aunts had warned "very") dangerous descent to the coast. Yolanda pulled up at a cantina, the thatched roof held up by several posts. Instead of a menu, there was a yellowing, grimy poster for Palmolive soap tacked on one of the posts with a picture of a blonde woman under a spraying shower, her head thrown back in seeming ecstasy, her mouth opened in a wordless cry. ("Palmolive"? Yolanda wondered.) She felt even thirstier and grimier looking at this lathered beauty after her hot day on the road.

An old woman emerged at last from a shack behind the cabana, buttoning up a torn housedress, and followed closely by a little boy, who kept ducking behind her whenever Yolanda smiled at him. Asking him his name just drove him further into the folds of the old woman's skirt.

"You must excuse him, Doña,"[5] she apologized. "He's not used to being among people." But Yolanda knew the old woman meant, not the people in the village, but the people with money who drove through Altamira to the beaches on the coast. "Your name," the old woman repeated, as if Yolanda hadn't asked him in Spanish. The little boy mumbled at the ground. "Speak up!" the old woman scolded, but her voice betrayed pride when she spoke up for him. "This little know-nothing is Jose Duarte Sanchez y Mella Garcia."

Yolanda laughed. Not only were those a lot of names for such a little boy, but they certainly were momentous: the surnames of the three liberators of the country!

"Can I serve the Doña in any way?" the woman asked. Yolanda gave the tree line beyond the woman's shack a glance. "You think you might have some guavas around?"

The old woman's face scrunched up. "Guavas?" she murmured and thought to herself a second. "Why, they're all around, Doña. But I can't say as I've seen any."

---

5. **Doña** (dō′ nyä) "Madam" (Spanish)

Literature in context History Connection

The Dominican Republic

Located in the West Indies, and occupying an area of 18,800 square miles, the Dominican Republic takes up the eastern two thirds of the island of Hispaniola. The country is bounded on the north by the Atlantic Ocean; on the east, by the Mona Passage, which separates it from Puerto Rico; on the south, by the Caribbean Sea; and on the west, by Haiti.

In Alvarez's story, Yolanda begins her journey in Santo Domingo, the capital city. Located on the country's southern coast, Santo Domingo was founded in 1496, four years after Christopher Columbus landed on the island. Yolanda's journey takes her into the Cordillera Central Range, which includes Pico Duarte, the highest mountain in the Caribbean at a height of 3,175 meters (over 10,000 feet). The slopes of many of these mountains are covered with dense semi-tropical forests, like those in which Yolanda searches for guavas.

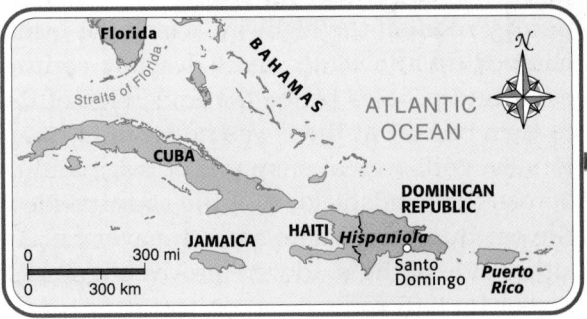

Reading Check

Who does Yolanda meet at the roadside cantina?

"With your permission—" Jose Duarte had joined a group of little boys who had come out of nowhere and were milling around the car, boasting how many automobiles they had ridden in. At Yolanda's mention of guavas, he sprung forward, pointing across the road towards the summit of the western hills. "I know where there's a whole grove of them." Behind him, his little companions nodded.

"Go on, then!" His grandmother stamped her foot as if she were scatting a little animal. "Get the Doña some."

A few boys dashed across the road and disappeared up a steep path on the hillside, but before Jose could follow, Yolanda called him back. She wanted to go along too. The little boy looked towards his grandmother, unsure of what to think. The old woman shook her head. The Doña would get hot, her nice clothes would get all dirty. Jose would get the Doña as many guavas as she was wanting.

"But they taste so much better when you've picked them yourself," Yolanda's voice had an edge, for suddenly, it was as if the woman had turned into the long arm of her family, keeping her away from seeing her country on her own.

The few boys who had stayed behind with Jose had congregated around the car. Each one claimed to be guarding it for the Doña. It occurred to Yolanda that there was a way to make this a treat all the way around. "What do you say we take the car?"

"*Sí, Sí, Sí*,"[6] the boys screamed in a riot of excitement.

The old woman hushed them but agreed that was not a bad idea if the Doña insisted on going. There was a dirt road up ahead she could follow a ways and then cross over onto the road that was paved all the way to the coffee barns. The woman pointed south in the direction of the big house. Many workers took that short cut to work.

They piled into the car, half a dozen boys in the back, and Jose as co-pilot in the passenger seat beside Yolanda. They turned onto a bumpy road off the highway, which got bumpier and bumpier, and climbed up into wilder, more desolate country. Branches scraped the sides and pebbles pelted the underside of the car. Yolanda wanted to turn back, but there was no room to maneuver the car around. Finally, with a great snapping of twigs and thrashing of branches across the windshield, as if the countryside were <u>loath</u> to release them, the car burst forth onto smooth pavement and the light of day. On either side of the road were groves of guava trees. Among them, the boys who had gone ahead on foot were already pulling down branches and shaking loose a rain of guavas. The fruit was definitely in season.

For the next hour or so, Yolanda and her crew scavenged the grove, the best of the pick going into the beach basket Yolanda had gotten out of the trunk, with the exception of the ones she ate right on the spot, relishing the slightly bumpy feel of the skin in her hand, devouring the crunchy, sweet, white meat. The boys watched her, surprised by her odd hunger.

---

6. *Sí, Sí, Sí* (sē) "Yes, Yes, Yes" (Spanish).

Reading Strategy
Identifying With a Character Can you identify with Yolanda's feelings as she responds to the old woman? Why or why not?

loath (lōth) *adj.* reluctant

▶ **Critical Viewing**
Do you think the people in this picture have more in common with Yolanda and her family or with the people she meets in the mountains? Explain. **[Analyze]**

Yolanda and Jose, partners, wandered far from the path that cut through the grove. Soon they were bent double to avoid getting entangled in the thick canopy of branches overhead. Each addition to the basket caused a spill from the stash already piled high above the brim. Finally, it was a case of abandoning the treasure in order to cart some of it home. With Jose hugging the basket to himself and Yolanda parting the wayward branches in front of them, they headed back toward the car.

When they finally cleared the thicket of guava branches, the sun was low on the western horizon. There was no sign of the other boys. "They must have gone to round up the goats," Jose observed.

Yolanda glanced at her watch: it was past six o'clock. She'd never make the north coast by nightfall, but at least she could get off the dangerous mountain roads while it was still light. She hurried Jose back to the car, where they found a heap of guavas the other boys had left behind on the shoulder of the road. Enough guavas to <u>appease</u> even the greediest island spirit for life!

They packed the guavas in the trunk quickly and climbed in, but the car had not gone a foot before it lurched forward with a horrible hobble. Yolanda closed her eyes and laid her head down on the wheel, then glanced over at Jose. The way his eyes were searching

appease (ə pēz´) *v.* satisfy

✔**Reading Check**

What do Jose and his friends help Yolanda to gather?

the inside of the car for a clue as to what could have happened, she could tell he didn't know how to change a flat tire either.

It was no use regretting having brought the car up that bad stretch of road. The thing to do now was to act quickly. Soon the sun would set and night would fall swiftly, no lingering dusk as in the States. She explained to Jose that they had a flat tire and had to hike back to town and send for help down the road to the big house. Whoever tended to the brown Mercedes would know how to change the tire on her car.

"With your permission," Jose offered meekly. He pointed down the paved road. "This goes directly to the big house." The Doña could just wait in the car and he would be back in no time with someone from the Miranda place.

She did not like the idea of staying behind in the car, but Jose could probably go and come back much quicker without her. "All right," she said to the boy. "I'll tell you what." She pointed to her watch. It was almost six thirty. "If you're back by the time this hand is over here, I'll give you"—she held up one finger "a dollar." The boy's mouth fell open. In no time, he had shot out of his side of the car and was headed at a run toward the Miranda place. Yolanda climbed out as well and walked down a pace, until the boy had disappeared in one of the turnings of the road.

Suddenly, the countryside was so very quiet. She looked up at the purple sky. A breeze was blowing through the grove, rustling the leaves, so they whispered like voices, something indistinct. Here and there a light flickered on the hills, a *campesino* living out his solitary life. This was what she had been missing without really knowing that she was missing it all these years. She had never felt at home in the States, never, though she knew she was lucky to have a job, so she could afford her own life and not be run by her family. But independence didn't have to be exile. She could come home, home to places like these very hills, and live here on her own terms.

Heading back to the car, Yolanda stopped. She had heard footsteps in the grove. Could Jose be back already? Branches were being thrust aside, twigs snapped. Suddenly, a short, dark man, and then a slender, light-skin man emerged from a footpath on the opposite side of the grove from the one she and Jose had scavenged. They wore ragged work clothes stained with patches of sweat; their faces were drawn and tired. Yolanda's glance fell on the <u>machetes</u> that hung from their belts.

The men's faces snapped awake from their stupor at the sight of her. They looked beyond her at the car. "Yours?" the darker man spoke first. It struck her, even then, as an absurd question. Who else's would it be here in the middle of nowhere?

"Is there some problem?" the darker man spoke up again. The taller one was looking her up and down with interest. They were now both in front of her on the road, blocking her escape. Both—she had looked them up and down as well—were strong and quite capable of catching her if she made a run for the Miranda's. Not that she could have moved, for her legs seemed suddenly to have been hammered

machetes (mə shet′ ēz) *n.* large heavy knives with broad blades

into the ground beneath her. She thought of explaining that she was just out for a drive before dinner at the big house, so that these men would think someone knew where she was, someone would come looking for her if they tried to carry her off. But she found she could not speak. Her tongue felt as if it'd been stuffed in her mouth like a rag to keep her quiet.

The men exchanged a look—it seemed to Yolanda of <u>collusion</u>. Then the shorter, darker one spoke up again, "Señorita,[7] are you all right?" He peered at her. The darkness of his complexion in the growing darkness of the evening made it difficult to distinguish an expression. He was no taller than Yolanda, but he gave the impression of being quite large, for he was broad and solid, like something not yet completely carved out of a piece of wood. His companion was tall and of a rich honey-brown color that matched his honey-brown eyes. Anywhere else, Yolanda would have found him extremely attractive, but here on a lonely road, with the sky growing darker by seconds, his good looks seemed dangerous, a lure to catch her off her guard.

"Can we help you?" the shorter man repeated.

The handsome one smiled knowingly. Two long, deep dimples appeared like gashes on either side of his mouth. "*Americana*," he said to the other in Spanish, pointing to the car. "She doesn't understand."

The darker man narrowed his eyes and studied Yolanda a moment. "*Americana?*" he asked her as if not quite sure what to make of her.

She had been too frightened to carry out any strategy, but now a road was opening before her. She laid her hand on her chest—she could feel her pounding heart—and nodded. Then, as if the admission itself loosened her tongue, she explained in English how it came that she was on a back road by herself, her craving for guavas, her never having learned to change a flat. The two men stared at her, uncomprehendingly, rendered <u>docile</u> by her gibberish. Strangely enough, it soothed her to hear herself speaking something they could not understand. She thought of something her teacher used to say to her when as a young immigrant girl she was learning English, "Language is power." It was her only defense now.

Yolanda made the motions of pumping. The darker man looked at the other, who had shown better luck at understanding the foreign lady. But his companion shrugged, baffled as well. "I'll show you," Yolanda waved for them to follow her. And suddenly, as if after pulling and pulling at roots, she had finally managed to yank them free of the soil they had clung to, she found she could move her own feet forward to the car.

The small group stood staring at the sagging tire a moment, the two men kicking at it as if punishing it for having failed the Señorita. They squatted by the passenger's side, conversing in low tones. Yolanda led them to the rear of the car, where the men lifted the spare out of its sunken nest—then set to work, fitting the interlocking pieces of the

---

7. **Señorita** (se´ nyō rē´ tä) "Miss" (Spanish).

collusion (kə lōō´ zhən) *n.* secret agreement; conspiracy

Literary Analysis
Plot In what ways is Yolanda's conflict growing more intense and complex?

docile (däs´ əl) *adj.* easy to direct or manage; obedient

**Reading Check**
What does Yolanda pretend when she is approached by the two men?

jack, unpacking the tools from the deeper hollows of the trunk. They laid their machetes down on the side of the road, out of the way. Yolanda turned on the headlights to help them see in the growing darkness. Above the small group, the sky was purple with twilight.

There was a problem with the jack. It squeaked and labored, but the car would not rise. The shorter man squirmed his way underneath and placed the mechanism deeper under the bowels of the car. There, he pumped vigorously, his friend bracing him by holding him down by the ankles. Slowly, the car rose until the wheel hung suspended. When the man came out from under the car, his hand was bloody where his knuckles had scraped against the pavement.

Yolanda pointed to the man's hand. She had been sure that if any blood were going to be spilled tonight, it would be hers. She offered him the towel she kept draped on her car seat to absorb her perspiration. But he waved it away and sucked his knuckles to make the bleeding stop.

Once the flat had been replaced with the spare, the two men lifted the deflated tire into the trunk and put away the tools. They handed Yolanda her keys. There was still no sign of Jose and the Miranda's.

▲ Critical Viewing
In what ways might these boys' reactions to the photographer taking their picture be similar to Jose's reaction to Yolanda in the story?
[Connect]

Yolanda was relieved. As she had waited, watching the two men hard at work, she had begun to dread the boy's return with help. The two men would realize she spoke Spanish. It was too late to admit that she had tricked them, to explain she had done so only because she thought her survival was on the line. The least she could do now was to try and repay them, handsomely, for their trouble.

"I'd like to give you something," she began reaching for the purse she'd retrieved from the trunk. The English words sounded hollow on her tongue. She rolled up a couple of American bills and offered them to the men. The shorter man held up his hand. Yolanda could see where the blood had dried dark streaks on his palm. "No, no, Señorita. *Nuestro placer.*"[8] Our pleasure.

Yolanda turned to the other man, who had struck her as more pliant than his sterner companion. "Please," she urged the bills on him. But he too looked down at the ground with the bashfulness she had observed in Jose of country people not wanting to offend. She felt the poverty of her response and stuffed the bills quickly into his pocket.

The two men picked up their machetes and raised them to their shoulders like soldiers their guns. The tall man motioned towards the big house. "*Directo, directo,*"[9] he <u>enunciated</u> the words carefully. Yolanda looked in the direction of his hand. In the faint light of what was left of day, she could barely make out the road ahead. It was as if the guava grove had overgrown into the road and woven its mat of branches so securely and tightly in all directions, she would not be able to escape.

But finally, she was off! While the two men waited a moment on the shoulder to see if the tire would hold, Yolanda drove a few yards, poking her head out the window before speeding up. "*Gracias!*"[10] she called, and they waved, appreciatively, at the foreign lady making an effort in their native tongue. When she looked for them in her rear-view mirror, they had disappeared into the darkness of the guava grove.

Just ahead, her lights described the figure of a small boy: Jose was walking alone, listlessly, as if he did not particularly want to get to where he was going.

Yolanda leaned over and opened the door for him. The small overhead light came on; she saw that the boy's face was streaked with tears.

"Why, what's wrong, Jose?"

The boy swallowed hard. "They would not come. They didn't believe me." He took little breaths between words to keep his tears at bay. He had lost his chance at a whole dollar. "And the guard, he said if I didn't stop telling stories, he was going to whip me."

"What did you tell him, Jose?"

"I told him you had broken your car and you needed help fixing it."

---

8. *Nuestro placer* (noō es´ trō plä ser´) "Our pleasure" (Spanish).
9. *Directo, directo* (dē rek´ tō) "Straight, straight" (Spanish).
10. *Gracias* (grä´ sē äs) "Thank you" (Spanish).

Literary Analysis

Plot Is Yolanda's problem fully addressed now that the men have fixed her tire? What is still unresolved?

enunciated (ē nun´ sē āt´ əd) v. pronounced; stated precisely

✓ Reading Check

What do the two men do to help Yolanda?

She should have gone along with Jose to the Miranda's. Given all the trouble in the country, they would be suspicious of a boy coming to their door at nightfall with some story about a lady on a back road with a broken car. "Don't you worry, Jose," Yolanda patted the boy. She could feel the bony shoulder through the thin fabric of his worn shirt. "You can still have your dollar. You did your part."

But the shame of being suspected of lying seemed to have obscured any immediate pleasure he might feel in her offer. Yolanda tried to distract him by asking what he would buy with his money, what he most craved, thinking that on a subsequent trip, she might bring him his little *antojo*. But Jose Duarte Sanchez y Mella said nothing, except a bashful thank you when she left him off at the cantina with his promised dollar. In the glow of the headlights, Yolanda made out the figure of the old woman in the black square of her doorway, waving good-bye. Above the picnic table on a near post, the Palmolive woman's skin shone; her head was thrown back, her mouth opened as if she were calling someone over a great distance.

Review and Assess

Thinking About the Selection

1. **Respond:** Did this story surprise you in any way? Explain.

2. **(a) Recall:** What warnings do her aunts give Yolanda before she starts on her journey? **(b) Interpret:** How do these warnings anticipate, or foreshadow, Yolanda's experiences on her trip?

3. **(a) Recall:** With what emotions do her aunts react to Yolanda's announcement that she plans to drive north on her own? **(b) Compare and Contrast:** In what ways is Yolanda different from her aunts? **(c) Speculate:** What factors might account for the differences between Yolanda and her aunts?

4. **(a) Recall:** What are *antojos*? **(b) Connect:** What theme does the title of the story stress?

5. **(a) Recall:** How does the boy Jose react to Yolanda's promise of a dollar? **(b) Infer:** What is suggested about the country's political situation by the idea of a "hunger march" taking place in the capital? **(c) Analyze:** What role do issues of money and social inequity play in this story?

6. **(a) Interpret:** When Yolanda first sees the two men what emotions does she experience? **(b) Analyze:** Why does Yolanda pretend not to speak Spanish?

7. **(a) Evaluate:** Does Yolanda learn or grow in the story? Explain. **(b) Speculate:** How might Yolanda describe her experiences to her family when she returns from her trip?

Review and Assess

Literary Analysis

Plot

1. Use a chart like the one shown to analyze the **plot** and answer the following questions: (a) What events in the story form the rising action? (b) What events form the falling action? (c) What is the story's main conflict? (d) How does it resolve?

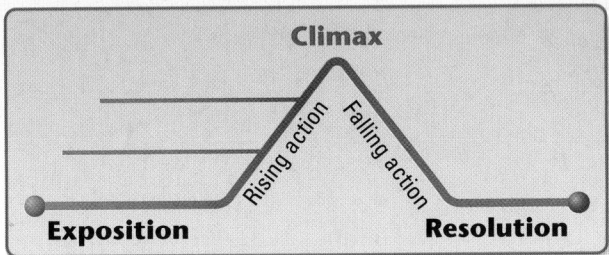

2. In what ways does the story's central conflict mirror other, deeper conflicts that may not be so easily resolved?

Connecting Literary Elements

3. (a) What does the **flashback** to Yolanda's visit with her aunts reveal about her family's social and economic circumstances? (b) What does the flashback reveal about Yolanda's reasons for traveling north?

4. (a) How else might Alvarez have conveyed the information given in the flashback? (b) Is her use of flashback more or less effective than another technique might be? Explain.

Reading Strategy

Identifying With a Character

5. (a) Examine Yolanda's attitudes and behavior toward her aunts, Jose, and the two men who approach her. (b) Do you **identify** with Yolanda in her dealings with these people? Explain.

6. (a) What information about the country's political turmoil adds to the weight of Yolanda's feelings about the two men? (b) How might her aunts' feelings about solo travel have affected Yolanda?

Extend Understanding

7. **Cultural Connection:** How might it feel to return to one's country of origin after a long absence? Respond from your own experience, or interview a family member, friend, or neighbor to find out.

Quick Review

Plot is the sequence of events in narrative writing. The sequence of a plot follows these stages: the **exposition,** when the basic situation is introduced; the **inciting incident,** when the conflict is revealed; the **development,** when the conflict intensifies; the **climax,** when the conflict reaches its most intense point; the **denouement,** when information about events that occur after the climax are revealed; and the **resolution,** when the conflict is resolved and changes or insights are noted.

A **flashback** is an interruption in the chronological narrative that is used to present a scene or an event from an earlier time.

To **identify with a character,** think about character traits and experiences you share.

 Take It to the Net
www.phschool.com

Take the interactive self-test online to check your understanding of the selection.

Integrate Language Skills

Vocabulary Development Lesson

Concept Development: Words From Spanish

Many words, such as *machete, tortilla*, and *sombrero*, come to English directly from Spanish. Use the story context to help you answer these questions about three other Spanish words.

1. Which English word used in the story probably comes from *guayaba*, the Spanish name for the same tropical fruit?

2. *Cantina*, from the Spanish for "bar" or "tavern," is related to an Italian word for "wine cellar." Which English word probably has a similar origin?

3. In English, a *cabana* or *cabaña* is usually a small building at a swimming pool or beach. Is that the word's meaning on page 1085 in the story? Explain.

Concept Development: Synonyms or Antonyms

Classify each of the following pairs of words as either synonyms or antonyms.

1. dissuade, discourage
2. loath, eager
3. appease, arouse
4. machetes, knives
5. collusion, plotting
6. docile, cantankerous
7. enunciated, slurred

Spelling Strategy

For words ending in silent *e*, drop the *e* before adding a suffix beginning with a vowel (*enunciate +-ed = enunciated*). Correctly add the indicated suffix to each word listed.

1. skate (*-ed*)   2. define (*-ing*)   3. capture (*-ed*)

Grammar and Style Lesson

Absolute Phrases

An **absolute phrase** consists of a noun or noun phrase modified by a participle or participial phrase. Though it modifies the clause to which it is attached, it is not part of the subject or predicate and is set off from the rest of the sentence by commas.

> **Example:** A bus came lurching around the curve, *the driver saluting.*

Practice Identify the absolute phrases in the following sentences.

1. It was an old army bus, the official name brushed over with paint.

2. She speeded up and left them behind, the small compact climbing easily.
3. Yolanda pulled up at a cantina, the thatched roof held up by several posts.
4. Yolanda and her crew scavenged the grove, the best of the pick going into the basket.
5. The small group stared at the sagging tire, the two men kicking it.

Writing Application Write a one-paragraph description of an important childhood memory. Include at least three absolute phrases in your account to add descriptive detail.

W͟G Prentice Hall Writing and Grammar Connection: Chapter 19, Section 2

Writing Lesson

New Version of the Story

In both literature and life, stories are shaped by the points of view of those who tell them. For example, in this story you see events and people through Yolanda's eyes. You can only speculate about the thoughts of the people she encounters. Write a new version of the story from the point of view of one of the men who changes Yolanda's tire.

Prewriting Choose the character whose point of view you will use and reread the story considering that perspective. Note details to incorporate and develop. Then, write a brief outline of your new version.

Drafting Write the story from the new point of view you have selected. Use sensory details, flashbacks, and dialogue to provide background and flesh out the character's world.

Model: Using Details to Create A Vivid Portrayal

Paulo saw a small, white car stuck in the foliage. The tire was busted, and a lady stood there. Her eyes were nervous and black. She reminded Paulo of a cornered chihuahua, and he thought she might bite. He laughed at the thought. "How can we help you, Doña?" he asked.

> The inclusion of dialogue and a character's inner thoughts add to the vividness of a narrative.

Revising Reread your story, and look for points where you may have strayed from the perspective you have chosen. Delete details the character might not know, and add information to strengthen your use of point of view.

Prentice Hall Writing and Grammar Connection: Chapter 5, Section 4

Extension Activities

Listening and Speaking Create a **cause-and-effect flowchart** that examines the series of decisions each character makes. Use the flowchart as the basis for a class presentation. Use these tips to prepare:

- Diagram the characters' choices in each situation.
- Note how the decisions made by Yolanda and other characters affect the plot.

After your presentation, lead a discussion about the conflicts and decisions portrayed in this story.

Research and Technology Work with several classmates to prepare a **multimedia report** about the Dominican Republic. Choose one area to research—for example, geography, or economics. Add music and images, and report your findings in a presentation. **[Group Activity]**

 **Take It to the Net** www.phschool.com

Go online for an additional research activity using the Internet.

Prepare to Read

Freeway 280 ◆ Who Burns for the Perfection of Paper ◆ Most Satisfied by Snow ◆ Hunger in New York City ◆ What For

Lorna Dee Cervantes (b. 1954)

California native Lorna Dee Cervantes has been writing poetry since she was eight years old. A committed feminist and Hispanic rights activist, she founded her own small press in 1976 "to broaden not only the horizons but also the definitions of what was Chicana literature." Cervantes published her own first book of poetry, *Emplumada*, in 1981. She also established the literary magazine *Mango* to help nurture other Hispanic American writers. Despite her commitment to the Chicano community, she writes in English to give her work a greater political reach.

Martín Espada (b. 1957)

Not many lawyers pursue simultaneous careers as poets, but, until 1993, Martín Espada was an exception. Espada's creativity was inspired by his father, a talented photographer based in Brooklyn, New York. Father and son worked together on a 1981 photo documentary called *The Puerto Rican Diaspora Documentary Project*. A year later, Espada published his first volume of poetry, *The Immigrant Iceboy's Bolero*. He now teaches poetry at the University of Massachusetts at Amherst.

Diana Chang (b. 1934)

Born in New York City, Diana Chang spent most of her childhood in China. She returned to the United States after World War II and attended Barnard College in New York. In addition to writing poetry, she has written several novels, including *The Frontiers of Love* (1993). Chang's spare, introspective poetry, collected in volumes such as *What Matisse Is After* (1984), shows the influence of traditional Asian verse forms. She has also translated Asian writings into English. Perhaps due to the many views and voices in her experience, Chang's work "moves beyond ethnicity" to examine "identity and self."

Simon Ortiz (b. 1941)

A native of the Acoma Pueblo in New Mexico, Simon Ortiz grew up steeped in the oral tradition of his people. Writing came naturally to him, and in 1980 he was honored at a White House "Salute to Poetry and American Poets." Ortiz has published more than a dozen books of poetry and prose, including *Men on the Moon: Collected Short Stories* (1999) and *From Sand Creek* (2000). He edits the literary magazine *Wanbli Ho.*

Garrett Hongo (b. 1951)

One of the stars among contemporary Asian American poets, Garrett Hongo is a fourth-generation Japanese American who spent his early childhood in Hawaii. His father, an electrical technician, figures prominently in Hongo's poems and is profiled in his book *Volcano: A Memoir of Hawaii* (1995). Hongo has won numerous awards, including fellowships from the Thomas Watson and Guggenheim foundations. Among Hongo's other works are *Yellow Light* (1982) and *The River of Heaven* (1988).

Preview
Connecting to the Literature

The poets whose work appears here represent some of the many distinct cultural groups that make up the American fabric. As you read, think about the role that family and cultural heritage plays in your life.

Literary Analysis
Voice

Just as each person has a distinctive way of speaking, every poet has a unique **voice,** or literary personality. A poet's voice is based on word choice, tone, sound devices, rhyme (or its absence), pace, attitude, and even the patterns of vowels and consonants. Consider these examples:

Cervantes: Viejitas come here with paper bags to gather greens . . .
Chang: Against my windows, / fog knows / what to do, too

As you read these poems, note the distinctive voice each one reveals.

Comparing Literary Works

Issues of cultural and personal **alienation** are a common theme in American poetry of the late twentieth century. Alienation is the feeling of being separate, or detached from a group. Feelings of alienation arise from internal sources, such as questions of personal identity, or from external sources, such as clashes between cultures. As you read these poems, think about the poet's relationship to his or her subject, and whether or not it expresses acceptance or the more difficult feelings of alienation.

Reading Strategy
Summarizing

Sometimes, you can understand a poem better if you briefly restate the main points in a **summary.** A summary should match these criteria:

- It includes content from the beginning, middle, and end.
- It is concise—no longer than a single sentence.
- It is precise, clearly conveying the poem's essence.

Use a chart like the one shown to create summaries of each poem.

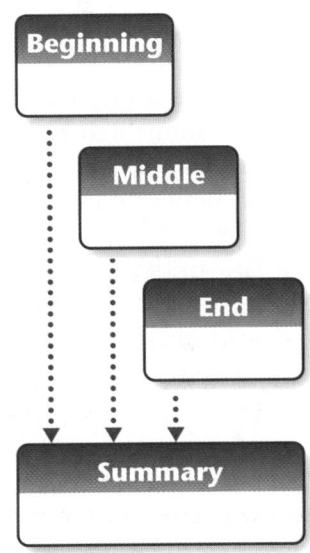

Vocabulary

crevices (krev´ is iz) *n.* narrow cracks or splits (p. 1100)

pervade (pər vād´) *v.* to spread throughout (p. 1101)

automation (ôt´ ə mā´ shən) *n.* manufacturing conducted with partly or fully self-operating machinery (p. 1102)

liturgy (lit´ ər jē) *n.* public religious ceremonies; religious ritual (p. 1103)

conjure (kun´ jər) *v.* to summon by magic or as if by magic; to call forth (p. 1103)

calligraphy (kə lig´ rə fē) *n.* artistic handwriting (p. 1104)

trough (trôf) *n.* a low point of a wave (p. 1104)

Freeway 280

Lorna Dee Cervantes

Untitled (detail), Peter Malone

Background

The poems you are about to read reflect the cultural roots of their authors. Cervantes writes of her Chicana heritage in a familiar California setting, a barrio near a freeway. Espada recalls the harsh physical labor of an after-school job. Ortiz describes how life in New York City prompts a hunger for his southwestern home. Chinese American writer Chang offers a poem whose subject and style are reminiscent of Asian verse. Hongo's poem draws on his heritage as one of many Japanese Americans in Hawaii, some of whom practice the Buddhist faith of their ancestors.

Las casitas[1] near the gray cannery,
nestled amid wild abrazos[2] of climbing roses
and man-high red geraniums
are gone now. The freeway conceals it
5 all beneath a raised scar.

But under the fake windsounds of the open lanes,
in the abandoned lots below, new grasses sprout,
wild mustard remembers, old gardens
come back stronger than they were,
10 trees have been left standing in their yards.
Albaricoqueros, cerezos, nogales . . .[3]

1. **Las casitas** (läs kä sē´ täs) "The little houses" (Spanish).
2. **abrazos** (ä brä´ sōs) "hugs" (Spanish).
3. **Albaricoqueros, cerezos, nogales** (äl bär´ rē kō ker´ ōs, se rē´ sōs, nō gä´ les) "Apricot trees, cherry trees, walnut trees" (Spanish).

▲ **Critical Viewing**
Is the red light in this painting suited to the ideas in Cervantes' poem? Why or why not? **[Connect]**

Viejitas[4] come here with paper bags to gather greens.
Espinaca, verdolagas, yerbabuena . . .[5]

I scramble over the wire fence
15 that would have kept me out.
Once, I wanted out, wanted the rigid lanes
to take me to a place without sun,
without the smell of tomatoes burning
on swing shift in the greasy summer air.

20 Maybe it's here
en los campos extraños de esta ciudad[6]
where I'll find it, that part of me
mown under
like a corpse
25 or a loose seed.

---

4. **Viejitas** (bye hē′ täs) "Old women" (Spanish).
5. **Espinaca, verdolagas, yerbabuena** (es pē nä′ kä, ber thō lä′ gäs, yer′ bä bwe′ nä) "Spinach, purslane, peppermint" (Spanish).
6. **en los campos extraños de esta ciudad** (en lōs käm′ pōs es trä′ nyōs de es′ tä syoō däd′) "In the strange fields of this city" (Spanish).

Review and Assess

Thinking About the Selection

1. **Respond:** In what way does the author's use of both Spanish and English affect your response to this poem? Explain.

2. **(a) Recall:** In the first stanza, which buildings does the speaker say are now gone? **(b) Classify:** What sort of neighborhood once stood at the site of the freeway? **(c) Interpret:** In what way is Freeway 280 like a scar?

3. **(a) Recall:** In lines 14–19, what does the speaker do? **(b) Interpret:** How do the speaker's actions represent a change in attitude toward this neighborhood?

4. **(a) Connect:** In lines 24–25, what does the speaker liken to a "corpse" and a "loose seed"? **(b) Interpret:** In your own words, what do you think the speaker is seeking? **(c) Analyze:** What details in lines 7–10 imply that the "loose seed" will take root?

5. **(a) Analyze:** What aspects of this poem challenge the idea that speed and progress are always beneficial? **(b) Take a Position:** Do you agree or disagree with the poet's position? Explain.

Who Burns for the Perfection of Paper

Martín Espada

At sixteen, I worked after high school hours
at a printing plant
that manufactured legal pads:
Yellow paper
5 stacked seven feet high
and leaning
as I slipped cardboard
between the pages,
then brushed red glue
10 up and down the stack.
No gloves: fingertips required
for the perfection of paper,
smoothing the exact rectangle.
Sluggish by 9 PM, the hands
15 would slide along suddenly sharp paper,
and gather slits thinner than the <u>crevices</u>
of the skin, hidden.
Then the glue would sting,
hands oozing
20 till both palms burned
at the punchclock.

Ten years later, in law school,
I knew that every legal pad
was glued with the sting of hidden cuts,
25 that every open lawbook
was a pair of hands
upturned and burning.

crevices (krev′ is iz) *n.*
narrow cracks or splits

MOST SATISFIED BY SNOW
Diana Chang

Against my windows,
fog knows
what to do, too

Spaces <u>pervade</u>
5   us, as well

But occupied by snow,
I see

Matter
matters

10   I, too,
flowering

▲ **Critical Viewing**
In what ways does this image of trees relate to the last two lines of the poem? **[Connect]**

pervade (pər vād´) v. to spread throughout

Review and Assess

Thinking About the Selections

1. **Respond:** In what ways were you surprised by these poems?

2. **(a) Recall:** In "Who Burns for the Perfection of Paper," what was the speaker's first experience with legal pads?
   (b) Recall: What were the speaker's later job with legal pads?
   (c) Interpret: What did the speaker learn from the first job?

3. **(a) Recall:** What word does the speaker use twice to describe cuts on the hands? **(b) Interpret:** What role does the idea of anonymity play in this poem?

4. **(a) Classify:** In "Most Satisfied by Snow," the speaker observes two kinds of weather. What are they?
   (b) Compare and Contrast: What differences between these two types of weather does the poem highlight?

5. **(a) Interpret:** What might the speaker mean by the comment that "spaces pervade us"? **(b) Interpret:** What is the relationship of "matter" to these "spaces"?

Hunger in New York City

Simon Ortiz

Hunger crawls into you
from somewhere out of your muscles
or the concrete or the land
or the wind pushing you.

5   It comes to you, asking
for food, words, wisdom, young memories
of places you ate at, drank cold spring water,
or held somebody's hand,
or home of the gentle, slow dances,
10   the songs, the strong gods, the world
you know.

That is, hunger searches you out.
It always asks you,
How are you, son? Where are you?
15   Have you eaten well?
Have you done what you as a person
of our people is supposed to do?

And the concrete of this city,
the oily wind, the blazing windows,
20   the shrieks of <u>automation</u> cannot,
truly cannot, answer for that hunger
although I have hungered,
truthfully and honestly, for them
to feed myself with.

25   So I sang to myself quietly:
I am feeding myself
with the humble presence
of all around me;
I am feeding myself
30   with your soul, my mother earth;
make me cool and humble.
Bless me.

▲ Critical Viewing
What words would you
use to describe the
emotions conveyed
by both the poem and
this photograph?
[Interpret]

automation (ôt´ ə mā´ shən)
n. manufacturing con-
ducted with partly or fully
self-operating machinery

Reading Strategy
Summarizing Summarize
the final stanza to determine what it reveals about
the speaker's struggle.

What For

GARRETT HONGO

At six I lived for spells:
how a few Hawaiian words could call
up the rain, could hymn like the sea
in the long swirl of chambers
5   curling in the nautilus of a shell,[1]
how Amida's[2] ballads of the Buddhaland
in the drone of the priest's <u>liturgy</u>
could <u>conjure</u> money from the poor
and give them nothing but mantras,[3]
10   the strange syllables that healed desire.

---

1. **nautilus** (nôt´ əl əs) **of a shell** spiral of a seashell such as the chambered nautilus or paper nautilus.
2. **Amida's** (ä mēd ä) referring to Amida, the great savior worshiped by members of the Pure Land sect of Buddhism popular in eastern Asia.
3. **mantras** (män´ trəz) sacred words repeated in prayers, hymns, or chants.

▲ **Critical Viewing** In the poem's final stanza, in what way does the poet use the image of the fragrant plumeria flower to communicate his desire to heal his father's pain? **[Analyze]**

liturgy (lit´ ər jē) *n.* public religious ceremonies; religious ritual

conjure (kän´ jər) *v.* to summon by magic or as if by magic; to call forth

I lived for stories about the war
my grandfather told over *hana* cards,[4]
slapping them down on the mats
with a sharp Japanese *kiai.*[5]

15 I lived for songs my grandmother sang
stirring curry into a thick stew,
weaving a <u>calligraphy</u> of Kannon's[6] love
into grass mats and straw sandals.

I lived for the red volcano dirt
20 staining my toes, the salt residue
of surf and sea wind in my hair,
the arc of a flat stone skipping
in the hollow <u>trough</u> of a wave.

I lived a child's world, waited
25 for my father to drag himself home,
dusted with blasts of sand, powdered rock,
and the strange ash of raw cement,
his deafness made worse by the clang
of pneumatic drills,[7] sore in his bones
30 from the buckings of a jackhammer.

He'd hand me a scarred lunchpail,
let me unlace the hightop G.I. boots,[8]
call him the new name I'd invented
that day in school, write it for him
35 on his newspaper. He'd rub my face
with hands that felt like gravel roads,
tell me to move, go play, and then he'd
walk to the laundry sink to scrub,
rinse the dirt of his long day
40 from a face brown and grained as koa wood.[9]

I wanted to take away the pain
in his legs, the swelling in his joints,
give him back his hearing,
clear and rare as crystal chimes,
45 the fins of glass that wrinkled
and sparked the air with their sound.

calligraphy (kə lig′ rə fē) *n.*
artistic handwriting

trough (trôf) *n.* a low
point of a wave

Reading Strategy
Summarizing Summarize
the father's daily
experience.

Literary Analysis
Voice In what way would
you describe the
speaker's voice in
lines 41–46?

---

4. *hana* (hä′ nä) **cards** cards with flower patterns that players try to pair up in a popular
   Japanese card game. *Hana* is Japanese for "flower."
5. *kiai* (kē ī′) Japanese word for the sound made by slapping down *hana* cards.
6. **Kannon's** (kä′ nənz) referring to an enlightened savior of Japanese Buddhism who,
   out of infinite compassion and mercy, forgoes the heavenly state of nirvana in order to
   save others.
7. **pneumatic** (noo mat′ ik) **drills** air drills used in construction.
8. **hightop G.I. boots** army boots.
9. **koa** (kō′ ə) **wood** grainy wood of the Hawaiian acacia tree.

I wanted to heal the sores that work
and war had sent to him,
let him play catch in the backyard
50   with me, tossing a tennis ball
past papaya trees without the shoulders
of pain shrugging back his arms.

I wanted to become a doctor of pure magic,
to string a necklace of sweet words
55   fragrant as pine needles and plumeria,[10]
fragrant as the bread my mother baked,
place it like a lei of cowrie shells[11]
and *pikake*[12] flowers around my father's neck,
and chant him a blessing, a sutra.[13]

---

10. **plumeria** (plōō mer′ ē ə) tropical tree bearing flowers known for their fragrance.
11. **lei** (lā) **of cowrie** (kou′ rē) **shells** garland made of brightly colored seashells found in the South Pacific.
12. *pikake* (pē kä′ kā) Hawaiian word for jasmine, a fragrant flowering shrub.
13. **sutra** (sōō′ trə) one of the sacred texts or scriptures of Buddhism.

Review and Assess

Thinking About the Selections

1. **Respond:** Do you think the speaker of "What For" had a happy childhood? Why or why not?

2. **(a) Recall:** In "Hunger in New York City," what four questions does hunger ask? **(b) Analyze:** What kind of hunger does the speaker mean?

3. **(a) Interpret:** What key words does the speaker use to paint a harsh portrait of New York City?
   (b) Compare and Contrast: In what ways is the city unlike the world the speaker has known—the world of his home?

4. **(a) Recall:** In the first four stanzas of "What For," what forms of communication did the speaker live for? **(b) Infer:** What do these forms of communication suggest about the child's relationship to adults?

5. **(a) Deduce:** From where did the father "drag himself home" each day? **(b) Analyze:** What values are expressed in the father's behavior?

6. **(a) Classify:** In what ways does the landscape of the poem change in the fifth stanza? **(b) Interpret:** Is this shift connected to the child's wish for the father in the final stanza? Explain.

7. **Evaluate:** Evaluate the title's relationship to the content of the poem. Is the title an effective one? Explain.

Review and Assess

Literary Analysis

Voice

1. (a) Use a chart like the one shown to select the adjective that best describes each poet's **voice.** (b) Then, choose another adjective that additionally characterizes each poet's voice.

> **Adjectives:** angry, meditative, remorseful, yearning, reverent

Poet	Voice	Evidence		Additional Adjectives
			···▶	

2. (a) What aspects of Hongo's and Cervantes's voices reflect their respective cultures? (b) In what ways do the voices of the other poets reflect their cultural backgrounds?

Comparing Literary Works

3. (a) Which of these poets express **alienation**? (b) In each case, what is the cause of that alienation?

4. (a) What traits do the freeway, the printing plant, the urban setting, and the construction site share? (b) What does each bring to the speakers in these poems? What does each take away?

5. Simon Ortiz notes that the "hunger" asks "Have you done what you as a person / of our people is supposed to do?" How does this question apply to the poems by Cervantes, Espada, and Hongo?

Reading Strategy

Summarizing

6. (a) Write a **summary** of "Hunger in New York City" and "Who Burns for the Perfection of Paper." (b) What poetic effects and meanings are lost in the summaries?

7. (a) Write a summary of stanzas 1–4 of "What For." (b) Write a summary of stanzas 5–8. (c) What do these summaries reveal to you about the poem's structure?

Extend Understanding

8. **Cultural Connection:** What aspects of American popular culture reflect the country's growing diversity?

Integrate Language Skills

Vocabulary Development Lesson

Word Analysis: Greek Prefix *auto-*

Explain how the meaning of *auto-*, defined as "self," is expressed in each of the following words:

1. automobile
2. autopilot
3. autograph
4. autobiography
5. automatic
6. autocratic

Spelling Strategy

The *shun* sound in a suffix is usually formed by the letters *sion* or *tion*, as in percus*sion* or automa*tion*. Add the suffix *-sion* or *-tion* to change each of the following verbs into a noun.

1. fascinate
2. extend
3. intervene
4. devote

Fluency: Definitions

Choose the definition that best matches each numbered word.

1. trough (a) high point of a wave, (b) low point of a wave, (c) surf
2. conjure (a) quickly follow, (b) harshly criticize, (c) magically summon
3. calligraphy (a) bright tapestry, (b) intricate hairdo, (c) artistic handwriting
4. liturgy (a) a religious ritual, (b) dinner menu, (c) architectural blueprint
5. automation (a) electrification, (b) mechanization, (c) termination
6. crevices (a) gorges, (b) rivers, (c) narrow cracks
7. pervade (a) spread, (b) withdraw, (c) request

Grammar and Style Lesson

Participial Phrases

A **participial phrase** is a participle—a verb form that can be used as an adjective—and the words that modify or complete it. The entire phrase works as an adjective to modify a noun or a pronoun.

> **Present Participle:** My hands, *smoothing the exact rectangle*, would slide along the paper. (modifies *hands*)
>
> **Past Participle:** *Reminded of the experience*, he winced. (modifies *he*)

Practice Identify the participial phrase in each sentence. Determine the noun or pronoun it modifies.

1. Seeking an after-school job, I found one at a printing plant.
2. I worked hard, slipping cardboard between the papers.
3. Cut by sharp edges, my hands were often stinging.
4. The glue, oozing over them, made the stinging worse.
5. I can still visualize my hands, upturned in pain.

Writing Application Write a paragraph about a place you know or can picture, using the following participial phrases:

1. nestled among climbing roses
2. sitting beside the freeway
3. abandoned in the open lots

W͜G *Prentice Hall Writing and Grammar Connection: Chapter 19, Section 2*

Writing Lesson

Comparison-and-Contrast Essay

The poems by Cervantes and Hongo present childhood in distinctly different ways. In a comparison-and-contrast essay, evaluate the sensory images each poet uses to generate a vivid sense of childhood. Compare and contrast the nature of the wisdom each speaker gains in adulthood.

Prewriting   Reread each poem and take notes about its language, meaning, and structure. Decide why each poem is effective on its own, and then compare the two.

Drafting   Introduce the poets and summarize the poems. Then, state your main ideas about the way each poem portrays childhood. As you draft, include modifiers that clearly express praise or criticism.

Revising   Review your essay to make sure you have expressed your points about each poem with conviction. Identify any weak or unclear modifiers and replace them with stronger choices.

Model: Elaborating for a Stronger Statement

elegantly   *and vivid*

Cervantes's poem is compact. Even though they describe tended

lush   *appropriate to childhood*

gardens, her images of flowers convey a feeling of wildness.

> Precise modifiers create a stronger piece of evaluative writing.

 *Prentice Hall Writing and Grammar Connection: Chapter 14, Section 4*

Extension Activities

Listening and Speaking You probably know someone whose life centers around his or her cultural heritage. With a classmate, conduct an **interview** with such a person. To prepare, use the following tips:

- Develop questions to establish the subject's background and personal history.
- Create a list of suitable follow-up questions.

Videotape or record the interview to share with classmates. [**Group Activity**]

Research and Technology Locate and gather Asian poetry in English translation, using library or Internet resources. Create an **anthology** of these poems. In a brief introduction to your anthology, explain how Diana Chang's "Most Satisfied by Snow" demonstrates the influence of Asian verse.

 **Take It to the Net**   www.phschool.com

Go online for an additional research activity using the Internet.

Focus on Literary Forms: Essay

My Mother's Book of Life, Lee Lawson

A nalytic, expository, satiric, or personal, the essay has been used for centuries to express ideas that range from personal reflection to national revolution. In the busy modern world, readers have embraced the essay form, which presents ideas in a limited space. From comedy to personal triumph, the essays in this section demonstrate the flexibility of the form.

Prepare to Read

from The Mortgaged Heart ◆ Onomatopoeia ◆ Coyote v. Acme

Carson McCullers (1917–1967)

Carson McCullers, whose writing has been praised as a brilliant fusion of the compassionate and the grotesque, led a troubled life marked by serious health problems. She was raised in Columbus, Georgia, a town that later formed the backdrop for all her fiction. At the age of seventeen, she moved to New York and married Reeves McCullers three years later. While still in her twenties, she suffered a series of strokes that incapacitated her for long periods. In later years, partial paralysis confined her to a wheelchair, yet she still managed to type new manuscripts. Her loneliness and suffering are reflected in her novels, which include *The Heart Is a Lonely Hunter* (1940), *The Member of the Wedding* (1946), and *Clock Without Hands* (1961).

William Safire (b. 1929)

When it comes to questions about the use—and misuse— of the English language, few people have more answers or observations than William Safire. A political commentator and the author of the "On Language" column of *The New York Times*, Safire is one of the world's most widely read writers on language in America today. The 1978 Pulitzer Prize winner for distinguished commentary, Safire was once a political speech writer for the Nixon White House. His books include *On Language* (1980), *What's the Good Word?* (1982), *I Stand Corrected* (1984), *Take My Word for It* (1986), *You Could Look It Up* (1988), and *Coming to Terms* (1991). He has also written four novels, *Full Disclosure* (1977), *Freedom* (1987), *Sleeper Spy* (1995), and *Scandalmonger* (2000).

Ian Frazier (b. 1951)

Known for humorous essays and affectionate descriptions of rural America, Ian Frazier brings "an antic sense of fun" to much of his work. He does have a serious side, too. For example, his nonfiction book, *Great Plains* (1989) explores the history of the American West to discover its meaning for today's Americans. His book *On The Rez* (2000), an exploration of life for today's Oglala Sioux Indians, followed.

Frazier was born in Cleveland, Ohio, and now lives in New York City, where he works as a staff writer for *The New Yorker* magazine. His humorous and often ironic essays are collected in a series of nonfiction books, including *Dating Your Mom* (1986), *Nobody Better, Better Than Nobody* (1987), *Family* (1994), *Coyote v. Acme* (1996), and *Lamentations of the Father* (2000). "Coyote v. Acme" is typical of his work: a ludicrous premise packaged in serious style.

Preview

Connecting to the Literature

Perhaps you explore subjects that matter to you, such as friendship or creativity, in a journal. Some writers use a more public form of writing—the essay—to discuss ideas they find important.

Literary Analysis

Essay

An **essay** is a short piece of nonfiction in which a writer expresses a personal view on a topic. The many types of essays include

- the **analytical essay,** which breaks down and interprets various elements of a topic.
- the **expository essay,** which explains a topic.
- the **satirical essay,** which uses irony, ridicule, or sarcasm to comment on a topic.

Look for the elements in these essays that will help you decide how to classify each one.

Comparing Literary Works

Different from one another in topic and mood, these selections illustrate the flexibility of the essay form. Yet their greatest difference lies in the concept of **tone,** or the author's attitude toward the subject, characters, or audience. You can hear the tone—humorous, critical, or serious—in each writer's choice of words and details. As you read, note how each author's tone contributes to the structure and meaning of each essay.

Reading Strategy

Identifying Line of Reasoning

When presenting an argument, an essayist offers a **line of reasoning** to convince readers of the soundness of his or her ideas. As you read these essays, identify the key points and note the reasons, facts, and examples that support them. Study the ways in which pieces of evidence are connected, noting any cause-and-effect relationships. Record each line of reasoning, and its evidence, in a chart like the one shown.

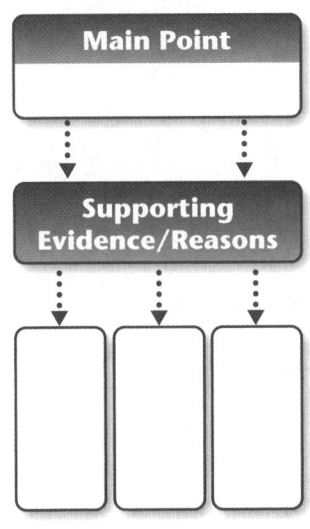

Vocabulary Development

pristine (pris´ tēn) *adj.* pure; uncorrupted (p. 1113)

corollary (kôr´ ə ler´ ē) *n.* easily drawn conclusion (p. 1113)

aesthetic (es thet´ ik) *adj.* pertaining to the study or theory of beauty (p. 1113)

maverick (mav´ ər ik) *n.* nonconformist (p. 1113)

contiguous (kən tig´ yōō əs) *adj.* bordering; adjacent (p. 1118)

precipitate (prē sip´ ə tit) *adj.* very sudden (p. 1119)

caveat (kā´ vē at´) *n.* formal notice; warning (p. 1120)

tensile (ten´ sil) *adj.* stretchable (p. 1121)

from The Mortgaged Heart
Carson McCullers

This city, New York—consider the people in it, the eight million of us. An English friend of mine, when asked why he lived in New York City, said that he liked it here because he could be so alone. While it was my friend's desire to be alone, the aloneness of many Americans who live in cities is an involuntary and fearful thing. It has been said that loneliness is the great American malady. What is the nature of this loneliness? It would seem essentially to be a quest for identity.

To the spectator, the amateur philosopher, no motive among the complex ricochets of our desires and rejections seems stronger or more enduring than the will of the individual to claim his identity and belong. From infancy to death, the human being is obsessed by these dual motives. During our first weeks of life, the question of identity shares urgency with the need for milk. The baby reaches for his toes, then

Literary Analysis
Essay In what ways does the question about the nature of loneliness signal to readers that this is an analytical essay?

explores the bars of his crib; again and again he compares the difference between his own body and the objects around him, and in the wavering, infant eyes there comes a <u>pristine</u> wonder.

Consciousness of self is the first abstract problem that the human being solves. Indeed, it is this self-consciousness that removes us from lower animals. This primitive grasp of identity develops with constantly shifting emphasis through all our years. Perhaps maturity is simply the history of those mutations that reveal to the individual the relation between himself and the world in which he finds himself.

After the first establishment of identity there comes the imperative need to lose this new-found sense of separateness and to belong to something larger and more powerful than the weak, lonely self. The sense of moral isolation is intolerable to us.

In *The Member of the Wedding*[1] the lonely twelve-year-old girl, Frankie Addams, articulates this universal need: "The trouble with me is that for a long time I have just been an *I* person. All people belong to a *We* except me. Not to belong to a *We* makes you too lonesome."

Love is the bridge that leads from the *I* sense to the *We*, and there is a paradox about personal love. Love of another individual opens a new relation between the personality and the world. The lover responds in a new way to nature and may even write poetry. Love is affirmation; it motivates the *yes* responses and the sense of wider communication. Love casts out fear, and in the security of this togetherness we find contentment, courage. We no longer fear the age-old haunting questions: "Who am I?" "Why am I?" "Where am I going?"—and having cast out fear, we can be honest and charitable.

For fear is a primary source of evil. And when the question "Who am I?" recurs and is unanswered, then fear and frustration project a negative attitude. The bewildered soul can answer only: "Since I do not understand 'Who I am,' I only know what I am *not*." The <u>corollary</u> of this emotional incertitude is snobbism, intolerance and racial hate. The xenophobic[2] individual can only reject and destroy, as the xenophobic nation inevitably makes war.

The loneliness of Americans does not have its source in xenophobia; as a nation we are an outgoing people, reaching always for immediate contacts, further experience. But we tend to seek out things as individuals, alone. The European, secure in his family ties and rigid class loyalties, knows little of the moral loneliness that is native to us Americans. While the European artists tend to form groups or <u>aesthetic</u> schools, the American artist is the eternal <u>maverick</u>—not only from society in the way of all creative minds, but within the orbit of his own art.

Thoreau took to the woods to seek the ultimate meaning of his life. His creed was simplicity and his *modus vivendi*[3] the deliberate stripping

---

1. *The Member of the Wedding* novel and play by Carson McCullers.
2. **xenophobic** (zen´ ə fō´ bik) *adj.* afraid of strangers or foreigners.
3. *modus vivendi* (mō´ dəs vi ven´ dī) "manner of living" (Latin).

Reading Strategy
Identifying Line of Reasoning What evidence does McCullers offer to support the connections between her ideas about identity and loneliness?

corollary (kôr´ ə ler´ ē) *n.* easily drawn conclusion

aesthetic (es *thet*´ ik) *adj.* pertaining to the study or theory of beauty

maverick (mav´ ər ik) *n.* nonconformist

**Reading Check**

According to McCullers, what is the bridge that leads from the sense of *I* to the sense of *We*?

of external life to the Spartan[4] necessities in order that his inward life could freely flourish. His objective, as he put it, was to back the world into a corner. And in that way did he discover "What a man thinks of himself, that it is which determines, or rather indicates, his fate."

On the other hand, Thomas Wolfe turned to the city, and in his wanderings around New York he continued his frenetic and lifelong search for the lost brother, the magic door. He too backed the world into a corner, and as he passed among the city's millions, returning their stares, he experienced "That silent meeting [that] is the summary of all the meetings of men's lives."

Whether in the pastoral joys of country life or in the labyrinthine city, we Americans are always seeking. We wander, question. But the answer waits in each separate heart—the answer of our own identity and the way by which we can master loneliness and feel that at last we belong.

---

4. **Spartan** (spär′ tən) *adj.* characteristic of the people of ancient Sparta: hardy, stoical, severe, frugal.

Review and Assess

Thinking About the Selection

1. **Respond:** If you could meet Carson McCullers, which of the observations in this essay would you most like to discuss with her? Explain your reasons for choosing this observation.

2. **(a) Recall:** Why does McCullers's English friend like living in New York City? **(b) Interpret:** In what way is his explanation seemingly contradictory or paradoxical?

3. **(a) Recall:** According to McCullers, what is "the great American malady"? **(b) Analyze:** When McCullers describes this American malady, she speaks of *moral* isolation and *moral* loneliness. What does she mean by these terms?

4. **(a) Recall:** What is a primary source of evil? **(b) Analyze Cause and Effect:** What are the consequences of evil? **(c) Speculate:** According to McCullers, how might the personal experience of love change society?

5. **(a) Distinguish:** What does McCullers say is the main difference between Europeans and Americans? **(b) Interpret:** In what ways does she believe this difference is expressed?

6. **(a) Define:** What is the *I* sense? **(b) Define:** What is the *We* sense? **(c) Interpret:** According to McCullers, how does love lead from one to the other?

7. **(a) Evaluate:** In what ways does McCullers think American individualism hurts people? **(b) Take a Position:** Do you see any positive effects of our emphasis on individualism? Explain.

ONOMATOPOEIA

William Safire

Blam, 1962, Roy Lichtenstein

▲ **Critical Viewing** What meaning does the onomatopoeia *Blam* convey in this image? **[Analyze]**

Background

The vocabulary of English is the largest of any language in the world. English readily incorporates new words from a wide variety of sources, including borrowing them from other languages. William Safire, a former Presidential speechwriter, describes another way in which English evolves. According to Safire, when we consider onomatopoeia—the figure of speech in which a word sounds like what it means—we discover that new words are not just based on what we experience, but on what we merely imagine.

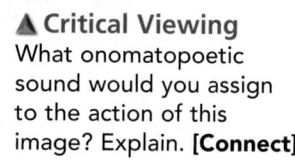

The word *onomatopoeia* was used above, and it had better be spelled right or one usage dictator and six copy editors will get zapped. That word is based on the Greek for "word making"—the *poe* is the same as in *poetry,* "something made"—and is synonymous with *imitative* and *echoic,* denoting words that are made by people making sounds like the action to be described. (The *poe* in *onomatopoeia* has its own rule for pronunciation. Whenever a vowel follows *poe,* the *oe* combination is pronounced as a long *e: onomato-PEE-ia.* Whenever a consonant follows, as in *poetry* and *onomatopoetic,* pronounce the long *o* of Edgar Allan's name.)

Henry Peacham, in his 1577 book on grammar and rhetoric called *The Garden of Eloquence,* first used *onomatopoeia* and defined it as "when we invent, devise, fayne, and make a name intimating the sound of that it signifieth, as *hurlyburly,* for an uprore and tumultuous stirre." He also gave *flibergib* to "a gossip," from which we derive *flibbertigibbet,* and the long-lost *clapperclaw* and *kickle-kackle.*

Since Willard Espy borrowed the title of Peacham's work for his rhetorical bestiary in 1983, the author went beyond the usual examples of *buzz, hiss, bobwhite* and *babble.* He pointed out that one speculation about the origin of language was the *bow-wow theory,* holding that words originated in imitation of natural sounds of animals and thunder. (Proponents of the *pooh-pooh theory* argued that interjections like *ow!* and *oof!* started us all yakking toward language. Other theories—arrgh!—abound.)

Reaching for an alliterative onomatope, the poet Milton chose "melodious *murmurs;*" Edgar Allan Poe one-upped him with "the *tintinnabulation* of the bells." When carried too far, an obsession with words is called *onomatomania;* in the crunch (a word imitating the sound of an icebreaker breaking through ice) Gertrude Stein turned into an *onomatomaniac.*

▲ **Critical Viewing**
What onomatopoetic sound would you assign to the action of this image? Explain. **[Connect]**

Literary Analysis
Essay What kind of essay do you think Safire is writing? Explain.

What makes a word like *zap* of particular interest is that it imitates an imaginary noise—the sound of a paralyzing ray gun. Thus we can see another way that the human mind creates new words: imitating what can be heard only in the mind's ear. The coinage filled a need for an unheard sound and—*pow!*—slammed the vocabulary right in the kisser. Steadily, surely, under the watchful eye of great lexicographers and with the encouragement of columnists and writers who ache for color in verbs, the creation of Buck Rogers's creator has blasted its way into the dictionaries. The verb will live long after superpowers agree to ban ray guns; no sound thunders or crackles like an imaginary sound turned into a new word.

Took me a while to get to the point today, but that is because I did not know what the point was when I started.

"I now zap all the commercials," says the merry Ellen Goodman. "I zap to the memory of white tornadoes past. I zap headaches, arthritis, bad breath and laundry detergent. I zap diet-drink maidens and hand-lotion mavens . . . Wiping out commercials could entirely and joyfully upend the TV industry. Take the word of The Boston Zapper."

Review and Assess

Thinking About the Selection

1. **Respond:** Had you ever noticed the connection between the onomatopoetic words Safire discusses and the sounds they describe?

2. **(a) Recall:** What is onomatopoeia? **(b) Classify:** What is the origin of this word?

3. **(a) Recall:** What is the *bow-wow theory* concerning the origin of language? **(b) Compare and Contrast:** Compare and contrast it with the *pooh-pooh theory* of language. **(c) Make a Judgment:** Do you think either of these terms is actually used by linguists? Explain.

4. **(a) Recall:** What does Safire find so interesting about the word *zap*? **(b) Analyze:** Why does he believe that this word will "live long after superpowers agree to ban ray guns"?

5. **(a) Infer:** Based on Safire's comment, what would you expect to find in Gertrude Stein's writing? **(b) Infer:** How do you think Safire views the use of onomatopoeia by writers?

6. **Evaluate:** Do you think Safire's humorous style is more or less effective than a factual explanation? Explain.

COYOTE V. ACME

Ian Frazier

Background

This essay is the fictional opening statement of a lawsuit by Mr. Wile E. Coyote, charging the Acme Company with the sale of defective merchandise. If these names sound familiar, you may have a childhood memory of watching Wile E. Coyote chase the Road Runner around the desert. The Warner Brothers cartoon "Road Runner and Coyote" made its debut in 1949; more than half a century later, both the coyote and the elusive bird are still going strong. Perhaps fifty years from now your grandchildren will be watching Coyote's ill-fated attempts—many involving Acme products—to capture the fleet-footed bird. As you read the essay, consider what Frazier is really satirizing—the cartoon character who is his subject or the legal profession.

**In the United States District Court,
Southwestern District,
Tempe, Arizona
Case No. B19294,
Judge Joan Kujava, Presiding**

WILE E. COYOTE, Plaintiff
—v.—
ACME COMPANY, Defendant

Opening Statement of Mr. Harold Schoff, attorney for Mr. Coyote: My client, Mr. Wile E. Coyote, a resident of Arizona and <u>contiguous</u> states, does hereby bring suit for damages against the Acme Company, manufacturer and retail distributor of assorted merchandise, incorporated in Delaware and doing business in every state, district, and territory. Mr. Coyote seeks compensation for personal injuries, loss of business income, and mental suffering caused as a direct result of the actions and/or gross negligence of said company, under Title 15 of the United States Code, Chapter 47, section 2072, subsection (a), relating to product liability.

contiguous (kən tig´ yo͞o əs) *adj.* bordering; adjacent

Mr. Coyote states that on eighty-five separate occasions he has purchased of the Acme Company (hereinafter, "Defendant"), through that company's mail-order department, certain products which did cause him bodily injury due to defects in manufacture or improper cautionary labeling. Sales slips made out to Mr. Coyote as proof of purchase are at present in the possession of the Court, marked Exhibit A. Such injuries sustained by Mr. Coyote have temporarily restricted his ability to make a living in his profession of predator. Mr. Coyote is self-employed and thus not eligible for Workmen's Compensation.[1]

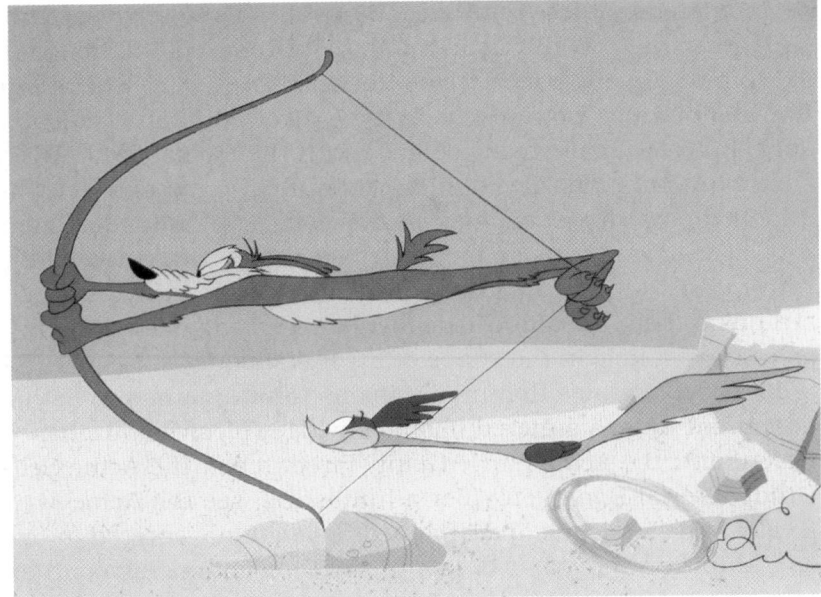

▲ Critical Viewing
Which word from the vocabulary list on page 1111 might be used to describe Coyote's bow? Explain. **[Connect]**

Mr. Coyote states that on December 13th he received of Defendant via parcel post one Acme Rocket Sled. The intention of Mr. Coyote was to use the Rocket Sled to aid him in pursuit of his prey. Upon receipt of the Rocket Sled Mr. Coyote removed it from its wooden shipping crate and, sighting his prey in the distance, activated the ignition. As Mr. Coyote gripped the handlebars, the Rocket Sled accelerated with such sudden and <u>precipitate</u> force as to stretch Mr. Coyote's forelimbs to a length of fifty feet. Subsequently, the rest of Mr. Coyote's body shot forward with a violent jolt, causing severe strain to his back and neck and placing him unexpectedly astride the Rocket Sled. Disappearing over the horizon at such speed as to leave a diminishing jet trail along its path, the Rocket Sled soon brought Mr. Coyote abreast of his prey. At that moment the animal he was pursuing veered sharply to the right. Mr. Coyote vigorously attempted to follow this maneuver but was unable to, due to poorly designed steering on the Rocket Sled and a faulty or nonexistent braking system. Shortly thereafter, the unchecked progress of the Rocket Sled brought it and Mr. Coyote into collision with the side of a mesa.[2]

precipitate (prē sip´ ə tit) *adj.* very sudden

Paragraph One of the Report of Attending Physician (Exhibit B), prepared by Dr. Ernest Grosscup, M.D., D.O., details the multiple fractures, contusions, and tissue damage suffered by Mr. Coyote as a result of this collision. Repair of the injuries required a full bandage around the head (excluding the ears), a neck brace, and full or partial casts on all four legs.

✔ Reading Check
For what three reasons does Mr. Coyote seek compensation from The Acme Company?

---

1. **Workmen's Compensation** form of disability insurance that provides income to workers who are unable to work due to injuries sustained on the job.
2. **mesa** (mā´ sə) *n.* small, high plateau with steep sides.

Hampered by these injuries, Mr. Coyote was nevertheless obliged to support himself. With this in mind, he purchased of Defendant as an aid to mobility one pair of Acme Rocket Skates. When he attempted to use this product, however, he became involved in an accident remarkably similar to that which occurred with the Rocket Sled. Again, Defendant sold over the counter, without <u>caveat</u>, a product which attached powerful jet engines (in this case, two) to inadequate vehicles, with little or no provision for passenger safety. Encumbered by his heavy casts, Mr. Coyote lost control of the Rocket Skates soon after strapping them on, and collided with a roadside billboard so violently as to leave a hole in the shape of his full silhouette.

Mr. Coyote states that on occasions too numerous to list in this document he has suffered mishaps with explosives purchased of Defendant: the Acme "Little Giant" Firecracker, the Acme Self-Guided Aerial Bomb, etc. (For a full listing, see the Acme Mail Order Explosives Catalogue and attached deposition,[3] entered in evidence as Exhibit C.) Indeed, it is safe to say that not once has an explosive purchased of Defendant by Mr. Coyote performed in an expected manner. To cite just one example: At the expense of much time and personal effort, Mr. Coyote constructed around the outer rim of a butte[4] a wooden trough beginning at the top of the butte and spiraling downward around it to some few feet above a black X painted on the desert floor. The trough was designed in such a way that a spherical explosive of the type sold by Defendant would roll easily and swiftly down to the point of detonation indicated by the X. Mr. Coyote placed a generous pile of birdseed directly on the X, and then, carrying the spherical Acme Bomb (Catalogue #78–832), climbed to the top of the butte. Mr. Coyote's prey, seeing the birdseed, approached, and Mr. Coyote proceeded to light the fuse. In an instant, the fuse burned down to the stem, causing the bomb to detonate.

In addition to reducing all Mr. Coyote's careful preparations to naught, the premature detonation of Defendant's product resulted in the following disfigurements to Mr. Coyote:

1. Severe singeing of the hair on the head, neck, and muzzle.
2. Sooty discoloration.
3. Fracture of the left ear at the stem, causing the ear to dangle in the aftershock with a creaking noise.
4. Full or partial combustion of whiskers producing kinking, frazzling, and ashy disintegration
5. Radical widening of the eyes, due to brow and lid charring.

caveat (kā´ vē at´) *n.* formal notice; warning

Literary Analysis
Essay and Tone How would you describe the tone created by the use of legal language to describe the exaggerated events of a cartoon?

---

3. **deposition** (dep´ ə zish´ ən) *n.* legal term for the written testimony of a witness.
4. **butte** (byo͞ot) *n.* steep hill standing alone in a plain.

We come now to the Acme Spring-Powered Shoes. The remains of a pair of these purchased by Mr. Coyote on June 23rd are Plaintiff's Exhibit D. Selected fragments have been shipped to the metallurgical laboratories of the University of California at Santa Barbara for analysis, but to date no explanation has been found for this product's sudden and extreme malfunction. As advertised by Defendant, this product is simplicity itself: two wood-and-metal sandals, each attached to milled-steel springs of high <u>tensile</u> strength and compressed in a tightly coiled position by a cocking device with a lanyard release. Mr. Coyote believed that this product would enable him to pounce upon his prey in the initial moments of the chase, when swift reflexes are at a premium.

To increase the shoes' thrusting still further, Mr. Coyote affixed them by their bottoms to the side of a large boulder. Adjacent to the boulder was a path which Mr. Coyote's prey was known to frequent. Mr. Coyote put his hind feet in the wood-and-metal sandals and crouched in readiness, his right forepaw holding firmly to the lanyard release. Within a short time Mr. Coyote's prey did indeed appear on the path coming toward him. Unsuspecting, the prey stopped near Mr. Coyote, well within range of the springs at full extension. Mr. Coyote gauged the distance with care and proceeded to pull the lanyard release.

At this point, Defendant's product should have thrust Mr. Coyote forward and away from the boulder. Instead, for reasons yet unknown, the Acme Spring-Powered Shoes thrust the boulder away from Mr. Coyote. As the intended prey looked on unharmed, Mr. Coyote hung suspended in air. Then the twin springs recoiled, bringing Mr. Coyote to a violent feet-first collision with the boulder, the full weight of his head and forequarters falling upon his lower extremities.

The force of this impact then caused the springs to rebound, whereupon Mr. Coyote was thrust skyward. A second recoil and collision followed. The boulder, meanwhile, which was roughly ovoid in shape, had begun to bounce down a hillside, the coiling and recoiling of the springs adding to its velocity. At each bounce, Mr. Coyote came into contact with the boulder, or the boulder came into contact with Mr. Coyote, or both came into contact with the ground. As the grade was a long one, this process continued for some time.

The sequence of collisions resulted in systemic physical damage to Mr. Coyote, viz., flattening of the cranium, sideways displacement of the tongue, reduction of length of legs and upper body, and compression of vertebrae from base of tail to head. Repetition of blows along a vertical axis produced a series of regular horizontal folds in Mr. Coyote's body tissues—a rare and painful condition which caused Mr. Coyote to expand upward and contract downward alternately as he walked, and to emit an off-key accordion-like wheezing with every step.

tensile (ten´ sil) *adj.*
stretchable

☑**Reading Check**

Have Acme products performed well for Mr. Coyote? Explain.

The distracting and embarrassing nature of this symptom has been a major impediment to Mr. Coyote's pursuit of a normal social life.

As the Court is no doubt aware, Defendant has a virtual monopoly of manufacture and sale of goods required by Mr. Coyote's work. It is our contention that Defendant has used its market advantage to the detriment of the consumer of such specialized products as itching powder, giant kites, Burmese tiger traps, anvils, and two-hundred-foot-long rubber bands. Much as he has come to mistrust Defendant's products, Mr. Coyote has no other domestic source of supply to which to turn. One can only wonder what our trading partners in Western Europe and Japan would make of such a situation, where a giant company is allowed to victimize the consumer in the most reckless and wrongful manner over and over again.

Mr. Coyote respectfully requests that the Court regard these larger economic implications and assess punitive damages in the amount of seventeen million dollars. In addition, Mr. Coyote seeks actual damages (missed meals, medical expenses, days lost from professional occupation) of one million dollars; general damages (mental suffering, injury to reputation) of twenty million dollars; and attorney's fees of seven hundred and fifty thousand dollars. Total damages: thirty-eight million seven hundred and fifty thousand dollars. By awarding Mr. Coyote the full amount, this Court will censure Defendant, its directors, officers, shareholders, successors, and assigns, in the only language they understand, and reaffirm the right of the individual predator to equal protection under the law.

Literary Analysis
Essay What aspects of the legal and business professions does the line about "our trading partners" satirize?

Review and Assess

Thinking About the Selection

1. **Respond:** As you read the attorney's statement, did you sympathize with Wile E. Coyote? Why or why not?

2. **(a) Recall:** What happens to Wile E. Coyote's forelimbs when he uses the Rocket Sled? **(b) Support:** What details in this essay suggest that Wile E. Coyote is a cartoon character?

3. **(a) Recall:** How often does Wile E. Coyote buy products from the Acme Company? **(b) Support:** Find evidence to explain why he maintains this relationship with Acme, despite the outcomes he has faced with their products.

4. **(a) Recall:** What action is Wile E. Coyote seeking from the court? **(b) Make a Judgment:** If you were a member of the jury in this case, what would your verdict be? Explain.

5. **Evaluate:** What do you believe was Frazier's purpose in writing this essay? Was he simply trying to be funny or was he making a point? Explain.

Review and Assess

Literary Analysis

Essay

1. (a) What type of **essay** is "The Mortgaged Heart"? (b) What aspects of loneliness does McCullers explore? (c) What is her main point?

2. (a) What is the main purpose of "Onomatopoeia"? (b) Give an example of an idea that Safire explains.

3. (a) In "Coyote v. Acme," in what ways does the use of humor convey a serious idea? (b) What is the main point of the essay?

Comparing Literary Works

4. (a) Use a chart like the one shown to analyze the first paragraph of each essay and determine the author's **tone**. (b) What attitude toward his or her subject is revealed in each author's tone?

Summary of first paragraph	Words/details that indicate tone		Tone
		...▶	

5. Both Safire's and Frazier's essays rely on humor, but of different kinds. In your own words, describe the kind of humor used in each essay.

6. Imagine these essays with different tones. What role does tone play in the overall effect of each one? Explain.

Reading Strategy

Identifying Line of Reasoning

7. In "The Mortgaged Heart," what supporting information does McCullers use to convince the reader that (a) loneliness stems from the quest for identity and (b) love is the means of overcoming loneliness? (c) Is her supporting evidence convincing?

8. (a) Summarize the attorney's case for Mr. Coyote in "Coyote v. Acme." (b) What is the connection between Exhibits A–D and the main points of the attorney's arguments?

Extend Understanding

9. **Social Studies Connection:** Do you think Americans today are likely to be more or less lonely than the early settlers? Explain the societal changes that prompted your answer.

Quick Review

In an **analytical essay,** writers explore and clarify a topic. In an **expository essay,** writers explain, or provide information about, a topic. In a **satirical essay,** writers use irony, ridicule, or sarcasm to comment on a topic.

A writer's **tone** reflects his or her attitude toward the topic, characters, or audience.

To **identify the line of reasoning,** note the author's main points and the connection between the supporting evidence.

 Take It to the Net
www.phschool.com
Take the interactive self-test online to check your understanding of these selections.

Integrate Language Skills

Vocabulary Development Lesson

Word Analysis: Latin Root *-ten-*

The word *tensile* contains the Latin root *-ten-*, meaning "to stretch tightly." Tensile springs would be "stretchable." The words below take their meaning from the root *-ten-*. Use at least four of the words to write a paragraph about a disastrous camping trip.

tension	tense	tent
extent	tendon	intensify

Spelling Strategy

When you add the suffix *-ic* to nouns ending in *e* or *y*, drop the final *e*, as in *aesthete* + *-ic* = *aesthetic*. Notice that the new word is an adjective. Add the suffix *-ic* to create the adjective form for each of the following words.

1. athlete   **2.** base   **3.** fantasy

Fluency: Definitions

Review the vocabulary list on page 1111. Then, choose the definition from the right column that best fits the word in the left column.

1. precipitate	**a.**	share a common border
2. tensile	**b.**	conclusion
3. contiguous	**c.**	sudden, abrupt
4. pristine	**d.**	formal warning
5. caveat	**e.**	nonconformist
6. aesthetic	**f.**	stretchable quality
7. corollary	**g.**	sense of beauty
8. maverick	**h.**	completely untouched

Grammar and Style Lesson

Pronouns With Appositives

McCullers observes that ". . . we Americans are always seeking." Notice that the pronoun *we* is followed by the noun *Americans* and acts as the subject of the clause. When a **pronoun** is followed by an **appositive**—a noun that renames the pronoun—choose the correct pronoun by mentally dropping the appositive.

Subject: We <u>players</u> had to win.
(We had to win.)

Object: It was up to us <u>players</u>.
(It was up to us.)

Use *I*, *he*, *she*, *we*, or *they* to rename subjects and *me*, *him*, *her*, *us*, or *them* to rename objects.

Practice For each of the sentences below, choose the correct form of the pronoun in parentheses. Then, rewrite the complete sentence correctly.

1. Loneliness is common among (we, us) Americans.

2. Love can help (us, you) and (I, me).

3. Two students, (she, her) and Carlos, were tied for the best grades.

4. (We, Us) cartoon lovers all know Wile E. Coyote.

5. He would like to gain sympathy amongst (us, we) predators.

Writing Application Write a paragraph in which you describe a sporting event. Use the correct form of pronouns with appositives at least three times.

W G *Prentice Hall Writing and Grammar Connection: Chapter 19, Section 1*

Writing Lesson

Analytical Essay

Carson McCullers describes the American artist as "the eternal maverick." In an analytical essay, explore the origin and current meaning of the word. Then, explain why being a maverick is or is not a uniquely American quality.

Prewriting Use a dictionary to trace the etymology of the word *maverick*. Compare the word's origins with its use today. Brainstorm for specific examples of people who demonstrate maverick traits.

Drafting Include the quote from McCullers's essay in your introduction, and state whether or not you agree with it. Use your body paragraphs to explain the origin and meaning of *maverick*, and to cite evidence for agreeing or disagreeing with McCullers.

Revising Review your essay and make sure you have clearly connected your ideas. Highlight transitional phrases you have used, and add any that may be needed.

Model: Using Transitions for Clarity

In comparison to the rest of the world, America is a young, brash country. *However,* we are not the only ones who value independent thinking. *For example,* Pablo Picasso was one of the great artists of the 20th century. He was a maverick, but he was not American.

> Transitional words and phrases help to establish a sound line of reasoning.

 Prentice Hall Writing and Grammar Connection: Chapter 3, Section 2

Extension Activities

Listening and Speaking Working in groups as teams of attorneys defending the Acme Company, develop a response to the arguments presented in "Coyote v. Acme." Present your **opening statement** for the defense to the class. Use these tips to prepare:

- Respond to each of the main arguments presented in the essay.
- Appeal both to logic and to the emotions.

Present your opening statements using appropriate body language. **[Group Activity]**

Research and Technology View episodes of the Roadrunner cartoon. As you watch, evaluate the various ways the cartoon makers present events and communicate characters' motivations. Then, write a short **essay** analyzing the cartoon and discussing the expository methods you identified. Exchange your essay with classmates and discuss points of agreement and disagreement.

 Take It to the Net   www.phschool.com

Go online for an additional research activity using the Internet.

Prepare to Read

Straw Into Gold ◆ For the Love of Books ◆ Mother Tongue

Sandra Cisneros (b. 1954)

Sandra Cisneros was born in Chicago into a large Mexican American family. Because her family was poor, Cisneros moved frequently and lived for the most part in small, cramped apartments. To cope with these conditions, she retreated into herself and spent much of her time reading fairy tales and classic literature. She attended Loyola University in Chicago and the Writer's Workshop at the University of Iowa. During her college years, Cisneros met writers from many other backgrounds. At first uncomfortable about her family's struggles, she soon realized that her heritage provided her with something unique. Cisneros began writing about her childhood in a book of connected short stories. *The House on Mango Street* (1984) was a modest success. However, her later book, *Woman Hollering Creek* (1991), won critical acclaim and earned Cisneros widespread recognition. Of her desire to write about her family and community, Cisneros has said "I'm trying to write stories that haven't been written. I feel like a cartographer; I'm determined to fill a literary void."

Rita Dove (b. 1952)

Now a famous poet, Rita Dove's first writing efforts—at the age of nine or ten—were comic books with female superheroes. Dove was born in Akron, Ohio, to highly educated parents. Her father, Ray A. Dove, was the first African American chemist to work in the tire and rubber industry. Dove attended Miami University in Oxford, Ohio, and later the University of Iowa. She has published six volumes of poetry, including the Pulitzer Prize-winning *Thomas and Beulah* (1986) and the critically acclaimed *On the Bus with Rosa Parks* (1999). Dove has also written a play, a novel, and a collection of short stories. In 1993, she was appointed Poet Laureate of the United States, becoming the first African American and the youngest person ever to hold that position. "Every time I write a poem," Dove has said, "I try to imagine the reader—the reader that I was—curled up on the couch, at the moment of opening a book and absolutely having my world fall away and entering into another one."

Amy Tan (b. 1952)

As a child starting school, Amy Tan—the daughter of Chinese immigrants—would answer her mother's Chinese questions in English. Growing up in Oakland, California, Tan continued to embrace typical American values and ideas, which she assumed defined her identity. These assumptions were upended when the thirty-five-year old Tan visited China with her mother. There she came to appreciate her Chinese roots. At the time, she was leaving a successful career as a business writer to become a fiction writer. When she returned to the United States, she began *The Joy Luck Club* (1989), a novel about four Chinese American women and their mothers. The book made Tan a celebrity. Although she struggled terribly with writer's block—beginning and discarding six novels—Tan triumphed with her second novel, *The Kitchen God's Wife* (1991). Her third novel, *The Hundred Secret Senses*, was published in 1995, and her fourth, *The Bonesetter's Daughter*, appeared in 2001.

Preview

Connecting to the Literature

Perhaps, like the writers of these essays when they were girls, you are not as confident as you would like to be. These writers discovered the world of books, and their love of reading led them to write. In writing, each found her own voice.

Literary Analysis

Reflective Essay

An essay is a short piece of nonfiction in which a writer expresses a personal view of a topic. In a **reflective essay,** the writer uses an informal tone to describe personal experiences or pivotal events. In her essay Rita Dove focuses on her love of books:

> . . . always, I have been passionate about books. . . . I loved to feel their heft in my hand . . .

An essay writer often explores an experience in order to arrive at a deeper understanding of its significance. To help you track each writer's reflections, use a chart like the one shown.

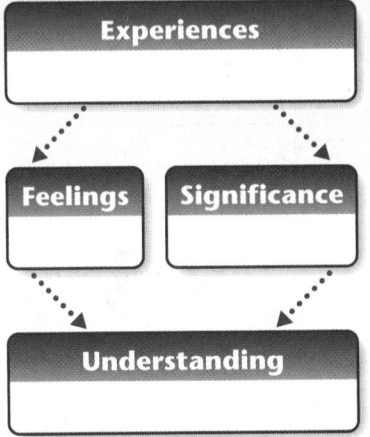

Comparing Literary Works

Each of these three writers discusses her struggle to create her own true sense of **identity.** As you read, examine how each writer describes the role played by other people in her creation of a genuine sense of self. Determine if a true sense of identity is to be discovered among our companions, in the recesses of our own privacy, or in some combination of the two.

Reading Strategy

Evaluating a Writer's Message

As a reader, your job is not only to get a writer's point, but also to decide what you think about it. When you **evaluate a writer's message,** you assess the validity of the writer's ideas and decide whether you agree or disagree with them. As you read these essays, identify and then evaluate the message of each writer.

Vocabulary Development

nomadic (nō mad´ ik) *adj.* wandering; leading the life of a nomad (p. 1130)

transcribed (tran skrībd´) *v.* wrote or typed a copy (p. 1137)

empirical (em pir´ i kəl) *adj.* derived from observation or experiment (p. 1138)

benign (bi nīn´) *adj.* not injurious or malignant; not cancerous (p. 1139)

semantic (sə man´ tik) *adj.* pertaining to meaning in language (p. 1140)

quandary (kwän´ də rē; kwän´ drē) *n.* state of uncertainty; dilemma (p. 1141)

nascent (nas´ ənt; nā´ sənt) *adj.* coming into existence; emerging (p. 1141)

STRAW INTO GOLD:
THE METAMORPHOSIS
OF THE EVERYDAY

Sandra Cisneros

Background

The term "essay" from the French *essai,* meaning "try," historically described an exploratory piece of writing that lacked finish. In 1597, Francis Bacon called his own *Essays* "grains of salt which will rather give an appetite than offend with satiety." Eventually, the essay lost its original "unfinished" sense and writers began to think of it as an elegant, logically reasoned, polished piece of writing. Today, the essay has become one of the most popular literary forms among writers and readers.

When I was living in an artists' colony in the south of France, some fellow Latin-Americans who taught at the university in Aix-en-Provence[1] invited me to share a home-cooked meal with them. I had been living abroad almost a year then on an NEA[2] grant, subsisting mainly on French bread and lentils while in France so that my money could last longer. So when the invitation to dinner arrived, I accepted without hesitation. Especially since they had promised Mexican food.

What I didn't realize when they made this invitation was that I was supposed to be involved in preparing this meal. I guess they assumed I knew how to cook Mexican food because I was Mexican. They wanted specifically tortillas, though I'd never made a tortilla in my life.

It's true I had witnessed my mother rolling the little armies of dough into perfect circles, but my mother's family is from Guanajuato,[3] *provinciales,*[4] country folk. They only know how to make flour tortillas. My father's family, on the other hand, is chilango,[5] from Mexico City.

1. **Aix-en-Provence** (eks än prō väns´) city in southeastern France.
2. **NEA** National Endowment for the Arts.
3. **Guanajuato** (gwä´ nä hwä´ tō) state in central Mexico.
4. **provinciales** (prō bēn sē ä´ läs) "country folk" (Spanish).
5. **chilango** (chē län´ gō) "city folk" (Spanish).

Biography, 1988, Marina Gutierrez, Courtesy of the artist

We ate corn tortillas but we didn't make them. Someone was sent to the corner tortilleria to buy some. I'd never seen anybody make corn tortillas. Ever.

Well, somehow my Latino hosts had gotten a hold of a packet of corn flour, and this is what they tossed my way with orders to produce tortillas. *Asi como sea.* Any ol' way, they said and went back to their cooking.

Why did I feel like the woman in the fairy tale who was locked in a room and ordered to spin straw into gold? I had the same sick feeling when I was required to write my critical essay for my MFA[6] exam—the only piece of noncreative writing necessary in order to get my graduate degree. How was I to start? There were rules involved here, unlike writing a poem or story, which I did intuitively. There was a step-by-step process needed and I had better know it. I felt as if making tortillas, or writing a critical paper for that matter, were tasks so impossible I wanted to break down into tears.

Somehow though, I managed to make those tortillas—crooked and burnt, but edible nonetheless. My hosts were absolutely ignorant when it came to Mexican food; they thought my tortillas were delicious. (I'm glad my mama wasn't there.) Thinking back and

6. **MFA** Master of Fine Arts.

▲ **Critical Viewing** This painting, titled *Biography*, challenges the viewer to piece together the experiences of a lifetime from a variety of small objects. What parallels can you draw between the picture and this essay? **[Connect]**

✔**Reading Check**

What Mexican dish was Cisneros asked to prepare?

looking at that photograph documenting the three of us consuming those lopsided circles I am amazed. Just as I am amazed I could finish my MFA exam (lopsided and crooked, but finished all the same). Didn't think I could do it. But I did.

I've managed to do a lot of things in my life I didn't think I was capable of and which many others didn't think me capable of either.

Especially because I am a woman, a Latina, an only daughter in a family of six men. My father would've liked to have seen me married long ago. In our culture, men and women don't leave their father's house except by way of marriage. I crossed my father's threshold with nothing carrying me but my own two feet. A woman whom no one came for and no one chased away.

To make matters worse, I had left before any of my six brothers had ventured away from home. I had broken a terrible taboo. Somehow, looking back at photos of myself as a child, I wonder if I was aware of having begun already my own quiet war.

I like to think that somehow my family, my Mexicanness, my poverty all had something to do with shaping me into a writer. I like to think my parents were preparing me all along for my life as an artist even though they didn't know it. From my father I inherited a love of wandering. He was born in Mexico City but as a young man he traveled into the U.S. vagabonding. He eventually was drafted and thus became a citizen. Some of the stories he has told about his first months in the U.S. with little or no English surface in my stories in *The House on Mango Street* as well as others I have in mind to write in the future. From him I inherited a sappy heart. (He still cries when he watches the Mexican soaps—especially if they deal with children who have forsaken their parents.)

My mother was born like me—in Chicago but of Mexican descent. It would be her tough, streetwise voice that would haunt all my stories and poems. An amazing woman who loves to draw and read books and can sing an opera. A smart cookie.

When I was a little girl we traveled to Mexico City so much I thought my grandparents' house on La Fortuna, Number 12, was home. It was the only constant in our <u>nomadic</u> ramblings from one Chicago flat to another. The house on Destiny Street, Number 12, in the colonia Tepeyac,[7] would be perhaps the only home I knew, and that nostalgia for a home would be a theme that would obsess me.

My brothers also figured greatly in my art. Especially the oldest two; I grew up in their shadows. Henry, the second oldest and my favorite, appears often in poems I have written and in stories which at times only borrow his nickname, Kiki. He played a major role in my childhood. We were bunkbed mates. We were co-conspirators. We were pals. Until my oldest brother came back from studying in Mexico and left me odd-woman-out for always.

What would my teachers say if they knew I was a writer? Who would've guessed it? I wasn't a very bright student. I didn't much like

---

7. **colonia Tepeyac** (cô lō′ nēä tā pä′ yäc) district of Mexico City.

Literary Analysis
Reflective Essay What words or phrases in this paragraph signal that this is a reflective essay on a personal topic?

nomadic (nō mad′ ik) *adj.* wandering; leading the life of a nomad

school because we moved so much and I was always new and funny-looking. In my fifth-grade report card, I have nothing but an avalanche of C's and D's, but I don't remember being that stupid. I was good at art and I read plenty of library books and Kiki laughed at all my jokes. At home I was fine, but at school I never opened my mouth except when the teacher called on me, the first time I'd speak all day.

When I think how I see myself, it would have to be at age eleven. I know I'm thirty-two on the outside, but inside I'm eleven. I'm the girl in the picture with skinny arms and a crumpled shirt and crooked hair. I didn't like school because all they saw was the outside me. School was lots of rules and sitting with your hands folded and being very afraid all the time. I liked looking out the window and thinking. I liked staring at the girl across the way writing her name over and over again in red ink. I wondered why the boy with the dirty collar in front of me didn't have a mama who took better care of him.

I think my mama and papa did the best they could to keep us warm and clean and never hungry. We had birthday and graduation parties and things like that, but there was another hunger that had to be fed. There was a hunger I didn't even have a name for. Was this when I began writing?

In 1966 we moved into a house, a real one, our first real home. This meant we didn't have to change schools and be the new kids on the block every couple of years. We could make friends and not be afraid we'd have to say goodbye to them and start all over. My brothers and the flock of boys they brought home would become important characters eventually for my stories—Louie and his cousins, Meme Ortiz and his dog with two names, one in English and one in Spanish.

My mother flourished in her own home. She took books out of the library and taught herself to garden, producing flowers so envied we had to put a lock on the gate to keep out the midnight flower thieves. My mother is still gardening to this day.

This was the period in my life, that slippery age when you are both child and woman and neither, I was to record in *The House on Mango Street*. I was still shy. I was a girl who couldn't come out of her shell.

How was I to know I would be recording and documenting the women who sat their sadness on an elbow and stared out a window? It would be the city streets of Chicago I would later record, but from a child's eyes.

I've done all kinds of things I didn't think I could do since then. I've gone to a prestigious university, studied with famous writers, and taken away an MFA degree. I've taught poetry in the schools in Illinois and Texas. I've gotten an NEA grant and run away with it as far as my courage would take me. I've seen the bleached and bitter mountains of the Peloponnesus.[8] I've lived on a Greek island. I've been to Venice[9]

---

8. **Peloponnesus** (pel´ ə pə nē´ səs) peninsula forming the southeastern part of the Greek mainland.
9. **Venice** (ven´ is) seaport in northern Italy.

Literary Analysis
Reflective Essay and Identity When she was a child, in what ways did Cisneros's inner life not communicate itself to those around her?

Reading Strategy
Evaluating a Writer's Message Why do you think Cisneros does not go into greater detail about the nature of her "hunger"?

**Reading Check**

In Cisneros's culture, under what circumstances do women usually leave home?

twice. In Rapallo, I met Ilona once and forever and took her sad heart with me across the south of France and into Spain.

I've lived in Yugoslavia. I've been to the famous Nice[10] flower market behind the opera house. I've lived in a village in the pre-Alps[11] and witnessed the daily parade of promenaders.

I've moved since Europe to the strange and wonderful country of Texas, land of polaroid-blue skies and big bugs. I met a mayor with my last name. I met famous Chicana/o artists and writers and *politicos*.[12]

Texas is another chapter in my life. It brought with it the Dobie-Paisano Fellowship, a six-month residency on a 265-acre ranch. But most important Texas brought Mexico back to me.

Sitting at my favorite people-watching spot, the snaky Woolworth's counter across the street from the Alamo,[13] I can't think of anything else I'd rather be than a writer. I've traveled and lectured from Cape Cod to San Francisco, to Spain, Yugoslavia, Greece, Mexico, France, Italy, and finally today to Seguin, Texas. Along the way there is straw for the taking. With a little imagination, it can be spun into gold.

---

10. **Nice** (nēs) seaport and resort in southeastern France.
11. **pre-Alps** foothills of the Alps, a mountain range in south-central Europe.
12. **politicos** (pō lē′ tē cōs) "politicians" (Spanish).
13. **the Alamo** (al′ ə mō′) mission in San Antonio, Texas, that was the scene of a famous battle between Texans and Mexican troops in 1836.

Review and Assess

Thinking About the Selection

1. **Respond:** Does Cisneros seem to be someone you would like to meet? Why or why not?

2. **(a) Recall:** Which experience reminds Cisneros of the story of the woman who had to spin straw into gold? **(b) Interpret:** What point is she trying to make through this anecdote? **(c) Connect:** What connections does Cisneros draw between this anecdote and the rest of her essay?

3. **(a) Recall:** What was the taboo Cisneros broke when she left her family home? **(b) Analyze:** Who was the enemy in the "quiet war" Cisneros had begun?

4. **(a) Recall:** How old is Cisneros "on the inside"? **(b) Analyze:** In what ways does her description of herself at that age represent a divide between her inner sense of self and her external realities?

5. **(a) Distinguish:** Which obstacles stood in the way of Cisneros's becoming a writer? **(b) Analyze:** What circumstances contributed to her literary success?

6. **(a) Draw Conclusions:** What is the main point of the essay? Support your answer. **(b) Apply:** In what ways could you apply Cisneros's message to your own life?

For the Love of BOOKS

—Rita Dove

When I am asked: "What made you want to be a writer?" my answer has always been: "Books." First and foremost, now, then, and always, I have been passionate about books. From the time I began to read, as a child, I loved to feel their heft in my hand and the warm spot caused by their intimate weight in my lap; I loved the crisp whisper of a page turning, the musky odor of old paper and the sharp inky whiff of new pages. Leather bindings sent me into ecstasy. I even loved to gaze at a closed book and daydream about the possibilities inside—it was like contemplating a genie's lamp. Of course, my favorite fairy tale was *A Thousand and One Nights*—imagine buying your life with stories!— and my favorite cartoons were those where animated characters popped out of books and partied while the unsuspecting humans slept. In books, I could travel anywhere, be anybody, understand worlds long past and imaginary colonies in the future. My idea of a bargain was to go to the public library, wander along the bookshelves, and emerge with a chin-high stack of books that were mine, all mine, for two weeks—free of charge!

What I remember most about long summer days is browsing the bookshelves in our solarium to see if there were any new additions. I grew up with those rows of books; I knew where each one was shelved and immediately spotted newcomers. And after months had gone by and there'd be no new books, I would think: Okay, I guess I'll try this one—and then discover that the very book I had been avoiding because of a drab cover or small print was actually a wonderful read. Louis Untermeyer's *Treasury of Best Loved Poems* had a sickeningly sweet lilac and gold cover and was forbiddingly thick, but I finally pulled it

☑ **Reading Check**

What made Dove want to be a writer?

off the shelf and discovered a cornucopia of emotional and linguistic delights, from "The Ballad of Barbara Fritchie," which I adored for its sheer length and rather numbing rhymes, to Langston Hughes's dazzlingly syncopated "Dream Boogie." Then there was Shakespeare—daunting for many years because it was his entire oeuvre,[1] in matching wine-red volumes that were so thick they looked more like over-sized bouillon cubes than books, and yet it was that ponderous title—*The Complete Works of William Shakespeare*—that enticed me, because here was a lifetime's work—a lifetime!—in two compact, dense packages. I began with the long poem "The Rape of Lucrece" . . . I sampled a few sonnets, which I found beautiful but rather adult; and finally wandered into the plays—first *Romeo and Juliet,* then *Macbeth, Julius Caesar, A Midsummer Night's Dream, Twelfth Night*—enthralled by the language, by the fact that poetry was spinning the story. Of course I did not understand every single word, but I was too young to know that this was supposed to be difficult; besides, no one was waiting to test me on anything, so, free from pressure, I dove in.

At the same time, my brother, two years my senior, had become a science fiction buff, so I'd read his *Analog* and *Fantasy* and Science Fiction magazines after he was finished with them. One story particularly fascinated me: A retarded boy in a small town begins building a sculpture in his backyard, using old and discarded materials—coke bottles, scrap iron, string, and bottle caps. Everyone laughs at him, but he continues building. Then one day he disappears. And when the neighbors investigate, they discover that the sculpture has been dragged onto the back porch and that the screen door is open. Somehow the narrator of the story figures out how to switch on the sculpture: The back door frame begins to glow, and when he steps through it, he's in an alternate universe, a town the mirror image of his own—even down to the colors, with green roses and an orange sky. And he walks through this town until he comes to the main square, where there is a statue erected to—who else?—the village idiot.

I loved this story, the idea that the dreamy, mild, scatter-brained boy of one world could be the hero of another. And in a way, I identified with that village idiot because in real life I was painfully shy and awkward; the place where I felt most alive was between the pages of a book.

Although I loved books, for a long time I had no aspirations to be a writer. The possibility was beyond my imagination. I liked to write, however—and on long summer days when I ran out of reading material or my legs had fallen asleep because I had been curled up on the couch for hours on end, I made up my own stories. Most were abandoned midway. Those that I did bring to a conclusion I neither showed to others nor considered saving.

My first piece of writing I thought enough of to keep was a novel called *Chaos,* which was about robots taking over the earth. I had

Reading Strategy
Evaluating a Writer's Message What point is Dove making about the value of reading when she notes that she did not understand every word she read?

Literary Analysis
Reflective Essay and Identity What sense of herself as a child does Dove's description of the boy in the story convey?

---

1. **oeuvre** (ĕ´ vrə) *n.* all the works, usually of a lifetime, of a particular writer, artist, or composer.

just entered third or fourth grade; the novel had forty-three chapters, and each chapter was twenty lines or less because I used each week's spelling list as the basis for each chapter, and there were twenty words per list. In the course of the year I wrote one installment per week, and I never knew what was going to happen next—the words led me, not the other way around.

At that time I didn't think of writing as an activity people admited doing. I had no living role models—a "real" writer was a long-dead white male, usually with a white beard to match. Much later, when I was in eleventh grade, my English teacher, Miss Oechsner, took me to a book-signing in a downtown hotel. She didn't ask me if I'd like to go—she asked my parents instead, signed me and a classmate (who is now a professor of literature) out of school one day, and took us to meet a writer. The writer was John Ciardi, a poet who also had translated Dante's *Divine Comedy*, which I had heard of, vaguely. At that moment I realized that writers were real people and how it was possible to write down a poem or story in the intimate sphere of one's own room and then share it with the world.

Review and Assess

Thinking About the Selection

1. **Respond:** Would you have been friends with Rita Dove if you had known her as a child? Why or why not?

2. **(a) Recall:** Which emotion did Dove feel in the presence of an unopened book? **(b) Interpret:** For Dove, what traits did an unopened book and a genie's lamp share? **(c) Analyze:** What attitude toward the imagination is suggested by this simile?

3. **(a) Recall:** What books does Dove note most delighted her as a child? **(b) Interpret:** What point is Dove making about the imaginative life of a child through this catalog of her favorite literature?

4. **(a) Recall:** What happens in the science fiction story that Dove enjoys so much? **(b) Connect:** Why is the story especially meaningful to Dove?

5. **(a) Recall:** Which experience made Dove realize that she could be a "real" writer? **(b) Speculate:** Do you think Dove would have gone on to become a writer if she had not had that experience? Why or why not?

6. **Take a Position:** When Dove started reading Shakespeare, she did not know that it "was supposed to be difficult" and so she loved it. What does this statement suggest about our expectations when approaching challenges?

Mother Tongue

Amy Tan

▲ **Critical Viewing**
Based on this photograph of Amy Tan and her mother, what kind of a relationship do you think they share? Explain.
[Infer]

Literary Analysis
Reflective Essay Which ideas in these opening paragraphs signal that this will be a reflective essay?

I am not a scholar of English or literature. I cannot give you much more than personal opinions on the English language and its variations in this country or others.

I am a writer. And by that definition, I am someone who has always loved language. I am fascinated by language in daily life. I spend a great deal of my time thinking about the power of language—the way it can evoke an emotion, a visual image, a complex idea, or a simple truth. Language is the tool of my trade. And I use them all—all the Englishes I grew up with.

Recently, I was made keenly aware of the different Englishes I do use. I was giving a talk to a large group of people, the same talk I had already given to half a dozen other groups. The nature of the talk was about my writing, my life, and my book, *The Joy Luck Club.* The talk was going along well enough, until I remembered one major difference that made the whole talk sound wrong. My mother was in the room. And it was perhaps the first time she had heard me give a lengthy speech, using the kind of English I have never used with her. I was saying things like, "The intersection of memory upon imagination" and "There is an aspect of my fiction that relates to thus-and-thus"—a speech filled with carefully wrought grammatical phrases, burdened, it suddenly seemed to me, with nominalized forms, past perfect tenses, conditional phrases, all the forms of standard English that I had learned in school and through books, the forms of English I did not use at home with my mother.

Just last week, I was walking down the street with my mother, and I again found myself conscious of the English I was using, the English I do use with her. We were talking about the price of new and used furniture and I heard myself saying this: "Not waste money that way." My husband was with us as well, and he didn't notice any switch in my English. And then I realized why. It's because over the twenty years we've been together I've often used the same kind of English with him, and sometimes he even uses it with me. It has become our language of intimacy, a different sort of English that relates to family talk, the language I grew up with.

So you'll have some idea of what this family talk I heard sounds like, I'll quote what my mother said during a recent conversation which I videotaped and then <u>transcribed</u>.

During this conversation, my mother was talking about a political gangster in Shanghai[1] who had the same last name as her family's, Du, and how the gangster in his early years wanted to be adopted by her family, which was rich by comparison. Later, the gangster became more powerful, far richer than my mother's family, and one day showed up at my mother's wedding to pay his respects. Here's what she said in part:

"Du Yusong having business like fruit stand. Like off the street kind. He is Du like Du Zong—but not Tsung-ming Island people. The local people call putong, the river east side, he belong to that side local people. That man want to ask Du Zong father take him in like become own family. Du Zong father wasn't look down on him, but didn't take seriously, until that man big like become a mafia. Now important person, very hard to inviting him. Chinese way, come only to show respect, don't stay for dinner. Respect for making big celebration, he shows up. Mean gives lots of respect. Chinese custom. Chinese social life that way. If too important won't have to stay too long. He come to my wedding. I didn't see, I heard it. I gone to boy's side, they have YMCA[2] dinner. Chinese age I was nineteen."

You should know that my mother's expressive command of English belies how much she actually understands. She reads the Forbes[3] report, listens to *Wall Street Week*,[4] converses daily with her stockbroker, reads all of Shirley MacLaine's[5] books with ease—all kinds

1. **Shanghai** (shaŋ´ hī´) seaport city in eastern China.
2. **YMCA** Young Men's Christian Association.
3. *Forbes* magazine of business and finance.
4. *Wall Street Week* weekly television program that reports business and investment news.
5. **Shirley MacLaine's** (mək länz´) Shirley MacLaine is an American actress who has written several books.

transcribed (tran skrībd´) *v.* wrote or typed a copy

Reading Check

How does Tan's language change when she gives her speech?

of things I can't begin to understand. Yet some of my friends tell me they understand 50 percent of what my mother says. Some say they understand 80 to 90 percent. Some say they understand none of it, as if she were speaking pure Chinese. But to me, my mother's English is perfectly clear, perfectly natural. It's my mother tongue. Her language, as I hear it, is vivid, direct, full of observation and imagery. That was the language that helped shape the way I saw things, expressed things, made sense of the world.

Lately, I've been giving more thought to the kind of English my mother speaks. Like others, I have described it to people as "broken," or "fractured" English. But I wince when I say that. It has always bothered me that I can think of no way to describe it other than "broken," as if it were damaged and needed to be fixed, as if it lacked a certain wholeness and soundness. I've heard other terms used, "limited English," for example. But they seem just as bad, as if everything is limited, including people's perceptions of the limited English speaker.

Literary Analysis
Reflective Essay
What language in this paragraph reinforces the idea that the essay is reflective?

I know this for a fact, because when I was growing up, my mother's "limited" English limited my perception of her. I was ashamed of her English. I believed that her English reflected the quality of what she had to say. That is, because she expressed them imperfectly her thoughts were imperfect. And I had plenty of <u>empirical</u> evidence to support me: the fact that people in department stores, at banks, and at restaurants did not take her seriously, did not give her good service, pretended not to understand her, or even acted as if they did not hear her.

empirical (em pir′ i kəl) *adj.* derived from observation or experiment

My mother has long realized the limitations of her English as well. When I was fifteen, she used to have me call people on the phone to pretend I was she. In this guise, I was forced to ask for information or even to complain and yell at people who had been rude to her. One time it was a call to her stockbroker in New York. She had cashed out her small portfolio and it just so happened we were going to go to New York the next week, our very first trip outside California. I had to get on the phone and say in an adolescent voice that was not very convincing, "This is Mrs. Tan."

And my mother was standing in the back whispering loudly, "Why he don't send me check, already two weeks late. So mad he lie to me, losing me money."

And then I said in perfect English, "Yes, I'm getting rather concerned. You had agreed to send the check two weeks ago, but it hasn't arrived."

Reading Strategy
Evaluating a Writer's Message What point does Tan make through this anecdote about speaking for her mother? Do you find her point valid? Explain.

Then she began to talk more loudly. "What he want, I come to New York tell him front of his boss, you cheating me?" And I was trying to calm her down, make her be quiet, while telling the stockbroker, "I can't tolerate any more excuses. If I don't receive the check immediately, I am going to have to speak to your manager when I'm in New York next week." And sure enough, the following week there we were in front of this astonished stockbroker, and I was sitting there red-faced and quiet, and my mother, the real Mrs. Tan, was shouting at his boss in her impeccable broken English.

We used a similar routine just five days ago, for a situation that was far less humorous. My mother had gone to the hospital for an appointment, to find out about a <u>benign</u> brain tumor a CAT scan[6] had revealed a month ago. She said she had spoken very good English, her best English, no mistakes. Still, she said, the hospital did not apologize when they said they had lost the CAT scan and she had come for nothing. She said they did not seem to have any sympathy when she told them she was anxious to know the exact diagnosis, since her husband and son had both died of brain tumors. She said they would not give her any more information until the next time and she would have to make another appointment for that. So she said she would not leave until the doctor called her daughter. She wouldn't budge. And when the doctor finally called her daughter, me, who spoke in perfect English—lo and behold—we had assurances the CAT scan would be found, promises that a conference call on Monday would be held, and apologies for any suffering my mother had gone through for a most regrettable mistake.

I think my mother's English almost had an effect on limiting my possibilities in life as well. Sociologists and linguists probably will tell you that a person's developing language skills are more influenced by peers. But I do think that the language spoken in the family, especially in immigrant families which are more insular, plays a large role in shaping the language of the child. And I believe that it affected my results on achievement tests, IQ tests, and the SAT.[7] While my English skills were never judged as poor, compared to math, English could not be considered my strong suit. In grade school I did moderately well, getting perhaps B's, sometimes B-pluses, in English and scoring perhaps in the sixtieth or seventieth percentile on achievement tests. But those scores were not good enough to override the opinion that my true abilities lay in math and science, because in those areas I achieved A's and scored in the ninetieth percentile or higher.

This was understandable. Math is precise; there is only one correct answer. Whereas, for me at least, the answers on English tests were always a judgment call, a matter of opinion and personal experience. Those tests were constructed around items like fill-in-the-blank sentence completion, such as, "Even though Tom was

benign (bi nīn´) *adj.* not injurious or malignant; not cancerous

---

6. **CAT scan** method used by doctors to diagnose brain disorders.
7. **SAT** Scholastic Aptitude Test; national college entrance exam.

▶Critical Viewing Is the language on these signs in San Francisco's Chinatown district the "mother tongue" to which Tan refers? Explain. **[Distinguish]**

_____, Mary thought he was _____." And the correct answer always seemed to be the most bland combinations of thoughts, for example, "Even though Tom was shy, Mary thought he was charming," with the grammatical structure "even though" limiting the correct answer to some sort of <u>semantic</u> opposites, so you wouldn't get answers like, "Even though Tom was foolish, Mary thought he was ridiculous." Well, according to my mother, there were very few limitations as to what Tom could have been and what Mary might have thought of him. So I never did well on tests like that.

semantic (sə man´ tik) *adj.* pertaining to meaning in language

The same was true with word analogies, pairs of words in which you were supposed to find some sort of logical, semantic relationship—for example, "*Sunset* is to *nightfall* as _____ is to _____." And here you would be presented with a list of four possible pairs, one of which showed the same kind of relationship: *red* is to *stoplight, bus* is to *arrival, chills* is to *fever, yawn* is to *boring.* Well, I could never think that way. I knew what the tests were asking, but I could not block out of my mind the images already created by the first pair, "*sunset* is to *nightfall*"—and I would see a burst of colors against a darkening sky, the moon rising, the lowering of a curtain of stars. And all the other pairs of words—red, bus, stoplight, boring—just threw up a mass of confusing images, making it impossible for me to sort out something as logical as saying: "A sunset precedes nightfall" is the same as "a chill precedes a fever." The only way I would have gotten that answer right would have been to imagine an associative situation, for example, my being disobedient and staying out past sunset, catching a chill at night, which turns into feverish pneumonia as punishment, which indeed did happen to me.

I have been thinking about all this lately, about my mother's English, about achievement tests. Because lately I've been asked, as a writer, why there are not more Asian Americans represented in American literature. Why are there few Asian Americans enrolled in creative writing programs? Why do so many Chinese students go into engineering? Well, these are broad sociological questions I can't begin to answer. But I have noticed in surveys—in fact, just last week—that Asian students, as a whole, always do significantly better on math achievement tests than in English. And this makes me think that there are other Asian-American students whose English spoken in the home might also be described as "broken" or "limited." And perhaps they also have teachers who are steering them away from writing and into math and science, which is what happened to me.

Fortunately, I happen to be rebellious in nature and enjoy the challenge of disproving assumptions made about me. I became an English major my first year in college, after being enrolled as pre-med. I started writing nonfiction as a freelancer the week after I was told by my former boss that writing was my worst skill and I should hone my talents toward account management.

But it wasn't until 1985 that I finally began to write fiction. And at first I wrote using what I thought to be wittily crafted sentences,

Literary Analysis
Reflective Essay and Identity What conflict between her personal sensibilities and the values of society does Tan highlight in this discussion of her struggles in English classes?

Reading Strategy
Evaluating a Writer's Message What point about defying expectations is Tan making? Do you agree with her?

sentences that would finally prove I had mastery over the English language. Here's an example from the first draft of a story that later made its way into *The Joy Luck Club*, but without this line: "That was my mental <u>quandary</u> in its <u>nascent</u> state." A terrible line, which I can barely pronounce.

Fortunately, for reasons I won't get into today, I later decided I should envision a reader for the stories I would write. And the reader I decided upon was my mother, because these were stories about mothers. So with this reader in mind—and in fact she did read my early drafts—I began to write stories using all the Englishes I grew up with: the English I spoke to my mother, which for lack of a better term might be described as "simple"; the English she used with me, which for lack of a better term might be described as "broken"; my translation of her Chinese, which could certainly be described as "watered down"; and what I imagined to be her translation of her Chinese if she could speak in perfect English, her internal language, and for that I sought to preserve the essence, but neither an English nor a Chinese structure. I wanted to capture what language ability tests can never reveal: her intent, her passion, her imagery, the rhythms of her speech and the nature of her thoughts.

Apart from what any critic had to say about my writing, I knew I had succeeded where it counted when my mother finished reading my book and gave me her verdict: "So easy to read."

quandary (kwän′ dä rē) *n.* state of uncertainty; dilemma

nascent (nas′ ənt, nā′ sənt) *adj.* coming into existence; emerging

Review and Assess

Thinking About the Selection

1. **Respond:** Having read this essay, what are your feelings about Tan and her mother? Explain.

2. **(a) Recall:** What does Tan realize while speaking to an audience that includes her mother? **(b) Infer:** What circumstances account for Tan's having developed more than one "English"?

3. **(a) Recall:** According to Tan, in what ways do math skills differ from language skills? **(b) Interpret:** In what ways did Tan's sense of different "Englishes" prevent her from answering correctly on grammar tests?

4. **(a) Summarize:** Summarize one experience Tan had involving her mother's difficulty with Standard English.
   (b) Compare and Contrast: In what ways does Tan's sense of her mother's English differ from the perceptions of strangers?
   (c) Analyze: What influence has Tan's mother had on her daughter's writing? Support your answer.

5. **Speculate:** What would it be like to live in a place where a language barrier made it difficult for you to communicate with others? What actions might you take to overcome the barrier?

Review and Assess

Literary Analysis

Reflective Essay

1. (a) What does Cisneros's list of accomplishments reveal about her values? (b) Does the last paragraph confirm or contradict that idea? Explain.

2. (a) What kind of child does Dove say she was? (b) How do you think Dove feels about her childhood?

3. In what ways has Tan's attitude toward her mother changed as she has grown older? Explain.

4. Based on these examples, why might an author use a **reflective essay** instead of fiction or poetry to explore a specific subject?

Comparing Literary Works

5. (a) Compare and contrast Dove's and Cisneros's childhoods and the paths each took to become writers. (b) In what ways do you think their backgrounds might be expressed in their fiction?

6. What evidence do you find in these essays that each writer struggled or sacrificed to create a true sense of **identity**?

7. (a) In what ways do these author's inner lives contrast—or conflict—with the outside world? (b) What role does writing play in the relationship between each writer's inner and outer life?

Reading Strategy

Evaluating a Writer's Message

8. Use a chart like the one shown to answer the following questions: (a) What does Dove believe about the power of books? (b) What does Tan's essay reveal about how language differences can lead to misconceptions? (c) For each essay, explain whether you do or do not agree with the author's message.

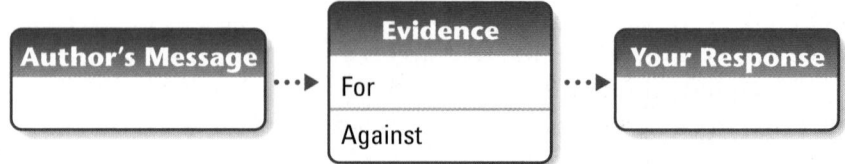

Extend Understanding

9. **Community Connection:** Amy Tan's mother struggled to communicate effectively in the United States. What services can a community provide to people with limited abilities in English?

Integrate Language Skills

Vocabulary Development Lesson

Word Analysis: Latin Root -scrib-, -script-

The word *transcribe*, which means "write out or type out in full," is formed from the Latin root *-scrib-*, which means "write." Using each pair of words below, write a sentence that demonstrates the meaning of this root.

1. scribble, child
2. prescription, doctor
3. inscription, trophy
4. author, manuscript

Spelling Strategy

When adding a suffix beginning with a vowel to words of more than one syllable ending with a single consonant, do not double the final consonant: *nomad + -ic = nomadic*. Often, however, when a word's final syllable has the accent, the final consonant is doubled: *regrettable*. Correctly add the indicated suffix to each word below.

1. benefit + *-ed*   2. refer + *-ing*   3. travel + *-er*

Fluency: Sentence Completions

Complete each sentence by filling in each blank with a vocabulary word from the list on page 1127.

1. The wandering tribe led a ___?___ life in the desert.
2. A person who loves language might pursue ___?___ studies.
3. The kindly old woman had a ___?___ influence on her children.
4. Her ___?___ social extroversion revealed itself before she could talk.
5. The archaeologist ___?___ the message that was carved on the wall of the tomb.
6. Having accepted two invitations, he found himself in a social ___?___.
7. Scientists use ___?___ evidence to prove or disprove a hypothesis.

Grammar and Style Lesson

Varying Sentence Structure

Simple sentences—those consisting of one independent clause—convey ideas concisely and directly. **Compound sentences** contain two or more independent clauses. **Complex sentences** contain an independent clause and one or more subordinate clauses. In this example, Sandra Cisneros follows a complex sentence with a simple one:

> **Example:** To make matters worse, I had left before any of my six brothers had ventured away from home. I had broken a terrible taboo.

Looking at Style Compare Amy Tan's first two paragraphs with the rest of her essay.

1. What do you notice about the sentence structure?
2. What affect does her choice of sentence structure have on the rhythm of her writing?
3. How does Tan's style relate to her message?

Writing Application Using a variety of sentence structures, write a paragraph in which you discuss the essay you enjoyed most. In your writing, explain your choice.

WG Prentice Hall Writing and Grammar Connection: Chapter 20, Section 3

Writing Lesson

Letter to the Author

Because they seem so personal and are written in a conversational style, these reflective essays invite response. Write a letter to the author of the essay you found most interesting. Explain what you liked, what you did not like, and ask any questions you might have.

Prewriting   Choose the essay you wish to discuss and reread it. Take notes about the author's message and style. List statements and images that you like, or that disturb you in some way.

Drafting   In your opening paragraph, state how much you enjoyed the essay and why. In the body paragraphs, go into greater detail, and ask any relevant questions. Consider drawing parallels to your own life.

Revising   Review your letter, and determine whether or not you have used the best language to communicate your thoughts. Highlight and replace any vague words with more specific ones.

Model: Revising to Include Precise Language

captured

I enjoyed the way you ~~stated~~ your mother's English in

This example of her speech

the anecdote of the Shanghai gangster. ~~It~~ helped me to

incident

see my own prejudices. The ~~point~~ with the stockbroker

described

you ~~added~~ made your mother's struggle very clear.

> Replacing vague references with more accurate words and phrases more accurately conveys ideas.

W/G Prentice Hall Writing and Grammar Connection: Chapter 14, Section 4

Extension Activities

Listening and Speaking   Write and deliver a **speech** that Cisneros, Dove, or Tan might present to aspiring young authors. Keep the following tips in mind as you prepare:

- List each main point on an index card for easy reference.
- Practice until you refer only occasionally to your index cards.

As you deliver your speech, speak slowly and clearly, maintaining eye contact with the audience.

Research and Technology   Both Tan and Cisneros grew up with more than one language. In a group, research the ways in which multilingual environments affect the development of language skills. Then, deliver a **team report** arguing either for or against language studies for young children. **[Group Activity]**

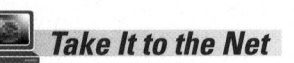 **Take It to the Net**   www.phschool.com

Go online for an additional research activity using the Internet.

Social Protest

Choke, 1964, Robert Rauschenberg, Oil and screenprint on canvas, 60" x 48", Washington University Gallery of Art, St. Louis, © Robert Rauschenberg/Licensed by VAGA, New York, NY

Prepare to Read

The Rockpile

James Baldwin (1924–1987)

James Baldwin once told an interviewer that he "never had a childhood." Because his stepfather worked long hours as both a preacher and a factory hand, Baldwin was given much of the responsibility for raising his eight half brothers and half sisters. The only leisure activity he was able to pursue was reading. He explained, "As [my half brothers and half sisters] were born, I took them over with one hand and held a book with the other. . . . In this way I read *Uncle Tom's Cabin* and *A Tale of Two Cities* over and over again; in this way, in fact, I read just about everything I could get my hands on." Baldwin's early love for reading deepened his imagination, planting the seeds of inspiration for his later success as a writer.

A Harlem Childhood Baldwin was born in Harlem, the New York community that served as a cultural center for African Americans during the 1920s and 30s. Even as a young boy, it was clear that he had a gift for words. He published his first short story in a church newspaper when he was twelve years old. Despite his obvious gift, Baldwin's deeply religious parents disapproved of his interest in literature. At age fourteen, Baldwin followed their wishes and became a preacher, earning a degree of fame in churches around Harlem, but he continued to pursue his literary ambitions.

Baldwin was encouraged by African American poet Countee Cullen, who taught in his junior high school. With Cullen's support, he wrote poetry and worked on his school's literary magazine. Inspired by the success of Richard Wright's novel *Native Son,* which proved to him that an African American could have success as a writer, Baldwin eventually decided to abandon preaching and devote his life to writing.

The Road to "Writer" For several years, Baldwin worked at odd jobs while writing and reading in his spare time. He wrote book reviews and essays, which were published in several New York journals. Some of these articles were later collected in *Notes of a Native Son* (1955). When he was twenty-four, Baldwin won a fellowship that enabled him to travel to Europe and write. He lived in Paris for the next four years, where he completed his first novel, *Go Tell It on the Mountain* (1953). The novel marked the beginning of a distinguished literary career that included the novels *Giovanni's Room* (1956), *Another Country* (1962), *The Fire Next Time* (1963), and *Tell Me How Long the Train's Been Gone* (1968); a play set in the American South called *Blues for Mr. Charlie* (1964); a collection of short stories titled *Going to Meet the Man* (1965); and several successful collections of essays.

A Powerful Witness Baldwin once said, "One writes out of one thing only—one's own experience. Everything depends on how relentlessly one forces from this experience the last drop, sweet or bitter, it can possibly give." Baldwin's work bears powerful witness to his own experience as an African American. In his writing, he expresses the need for social justice as well as the universal desire for love. Because his books dig deeply into contemporary life, they are sometimes painful to read, but the pain is always tempered by hope, and by Baldwin's magnificent language. Of Baldwin's essays, the poet Langston Hughes once wrote, "He uses words like the sea uses waves, to flow and beat, advance and retreat, rise and take a bow in disappearing." In interviews throughout his life, Baldwin often repeated one phrase: "People can be better than they are." This simple idea is woven into everything he wrote.

Preview

Connecting to the Literature

This story centers on a family living in a poor neighborhood where the setting itself presents a conflict. The children of the family are caught between two sources of danger—the street life they are forbidden to join and the tensions between their parents.

Literary Analysis

Setting

The **setting** of a story is the time and place in which it occurs, and may include details about the weather, physical features of the landscape, and other elements of an environment. "The Rockpile" is set in Harlem during the 1930s. Life in that place and time was influenced by the difficult economic and social realities that people faced. As you read, think about how the setting helps to shape the characters' personalities and actions.

Connecting Literary Elements

A **symbol** is a person, place, or object that has a meaning in itself but also suggests a larger meaning. For example, in this story, the rockpile represents both failure in the community and conflict within the family.

> They fought on the rockpile. Sure footed, dangerous, and reckless, they rushed each other and grappled on the heights . . .

As you read, note the ways in which the rockpile is described, the characters associated with it, and the events that take place there. These details will help reveal the symbolic meaning of the rockpile.

Reading Strategy

Identifying Cause and Effect

In this story, a child's disobedience reveals a complicated family dynamic. You will understand the characters in the story better if you **identify cause-and-effect** relationships among them. Use a chart like the one shown to determine the motives for characters' actions and their effects on others.

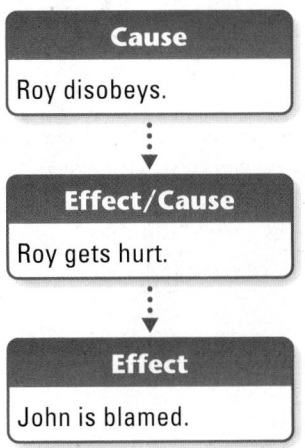

Cause
Roy disobeys.

Effect/Cause
Roy gets hurt.

Effect
John is blamed.

Vocabulary Development

intriguing (in trē´ gin) *adj.* interesting or curious (p. 1149)

benevolent (bə nev´ ə lənt) *adj.* kindly; charitable (p. 1150)

decorously (dek´ ə rəs lē) *adv.* characterized by or showing decorum and good taste (p. 1150)

latent (lāt´ 'nt) *adj.* present but invisible or inactive (p. 1150)

engrossed (en grōst´) *adj.* occupied wholly; absorbed (p. 1151)

jubilant (jōō´ bə lənt) *adj.* joyful and triumphant (p. 1151)

arrested (ə res´ tid) *adj.* stopped (p. 1152)

malevolence (mə lev´ ə ləns) *n.* malice; spitefulness (p. 1156)

perdition (pər dish´ ən) *n.* complete and irreparable loss; ruin (p. 1156)

The Rock Pile

James Baldwin

Background

Even though he spent most of his adult life in Europe, James Baldwin's impassioned voice is full of the rhythms and details of life in Harlem, the New York City neighborhood where he grew up. This story, about a struggling Harlem family, is a strong example of Baldwin's connection to the place that shaped him both as a writer and as a person.

Across the street from their house, in an empty lot between two houses, stood the rockpile. It was a strange place to find a mass of natural rock jutting out of the ground; and someone, probably Aunt Florence, had once told them that the rock was there and could not be taken away because without it the subway cars underground would fly apart, killing all the people. This, touching on some natural mystery concerning the surface and the center of the earth, was far too <u>intriguing</u> an explanation to be challenged, and it invested the rockpile, moreover, with such mysterious importance that Roy felt it to be his right, not to say his duty, to play there.

Other boys were to be seen there each afternoon after school and all day Saturday and Sunday. They fought on the rockpile. Sure footed, dangerous, and reckless, they rushed each other and grappled on the

Push to Walk, (collage 48" x 48"), Phoebe Beasley

Literary Analysis

Setting and Symbol
Which unique features of the rockpile are described in the opening paragraph?

intriguing (in trē′ gin) *adj.* interesting or curious

✔Reading Check

Where is the rockpile located?

◀ **Critical Viewing** What details shown in this painting connect to Baldwin's story? **[Connect]**

heights, sometimes disappearing down the other side in a confusion of dust and screams and upended, flying feet. "It's a wonder they don't kill themselves," their mother said, watching sometimes from the fire escape. "You children stay away from there, you hear me?" Though she said "children" she was looking at Roy, where he sat beside John on the fire escape. "The good Lord knows," she continued, "I don't want you to come home bleeding like a hog every day the Lord sends." Roy shifted impatiently, and continued to stare at the street, as though in this gazing he might somehow acquire wings. John said nothing. He had not really been spoken to: he was afraid of the rockpile and of the boys who played there.

Each Saturday morning John and Roy sat on the fire escape and watched the forbidden street below. Sometimes their mother sat in the room behind them, sewing, or dressing their younger sister, or nursing the baby, Paul. The sun fell across them and across the fire escape with a high, <u>benevolent</u> indifference; below them, men and women, and boys and girls, sinners all, loitered; sometimes one of the church-members passed and saw them and waved. Then, for the moment that they waved <u>decorously</u> back, they were intimidated. They watched the saint, man or woman, until he or she had disappeared from sight. The passage of one of the redeemed made them consider, however vacantly, the wickedness of the street, their own <u>latent</u> wickedness in sitting where they sat; and made them think of their father, who came home early on Saturdays and who would soon be turning this corner and entering the dark hall below them.

But until he came to end their freedom, they sat, watching and longing above the street. At the end of the street nearest their house was the bridge which spanned the Harlem River[1] and led to a city called the Bronx; which was where Aunt Florence lived. Nevertheless, when they saw her coming, she did not come from the bridge, but from the opposite end of the street. This, weakly, to their minds, she explained by saying that she had taken the subway, not wishing to walk, and that, besides, she did not live in that section of the Bronx. Knowing that the Bronx was across the river, they did not believe this story ever, but, adopting toward her their father's attitude, assumed that she had just left some sinful place which she dared not name, as, for example, a movie palace.

In the summertime boys swam in the river, diving off the wooden dock, or wading in from the garbage-heavy bank. Once a boy, whose name was Richard, drowned in the river. His mother had not known where he was; she had even come to their house, to ask if he was there. Then, in the evening, at six o'clock, they had heard from the street a woman screaming and wailing; and they ran to the windows and looked out. Down the street came the woman, Richard's mother, screaming, her face raised to the sky and tears running down her face. A woman walked beside her, trying to make her quiet and trying

---

1. **Harlem River** river that separates Manhattan Island from the Bronx in New York City.

Literary Analysis
Setting and Symbol
What does the rockpile represent to the neighborhood children? What does it represent to Roy's mother?

benelovent (bə nev′ ə lənt) *adj.* kindly; charitable

decorously (dek′ ər əs lē) *adv.* characterized by or showing decorum and good taste

latent (lāt′ ənt) *adj.* present but invisible or inactive

Literary Analysis
Setting and Symbol Can the tragedy of the boy's drowning in the river be seen as a symbol? If so, of what?

to hold her up. Behind them walked a man, Richard's father, with Richard's body in his arms. There were two white policemen walking in the gutter, who did not seem to know what should be done. Richard's father and Richard were wet, and Richard's body lay across his father's arms like a cotton baby. The woman's screaming filled all the street; cars slowed down and the people in the cars stared; people opened their windows and looked out and came rushing out of doors to stand in the gutter, watching. Then the small procession disappeared within the house which stood beside the rockpile. Then, *"Lord, Lord, Lord!"* cried Elizabeth, their mother, and slammed the window down.

One Saturday, an hour before his father would be coming home, Roy was wounded on the rockpile and brought screaming upstairs. He and John had been sitting on the fire escape and their mother had gone into the kitchen to sip tea with Sister McCandless. By and by Roy became bored and sat beside John in restless silence; and John began drawing into his schoolbook a newspaper advertisement which featured a new electric locomotive. Some friends of Roy passed beneath the fire escape and called him. Roy began to fidget, yelling down to them through the bars. Then a silence fell. John looked up. Roy stood looking at him.

"I'm going downstairs," he said.

"You better stay where you is, boy. You know Mama don't want you going downstairs."

"I be right *back*. She won't even know I'm gone, less you run and tell her."

"I ain't *got* to tell her. What's going to stop her from coming in here and looking out the window?"

"She's talking," Roy said. He started into the house.

"But Daddy's going to be home soon!"

"I be back before *that*. What you all the time got to be so *scared* for?" He was already in the house and he now turned, leaning on the windowsill, to swear impatiently, "I be back in *five* minutes."

John watched him sourly as he carefully unlocked the door and disappeared. In a moment he saw him on the sidewalk with his friends. He did not dare to go and tell his mother that Roy had left the fire escape because he had practically promised not to.

He started to shout, *Remember, you said five minutes!* but one of Roy's friends was looking up at the fire escape. John looked down at his schoolbook: he became <u>engrossed</u> again in the problem of the locomotive.

When he looked up again he did not know how much time had passed, but now there was a gang fight on the rockpile. Dozens of boys fought each other in the harsh sun: clambering up the rocks and battling hand to hand, scuffed shoes sliding on the slippery rock; filling the bright air with curses and <u>jubilant</u> cries. They filled the air, too, with flying weapons: stones, sticks, tin cans, garbage, whatever could be picked up and thrown. John watched in a kind of absent amazement—until he remembered that Roy was still downstairs, and that he was one of the

Reading Strategy
Identifying Cause and Effect What causes Roy to go down to the street?

engrossed (en grōst´) *adj.* occupied wholly; absorbed

jubilant (jōō´ bəl ənt) *adj.* joyful and triumphant

Reading Check

Does Roy obey the instructions his mother gives him regarding the rockpile?

boys on the rockpile. Then he was afraid; he could not see his brother among the figures in the sun; and he stood up, leaning over the fire-escape railing. Then Roy appeared from the other side of the rocks; John saw that his shirt was torn; he was laughing. He moved until he stood at the very top of the rockpile. Then, something, an empty tin can, flew out of the air and hit him on the forehead, just above the eye. Immediately, one side of Roy's face ran with blood, he fell and rolled on his face down the rocks. Then for a moment there was no movement at all, no sound, the sun, arrested, lay on the street and the sidewalk and the <u>arrested</u> boys. Then someone screamed or shouted; boys began to run away, down the street, toward the bridge. The figure on the ground, having caught its breath and felt its own blood, began to shout. John cried, "Mama! Mama!" and ran inside.

"Don't fret, don't fret," panted Sister McCandless as they rushed down the dark, narrow, swaying stairs, "don't fret. Ain't a boy been born don't get his knocks every now and again. *Lord!*" they hurried into the sun. A man had picked Roy up and now walked slowly toward them. One or two boys sat silent on their stoops; at either end of the street there was a group of boys watching. "He ain't hurt bad," the man said, "wouldn't be making this kind of noise if he was hurt real bad."

Elizabeth, trembling, reached out to take Roy, but Sister McCandless, bigger, calmer, took him from the man and threw him over her shoulder as she once might have handled a sack of cotton. "God bless you," she said to the man, "God bless you, son." Roy was still screaming. Elizabeth stood behind Sister McCandless to stare at his bloody face.

"It's just a flesh wound," the man kept saying, "just broke the skin, that's all." They were moving across the sidewalk, toward the house. John, not now afraid of the staring boys, looked toward the corner to see if his father was yet in sight.

Upstairs, they hushed Roy's crying. They bathed the blood away, to find, just above the left eyebrow, the jagged, superficial scar. "Lord, have mercy," murmured Elizabeth, "another inch and it would've been his eye." And she looked with apprehension toward the clock. "Ain't it the truth," said Sister McCandless, busy with bandages and iodine.

"When did he go downstairs?" his mother asked at last.

Sister McCandless now sat fanning herself in the easy chair, at the head of the sofa where Roy lay, bound and silent. She paused for a moment to look sharply at John. John stood near the window, holding the newspaper advertisement and the drawing he had done.

"We was sitting on the fire escape," he said. "Some boys he knew called him."

"When?"

"He said he'd be back in five minutes."

"Why didn't you tell me he was downstairs?"

He looked at his hands, clasping his notebook, and did not answer.

"Boy," said Sister McCandless, "you hear your mother a-talking to you?"

Literary Analysis
Setting Which details of Roy's accident reflect the difficulties of life in this place?

arrested (ə rest′ id) *adj.* stopped

He looked at his mother. He repeated:

"He said he'd be back in five minutes."

"He said he'd be back in five minutes," said Sister McCandless with scorn, "don't look to me like that's no right answer. You's the man of the house, you supposed to look after your baby brothers and sisters—you ain't supposed to let them run off and get half-killed. But I expect," she added, rising from the chair, dropping the cardboard fan, "your Daddy'll make you tell the truth. Your Ma's way too soft with you."

He did not look at her, but at the fan where it lay in the dark red, depressed seat where she had been. The fan advertised a pomade[2] for the hair and showed a brown woman and her baby, both with glistening hair, smiling happily at each other.

"Honey," said Sister McCandless, "I got to be moving along. Maybe I drop in later tonight. I don't reckon you going to be at Tarry Service tonight?"

Tarry Service was the prayer meeting held every Saturday night at church to strengthen believers and prepare the church for the coming of the Holy Ghost on Sunday.

"I don't reckon," said Elizabeth. She stood up; she and Sister McCandless kissed each other on the cheek. "But you be sure to remember me in your prayers."

"I surely will do that." She paused, with her hand on the door knob, and looked down at Roy and laughed. "Poor little man," she said, "reckon he'll be content to sit on the fire escape *now*."

Elizabeth laughed with her. "It sure ought to be a lesson to him. You don't reckon," she asked nervously, still smiling, "he going to keep that scar, do you?"

"Lord, no," said Sister McCandless, "ain't nothing but a scratch. I declare, Sister Grimes, you worse than a child. Another couple of weeks and you won't be able to *see* no scar. No, you go on about your housework, honey, and thank the Lord it weren't no worse." She opened the door; they heard the sound of feet on the stairs. "I expect that's the Reverend," said Sister McCandless, placidly, "I *bet* he going to raise cain."[3]

"Maybe it's Florence," Elizabeth said. "Sometimes she get here about this time." They stood in the doorway, staring, while the steps reached the landing below and began again climbing to their floor. "No," said Elizabeth then, "that ain't her walk. That's Gabriel."

"Well, I'll just go on," said Sister McCandless, "and kind of prepare his mind." She pressed Elizabeth's hand as she spoke and started into the hall, leaving the door behind her slightly ajar. Elizabeth turned slowly back into the room. Roy did not open his eyes, or move; but she knew that he was not sleeping; he wished to delay until the last possible moment any contact with his father. John put

---

2. **pomade** (päm ād´) *n.* perfumed ointment.
3. **raise cain** slang for "cause trouble."

✓Reading Check

What happens to Roy on the rockpile?

his newspaper and his notebook on the table and stood, leaning on the table, staring at her.

"It wasn't my fault," he said. "I couldn't stop him from going downstairs."

"No," she said, "you ain't got nothing to worry about. You just tell your Daddy the truth."

He looked directly at her, and she turned to the window, staring into the street. What was Sister McCandless saying? Then from her bedroom she heard Delilah's thin wail and she turned, frowning, looking toward the bedroom and toward the still open door. She knew that John was watching her. Delilah continued to wail, she thought, angrily, *Now that girl's getting too big for that,* but she feared that Delilah would awaken Paul and she hurried into the bedroom. She tried to soothe Delilah back to sleep. Then she heard the front door open and close—too loud, Delilah raised her voice, with an exasperated sigh Elizabeth picked the child up. Her child and Gabriel's, her children and Gabriel's: Roy, Delilah, Paul. Only John was nameless and a stranger, living, unalterable testimony to his mother's days in sin.

"What happened?" Gabriel demanded. He stood, enormous, in the center of the room, his black lunchbox dangling from his hand, staring at the sofa where Roy lay. John stood just before him, it seemed to her astonished vision just below him, beneath his fist, his heavy shoe.

The child stared at the man in fascination and terror—when a girl down home she had seen rabbits stand so paralyzed before the barking dog. She hurried past Gabriel to the sofa, feeling the weight of Delilah in her arms like the weight of a shield, and stood over Roy, saying:

"Now, ain't a thing to get upset about, Gabriel. This boy sneaked downstairs while I had my back turned and got hisself hurt a little. He's alright now."

Roy, as though in confirmation, now opened his eyes and looked gravely at his father. Gabriel dropped his lunchbox with a clatter and knelt by the sofa.

"How you feel, son? Tell your Daddy what happened?"

Roy opened his mouth to speak and then, relapsing into panic, began to cry. His father held him by the shoulder.

"You don't want to cry. You's Daddy's little man. Tell your Daddy what happened."

"He went downstairs," said Elizabeth, "where he didn't have no business to be, and got to fighting with them bad boys playing on the rockpile. That's what happened and it's a mercy it weren't nothing worse."

He looked up at her. "Can't you let this boy answer me for hisself?"

Ignoring this, she went on, more gently: "He got cut on the forehead, but it ain't nothing to worry about."

Reading Strategy
Identifying Cause and Effect How does Gabriel react to Roy's tears?

"You call a doctor? How you know it ain't nothing to worry about?"

"Is you got money to be throwing away on doctors? No, I ain't called no doctor. Ain't nothing wrong with my eyes that I can't tell whether he's hurt bad or not. He got a fright more'n anything else, and you ought to pray God it teaches him a lesson."

"You got a lot to say now," he said, "but I'll have *me* something to say in a minute. I'll be wanting to know when all this happened, what you was doing with your eyes *then*." He turned back to Roy, who had lain quietly sobbing eyes wide open and body held rigid: and who now, at his father's touch, remembered the height, the sharp, sliding rock beneath his feet, the sun, the explosion of the sun, his plunge into darkness and his salty blood; and recoiled, beginning to scream, as his father touched his forehead. "Hold still, hold still," crooned his father, shaking, "hold still. Don't cry. Daddy ain't going to hurt you, he just wants to see this bandage, see what they've done to his little man." But Roy continued to scream and would not be still and Gabriel dared not lift the bandage for fear of hurting him more. And he looked at Elizabeth in fury: "Can't you put that child down and help me with this boy? John, take your baby sister from your mother—don't look like neither of you got good sense."

John took Delilah and sat down with her in the easy chair. His mother bent over Roy, and held him still, while his father, carefully— but still Roy screamed—lifted the bandage and stared at the wound. Roy's sobs began to lessen. Gabriel readjusted the bandage. "You see," said Elizabeth, finally, "he ain't nowhere near dead."

"It sure ain't your fault that he ain't dead." He and Elizabeth considered each other for a moment in silence. "He came mightly close to losing an eye. Course, his eyes ain't as big as your'n, so I reckon you don't think it matters so much." At this her face hardened; he smiled. "Lord, have mercy," he said, "you think you ever going to learn to do right? Where was you when all this happened? Who let him go downstairs?"

"Ain't nobody let him go downstairs, he just went. He got a head just like his father, it got to be broken before it'll bow. I was in the kitchen."

"Where was Johnnie?"

"He was in here."

"Where?"

"He was on the fire escape."

"Didn't he know Roy was downstairs?"

"I reckon."

"What you mean, you reckon? He ain't got your big eyes for nothing, does he?" He looked over at John. "Boy, you see your brother go downstairs?"

"Gabriel, ain't no sense in trying to blame Johnnie. You know right well if you have trouble making Roy behave, he ain't going to listen to his brother. He don't hardly listen to me."

"How come you didn't tell your mother Roy was downstairs?"

John said nothing, staring at the blanket which covered Delilah.

Reading Strategy
Identifying Cause and Effect What is Gabriel's reaction to Elizabeth's efforts to downplay the incident?

Reading Check

On whom does Gabriel attempt to pin the blame for Roy's accident?

"Boy, you hear me? You want me to take a strap to you?"

"No, you ain't," she said. "You ain't going to taken no strap to this boy, not today you ain't. Ain't a soul to blame for Roy's lying up there now but you—you because you done spoiled him so that he thinks he can do just anything and get away with it. I'm here to tell you that ain't no way to raise no child. You don't pray to the Lord to help you do better than you been doing, you going to live to shed bitter tears that the Lord didn't take his soul today." And she was trembling. She moved, unseeing, toward John and took Delilah from his arms. She looked back at Gabriel, who had risen, who stood near the sofa, staring at her. And she found in his face not fury alone, which would not have surprised her; but hatred so deep as to become insupportable in its lack of personality. His eyes were struck alive, unmoving, blind with <u>malevolence</u> —she felt, like the pull of the earth at her feet, his longing to witness her <u>perdition</u>. Again, as though it might be propitiation, she moved the child in her arms. And at this his eyes changed, he looked at Elizabeth, the mother of his children, the helpmeet given by the Lord. Then her eyes clouded; she moved to leave the room; her foot struck the lunchbox lying on the floor.

"John," she said, "pick up your father's lunchbox like a good boy."

She heard, behind her, his scrambling movement as he left the easy chair, the scrape and jangle of the lunchbox as he picked it up, bending his dark head near the toe of his father's heavy shoe.

malevolence (mə lev′ ə ləns) *n.* malice; spitefulness

perdition (pər dish′ ən) *n.* complete and irreparable loss; ruin

Review and Assess

Thinking About the Selection

1. **Respond:** Does this story call to mind any of your own childhood experiences? Explain.

2. **(a) Recall:** What do John and Roy do each Saturday morning? **(b) Deduce:** Why is the street "forbidden"?

3. **(a) Recall:** How is John related to Gabriel? **(b) Support:** What evidence is there that Gabriel's relationship with John is different from his relationship with the other children?

4. **(a) Recall:** What happens to the boy, Richard, at the river? **(b) Analyze:** Through this anecdote, what is Baldwin saying about this family's relationship to their community?

5. **(a) Recall:** Whom does Gabriel blame for Roy's injury? **(b) Draw Conclusions:** What conclusions can you draw about Gabriel's relationship with Elizabeth? Explain. **(c) Speculate:** Why do Gabriel's feelings toward Elizabeth soften at the end of the story?

6. **Make a Judgment:** Who do you think is responsible for Roy's injury?

Review and Assess

Literary Analysis

Setting

1. Find three details that describe the psychological environment of the story's **setting**—the mood and atmosphere of the neighborhood.

2. Find three details that describe the physical environment—the landmarks of the neighborhood.

3. What are some of the potential dangers the setting presents?

4. In what ways do you think the setting has influenced Gabriel's and Elizabeth's decisions about how to raise their children?

Connecting Literary Elements

5. (a) Use a chart like the one shown to analyze the rockpile, the main **symbol** in this story. (b) What does the rockpile represent?

The Rockpile				What it Means
What people say about it	Events linked with it	Details used to describe it	···▶ ···▶	

6. (a) What does "the toe of his father's heavy shoe," mentioned at the end of the story, symbolize? (b) In what way does this image capture John's relationship to Gabriel? (c) How would you define their relationship?

Reading Strategy

Identifying Cause and Effect

7. (a) What **causes** John to avoid telling his mother that Roy went to the rockpile? (b) What is the **effect** of his delay?

8. (a) What are the causes of Elizabeth's protectiveness toward John? (b) What is the effect on Gabriel of this protectiveness?

Extend Understanding

9. **Psychology Connection:** In this story, John is given a heavy responsibility: monitoring his brother's behavior. What problems might such responsibility create for a young boy like John?

Quick Review

The **setting** of a story is the time and place in which it occurs.

A **symbol** is a person, place, or object that has a meaning in itself but suggests other meanings as well.

To **identify cause-and-effect** relationships, note the circumstances that cause characters' actions and the effects their actions have on others.

 Take It to the Net
www.phschool.com
Take the interactive self-test online to check your understanding of the selection.

Integrate Language Skills

Vocabulary Development Lesson

Word Analysis: Latin Prefix *mal-*

The Latin prefix *mal-* means "bad," "wrong," or "ill." Combined with the root *-vol-*, meaning "wish," *malevolence* means "ill will." Use this root to determine the meaning of each of these words.

1. malfunction
2. malodorous
3. maladjusted
4. malnutrition

Spelling Strategy

If a word ends in a double consonant, do not make a change when you add a suffix. For example, *engross* + *-ed* = *engrossed*. Correctly add the indicated suffix to the following words.

1. reckless + *-ly*   2. dress + *-ing*   3. pass + *-ed*

Concept Development: Synonyms or Antonyms

Identify each of the following pairs of words as either synonyms or antonyms.

1. intriguing, boring
2. benevolent, charitable
3. decorously, tastefully
4. latent, obvious
5. engrossed, detached
6. jubilant, despondent
7. arrested, halted
8. malevolence, kindness
9. perdition, salvation

Grammar and Style Lesson

Restrictive and Nonrestrictive Adjective Clauses

Containing both a subject and a verb, **adjective clauses** add information about nouns in the main part of a sentence.

A **restrictive adjective clause** is necessary to complete the meaning of the noun or pronoun it modifies.

> **Restrictive:** He was afraid of the rockpile and the boys *who played there.* (essential; tells which *boys*)

A **nonrestrictive adjective clause** provides additional but inessential information and must be set off by commas.

> **Nonrestrictive:** Once a boy, whose name was Richard, drowned in the river. (nonessential; modifies *boy*)

Practice Identify the adjective clause(s), and indicate the word it modifies. Then, state whether it is restrictive or nonrestrictive.

1. There were two white policemen, who seemed at a loss, walking in the street.
2. At the end of the street nearest the house was the bridge which spanned the river . . .
3. . . . made them think of their father, who came home early on Saturdays . . .
4. Then the small procession disappeared into the house which stood beside the rockpile.
5. He did not look at her, but at the fan where it lay in the seat where she had been.

Writing Application Write two sentences. In the first, use a restrictive adjective clause. In the second, use a nonrestrictive adjective clause.

W̶G̶ Prentice Hall Writing and Grammar Connection: Chapter 19, Section 3

Writing Lesson

Roy's Journal

In "The Rockpile," Roy's actions spark a family crisis in which much is revealed about the family as a whole, but very little about Roy himself. Write a journal entry for Roy in which he discusses his inner thoughts and conflicts. Use appropriate language to express the genuine thoughts and feelings of a young boy.

Prewriting   Reread the story to create a timeline of events. Then, for each point on the line, jot down ideas about Roy's thoughts and feelings.

Drafting   As you draft Roy's journal, refer to your notes for detail. Keep the language personal and informal.

Revising   Look for opportunities to make the tone of the journal more personal. Replace words that may be too formal with more appropriate choices. Determine whether or not your writing provides new insight into Roy's behavior.

Model: Revising to Achieve a Personal Tone

When I heard my daddy coming up the stairs, I got real

snuck out

scared. I didn't want him to know I had ~~escaped my home~~.

a good man

He's big, and he's ~~devout~~, and gets so mad.

> Replacing formal words with informal ones creates a personal tone.

WG   *Prentice Hall Writing and Grammar Connection: Chapter 14, Section 3*

Extension Activities

Listening and Speaking   In a group, adapt "The Rockpile" as a **radio play.** Divide the story into scenes and develop a script. Keep the following tips in mind as you write and rehearse:

- Assign one person to be the narrator.

- Choose appropriate sound effects and music that evokes the time and place of the story.

Rehearse the play until you are satisfied that you are presenting it as effectively as possible. Then, perform it for the class. **[Group Activity]**

Research and Technology   Using a wide range of sources, including the Internet, prepare an **illustrated report** comparing Harlem today with Harlem in the 1930s. Explain the reasons for any similarities and differences between Harlem past and Harlem present. Share your report with the class.

 **Take It to the Net**   www.phschool.com

Go online for an additional research activity using the Internet.

Prepare to Read

from Hiroshima ◆ Losses ◆
The Death of the Ball Turret Gunner

John Hersey (1914–1993)

Born in China to American parents and raised there until age ten, John Hersey returned repeatedly to East Asia during his long career as a war correspondent, novelist, and essayist.

In his twenty-five books and countless articles, Hersey combined a profound moral sensibility with the highest artistry. His novels and essays not only examine the moral implications of the major political and historical events of his day, they do so with high literary grace. In 1945, Hersey won a Pulitzer Prize for his novel *A Bell for Adano,* in which an American major discovers the human dignity of the Italian villagers who were his enemies in World War II.

The Atomic Bomb During the 1940s, Hersey traveled to China and Japan as a correspondent for *The New Yorker* and *Time* magazines. He also used these visits to gather material for his most famous and acclaimed book, *Hiroshima* (1946), a shocking, graphic depiction of the devastation caused by the atomic bomb that was dropped on the Japanese city of Hiroshima at the end of World War II. This remarkable report first appeared in *The New Yorker* on August 31, 1946. Wallace Shawn, then editor of *The New Yorker,* made the unprecedented decision to bump all of the magazine's other editorial content in order to publish Hersey's four-part article.

Stories of Inhumanity and Courage In 1950, Hersey published the novel *The Wall,* which tells of the extinction of the Warsaw ghetto by the Germans during World War II. Hersey's later works include *A Single Pebble* (1956), *The War Lover* (1959), *The Child Buyer* (1960), *The Algiers Motel Incident* (1968), *The Writer's Craft* (1974), *Blues* (1987), and *Fling and Other Stories* (1990).

Randall Jarrell (1914–1965)

Randall Jarrell was a talented poet, literary critic, and teacher whose work was praised by both writers and critics. His literary essays, many of which appear in his book *Poetry and the Age* (1953), have been credited with changing the critical tastes and trends of his time.

Literary Ambitions Born in Nashville, Tennessee, Jarrell graduated from Vanderbilt University, where he studied under writers Robert Penn Warren, Allen Tate, and John Crowe Ransom. All of these men would prove helpful in promoting Jarrell's career. Warren and Tate published Jarrell's early poetry and criticism, and Tate helped land Jarrell his first teaching job at Kenyon College.

During World War II, Jarrell enlisted in the U.S. Air Force. He served only briefly as a pilot, and spent the remaining war years as an aviation instructor, training pilots to fly the famed B-29 bombers that helped secure victory. Jarrell's war experiences provided him with the material for the poems in his books *Little Friend, Little Friend* (1945) and *Losses* (1948). These books rank among the finest literature to emerge from the war.

American Language Jarrell was a great admirer of the poetry of Robert Frost, and, like Frost, he wrote poems based on the sounds and rhythms of American speech. Jarrell's collections *The Seven-League Crutches* (1951) and *The Lost World* (1965) focus on childhood and innocence. *The Woman at the Washington Zoo* (1960) deals with the theme of aging and loneliness. "The Death of the Ball Turret Gunner"—a brief poem told in the first person of a soldier experiencing his last moments in a World War II bomber plane—is one of Jarrell's most famous works.

Preview

Connecting to the Literature

You may have seen movies about World War II. You may even have a relative who experienced the war firsthand. Yet, it is probably still difficult for you to imagine what it was like to live through a conflict of such immensity. These selections will give you a better sense of the war and provide a picture of events that changed the world forever.

Literary Analysis

Implied Theme

The **theme** is the central idea that a writer conveys in a work of literature. Most often a theme is **implied,** or revealed indirectly, through the writer's choice of details, portrayal of characters and events, and use of literary devices. These selections all present implied themes about war.

Comparing Literary Works

Usually, we expect works of journalism to be objective, while we expect poems to be subjective. These selections, however, challenge our expectations.

- An **objective account** of a story is one in which the narrator is an outside observer who reports events without emotion or bias.

  Hersey: A hundred thousand people were killed by the atomic bomb . . .

- A **subjective account** is one in which the narrator reveals his or her feelings about the events described.

  Jarrell: I woke to black flak and the nightmare fighters.

As you read these powerful pieces, compare how the authors mix objectivity and subjectivity in surprising and effective ways.

Reading Strategy

Drawing Inferences About Theme

When the theme of a literary work is conveyed indirectly, it is up to the reader to **draw inferences,** or conclusions, by looking closely at the writer's choice of details, events, and characters. As you read, use a chart like the one shown to note important details that point to an implied theme.

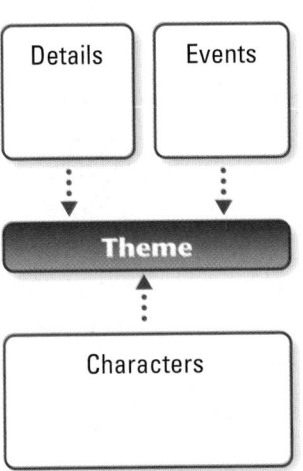

Vocabulary Development

evacuated (ē vak′ yoō āt′ id) *v.* to have made empty; withdrawn (p. 1163)

volition (vō lish′ ən) *n.* act of using the will (p. 1163)

rendezvous (rän′ dā voō′) *n.* meeting place (p. 1164)

philanthropies (fə lan′ thrə pēz) *n.* charitable acts or gifts (p. 1165)

incessant (in ses′ ənt) *adj.* constant; continuing or repeating in a way that seems endless (p. 1170)

convivial (kən viv′ ē əl) *adj.* fond of good company; sociable (p. 1171)

FROM HIROSHIMA

John Hersey

Background

In August 1945, American President Harry Truman was faced with a terrible decision. The world had been at war for six years. Germany had surrendered in May, but Japan refused to give up. The United States had just finished developing an atomic bomb. President Truman had to decide whether or not to use this new technology to bring an end to the war. On August 6, Truman ordered that the atomic bomb be dropped on the Japanese city of Hiroshima. Three days later, another bomb was dropped on Nagasaki. These two bombs killed more than 200,000 people and forced the Japanese surrender. Like so many events of World War II, the atomic bomb gave the world a new horror, as John Hersey so carefully documents in this selection.

At exactly fifteen minutes past eight in the morning, on August 6, 1945, Japanese time, at the moment when the atomic bomb flashed above Hiroshima, Miss Toshiko Sasaki, a clerk in the personnel department of the East Asia Tin Works, had just sat down at her place in the plant office and was turning her head to speak to the girl at the next desk. At that same moment, Dr. Masakazu Fujii was settling down cross-legged to read the Osaka *Asahi* on the porch of his private hospital, overhanging one of the seven deltaic rivers which divide Hiroshima; Mrs. Hatsuyo Nakamura, a tailor's widow, stood by the window of her kitchen, watching a neighbor tearing down his house because it lay in the path of an air-raid-defense fire lane . . . and the Reverend Mr. Kiyoshi Tanimoto, pastor of the Hiroshima Methodist Church, paused at the door of a rich man's house in Koi, the city's western suburb, and prepared to unload a handcart full of things he had evacuated from town in fear of the massive B-29 raid which everyone expected Hiroshima to suffer. A hundred thousand people were killed by the atomic bomb, and these [four] were among the survivors. They still wonder why they lived when so many others died. Each of them counts many small items of chance or volition—a step taken in time, a decision to go indoors, catching one streetcar instead of the next—that spared him. And now each knows that in the act of survival he lived a dozen lives and saw more death than he ever thought he would see. At the time, none of them knew anything.

The Reverend Mr. Tanimoto got up at five o'clock that morning. He was alone in the parsonage, because for some time his wife had been commuting with their year-old baby to spend nights with a friend in Ushida, a suburb to the north. Of all the important cities of Japan, only two, Kyoto and Hiroshima, had not been visited in strength by *B-san*, or Mr. B, as the Japanese, with a mixture of respect

evacuated (ē vak´ yoo āt´ əd) *v.* to have made empty; withdrawn

volition (vō lish´ ən) *n.* act of using the will

☑ **Reading Check**
What happened at exactly 8:15 in the morning on August 6, 1945?

◀ **Critical Viewing** How effectively do these remains of the sacred tree of a Hiroshima temple convey the physical and emotional devastation of the blast? Explain. **[Evaluate]**

and unhappy familiarity, called the B-29[*]; and Mr. Tanimoto, like all his neighbors and friends, was almost sick with anxiety. He had heard uncomfortably detailed accounts of mass raids on Kure, Iwakuni, Tokuyama, and other nearby towns; he was sure Hiroshima's turn would come soon. He had slept badly the night before, because there had been several air-raid warnings. Hiroshima had been getting such warnings almost every night for weeks, for at that time the B-29s were using Lake Biwa, northeast of Hiroshima, as a <u>rendezvous</u> point, and no matter what city the Americans planned to hit, the Super-fortresses streamed in over the coast near Hiroshima. The frequency of the warning and the continued abstinence of Mr. B with respect to Hiroshima had made its citizens jittery; a rumor was going around that the Americans were saving something special for the city.

Mr. Tanimoto was a small man, quick to talk, laugh, and cry. He wore his black hair parted in the middle and rather long; the prominence of the frontal bones just above his eyebrows and the smallness of his mustache, mouth, and chin gave him a strange old-young look, boyish and yet wise, weak and yet fiery. He moved nervously and fast, but with a restraint which suggested that he is a cautious, thoughtful man. He showed, indeed, just those qualities in the uneasy days before the bomb fell. Mr. Tanimoto had been carrying all the portable things from his church, in the close-packed residential district called Nagaragawa, to a house that belonged to a rayon manufacturer in Koi, two miles from the center of town. The rayon man, a Mr. Matsui, had opened his then unoccupied estate to a large number of his friends and acquaintances, so that they might evacuate whatever they wished to a safe distance from the probable target area. Mr. Tanimoto had had no difficulty in moving chairs, hymnals, Bibles, altar gear, and church records by pushcart himself, but the organ console and an upright piano required some aid. A friend of his named Matsuo had, the day before, helped him get the piano out to Koi; in return, he had promised this day to assist Mr. Matsuo in hauling out a daughter's belongings. That is why he had risen so early.

Mr. Tanimoto cooked his own breakfast. He felt awfully tired. The effort of moving the piano the day before, a sleepless night, weeks of worry and unbalanced diet, the cares of his parish—all combined to make him feel hardly adequate to the new day's work. There was another thing, too: Mr. Tanimoto had studied theology at Emory College, in Atlanta, Georgia; he had graduated in 1940; he spoke excellent English; he dressed in American clothes; he had corresponded with many American friends right up to the time the war began; and among a people obsessed with a fear of being spied upon— perhaps almost obsessed himself—he found himself growing increasingly uneasy. The police had questioned

rendezvous (rän′dā voo′) *n.* meeting place

Literature in context History Connection

♦ *B-29 Bombers*
The Second World War saw major advances in the technology of mechanized warfare—warfare that relied heavily on machines. The B-29 Superfortress bomber that Hersey mentions was an aircraft capable of long-range, heavy bombing runs. It was used frequently against Japan during 1944 and 1945. Firebomb B-29 raids against industrial cities in Japan totaled nearly 7,000 flights and dropped 41,600 tons of bombs.

him several times, and just a few days before, he had heard that an influential acquaintance, a Mr. Tanaka, a retired officer of the Toyo Kisen Kaisha steamship line, an anti-Christian, a man famous in Hiroshima for his showy <u>philanthropies</u> and notorious for his personal tyrannies, had been telling people that Tanimoto should not be trusted. In compensation, to show himself publicly a good Japanese, Mr. Tanimoto had taken on the chairmanship of his local *tonarigumi*, or Neighborhood Association, and to his other duties and concerns this position had added the business of organizing air-raid defense for about twenty families.

Before six o'clock that morning, Mr. Tanimoto started for Mr. Matsuo's house. There he found that their burden was to be a *tansu*, a large Japanese cabinet, full of clothing and household goods. The two men set out. The morning was perfectly clear and so warm that the day promised to be uncomfortable. A few minutes after they started, the air-raid siren went off—a minute-long blast that warned of approaching planes but indicated to the people of Hiroshima only a slight degree of danger, since it sounded every morning at this time, when an American weather plane came over. The two men pulled and pushed the handcart through the city streets. Hiroshima was a fan-shaped city, lying mostly on the six islands formed by the seven estuarial rivers that branch out from the Ota River; its main commercial and residential districts, covering about four square miles in the center of the city, contained three-quarters of its population, which had been reduced by several evacuation programs from a wartime peak of 380,000 to about 245,000. Factories and other residential districts, or suburbs, lay compactly around the edges of the city. To the south were the docks, an airport, and the island-studded Inland Sea. A rim of mountains runs around the other three sides of the delta. Mr. Tanimoto and Mr. Matsuo took their way through the shopping center, already full of people, and across two of the rivers to the sloping streets of Koi, and up them to the outskirts and foothills. As they started up a valley away from the tight-ranked houses, the all-clear sounded. (The Japanese radar operators, detecting only three planes, supposed that they comprised a reconnaissance.) Pushing the handcart up to the rayon man's house was tiring, and the men, after they had maneuvered their load into the driveway and to the front steps, paused to rest awhile. They stood with a wing of the house between them and the city. Like most homes in this part of Japan, the house consisted of a wooden frame and wooden walls supporting a heavy tile roof. Its front hall, packed with rolls of bedding and clothing, looked like a cool cave full of fat cushions. Opposite the house, to the right of the front door, there was a large, finicky rock garden. There was no sound of planes. The morning was still; the place was cool and pleasant.

Then a tremendous flash of light cut across the sky. Mr. Tanimoto has a distinct recollection that it travelled from east to west, from the city toward the hills. It seemed a sheet of sun. Both he and Mr. Matsuo reacted in terror—and both had time to react (for they were 3,500 yards, or two miles, from the center of the explosion). Mr. Matsuo dashed up

philanthropies (fə lan´ thrə pēz) *n.* charitable acts or gifts

Literary Analysis
Implied Theme In light of the bombing, what is ironic about an air-raid siren indicating only a "slight degree of danger"?

☑ **Reading Check**

Why does Mr. Tanimoto move all the portable things in his church to a home farther from the town center?

the front steps into the house and dived among the bedrolls and buried himself there. Mr. Tanimoto took four or five steps and threw himself between two big rocks in the garden. He bellied up very hard against one of them. As his face was against the stone, he did not see what happened. He felt a sudden pressure, and then splinters and pieces of board and fragments of tile fell on him. He heard no roar. (Almost no one in Hiroshima recalls hearing any noise of the bomb. But a fisherman in his sampan on the Inland Sea near Tsuzu, the man with whom Mr. Tanimoto's mother-in-law and sister-in-law were living, saw the flash and heard a tremendous explosion; he was nearly twenty miles from Hiroshima, but the thunder was greater than when the B-29s hit Iwakuni, only five miles away.)

When he dared, Mr. Tanimoto raised his head and saw that the rayon man's house had collapsed. He thought a bomb had fallen directly on it. Such clouds of dust had risen that there was a sort of twilight around. In panic, not thinking for the moment of Mr. Matsuo under the ruins, he dashed out into the street. He noticed as he ran that the concrete wall of the estate had fallen over—toward the house rather than away from it. In the street, the first thing he saw was a squad of soldiers who had been burrowing into the hillside opposite, making one

▲ **Critical Viewing**
You may have seen photographs like this one of the aftermath of the Hiroshima bombing. Does Hersey's account change the way you view such pictures? Explain. **[Relate]**

of the thousands of dugouts in which the Japanese apparently intended to resist invasion, hill by hill, life for life; the soldiers were coming out of the hole, where they should have been safe, and blood was running from their heads, chests, and backs. They were silent and dazed.

Under what seemed to be a local dust cloud, the day grew darker and darker.

Reading Strategy
Drawing Inferences About Theme What does the detail about the bleeding, dazed soldiers imply about the catastrophe that has just taken place?

At nearly midnight, the night before the bomb was dropped, an announcer on the city's radio station said that about two hundred B-29s were approaching southern Honshu and advised the population of Hiroshima to evacuate to their designated "safe areas." Mrs. Hatsuyo Nakamura, the tailor's widow, who lived in the section called Nobori-cho and who had long had a habit of doing as she was told, got her three children—a ten-year-old boy, Toshio, an eight-year-old girl, Yaeko, and a five-year-old girl, Myeko—out of bed and dressed them and walked with them to the military area known as the East Parade Ground, on the northeast edge of the city. There she unrolled some mats and the children lay down on them. They slept until about two, when they were awakened by the roar of the planes going over Hiroshima.

As soon as the planes had passed, Mrs. Nakamura started back with her children. They reached home a little after two-thirty and she immediately turned on the radio, which, to her distress, was just then broadcasting a fresh warning. When she looked at the children and saw how tired they were, and when she thought of the number of trips they had made in past weeks, all to no purpose, to the East Parade Ground, she decided that in spite of the instructions on the radio, she simply could not face starting out all over again. She put the children in their bedrolls on the floor, lay down herself at three o'clock, and fell asleep at once, so soundly that when planes passed over later, she did not waken to their sound.

Literary Analysis
Implied Theme and Objective/Subjective Accounts What do the details about Mrs. Nakamura's tired children suggest about the author's objectivity?

The siren jarred her awake at about seven. She arose, dressed quickly, and hurried to the house of Mr. Nakamoto, the head of her Neighborhood Association, and asked him what she should do. He said that she should remain at home unless an urgent warning—a series of intermittent blasts of the siren—was sounded. She returned home, lit the stove in the kitchen, set some rice to cook, and sat down to read that morning's Hiroshima *Chugoku.* To her relief, the all-clear sounded at eight o'clock. She heard the children stirring, so she went and gave each of them a handful of peanuts and told them to stay in their bedrolls, because they were tired from the night's walk. She had hoped that they would go back to sleep, but the man in the house directly to the south began to make a terrible hullabaloo of hammering, wedging, ripping, and splitting. The prefectural government,[1] convinced, as everyone in Hiroshima was, that the city would be attacked soon, had begun to press with threats and warnings for the completion of wide

---

1. **prefectural government** regional districts of Japan which are administered by a governor.

Reading Check

Why are Mrs. Nakamura's children so tired?

fire lanes, which, it was hoped, might act in conjunction with the rivers to localize any fires started by an incendiary[2] raid; and the neighbor was reluctantly sacrificing his home to the city's safety. Just the day before, the prefecture had ordered all able-bodied girls from the secondary schools to spend a few days helping to clear these lanes, and they started work soon after the all-clear sounded.

Mrs. Nakamura went back to the kitchen, looked at the rice, and began watching the man next door. At first, she was annoyed with him for making so much noise, but then she was moved almost to tears by pity. Her emotion was specifically directed toward her neighbor, tearing down his home, board by board, at a time when there was so much unavoidable destruction, but undoubtedly she also felt a generalized, community pity, to say nothing of self-pity. She had not had an easy time. Her husband, Isawa, had gone into the Army just after Myeko was born, and she had heard nothing from or of him for a long time, until, on March 5, 1942, she received a seven-word telegram: "Isawa died an honorable death at Singapore." She learned later that he had died on February 15th, the day Singapore fell, and that he had been a

Literary Analysis
Implied Theme Why do you think the author included information about the citizens' attempts to defend their city and its population?

---

2. **incendiary** (in sen′ dē er′ ē) *adj.* designed to cause fires.

◀ **Critical Viewing**
There are no people shown
in this photograph—nor in
many others—depicting
the devastation wrought
by the Hiroshima bomb.
Does the lack of humanity
lessen or intensify the
power of the image?
Explain. **[Assess]**

corporal. Isawa had been a not particularly prosperous tailor, and
his only capital was a Sankoku sewing machine. After his death, when
his allotments stopped coming, Mrs. Nakamura got out the machine
and began to take in piecework herself, and since then had supported
the children, but poorly, by sewing.

As Mrs. Nakamura stood watching her neighbor, everything flashed
whiter than any white she had ever seen. She did not notice what
happened to the man next door; the reflex of a mother set her in
motion toward her children. She had taken a single step (the house
was 1,350 yards, or three-quarters of a mile, from the center of the
explosion) when something picked her up and she seemed to fly into
the next room over the raised sleeping platform, pursued by parts of
her house.

Timbers fell around her as she landed, and a shower of tiles pom-
melled her; everything became dark, for she was buried. The debris
did not cover her deeply. She rose up and freed herself. She heard
a child cry, "Mother, help me!" and saw her youngest—Myeko, the
five-year-old—buried up to her breast and unable to move. As Mrs.
Nakamura started frantically to claw her way toward the baby, she
could see or hear nothing of her other children.

✔ **Reading Check**

What happens as Mrs.
Nakamura stands
watching her neighbor?

In the days right before the bombing, Dr. Masakazu Fujii, being prosperous, hedonistic,[3] and at the time not too busy, had been allowing himself the luxury of sleeping until nine or nine-thirty, but fortunately he had to get up early the morning the bomb was dropped to see a house guest off on a train. He rose at six, and half an hour later walked with his friend to the station, not far away, across two of the rivers. He was back home by seven, just as the siren sounded its sustained warning. He ate breakfast and then, because the morning was already hot, undressed down to his underwear and went out on the porch to read the paper. This porch—in fact, the whole building—was curiously constructed. Dr. Fujii was the proprietor of a peculiarly Japanese institution; a private, single-doctor hospital. This building, perched beside and over the water of the Kyo River, and next to the bridge of the same name, contained thirty rooms for thirty patients and their kinfolk—for, according to Japanese custom, when a person falls sick and goes to a hospital, one or more members of his family go and live there with him, to cook for him, bathe, massage, and read to him, and to offer <u>incessant</u> familial sympathy, without which a Japanese patient would be miserable indeed. Dr. Fujii had no beds—only straw mats—for his patients. He did, however, have all sorts of modern equipment: an X-ray machine, diathermy[4] apparatus, and a fine tiled laboratory. The structure rested two-thirds on the land, one-third on piles over the tidal waters of the Kyo. This overhang, the part of the building where Dr. Fujii lived, was queer-looking, but it was cool in summer and from the porch, which faced away from the center of the city, the prospect of the river, with pleasure boats drifting up and down it, was always refreshing. Dr. Fujii had occasionally had anxious moments when the Ota and its mouth branches rose to flood, but the piling was apparently firm enough and the house had always held.

Dr. Fujii had been relatively idle for about a month because in July, as the number of untouched cities in Japan dwindled and as Hiroshima seemed more and more inevitably a target, he began turning patients away, on the ground that in case of a fire raid he would not be able to evacuate them. Now he had only two patients left—a woman from Yano, injured in the shoulder, and a young man of twenty-five recovering from burns he had suffered when the steel factory near Hiroshima in which he worked had been hit. Dr. Fujii had six nurses to tend his patients. His wife and children were safe; his wife and one son were living outside Osaka, and another son and two daughters were in the country on Kyushu. A niece was living with him,

3. **hedonistic** (he de nis´ tik) *adj.* indulgently seeking out pleasure.
4. **diathermy** (dī´ ə thʉr´ mē) *n.* medical treatment in which heat is produced beneath the skin to warm or destroy tissue.

and a maid and a manservant. He had little to do and did not mind, for he had saved some money. At fifty, he was healthy, <u>convivial</u>, and calm, and he was pleased to pass the evenings drinking whiskey with friends, always sensibly and for the sake of conversation. Before the war, he had affected brands imported from Scotland and America; now he was perfectly satisfied with the best Japanese brand, Suntory.

Dr. Fujii sat down cross-legged in his underwear on the spotless matting of the porch, put on his glasses, and started reading the Osaka *Asahi.* He liked to read the Osaka news because his wife was there. He saw the flash. To him—faced away from the center and looking at his paper—it seemed a brilliant yellow. Startled, he began to rise to his feet. In that moment (he was 1,550 yards from the center), the hospital leaned behind his rising and, with a terrible ripping noise, toppled into the river. The Doctor, still in the act of getting to his feet, was thrown forward and around and over; he was buffeted and gripped; he lost track of everything, because things were so speeded up; he felt the water.

Dr. Fujii hardly had time to think that he was dying before he realized that he was alive, squeezed tightly by two long timbers in a V across his chest, like a morsel suspended between two huge chopsticks—held upright, so that he could not move, with his head miraculously above water and his torso and legs in it. The remains of his hospital were all around him in a mad assortment of splintered lumber and materials for the relief of pain. His left shoulder hurt terribly. His glasses were gone. . . .

Miss Toshiko Sasaki, the East Asia Tin Works clerk, . . . got up at three o'clock in the morning on the day the bomb fell. There was extra housework to do. Her eleven-month-old brother, Akio, had come down the day before with a serious stomach upset; her mother had taken him to the Tamura Pediatric Hospital and was staying there with him. Miss Sasaki, who was about twenty, had to cook breakfast for her father, a brother, a sister, and herself, and—since the hospital, because of the war, was unable to provide food—to prepare a whole day's meals for her mother and the baby, in time for her father, who worked in a factory making rubber earplugs for artillery crews, to take the food by on his way to the plant. When she had finished and had cleaned and put away the cooking things, it was nearly seven. The family lived in Koi, and she had a forty-five-minute trip to the tin works, in the section of town called Kannonmachi. She was in charge of the personnel records in the factory. She left Koi at seven, and as soon as she reached the plant, she went with some of the other girls from the personnel department to the factory auditorium. A prominent local Navy man, a former employee, had committed suicide the day before by throwing himself under a train—a death considered honorable enough to warrant a memorial service, which was to be held at the tin works at ten o'clock that morning. In the large hall, Miss Sasaki and the others made suitable preparations for the meeting. This work took about twenty minutes.

convivial (kən viv′ ē əl) *adj.* fond of good company; sociable

Literary Analysis
Implied Theme and Objective/Subjective Accounts Is Hersey's description of Dr. Fujii objective or subjective? Explain.

Reading Check
Where is Dr. Fujii when the bomb hits?

Miss Sasaki went back to her office and sat down at her desk. She was quite far from the windows, which were off to her left, and behind her were a couple of tall bookcases containing all the books of the factory library, which the personnel department had organized. She settled herself at her desk, put some things in a drawer, and shifted papers. She thought that before she began to make entries in her lists of new employees, discharges, and departures for the Army, she would chat for a moment with the girl at her right. Just as she turned her head away from the windows, the room was filled with a blinding light. She was paralyzed by fear, fixed still in her chair for a long moment (the plant was 1,600 yards from the center).

Everything fell, and Miss Sasaki lost consciousness. The ceiling dropped suddenly and the wooden floor above collapsed in splinters and the people up there came down and the roof above them gave way; but principally and first of all, the bookcases right behind her swooped forward and the contents threw her down, with her left leg horribly twisted and breaking underneath her. There, in the tin factory, in the first moment of the atomic age, a human being was crushed by books.

Review and Assess

Thinking About the Selection

1. **Respond:** What thoughts remain with you after reading this account of the bombing of Hiroshima?

2. **(a) Recall:** At what time and on what day was the bomb dropped on Hiroshima? **(b) Draw Conclusions:** Why do you think Hersey is so precise in noting the exact date and time?

3. **(a) Recall:** In describing each individual's experience, which moment does Hersey refer to again and again?
   (b) Interpret: What is the effect of Hersey's returning to this moment repeatedly?

4. **(a) Recall:** Note three details describing the city of Hiroshima in the hours preceding the bomb. **(b) Analyze:** Why does Hersey spend so much time describing the city before the blast?

5. **(a) Recall:** By what is Miss Sasaki crushed? **(b) Infer:** What effect do you think Hersey intended when he described Miss Sasaki's experience?

6. **(a) Classify:** Are the people Hersey portrays important decision makers or merely ordinary citizens?
   (b) Draw Conclusions: What is Hersey implying about the fates of individuals in the midst of war?

7. **Take a Position:** President Truman's hope that the atomic bomb would end the war proved true but at a huge cost. Do you think he made the right decision? Why or why not?

Losses

Randall Jarrell

It was not dying: everybody died.
It was not dying: we had died before
In the routine crashes—and our fields
Called up the papers, wrote home to our folks,
5 And the rates rose, all because of us.
We died on the wrong page of the almanac,
Scattered on mountains fifty miles away;
Diving on haystacks, fighting with a friend,
We blazed up on the lines we never saw.
10 We died like aunts or pets or foreigners.
(When we left high school nothing else had died
For us to figure we had died like.)

In our new planes, with our new crews, we bombed
The ranges by the desert or the shore,
15 Fired at towed targets, waited for our scores—
And turned into replacements and woke up
One morning, over England, operational.
It wasn't different: but if we died
It was not an accident but a mistake
20 (But an easy one for anyone to make).
We read our mail and counted up our missions—
In bombers named for girls, we burned
The cities we had learned about in school—
Till our lives wore out; our bodies lay among
25 The people we had killed and never seen.
When we lasted long enough they gave us medals;
When we died they said, "Our casualties were low."

Reading Strategy
Drawing Inferences About Theme In lines 1–2, what surprising comments does the poet make about death?

✔**Reading Check**

Who is speaking? Who are "we"?

The Death of the Ball Turret Gunner

Randall Jarrell

A ball turret was a plexiglass sphere, or circular capsule, in the underside of certain World War II bombers; it held a small man and two machine guns. When the bomber was attacked by a plane below, the gunner, hunched in his little sphere, would revolve with the turret to fire his guns from an upside-down position.

From my mother's sleep I fell into the State,
And I hunched in its belly till my wet fur froze.
Six miles from earth, loosed from its dream of life,
I woke to black flak[1] and the nightmare fighters.
5   When I died they washed me out of the turret with a hose.

---

1. flak *n.* anti-aircraft fire.

Review and Assess

Thinking About the Selections

1. **Respond:** Do you share the poet's attitude toward war as he expresses it in "Losses"? Why or why not?

2. **(a) Recall:** In the first stanza of "Losses," in what variety of ways do the pilots die? **(b) Interpret:** What do these descriptions suggest about the pilots' attitude toward death?

3. **(a) Recall:** Do the pilots see the people they kill? **(b) Analyze:** What is the poet suggesting about the horror of modern warfare?

4. **(a) Recall:** In "The Death of the Ball Turret Gunner," which words does the gunner use to describe his view of life on Earth? **(b) Analyze:** In what way is this view of life related to the "nightmare" in the turret?

5. **(a) Interpret:** To what does the word "State" refer? **(b) Draw Conclusions:** What is the poet suggesting about the relationship between a soldier in a war and the government?

6. **Take a Position:** Jarrell based his poems on observations of World War II, a war that has been called "the good war." Is there such a thing as a "good war"? Explain.

Review and Assess

Literary Analysis

Implied Theme

1. (a) Which details in *Hiroshima* give clues to the **implied theme**? (b) What is that theme?

2. (a) In "Losses," what does line 26 imply about the value of the medals? (b) What is the poet saying about honor and valor in war?

3. In "The Death of the Ball Turret Gunner," what is the poet saying about the value of human life during war?

4. (a) Use a chart like the one shown to explore similarities and differences in Hersey's and Jarrell's portrayals of victims in war. (b) Do the three pieces share a common theme? Explain.

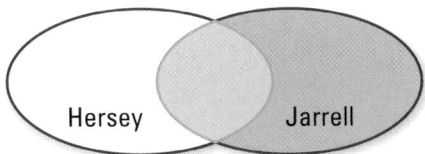

Comparing Literary Works

5. (a) In *Hiroshima*, which descriptions evoke the strongest emotions in you? (b) Is Hersey writing an **objective account** as a reporter or a **subjective account** as a commentator? Explain.

6. (a) Which lines in Jarrell's poems are stated as pure fact, seemingly without emotional bias? (b) What is the effect?

Reading Strategy

Drawing Inferences About Theme

7. (a) Explain the underlying meaning of this line from *Hiroshima*:

    . . . the night before the bomb was dropped, an announcer . . . advised the population . . . to evacuate to their designated 'safe areas.'

    (b) In what ways does that line help to communicate the theme?

8. In "Losses," the speaker notes, "We died like aunts or pets or foreigners." What does this line suggest about the poem's theme?

Extend Understanding

9. **Science Connection:** When the atom bomb was dropped on Hiroshima, no one knew about fallout, radiation sickness, or long-term contamination of the land. How might such knowledge have changed the decision to drop the bomb?

Quick Review

An **implied theme** is the message the author suggests through details, characterization, and events but does not directly state.

In an **objective account,** the narrator is an outside observer who comments on the events without emotion. In a **subjective account,** the narrator reveals his or her feelings about the events described.

To **draw inferences about theme,** examine clues from the work for their underlying meanings.

 **Take It to the Net**
www.phschool.com
Take the interactive self-test online to check your understanding of these selections.

Integrate Language Skills

Vocabulary Development Lesson

Word Analysis: Latin Root *-vol-*

The meaning of the word *volition*, "the act of using the will," is derived from the Latin root *-vol-*, meaning "to will" or "to wish." Using your knowledge of the roots, define each of the following words. Then, check your answers in a dictionary.

1. volunteer
2. malevolence
3. benevolence
4. involuntary

Spelling Strategy

The plural of words ending in *z, x, sh, ch,* or *s* is usually formed by adding *-es* to the base word. For example, *porch + -es = porches*. Write the plural of each of the following words.

1. loss
2. parish
3. crash
4. reflex
5. church
6. glass

Grammar and Style

Transitions and Transitional Phrases

Transitions are words that show chronological, spatial, comparison and contrast, cause and effect, and order of importance relationships among ideas. Groups of words that function in the same way are called **transitional phrases.**

> **Transition:** *Then*, a tremendous flash of light cut across the sky.
>
> **Transitional phrase:** *At the time*, none of them knew anything.

Common transitions like *because, as a result, if, therefore, in addition, although, next, in contrast, similarly, despite,* and *recently* can clarify the connections between ideas.

Fluency: Sentence Completion

Select the word from the vocabulary list on p. 1161 that best completes each of these sentences.

1. The birds ___?___ their nest and never returned to it.
2. She did extra homework of her own ___?___.
3. Let's establish a ___?___ point, so we don't miss each other.
4. Among the financier's ___?___ was a fund to send young musicians to music camp.
5. The child's ___?___ whining bothered fellow train passengers.
6. The ___?___ friends attend parties together often.

Practice Add transitions or transitional phrases to the following paragraph.

> Mr. Tanimoto cooked his own breakfast. He started for Mr. Matsuo's house. The two men set out. An air-raid siren went off. The all-clear sounded. There was no sound of planes. A tremendous flash of light cut across the sky. Both Mr. Tanimoto and Mr. Matsuo reacted in terror.

Writing Application Write a series of sentences summarizing your activities during a typical day. Use transitions and transitional phrases to link ideas.

WG Prentice Hall Writing and Grammar Connection: Chapter 3, Section 2

Writing Lesson

Book Review

John Hersey's book *Hiroshima* was published in 1946. Imagine that, more than fifty years later, you have been asked to write a review of the book celebrating its anniversary. In your review, discuss the book as both a work of literature and an important historical document.

Prewriting   Reread the excerpt from *Hiroshima*. Speculate about the effect the book had on its first readers who were just learning about the power of nuclear weapons. Take notes about Hersey's use of description, and identify his attitude toward his subject.

Drafting   Begin with a vivid opening sentence. Then, describe the book and state why it is both a moving and an important piece of writing. Present point-by-point detail in your body paragraphs, and write a conclusion that reinforces Hersey's insights for modern readers.

Revising   Read your review to make sure you have conveyed a clear sense of the book. Determine whether you have appropriately targeted the knowledge level of your expected audience.

Model: Revising for Knowledge Level of Readers

the Japanese city of   *on August 6, 1945*
When the United States bombed Hiroshima, a catastrophic power was unleashed. This event contributed to a fear of nuclear war that would last for decades.

> An audience unfamiliar with an event requires the basic information added in revision.

WG *Prentice Hall Writing and Grammar Connection: Chapter 13, Section 2*

Extension Activities

Listening and Speaking Present a **dramatic reading** of one of Randall Jarrell's poems. To prepare, try the following tips:

- Supplement the reading with evocative music and appropriate sound effects.
- Vary your tone of voice to draw out shades of meaning.
- Include visual aids, such as a photograph of a World War II bomber, to accompany your reading.

Research and Technology Using library and Internet sources, conduct research on the city of Hiroshima. Focus your investigation on the state of the city just before and after August 1945, when the bomb was dropped. Gather your findings in a **written report**.

 **Take It to the Net**   www.phschool.com

Go online for an additional research activity using the Internet.

Prepare to Read

Mirror ◆ In a Classroom ◆ The Explorer ◆ Frederick Douglass ◆ Runagate Runagate

Sylvia Plath (1932–1963)

Despite her success as a writer, Sylvia Plath lived a short, unhappy life. In many of her poems, she expresses intense feelings of despair and deep inner pain. Born in Boston, Plath wrote poetry and received scholastic and literary awards as a youth. Although she suffered a nervous breakdown in her junior year, she graduated with highest honors from Smith College. She also studied at Cambridge University in England, where she met and married poet Ted Hughes in 1956. Her first book of verse, *The Colossus and Other Poems* (1960), was the only one published during her lifetime. Four more books of poetry and a novel, *The Bell Jar* (1963), were published posthumously.

Adrienne Rich (b. 1929)

Born in Baltimore, Maryland, Adrienne Rich is a poet and an essayist who is best known for her examination of women in society. Rich's career as a poet can be divided into two distinct stages. In the early part of her career, she wrote neatly crafted traditional verse. In contrast, her later poems are written in free verse and often explore deep personal feelings. Her first volume of poetry, *A Change of World* (1951), was published just after she graduated from Radcliffe College. Her most recent books are *Dark Fields of the Republic (Poems 1991–1995)* and *Midnight Salvage (Poems 1995–1998)*. A new selection of her essays, *Arts of the Possible: Essays and Conversations*, and a new volume of poems, *Fox (Poems 1998–2000)*, appeared in 2001.

Gwendolyn Brooks (1917–2000)

Gwendolyn Brooks was raised in a Chicago neighborhood known as "Bronzeville"—the setting for her first book, *A Street in Bronzeville* (1945). Although her early poems focus on suffering urban blacks who feel uprooted and are unable to make a living, Brooks's own youth was quite different. Her home was warm and her family loving, supportive, and confident that Brooks would find success as a writer. Brooks began writing poetry at the age of seven. In 1950, she became the first African American writer to win a Pulitzer Prize. After that, her reputation grew steadily, and she became one of the most highly regarded poets of our time.

Robert Hayden (1913–1980)

Born in Detroit, Robert Hayden was a young, politically active writer in the 1930s who protested not only the social and economic conditions of African Americans but also what he saw as the nation's inadequate care of the poor. Hayden was an extremely versatile writer who used a variety of poetic forms and techniques, focusing on a wide range of subjects. He published several collections of poetry, including *Heart-Shape in the Dust* (1940), *The Lion and the Archer* (1948), and *The Night-Blooming Cereus* (1972). His collection *A Ballad of Remembrance* received the Grand Prize for Poetry at the First World Festival for Negro Arts in 1966.

Preview

Connecting to the Literature

It is human nature to find fault with the situations, policies, and attitudes we experience in everyday life. While you may discuss your social concerns with your family and friends, some poets use their writing as a means of expressing their views.

Literary Analysis

Theme

A poem's **theme** is the central idea it conveys. Poets suggest themes through the connotations of the words and images they choose. For example, in these lines about aging by Sylvia Plath, the words *drowned* and *terrible* have negative associations; thus, you can infer that the theme has something to do with the fear of growing old:

> In me she has drowned a young girl, and in me an old woman
> Rises toward her day after day, like a terrible fish.

As you read these poems, find clues to the themes in words and images that evoke either negative or positive responses.

Comparing Literary Works

Poetry has long been a vehicle for **social criticism.** In some poems, the social critique addresses topics we usually categorize as personal. In the poet's message, however, the personal takes on larger meaning. Other poems address large social themes and show the ways in which broad social problems affect the lives of individuals. All the poems you are about to read carry messages of social critique. As you read, examine the ways in which each one explores the intersection between the individual and the society of which he or she is part.

Reading Strategy

Interpreting

In most poems, the central message is not directly stated. It is up to you to **interpret** it by looking for an underlying meaning in the words and images. Consider the connotations of the words and the associations they call to mind, and then try to determine what common thread ties them together. Use an organizer like the one shown to record words and images that will help you interpret the theme.

Words and Images	Potential Meaning

Vocabulary Development

preconceptions (prē´ kən sep´ shənz) *n.* ideas formed beforehand (p. 1180)

meditate (med´ ə tāt´) *v.* think deeply; ponder (p. 1180)

din (din) *n.* loud, continuous noise; uproar or clamor (p. 1182)

wily (wī´ lē) *adj.* sly; cunning (p. 1182)

Mirror

Sylvia Plath

Mirror II, George Tooker, © Addison Gallery of American Art, Phillips Academy, Andover, Massachusetts

◀ **Critical Viewing** The artist titled this painting *Mirror II*. What ideas are common to both the painting and poem? **[Connect]**

I am silver and exact. I have no <u>preconceptions</u>.
Whatever I see I swallow immediately
Just as it is, unmisted by love or dislike.
I am not cruel, only truthful—
5   The eye of a little god, four-cornered.
Most of the time I <u>meditate</u> on the opposite wall.
It is pink, with speckles. I have looked at it so long
I think it is a part of my heart. But it flickers.
Faces and darkness separate us over and over.
10 Now I am a lake. A woman bends over me,
Searching my reaches for what she really is.
Then she turns to those liars, the candles or the moon.
I see her back, and reflect it faithfully.
She rewards me with tears and an agitation of hands.
15 I am important to her. She comes and goes.
Each morning it is her face that replaces the darkness.
In me she has drowned a young girl, and in me an old woman
Rises toward her day after day, like a terrible fish.

preconceptions (prē´ kən sep´ shənz) *n.* ideas formed beforehand

meditate (med´ ə tāt´) *v.* think deeply; ponder

IN A CLASSROOM

Adrienne Rich

    Talking of poetry, hauling the books
    arm-full to the table where the heads
    bend or gaze upward, listening, reading aloud,
    talking of consonants, elision,[1]
5 caught in the how, oblivious of why:
    I look in your face, Jude,
    neither frowning nor nodding,
    opaque in the slant of dust-motes over the table:
    a presence like a stone, if a stone were thinking
10 *What I cannot say, is me. For that I came.*

---

1. **elision** (ē lizh´ ən) *n.* omission or slurring over of a vowel or syllable; often used in poetry to preserve meter.

Review and Assess

Thinking About the Selections

1. **Respond:** The speaker of "Mirror" maintains, "I am not cruel, only truthful—." If the truth hurts, do you think being truthful is cruel? Explain.

2. **(a) Recall:** What two reflecting surfaces does the speaker name? **(b) Infer:** Who is the speaker?

3. **(a) Recall:** In what way does the woman "reward" the speaker? **(b) Interpret:** Explain why she reacts this way.

4. **(a) Recall:** To whom does the woman turn? **(b) Interpret:** Why are they called liars?

5. **Infer:** Who is the "old woman"? **(b) Draw Conclusions:** What are the woman's feelings about aging?

6. **Extend:** The woman searches the mirror for "what she really is." Can one's true self be seen in a mirror? Explain.

The Explorer
Gwendolyn Brooks

Somehow to find a still spot in the noise
Was the frayed inner want, the winding, the frayed hope
Whose tatters he kept hunting through the <u>din</u>.
A satin peace somewhere.
5 A room of <u>wily</u> hush somewhere within.

So tipping down the scrambled halls he set
Vague hands on throbbing knobs. There were behind
Only spiraling, high human voices,
The scream of nervous affairs,
10 Wee griefs,
Grand griefs. And choices.

He feared most of all the choices, that cried to be taken.

There were no bourns.[1]
There were no quiet rooms.

din (din) *n.* loud, continuous noise; uproar or clamor

wily (wī´ lē) *adj.* sly; cunning

---

1. bourns (bōrnz) *n.* limits; boundaries

Review and Assess

Thinking About the Selection

1. **Respond:** What did you see and hear as you read this poem?
2. **(a) Recall:** What is the "inner want" the poem's speaker expresses? **(b) Interpret:** In what way does the title of the poem relate to the "inner want"?
3. **(a) Recall:** Where is the explorer searching for the "inner want"? **(b) Assess:** Does he find it?
4. **(a) Interpret:** What might the explorer's apartment building symbolize? **(b) Interpret:** What might the explorer's actions and feelings symbolize?
5. **Apply:** Why do you think people often fear having to make choices?

Frederick Douglass[1]

Robert Hayden

When it is finally ours, this freedom, this liberty,
   this beautiful
and terrible thing, needful to man as air,
usable as earth; when it belongs at last to all,
when it is truly instinct, brain matter, diastole, systole,[2]
5 reflex action; when it is finally won; when it is more
than the gaudy mumbo jumbo of politicians:
this man, this Douglass, this former slave, this Negro
beaten to his knees, exiled, visioning a world
where none is lonely, none hunted, alien,
10 this man, superb in love and logic, this man
shall be remembered. Oh, not with statues' rhetoric,
not with legends and poems and wreaths of bronze alone,
but with the lives grown out of his life, the lives
fleshing his dream of the beautiful, needful thing.

Part II, The Free Man, No. 30, The Frederick Douglass Series, Jacob Lawrence, Hampton University Museum, Hampton, Virginia

▲ **Critical Viewing**
What impression of
Douglass does this
painting convey?
[Analyze]

---

1. **Frederick Douglass** American abolitionist (1817?–1895).
2. **diastole** (dī as´ tə lē´), **systole** (sis´ tə lē´) Diastole is the normal rhythmic dilation, or
opening, of the heart. Systole is the normal rhythmic closing of the heart.

Review and Assess

Thinking About the Selection

1. **Respond:** What impression do you have of Frederick Douglass after reading this poem? What kind of person was he?

2. **(a) Recall:** What is the "beautiful and terrible" thing?
   (b) Infer: To whom does it not yet belong?

3. **(a) Recall:** In what ways does the speaker say that Douglass will not be remembered? **(b) Infer:** What does the speaker think are the limitations of statues and memorials?

4. **(a) Interpret:** In what way does the speaker say Douglass truly will be remembered? **(b) Analyze:** What does the speaker mean by "the lives fleshing his dream of the beautiful, needful thing"?

5. **Apply:** How do you think Frederick Douglass would respond to this poem? Explain.

Runagate Runagate

Robert Hayden

Background

Although Robert Hayden's poetry spans the range of human experience, much of it reflects his passionate, lifelong interest in African American history. His first job after graduating from Detroit City College was to research local African American history with Detroit's Federal Writer's Project. Throughout his career as a professor of literature, Hayden continued to research and write about his heritage. In "Frederick Douglass," he pays tribute to the famous African American abolitionist. "Runagate Runagate" brings the experiences of the Underground Railroad vividly to life.

I

Runs falls rises stumbles on from darkness into darkness
and the darkness thicketed with shapes of terror
and the hunters pursuing and the hounds pursuing
and the night cold and the night long and the river
5 to cross and the jack-muh-lanterns beckoning beckoning
and blackness ahead and when shall I reach that somewhere
morning and keep on going and never turn back and keep on going

Reading Strategy
Interpreting How do the words in lines 1–7 capture the feeling of running?

          Runagate[1]
               Runagate
10   Runagate

Many thousands rise and go
many thousands crossing over

                  O mythic North
           O star-shaped yonder Bible city[2]

15 Some go weeping and some rejoicing
some in coffins and some in carriages
some in silks and some in shackles

        Rise and go or fare you well

No more auction block for me
20 no more driver's lash for me

---

1. **Runagate** (run´ ə gāt) runaway; fugitive.
2. **star-shaped yonder Bible city** Bethlehem, a town in the free state of Pennsylvania.

If you see my Pompey, 30 yrs of age,
new breeches, plain stockings, negro shoes;
if you see my Anna, likely young mulatto
branded E on the right cheek, R on the left,
25   catch them if you can and notify subscriber.[3]
Catch them if you can, but it won't be easy.
They'll dart underground when you try to catch them,
plunge into quicksand, whirlpools, mazes,
turn into scorpions when you try to catch them.

30   And before I'll be a slave
I'll be buried in my grave

North star and bonanza gold
I'm bound for the freedom, freedom-bound
and oh Susyanna don't you cry for me.

35   Runagate

                        Runagate

II

Rises from their anguish and their power,

                Harriet Tubman,[4]

                woman of earth, whipscarred,
40   a summoning, a shining

                Mean to be free

And this was the way of it, brethren brethren,
way we journeyed from Can't to Can.
Moon so bright and no place to hide,
45   the cry up and the patterollers[5] riding,
hound dogs belling in bladed air.
And fear starts a-murbling, Never make it,
we'll never make it. *Hush that now,*
and she's turned upon us, leveled pistol
50   glinting in the moonlight:
Dead folks can't jaybird-talk, she says;
you keep on going now or die, she says.

Wanted   Harriet Tubman   alias The General
alias Moses   Stealer of Slaves
55 In league with Garrison   Alcott   Emerson
Garrett   Douglass   Thoreau   John Brown[6]

---

3. **subscriber** slave holder from whom the slaves are fleeing.
4. **Harriet Tubman** (c. 1820–1913) African American slave who escaped and led other slaves to safety in the North.
5. **patterollers** patrollers, hunting the escaped slaves.
6. **Garrison . . . John Brown** prominent abolitionists.

▲ **Critical Viewing**
What inspiration might the moon have offered runaways? **[Hypothesize]**

✔**Reading Check**
To where is the speaker journeying? Why?

Armed and known to be Dangerous

Wanted   Reward   Dead or Alive

    Tell me, Ezekiel, oh tell me do you see
60   mailed Jehovah[7] coming to deliver me?

Hoot-owl calling in the ghosted air,
five times calling to the hants[8] in the air.
Shadow of a face in the scary leaves,
shadow of a voice in the talking leaves:

65   Come ride-a my train

Oh that train, ghost-story train
through swamp and savanna movering movering,
over trestles of dew, through caves of the wish,
Midnight Special on a sabre track movering movering,
first stop Mercy and the last Hallelujah.

Come ride-a my train

    Mean mean mean to be free.

---

7. Ezekiel (ē zē′ kē əl) **. . . Jehovah** (ji hō′ və) Ezekiel was a sixth-century B.C. Hebrew prophet; Jehovah is an Old Testament name for the Judeo-Christian God.
8. hants haunts; ghosts.

Review and Assess

Thinking About the Selection

1. **Respond:** How did your response change as the poem moved from stanza to stanza?

2. **(a) Recall:** What is being described in this poem?
   (b) Interpret: What feeling do the words "Runagate, Runagate, Runagate" convey? Explain.

3. **(a) Recall:** Who "rises from their anguish and their power"?
   (b) Interpret: In what ways does this person prevent the frightened fugitives from giving themselves up?

4. **(a) Draw Conclusions:** Whom do you think is wanted dead or alive? **(b) Draw Conclusions:** Who will pay the reward?

5. **(a) Interpret:** Do you think this poem reflects the experiences of a single speaker, or does it reflect a chorus of voices? Explain.
   (b) Interpret: If there is more than one voice, whose voices are they? Support your answers with examples from the poem.

6. **(a) Apply:** What do you think were some of the risks involved in the struggle for freedom? **(b) Take a Position:** If you had been in the situation of a "runagate," would you have put yourself at such risk? Explain.

Review and Assess

Literary Analysis

Theme

1. (a) Using a chart like the one shown, list the sensory images used in "Runagate Runagate." (b) Explain how the words you have listed express the **theme** that a journey on the Underground Railroad was full of risk, danger, reward, and emotion.

Sight	Hearing	Smell	Touch	Taste

2. List three images in "The Explorer" that help to identify the theme.

3. (a) In "Frederick Douglass," what words does Hayden use to describe Douglass and his work? (b) Based on these words, what would you say is the theme of the poem?

4. In "Mirror," what does the line "I am important to her" suggest about the theme of the poem?

Comparing Literary Works

5. (a) In what ways do both "The Explorer" and "Frederick Douglass" express the longing for an end to struggle? (b) What are the struggles each poem addresses?

6. (a) In what way can "Mirror" be read as a poem of social critique? (b) What social change, if any, does the poem advocate?

7. (a) How does "Runagate Runagate" demonstrate the suffering of individuals caused by a social injustice? (b) Does the poem propose a specific social change, or not? Explain.

Reading Strategy

Interpreting

8. (a) In "Mirror," what is the significance of the word *swallow*? (b) How does this word contribute to the message of the poem?

9. What is the significance of the medical terms Hayden uses to describe a time when freedom is "diastole, systole, reflex action"?

Extend Understanding

10. **Cultural Connection:** Do you think most people share the attitude toward aging that the woman in "Mirror" has? Why or why not?

Integrate Language Skills

Vocabulary Development Lesson

Word Analysis: Latin Root *-cep-/-cept-*

The word *preconception*, like other English words such as *deception, inception, conception, concept, reception,* and *intercept,* derives from the Latin root *-cep-/-cept-*, meaning "to take, hold, or seize." Using these words, write a reflective poem about an experience you have had.

Spelling Strategy

A prefix added to a word does not affect the spelling of the original word. For example, when you add the prefix *pre-* to the word *conceptions*, you create *preconceptions*. Use the prefixes given with a word root you know to make new words.

1. *dis-*   3. *re-*
2. *pre-*   4. *mis-*

Fluency: Sentence Completion

Review the list of vocabulary words on page 1179. Then, select the word that best completes each sentence below.

1. The guru will ___?___ on the question I posed.

2. To keep the trial fair, the jurors had no ___?___ about the case.

3. The ___?___ of the machines was ear-splitting.

4. The raccoon is one of the most ___?___ of animals.

Grammar and Style Lesson

Parallel Structure

Parallel structure is the expression of similar ideas in similar grammatical forms. Parallelism is especially helpful in poetry where it can add to the rhythm and sound of a poem. When writing, be careful to avoid faulty parallelism—the use of dissimilar grammatical structures to express similar ideas.

> **Example:** *when it is* truly instinct . . . / *when it is* finally won; *when it is* more / than the gaudy mumbo jumbo . . .

Practice Rewrite the following sentences using correct parallel structure.

1. The woman rewards the mirror's faithful accuracy with tears, tantrums, and getting depressed.

2. High human voices are heard in one room, and from another room comes the scream of nervous affairs.

3. There is no quiet place for the explorer and he's not finding any peace.

4. The runagates escaped from slavery, some in coffins, some in carriages, some in silks, and some were wearing shackles.

5. They saw the shadow of a face in the scary leaves and heard the shadow of a voice in the leaves that were talking.

Writing Application Write three sentences about a hero whose actions or attitudes you admire. In each sentence, use parallel structure to express your ideas eloquently.

WG *Prentice Hall Writing and Grammar Connection: Chapter 8, Section 4*

Writing Lesson

Literary Analysis

The purpose of a literary analysis is to show how various elements of a work of literature combine to convey an overall meaning or effect. Write a literary analysis of one of the poems you have just read.

Prewriting   Select a poem and read it several times, taking notes on how you will describe its overall effect or meaning. Gather examples of the poet's use of various elements such as imagery, personification, or metaphor to achieve this effect.

Drafting   Begin your analysis with a general statement about the poem and the points you will cover. Then, in a separate paragraph, support each point with examples and quotations from the poem. Conclude a well-phrased summary of your analysis.

Revising   Identify places in your draft at which you make important general statements about the poem. Strengthen your analysis by adding accurate quotations from the poem to support your interpretation.

Model: Using Quotations to Support Interpretation

Plath personifies the inanimate objects and contrasts them, giving them positive and negative human traits:

The mirror says, "I am not cruel, only truthful," but Plath adds, "Then she turns to those liars, the candles or the moon."

> Using direct quotations supports the interpretation of the poem.

W͞G Prentice Hall Writing and Grammar Connection: Chapter 14, Section 4

Extension Activities

Listening and Speaking With a group of classmates, stage a **debate** that answers these questions: What does freedom mean to you? Do you believe that everyone in present-day America is free? As you explore the issues raised by the questions, be sure to follow these rules:

- Allow each side to speak without interruption.
- Provide facts to support your ideas.

After both sides speak, give each one a chance for rebuttal. **[Group Activity]**

Research and Technology In "Mirror," a woman is preoccupied with her appearance and upset at the signs of aging. With a partner, use magazine ads, song tracks, and oral commentary to create a **multimedia presentation** exploring our culture's emphasis on youth.

 **Take It to the Net**   www.phschool.com

Go online for an additional research activity using the Internet.

Prepare to Read

For My Children ◆ Bidwell Ghost

Colleen McElroy (b. 1935)

Like a modern-day explorer, Colleen McElroy enjoys experiencing new places and has traveled widely throughout the United States and abroad. This wandering spirit is reflected in many of her poems, which are inspired by people and scenes she has discovered during her travels. McElroy's love of travel has led her to embark on ancestral searches. Her many adventures on these searches have included island hopping in Fiji, exploring Malaysia, climbing Machu Picchu, and riding a motorcycle at age 58 across the Australian desert where she encountered aborigines. In her poetry, she often delves into her rich African American and Pacific Islander heritage to find connections between experiences of the past, realities of the present, and hopes for the future.

A Prolific Writer After growing up in St. Louis, Missouri, McElroy graduated from Kansas State University and earned a doctorate from the University of Washington, where she is now a professor of English. A prolific writer, she has published several collections of poetry, including *The Mules Done Long Since Gone* (1973), *Music from Home: Selected Poems* (1976), *Bone Flames* (1987), and *What Madness Brought Me Here* (1990). She has also published numerous short stories, as well as a travel memoir entitled *A Long Way from St. Louie* (1997).

She has received many awards and honors, including two fellowships from the National Endowment for the Arts, two Fulbright Creative Writing fellowships, a Jesse Ball DuPont Distinguished Black Scholar Fellowship, the Before Columbus American Book Award, and the Pushcart Prize.

In "For My Children," McElroy uses rich metaphors of her culture both past and present.

Louise Erdrich (b. 1954)

Louise Erdrich, whose Chippewa ancestry has shaped her identity, was born in Little Falls, Minnesota, the first of seven children. Her mother was of Chippewa and French descent, and her father was German American. Both of her parents were teachers at the Bureau of Indian Affairs school in Wahpeton, North Dakota, and they strongly encouraged Erdrich's storytelling skills.

A Writer's Education Erdrich entered Dartmouth College in 1972 as part of the school's first coeducational class. After receiving her undergraduate degree from Dartmouth, she taught poetry and writing to young people through a position at the State Arts Council of North Dakota. She then attended Johns Hopkins University, where she earned a master's degree in creative writing.

A Critically Acclaimed Writer Erdrich settled in central New Hampshire and published her first volume of poems, *Jacklight* (1984). Her debut novel, *Love Medicine* (1984), is the story of three Chippewa families living on a North Dakota reservation in the early part of the twentieth century. The novel, planned and written as part of a four-novel series set between 1912 and 1984, enjoyed great critical and commercial success. Erdrich's reputation grew with the publication of three sequels to the book, *The Beet Queen* (1986), *Tracks* (1988), and *The Bingo Palace* (1994). Her novel *The Antelope Wife* was published in 1998.

A Fruitful Career In 1989, Erdrich released a second volume of poetry, *Baptism of Fire*, and in 1991 she co-wrote *The Crown of Columbus*, which offers a Native American perspective of American historical events. Erdrich's most recent novel is *The Last Report on the Miracles at Little No Horse* (2001).

Preview

Connecting to the Literature

The stories we hear from relatives, family friends, and neighbors help shape our awareness of our heritage. In different ways, both of these poems explore the mythic power of cultural heritage.

Literary Analysis

Lyric Poetry

Lyric poetry is melodic poetry that expresses the observations and feelings of a single speaker. Lyric poems were originally sung to the accompaniment of a stringed instrument called a lyre. Though rarely set to music today, lyric poems are still brief and melodic. Unlike narrative poems that tell stories, lyric poems focus on producing a single effect. In these lines from "Bidwell Ghost," for example, the speaker recalls vivid impressions of a fiery tragedy.

> It has been twenty years
>
> since her house surged and burst in the dark trees

As you read each poem, use a chart like the one shown to record the words and phrases that contribute to a single unifying effect.

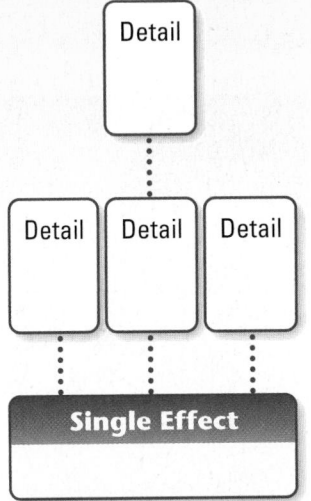

Comparing Literary Works

Both of these poems speak about the past and its relation to the present. In "For My Children," the past is presented in a positive light, a pleasant place that holds a family's history. In "Bidwell Ghost," the past is seen in a terrifying light, as a dangerous place where the character experienced a great tragedy. Poets often use **flashbacks** to move back and forth in time. As you read, compare the use of this device to express the observations and feelings of a single speaker.

Reading Strategy

Reading in Sentences

Like prose, many poems are written in sentences. They are also written in lines, but poets do not always complete sentences at the end of a line. Instead, a sentence may extend for several lines and then end in the middle of a line so that the poet can keep to a chosen rhythm and rhyme scheme. To understand the meaning of a poem, **read in sentences**. Notice the punctuation. Do not make a full stop at the end of a line unless there is a period, comma, colon, semicolon, or dash.

Vocabulary Development

shackles (shak´ əlz) *n.* restraints on freedom of expression or action (p. 1193)

heritage (her´ i tij´) *n.* something handed down from one's ancestors or from the past (p. 1193)

effigies (ef´ i jēz) *n.* likenesses; figures, such as dolls or statues (p. 1193)

FOR MY CHILDREN

Colleen McElroy

▲ **Critical Viewing** In what ways does this painting reflect the heritage that the speaker seeks to hand on to her children? Explain. **[Analyze]**

Background

In recent years, many Americans have become fascinated by oral history—the information gathered through interviews with individuals who can recall events and people of years past. Oral histories of families and communities are especially popular.

In societies without a written language, oral information that was passed down from one generation to the next took the place of written historical accounts. The speaker of "For My Children" is a collector of the oral history of her people. In telling this poem, she sifts through many facts and images of the past and passes on to the reader those she finds most striking.

I have stored up tales for you, my children
  My favorite children, my only children;
Of <u>shackles</u> and slaves and a bill of rights.
But skin of honey and beauty of ebony begins
5   In the land called Bilad as-Sudan,[1]
So I search for a <u>heritage</u> beyond St. Louis.

My memory floats down a long narrow hall,
  A calabash[2] of history.
Grandpa stood high in Watusi[3] shadows
10   In this land of yearly rituals for alabaster beauty;
Where <u>effigies</u> of my ancestors are captured
  In Beatle tunes,
And crowns never touch Bantu[4] heads.

My past is a slender dancer reflected briefly
15   Like a leopard in fingers of fire.
The future of Dahomey[5] is a house of 16 doors,
The totem of the Burundi[6] counts 17 warriors—
  In reverse generations.
While I cling to one stray Seminole.[7]

---

1. **Bilad as-Sudan** (bē lād´ äs sōō dan´) "land of the blacks," an Arabic expression by which Arab geographers referred to the settled African countries north of the southern edge of the Sahara.
2. **calabash** (kal´ ə bash´) n. dried, hollow shell of a gourd, used as a bowl or a cup.
3. **Watusi** (wä tōō´ sē) people of east-central Africa.
4. **Bantu** (ban´ tōō) Bantu-speaking peoples of southern Africa.
5. **Dahomey** (də hō´ mē) old name for Benin, in west-central Africa.
6. **Burundi** (bōō rōōn´ dē) country in east-central Africa.
7. **Seminole** (sem´ ə nōl´) Native American people from Florida.

shackles (shak´ əlz) n. restraints on freedom of expression or action

heritage (her´ i tij´) n. something handed down from one's ancestors or from the past

effigies (ef´ i jēz) n. likenesses; figures, such as dolls or statues

Reading Check

What has the speaker stored up for her children?

20 My thoughts grow thin in the urge to travel
        Beyond Grandma's tale
Of why cat fur is for kitten britches;
Past the wrought-iron rail of first stairs
        In baby white shoes,
25 To Ashanti[8] mysteries and rituals.

Back in the narrow hallway of my childhood.
        I cradled my knees
In limbs as smooth and long as the neck of a bud vase,
I began this ancestral search that you children yield now
30   In profile and bust
By common invention, in being and belonging.

The line of your cheeks recalls Ibo[9] melodies
        As surely as oboe and flute.
The sun dances a honey and cocoa duet on your faces.
35 I see smiles that mirror schoolboy smiles
        In the land called Bilad as-Sudan;
I see the link between the Mississippi and the Congo.

---

8. **Ashanti** (ə shän′ tə) people of western Africa.
9. **Ibo** (ē′ bō′) African people of southeastern Nigeria.

Review and Assess

Thinking About the Selection

1. **Respond:** Does this poem stir up thoughts about your own ancestors and cultural traditions? Why or why not?

2. **(a) Recall:** To whom does the speaker address this poem? **(b) Infer:** What is the speaker's reason for addressing the poem to them?

3. **(a) Recall:** Identify the cultures in which the speaker searches for evidence of her heritage. **(b) Analyze:** In the second and third stanzas, what impressions of her ancestors does the speaker convey? **(c) Analyze:** What images shape these impressions?

4. **(a) Recall:** Which two rivers does the speaker mention in the last stanza? **(b) Interpret:** Why might these two rivers be important to the speaker and to her children?

5. **(a) Interpret:** What is the poem's theme, or central message? **(b) Support:** What details or ideas in the poem support your interpretation?

6. **Apply:** In what specific ways might educating children about their heritage affect the choices they make in life?

BIDWELL GHOST

Louise Erdrich

Winter, Ozz Franca

◀ **Critical Viewing**
What features of this painting are reminiscent of phrases from the poem? Explain. [**Connect**]

Each night she waits by the road
in a thin white dress
embroidered with fire.

It has been twenty years
5 since her house surged and burst in the dark trees.
Still nobody goes there.

The heat charred the branches
of the apple trees,
but nothing can kill that wood.

☑ **Reading Check**

What is remarkable about the apple trees?

10   She will climb into your car
     but not say where she is going
     and you shouldn't ask.

     Nor should you try to comb the blackened nest of hair
     or press the agates of tears
15   back into her eyes.

     First the orchard bowed low and complained
     of the unpicked fruit,
     then the branches cracked apart and fell.

     The windfalls sweetened to wine
20   beneath the ruined arms and snow.
     Each spring now, in the grass, buds form on the tattered wood.

     The child, the child, why is she so persistent
     in her need? Is it so terrible
     to be alone when the cold white blossoms
25   come to life and burn?

Review and Assess

Thinking About the Selection

1. **Respond:** What questions arose in your mind as you read this poem? Were they all answered? Explain.

2. **(a) Recall:** What occurred twenty years ago? **(b) Draw Conclusions:** Who or what was affected by that event?

3. **(a) Recall:** What does the Bidwell ghost do each night? **(b) Interpret:** How would you describe the Bidwell ghost's attitude or behavior? **(c) Speculate:** Why might the ghost feel or behave this way?

4. **(a) Recall:** What happens to the apple trees each spring? **(b) Analyze:** What does this image suggest about nature's resilience?

5. **(a) Analyze:** Who is "the child" in the final stanza? **(b) Speculate:** Why do you think the speaker uses this term?

6. **Speculate:** Why do you think people from so many cultures are fascinated with ghosts?

7. **(a) Interpret:** What does the poet suggest about the lasting impact of tragedy? **(b) Take a Position:** Do you agree with this idea? Explain.

Review and Assess

Literary Analysis

Lyric Poetry

1. Describe, in your own words, the thoughts that the speaker expresses in the opening stanza of "For My Children."
2. In what way would you describe the "observations and feelings" the speaker expresses in "Bidwell Ghost"?
3. What is the single effect in (a) "For My Children" and (b) "Bidwell Ghost"?

Comparing Literary Works

4. In what ways are the Bidwell ghost and the apple trees alike?
5. Explain where the speaker's thoughts are "traveling" in the fourth stanza of "For My Children."
6. In "Bidwell Ghost," analyze the effect that the past has on the present. What connection can you find between the ghost and the people who see her? Use evidence from the poem for support.
7. Both "For My Children" and "Bidwell Ghost" consider the past as it affects the present. Does one of these poems seem more optimistic about the future? Explain.

Reading Strategy

Reading in Sentences

8. (a) By focusing on Louise Erdrich's use of punctuation, what do you notice about every stanza? (b) Why do you think Erdich chose to punctuate this poem as she did?
9. (a) Using a chart like the one shown, identify the figurative language in the last stanza of "For My Children." (b) Did reading the poem in sentences help you to understand the figurative language? Explain.

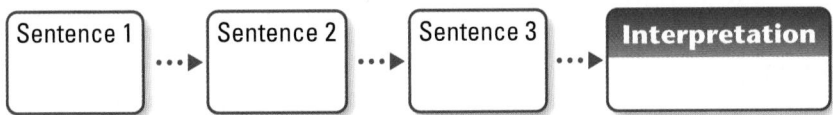

| Sentence 1 | Sentence 2 | Sentence 3 | **Interpretation** |

Extend Understanding

10. **Cultural Connection:** Could each poet's ancestral search be understood as a form of social protest? Explain.

Quick Review

Lyric poetry is melodic poetry that expresses the observations and feelings of a single speaker.

A **flashback** interrupts the chronological presentation of a narrative to relate an event of an earlier time.

To understand a poem's meaning, **read it in sentences,** pausing according to the punctuation rather than stopping automatically at the end of every line.

 Take It to the Net
www.phschool.com
Take the interactive self-test online to check your understanding of these selections.

Integrate Language Skills

Vocabulary Development Lesson

Related Words: *heritage*

The word *heritage* means "something handed down from ancestors." It derives from the Latin word *heres*, meaning "heir," and usually refers more to cultural ideas, values, and tales than to objects or artifacts. Several English words, such as *heredity*, *inherit*, and *inheritance*, are related to this word. Use these four related words to complete the sentences below.

1. His slender physique is a result of ___?___.
2. The siblings' ___?___ included their uncle's prized collection of hand tools.
3. My twin cousins are very proud of their Scandinavian ___?___.
4. Children ___?___ physical characteristics from both parents.

Fluency: Synonyms

A synonym is a word that has a meaning similar to that of another word. Choose the best synonym for each of the first words.

1. effigies: (a) representations, (b) toys, (c) machines
2. shackles: (a) imprisoned, (b) worries, (c) chains
3. heritage: (a) folk art, (b) traditions, (c) society

Spelling Strategy

When forming the plural of a word that ends in a consonant plus *y*, change the *y* to *i* and add *es*. *Effigy* thus becomes *effigies*. Write the plural form of these words.

1. memory   2. melody   3. mystery

Grammar and Style Lesson

Sequence of Tenses

Using the correct **sequence of verb tenses** allows you to show the relationship of events in time. The *present tense* shows action that exists in the present. *The present-perfect tense* indicates something that began in the past and continues to the present. The *past tense* shows action that began and ended at a given time in the past.

Present: So I **search** for a heritage beyond St. Louis . . .

Present-Perfect: I **have stored** up tales for you . . .

Past: First the orchard **bowed** low and **complained** . . .

Practice Identify the tense of the italicized verbs in the following sentences, and then explain the relationship of events in time that the verbs express.

1. Each night she *waits* by the road.
2. The heat *charred* the branches of the trees.
3. Each spring now, in the grass, buds *form* on the tattered wood.
4. Is it so terrible to be alone when the cold white blossoms *come* to life and *burn*?
5. She *has wondered* about this all her life.

Writing Application Write three sentences about your own heritage. In the first sentence, use a verb in the present tense. In the second, use a verb in the present-perfect tense. In the third, use a verb in the past tense.

W͏G Prentice Hall Writing and Grammar Connection: Chapter 21, Section 2

Writing Lesson

Ghost Story

Ghost stories are common in Gothic fiction, folk literature, legends, and oral histories. Almost all ghost stories contain an element of mystery and eeriness; some also feature a noticeable air of humor or melancholy. Write a ghost story based on "The Bidwell Ghost."

Prewriting Reread the poem and take notes about the characteristics of the Bidwell ghost. Use a chart like the one shown to organize the poem's sensory details into categories. Then, decide which elements will best convey an aura of mystery.

Model: Categorizing Sensory Details

Sight	Hearing	Touch	Taste	Smell

Drafting Grab your audience's interest from the start with a vivid description of the setting or a description of an eerie event. As you develop your story, focus on building suspense by including descriptions, events, or hints that raise questions for readers. Be sure to answer most questions by the story's end.

Revising Read your story several times, both silently and aloud. Revise it to make it more suspenseful, adding or deleting as needed.

 Prentice Hall Writing and Grammar Connection: Chapter 5, Section 3

Extension Activities

Listening and Speaking Think of a tale or legend that you remember from childhood—or create one yourself—and share it in a **dramatic presentation.** Follow this procedure:

- Prepare by writing the story down and rehearsing your delivery without notes.
- When you practice the story, speak with emotion.
- Use pacing and gestures to heighten the story's suspense or interest level.

After you have practiced, give the presentation to the class.

Research and Technology In a small group, research and deliver a short **multimedia cultural presentation** about one of the African cultures mentioned in "For My Children"—Watusi, Bantu, Dahomey, Burundi, Ashanti, or Ibo. Describe the culture, and include posters, photographs, art, and music to present the culture in an interesting way. **[Group Activity]**

 Take It to the Net   www.phschool.com

Go online for an additional research activity using the Internet.

Prepare to Read

The Writer in the Family

E. L. Doctorow (b. 1931)

The literary work of Edgar Lawrence Doctorow defies strict categorization. It is distinguished by a unique and authoritative blend of fact and fiction—sometimes called "faction," a term first coined to describe Doctorow's work. Doctorow has always been fascinated by the political unrest, social rootlessness, and constant motion of his time; his literary experimentation, which pushes the limits of style, form, and content, both responds to and reflects an era brimming with contradiction and irony.

Early Years The son of a record store owner, Doctorow attended the respected Bronx High School of Science. He later studied philosophy and drama, which perhaps gave Doctorow a sense of staging and an understanding of character.

Rising to a Challenge As a reader for Columbia Pictures, Doctorow was dismayed at the inferior scripts he read. Certain he could create better stories, he began writing. In his first novel, *Welcome to Hard Times* (1960), Doctorow focused on stretching the boundaries of fiction set in the Old West by addressing serious themes of a kind not usually treated in such literature. During these early professional years, Doctorow combined writing with a successful career in book publishing. Editing the works of landmark authors such as Norman Mailer and James Baldwin added literary knowledge and versatility to Doctorow's own talents. He continued writing, producing novels, short stories, essays, plays, and screen adaptations that exhibit the same type of inventiveness demonstrated in his first novel.

Mixing Fact and Fiction Doctorow frequently incorporates fact and fiction into his writing to create powerful dramatic effects. *The Book of Daniel* (1971), for example, weaves factual details about Ethel and Julius Rosenberg—communists found guilty of treason and sentenced to die—into a story centering on the lives of fictional children parted from their parents amid political scandal.

Similarly Doctorow's 1975 novel, *Ragtime*, blends fictional characters with the invented and real experiences of historical figures such as Harry Houdini and J. P. Morgan. In his later books, including *In Loon Lake* (1980), *Waterworks* (1994), and *City of God* (2000), Doctrow continued his experimentations with narrative structure and content.

Acclaim and Success Unlike the work of many other experimental writers, Doctorow's books are crowd-pleasers. He does not sacrifice the elements of entertainment for the sake of aesthetic experiment. His books remain readable, rich, and enjoyable even as they challenge accepted ideas about the nature of literature. Perhaps this is the reason Doctorow has enjoyed both critical and popular success. He has won two National Book Critic Circle Awards, one for *Ragtime* and another for *Billy Bathgate* (1989). His memoir *World's Fair* (1986) won the American Book Award. Four of his novels have been made into major motion pictures, and a successful adaptation of *Ragtime* opened on Broadway in 1998.

The Creative Process As a best-selling novelist and professor of English at New York University, Doctorow has often spoken about fiction writing. In a 1990 lecture at the New York Public Library, he said of the creative process, "The writer sits alone in a room creating alternate worlds. . . . He does not just give the intellect, but the whole being of [a] character." Doctorow's short story "The Writer in the Family" gives additional insight into this remark: It is written from the point of view of a young writer who must invent his own father as a fictional character.

Preview

Connecting to the Literature

One of the most difficult aspects of life is coping with the loss of loved ones. In this story, the characters deal with such a loss in a complicated way that will probably surprise you.

Literary Analysis

Static and Dynamic Characters

Doctorow uses static and dynamic characters to create a heightened sense of contrast in his story.

- A **static character** is one whose attitudes and behavior remain essentially stable throughout a literary work.
- **Dynamic characters** experience a shift or change in attitude and behavior during the course of a work.

As you read "The Writer in the Family," organize a character list like the one shown, identifying each of the characters as either static or dynamic. Consider how the contrasts between these character types add to the story's impact.

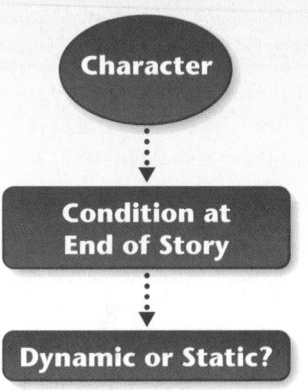

Character

↓

Condition at End of Story

↓

Dynamic or Static?

Connecting Literary Elements

Characters arise in part from their **cultural context,** the economic and social environment that they inhabit. In this story, that context is the Bronx, a borough of New York City that includes a community of recent Jewish immigrants and their descendants. Set in the 1950s, the story focuses on a family for which "the journey . . . from the working class to the professional class" is the central goal. As you read, notice how the cultural context influences the characters' goals, aspirations, and values. Consider the impact that the aspirations of parents have on the lives of their children.

Reading Strategy

Judging Characters' Actions

The characters in this story bend the rules relating to a pivotal event in their lives—the death of a family member. Think about how you would behave if faced with similar circumstances. When you **judge the characters' actions,** you evaluate their behavior against moral or other criteria. While reading the story, consider the actions of each character. Then, decide whether or not you find them morally defensible.

Vocabulary Development

bronchitis (brän kīt´ is) *n.* inflammation of the lining of the major air passageways of the lungs (p. 1202)

cronies (krō nēz) *n.* close companions (p. 1202)

barometer (bə räm´ ət ər) *n.* instrument for measuring atmospheric pressure (p. 1204)

anthology (an thäl´ ə jē) *n.* collection of poems, stories, and so on (p. 1207)

The Writer in the Family

E. L. Doctorow

Background

Most cultures have unique mourning rituals. For Jews, that ritual is called "shi'va." After a death, the family observes shi'va for seven days, during which time the mourners follow certain traditional rules. They remain at home and do not conduct business. Mirrors are covered, and comfortable furniture is exchanged for seating on low stools or the floor. Men and women neither shave nor cut their hair. Mourners do not wear new clothing or leather footwear. Traditionally, friends and fellow mourners join the family in their home to express sympathy and recite prayers. In "The Writer in the Family," the shi'va's ritual acknowledgment of death contrasts sharply with the pretense at the story's center.

In 1955 my father died with his ancient mother still alive in a nursing home. The old lady was ninety and hadn't even known he was ill. Thinking the shock might kill her, my aunts told her that he had moved to Arizona for his <u>bronchitis</u>. To the immigrant generation of my grandmother, Arizona was the American equivalent of the Alps, it was where you went for your health. More accurately, it was where you went if you had the money. Since my father had failed in all the business enterprises of his life, this was the aspect of the news my grandmother dwelled on, that he had finally had some success. And so it came about that as we mourned him at home in our stocking feet,[1] my grandmother was bragging to her <u>cronies</u> about her son's new life in the dry air of the desert.

My aunts had decided on their course of action without consulting us. It meant neither my mother nor my brother nor I could visit Grandma because we were supposed to have moved west too, a family, after all. My brother Harold and I didn't mind—it was

bronchitis (brän kīt′ is) *n.* inflammation of the lining of the major air passageways of the lungs

cronies (krō′ nēz) *n.* close companions

---

1. **as we mourned . . . in our stocking feet** refers to the Jewish custom of not wearing leather footwear during the traditional mourning period known as shi'va.

Laurence Typing, 1952, Fairfield Porter, Oil on canvas 40" x 30 1/8", The Parrish Art Museum, Southampton, New York, Gift of the Estate of Fairfield Porter

▲ **Critical Viewing** How might the boy in this picture use the familiar surroundings to help him concoct a believable letter? **[Connect]**

always a nightmare at the old people's home, where they all sat around staring at us while we tried to make conversation with Grandma. She looked terrible, had numbers of ailments, and her mind wandered. Not seeing her was no disappointment either for my mother, who had never gotten along with the old woman and did not visit when she could have. But what was disturbing was that my aunts had acted in the manner of that side of the family of making government on everyone's behalf, the true citizens by blood and the lesser citizens by marriage. It was exactly this attitude that had tormented my mother all her married life. She claimed Jack's family had never accepted her. She had battled them for twenty-five years as an outsider.

A few weeks after the end of our ritual mourning my Aunt Frances phoned us from her home in Larchmont. Aunt Frances was the wealthier of my father's sisters. Her husband was a lawyer, and both her sons were at Amherst.[2] She had called to say that Grandma was asking why she didn't hear from Jack. I had answered the phone. "You're the writer in the family," my aunt said. "Your father had so much faith in you. Would you mind making up something? Send it to me and I'll read it to her. She won't know the difference."

That evening, at the kitchen table, I pushed my homework aside and composed a letter. I tried to imagine my father's response to his new life. He had never been west. He had never traveled anywhere. In his generation the great journey was from the working class to the professional class. He hadn't managed that either. But he loved New York, where he had been born and lived all his life, and he was always discovering new things about it. He especially loved the old parts of the city below Canal Street, where he would find ships' chandlers or firms that wholesaled in spices and teas. He was a salesman for an appliance jobber[3] with accounts all over the city. He liked to bring home rare cheeses or exotic foreign vegetables that were sold only in certain neighborhoods. Once he brought home a <u>barometer</u>, another time an antique ship's telescope in a wooden case with a brass snap.

"Dear Mama," I wrote. "Arizona is beautiful. The sun shines all day and the air is warm and I feel better then I have in years. The desert is not as barren as you would expect, but filled with wildflowers and cactus plants and peculiar crooked trees that look like men holding their arms out. You can see great distances in whatever direction you turn and to the west is a range of mountains maybe fifty miles from here, but in the morning with the sun on them you can see the snow on their crests."

My aunt called some days later and told me it was when she read this letter aloud to the old lady that the full effect of Jack's death came over her. She had to excuse herself and went out in the parking lot to cry. "I wept so," she said. "I felt such terrible longing for him. You're so right, he loved to go places, he loved life, he loved everything."

Reading Strategy
Judging the Characters' Actions Which of the aunt's actions are controlling or manipulative? Explain.

barometer (bə räm′ ət ər) *n.* instrument for measuring atmospheric pressure

---

2. **Amherst** Amherst College in Amherst, Massachusetts.
3. **jobber** industry jargon for a person who buys goods in quantity from manufacturers and sells them to dealers; a wholesaler or middleman.

We began trying to organize our lives. My father had borrowed money against his insurance and there was very little left. Some commissions were still due but it didn't look as if his firm would honor them. There was a couple of thousand dollars in a savings bank that had to be maintained there until the estate was settled. The lawyer involved was Aunt Frances' husband and he was very proper. "The estate!" my mother muttered, gesturing as if to pull out her hair. "The estate!" She applied for a job part-time in the admissions office of the hospital where my father's terminal illness had been diagnosed, and where he had spent some months until they had sent him home to die. She knew a lot of the doctors and staff and she had learned "from bitter experience," as she told them, about the hospital routine. She was hired.

I hated that hospital, it was dark and grim and full of tortured people. I thought it was masochistic[4] of my mother to seek out a job there, but did not tell her so.

We lived in an apartment on the corner of 175th Street and the Grand Concourse, one flight up. Three rooms. I shared the bedroom with my brother. It was jammed with furniture because when my father had required a hospital bed in the last weeks of his illness we had moved some of the living-room pieces into the bedroom and made over the living room for him. We had to navigate bookcases, beds, a gateleg table, bureaus, a record player and radio console, stacks of 78 albums, my brother's trombone and music stand, and so on. My mother continued to sleep on the convertible sofa in the living room that had been their bed before his illness. The two rooms were connected by a narrow hall made even narrower by bookcases along the wall. Off the hall were a small kitchen and dinette and a bathroom. There were lots of appliances in the kitchen—broiler, toaster, pressure cooker, counter-top dishwasher, blender—that my father had gotten through his job, at cost. A treasured phrase in our house: *at cost.* But most of these fixtures went unused because my mother did not care for them. Chromium devices with timers or gauges that required the reading of elaborate instructions were not for her. They

4. **masochistic** (mas′ ə kis′ tik) *adj.* deriving pleasure from physical or psychological pain.

Literary Analysis

Static and Dynamic Characters and Cultural Context What does this passage tell you about the cultural context of the speaker's family life?

✔**Reading Check**

How did the family manage financially after the father died?

were in part responsible for the awful clutter of our lives and now she wanted to get rid of them. "We're being buried," she said. "Who needs them!"

So we agreed to throw out or sell anything inessential. While I found boxes for the appliances and my brother tied the boxes with twine, my mother opened my father's closet and took out his clothes. He had several suits because as a salesman he needed to look his best. My mother wanted us to try on his suits to see which of them could be altered and used. My brother refused to try them on. I tried on one jacket which was too large for me. The lining inside the sleeves chilled my arms and the vaguest scent of my father's being came to me.

"This is way too big," I said.

"Don't worry," my mother said. "I had it cleaned. Would I let you wear it if I hadn't?"

It was the evening, the end of winter, and snow was coming down on the windowsill and melting as it settled. The ceiling bulb glared on a pile of my father's suits and trousers on hangers flung across the bed in the shape of a dead man. We refused to try on anything more, and my mother began to cry.

"What are you crying for?" my brother shouted. "You wanted to get rid of things, didn't you?"

A few weeks later my aunt phoned again and said she thought it would be necessary to have another letter from Jack. Grandma had fallen out of her chair and bruised herself and was very depressed.

"How long does this go on?" my mother said.

"It's not so terrible," my aunt said, "for the little time left to make things easier for her."

My mother slammed down the phone. "He can't even die when he wants to!" she cried. "Even death comes second to Mama! What are they afraid of, the shock will kill her? Nothing can kill her. She's indestructible! A stake through the heart couldn't kill her!"

When I sat down in the kitchen to write the letter I found it more difficult than the first one. "Don't watch me," I said to my brother. "It's hard enough."

"You don't have to do something just because someone wants you to," Harold said. He was two years older than me and had started at City College; but when my father became ill he had switched to night school and gotten a job in a record store.

"Dear Mama," I wrote. "I hope you're feeling well. We're all fit as a fiddle. The life here is good and the people are very friendly and informal. Nobody wears suits and ties here. Just a pair of slacks and a short-sleeved shirt. Perhaps a sweater in the evening. I have bought into a very successful radio and record business and I'm doing very well. You remember Jack's Electric, my old place on Forty-third Street? Well, now it's Jack's Arizona Electric and we have a line of television sets as well."

I sent that letter off to my Aunt Frances, and as we all knew she would, she phoned soon after. My brother held his hand over the mouthpiece. "It's Frances with her latest review," he said.

"Jonathan? You're a very talented young man. I just wanted to tell you what a blessing your letter was. Her whole face lit up when I read the part about Jack's store. That would be an excellent way to continue."

"Well, I hope I don't have to do this anymore, Aunt Frances. It's not very honest."

Her tone changed. "Is your mother there? Let me talk to her."

"She's not here," I said.

"Tell her not to worry," my aunt said. "A poor old lady who has never wished anything but the best for her will soon die."

I did not repeat this to my mother, for whom it would have been one more in the family <u>anthology</u> of unforgivable remarks. But then I had to suffer it myself for the possible truth it might embody. Each side defended its position with rhetoric, but I, who wanted peace, rationalized the snubs and rebuffs each inflicted on the other, taking no stands, like my father himself. Years ago his life had fallen into a pattern of business failures and missed opportunities. The great debate between his family on one side, and my mother Ruth on the other, was this: who was responsible for the fact that he had not lived up to anyone's expectations?

As to the prophecies, when spring came my mother's prevailed. Grandma was still alive.

One balmy Sunday my mother and brother and I took the bus to the Beth El cemetery in New Jersey to visit my father's grave. It was situated on a slight rise. We stood looking over rolling fields embedded with monuments. Here and there processions of black cars wound their way through the lanes, or clusters of people stood at open graves. My father's grave was planted with tiny shoots of evergreen but it lacked a headstone. We had chosen one and paid for it and then the stonecutters had gone on strike. Without a headstone my father did not seem to be honorably dead. He didn't seem to me properly buried.

My mother gazed at the plot beside his, reserved for her coffin. "They were always too fine for other people," she said. "Even in the old days on Stanton Street. They put on airs. Nobody was ever good enough for

Reading Strategy
Judging the Characters' Actions Do you agree with the narrator's statement that the letter-writing is dishonest? Why or why not?

anthology (an thäl′ ə jē) n. collection of poems, stories, and so on

**Reading Check**

In what way does the narrator deal with his aunt's inconsiderate remarks?

them. Finally Jack himself was not good enough for them. Except to get them things wholesale. Then he was good enough for them."

"Mom, please," my brother said.

"If I had known. Before I ever met him he was tied to his mama's apron strings. And Essie's apron strings were like chains, let me tell you. We had to live where we could be near them for the Sunday visits. Every Sunday, that was my life, a visit to mamaleh. Whatever she knew I wanted, a better apartment, a stick of furniture, a summer camp for the boys, she spoke against it. You know your father, every decision had to be considered and reconsidered. And nothing changed. Nothing ever changed."

She began to cry. We sat her down on a nearby bench. My brother walked off and read the names on stones. I looked at my mother, who was crying, and I went off after my brother.

"Mom's still crying," I said. "Shouldn't we do something?"

"It's all right," he said. "It's what she came here for."

"Yes," I said, and then a sob escaped from my throat. "But I feel like crying too."

My brother Harold put his arm around me. "Look at this old black stone here," he said. "The way it's carved. You can see the changing fashion in monuments—just like everything else."

Somewhere in this time I began dreaming of my father. Not the robust father of my childhood, the handsome man with healthy pink skin and brown eyes and a mustache and the thinning hair parted in the middle. My dead father. We were taking him home from the hospital. It was understood that he had come back from death. This was amazing and joyous. On the other hand, he was terribly mysteriously damaged, or, more accurately, spoiled and unclean. He was very yellowed and debilitated by his death, and there were no guarantees that he wouldn't soon die again. He seemed aware of this and his entire personality was changed. He was angry and impatient with all of us. We were trying to help him in some way, struggling to get him home, but something prevented us, something we had to fix, a tattered suitcase that had sprung open, some mechanical thing: he had a car but it wouldn't start; or the car was made of wood; or his clothes, which had become too large for him, had caught in the door. In one version he was all bandaged and as we tried to lift him from his wheelchair into a taxi the bandage began to unroll and catch in the spokes of the wheelchair. This seemed to be some unreasonableness on his part. My mother looked on sadly and tried to get him to cooperate.

Letters and Postcards, Reid Christman, Courtesy of the artist.

▲ **Critical Viewing**
Describe how a person who saves letters and mementos like these might feel about the narrator of this story. **[Infer]**

That was the dream. I shared it with no one. Once when I woke, crying out, my brother turned on the light. He wanted to know what I'd been dreaming but I pretended I didn't remember. The dream made me feel guilty. I felt guilty in the dream too because my enraged father knew we didn't want to live with him. The dream represented us taking him home, or trying to, but it was nevertheless understood by all of us that he was to live alone. He was this derelict back from death, but what we were doing was taking him to some place where he would live by himself without help from anyone until he died again.

At one point I became so fearful of this dream that I tried not to go to sleep. I tried to think of good things about my father and to remember him before his illness. He used to call me "matey." "Hello, matey," he would say when he came home from work. He always wanted us to go someplace—to the store, to the park, to a ball game. He loved to walk. When I went walking with him he would say: "Hold your shoulders back, don't slump. Hold your head up and look at the world. Walk as if you meant it!" As he strode down the street his shoulders moved from side to side, as if he was hearing some kind of cakewalk. He moved with a bounce. He was always eager to see what was around the corner.

The next request for a letter coincided with a special occasion in the house. My brother Harold had met a girl he liked and had gone out with her several times. Now she was coming to our house for dinner. We had prepared for this for days, cleaning everything in sight, giving the house a going-over, washing the dust of disuse from the glasses and good dishes. My mother came home early from work to get the dinner going. We opened the gateleg table in the living room and brought in the kitchen chairs. My mother spread the table with a laundered white cloth and put out her silver. It was the first family occasion since my father's illness.

I liked my brother's girlfriend a lot. She was a thin girl with very straight hair and she had a terrific smile. Her presence seemed to excite the air. It was amazing to have a living breathing girl in our house. She looked around and what she said was: "Oh, I've never seen so many books!" While she and my brother sat at the table my mother was in the kitchen putting the food into serving bowls and I was going from the kitchen to the living room, kidding around like a waiter, with a white cloth over my arm and a high style of service, placing the serving dish of green beans on the table with a flourish. In the kitchen my mother's eyes were sparkling. She looked at me and nodded and mimed the words: "She's adorable!"

My brother suffered himself to be waited on. He was wary of what we might say. He kept glancing at the girl—her name was Susan—to see if we met with her approval. She worked in an insurance office and was taking courses in accounting at City College. Harold was under a terrible strain but he was excited and happy too. He had bought a bottle of Concord-grape wine to go with the roast chicken. He held up his glass and proposed a toast. My mother said: "To good health and happiness,"

Literary Analysis
Static and Dynamic Characters Judging by Jonathan's guilty reaction would you say he is a static or a dynamic character?

Literary Analysis
Static and Dynamic Characters and Cultural Context What does this passage reveal about the family's cultural context?

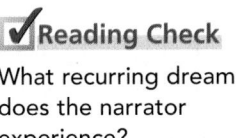**Reading Check**

What recurring dream does the narrator experience?

and we all drank, even I. At that moment the phone rang and I went into the bedroom to get it.

"Jonathan? This is your Aunt Frances. How is everyone?"

"Fine, thank you."

"I want to ask one last favor of you. I need a letter from Jack. Your grandma's very ill. Do you think you can?"

"Who is it?" my mother called from the living room.

"OK, Aunt Frances," I said quickly. "I have to go now, we're eating dinner." And I hung up the phone.

"It was my friend Louie," I said, sitting back down. "He didn't know the math pages to review."

The dinner was very fine. Harold and Susan washed the dishes and by the time they were done my mother and I had folded up the gateleg table and put it back against the wall and I had swept the crumbs up with the carpet sweeper. We all sat and talked and listened to records for a while and then my brother took Susan home. The evening had gone very well.

Once when my mother wasn't home my brother had pointed out something: the letters from Jack weren't really necessary. "What is this ritual?" he said, holding his palms up. "Grandma is almost totally blind, she's half deaf and crippled. Does the situation really call for a literary composition? Does it need verisimilitude? Would the old lady know the difference if she was read the phone book?"

"Then why did Aunt Frances ask me?"

"That is the question, Jonathan. Why did she? After all, she could write the letter herself—what difference would it make? And if not Frances, why not Frances' sons, the Amherst students? They should have learned by now to write."

"But they're not Jack's sons," I said.

"That's exactly the point," my brother said. "The idea is *service*. Dad used to break his back getting them things wholesale, getting them deals on things. Frances of Westchester really needed things at cost. And Aunt Molly. And Aunt Molly's husband, and Aunt Molly's ex-husband. Grandma, if she needed an errand done. He was always on the hook for something. They never thought his time was important. They never thought every favor he got was one he had to pay back. Appliances, records, watches, china, opera tickets, . . . anything. Call Jack."

"It was a matter of pride to him to be able to do things for them," I said. "To have connections."

"Yeah, I wonder why," my brother said. He looked out the window.

Then suddenly it dawned on me that I was being implicated.

"You should use your head more," my brother said.

Literature in context Social Studies Connection

Higher Education

The City College that Harold and his girlfriend attend revolutionized higher education for both immigrant and working-class New York families. An outgrowth of the Free Academy founded in 1847, City College proclaimed a mission to "let the children of the rich and poor take seats together. . . ." Low tuition costs made it possible for upwardly mobile students like Harold to gain the education they needed for access to the professional class. Today, a much larger CUNY (City University of New York) carries forth founder Townsend Harris's legacy to educate immigrant students from 145 countries, along with ethnically diverse native New Yorkers.

Yet I had agreed once again to write a letter from the desert and so I did. I mailed it off to Aunt Frances. A few days later, when I came home from school, I thought I saw her sitting in her car in front of our house. She drove a black Buick Roadmaster, a very large clean car with whitewall tires. It was Aunt Frances all right. She blew the horn when she saw me. I went over and leaned in at the window.

"Hello, Jonathan," she said. "I haven't long. Can you get in the car?"

"Mom's not home," I said. "She's working."

"I know that. I came to talk to you."

"Would you like to come upstairs?"

"I can't, I have to get back to Larchmont. Can you get in for a moment, please?"

I got in the car. My Aunt Frances was a very pretty white-haired woman, very elegant, and she wore tasteful clothes. I had always liked her and from the time I was a child she had enjoyed pointing out to everyone that I looked more like her son than Jack's. She wore white gloves and held the steering wheel and looked straight ahead as she talked, as if the car was in traffic and not sitting at the curb.

"Jonathan," she said, "there is your letter on the seat. Needless to say I didn't read it to Grandma. I'm giving it back to you and I won't ever say a word to anyone. This is just between us. I never expected cruelty from you. I never thought you were capable of doing something so deliberately cruel and perverse."

I said nothing.

"Your mother has very bitter feelings and now I see she has poisoned you with them. She has always resented the family. She is a very strong-willed, selfish person."

"No she isn't," I said.

"I wouldn't expect you to agree. She drove poor Jack crazy with her demands. She always had the highest aspirations and he could never fulfill them to her satisfaction. When he still had his store he kept your mother's brother . . . on salary. After the war when he began to make a little money he had to buy Ruth a mink jacket because she was so desperate to have one. He had debts to pay but she wanted a mink. He was a very special person, my brother, he should have accomplished something special, but he loved your mother and devoted his life to her. And all she ever thought about was keeping up with the Joneses."

I watched the traffic going up the Grand Concourse. A bunch of kids were waiting at the bus stop at the corner. They had put their books on the ground and were horsing around.

"I'm sorry I have to descend to this," Aunt Frances said. "I don't like talking about people this way. If I have nothing good to say about someone, I'd rather not say anything. How is Harold?"

"Fine."

"Did he help you write this marvelous letter?"

"No."

Literary Analysis
Static and Dynamic Characters In what ways do Aunt Frances's comments reveal that she is a static character?

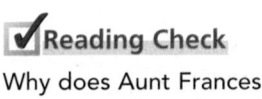**Reading Check**

Why does Aunt Frances return Jonathan's letter?

After a moment she said more softly: "How are you all getting along?"

"Fine."

"I would invite you up for Passover if I thought your mother would accept."

I didn't answer.

She turned on the engine. "I'll say good-bye now, Jonathan. Take your letter. I hope you give some time to thinking about what you've done."

That evening when my mother came home from work I saw that she wasn't as pretty as my Aunt Frances. I usually thought my mother was a good-looking woman, but I saw now that she was too heavy and that her hair was undistinguished.

"Why are you looking at me?" she said.

"I'm not."

"I learned something interesting today," my mother said. "We may be eligible for a V.A. pension because of the time your father spent in the Navy."

That took me by surprise. Nobody had ever told me my father was in the Navy. "In World War I," she said, "he went to Webb's Naval Academy on the Harlem River. He was training to be an ensign. But the war ended and he never got his commission."

After dinner the three of us went through the closets looking for my father's papers, hoping to find some proof that could be filed with the Veterans Administration. We came up with two things, a Victory medal, which my brother said everyone got for being in the service during the Great War, and an astounding sepia photograph of my father and his shipmates on the deck of a ship. They were dressed in bell-bottoms and T-shirts and armed with mops and pails, brooms and brushes.

"I never knew this," I found myself saying.

"I never knew this."

"You just don't remember," my brother said.

I was able to pick out my father. He stood at the end of the row, a thin, handsome boy with a full head of hair, a mustache, and an intelligent smiling countenance. . . .

Neither the picture nor the medal was proof of anything, but my brother thought a duplicate of my father's service record had to be in Washington somewhere and that it was just a matter of learning how to go about finding it.

"The pension wouldn't amount to much," my mother said. "Twenty or thirty dollars. But it would certainly help."

I took the picture of my father and his shipmates and propped it against the lamp at my bedside. I looked into his youthful face and tried

▼ **Critical Viewing**
Affluent Aunt Frances drives a Buick Roadmaster like the one shown here. Judging from this image, why might she have chosen such a car?
[Connect]

to relate it to the Father I knew. I looked at the picture a long time. Only gradually did my eye connect it to the set of Great Sea Novels in the bottom shelf of the bookcase a few feet away. My father had given that set to me: it was uniformly bound in green with gilt lettering and it included works by Melville, Conrad, Victor Hugo and Captain Marryat. And lying across the top of the books, jammed in under the sagging shelf above, was his old ship's telescope in its wooden case with the brass snap.

I thought how stupid, and imperceptive, and self-centered I had been never to have understood while he was alive what my father's dream for his life had been.

Literary Analysis
Static and Dynamic Characters In what ways has Jonathan changed since the story's opening scene?

✔**Reading Check**

What new information does Jonathan learn about his father's life?

On the other hand, I had written in my last letter from Arizona—the one that had so angered Aunt Frances—something that might allow me, the writer in the family, to soften my judgment of myself. I will conclude by giving the letter here in its entirety.

Dear Mama,

This will be my final letter to you since I have been told by the doctors that I am dying.

I have sold my store at a very fine profit and am sending Frances a check for five thousand dollars to be deposited in your account. My present to you, Mamaleh. Let Frances show you the passbook.

As for the nature of my ailment, the doctors haven't told me what it is, but I know that I am simply dying of the wrong life. I should never have come to the desert. It wasn't the place for me. I have asked Ruth and the boys to have my body cremated and the ashes scattered in the ocean.

      Your loving son,
      Jack

Review and Assess

Thinking About the Selection

1. **Respond:** What did you find admirable or disappointing about the narrator?

2. **(a) Recall:** What has happened to Jonathan's father? **(b) Recall:** What is Jonathan's grandmother told about his father? **(c) Interpret:** What might happen to the grandmother if she were told the truth?

3. **(a) Recall:** What key decision is made about communicating with the narrator's grandmother? **(b) Analyze:** What does Aunt Frances's desire to conceal Jack's situation from their mother reveal about her character?

4. **(a) Recall:** What does Jonathan do to help his Aunt Frances with her plan? **(b) Infer:** How does Jonathan's mother feel about deceiving Grandma? **(c) Interpret:** What do these feelings suggest about her?

5. **(a) Interpret:** Why does Jonathan ultimately change his mind about what he is doing? **(b) Generalize:** What message does his change suggest? **(c) Hypothesize:** How do you think Jonathan will apply this insight to his life?

6. **Evaluate:** Do you think Doctorow's portrayal of a family in mourning is realistic? Explain.

7. **Take a Position:** How would you have responded had you been asked to write such letters? Explain.

Review and Assess

Literary Analysis

Static and Dynamic Characters

1. (a) Is Jonathan a **dynamic character**? (b) Cite three examples from the story to support your answer.
2. From the narrator's view, is the father a **static** or a **dynamic character**? Explain.
3. Identify Aunt Frances as either a static or a dynamic character. Support your answer.

Connecting Literary Elements

4. Use the **cultural context** of Jack's family to explain why Aunt Frances chooses Arizona as the fictional place for Jack's move.
5. (a) What cultural rituals and values bind the family together? (b) Which one divides them?
6. In what ways does the cultural context in which Jonathan lives contrast with that of Aunt Frances and her children?

Reading Strategy

Judging the Characters' Actions

7. (a) What do you think of Aunt Frances's behavior over the years? (b) In what way might her actions have contributed to her sister-in-law's bitterness toward the family?
8. (a) Contrast Aunt Frances's and Ruth's approach to death. (b) What values does each approach express? Record your answers and evidence in a chart like the one shown.

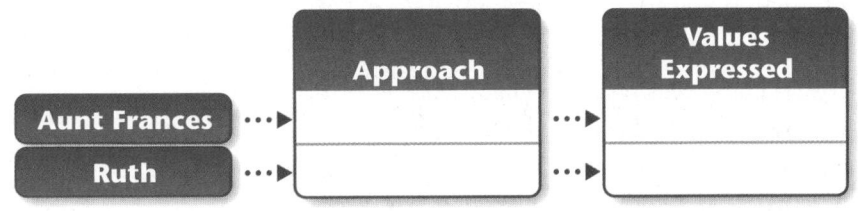

9. Who do you think was "right" at the end of the story? Why?

Extend Understanding

10. **Cultural Connection:** In today's society, doctors sometimes spare patients by not informing them of their terminal illnesses. Do you agree with this approach? Why or why not?

Quick Review

A **static character** is one whose attitudes and behavior remain essentially stable throughout a literary work.

A **dynamic character** experiences a shift or change in attitude and behavior during the course of a work.

Cultural context is the social and economic environment that the characters inhabit.

To **judge the characters' actions,** evaluate their behaviors and actions according to your standards of right and wrong.

 Take It to the Net
www.phschool.com
Take the interactive self-test online to check your understanding of the selection.

Integrate Language Skills

Vocabulary Development Lesson

Word Analysis: Greek Suffix -itis

The Greek suffix -itis means "disease" or "inflammation." *Bronchitis* means "inflammation of the bronchial tubes." With this knowledge, define each of the following words.

1. sinusitis
2. appendicitis
3. tendonitis
4. tonsillitis

Spelling Strategy

The "k" sound can be spelled with *ck*, *ch*, *cq*, or *q*. For example, in *bronchitis*, *ch* spells the "k" sound. When you are uncertain about the spelling of a word with the "k" sound, consult a dictionary. Complete the spelling of each word.

1. bea__on
2. bi__ered
3. wa__en
4. __orus

Concept Development: Sentence Completions

Review the vocabulary list on page 1201 and review the way each word is used in the context of the story. Then, select the vocabulary word that fits best in each of the following sentences.

1. According to the ___?___, it will probably rain in a day or two.

2. Grandpa and his ___?___ play golf every week.

3. My bout with ___?___ left me coughing for weeks.

4. We developed an ___?___ of short stories to share with the children.

Grammar and Style Lesson

Commonly Confused Words: *affect* and *effect*

Affect and *effect* are two examples of commonly confused words that look or sound alike but have different meanings. The word **effect** is most often used as a noun that describes the result of an action. **Affect** is most often used as a verb meaning "to act upon."

Correct use of *effect*: . . . it was when she read this letter aloud to the old lady that the full **effect** of Jack's death came over her. (Here, *effect* is a noun meaning the full result.)

Correct use of *affect*: Aunt Frances tried to **affect** every decision in the family. (Here, *affect* is a verb meaning "to influence.")

Practice Name the part of speech for each italicized word, and explain whether or not the word is used correctly.

1. How did her husband's death *affect* Ruth?
2. Jack's illness had a serious *effect* on his business.
3. How was Jonathan *effected* by his family?
4. What *affect* might Arizona's climate have on bronchitis?
5. Aunt Frances was very *affected* by hearing Jonathan's first letter.

Writing Application Write a paragraph explaining the impact you think Jack's death had on Jonathan, using *affect* and *effect* at least once.

WG *Prentice Hall Writing and Grammar Connection: Chapter 25, Section 2*

Writing Lesson

Advice Column

Doctorow's story explores Jonathan's difficult dilemma of how to handle the odd situation with his Aunt Frances. Write an advice column in response to a brief letter from Jonathan. As the columnist, propose specific actions and support your argument with solid reasoning and evidence.

Prewriting   First, list the elements of Jonathan's dilemma. Then, decide on the best advice. Identify several reasons to persuade Jonathan to follow your advice. Support your reasons with researched facts about the mechanisms people use to cope with grief.

Drafting   Begin your response by expressing sympathy for Jonathan's problem. Then, summarize your proposed action. Elaborate each point with logical arguments, reasons, or facts.

Model: Elaborating to Support an Argument

Tell your grandmother about your father's death because it is the honest thing to do. According to Dr. Sam Keigler, older people face death far more easily than do young people.

> Coherent reasons and expert evidence help support an argument.

Revising   Reread your column to be sure that Jonathan's problem and your response are clearly stated. Look for ways to strengthen your argument. Consider additional reasons and support you might add.

W̶G̶ Prentice Hall Writing and Grammar Connection: Chapter 11, Connected Assignment

Extension Activities

Listening and Speaking As Jonathan, write and deliver a **eulogy** for his father's memorial service. Focus on the unique value of his father's life. Use the following tips as a guide:

- Identify two or three of Jack's special qualities.
- Give examples from his life.
- Explain how his father's presence enhanced Jonathan's life.

After you have rehearsed, present the eulogy to your class.

Research and Technology This story takes place in the 1950s. To prepare **a costume proposal** for a dramatic adaptation, conduct research to learn how the characters might have dressed and styled their hair. In a small group, look for photographs, illustrations, or actual clothing from older family members. Present your findings to the class. **[Group Activity]**

 Take It to the Net   www.phschool.com

Go online for an additional research activity using the Internet.

Prepare to Read

Camouflaging the Chimera ◆ Ambush
from The Things They Carried

Yusef Komunyakaa (b. 1947)

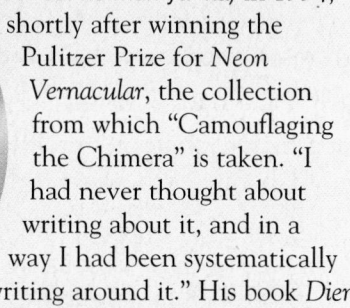

"It took me fourteen years to write poems about Vietnam," said Yusef Komunyakaa (yōō´ sef kō mun yä´ kä) in 1994, shortly after winning the Pulitzer Prize for *Neon Vernacular*, the collection from which "Camouflaging the Chimera" is taken. "I had never thought about writing about it, and in a way I had been systematically writing around it." His book *Dien Cai Dau*, which is Vietnamese for "crazy," is also about Vietnam.

Opening the Creative Gates Komunyakaa was born in Bogalusa, Louisiana. He joined the army and went to Vietnam in 1965. Serving as an "information specialist," he reported from the front lines, edited a military newspaper called *The Southern Cross*, and earned a Bronze Star. After the war, he pursued his education, earning a B.A. at the University of Colorado, an M.A. at Colorado State University, and an M.F.A. at the University of California, Irvine. He then took a variety of teaching jobs and, in 1977, published his first collection of poetry. In 1983, he returned to his native Louisiana, working as a poet-in-the-schools in New Orleans. During this time, he let Vietnam resurface in his consciousness. "And it was as if I had uncapped some hidden place in me," Komunyakaa said. "Poem after poem came spilling out."

To date, Komunyakaa has published twelve poetry collections, as well as a collection of essays entitled *Blues Notes* (2000), and a libretto for an opera by composer T. J. Anderson. Komunyakaa teaches at Princeton University and is Chancellor of the Academy of American Poets.

Tim O'Brien (b. 1946)

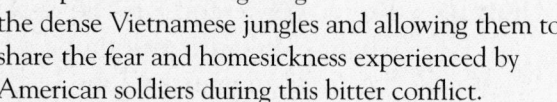

No writer has more effectively captured the Vietnam War than Tim O'Brien. O'Brien has written five books that focus on the war, providing readers with vivid pictures of the fighting in the dense Vietnamese jungles and allowing them to share the fear and homesickness experienced by American soldiers during this bitter conflict.

The Essence of Things Born in Austin, Minnesota, O'Brien was drafted a month after graduating from college. Even though he was against the war, O'Brien reported for duty and was sent to Vietnam. He arrived in January 1969 and served near the village of My Lai, just months after an infamous massacre of its inhabitants by American soldiers. (The My Lai massacre plays an important part in his novel *In the Lake of the Woods*, published in 1994.)

After coming home in 1970, O'Brien attended graduate school at Harvard, and began writing essays about his experiences in Vietnam. His first published work, *If I Die in a Combat Zone, Box Me Up and Ship Me Home* (1973), is a memoir. Several subsequent novels include the National Book Award winner, *Going After Cacciato* (1978), and the widely praised *The Things They Carried* (1990), from which "Ambush" is taken. In this fictional memoir of Vietnam, the author artfully straddles the line between fact and fiction. The collection of interrelated stories centers around the men of Alpha Company, an infantry platoon. The book explores the very nature of storytelling and memory, and examines how the truths of fiction are sometimes more profound than those of life. O'Brien has said that he writes fiction ". . . to get at the essence of things, not merely the surface."

Preview

Connecting to the Literature

Most soldiers who went to Vietnam were only a few years older than you are now. Imagine finding yourself in a jungle, far from home, where you might have to kill or be killed. This is the reality that faces the narrators of these works.

Literary Analysis

First-Person Narrator

Sometimes, the most compelling stories are those told in the **first person,** by a narrator who uses the pronouns *I* and *we* and participates in the action. In these lines from "Ambush," the speaker describes hiding in wait for an enemy soldier:

> I did not hate the young man; I did not see him as the enemy; . . .
> I crouched and kept my head low.

As you read, notice how the use of the first-person point of view pulls you inside the narrator's mind, creating an intimate connection to the story.

Comparing Literary Works

These selections have many similarities. Both are narrated in the first person, describe soldiers waiting in ambush, and communicate the terror and moral ambiguity of war. However, one is a lyric poem, and the other is a story. An author's choice of form is one of the first and most important decisions he or she makes. **Form** creates the basic structure on which all matters of meaning and content are built. As you read these works, explore the ways in which the form of each one contributes to its power and meaning.

Reading Strategy

Picturing the Action

Set during wartime in remote jungles, these selections are especially dramatic and vivid. Use the details the writers provide to **picture the action,** or form a mental image of what you are reading. When Komunyakaa writes, "We painted our faces & rifles/with mud from a riverbank," picture doing what he describes. These mental images will help the writing come alive. Record especially vivid details in a chart like the one shown.

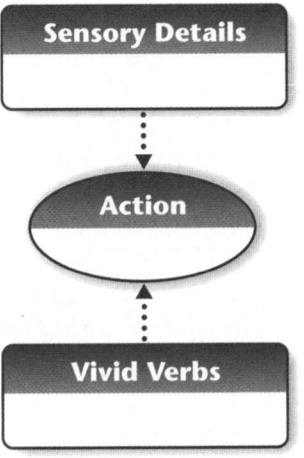

Vocabulary Development

refuge (ref´ yōōj) *n.* shelter or protection from danger (p. 1221)

ambush (am´ bŏŏsh´) *n.* lying in wait to attack by surprise (p. 1222)

ammunition (am´ yōō nish´ ən) *n.* anything hurled by a weapon or exploded as a weapon (p. 1223)

muzzle (muz´ əl) *n.* front end of a barrel of a gun; the snout of an animal (p. 1223)

gape (gāp) *v.* stare, open-mouthed (p. 1124)

Camouflaging the Chimera[1]

Yusef Komunyakaa

> ## Background
> American involvement in the Vietnam War lasted from 1961 to 1973. The war presented American military forces with the frustrating and terrifying problem of how to fight in dense jungle against the Viet Cong (or VC), an enemy capable of magically "merging" with the landscape. As these selections demonstrate, part of the answer to this problem involved sending small groups of American soldiers into the jungle to wait in ambush for the elusive enemy.

We tied branches to our helmets.
We painted our faces & rifles
with mud from a riverbank,

blades of grass hung from the pockets
5 of our tiger suits. We wove
ourselves into the terrain,
content to be a hummingbird's target.

We hugged bamboo & leaned
against a breeze off the river,
10 slow-dragging with ghosts

from Saigon to Bangkok,
with women left in doorways

---

1. **Chimera** (kĭ´ mir´ ə) from Greek mythology, a firebreathing monster with a lion's head, a goat's body, and a serpent's tail.

Literary Analysis
First-Person Narrator
Who is the first-person narrator or speaker of this poem?

reaching in from America.
We aimed at dark-hearted songbirds.

15 In our way station of shadows
rock apes tried to blow our cover,
throwing stones at the sunset. Chameleons

crawled our spines, changing from day
to night: green to gold,
20 gold to black. But we waited
till the moon touched metal,

till something almost broke
inside us. VC struggled
with the hillside, like black silk

25 wrestling iron through grass.
We weren't there. The river ran
through our bones. Small animals took <u>refuge</u>
against our bodies; we held our breath,

ready to spring the L-shaped
30 ambush, as a world revolved
under each man's eyelid.

refuge (ref´ yōōj) *n.*
shelter or protection
from danger

Review and Assess

Thinking About the Selection

1. **Respond:** What emotions did this poem evoke in you? Explain.

2. **(a) Recall:** Where does this poem take place?
   (b) Analyze: What obstacles and burdens does the speaker face?

3. **(a) Recall:** What runs through the soldiers' bones?
   (b) Support: What other images suggest that the speaker is merging with his surroundings? **(c) Interpret:** What does the speaker mean by his observation that "We weren't there"?

4. **(a) Interpret:** How would you describe the speaker's feelings toward the VC? Support your answer. **(b) Analyze:** Do the images in this poem suggest that the speaker is opposed to the war? Explain.

5. **(a) Define:** What is a chimera? **(b) Interpret:** What effect does the title have on your interpretation of the poem? Explain.

6. **Evaluate:** Komunyakaa has said, "I like connecting the abstract to the concrete." Has he succeeded in this poem? Explain.

AMBUSH
from The Things They Carried
Tim O'Brien

When she was nine, my daughter Kathleen asked if I had ever killed anyone. She knew about the war; she knew I'd been a soldier. "You keep writing these war stories," she said, "so I guess you must've killed somebody." It was a difficult moment, but I did what seemed right, which was to say, "Of course not," and then to take her onto my lap and hold her for a while. Someday, I hope, she'll ask again. But here I want to pretend she's a grown-up. I want to tell her exactly what happened, or what I remember happening, and then I want to say to her that as a little girl she was absolutely right. This is why I keep writing war stories:

He was a short, slender young man of about twenty. I was afraid of him—afraid of something—and as he passed me on the trail I threw a grenade that exploded at his feet and killed him.

Or to go back:

Shortly after midnight we moved into the <u>ambush</u> site outside My Khe. The whole platoon was there, spread out in the dense brush along the trail, and for five hours nothing at all happened. We were working in two-man teams—one man on guard while the other slept, switching off every two hours—and I remember it was still dark when Kiowa shook me awake for the final watch. The night was foggy and hot. For the first few moments I felt lost, not sure about directions, groping for my helmet and weapon. I reached out and found three grenades and lined them up in front of me; the pins had already been straightened for quick throwing. And then for maybe half an hour I knelt there and waited. Very gradually, in tiny slivers, dawn began to break through the fog, and from my position in the brush I could see ten or fifteen meters up the trail. The mosquitoes were fierce. I remember slapping at them, wondering if I should wake up Kiowa and ask for some repellent, then thinking it was a bad idea, then looking up and seeing the young man come out of the fog. He wore black clothing and rubber sandals and a gray <u>ammunition</u> belt. His shoulders were slightly stooped, his head cocked to the side as if listening for something. He seemed at ease. He carried his weapon in one hand, <u>muzzle</u> down, moving without any hurry up the center of the trail. There was no sound at all—none that I can remember. In a way, it seemed, he was part of the morning fog, or my own imagination, but there was also the reality of what was happening in my stomach. I had already pulled the pin on a grenade. I had come up to a crouch. It was entirely automatic. I did not hate the young man; I did not see him as the enemy; I did not ponder issues of morality or politics or military duty. I crouched and kept my head low. I tried to swallow whatever was rising from my stomach, which tasted like lemonade, something fruity and sour. I was terrified. There were no thoughts about killing. The grenade was to make him go away—just evaporate—and I leaned back and felt my mind go empty and then felt it fill up again. I had already thrown the grenade before telling myself to throw it. The brush was thick and I had to lob it high, not aiming, and I remember the grenade seeming to freeze above me for an instant, as if a camera had clicked, and I remember ducking down and holding my breath and seeing little wisps of fog rise from the earth. The grenade bounced once and rolled across the trail. I did not hear it, but there must've been a sound, because the young man dropped his weapon and began to run, just two or three quick steps, then he hesitated, swiveling to his right, and he glanced down at the grenade and tried to cover his head but never did. It occurred to me then that he was about

ammunition (am´ yōō nish´ ən) *n.* anything hurled by a weapon or exploded as a weapon

muzzle (muz´ əl) *n.* front end of a barrel of a gun; the snout of an animal

**Reading Check**

What does the speaker do when he sees the young man on the path?

to die. I wanted to warn him. The grenade made a popping noise—not soft but not loud either—not what I'd expected—and there was a puff of dust and smoke—a small white puff—and the young man seemed to jerk upward as if pulled by invisible wires. He fell on his back. His rubber sandals had been blown off. There was no wind. He lay at the center of the trail, his right leg bent beneath him, his one eye shut, his other eye a huge star-shaped hole.

It was not a matter of live or die. There was no real peril. Almost certainly the young man would have passed by. And it will always be that way.

Later, I remember, Kiowa tried to tell me that the man would've died anyway. He told me that it was a good kill, that I was a soldier and this was a war, that I should shape up and stop staring and ask myself what the dead man would've done if things were reversed.

None of it mattered. The words seemed far too complicated. All I could do was gape at the fact of the young man's body.

Even now I haven't finished sorting it out. Sometimes I forgive myself, other times I don't. In the ordinary hours of life I try not to dwell on it, but now and then, when I'm reading a newspaper or just sitting alone in a room, I'll look up and see the young man coming out of the morning fog. I'll watch him walk toward me, his shoulders slightly stooped, his head cocked to the side, and he'll pass within a few yards of me and suddenly smile at some secret thought and then continue up the trail to where it bends back into the fog.

Reading Strategy
Picturing the Action
Which images and words help you to imagine the action here?

gape (gāp) *v.* stare, open-mouthed

Review and Assess

Thinking About the Selection

1. **Respond:** If you had been the narrator, would you have told your nine-year-old this story? Why or why not?

2. **(a) Recall:** What does the narrator say to describe the degree of danger he faced? **(b) Interpret:** What does he mean when he says "And it will always be that way"?

3. **(a) Deduce:** How does the narrator react to the killing? **(b) Interpret:** In what way does Kiowa respond to the narrator's reaction?

4. **(a) Recall:** At the end of the story, what does the narrator fantasize? **(b) Interpret:** In what ways does this fantasy add to the story's meaning?

5. **(a) Compare and Contrast:** The narrator tells his story twice. Compare and contrast the short and long versions. **(b) Speculate:** Why do you think the author chose this narrative device?

6. **Make a Judgment:** Kiowa uses the expression "a good kill." Is there such a thing? Explain.

Review and Assess

Literary Analysis

First-Person Narrator

1. In what specific ways does Komunyakaa's use of the **first-person narrator** help you enter the poem as a participant?
2. Do you think O'Brien's use of a first-person narrator makes you more sympathetic to the protagonist? Why or why not?

Comparing Literary Works

3. (a) Which of these works is informal and uses everyday speech? (b) Which is formal and uses complex imagery? (c) Can these differences be explained by the **form** of each work? Explain.
4. Despite the differences in form, what similarities do you find in the meaning of these two works? Record both similarities and differences in a diagram like the one shown.

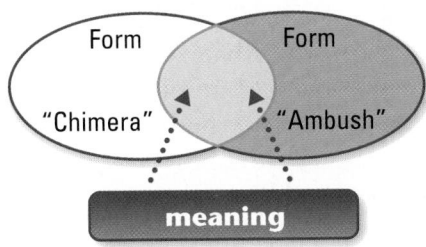

5. (a) How would you expect a poem to convey meaning in comparison with a story? (b) Are your expectations met by these works? Explain.

Reading Strategy

Picturing the Action

6. Explain how your ability to **picture the action** in this passage draws you into Tim O'Brien's world.

    . . . I remember the grenade seeming to freeze above me for an instant as if a camera had clicked, and I remember ducking down . . .

7. When you **picture** images such as "We hugged bamboo & leaned/against a breeze off the river" do you better understand and appreciate "Camouflaging the Chimera"? Explain.

Extend Understanding

8. **History Connection:** (a) What role does the jungle setting play in these works? (b) What role has the landscape played in other wars that Americans have fought?

Quick Review

A **first-person narrator** uses the pronouns *I* and *we*, participates in the action of a literary work, and reveals his or her private thoughts, feelings, and perceptions.

The **form** of a work is its essential structure, for example, a lyric poem, short story, or one-act play. Form helps to shape the **meaning** and message of a work of literature.

To **picture the action,** use details from the work to see the events in your mind.

 Take It to the Net
www.phschool.com
Take the interactive self-test online to check your understanding of these selections.

Integrate Language Skills

Vocabulary Development Lesson

Concept Development: Words From War

Each war produces unique terms. World War I, for example, gave us *doughboy, over the top,* and *no man's land.* Many words of war, such as *ambush* and *ammunition,* have long since entered everyday language. Write a paragraph about a military practice maneuver using these words: *ammunition, ambush, platoon, grenade.*

Spelling Strategy

English words almost never end with the letter *j,* except for a few foreign derivatives. If a word ends with the *j* sound, always use *ge,* as in *refuge.* In your notebook, complete the spelling of these words.

1. dosa__   3. villa__
2. enra__   4. folia__

Fluency: Context

Write a sentence responding to each of the following instructions. Include one vocabulary word from the list on page 1219 in each sentence.

1. Tell what you would do if you were caught outside in a thunderstorm.
2. Tell how a drill sergeant might instruct new recruits to hold a gun correctly when standing at ease.
3. Describe your reaction when your best friend reveals that she is from Mars.
4. Explain your strategy for capturing the leader of a rival team at camp.
5. Make a rule that would prevent children from injuring themselves with guns found in the home.

Grammar and Style Lesson

Noun Clauses

A subordinate clause is a group of words with a subject and a verb that cannot stand by itself as a sentence. A **noun clause** is a subordinate clause that functions as a noun. Words that introduce noun clauses include *that, which, what, if, how, when, where, why, whatever, whoever,* and *whether.*

> **Subject:** *Whoever knows this* is wise.
>
> **Direct Object:** My daughter Kathleen asked *if I had ever killed anyone.*

In some cases, the word that introduces a noun clause is implied. For example, in the sentence "She knew I'd been a soldier," the introductory word *that* is implied.

Practice Identify the noun clause in each sentence.

1. This is why I keep writing war stories.
2. . . . but there was also the reality of what was happening in my stomach.
3. I tried to swallow whatever was rising from my stomach. . . .
4. Later, I remember, Kiowa would try to tell me that the man would've died anyway.
5. . . . she said, "so I guess you must've killed somebody."

Writing Application Write a paragraph in response to these war writings by Komunyakaa and O'Brien. Use and identify at least three noun clauses.

 Prentice Hall Writing and Grammar Connection: Chapter 19, Section 3

Writing Lesson

Newspaper Article

The Vietnam War received intense journalistic coverage. Reporters from all media went to the jungle to gather stories for a public that was deeply divided about the war. As a newspaper reporter, write an article about the events Tim O'Brien relates in "Ambush."

Prewriting A newspaper article is supposed to be objective, even when relating the horrors of war. However, by stating clearly what they see and hear, reporters often communicate emotions as well. Reread "Ambush," and create an outline of the series of events that it describes.

Drafting Begin with a strong first paragraph, or lead, to hook your readers. Follow with a thorough description of the events.

Model: Drafting With Objectivity

The platoon waited in the dark all night. Mosquitoes swarmed, but otherwise, there was nothing but silence. Then, a young Viet Cong soldier appeared on the path. Tim lobbed a grenade. It was over quickly.

> A newspaper article sticks to the facts.

Revising Review your account, and note language that too clearly reveals a bias. Replace any emotional language with simple and clear observations of events.

 Prentice Hall Writing and Grammar Connection: Chapter 5, Section 3

Extension Activities

Listening and Speaking Conduct an **interview** with a Vietnam War veteran about his or her experiences during the war. Use these tips to prepare:

- Choose a focus for your interview.
- Ask questions requiring in-depth, not "yes" or "no," responses.
- Ask questions about lessons that he or she feels can be learned from the war.

Record the interview on audio- or videotape, and share highlights with the class.

Research and Technology The Vietnam War was the first televised war. In a group, investigate the effect that media reports had on politics and protests in the 1960s. Then, create a **multimedia presentation** about the war. Use newspaper and magazine articles, photographs, political cartoons, television news reports, and protest songs. **[Group Activity]**

 Take It to the Net www.phschool.com

Go online for an additional research activity using the Internet.

A Closer Look

Twentieth Century Drama: America on Stage

O'Neill, Hellman, Williams, and a host of American playwrights rewrote the rules of the theater.

It is opening night at a major American theater. You check your coat, find your seat, and flip through the *Playbill*. As the curtain rises, you are filled with anticipation of a bold, exciting, new play, like nothing you have ever seen.

No, it is not a big-budget musical with elaborate sets and fancy costumes. It is a night of talk—sometimes loud and angry, sometimes hushed and mournful, but always riveting.

For much of the twentieth century, the American theater was the center of the intellectual world. Great plays offered thrilling stories, crackling dialogue, and philosophical truth. The best American playwrights of the twentieth century chronicled different aspects of the American experience.

- **Thornton Wilder** (1897–1975), best known for the Pulitzer Prize-winning play *Our Town* (1938), revealed the secrets of small-town America.
- **Arthur Miller** (b. 1915) combined politics and realism to give America some of its most moving plays, including *Death of a Salesman* (1949) and *The Crucible* (1953) (see page 1232).
- **Lorraine Hansberry** (1930–1965) filled theaters with the stories of African Americans. Her play *A Raisin in the Sun* (1959) was the first drama by a black woman to be produced on Broadway.
- **Edward Albee** (b. 1928) shocked audiences with his psychological dramas, including the harsh and powerful *Who's Afraid of Virginia Woolf* (1962).

The American theater had not always been such a powerful forum. Before the 1920s, the American stage was known for light, escapist fare, and was a showcase for actors, not writers. It was Eugene O'Neill who introduced a new level of seriousness and ushered in a century of great drama.

America's First Great Playwright "I want to be an artist or nothing," Eugene O'Neill said at the age of twenty-five. He pursued that goal relentlessly. When he died forty years later, he had written more than fifty plays, and won the Nobel Prize and four Pulitzer Prizes.

▼ **Critical Viewing**
This photograph shows Vivien Leigh as Blanche Dubois and Marlon Brando as Stanley Kowalski in Tennesse Williams's *A Streetcar named Desire.* In what ways does this scene depict the "raw power of human emotion"? **[Interpret]**

Nearly all of O'Neill's work reflects his troubled childhood, and the rough-and-tumble experiences of his youth. When he was in his mid-twenties, hard living landed him in the hospital, where he pondered his life for the first time. "It was in this enforced period of reflection that the urge to write first came to me," he said.

O'Neill experimented with different styles—sometimes realistic, sometimes symbolic, and sometimes political. *Beyond the Horizon* (1920), his first play produced on Broadway, was a smash hit. *The Iceman Cometh* (1946) told the stories of dreamers and losers who frequent a waterfront saloon. *A Long Day's Journey Into Night* (1956), O'Neill's greatest play, recounted the playwright's traumatic childhood. It was not produced until after his death in 1953.

A Woman's Voice Lillian Hellman was born in 1905 in New Orleans, the daughter of a shoe salesman and a socialite. She became the most influential female playwright of the twentieth century.

In 1930, Hellman met detective novelist Dashiell Hammet, who was famous for stylish books like the *Thin Man* and *The Maltese Falcon*. Hammett became Hellman's mentor and encouraged her to shun cheap success for honest drama. Hellman's first play, *The Children's Hour*, appeared on Broadway in 1934. The tale of two female teachers whose lives are ruined by rumor and innuendo both captivated and shocked audiences.

From the late 1930s through the late 1940s, Hellman helped to shape a golden age of American theater. Her best-known work, *The Little Foxes* (1939), takes a harsh look at a rich and powerful Southern family. Her political drama *Watch on the Rhine* (1941) warned the world of the dangers of Nazism. By the time of her death in 1984, Hellman had paved the way for women writers to exert influence and express powerful views.

The Raw Power of Human Emotion Born in 1911, in rural Mississippi, Tennessee Williams was the son of a traveling salesman and a minister's daughter. While still a teenager, Williams became determined to be a writer.

Williams's first major play, *The Glass Menagerie*, appeared on Broadway in 1945, and was a huge hit. Based loosely on his own family, the play moved audiences with its compassion for a mother and sister who cling to their ever-fading dreams.

In 1947, the shy, sensitive Williams shocked audiences with the intensity of his play *A Streetcar Named Desire*. The play presented a hard-hitting story, filled with cruelty but also with beauty. Its effect on audiences was so great that it inspired dozens of writers to imitate it.

Williams wrote more than 60 plays. By the time he died in 1983, he had become one of the most influential—and imitated—writers of all time.

Prepare to Read

The Crucible

Arthur Miller (b. 1915)

A living legend of the American theater, Arthur Miller has chronicled the dilemmas of common people pitted against powerful and unyielding social forces. A native New Yorker, Miller has known bad times as well as good.

During the Depression, his family lost its money and was forced to move from Manhattan to more modest living quarters in Brooklyn. Although Miller graduated from Abraham Lincoln High School in 1932, he was forced to delay his enrollment at the University of Michigan for more than two years in order to raise money for tuition. He did so by working at a variety of jobs, including singing for a local radio station, driving a truck, and working as a stock clerk in an automobile parts warehouse.

Promising Playwright Miller first began writing drama while still in college. In 1947, his play *All My Sons* opened on Broadway to immediate acclaim, establishing Miller as a bright new talent. Two years later, he won international fame and a Pulitzer Prize for *Death of a Salesman* (1949), which critics hailed as a modern American tragedy.

His next play, *The Crucible* (1953), was less warmly received, because it uses the Salem witchcraft trials of 1692 as a means of attacking the anti-communist "witch hunts" in Congress in the 1950s. Miller believed that the hysteria surrounding the witchcraft trials in Puritan New England paralleled the contemporary climate of McCarthyism—Senator Joseph McCarthy's obsessive quest to uncover Communist party infiltration of American institutions.

In the introduction to his *Collected Plays* (1957), Miller described his perceptions of the atmosphere during the McCarthy era and the way in which those perceptions influenced the writing of *The Crucible*. He said, "It was as though the whole country had been born anew, without a memory even of certain elemental decencies which a year or two earlier no one would have imagined could be altered, let alone forgotten. Astounded, I watched men pass me by without a nod whom I had known rather well for years; and again, the astonishment was produced by my knowledge, which I could not give up, that the terror in these people was being knowingly planned and consciously engineered, and yet that all they knew was terror. That so interior and subjective an emotion could have been so manifestly created from without was a marvel to me. It underlies every word in *The Crucible*."

In the Shadows of McCarthyism During the two years following the publication and production of *The Crucible*, Miller was investigated for possible associations with the Communist party. In 1956, he was called to testify before the House Committee on Un-American Activities. Although he never became a member of the Communist party, Miller, like so many of his contemporaries, had advocated principles of social justice and equality among the classes. He had become disillusioned, however, by the reality of communism as practiced in the Soviet Union. At the hearings, he testified about his own experiences, but he refused to discuss his colleagues and associates. He was found guilty of contempt of Congress for his refusal, but the sentence was later overturned.

Hollywood Glamour In 1956, the spotlight was focused on Miller's personal life when he married glamorous film star Marilyn Monroe. Although he did little writing during their five-year marriage, he did pen the screenplay for a film, *The Misfits* (1961), in which Monroe starred. After their divorce, Miller wrote other noteworthy plays, including *The Price* (1968) and *The Last Yankee* (1993).

Background

In 1692, the British colony of Massachusetts was swept by a witchcraft hysteria that resulted in the execution of twenty people and the jailing of at least 150 others. The incident was not isolated. It is estimated that between 1 million and 9 million Europeans were accused of being witches and then executed in the sixteenth and seventeenth centuries. Many of these people were merely practicing folk customs that had survived in Europe since pre-Christian times. In addition, in an era when religion and politics were closely allied, witch hunts were often politically motivated. England's James I, for example, wrote a treatise on witchcraft and sometimes accused his enemies of practicing the black arts. It was a cry that resonated well among a superstitious populace.

For the New England colonies, however, the witchcraft episode was unusual, though perhaps inevitable. The colonists endured harsh conditions and punishing hardship in their lives. Finding themselves at the mercy of forces beyond their control—bitter weather, sickness and death, devastating fires, drought, and insect infestations that killed their crops—many colonists attributed their misfortunes to the Devil. They were fearful (some would say paranoid) people, and their Puritan faith stressed the biblical teaching that witches were real and dangerous.

In the small parish of Salem Village, many were quick to blame witchcraft when the minister's daughter and several other girls were afflicted by seizures and lapses into unconsciousness, especially after it was learned that the girls had been dabbling in fortunetelling with the minister's slave, Tituba. (They were not dancing in the woods, as portrayed in the play.) At first, only Tituba and two elderly women were called witches, but then the hunt spread until some of the colony's most prominent citizens stood accused. Many historians have seen a pattern of social and economic

animosity behind the accusations, but most feel that mass hysteria was also a strong contributing factor.

When *The Crucible* was first published, Arthur Miller added a note about the play's historical accuracy: "This play is not history in the sense in which the word is used by the academic historian. Dramatic purposes have sometimes required many characters to be fused into one; the number of girls involved in the 'crying-out' has been reduced; Abigail's age has been raised; while there were several judges of almost equal authority, I have symbolized them in Hathorne and Danforth. However, I believe that the reader will discover here the essential nature of one of the strangest and most awful chapters in human history. The fate of each character is exactly that of his historical model, and there is no one in the drama who did not play a similar—and in some cases exactly the same—role in history."

Preview

Connecting to the Literature

If you have ever observed the way a rumor spreads through your school or helped to spread one yourself, you know how easy it is to be swept along with a crowd, believing blindly rather than using your own judgment.

Literary Analysis

Dialogue and Stage Directions

The written script of a drama consists of dialogue and stage directions.

- **Dialogue** refers to the words characters speak. Dialogue both advances the plot and reveals the characters' personalities and backgrounds.
- **Stage directions** usually indicate where a scene takes place, what it should look like, and how the characters should move and speak. Stage directions are usually set in italic type to distinguish them from dialogue.

As you read Act I of *The Crucible*, look for information about characters and events in the stage directions as well as in the dialogue.

Connecting Literary Elements

Dramatic exposition conveys critical information about a play's settings, props, characters, and even historical or social context. Most playwrights provide such information in the dialogue or stage directions. In *The Crucible*, Arthur Miller does something quite different, interjecting lengthy prose commentaries that contain a wealth of dramatic exposition. As you read Act I, gather details from these essay-like passages to help you enter the world of the play.

Reading Strategy

Questioning the Characters' Motives

Like people in real life, characters in plays are not always what they seem. Often, we must **question the characters' motives**—their reasons for behaving as they do. Fear, greed, guilt, love, loyalty, and revenge are some of the driving forces behind human behavior. Use a chart like the one shown to examine the motives of each character in Act I.

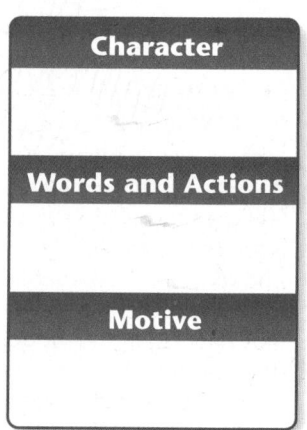

Character

Words and Actions

Motive

Vocabulary Development

predilection (pred´ ə lek´ shən) *n.* pre-existing preference (p. 1235)

ingratiating (in grā´ shē āt´ iŋ) *adj.* charming or flattering (p. 1236)

dissembling (di sem´ bliŋ) *n.* disguising one's real nature or motives (p. 1238)

calumny (kal´ əm nē) *n.* false accusation; slander (p. 1245)

inculcation (in´ kul kā´ shən) *n.* teaching by repetition and urging (p. 1253)

propitiation (prə pish´ ē ā´ shən) *n.* action designed to soothe or satisfy a person, a cause, etc. (p. 1254)

licentious (lī sen´ shəs) *adj.* lacking moral restraint (p. 1258)

The CRUCIBLE[1]

Arthur Miller

---

1. crucible (kr$\overline{oo}'$ sə bəl) *n.* heat-resistant container in which metals are melted or fused at very high temperatures; thus, a severe trial or test.

CHARACTERS

REVEREND PARRIS	MARTHA COREY
BETTY PARRIS	REVEREND JOHN HALE
TITUBA	ELIZABETH PROCTOR
ABIGAIL WILLIAMS	FRANCIS NURSE
SUSANNA WALCOTT	EZEKIEL CHEEVER
MRS. ANN PUTNAM	MARSHAL HERRICK
THOMAS PUTNAM	JUDGE HATHORNE
MERCY LEWIS	DEPUTY GOVERNOR
MARY WARREN	DANFORTH
JOHN PROCTOR	SARAH GOOD
REBECCA NURSE	HOPKINS
GILES COREY	

ACT I

(An Overture)

A small upper bedroom in the home of REVEREND SAMUEL PARRIS, *Salem, Massachusetts, in the spring of the year 1692.*

There is a narrow window at the left. Through its leaded panes the morning sunlight streams. A candle still burns near the bed, which is at the right. A chest, a chair, and a small table are the other furnishings. At the back a door opens on the landing of the stairway to the ground floor. The room gives off an air of clean spareness. The roof rafters are exposed, and the wood colors are raw and unmellowed.

As the curtain rises, REVEREND PARRIS *is discovered kneeling beside the bed, evidently in prayer. His daughter,* BETTY PARRIS, *aged ten, is lying on the bed, inert.*

At the time of these events Parris was in his middle forties. In history he cut a villainous path, and there is very little good to be said for him. He believed he was being persecuted wherever he went, despite his best efforts to win people and God to his side. In meeting, he felt insulted if someone rose to shut the door without first asking his permission. He was a widower with no interest in children, or talent with them. He regarded them as young adults, and until this strange crisis he, like the rest of Salem, never conceived that the children were anything but thankful for being permitted to walk straight, eyes slightly lowered, arms at the sides, and mouths shut until bidden to speak.

His house stood in the "town"—but we today would hardly call it a village. The meeting house was nearby, and from this point outward—toward the bay or inland—there were a few small-windowed, dark houses snuggling against the raw Massachusetts winter. Salem had been established hardly forty years before. To the European world the whole province was a barbaric frontier inhabited by a sect of fanatics who, nevertheless, were shipping out products of slowly increasing quantity and value.

Literary Analysis
Dialogue and Stage Directions What important information is revealed in the third paragraph of the stage direction?

No one can really know what their lives were like. They had no novel-ists—and would not have permitted anyone to read a novel if one were handy. Their creed forbade anything resembling a theater or "vain enjoyment." They did not celebrate Christmas, and a holiday from work meant only that they must concentrate even more upon prayer.

Which is not to say that nothing broke into this strict and somber way of life. When a new farmhouse was built, friends assembled to "raise the roof," and there would be special foods cooked and probably some potent cider passed around. There was a good supply of ne'er-do-wells in Salem, who dallied at the shovelboard[2] in Bridget Bishop's tavern. Probably more than the creed, hard work kept the morals of the place from spoiling, for the people were forced to fight the land like heroes for every grain of corn, and no man had very much time for fooling around.

That there were some jokers, however, is indicated by the practice of appointing a two-man patrol whose duty was to "walk forth in the time of God's worship to take notice of such as either lie about the meet-ing house, without attending to the word and ordinances, or that lie at home or in the fields without giving good account thereof, and to take the names of such persons, and to present them to the magistrates, whereby they may be accordingly proceeded against." This <u>predilection</u> for minding other people's business was time-honored among the people of Salem, and it undoubtedly created many of the suspicions which were to feed the coming madness. It was also, in my opinion, one of the things that a John Proctor would rebel against, for the time of the armed camp had almost passed, and since the country was reasonably— although not wholly—safe, the old disciplines were beginning to rankle. But, as in all such matters, the issue was not clear-cut, for danger was still a possibility, and in unity still lay the best promise of safety.

The edge of the wilderness was close by. The American continent stretched endlessly west, and it was full of mystery for them. It stood, dark and threatening, over their shoulders night and day, for out of it Indian tribes marauded from time to time, and Reverend Parris had parishioners who had lost relatives to these heathen.

The parochial snobbery of these people was partly responsible for their failure to convert the Indians. Probably they also preferred to take land from heathens rather than from fellow Christians. At any rate, very few Indians were converted, and the Salem folk believed that the virgin forest was the Devil's last preserve, his home base and the citadel of his final stand. To the best of their knowledge the American forest was the last place on earth that was not paying homage to God.

For these reasons, among others, they carried about an air of innate resistance, even of persecution. Their fathers had, of course, been per-secuted in England. So now they and their church found it necessary to deny any other sect its freedom, lest their New Jerusalem[3] be defiled and corrupted by wrong ways and deceitful ideas.

---

2. **shovelboard** game in which a coin or other disk is driven with the hand along a highly polished board, floor, or table marked with transverse lines.
3. **New Jerusalem** in the Bible, the holy city of heaven.

Literary Analysis
Dialogue, Stage Directions, and Dramatic Exposition In what way does the information Miller provides in these essay-like passages differ from the typical stage direction or dialogue?

predilection (pred′ əl ek′ shən) *n.* preexisting preference

Literary Analysis
Dialogue, Stage Directions, and Dramatic Exposition Why is this background information about Salem important to your understanding of the play?

Reading Check

What is a time-honored activity among the people of Salem?

They believed, in short, that they held in their steady hands the candle that would light the world. We have inherited this belief, and it has helped and hurt us. It helped them with the discipline it gave them. They were a dedicated folk, by and large, and they had to be to survive the life they had chosen or been born into in this country.

The proof of their belief's value to them may be taken from the opposite character of the first Jamestown settlement, farther south, in Virginia. The Englishmen who landed there were motivated mainly by a hunt for profit. They had thought to pick off the wealth of the new country and then return rich to England. They were a band of individualists, and a much more <u>ingratiating</u> group than the Massachusetts men. But Virginia destroyed them. Massachusetts tried to kill off the Puritans, but they combined; they set up a communal society which, in the beginning, was little more than an armed camp with an autocratic and very devoted leadership. It was, however, an autocracy by consent, for they were united from top to bottom by a commonly held ideology whose perpetuation was the reason and justification for all their sufferings. So their self-denial, their purposefulness, their suspicion of all vain pursuits, their hard-handed justice, were altogether perfect instruments for the conquest of this space so antagonistic to man.

But the people of Salem in 1692 were not quite the dedicated folk that arrived on the *Mayflower.* A vast differentiation had taken place, and in their own time a revolution had unseated the royal government and substituted a junta[4] which was at this moment in power. The times, to their eyes, must have been out of joint, and to the common folk must have seemed as insoluble and complicated as do ours today. It is not hard to see how easily many could have been led to believe that the time of confusion had been brought upon them by deep and darkling forces. No hint of such speculation appears on the court record, but social disorder in any age breeds such mystical suspicions, and when, as in Salem, wonders are brought forth from below the social surface, it is too much to expect people to hold back very long from laying on the victims with all the force of their frustrations.

The Salem tragedy, which is about to begin in these pages, developed from a paradox. It is a paradox in whose grip we still live, and there is no prospect yet that we will discover its resolution. Simply, it was this: for good purposes, even high purposes, the people of Salem developed a theocracy, a combine of state and religious power whose function was to keep the community together, and to prevent any kind of disunity that might open it to destruction by material or ideological enemies. It was forged for a necessary purpose and accomplished that purpose. But all organization is and must be grounded on the idea of exclusion and prohibition, just as two objects

---

4. **junta** (hoon' tə) *n.* assembly or council.

ingratiating (in grā′ shē āt′ in) *adj.* charming or flattering

The Execution of Stephen Burroughs for Witchcraft at Salem, Massachusetts in 1692, 19th-CenturyEngraving

▲ **Critical Viewing**
This nineteenth-century engraving shows the hanging of the Reverend Stephen Burroughs during the Salem witchcraft trials. What does this image suggest about the condemned man's state of mind? **[Infer]**

cannot occupy the same space. Evidently the time came in New England when the repressions of order were heavier than seemed warranted by the dangers against which the order was organized. The witch-hunt was a perverse manifestation of the panic which set in among all classes when the balance began to turn toward greater individual freedom.

When one rises above the individual villainy displayed, one can only pity them all, just as we shall be pitied someday. It is still impossible for man to organize his social life without repressions, and the balance has yet to be struck between order and freedom.

The witch-hunt was not, however, a mere repression. It was also, and as importantly, a long overdue opportunity for everyone so inclined to express publicly his guilt and sins, under the cover of accusations against the victims. It suddenly became possible—and patriotic and holy—for a man to say that Martha Corey had come into his bedroom at night, and that, while his wife was sleeping at his side, Martha laid herself down on his chest and "nearly suffocated him." Of course it was her spirit only, but his satisfaction at confessing himself was no lighter than if it had been Martha herself. One could not ordinarily speak such things in public.

Long-held hatreds of neighbors could now be openly expressed, and vengeance taken, despite the Bible's charitable injunctions. Land-lust which had been expressed before by constant bickering over boundaries and deeds, could now be elevated to the arena of morality; one could cry witch against one's neighbor and feel perfectly justified in the bargain. Old scores could be settled on a plane of heavenly combat between Lucifer[5] and the Lord; suspicions and the envy of the miserable toward the happy could and did burst out in the general revenge.

REVEREND PARRIS *is praying now, and, though we cannot hear his words, a sense of his confusion hangs about him. He mumbles, then seems about to weep; then he weeps, then prays again; but his daughter does not stir on the bed.*

The door opens, and his Negro slave enters. TITUBA *is in her forties.* PARRIS *brought her with him from Barbados, where he spent some years as a merchant before entering the ministry. She enters as one does who can no longer bear to be barred from the sight of her beloved, but she is also very frightened because her slave sense has warned her that, as always, trouble in this house eventually lands on her back.*

TITUBA, *already taking a step backward:* My Betty be hearty soon?

PARRIS: Out of here!

TITUBA, *backing to the door:* My Betty not goin' die . . .

PARRIS, *scrambling to his feet in a fury:* Out of my sight! *She is gone.* Out of my— *He is overcome with sobs. He clamps his teeth against them and closes the door and leans against it, exhausted.* Oh, my God! God help me! *Quaking with fear, mumbling to himself through his sobs, he goes to the bed and gently takes* BETTY'S *hand.* Betty. Child. Dear child. Will you wake, will you open up your eyes! Betty, little one . . .

---

5. **Lucifer** (lōō′ sə fər) the Devil.

Reading Strategy
Questioning the Characters' Motives
What do you learn here about Tituba's motives?

✓**Reading Check**
What accusation surfaces among the residents of Salem?

He is bending to kneel again when his niece, ABIGAIL WILLIAMS, *seventeen, enters—a strikingly beautiful girl, an orphan, with an endless capacity for* dissembling. *Now she is all worry and apprehension and propriety.*

ABIGAIL: Uncle? *He looks to her.* Susanna Walcott's here from Doctor Griggs.

PARRIS: Oh? Let her come, let her come.

ABIGAIL, *leaning out the door to call to Susanna, who is down the hall a few steps:* Come in, Susanna.

SUSANNA WALCOTT, *a little younger than Abigail, a nervous, hurried girl, enters.*

PARRIS, *eagerly:* What does the doctor say, child?

SUSANNA, *craning around* PARRIS *to get a look at* BETTY: He bid me come and tell you, reverend sir, that he cannot discover no medicine for it in his books.

PARRIS: Then he must search on.

SUSANNA: Aye, sir, he have been searchin' his books since he left you, sir. But he bid me tell you, that you might look to unnatural things for the cause of it.

PARRIS, *his eyes going wide:* No—no. There be no unnatural cause here. Tell him I have sent for Reverend Hale of Beverly, and Mr. Hale will surely confirm that. Let him look to medicine and put out all thought of unnatural causes here. There be none.

SUSANNA: Aye, sir. He bid me tell you. *She turns to go.*

ABIGAIL: Speak nothin' of it in the village, Susanna.

PARRIS: Go directly home and speak nothing of unnatural causes.

SUSANNA: Aye, sir. I pray for her. *She goes out.*

ABIGAIL: Uncle, the rumor of witchcraft is all about; I think you'd best go down and deny it yourself. The parlor's packed with people, sir. I'll sit with her.

PARRIS, *pressed, turns on her:* And what shall I say to them? That my daughter and my niece I discovered dancing like heathen in the forest?

ABIGAIL: Uncle, we did dance; let you tell them I confessed it—and I'll be whipped if I must be. But they're speakin' of witchcraft. Betty's not witched.

PARRIS: Abigail, I cannot go before the congregation when I know you have not opened with me. What did you do with her in the forest?

ABIGAIL: We did dance, uncle, and when you leaped out of the bush so suddenly, Betty was frightened and then she fainted. And there's the whole of it.

PARRIS: Child. Sit you down.

ABIGAIL, *quavering, as she sits:* I would never hurt Betty. I love her dearly.

PARRIS: Now look you, child, your punishment will come in its time. But if you trafficked with spirits in the forest I must know it now, for surely my enemies will, and they will ruin me with it.

ABIGAIL: But we never conjured spirits.

dissembling (di sem´ blin) *n.* disguising one's real nature or motives

Reading Strategy
Questioning the Characters' Motives Based on what stage directions have revealed about Abigail's personality, what can you conclude about her "worry" and "apprehension"?

Reading Strategy
Questioning the Characters' Motives Why is Parris so quick to dismiss the possibility that Betty's ailment is the result of "unnatural causes"?

PARRIS: Then why can she not move herself since midnight? This child is desperate! *Abigail lowers her eyes.* It must come out—my enemies will bring it out. Let me know what you done there. Abigail, do you understand that I have many enemies?

ABIGAIL: I have heard of it, uncle.

PARRIS: There is a faction that is sworn to drive me from my pulpit. Do you understand that?

ABIGAIL: I think so, sir.

PARRIS: Now then, in the midst of such disruption, my own household is discovered to be the very center of some obscene practice. Abominations are done in the forest—

ABIGAIL: It were sport, uncle!

PARRIS, *pointing at* BETTY: You call this sport? *She lowers her eyes. He pleads:* Abigail, if you know something that may help the doctor, for God's sake tell it to me. *She is silent.* I saw Tituba waving her arms over the fire when I came on you. Why was she doing that? And I heard a screeching and gibberish coming from her mouth. She were swaying like a dumb beast over that fire!

ABIGAIL: She always sings her Barbados songs, and we dance.

PARRIS: I cannot blink what I saw, Abigail, for my enemies will not blink it. I saw a dress lying on the grass.

ABIGAIL, *innocently:* A dress?

PARRIS—*it is very hard to say:* Aye, a dress. And I thought I saw—someone naked running through the trees!

ABIGAIL, *in terror:* No one was naked! You mistake yourself, uncle!

PARRIS, *with anger:* I saw it! *He moves from her. Then, resolved:* Now tell me true, Abigail. And I pray you feel the weight of truth upon you, for now my ministry's at stake, my ministry and perhaps your cousin's life. Whatever abomination you have done, give me all of it now, for I dare not be taken unaware when I go before them down there.

ABIGAIL: There is nothin' more. I swear it, uncle.

PARRIS, *studies her, then nods, half convinced:* Abigail, I have fought here three long years to bend these stiff-necked people to me, and now, just now when some good respect is rising for me in the parish, you compromise my very character. I have given you a home, child, I have put clothes upon your back—now give me upright answer. Your name in the town—it is entirely white, is it not?

ABIGAIL, *with an edge of resentment:* Why, I am sure it is, sir. There be no blush about my name.

PARRIS, *to the point:* Abigail, is there any other cause than you have told me, for your being discharged from Goody[6] Proctor's service? I have heard it said, and I tell you as I heard it, that she comes so rarely to the church this year for she will not sit so close to something soiled. What signified that remark?

---

6. **Goody** title used for a married woman; short for Goodwife.

Literary Analysis
Dialogue What do his references to his "enemies" reveal about Parris's personality?

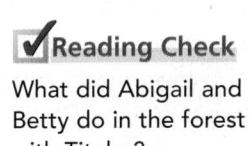

Reading Check
What did Abigail and Betty do in the forest with Tituba?

The Crucible, Act I ◆ 1239

ABIGAIL: She hates me, uncle, she must, for I would not be her slave. It's a bitter woman, a lying, cold, sniveling woman, and I will not work for such a woman!

PARRIS: She may be. And yet it has troubled me that you are now seven month out of their house, and in all this time no other family has ever called for your service.

ABIGAIL: They want slaves, not such as I. Let them send to Barbados for that. I will not black my face for any of them! *With ill-concealed resentment at him:* Do you begrudge my bed, uncle?

PARRIS: No—no.

ABIGAIL, *in a temper:* My name is good in the village! I will not have it said my name is soiled! Goody Proctor is a gossiping liar!

Enter MRS. ANN PUTNAM. *She is a twisted soul of forty-five, a death-ridden woman, haunted by dreams.*

PARRIS, *as soon as the door begins to open:* No—no, I cannot have anyone. *He sees her, and a certain deference springs into him, although his worry remains.* Why, Goody Putnam, come in.

MRS. PUTNAM, *full of breath, shiny-eyed:* It is a marvel. It is surely a stroke of hell upon you.

PARRIS: No, Goody Putnam, it is—

MRS. PUTNAM, *glancing at* BETTY: How high did she fly, how high?

PARRIS: No, no, she never flew—

MRS. PUTNAM, *very pleased with it:* Why, it's sure she did. Mr. Collins saw her goin' over Ingersoll's barn, and come down light as bird, he says!

PARRIS: Now, look you, Goody Putnam, she never—*Enter* THOMAS PUTNAM, *a well-to-do, hard-handed landowner, near fifty.* Oh, good morning, Mr. Putnam.

PUTNAM: It is a providence the thing is out now! It is a providence. *He goes directly to the bed.*

PARRIS: What's out, sir, what's—?

MRS. PUTNAM *goes to the bed.*

PUTNAM, *looking down at* BETTY: Why, her eyes is closed! Look you, Ann.

MRS. PUTNAM: Why, that's strange. *To* PARRIS: Ours is open.

PARRIS, *shocked:* Your Ruth is sick?

MRS. PUTNAM, *with vicious certainty:* I'd not call it sick; the Devil's touch is heavier than sick. It's death, y'know, it's death drivin' into them, forked and hoofed.

PARRIS: Oh, pray not! Why, how does Ruth ail?

MRS. PUTNAM: She ails as she must—she never waked this morning, but her eyes open and she walks, and hears naught, sees naught, and cannot eat. Her soul is taken, surely.

PARRIS *is struck.*

PUTNAM, *as though for further details:* They say you've sent for Reverend Hale of Beverly?

PARRIS *with dwindling conviction now:* A precaution only. He has much experience in all demonic arts, and I—

MRS. PUTNAM: He has indeed; and found a witch in Beverly last year, and let you remember that.

PARRIS: Now, Goody Ann, they only thought that were a witch, and I am certain there be no element of witchcraft here.

PUTNAM: No witchcraft! Now look you, Mr. Parris—

PARRIS: Thomas, Thomas, I pray you, leap not to witchcraft. I know that you—you least of all, Thomas, would ever wish so disastrous a charge laid upon me. We cannot leap to witchcraft. They will howl me out of Salem for such corruption in my house.

A word about Thomas Putnam. He was a man with many grievances, at least one of which appears justified. Some time before, his wife's brother-in-law, James Bayley, had been turned down as minister at Salem. Bayley had all the qualifications, and a two-thirds vote into the bargain, but a faction stopped his acceptance, for reasons that are not clear.

Thomas Putnam was the eldest son of the richest man in the village. He had fought the Indians at Narragansett, and was deeply interested in parish affairs. He undoubtedly felt it poor payment that the village should so blatantly disregard his candidate for one of its more important offices, especially since he regarded himself as the intellectual superior of most of the people around him.

His vindictive nature was demonstrated long before the witchcraft began. Another former Salem minister, George Burroughs, had had to borrow money to pay for his wife's funeral, and, since the parish was remiss in his salary, he was soon bankrupt. Thomas and his brother John had Burroughs jailed for debts the man did not owe. The incident is important only in that Burroughs succeeded in becoming minister where Bayley, Thomas Putnam's brother-in-law, had been rejected; the motif of resentment is clear here. Thomas Putnam felt that his own name and the honor of his family had been smirched by the village, and he meant to right matters however he could.

Another reason to believe him a deeply embittered man was his attempt to break his father's will, which left a disproportionate amount to a stepbrother. As with every other public cause in which he tried to force his way, he failed in this.

So it is not surprising to find that so many accusations against people are in the handwriting of Thomas Putnam, or that his name is so often found as a witness corroborating the supernatural testimony, or that his daughter led the crying-out at the most opportune junctures of the trials, especially when—But we'll speak of that when we come to it.

PUTNAM—*at the moment he is intent upon getting* PARRIS, *for whom he has only contempt, to move toward the abyss:*[7] Mr. Parris, I have taken your

---

7. **abyss** (ə bis´) *n.* deep crack in the Earth.

✔Reading Check

Why has Parris sent for Reverend Hale?

part in all contention here, and I would continue; but I cannot if you hold back in this. There are hurtful, vengeful spirits layin' hands on these children.

PARRIS: But, Thomas, you cannot—

PUTNAM: Ann! Tell Mr. Parris what you have done.

MRS. PUTNAM: Reverend Parris, I have laid seven babies unbaptized in the earth. Believe me, sir, you never saw more hearty babies born. And yet, each would wither in my arms the very night of their birth. I have spoke nothin', but my heart has clamored intimations. And now, this year, my Ruth, my only—I see her turning strange. A secret child she has become this year, and shrivels like a sucking mouth were pullin' on her life too. And so I thought to send her to your Tituba—

PARRIS: To Tituba! What may Tituba—?

MRS. PUTNAM: Tituba knows how to speak to the dead, Mr. Parris.

PARRIS: Goody Ann, it is a formidable sin to conjure up the dead!

MRS. PUTNAM: I take it on my soul, but who else may surely tell us what person murdered my babies?

PARRIS, *horrified:* Woman!

MRS. PUTNAM: They were murdered, Mr. Parris! And mark this proof! Mark it! Last night my Ruth were ever so close to their little spirits; I know it, sir. For how else is she struck dumb now except some power of darkness would stop her mouth? It is a marvelous sign, Mr. Parris!

PUTNAM: Don't you understand it, sir? There is a murdering witch among us, bound to keep herself in the dark. PARRIS *turns to* BETTY, *a frantic terror rising in him.* Let your names make of it what they will, you cannot blink it more.

PARRIS, *to* ABIGAIL: Then you were conjuring spirits last night.

ABIGAIL, *whispering:* Not I, sir—Tituba and Ruth.

PARRIS *turns now, with new fear, and goes to* BETTY, *looks down at her, and then, gazing off:* Oh, Abigail, what proper payment for my charity! Now I am undone.

PUTNAM: You are not undone! Let you take hold here. Wait for no one to charge you—declare it yourself. You have discovered witchcraft—

PARRIS: In my house? In my house, Thomas? They will topple me with this! They will make of it a—

Enter MERCY LEWIS, *the Putnams' servant, a fat, sly, merciless girl of eighteen.*

MERCY: Your pardons. I only thought to see how Betty is.

PUTNAM: Why aren't you home? Who's with Ruth?

MERCY: Her grandma come. She's improved a little, I think—she give a powerful sneeze before.

MRS. PUTNAM: Ah, there's a sign of life!

▼ **Critical Viewing**
Abigail Williams has accused Tituba of conjuring up spirits. What can you infer about Tituba's reaction from her expression here? **[Infer]**

MERCY: I'd fear no more, Goody Putnam. It were a grand sneeze; another like it will shake her wits together, I'm sure. *She goes to the bed to look.*

PARRIS: Will you leave me now, Thomas? I would pray a while alone.

ABIGAIL: Uncle, you've prayed since midnight. Why do you not go down and—

PARRIS: No—no. *To* PUTNAM: I have no answer for that crowd. I'll wait till Mr. Hale arrives. *To get* MRS. PUTNAM *to leave:* If you will, Goody Ann . . .

PUTNAM: Now look you, sir. Let you strike out against the Devil, and the village will bless you for it! Come down, speak to them—pray with them. They're thirsting for your word, Mister! Surely you'll pray with them.

PARRIS, *swayed:* I'll lead them in a psalm, but let you say nothing of witchcraft yet. I will not discuss it. The cause is yet unknown. I have had enough contention since I came; I want no more.

MRS. PUTNAM: Mercy, you go home to Ruth, d'y'hear?

MERCY: Aye, mum.

MRS. PUTNAM *goes out.*

PARRIS, *to* ABIGAIL: If she starts for the window, cry for me at once.

ABIGAIL: I will, uncle.

PARRIS, *to* PUTNAM: There is a terrible power in her arms today. *He goes out with* PUTNAM.

ABIGAIL, *with hushed trepidation:* How is Ruth sick?

MERCY: It's weirdish, I know not—she seems to walk like a dead one since last night.

ABIGAIL, *turns at once and goes to* BETTY, *and now, with fear in her voice:* Betty? BETTY *doesn't move. She shakes her.* Now stop this! Betty! Sit up now!

BETTY *doesn't stir.* MERCY *comes over.*

MERCY: Have you tried beatin' her? I gave Ruth a good one and it waked her for a minute. Here, let me have her.

ABIGAIL, *holding* MERCY *back:* No, he'll be comin' up. Listen, now; if they be questioning us, tell them we danced—I told him as much already.

MERCY: Aye. And what more?

ABIGAIL: He knows Tituba conjured Ruth's sisters to come out of the grave.

MERCY: And what more?

ABIGAIL: He saw you naked.

MERCY: *clapping her hands together with a frightened laugh:* Oh, Jesus! *Enter* MARY WARREN, *breathless. She is seventeen, a subservient, naive, lonely girl.*

MARY WARREN: What'll we do? The village is out! I just come from the farm; the whole country's talkin' witchcraft! They'll be callin' us witches, Abby!

MERCY, *pointing and looking at* MARY WARREN: She means to tell, I know it.

Literary Analysis
Dialogue and Stage Directions What does this conversation reveal about the two young women?

Literary Analysis
Dialogue and Stage Directions What are the contrasting character traits of Mary Warren and of Mercy Lewis?

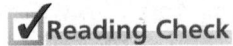**Reading Check**

Why do the Putnams believe there is witchcraft in Salem Village?

MARY WARREN: Abby, we've got to tell. Witchery's a hangin' error, a hangin' like they done in Boston two year ago! We must tell the truth, Abby! You'll only be whipped for dancin', and the other things!

ABIGAIL: Oh, *we'll* be whipped!

MARY WARREN: I never done none of it, Abby. I only looked!

MERCY, *moving menacingly toward* MARY: Oh, you're a great one for lookin', aren't you, Mary Warren? What a grand peeping courage you have!

BETTY, *on the bed, whimpers.* ABIGAIL *turns to her at once.*

ABIGAIL: Betty? *She goes to* BETTY. Now, Betty, dear, wake up now. It's Abigail. *She sits* BETTY *up and furiously shakes her.* I'll beat you, Betty! BETTY *whimpers.* My, you seem improving. I talked to your papa and I told him everything. So there's nothing to—

BETTY, *darts off the bed, frightened of* ABIGAIL, *and flattens herself against the wall:* I want my mama!

ABIGAIL, *with alarm, as she cautiously approaches* BETTY: What ails you, Betty? Your mama's dead and buried.

BETTY: I'll fly to Mama. Let me fly! *She raises her arms as though to fly, and streaks for the window, gets one leg out.*

ABIGAIL, *pulling her away from the window:* I told him everything; he knows now, he knows everything we—

BETTY: You drank blood, Abby! You didn't tell him that!

ABIGAIL: Betty, you never say that again! You will never—

BETTY: You did, you did! You drank a charm to kill John Proctor's wife! You drank a charm to kill Goody Proctor!

ABIGAIL, *smashes her across the face:* Shut it! Now shut it!

BETTY: *collapsing on the bed:* Mama, Mama! *She dissolves into sobs.*

ABIGAIL: Now look you. All of you. We danced. And Tituba conjured Ruth Putnam's dead sisters. And that is all. And mark this. Let either of you breathe a word, or the edge of a word, about the other things, and I will come to you in the black of some terrible night and I will bring a pointy reckoning that will shudder you. And you know I can do it; I saw Indians smash my dear parents' heads on the pillow next to mine, and I have seen some reddish work done at night, and I can make you wish you had never seen the sun go down! *She goes to* BETTY *and roughly sits her up.* Now, you—sit up and stop this!

But BETTY *collapses in her hands and lies inert on the bed.*

▲ **Critical Viewing**
What emotion is conveyed in this image of Betty Parris's attempt to fly? Explain. **[Interpret]**

MARY WARREN, *with hysterical fright:* What's got her? ABIGAIL *stares in fright at* BETTY. Abby, she's going to die! It's a sin to conjure, and we—

ABIGAIL, *starting for* MARY: I say shut it, Mary Warren!

Enter JOHN PROCTOR. *On seeing him.* MARY WARREN *leaps in fright.*

Proctor was a farmer in his middle thirties. He need not have been a partisan of any faction in the town, but there is evidence to suggest that he had a sharp and biting way with hypocrites. He was the kind of man—powerful of body, even-tempered, and not easily led—who cannot refuse support to partisans without drawing their deepest resentment. In Proctor's presence a fool felt his foolishness instantly—and a Proctor is always marked for <u>calumny</u> therefore.

But as we shall see, the steady manner he displays does not spring from an untroubled soul. He is a sinner, a sinner not only against the moral fashion of the time, but against his own vision of decent conduct. These people had no ritual for the washing away of sins. It is another trait we inherited from them, and it has helped to discipline us as well as to breed hypocrisy among us. Proctor, respected and even feared in Salem, has come to regard himself as a kind of fraud. But no hint of this has yet appeared on the surface, and as he enters from the crowded parlor below it is a man in his prime we see, with a quiet confidence and an unexpressed, hidden force. Mary Warren, his servant, can barely speak for embarrassment and fear.

MARY WARREN: Oh! I'm just going home, Mr. Proctor.

PROCTOR: Be you foolish, Mary Warren? Be you deaf? I forbid you leave the house, did I not? Why shall I pay you? I am looking for you more often than my cows!

MARY WARREN: I only come to see the great doings in the world.

PROCTOR: I'll show you a great doin' on your arse one of these days. Now get you home; my wife is waitin' with your work! *Trying to retain a shred of dignity, she goes slowly out.*

MERCY LEWIS, *both afraid of him and strangely titillated:* I'd best be off. I have my Ruth to watch. Good morning, Mr. Proctor.

MERCY *sidles out. Since* PROCTOR'S *entrance,* ABIGAIL *has stood as though on tiptoe, absorbing his presence, wide-eyed. He glances at her then goes to* BETTY *on the bed.*

ABIGAIL: Gad. I'd almost forgot how strong you are, John Proctor!

PROCTOR, *looking at* ABIGAIL *now, the faintest suggestion of a knowing smile on his face:* What's this mischief here?

ABIGAIL, *with a nervous laugh:* Oh, she's only gone silly somehow.

PROCTOR: The road past my house is a pilgrimage to Salem all morning. The town's mumbling witchcraft.

ABIGAIL: Oh, posh! *Winningly she comes a little closer, with a confidential, wicked air.* We were dancin' in the woods last night, and my uncle leaped in on us. She took fright, is all.

PROCTOR, *his smile widening:* Ah, you're wicked yet, aren't y'! *A trill of expectant laughter escapes her, and she dares come closer, feverishly*

Literary Analysis
Dialogue, Stage Directions, and Dramatic Exposition What does Miller reveal about Proctor through this dramatic exposition?

calumny (kal′ əm nē) *n.* false accusation; slander

✓**Reading Check**
What does Mary Warren insist the girls do? How does Abigail react?

looking into his eyes. You'll be clapped in the stocks before you're twenty. *He takes a step to go, and she springs into his path.*

ABIGAIL: Give me a word, John. A soft word. *Her concentrated desire destroys his smile.*

PROCTOR: No, no, Abby. That's done with.

ABIGAIL, *tauntingly:* You come five mile to see a silly girl fly? I know you better.

PROCTOR, *setting her firmly out of his path:* I come to see what mischief your uncle's brewin' now. *With final emphasis:* Put it out of mind, Abby.

ABIGAIL, *grasping his hand before he can release her:* John—I am waitin' for you every night.

PROCTOR: Abby, I never give you hope to wait for me.

ABIGAIL, *now beginning to anger—she can't believe it:* I have something better than hope, I think!

PROCTOR: Abby, you'll put it out of mind. I'll not be comin' for you more.

ABIGAIL: You're surely sportin' with me.

PROCTOR: You know me better.

ABIGAIL: I know how you clutched my back behind your house and sweated like a stallion whenever I come near! Or did I dream that? It's she put me out, you cannot pretend it were you. I saw your face when she put me out, and you loved me then and you do now!

PROCTOR: Abby, that's a wild thing to say—

ABIGAIL: A wild thing may say wild things. But not so wild, I think. I have seen you since she put me out; I have seen you nights.

PROCTOR: I have hardly stepped off my farm this seven-month.

ABIGAIL: I have a sense for heat, John, and yours has drawn me to my window, and I have seen you looking up, burning in your loneliness. Do you tell me you've never looked up at my window?

PROCTOR: I may have looked up.

ABIGAIL, *now softening:* And you must. You are no wintry man. I know you, John. I *know* you. *She is weeping.* I cannot sleep for dreamin'; I cannot dream but I wake and walk about the house as though I'd find you comin' through some door. *She clutches him desperately.*

PROCTOR, *gently pressing her from him, with great sympathy but firmly:* Child—

ABIGAIL, *with a flash of anger:* How do you call me child!

PROCTOR: Abby, I may think of you softly from time to time. But I will cut off my hand before I'll ever reach for you again. Wipe it out of mind. We never touched, Abby.

ABIGAIL: Aye, but we did.

PROCTOR: Aye, but we did not.

ABIGAIL, *with a bitter anger:* Oh, I marvel how such a strong man may let such a sickly wife be—

PROCTOR, *angered—at himself as well:* You'll speak nothin' of Elizabeth!

Literary Analysis
Dialogue and Stage Directions What important information about Abigail's behavior and emotions is conveyed through these stage directions?

Reading Strategy
Questioning the Characters' Motives What does this paragraph reveal about Abigail's motivations?

ABIGAIL: She is blackening my name in the village! She is telling lies about me! She is a cold, sniveling woman, and you bend to her! Let her turn you like a—

PROCTOR, *shaking her:* Do you look for whippin'?

A psalm is heard being sung below.

ABIGAIL, *in tears:* I look for John Proctor that took me from my sleep and put knowledge in my heart! I never knew what pretense Salem was, I never knew the lying lessons I was taught by all these Christian women and their covenanted men! And now you bid me tear the light out of my eyes? I will not, I cannot! You loved me, John Proctor, and whatever sin it is, you love me yet! *He turns abruptly to go out. She rushes to him.* John, pity me, pity me!

The words "going up to Jesus" are heard in the psalm, and BETTY *claps her ears suddenly and whines loudly.*

ABIGAIL: Betty? *She hurries to* BETTY, *who is now sitting up and screaming.* PROCTOR *goes to* BETTY *as* ABIGAIL *is trying to pull her hands down, calling "Betty!"*

PROCTOR, *growing unnerved:* What's she doing? Girl, what ails you? Stop that wailing!

The singing has stopped in the midst of this, and now PARRIS *rushes in.*

PARRIS: What happened? What are you doing to her? Betty! *He rushes to the bed, crying, "Betty, Betty!"* MRS. PUTNAM *enters, feverish with curiosity, and with her* PUTNAM *and* MERCY LEWIS. PARRIS, *at the bed, keeps lightly slapping* BETTY'S *face, while she moans and tries to get up.*

ABIGAIL: She heard you singin' and suddenly she's up and screamin'.

MRS. PUTNAM: The psalm! The psalm! She cannot bear to hear the Lord's name!

PARRIS: No, God forbid. Mercy, run to the doctor! Tell him what's happened here! MERCY LEWIS *rushes out.*

MRS. PUTNAM: Mark it for a sign, mark it!

REBECCA NURSE, *seventy-two, enters. She is white-haired, leaning upon her walking-stick.*

PUTNAM, *pointing at the whimpering* BETTY: That is a notorious sign of witchcraft afoot, Goody Nurse, a prodigious sign!

MRS. PUTNAM: My mother told me that! When they cannot bear to hear the name of—

PARRIS, *trembling:* Rebecca, Rebecca, go to her, we're lost. She suddenly cannot bear to hear the Lord's—

GILES COREY, *eighty-three, enters. He is knotted with muscle, canny, inquisitive, and still powerful.*

REBECCA: There is hard sickness here, Giles Corey, so please to keep the quiet.

GILES: I've not said a word. No one here can testify I've said a word. Is she going to fly again? I hear she flies.

PUTNAM: Man, be quiet now!

Literary Analysis
Dialogue and Stage Directions What do these lines reveal about Mrs. Putnam's eagerness to see signs of witchcraft?

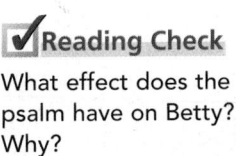Reading Check

What effect does the psalm have on Betty? Why?

Everything is quiet. REBECCA *walks across the room to the bed.*
Gentleness exudes from her. BETTY *is quietly whimpering, eyes shut.*
REBECCA *simply stands over the child, who gradually quiets.*

And while they are so absorbed, we may put a word in for Rebecca.
Rebecca was the wife of Francis Nurse, who, from all accounts, was one
of those men for whom both sides of the argument had to have respect.
He was called upon to arbitrate disputes as though he were an unofficial judge, and Rebecca also enjoyed the high opinion most people had
for him. By the time of the delusion, they had three hundred acres, and
their children were settled in separate homesteads within the same
estate. However, Francis had originally rented the land, and one theory
has it that, as he gradually paid for it and raised his social status, there
were those who resented his rise.

Another suggestion to explain the systematic campaign against
Rebecca, and inferentially against Francis, is the land war he fought
with his neighbors, one of whom was a Putnam. This squabble grew to
the proportions of a battle in the woods between partisans of both
sides, and it is said to have lasted for two days. As for Rebecca herself,
the general opinion of her character was so high that to explain how
anyone dared cry her out for a witch—and more, how adults could
bring themselves to lay hands on her—we must look to the fields and
boundaries of that time.

As we have seen, Thomas Putnam's man for the Salem ministry was
Bayley. The Nurse clan had been in the faction that prevented Bayley's
taking office. In addition, certain families allied to the Nurses by blood
or friendship, and whose farms were contiguous with the Nurse farm
or close to it, combined to break away from the Salem town
authority and set up Topsfield, a new and independent
entity whose existence was resented by old Salemites.

That the guiding hand behind the outcry was
Putnam's is indicated by the fact that, as soon as it
began, this Topsfield-Nurse faction absented themselves
from church in protest and disbelief. It was Edward and
Jonathan Putnam who signed the first complaint against
Rebecca; and Thomas Putnam's little daughter was the one
who fell into a fit at the hearing and pointed to Rebecca
as her attacker. To top it all, Mrs. Putnam—who is now
staring at the bewitched child on the bed—soon accused
Rebecca's spirit of "tempting her to iniquity," a charge
that had more truth in it than Mrs. Putnam could know.

MRS. PUTNAM, *astonished:* What have you done?

REBECCA, *in thought, now leaves the bedside and sits.*

PARRIS, *wondrous and relieved:* What do you make of it,
Rebecca?

PUTNAM, *eagerly:* Goody Nurse, will you go to my Ruth
and see if you can wake her?

REBECCA, *sitting:* I think she'll wake in time. Pray calm
yourselves. I have eleven children, and I am twenty-six

▼ **Critical Viewing**
Abigail calls John Proctor
a "strong man." What
details in this photograph
support that idea?
[Interpret]

times a grandma, and I have seen them all through their silly seasons, and when it come on them they will run the Devil bowlegged keeping up with their mischief. I think she'll wake when she tires of it. A child's spirit is like a child, you can never catch it by running after it; you must stand still, and, for love, it will soon itself come back.

PROCTOR: Aye, that's the truth of it, Rebecca.

MRS. PUTNAM: This is no silly season, Rebecca. My Ruth is bewildered, Rebecca; she cannot eat.

REBECCA: Perhaps she is not hungered yet. *To* PARRIS: I hope you are not decided to go in search of loose spirits, Mr. Parris. I've heard promise of that outside.

PARRIS: A wide opinion's running in the parish that the Devil may be among us, and I would satisfy them that they are wrong.

PROCTOR: Then let you come out and call them wrong. Did you consult the wardens before you called this minister to look for devils?

PARRIS: He is not coming to look for devils!

PROCTOR: Then what's he coming for?

PUTNAM: There be children dyin' in the village, Mister!

PROCTOR: I seen none dyin'. This society will not be a bag to swing around your head, Mr. Putnam. *To Parris:* Did you call a meeting before you—?

PUTNAM: I am sick of meetings; cannot the man turn his head without he have a meeting?

PROCTOR: He may turn his head, but not to Hell!

REBECCA: Pray, John, be calm. *Pause. He defers to her.* Mr. Parris, I think you'd best send Reverend Hale back as soon as he come. This will set us all to arguin' again in the society, and we thought to have peace this year. I think we ought rely on the doctor now, and good prayer.

MRS. PUTNAM: Rebecca, the doctor's baffled!

REBECCA: If so he is, then let us go to God for the cause of it. There is prodigious danger in the seeking of loose spirits. I fear it, I fear it. Let us rather blame ourselves and—

PUTNAM: How may we blame ourselves? I am one of nine sons; the Putnam seed have peopled this province. And yet I have but one child left of eight—and now she shrivels!

REBECCA: I cannot fathom that.

MRS. PUTNAM, *with a growing edge of sarcasm:* But I must! You think it God's work you should never lose a child, nor grandchild either, and I bury all but one? There are wheels within wheels in this village, and fires within fires!

PUTNAM, *to* PARRIS: When Reverend Hale comes, you will proceed to look for signs of witchcraft here.

PROCTOR, *to* PUTNAM: You cannot command Mr. Parris. We vote by name in this society, not by acreage.

Reading Strategy
Questioning the Characters' Motives
What do the Putnams suggest by their remarks?

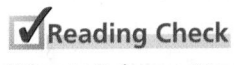Reading Check

What is Rebecca Nurse's effect on Betty? Why?

The Crucible, Act I ◆ *1249*

PUTNAM: I never heard you worried so on this society, Mr. Proctor. I do not think I saw you at Sabbath meeting since snow flew.

PROCTOR: I have trouble enough without I come five mile to hear him preach only hellfire and bloody damnation. Take it to heart, Mr. Parris. There are many others who stay away from church these days because you hardly ever mention God any more.

PARRIS, *now aroused:* Why, that's a drastic charge!

REBECCA: It's somewhat true; there are many that quail to bring their children—

PARRIS: I do not preach for children, Rebecca. It is not the children who are unmindful of their obligations toward this ministry.

REBECCA: Are there really those unmindful?

PARRIS: I should say the better half of Salem village—

PUTNAM: And more than that!

PARRIS: Where is my wood? My contract provides I be supplied with all my firewood. I am waiting since November for a stick, and even in November I had to show my frostbitten hands like some London beggar!

GILES: You are allowed six pound a year to buy your wood, Mr. Parris.

PARRIS: I regard that six pound as part of my salary. I am paid little enough without I spend six pound on firewood.

PROCTOR: Sixty, plus six for firewood—

PARRIS: The salary is sixty-six pound, Mr. Proctor! I am not some preaching farmer with a book under my arm; I am a graduate of Harvard College.

GILES: Aye, and well instructed in arithmetic!

PARRIS: Mr. Corey, you will look far for a man of my kind at sixty pound a year! I am not used to this poverty; I left a thrifty business in the Barbados to serve the Lord. I do not fathom it, why am I persecuted here? I cannot offer one proposition but there be a howling riot of argument. I have often wondered if the Devil be in it somewhere; I cannot understand you people otherwise.

PROCTOR: Mr. Parris, you are the first minister ever did demand the deed to this house—

PARRIS: Man! Don't a minister deserve a house to live in?

PROCTOR: To live in, yes. But to ask ownership is like you shall own the meeting house itself; the last meeting I were at you spoke so long on deeds and mortgages I thought it were an auction.

PARRIS: I want a mark of confidence, is all! I am your third preacher in seven years. I do not wish to be put out like the cat whenever some majority feels the whim. You people seem not to comprehend that a minister is the Lord's man in the parish; a minister is not to be so lightly crossed and contradicted—

PUTNAM: Aye!

PARRIS: There is either obedience or the church will burn like Hell is burning!

Reading Strategy
Questioning the Characters' Motives Of what charge does Parris accuse members of his congregation? What does this accusation reveal about him?

Literary Analysis
Dialogue and Stage Direction How does the playwright indicate that Parris interrupts Proctor?

PROCTOR: Can you speak one minute without we land in Hell again? I am sick of Hell!

PARRIS: It is not for you to say what is good for you to hear!

PROCTOR: I may speak my heart, I think!

PARRIS, *in a fury:* What, are we Quakers?[8] We are not Quakers here yet, Mr. Proctor. And you may tell that to your followers!

PROCTOR: My followers!

PARRIS—*now he's out with it:* There is a party in this church. I am not blind; there is a faction and a party.

PROCTOR: Against you?

PUTNAM: Against him and all authority!

PROCTOR: Why, then I must find it and join it.

There is shock among the others.

REBECCA: He does not mean that.

PUTNAM: He confessed it now!

PROCTOR: I mean it solemnly, Rebecca; I like not the smell of this "authority."

REBECCA: No, you cannot break charity with your minister. You are another kind, John. Clasp his hand, make your peace.

PROCTOR: I have a crop to sow and lumber to drag home. *He goes angrily to the door and turns to* COREY *with a smile.* What say you, Giles, let's find the party. He says there's a party.

GILES: I've changed my opinion of this man, John. Mr. Parris, I beg your pardon. I never thought you had so much iron in you.

PARRIS, *surprised:* Why, thank you, Giles!

GILES: It suggests to the mind what the trouble be among us all these years. *To all:* Think on it. Wherefore is everybody suing everybody else? Think on it now, it's a deep thing, and dark as a pit. I have been six time in court this year—

PROCTOR, *familiarly, with warmth, although he knows he is approaching the edge of Giles' tolerance with this:* Is it the Devil's fault that a man cannot say you good morning without you clap him for defamation? You're old, Giles, and you're not hearin' so well as you did.

GILES—*he cannot be crossed:* John Proctor, I have only last month collected four pound damages for you publicly sayin' I burned the roof off your house, and I—

PROCTOR, *laughing:* I never said no such thing, but I've paid you for it, so I hope I can call you deaf without charge. Now come along, Giles, and help me drag my lumber home.

PUTNAM: A moment, Mr. Proctor. What lumber is that you're draggin', if I may ask you?

---

8. **Quakers** members of the Society of Friends, a Christian religious sect that was founded in the mid-17th century and has no formal creed, rites, or priesthood. Unlike the Quakers, the Puritans had a rigid code of conduct and were expected to heed the words of their ministers.

Literary Analysis
Dialogue and Stage Directions What does this dialogue between Proctor and Giles reveal about the mood and atmosphere in Salem?

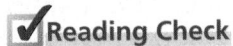

Reading Check

How do Proctor's and Parris's beliefs about authority differ?

PROCTOR: My lumber. From out my forest by the riverside.

PUTNAM: Why, we are surely gone wild this year. What anarchy is this? That tract is in my bounds, it's in my bounds, Mr. Proctor.

PROCTOR: In your bounds! *Indicating* REBECCA: I bought that tract from Goody Nurse's husband five months ago.

PUTNAM: He had no right to sell it. It stands clear in my grandfather's will that all the land between the river and—

PROCTOR: Your grandfather had a habit of willing land that never belonged to him, if I may say it plain.

GILES: That's God's truth; he nearly willed away my north pasture but he knew I'd break his fingers before he'd set his name to it. Let's get your lumber home, John. I feel a sudden will to work coming on.

PUTNAM: You load one oak of mine and you'll fight to drag it home!

GILES: Aye, and we'll win too, Putnam—this fool and I. Come on! *He turns to* PROCTOR *and starts out.*

PUTNAM: I'll have my men on you, Corey! I'll clap a writ on you!

Enter REVEREND JOHN HALE *of Beverly.*

Mr. Hale is nearing forty, a tight-skinned, eager-eyed intellectual. This is a beloved errand for him; on being called here to ascertain witchcraft he felt the pride of the specialist whose unique knowledge has at last been publicly called for. Like almost all men of learning, he spent a good deal of time pondering the invisible world, especially since he had himself encountered a witch in his parish not long before. That woman, however, turned into a mere pest under his searching scrutiny, and the child she had allegedly been afflicting recovered her normal behavior after Hale had given her his kindness and a few days of rest in his own house. However, that experience never raised a doubt in his mind as to the reality of the underworld or the existence of Lucifer's many-faced lieutenants. And his belief is not to his discredit. Better minds than Hale's were—and still are—convinced that there is a society of spirits beyond our ken. One cannot help noting that one of his lines has never yet raised a laugh in any audience that has seen this play; it is his assurance that "We cannot look to superstition in this. The Devil is precise." Evidently we are not quite certain even now whether diabolism is holy and not to be scoffed at. And it is no accident that we should be so bemused.

Like Reverend Hale and the others on this stage, we conceive the Devil as a necessary part of a respectable view of cosmology. Ours is a divided empire in which certain ideas and emotions and actions are of God, and their opposites are of Lucifer. It is as impossible for most men to conceive of a morality without sin as of an earth without "sky." Since 1692 a great but superficial change has wiped out God's beard and the Devil's horns, but the world is still gripped between two diametrically opposed absolutes. The concept of unity, in which positive and negative are attributes of the same force, in which good and evil are relative, ever-changing, and always joined to the same phenomenon—such a

Reading Strategy
Questioning the Characters' Motives Why does Giles feel a "sudden will to work"?

Literary Analysis
Dialogue, Stage Directions, and Dramatic Exposition What important information does Miller provide about his view of the world?

concept is still reserved to the physical sciences and to the few who have grasped the history of ideas. When it is recalled that until the Christian era the underworld was never regarded as a hostile area, that all gods were useful and essentially friendly to man despite occasional lapses; when we see the steady and methodical <u>inculcation</u> into humanity of the idea of man's worthlessness—until redeemed—the necessity of the Devil may become evident as a weapon, a weapon designed and used time and time again in every age to whip men into a surrender to a particular church or church-state.

Our difficulty in believing the—for want of a better word—political inspiration of the Devil is due in great part to the fact that he is called up and damned not only by our social antagonists but by our own side, whatever it may be. The Catholic Church, through its Inquisition,♦ is famous for cultivating Lucifer as the arch-fiend, but the Church's enemies relied no less upon the Old Boy to keep the human mind enthralled. Luther[9] was himself accused of alliance with Hell, and he in turn accused his enemies. To complicate matters further, he believed that he had had contact with the Devil and had argued theology with him. I am not surprised at this, for at my own university a professor of history—a Lutheran,[10] by the way—used to assemble his graduate students, draw the shades, and commune in the classroom with Erasmus.[11] He was never, to my knowledge, officially scoffed at for this, the reason being that the university officials, like most of us, are the children of a history which still sucks at the Devil's teats. At this writing, only England has held back before the temptations of contemporary diabolism. In the countries of the Communist ideology, all resistance of any import is linked to the totally malign capitalist succubi,[12] and in America any man who is not reactionary in his views is open to the charge of alliance with the Red hell. Political opposition, thereby, is given an inhumane overlay which then justifies the abrogation[13] of all normally applied customs of civilized intercourse. A political policy is equated with moral right, and opposition to it with diabolical malevolence. Once such an equation is effectively made, society becomes a congerie[14] of plots and counterplots, and the main role of government changes from that of the arbiter to that of the scourge of God.

The results of this process are no different now from what they ever were, except sometimes in the degree of

---

9. **Luther** Martin Luther (1483–1546), German theologian who led the Protestant Reformation.
10. **Lutheran** member of the Protestant denomination founded by Martin Luther.
11. **Erasmus Desiderius** Erasmus (1466?–1536), Dutch humanist, scholar, and theologian.
12. **succubi** (suk´ yoo bī) female demons thought to lie on sleeping men.
13. **abrogation** (ab´ rō gā´ shən) abolishment.
14. **congerie** (kän´ jə rē´) heap; pile.

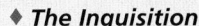

Literature in context   History Connection

♦ The Inquisition

Although Miller alludes to the Inquisition, a "court of justice" established by the Catholic Church during the 13th century, he does not describe it in the script of *The Crucible*. The Inquisition bears a close resemblance to the Salem witch hunts of the 1690s and to the Red Scare in the United States during the 1950s. In each case, a panel of judges decided allegations of heresy or treason. The Salem judges sentenced some individuals to death, as had the Catholic judges of the Middle Ages.

No one died in the 1950s as a result of Senator Joseph McCarthy's interrogations and accusations of communism. However, many suffered great damage to their personal and professional reputations and were unable to continue their careers and even their social lives for many years.

inculcation (in´ kul kā´ shən) *n.* teaching by repetition and urging

✓ Reading Check

What is Reverend Hale's experience with witchcraft?

cruelty inflicted, and not always even in that department. Normally, the actions and deeds of a man were all that society felt comfortable in judging. The secret intent of an action was left to the ministers, priests, and rabbis to deal with. When diabolism rises, however, actions are the least important manifests of the true nature of a man. The Devil, as Reverend Hale said, is a wily one, and until an hour before he fell, even God thought him beautiful in Heaven.

The analogy, however, seems to falter when one considers that, while there were no witches then, there are Communists and capitalists now, and in each camp there is certain proof that spies of each side are at work undermining the other. But this is a snobbish objection and not at all warranted by the facts. I have no doubt that people *were* communing with, and even worshiping, the Devil in Salem, and if the whole truth could be known in this case, as it is in others, we should discover a regular and conventionalized <u>propitiation</u> of the dark spirit. One certain evidence of this is the confession of Tituba, the slave of Reverend Parris, and another is the behavior of the children who were known to have indulged in sorceries with her.

There are accounts of similar *klatches*[15] in Europe, where the daughters of the towns would assemble at night and, sometimes with fetishes,[16] sometimes with a selected young man, give themselves to love, with some bastardly results. The Church, sharp-eyed as it must be when gods long dead are brought to life, condemned these orgies as witchcraft and interpreted them, rightly, as a resurgence of the Dionysiac[17] forces it had crushed long before. Sex, sin, and the Devil were early linked, and so they continued to be in Salem, and are today. From all accounts there are no more puritanical mores in the world than those enforced by the Communists in Russia, where women's fashions, for instance, are as prudent and all-covering as any American Baptist would desire. The divorce laws lay a tremendous responsibility on the father for the care of his children. Even the laxity of divorce regulations in the early years of the revolution was undoubtedly a revulsion from the nineteenth-century Victorian[18] immobility of marriage and the consequent hypocrisy that developed from it. If for no other reasons, a state so powerful, so jealous of the uniformity of its citizens, cannot long tolerate the atomization of the family. And yet, in American eyes at least, there

propitiation (prə pish´ ē ā´ shən) *n.* action designed to soothe or satisfy a person, a cause, etc.

---

15. *klatches* (klächz) informal gatherings.
16. **fetishes** (fet´ ish iz) objects believed to have magical power.
17. **Dionysiac** (dī´ ə nis´ ē ak´) characteristic of Dionysus, Greek god of wine and revelry; thus, wild, frenzied, sensuous.
18. **Victorian** characteristic of the time when Victoria was queen of England (1837–1901), an era associated with respectability, prudery, and hypocrisy.

remains the conviction that the Russian attitude toward women is lascivious. It is the Devil working again, just as he is working within the Slav who is shocked at the very idea of a woman's disrobing herself in a burlesque show. Our opposites are always robed in sexual sin, and it is from this unconscious conviction that demonology gains both its attractive sensuality and its capacity to infuriate and frighten.

Coming into Salem now, Reverend Hale conceives of himself much as a young doctor on his first call. His painfully acquired armory of symptoms, catchwords, and diagnostic procedures are now to be put to use at last. The road from Beverly is unusually busy this morning, and he has passed a hundred rumors that make him smile at the ignorance of the yeomanry in this most precise science. He feels himself allied with the best minds of Europe—kings, philosophers, scientists, and ecclesiasts of all churches. His goal is light, goodness and its preservation, and he knows the exaltation of the blessed whose intelligence, sharpened by minute examinations of enormous tracts, is finally called upon to face what may be a bloody fight with the Fiend himself.

He appears loaded down with half a dozen heavy books.

HALE: Pray you, someone take these!

PARRIS, *delighted:* Mr. Hale! Oh! it's good to see you again! *Taking some books:* My, they're heavy!

HALE, *setting down his books:* They must be; they are weighted with authority.

PARRIS, *a little scared:* Well, you do come prepared!

HALE: We shall need hard study if it comes to tracking down the Old Boy. *Noticing* REBECCA: You cannot be Rebecca Nurse?

REBECCA: I am, sir. Do you know me?

HALE: It's strange how I knew you, but I suppose you look as such a good soul should. We have all heard of your great charities in Beverly.

PARRIS: Do you know this gentleman? Mr. Thomas Putnam. And his good wife Ann.

HALE: Putnam! I had not expected such distinguished company, sir.

PUTNAM, *pleased:* It does seem to help us today, Mr. Hale. We look to you to come to our house and save our child.

HALE: Your child ails too?

MRS. PUTNAM: Her soul, her soul seems flown away. She sleeps and yet she walks . . .

PUTNAM: She cannot eat.

HALE: Cannot eat! *Thinks on it. Then, to* PROCTOR *and* GILES COREY: Do you men have afflicted children?

PARRIS: No, no, these are farmers. John Proctor—

GILES COREY: He don't believe in witches.

Reading Strategy
Questioning the Characters' Motives
According to this passage, what motivates Reverend Hale to study and expose witchcraft?

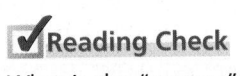Reading Check

What is the "armory" Hale brings with him to Salem?

PROCTOR, *to* HALE: I never spoke on witches one way or the other. Will you come, Giles?

GILES: No—no, John, I think not. I have some few queer questions of my own to ask this fellow.

PROCTOR: I've heard you to be a sensible man, Mr. Hale. I hope you'll leave some of it in Salem.

PROCTOR *goes.* HALE *stands embarrassed for an instant.*

PARRIS, *quickly:* Will you look at my daughter, sir? *Leads* HALE *to the bed.* She has tried to leap out the window; we discovered her this morning on the highroad, waving her arms as though she'd fly.

HALE, *narrowing his eyes:* Tries to fly.

PUTNAM: She cannot bear to hear the Lord's name, Mr. Hale; that's a sure sign of witchcraft afloat.

HALE, *holding up his hands:* No, no. Now let me instruct you. We cannot look to superstition in this. The Devil is precise; the marks of his presence are definite as stone, and I must tell you all that I shall not proceed unless you are prepared to believe me if I should find no bruise of hell upon her.

PARRIS: It is agreed, sir—it is agreed—we will abide by your judgment.

HALE: Good then. *He goes to the bed, looks down at* BETTY. *To* PARRIS: Now, sir, what were your first warning of this strangeness?

PARRIS: Why, sir—I discovered her—*indicating* ABIGAIL—and my niece and ten or twelve of the other girls, dancing in the forest last night.

HALE, *surprised:* You permit dancing?

PARRIS: No, no, it were secret—

MRS. PUTNAM, *unable to wait:* Mr. Parris's slave has knowledge of conjurin', sir.

PARRIS, *to* MRS. PUTNAM: We cannot be sure of that, Goody Ann—

MRS. PUTNAM, *frightened, very softly:* I know it, sir. I sent my child—she should learn from Tituba who murdered her sisters.

REBECCA, *horrified:* Goody Ann! You sent a child to conjure up the dead?

MRS. PUTNAM: Let God blame me, not you, not you, Rebecca! I'll not have you judging me any more! *To* HALE: Is it a natural work to lose seven children before they live a day?

PARRIS: Sssh!

REBECCA, *with great pain, turns her face away. There is a pause.*

HALE: Seven dead in childbirth.

MRS. PUTNAM, *softly:* Aye. *Her voice breaks; she looks up at him. Silence.* HALE *is impressed.* PARRIS *looks to him. He goes to his books, opens one, turns pages, then reads. All wait, avidly.*

PARRIS, *hushed:* What book is that?

MRS. PUTNAM: What's there, sir?

Literary Analysis

Dialogue and Stage Directions What does this speech about the devil's precision reveal about Hale's understanding of human nature?

Literary Analysis

Dialogue and Stage Directions What does this dialogue reveal about Ann Putnam's character and judgment?

HALE, *with a tasty love of intellectual pursuit:* Here is all the invisible world, caught, defined, and calculated. In these books the Devil stands stripped of all his brute disguises. Here are all your familiar spirits—your incubi[19] and succubi, your witches that go by land, by air, and by sea; your wizards of the night and of the day. Have no fear now—we shall find him out if he has come among us, and I mean to crush him utterly if he has shown his face! *He starts for the bed.*

REBECCA: Will it hurt the child, sir?

HALE: I cannot tell. If she is truly in the Devil's grip we may have to rip and tear to get her free.

REBECCA: I think I'll go, then. I am too old for this. *She rises.*

PARRIS, *striving for conviction:* Why, Rebecca, we may open up the boil of all our troubles today!

REBECCA: Let us hope for that. I go to God for you, sir.

PARRIS, *with trepidation—and resentment:* I hope you do not mean to go to Satan here! *Slight pause.*

REBECCA: I wish I knew. *She goes out; they feel resentful of her note of moral superiority.*

PUTNAM, *abruptly:* Come, Mr. Hale, let's get on. Sit you here.

GILES: Mr. Hale, I have always wanted to ask a learned man—what signifies the readin' of strange books?

HALE: What books?

GILES: I cannot tell; she hides them.

HALE: Who does this?

GILES: Martha, my wife. I have waked at night many a time and found her in a corner, readin' of a book. Now what do you make of that?

HALE: Why, that's not necessarily—

GILES: It discomfits me! Last night—mark this—I tried and tried and could not say my prayers. And then she close her book and walks out of the house, and suddenly—mark this—I could pray again!

Old Giles must be spoken for, if only because his fate was to be so remarkable and so different from that of all the others. He was in his early eighties at this time, and was the most comical hero in the history. No man has ever been blamed for so much. If a cow was missed, the first thought was to look for her around Corey's house; a fire blazing up at night brought suspicion of arson to his door. He didn't give a hoot for public opinion, and only in his last years—after he had married Martha—did he bother much with the church. That she stopped his prayer is very probable, but he forgot to say that he'd only recently learned any prayers and it didn't take much to make him stumble over them. He was a crank and a nuisance, but withal a deeply innocent and brave man. In court, once, he was asked if it were true that he had been frightened by the strange behavior of a hog and had then said he knew it to be the Devil in an animal's shape. "What frighted you?" he

---

Literary Analysis

Dialogue, Stage Directions, and Dramatic Exposition Which details given in this background information explain Giles Corey's remarks about his wife, Martha?

**Reading Check**

How does Rebecca's concern for the children compare to Hale's and Parris's?

---

19. incubi (in´ kyoo bī) spirits or demons thought to lie on sleeping women.

was asked. He forgot everything but the word "frighted," and instantly replied, "I do not know that I ever spoke that word in my life."

HALE: Ah! The stoppage of prayer—that is strange. I'll speak further on that with you.

GILES: I'm not sayin' she's touched the Devil, now, but I'd admire to know what books she reads and why she hides them. She'll not answer me, y' see.

HALE: Aye, we'll discuss it. To all: Now mark me, if the Devil is in her you will witness some frightful wonders in this room, so please to keep your wits about you. Mr. Putnam, stand close in case she flies. Now, Betty, dear, will you sit up? PUTNAM *comes in closer, ready-handed.* HALE *sits* BETTY *up, but she hangs limp in his hands.* Hmmm. *He observes her carefully. The others watch breathlessly.* Can you hear me? I am John Hale, minister of Beverly. I have come to help you, dear. Do you remember my two little girls in Beverly? *She does not stir in his hands.*

PARRIS, *in fright:* How can it be the Devil? Why would he choose my house to strike? We have all manner of <u>licentious</u> people in the village!

HALE: What victory would the Devil have to win a soul already bad? It is the best the Devil wants, and who is better than the minister?

GILES: That's deep, Mr. Parris, deep, deep!

PARRIS, *with resolution now:* Betty! Answer Mr. Hale! Betty!

HALE: Does someone afflict you, child? It need not be a woman, mind you, or a man. Perhaps some bird invisible to others comes to you—perhaps a pig, a mouse, or any beast at all. Is there some figure bids you fly? *The child remains limp in his hands. In silence he lays her back on the pillow. Now, holding out his hands toward her, he intones:* In nomine Domini Sabaoth sui filiique ite ad infernos.[20] *She does not stir. He turns to* ABIGAIL, *his eyes narrowing.* Abigail, what sort of dancing were you doing with her in the forest?

ABIGAIL: Why—common dancing is all.

PARRIS: I think I ought to say that I—I saw a kettle in the grass where they were dancing.

ABIGAIL: That were only soup.

HALE: What sort of soup were in this kettle, Abigail?

ABIGAIL: Why, it were beans—and lentils, I think, and—

HALE: Mr. Parris, you did not notice, did you, any living thing in the kettle? A mouse, perhaps, a spider, a frog—?

PARRIS, *fearfully:* I—do believe there were some movement—in the soup.

ABIGAIL: That jumped in, we never put it in!

HALE, *quickly:* What jumped in?

ABIGAIL: Why, a very little frog jumped—

PARRIS: A frog, Abby!

licentious (lī sen′ shəs) *adj.* lacking moral restraint

Literary Analysis
Dialogue and Stage Directions In what way do Hale's questions to Betty suggest the answers he wants to hear?

▶ **Critical Viewing**
Based on this photograph of Abigail and Tituba surrounded by other girls of Salem, how would you describe what actually happened in the woods? **[Interpret]**

---

20. In nomine Domini Sabaoth sui filiique ite ad infernos (in nō′mē nā dō′ mē nē sab′ ā äth sōō′ ē fē′ lēē kwā ē′ tā äd in fur′ nōs) "In the name of the lord of hosts and his son, get thee to the lower world" (Latin).

HALE, *grasping* ABIGAIL: Abigail, it may be your cousin is dying. Did you call the Devil last night?

ABIGAIL: I never called him! Tituba, Tituba . . .

PARRIS, *blanched:* She called the Devil?

HALE: I should like to speak with Tituba.

PARRIS: Goody Ann, will you bring her up? MRS. PUTNAM *exits.*

HALE: How did she call him?

ABIGAIL: I know not—she spoke Barbados.

HALE: Did you feel any strangeness when she called him? A sudden cold wind, perhaps? A trembling below the ground?

ABIGAIL: I didn't see no Devil! *Shaking* BETTY: Betty, wake up. Betty! Betty!

HALE: You cannot evade me, Abigail. Did your cousin drink any of the brew in that kettle?

ABIGAIL: She never drank it!

HALE: Did you drink it?

ABIGAIL: No, sir!

HALE: Did Tituba ask you to drink it?

ABIGAIL: She tried, but I refused.

HALE: Why are you concealing? Have you sold yourself to Lucifer?

ABIGAIL: I never sold myself! I'm a good girl! I'm a proper girl!

MRS. PUTNAM *enters with* TITUBA, *and instantly* ABIGAIL *points at* TITUBA.

Reading Strategy
Questioning the Characters' Motives Why does Hale want to speak with Tituba?

Reading Check

What important details does Parris add to Abigail's story? How does she explain them?

ABIGAIL: She made me do it! She made Betty do it!

TITUBA, *shocked and angry:* Abby!

ABIGAIL: She makes me drink blood!

PARRIS: Blood!!

MRS. PUTNAM: My baby's blood?

TITUBA: No, no, chicken blood. I give she chicken blood!

HALE: Woman, have you enlisted these children for the Devil?

TITUBA: No, no, sir, I don't truck with no Devil!

HALE: Why can she not wake? Are you silencing this child?

TITUBA: I love me Betty!

HALE: You have sent your spirit out upon this child, have you not? Are you gathering souls for the Devil?

ABIGAIL: She sends her spirit on me in church; she makes me laugh at prayer!

PARRIS: She have often laughed at prayer!

ABIGAIL: She comes to me every night to go and drink blood!

TITUBA: You beg *me* to conjure! She beg *me* make charm—

ABIGAIL: Don't lie! *To* HALE: She comes to me while I sleep; she's always making me dream corruptions!

TITUBA: Why you say that, Abby?

ABIGAIL: Sometimes I wake and find myself standing in the open doorway and not a stitch on my body! I always hear her laughing in my sleep. I hear her singing her Barbados songs and tempting me with—

TITUBA: Mister Reverend, I never—

HALE, *resolved now:* Tituba, I want you to wake this child.

TITUBA: I have no power on this child, sir.

HALE: You most certainly do, and you will free her from it now! When did you compact with the Devil?

TITUBA: I don't compact with no Devil!

PARRIS: You will confess yourself or I will take you out and whip you to your death, Tituba!

PUTNAM: This woman must be hanged! She must be taken and hanged!

TITUBA, *terrified, falls to her knees:* No, no, don't hang Tituba! I tell him I don't desire to work for him, sir.

PARRIS: The Devil?

HALE: Then you saw him! TITUBA *weeps.* Now Tituba, I know that when we bind ourselves to Hell it is very hard to break with it. We are going to help you tear yourself free—

TITUBA, *frightened by the coming process:* Mister Reverend, I do believe somebody else be witchin' these children.

HALE: Who?

TITUBA: I don't know, sir, but the Devil got him numerous witches.

Reading Strategy

Questioning the Characters' Motives
What do you think Abigail is trying to do in accusing Tituba of making her "laugh at prayer"?

Reading Strategy

Questioning the Characters' Motives
What does this dialogue reveal about the motives for Tituba's sudden confession?

HALE: Does he! *It is a clue.* Tituba, look into my eyes. Come, look into me. *She raises her eyes to his fearfully.* You would be a good Christian woman, would you not, Tituba?

TITUBA: Aye, sir, a good Christian woman.

HALE: And you love these little children?

TITUBA: Oh, yes, sir, I don't desire to hurt little children.

HALE: And you love God, Tituba?

TITUBA: I love God with all my bein'.

HALE: Now, in God's holy name—

TITUBA: Bless Him. Bless Him. *She is rocking on her knees, sobbing in terror.*

HALE: And to His glory—

TITUBA: Eternal glory. Bless Him—bless God . . .

HALE: Open yourself, Tituba—open yourself and let God's holy light shine on you.

TITUBA: Oh, bless the Lord.

HALE: When the Devil come to you does he ever come—with another person? *She stares up into his face.* Perhaps another person in the village? Someone you know.

PARRIS: Who came with him?

PUTNAM: Sarah Good? Did you ever see Sarah Good with him? Or Osburn?

PARRIS: Was it man or woman came with him?

TITUBA: Man or woman. Was—was woman.

PARRIS: What woman? A woman, you said. What woman?

TITUBA: It was black dark, and I—

PARRIS: You could see him, why could you not see her?

TITUBA: Well, they was always talking; they was always runnin' round and carryin' on—

PARRIS: You mean out of Salem? Salem witches?

TITUBA: I believe so, yes, sir.

Now HALE *takes her hand. She is surprised.*

HALE: Tituba. You must have no fear to tell us who they are, do you understand? We will protect you. The Devil can never overcome a minister. You know that, do you not?

TITUBA, *kisses* HALE's *hand:* Aye, sir, oh, I do.

HALE: You have confessed yourself to witchcraft, and that speaks a wish to come to Heaven's side. And we will bless you, Tituba.

TITUBA, *deeply relieved:* Oh, God bless you, Mr. Hale!

HALE, *with rising exaltation:* You are God's instrument put in our hands to discover the Devil's agent among us. You are selected, Tituba, you are chosen to help us cleanse our village. So speak utterly, Tituba,

Literary Analysis

Dialogue and Stage Directions What techniques does Miller use to indicate that Tituba is making things up?

Literary Analysis

Dialogue and Stage Directions To what does Tituba confess in this dialogue?

**Reading Check**

Who is the first person to name specific individuals?

turn your back on him and face God—face God, Tituba, and God will protect you.

TITUBA, *joining with him:* Oh, God, protect Tituba!

HALE, *kindly:* Who came to you with the Devil? Two? Three? Four? How many?

Tituba pants, and begins rocking back and forth again, staring ahead.

TITUBA: There was four. There was four.

PARRIS, *pressing in on her:* Who? Who? Their names, their names!

TITUBA, *suddenly bursting out:* Oh, how many times he bid me kill you, Mr. Parris!

PARRIS: Kill me!

TITUBA, *in a fury:* He say Mr. Parris must be kill! Mr. Parris no goodly man, Mr. Parris mean man and no gentle man, and he bid me rise out of my bed and cut your throat! *They gasp.* But I tell him "No! I don't hate that man. I don't want kill that man." But he say, "You work for me, Tituba, and I make you free! I give you pretty dress to wear, and put you way high up in the air, and you gone fly back to Barbados!" And I say, "You lie, Devil, you lie!" And then he come one stormy night to me, and he say, "Look! I have *white* people belong to me." And I look—and there was Goody Good.

PARRIS: Sarah Good!

TITUBA, *rocking and weeping:* Aye, sir, and Goody Osburn.

MRS. PUTNAM: I knew it! Goody Osburn were midwife to me three times. I begged you, Thomas, did I not? I begged him not to call Osburn because I feared her. My babies always shriveled in her hands!

HALE: Take courage, you must give us all their names. How can you bear to see this child suffering? Look at her, Tituba. *He is indicating* BETTY *on the bed.* Look at her God-given innocence; her soul is so tender; we must protect her, Tituba; the Devil is out and preying on her like a beast upon the flesh of the pure lamb. God will bless you for your help.

ABIGAIL *rises, staring as though inspired, and cries out.*

ABIGAIL: I want to open myself! *They turn to her, startled. She is enraptured, as though in a pearly light.* I want the light of God, I want the sweet love of Jesus! I danced for the Devil; I saw him; I wrote in his book; I go back to Jesus; I kiss His hand. I saw Sarah Good with the Devil! I saw Goody Osburn with the Devil! I saw Bridget Bishop with the Devil!

As she is speaking, BETTY *is rising from the bed, a fever in her eyes, and picks up the chant.*

BETTY, *staring too:* I saw George Jacobs with the Devil! I saw Goody Howe with the Devil!

PARRIS: She speaks! *He rushes to embrace* BETTY. She speaks!

HALE: Glory to God! It is broken, they are free!

Reading Strategy
Questioning the Characters' Motives
What do you think motivates Hale to speak "kindly" to Tituba?

BETTY, *calling out hysterically and with great relief:* I saw Martha Bellows with the Devil!

ABIGAIL: I saw Goody Sibber with the Devil! *It is rising to a great glee.*

PUTNAM: The marshal, I'll call the marshal!

PARRIS *is shouting a prayer of thanksgiving.*

BETTY: I saw Alice Barrow with the Devil!

The curtain begins to fall.

HALE, *as* PUTNAM *goes out:* Let the marshal bring irons!

ABIGAIL: I saw Goody Hawkins with the Devil!

BETTY: I saw Goody Bibber with the Devil!

ABIGAIL: I saw Goody Booth with the Devil!

On their ecstatic cries—

THE CURTAIN FALLS

Review and Assess

Thinking About Act I

1. **Respond:** Were you surprised when the accusations against specific individuals multiplied? Explain.

2. **(a) Recall:** What is Betty's condition when the play opens? **(b) Recall:** What does Abigail say that she and Betty were doing in the forest? **(c) Infer:** What seems to be the main motivation for Reverend Parris's concern about the girls' behavior in the forest?

3. **(a) Recall:** What do Abigail, Betty, Mercy, and Mary discuss after Reverend Parris leaves his daughter's room? **(b) Interpret:** What events does this scene suggest may occur later in the play?

4. **(a) Recall:** Who is Reverend Hale? **(b) Recall:** Why is he contacted? **(c) Evaluate:** Do you think he is being fair and impartial so far? Why or why not?

5. **(a) Summarize:** Summarize Abigail's prior relationship with the Proctors. **(b) Interpret:** What does Betty's revelation about Abigail's actions in the forest suggest about Abigail's feelings for Goody Proctor?

6. **(a) Support:** What evidence suggests that sharp divisions exist among the people of Salem Village? **(b) Apply:** Name two others who may be accused. Explain your choices.

7. **Evaluate:** Which situations, if any, in contemporary life might cause an American town to be afflicted with a general hysteria? Explain.

Review and Assess

Literary Analysis

Dialogue and Stage Directions

1. Use a chart like the one shown to analyze the character of Abigail Williams. To respond, combine details from her **dialogue** with Miller's descriptions of her in the **stage directions.**

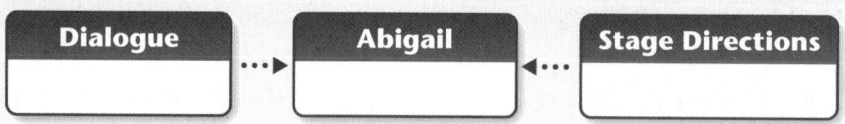

2. In the scene between Abigail and John Proctor, in what ways do the stage directions add to your understanding of their relationship?

Connecting Literary Elements

3. (a) Why does Miller include such extensive background information about seventeenth-century Salem and its inhabitants? (b) To whom is this information addressed? Explain.

4. What information is conveyed about the play's basic situation in the first three paragraphs of stage directions?

5. What technique does Miller use to provide important information about the recent activities of several village girls? Explain.

6. When Reverend Hale enters the scene, what two historic events does Miller compare in his **dramatic exposition**?

Reading Strategy

Questioning the Characters' Motives

7. What do Reverend Parris's comments and actions reveal about his **motivations**?

8. What do Abigail's actions in the forest and her threat to the girls reveal about her motives?

9. What is Putnam's motive for asking Tituba whether she saw Sarah Good or Goody Osburn in the woods?

Extend Understanding

10. **Cultural Connection:** Which elements of society does Miller seem to be criticizing through the characters of Reverend Parris and the Putnams? Explain.

Quick Review

Dialogue refers to the words characters speak; it reveals characters' personalities and backgrounds.

Stage directions are the instructions the playwright provides for the director, actors, and technicians involved in putting on the play.

Dramatic exposition conveys important background information about the setting and characters.

To better understand a plot, **question characters' motives** by identifying the reasons behind their actions.

 Take It to the Net
www.phschool.com

Take the interactive self-test online to check your understanding of this selection.

Integrate Language Skills

Vocabulary Development Lesson

Word Analysis: Latin Root -grat-

From *gratus*, Latin for "pleasing," comes the root -grat-, which means "pleasing" or "agreeable." An *ingratiating* attitude, for example, is one designed to please others. Explain how -grat- relates to the meaning of these words.

   1. gratify   **2.** grateful   **3.** congratulate

Spelling Strategy

When adding a suffix that begins with a vowel to a word that ends in a silent *e*, drop the *e* and then add the suffix: *ingratiate* becomes *ingratiating*. For each word below, add the suffix given to form a new word.

   1. ignite (*-ion*)   **2.** observe (*-ance*)

Concept Development: Context

Complete each of the following sentences with the appropriate vocabulary word from page 1232.

1. ____?____ can destroy a person's reputation.
2. Months of ____?____ helped me to learn.
3. He hid his true nature by ____?____.
4. His ____?____ behavior was scandalous.
5. To soothe their gods, they made sacrifices as an act of ____?____.
6. Her ____?____ manner pleased the customers.
7. With my ____?____ for history I knew I would enjoy *The Crucible*.

Grammar and Style Lesson

Pronoun Case in Incomplete Constructions

In an **incomplete construction,** you may be uncertain about which form of pronoun to use. To decide, mentally complete the construction by inserting the missing words.

> **Example:** They want slaves, not such as *I*.
>   (complete construction: *as I am.*)

Practice Choose the pronoun that best completes each sentence.

   1. Proctor is not more sinful than (he, him).

2. Proctor has some affection for Abigail but cares more for his wife than (she, her).
3. Betty lies, but Abigail is craftier than (she, her).
4. "Blame her more than (I, me)," she says.
5. Abigail is manipulative, but Mercy Lewis is more cruel than (she, her).

Writing Application Write three sentences in which you compare two people. Use both proper nouns and correct pronouns in your sentences.

W/G *Prentice Hall Writing and Grammar Connection: Chapter 22, Section 2*

Extension Activities

Writing Write a series of **news accounts** of the events in Salem as they might be described in a Boston newspaper of the day.

Listening and Speaking Working in a group, research and then report on the belief in witches in seventeenth-century Europe. Present your findings in an **oral report. [Group Activity]**

Prepare to Read

The Crucible, Act II

Literary Analysis

Allusion

An **allusion** is a brief reference within a work to something outside
the work. Usually, an allusion relates to one of the following:

- Another literary work
- A well-known person
- A place
- A historical event

The Crucible makes many biblical allusions. For example, Act I
contains a reference to the New Jerusalem, a term for the holy
city of heaven. Use a chart like the one shown to record biblical
allusions in Act II.

Connecting Literary Elements

To bring the Puritans to life on stage, Miller incorporates details of
historical context, the key factors of life in the time period in which a
literary work is set. Biblical allusions are one aspect of this re-creation
of a historic time and place; the Puritans were a deeply religious people
whose convictions help to set the play's action in motion. As you read,
notice the ways in which Puritan ideas influence the action.

```
   Biblical
   Allusion
      |
      v
 What It Means

      |
      v
 Value to Text
```

Reading Strategy

Reading Drama

When you **read a drama** instead of watching the action and staging,
you read the stage directions. Stage directions often interrupt the dialogue,
but they provide critical information. As you read, pay close attention
to the stage directions to understand the thoughts, attitudes, and behavior of the characters.

Vocabulary Development

pallor (pal´ ər) *n.* paleness (p. 1271)

ameliorate (ə mēl´ yə rāt) *v.* make better
(p. 1271)

avidly (av´ id lē) *adv.* eagerly (p. 1272)

base (bās) *adj.* low; mean (p. 1275)

deference (def´ ər əns) *n.* courteous
regard or respect (p. 1275)

theology (thē äl´ ə jē) *n.* the study
of religion (p. 1276)

quail (kwāl) *v.* cringe from (p. 1280)

gingerly (jin´ jər´ lē) *adv.* cautiously
(p. 1281)

abomination (ə bäm´ ə nā´ shən) *n.*
something that causes great horror
or disgust (p. 1286)

blasphemy (blas´ fə mē´) *n.* sinful act
or remark (p. 1286)

Review and Anticipate

As Act I draws to a close, Salem is in the grip of mounting hysteria. What had begun as concern over the strange behavior of Betty—a reaction that may have stemmed from guilty feelings about her activities in the woods the night before—had swelled by the Act's end to a mass hysteria in which accusations of witchcraft were being made and accepted against a growing number of Salem's citizens. Which characters do you think will believe the accusations? Who do you think will be accused next?

ACT II

The common room of PROCTOR'*s house, eight days later.*

At the right is a door opening on the fields outside.
A fireplace is at the left, and behind it a stairway leading upstairs. It is the low, dark, and rather long living room of the time. As the curtain rises, the room is empty. From above, ELIZABETH *is heard softly singing to the children. Presently the door opens and* JOHN PROCTOR *enters, carrying his gun. He glances about the room as he comes toward the fireplace, then halts for an instant as he hears her singing. He continues on to the fireplace, leans the gun against the wall as he swings a pot out of the fire and smells it. Then he lifts out the ladle and tastes. He is not quite pleased. He reaches to a cupboard, takes a pinch of salt, and drops it into the pot. As he is tasting again, her footsteps are heard on the stair. He swings the pot into the fireplace and goes to a basin and washes his hands and face.* ELIZABETH *enters.*

ELIZABETH: What keeps you so late? It's almost dark.

PROCTOR: I were planting far out to the forest edge.

ELIZABETH: Oh, you're done then.

PROCTOR: Aye, the farm is seeded. The boys asleep?

ELIZABETH: They will be soon. *And she goes to the fireplace, proceeds to ladle up stew in a dish.*

PROCTOR: Pray now for a fair summer.

ELIZABETH: Aye.

PROCTOR: Are you well today?

ELIZABETH: I am. *She brings the plate to the table, and, indicating the food:* It is a rabbit.

PROCTOR, *going to the table:* Oh, is it! In Jonathan's trap?

ELIZABETH: No, she walked into the house this afternoon; I found her sittin' in the corner like she come to visit.

PROCTOR: Oh, that's a good sign walkin' in.

ELIZABETH: Pray God. It hurt my heart to strip her, poor rabbit. *She sits and watches him taste it.*

Reading Strategy

Reading Drama What important information do you learn about the amount of time passed between Act I and Act II?

✔**Reading Check**

At what time of day does this scene take place?

PROCTOR: It's well seasoned.

ELIZABETH, *blushing with pleasure:* I took great care. She's tender?

PROCTOR: Aye. *He eats. She watches him.* I think we'll see green fields soon. It's warm as blood beneath the clods.

ELIZABETH: That's well.

PROCTOR *eats, then looks up.*

PROCTOR: If the crop is good I'll buy George Jacob's heifer. How would that please you?

ELIZABETH: Aye, it would.

PROCTOR, *with a grin:* I mean to please you, Elizabeth.

ELIZABETH—*it is hard to say:* I know it, John.

He gets up, goes to her, kisses her. She receives it. With a certain disappointment, he returns to the table.

PROCTOR, *as gently as he can:* Cider?

ELIZABETH, *with a sense of reprimanding herself for having forgot:* Aye! *She gets up and goes and pours a glass for him. He now arches his back.*

PROCTOR: This farm's a continent when you go foot by foot droppin' seeds in it.

ELIZABETH, *coming with the cider:* It must be.

PROCTOR, *drinks a long draught, then, putting the glass down:* You ought to bring some flowers in the house.

ELIZABETH: Oh! I forgot! I will tomorrow.

PROCTOR: It's winter in here yet. On Sunday let you come with me, and we'll walk the farm together; I never see such a load of flowers on the earth. *With good feeling he goes and looks up at the sky through the open doorway.* Lilacs have a purple smell. Lilac is the smell of nightfall, I think. Massachusetts is a beauty in the spring!

ELIZABETH: Aye, it is.

There is a pause. She is watching him from the table as he stands there absorbing the night. It is as though she would speak but cannot. Instead, now, she takes up his plate and glass and fork and goes with them to the basin. Her back is turned to him. He turns to her and watches her. A sense of their separation rises.

PROCTOR: I think you're sad again. Are you?

ELIZABETH—*she doesn't want friction, and yet she must:* You come so late I thought you'd gone to Salem this afternoon.

PROCTOR: Why? I have no business in Salem.

ELIZABETH: You did speak of going, earlier this week.

PROCTOR—*he knows what she means:* I thought better of it since.

ELIZABETH: Mary Warren's there today.

PROCTOR: Why'd you let her? You heard me forbid her go to Salem any more!

ELIZABETH: I couldn't stop her.

Reading Strategy
Reading Drama What do you learn about Elizabeth's feelings toward her husband from these stage directions?

Reading Strategy
Reading Drama How do these stage directions help prepare you for Proctor's remark that Elizabeth seems sad?

PROCTOR, *holding back a full condemnation of her:* It is a fault, it is a fault, Elizabeth—you're the mistress here, not Mary Warren.

ELIZABETH: She frightened all my strength away.

PROCTOR: How may that mouse frighten you, Elizabeth? You—

ELIZABETH: It is a mouse no more. I forbid her go, and she raises up her chin like the daughter of a prince and says to me, "I must go to Salem, Goody Proctor; I am an official of the court!"

PROCTOR: Court! What court?

ELIZABETH: Aye, it is a proper court they have now. They've sent four judges out of Boston, she says, weighty magistrates of the General Court, and at the head sits the Deputy Governor of the Province.

PROCTOR, *astonished:* Why, she's mad.

ELIZABETH: I would to God she were. There be fourteen people in the jail now, she says. PROCTOR *simply looks at her, unable to grasp it.* And they'll be tried, and the court have power to hang them too, she says.

PROCTOR, *scoffing but without conviction:* Ah, they'd never hang—

ELIZABETH: The Deputy Governor promise hangin' if they'll not confess, John. The town's gone wild, I think. She speak of Abigail, and I thought she were a saint, to hear her. Abigail brings the other girls into the court, and where she walks the crowd will part like the sea for Israel.[1] And folks are brought before them, and if they scream and howl and fall to the floor—the person's clapped in the jail for bewitchin' them.

PROCTOR, *wide-eyed:* Oh, it is a black mischief.

ELIZABETH: I think you must go to Salem, John. *He turns to her.* I think so. You must tell them it is a fraud.

PROCTOR, *thinking beyond this:* Aye, it is, it is surely.

ELIZABETH: Let you go to Ezekiel Cheever—he knows you well. And tell him what she said to you last week in her uncle's house. She said it had naught to do with witchcraft, did she not?

PROCTOR, *in thought:* Aye, she did, she did. *Now, a pause.*

ELIZABETH, *quietly, fearing to anger him by prodding:* God forbid you keep that from the court, John. I think they must be told.

PROCTOR, *quietly, struggling with his thought:* Aye, they must, they must. It is a wonder they do believe her.

ELIZABETH: I would go to Salem now, John—let you go tonight.

PROCTOR: I'll think on it.

ELIZABETH, *with her courage now:* You cannot keep it, John.

PROCTOR, *angering:* I know I cannot keep it. I say I will think on it!

ELIZABETH, *hurt, and very coldly:* Good, then, let you think on it. *She stands and starts to walk out of the room.*

PROCTOR: I am only wondering how I may prove what she told me, Elizabeth. If the girl's a saint now, I think it is not easy to prove she's

---

1. **part like . . . Israel** In the Bible, God commanded Moses, the leader of the Jews, to part the Red Sea to enable the Jews to escape from the Egyptians into Canaan.

Literary Analysis
Allusion What does Elizabeth's allusion to Moses' parting of the Red Sea reveal about Abigail's new standing in the community?

Reading Strategy
Reading Drama How would you describe Elizabeth's changing emotions as she challenges John?

Reading Check
What does Elizabeth want John to do?

fraud, and the town gone so silly. She told it to me in a room alone—I have no proof for it.

ELIZABETH: You were alone with her?

PROCTOR, *stubbornly:* For a moment alone, aye.

ELIZABETH: Why, then, it is not as you told me.

PROCTOR, *his anger rising:* For a moment, I say. The others come in soon after.

ELIZABETH, *quietly—she has suddenly lost all faith in him:* Do as you wish, then. *She starts to turn.*

PROCTOR: Woman. *She turns to him.* I'll not have your suspicion any more.

ELIZABETH, *a little loftily:* I have no—

PROCTOR: I'll not have it!

ELIZABETH: Then let you not earn it.

PROCTOR, *with a violent undertone:* You doubt me yet?

ELIZABETH, *with a smile, to keep her dignity:* John, if it were not Abigail that you must go to hurt, would you falter now? I think not.

PROCTOR: Now look you—

ELIZABETH: I see what I see, John.

PROCTOR, *with solemn warning:* You will not judge me more, Elizabeth. I have good reason to think before I charge fraud on Abigail, and I will think on it. Let you look to your own improvement before you go to judge your husband any more. I have forgot Abigail, and—

ELIZABETH: And I.

PROCTOR: Spare me! You forget nothin' and forgive nothin'. Learn charity, woman. I have gone tiptoe in this house all seven month since she is gone. I have not moved from there to there without I think to please you, and still an everlasting funeral marches round your heart. I cannot speak but I am doubted, every moment judged for lies, as though I come into a court when I come into this house!

ELIZABETH: John, you are not open with me. You saw her with a crowd, you said. Now you—

PROCTOR: I'll plead my honesty no more, Elizabeth.

ELIZABETH—*now she would justify herself:* John, I am only—

PROCTOR: No more! I should have roared you down when first you told me your suspicion. But I wilted, and, like a Christian, I confessed. Confessed! Some dream I had must have mistaken you for God that day. But you're not, you're not, and let you remember it! Let you look sometimes for the goodness in me, and judge me not.

▲ **Critical Viewing**
What aspects of the Proctor's lives early in the play seem likely to result in the emotional intensity shown on John Proctor's face in this photo?
[Anticipate]

ELIZABETH: I do not judge you. The magistrate sits in your heart that judges you. I never thought you but a good man, John—*with a smile—only somewhat bewildered.*

PROCTOR, *laughing bitterly:* Oh, Elizabeth, your justice would freeze beer! *He turns suddenly toward a sound outside. He starts for the door as* MARY WARREN *enters. As soon as he sees her, he goes directly to her and grabs her by the cloak, furious.* How do you go to Salem when I forbid it? Do you mock me? *Shaking her.* I'll whip you if you dare leave this house again!

Strangely, she doesn't resist him, but hangs limply by his grip.

MARY WARREN: I am sick, I am sick, Mr. Proctor. Pray, pray, hurt me not. *Her strangeness throws him off, and her evident <u>pallor</u> and weakness. He frees her.* My insides are all shuddery; I am in the proceedings all day, sir.

PROCTOR, *with draining anger—his curiosity is draining it:* And what of these proceedings here? When will you proceed to keep this house, as you are paid nine pound a year to do—and my wife not wholly well?

As though to compensate, MARY WARREN *goes to* ELIZABETH *with a small rag doll.*

MARY WARREN: I made a gift for you today, Goody Proctor. I had to sit long hours in a chair, and passed the time with sewing.

ELIZABETH, *perplexed, looking at the doll:* Why, thank you, it's a fair poppet.[2]

MARY WARREN, *with a trembling, decayed voice:* We must all love each other now, Goody Proctor.

ELIZABETH, *amazed at her strangeness:* Aye, indeed we must.

MARY WARREN, *glancing at the room:* I'll get up early in the morning and clean the house. I must sleep now. *She turns and starts off.*

PROCTOR: Mary. *She halts.* Is it true? There be fourteen women arrested?

MARY WARREN: No, sir. There be thirty-nine now— *She suddenly breaks off and sobs and sits down, exhausted.*

ELIZABETH: Why, she's weepin'! What ails you, child?

MARY WARREN: Goody Osburn—will hang!

There is a shocked pause, while she sobs.

PROCTOR: Hang! *He calls into her face.* Hang, y'say?

MARY WARREN, *through her weeping:* Aye.

PROCTOR: The Deputy Governor will permit it?

MARY WARREN: He sentenced her. He must. *To <u>ameliorate</u> it:* But not Sarah Good. For Sarah Good confessed, y'see.

PROCTOR: Confessed! To what?

MARY WARREN: That she—*in horror at the memory*—she sometimes made a compact with Lucifer, and wrote her name in his black book—with

---

2. **poppet** doll.

pallor (pal′ ər) *n.* paleness

Reading Strategy
Reading Drama
What do these stage directions clarify?

ameliorate (ə mēl′ yə rāt′) *v.* make better

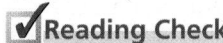**Reading Check**

What are John and Elizabeth Proctor arguing about?

her blood—and bound herself to torment Christians till God's thrown down—and we all must worship Hell forevermore.

Pause.

PROCTOR: But—surely you know what a jabberer she is. Did you tell them that?

MARY WARREN: Mr. Proctor, in open court she near to choked us all to death.

PROCTOR: How, choked you?

MARY WARREN: She sent her spirit out.

ELIZABETH: Oh, Mary, Mary, surely you—

MARY WARREN, *with an indignant edge:* She tried to kill me many times, Goody Proctor!

ELIZABETH: Why, I never heard you mention that before.

MARY WARREN: I never knew it before. I never knew anything before. When she come into the court I say to myself, I must not accuse this woman, for she sleep in ditches, and so very old and poor. But then—then she sit there, denying and denying, and I feel a misty coldness climbin' up my back, and the skin on my skull begin to creep, and I feel a clamp around my neck and I cannot breathe air; and then—*entranced*—I hear a voice, a screamin' voice, and it were my voice—and all at once I remembered everything she done to me!

PROCTOR: Why? What did she do to you?

MARY WARREN, *like one awakened to a marvelous secret insight:* So many time, Mr. Proctor, she come to this very door, beggin' bread and a cup of cider—and mark this: whenever I turned her away empty, she *mumbled.*

ELIZABETH: Mumbled! She may mumble if she's hungry.

MARY WARREN: But *what* does she mumble? You must remember, Goody Proctor. Last month—a Monday, I think—she walked away, and I thought my guts would burst for two days after. Do you remember it?

ELIZABETH: Why—I do, I think, but—

MARY WARREN: And so I told that to Judge Hathorne, and he asks her so. "Goody Osburn," says he, "what curse do you mumble that this girl must fall sick after turning you away?" And then she replies—*mimicking an old crone*—"Why, your excellence, no curse at all. I only say my commandments; I hope I may say my commandments," says she!

ELIZABETH: And that's an upright answer.

MARY WARREN: Aye, but then Judge Hathorne say, "Recite for us your commandments!"—*leaning avidly toward them*—and of all the ten she could not say a single one. She never knew no commandments, and they had her in a flat lie!

PROCTOR: And so condemned her?

MARY WARREN, *now a little strained, seeing his stubborn doubt:* Why, they must when she condemned herself.

avidly (av′ id lē) *adv.* eagerly

PROCTOR: But the proof, the proof!

MARY WARREN, *with greater impatience with him:* I told you the proof. It's hard proof, hard as rock, the judges said.

PROCTOR, *pauses an instant, then:* You will not go to court again, Mary Warren.

MARY WARREN: I must tell you, sir, I will be gone every day now. I am amazed you do not see what weighty work we do.

PROCTOR: What work you do! It's strange work for a Christian girl to hang old women!

MARY WARREN: But, Mr. Proctor, they will not hang them if they confess. Sarah Good will only sit in jail some time—*recalling*—and here's a wonder for you; think on this. Goody Good is pregnant!

ELIZABETH: Pregnant! Are they mad? The woman's near to sixty!

MARY WARREN: They had Doctor Griggs examine her, and she's full to the brim. And smokin' a pipe all these years, and no husband either! But she's safe, thank God, for they'll not hurt the innocent child. But be that not a marvel? You must see it, sir, it's God's work we do. So I'll be gone every day for some time. I'm—I am an official of the court, they say, and I—*She has been edging toward offstage.*

PROCTOR: I'll official you! *He strides to the mantel, takes down the whip hanging there.*

MARY WARREN, *terrified, but coming erect, striving for her authority:* I'll not stand whipping any more!

ELIZABETH, *hurriedly, as* PROCTOR *approaches:* Mary, promise you'll stay at home—

MARY WARREN, *backing from him, but keeping her erect posture, striving, striving for her way:* The Devil's loose in Salem, Mr. Proctor; we must discover where he's hiding!

PROCTOR: I'll whip the Devil out of you! *With whip raised he reaches out for her, and she streaks away and yells.*

MARY WARREN, *pointing at* ELIZABETH: I saved her life today!

Silence. His whip comes down.

ELIZABETH, *softly:* I am accused?

MARY WARREN, *quaking:* Somewhat mentioned. But I said I never see no sign you ever sent your spirit out to hurt no one, and seeing I do live so closely with you, they dismissed it.

ELIZABETH: Who accused me?

MARY WARREN: I am bound by law, I cannot tell it. *To* PROCTOR: I only hope you'll not be so sarcastical no more. Four judges and the King's deputy sat to dinner with us but an hour ago. I—I would have you speak civilly to me, from this out.

PROCTOR, *in horror, muttering in disgust at her:* Go to bed.

MARY WARREN, *with a stamp of her foot:* I'll not be ordered to bed no more, Mr. Proctor! I am eighteen and a woman, however single!

Reading Strategy
Reading Drama What change has Mary's participation in the court proceedings brought in her attitude toward the Proctors?

**Reading Check**

What evidence does Mary Warren use to prove that Goody Osborn is a witch?

PROCTOR: Do you wish to sit up? Then sit up.

MARY WARREN: I wish to go to bed!

PROCTOR, *in anger:* Good night, then!

MARY WARREN: Good night. *Dissatisfied, uncertain of herself, she goes out. Wide-eyed, both* PROCTOR *and* ELIZABETH *stand staring.*

ELIZABETH, *quietly:* Oh, the noose, the noose is up!

PROCTOR: There'll be no noose.

ELIZABETH: She wants me dead. I knew all week it would come to this!

PROCTOR, *without conviction:* They dismissed it. You heard her say—

ELIZABETH: And what of tomorrow? She will cry me out until they take me!

PROCTOR: Sit you down.

ELIZABETH: She wants me dead, John, you know it!

PROCTOR: I say sit down! *She sits, trembling. He speaks quickly, trying to keep his wits.* Now we must be wise, Elizabeth.

ELIZABETH, *with sarcasm, and a sense of being lost:* Oh, indeed, indeed!

PROCTOR: Fear nothing. I'll find Ezekiel Cheever. I'll tell him she said it were all sport.

ELIZABETH: John, with so many in the jail, more than Cheever's help is needed now, I think. Would you favor me with this? Go to Abigail.

PROCTOR, *his soul hardening as he senses . . .:* What have I to say to Abigail?

ELIZABETH, *delicately:* John—grant me this. You have a faulty understanding of young girls. There is a promise made in any bed—

PROCTOR, *striving against his anger:* What promise!

ELIZABETH: Spoke or silent, a promise is surely made. And she may dote on it now—I am sure she does—and thinks to kill me, then to take my place.

PROCTOR'S *anger is rising; he cannot speak.*

ELIZABETH: It is her dearest hope, John, I know it. There be a thousand names; why does she call mine? There be a certain danger in calling such a name—I am no Goody Good that sleeps in ditches, nor Osburn, drunk and half-witted. She'd dare not call out such a farmer's wife but there be monstrous profit in it. She thinks to take my place, John.

PROCTOR: She cannot think it! *He knows it is true.*

ELIZABETH, *"reasonably":* John, have you ever shown her somewhat of contempt? She cannot pass you in the church but you will blush—

PROCTOR: I may blush for my sin.

ELIZABETH: I think she sees another meaning in that blush.

PROCTOR: And what see you? What see you, Elizabeth?

ELIZABETH, *"conceding":* I think you be somewhat ashamed, for I am there, and she so close.

PROCTOR: When will you know me, woman? Were I stone I would have cracked for shame this seven month!

Reading Strategy
Reading Drama How do the stage directions indicating that Proctor speaks "without conviction" affect your understanding of his line?

ELIZABETH: Then go and tell her she's a whore. Whatever promise she may sense—break it, John, break it.

PROCTOR, *between his teeth:* Good, then. I'll go. *He starts for his rifle.*

ELIZABETH, *trembling, fearfully:* Oh, how unwillingly!

PROCTOR, *turning on her, rifle in hand:* I will curse her hotter than the oldest cinder in hell. But pray, begrudge me not my anger!

ELIZABETH: Your anger! I only ask you—

PROCTOR: Woman, am I so <u>base</u>? Do you truly think me base?

ELIZABETH: I never called you base.

PROCTOR: Then how do you charge me with such a promise? The promise that a stallion gives a mare I gave that girl!

ELIZABETH: Then why do you anger with me when I bid you break it?

PROCTOR: Because it speaks deceit, and I am honest! But I'll plead no more! I see now your spirit twists around the single error of my life, and I will never tear it free!

ELIZABETH, *crying out:* You'll tear it free—when you come to know that I will be your only wife, or no wife at all! She has an arrow in you yet, John Proctor, and you know it well!

Quite suddenly, as though from the air, a figure appears in the doorway. They start slightly. It is MR. HALE. *He is different now—drawn a little, and there is a quality of <u>deference</u>, even of guilt, about his manner now.*

HALE: Good evening.

PROCTOR, *still in his shock:* Why, Mr. Hale! Good evening to you, sir. Come in, come in.

HALE, *to Elizabeth:* I hope I do not startle you.

ELIZABETH: No, no, it's only that I heard no horse—

HALE: You are Goodwife Proctor.

PROCTOR: Aye; Elizabeth.

HALE, *nods, then:* I hope you're not off to bed yet.

PROCTOR, *setting down his gun:* No, no. HALE *comes further into the room. And* PROCTOR, *to explain his nervousness:* We are not used to visitors after dark, but you're welcome here. Will you sit you down, sir?

HALE: I will. *He sits.* Let you sit, Goodwife Proctor.

She does, never letting him out of her sight. There is a pause as HALE *looks about the room.*

PROCTOR, *to break the silence:* Will you drink cider, Mr. Hale?

HALE: No, it rebels my stomach; I have some further traveling yet tonight. Sit you down, sir. PROCTOR *sits.* I will not keep you long, but I have some business with you.

PROCTOR: Business of the court?

HALE: No—no, I come of my own, without the court's authority. Hear me. *He wets his lips.* I know not if you are aware, but your wife's name is—mentioned in the court.

---

base (bās) *adj.* low; mean

deference (def´ ər əns) *n.* courteous regard or respect

Reading Strategy

Reading Drama Why is the silent pause indicated by the stage directions important?

**Reading Check**

What does Elizabeth fear that Abigail will do to her?

PROCTOR: We know it, sir. Our Mary Warren told us. We are entirely amazed.

HALE: I am a stranger here, as you know. And in my ignorance I find it hard to draw a clear opinion of them that come accused before the court. And so this afternoon, and now tonight, I go from house to house—I come now from Rebecca Nurse's house and—

ELIZABETH, *shocked:* Rebecca's charged!

HALE: God forbid such a one be charged. She is, however—mentioned somewhat.

ELIZABETH, *with an attempt at a laugh:* You will never believe, I hope, that Rebecca trafficked with the Devil.

HALE: Woman, it is possible.

PROCTOR, *taken aback:* Surely you cannot think so.

HALE: This is a strange time, Mister. No man may longer doubt the powers of the dark are gathered in monstrous attack upon this village. There is too much evidence now to deny it. You will agree, sir?

PROCTOR, *evading:* I—have no knowledge in that line. But it's hard to think so pious a woman be secretly a Devil's bitch after seventy year of such good prayer.

HALE: Aye. But the Devil is a wily one, you cannot deny it. However, she is far from accused, and I know she will not be. *Pause.* I thought, sir, to put some questions as to the Christian character of this house, if you'll permit me.

PROCTOR, *coldly, resentful:* Why, we—have no fear of questions, sir.

HALE: Good, then. *He makes himself more comfortable.* In the book of record that Mr. Parris keeps, I note that you are rarely in the church on Sabbath Day.

PROCTOR: No, sir, you are mistaken.

HALE: Twenty-six time in seventeen month, sir. I must call that rare. Will you tell me why you are so absent?

PROCTOR: Mr. Hale, I never knew I must account to that man for I come to church or stay at home. My wife were sick this winter.

HALE: So I am told. But you, Mister, why could you not come alone?

PROCTOR: I surely did come when I could, and when I could not I prayed in this house.

HALE: Mr. Proctor, your house is not a church; your <u>theology</u> must tell you that.

PROCTOR: It does, sir, it does; and it tells me that a minister may pray to God without he have golden candlesticks upon the altar.

HALE: What golden candlesticks?

PROCTOR: Since we built the church there were pewter candlesticks upon the altar; Francis Nurse made them y'know, and a sweeter hand never touched the metal. But Parris came, and for twenty week he preach nothin' but golden candlesticks until he had them. I labor the earth from dawn of day to blink of night, and I tell you true when I look

Reading Strategy
Reading Drama What do the stage directions here reveal about Elizabeth's true emotions?

theology (thē äl′ ə jē) *n.* the study of religion

Literary Analysis
Allusion and Historical Context What do you know about the Puritans and their "plain style" that affects your interpretation of the golden candlesticks?

to heaven and see my money glaring at his elbows—it hurt my prayer, sir, it hurt my prayer. I think, sometimes, the man dreams cathedrals, not clapboard meetin' houses.

HALE, *thinks, then:* And yet, Mister, a Christian on Sabbath Day must be in church. *Pause.* Tell me—you have three children?

PROCTOR: Aye. Boys.

HALE: How comes it that only two are baptized?

PROCTOR, *starts to speak, then stops, then, as though unable to restrain this:* I like it not that Mr. Parris should lay his hand upon my baby. I see no light of God in that man. I'll not conceal it.

HALE: I must say it, Mr. Proctor; that is not for you to decide. The man's ordained, therefore the light of God is in him.

PROCTOR, *flushed with resentment but trying to smile:* What's your suspicion, Mr. Hale?

HALE: No, no, I have no—

PROCTOR: I nailed the roof upon the church, I hung the door—

HALE: Oh, did you! That's a good sign, then.

PROCTOR: It may be I have been too quick to bring the man to book, but you cannot think we ever desired the destruction of religion. I think that's in your mind, is it not?

HALE, *not altogether giving way:* I—have—there is a softness in your record, sir, a softness.

ELIZABETH: I think, maybe, we have been too hard with Mr. Parris. I think so. But sure we never loved the Devil here.

HALE, *nods, deliberating this. Then, with the voice of one administering a secret test:* Do you know your Commandments, Elizabeth?

ELIZABETH, *without hesitation, even eagerly:* I surely do. There be no mark of blame upon my life, Mr. Hale. I am a covenanted Christian woman.

HALE: And you, Mister?

PROCTOR, *a trifle unsteadily:* I—am sure I do, sir.

HALE, *glances at her open face, then at* JOHN, *then:* Let you repeat them, if you will.

PROCTOR: The Commandments.

HALE: Aye.

PROCTOR, *looking off, beginning to sweat:* Thou shalt not kill.

HALE: Aye.

PROCTOR, *counting on his fingers:* Thou shalt not steal. Thou shalt not covet thy neighbor's goods, nor make unto thee any graven image. Thou shalt not take the name of the Lord in vain; thou shalt have no other gods before me. *With some hesitation:* Thou shalt remember the Sabbath Day and keep it holy. *Pause. Then:* Thou shalt honor thy father and mother. Thou shalt not bear false witness. *He is stuck. He counts back on his fingers, knowing one is missing.* Thou shalt not make unto thee any graven image.

Reading Strategy
Reading Drama What does this passage reveal about Proctor's attitude toward Parris as a minister.

Reading Check

What aspects of the Proctor household does Hale question?

HALE: You have said that twice, sir.

PROCTOR, *lost:* Aye. *He is flailing for it.*

ELIZABETH, *delicately:* Adultery, John.

PROCTOR, *as though a secret arrow had pained his heart:* Aye. *Trying to grin it away—to* HALE: You see, sir, between the two of us we do know them all. HALE *only looks at* PROCTOR, *deep in his attempt to define this man.* PROCTOR *grows more uneasy.* I think it be a small fault.

HALE: Theology, sir, is a fortress; no crack in a fortress may be accounted small. *He rises; he seems worried now. He paces a little, in deep thought.*

PROCTOR: There be no love for Satan in this house, Mister.

HALE: I pray it, I pray it dearly. *He looks to both of them, an attempt at a smile on his face, but his misgivings are clear.* Well, then—I'll bid you good night.

ELIZABETH, *unable to restrain herself:* Mr. Hale. *He turns.* I do think you are suspecting me somewhat? Are you not?

HALE, *obviously disturbed—and evasive:* Goody Proctor, I do not judge you. My duty is to add what I may to the godly wisdom of the court. I pray you both good health and good fortune. *To* JOHN: Good night, sir. *He starts out.*

ELIZABETH, *with a note of desperation:* I think you must tell him, John.

HALE: What's that?

ELIZABETH, *restraining a call:* Will you tell him?

Slight pause. HALE *looks questioningly at* JOHN.

PROCTOR, *with difficulty:* I—I have no witness and cannot prove it, except my word be taken. But I know the children's sickness had naught to do with witchcraft.

HALE, *stopped, struck:* Naught to do—?

PROCTOR: Mr. Parris discovered them sportin' in the woods. They were startled and took sick.

Pause.

HALE: Who told you this?

PROCTOR, *hesitates, then:* Abigail Williams.

HALE: Abigail.

PROCTOR: Aye.

HALE, *his eyes wide:* Abigail Williams told you it had naught to do with witchcraft!

PROCTOR: She told me the day you came, sir.

HALE, *suspiciously:* Why—why did you keep this?

PROCTOR: I never knew until tonight that the world is gone daft with this nonsense.

HALE: Nonsense! Mister, I have myself examined Tituba, Sarah Good, and numerous others that have confessed to dealing with the Devil. They have *confessed* it.

Reading Strategy
Reading Drama How can you tell that Hale is beginning to grow suspicious of the Proctors?

PROCTOR: And why not, if they must hang for denyin' it? There are them that will swear to anything before they'll hang; have you never thought of that?

HALE: I have. I—I have indeed. *It is his own suspicion, but he resists it. He glances at* ELIZABETH, *then at* JOHN. And you—would you testify to this in court?

PROCTOR: I—had not reckoned with goin' into court. But if I must I will.

HALE: Do you falter here?

PROCTOR: I falter nothing, but I may wonder if my story will be credited in such a court. I do wonder on it, when such a steady-minded minister as you will suspicion such a woman that never lied, and cannot, and the world knows she cannot! I may falter somewhat, Mister; I am no fool.

HALE, *quietly—it has impressed him:* Proctor, let you open with me now, for I have a rumor that troubles me. It's said you hold no belief that there may even be witches in the world. Is that true, sir?

PROCTOR—*he knows this is critical, and is striving against his disgust with* HALE *and with himself for even answering:* I know not what I have said, I may have said it. I have wondered if there be witches in the world—although I cannot believe they come among us now.

HALE: Then you do not believe—

PROCTOR: I have no knowledge of it; the Bible speaks of witches, and I will not deny them.

HALE: And you, woman?

ELIZABETH: I—I cannot believe it.

HALE, *shocked:* You cannot!

PROCTOR: Elizabeth, you bewilder him!

ELIZABETH, *to* HALE: I cannot think the Devil may own a woman's soul, Mr. Hale, when she keeps an upright way, as I have. I am a good woman, I know it; and if you believe I may do only good work in the world, and yet be secretly bound to Satan, then I must tell you, sir, I do not believe it.

HALE: But, woman, you do believe there are witches in—

ELIZABETH: If you think that I am one, then I say there are none.

HALE: You surely do not fly against the Gospel, the Gospel—

PROCTOR: She believe in the Gospel, every word!

ELIZABETH: Question Abigail Williams about the Gospel, not myself!

HALE *stares at her.*

PROCTOR: She do not mean to doubt the Gospel, sir, you cannot think it. This be a Christian house, sir, a Christian house.

HALE: God keep you both; let the third child be quickly baptized, and go you without fail each Sunday to Sabbath prayer; and keep a solemn, quiet way among you. I think—

GILES COREY *appears in doorway.*

GILES: John!

Reading Strategy

Reading Drama In what way do the stage directions help you to understand that Hale wants to believe that the Proctors are good people?

**Reading Check**

What does John Proctor tell Reverend Hale about Abigail Williams?

PROCTOR: Giles! What's the matter?

GILES: They take my wife.

FRANCIS NURSE *enters.*

GILES: And his Rebecca!

PROCTOR, *to* FRANCIS: Rebecca's in the *jail!*

FRANCIS: Aye, Cheever come and take her in his wagon. We've only now come from the jail, and they'll not even let us in to see them.

ELIZABETH: They've surely gone wild now, Mr. Hale!

FRANCIS, *going to* HALE: Reverend Hale! Can you not speak to the Deputy Governor? I'm sure he mistakes these people—

HALE: Pray calm yourself, Mr. Nurse.

FRANCIS: My wife is the very brick and mortar of the church, Mr. Hale—*indicating* GILES—and Martha Corey, there cannot be a woman closer yet to God than Martha.

HALE: How is Rebecca charged, Mr. Nurse?

FRANCIS, *with a mocking, half-hearted laugh:* For murder, she's charged! *Mockingly quoting the warrant:* "For the marvelous and supernatural murder of Goody Putnam's babies." What am I to do, Mr. Hale?

HALE, *turns from* FRANCIS, *deeply troubled, then:* Believe me, Mr. Nurse, if Rebecca Nurse be tainted, then nothing's left to stop the whole green world from burning. Let you rest upon the justice of the court; the court will send her home. I know it.

FRANCIS: You cannot mean she will be tried in court!

HALE, *pleading:* Nurse, though our hearts break, we cannot flinch; these are new times, sir. There is a misty plot afoot so subtle we should be criminal to cling to old respects and ancient friendships. I have seen too many frightful proofs in court—the Devil is alive in Salem, and we dare not <u>quail</u> to follow wherever the accusing finger points!

PROCTOR, *angered:* How may such a woman murder children?

HALE, *in great pain:* Man, remember, until an hour before the Devil fell, God thought him beautiful in Heaven.

GILES: I never said my wife were a witch, Mr. Hale; I only said she were reading books!

HALE: Mr. Corey, exactly what complaint were made on your wife?

GILES: That bloody mongrel Walcott charge her. Y'see, he buy a pig of my wife four or five years ago, and the pig died soon after. So he come dancin' in for his money back. So my Martha, she says to him, "Walcott, if you haven't the wit to feed a pig properly, you'll not live to own many," she says. Now he goes to court and claims that from that day to this he cannot keep a pig alive for more than four weeks because my Martha bewitch them with her books!

Enter EZEKIEL CHEEVER. *A shocked silence.*

CHEEVER: Good evening to you, Proctor.

PROCTOR: Why, Mr. Cheever. Good evening.

quail (kwāl) *v.* cringe from

Literary Analysis
Allusion What is the meaning of this allusion to the Devil?

CHEEVER: Good evening, all. Good evening, Mr. Hale.

PROCTOR: I hope you come not on business of the court.

CHEEVER: I do, Proctor, aye. I am clerk of the court now, y'know.

Enter MARSHAL HERRICK, *a man in his early thirties, who is somewhat shamefaced at the moment.*

GILES: It's a pity, Ezekiel, that an honest tailor might have gone to Heaven must burn in Hell. You'll burn for this, do you know it?

CHEEVER: You know yourself I must do as I'm told. You surely know that, Giles. And I'd as lief[3] you'd not be sending me to Hell. I like not the sound of it, I tell you; I like not the sound of it. *He fears* PROCTOR, *but starts to reach inside his coat.* Now believe me, Proctor, how heavy be the law, all its tonnage I do carry on my back tonight. *He takes out a warrant.* I have a warrant for your wife.

PROCTOR, *to* HALE: You said she were not charged!

HALE: I know nothin' of it. *To* CHEEVER: When were she charged?

CHEEVER: I am given sixteen warrant tonight, sir, and she is one.

PROCTOR: Who charged her?

CHEEVER: Why, Abigail Williams charge her.

PROCTOR: On what proof, what proof?

CHEEVER, *looking about the room:* Mr. Proctor, I have little time. The court bid me search your house, but I like not to search a house. So will you hand me any poppets that your wife may keep here?

PROCTOR: Poppets?

ELIZABETH: I never kept no poppets, not since I were a girl.

CHEEVER, *embarrassed, glancing toward the mantel where sits* MARY WARREN'S *poppet:* I spy a poppet, Goody Proctor.

ELIZABETH: Oh! *Going for it:* Why, this is Mary's.

CHEEVER, *shyly:* Would you please to give it to me?

ELIZABETH, *handing it to him, asks* HALE: Has the court discovered a text in poppets now?

CHEEVER, *carefully holding the poppet:* Do you keep any others in this house?

PROCTOR: No, nor this one either till tonight. What signifies a poppet?

CHEEVER: Why, a poppet—*he gingerly turns the poppet over*—a poppet may signify—Now, woman, will you please to come with me?

PROCTOR: She will not! *To* ELIZABETH: Fetch Mary here.

CHEEVER, *ineptly reaching toward* ELIZABETH: No, no, I am forbid to leave her from my sight.

PROCTOR, *pushing his arm away:* You'll leave her out of sight and out of mind, Mister. Fetch Mary, Elizabeth. ELIZABETH *goes upstairs.*

HALE: What signifies a poppet, Mr. Cheever?

---

3. as lief (as lēf) *adv.* rather.

The Crucible, Act II ◆ 1281

CHEEVER, *turning the poppet over in his hands:* Why, they say it may signify that she—*he has lifted the poppet's skirt, and his eyes widen in astonished fear.* Why, this, this—

PROCTOR, *reaching for the poppet:* What's there?

CHEEVER: Why—*He draws out a long needle from the poppet*—it is a needle! Herrick, Herrick, it is a needle!

HERRICK *comes toward him.*

PROCTOR, *angrily, bewildered:* And what signifies a needle!

CHEEVER, *his hands shaking:* Why, this go hard with her, Proctor, this—I had my doubts, Proctor, I had my doubts, but here's calamity. *To* HALE, *showing the needle:* You see it, sir, it is a needle!

HALE: Why? What meanin' has it?

CHEEVER, *wide-eyed, trembling:* The girl, the Williams girl, Abigail Williams, sir. She sat to dinner in Reverend Parris's house tonight, and without word nor warnin' she falls to the floor. Like a struck beast, he says, and screamed a scream that a bull would weep to hear. And he goes to save her, and, stuck two inches in the flesh of her belly, he draw a needle out. And demandin' of her how she come to be so stabbed, she—*to* PROCTOR *now*—testify it were your wife's familiar spirit pushed it in.

PROCTOR: Why, she done it herself! *To* HALE: I hope you're not takin' this for proof, Mister!

HALE, *struck by the proof, is silent.*

CHEEVER: 'Tis hard proof! *To* HALE: I find here a poppet Goody Proctor keeps. I have found it, sir. And in the belly of the poppet a needle's stuck. I tell you true, Proctor, I never warranted to see such proof of Hell, and I bid you obstruct me not, for I—

Enter ELIZABETH *with* MARY WARREN. PROCTOR, *seeing* MARY WARREN, *draws her by the arm to* HALE.

PROCTOR: Here now! Mary, how did this poppet come into my house?

MARY WARREN, *frightened for herself, her voice very small:* What poppet's that, sir?

PROCTOR, *impatiently, points at the doll in* CHEEVER's *hand:* This poppet, this poppet.

MARY WARREN, *evasively, looking at it:* Why, I—I think it is mine.

PROCTOR: It is your poppet, is it not?

MARY WARREN, *not understanding the direction of this:* It—is, sir.

PROCTOR: And how did it come into this house?

MARY WARREN, *glancing about at the avid faces:* Why—I made it in the court, sir, and—give it to Goody Proctor tonight.

PROCTOR, *to* HALE: Now, sir—do you have it?

HALE: Mary Warren, a needle have been found inside this poppet.

MARY WARREN, *bewildered:* Why, I meant no harm by it, sir.

PROCTOR, *quickly:* You stuck that needle in yourself?

Reading Strategy
Reading Drama What do these stage directions reveal about Hale's true thoughts?

MARY WARREN: I—I believe I did, sir, I—

PROCTOR, *to* HALE: What say you now?

HALE, *watching* MARY WARREN *closely:* Child, you are certain this be your natural memory? May it be, perhaps that someone conjures you even now to say this?

MARY WARREN: Conjures me? Why, no, sir, I am entirely myself, I think. Let you ask Susanna Walcott—she saw me sewin' it in court. *Or better still:* Ask Abby, Abby sat beside me when I made it.

PROCTOR, *to* HALE, *of* CHEEVER: Bid him begone. Your mind is surely settled now. Bid him out, Mr. Hale.

ELIZABETH: What signifies a needle?

HALE: Mary—you charge a cold and cruel murder on Abigail.

MARY WARREN: Murder! I charge no—

HALE: Abigail were stabbed tonight; a needle were found stuck into her belly—

ELIZABETH: And she charges me?

HALE: Aye.

ELIZABETH, *her breath knocked out:* Why—! The girl is murder! She must be ripped out of the world!

CHEEVER, *pointing at* ELIZABETH: You've heard that, sir! Ripped out of the world! Herrick, you heard it!

PROCTOR, *suddenly snatching the warrant out of* CHEEVER'S *hands:* Out with you.

CHEEVER: Proctor, you dare not touch the warrant.

PROCTOR, *ripping the warrant:* Out with you!

CHEEVER: You've ripped the Deputy Governor's warrant, man!

PROCTOR: Damn the Deputy Governor! Out of my house!

HALE: Now, Proctor, Proctor!

PROCTOR: Get y'gone with them! You are a broken minister.

HALE: Proctor, if she is innocent, the court—

PROCTOR: If *she* is innocent! Why do you never wonder if Parris be innocent, or Abigail? Is the accuser always holy now? Were they born this morning as clean as God's fingers? I'll tell you what's walking Salem—vengeance is walking Salem. We are what we always were in Salem, but now the little crazy children are jangling the keys of the kingdom, and common vengeance writes the law! This warrant's vengeance! I'll not give my wife to vengeance!

ELIZABETH: I'll go, John—

PROCTOR: You will not go!

HERRICK: I have nine men outside. You cannot keep her. The law binds me, John, I cannot budge.

PROCTOR, *to* HALE, *ready to break him:* Will you see her taken?

HALE: Proctor, the court is just—

Reading Strategy

Reading Drama What do the stage directions and Hale's comment reveal about his trust in Mary Warren?

Reading Check

What does Cheever discover in the Proctor's home?

PROCTOR: Pontius Pilate![4] God will not let you wash your hands of this!

ELIZABETH: John—I think I must go with them. *He cannot bear to look at her.* Mary, there is bread enough for the morning; you will bake, in the afternoon. Help Mr. Proctor as you were his daughter—you owe me that, and much more. *She is fighting her weeping. To* PROCTOR: When the children wake, speak nothing of witchcraft— it will frighten them. *She cannot go on.*

PROCTOR: I will bring you home. I will bring you soon.

ELIZABETH: Oh, John, bring me soon!

PROCTOR: I will fall like an ocean on that court! Fear nothing, Elizabeth.

ELIZABETH, *with great fear:* I will fear nothing. *She looks about the room, as though to fix it in her mind.* Tell the children I have gone to visit someone sick.

She walks out the door, HERRICK *and* CHEEVER *behind her. For a moment,* PROCTOR *watches from the doorway. The clank of chain is heard.*

PROCTOR: Herrick! Herrick, don't chain her! *He rushes out the door. From outside:* Damn you, man, you will not chain her! Off with them! I'll not have it! I will not have her chained!

There are other men's voices against his. HALE, *in a fever of guilt and uncertainty, turns from the door to avoid the sight:* MARY WARREN *bursts into tears and sits weeping.* GILES COREY *calls to* HALE.

GILES: And yet silent, minister? It is fraud, you know it is fraud! What keeps you, man?

PROCTOR *is half braced, half pushed into the room by two deputies and* HERRICK.

PROCTOR: I'll pay you, Herrick, I will surely pay you!

HERRICK, *panting:* In God's name, John, I cannot help myself. I must chain them all. Now let you keep inside this house till I am gone! *He goes out with his deputies.*

PROCTOR *stands there, gulping air. Horses and a wagon creaking are heard.*

---

4. **Pontius** (pän´ shəs) **Pilate** (pī´ lət) Roman leader who condemned Jesus to be crucified.

Literary Analysis
Allusion To what biblical event, key to Puritan belief, does Proctor refer when he alludes to Pontius Pilate?

◄ **Critical Viewing**
What thoughts or feelings do the facial expressions of Elizabeth Proctor, Reverend Parris, and the deputy convey in this photo? **[Analyze]**

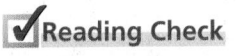**Reading Check**
What happens to Elizabeth Proctor?

HALE, *in great uncertainty:* Mr. Proctor—

PROCTOR: Out of my sight!

HALE: Charity, Proctor, charity. What I have heard in her favor, I will not fear to testify in court. God help me, I cannot judge her guilty or innocent—I know not. Only this consider: the world goes mad, and it profit nothing you should lay the cause to the vengeance of a little girl.

PROCTOR: You are a coward! Though you be ordained in God's own tears, you are a coward now!

HALE: Proctor, I cannot think God be provoked so grandly by such a petty cause. The jails are packed—our greatest judges sit in Salem now—and hangin's promised. Man, we must look to cause proportionate. Were there murder done, perhaps, and never brought to light? Abomination? Some secret blasphemy that stinks to Heaven? Think on cause, man, and let you help me to discover it. For there's your way, believe it, there is your only way, when such confusion strikes upon the world. *He goes to* GILES *and* FRANCIS. Let you counsel among yourselves; think on your village and what may have drawn from heaven such thundering wrath upon you all. I shall pray God open up our eyes.

HALE *goes out.*

FRANCIS, *struck by* HALE'S *mood:* I never heard no murder done in Salem.

PROCTOR—*he has been reached by* HALE'S *words:* Leave me, Francis, leave me.

GILES, *shaken:* John—tell me, are we lost?

PROCTOR: Go home now, Giles. We'll speak on it tomorrow.

GILES: Let you think on it. We'll come early, eh?

PROCTOR: Aye. Go now, Giles.

GILES: Good night, then.

GILES COREY *goes out. After a moment:*

MARY WARREN, *in a fearful squeak of a voice:* Mr. Proctor, very likely they'll let her come home once they're given proper evidence.

PROCTOR: You're coming to the court with me, Mary. You will tell it in the court.

MARY WARREN: I cannot charge murder on Abigail.

PROCTOR, *moving menacingly toward her:* You will tell the court how that poppet come here and who stuck the needle in.

MARY WARREN: She'll kill me for sayin' that! PROCTOR *continues toward her.* Abby'll charge lechery[5] on you, Mr. Proctor!

PROCTOR, *halting:* She's told you!

MARY WARREN: I have known it, sir. She'll ruin you with it, I know she will.

abomination (ə bäm´ ə nā´ shən) *n.* something that causes great horror or disgust

blasphemy (blas´ fə mē´) *n.* sinful act or remark

---

5. **lechery** (lech´ ər ē) *n.* lust; adultery—a charge almost as serious as witchcraft in this Puritan community.

PROCTOR, *hesitating, and with deep hatred of himself:* Good. Then her saintliness is done with. MARY *backs from him.* We will slide together into our pit; you will tell the court what you know.

MARY WARREN, *in terror:* I cannot, they'll turn on me—

PROCTOR *strides and catches her, and she is repeating, "I cannot, I cannot!"*

PROCTOR: My wife will never die for me! I will bring your guts into your mouth but that goodness will not die for me!

MARY WARREN, *struggling to escape him:* I cannot do it. I cannot!

PROCTOR, *grasping her by the throat as though he would strangle her:* Make your peace with it! Now Hell and Heaven grapple on our backs, and all our pretense is ripped away—make your peace! *He throws her to the floor, where she sobs, "I cannot, I cannot . . ." And now, half to himself, staring, and turning to the open door:* Peace. It is a providence, and no great change; we are only what we always were, but naked now. *He walks as though toward a great horror, facing the open sky.* Aye, naked! And the wind, God's icy wind, will blow!

And she is over and over again sobbing, "I cannot, I cannot, I cannot."

Review and Assess

Thinking About Act II

1. **Respond:** Which character do you find the most intriguing? Why?

2. **(a) Recall:** What does Mary Warren bring home to Elizabeth Proctor? **(b) Interpret:** What is the significance of this gift?

3. **(a) Recall:** What evidence is used to support Abigail Williams's assertion that Elizabeth Proctor is guilty of witchcraft? **(b) Assess:** Do you think the evidence is compelling? Why or why not?

4. **(a) Recall:** What does Sarah Good do to save herself from hanging? **(b) Draw Conclusions:** Why would such an action save her?

5. **(a) Recall:** According to John Proctor, what is "walking Salem" and writing the law in the community? **(b) Support:** What evidence would support Proctor's assertion?

6. **(a) Recall:** Who says the witchcraft trials are "a black mischief"? **(b) Analyze:** What is ironic about that remark?

7. **Analyze:** Why is it surprising that Rebecca Nurse is charged with witchcraft?

8. **Evaluate:** Do you find any irony in the fact that Ezekiel Cheever is the one who arrests Elizabeth Proctor? Why or why not?

Review and Assess

Literary Analysis

Allusion

1. What does the biblical **allusion** to Moses and the parting of the Red Sea on page 1269 suggest about how the crowd views Abigail?
2. (a) What does John Proctor's allusion to Pontius Pilate on page 1285 imply about Proctor's opinion of Reverend Hale? (b) What does the allusion to Pontius Pilate imply about the witchcraft proceedings in Salem?

Connecting Literary Elements

3. In what way do details of **historical context,** including the status of women, explain why women were accused of witchcraft?
4. Knowing that keeping the Sabbath and attending church services were strictly enforced by the Puritans, how do you interpret John Proctor's exchange with Reverend Hale about the baptism of Proctor's sons? Explain.
5. The Puritans lacked laws to protect people from illegal searches and arrests. How does this fact add to your appreciation of the scene in which Elizabeth Proctor is apprehended?

Reading Strategy

Reading Drama

6. Using a chart like the one shown here, cite three examples of dialogue in which a character's attitudes would have been unclear to you if you had not read the stage directions.

Dialogue	Attitude Revealed in Stage Direction

7. In addition to characters' attitudes, what other significant information do the stage directions in Act II reveal to you?

Extend Understanding

8. **Social Studies Connection:** How are legal principles and evidence-gathering procedures different in America today than they were in the time in which the play is set? Explain.

Integrate Language Skills

Vocabulary Development Lesson

Word Analysis: Greek Suffix -logy

The Greek suffix -logy means "the science, theory, or study of." When combined with the Greek root -theo-, meaning "god," the word theology means "the study of religion." For each item below, identify a word that combines a root with the suffix -logy.

1. "star" __logy
2. "life" __logy
3. "earth" __ logy
4. "social" __logy

Spelling Strategy

For verbs that end in -er, add the suffix -ence to form nouns. For each of these words, use the suffix -ence to generate a noun.

1. differ
2. confer
3. prefer

Fluency: Words in Context

Explain why each statement is true or false.

1. Lying is base behavior.
2. To step gingerly is to stomp.
3. Someone who watches sports avidly probably knows very little about them.
4. Rude youngsters show deference to elders.
5. Puritans think witchcraft is an abomination.
6. A fearful animal may quail at the sight of a whip.
7. A minister is pleased to hear blasphemy.
8. A blushing person exhibits pallor.
9. The Puritans questioned their theology.
10. To ameliorate a situation is to make it better.

Grammar and Style Lesson

Commas After Introductory Words

Use a **comma** to set off a mild interjection or another interrupter that introduces a sentence.

> **Examples:** *Oh,* you're not done then.
> *Aye,* the farm is seeded.

Practice Add commas to set off introductory words. If a sentence is correct as is, write *Correct*.

1. Hey did you ever see *The Crucible*?
2. Yes I saw a local theater group's production.
3. Well which characters are sympathetic?
4. I must admit that I found it unpleasant.
5. Perhaps but the problem could have been with the performance you saw.

Writing Application Write a brief scene using dialogue that involves two or more characters. Use commas to set off at least three introductory words.

Extension Activities

Writing Imagine that one of the citizens accused of witchcraft has disappeared. In a group, design a **wanted poster** that describes the individual and the reason he or she should be apprehended. **[Group Activity]**

Listening and Speaking Write and perform a **scene** that dramatizes the arrest of Rebecca Nurse. Make the style of your scene consistent with that of the rest of the play. Present the scene to your class.

WG *Prentice Hall Writing and Grammar Connection: Chapter 27, Section 2*

Prepare to Read

The Crucible, Act III

Literary Analysis
Dramatic and Verbal Irony

Irony involves a contrast between what is stated and what is meant, or between what is expected to happen and what actually happens.

- In **dramatic irony,** there is a contradiction between what a character thinks and what the audience knows to be true.
- In **verbal irony,** a character says one thing but means something quite different.

Look for both forms of irony as you read Act III.

Connecting Literary Elements

In this act of the play, Miller challenges audiences to think critically. Beyond maintaining an awareness of irony, the audience must also weigh the logic presented in the court scene. There, Miller introduces a **logical fallacy,** an idea or argument that appears logical though it is based on a completely faulty premise. Judge Danforth explains his reasoning for believing the accusations of witchcraft. Though his thoughts seem logical, read them critically—all are based on a mistaken premise.

Reading Strategy
Categorizing Characters by Role

The introduction of many characters in a drama can become confusing. It may be helpful to **categorize the characters**. One way you can classify characters in *The Crucible* is by the roles they play in the community. Using a chart like the one shown, identify the characters and their positions in Salem Village.

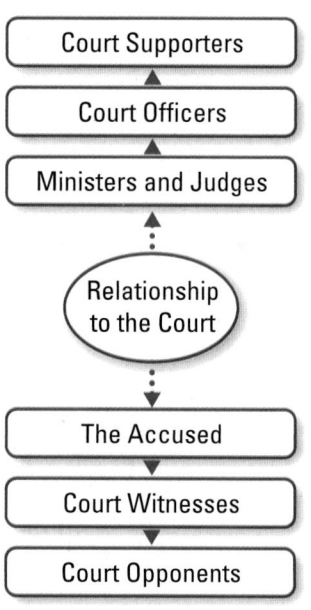

Court Supporters

Court Officers

Ministers and Judges

Relationship to the Court

The Accused

Court Witnesses

Court Opponents

Vocabulary Development

contentious (kən ten´ shəs) *adj.* argumentative (p. 1292)

deposition (dep´ ə zish´ ən) *n.* the testimony of a witness made under oath but not in open court (p. 1294)

imperceptible (im´ pər sep´ tə bəl) *adj.* barely noticeable (p. 1296)

deferentially (def´ ər en´ shəl lē) *adv.* in a manner that bows to another's wishes; very respectfully (p. 1297)

anonymity (an´ ə nim´ ə tē) *n.* the condition of being unknown (p. 1299)

prodigious (prə dij´ əs) *adj.* of great size, power, or extent (p. 1300)

effrontery (e frun´ tər ē) *n.* shameless boldness (p. 1300)

confounded (kən found´ id) *v.* confused; dismayed (p. 1301)

incredulously (in krej´ o͞o ləs lē) *adv.* skeptically (p. 1304)

blanched (blancht) *adj.* paled; whitened (p. 1309)

Review and Anticipate

Act II ends as Elizabeth Proctor is accused of witchcraft and carted off to jail as a result of the connivance of Abigail Williams. John Proctor demands that Mary Warren tell the court the truth; Mary, though aware of Abigail's ploys, is terrified of exposing her. Do you think John will convince Mary to overcome her fears and testify against Abigail? If he does convince her, how will the judges receive Mary Warren's testimony? Read Act III to see what happens in the Salem courtroom.

ACT III

The vestry room of the Salem meeting house, now serving as the anteroom of the General Court.

As the curtain rises, the room is empty, but for sunlight pouring through two high windows in the back wall. The room is solemn, even forbidding. Heavy beams jut out, boards of random widths make up the walls. At the right are two doors leading into the meeting house proper, where the court is being held. At the left another door leads outside.

There is a plain bench at the left, and another at the right. In the center a rather long meeting table, with stools and a considerable armchair snugged up to it.

Through the partitioning wall at the right we hear a prosecutor's voice, JUDGE HATHORNE's, *asking a question; then a woman's voice,* MARTHA COREY's, *replying.*

HATHORNE'S VOICE: Now, Martha Corey, there is abundant evidence in our hands to show that you have given yourself to the reading of fortunes. Do you deny it?

MARTHA COREY'S VOICE: I am innocent to a witch. I know not what a witch is.

HATHORNE'S VOICE: How do you know, then, that you are not a witch?

MARTHA COREY'S VOICE: If I were, I would know it.

HATHORNE'S VOICE: Why do you hurt these children?

MARTHA COREY'S VOICE: I do not hurt them. I scorn it!

GILES'S VOICE, *roaring:* I have evidence for the court!

Voices of townspeople rise in excitement.

DANFORTH'S VOICE: You will keep your seat!

GILES' VOICE: Thomas Putnam is reaching out for land!

DANFORTH'S VOICE: Remove that man, Marshal!

GILES' VOICE: You're hearing lies, lies!

A roaring goes up from the people.

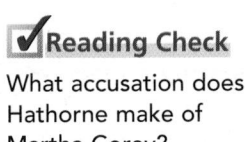

✔ **Reading Check**
What accusation does Hathorne make of Martha Corey?

HATHORNE'S VOICE: Arrest him, excellency!

GILES' VOICE: I have evidence. Why will you not hear my evidence?

The door opens and GILES *is half carried into the vestry room by* HERRICK.

GILES: Hands off, damn you, let me go!

HERRICK: Giles, Giles!

GILES: Out of my way, Herrick! I bring evidence—

HERRICK: You cannot go in there, Giles; it's a court!

Enter HALE *from the court.*

HALE: Pray be calm a moment.

GILES: You, Mr. Hale, go in there and demand I speak.

HALE: A moment, sir, a moment.

GILES: They'll be hangin' my wife!

JUDGE HATHORNE *enters. He is in his sixties, a bitter, remorseless Salem judge.*

HATHORNE: How do you dare come roarin' into this court! Are you gone daft, Corey?

GILES: You're not a Boston judge, Hathorne. You'll not call me daft!

Enter DEPUTY GOVERNOR DANFORTH *and, behind him,* EZEKIEL CHEEVER *and* PARRIS. *On his appearance, silence falls.* DANFORTH *is a grave man in his sixties, of some humor and sophistication that does not, however, interfere with an exact loyalty to his position and his cause. He comes down to* GILES, *who awaits his wrath.*

DANFORTH, *looking directly at* GILES: Who is this man?

PARRIS: Giles Corey, sir, and a more <u>contentious</u>—

GILES, *to* PARRIS: I am asked the question, and I am old enough to answer it! *To* DANFORTH, *who impresses him and to whom he smiles through his strain:* My name is Corey, sir, Giles Corey. I have six hundred acres, and timber in addition. It is my wife you be condemning now. *He indicates the courtroom.*

DANFORTH: And how do you imagine to help her cause with such contemptuous riot? Now be gone. Your old age alone keeps you out of jail for this.

GILES, *beginning to plead:* They be tellin' lies about my wife, sir, I—

DANFORTH: Do you take it upon yourself to determine what this court shall believe and what it shall set aside?

GILES: Your Excellency, we mean no disrespect for—

DANFORTH: Disrespect indeed! It is disruption, Mister. This is the highest court of the supreme government of this province, do you know it?

GILES, *beginning to weep:* Your Excellency, I only said she were readin' books, sir, and they come and take her out of my house for—

DANFORTH, *mystified:* Books! What books?

GILES, *through helpless sobs:* It is my third wife, sir; I never had no wife that be so taken with books, and I thought to find the cause of it, d'y'see, but it were no witch I blamed her for. *He is openly weeping.*

Reading Strategy

Categorizing Characters by Role Why do you think Giles makes this statement about Hathorne's status as a judge?

contentious (kən ten′ shəs) *adj.* argumentative

I have broke charity with the woman, I have broke charity with her. *He covers his face, ashamed.* DANFORTH *is respectfully silent.*

HALE: Excellency, he claims hard evidence for his wife's defense. I think that in all justice you must—

DANFORTH: Then let him submit his evidence in proper affidavit.[1] You are certainly aware of our procedure here, Mr. Hale. *To* HERRICK: Clear this room.

HERRICK: Come now, Giles. *He gently pushes* COREY *out.*

FRANCIS: We are desperate, sir; we come here three days now and cannot be heard.

DANFORTH: Who is this man?

FRANCIS: Francis Nurse, Your Excellency.

HALE: His wife's Rebecca that were condemned this morning.

DANFORTH: Indeed! I am amazed to find you in such uproar. I have only good report of your character, Mr. Nurse.

HERRICK: I think they must both be arrested in contempt, sir.

DANFORTH, *to* FRANCIS: Let you write your plea, and in due time I will—

FRANCIS: Excellency, we have proof for your eyes; God forbid you shut them to it. The girls, sir, the girls are frauds.

DANFORTH: What's that?

FRANCIS: We have proof of it, sir. They are all deceiving you.

DANFORTH *is shocked, but studying* FRANCIS.

HATHORNE: This is contempt, sir, contempt!

DANFORTH: Peace, Judge Hathorne. Do you know who I am, Mr. Nurse?

FRANCIS: I surely do, sir, and I think you must be a wise judge to be what you are.

DANFORTH: And do you know that near to four hundred are in the jails from Marblehead to Lynn, and upon my signature?

FRANCIS: I—

DANFORTH: And seventy-two condemned to hang by that signature?

FRANCIS: Excellency, I never thought to say it to such a weighty judge, but you are deceived.

Enter GILES COREY *from left. All turn to see as he beckons in* MARY WARREN *with* PROCTOR. MARY *is keeping her eyes to the ground;* PROCTOR *has her elbow as though she were near collapse.*

PARRIS, *on seeing her, in shock:* Mary Warren! *He goes directly to bend close to her face.* What are you about here?

PROCTOR, *pressing* PARRIS *away from her with a gentle but firm motion of protectiveness:* She would speak with the Deputy Governor.

DANFORTH, *shocked by this, turns to* HERRICK: Did you not tell me Mary Warren were sick in bed?

---

1. affidavit (af´ ə dā´ vit) *n.* written statement made under oath.

Literary Analysis
Dramatic and Verbal Irony and Logical Fallacy
What is illogical about Danforth's statement to Francis Nurse?

Reading Strategy
Categorizing Characters by Role In what sense could Danforth and Hathorne be classified together?

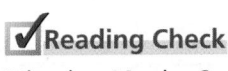Reading Check

What has Martha Corey done that results in her arrest?

HERRICK: She were, Your Honor. When I go to fetch her to the court last week, she said she were sick.

GILES: She has been strivin' with her soul all week, Your Honor; she comes now to tell the truth of this to you.

DANFORTH: Who is this?

PROCTOR: John Proctor, sir. Elizabeth Proctor is my wife.

PARRIS: Beware this man, Your Excellency, this man is mischief.

HALE, *excitedly:* I think you must hear the girl, sir, she—

DANFORTH, *who has become very interested in* MARY WARREN *and only raises a hand toward* HALE: Peace. What would you tell us, Mary Warren?

PROCTOR *looks at her, but she cannot speak.*

PROCTOR: She never saw no spirits, sir.

DANFORTH, *with great alarm and surprise, to* MARY: Never saw no spirits!

GILES, *eagerly:* Never.

PROCTOR, *reaching into his jacket:* She has signed a <u>deposition</u>, sir—

DANFORTH, *instantly:* No, no, I accept no depositions. *He is rapidly calculating this; he turns from her to* PROCTOR. Tell me, Mr. Proctor, have you given out this story in the village?

PROCTOR: We have not.

PARRIS: They've come to overthrow the court, sir! This man is—

DANFORTH: I pray you, Mr. Parris. Do you know, Mr. Proctor that the entire contention of the state in these trials is that the voice of Heaven is speaking through the children?

PROCTOR: I know that, sir.

DANFORTH, *thinks, staring at* PROCTOR, *then turns to* MARY WARREN: And you, Mary Warren, how come you to cry out people for sending their spirits, against you?

MARY WARREN: It were pretense, sir.

DANFORTH: I cannot hear you.

PROCTOR: It were pretense, she says.

DANFORTH: Ah? And the other girls? Susanna Walcott, and—the others? They are also pretending?

MARY WARREN: Aye, sir.

DANFORTH, *wide-eyed:* Indeed. *Pause. He is baffled by this. He turns to study* PROCTOR'S *face.*

PARRIS, *in a sweat:* Excellency, you surely cannot think to let so vile a lie be spread in open court.

DANFORTH: Indeed not, but it strike hard upon me that she will dare come here with such a tale. Now, Mr. Proctor, before I decide whether I shall hear you or not, it is my duty to tell you this. We burn a hot fire here; it melts down all concealment.

PROCTOR: I know that, sir.

deposition (dep´ ə zish´ ən) *n.* the testimony of a witness made under oath but not in open court

Reading Strategy
Categorizing Characters by Role Would Parris be so concerned about Mary Warren's testimony being heard in open court if he were not a community leader?

DANFORTH: Let me continue. I understand well, a husband's tenderness may drive him to extravagance in defense of a wife. Are you certain in your conscience, Mister, that your evidence is the truth?

PROCTOR: It is. And you will surely know it.

DANFORTH: And you thought to declare this revelation in the open court before the public?

PROCTOR: I thought I would, aye—with your permission.

DANFORTH, *his eyes narrowing:* Now, sir, what is your purpose in so doing?

PROCTOR: Why, I—I would free my wife, sir.

DANFORTH: There lurks nowhere in your heart, nor hidden in your spirit, any desire to undermine this court?

PROCTOR, *with the faintest faltering:* Why, no, sir.

CHEEVER, *clears his throat, awakening:* I—Your Excellency.

DANFORTH: Mr. Cheever.

CHEEVER: I think it be my duty, sir—*Kindly, to* PROCTOR: You'll not deny it, John. *To* DANFORTH: When we come to take his wife, he damned the court and ripped your warrant.

PARRIS: Now you have it!

DANFORTH: He did that, Mr. Hale?

HALE, *takes a breath:* Aye, he did.

PROCTOR: It were a temper, sir. I knew not what I did.

DANFORTH, *studying him:* Mr. Proctor.

PROCTOR: Aye, sir.

DANFORTH, *straight into his eyes:* Have you ever seen the Devil?

PROCTOR: No, sir.

DANFORTH: You are in all respects a Gospel Christian?

PROCTOR: I am, sir.

PARRIS: Such a Christian that will not come to church but once in a month!

DANFORTH, *restrained—he is curious:* Not come to church?

PROCTOR: I—I have no love for Mr. Parris. It is no secret. But God I surely love.

CHEEVER: He plow on Sunday, sir.

DANFORTH: Plow on Sunday!

CHEEVER, *apologetically:* I think it be evidence, John. I am an official of the court, I cannot keep it.

PROCTOR: I—I have once or twice plowed on Sunday. I have three children, sir, and until last year my land give little.

GILES: You'll find other Christians that do plow on Sunday if the truth be known.

HALE: Your Honor, I cannot think you may judge the man on such evidence.

Reading Strategy
Categorizing Characters by Role Would you classify either Parris or Danforth as a villain? Why or why not?

Reading Check

What new testimony does Mary Warren give?

DANFORTH: I judge nothing. *Pause. He keeps watching* PROCTOR, *who tries to meet his gaze.* I tell you straight, Mister—I have seen marvels in this court. I have seen people choked before my eyes by spirits; I have seen them stuck by pins and slashed by daggers. I have until this moment not the slightest reason to suspect that the children may be deceiving me. Do you understand my meaning?

PROCTOR: Excellency, does it not strike upon you that so many of these women have lived so long with such upright reputation, and—

PARRIS: Do you read the Gospel, Mr. Proctor?

PROCTOR: I read the Gospel.

PARRIS: I think not, or you should surely know that Cain were an upright man, and yet he did kill Abel.[2]

PROCTOR: Aye, God tells us that. *To* DANFORTH: But who tells us Rebecca Nurse murdered seven babies by sending out her spirit on them? It is the children only, and this one will swear she lied to you.

DANFORTH *considers, then beckons* HATHORNE *to him.* HATHORNE *leans in, and he speaks in his ear.* HATHORNE *nods.*

HERRICK: Aye, she's the one.

DANFORTH: Mr. Proctor, this morning, your wife send me a claim in which she states that she is pregnant now.

PROCTOR: My wife pregnant!

DANFORTH: There be no sign of it—we have examined her body.

PROCTOR: But if she say she is pregnant, then she must be! That woman will never lie, Mr. Danforth.

DANFORTH: She will not?

PROCTOR: Never, sir, never.

DANFORTH: We have thought it too convenient to be credited. However, if I should tell you now that I will let her be kept another month; and if she begin to show her natural signs, you shall have her living yet another year until she is delivered—what say you to that? JOHN PROCTOR *is struck silent.* Come now. You say your only purpose is to save your wife. Good, then, she is saved at least this year, and a year is long. What say you, sir? It is done now. *In conflict,* PROCTOR *glances at* FRANCIS *and* GILES. Will you drop this charge?

PROCTOR: I—I think I cannot.

DANFORTH, *now an almost imperceptible hardness in his voice:* Then your purpose is somewhat larger.

PARRIS: He's come to overthrow this court, Your Honor!

PROCTOR: These are my friends. Their wives are also accused—

DANFORTH, *with a sudden briskness of manner:* I judge you not, sir. I am ready to hear your evidence.

PROCTOR: I come not to hurt the court; I only—

Literary Analysis
Dramatic and Verbal Irony and Logical Fallacy
In what way does Danforth's statement represent a logical fallacy?

imperceptible (im´ pər sep´ tə bəl) *adj.* barely noticeable

---

2. Cain . . . Abel In the Bible, Cain, the oldest son of Adam and Eve, killed his brother, Abel.

DANFORTH, *cutting him off:* Marshal, go into the court and bid Judge Stoughton and Judge Sewall declare recess for one hour. And let them go to the tavern, if they will. All witnesses and prisoners are to be kept in the building.

HERRICK: Aye, sir. *Very deferentially:* If I may say it, sir. I know this man all my life. It is a good man, sir.

DANFORTH—*it is the reflection on himself he resents:* I am sure of it, Marshal. HERRICK *nods, then goes out.* Now, what deposition do you have for us, Mr. Proctor? And I beg you be clear, open as the sky, and honest.

PROCTOR, *as he takes out several papers:* I am no lawyer, so I'll—

DANFORTH: The pure in heart need no lawyers. Proceed as you will.

PROCTOR, *handing* DANFORTH *a paper:* Will you read this first, sir? It's a sort of testament. The people signing it declare their good opinion of Rebecca, and my wife, and Martha Corey.

DANFORTH *looks down at the paper.*

PARRIS, *to enlist* DANFORTH's *sarcasm:* Their good opinion! *But* DANFORTH *goes on reading, and* PROCTOR *is heartened.*

PROCTOR: These are all landholding farmers, members of the church. *Delicately, trying to point out a paragraph:* If you'll notice, sir—they've known the women many years and never saw no sign they had dealings with the Devil.

PARRIS *nervously moves over and reads over* DANFORTH's *shoulder.*

DANFORTH, *glancing down a long list:* How many names are here?

FRANCIS: Ninety-one, Your Excellency.

PARRIS, *sweating:* These people should be summoned. DANFORTH *looks up at him questioningly.* For questioning.

FRANCIS. *trembling with anger:* Mr. Danforth, I gave them all my word no harm would come to them for signing this.

PARRIS: This is a clear attack upon the court!

HALE, *to* PARRIS, *trying to contain himself:* Is every defense an attack upon the court? Can no one—?

PARRIS: All innocent and Christian people are happy for the courts in Salem! These people are gloomy for it. *To* DANFORTH *directly:* And I think you will want to know, from each and every one of them, what discontents them with you!

HERRICK: I think they ought to be examined, sir.

DANFORTH: It is not necessarily an attack, I think. Yet—

FRANCIS: These are all covenanted Christians, sir.

DANFORTH: Then I am sure they may have nothing to fear. *Hands* CHEEVER *the paper.* Mr. Cheever, have warrants drawn for all of these—arrest for examination. *To* PROCTOR: Now, Mister, what other information do you have for us? FRANCIS *is still standing, horrified.* You may sit, Mr. Nurse.

FRANCIS: I have brought trouble on these people: I have—

---

deferentially (def′ ər en′ shəl lē) *adv.* in a manner that bows to another's wishes; very respectfully

Literary Analysis
Dramatic and Verbal Irony
What makes Danforth's statement about the "pure in heart" an example of verbal irony?

Reading Check
What document does Proctor present to the count?

DANFORTH: No, old man, you have not hurt these people if they are of good conscience. But you must understand, sir, that a person is either with this court or he must be counted against it, there be no road between. This is a sharp time, now, a precise time—we live no longer in the dusky afternoon when evil mixed itself with good and befuddled the world. Now, by God's grace, the shining sun is up, and them that fear not light will surely praise it. I hope you will be one of those. MARY WAR-REN *suddenly sobs.* She's not hearty, I see.

PROCTOR: No, she's not, sir. *To* MARY, *bending to her, holding her hand, quietly:* Now remember what the angel Raphael said to the boy Tobias.[3] Remember it.

MARY WARREN, *hardly audible:* Aye.

PROCTOR: "Do that which is good, and no harm shall come to thee."

MARY WARREN: Aye.

DANFORTH: Come, man, we wait you.

MARSHAL HERRICK *returns, and takes his post at the door.*

GILES: John, my deposition, give him mine.

PROCTOR: Aye. *He hands* DANFORTH *another paper.* This is Mr. Corey's deposition.

DANFORTH: Oh? *He looks down at it. Now* HATHORNE *comes behind him and reads with him.*

HATHORNE, *suspiciously:* What lawyer drew this, Corey?

GILES: You know I never hired a lawyer in my life, Hathorne.

DANFORTH, *finishing the reading:* It is very well phrased. My compliments. Mr. Parris, if Mr. Putnam is in the court, will you bring him in? HATHORNE *takes the deposition, and walks to the window with it.* PARRIS *goes into the court.* You have no legal training, Mr. Corey?

GILES, *very pleased:* I have the best, sir—I am thirty-three time in court in my life. And always plaintiff, too.

DANFORTH: Oh, then you're much put-upon.

GILES: I am never put-upon; I know my rights, sir, and I will have them. You know, your father tried a case of mine—might be thirty-five year ago, I think.

DANFORTH: Indeed.

GILES: He never spoke to you of it?

DANFORTH: No, I cannot recall it.

GILES: That's strange, he gave me nine pound damages. He were a fair judge, your father. Y'see, I had a white mare that time, and this fellow come to borrow the mare—*Enter* PARRIS *with* THOMAS PUTNAM. *When he*

<aside>
Literary Analysis
Dramatic and Verbal Irony In what sense is Proctor's quotation from the bible ironic?
</aside>

---

3. **Raphael. . .Tobias** In the Bible, Tobias is guided by the archangel Raphael to save two people who have prayed for their deaths. One of the two is Tobias's father, Tobit, who has prayed for his death because he has lost his sight; the other is Sara, a woman who is afflicted by a demon and has killed her seven husbands on their wedding day. With Raphael's assistance, Tobias exorcises the devil from Sara and cures his father of blindness.

sees PUTNAM, GILES' *ease goes; he is hard.* Aye, there he is.

DANFORTH: Mr. Putnam, I have here an accusation by Mr. Corey against you. He states that you coldly prompted your daughter to cry witchery upon George Jacobs that is now in jail.

PUTNAM: It is a lie.

DANFORTH, *turning to* GILES: Mr. Putnam states your charge is a lie. What say you to that?

GILES, *furious, his fists clenched:* A fart on Thomas Putnam, that is what I say to that!

DANFORTH: What proof do you submit for your charge, sir?

GILES: My proof is there! *Pointing to the paper.* If Jacobs hangs for a witch he forfeit up his property—that's law! And there is none but Putnam with the coin to buy so great a piece. This man is killing his neighbors for their land!

DANFORTH: But proof, sir, proof.

GILES, *pointing at his deposition:* The proof is there! I have it from an honest man who heard Putnam say it! The day his daughter cried out on Jacobs, he said she'd given him a fair gift of land.

HATHORNE: And the name of this man?

GILES, *taken aback:* What name?

HATHORNE: The man that give you this information.

GILES, *hesitates, then:* Why, I—I cannot give you his name.

HATHORNE: And why not?

GILES, *hesitates, then bursts out:* You know well why not! He'll lay in jail if I give his name!

HATHORNE: This is contempt of the court, Mr. Danforth!

DANFORTH, *to avoid that:* You will surely tell us the name.

GILES: I will not give you no name. I mentioned my wife's name once and I'll burn in hell long enough for that. I stand mute.

DANFORTH: In that case, I have no choice but to arrest you for contempt of this court, do you know that?

GILES: This is a hearing; you cannot clap me for contempt of a hearing.

DANFORTH: Oh, it is a proper lawyer! Do you wish me to declare the court in full session here? Or will you give me good reply?

GILES, *faltering:* I cannot give you no name, sir, I cannot.

DANFORTH: You are a foolish old man. Mr. Cheever, begin the record. The court is now in session. I ask you, Mr. Corey—

PROCTOR, *breaking in:* Your Honor—he has the story in confidence, sir, and he—

PARRIS: The Devil lives on such confidences! *To* DANFORTH: Without confidences there could be no conspiracy, Your Honor!

HATHORNE: I think it must be broken, sir.

DANFORTH, *to* GILES: Old man, if your informant tells the truth let him come here openly like a decent man. But if he hide in <u>anonymity</u> I

Reading Strategies
Categorizing Characters by Role In which segment of the community would you classify Giles? Why?

anonymity (an´ ə nim´ ə tē) *n.* the condition of being unknown

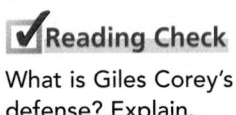
Reading Check

What is Giles Corey's defense? Explain.

must know why. Now sir, the government and central church demand of you the name of him who reported Mr. Thomas Putnam a common murderer.

HALE: Excellency—

DANFORTH: Mr. Hale.

HALE: We cannot blink it more. There is a <u>prodigious</u> fear of this court in the country—

DANFORTH: Then there is a prodigious guilt in the country. Are you afraid to be questioned here?

HALE: I may only fear the Lord, sir, but there is fear in the country nevertheless.

DANFORTH, *angered now:* Reproach me not with the fear in the country; there is fear in the country because there is a moving plot to topple Christ in the country!

HALE: But it does not follow that everyone accused is part of it.

DANFORTH: No uncorrupted man may fear this court, Mr. Hale! None! *To* GILES: You are under arrest in contempt of this court. Now sit you down and take counsel with yourself, or you will be set in the jail until you decide to answer all questions.

GILES COREY *makes a rush for* PUTNAM. PROCTOR *lunges and holds him.*

PROCTOR: No, Giles!

GILES, *over proctor's shoulder at* PUTNAM: I'll cut your throat, Putnam, I'll kill you yet!

PROCTOR, *forcing him into a chair:* Peace, Giles, peace. *Releasing him.* We'll prove ourselves. Now we will. *He starts to turn to* DANFORTH.

GILES: Say nothin' more, John. *Pointing at* DANFORTH: He's only playin' you! He means to hang us all!

MARY WARREN *bursts into sobs.*

DANFORTH: This is a court of law, Mister. I'll have no <u>effrontery</u> here!

PROCTOR: Forgive him, sir, for his old age. Peace, Giles, we'll prove it all now. *He lifts up* MARY'S *chin.* You cannot weep, Mary. Remember the angel, what he say to the boy. Hold to it, now; there is your rock. MARY *quiets. He takes out a paper, and turns to* DANFORTH. This is Mary Warren's deposition. I—I would ask you remember, sir, while you read it, that until two week ago she were no different than the other children are today. *He is speaking reasonably, restraining all his fears, his anger, his anxiety.* You saw her scream, she howled, she swore familiar spirits choked her; she even testified that Satan, in the form of women now in jail, tried to win her soul away, and then when she refused—

DANFORTH: We know all this.

PROCTOR: Aye, sir. She swears now that she never saw Satan; nor any spirit, vague or clear, that Satan may have sent to hurt her. And she declares her friends are lying now.

PROCTOR *starts to hand* DANFORTH *the deposition, and* HALE *comes up to* DANFORTH *in a trembling state.*

prodigious (prə dij´ əs) *adj.* of great size, power, or extent

effrontery (e frunt´ ər ē) *n.* shameless boldness

HALE: Excellency, a moment. I think this goes to the heart of the matter.

DANFORTH, *with deep misgivings:* It surely does.

HALE: I cannot say he is an honest man; I know him little. But in all justice, sir, a claim so weighty cannot be argued by a farmer. In God's name, sir, stop here; send him home and let him come again with a lawyer—

DANFORTH, *patiently:* Now look you, Mr. Hale—

HALE: Excellency, I have signed seventy-two death warrants; I am a minister of the Lord, and I dare not take a life without there be a proof so immaculate no slightest qualm of conscience may doubt it.

DANFORTH: Mr. Hale, you surely do not doubt my justice.

HALE: I have this morning signed away the soul of Rebecca Nurse, Your Honor. I'll not conceal it, my hand shakes yet as with a wound! I pray you, sir, *this* argument let lawyers present to you.

DANFORTH: Mr. Hale, believe me; for a man of such terrible learning you are most bewildered—I hope you will forgive me. I have been thirty-two year at the bar, sir, and I should be <u>confounded</u> were I called upon to defend these people. Let you consider, now—*To* PROCTOR *and the others:* And I bid you all do likewise. In an ordinary crime, how does one defend the accused? One calls up witnesses to prove his innocence. But witchcraft is *ipso facto,*[4] on its face and by its nature, an invisible crime, is it not? Therefore, who may possibly be witness to it? The witch and the victim. None other. Now we cannot hope the witch will accuse herself; granted? Therefore, we must rely upon her victims—and they do testify, the children certainly do testify. As for the witches, none will deny that we are most eager for all their confessions. Therefore, what is left for a lawyer to bring out? I think I have made my point. Have I not?

HALE: But this child claims the girls are not truthful, and if they are not—

DANFORTH: That is precisely what I am about to consider, sir. What more may you ask of me? Unless you doubt my probity?[5]

HALE, *defeated:* I surely do not, sir. Let you consider it, then.

DANFORTH: And let you put your heart to rest. Her deposition, Mr. Proctor.

PROCTOR *hands it to him.* HATHORNE *rises, goes beside* DANFORTH, *and starts reading.* PARRIS *comes to his other side.* DANFORTH *looks at* JOHN PROCTOR, *then proceeds to read.* HALE *gets up, finds position near the judge, reads too.* PROCTOR *glances at* GILES. FRANCIS *prays silently, hands pressed together.* CHEEVER *waits placidly, the sublime official, dutiful.* MARY WARREN *sobs once.* JOHN PROCTOR *touches her hand reassuringly. Presently* DANFORTH *lifts his eyes, stands up, takes out a kerchief and blows his nose. The others stand aside as he moves in thought toward the window.*

PARRIS, *hardly able to contain his anger and fear:* I should like to question—

---

4. **ipso facto** (ip' sō fak' tō) "by that very fact"; "therefore" (Latin).
5. **probity** (prō' bə tē) *n.* complete honesty: integrity.

> **confounded** (kən found' id) *v.* confused; dismayed
>
> **Literary Analysis**
> **Dramatic and Verbal Irony and Logical Fallacy** In what ways is Danforth's entire argument based on a faulty premise?
>
> **Reading Strategy**
> **Categorizing Characters by Role** Based on this scene, how would you classify Danforth?
>
> **Reading Check**
> What is Danforth's basic argument about witnesses and witchcraft?

DANFORTH—*his first real outburst, in which his contempt for* PARRIS *is clear:* Mr. Parris, I bid you be silent! *He stands in silence, looking out the window. Now, having established that he will set the gait:* Mr. Cheever, will you go into the court and bring the children here? CHEEVER *gets up and goes out upstage.* DANFORTH *now turns to* MARY. Mary Warren, how came you to this turnabout? Has Mr. Proctor threatened you for this deposition?

MARY WARREN: No, sir.

DANFORTH: Has he ever threatened you?

MARY WARREN, *weaker:* No, sir.

DANFORTH, *sensing a weakening:* Has he threatened you?

MARY WARREN: No, sir.

DANFORTH: Then you tell me that you sat in my court, callously lying, when you knew that people would hang by your evidence? *She does not answer.* Answer me!

MARY WARREN, *almost inaudibly:* I did, sir.

DANFORTH: How were you instructed in your life? Do you not know that God damns all liars? *She cannot speak.* Or is it now that you lie?

▼ **Critical Viewing**
In this movie still, Danforth conveys a feeling of sympathy or understanding for Mary Warren. Compare this portrayal with your own image of Danforth. **[Compare]**

MARY WARREN: No, sir—I am with God now.

DANFORTH: You are with God now.

MARY WARREN: Aye, sir.

DANFORTH, *containing himself:* I will tell you this—you are either lying now, or you were lying in the court, and in either case you have committed perjury and you will go to jail for it. You cannot lightly say you lied, Mary. Do you know that?

MARY WARREN: I cannot lie no more. I am with God, I am with God.

But she breaks into sobs at the thought of it, and the right door opens, and enter SUSANNA WALCOTT, MERCY LEWIS, BETTY PARRIS, *and finally* ABIGAIL. CHEEVER *comes to* DANFORTH.

CHEEVER: Ruth Putnam's not in the court, sir, nor the other children.

DANFORTH: These will be sufficient. Sit you down, children. *Silently they sit.* Your friend, Mary Warren, has given us a deposition. In which she swears that she never saw familiar spirits, apparitions, nor any manifest of the Devil. She claims as well that none of you have seen these things either. *Slight pause.* Now, children, this is a court of law. The law, based upon the Bible, and the Bible, writ by Almighty God, forbid the practice of witchcraft, and describe death as the penalty thereof. But likewise, children, the law and Bible damn all bearers of false witness. *Slight pause.* Now then. It does not escape me that this deposition may be devised to blind us; it may well be that Mary Warren has been conquered by Satan, who sends her here to distract our sacred purpose. If so, her neck will break for it. But if she speak true, I bid you now drop your guile and confess your pretense, for a quick confession will go easier with you. *Pause.* Abigail Williams, rise. ABIGAIL *slowly rises.* Is there any truth in this?

ABIGAIL: No, sir.

DANFORTH, *thinks, glances at* MARY *then back to* ABIGAIL: Children, a very augur bit[6] will now be turned into your souls until your honesty is proved. Will either of you change your positions now, or do you force me to hard questioning?

ABIGAIL: I have naught to change, sir. She lies.

DANFORTH, *to* MARY: You would still go on with this?

MARY WARREN, *faintly:* Aye, sir.

DANFORTH, *turning to* ABIGAIL: A poppet were discovered in Mr. Proctor's house, stabbed by a needle. Mary Warren claims that you sat beside her in the court when she made it, and that you saw her make it and witnessed how she herself stuck the needle into it for safe-keeping. What say you to that?

ABIGAIL, *with a slight note of indignation:* It is a lie, sir.

DANFORTH, *after a slight pause:* While you worked for Mr. Proctor, did you see poppets in that house?

ABIGAIL: Goody Proctor always kept poppets.

---

6. **augur bit** sharp point of an augur, a tool used for boring holes.

Literary Analysis
Dramatic and Verbal Irony In what ways are Danforth's statements examples of dramatic irony?

**Reading Check**

According to Danforth, what is Mary Warren's fate—regardless of what she testifies? Why?

PROCTOR: Your Honor, my wife never kept no poppets. Mary Warren confesses it was her poppet.

CHEEVER: Your Excellency.

DANFORTH: Mr. Cheever.

CHEEVER: When I spoke with Goody Proctor in that house, she said she never kept no poppets. But she said she did keep poppets when she were a girl.

PROCTOR: She has not been a girl these fifteen years, Your Honor.

HATHORNE: But a poppet will keep fifteen years, will it not?

PROCTOR: It will keep if it is kept, but Mary Warren swears she never saw no poppets in my house, nor anyone else.

PARRIS: Why could there not have been poppets hid where no one ever saw them?

PROCTOR, *furious:* There might also be a dragon with five legs in my house, but no one has ever seen it.

PARRIS: We are here, Your Honor, precisely to discover what no one has ever seen.

PROCTOR: Mr. Danforth, what profit this girl to turn herself about? What may Mary Warren gain but hard questioning and worse?

DANFORTH: You are charging Abigail Williams with a marvelous cool plot to murder, do you understand that?

PROCTOR: I do, sir. I believe she means to murder.

DANFORTH, *pointing at* ABIGAIL, *incredulously:* This child would murder your wife?

PROCTOR: It is not a child. Now hear me, sir. In the sight of the congregation she were twice this year put out of this meetin' house for laughter during prayer.

DANFORTH, *shocked, turning to* ABIGAIL: What's this? Laughter during—!

PARRIS: Excellency, she were under Tituba's power at that time, but she is solemn now.

GILES: Aye, now she is solemn and goes to hang people!

DANFORTH: Quiet, man.

HATHORNE: Surely it have no bearing on the question, sir. He charges contemplation of murder.

DANFORTH: Aye. *He studies* ABIGAIL *for a moment, then:* Continue, Mr. Proctor.

PROCTOR: Mary. Now tell the Governor how you danced in the woods.

PARRIS, *instantly:* Excellency, since I come to Salem this man is blackening my name. He—

DANFORTH: In a moment, sir. *To* MARY WARREN, *sternly, and surprised.* What is this dancing?

MARY WARREN: I—*She glances at* ABIGAIL, *who is staring down at her remorselessly. Then, appealing to* PROCTOR: Mr. Proctor—

Reading Strategy
Categorizing Characters by Role How might Proctor classify Mary Warren? Why?

incredulously (in krej´ o͞o ləs lē) *adv.* skeptically

Reading Strategy
Categorizing Characters by Role In what category would you place Hathorne? Explain.

PROCTOR, *taking it right up:* Abigail leads the girls to the woods, Your Honor, and they have danced there naked—

PARRIS: Your Honor, this—

PROCTOR, *at once:* Mr. Parris discovered them himself in the dead of night! There's the "child" she is!

DANFORTH—*it is growing into a nightmare, and he turns, astonished, to* PARRIS: Mr. Parris—

PARRIS: I can only say, sir, that I never found any of them naked, and this man is—

DANFORTH: But you discovered them dancing in the woods? *Eyes on* PARRIS, *he points at* ABIGAIL. Abigail?

HALE: Excellency, when I first arrived from Beverly, Mr. Parris told me that.

DANFORTH: Do you deny it, Mr. Parris?

PARRIS: I do not, sir, but I never saw any of them naked.

DANFORTH: But she have *danced?*

PARRIS, *unwillingly:* Aye, sir.

DANFORTH, *as though with new eyes, looks at* ABIGAIL.

HATHORNE: Excellency, will you permit me? *He points at* MARY WARREN.

DANFORTH, *with great worry:* Pray, proceed.

HATHORNE: You say you never saw no spirits, Mary, were never threatened or afflicted by any manifest of the Devil or the Devil's agents.

MARY WARREN, *very faintly:* No, sir.

HATHORNE, *with a gleam of victory:* And yet, when people accused of witchery confronted you in court, you would faint, saying their spirits came out of their bodies and choked you—

MARY WARREN: That were pretense, sir.

DANFORTH: I cannot hear you.

MARY WARREN: Pretense, sir.

PARRIS: But you did turn cold, did you not? I myself picked you up many times, and your skin were icy. Mr. Danforth, you—

DANFORTH: I saw that many times.

PROCTOR: She only pretended to faint, Your Excellency. They're all marvelous pretenders.

HATHORNE: Then can she pretend to faint now?

PROCTOR: Now?

PARRIS: Why not? Now there are no spirits attacking her, for none in this room is accused of witchcraft. So let her turn herself cold now, let her pretend she is attacked now, let her faint. *He turns to* MARY WARREN. Faint!

MARY WARREN: Faint?

PARRIS: Aye, faint. Prove to us how you pretended in the court so many times.

Reading Strategy
Categorizing Characters by Role In what category is Parris? Explain your choice.

Reading Check

What information about Abigail does Danforth find shocking?

MARY WARREN, *looking to* PROCTOR: I—cannot faint now, sir.

PROCTOR, *alarmed, quietly:* Can you not pretend it?

MARY WARREN: I—*She looks about as though searching for the passion to faint.* I—have no *sense* of it now, I—

DANFORTH: Why? What is lacking now?

MARY WARREN: I—cannot tell, sir, I—

DANFORTH: Might it be that here we have no afflicting spirit loose, but in the court there were some?

MARY WARREN: I never saw no spirits.

PARRIS: Then see no spirits now, and prove to us that you can faint by your own will, as you claim.

MARY WARREN, *stares, searching for the emotion of it, and then shakes her head:* I— cannot do it.

PARRIS: Then you will confess, will you not? It were attacking spirits made you faint!

MARY WARREN: No, sir, I—

PARRIS: Your Excellency, this is a trick to blind the court!

MARY WARREN: It's not a trick! *She stands.* I—I used to faint because I— I thought I saw spirits.

DANFORTH: *Thought* you saw them!

MARY WARREN: But I did not, Your Honor.

HATHORNE: How could you think you saw them unless you saw them?

MARY WARREN: I—I cannot tell how, but I did. I—I heard the other girls screaming, and you, Your Honor, you seemed to believe them, and I—It

Literary Analysis
Dramatic and Visual Irony and Logical Fallacy
In what sense does Danforth's question express a logical fallacy?

▼ **Critical Viewing**
In this scene, Parris and Danforth order Mary to pretend to faint. Analyze this movie still and describe the emotions conveyed by Parris, Danforth, Mary, and the girls. **[Analyze]**

were only sport in the beginning, sir, but then the whole world cried spirits, spirits, and I—I promise you, Mr. Danforth, I only thought I saw them but I did not.

DANFORTH *peers at her.*

PARRIS, *smiling, but nervous because* DANFORTH *seems to be struck by* MARY WARREN'S *story:* Surely Your Excellency is not taken by this simple lie.

DANFORTH, *turning worriedly to* ABIGAIL: Abigail. I bid you now search your heart and tell me this—and beware of it, child, to God every soul is precious and His vengeance is terrible on them that take life without cause. Is it possible, child, that the spirits you have seen are illusion only, some deception that may cross your mind when—

ABIGAIL: Why, this—this—is a base question, sir.

DANFORTH: Child, I would have you consider it—

ABIGAIL: I have been hurt, Mr. Danforth; I have seen my blood runnin' out! I have been near to murdered every day because I done my duty pointing out the Devil's people—and this is my reward? To be mistrusted, denied, questioned like a—

DANFORTH, *weakening:* Child, I do not mistrust you—

ABIGAIL, *in an open threat:* Let you beware, Mr. Danforth. Think you to be so mighty that the power of Hell may not turn *your* wits? Beware of it! There is—*Suddenly, from an accusatory attitude, her face turns, looking into the air above—it is truly frightened.*

DANFORTH, *apprehensively:* What is it, child?

ABIGAIL, *looking about in the air, clasping her arms about her as though cold:* I—I know not. A wind, a cold wind, has come. *Her eyes fall on* MARY WARREN.

MARY WARREN, *terrified, pleading:* Abby!

MERCY LEWIS, *shivering:* Your Honor, I freeze!

PROCTOR: They're pretending!

HATHORNE, *touching* ABIGAIL'S *hand:* She is cold, Your Honor, touch her!

MERCY LEWIS, *through chattering teeth:* Mary, do you send this shadow on me?

MARY WARREN: Lord, save me!

SUSANNA WALCOTT: I freeze, I freeze!

ABIGAIL, *shivering, visibly:* It is a wind, a wind!

MARY WARREN: Abby, don't do that!

DANFORTH, *himself engaged and entered by* ABIGAIL: Mary Warren, do you witch her? I say to you, do you send your spirit out?

With a hysterical cry MARY WARREN *starts to run.* PROCTOR *catches her.*

MARY WARREN, *almost collapsing:* Let me go, Mr. Proctor, I cannot, I cannot—

ABIGAIL, *crying to Heaven:* Oh, Heavenly Father, take away this shadow!

Without warning or hesitation, PROCTOR *leaps at* ABIGAIL *and, grabbing*

Literary Analysis
Dramatic and Verbal Irony Which kind of irony does Abigail's speech about her "blood runnin' out" demonstrate? Explain.

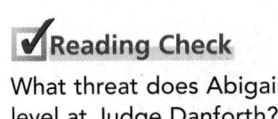

Reading Check
What threat does Abigail level at Judge Danforth?

her by the hair, pulls her to her feet. She screams in pain. DANFORTH,
astonished, cries, "What are you about?" and HATHORNE and PARRIS call,
"Take your hands off her!" and out of it all comes PROCTOR's roaring voice.

PROCTOR: How do you call Heaven! Whore! Whore!

HERRICK breaks PROCTOR from her.

HERRICK: John!

▲ **Critical Viewing**
Abigail pretends to be
under the control of
spirits. Does this scene
from the movie effectively
portray the scene in the
play? **[Connect]**

DANFORTH: Man! Man, what do you—

PROCTOR, *breathless and in agony:* It is a whore!

DANFORTH, *dumfounded:* You charge—?

ABIGAIL: Mr. Danforth, he is lying!

PROCTOR: Mark her! Now she'll suck a scream to stab me with, but—

DANFORTH: You will prove this! This will not pass!

PROCTOR, *trembling, his life collapsing about him:* I have known her, sir. I have known her.

DANFORTH: You—you are a lecher?

FRANCIS, *horrified:* John, you cannot say such a—

PROCTOR: Oh, Francis, I wish you had some evil in you that you might know me! *To* DANFORTH: A man will not cast away his good name. You surely know that.

DANFORTH, *dumfounded:* In—in what time? In what place?

PROCTOR, *his voice about to break, and his shame great:* In the proper place—where my beasts are bedded. On the last night of my joy, some eight months past. She used to serve me in my house, sir. *He has to clamp his jaw to keep from weeping.* A man may think God sleeps, but God sees everything. I know it now. I beg you, sir, I beg you—see her what she is. My wife, my dear good wife, took this girl soon after, sir, and put her out on the highroad. And being what she is, a lump of vanity, sir—*He is being overcome.* Excellency, forgive me, forgive me. *Angrily against himself, he turns away from the* GOVERNOR *for a moment. Then, as though to cry out is his only means of speech left:* She thinks to dance with me on my wife's grave! And well she might, for I thought of her softly. God help me, I lusted, and there *is* a promise in such sweat. But it is a whore's vengeance, and you must see it; I set myself entirely in your hands. I know you must see it now.

DANFORTH, <u>blanched</u>, *in horror, turning to* ABIGAIL: You deny every scrap and tittle of this?

ABIGAIL: If I must answer that, I will leave and I will not come back again!

DANFORTH *seems unsteady.*

PROCTOR: I have made a bell of my honor! I have rung the doom of my good name—you will believe me, Mr. Danforth! My wife is innocent, except she knew a whore when she saw one!

ABIGAIL, *stepping up to* DANFORTH: What look do you give me? DANFORTH *cannot speak.* I'll not have such looks! *She turns and starts for the door.*

DANFORTH: You will remain where you are! HERRICK *steps into her path. She comes up short, fire in her eyes.* Mr. Parris, go into the court and bring Goodwife Proctor out.

PARRIS, *objecting:* Your Honor, this is all a—

DANFORTH, *sharply to* PARRIS: Bring her out! And tell her not one word of what's been spoken here. And let you knock before you enter. PARRIS *goes out.* Now we shall touch the bottom of this swamp. *To* PROCTOR:

Reading Strategy
Categorizing Characters by Role Does Proctor's confession cause you to change the category to which you have assigned him? Why or why not?

blanched (blancht) *adj.* paled; whitened

**Reading Check**

What does John Proctor reveal about Abigail Williams?

Your wife, you say, is an honest woman.

PROCTOR: In her life, sir, she have never lied. There are them that cannot sing, and them that cannot weep—my wife cannot lie. I have paid much to learn it, sir.

DANFORTH: And when she put this girl out of your house, she put her out for a harlot?

PROCTOR: Aye, sir.

DANFORTH: And knew her for a harlot?

PROCTOR: Aye, sir, she knew her for a harlot.

DANFORTH: Good then. *To* ABIGAIL: And if she tell me, child, it were for harlotry, may God spread His mercy on you! *There is a knock. He calls to the door.* Hold! *To* ABIGAIL: Turn your back. Turn your back. *To* PROCTOR: Do likewise. *Both turn their backs—*ABIGAIL *with indignant slowness.* Now let neither of you turn to face Goody Proctor. No one in this room is to speak one word, or raise a gesture aye or nay. *He turns toward the door, calls:* Enter! *The door opens.* ELIZABETH *enters with* PARRIS. PARRIS *leaves her. She stands alone, her eyes looking for* PROCTOR. Mr. Cheever, report this testimony in all exactness. Are you ready?

CHEEVER: Ready, sir.

DANFORTH: Come here, woman. ELIZABETH *comes to him, glancing at* PROCTOR'S *back.* Look at me only, not at your husband. In my eyes only.

ELIZABETH, *faintly:* Good, sir.

DANFORTH: We are given to understand that at one time you dismissed your servant, Abigail Williams.

ELIZABETH: That is true, sir.

DANFORTH: For what cause did you dismiss her? *Slight pause. Then* ELIZABETH *tries to glance at* PROCTOR. You will look in my eyes only and not at your husband. The answer is in your memory and you need no help to give it to me. Why did you dismiss Abigail Williams?

ELIZABETH, *not knowing what to say, sensing a situation, wetting her lips to stall for time:* She—dissatisfied me. *Pause.* And my husband.

DANFORTH: In what way dissatisfied you?

ELIZABETH: She were—*She glances at* PROCTOR *for a cue.*

DANFORTH: Woman, look at me? ELIZABETH *does.* Were she slovenly? Lazy? What disturbance did she cause?

ELIZABETH: Your Honor, I—in that time I were sick. And I—My husband is a good and righteous man. He is never drunk as some are, nor wastin' his time at the shovelboard, but always at his work. But in my sickness—you see, sir, I were a long time sick after my last baby, and I thought I saw my husband somewhat turning from me. And this girl—*She turns to* ABIGAIL.

DANFORTH: Look at me.

ELIZABETH: Aye, sir. Abigail Williams—*She breaks off.*

Literary Analysis
Dramatic and Verbal Irony Which details in Elizabeth's exchange with Danforth reveal the dramatic irony at work in this scene?

DANFORTH: What of Abigail Williams?

ELIZABETH: I came to think he fancied her. And so one night I lost my wits, I think, and put her out on the highroad.

DANFORTH: Your husband—did he indeed turn from you?

ELIZABETH, *in agony:* My husband—is a goodly man, sir.

DANFORTH: Then he did not turn from you.

ELIZABETH, *starting to glance at* PROCTOR: He—

DANFORTH, *reaches out and holds her face, then:* Look at me! To your own knowledge, has John Proctor ever committed the crime of lechery? *In a crisis of indecision she cannot speak.* Answer my question! Is your husband a lecher!

ELIZABETH, *faintly:* No, sir.

DANFORTH: Remove her, Marshal.

PROCTOR: Elizabeth, tell the truth!

DANFORTH: She has spoken. Remove her!

PROCTOR, *crying out:* Elizabeth, I have confessed it!

ELIZABETH: Oh, God! *The door closes behind her.*

PROCTOR: She only thought to save my name!

HALE: Excellency, it is a natural lie to tell; I beg you, stop now before another is condemned! I may shut my conscience to it no more—private vengeance is working through this testimony! From the beginning this man has struck me true. By my oath to Heaven, I believe him now, and I pray you call back his wife before we—

DANFORTH: She spoke nothing of lechery, and this man has lied!

HALE: I believe him! *Pointing at* ABIGAIL: This girl has always struck me false! She has—

ABIGAIL, *with a weird, wild, chilling cry, screams up to the ceiling.*

ABIGAIL: You will not! Begone! Begone, I say!

DANFORTH: What is it, child? *But* ABIGAIL, *pointing with fear, is now raising up her frightened eyes, her awed face, toward the ceiling—the girls are doing the same—and now* HATHORNE, HALE, PUTNAM, CHEEVER, HERRICK, *and* DANFORTH *do the same. What's there? He lowers his eyes from the ceiling, and now he is frightened; there is real tension in his voice.* Child! *She is transfixed—with all the girls, she is whimpering, openmouthed, agape at the ceiling.* Girls! Why do you—?

MERCY LEWIS, *pointing:* It's on the beam! Behind the rafter!

DANFORTH, *looking up:* Where!

ABIGAIL: Why—? *She gulps.* Why do you come, yellow bird?

PROCTOR: Where's a bird? I see no bird!

ABIGAIL, *to the ceiling:* My face? My face?

PROCTOR: Mr. Hale—

DANFORTH: Be quiet!

PROCTOR, *to* HALE: Do you see a bird?

DANFORTH: Be quiet!!

ABIGAIL, *to the ceiling, in a genuine conversation with the "bird," as though trying to talk it out of attacking her:* But God made my face; you cannot want to tear my face. Envy is a deadly sin, Mary.

MARY WARREN, *on her feet with a spring, and horrified, pleading:* Abby!

ABIGAIL, *unperturbed, continuing to the "bird":* Oh, Mary, this is a black art to change your shape. No, I cannot, I cannot stop my mouth; it's God's work I do.

MARY WARREN: Abby, I'm *here!*

PROCTOR, *frantically:* They're pretending, Mr. Danforth!

ABIGAIL—*now she takes a backward step, as though in fear the bird will swoop down momentarily:* Oh, please, Mary! Don't come down.

SUSANNA WALCOTT: Her claws, she's stretching her claws!

PROCTOR: Lies, lies.

ABIGAIL, *backing further, eyes still fixed above:* Mary, please don't hurt me!

MARY WARREN, *to* DANFORTH: I'm not hurting her!

DANFORTH, *to* MARY WARREN: Why does she see this vision?

MARY WARREN: She sees nothin'!

ABIGAIL, *now staring full front as though hypnotized, and mimicking the exact tone of* MARY WARREN'S *cry:* She sees nothin'!

MARY WARREN, *pleading:* Abby, you mustn't!

ABIGAIL AND ALL THE GIRLS, *all transfixed:* Abby, you mustn't!

MARY WARREN, *to all the girls:* I'm here, I'm here!

GIRLS: I'm here, I'm here!

DANFORTH, *horrified:* Mary Warren! Draw back your spirit out of them!

MARY WARREN: Mr. Danforth!

GIRLS, *cutting her off:* Mr. Danforth!

DANFORTH: Have you compacted with the Devil? Have you?

MARY WARREN: Never, never!

GIRLS: Never, never!

DANFORTH, *growing hysterical:* Why can they only repeat you?

PROCTOR: Give me a whip—I'll stop it!

MARY WARREN: They're sporting. They—!

GIRLS: They're sporting!

MARY WARREN, *turning on them all hysterically and stamping her feet:* Abby, stop it!

GIRLS, *stamping their feet:* Abby, stop it!

MARY WARREN: Stop it!

GIRLS: Stop it!

MARY WARREN, *screaming it out at the top of her lungs, and raising her fists:* Stop it!!

GIRLS, *raising their fists:* Stop it!!

MARY WARREN, *utterly confounded, and becoming overwhelmed by* ABIGAIL'S *—and the girls'—utter conviction, starts to whimper, hands half raised, powerless, and all the girls begin whimpering exactly as she does.*

DANFORTH: A little while ago you were afflicted. Now it seems you afflict others; where did you find this power?

MARY WARREN, *staring at* ABIGAIL: I—have no power.

GIRLS: I have no power.

PROCTOR: They're gulling[7] you, Mister!

DANFORTH: Why did you turn about this past two weeks? You have seen the Devil, have you not?

HALE, *indicating* ABIGAIL *and the* GIRLS: You cannot believe them!

MARY WARREN: I—

PROCTOR, *sensing her weakening:* Mary, God damns all liars!

DANFORTH, *pounding it into her:* You have seen the Devil, you have made compact with Lucifer, have you not?

PROCTOR: God damns liars, Mary!

MARY *utters something unintelligible, staring at* ABIGAIL, *who keeps watching the "bird" above.*

DANFORTH: I cannot hear you. What do you say? MARY *utters again unintelligibly.* You will confess yourself or you will hang! *He turns her roughly to face him.* Do you know who I am? I say you will hang if you do not open with me!

PROCTOR: Mary, remember the angel Raphael—do that which is good and—

ABIGAIL, *pointing upward:* The wings! Her wings are spreading! Mary, please, don't, don't—!

HALE: I see nothing, Your Honor!

DANFORTH: Do you confess this power! *He is an inch from her face.* Speak!

ABIGAIL: She's going to come down! She's walking the beam!

DANFORTH: Will you speak!

MARY WARREN, *staring in horror:* I cannot!

GIRLS: I cannot!

PARRIS: Cast the Devil out! Look him in the face! Trample him! We'll save you, Mary, only stand fast against him and—

ABIGAIL, *looking up:* Look out! She's coming down!

---

7. gulling fooling.

Literary Analysis

Dramatic and Verbal Irony In what ways does the idea of Abigail's "utter conviction" serve as an ironic statement?

**Reading Check**

What do the girls do to undermine Mary Warren's testimony?

She and all the girls run to one wall, shielding their eyes. And now, as though cornered, they let out a gigantic scream, and MARY, *as though infected, opens her mouth and screams with them. Gradually* ABIGAIL *and the girls leave off, until only* MARY *is left there, staring up at the "bird," screaming madly. All watch her, horrified by this evident fit.* PROCTOR *strides to her.*

PROCTOR: Mary, tell the Governor what they—*He has hardly got a word out, when, seeing him coming for her, she rushes out of his reach, screaming in horror.*

MARY WARREN: Don't touch me—don't touch me! *At which the girls halt at the door.*

PROCTOR, *astonished:* Mary!

MARY WARREN, *pointing at* PROCTOR: You're the Devil's man!

He is stopped in his tracks.

PARRIS: Praise God!

GIRLS: Praise God!

PROCTOR, *numbed:* Mary, how— ?

MARY WARREN: I'll not hang with you! I love God, I love God.

DANFORTH, *to* MARY: He bid you do the Devil's work?

MARY WARREN, *hysterically, indicating* PROCTOR: He come at me by night and every day to sign, to sign, to—

DANFORTH: Sign what?

PARRIS: The Devil's book? He come with a book?

MARY WARREN, *hysterically, pointing at* PROCTOR, *fearful of him:* My name, he want my name. "I'll murder you," he says, "if my wife hangs! We must go and overthrow the court," he says!

DANFORTH'S *head jerks toward* PROCTOR, *shock and horror in his face.*

PROCTOR, *turning, appealing to* HALE: Mr. Hale!

MARY WARREN, *her sobs beginning:* He wake me every night, his eyes were like coals and his fingers claw my neck, and I sign, I sign . . .

HALE: Excellency, this child's gone wild!

PROCTOR, *as* DANFORTH'S *wide eyes pour on him:* Mary, Mary!

MARY WARREN, *screaming at him:* No, I love God; I go your way no more. I love God, I bless God. *Sobbing, she rushes to* ABIGAIL. Abby, Abby, I'll never hurt you more! *They all watch, as* ABIGAIL, *out of her infinite charity, reaches out and draws the sobbing* MARY *to her, and then looks up to* DANFORTH.

DANFORTH, *to* PROCTOR: What are you? PROCTOR *is beyond speech in his anger.* You are combined with anti-Christ,[8] are you not? I have seen your power; you will not deny it! What say you, Mister?

HALE: Excellency—

Literary Analysis
Dramatic and Verbal Irony Which two words in these stage directions describing Abigail and Mary are an example of verbal irony?

---

8. anti-Christ In the Bible, the great antagonist of Christ expected to spread universal evil.

DANFORTH: I will have nothing from you, Mr. Hale! *To* PROCTOR: Will you confess yourself befouled with Hell, or do you keep that black allegiance yet? What say you?

PROCTOR, *his mind wild, breathless:* I say—I say—God is dead!

PARRIS: Hear it, hear it!

PROCTOR, *laughs insanely, then:* A fire, a fire is burning! I hear the boot of Lucifer, I see his filthy face! And it is my face, and yours, Danforth! For them that quail to bring men out of ignorance, as I have quailed, and as you quail now when you know in all your black hearts that this be fraud—God damns our kind especially, and we will burn, we will burn together.

DANFORTH: Marshal! Take him and Corey with him to the jail!

HALE, *staring across to the door:* I denounce these proceedings!

PROCTOR: You are pulling Heaven down and raising up a whore!

HALE: I denounce these proceedings, I quit this court! *He slams the door to the outside behind him.*

DANFORTH, *calling to him in a fury:* Mr. Hale! Mr. Hale!

Review and Assess
Thinking About Act III

1. **Respond:** Which incident in Act III provoked the strongest emotional response in you? Why?

2. **(a) Recall:** Which three depositions are presented to the judges and on whose behalf? **(b) Analyze:** How do the judges discourage defenses of the accused?

3. **(a) Recall:** What does John Proctor confess to Danforth? **(b) Interpret:** Why does Proctor make this confession? **(c) Infer:** What does his confession reveal about his character?

4. **(a) Recall:** What is the lie Elizabeth Proctor tells Danforth? **(b) Analyze:** What are the consequences of her lie?

5. **(a) Recall:** What truth does Mary Warren reveal about her involvement with "spirits"? **(b) Analyze:** Why does she change her testimony and turn on John Proctor?

6. **(a) Recall:** What does Hale denounce at the end of Act III? **(b) Evaluate:** Do you find Hale sympathetic? Why or why not?

7. **Apply:** Imagine that Elizabeth Proctor had told Danforth the truth. In what way might the outcome of the trials have been different?

8. **Assess:** Who bears the most guilt for the fate of those hanged in the Salem witch trials—the girls who accused innocent people or the judges who sentenced them to death?

Review and Assess

Literary Analysis

Dramatic and Verbal Irony

1. Using a chart like the one shown, list three examples of **dramatic and verbal irony** from Act III. Identify the type of irony and explain what each speaker really means.

Passage		Type of Irony	Analysis
	...▶		

2. What does the audience know that Elizabeth does not know when she testifies about her husband's behavior?
3. Why is the effect of Elizabeth's testimony ironic?
4. What is ironic about Mary Warren's statement, "I—have no power," when she is being interrogated in front of Abigail Williams?

Connecting Literary Elements

5. In Judge Danforth's dramatic exchange with Reverend Hale, what erroneous idea underlies all his reasoning about the legal proceedings? Explain.
6. In what sense does Danforth's **logical fallacy** have ramifications far beyond the conviction of John Proctor?

Reading Strategy

Categorizing Characters by Role

7. (a) Compare and contrast Reverend Parris with Reverend Hale. (b) How would you **categorize** the effectiveness of each in his role as minister?
8. (a) Which character traits would you ascribe to Betty Parris, Sarah Good, and Mercy Lewis? (b) Do you have sympathy for them? Why or why not?
9. Which characters would you classify as static (unchanging), and which would you classify as dynamic (changing or growing)? Why?
10. What other categories do you think would be useful for classifying the characters? Explain.

Extend Understanding

11. **Career Connection:** Which qualities of a good judge do you think are lacking in Hathorne and Danforth? Explain.

Quick Review

Dramatic irony occurs when there is a contradiction between what a character thinks and what the audience knows to be true.

Verbal irony occurs when a character says one thing but means something else.

A **logical fallacy** is an argument that appears logical but is based on a faulty premise.

To understand the characters' roles in a play, **categorize the characters** in meaningful ways.

 Take It to the Net
www.phschool.com
Take the interactive self-test online to check your understanding of this selection.

Integrate Language Skills

Vocabulary Development Lesson

Concept Development: Legal Terms

The Crucible contains a number of legal terms. For example, a *deposition* is a legal document that contains the written testimony of a witness. Determine the meaning of each of these words from the context in which it appears in Act III. Then, use each word in a sentence.

1. prosecutor **2.** contempt **3.** perjury

Spelling Strategy

When adding an *-ly* suffix to a word that ends in a consonant, do not double or change the consonant. The words *deferentially* and *incredulously* follow this rule. Change each of the following adjectives into adverbs by adding the suffix *-ly:*

1. dubious **2.** bountiful **3.** obvious

Grammar and Style Lesson

Subject and Verb Agreement in Inverted Sentences

In most sentences, the subject precedes the verb, but in an **inverted sentence** the verb comes first. Notice how the verb **agrees** in number with the subject of the following inverted sentences.

> V   S
> **Plural:** Now there <u>are</u> no <u>spirits</u> attacking her.

Practice Complete each sentence by choosing the correct form of the verb in parentheses.

1. There (is, are) a courtroom scene in Act III.

Concept Development: Relationships

Review the vocabulary list on page 1290. Then, for each item below, indicate whether the paired words are synonyms or antonyms.

1. contentious, combative
2. deposition, testimony
3. imperceptible, obvious
4. deferentially, politely
5. anonymity, notoriety
6. prodigious, minuscule
7. effrontery, timidity
8. confounded, puzzled
9. incredulously, disbelievingly
10. blanched, darkened

2. In the courtroom (sits, sit) many people.
3. Hearing the case (is, are) Danforth and Hathorne.
4. Here (is, are) Abigail and her cohorts.
5. Under suspicion (is, are) dozens of citizens.

Writing Application As Reverend Hale, write a letter to the editor of the Salem newspaper explaining why you now oppose the court's actions. Use three inverted sentences, and make your subjects and verbs agree in number.

W∕G *Prentice Hall Writing and Grammar Connection: Chapter 23, Section 1*

Extension Activities

Writing Write a **character sketch** of Mary Warren in which you evaluate her strengths and weaknesses.

Listening and Speaking Draft and perform the monologue Elizabeth might give at the moment she learns the effect of her lie in court.

Prepare to Read

The Crucible, Act IV

Literary Analysis

Theme

A **theme** is the central idea or insight into life that a writer strives to convey in a work of literature. Like most longer works, *The Crucible* has several themes. One theme is that fear and suspicion are infectious and can turn into mass hysteria. Miller also touches upon the destructive power of guilt, revenge, and the failure of a judicial system fueled by ideology instead of justice. As you read Act IV, use a chart like the one shown to consider these and other themes that Miller conveys.

Connecting Literary Elements

An **extended metaphor** is a comparison that is developed throughout the course of a literary work. Miller's imagery of the seventeenth-century witch hunt in Salem builds a comparison to the events of the late 1940s and early 1950s in America, a time characterized by these intensified emotions:

- Fear of communism and a widespread hysteria that Communists had infiltrated the State Department.
- Panic based on witch hunt tactics—those who opposed McCarthy's hearings were charged with Communism themselves.

Notice Miller's ability to explore the events of his own era within the parallel context of the Salem witchcraft trials.

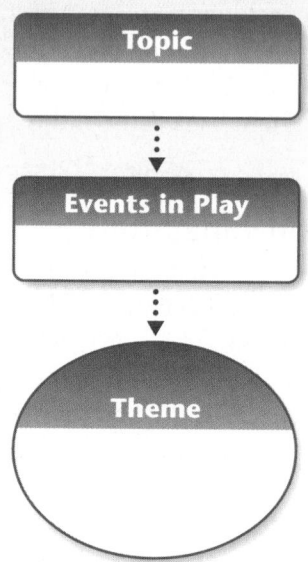

Reading Strategy

Applying Themes to Contemporary Events

The parallel between the events in Salem, as Miller depicts them, and ongoing events in Congress at the time Miller wrote the play are clear. As you read Act IV, think about what themes or messages Miller was conveying that specifically related to contemporary events.

Vocabulary Development

agape (ə gāp´) *adj.* wide open (p. 1322)

conciliatory (kən sil´ ē ə tôr´ ē) *adj.* tending to soothe anger (p. 1324)

beguile (bē gīl´) *v.* trick (p. 1324)

floundering (floun´ də riŋ) *n.* awkward struggling (p. 1324)

retaliation (ri ta´ lē ā´ shən) *n.* act of returning an injury or wrong (p. 1324)

adamant (ad´ ə mənt) adj. firm; unyielding (p. 1324)

cleave (klēv) *v.* adhere; cling (p. 1326)

sibilance (sib´ əl əns) *n.* hissing sound (p. 1326)

tantalized (tan´ tə līzd) *adj.* tormented; frustrated (p. 1329)

purged (pʉrjd) *v.* cleansed (p. 1331)

Review and Anticipate

"Is every defense an attack upon the court?" Hale asks in Act III. Danforth observes, "A person is either with this court or he must be counted against it." Such remarks stress the powerlessness of people like John Proctor and Giles Corey against the mounting injustices in Salem. In pursuing justice, their efforts backfire, and their own names join the list of those accused. What do you think the final outcome will be? Who will survive, and who will perish? Read the final act to see if your predictions are correct.

ACT IV

A cell in Salem jail, that fall.

At the back is a high barred window; near it, a great, heavy door. Along the walls are two benches.

The place is in darkness but for the moonlight seeping through the bars. It appears empty. Presently footsteps are heard coming down a corridor beyond the wall, keys rattle, and the door swings open. MARSHAL HERRICK *enters with a lantern.*

He is nearly drunk, and heavy-footed. He goes to a bench and nudges a bundle of rags lying on it.

HERRICK: Sarah, wake up! Sarah Good! *He then crosses to the other benches.*

SARAH GOOD, *rising in her rags:* Oh, Majesty! Comin',comin'! Tituba, he's here, His Majesty's come!

HERRICK: Go to the north cell; this place is wanted now. *He hangs his lantern on the wall.* TITUBA *sits up.*

TITUBA: That don't look to me like His Majesty; look to me like the marshal.

HERRICK, *taking out a flask:* Get along with you now, clear this place. *He drinks, and* SARAH GOOD *comes and peers up into his face.*

SARAH GOOD: Oh, is it you, Marshal! I thought sure you be the devil comin' for us. Could I have a sip of cider for me goin'-away?

HERRICK, *handing her the flask:* And where are you off to, Sarah?

TITUBA, *as* SARAH *drinks:* We goin' to Barbados, soon the Devil gits here with the feathers and the wings.

HERRICK: Oh? A happy voyage to you.

SARAH GOOD: A pair of bluebirds wingin' southerly, the two of us! Oh, it be a grand transformation, Marshal! *She raises the flask to drink again.*

HERRICK, *taking the flask from her lips:* You'd best give me that or you'll never rise off the ground. Come along now.

Literary Analysis
Theme In what ways do these stage directions describing an empty cell help to convey a theme?

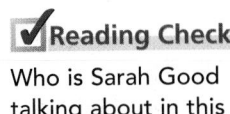

✔Reading Check
Who is Sarah Good talking about in this scene?

TITUBA: I'll speak to him for you, if you desires to come along, Marshal.

HERRICK: I'd not refuse it, Tituba; it's the proper morning to fly into Hell.

TITUBA: Oh, it be no Hell in Barbados. Devil, him be pleasure man in Barbados, him be singin' and dancin' in Barbados. It's you folks—you riles him up 'round here; it be too cold 'round here for that Old Boy. He freeze his soul in Massachusetts, but in Barbados he just as sweet and—*A bellowing cow is heard, and* TITUBA *leaps up and calls to the window:* Aye, sir! That's him, Sarah!

SARAH GOOD: I'm here, Majesty! *They hurriedly pick up their rags as* HOPKINS, *a guard, enters.*

HOPKINS: The Deputy Governor's arrived.

HERRICK, *grabbing* TITUBA: Come along, come along.

TITUBA, *resisting him:* No, he comin' for me. I goin' home!

HERRICK, *pulling her to the door:* That's not Satan, just a poor old cow with a hatful of milk. Come along now, out with you!

TITUBA, *calling to the window:* Take me home, Devil! Take me home!

SARAH GOOD, *following the shouting* TITUBA *out:* Tell him I'm goin', Tituba! Now you tell him Sarah Good is goin' too!

In the corridor outside TITUBA *calls on—"Take me home, Devil: Devil take me home!" and* HOPKINS' *voice orders her to move on.* HERRICK *returns and begins to push old rags and straw into a corner. Hearing footsteps, he turns, and enter* DANFORTH *and* JUDGE HATHORNE. *They are in greatcoats and wear hats against the bitter cold. They are followed in by* CHEEVER, *who carries a dispatch case and a flat wooden box containing his writing materials.*

HERRICK: Good morning, Excellency.

DANFORTH: Where is Mr. Parris?

HERRICK: I'll fetch him. *He starts for the door.*

DANFORTH: Marshal. HERRICK *stops.* When did Reverend Hale arrive?

HERRICK: It were toward midnight, I think.

DANFORTH, *suspiciously:* What is he about here?

HERRICK: He goes among them that will hang, sir. And he prays with them. He sits with Goody Nurse now. And Mr. Parris with him.

DANFORTH: Indeed. That man have no authority to enter here, Marshal. Why have you let him in?

HERRICK: Why, Mr. Parris command me, sir. I cannot deny him.

DANFORTH: Are you drunk, Marshal?

HERRICK: No, sir; it is a bitter night, and I have no fire here.

DANFORTH, *containing his anger:* Fetch Mr. Parris.

HERRICK: Aye, sir.

DANFORTH: There is a prodigious stench in this place.

HERRICK: I have only now cleared the people out for you.

DANFORTH: Beware hard drink, Marshal.

Literary Analysis
Theme What theme do you think Herrick's drunkenness on execution day implies?

HERRICK: Aye, sir. *He waits an instant for further orders. But* DANFORTH, *in dissatisfaction, turns his back on him, and* HERRICK *goes out. There is a pause.* DANFORTH *stands in thought.*

HATHORNE: Let you question Hale, Excellency; I should not be surprised he have been preaching in Andover[1] lately.

DANFORTH: We'll come to that; speak nothing of Andover. Parris prays with him. That's strange. *He blows on his hands, moves toward the window, and looks out.*

HATHORNE: Excellency, I wonder if it be wise to let Mr. Parris so continuously with the prisoners. DANFORTH *turns to him, interested.* I think, sometimes, the man has a mad look these days.

DANFORTH: Mad?

HATHORNE: I met him yesterday coming out of his house, and I bid him good morning—and he wept and went his way. I think it is not well the village sees him so unsteady.

DANFORTH: Perhaps he have some sorrow.

CHEEVER, *stamping his feet against the cold:* I think it be the cows, sir.

DANFORTH: Cows?

CHEEVER: There be so many cows wanderin' the highroads, now their masters are in the jails, and much disagreement who they will belong to now. I know Mr. Parris be arguin' with farmers all yesterday—there is great contention, sir, about the cows. Contention make him weep, sir; it were always a man that weep for contention. *He turns, as do* HATHORNE *and* DANFORTH *hearing someone coming up the corridor.* DANFORTH *raises his head as* PARRIS *enters. He is gaunt, frightened, and sweating in his greatcoat.*

PARRIS, *to* DANFORTH, *instantly:* Oh, good morning, sir, thank you for coming. I beg your pardon wakin' you so early. Good morning, Judge Hathorne.

DANFORTH: Reverend Hale have no right to enter this—

PARRIS: Excellency, a moment. *He hurries back and shuts the door.*

HATHORNE: Do you leave him alone with the prisoners?

DANFORTH: What's his business here?

PARRIS, *prayerfully holding up his hands:* Excellency, hear me. It is a providence. Reverend Hale has returned to bring Rebecca Nurse to God.

DANFORTH, *surprised:* He bids her confess?

PARRIS, *sitting:* Hear me. Rebecca have not given me a word this three month since she came. Now she sits with him, and her sister and Martha Corey and two or three others, and he pleads with them, confess their crimes and save their lives.

---

1. **Andover** During the height of the terror in Salem Village, a similar hysteria broke out in the nearby town of Andover. There, many respected people were accused of practicing witchcraft and confessed to escape death. However, in Andover people soon began questioning the reality of the situation and the hysteria quickly subsided.

Literary Analysis
Theme What theme does Miller convey through Hathorne's description of Parris?

Reading Strategy
Applying Themes to Contemporary Events What warning might the details about changes in Salem convey about the growing anti-Communist fear and suspicion in Miller's own time?

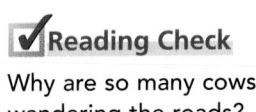Reading Check

Why are so many cows wandering the roads?

DANFORTH: Why—this is indeed a providence. And they soften, they soften?

PARRIS: Not yet, not yet. But I thought to summon you, sir, that we might think on whether it be not wise, to—*He dares not say it.* I had thought to put a question, sir, and I hope you will not—

DANFORTH: Mr. Parris, be plain, what troubles you?

PARRIS: There is news, sir, that the court—the court must reckon with. My niece, sir, my niece—I believe she has vanished.

DANFORTH: Vanished!

PARRIS: I had thought to advise you of it earlier in the week, but—

DANFORTH: Why? How long is she gone?

PARRIS: This be the third night. You see, sir, she told me she would stay a night with Mercy Lewis. And next day, when she does not return, I send to Mr. Lewis to inquire. Mercy told him she would sleep in *my* house for a night.

DANFORTH: They are both gone?!

PARRIS, *in fear of him:* They are, sir.

DANFORTH, *alarmed:* I will send a party for them. Where may they be?

PARRIS: Excellency, I think they be aboard a ship. DANFORTH *stands agape.* My daughter tells me how she heard them speaking of ships last week, and tonight I discover my—my strongbox is broke into. *He presses his fingers against his eyes to keep back tears.*

HATHORNE, *astonished:* She have robbed you?

PARRIS: Thirty-one pound is gone. I am penniless. *He covers his face and sobs.*

DANFORTH: Mr. Parris, you are a brainless man! *He walks in thought, deeply worried.*

PARRIS: Excellency, it profit nothing you should blame me. I cannot think they would run off except they fear to keep in Salem any more. *He is pleading.* Mark it, sir, Abigail had close knowledge of the town, and since the news of Andover has broken here—

DANFORTH: Andover is remedied. The court returns there on Friday, and will resume examinations.

PARRIS: I am sure of it, sir. But the rumor here speaks rebellion in Andover, and it—

DANFORTH: There is no rebellion in Andover!

PARRIS: I tell you what is said here, sir. Andover have thrown out the court, they say, and will have no part of witchcraft. There be a faction here, feeding on that news, and I tell you true, sir, I fear there will be riot here.

HATHORNE: Riot! Why at every execution I have seen naught but high satisfaction in the town.

PARRIS: Judge Hathorne—it were another sort that hanged till now. Rebecca Nurse is no Bridget that lived three year with Bishop before she married him. John Proctor is not Isaac Ward that drank his

agape (ə gāp′) *adj.* wide open

▶ **Critical Viewing**
In this court scene from execution day what might Parris be saying to Judge Danforth? **[Speculate]**

family to ruin. *To* DANFORTH: I would to God it were not so, Excellency, but these people have great weight yet in the town. Let Rebecca stand upon the gibbet[2] and send up some righteous prayer, and I fear she'll wake a vengeance on you.

HATHORNE: Excellency, she is condemned a witch. The court have—

DANFORTH, *in deep concern, raising a hand to* HATHORNE: Pray you. *To* PARRIS: How do you propose, then?

PARRIS: Excellency, I would postpone these hangin's for a time.

DANFORTH: There will be no postponement.

PARRIS: Now Mr. Hale's returned, there is hope, I think—for if he bring even one of these to God, that confession surely damns the others in the public eye, and none may doubt more that they are all linked to Hell. This way, unconfessed and claiming innocence, doubts are multiplied, many honest people will weep for them, and our good purpose is lost in their tears.

DANFORTH, *after thinking a moment, then going to* CHEEVER: Give me the list.

CHEEVER *opens the dispatch case, searches.*

PARRIS: It cannot be forgot, sir, that when I summoned the congregation for John Proctor's excommunication there were hardly thirty people come to hear it. That speak a discontent, I think, and—

DANFORTH, *studying the list:* There will be no postponement.

PARRIS: Excellency—

DANFORTH: Now, sir—which of these in your opinion may be brought to God? I will myself strive with him till dawn. *He hands the list to* PARRIS, *who merely glances at it.*

---

2. **gibbet** (jib′ it) *n.* gallows.

Reading Strategy
Applying Themes to Contemporary Events
What might have happened if the McCarthy hearings had been postponed?

✔ **Reading Check**
What has happened to Abigail?

The Crucible, Act IV ◆ 1323

PARRIS: There is not sufficient time till dawn.

DANFORTH: I shall do my utmost. Which of them do you have hope for?

PARRIS, *not even glancing at the list now, and in a quavering voice, quietly:* Excellency—a dagger—*He chokes up.*

DANFORTH: What do you say?

PARRIS: Tonight, when I open my door to leave my house—a dagger clattered to the ground. *Silence.* DANFORTH *absorbs this. Now* PARRIS *cries out:* You cannot hang this sort. There is danger for me. I dare not step outside at night!

REVEREND HALE *enters. They look at him for an instant in silence. He is steeped in sorrow, exhausted, and more direct than he ever was.*

DANFORTH: Accept my congratulations, Reverend Hale; we are gladdened to see you returned to your good work.

HALE, *coming to* DANFORTH *now:* You must pardon them. They will not budge.

HERRICK *enters, waits.*

DANFORTH, *conciliatory:* You misunderstand, sir; I cannot pardon these when twelve are already hanged for the same crime. It is not just.

PARRIS, *with failing heart:* Rebecca will not confess?

HALE: The sun will rise in a few minutes. Excellency, I must have more time.

DANFORTH: Now hear me, and beguile yourselves no more. I will not receive a single plea for pardon or postponement. Them that will not confess will hang. Twelve are already executed; the names of these seven are given out, and the village expects to see them die this morning. Postponement now speaks a floundering on my part; reprieve or pardon must cast doubt upon the guilt of them that died till now. While I speak God's law, I will not crack its voice with whimpering. If retaliation is your fear, know this—I should hang ten thousand that dared to rise against the law, and an ocean of salt tears could not melt the resolution of the statutes. Now draw yourselves up like men and help me, as you are bound by Heaven to do. Have you spoken with them all, Mr. Hale?

HALE: All but Proctor. He is in the dungeon.

DANFORTH, *to* HERRICK: What's Proctor's way now?

HERRICK: He sits like some great bird; you'd not know he lived except he will take food from time to time.

DANFORTH, *after thinking a moment:* His wife—his wife must be well on with child now.

HERRICK: She is, sir.

DANFORTH: What think you, Mr. Parris? You have closer knowledge of this man; might her presence soften him?

PARRIS: It is possible, sir. He have not laid eyes on her these three months. I should summon her.

DANFORTH, *to* HERRICK: Is he yet adamant? Has he struck at you again?

conciliatory (kən sil′ ē ə tôr′ ē) *adj.* tending to soothe anger

beguile (bē gīl′) *v.* trick

floundering (floun′ dər in) *n.* awkward struggling

retaliation (ri tal′ ē ā′ shən) *n.* act of returning an injury or wrong

adamant (ad′ ə mənt) *adj.* firm; unyielding

HERRICK: He cannot, sir, he is chained to the wall now.

DANFORTH, *after thinking on it:* Fetch Goody Proctor to me. Then let you bring him up.

HERRICK: Aye, sir. HERRICK *goes. There is silence.*

HALE: Excellency, if you postpone a week and publish to the town that you are striving for their confessions, that speak mercy on your part, not faltering.

DANFORTH: Mr. Hale, as God have not empowered me like Joshua to stop this sun from rising,[3] so I cannot withhold from them the perfection of their punishment.

HALE, *harder now:* If you think God wills you to raise rebellion, Mr. Danforth, you are mistaken!

DANFORTH, *instantly:* You have heard rebellion spoken in the town?

HALE: Excellency, there are orphans wandering from house to house; abandoned cattle bellow on the highroads, the stink of rotting crops hangs everywhere, and no man knows when the harlots' cry will end his life—and you wonder yet if rebellion's spoke? Better you should marvel how they do not burn your province!

DANFORTH: Mr. Hale, have you preached in Andover this month?

HALE: Thank God they have no need of me in Andover.

DANFORTH: You baffle me, sir. Why have you returned here?

HALE: Why, it is all simple. I come to do the Devil's work. I come to counsel Christians they should belie themselves. *His sarcasm collapses.* There is blood on my head! Can you not see the blood on my head!!

PARRIS: Hush! *For he has heard footsteps. They all face the door.* HERRICK *enters with* ELIZABETH. *Her wrists are linked by heavy chain, which* HERRICK *now removes. Her clothes are dirty; her face is pale and gaunt.* HERRICK *goes out.*

DANFORTH, *very politely:* Goody Proctor. *She is silent.* I hope you are hearty?

ELIZABETH, *as a warning reminder:* I am yet six months before my time.

DANFORTH: Pray be at your ease, we come not for your life. We— *uncertain how to plead, for he is not accustomed to it.* Mr. Hale, will you speak with the woman?

HALE: Goody Proctor, your husband is marked to hang this morning *Pause.*

ELIZABETH, *quietly:* I have heard it.

HALE: You know, do you not, that I have no connection with the court? *She seems to doubt it.* I come of my own, Goody Proctor. I would save your husband's life, for if he is taken I count myself his murderer. Do you understand me?

---

3. **Joshua . . . rising** In the Bible, Joshua, leader of the Jews after the death of Moses, asks God to make the sun and the moon stand still during a battle, and his request is granted.

Literary Analysis
Theme What themes do these descriptions of abandonment convey?

**Reading Check**
Why does Hale say he has returned to Salem?

ELIZABETH: What do you want of me?

HALE: Goody Proctor, I have gone this three month like our Lord into the wilderness. I have sought a Christian way, for damnation's doubled on a minister who counsels men to lie.

HATHORNE: It is no lie, you cannot speak of lies.

HALE: It is a lie! They are innocent!

DANFORTH: I'll hear no more of that!

HALE, *continuing to* ELIZABETH: Let you not mistake your duty as I mistook my own. I came into this village like a bridegroom to his beloved, bearing gifts of high religion; the very crowns of holy law I brought, and what I touched with my bright confidence, it died; and where I turned the eye of my great faith, blood flowed up. Beware, Goody Proctor— <u>cleave</u> to no faith when faith brings blood. It is mistaken law that leads you to sacrifice. Life, woman, life is God's most precious gift; no principle, however glorious, may justify the taking of it. I beg you, woman, prevail upon your husband to confess. Let him give his lie. Quail not before God's judgment in this, for it may well be God damns a liar less than he that throws his life away for pride. Will you plead with him? I cannot think he will listen to another.

ELIZABETH, *quietly:* I think that be the Devil's argument.

HALE, *with a climactic desperation:* Woman, before the laws of God we are as swine! We cannot read His will!

ELIZABETH: I cannot dispute with you, sir; I lack learning for it.

DANFORTH, *going to her:* Goody Proctor, you are not summoned here for disputation. Be there no wifely tenderness within you? He will die with the sunrise. Your husband. Do you understand it? *She only looks at him.* What say you? Will you contend with him? *She is silent.* Are you stone? I tell you true, woman, had I no other proof of your unnatural life, your dry eyes now would be sufficient evidence that you delivered up your soul to Hell! A very ape would weep at such calamity! Have the devil dried up any tear of pity in you? *She is silent.* Take her out. It profit nothing she should speak to him!

ELIZABETH, *quietly:* Let me speak with him, Excellency.

PARRIS, *with hope:* You'll strive with him? *She hesitates.*

DANFORTH: Will you plead for his confession or will you not?

ELIZABETH: I promise nothing. Let me speak with him.

A sound—the <u>sibilance</u> *of dragging feet on stone. They turn. A pause.* HERRICK *enters with* JOHN PROCTOR. *His wrists are chained. He is another man, bearded, filthy, his*

Literary Analysis
Theme What theme or themes does Reverend Hale state in this speech?

cleave (klēv) *v.* adhere; cling

sibilance (sib′ əl əns) *n.* hissing sound

▼ Critical Viewing
From this movie still, what emotions do you imagine that John and Elizabeth Proctor are experiencing at this point? **[Infer]**

eyes misty as though webs had overgrown them. He halts inside the doorway, his eyes caught by the sight of ELIZABETH. *The emotion flowing between them prevents anyone from speaking for an instant. Now* HALE, *visibly affected, goes to* DANFORTH *and speaks quietly.*

HALE: Pray, leave them Excellency.

DANFORTH, *pressing* HALE *impatiently aside:* Mr. Proctor, you have been notified, have you not? PROCTOR *is silent, staring at* ELIZABETH. I see light in the sky, Mister; let you counsel with your wife, and may God help you turn your back on Hell. PROCTOR *is silent, staring at* ELIZABETH.

HALE, *quietly:* Excellency, let—

DANFORTH *brushes past* HALE *and walks out.* HALE *follows.* CHEEVER *stands and follows,* HATHORNE *behind.* HERRICK *goes.* PARRIS, *from a safe distance, offers:*

PARRIS: If you desire a cup of cider, Mr. Proctor, I am sure I—PROCTOR *turns an icy stare at him, and he breaks off.* PARRIS *raises his palms toward* PROCTOR. God lead you now. PARRIS *goes out.*

Alone, PROCTOR *walks to her, halts. It is as though they stood in a spinning world. It is beyond sorrow, above it. He reaches out his hand as though toward an embodiment not quite real, and as he touches her, a strange soft sound, half laughter, half amazement, comes from his throat. He pats her hand. She covers his hand with hers. And then, weak, he sits. Then she sits, facing him.*

PROCTOR: The child?

ELIZABETH: It grows.

PROCTOR: There is no word of the boys?

ELIZABETH: They're well. Rebecca's Samuel keeps them.

PROCTOR: You have not seen them?

ELIZABETH: I have not. *She catches a weakening in herself and downs it.*

PROCTOR: You are a—marvel, Elizabeth.

ELIZABETH: You—have been tortured?

PROCTOR: Aye. *Pause. She will not let herself be drowned in the sea that threatens her.* They come for my life now.

ELIZABETH: I know it.

Pause.

PROCTOR: None—have yet confessed?

ELIZABETH: There be many confessed.

PROCTOR: Who are they?

ELIZABETH: There be a hundred or more, they say. Goody Ballard is one; Isaiah Goodkind is one. There be many.

PROCTOR: Rebecca?

ELIZABETH: Not Rebecca. She is one foot in Heaven now; naught may hurt her more.

PROCTOR: And Giles?

ELIZABETH: You have not heard of it?

Literary Analysis
Theme How does Miller's depiction of Elizabeth's attitude and behavior support his theme?

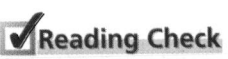
Reading Check

What does Hale urge Elizabeth Proctor to do?

PROCTOR: I hear nothin', where I am kept.

ELIZABETH: Giles is dead.

He looks at her incredulously.

PROCTOR: When were he hanged?

ELIZABETH, *quietly, factually:* He were not hanged. He would not answer aye or nay to his indictment; for if he denied the charge they'd hang him surely, and auction out his property. So he stand mute, and died Christian under the law. And so his sons will have his farm. It is the law, for he could not be condemned a wizard without he answer the indictment, aye or nay.

PROCTOR: Then how does he die?

ELIZABETH, *gently:* They press him, John.

PROCTOR: Press?

ELIZABETH: Great stones they lay upon his chest until he plead aye or nay. *With a tender smile for the old man:* They say he give them but two words. "More weight," he says. And died.

PROCTOR, *numbed—a thread to weave into his agony:* "More weight."

ELIZABETH: Aye. It were a fearsome man, Giles Corey.

Pause.

PROCTOR, *with great force of will, but not quite looking at her:* I have been thinking I would confess to them, Elizabeth. *She shows nothing.* What say you? If I give them that?

ELIZABETH: I cannot judge you, John.

Pause.

PROCTOR, *simply—a pure question:* What would you have me do?

ELIZABETH: As you will, I would have it. *Slight pause:* I want you living, John. That's sure.

PROCTOR, *pauses, then with a flailing of hope:* Giles' wife? Have she confessed?

ELIZABETH: She will not.

Pause.

PROCTOR: It is a pretense, Elizabeth.

ELIZABETH: What is?

PROCTOR: I cannot mount the gibbet like a saint. It is a fraud. I am not that man. *She is silent.* My honesty is broke, Elizabeth; I am no good man. Nothing's spoiled by giving them this lie that were not rotten long before.

ELIZABETH: And yet you've not confessed till now. That speak goodness in you.

PROCTOR: Spite only keeps me silent. It is hard to give a lie to dogs. *Pause, for the first time he turns directly to her.* I would have your forgiveness, Elizabeth.

ELIZABETH: It is not for me to give, John, I am—

PROCTOR: I'd have you see some honesty in it. Let them that never lied die now to keep their souls. It is pretense for me, a vanity that will not blind God nor keep my children out of the wind. *Pause.* What say you?

ELIZABETH, *upon a heaving sob that always threatens:* John, it come to naught that I should forgive you, if you'll not forgive yourself. *Now he turns away a little, in great agony.* It is not my soul, John, it is yours. *He stands, as though in physical pain, slowly rising to his feet with a great immortal longing to find his answer. It is difficult to say, and she is on the verge of tears.* Only be sure of this, for I know it now: Whatever you will do, it is a good man does it. *He turns his doubting, searching gaze upon her.* I have read my heart this three month, John. *Pause.* I have sins of my own to count. It needs a cold wife to prompt lechery.

PROCTOR, *in great pain:* Enough, enough—

ELIZABETH, *now pouring out her heart:* Better you should know me!

PROCTOR: I will not hear it! I know you!

ELIZABETH: You take my sins upon you, John—

PROCTOR, *in agony:* No, I take my own, my own!

ELIZABETH: John, I counted myself so plain, so poorly made, no honest love could come to me! Suspicion kissed you when I did; I never knew how I should say my love. It were a cold house I kept! *In fright, she swerves, as* HATHORNE *enters.*

HATHORNE: What say you Proctor? The sun is soon up.

PROCTOR, *his chest heaving, stares, turns to* ELIZABETH. *She comes to him as though to plead, her voice quaking.*

ELIZABETH: Do what you will. But let none be your judge. There be no higher judge under Heaven than Proctor is! Forgive me, forgive me, John—I never knew such goodness in the world! *She covers her face, weeping.*

PROCTOR *turns from her to* HATHORNE; *he is off the earth, his voice hollow.*

PROCTOR: I want my life.

HATHORNE *electrified, surprised:* You'll confess yourself?

PROCTOR: I will have my life.

HATHORNE, *with a mystical tone:* God be praised! It is a providence! *He rushes out the door, and his voice is heard calling down the corridor:* He will confess! Proctor will confess!

PROCTOR, *with a cry, as he strides to the door:* Why do you cry it? *In great pain he turns back to her.* It is evil, is it not? It is evil.

ELIZABETH, *in terror, weeping:* I cannot judge you, John, I cannot!

PROCTOR: Then who will judge me? *Suddenly clasping his hands:* God in Heaven, what is John Proctor, what is John Proctor? *He moves as an animal, and a fury is riding in him, a <u>tantalized</u> search.* I think it is honest, I think so; I am no saint. *As though she had denied this he calls angrily at her:* Let Rebecca go like a saint; for me it is fraud!

Literary Analysis
Theme What theme does Miller convey through John Proctor's statement about honesty?

tantalized (tan´ tə līzd) *adj.* tormented; frustrated

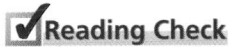**Reading Check**

What sins does Elizabeth think she has committed?

Voices are heard in the hall, speaking together in suppressed excitement.

ELIZABETH: I am not your judge, I cannot be. *As though giving him release:* Do as you will, do as you will!

PROCTOR: Would you give them such a lie? Say it. Would you ever give them this? *She cannot answer.* You would not; if tongs of fire were singeing you you would not! It is evil. Good, then—it is evil, and I do it!

HATHORNE *enters with* DANFORTH, *and, with them,* CHEEVER, PARRIS, *and* HALE. *It is a businesslike, rapid entrance, as though the ice had been broken.*

DANFORTH, *with great relief and gratitude:* Praise to God, man, praise to God; you shall be blessed in Heaven for this. CHEEVER *has hurried to the bench with pen, ink, and paper.* PROCTOR *watches him.* Now then, let us have it. Are you ready, Mr. Cheever?

PROCTOR, *with a cold, cold horror at their efficiency:* Why must it be written?

DANFORTH: Why, for the good instruction of the village, Mister; this we shall post upon the church door! *To* PARRIS, *urgently:* Where is the marshal?

PARRIS, *runs to the door and calls down the corridor:* Marshal! Hurry!

DANFORTH: Now, then, Mister, will you speak slowly, and directly to the point, for Mr. Cheever's sake. *He is on record now, and is really dictating to* CHEEVER, *who writes.* Mr. Proctor, have you seen the Devil in your life? PROCTOR'S *jaws lock.* Come, man, there is light in the sky; the town waits at the scaffold; I would give out this news. Did you see the Devil?

PROCTOR: I did.

PARRIS: Praise God!

DANFORTH: And when he come to you, what were his demand?

PROCTOR *is silent.* DANFORTH *helps.* Did he bid you to do his work upon the earth?

PROCTOR: He did.

DANFORTH: And you bound yourself to his service? DANFORTH *turns, as* REBECCA *Nurse enters, with* HERRICK *helping to support her. She is barely able to walk.* Come in, come in, woman!

REBECCA, *brightening as she sees* PROCTOR: Ah, John! You are well, then, eh?

PROCTOR *turns his face to the wall.*

DANFORTH: Courage, man, courage—let her witness your good example that she may come to God herself. Now hear it, Goody Nurse! Say on, Mr. Proctor. Did you bind yourself to the Devil's service?

REBECCA, *astonished:* Why, John!

PROCTOR, *through his teeth, his face turned from* REBECCA: I did.

DANFORTH: Now, woman, you surely see it profit nothin' to keep this conspiracy any further. Will you confess yourself with him?

REBECCA: Oh, John—God send his mercy on you!

DANFORTH: I say, will you confess yourself, Goody Nurse?

Literary Analysis
Theme Which details of Rebecca Nurse's character reinforce the theme of courage and personal integrity?

REBECCA: Why, it is a lie, it is a lie; how may I damn myself? I cannot, I cannot.

DANFORTH: Mr. Proctor. When the Devil came to you did you see Rebecca Nurse in his company? PROCTOR *is silent.* Come, man, take courage—did you ever see her with the Devil?

PROCTOR, *almost inaudibly:* No.

DANFORTH, *now sensing trouble, glances at* JOHN *and goes to the table, and picks up a sheet—the list of condemned.*

DANFORTH: Did you ever see her sister, Mary Easty, with the Devil?

PROCTOR: No, I did not.

DANFORTH, *his eyes narrow on* PROCTOR: Did you ever see Martha Corey with the Devil?

PROCTOR: I did not.

DANFORTH, *realizing, slowly putting the sheet down:* Did you ever see anyone with the Devil?

PROCTOR: I did not.

DANFORTH: Proctor, you mistake me. I am not empowered to trade your life for a lie. You have most certainly seen some person with the Devil. PROCTOR *is silent.* Mr. Proctor, a score of people have already testified they saw this woman with the Devil.

PROCTOR: Then it is proved. Why must I say it?

DANFORTH: Why "must" you say it! Why, you should rejoice to say it if your soul is truly <u>purged</u> of any love for Hell!

PROCTOR: They think to go like saints. I like not to spoil their names.

DANFORTH, *inquiring, incredulous:* Mr. Proctor, do you think they go like saints?

PROCTOR, *evading:* This woman never thought she done the Devil's work.

DANFORTH: Look you, sir. I think you mistake your duty here. It matter nothing what she thought—she is convicted of the unnatural murder of children, and you for sending your spirit out upon Mary Warren. Your soul alone is the issue here, Mister, and you will prove its whiteness or you cannot live in a Christian country. Will you tell me now what persons conspired with you in the Devil's company? PROCTOR *is silent.* To your knowledge was Rebecca Nurse ever—

PROCTOR: I speak my own sins; I cannot judge another. *Crying out, with hatred:* I have no tongue for it.

HALE, *quickly to* DANFORTH: Excellency, it is enough he confess himself. Let him sign it, let him sign it.

PARRIS, *feverishly:* It is a great service, sir. It is a weighty name; it will strike the village that Proctor confess. I beg you, let him sign it. The sun is up, Excellency!

DANFORTH, *considers; then with dissatisfaction:* Come, then, sign your testimony. *To* CHEEVER: Give it to him. CHEEVER *goes to* PROCTOR, *the confession and a pen in hand.* PROCTOR *does not look at it.* Come, man, sign it.

purged (purjd) *v.* cleansed

Literary Analysis
Theme and Extended Metaphor How might Proctor's refusal to incriminate others relate to the McCarthy hearings of the 1950s?

**Reading Check**

What does Danforth want Proctor to do?

PROCTOR, *after glancing at the confession:* You have all witnessed it— it is enough.

DANFORTH: You will not sign it?

PROCTOR: You have all witnessed it; what more is needed?

DANFORTH: Do you sport with me? You will sign your name or it is no confession, Mister! *His breast heaving with agonized breathing,* PROCTOR *now lays the paper down and signs his name.*

PARRIS: Praise be to the Lord!

PROCTOR *has just finished signing when* DANFORTH *reaches for the paper. But* PROCTOR *snatches it up, and now a wild terror is rising in him, and a boundless anger.*

DANFORTH, *perplexed, but politely extending his hand:* If you please, sir.

PROCTOR: No.

DANFORTH, *as though* PROCTOR *did not understand:* Mr. Proctor, I must have—

PROCTOR: No, no. I have signed it. You have seen me. It is done! You have no need for this.

PARRIS: Proctor, the village must have proof that—

PROCTOR: Damn the village! I confess to God, and God has seen my name on this! It is enough!

DANFORTH: No, sir, it is—

PROCTOR: You came to save my soul, did you not? Here! I have confessed myself; it is enough!

DANFORTH: You have not con—

PROCTOR: I have confessed myself! Is there no good penitence but it be public? God does not need my name nailed upon the church! God sees my name; God knows how black my sins are! It is enough!

DANFORTH: Mr. Proctor—

PROCTOR: You will not use me! I am no Sarah Good or Tituba, I am John Proctor! You will not use me! It is no part of salvation that you should use me!

DANFORTH: I do not wish to—

PROCTOR: I have three children—how may I teach them to walk like men in the world, and I sold my friends?

DANFORTH: You have not sold your friends—

PROCTOR: Beguile me not! I blacken all of them when this is nailed to the church the very day they hang for silence!

DANFORTH: Mr. Proctor, I must have good and legal proof that you—

PROCTOR: You are the high court, your word is good enough! Tell them I confessed myself; say Proctor broke his knees and wept like a woman; say what you will, but my name cannot—

DANFORTH, *with suspicion:* It is the same, is it not? If I report it or you sign to it?

Reading Strategy
Applying Themes to Contemporary Events
Which notorious aspect of the McCarthy hearings might Miller be suggesting here?

PROCTOR—*he knows it is insane:* No, it is not the same! What others say and what I sign to is not the same!

DANFORTH: Why? Do you mean to deny this confession when you are free?

PROCTOR: I mean to deny nothing!

DANFORTH: Then explain to me, Mr. Proctor, why you will not let—

PROCTOR, *with a cry of his whole soul:* Because it is my name! Because I cannot have another in my life! Because I lie and sign myself to lies! Because I am not worth the dust on the feet of them that hang! How may I live without my name? I have given you my soul; leave me my name!

DANFORTH, *pointing at the confession in* PROCTOR'S *hand:* Is that document a lie? If it is a lie I will not accept it! What say you? I will not deal in lies, Mister! PROCTOR *is motionless.* You will give me your honest confession in my hand, or I cannot keep you from the rope. PROCTOR *does not reply.* What way do you go, Mister?

His breast heaving, his eyes staring, PROCTOR *tears the paper and crumples it, and he is weeping in fury, but erect.*

DANFORTH: Marshal!

PARRIS, *hysterically, as though the tearing paper were his life:* Proctor, Proctor!

HALE: Man, you will hang! You cannot!

PROCTOR, *his eyes full of tears:* I can. And there's your first marvel, that I can. You have made your magic now, for now I do think I see some shred of goodness in John Proctor. Not enough to weave a banner with, but white enough to keep it from such dogs. ELIZABETH, *in a burst of terror, rushes to him and weeps against his hand.* Give them no tear! Tears pleasure them! Show honor now, show a stony heart and sink them with it! *He has lifted her, and kisses her now with great passion.*

REBECCA: Let you fear nothing! Another judgment waits us all!

DANFORTH: Hang them high over the town! Who weeps for these, weeps for corruption! *He sweeps out past them.* HERRICK *starts to lead* REBECCA, *who almost collapses, but* PROCTOR *catches her, and she glances up at him apologetically.*

REBECCA: I've had no breakfast.

▲ **Critical Viewing**
Judge Danforth says, "He who weeps for these weeps for corruption." What do you think the people surrounding the condemned are thinking? **[Analyze]**

Literary Analysis
Theme In what way does Proctor's change of heart reflect the themes of integrity and courage?

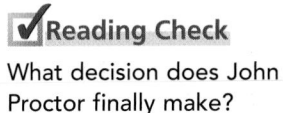**Reading Check**

What decision does John Proctor finally make?

HERRICK: Come, man.

HERRICK *escorts them out,* HATHORNE *and* CHEEVER *behind them.* ELIZABETH *stands staring at the empty doorway.*

PARRIS, *in deadly fear, to* ELIZABETH: Go to him, Goody Proctor! There is yet time!

From outside a drumroll strikes the air. PARRIS *is startled.* ELIZABETH *jerks about toward the window.*

PARRIS: Go to him! *He rushes out the door, as though to hold back his fate.* Proctor! Proctor!

Again, a short burst of drums.

HALE: Woman, plead with him! *He starts to rush out the door, and then goes back to her.* Woman! It is pride, it is vanity. *She avoids his eyes, and moves to the window. He drops to his knees.* Be his helper!—What profit him to bleed? Shall the dust praise him? Shall the worms declare his truth? Go to him, take his shame away!

ELIZABETH, *supporting herself against collapse, grips the bars of the window, and with a cry:* He have his goodness now. God forbid I take it from him!

The final drumroll crashes, then heightens violently. HALE *weeps in frantic prayer, and the new sun is pouring in upon her face, and the drums rattle like bones in the morning air.*

Review and Assess

Thinking About Act IV

1. **(a) Respond:** How did you react to the ending of the play?
   (b) Extend: Would you recommend the play to a friend? Why or why not?

2. **(a) Recall:** Who seeks confessions from Rebecca Nurse and other condemned prisoners? **(b) Infer:** What motivates this person—or people—to seek these confessions?

3. **(a) Recall:** What unexpected action does Abigail take in this act? **(b) Draw Conclusions:** Why do you think she does this?

4. **(a) Recall:** What decision torments John Proctor?
   (b) Interpret: What conflict does Elizabeth experience as her husband seeks her guidance?

5. **(a) Recall:** What does John Proctor have "no tongue for"?
   (b) Analyze: Why does Proctor confess and then retract his confession?

6. **Interpret:** Why does Elizabeth say her husband has "his goodness" as he is about to be hanged?

7. **Evaluate:** Do you think John Proctor made the right decision? Why or why not?

Review and Assess

Literary Analysis

Theme

1. Use evidence from the play to show how Arthur Miller conveys the **theme** that fear and suspicion are infectious and can produce a mass hysteria that destroys public order and rationality.

2. Cite evidence from the play that supports the theme that it is more noble to die with integrity than to live with compromised principles that harm others.

3. (a) In what ways do Hale's reactions to events compare to those of the other ministers and court officers? (b) What do these differences suggest about the ideas of integrity, pride, and vanity?

4. State and support another theme that you believe is central to the meaning of the play.

Connecting Literary Elements

5. Using a chart like the one shown, cite examples from the text that show how ideas such as witchcraft and "the work of the Devil" function in *The Crucible* as **extended metaphors** for Communism.

Passage From the Text	How It Relates to Communism

6. (a) What does the ending of the play suggest about the value of integrity and of holding fast to principles? (b) How might this idea relate to the McCarthy era?

Reading Strategy

Applying Themes to Contemporary Events

7. Based on the play's details, what criticisms might Miller be making about the way McCarthy's Senate committee dealt with those it questioned and those who criticized it?

8. What does the play suggest about the motives behind Senator Joseph McCarthy's political "witch hunts"? Explain.

Extend Understanding

9. **Social Studies Connection:** Given the nation's experience with McCarthyism, do you think a tragedy like the Salem witchcraft trials could occur today? Explain.

Quick Review

A **theme** is a central idea or insight about life revealed by a literary work.

An **extended metaphor** is a comparison that is developed through the course of a literary work.

To **apply a theme to a contemporary event,** draw a parallel between the central idea of a story and a current event.

 Take It to the Net
www.phschool.com
Take the interactive self-test online to check your understanding of this selection.

Integrate Language Skills

Vocabulary Development Lesson

Concept Development: Words From Myths

The word *tantalize* comes from the Greek myth about Tantalus a man tormented by the gods. Review the list of mythological figures below. Write a sentence for each, using the word in parentheses.

1. Ceres: The goddess of the harvest (*cereal*)
2. Titan: A race of giants with brute strength (*titanic*)
3. Narcissus: A boy punished by the gods for vanity (*narcissistic*)

Spelling Strategy

When you add a suffix beginning with a vowel to a word that ends in a silent *e*, drop the *e* before adding the suffix. For example, *tantalize* +*-ing* = *tantalizing*. For each word below, add the suffix indicated.

1. baste (*-ing*) 2. pure (*-ify*) 3. serene (*-ity*)

Concept Development: Synonyms

Select the letter of the word that is the closest in meaning to the first word.

1. agape: (a) dark, (b) open, (c) shocking
2. conciliatory: (a) soothing, (b) rude, (c) vengeful
3. beguile: (a) plead, (b) fool, (c) straighten
4. floundering: (a) groping, (b) jogging, (c) smelling
5. retaliation: (a) narration, (b) restatement, (c) revenge
6. adamant: (a) calm, (b) first, (c) stubborn
7. cleave: (a) depart, (b) grow, (c) adhere
8. sibilance: (a) hissing, (b) humming, (c) screaming
9. tantalized: (a) freed, (b) tempted, (c) danced
10. purged: (a) soothed, (b) washed, (c) filled

Grammar and Style Lesson

Commonly Confused Words:
raise and *rise*

Some words in English sound similar but function differently. For example, to *raise* means "to lift up"; it takes a direct object (a noun or pronoun that receives the action of the verb). To *rise* means "to go up or get up," and it does not take a direct object.

Verb	Present	Present Participle	Past	Past Participle
raise	raise, raises	raising	raised	(have) raised
rise	rise, rises	rising	rose	(have) risen

Practice Complete each sentence with the correct form of *rise* or *raise* in the tense indicated.

1. All (*past*) when the judge entered.
2. They were (*present participle*) the flag outside the courthouse.
3. Cries of witchcraft (*past*) a ruckus.
4. Spirits were reported to have (*past participle*) to the courtroom ceiling.
5. Citizens had (*past participle*) a rebellion.

Writing Application Write a paragraph in which you use the verbs *raise* and *rise* correctly.

W̶G̶ Prentice Hall Writing and Grammar Connection: Chapter 21, Section 1

Writing Lesson

Defense of a Character's Actions

Write an essay in which you defend the actions of an accused character in *The Crucible*. Like a good trial lawyer, you need not agree with your client's actions, but you must present the best defense possible to prove why he or she should not be found guilty.

Prewriting   Skim the play to decide which character's actions you will defend. Record possible "pros" and "cons" in a two-column chart. You might discuss the character with others to come up with as complete a list of pros and cons as possible.

Model: Analyzing the Evidence

"Pros"	"Cons"
He is honest.	He angers quickly.
He is trustworthy.	He made a mistake.
He is loyal.	He is stubborn.

Drafting   Begin by presenting the negative aspects of your character's actions. Then, move on to the positive aspects. In each case, cite specific evidence from the play. Use forceful, persuasive language to explain why the pros outweigh the cons.

Revising   Make sure you have effectively refuted the negatives and included enough positive ideas to support the defense. Also, be sure that your word choice is clear, precise, and persuasive.

 Prentice Hall Writing and Grammar Connection: Chapter 7, Section 2

Extension Activities

Listening and Speaking Stage a **mock trial** to determine whether Danforth and Hathorne are guilty of murder for their roles in the Salem witch trials. Appoint a prosecutor, a defense attorney, defendants, witnesses, a jury, and a fair judge. Consider the following:

- Select prosecution and defense witnesses.
- Have both the defense attorney and the prosecutor give summations.

Present the trial to the class. [**Group Activity**]

Research and Technology Research the facts of the Salem witchcraft trials. Then, present a **comparison-and-contrast chart,** listing differences between the trials and the events in this play. For each difference, provide reasons Miller might have had for making those changes.

 Take It to the Net   www.phschool.com

Go online for an additional research activity using the Internet.

READING INFORMATIONAL MATERIALS

Critical Commentaries

About Critical Commentaries

A critical commentary is a piece of writing that analyzes and evaluates a work of art, an artistic performance, or a piece of literature.

- Some critical commentaries address the work itself—for example, discussing the strengths and weaknesses of a novel or a symphony.
- Other critical commentaries, like this piece by Arthur Miller, use the work as a springboard to a larger discussion. They might discuss particular works but then go on to offer the author's view of trends in society, of contemporary values, or of another issue of significance.

As the name suggests, critical commentaries express strong opinions. This does not mean, however, that they are not carefully planned and supported. Indeed, critical commentaries tend to be detailed and precise. Since their intent is largely persuasive, however, expect to find argumentative presentations and powerful use of language.

Reading Strategy

Interpreting an Author's Arguments

To gain the most from a critical commentary, interpret its arguments—the major points the author makes and the support he or she gives them. To interpret an argument, determine its meaning and importance, and then share it in terms that others can understand even if they have not read the work. While you may not choose to write about a commentary, deciding how to share its meaning is a good way to check your comprehension. These strategies can build your interpretive skills:

HOW TO	
Determine the Meaning	**Share the Meaning**
• After you read the commentary, write a sentence that asserts its main point. • Make sure your sentence is supported by the text. • List the evidence—examples, quotations, or other details—the author provides to support his or her view. • Notice how the author's word choice affects the message.	• Rewrite the main point as if you were sharing it with someone who had not read the commentary. • Summarize the author's argument. • Prepare a two-minute talk about the commentary. Explain its meaning and why it is important.

from On Social Plays
Arthur Miller

Time is moving; there is a world to make, a civilization to create that will move toward the only goal the humanistic, democratic mind can ever accept with honor. It is a world in which the human being can live as a naturally political, naturally private, naturally engaged person, a world in which once again a true tragic victory may be scored.

But that victory is not really possible unless the individual is more than theoretically capable of being recognized by the powers that lead society. Specifically, when men live, as they do under any industrialized system, as integers[1] who have no weight, no *person*, excepting as cus-tomers, draftees, machine tenders, ideologists, or whatever, it is unlikely (and in my opinion impossible) that a dramatic picture of them can really overcome the public knowledge of their nature in real life. In such a society, be it communistic or capi-talistic, man is not tragic, he is pathetic.[2] The tragic figure must have certain innate powers which he uses to pass over the boundaries of the known social law—the accepted mores[3] of his people—in order to test and discover necessity. Such a quest implies that the individual who has moved onto that course must be somehow recognized by the law,

> Here, Miller states his view. Notice how he uses such emotion-laden words as *impossible, overcome,* and *pathetic.*

---

1. **integers** (in´ tə jerz) *n.* numbers.

2. **pathetic** (pə the´ tik) *adj.* arousing pity.
3. **mores** (mōr´ āz´) *n.* customs; unwritten laws.

by the mores, by the powers that design—be they anthropomorphic[4] gods or economic and political laws—as having the worth, the innate value, of a whole people asking a basic question and demanding its answer. We are so atomized[5] socially that no character in a play can conceivably stand as our vanguard,[6] as our heroic questioner.

Our society—and I am speaking of every industrialized society in the world—is so complex, each person being so specialized an integer, that the moment any individual is dramatically characterized and set forth as a hero, our common sense reduces him to the size of a complainer, a misfit. For deep down we no longer believe in the rules of the tragic contest; we no longer believe that some ultimate sense can in fact be made of social causation,[7] or in the possibility that any individual can, by a heroic effort, make sense of it. Thus the man that is driven to question the moral chaos in which we live ends up in our estimate as a possibly commendable but definitely odd fellow, and probably as a compulsively driven neurotic.[8] In place of a social aim which called an all-around excellence—physical, intellectual, and moral—the ultimate good, we have set up a goal which can best be characterized as

"happiness"—namely, staying out of trouble.[9] This concept is the end result of the truce which all of us have made with society. And a truce implies two enemies. When the truce is broken it means either that the individual has broken out of his ordained[10] place as an integer, or that the society has broken the law by harming him unjustly—that is, it has not left him alone to be a peaceful integer. In the heroic and tragic time the act of questioning the-way-things-are implied that a quest was being carried on to discover an ultimate law or way of life which would yield excellence; in the present time the quest is that of a man made unhappy by rootlessness and, in every important modern play, by a man who is essentially a victim. We have abstracted[11] from the Greek drama its air of doom, its physical destruction of the hero, but its victory escapes us. Thus it has even become difficult to separate in our minds the ideas of the pathetic and of the tragic. And behind this melting of the two lies the overwhelming power of the modern industrial state, the ignorance of each person in it of anything but his own technique as an economic integer, and the elevation of that state to a holy, quite religious sphere.

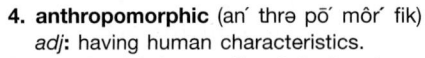

> **Miller offers this reasoning, whether based on his research or his personal observations, to support his view.**

> **The use of words like *industrial* and *integer* helps tie this point to the view that Miller stated earlier.**

---

4. **anthropomorphic** (an´ thrə pō´ môr´ fik) *adj*: having human characteristics.
5. **atomized** (at´ ə mīzd´) *adj*. broken into small, disconnected pieces.
6. **vanguard** (van´ gärd´) *n*. leading part of an army or other group.
7. **social causation** social forces.
8. **neurotic** (nо͞о rät´ ik) *n*. person suffering from mental or emotional imbalance.

9. **a social aim . . . staying out of trouble** Miller is contrasting the ancient Greek ideal of *areté* (excellence; virtue) with the modern drives for conformity and comfort.
10. **ordained** (ôr dānd´) *adj*. assigned; appointed.
11. **abstracted** (ab strak´ tid) *v*. taken; separated.

Check Your Comprehension

1. What does Miller mean when he calls people "integers"?
2. According to Miller, what must happen before a person can achieve "a true tragic victory" in the world?
3. Why does Miller disapprove of happiness as a goal?

Applying the Reading Strategy

Interpreting an Author's Arguments

4. When you interpret an argument, you must also determine its importance. Use a chart like the one shown to analyze your thoughts about Miller's commentary in "On Social Plays."

This critical commentary is important to . . .	
my understanding of *The Crucible* because . . .	my understanding of Arthur Miller as a writer because . . .
1. 2.	1. 2.

Activity

Writing a Critical Commentary

Select a story that you have recently read or a movie that you have recently seen. Identify which of the following statements most accurately represents your reaction to the story or film.

- "Life certainly is like that because . . ."
- "That was not true to life. In real life . . ."

In a brief critical commentary, use the story or movie as a springboard for sharing your views about some aspect of life.

Comparing Informational Materials

Critical Commentaries and Theater Reviews

Find a review of *The Crucible*. You might select a theater review from the play's debut in 1953 or a review of the 1996 film version. Analyze the ways in which the reviewer's comments about the society that Miller depicts differ from Miller's views as stated in "On Social Plays." Write a paragraph to compare and contrast the two commentaries.

Writing About Literature

Analyze Literary Trends

During the period covered by this unit, issues of identity became a preoccupation in American life and literature. The changing role of women and the awareness that America is home to people of many cultural backgrounds added resonance to this preoccupation. Writers ask questions of identity in very personal ways: Who am I? Where do I come from? What is my role in my family and community?

To explore the variety of ways in which writers have answered these questions, complete the assignment outlined in the yellow box at right.

Prewriting

Find a focus. Use a chart like the one below to choose the characters and ideas that you want to analyze. Narrow your focus by answering these questions:

- Are the goals of the characters at odds with those of others?
- Are the beliefs of the characters in conflict with those of others?
- Do the actions of the characters reflect personal desires or the desires of others?

Use a self-sticking note to jot down ideas for the focus of your essay.

**Assignment:
A Question of Identity**

Write an analytical essay that examines the fate of the individual within the family and community as it is depicted in at least three pieces of fiction from this unit.

Criteria:

- Analyze elements of plot and characterization from at least three stories.
- Identify larger trends or social forces to which characters are responding.
- Approximate length: 1,500 words.

Model: Listing to Find a Focus

Possible focus: Explore conflict between materialism (status) and traditional values.

Story	Individual Characters	Family and Community	Notes
"The First Seven Years" p. 988	Miriam	Feld; Sobel; Max; aspiration for a better life; how is "better" measured?	Story shows conflict of values between materialism and depth of soul.
"Everyday Use" p. 1056	Dee	Dee is educated, sophisticated. Mother and Maggie are poor, uneducated.	Dee has "escaped," but she is the story's villain.

Gather details. Collect detailed information about the characters, including dialogue and descriptions. Note page numbers for future reference. These details will help you formulate your ideas.

Write a working thesis. A thesis is the focus, or main point, of your essay—the argument that you intend to prove. Your thesis may change as you write, but you need to have an idea of your intentions when you begin. Review your notes and write a thesis sentence.

Read to Write

Reread the texts to identify each character's goals and desires.

Drafting

Organize. Create an informal outline like the one shown below, and note where you will include quotations from the literature. Like your thesis, your outline may change as you clarify your ideas and determine the best way to present them.

Model: Creating an Informal Outline

    I. Introduction/thesis: In these stories, those who seek new identities challenge traditional values.

    II. Example: Feld wants Miriam to have a "better" life.

    III. Example: Dee escapes the "backward" life of her family.

    IV. Conclusion: To Dee, the quilt is an artifact, not something to use every day. In the same way, traditional values become quaint artifacts when abandoned by those seeking status.

Frame your ideas. Write an introduction that will grab the reader's attention. Consider beginning with a compelling quotation or detail. Then, write a strong conclusion that ends your essay with a memorable image or a statement that reinforces your main idea.

Revising and Editing

Review content: Revise to ensure a powerful argument. Make sure that your thesis is clearly stated and that you have proved it with evidence from the reading. Underline main ideas in your paper and confirm that each one is supported. Add more proof as needed.

Review style: Revise to cut wordy language. Check that you have found the clearest, simplest way to communicate your ideas. Omit unnecessary words.

> **Wordy:** Miriam is not interested in or attracted to Max, but Feld pushes her to date him because he believes that Max, a college student, will be willing and able to give Miriam a life filled with luxury, wealth, and material comfort.
>
> **Revised:** Miriam is not interested in the sullen Max, but Feld dreams that the college student will give her a comfortable life.

Publishing and Presenting

Give an oral presentation. Develop a brief talk for your class in which you detail your thesis. After your presentation, ask for questions and comments from your listeners.

$\mathcal{W}_G$ *Prentice Hall Writing and Grammar Connection: Chapter 14*

Write to Learn
Writing is a tool for discovery, a way to figure out what you think and feel. This means that you may change your mind or get new ideas as you work. Allowing for this will improve your final draft.

Write to Explain
Do not simply summarize selections. Give examples from the reading to support your ideas.

Writing WORKSHOP

Workplace Writing: Job Portfolio

The **job portfolio** candidates submit to prospective employers usually consists of two main components—the **résumé**, which is a summary of one's qualifications and experience, and a cover letter that introduces the job seeker. Other elements of a job portfolio may include a list of references, a salary history, and writing or work samples. In this workshop, you will write a résumé designed to best show your strengths as a candidate for a job.

Assignment Criteria Your résumé should demonstrate the following characteristics:

- Name, address, and contact information provided in a highly visible format
- Clear summaries of the writer's work history, education, and related experience
- Information logically organized and provided in labeled sections and limited to one page
- Conventional formats, fonts, style, and spacing
- Formal and consistent use of language

To preview the criteria on which your résumé may be assessed, see the Rubric on page 1347.

Prewriting

Gather elements. Brainstorm for a **list** that thoroughly represents your work experience, education, honors, hobbies, interests, and extracurricular activities. The list may be messy and long; as you cut and focus your résumé you will not include every item, but it is helpful to begin by examining all the possibilities.

Select elements. Use a chart like the one shown to assess your list of items. Place a check beside those that best express your experience and skills. Then, select an appropriate category, such as work experience, activities, or skills, for each item. Note that many high school students do not have extensive work histories, but other activities, including experience on school clubs or responsibilities at home, can be mined for skills valuable to an employer.

Model: Selecting and Categorizing Experience

Include?	Item	Category
✓	Videographer	Work experience
✓	Mock Trial Team	Activities
✗	Mow Lawn	
✓	Speak Hebrew	Skills

Organize the timeline. Because you are a high school student, most employers will not look for a seamless work history, as they may with adult job seekers. However, it is useful to arrange items on your résumé to reflect an easily identifiable chronology.

Student Model

Before you begin writing, read this student model and review the characteristics of an effective résumé.

Mark Israel Schilsky
123 Any Street
West Orange, New Jersey 00000
Telephone: (973) 555-5555 • E-Mail: mis@---.com

> Name and contact information are placed prominently at the top of the page and set in a larger font size.

OVERVIEW

Academically focused, hard-working, reliable high school student with strong interest in biology, seeking a laboratory internship for the summer; available from June 20 through August 25.

EDUCATION

West Orange High School, West Orange, NJ; will graduate in June 200-

HONORS

NMSQT Commended Scholar, Biology II NJ Science League Sixth individually in all of NJ, Finalist NJ Governors School in the Sciences, Nominated to attend NJ Boys' State, Red Cross CPR/Lifeguard Certified, National Association of Biology Teachers Award for Excellence, National Youth Leadership Forum on Medicine Invitee, Recipient of Edward J. Bloustein Award for Academics, Eagle Scout Rank

> Clear labels like *Education* and *Honors* organize background and experience.

WORK EXPERIENCE

Summer 2001	**Laboratory Technician,** Duke University, Durham, NC *Performed PCR reactions, obtained DNA samples, and photographed electrophoresis gels.*
9/99–present	**Videographer,** Temple Sharey-Tefilo, South Orange, NJ *Videotape celebrations, meetings, drama programs, and other special events; edit tapes, add special effects.*
9/00–present	**Student Aide/Hebrew Teacher,** Temple Sharey-Tefilo, South Orange, NJ *Assist after-school teachers with children ages 5–7. Lead games and sports activities. Teach Hebrew to students, ages 9–11, 3–5 hours per week.*

> Mark included dates, clearly set off to focus information.

SKILLS

• Computers: word processing, spreadsheets, graphics, HTML
• Microbiology laboratory procedures
• Knowledge Hebrew and Spanish

ACTIVITIES

• Mock Trial team
• Marching Band: Alto Sax Section Leader (1 yr)
• Varsity Spring Track
• School Musical: Program Editor, Stage Crew
• National Honor Society

> Mark provides a more complete picture of his personality by including information about his activities.

Drafting

Select a style. Choose a style with which to convey information and apply it consistently as you draft. For example, use either whole sentences or phrases in your experience descriptions, but do not mix the two.

- **Whole sentences:** I edit videotapes and add special effects.
- **Phrases:** Edit videotapes; add special effects.

Adhere to standards. As you draft, use a checklist like the one shown to verify that you have included all standard and expected elements. Add any element that you may have overlooked.

Play to your strengths. If you, like many high school students, have had only limited work experience, use your résumé to emphasize academic and life experiences that show your capabilities. Stress skills related to the job for which you are applying.

Résumé Conventions

- ☐ **Heading** indicates name, address and contact information of the candidate.

- ☐ **Overview or Summary** provides a brief statement about the candidate.

- ☐ **Experience** lists details of work history.

- ☐ **Education** provides history of candidate's schooling and other training.

- ☐ **Skills** notes special abilities, such as computer training or fluency in a foreign language.

- ☐ **Honors/Awards/Activities/Memberships** is a flexible category used to show interests or hobbies.

Revising

Revise to make your format consistent. Make sure that you have followed a consistent organizational strategy throughout the résumé.

1. Check that your categories are clearly labeled, and the experience descriptions placed under the proper sections.

2. Check that all elements of the résumé are uniform. For example, the dates of your activities should be clearly indicated, and given in a consistent fashion—do not switch back and forth between styles.

3. Make sure that your résumé is only one page long. If it is too long, edit it so that it fits.

Model: Revising to Maintain Organizational Strategy

Summer 2001	**Laboratory Technician**, Duke University, Durham, NC
	Performed PCR reactions, obtained DNA samples, and photographed electrophoresis gels.
9/99-present	**Mock Trial Team,** West Orange High School, West Orange, NJ
	Served as defense attorney for mock trial cases.
	Honed research, public speaking, and team
move to **Activities**	building skills.

Mark moved the description of his participation in the Mock Trial Team out of *Work Experience,* where it did not belong. He then edited it for length and placed it under *Activities.*

Revise to include active and specific language. The language you use in your résumé reveals your attitudes and seriousness of purpose. Avoid the use of unspecific or passive language. Use active verbs and specific descriptions.

Unspecific: Made brochures for public relations firm.

Specific: Researched, wrote, and edited four-color brochures for public relations firm.

Compare the model and the nonmodel. Why is the model more effective?

Nonmodel	Model
Watch children at after-school program.	Lead games and sports activities. Teach Hebrew to students ages 9–11.

Publishing and Presenting

Consider the following strategy to share your résumé with a wider audience.

Submit your résumé to an employer. Print your résumé on good-quality paper in a neutral color, such as white or ivory. When you read about a job you would like to pursue, send your résumé, along with a cover letter using standard business format. In your cover letter, you may wish to introduce yourself and elaborate on any talents or experiences that make you an excellent job candidate.

 Prentice Hall Writing and Grammar Connection: Chapter 16

Rubric for Self-Assessment

Evaluate your résumé using the following criteria and rating scale:

Criteria	Rating Scale Not very				Very
How visibly does the résumé present the writer's name, address, and contact information?	1	2	3	4	5
How clear are the summaries of the writer's work history, education, and other experience?	1	2	3	4	5
How well organized is the résumé?	1	2	3	4	5
How well does the writer apply conventional formats, fonts, style, and spacing?	1	2	3	4	5
How formal and consistent is the writer's use of language?	1	2	3	4	5

Listening and Speaking WORKSHOP

Analyze the Impact of the Media

Both print and broadcast media can have a dramatic effect on the unfolding of the democratic process. As a potential voter, you must develop critical listening and viewing skills in order to analyze media activities and evaluate their effects. The strategies outlined below will help you understand some common points of media influence. The form on this page offers a starting point for actual analysis.

Analyze Explicit Influence

Journalists and media makers often hold strong views and sometimes seek to affect the political process by expressing their beliefs. Familiarize yourself with the usual forums for such statements of opinion.

Identify editorials. Talk-show hosts and journalists may deliver editorials that are intended to express opinions. Likewise, news shows may host discussions in which a variety of participants express opinions. Listen carefully as a participant is introduced. Words such as "views," "thoughts," or "comments" signal an opinion that listeners should evaluate.

Recognize opinion forums. Debate forums in which journalists express opposing views offer you the opportunity to hear many opinions. Note, however, that each speaker hopes to influence you to share a particular view.

Analyze Implicit Influence

Often, media makers exert indirect influence on elections or public opinion. Pay attention to these avenues of influence.

- **Images of leaders** When the media shows a candidate looking strong, it sends a positive message about that candidate. If the candidate looks tired or confused, the media has telegraphed a lack of support.

- **Reporting priorities** Media makers exert influence through the stories they report *and* the sequence in which they present them. The lead story of a television news show usually gets the largest audience, while stories reported later may reach a tiny audience. The placement of a story in the sequence may affect public perception.

- **Shaping attitudes** When journalists conduct interviews, the questions they ask influence the information you receive. To avoid accepting biased information, compare news sources.

Activity: Listen and Analyze For a week, analyze the coverage of an important story in at least one form of media. Use the feedback form shown here to analyze the impact of the coverage each day.

Feedback Form for Evaluating Media Influence

Rating System
+ = Present   – = Omitted

Explicit Influence of Reports
Editorial _____
Opinion Forum _____
How did these reports exert influence? What signals suggested opinion?

Implicit Influence of Reports
Persuasive images _____
Reporting priorities _____
Questioning priorities _____
Time issues _____

Answer the following question:
How might the media choices or elements that you noted affect the audience or even influence the outcome of a story?

Punctuation, Usage, and Sentence Structure

The writing sections of some tests examine your knowledge of the usage and mechanics of Standard Written English. Use the following strategies to help you answer test questions regarding punctuation, grammar and usage, and sentence structure:

- You can often identify errors by reading the sentence aloud, as if it were being spoken. Incorrect English usually sounds wrong, and you can learn to hear errors.
- Remember that punctuation marks act as symbols to readers, telling them where to stop, pause, read with a questioning tone, or read with excitement.
- Memorize the rules for specific grammatical structures, such as the use of *its* or *it's,* and the use of *who* and *whom,* that are a common source of errors.
- As you read, recognize correct and incorrect grammar— especially subject-verb agreement and pronoun usage.
- Learn to recognize structural errors, such as run-on sentences, sentence fragments, and misplaced modifiers.

Test-Taking Strategies

- Look carefully at all punctuation in each passage.
- Remember that there may be more than one error in each passage.
- Choose the answer that corrects *all* of the errors in the passage.

Sample Test Question

Directions: Read the sentence, and then choose the letter of the best answer to the question.

Some automobiles require diesel fuel to run properly, some do not.

1. Which of the following choices is the best revision to the underlined passage?

   A properly; some do not
   B properly . . . some do not
   C properly: some do not
   D Correct as is.

Answer and Explanation

The correct answer is *A.* A semicolon should be used to separate two independent clauses.

Practice

Directions: Read the passage, and then choose the letter of the best answer to the question.

(1) It had been a long and hard-fought campaign, the voters were ready to make a choice. (2) With the qualifications of all the candidates in mind, the voters chose Dan O'Neill to be mayor. (3) Voters claimed that they were impressed with the full range of his positive attributes.

1. How would you correct sentence 1?

   A campaign: the voters
   B campaign; the voters
   C campaign The voters
   D Correct as is

RESOURCES

Following are some suggestions for longer works that will give you the opportunity to experience the fun of sustained reading. Each of the suggestions explores one of the time periods, themes, or literary movements in this book. Many of the titles are included in the **Prentice Hall Literature Library**, featuring the **Penguin Literature Library**.

You may want to consult your teacher before choosing one of these longer works.

Unit 1: Beginnings–1750

The Interesting Narrative and Other Writings
Olaudah Equiano
Penguin Books, 1995

In the mid-eighteenth century, the young West African Olaudah Equiano was sold into slavery and shipped to the West Indies. There, his intelligence and curiosity enabled him to benefit from his travels with his master and from the education he received. After gaining his freedom, he traveled to England and joined the abolitionist cause, lecturing on the evils of slavery. It was British abolitionists who helped him publish his autobiography, *The Interesting Narrative of Olaudah Equiano.* This book and his other writings are not only a compelling argument against slavery, but also the "interesting" record of a compassionate and gifted man.

American Colonies: The Settling of North America
Alan Taylor
Penguin Books, 2001

The settling of the American colonies was not a simple, straightforward story but an interweaving of many narratives. Pulitzer Prize-winning author Alan Taylor does justice to this multifaceted history by explaining the roles that different peoples played in this process: enslaved Africans, Native American tribes, and European colonizers from England, the Netherlands, Spain, Russia, and France. In addition, Taylor expands his focus to include regions of the continent beyond the Eastern seaboard as well as ecological factors influencing colonial settlement.

The Four Voyages
Christopher Columbus, edited and translated by J. M. Cohen
Penguin Books, 1969

Imagine standing beside Christopher Columbus when, after a long and risky voyage across the Atlantic, he first arrived at the island of San Salvador. Readers can have this and other equally exciting experiences as they "travel" through *The Four Voyages.* This volume combines material from Columbus's own logbook and letters with contemporary biographies of him and letters from others who participated in his expeditions.

Chronicle of the Narváez Expedition
Alvar Núñez Cabeza de Vaca, translated by Fanny Bandelier
Penguin Books, 2002

In the early sixteenth century, Spain sent the Narváez expedition to the southern United States to claim vast territories for the Spanish empire. Cabeza de Vaca, who went on this journey, describes the fascinating but sad fate of this expedition. After being shipwrecked, members of the expedition traveled by foot all the way from Florida to California. Their numbers diminished until, by the end of the 9-year ordeal, only Cabeza de Vaca and three others remained.

Native American Literature
Prentice Hall
Pearson Prentice Hall, 2000

The literature of Native Americans from the Northeast through Central America is a rich and varied collection of myths and legends, poems, tribal histories, personal experiences, dreams, and songs. More than fifty such selections are collected in this anthology. This collection of Native American literature offers several perspectives on history, nature, Native American heritage and culture, and the relationships between humans and the spirit world. Through this anthology, readers can experience a wealth of information and tradition as told by Native American writers of the past and present.

Unit 2: A Nation Is Born (1750–1800)

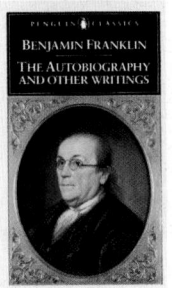

The Autobiography and Other Writings
Benjamin Franklin
Penguin Books, 1986

Benjamin Franklin is one of America's best-loved Founding Fathers. He was a member of the Second Continental Congress and served on the committee that drafted the Declaration of Independence. Besides helping to establish the nation itself, he created many institutions—for example, a hospital, an academy, and a fire company—that were often the first ones of their type in the New World. In his *Autobiography,* Franklin reveals the qualities that enabled him to achieve success as a publisher, scientist, writer, politician, and diplomat.

Complete Writings
Phillis Wheatley
Penguin Books, 2001

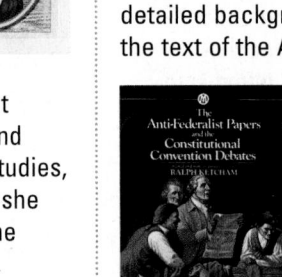

Phillis Wheatley was an enslaved African who was brought to the United States as a child in 1761. She received her name from John Wheatley, the Boston tailor who purchased her. Wheatley and his wife realized Phillis's intelligence and provided her with an education that included such subjects as Latin, Greek, the Bible, and English and classical literature. Stimulated by her studies, Phillis won fame by publishing her first poem when she was just fourteen years old. She went on to write the many poems, translations, and letters in this volume, becoming America's first important black woman poet.

Rights of Man
Thomas Paine
Penguin Books, 1984

Thomas Paine was one of the most eloquent and widely read political authors of all time. His pamphlet "Common Sense" helped inspire the Declaration of Independence, and the first installment of his *Crisis* papers encouraged George Washington's army when it was enduring a difficult winter at Valley Forge. After the American Revolution,

Paine traveled to Europe and wrote *Rights of Man,* his defense of the French Revolution. In it, he argues against monarchy and for a republican form of government. He also sets forth ideas for curing society's ills, including a progressive income tax, popular education, and pensions. This book so infuriated the British government that it was banned. Today's readers, however, will marvel at Paine's prophetic insights.

The Federalist Papers
Alexander Hamilton, James Madison, and John Jay
Mentor, 1999

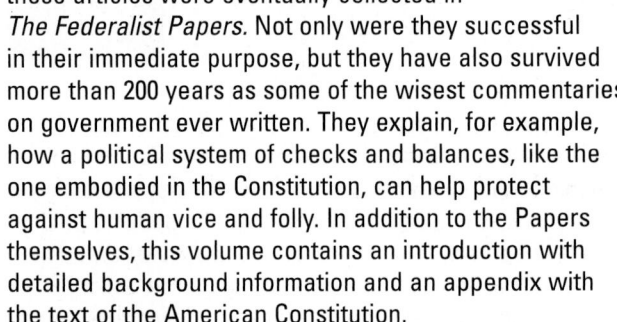

In 1787 and 1788, Alexander Hamilton, James Madison, and John Jay wrote eighty-five essays to persuade New Yorkers to adopt the new national Constitution. First published in newspapers, these articles were eventually collected in *The Federalist Papers.* Not only were they successful in their immediate purpose, but they have also survived more than 200 years as some of the wisest commentaries on government ever written. They explain, for example, how a political system of checks and balances, like the one embodied in the Constitution, can help protect against human vice and folly. In addition to the Papers themselves, this volume contains an introduction with detailed background information and an appendix with the text of the American Constitution.

The Anti-Federalist Papers and the Constitutional Convention Debates
Edited by Ralph Ketcham
Mentor, 1986

The perfect companion to *The Federalist Papers,* this volume provides a context for the debate surrounding the ratification of the Constitution. The introduction, for example, outlines both federalist principles and antifederalist political thought. It also provides a chronology of documents and important events. The many primary documents in the book itself are grouped into two sections: Part I, The Federal Convention of 1787, and Part II, Ratification of the Constitution. Readers can experience the birth of the nation as they follow debates on such essential issues as "State Equality in the Senate" and "Election and Term of Office of the National Executive."

Unit 3: A Growing Nation (1800–1870)

The Journals of Lewis and Clark
Edited by John Bakeless
Mentor, 1964

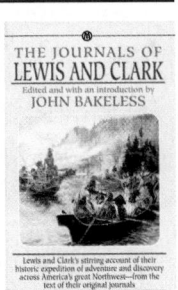

In 1803, Thomas Jefferson doubled the size of the United States by purchasing a tract of land west of the Mississippi River. Jefferson then sent Captains Meriwether Lewis and William Clark on an expedition to explore this vast, new territory. Readers will feel as if they are accompanying this historic expedition every step of the way as they read the journal entries of its two leaders. On this trek from the Missouri River to the Pacific coast, encounters with friendly and unfriendly Native Americans, awe-inspiring scenery, and grizzly bears are part of the daily routine.

The Scarlet Letter
Nathaniel Hawthorne
Pearson Prentice Hall, 2000

They were very few in number, but their courage, hard work, and intense perseverance enabled the Puritans who landed at Plymouth in 1620 to establish a colony. Though *The Scarlet Letter* was published in 1850, Nathaniel Hawthorne chose this setting—a world in which people lived simple lives and followed a strict moral code—for his masterpiece. The novel tells the story of Hester Prynne, who is branded as an outcast and struggles to create her own redemption.

Selected Writings of Ralph Waldo Emerson
Edited by William H. Gilman
Signet Classic, 1965

New England philosopher and poet Ralph Waldo Emerson was perhaps the most eloquent and influential author of nineteenth-century America. He was the leading advocate of Transcendentalism, a philosophy that stressed individualism. In his essay "Self-Reliance," for example, he writes, "Whoso would be a man must be a nonconformist." This volume contains a selection from Emerson's journals and letters; famous essays such as "Nature," "The American Scholar," and "Self-Reliance"; and Emerson's best poems, including "The Rhodora," "The Snow-Storm," and "Brahma." In addition, the editor, William H. Gilman, provides a foreword and a chronology of Emerson's life.

Walden and Civil Disobedience
Henry David Thoreau
Signet Classic, 1999

If Ralph Waldo Emerson was the leading advocate of Transcendentalism, his friend Henry David Thoreau was probably its leading practitioner. He lived the truths in which he believed. In 1845, for example, he built a wooden hut on the banks of Walden Pond near Concord, Massachusetts, and settled there for about two and a half years. *Walden* is the account of this attempt to live simply and independently. This grab bag of eloquence contains everything from vivid descriptions of nature to poems to a balance sheet of purchases. The essay "On the Duty of Civil Disobedience," prompted by Thoreau's opposition to slavery and to the war against Mexico, affirms that an individual's conscience has more authority than an unjust law. Its ideas still seem radical today.

Leaves of Grass
Walt Whitman
Signet Classic, 2000

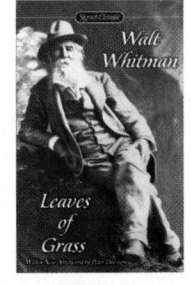

Walt Whitman invented American poetry by breaking free of British influence. While other American poets modeled their work on that of British writers, Whitman drew on unexpected sources such as opera, the newspaper, the Bible, and public oratory. The result was an expansive, unrhymed free verse that sounded thoroughly American. *Leaves of Grass* is the volume of poetry that Whitman first published in 1855 and then kept revising throughout his life. This volume is the ninth edition of the book, published in 1892.

Unit 4: Division, Reconciliation, and Expansion (1850–1914)

Narrative of the Life of Frederick Douglass
Frederick Douglass
Signet Classic, 1997

Frederick Douglass was born a slave in Maryland in the early 1800s. Intelligent, courageous, and persistent, he learned how to read and write even though the conditions of his servitude made it extremely difficult to gain such skills. After experiencing a number of masters and mistresses, both good and bad, Douglass escaped to New York and freedom. From there, he traveled to New Bedford, Massachusetts, where he found employment. He began to read the abolitionist publication the "Liberator," and soon launched a career as an antislavery speaker. In this narrative, Douglass not only conveys the facts of his early life, he also reveals the soul-destroying effects of slavery on master and slave alike.

The Adventures of Huckleberry Finn
Mark Twain
Pearson Prentice Hall, 2000

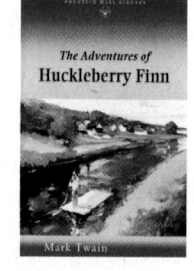

Ernest Hemingway once wrote that "all modern American literature comes from one book by Mark Twain called *Huckleberry Finn.*" The most important part of this influential novel concerns the adventures of two "runaways" on the great Mississippi River. One is Huck Finn, the hero of the novel, who is escaping from his abusive father. The other is Jim, an enslaved African trying to gain his freedom. In the course of their travels, they meet a variety of memorable characters, and Huck experiences a conflict about the morality of slavery. Twain's novel has earned its place of honor in American literature through its skillful use of dialect, its vivid depiction of American life, and its compassionate analysis of race relations.

Spoon River Anthology
Edgar Lee Masters
Signet Classic, 1992

Edgar Lee Masters fled the small towns of his Illinois boyhood to become a big-city lawyer in Chicago. Yet in writing the poems of *Spoon River Anthology,* his most successful book, he drew heavily on his boyhood experiences. An interesting twist, however, is that the more than 200 townspeople in the book are all dead! They speak their free-verse poems from the graveyard, summing up their lives and expressing their angers, disappointments, ideas, dreams, and loves. Together, they provide a realistic picture of life in a small American town, a picture that is fascinating but not always pretty.

My Ántonia
Willa Cather
Pearson Prentice Hall, 2000

Willa Cather drew on her girlhood experiences to write *My Ántonia.* The book's heroine, Ántonia, is a self-reliant and spirited young Bohemian woman growing up on the Nebraska frontier. The narrator of the story is Jim Burden, who after having lost both his parents, travels to Nebraska to live with his grandparents. Cather provides vivid descriptions of the prairie through Jim's eyes. She also chronicles the friendship between Jim and Ántonia as they grow, experience pains and joys, lose sight of each other for twenty years, and renew their relationship. This novel celebrates the pioneer spirit and realistically portrays both the beauty and hardship of life on the American frontier.

The Sea-Wolf and Selected Stories
Jack London
Signet Classic, 1964

Fascinated by the conflict between wildness and civilization, Jack London wrote about this theme in many novels and tales. In his adventure story *The Sea-Wolf,* this conflict takes the form of a struggle between Wolf Larsen and Humphrey Van Weyden. Larsen is the captain of a seal-hunting ship, and as his first name suggests, he is fierce and cruel. Yet this complex man is also a student of philosophy. Van Weyden, who reluctantly becomes a crewman on the ship, is a believer in the value of civilization. The struggle between them takes place as the ship cruises the Pacific in search of seal herds. In addition to *The Sea-Wolf,* the book contains four stories by London, including "The Law of Life" and "All Gold Canyon."

Unit 5: Disillusion, Defiance, and Discontent (1914–1946)

The Great Gatsby
F. Scott Fitzgerald
Scribner, 1992

Fitzgerald's celebrated novel incorporates all of the glamour and decadence that characterized America in the 1920s. This tragic tale of broken dreams and ruined lives explores self-made millionaire Jay Gatsby's quest to win the love of the wealthy, beautiful—and married—Daisy Buchanan. The narrator of the story is Nick Carraway, a young Midwesterner who becomes Gatsby's neighbor on Long Island one summer. Nick is caught up in the dazzling lives of Gatsby, Daisy, and their wealthy friends until tragic circumstances reveal the emptiness of their values. The mysterious Gatsby, an impure man with a pure dream, is the perfect symbol of America in the Jazz Age.

The Grapes of Wrath
John Steinbeck
Penguin Books, 1967

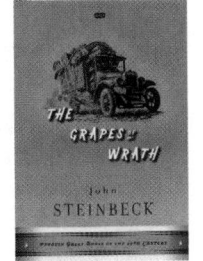

This powerful and moving novel is set during the period of severe economic hardship known as the Great Depression. It recounts the Joad family's journey from the Oklahoma Dust Bowl in search of a better life in California's "promised land." Harsh yet uplifting, this story affirms the strength of America's common people in the face of adversity and injustice.

Winesburg, Ohio
Sherwood Anderson
Penguin Books, 1960

Inspired by Edgar Lee Master's *Spoon River Anthology,* Sherwood Anderson started to write a group of related stories about small-town life that became *Winesburg, Ohio.* He based his fictional town of Winesburg on his own hometown of Clyde, Ohio. Central to the book is young George Willard, the sympathetic character to whom others try to explain themselves. The characters who open up to George are isolated people who usually have trouble communicating. Among them are Dr. Parcival, a failed writer, and Enoch Robinson, who "was always a child." When George's mother dies and he begins to become a man, he is ready to leave Winesburg for "his future life in the city."

Poems by Robert Frost: A Boy's Will and North of Boston
Robert Frost
Signet Classic, 2001

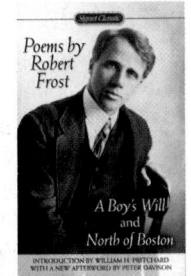

This volume contains Frost's first two published books in their original form, *A Boy's Will* (1913) and *North of Boston* (1914). These books, which introduced Frost's distinctively New England voice and established him as a major poet, contain some of his best poems: "Mowing," "The Trial by Existence," "Mending Wall," and "After Apple-Picking," among others. *North of Boston* has many of the dramatic monologues that reveal Frost's skill in capturing memorable thoughts in down-to-earth speech.

Black Voices: An Anthology of African-American Literature
Edited by Abraham Chapman
Signet Classic, 2001

This volume collects the best African American literature of the twentieth century in a variety of genres: fiction, autobiography, poetry, and literary criticism.
The fiction includes, among other works, Langston Hughes's humorous *Tales of Simple* and the dramatic prologue to Ralph Ellison's novel *Invisible Man.* Appearing in the autobiography section are such famous figures as Frederick Douglass, James Baldwin, and Malcolm X. The poetry section includes work by the Harlem Renaissance poets Langston Hughes, Claude McKay, and Countee Cullen, as well as the major post–World War II poets Robert Hayden and Gwendolyn Brooks. The last section features literary criticism by W.E.B. Du Bois, Alain Locke, Clarence Major, and others.

Unit 6: Prosperity and Protest (1946–Present)

The Joy Luck Club
Amy Tan
Putnam, 1989

Organized as a group of sixteen related stories, *The Joy Luck Club* deals with mother-daughter relationships in the Chinese immigrant community of San Francisco. The title refers to the name of a club begun in 1949 by four immigrant Chinese women. Meeting regularly to play the Chinese game of mah jong, they snack, gossip, and tell one another their hopes and fears. The book is divided into four sections, two in which the mothers speak and two in which their American-raised daughters express themselves. Unexpectedly, one mother's sad family secret helps bridge the distance between the generations.

Breathing Lessons
Anne Tyler
Berkley, 1988

The main characters in *Breathing Lessons*, Maggie and Ira Moran, could be your next-door neighbors. Maggie is a mother and wife who is preoccupied with solving the complex problems of her family. Ira is a patient husband who accepts his wife's quirks with good humor. Maggie and Ira start off on what should be a short journey to a funeral. Instead, a series of detours turns the trip into an unexpected odyssey that forces them to reexamine their own seemingly normal lives. This Pulitzer Prize-winning novel is full of insights and humorous moments that show that humdrum reality is rarely what it seems.

On Nature: Great Writers on the Great Outdoors
Edited by Lee Gutkind
Most Tarcher/Putnam, 2002

This book of contemporary nature essays will appeal to those who love outdoor activities as well as to those who prefer mental exercise in an armchair. It features nonfiction by some of America's best contemporary authors: Joyce Carol Oates, Barry Lopez, Mark Doty, Diane Ackerman, John McPhee, and Bill Bryson, among others. Just a sample of the essay titles conveys the adventures that this book holds in store: "Killing Wolves," "Plain Scared," "The Spray and the Slamming Sea," "Love, War, and Deer Hunting," and "The Moon by the Whale Light."

Twentieth-Century American Drama
Prentice Hall
Pearson Prentice Hall, 2000

The plays in this volume represent some of the best work by America's greatest twentieth-century playwrights: *Our Town*, by Thornton Wilder; *The Glass Menagerie*, by Tennessee Williams; *Death of a Salesman* and *The Crucible*, by Arthur Miller; and *A Raisin in the Sun*, by Lorraine Hansberry. Wilder's innovative play, with its stage manager who addresses the audience, reveals the preciousness of everyday life in a typical American town. In Williams's poetic drama, harsh realities threaten the fantasies of a mother and daughter. Miller's *Death of a Salesman*, the tragedy of a common man, is as powerful as an ancient Greek tragedy about the downfall of a king. Hansberry documents several weeks in the life of an African American family, revealing the conflicting dreams of her characters.

Nonfiction Readings Across the Curriculum
Prentice Hall
Pearson Prentice Hall, 2000

These essays by well-known authors provide new and exciting ways of thinking about many subjects including literature, science, social studies, mathematics, sports, and the arts. This list, however, cannot do justice to the variety and liveliness of the essays. In a memoir, for example, author Beverly Cleary tells how she got started in her career and recalls some of the real-life people on whom she based her characters. Football great Joe Namath gives players a pep talk in his how-to essay from *Football for Young Players and Parents*. Readers will find that the enthusiasm of the writers in this volume is contagious.

abeyance (ə bā´ əns) n.: Temporary suspension

ablutions (ab lōō´ shənz) n.: Washing or cleansing the body as part of a religious rite

abundance (ə bun´ dəns) n.: A great supply; more than enough

acquiesce (ak´ wē es´) v.: Agree without protest

admonitory (ad män´ i tôr´ ē) adj.: Warning

adversary (ad´ vər ser´ ē) n.: Opponent; enemy

affliction (ə flik´ shən) n.: Something causing pain or suffering

aggregation (ag´ grə gā´ shən) n.: Group or mass of distinct objects or individuals

aggrieved (ə grēvd´) adj.: Offended; wronged

agues (ā´ gyōōz) n.: Fits of shivering

alacrity (ə lak´ rə tē) n.: Speed

alliance (ə lī´ əns) n.: Union of nations for a specific purpose

anarchy (an´ ər kē) n.: Absence of government

anathema (ə nath´ ə mə) n.: Curse

anomalous (ə näm´ ə ləs) adj.: Abnormal

antagonism (an tag´ ə niz´ əm) n.: Hostility

apparition (ap´ ə rish´ ən) n.: The act of appearing or becoming visible

appellation (ap´ ə lā´ shən) n.: Name or title

apprised (ə prīzd´) v.: Informed; notified

arduous (är´ jōō wəs) adj.: Difficult

arrested (ə rest´ id) adj.: Stopped

aspiration (as´pə rā´shən) n.: Strong ambition

asylum (ə sī´ ləm) n.: Place of refuge

audaciously (ô dā´ shəs lē) adv.: Boldly or daringly

autonomous (ô tän´ ə məs) adj.: Independent

avarice (av´ ər is) n.: Greed for riches

aversion (ə vur´ zhən) n.: Object arousing an intense or definite dislike

avuncular (ə vuŋ´ kyōō lər) adj.: Having traits considered typical of uncles: jolly, indulgent, stodgy

bastions (bas´ chənz) n.: Fortifications

bayou (bī´ ōō) n.: Sluggish, marshy inlet

beguile (bē gīl´) v.: Charm or delight

bellicose (bel´ ə kōs) adj.: Quarrelsome

benevolent (bə nev´ ə lənt) adj.: Kindly; charitable

bivouac (biv´ wak) n.: Temporary encampment

blaspheming (blas fēm´ iŋ) v.: Cursing

blithe (blīth) adj.: Carefree

brazenness (brā´ zən nis) n.: Shamelessness; boldness; impudence

brutal (brōōt´ əl) adj.: Cruel and without feeling; savage; violent

buck (buk) n.: Male animal, especially a male deer

cacophony (kə käf´ ə nē) n.: Harsh, jarring sound

caper (kā´ pər) n.: Prank

capitulate (kə pich´ ə lāt´) v.: Surrender conditionally

celestial (sə les´ chəl) adj.: Of the heavens

chaos (kā´ äs) n.: Disorder of formless matter and infinite space, supposed to have existed before the ordered universe

claustrophobia (klôs´ trə fō´ bē ə) n.: Fear of being in a confined space

commiseration (kə miz´ ər ā´ shən) n.: Sympathy; condolence

conceits (kən sētz´) n.: Strange or fanciful ideas

confederate (kən fed´ ər it) adj.: United with others for a common purpose

conflagration (kän´ flə grā´ shən) n.: Big, destructive fire

congealed (kən jēld´) v.: Thickened or solidified

congenial (kən jēn´ yəl) adj.: Agreeable

conjectural (kən jek´ chər əl) adj.: Based on guesswork

conjectured (kən jek´ chərd) v.: Guessed

connate (kän āt´) adj.: Existing naturally; innate

consanguinity (kän´ saŋ gwin´ ə tē) n.: Kinship

consecrate (kän´ sə krāt´) v.: Cause to be revered or honored

conspicuous (kən spik´ yōō əs) adj.: Obvious; easy to see or perceive

consternation (kän´ stər nā´ shən) n.: Great fear or shock that makes one feel helpless or bewildered

contrition (kən trish´ ən) n.: Remorse for having done wrong

copious (kō´ pē əs) adj.: Plentiful; abundant

cornice (kôr´ nis) n.: Projecting decorative molding along the top of a building

cosmopolitan (käz´ mə päl´ ə tən) adj.: Common to or representative of all or many parts of the world

countenance (koun´ tə nəns) v.: Approve; tolerate

covertly (kō vərt´ lē) adv.: Secretly; surreptitiously

craven (krā´ vən) adj.: Very cowardly

crux (kruks) n.: Essential point

cunning (kun´ iŋ) adj.: Skillful in deception; crafty; sly

deference (def´ ər əns) n.: Respect; courtesy; regard

degenerate (dē jen´ ər it) adj.: Morally corrupt

deliberation (di lib´ ə rā´ shən) n.: Careful consideration

demarcation (dē´ mär kā´ shən) n.: Separation

depravity (di prav´ ə tē) n.: Corruption; wickedness

deprecated (dep´ rə kāt´ id) v.: Expressed disapproval of; pleaded against

depredations (dep´ rə dā´ shənz) n.: Acts of robbing or plundering

derivative (də riv´ ə tiv) adj.: Not original; based on something else

despotic (de spät´ ik) adj.: Harsh; cruel; unjust

despotism (des´ pət iz´ əm) n.: Government by absolute rule; tyranny

dictum (dik´ təm) n.: Formal statement of fact or opinion

digress (dī gres´) v.: Depart temporarily from the main subject

dilapidated (di lap´ ə dā tid) adj.: In disrepair

discern (di surn´) v.: Perceive or recognize; make out clearly

disdainfully (dis dān´ fəl ē) adv.: Showing scorn or contempt

dispatched (dis pacht´) v.: Sent off on a specific assignment

disposition (dis´ pə zish´ ən) n.: Inclination or tendency

distillery (dis til´ ə rē) n.: Place where alcoholic liquors are distilled

divines (də vīnz´) n.: Clergy

dogma (dôg´ mə) n.: Formalized and authoritative doctrines or beliefs

dolorous (dō´ lər əs) adj.: Sad; mournful

dominion (də min´ yən) n.: Power to rule

dusky (dus´ kē) adj.: Dim; shadowy

dyspepsia (dis pep´ shə) n.: Indigestion

efface (ə fās´) v.: Erase; wipe out

effaced (ə fāsd´) adj.: Erased; wiped out

effuse (ə fyōōz´) v.: Spread out; diffuse

elusive (ē lōō´ siv) adj.: Hard to grasp

embankment (em baŋk´ mənt) n.: Mound of earth or stone built to hold back water or support a roadway

emigrants (em´ i grəntz) n.: People who leave one area to move to another

eminence (em´ ə nəns) n.: Greatness; celebrity

engrossed (en grōst´) adj.: Occupied wholly; absorbed

entreated (en trēt´ id) v.: Begged; pleaded

epitaph (ep´ ə taf) n.: Inscription on a tombstone or grave marker

equanimity (ek´ wə nim´ ə tē) n.: Composure

equivocal (i kwiv´ ə kəl) adj.: Having more than one possible interpretation; uncertain

eradicate (e rad´ i kāt´) v.: Get rid of; wipe out; destroy

etiquette (et´ i kit) n.: Appropriate behavior and ceremonies

evitable (ev´ ə tə bəl) adj.: Avoidable

exalted (eg zôlt´ id) *adj.:* Filled with joy or pride; elated

excavated (eks´ kə vā tid) *v.:* Dug out; made a hole

expatriated (eks pā´ trē āt´ id) *adj.:* Deported; driven from one's native land

expedient (ik spē´ dē ənt) *n.:* Resource

exquisite (eks´ kwi zit) *adj.:* Very beautiful; delicate; carefully wrought

extort (eks tôrt´) *v.:* Obtain by threat or violence

extricate (eks´ tri kāt´) *v.:* Set free

fallowness (fal´ ō nis) *n.:* Inactivity

fasting (fast´ iŋ) *v.:* Eating very little or nothing

feigned (fānd) *v.:* Pretended; faked

felicity (fə lis´ ə tē) *n.:* Happiness; bliss

finite (fī´ nīt) *adj.:* Having measurable or definable limits

flagrant (flā´ grənt) *adj.:* Glaring; outrageous

foppery (fäp´ ər ē) *n.:* Foolishness

foreboding (fôr bōd´ iŋ) *n.:* Presentiment

foreknowledge (fôr´ näl´ ij) *n.:* Awareness of something before it happens or exists

forestall (fôr stôl´) *v.:* Prevent by acting ahead of time

fortuitous (fôr tōō´ ə təs) *adj.:* Fortunate

frippery (frip´ ər ē) *n.:* Showy display of elegance

galvanic (gal van´ ik) *adj.:* Startling; stimulating as if by electric current

garrulous (gar´ ə ləs) *adj.:* Talking too much

genial (jēn´ yəl) *adj.:* Cheerful; friendly

geography (jē ôg´ rə fē) *n.:* The study of the surface of the Earth

glade (glād) *n.:* Open space in a wood or forest

glean (glēn) *v.:* Collect the remaining grain after reaping

gloaming (glō´ miŋ) *n.:* Evening dusk; twilight

grave (grāv) *adj.:* Serious; solemn

gregarious (grə ger´ ē əs) *adj.:* Sociable

guile (gīl) *n.:* Craftiness

hallow (hal´ ō) *v.:* Honor as sacred

heirs (erz) *n.:* People who carry on the tradition of predecessors

impelled (im peld´) *v.:* Moved; forced

imperially (im pir´ ē əl ē) *adv.:* Majestically

imperious (im pir´ ē əs) *adj.:* Urgent; imperative

impertinent (im pʉr´ tən ənt) *adj.:* Not showing proper respect

impious (im´ pē əs) *adj.:* Lacking reverence for God

importunate (im pôr´ choo nit) *adj.:* Insistent

importunities (im´ pôr tōōn´ ə tēz) *n.:* Persistent requests or demands

imprecations (im´ prə kā´ shənz) *n.:* Curses

improvident (im präv´ ə dənt) *adj.:* Shortsighted; failing to provide for the future

increment (in´ krə mənt) *n.:* Increase, as in a series

indecorous (in dek´ ər əs) *adj.:* Improper

indications (in´ di kā´ shənz) *n.:* Signs; things that point out or signify

ineffable (in ef´ ə bəl) *adj.:* Inexpressible; unable to be spoken

inert (in ʉrt´) *adj.:* Motionless

infallibility (in fal´ ə bil´ ə tē) *n.:* Inability to be wrong; reliability

infidel (in´ fə dəl) *n.:* Person who holds no religious belief

infinity (in fin´ i tē) *n.:* Endless or unlimited space, time, or distance

iniquity (in ik´ wə tē) *n.:* Sin

insatiable (in sā´ shə bəl) *adj.:* Constantly wanting more; unable to be satisfied

inscrutable (in skrōōt´ ə bəl) *adj.:* Not able to be easily understood

insidious (in sid´ ē əs) *adj.:* Secretly treacherous

insurgents (in sʉr´ jənts) *n.:* Rebels; those who revolt against established authority

interminable (in tʉr´ mi nə bəl) *adj.:* Seeming to last forever

intuitively (in tōō´ i tiv lē) *adv.:* Instinctively

invalided (in´ və lid´ id) *v.:* Released because of illness or disability

invective (in vek´ tiv) *n.:* Verbal attack; strong criticism

invoke (in vōk´) *v.:* Call on for help, inspiration, or support

jettisoned (jet´ ə sənd) *v.:* Thrown overboard to lighten the weight of a ship

jocularity (jäk´ yə lar´ ə tē) *n.:* Joking good humor

jubilant (jōō´ bəl ənt) *adj.:* Joyful and triumphant

labyrinth (lab´ ə rinth´) *n.:* Intricate network of winding passages; maze

liberty (lib´ ər tē) *n.:* The condition of being free from control by others

limber (lim´ bər) *adj.:* Flexible

literalists (lit´ ər əl ists) *n.:* People who insist on taking words at their exact meaning

loath (lōth) *adj.:* Reluctant; unwilling

loathsome (lōth´ səm) *adj.:* Hateful; detestable

lulled (luld) *v.:* Calmed or soothed by a gentle sound or motion

luminary (lōō´ mə ner´ ē) *adj.:* Giving off light

magnanimity (mag´ nə nim´ ə tē) *n.:* Ability to rise above pettiness or meanness

maledictions (mal´ ə dik´ shənz) *n.:* Curses

malevolence (mə lev´ ə ləns) *n.:* Malice; spitefulness

malevolent (mə lev´ ə lənt) *adj.:* Mean-spirited; showing ill will

malice (mal´ is) *n.:* Ill will; spite

malign (mə līn´) *adj.:* Malicious; very harmful

malingered (mə liŋ´ gərd) *v.:* Escaped work or duty by pretending to be ill

manifest (man´ ə fest´) *adj.:* Evident; obvious; clear

manifold (man´ ə fōld´) *adj.:* In many ways

manuscript (man´ yōō skript´) *n.:* Written or typed document, especially one submitted to a publisher or printer

meticulous (mə tik´ yōō ləs) *adj.:* Extremely careful about details

moiling (moi´ liŋ) *v.:* Churning; swirling

mollified (mäl´ ə fīd´) *v.:* Soothed; calmed

monotonous (mə nät´ ən əs) *adj.:* Tiresome because unvarying

monotony (mə nät´ ən ē) *n.:* Tiresome, unchanging sameness; lack of variety

mortality (môr tal´ ə tē) *n.:* Death on a large scale, as from disease or war

motives (mōt´ ivz) *n.:* Reasons for action; inner drives

multifarious (mul´ tə far´ ē əs) *adj.:* Having many parts or elements; diverse

multitudinous (mul´ tə tōōd´ ən əs) *adj.:* Numerous

mundane (mun dān´) *adj.:* Commonplace; ordinary

munificent (myōō nif´ ə sənt) *adj.:* Generous

myriad (mir´ ē əd) *n.:* Countless

negligence (neg´ li jəns) *n.:* Instance of failure, carelessness, or indifference

nonplused (nän´ plüsd´) *adj.:* Bewildered; perplexed

obeisance (ō bā´ səns) *n.:* Gesture of respect

obliterated (ə blit´ ər āt´ id) *v.:* Blotted out; destroyed

obstinacy (äb´ stə nə sē) *n.:* Stubbornness

obstinate (äb´ stə nit) *adj.:* Stubborn

obtuse (äb tōōs´) *adj.:* Slow to understand or perceive

ominous (äm´ ə nəs) *adj.:* Threatening

omnipotent (äm nip´ ə tənt) *adj.:* All-powerful

oppressed (ə prest´) *v.:* Kept down by cruel or unjust power or authority

oppresses (ə pres´ əz) *v.:* Weighs heavily on the mind

ornery (ôr´ nər ē) *adj.:* Having a mean disposition

oscillation (äs´ ə lā´ shən) *n.:* Act of swinging or moving regularly back and forth

ostentation (äs´ tən tā´ shən) *n.:* Boastful display

ostentatious (äs´ tən tā´ shəs) *adj.:* Intended to attract notice

pacify (pas´ ə fī´) *v.:* Calm; soothe

palisades (pal´ ə sādz´) *n.:* Large, pointed stakes set in the ground to form a fence used for defense

palpable (pal´ pə bəl) *adj.:* Able to be touched, felt, or handled

parsimony (pär´ sə mō´ nē) *n.:* Stinginess

patriarch (pā´ trē ärk´) *n.:* Father and ruler of a family or tribe

pensive (pen′ siv) *adj.:* Thinking deeply or seriously

penury (pen′ yə rē) *n.:* Lack of money, property, or necessities

perdition (pər dish′ ən) *n.:* Complete and irreparable loss; ruin

peremptorily (pər emp′ tər ə lē) *adv.:* Decisively; commandingly

perfidy (pur′ fə dē) *n.:* Betrayal of trust

peril (per′ əl) *n.:* Danger

persevere (pur sə vir′) *v.:* Persist; be steadfast in purpose

pertinaciously (pur′ tə nā′ shəs lē) *adv.:* Holding firmly to some purpose

pervading (pər vād′ iŋ) *adj.:* Spreading throughout

pestilential (pes′ tə len′ shəl) *adj.:* Likely to cause disease

piety (pī′ ə tē) *n.:* Devotion to religious duties

pilfer (pil′ fər) *v.:* Steal

placid (plas′ id) *adj.:* Tranquil; calm; quiet

poignant (poin′ yənt) *adj.:* Sharply painful to the feelings

poise (poiz) *n.:* Balance; stability

posterity (päs ter′ ə tē) *n.:* All succeeding generations

precipitate (prē sip′ ə tāt′) *v.:* Cause to happen before expected or desired

prelude (prel′ yood) *n.:* Introductory section or movement of a suite, fugue, or work of music

preposterous (pri päs′ tər əs) *adj.:* Ridiculous

prescient (presh′ ənt) *adj.:* Having fore-knowledge

prodigious (prə dij′ əs) *adj.:* Of great power or size

profundity (prō fun′ də tē) *n.:* Intellectual depth

profusion (prō fyoo′ zhən) *n.:* Abundance; rich supply

propitious (prō pish′ əs) *adj.:* Favorably inclined or disposed

protruded (prō trood′ id) *v.:* Jutted out

psychology (sī käl′ ə jē) *n.:* The science dealing with the mind and with mental and emotional processes

pugilistic (pyoo′ jə lis′ tik) *adj.:* Looking for a fight

querulous (kwer′ ə ləs) *adj.:* Inclined to find fault

radiant (rā′ dē ənt) *adj.:* Shining brightly

reaping (rēp′ iŋ) *v.:* Cutting or harvesting grain from a field

recompense (rek′ əm pens′) *n.:* Reward; repayment

recumbent (ri kum′ bənt) *adj.:* Resting

redolent (red′ əl ənt) *adj.:* Suggestive

redress (ri′ dres) *n.:* Atonement; rectification

refluent (ref′ loo ənt) *adj.:* Flowing back

refulgent (ri ful′ jənt) *adj.:* Radiant; shining

repose (ri pōz′) *n.:* State of being at rest

repression (ri presh′ ən) *n.:* Restraint

retrospective (re trə spek′ tiv) *adj.:* Looking back on or directed to the past

reverential (rev′ ə ren′ shəl) *adj.:* Showing or caused by a feeling of deep respect, love, and awe

rueful (roo′ fəl) *adj.:* Feeling or showing sorrow or pity

sagacious (sə gā′ shəs) *adj.:* Shrewd

salient (sāl′ yənt) *adj.:* Standing out from the rest

sallow (sal′ ō) *adj.:* Sickly; pale yellow

salutary (sal′ yoo ter′ ē) *adj.:* Beneficial; promoting a good purpose

scepter (sep′ tər) *n.:* Rod or staff held by rulers as a symbol of sovereignty

scintillating (sint′ əl āt′ iŋ) *adj.:* Sparkling

scourge (skurj) *n.:* Cause of serious trouble or affliction

scrabbling (skrab′ liŋ) *v.:* Scrambling

semi-somnambulant (sem′ i säm nam′ byoo lənt) *adj.:* Half-sleepwalking

sentience (sen′ shəns) *n.:* Capacity of feeling

sepulcher (sep′ əl kər) *n.:* Grave; tomb

serenity (sə ren′ ə tē) *n.:* Calmness

sinuous (sin′ yoo wəs) *adj.:* Moving in and out; wavy

slovenly (sluv′ ən lē) *adj.:* Untidy

smite (smīt) *v.:* Kill by a powerful blow

somnolent (säm′ nə lənt) *adj.:* Sleepy; drowsy

specious (spē′ shəs) *adj.:* Seeming to be good or sound without actually being so

squander (skwän′ dər) *v.:* Spend or use wastefully

stark (stärk) *adj.:* Stiff or rigid, as a corpse; severe

statistics (sta tis′ tiks) *n.:* The science of collecting and arranging facts about a particular subject in the form of numbers

stringency (strin′ jən sē) *n.:* Strictness; severity

subjugation (sub′ jə gā′ shən) *n.:* The act of conquering

sublime (sə blīm′) *adj.:* Inspiring awe or admiration through grandeur or beauty

subsistence (səb sis′ təns) *n.:* Means of support

subterranean (sub′ tə rā′ nē ən) *adj.:* Underground

suffice (sə fīs′) *v.:* Be adequate; meet the needs of

suffrage (suf′ rij) *n.:* Vote or voting

sullen (sul′ ən) *adj.:* Sulky; glum

summarily (sə mer′ ə lē) *adv.:* Promptly and without formality

sundry (sun′ drē) *adj.:* Various; different

superfluous (soo pur′ floo wəs) *adj.:* Excessive; not necessary

surmised (sər mīzd′) *v.:* Guessed

swag (swag) *n.:* Suspended cluster of branches

switch (swich) *n.:* Slender, flexible twig or whip

tempest (tem′ pist) *n.:* Violent storm

tempo (tem′ pō) *n.:* Rate of activity of a sound or motion; pace

terra firma (ter′ ə fur′ mə) *n.:* Firm earth; solid ground (Latin)

timorous (tim′ ər əs) *adj.:* Full of fear

trajectory (trə jek′ tə rē) *n.:* Curved path of an object hurtling through space

transient (tran′ zē ənt) *adj.:* Not permanent

tremulous (trem′ yoo ləs) *adj.:* Characterized by trembling

tremulously (trem′ yoo ləs lē) *adv.:* Fearfully; timidly

tumultuous (too mult′ choo wəs) *adj.:* Rough; stormy

tumultuously (too mul′ choo wəs lē) *adv.:* In an agitated way

tyranny (tir′ ə nē) *n.:* Oppressive and unjust government

unalienable (un āl′ yən ə bəl) *adj.:* Not to be taken away

unanimity (yoo′ nə nim′ ə tē) *n.:* Complete agreement

untoward (un tō′ ərd) *adj.:* Inappropriate or improper

unwonted (un wän′ tid) *adj.:* Unusual; unfamiliar

usurers (yoo′ zhərz) *n.:* Moneylenders who charge very high interest

usurpations (yoo′ sər pā′ shənz) *n.:* Unlawful seizures of rights or privileges

vagary (və ger′ ē) *n.:* Unpredictable occurrence

venerable (ven′ ər ə bəl) *adj.:* Worthy of respect

vigilance (vij′ ə ləns) *n.:* Watchfulness

vigilant (vij′ ə lənt) *adj.:* Alert to danger

visage (viz′ ij) *n.:* Appearance

vitality (vī tal′ ə tē) *n.:* Power to endure or survive; life force

vituperative (vī too′ pər ə tiv) *adj.:* Spoken abusively

vociferation (vō sif′ ər ā′ shən) *n.:* Loud or vehement shouting

voluminous (və loom′ ə nəs) *adj.:* Of enough material to fill volumes

waggery (wag′ ər ē) *n.:* Mischievous humor

wanton (wän′ tən) *adj.:* Senseless; unjustified

When you were younger, you learned to read. Then, you read to expand your experiences or for pure enjoyment. Now, you are expected to read to learn. As you progress in school, you are given more and more material to read. The tips on these pages will help you improve your reading fluency, or your ability to read easily, smoothly, and expressively.

Keeping Your Concentration

One common problem that readers face is the loss of concentration. When you are reading an assignment, you might find yourself rereading the same sentence several times without really understanding it. The first step in changing this behavior is to notice that you do it. Becoming an active, aware reader will help you get the most from your assignments. Practice using these strategies:

- Cover what you have already read with a note card as you go along. Then, you will not be able to reread without noticing that you are doing it.

- Set a purpose for reading beyond just completing the assignment. Then, read actively by pausing to ask yourself questions about the material as you read.

- Use the Reading Strategy instruction and notes that appear with each selection in this textbook.

- Stop reading after a specified period of time (for example, 5 minutes) and summarize what you have read. To help you with this strategy, use the Reading Check questions that appear with each selection in this textbook. Reread to find any answers you do not know.

Reading Phrases

Fluent readers read phrases rather than individual words. Reading this way will speed up your reading and improve your comprehension. Here are some useful ideas:

- Experts recommend rereading as a strategy to increase fluency. Choose a passage of text that is neither too hard nor too easy. Read the same passage aloud several times until you can read it smoothly. When you can read the passage fluently, pick another passage and keep practicing.

- Read aloud into a tape recorder. Then, listen to the recording, noting your accuracy, pacing, and expression. You can also read aloud and share feedback with a partner.

- Use the *Prentice Hall Listening to Literature* audiotapes or CDs to hear the selections read aloud. Read along silently in your textbook, noticing how the reader uses his or her voice and emphasizes certain words and phrases.

Reading Check

What common problem do many readers face?

Reading Check

In what ways will reading phrases rather than individual words affect your reading?

Understanding Key Vocabulary

If you do not understand some of the words in an assignment, you may miss out on important concepts. Therefore, it is helpful to keep a dictionary nearby when you are reading. Follow these steps:

- Before you begin reading, scan the text for unfamiliar words or terms. Find out what those words mean before you begin reading.
- Use context—the surrounding words, phrases, and sentences—to help you determine the meanings of unfamiliar words.
- If you are unable to understand the meaning through context, refer to the dictionary.

Paying Attention to Punctuation

When you read, pay attention to punctuation. Commas, periods, exclamation points, semicolons, and colons tell you when to pause or stop. They also indicate relationships between groups of words. When you recognize these relationships you will read with greater understanding and expression. Look at the chart below.

Punctuation Mark	Meaning
comma	brief pause
period	pause at the end of a thought
exclamation point	pause that indicates emphasis
semicolon	pause between related but distinct thoughts
colon	pause before giving explanation or examples

☑ **Reading Check**

Why should you look up words you do not know when reading an assignment?

Using the Reading Fluency Checklist

Use the checklist below each time you read a selection in this textbook. In your Language Arts journal or notebook, note which skills you need to work on and chart your progress each week.

Reading Fluency Checklist

❏ Preview the text to check for difficult or unfamiliar words.
❏ Practice reading aloud.
❏ Read according to punctuation.
❏ Break down long sentences into the subject and its meaning.
❏ Read groups of words for meaning rather than reading single words.
❏ Read with expression (change your tone of voice to add meaning to the word).

Reading is a skill that can be improved with practice. The key to improving your fluency is to read. The more you read, the better your reading will become.

ALLEGORY An *allegory* is a story or tale with two or more levels of meaning—a literal level and one or more symbolic levels. The events, setting, and characters in an allegory are symbols for ideas or qualities. Many of Nathaniel Hawthorne's short stories, such as "The Minister's Black Veil" (p. 336), are allegories.

ALLITERATION *Alliteration* is the repetition of consonant sounds at the beginning of words or accented syllables. Sara Teasdale uses alliteration in these lines from her poem "Understanding":

> Your spirit's secret hides like gold
> Sunk in a Spanish galleon

ALLUSION An *allusion* is a reference to a well-known person, place, event, literary work, or work of art. Writers often make allusions to stories from the Bible, to Greek and Roman myths, to plays by Shakespeare, to political and historical events, and to other materials with which they can expect their readers to be familiar. In "The Love Song of J. Alfred Prufrock" (p. 718), T. S. Eliot alludes to, among other things, Dante's *Inferno*, Italian artist Michelangelo, Shakespeare's *Hamlet*, and the Bible. By using allusions, writers can suggest complex ideas simply and easily.

AMBIGUITY *Ambiguity* is the effect created when words suggest and support two or more divergent interpretations. Ambiguity may be used in literature to express experiences or truths that are complex or contradictory. Ambiguity often derives from the fact that words have multiple meanings.
See also Irony.

ANALOGY An *analogy* is an extended comparison of relationships. It is based on the idea that the relationship between one pair of things is like the relationship between another pair. Unlike a metaphor, an analogy involves an explicit comparison, often using the words *like* or *as*.
See also Metaphor, Simile.

ANECDOTE An *anecdote* is a brief story about an interesting, amusing, or strange event. An anecdote is told to entertain or to make a point. In the excerpt from *Life on the Mississippi* (p. 564), Mark Twain tells several anecdotes about his experiences on the Mississippi River.

ANTAGONIST An *antagonist* is a character or force in conflict with a main character, or protagonist. In Jack London's "To Build a Fire" (p. 608), the antagonist is neither a person nor an animal but rather the extreme cold. In many stories, the conflict between the antagonist and the protagonist is the basis for the plot.

See also Conflict, Plot, *and* Protagonist.

APHORISM An *aphorism* is a general truth or observation about life, usually stated concisely. Often witty and wise, aphorisms appear in many kinds of works. An essay writer may have an aphoristic style, making many such statements. Ralph Waldo Emerson was famous for his aphoristic style. His essay entitled "Fate" contains the following aphorisms:

> Nature is what you may do.
> So far as a man thinks, he is free.
> A man's fortunes are the fruit of his character.

Used in an essay, an aphorism can be a memorable way to sum up or to reinforce a point or an argument.

APOSTROPHE An *apostrophe* is a figure of speech in which a speaker directly addresses an absent person or a personified quality, object, or idea. Phillis Wheatley uses apostrophe in this line from "To the University of Cambridge, in New England":

> Students, to you 'tis given to scan the heights

See also Figurative Language.

ARCHETYPAL LITERARY ELEMENTS *Archetypal literary elements* are patterns in literature found around the world. For instance, the occurrence of events in threes is an archetypal element of fairy tales. Certain character types, such as mysterious guides, are also archetypal elements of such traditional stories. Archetypal elements make stories easier to remember and retell. In *Moby-Dick* (p. 354), Melville uses the archetype of a whale—like the biblical mammal in conflict with Jonah—to address man's conflict with nature.

ASSONANCE *Assonance* is the repetition of vowel sounds in conjunction with dissimilar consonant sounds. Emily Dickinson uses assonance in the line "The mountain at a given distance." The *i* sound is repeated in *given* and *distance*, in the context of the dissimilar consonant sounds *g–v* and *d–s*.

ATMOSPHERE *See* Mood.

AUTOBIOGRAPHY An *autobiography* is a form of nonfiction in which a person tells his or her own life story. Notable examples of autobiographies include those by Benjamin Franklin and Frederick Douglass. *Memoirs*, first-person accounts of personally or historically significant events in which the writer was a participant or an eyewitness, are a form of autobiographical writing.
See also Biography *and* Journal.

BALLAD A *ballad* is a songlike poem that tells a story, often one dealing with adventure and romance. Most ballads include simple language, four- or six-line stanzas, rhyme, and regular meter.

BIOGRAPHY A *biography* is a form of nonfiction in which a writer tells the life story of another person. Carl Sandburg's *Abe Lincoln Grows Up* is a biography of President Lincoln.
See also Autobiography.

BLANK VERSE *Blank verse* is poetry written in unrhymed iambic pentameter. An iamb is a poetic foot consisting of one weak stress followed by one strong stress. A pentameter line has five poetic feet. Robert Frost's "Birches" (p. 882) is written in blank verse.

CHARACTER A *character* is a person or an animal that takes part in the action of a literary work. The following are some terms used to describe various types of characters:

The *main character* in a literary work is the one on whom the work focuses. *Major characters* in a literary work include the main character and any other characters who play significant roles. A *minor character* is one who does not play a significant role. A *round character* is one who is complex and multifaceted, like a real person. A *flat character* is one who is one-dimensional. A *dynamic character* is one who changes in the course of a work. A *static character* is one who does not change in the course of a work.
See also Characterization *and* Motivation.

CHARACTERIZATION *Characterization* is the act of creating and developing a character. In *direct characterization*, a writer simply states a character's traits, as when F. Scott Fitzgerald writes of the main character in his story "Winter Dreams" (p. 744), "He wanted not association with glittering things and glittering people—he wanted the glittering things themselves." In *indirect characterization*, character is revealed through one of the following means:

1. words, thoughts, or actions of the character
2. descriptions of the character's appearance or background
3. what other characters say about the character
4. the ways in which other characters react to the character
See also Character.

CINQUAIN *See* Stanza.

CLASSICISM *Classicism* is an approach to literature and the other arts that stresses reason, balance, clarity, ideal beauty, and orderly form in imitation of the arts of ancient Greece and Rome. Classicism is often contrasted with *Romanticism*, which stresses imagination, emotion, and individualism.

Classicism also differs from *Realism*, which stresses the actual rather than the ideal.
See also Realism *and* Romanticism.

CLIMAX The *climax* is the high point of interest or suspense in a literary work. For example, Jack London's "To Build a Fire" (p. 608) reaches its climax when the man realizes that he is going to freeze to death. The climax generally appears near the end of a story, play, or narrative poem.
See also Plot.

CONFLICT A *conflict* is a struggle between opposing forces. Sometimes this struggle is internal, or within a character, as in Bernard Malamud's "The First Seven Years" (p. 988). At other times, this struggle is external, or between a character and an outside force, as in Jack London's "To Build a Fire" (p. 608). Conflict is one of the primary elements of narrative literature because most plots develop from conflicts.
See also Antagonist, Plot, *and* Protagonist.

CONNOTATION A *connotation* is an association that a word calls to mind in addition to the dictionary meaning of the word. Many words that are similar in their dictionary meanings, or denotations, are quite different in their connotations. Consider, for example, José García Villa's line, "Be beautiful, noble, like the antique ant." This line would have a very different effect if it were "Be pretty, classy, like the old ant." Poets and other writers choose their words carefully so that the connotations of those words will be appropriate.
See also Denotation.

CONSONANCE *Consonance* is the repetition of similar final consonant sounds at the ends of words or accented syllables. Emily Dickinson uses consonance in these lines:

But if he ask where you are hid
Until to-morrow,—happy letter!
Gesture, coquette, and shake your head!

COUPLET *See* Stanza.

CRISIS In the plot of a narrative, the *crisis* is the turning point for the protagonist—the point at which the protagonist's situation or understanding changes dramatically. In Bernard Malamud's "The First Seven Years" (p. 988), the crisis occurs when Feld recognizes that Sobel loves Miriam.

DENOTATION The *denotation* of a word is its objective meaning, independent of other associations that the word brings to mind.
See also Connotation.

DENOUEMENT *See* Plot.

DESCRIPTION A *description* is a portrayal, in words, of something that can be perceived by the senses. Writers create descriptions by using images, as John Wesley Powell does in this passage from "The Most Sublime Spectacle on Earth," his description of the Grand Canyon (p. 289):

> Clouds creep out of canyons and wind into other canyons. The heavens seem to be alive, not moving as move the heavens over a plain, in one direction with the wind, but following the multiplied courses of these gorges.

See also Image.

DEVELOPMENT *See* Plot.

DIALECT A *dialect* is the form of a language spoken by people in a particular region or group. Writers often use dialect to make their characters seem realistic and to create local color. See, for example, Mark Twain's "The Notorious Jumping Frog of Calaveras County" (p. 569).
See also Local Color.

DIALOGUE A *dialogue* is a conversation between characters. Writers use dialogue to reveal character, to present events, to add variety to narratives, and to arouse their readers' interest.
See also Drama.

DICTION *Diction* is a writer's or speaker's word choice. Diction is part of a writer's style and may be described as formal or informal, plain or ornate, common or technical, abstract or concrete.
See also Style.

DRAMA A *drama* is a story written to be performed by actors. The playwright supplies dialogue for the characters to speak, as well as stage directions that give information about costumes, lighting, scenery, properties, the setting, and the characters' movements and ways of speaking. Dramatic conventions include soliloquies, asides, or the passage of time between acts or scenes.
See also Genre.

DRAMATIC MONOLOGUE A *dramatic monologue* is a poem or speech in which an imaginary character speaks to a silent listener. T. S. Eliot's "The Love Song of J. Alfred Prufrock" (p. 718) is a dramatic monologue.
See also Dramatic Poem *and* Monologue.

DRAMATIC POEM A *dramatic poem* is one that makes use of the conventions of drama. Such poems may be monologues or dialogues or may present the speech of many characters. Robert Frost's "The Death of the Hired Man" is a famous example of a dramatic poem.
See also Dramatic Monologue.

DYNAMIC CHARACTER *See* Character.

EPIGRAM An *epigram* is a brief, pointed statement, in prose or in verse. Benjamin Franklin was famous for his epigrams, which include "Fools make feasts, and wise men eat them," and "A plowman on his legs is higher than a gentleman on his knees."

EPIPHANY An *epiphany* is a sudden revelation or flash of insight. The shoemaker in Bernard Malamud's "The First Seven Years" (p. 988) experiences an epiphany when he suddenly and thoroughly comprehends that the actions of his apprentice, Sobel, are motivated by his secret love for Miriam.

ESSAY An *essay* is a short nonfiction work about a particular subject. Essays can be classified as *formal* or *informal*, *personal* or *impersonal*. They can also be classified according to purpose, such as *analytical* (see the excerpt from *The Mortgaged Heart* on p. 1112), *satirical* (see "Coyote v. Acme" on p. 1118), or *reflective* (see Amy Tan's "Mother Tongue" on p. 1136). Modes of discourse, such as *expository*, *descriptive*, *persuasive*, or *narrative*, are other means of classifying essays.
See also Satire, Exposition, Description, Persuasion, *and* Narration.

EXPOSITION *Exposition* is writing or speech that explains, informs, or presents information. The main techniques of expository writing include analysis, classification, comparison and contrast, definition, and exemplification, or illustration. An essay may be primarily expository, as is William Safire's "Onomatopoeia" (p. 1115), or it may use exposition to support another purpose, such as persuasion or argumentation, as in Ian Frazier's satirical essay "Coyote v. Acme" (p. 1118).

In a story or play, the exposition is that part of the plot that introduces the characters, the setting, and the basic situation.
See also Plot.

FALLING ACTION *See* Plot.

FICTION *Fiction* is prose writing that tells about imaginary characters and events. Short stories and novels are works of fiction.
See also Genre, Narrative, Nonfiction, *and* Prose.

FIGURATIVE LANGUAGE *Figurative language* is writing or speech not meant to be taken literally. Writers use figurative language to express ideas in vivid and imaginative ways. For example, Emily Dickinson begins one poem with the following description of snow:

> It sifts from leaden sieves, / It powders all the wood

By describing the snow as if it were flour, Dickinson renders a precise and compelling picture of it.
See also Figure of Speech.

FIGURE OF SPEECH A *figure of speech* is an expression or a word used imaginatively rather than literally.

See also Figurative Language.

FLASHBACK A *flashback* is a section of a literary work that interrupts the chronological presentation of events to relate an event from an earlier time. A writer may present a flashback as a character's memory or recollection, as part of an account or story told by a character, as a dream or a day-dream, or simply by having the narrator switch to a time in the past.

FLAT CHARACTER *See* Character.

FOIL A *foil* is a character who provides a contrast to another character. In F. Scott Fitzgerald's "Winter Dreams" (p. 744), Irene Scheerer is a foil for the tantalizing Judy Jones.

FOLK LITERATURE *Folk literature* is the body of stories, legends, myths, ballads, songs, riddles, sayings, and other works arising out of the oral traditions of peoples around the globe. The folk literature traditions of the United States, including those of Native Americans and of the American pioneers, are especially rich.

FOOT *See* Meter.

FORESHADOWING *Foreshadowing* in a literary work is the use of clues to suggest events that have yet to occur.

FREE VERSE *Free verse* is poetry that lacks a regular rhythmical pattern, or meter. A writer of free verse is at liberty to use any rhythms that are appropriate to what he or she is saying. Free verse has been widely used by twentieth-century poets such as Leslie Marmon Silko, who begins "Where Mountain Lion Lay Down With Deer" with these lines:

> I climb the black rock mountain
>> stepping from day to day
>>> silently.

See also Meter.

GENRE A *genre* is a division, or type, of literature. Literature is commonly divided into three major genres: poetry, prose, and drama. Each major genre can in turn be divided into smaller genres. Poetry can be divided into lyric, concrete, dramatic, narrative, and epic poetry. Prose can be divided into fiction and nonfiction. Drama can be divided into serious drama, tragedy, comic drama, melodrama, and farce.

See also Drama, Poetry, *and* Prose.

GOTHIC *Gothic* refers to the use of primitive, medieval, wild, or mysterious elements in literature. Gothic novels feature places like mysterious and gloomy castles, where horrifying, supernatural events take place. Their influence on Edgar Allan Poe is evident in "The Fall of the House of Usher" (p. 308).

GROTESQUE *Grotesque* refers to the use of bizarre, absurd, or fantastic elements in literature. The grotesque is generally characterized by distortions or striking incongruities. *Grotesque characters*, like those in Flannery O'Connor's "The Life You Save May Be Your Own" (p. 972), are characters who have become bizarre through their obsession with an idea or a value or as a result of an emotional problem.

HARLEM RENAISSANCE The *Harlem Renaissance*, which occurred during the 1920s, was a time of African American artistic creativity centered in Harlem, in New York City. Writers of the Harlem Renaissance include Countee Cullen, Claude McKay, Jean Toomer, and Langston Hughes.

HYPERBOLE *Hyperbole* is a deliberate exaggeration or overstatement, often used for comic effect. In Mark Twain's "The Notorious Jumping Frog of Calaveras County" (p. 569), the claim that Jim Smiley would follow a bug as far as Mexico to win a bet is hyperbole.

IAMBIC PENTAMETER *Iambic pentameter* is a line of poetry with five iambic feet, each containing one unstressed syllable followed by one stressed syllable (˘ ´). Iambic pentameter may be rhymed or unrhymed. Unrhymed iambic pentameter is called blank verse. These lines from Anne Bradstreet's "The Author to Her Book" are in iambic pentameter:

> And for thy, Mother, she alas is poor,
> Which caused her thus to send thee out
>> of door.

See also Blank Verse *and* Meter.

IDYLL An *idyll* is a poem or part of a poem that describes and idealizes country life. John Greenleaf Whittier's "Snowbound" (p. 274) is an idyll.

IMAGE An *image* is a word or phrase that appeals to one or more of the five senses—sight, hearing, touch, taste, or smell.

See also Imagery.

IMAGERY *Imagery* is the descriptive or figurative language used in literature to create word pictures for the reader. These pictures, or images, are created by details of sight, sound, taste, touch, smell, or movement.

IMAGISM *Imagism* was a literary movement that flourished between 1912 and 1927. Led by Ezra Pound and Amy Lowell, the Imagist poets rejected nineteenth-century poetic forms and language. Instead, they wrote short poems that used ordinary language and free verse to create sharp, exact, concentrated pictures. Pound's poetry (p. 732) provides examples of Imagism.

IRONY *Irony* is a contrast between what is stated and what is meant, or between what is expected to happen and what actually happens. In *verbal irony*, a word or a phrase is used to suggest the opposite of its usual meaning. In *dramatic irony*, there is a contradiction between what a character thinks and what the reader or audience knows. In *irony of situation*, an event occurs that contradicts the expectations of the characters, of the reader, or of the audience.

JOURNAL A *journal* is a daily autobiographical account of events and personal reactions. For example, Mary Chesnut's journal (p. 536) records events during the Civil War.

LEGEND A *legend* is a traditional story. Usually a legend deals with a particular person—a hero, a saint, or a national leader. Often legends reflect a people's cultural values. American legends include those of the early Native Americans and those about folk heroes such as Davy Crockett.

See also Myth.

LETTER A *letter* is a written message or communication addressed to a reader or readers and is generally sent by mail. Letters may be *private* or *public*, depending on their intended audience. A *public letter*, also called a *literary letter* or *epistle*, is a work of literature written in the form of a personal letter but created for publication. Michel-Guillaume Jean de Crèvecoeur's "Letters From an American Farmer," excerpted on page 208, are public letters.

LOCAL COLOR *Local color* is the use in a literary work of characters and details unique to a particular geographic area. It can be created by the use of dialect and by descriptions of customs, clothing, manners, attitudes, and landscape. Local-color stories were especially popular after the Civil War, bringing readers the West of Bret Harte and the Mississippi River of Mark Twain.

See also Realism *and* Regionalism.

LYRIC POEM A lyric poem is a melodic poem that expresses the observations and feelings of a single speaker. Unlike a narrative poem, a lyric poem focuses on producing a single, unified effect. Types of lyric poems include the *elegy*, the *ode*, and the *sonnet*. Among contemporary American poets, the lyric is the most common poetic form.

MAIN CHARACTER *See* Character.

METAPHOR A *metaphor* is a figure of speech in which one thing is spoken of as though it were something else. The identification suggests a comparison between the two things that are identified, as in "death is a long sleep."

A *mixed metaphor* occurs when two metaphors are jumbled together. For example, thorns and rain are illogically mixed in "the thorns of life rained down on him." A *dead metaphor* is one that has been overused and has become a common expression, such as "the arm of the chair" or "nightfall."

METER The *meter* of a poem is its rhythmical pattern. This pattern is determined by the number and types of stresses, or beats, in each line. To describe the meter of a poem, you must scan its lines. *Scanning* involves marking the stressed and unstressed syllables, as follows:

> Soon as | the sun | forsook | the eas|tern main
> The peal | ing thun | der shook | the heav'n | ly plain;
> — "An Hymn to the Evening," p. 172

As the example shows, each strong stress is marked with a slanted line (´) and each weak stress with a horseshoe symbol (˘). The weak and strong stresses are then divided by vertical lines (|) into groups called feet. The following types of feet are common in poetry written in English:

1. *Iamb:* a foot with one unstressed syllable followed by one stressed syllable, as in the word "around"
2. *Trochee:* a foot with one stressed syllable followed by one unstressed syllable, as in the word "broken"
3. *Anapest:* a foot with two unstressed syllables followed by one stressed syllable, as in the phrase "in a flash"
4. *Dactyl:* a foot with one stressed syllable followed by two unstressed syllables, as in the word "argument"
5. *Spondee:* a foot with two stressed syllables, as in the word "airship"
6. *Pyrrhic:* a foot with two unstressed syllables, as in the last foot of the word "imag|ining"

Lines of poetry are often described as *iambic*, *trochaic*, *anapestic*, or *dactylic*. Lines are also described in terms of the number of feet that occur in them, as follows:

1. *Monometer:* verse written in one-foot lines
   > Evil
   > Begets
   > Evil
   >   —Anonymous

2. *Dimeter:* verse written in two-foot lines
   > This is | the time
   > of the trag|ic man
   >   —"Visits to St. Elizabeth's," Elizabeth Bishop

3. *Trimeter:* verse written in three-foot lines:
   > Over | the win|ter glaciers
   >   I see | the sum|mer glow,
   > And through | the wild-|piled snowdrift
   >   The warm | rosebuds | below.
   >   —"Beyond Winter," Ralph Waldo Emerson

4. *Tetrameter:* verse written in four-foot lines:

The sún | that bríef | Decém|ber dáy
Rose chéer|less ov̆|er hílls | of gráy
                                    —"Snowbound," p. 274

5. *Pentameter:* verse written in five-foot lines:

I doubt | not Gŏd | is góod, | well-méan|ing, kínd,
And díd | He stóop | to quíb|ble cóuld | tell whý
The lít|tle búr|ied móle | contín|ues blínd
                        —"Yet Do I Marvel," Countee Cullen

A complete description of the meter of a line tells both how many feet there are in the line and what kind of foot is most common. Thus, the lines from Countee Cullen's poem would be described as *iambic pentameter. Blank verse* is poetry written in unrhymed iambic pentameter. Poetry that does not have a regular meter is called *free verse.*

MONOLOGUE
A *monologue* is a speech delivered entirely by one person or character.

See also Dramatic Monologue.

MOOD
Mood, or atmosphere, is the feeling created in the reader by a literary work or passage. Elements that can influence the mood of a work include its setting, tone, and events.

See also Setting *and* Tone.

MOTIVATION
A *motivation* is a reason that explains a character's thoughts, feelings, actions, or speech. Characters are motivated by their values and by their wants, desires, dreams, wishes, and needs. Sometimes the reasons for a character's actions are stated directly, as in Willa Cather's "A Wagner Matinée" (p. 676), when Clark explains his reception of his aunt by saying, "I owed to this woman most of the good that ever came my way in my boyhood." At other times, the writer will just suggest a character's motivation.

MYTH
A *myth* is a fictional tale that explains the actions of gods or heroes or the causes of natural phenomena. Myths that explain the origins of earthly life, as do the Onondaga, Najavo, and Modoc myths in this text, are known as origin myths. Other myths express the central values of the people who created them.

NARRATION
Narration is writing that tells a story. The act of telling a story is also called *narration.* The *narrative,* or story, is told by a storyteller called the *narrator.* A story is usually told chronologically, in the order in which events take place in time, though it may include flashbacks and foreshadowing. Narratives may be true, like the events recorded in Mary Chesnut's journal (p. 536), or fictional, like the events in Flannery O'Connor's "The Life You Save May Be Your Own" (p. 972).

Narration is one of the forms of discourse and is used in novels, short stories, plays, narrative poems, anecdotes, autobiographies, biographies, and reports.

See also Narrative Poem *and* Narrator.

NARRATIVE
A *narrative* is a story told in fiction, nonfiction, poetry, or drama. Narratives are often classified by their content or purpose. An *exploration narrative* is a firsthand account of an explorer's travels in a new land. Alvar Núñez Cabeza de Vaca's account of his exploration of the wilderness that is now Texas, "A Journey Through Texas," appears on page 32. "The Interesting Narrative of the Life of Olaudah Equiano" (p. 44) is a *slave narrative,* an account of the experiences of an enslaved person. A *historical narrative* is a narrative account of significant historical events, such as John Smith's *The General History of Virginia* (p. 72).

See also Narration.

NARRATIVE POEM
A *narrative poem* tells a story in verse. Three traditional types of narrative verse are *ballads,* songlike poems that tell stories; *epics,* long poems about the deeds of gods or heroes; and *metrical romances,* poems that tell tales of love and chivalry.

See also Ballad.

NARRATOR
A *narrator* is a speaker or character who tells a story. A story or novel may be narrated by a main character, by a minor character, or by someone uninvolved in the story. The narrator may speak in the first person or in the third person. An *omniscient narrator* is all-knowing, while a *limited narrator* knows only what one character does.

See also Point of View.

NATURALISM
Naturalism was a literary movement among novelists at the end of the nineteenth century and during the early decades of the twentieth century. The Naturalists tended to view people as hapless victims of immutable natural laws. Early exponents of Naturalism included Stephen Crane, Jack London, and Theodore Dreiser.

See also Realism.

NONFICTION
Nonfiction is prose writing that presents and explains ideas or that tells about real people, places, objects, or events. Essays, biographies, autobiographies, journals, and reports are all examples of nonfiction.

See also Fiction *and* Genre.

NOVEL
A *novel* is a long work of fiction. A novel often has a complicated plot, many major and minor characters, a significant theme, and several varied settings. Novels can be classified in many ways, based on the historical periods in which they are written, the subjects and themes that they treat, the

techniques that are used in them, and the literary movements that inspired them. Classic nineteenth-century novels include Herman Melville's *Moby-Dick* (p. 354) and Nathaniel Hawthorne's *The Scarlet Letter* (an extended reading suggestion). Well-known twentieth-century novels include F. Scott Fitzgerald's *The Great Gatsby* and Edith Wharton's *Ethan Frome* (recommended selections for extended reading). A *novella* is not as long as a novel but is longer than a short story. Ernest Hemingway's *The Old Man and the Sea* is a novella.

ODE An *ode* is a long, formal lyric poem with a serious theme that may have a traditional stanza structure. Odes often honor people, commemorate events, respond to natural scenes, or consider serious human problems.

See also Lyric Poem.

OMNISCIENT NARRATOR *See* Narrator *and* Point of View.

ONOMATOPOEIA *Onomatopoeia* is the use of words that imitate sounds. Examples of such words are *buzz, hiss, murmur,* and *rustle.*

ORAL TRADITION *Oral tradition* is the passing of songs, stories, and poems from generation to generation by word of mouth. The oral tradition in America has preserved Native American myths and legends, spirituals, folk ballads, and other works originally heard and memorized rather than written down.

See also Ballad, Folk Literature, Legend, Myth, *and* Spiritual.

ORATORY *Oratory* is public speaking that is formal, persuasive, and emotionally appealing. Patrick Henry's "Speech in the Virginia Convention" (p. 186) is an example of oratory.

OXYMORON An *oxymoron* is a figure of speech that combines two opposing or contradictory ideas. An oxymoron, such as "freezing fire," suggests a paradox in just a few words.

See also Figurative Language *and* Paradox.

PARADOX A *paradox* is a statement that seems to be contradictory but that actually presents a truth. Marianne Moore uses paradox in "Nevertheless" when she says, "Victory won't come / to me unless I go / to it." Because a paradox is surprising, it draws the reader's attention to what is being said.

See also Figurative Language *and* Oxymoron.

PARALLELISM *Parallelism* is the repetition of a grammatical structure. Robert Hayden concludes his poem "Astronauts" with these questions in parallel form:

What do we want of these men?
What do we want of ourselves?

Parallelism is used in poetry and in other writing to emphasize and to link related ideas.

PARODY A *parody* is a humorous imitation of a literary work, one that exaggerates or distorts the characteristic features of the original.

PASTORAL *Pastoral* poems deal with rural settings, including shepherds and rustic life. Traditionally, pastoral poems have presented idealized views of rural life. In twentieth-century pastorals, however, poets like Robert Frost introduced ethical complexity into an otherwise simple landsape.

PERSONIFICATION *Personification* is a figure of speech in which a nonhuman subject is given human characteristics. In "April Rain Song," Langston Hughes personifies the rain:

Let the rain sing you a lullaby.

Effective personification of things or ideas makes them seem vital and alive, as if they were human.

See also Figurative Language.

PERSUASION *Persuasion* is writing or speech that attempts to convince a reader to think or act in a particular way. During the Revolutionary War period, leaders such as Patrick Henry, Thomas Paine, and Thomas Jefferson used persuasion in their political arguments. Persuasion is also used in advertising, in editorials, in sermons, and in political speeches.

PLAIN STYLE *Plain style* is a type of writing in which uncomplicated sentences and ordinary words are used to make simple, direct statements. This style was favored by those Puritans who wanted to express themselves clearly, in accordance with their religious beliefs. In the twentieth century, Ernest Hemingway was a master of plain style.

See also Style.

PLOT *Plot* is the sequence of events in a literary work. In most fiction, the plot involves both characters and a central conflict. The plot usually begins with an *exposition* that introduces the setting, the characters, and the basic situation. This is followed by the *inciting incident*, which introduces the central conflict. The conflict then increases during the *development* until it reaches a high point of interest or suspense, the *climax*. The climax is followed by the end, or *resolution*, of the central conflict. Any events that occur after the resolution make up the *denouement*. The events that lead up to the climax make up the *rising action*. The events that follow the climax make up the *falling action*.

See also Conflict.

POETRY *Poetry* is one of the three major types of literature. In poetry, form and content are closely connected, like the two faces of a single coin. Poems are often divided into lines and stanzas and often employ regular rhythmical patterns, or meters. Most poems use highly concise, musical, and emotionally charged language. Many also make use of imagery, figurative language, and special devices such as rhyme.
See also Genre.

POINT OF VIEW *Point of view* is the perspective, or vantage point, from which a story is told. Three commonly used points of view are first person, omniscient third person, and limited third person.

In the *first-person point of view*, the narrator is a character in the story and refers to himself or herself with the first-person pronoun "I." "The Fall of the House of Usher" (p. 308) is told by a first-person narrator.

The two kinds of third-person point of view, limited and omniscient, are called "third person" because the narrator uses third-person pronouns such as "he" and "she" to refer to the characters. There is no "I" telling the story.

In stories told from the *omniscient third-person point of view*, the narrator knows and tells about what each character feels and thinks. "The Devil and Tom Walker" (p. 242) is written from the omniscient third-person point of view.

In stories told from the *limited third-person point of view*, the narrator relates the inner thoughts and feelings of only one character, and everything is viewed from this character's perspective. "An Occurrence at Owl Creek Bridge" (p. 508) is written from the limited third-person point of view.
See also Narrator.

PROSE *Prose* is the ordinary form of written language. Most writing that is not poetry, drama, or song is considered prose. Prose is one of the major genres of literature. It occurs in two forms: fiction and nonfiction.
See also Fiction, Genre, *and* Nonfiction.

PROTAGONIST The *protagonist* is the main character in a literary work. In "The Jilting of Granny Weatherall" (p. 846), the protagonist is the dying grandmother.
See also Antagonist.

QUATRAIN *See* Stanza.

REALISM *Realism* is the presentation in art of the details of actual life. Realism was also a literary movement that began during the nineteenth century and stressed the actual as opposed to the imagined or the fanciful. The Realists tried to write objectively about ordinary characters in ordinary situations. They reacted against Romanticism, rejecting heroic,

adventurous, or unfamiliar subjects. Naturalists, who followed the Realists, traced the effects of heredity and environment on people helpless to change their situations.
See also Local Color, Naturalism, *and* Romanticism.

REFRAIN A *refrain* is a repeated line or group of lines in a poem or song. Most refrains end stanzas, as does "And the tide rises, the tide falls," the refrain in Henry Wadsworth Longfellow's poem (p. 260), or "Coming for to carry me home," the refrain in "Swing Low, Sweet Chariot" (p. 488). Although some refrains are nonsense lines, many increase suspense or emphasize character and theme.

REGIONALISM Regionalism in literature is the tendency among certain authors to write about specific geographical areas. Regional writers, like Willa Cather and William Faulkner, present the distinct culture of an area, including its speech, customs, beliefs, and history. Local-color writing may be considered a type of Regionalism, but Regionalists, like the Southern writers of the 1920s, usually go beyond mere presentation of cultural idiosyncrasies and attempt, instead, a sophisticated sociological or anthropological treatment of the culture of a region.
See also Local Color *and* Setting.

RESOLUTION *See* Plot.

RHYME *Rhyme* is the repetition of sounds at the ends of words. Rhyming words have identical vowel sounds in their final accented syllables. The consonants before the vowels may be different, but any consonants occurring after these vowels are the same, as in *frog* and *bog* or *willow* and *pillow*. End rhyme occurs when rhyming words are repeated at the ends of lines. Internal rhyme occurs when rhyming words fall within a line. *Approximate*, or *slant*, *rhyme* occurs when the rhyming sounds are similar, but not exact, as in *prove* and *glove*.
See also Rhyme Scheme.

RHYME SCHEME A *rhyme scheme* is a regular pattern of rhyming words in a poem. To describe a rhyme scheme, one uses a letter of the alphabet to represent each rhyming sound in a poem or stanza. Consider how letters are used to represent the *abab* rhyme scheme rhymes in the following example:

With innocent wide penguin eyes, three	a
large fledgling mocking-birds below	b
the pussywillow tree,	a
stand in a row.	b

—"Bird-Witted," Marianne Moore

See also Rhyme.

RHYTHM *Rhythm* is the pattern of beats, or stresses, in spoken or written language. Prose and free verse are written in the irregular rhythmical patterns of everyday speech. Consider, for example, the rhythmical pattern in the following free-verse lines by Gwendolyn Brooks:

Life for my child is simple, and is good.

He knows his wish. Yes, but that is not all.

Because I know mine too.

Traditional poetry often follows a regular rhythmical pattern, as in the following lines by America's first great female poet, Anne Bradstreet:

In critic's hands beware thou dost not come,

And take thy way where yet thou art not known
                      —"The Author to Her Book"

See also Meter.

RISING ACTION *See* Plot.

ROMANTICISM *Romanticism* was a literary and artistic movement of the nineteenth century that arose in reaction against eighteenth-century Neoclassicism and placed a premium on imagination, emotion, nature, individuality, and exotica. Romantic elements can be found in the works of American writers as diverse as Cooper, Poe, Thoreau, Emerson, Dickinson, Hawthorne, and Melville. Romanticism is particularly evident in the works of the Transcendentalists.

See also Classicism *and* Transcendentalism.

ROUND CHARACTER *See* Character.

SATIRE *Satire* is writing that ridicules or criticizes individuals, ideas, institutions, social conventions, or other works of art or literature. The writer of a satire, the satirist, may use a tolerant, sympathetic tone or an angry, bitter tone. Some satire is written in prose and some, in poetry. Examples of satire in this text include W. H. Auden's "The Unknown Citizen" (p. 779) and Ian Frazier's "Coyote v. Acme" (p. 1118).

SCANSION *Scansion* is the process of analyzing a poem's metrical pattern. When a poem is scanned, its stressed and unstressed syllables are marked to show what poetic feet are used and how many feet appear in each line. The last two lines of Edna St. Vincent Millay's "I Shall Go Back Again to the Bleak Shore" may be scanned as follows:

But I | shall find | the sul|len rocks | and skies

Unchanged | from what | they were | when I | was young.

See also Meter.

SENSORY LANGUAGE *Sensory language* is writing or speech that appeals to one or more of the five senses.

See also Image.

SETTING The *setting* of a literary work is the time and place of the action. A setting may serve any of a number of functions. It may provide a background for the action. It may be a crucial element in the plot or central conflict. It may also create a certain emotional atmosphere, or mood.

SHORT STORY A *short story* is a brief work of fiction. The short story resembles the novel but generally has a simpler plot and setting. In addition, the short story tends to reveal character at a crucial moment rather than developing it through many incidents. For example, Thomas Wolfe's "The Far and the Near" (p. 786) concentrates on what happens to a train engineer when he visits people who had waved to him every day.

See also Fiction *and* Genre.

SIMILE A *simile* is a figure of speech that makes a direct comparison between two subjects, using either *like* or *as*. Here are two examples of similes:

The trees looked like pitch forks against the sullen sky.

Her hair was as red as a robin's breast.

See also Figurative Language.

SLANT RHYME *See* Rhyme.

SONNET A *sonnet* is a fourteen-line lyric poem focused on a single theme. Sonnets have many variations but are usually written in iambic pentameter, following one of two traditional patterns: the *Petrarchan*, or *Italian*, *sonnet*, which is divided into two parts, the eight-line octave and the six-line sestet; and the *Shakespearean*, or *English*, *sonnet*, which consists of three quatrains and a concluding couplet.

See also Lyric Poem.

SPEAKER The *speaker* is the voice of a poem. Although the speaker is often the poet, the speaker may also be a fictional character or even an inanimate object or another type of non-human entity. Interpreting a poem often depends upon recognizing who the speaker is, whom the speaker is addressing, and what the speaker's attitude, or tone, is.

See also Point of View.

SPIRITUAL A *spiritual* is a type of African American folk song dating from the period of slavery and Reconstruction. A typical spiritual deals both with religious freedom and, on an allegorical level, with political and economic freedom. In some spirituals the biblical river Jordan was used as a symbol for the Ohio River, which separated slave states from free states; and the biblical promised land, Canaan, was used as a symbol for the free northern United States. Most spirituals made use of repetition, parallelism, and rhyme. See "Swing Low, Sweet Chariot" (p. 488) and "Go Down, Moses" (p. 490).

STAGE DIRECTIONS *See* Drama.

STANZA A *stanza* is a group of lines in a poem that are considered to be a unit. Many poems are divided into stanzas that are separated by spaces. Stanzas often function just like paragraphs in prose. Each stanza states and develops a single main idea.

Stanzas are commonly named according to the number of lines found in them, as follows:

1. *Couplet:* a two-line stanza
2. *Tercet:* a three-line stanza
3. *Quatrain:* a four-line stanza
4. *Cinquain:* a five-line stanza
5. *Sestet:* a six-line stanza
6. *Heptastich:* a seven-line stanza
7. *Octave:* an eight-line stanza

STATIC CHARACTER *See* Character.

STREAM OF CONSCIOUSNESS *Stream of consciousness* is a narrative technique that presents thoughts as if they were coming directly from a character's mind. Instead of being arranged in chronological order, the events are presented from the character's point of view, mixed in with the character's thoughts just as they might spontaneously occur. Katherine Anne Porter uses this technique in "The Jilting of Granny Weatherall" (p. 846) to capture Granny's dying thoughts and feelings. Ambrose Bierce also uses the stream of consciousness technique in "An Occurrence at Owl Creek Bridge" (p. 508).

See also Point of View.

STYLE A writer's *style* includes word choice, tone, degree of formality, figurative language, rhythm, grammatical structure, sentence length, organization—in short, every feature of a writer's use of language. Ernest Hemingway, for example, is noted for a simple prose style that contrasts with Thomas Paine's aphoristic style and with N. Scott Momaday's reflective style.

See also Diction *and* Plain Style.

SUSPENSE *Suspense* is a feeling of growing uncertainty about the outcome of events. Writers create suspense by raising questions in the minds of their readers. Suspense builds until the climax of the plot, at which point the suspense reaches its peak.

See also Climax *and* Plot.

SYMBOL A *symbol* is anything that stands for or represents something else. A *conventional symbol* is one that is widely known and accepted, such as a voyage symbolizing life or a skull symbolizing death. A *personal symbol* is one developed for a particular work by a particular author. Examples in this textbook include Hawthorne's black veil and Melville's white whale.

SYMBOLISM *Symbolism* was a literary movement during the nineteenth century that influenced poets, including the Imagists and T. S. Eliot. Symbolists turned away from everyday, realistic details to express emotions by using a pattern of symbols.

See also Imagism *and* Realism.

THEME A *theme* is a central message or insight into life revealed by a literary work. An essay's theme is often directly stated in its thesis statement. In most works of fiction, the theme is only indirectly stated: A story, poem, or play most often has an *implied theme*. For example, in "A Worn Path" (p. 820), Eudora Welty does not directly say that Phoenix Jackson's difficult journey shows the power of love, but readers learn this indirectly by the end of the story.

TONE The tone of a literary work is the writer's attitude toward his or her subject, characters, or audience. A writer's tone may be formal or informal, friendly or distant, personal or pompous. For example, William Faulkner's tone in his "Nobel Prize Acceptance Speech" (p. 875) is earnest and serious, whereas James Thurber's tone in "The Night the Ghost Got In" (p. 898) is humorous and ironic.

See also Mood.

TRANSCENDENTALISM *Transcendentalism* was an American literary and philosophical movement of the nineteenth century. The Transcendentalists, who were based in New England, believed that intuition and the individual conscience "transcend" experience and thus are better guides to truth than are the senses and logical reason. Influenced by Romanticism, the Transcendentalists respected the individual spirit and the natural world, believing that divinity was present everywhere, in nature and in each person. The Transcendentalists included Ralph Waldo Emerson, Henry David Thoreau, Bronson Alcott, W. H. Channing, Margaret Fuller, and Elizabeth Peabody.

See also Romanticism.

GRAMMAR AND MECHANICS HANDBOOK

SUMMARY OF GRAMMAR

Nouns A **noun** names a person, place, or thing. A **common noun** names any one of a class of people, places, or things. A **proper noun** names a specific person, place, or thing.

Common Nouns	Proper Nouns
essayist	William Safire
city	New Orleans

Pronouns A **pronoun** is a word that stands for a noun or for words that take the place of a noun.

A **personal pronoun** refers to (1) the person speaking, (2) the person spoken to, or (3) the person, place, or thing spoken about.

	Singular	Plural
First Person	I, me, my, mine	we, us, our, ours
Second Person	you, your, yours	you, your, yours
Third Person	he, him, his, she, her, hers, it, its	they, them, their, theirs

A **reflexive pronoun** ends in -*self* or -*selves* and adds information to a sentence by pointing back to a noun or pronoun in the sentence.

> . . . They click upon *themselves*
> As the breeze rises, . . .
>
> — Frost, p. 882

An **intensive pronoun** ends in -*self* or -*selves* and simply adds emphasis to a noun or pronoun in the same sentence.

> The United States *themselves* are essentially the greatest poem.
>
> — Whitman, p. 434

Demonstrative pronouns (*this, these, that,* and *those*) direct attention to a specific person, place, or thing.

> *this* hat   *these* coats   *that* frame

A **relative pronoun** begins a subordinate (relative) clause and connects it to another idea in the sentence.

> The brave men, living and dead, *who* struggled here, have consecrated it . . .
>
> — Lincoln, p. 522

> I made a little book, in *which* I allotted a page for each of the virtues.
>
> — Franklin, p. 140

An **indefinite pronoun** refers to a noun or pronoun that is not specifically named.

> *Few* could refrain from twisting their heads toward the door; *many* stood upright and turned directly about; . . .
>
> — Hawthorne, p. 336

Verbs A **verb** is a word or group of words that expresses time while showing an action, a condition, or the fact that something exists.

An **action verb** is a verb that tells what action someone or something is performing.

> The sun that brief December day
> *Rose* cheerless over hills of gray, . . .
>
> — Whittier, p. 274

A **linking verb** is a verb that connects its subject with a word generally found near the end of the sentence. All linking verbs are intransitive.

> Her name *was* Phoenix Jackson.
>
> — Welty, p. 820

A **helping verb** is a verb that can be added to another verb to make a single verb phrase.

> Sir, we *have* done everything that could be done to avert the storm which is now coming on.
>
> —Henry, p. 186

Adjectives An **adjective** is a word used to describe a noun or pronoun or to give a noun or pronoun a more specific meaning. Adjectives answer these questions:

What kind?	*green* leaf, *tall* chimney
Which one?	*this* clock, *those* pictures
How many?	*six* days, *several* concerts
How much?	*more* effort, *enough* applause
Whose?	*Kennedy's* address, *my* name

The articles *the, a,* and *an* are adjectives. *An* is used before a word beginning with a vowel sound.

A noun or pronoun may sometimes be used as an adjective.

> *diamond* necklace   *summer* vacation

Adverbs An **adverb** is a word that modifies a verb, an adjective, or another adverb. Adverbs answer the questions *where, when, in what way,* or *to what extent.*

She came *yesterday*. (modifies verb *came*)

They were *completely* unaware. (modifies adjective *unaware*)

It rained *rather* often. (modifies adverb *often*)

Prepositions A **preposition** is a word that relates a noun or pronoun that appears with it to another word in the sentence. Prepositions are almost always followed by nouns or pronouns.

aboard the train   *among* us   *below* our plane

Conjunctions A **conjunction** is a word used to connect other words or groups of words.

A **coordinating conjunction** connects similar kinds or groups of words.

dogs *and* cats   friendly *but* dignified

Correlative conjunctions are used in pairs to connect similar words or groups of words.

both Prem *and* Sanjay   *neither* she *nor* I

A **subordinating conjunction** connects two complete ideas by placing one idea below the other in rank or importance.

Even before I asked, you knew . . .

A **conjunctive adverb** is an adverb used as a conjunction to connect complete ideas.

O'Connor portrayed social outcasts; *however*, she addresses society as a whole.

Interjections An **interjection** is a word that expresses feeling or emotion and functions independently of a sentence.

Oh, woe is me!

Subject and Verb Agreement To make a subject and verb agree, make sure that both are singular or both are plural.

He reads Hemingway.   *We read* Thoreau.

Phrases A **phrase** is a group of words, without a subject and verb, that functions in a sentence as one part of speech.

A **prepositional phrase** is a group of words that includes a preposition and a noun or pronoun.

beyond the horizon   inside the corral

An **adjective phrase** is a prepositional phrase that modifies a noun or pronoun by telling *what kind* or *which one*.

the book *on the table*   the size *of the classroom*

An **adverb phrase** is a prepositional phrase that modifies a verb, an adjective, or an adverb by pointing out *where, when, in what way,* or *to what extent*.

During the intermission before the second half of the concert, I questioned my aunt and found that the "Prize Song" was not new to her.

—Cather, p. 676

An **appositive phrase** is a noun or pronoun with modifiers, placed next to a noun or pronoun to add information and details.

I drop to Hawthorne, *the customs officer*, measuring coal . . .

—Lowell, p. 1014

A **participial phrase** is a participle that is modified by an adjective or adverb phrase or that has a complement. The entire phrase acts as an adjective.

Two or three men, *conversing earnestly together*, ceased as he approached, . . .

—Harte, p. 580

A **nominative absolute** is a noun or pronoun followed by a participle or participial phrase that functions independently of the rest of the sentence.

The preparations being complete, the two private soldiers stepped aside and each drew away the plank upon which he had been standing.

—Bierce, p. 508

An **infinitive phrase** is an infinitive with modifiers, complements, or a subject, all acting together as a single part of speech.

. . . some set *to mow*, others *to bind thatch*, some *to build houses*, others *to thatch them* . . .

—Smith, p. 72

Clauses A **clause** is a group of words with its own subject and verb.

An **independent clause** can stand by itself as a complete sentence. A **subordinate clause** cannot stand by itself as a complete sentence; it can only be part of a sentence.

An **adjective clause** is a subordinate clause that modifies a noun or pronoun by telling *what kind* or *which one*.

In compliance with the request of a friend of mine, *who wrote me from the East*, I called on good-natured, garrulous old Simon Wheeler . . .

—Twain, p. 569

A **subordinate adverb clause** modifies a verb, an adjective, an adverb, or a verbal by telling *where, when, in what way, to what extent, under what condition,* or *why.*

Whenever you like, please visit.

A **noun clause** is a subordinate clause that acts as a noun.

As I knew, or thought I knew, *what was right and wrong*, I did not see why I might not always do one and avoid the other.

—Franklin, p. 140

SUMMARY OF CAPITALIZATION AND PUNCTUATION

Capitalization

Capitalize the first word in sentences, interjections, and incomplete questions. Also, capitalize the first word in a quotation if the quotation is a complete sentence.

And then I said in perfect English, "Yes, I'm getting rather concerned."

—Tan, p. 1136

Capitalize all proper nouns and adjectives.

T. S. Eliot   Mississippi River   Harvard University
Turkish   November   Puerto Rican

Capitalize a person's title when it is followed by the person's name or when it is used in direct address.

Rev. Leonidas W. Smiley   General Robert E. Lee

Capitalize titles showing family relationships when they refer to a specific person, unless they are preceded by a possessive noun or pronoun.

Granny Weatherall   my grandfather Mammedaty

Capitalize the first word and all other key words in the titles of books, periodicals, poems, stories, plays, paintings, and other works of art.

The Crucible   "Anecdote of the Jar"

Capitalize the first word and all nouns in letter salutations and the first word in letter closings.

Dear Henry,   Yours truly,

Punctuation

End Marks Use a **period** to end a declarative sentence, a mild imperative sentence, an indirect question, and most abbreviations.

Pile the bodies high at Austerlitz and Waterloo.

—Sandburg, p. 840

Use a **question mark** to end an interrogative sentence, an incomplete question, or a statement that is intended as a question.

Was it even Kentucky or Tennessee?

—Warren, p. 1017

Use an **exclamation mark** after an exclamatory sentence, a forceful imperative sentence, or an interjection expressing strong emotion.

"Don't let him, sister!"

—Frost, p. 888

Commas Use a comma before the conjunction to separate two independent clauses in a compound sentence.

From my mother's sleep I fell into the State,
And I hunched in its belly till my wet fur froze.

—Jarrell, p. 1174

Use commas to separate three or more words, phrases, or clauses in a series.

I spun, I wove, I kept the house, I nursed the sick, . . .

—Masters, p. 669

Use commas to separate adjectives of equal rank. Do not use commas to separate adjectives that must stay in a specific order.

She carried a thin, small cane made from an umbrella . . .

—Welty, p. 820

Use a comma after an introductory word, phrase, or clause.

Finding Tom so squeamish on this point, he did not insist upon it, . . .

—Irving, p. 242

Use commas to set off parenthetical and nonessential expressions.

My poor aunt's figure, however, would have presented astonishing difficulties to any dressmaker.

—Cather, p. 676

Use commas with places, dates, and titles.

Boston, Massachusetts   November 17, 1915
Dr. Martin Luther King, Jr.

Use commas after items in addresses, after the salutation in a personal letter, after the closing in all letters, and in numbers of more than three digits.

Linden Lane, Princeton, N.J. Dear Marian,

Affectionately yours,   6,778

Use a comma to indicate words left out of an elliptical sentence and to set off a direct quotation.

In T. S. Eliot's poetry, allusions are perhaps the most prominent device; in Ezra Pound's, images.

"Well, Granny," he said, "you must be a hundred years old and scared of nothing."

    —Welty, p. 820

Semicolons Use a semicolon to join independent clauses that are not already joined by a conjunction.

The old woman didn't change her position until he was almost into her yard; then she rose with one hand fisted on her hip.

    —O'Connor, p. 972

Use semicolons to avoid confusion when independent clauses or items in a series already contain commas.

Before these events, the day was glorious with expectancy; after them, the day was a dead and empty thing.

    —Twain, p. 564

Colons Use a colon before a list of items following an independent clause.

Great literature provides us with many things: entertainment, enrichment, and inspiration.

Use a colon to introduce a formal or a lengthy quotation.

In *The Member of the Wedding*, the lonely twelve-year-old girl, Frankie Addams, articulates this universal need: "The trouble with me is that for a long time I have just been an *I* person."

    —McCullers, p. 1112

Quotation Marks A **direct quotation** represents a person's exact speech and is enclosed in quotation marks.

"Good," he said. "You will be able to play football again better than ever."

    —Hemingway, p. 809

An **indirect quotation** reports only the general meaning of what a person said and does not require quotation marks.

One day I had said that Italian seemed such an easy language to me . . .

    —Hemingway, p. 809

Always place a comma or a period inside the final quotation mark.

"Well, Missy, excuse me," Doctor Harry patted her cheek.

    —Porter, p. 846

Place a question mark or an exclamation mark inside the final quotation mark if the end mark is part of the quotation; if it is not part of the quotation, place it outside the final quotation mark.

"Cornelia! Cornelia!" No footsteps, but a sudden hand on her cheek. "Bless you, where have you been?"

    —Porter, p. 846

Use single quotation marks for a quotation within a quotation.

"'All right,' I say, 'I can't afford to pay
Any fixed wages, though I wish I could.'
'Someone else can.' 'Then someone else will
have to.'"

—"The Death of the Hired Man," Robert Frost

Underline or italicize the titles of long written works, movies, television and radio shows, lengthy works of music, paintings, and sculpture.

The Great Gatsby *Mary Poppins* Aida

Use quotation marks around the titles of short written works, episodes in a series, songs, and titles of works mentioned as parts of a collection.

"Winter Dreams" "Go Down, Moses"

Dashes Use dashes to indicate an abrupt change of thought, a dramatic interrupting idea, or a summary statement.

She'd had moments herself of picturing some kind of evil gene in her husband's ordinary, stocky body—a dark little egg like a black jelly bean, she imagined it.

    —Tyler, p. 1028

Use dashes to set off a nonessential appositive or modifier when it is long, when it is already punctuated, or when you want to be dramatic.

... for some reason he was not completely sure of—it may have been the cold and his fatigue—he decided not to insist on seeing him.

—Malamud, p. 988

Hyphens Use a hyphen with certain numbers, after certain prefixes, with two or more words used as one word, with a compound modifier coming before a noun, and within a word when a combination of letters might otherwise be confusing.

> fifty-four   daughter-in-law   up-to-date report

Apostrophes Add an apostrophe and *-s* to show the possessive case of most singular nouns.

> Taylor's poetry   a poet's career

Add an apostrophe to show the possessive case of plural nouns ending in *-s* and *-es.*

> the boys' ambition   the Cruzes' house

Add an apostrophe and *-s* to show the possessive case of plural nouns that do not end in *-s* or *-es.*

> the men's suits   the deer's antlers

Use an apostrophe in a contraction to indicate the position of the missing letter or letters.

> "You look like a saint, Doctor Harry, and I vow that's as near as you'll ever come to it."

—Porter, p. 846

GLOSSARY OF COMMON USAGE

adapt, adopt
Adapt is a verb meaning "to change." *Adopt* is a verb meaning "to take as one's own."

> Washington Irving *adapted* many characters and situations from folk tales for his short stories.
>
> Ezra Pound's followers *adopted* a spare style.

advice, advise
Advice is a noun meaning "an opinion." *Advise* is a verb meaning "to give an opinion."

> The man ignores the *advice* of the old-timer.
>
> How might you *advise* the younger generation?

affect, effect
Affect is almost always a verb meaning "to influence." *Effect* is usually a noun meaning "result." Effect can also be a verb meaning "to bring about" or "to cause."

> An understanding of T. S. Eliot's multiple allusions can *affect* one's appreciation of his poetry.
>
> In Cather's story, the concert has a profound *effect* on Aunt Georgiana.
>
> The aim of persuasive writing is often to *effect* a change in the attitudes of the audience.

among, between
Among is usually used with three or more items. *Between* is generally used with only two items.

> *Among* the writers of the Harlem Renaissance, Langston Hughes stands out.
>
> In Frost's "Mending Wall," the speaker reports a conversation *between* himself and his neighbor.

as, because, like, as to
The word *as* has several meanings and can function as several parts of speech. To avoid confusion, use *because* rather than *as* when you want to indicate cause and effect.

> *Because* Jonathan Edwards believed that his listeners' souls were in danger, he wanted them to repent.

Do not use the preposition *like* to introduce a clause that requires the conjunction *as.*

> The Puritans reacted to music and dancing *as* one might expect: They considered that such entertainments were dangerous occasions for sin.

The use of *as to* for *about* is awkward and should be avoided.

> Captain Ahab's bitter vehemence *about* the white whale must seem puzzling to the crew.

bad, badly
Use the predicate adjective *bad* after linking verbs such as *feel, look,* and *seem.* Use *badly* whenever an adverb is required.

> Although Granny Weatherall looks *bad,* she is not at all happy to see Doctor Harry.
>
> Elizabeth is *badly* shaken when Mr. Hooper refuses to remove the black veil.

because of, due to
Use *due to* if it can logically replace the phrase *caused by.* In introductory phrases, however, *because of* is better usage than *due to.*

> Farquhar's failure to recognize the scout's trap may be *due to* his eagerness to aid a cause.

Because of Masters's ability to sketch characters accurately, his work became popular.

being as, being that

Avoid using the expressions *being as* and *being that*. Use *because* or *since* instead.

> *Because* Whitman believed that new styles were needed in American poetry, he broke with traditional forms.

> *Since* Shiftlet is more interested in the car than in Lucynell, it is hardly surprising that he abandons her.

beside, besides

Beside is a preposition meaning "at the side of" or "close to." Do not confuse *beside* with *besides*, which means "in addition to." *Besides* can be a preposition or an adverb.

> When Clark sits *beside* Georgiana, he tries to imagine her emotions as she hears the music.

> *Besides* Mr. Oakhurst, which other characters are run out of town?

> Thomas Jefferson was the third president of the United States; he was a gifted architect, *besides*.

can, may

The verb *can* generally refers to the ability to do something. The verb *may* generally refers to being allowed or permitted to do something.

> One of Ralph Waldo Emerson's major themes is that human beings *can* acquire from nature a sense of their own potential and autonomy.

> *May* I borrow your copy of *The Grapes of Wrath*?

different from, different than

The preferred usage is *different from*.

> In her powerful exploration of women's consciousness, Kate Chopin was *different from* the vast majority of her contemporaries.

due to the fact that

Replace this awkward expression with *because* or *since*.

> *Because* Dexter Green cherishes his memories of the glamourous Judy Jones, it is not surprising that he is saddened by the knowledge that her youth and beauty have faded.

farther, further

Use *farther* when you refer to distance. Use *further* when you mean "to a greater degree."

> The *farther* Phoenix Jackson travels in Eudora Welty's story "A Worn Path," the more her determination to reach her goal grows.

> In his speech, Patrick Henry urges his countrymen to trust the British no *further*.

fewer, less

Use *fewer* for things that can be counted. Use *less* for amounts or quantities that cannot be counted.

> The poem "The Red Wheelbarrow" uses *fewer* words than many other poems.

> The train engineer felt *less* anticipation with each step.

good, well

Use the predicate adjective *good* after linking verbs such as *feel, look, smell, taste*, and *seem*. Use *well* whenever you need an adverb.

> At the end of "Winter Dreams," Devon implies that Judy does not look as *good* as she used to.

> Anne Tyler writes especially *well* about ordinary people and family relationships.

hopefully

You should not loosely attach this adverb to a sentence, as in "Hopefully, the rain will stop by noon." Rewrite the sentence so that *hopefully* modifies a specific verb. Other possible ways of revising such sentences include using the adjective *hopeful* or a phrase such as *everyone hopes that*.

> William Faulkner wrote *hopefully* about mankind's ability to endure and prevail.

> Mai was *hopeful* that she could locate some more biographical information about Jean Toomer.

> *Everyone hopes that* Diane will win the essay contest.

its, it's

Do not confuse the possessive pronoun *its* with the contraction *it's*, standing for "it is" or "it has."

> Perhaps the most memorable line in Emerson's poem "The Rhodora" is "Beauty is *its* own excuse for being."

> Wallace Stevens's "Anecdote of the Jar" suggests that *it's* impossible to mediate completely between the wilderness and the world of civilization.

kind of, sort of

In formal writing, you should not use these colloquial expressions. Instead, use a word such as *rather* or *somewhat*.

> Robert Lowell's train of thought in "Hawthorne" is *rather* difficult to follow.

> Mary Chesnut is accurate but *somewhat* emotional.

lay, lie

Do not confuse these verbs. *Lay* is a transitive verb meaning "to set or put something down." Its principal parts are *lay, laying, laid, laid. Lie* is an intransitive verb meaning "to recline." Its principal parts are *lie, lying, lay, lain*.

> Stream-of-consciousness narration *lays* a special responsibility on the reader.

> The speaker of "I heard a Fly buzz—when I died—" *lies* in a silent room as her life slips away.

many, much

Use *many* to refer to a specific quantity. Use *much* for an indefinite amount or for an abstract concept.

> *Many* of William Faulkner's novels deal with the themes of pride, guilt, and the search for identity.

> *Much* of Mark Twain's fiction was influenced by his boyhood along the Mississippi.

may be, maybe

Be careful not to confuse the verb phrase *may be* with the adverb *maybe* (meaning "perhaps").

> The speaker *may be* the poet herself; in others, the speaker is clearly a different persona.

> The most memorable, and *maybe* the most ineffectual, character in T. S. Eliot's poetry is Prufrock.

plurals that do not end in -s

The plurals of certain nouns from Greek and Latin are formed as they were in their original language. Words such as *criteria, media,* and *phenomena* are plural and should not be treated as if they were singular (*criterion, medium, phenomenon*).

> In "Ars Poetica," Archibald MacLeish seems to deny that meaning is the most important *criterion* for the evaluation of poetry.

> The *phenomena* discussed by the "learn'd astronomer" in Whitman's poem may have

included planetary orbits and the influence of the moon on the tides.

raise, rise

Raise is a transitive verb that usually takes a direct object. *Rise* is intransitive and never takes a direct object.

> Suspense *raises* readers' expectations.

> Flannery O'Connor published a collection entitled *Everything That Rises Must Converge.*

set, sit

Do not confuse these verbs. *Set* is a transitive verb meaning "to put (something) in a certain place." Its principal parts are *set, setting, set, set. Sit* is an intransitive verb meaning "to be seated." Its principal parts are *sit, sitting, sat, sat.*

> Phillis Wheatley's poem is so complimentary to Washington that it seems to *set* him on a pedestal.

> As Mrs. Mallard *sits* upstairs alone, she contemplates the death of her husband.

that, which, who

Use the relative pronoun *that* to refer to things or people. Use *which* only for things and *who* only for people.

> The poet *that* Lee liked best was Sylvia Plath.

> The Romantic movement, *which* emphasized emotions, took place during the early 1800s.

> The poet *who* was the first to read his work at a presidential inauguration was Robert Frost.

unique

Because *unique* means "one of a kind," you should not use it carelessly instead of the words "interesting" or "unusual." Avoid such illogical expressions as "most unique," "very unique," and "extremely unique."

> Some critics have argued that its themes make Herman Melville's *Moby-Dick unique* in literary history.

who, whom

In formal writing, use *who* only as a subject in clauses and sentences and *whom* only as an object.

> Walt Whitman, *who* grieved Lincoln's assassination, wrote a tribute to the slain president.

> F. Scott Fitzgerald, *whom* many have heralded as the voice of the Jazz Age, wrote *The Great Gatsby.*

Introduction to the Internet

The Internet is a series of networks that are interconnected all over the world. The Internet allows users to have almost unlimited access to information stored on the networks. Dr. Berners-Lee, a physicist, created the Internet in the 1980s by writing a small computer program that allowed pages to be linked together using key words. The Internet was mostly text-based until 1992, when a computer program called the NCSA Mosaic (National Center for Supercomputing Applications) was created at the University of Illinois. This program was the first Web browser. The development of Web browsers greatly eased the ability of the user to navigate through all the pages stored on the Web. Very soon, the appearance of the Web was altered as well. More appealing visuals were added, and sound, too, was implemented. This change made the Web more user-friendly and more appealing to the general public.

Using the Internet for Research

Key Word Search

Before you begin a search, you should identify your specific topic. To make searching easier, narrow your subject to a key word or a group of key words. These are your search terms, and they should be as specific as possible. For example, if you are looking for the latest concert dates for your favorite musical group, you might use the band's name as a key word. However, if you were to enter the name of the group in the query box of the search engine, you might be presented with thousands of links to information about the group that is unrelated to what you want to know. You might locate such information as band member biographies, the group's history, fan reviews of concerts, and hundreds of sites with related names containing information that is irrelevant to your search. Because you used such a broad key word, you might need to navigate through all that information before you could find a link or subheading for concert dates. In contrast, if you were to type in "Duplex Arena and [band name]," you would have a better chance of locating pages that contain this information.

How to Narrow Your Search

If you have a large group of key words and still do not know which ones to use, write out a list of all the words you are considering. Once you have completed the list, scrutinize it. Then, delete the words that are least important to your search, and highlight those that are most important.

These **key search connectors** can help you fine-tune your search:

AND: Narrows a search by retrieving documents that include both terms. For example: *baseball* AND *playoffs*

OR: Broadens a search by retrieving documents including any of the terms. For example: *playoffs* OR *championships*

NOT: Narrows a search by excluding documents containing certain words. For example: *baseball* NOT *history of*

Tips for an Effective Search

1. Remember that search engines can be case-sensitive. If your first attempt at searching fails, check your search terms for misspellings and try again.

2. If you are entering a group of key words, present them in order from the most important to the least important key word.

3. Avoid opening the link to every single page in your results list. Search engines present pages in descending order of relevancy. The most useful pages will be located at the top of the list. However, read the description of each link before you open the page.

4. Some search engines provide helpful tips for specializing your search. Take the opportunity to learn more about effective searching.

Other Ways to Search

Using Online Reference Sites How you search should be tailored to what you are hoping to find. If you are looking for data and facts, use reference sites before you jump onto a simple search engine. For example, you can find reference sites to provide definitions of words, statistics about almost any subject, biographies, maps, and concise information on many topics. Here are some useful online reference sites:

Online libraries

Online periodicals

Almanacs

Encyclopedias

You can find these sources using subject searches.

Conducting Subject Searches As you prepare to go online, consider your subject and the best way to find information to suit your needs. If you are looking for general information on a topic and you want your search results to be extensive, consider the subject search indexes on most search engines. These indexes, in the form of category and subject lists, often appear on the first page of a search engine. When you click on a specific highlighted word, you will be presented with a new screen containing subcategories of the topic you chose.

Evaluating the Reliability of Internet Resources

Just as you would evaluate the quality, bias, and validity of any other research material you locate, check the source of information you find online. Compare these two sites containing information about the poet and writer Langston Hughes:

Site A is a personal Web site constructed by a college student. It contains no bibliographic information or links to sites that he used. Included on the site are several poems by Langston Hughes and a student essay about the poet's use of symbolism. It has not been updated in more than six months.

Site B is a Web site constructed and maintained by the English Department of a major university. Information on Hughes is presented in a scholarly format, with a bibliography and credits for the writer. The site includes links to other sites and indicates new features that are added weekly.

For your own research, consider the information you find on Site B to be more reliable and accurate than that on Site A. Because it is maintained by experts in their field who are held accountable for their work, the university site will be a better research tool than the student-generated one.

Tips for Evaluating Internet Sources

1. Consider who constructed and who now maintains the Web page. Determine whether this author is a reputable source. Often, the URL endings indicate a source.
   - Sites ending in *.edu* are maintained by educational institutions.
   - Sites ending in *.gov* are maintained by government agencies (federal, state, or local).
   - Sites ending in *.org* are normally maintained by non-profit organizations and agencies.
   - Sites ending in *.com* are commercially or personally maintained.
2. Skim the official and trademarked Web pages first. It is safe to assume that the information you draw from Web pages of reputable institutions, online encyclopedias, online versions of major daily newspapers, or government-owned sites produce information as reliable as the material you would find in print. In contrast, unbranded sites or those generated by individuals tend to borrow information from other sources without providing documentation. As information travels from one source to another, it could have been muddled, misinterpreted, edited, or revised.
3. You can still find valuable information in the less "official" sites. Check for the writer's credentials, and then consider these factors:
   - Do not be misled by official-looking graphics or presentations.
   - Make sure that the information is updated enough to suit your needs. Many Web pages will indicate how recently they have been updated.
   - If the information is borrowed, notice whether you can trace it back to its original source.

Respecting Copyrighted Material

Because the Internet is a relatively new and quickly growing medium, issues of copyright and ownership arise almost daily. As laws begin to govern the use and reuse of material posted online, they may change the way that people can access or reprint material.

Text, photographs, music, and fine art printed online may not be reproduced without acknowledged permission of the copyright owner.

Citing Sources

In research writing, cite your sources. In the body of your paper, provide a footnote, an endnote, or a parenthetical citation, identifying the sources of facts, opinions, or quotations. At the end of your paper, provide a bibliography or a works-cited list, a list of all the sources you cite. Follow an established format, such as Modern Language Association (MLA) Style.

Works-Cited List (MLA Style)

A works-cited list must contain accurate information sufficient to enable a reader to locate each source you cite. The basic components of an entry are as follows:

- Name of the author, editor, translator, or group responsible for the work
- Title of the work
- Place and date of publication
- Publisher

For print materials, the information required for a citation generally appears on the copyright and title pages of a work. For the format of works-cited list entries, consult the examples at right and in the chart on page R32.

Parenthetical Citations (MLA Style)

A parenthetical citation briefly identifies the source from which you have taken a specific quotation, factual claim, or opinion. It refers the reader to one of the entries on your works-cited list. A parenthetical citation has the following features:

- It appears in parentheses.
- It identifies the source by the last name of the author, editor, or translator.
- It gives a page reference, identifying the page of the source on which the information cited can be found.

Punctuation A parenthetical citation generally falls outside a closing quotation mark but within the final punctuation of a clause or sentence. For a long quotation set off from the rest of your text, place the citation at the end of the excerpt without any punctuation following.

Special Cases

- If the author is an organization, use the organization's name, in a shortened version if necessary.
- If you cite more than one work by the same author, add the title or a shortened version of the title.

Sample Works-Cited Lists

Carwardine, Mark, Erich Hoyt, R. Ewan Fordyce, and Peter Gill. *The Nature Company Guides: Whales, Dolphins, and Porpoises.* New York: Time-Life Books, 1998.
Whales in Danger. "Discovering Whales." 18 Oct. 1999. <http://whales.magna.com.au/DISCOVER>

Neruda, Pablo. "Ode to Spring." *Odes to Opposites.* Trans. Ken Krabbenhoft. Ed. and illus. Ferris Cook. Boston: Little, Brown and Company, 1995.
The Saga of the Volsungs. Trans. Jesse L. Byock. London: Penguin Books, 1990.

An anonymous work is listed by title.

Both the title of the work and of the collection in which it is found are listed.

Sample Parenthetical Citations

It makes sense that baleen whales such as the blue whale, the bowhead whale, the humpback whale, and the sei whale (to name just a few) grow to immense sizes (Carwardine, Hoyt, and Fordyce 19–21). The blue whale has grooves running from under its chin to partway along the length of its underbelly. As in some other whales, these grooves expand and allow even more food and water to be taken in (Ellis 18–21).

Author's last name

Page numbers where information can be found

MLA Style for Listing Sources

Book with one author	Pyles, Thomas. *The Origins and Development of the English Language.* 2nd ed. New York: Harcourt Brace Jovanovich, Inc., 1971.
Book with two or three authors	McCrum, Robert, William Cran, and Robert MacNeil. *The Story of English.* New York: Penguin Books, 1987.
Book with an editor	Truth, Sojourner. *Narrative of Sojourner Truth.* Ed. Margaret Washington. New York: Vintage Books, 1993.
Book with more than three authors or editors	Donald, Robert B., et al. *Writing Clear Essays.* Upper Saddle River, NJ: Prentice-Hall, Inc., 1996.
Single work from an anthology	Hawthorne, Nathaniel. "Young Goodman Brown." *Literature: An Introduction to Reading and Writing.* Ed. Edgar V. Roberts and Henry E. Jacobs. Upper Saddle River, NJ: Prentice-Hall, Inc., 1998. 376–385. [Indicate pages for the entire selection.]
Introduction in a published edition	Washington, Margaret. Introduction. *Narrative of Sojourner Truth.* By Sojourner Truth. Ed. Washington. New York: Vintage Books, 1993. v–xi.
Signed article in a weekly magazine	Wallace, Charles. "A Vodacious Deal." *Time* 14 Feb. 2000: 63.
Signed article in a monthly magazine	Gustaitis, Joseph. "The Sticky History of Chewing Gum." *American History* Oct. 1998: 30–38.
Unsigned editorial or story	"Selective Silence." Editorial. *Wall Street Journal* 11 Feb. 2000: A14. [If the editorial or story is signed, begin with the author's name.]
Signed pamphlet	[Treat the pamphlet as though it were a book.]
Pamphlet with no author, publisher, or date	*Are You at Risk of Heart Attack?* n.p. n.d. [n.p. n.d. indicates that there is no known publisher or date]
Filmstrips, slide programs, videocassettes, DVDs, and other audiovisual media	*The Diary of Anne Frank.* Dir. George Stevens. Perf. Millie Perkins, Shelley Winters, Joseph Schildkraut, Lou Jacobi, and Richard Beymer. 1959. DVD. Twentieth Century Fox, 2004.
Radio or television program transcript	"Washington's Crossing of the Delaware." Host Liane Hansen, Guest David Hackett Fischer, *Weekend Edition Sunday,* Natl. Public Radio, WNYC, New York City. 23 Dec. 2003. Transcript.
Internet	"Fun Facts About Gum." NACGM site. National Association of Chewing Gum Manufacturers. 19 Dec, 1999. <http://www.nacgm.org/consumer/funfacts.html> [Indicate the date you accessed the information. Content and addresses at Web sites change frequently.]
Newspaper	Thurow, Roger. "South Africans Who Fought for Sanctions Now Scrap for Investors." *Wall Street Journal* 11 Feb. 2000: A1+. [For a multipage article that does not appear on consecutive pages write only the first page number on which it appears, followed by a plus sign.]
Personal interview	Smith, Jane. Personal interview. 10 Feb. 2000.
CD (with multiple publishers)	Simms, James, ed. *Romeo and Juliet.* By William Shakespeare. CD-ROM. Oxford: Attica Cybernetics Ltd.; London: BBC Education; London: HarperCollins Publishers, 1995.
Signed article from an encyclopedia	Askeland, Donald R. "Welding." *World Book Encyclopedia.* 1991 ed.

RUBRICS

What is a rubric?

A rubric is a tool, often in the form of a chart or a grid, that helps you assess your work. Rubrics are particularly helpful for writing and speaking assignments.

To help you or others assess, or evaluate, your work, a rubric offers several specific criteria to be applied to your work. Then the rubric helps you or an evaluator indicate your range of success or failure according to those specific criteria. Rubrics are often used to evaluate writing for standardized tests.

Using a rubric will save you time, focus your learning, and improve the work you do. When you know what the rubric will be before you begin writing a persuasive essay, for example, you will be aware as you write of specific criteria that are important in that kind of an essay. As you evaluate the essay before giving it to your teacher, you will focus on the specific areas that your teacher wants you to master— or on areas that you know present challenges for you. Instead of searching through your work randomly for any way to improve it or correct its errors, you will have a clear and helpful focus on specific criteria.

How are rubrics constructed?

Rubrics can be constructed in several ways.

- Your teacher may assign a rubric for a specific assignment.
- Your teacher may direct you to a rubric in your textbook.
- Your teacher and your class may construct a rubric for a particular assignment together.
- You and your classmates may construct a rubric together.
- You may create your own rubric with criteria you want to evaluate in your work.

How will a rubric help me?

A rubric will help you assess your work on a scale. Scales vary from rubric to rubric but usually range from 6 to 1, 5 to 1, or 4 to 1, with 6, 5, or 4 being the highest score and 1 being the lowest. If someone else is using the rubric to assess your work, the rubric will give your evaluator a clear range within which to place your work. If you are using the rubric yourself, it will help you make improvements to your work.

What are the types of rubrics?

- A **holistic rubric** has general criteria that can apply to a variety of assignments. See p. R35 for an example of a holistic rubric.
- An **analytic rubric** is specific to a particular assignment. The criteria for evaluation address the specific issues important in that assignment. See p. R34 for examples of analytic rubrics.

SAMPLE ANALYTIC RUBRICS

Rubric With a 4-point Scale

*The following analytic rubric is an example of a rubric to assess a persuasive essay.
It will help you evaluate audience and purpose, organization, elaboration, and use of language.*

	Audience/Purpose	Organization	Elaboration	Use of Language
4	Demonstrates highly effective word choice; clearly focused on task.	Uses clear, consistent organizational strategy.	Provides convincing, well-elaborated reasons to support the position.	Incorporates transitions; includes very few mechanical errors.
3	Demonstrates good word choice; stays focused on persuasive task.	Uses clear organizational strategy with occasional inconsistencies.	Provides two or more moderately elaborated reasons to support the position.	Incorporates some transitions; includes few mechanical errors.
2	Shows some good word choices; minimally stays focused on persuasive task.	Uses inconsistent organizational strategy; presentation is not logical.	Provides several reasons, but few are elaborated.	Incorporates few transitions; includes many mechanical errors.
1	Shows lack of attention to persuasive task.	Demonstrates lack of organizational strategy.	Provides no specific reasons or does not elaborate.	Does not connect ideas; includes many mechanical errors.

Rubric With a 6-point Scale

*The following analytic rubric is an example of a rubric to assess a persuasive essay.
It will help you evaluate presentation, position, evidence, and arguments.*

	Presentation	Position	Evidence	Arguments
6	Essay clearly and effectively addresses an issue with more than one side.	Essay clearly states a supportable position on the issue.	All evidence is logically organized, well presented, and supports the position.	All reader concerns and counterarguments are effectively addressed.
5	Most of essay addresses an issue that has more than one side.	Essay clearly states a position on the issue.	Most evidence is logically organized, well presented, and supports the position.	Most reader concerns and counterarguments are effectively addressed.
4	Essay adequately addresses issue that has more than one side.	Essay adequately states a position on the issue.	Many parts of evidence support the position; some evidence is out of order.	Many reader concerns and counterarguments are adequately addressed.
3	Essay addresses issue with two sides but does not present second side clearly.	Essay states a position on the issue, but the position is difficult to support.	Some evidence supports the position, but some evidence is out of order.	Some reader concerns and counterarguments are addressed.
2	Essay addresses issue with two sides but does not present second side.	Essay states a position on the issue, but the position is not supportable.	Not much evidence supports the position, and what is included is out of order.	A few reader concerns and counterarguments are addressed.
1	Essay does not address issue with more than one side.	Essay does not state a position on the issue.	No evidence supports the position.	No reader concerns or counterarguments are addressed.

SAMPLE HOLISTIC RUBRIC

Holistic rubrics such as this one are sometimes used to assess writing assignments on standardized tests. Notice that the criteria for evaluation are focus, organization, support, and use of conventions.

Points	Criteria
6 Points	• The writing is strongly focused and shows fresh insight into the writing task. • The writing is marked by a sense of completeness and coherence and is organized with a logical progression of ideas. • A main idea is fully developed, and support is specific and substantial. • A mature command of the language is evident, and the writing may employ characteristic creative writing strategies. • Sentence structure is varied, and writing is free of all but purposefully used fragments. • Virtually no errors in writing conventions appear.
5 Points	• The writing is clearly focused on the task. • The writing is well organized and has a logical progression of ideas, though there may be occasional lapses. • A main idea is well developed and supported with relevant detail. • Command of the language is mature. • Sentence structure is varied, and the writing is free of fragments, except when used purposefully. • Writing conventions are followed correctly.
4 Points	• The writing is clearly focused on the task, but extraneous material may intrude at times. • A clear organizational pattern is present, though lapses may occur. • A main idea is adequately supported, but development may be uneven. • Sentence structure is generally fragment free but shows little variation. • Writing conventions are generally followed correctly.
3 Points	• Writing is generally focused on the task, but extraneous material may intrude at times. • An organizational pattern is evident, but writing may lack a logical progression of ideas. • Support for the main idea is generally present but is sometimes illogical. • Sentence structure is generally free of fragments, but there is almost no variation. • The work generally demonstrates a knowledge of writing conventions, with occasional misspellings.
2 Points	• The writing is related to the task but generally lacks focus. • There is little evidence of organizational pattern, and there is little sense of cohesion. • Support for the main idea is generally inadequate, illogical, or absent. • Sentence structure is unvaried, and serious errors may occur. • Errors in writing conventions and spelling are frequent.
1 Point	• The writing may have little connection to the task and is generally unfocused. • There has been little attempt at organization or development. • The paper seems fragmented, with no clear main idea. • Sentence structure is unvaried, and serious errors appear. • Poor word choice and poor command of the language obscure meaning. • Errors in writing conventions and spelling are frequent.
Unscorable	The paper is considered unscorable if • The response is unrelated to the task or is simply a rewording of the prompt. • The response has been copied from a published work. • The student did not write a response. • The response is illegible. • The words in the response are arranged with no meaning. • There is an insufficient amount of writing to score.

STUDENT MODEL

Persuasive Writing

This persuasive letter, which would receive a top score according to a persuasive rubric, is a response to the following writing prompt, or assignment:

Write a letter to a government official strongly supporting an environmental issue that is important to you and urging the official to take a specific action that supports your cause.

Dear Secretary of the Interior:

It's a normal, carefree day in the forest. The birds are singing and all of the animals are relaxing under the refreshing glow of the sun. But suddenly the thunderous sound of a chain saw echoes throughout the woodlands, and trees fall violently. The creatures of the forest run in terror. Many of these beautiful creatures will starve to death slowly and painfully as their homes are destroyed, and this precious ecosystem will not be able to regrow to its previous greatness for many years to come.

> A descriptive and interesting introduction grabs the reader's attention and shows a persuasive focus.

This sad story is a true one in many places around the globe. We must slow deforestation and replant trees immediately to save our breathable air, fertile topsoil, and fragile ecosystems.

If entire forests continue to be obliterated, less oxygen will be produced and more CO_2 emitted. In fact, deforestation accounts for a quarter of the CO_2 released into the atmosphere each year: about 1–2 billion tons. Forests provide the majority of the oxygen on earth, and if these forests disappear our air will soon be unbreathable.

Second, deforestation results in a loss of topsoil. Many of the companies who are involved in deforestation claim that the land is needed for farms, but deforestation makes the land much less fertile because it accelerates the process of erosion. According to the UN Food and Agriculture Organization, deforestation has damaged almost 6 million square kilometers of soil.

> The writer supports the argument with facts and evidence, and also uses the persuasive technique of appealing to the reader's emotions.

Finally, if cutting doesn't slow, many species will die off and many ecosystems will be destroyed. The 2000 UN Global Environment Outlook says that forests and rain forests have the most diverse plant and animal life in the world. The GEO also notes that there are more than 1,000 threatened species living in the world's forests. Imagine someone destroying all of the houses in your neighborhood and leaving all of the residents homeless. This is how it is for the organisms that live in the forests.

In conclusion, deforestation must slow and trees must be replanted immediately, or we will lose clean air, topsoil, and many precious organisms. Furthermore, a loss in forests will result in a generation that knows very little about nature. So, to prevent the chaotic disturbance of peace in the forests, please do whatever you can to prevent deforestation. Vote YES on any UN bills that would help the condition of our world's forests.

> The conclusion restates the argument and presents a call to action.

Sincerely yours,

Jamil Khouri

Success on college aptitude and achievement tests depends in a large part on the work you have done throughout your school career. By investing a sensible amount of time in preparing for a college entrance or AP exam, however, you can ensure that you obtain the highest score of which you are capable. Follow the strategies in this workshop for college-entrance test preparation.

PREPARING FOR THE TEST

Choose and Register for Tests

To decide which tests you will take, find out from the colleges to which you are applying which tests they require and which tests they encourage. Then, consult with guidance counselors, search the Web, or use library resources to determine the registration deadline and fees, the exact location of the test site, and the time each test will be given. Register in advance to take the test at a convenient location and date.

Familiarize Yourself With the Test

To focus your studies for the test, use available resources, such as the College Board Web site or the most recent edition of a reputable prep book to determine the following:

- the topics and skills covered on the test
- the time each section of the test will take
- the number and type of questions in each section
- how the test is scored

Study for the Test

Begin preparing for the test well in advance of the date on which you will take it. Read through a guide or two on the test, determine what study suggestions will work for you, and take a practice exam or two.

Subject-Area Tests If you are taking an AP or SAT II exam, review class notes, textbooks, and papers that you have written.

Aptitude Tests for College Admission

PSAT/NMSQT	Preliminary Scholastic Aptitude Test / National Merit Scholarship Qualifying Test **General Description** A two-hour version of the SAT, covering verbal and math skills and including a writing section. **Why Take It** Most often taken by juniors to prepare for the SAT, to make contact with colleges, and to qualify for the National Merit Scholarship.
SAT	Scholastic Aptitude Test **General Description** An aptitude test of vocabulary, math, and reasoning skills. Mostly multiple-choice questions. **Why Take It** Most colleges require that applicants submit either SAT or ACT scores. **Sections** Three Verbal sections — 78 questions total; 1 hour 15 minutes. Three Math sections—60 questions total; 1 hour 15 minutes. One additional, 30-question "equating section" that is not counted toward score.
ACT	American College Test **General Description** An aptitude test of English, math, and science reasoning skills. More content-based than the SAT. Multiple-choice questions only. **Why Take It** Most colleges require that applicants submit either SAT or ACT scores. **Sections** One English section—75 questions; 45 minutes. One Math section—60 questions; 60 minutes. One Reading section—40 questions; 35 minutes. One Science Reasoning section—40 questions; 35 minutes.

The AP English Open Response Question

Use your knowledge of the structure of the test to aid you in preparing. For instance, the AP English Literature and Composition test traditionally offers an "open response" question. You must choose a work to comment on in response to the question asked.

For this case, you should prepare to address two to four classic novels or plays in advance. Select diverse works to make sure that if the question does not apply to one there is a good chance that it will apply to the other. (Consult with your teacher or other resources for a list of recommended works).

Review your notes on the works you select and reread significant passages. Reread any papers you have written on them. Then, write a paragraph or two introducing the core themes of each work and the means by which the writer conveys them. By writing on the works in advance, you store ideas and connections to explore on the test. You ensure that your ideas will flow well when you write the actual test essay.

Practice

A standardized test tests your ability to apply knowledge or insight—within definite time limits. You can practice this skill by timing yourself as you take practice tests.

Practice as if you are taking the actual test. You can find practice copies of tests online or in test prep books. Each time you take a practice test, set aside the amount of time you will be given to take the actual test. Set a timer or alarm clock to warn you ten minutes before time is up. As you take the test, practice the strategies recommended in the Use Basic Test-Taking Strategies section below.

Analyze your practice results. Taking a practice test will sharpen your test-taking skills only if you understand your results. After scoring your practice test, review your responses to the questions. If you chose the correct answer for a question, jot a note explaining why it is the right answer. If you chose the wrong answer, note why it is wrong and why the correct answer is the best choice. By analyzing your answers—correct or incorrect—you will begin to "think like the test" and will be able to answer questions more effectively.

USE BASIC TEST-TAKING STRATEGIES

The following strategies can help you get the best score of which you are capable on any standardized test.

Manage Time on the Test

Analyze the test. Find out in advance how much time is allowed for each section of the test. Then, calculate how much time it should take to complete one quarter or one third of each section.

Keep track of time. Bring a watch with you to the test. As you work, check the time at reasonable intervals. You might check the time after completing the first ten multiple-choice questions out of thirty or after completing the first essay.

Subject-Area Tests for College Placement

SAT II	**General Description** Discipline-specific tests measuring command of a subject.
	Why Take It Some colleges may require SAT IIs for admission. Others use the scores to place students appropriately.
	Specifics All SAT II tests except the Writing test are multiple choice. Each takes an hour. The SAT II: Literature test divides 60 questions among 6 to 8 reading passages, covering poetry and prose from a broad range of periods.
AP exams	**General Description** Discipline-specific tests measuring command of a subject.
	Why Take It Participating colleges will award students college credit for achieving or bettering a given score.
	Specifics Formats vary with subject. The AP English Literature and Composition test traditionally features 50 to 55 multiple-choice questions divided among 4 to 5 reading passages (60 minutes) and 3 essay questions, including one "open response" (120 minutes total). Passages cover poetry and prose from a broad range of periods.

Adjust your pace. If you look at your watch after completing one third of a section and find out that you have used up half of your time, you should adjust your pace. Pick up speed—but do not rush. Remember, you do not need to answer every question to earn a respectable score.

Prioritize questions. Every question in a section counts for the same number of points, regardless of how difficult it may be. Prioritize questions. For a series of individual questions, as on the Analogies section of the SAT, you might simply skip the most difficult items and return to them later. On a test that features reading passages, quickly identify those passages that you are most confident you can analyze well, and work on the questions for these passages first. Return to the more difficult items when you have finished the easier ones.

Strategies for Answering Questions

The following strategies will aid you in answering the specific questions on the test.

Read passages effectively. First, skim a reading passage to get a general idea of its content. Then, read it carefully. When you encounter a word or idea that you do not understand, register it and move on. You may find a detail that clarifies it later.

The key to effective reading is to keep your focus. You need not understand everything in the passage. You do need to follow the main idea as it is developed from beginning to end. If you find your mind wandering—your eyes just running down the page without absorbing information—stop. Focus your attention, and keep reading.

After reading the passage, mentally sum up the main idea. When answering the questions on the passage, refer to the passage whenever necessary to confirm answers.

Read questions carefully. To test your reasoning skills, standardized tests ask questions that call on your ability to distinguish shades of meaning or make complex connections. For this reason, you must read every question with care, restating it in your own words to make sure you have understood it.

- Eliminate answer choices that are obviously wrong.
- Eliminate answer choices that contain a part that is obviously wrong.
- After eliminating one or more answer choices, choose the remaining answer that you think is likeliest to be correct.

Strategies for Essay Questions

To ensure that any essay you are called on to write for a test will command the attention of the person who will score it, use the following strategies.

Adapt your thesis from the question. The materials for the thesis of a test essay are right there in the test question. Read the question carefully. Then, jot down a thesis statement that mirrors the question, using key terms from the question, as in the example in the chart.

Motivate your thesis. To capture the attention of the person grading your essay, connect your thesis to a fundamental theme or issue. By doing so, you are showing your reader why he or she should care about your point.

For instance, you might face an essay question on Shakespeare's *The Tempest*. In your senior thesis, you may have written that the essential meaning of the play is to dramatize and reconcile opposing aspects of the human spirit. Imagination (Ariel), appetite (Caliban), revenge, and love all have their moment and are put in their proper place.

In the introduction to your test essay, you should restate that fundamental insight and say it in dramatic terms. Once you have stated the essential meaning or most important feature of the work, you can then motivate your thesis, as in the example below.

Sample question: In some works of literature, contrasts between characters are used to develop the central theme. Choose a work of literary merit and write a well-organized essay discussing how the writer uses character contrasts.

Sample preliminary thesis statement: In *The Tempest,* Shakespeare uses <u>contrasts between characters</u> such as Caliban and Ariel <u>to convey his theme</u> of the sorting out of oppositions in the human spirit.
[Thesis statement incorporates key terms from the question.]

Sample introduction (thesis plus motivation): In *The Tempest,* characters come in pairs. Each pair reflects a duality or conflict that defines the human spirit, from the quarrel between mind and body to the war of the sexes. Shakespeare uses contrasts between characters such as Caliban and Ariel to dramatize these dualities and, in the end, to reconcile them or at least to restore order to them.
[Motivates the thesis by connecting it to the meaning of the work as a whole]

Use precise and vivid language. As in any writing you do, choose words in your test essays that convey meaning precisely and create vivid images. If you are discussing Brutus's decision to join the conspirators in *Julius Caesar*, you might use the word *torn* instead of the word *undecided*.

If you are applying for admission to a college, you will probably need to submit an essay as part of your application. This essay is your introduction to a college applications committee. It will help committee members get a sense of you as a person and as a student. Review the chart at right for general strategies, and then follow the guidelines below to ensure that your college application essay does the best job presenting you.

Selecting a Topic

Read the essay question on the application form with care. Mark key criteria and direction words such as *describe* and *explain*. After you have written a first draft, check to make sure you have met all of the requirements of the question. Your essay has a better chance of succeeding if it meets the requirements exactly.

General Questions About You

The essay question on a college application may be as general as "Describe a significant experience or event in your life and explain its consequences for you." To choose the right topic for such a question, think of an event or experience that truly is meaningful to you—a camping trip, a volunteer event, a family reunion. Test the subject by drafting a letter about it to a good friend or relative. If you find that your enthusiasm for the subject grows as you write, and if your discussion reveals something about your growth or your outlook on life, the topic may be the right one for your essay.

Directed Questions

The essay question on an application may be more directed than a simple "tell us about yourself." For instance, you may be asked to select three figures from history you would like to meet and to explain your choices.

In such cases, do not give an answer just because you think it will please reviewers. Instead, consult your own interests and instincts. Your most convincing writing will come from genuine interest in the subject. You might discover the best topic by jotting down a diary entry or a letter to a friend in which you discuss possible subjects.

Style

Though an essay is a chance to tell something about yourself, it is also a formal document addressed to

---

> ### Strategies for Writing an Effective College Application Essay
>
> - **Choose the right topic.** If you have a choice of essay topics, choose the one that interests you.
> - **Organize.** Use a strong organization that carries the reader from introduction to conclusion.
> - **Begin with a bang.** Open with an introduction that has a good chance of sparking the reader's interest.
> - **Elaborate.** Be sure to explain why the experiences you discuss are important to you or what you learned from them.
> - **Show style.** Bring life to your essay through vivid descriptions, precise word choice, and sophisticated sentence structure, such as parallelism. Consider including dialogue where appropriate.
> - **Close with a clincher.** Write a conclusion that effectively sums up your ideas.
> - **Do a clean job.** Proofread your essay carefully to ensure that it is error-free.

---

strangers. Use a formal to semiformal style. Avoid incomplete sentences and slang unless you are using them for clear stylistic effect. Use words with precision, selecting one or two accurate words for what you mean, rather than piling up words in the hope that one of them will hit the mark.

Format

Most applications limit the length of essays. Do not exceed the allowed space or number of words. Your college application essay should be neatly typed or printed, using adequate margins. Proofread your final draft carefully. If you submit a separate copy of the essay (rather than writing on the application form), number the pages and include your name and contact information on each page.

Reusing Your Essay

Most students apply to a number of different colleges in order to ensure their admission to a school. Once you have written a strong essay for one application, you should consider adapting it for others.

Do not submit a single essay to several schools blindly. Always read the application essay question carefully to ensure that the essay you submit fulfills all of its requirements.

By writing **criticism**—writing that analyzes literature—readers share their responses to a written work. Criticism is also a way for a reader to deepen his or her own understanding and appreciation of the work, and to help others to deepen theirs.

The information in this handbook will guide you through the process of writing criticism. In addition, it will help you to refine your critical perceptions to ensure that you are ready to produce work at the college level.

Understanding Criticism

There are a few different types of criticism. Each can enhance understanding and deepen appreciation of literature in a distinctive way. All types share similar functions.

The Types of Criticism

Analysis Students are frequently asked to analyze, or break into parts and examine, a passage or a work. When you write an analysis, you must support your ideas with references to the text, as in this example:

> **Conclusion:** In "Heat," the poet H.D. creates an enduring image of heat. There is no deeper meaning here; her task is to commemorate physical experience in words.
>
> **Support:** The poem's imagery gives heat solidity and depth. In the first stanza, the speaker asks the wind to "cut apart the heat" and, in the third stanza, to "plow through it," as if heat were a thick substance like earth.

Biographical Criticism Biographical criticism uses information about a writer's life to shed light on his or her work, as in this passage by Kenneth Silverman:

> Much of [Poe's] later writing, despite its variety of forms and styles, places and characters, is driven by the question of whether the dead remain dead. . . . [C]hildren who lose a parent at an early age, as Edgar lost Eliza Poe [his mother], invest more feeling in and magnify the parent's image. . . . The young child . . . cannot comprehend the finality of death. . . .

Historical Criticism Historical criticism traces connections between an author's work and the events, circumstances, or ideas that shaped the writer's historical era. For example, Jean H. Hagstrum analyzes William Blake's character of Urizen by showing how the character symbolizes the Enlightenment ideas of the scientist Isaac Newton and the philosopher John Locke.

> Urizen is also an active force. Dividing, partitioning, dropping the plummet line, applying Newton's compasses to the world, he creates abstract mathematical forms. Like Locke, he shrinks the senses, narrows the perceptions, binds man to the natural fact.

The Functions of Criticism

In each of the previous examples of criticism, you can find evidence of the following critical functions:

Making Connections All criticism makes connections between two or more things. For instance, the analysis of H.D.'s poetry connects different parts of a poem (the images of heat being cut or parted by a plow).

Making Distinctions Criticism must make distinctions as well as connections. In the analysis of "Heat," the critic distinguishes between two possible purposes for poetry: first, to create an enduring image and, second, to present a deeper meaning.

Achieving Insight By making connections and distinctions, criticism achieves insight. The analysis of H.D.'s poem reaches the insight that the poem stands on its own as a work of beauty apart from any deeper meaning.

Making a Judgment Assessing the value of a work is an important function of criticism. A critic may assess a work by comparing it with other works and by using a standard such as enjoyment, insight, or beauty.

"Placing" the Work Critics guide readers not by telling them *what* to think but by giving them *terms in which to think.* In the passage quoted above, Hagstrum helps us "place" Urizen. We cannot respond to Urizen, she reminds us, as if he were an individual like Macbeth or Holden Caufield. Instead, we respond to him best by perceiving him as a historical force—the pursuit of reason—personified. The terms on which we appreciate and understand each of these characters are different.

Writing Criticism

Like all solid writing, a work of criticism presents a thesis (a central idea) and supports it with arguments and evidence. Follow the strategies below to develop a critical thesis and gather support for it.

Formulate a Working Thesis

Once you have chosen a work or works on which to write, formulate a working thesis. First, ask yourself questions like these:

- What strikes you most about the work or the writer that your paper will address? What puzzles you most?
- In what ways is the work unlike others you have read?
- What makes the techniques used by the writer so well-suited to (or so poorly chosen for) conveying the theme of the work?

Jot down notes answering your questions. Then, reread passages that illustrate your answers, jotting down notes about what each passage contributes to the work. Review your notes, and write a sentence that draws a conclusion about the work.

Gather Support

Taking Notes From the Work Once you have a working thesis, take notes on passages in the work that confirm it. To aid your search for support, consider the type of support suited to your thesis, as in the chart.

Conducting Additional Research If you are writing biographical or historical criticism, you will need to consult sources on the writer's life and era. Even if you are writing a close analysis of a poem, you should consider consulting the works of critics to benefit from their insights and understanding. For a more detailed explanation of the research process, see pages 694–699.

Take Notes

Consider recording notes from the works you are analyzing, as well as from any critical works you consult, on a set of note cards. A good set of note cards enables you to recall details accurately, to organize your ideas effectively, and to see connections between ideas.

If your thesis concerns . . .	look for support in the form of . . .
Character	• dialogue • character's actions • writer's descriptions of the character • other characters' reactions to the character
Theme	• fate of characters • patterns and contrasts of imagery, character, or events • mood • writer's attitude toward the action
Style	• memorable descriptions, observations • passages that "sound like" the writer • examples of rhetorical devices, such as exaggeration and irony
Historical Context	• references to historical events and personalities • evidence of social or political pressures on characters • socially significant contrasts between characters (for example, between the rich and the poor)
Literary Influences	• writer's chosen form or genre • passages that "sound like" another writer • events or situations that resemble those in other works • evidence of an outlook similar to that of another writer

One Card, One Idea If you use note cards while researching, record each key passage, theme, critical opinion, or fact on a separate note card. A good note card includes a brief quotation or summary of an idea and a record of the source, including the page number, in which you found the information. When copying a sentence from a work, use quotation marks and check to make sure you have copied it correctly.

Coding Sources Keep a working bibliography, a list of all works you consult, as you conduct research. Assign a code, such as a letter, to each work on the list. For each note you take, include the code for the source.

Coding Cards Organize your note cards by labeling each with the subtopic it concerns.

Present Support Appropriately

As you draft, consider how much support you need for each point and the form that support should take. You can provide support in the following forms:

- **Summaries** are short accounts in your own words of important elements of the work, such as events, a character's traits, or the writer's ideas. They are appropriate for background information.
- **Paraphrases** are restatements of passages from a work in your own words. They are appropriate for background and for information incidental to your main point.
- **Quotations of key passages** are direct transcriptions of the writer's words, enclosed in quotation marks or, if longer than three lines, set as indented text. If a passage is crucial to your thesis, you should quote it directly and at whatever length is necessary.

Quotations of multiple examples are required to support claims about general features of a work, such as a claim about the writer's ironic style or use of cartoonlike characters.

Revise Ideas as You Draft

When writing criticism, do not be afraid to revise your early ideas based on what you learn as you research or write further. As you draft, allow the insights—or the difficulties—that emerge to guide you back to the writer's works or other sources for clarification or support. What you discover may lead you to modify your thesis.

The chart above presents an example of the way this circular process can work.

DO's and DON'T's of Academic Writing

Avoid gender and cultural bias. Certain terms and usages reflect the bias of past generations. To eliminate bias in any academic work you do, edit with the following rules in mind:

- **Pronoun usage** When referring to an unspecified individual in a case in which his or her gender is irrelevant, use forms of the pronoun phrase *he or she*. Example: "A lawyer is trained to use <u>his or her</u> mind."

Stage of the Writing Process	The Developing Thesis Statement
Prewriting: A student rereads Sartre's story "The Wall" to find passages that support her thesis.	**First formulation:** "In his short story 'The Wall,' Sartre illustrates the belief that human life is ruled by inescapable fate."
Drafting: As the student summarizes the story's ending, she is struck by the fact that the narrator's final act has exactly the opposite effect from what he intended. She revises her thesis statement.	**Second formulation:** "In his short story 'The Wall,' Sartre demonstrates the power of fate by showing how the effects of a person's actions can completely contradict the person's intentions."
Revising: As the student rereads her first draft, she grows dissatisfied with her explanation of the story's ending. Why does the writer spend so much time showing the narrator's resignation to fate, only to have fate strike unexpectedly? She reworks her paper to support a new thesis statement.	**Final formulation:** "In his short story 'The Wall,' Sartre shows that 'fate' is a myth: However hard we try to resign ourselves to fate, we can never eliminate our responsibility for our own actions."

- **"Culture-centric" terms** Replace terms that reflect a bias toward one culture with more generally accepted synonyms. For instance, replace terms such as *primitive* (used of hunting-gathering peoples), *the Orient* (used to refer to Asia), and *Indians* (used of Native Americans), all of which suggest a view of the world centered in Western European culture.

Avoid plagiarism. Presenting someone else's ideas, research, or exact words as your own is plagiarism, the equivalent of stealing or fraud. Laws protect the rights of writers and researchers in cases of commercial plagiarism. Academic standards protect their rights in cases of academic plagiarism.

To avoid plagiarism, follow these practices:

- Read from several sources.
- Synthesize what you learn.
- Let the ideas of experts help you draw your own conclusions.
- Always credit your sources properly when using someone else's ideas to support your view.

By following these guidelines, you will also push yourself to think independently.

Forming Your Critical Vocabulary

To enhance your critical perceptions—the connections you find and the distinctions you make—improve your critical vocabulary. The following glossary shows contrasting pairs of critical terms. Some of these pairs define a spectrum along which you can place a work; others define simple opposites.

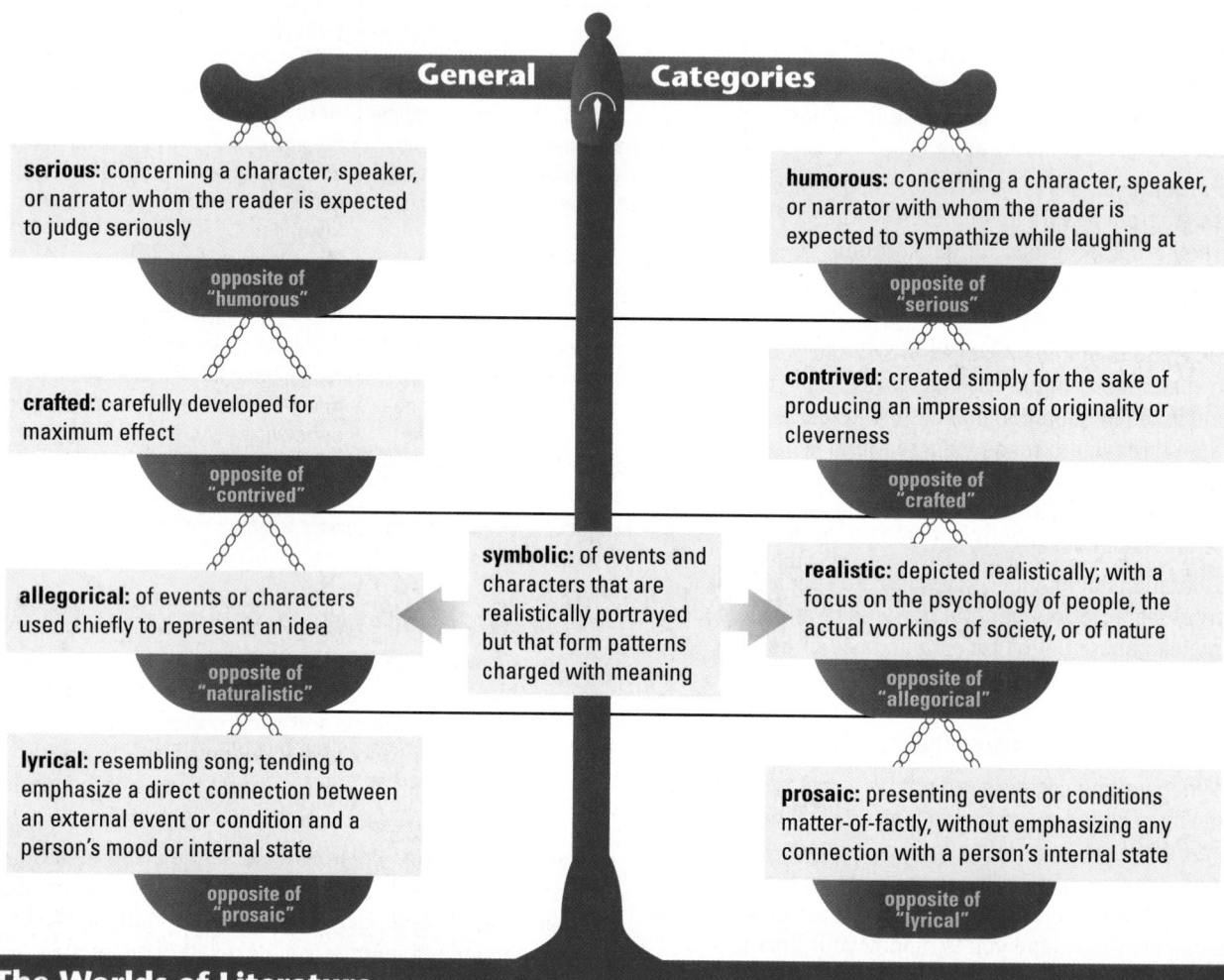

General Categories

serious: concerning a character, speaker, or narrator whom the reader is expected to judge seriously

opposite of "humorous"

humorous: concerning a character, speaker, or narrator with whom the reader is expected to sympathize while laughing at

opposite of "serious"

crafted: carefully developed for maximum effect

opposite of "contrived"

contrived: created simply for the sake of producing an impression of originality or cleverness

opposite of "crafted"

allegorical: of events or characters used chiefly to represent an idea

opposite of "naturalistic"

symbolic: of events and characters that are realistically portrayed but that form patterns charged with meaning

realistic: depicted realistically; with a focus on the psychology of people, the actual workings of society, or of nature

opposite of "allegorical"

lyrical: resembling song; tending to emphasize a direct connection between an external event or condition and a person's mood or internal state

opposite of "prosaic"

prosaic: presenting events or conditions matter-of-factly, without emphasizing any connection with a person's internal state

opposite of "lyrical"

The Worlds of Literature

In addition to categorizing elements and qualities of a work, critics categorize the imaginative world it assumes—the "rules" that govern actions and events in the work. Historically, the earliest literature projects a heroic world.

heroic, epic, or **tragic world:** a stern world governed by codes of conduct and divine judgments; characters are defined by moral qualities and are capable of significant, memorable actions (deeds)	**comic world:** a benevolent world temporarily disordered by confusions between appearance and reality, such as mistaken identity; characters are tested by the confusion, and order is restored	**naturalistic world:** a world in which the actions of characters are of limited significance and the rules of reality are objective and unalterable, strictly limiting what is possible	**farcical** or **absurd world:** a world in which characters are defined by ridiculous, exaggerated qualities and reality is replaced by mechanical, meaningless situations in which characters are trapped

Character

the people, animals, or other beings who perform or receive the action of a story

flat: marked by one dominant characteristic	**rounded:** having a complex set of characteristics
static: unchanging	**dynamic:** developing and growing
self-aware: acting with an understanding of his or her own motives and the consequences of his or her actions	**blind** or **fated:** acting with no understanding of his or her own motives or of the consequences of his or her actions

Plot

the narrated sequence of events in a work; the storyline, usually divided into an exposition (in which situation and characters are introduced), the rising action, the climax (or moment of greatest tension), the falling action, and the resolution

simple: telling of a single stream of events; each event affects the same set of characters	**complex:** telling of a number of streams of events, each involving a different set of characters (sets of characters may overlap)
dramatic: events unfold to build a maximum of tension or suspense, leading to a resolution	**episodic:** a series of loosely connected events occur, without building to a single, central climax or resolution
plot as driver: the question of "what happens next?" is intended to be the reader's primary interest in the work	**plot as vehicle:** the plot serves primarily to express a theme, display a character, or link together descriptions

Imagery

language used to suggest sensory experience, especially sensory experience linked by association to emotions and ideas

original: unique to the writer; distinctive	**conventional:** expected; patterned after previous work
sensual: devoted to recreating sensory experience	**metaphysical:** devoted to expressing abstract ideas or complicated analogies
effusive: pouring out; piled up	**patterned:** structured; controlled

Style

the distinctive features of a writer's choice of words and imagery, sentence length and structure, rhythm, and so on

elaborate: characterized by complex detail	**direct:** simple; to the point
sincere: attempting to convey ideas without drawing attention to the style of their presentation	**parodic:** drawing attention to style in order to mock a style that other writers' use seriously
straightforward: attempting to convey ideas directly	**ironic:** conveying ideas or attitudes by stating their opposites
conversational: resembling the style in which one friend might address another	**oracular:** suggesting that the writer is pronouncing deep truths without any particular concern that he or she be understood

Formatting Business Letters

Business letters follow one of several acceptable formats. In **block format** each part of the letter begins at the left margin. A double space is used between paragraphs. In **modified block format,** some parts of the letter are indented to the center of the page. No matter which format is used, all letters in business format have a heading, an inside address, a salutation, or greeting, a body, a closing, and a signature. These parts are shown and annotated on the model business letter below, formatted in modified block style.

Model Business Letter

In this letter, Yolanda Dodson uses modified block format to request information.

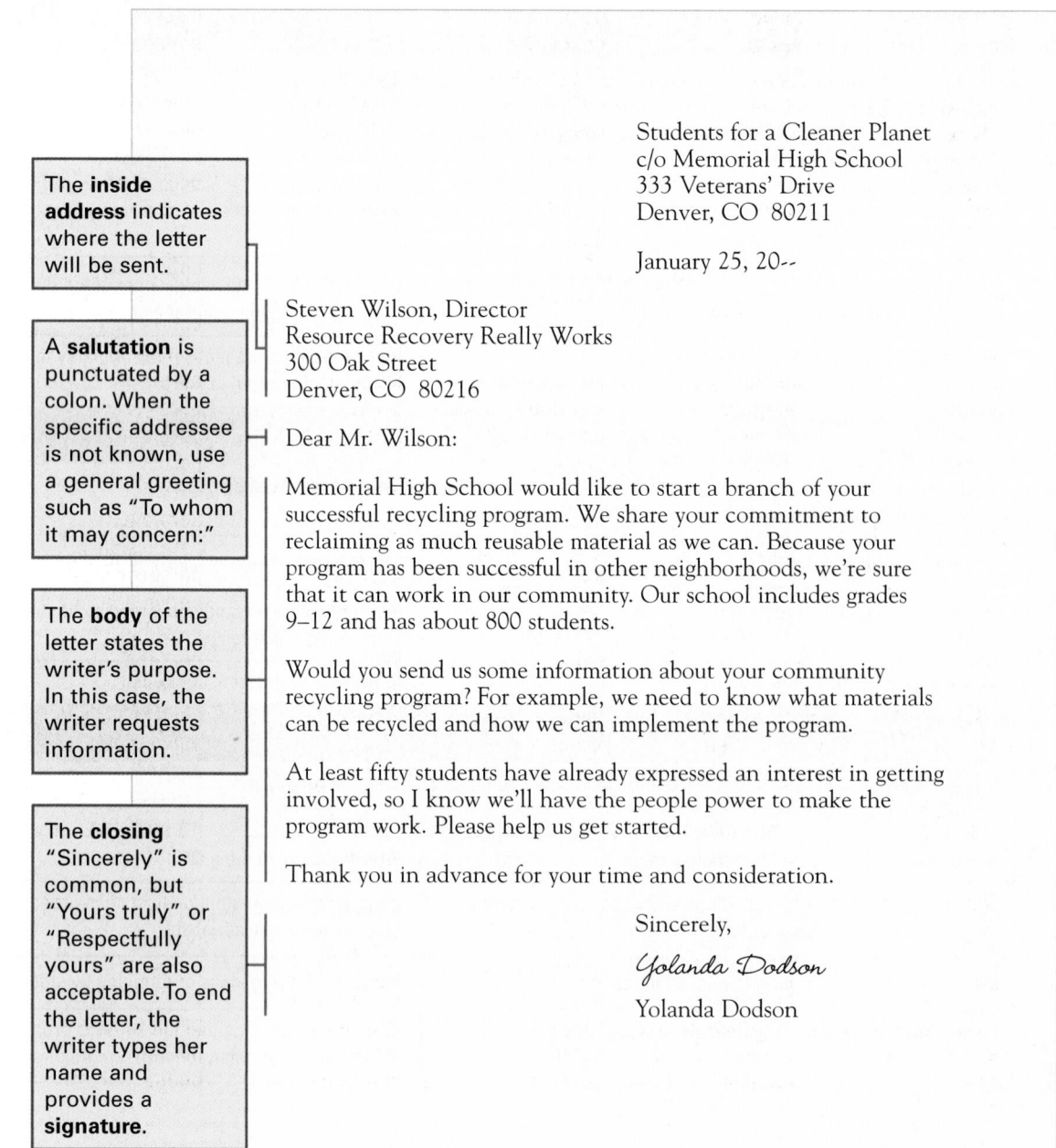

The **inside address** indicates where the letter will be sent.

A **salutation** is punctuated by a colon. When the specific addressee is not known, use a general greeting such as "To whom it may concern:"

The **body** of the letter states the writer's purpose. In this case, the writer requests information.

The **closing** "Sincerely" is common, but "Yours truly" or "Respectfully yours" are also acceptable. To end the letter, the writer types her name and provides a **signature.**

Students for a Cleaner Planet
c/o Memorial High School
333 Veterans' Drive
Denver, CO 80211

January 25, 20--

Steven Wilson, Director
Resource Recovery Really Works
300 Oak Street
Denver, CO 80216

Dear Mr. Wilson:

Memorial High School would like to start a branch of your successful recycling program. We share your commitment to reclaiming as much reusable material as we can. Because your program has been successful in other neighborhoods, we're sure that it can work in our community. Our school includes grades 9–12 and has about 800 students.

Would you send us some information about your community recycling program? For example, we need to know what materials can be recycled and how we can implement the program.

At least fifty students have already expressed an interest in getting involved, so I know we'll have the people power to make the program work. Please help us get started.

Thank you in advance for your time and consideration.

Sincerely,

Yolanda Dodson

Yolanda Dodson

Commonly Misspelled Words

The words on this page are ones that cause spelling problems for many people. As you review the list, check to see how many of the words give you trouble in your own writing.

abbreviate	bicycle	criticize	grammar	naturally	realize
absence	bookkeeper	cylinder	grievance	necessary	really
absolutely	boulevard	deceive	guarantee	negotiate	receipt
accelerate	brief	decision	guard	neighbor	recipe
accidentally	brilliant	defendant	guidance	neutral	recognize
accurate	bruise	definitely	handkerchief	nickel	recommend
ache	bulletin	delinquent	harass	niece	rehearse
achievement	buoy	dependent	height	ninety	relevant
acquaintance	bureau	descendant	humorous	noticeable	reminiscence
adequate	bury	description	hygiene	nuclear	renowned
advertisement	buses	desirable	immediately	nuisance	repetition
aerial	business	dessert	immigrant	obstacle	restaurant
aggravate	cafeteria	dining	independent	occasion	rhythm
agreeable	calendar	disappoint	individual	occurrence	ridiculous
aisle	campaign	disastrous	inflammable	omitted	sandwich
all right	canceled	discipline	interfere	opinion	satellite
aluminum	candidate	eighth	irritable	opportunity	schedule
amateur	captain	eligible	jewelry	optimistic	scissors
analysis	career	embarrass	judgment	outrageous	secretary
analyze	carriage	enthusiastic	knowledge	pamphlet	siege
ancient	cashier	entrepreneur	laboratory	parallel	sincerely
anecdote	category	envelope	lawyer	paralyze	solely
anniversary	ceiling	environment	legible	parentheses	sponsor
anonymous	cemetery	equipped	legislature	particularly	subtle
answer	census	equivalent	leisure	patience	superintendent
anxiety	certain	especially	liable	permanent	surveillance
apologize	characteristic	exaggerate	library	permissible	susceptible
appall	chauffeur	excel	license	perseverance	tariff
appearance	clothes	excellent	lieutenant	persistent	temperamental
appreciate	colonel	exercise	lightning	perspiration	theater
appropriate	column	existence	likable	persuade	threshold
architecture	commercial	extraordinary	liquefy	phenomenon	truly
argument	commitment	familiar	literature	physician	unmanageable
associate	committee	fascinating	maintenance	pneumonia	unwieldy
athletic	competitor	February	marriage	possession	usage
attendance	condemn	fiery	mathematics	prairie	usually
awkward	congratulate	financial	maximum	preferable	valuable
banquet	conscience	fluorescent	meanness	prejudice	various
bargain	conscious	foreign	mediocre	prerogative	vegetable
barrel	convenience	forfeit	mileage	privilege	voluntary
battery	cooperate	fourth	millionaire	probably	volunteer
beautiful	correspondence	fragile	minuscule	procedure	weight
beggar	counterfeit	gauge	miscellaneous	pronunciation	weird
beginning	courageous	genius	mischievous	psychology	whale
behavior	courteous	genuine	misspell	pursue	wield
benefit	criticism	government	mortgage	questionnaire	yield

Index of Authors and Titles
Page numbers in *italics* refer to biographical information.

Index of Skills

Literary Analysis

Reading Strategies

Grammar and Style

Writing
Writing Applications

Writing Strategies

Index of Features

Assessment Workshop

Closer Look, A

Connections

Listening and Speaking Workshops

Literature in Context

Reading Informational Materials

Writing Workshops

ACKNOWLEDGMENTS (CONTINUED)

Estate of Gwendolyn Brooks "The Explorer" from *Blacks by Gwendolyn Brooks,* published by The David Company, Chicago, IL. Copyright © 1987, renewed by Third World Press, Chicago, IL, 1991. Used by permission of The Estate of Gwendolyn Brooks.

Diana Chang "Most Satisfied by Snow" from *Most Satisfied by Snow* by Diana Chang. Copyright by Diana Chang. Used by permission of the author.

Sandra Dijkstra Literary Agency for Amy Tan "Mother Tongue" by Amy Tan. Copyright © 1990 by Amy Tan. First appeared in *Threepenny Review.* Reprinted by permission of the author and Sandra Dijkstra Literary Agency.

Doubleday, A division of Random House, Inc. "The Adamant" and "The Light Comes Brighter," copyright 1938 by Theodore Roethke, from *The Collected Poems of Theodore Roethke* by Theodore Roethke. From *Roots* by Alex Haley, copyright © 1976 by Alex Haley. Used by permission of Doubleday, a division of Random House, Inc.

Rita Dove Rita Dove, "For the Love of Books," first published as part of the *Introduction to Selected Poems,* Pantheon Books/Vintage Books, © 1993 by Rita Dove.

Farrar, Straus & Giroux, Inc. "Coyote v. Acme" from *Coyote V. Acme* by Ian Frazier. Copyright © 1996 by Ian Frazier. "The Death of the Ball Turret Gunner" and "Losses" from *The Complete Poems* by Randall Jarrell. Copyright © 1969 by Mrs. Randall Jarrell. "Hawthorne" from *The Union Dead* by Robert Lowell. Copyright © 1959 by Robert Lowell. Copyright renewed © 1987 by Harriot Lowell, Caroline Lowell, and Sheridan Lowell. "The First Seven Years" from *The Magic Barrel* by Bernard Malamud. Copyright © 1950, 1958 and copyright renewed © 1977, 1986 by Bernard Malamud. Excerpt from *The Right Stuff* by Tom Wolfe. Copyright © 1979 by Tom Wolfe. From "Homage to Mistress Bradstreet" by John Berryman from *Homage to Mistress Bradstreet and Other Poems.* Copyright © 1948, 1956, 1958, 1959, 1967, 1968 by John Berryman.

Fulcrum Publishing "The Earth on Turtle's Back" from *Keepers of the Earth: Native American Stories and Environmental Activities for Children,* by Michael J. Caduto and Joseph Bruchac (© 1988) Fulcrum Publishing, 350 Indiana St., #350, Golden, CO 80401, 800-992-2908. Used by permission.

Graywolf Press "Traveling through the Dark" copyright 1962, 1998 by the Estate of William Stafford. Reprinted from *The Way It Is: New and Selected Poems* with the permission of Graywolf Press, Saint Paul, Minnesota.

Harcourt Brace & Company "A Worn Path" from A *Curtain of Green and Other Stories,* copyright 1941 and renewed 1969 by Eudora Welty. "The Jilting of Granny Weatherall" from *Flowering Judas And Other Stories,* copyright 1930 and renewed 1958 by Katherine Anne Porter. "Chicago" and "Grass" from *Chicago Poems* by Carl Sandburg, copyright 1916 by Holt, Rinehart and Winston, Inc.; renewed 1944 by Carl Sandburg. "The Life You Save May Be Your Own" from *A Good Man Is Hard To Find And Other Stories,* copyright © 1953 by Flannery O'Connor and renewed 1981 by Regina O'Connor. This material may not be reproduced in any form or by any means without the prior written permission of the publisher. "Everyday Use" from *In Love & Trouble: Stories of Black Women,* copyright © 1973 by Alice Walker. Reprinted by permission of Harcourt Brace & Company.

Joy Harjo "Suspended" by Joy Harjo from *In Short: A Collection of Brief Creative Nonfiction,* edited by Judith Kitchen and Mary Paumier Jones. Copyright © 1996. Reprinted by permission of the author.

HarperCollins Publishers, Inc. "Bidwell Ghost" from *Baptism of Desire* by Louise Erdrich. Copyright © 1990 by Louise Erdrich. "Seeing" from *Pilgrim at Tinker Creek* by Annie Dillard. Copyright © 1974 by Annie Dillard. Used by permission of HarperCollins Publishers, Inc. "Where Is Here" taken from *Where Is Here?* by Joyce Carol Oates. Copyright © 1992 by The Ontario Review, Inc. First published by The Ecco Press in 1992. From *Dust Tracks On a Road* by Zora Neale Hurston. Copyright 1942 by Zora Neale Hurston. Copyright renewed 1970 by John C. Hurston. Used by permission.

HarperCollins Publishers, Inc. and Faber & Faber Ltd. "Mirror" from *Crossing the Water* by Sylvia Plath. Copyright © 1963 by Ted Hughes. Originally appeared in *The New Yorker.* Used by permission of HarperCollins Publishers, Inc.

HarperTorch, An imprint of HarperCollins Publishers, Inc. "Old-Time Cowboys in the Modern World" by John Graves from *A JOHN GRAVES READER.*

John Bret-Harte "The Outcasts of Poker Flat" by Bret Harte from *SELECTED STORIES OF BRET HARTE.*

Harvard University Press "There's a certain Slant of light" (#258), "Because I could not stop for Death" (#712), "There is a solitude of space" (#1695), "My life closed twice before its close—" (#1732), "I heard a Fly buzz—when I died" (#465), and "The Soul selects her own Society" (#303) by Emily Dickinson from *The Poems of Emily Dickinson,* Thomas H. Johnson, ed., Cambridge, Mass.: The Belknap Press of Harvard University Press, Copyright (c) 1951, 1955, 1979 by the Presidents and Fellows of Harvard College. Reprinted by permission of the publishers and the Trustees of Amherst College.

Henry Holt and Company, Inc. "Acquainted with the Night" and "The Gift Outright" from *The Poetry of Robert Frost* edited by Edward Connery Latham, Copyright 1928, © 1969 by Henry Holt and Co., © 1970 by Lesley Frost Ballantine, © 1942, 1956 by Robert Frost. Reprinted by permission of Henry Holt and Company, LLC. "Out, Out—" and "Mending Wall" from *The Poetry of Robert Frost* edited by Edward Connery Lathem. Copyright 1944, © 1958 by Robert Frost, © 1967 by Lesley Frost Ballantine, Copyright 1916, 1930, 1939, © 1969 by Henry Holt and Company, Inc.

Houghton Mifflin Company "Ars Poetica" by Archibald MacLeish from *NEW AND COLLECTED POEMS,* 1917–1982. Copyright © 1985 by the Estate of Archibald MacLeish. Reprinted by permission of Houghton Mifflin Company. All rights reserved.

Houghton Mifflin Company and The Estate of Carson McCullers From *The Mortgaged Heart* by Carson McCullers. Copyright 1940, 1941, 1942, 1945, 1948, 1949, 1953, © 1956, 1959, 1963, 1971 by Floria V. Lasky, Executrix of The Estate of Carson McCullers. Used by permission of Houghton Mifflin Company and The Estate of Carson McCullers.

International Creative Management, Inc. "Ambush" by Tim O'Brien from THE THINGS THEY CARRIED.

The Estate of Martin Luther King, Jr., c/o Writer's House Inc. "Letter from Birmingham City Jail " ("Why We Can't Wait") by Martin Luther King, Jr. Reprinted by arrangement with The Heirs to the Estate of Martin Luther King, Jr. c/o Writers House as agent for the proprietor. Copyright 1963 Martin Luther King, Jr., renewed 1991 by Coretta Scott King.

Alfred A. Knopf, Inc., a division of Random House, Inc. "The Brown Chest" from *The Afterlife: and Other Stories* by John Updike, copyright © 1994 by John Updike. "I, Too," "Refugee in America," "Dream Variations," "The Negro Speaks of Rivers," and "Ardella" from *The Collected Poems of Langston Hughes* by Langston Hughes, copyright © 1994 by The Estate of Langston Hughes. "A Noiseless Flash" from *Hiroshima* by John Hersey, copyright 1946 and renewed 1974 by John Hersey. "Ancedote of the Jar" from *The Collected Poems of Wallace Stevens* by Wallace Stevens, copyright 1954 by Wallace Stevens. From *The Woman Warrior* by Maxine Hong Kingston, copyright © 1975, 1976 by Maxine Hong Kingston. From *Of Plymouth Plantation 1620–1647* by William Bradford, edited by Samuel Eliot Morison. Copyright 1952 by Samuel Eliot Morison and renewed 1980 by Emily M. Beck. Used by permission of Alfred A. Knopf, a division of Random House, Inc.

Latin American Literary Review Press, "Freeway 280" by Lorna Dee Cervantes from *Freeway 280*. Copyright by Latin American Literary Review, Volume V, Number 10. Used by permission.

Liveright Publishing Corporation, a subsidiary of W. W. Norton & Company, Inc. "Frederick Douglass." Copyright © 1966 by Robert Hayden, from *Collected Poems of Robert Hayden* by Robert Hayden, edited by Frederick Glaysher. "Storm Ending," from *Cane* by Jean Toomer. Copyright 1923 by Boni & Liveright, renewed 1951 by Jean Toomer. "Runagate Runagate." Copyright © 1966 by Robert Hayden, from *Collected Poems of Robert Hayden* by Robert Hayden, edited by Frederick Glaysher. "anyone lived in a pretty how town." Copyright 1940, © 1968, 1991 by the Trustees for the E.E. Cummings Trust, "old age sticks." Copyright © 1958, 1986, 1991 by the Trustees for the E.E. Cummings Trust, from *COMPLETE POEMS: 1904–1962* by E.E. Cummings, edited by Fumage. Used by permission of Liveright Publishing Corporation.

Louisiana State University Press, "Dunbar" by Anne Spencer from *Time's Unfading Garden: Anne Spencer's Life and Poetry,* edited by J. Lee Greene. Copyright © 1977 by Lousiana State University Press. Reprinted by permission of Louisiana State University Press.

Archives of Claude McKay "The Tropics in New York" from *The Poems of Claude McKay* by Claude McKay, Harcourt Brace, publisher, copyright © 1981.

Elaine Markson Literary Agency, Inc. "Anxiety" from *Later the Same Day* by Grace Paley (Farrar, Straus and Giroux, 1985). Copyright © 1985 by Grace Paley. All rights reserved.

Ellen C. Masters, c/o Hillary Masters, POA "Richard Bone" and "Lucinda Matlock" from *Spoon River Anthology* by Edgar Lee Masters, published by Macmillan Co. Used by permission.

N. Scott Momaday From *The Names: A Memoir by N. Scott Momaday* published by Harper & Row Publishers, Inc. Copyright © 1976 by N. Scott Momaday. Reprinted by permission of the author.

William Morris Agency, Inc. "Gold Glade" by Robert Penn Warren from *New and Selected Poems*. Copyright © 1985 by Robert Penn Warren. Reprinted by permission of William Morris Agency, Inc., on behalf of the author.

New Directions Publishing Corporation "Heat" and "Pear Tree" by H. Doolittle, *Collected Poems, 1912–1944*. Copyright © 1982 by the Estate of Hilda Doolittle. "In a Station of the Metro" and "The River-Merchant's Wife: A Letter" by Ezra Pound, from *Personae*. Copyright © 1926 by Ezra Pound. "The Great Figure," "The Red Wheelbar-row," and "This is Just to Say" by William Carlos Williams, from *Collected Poems Volume 1: 1909–1939*. Copyright 1938 by New Directions Publishing Corporation. Used by permission of New Directions Publishing Corporation. Excerpts form "The Imagist Manifesto" from *Literary Essays of Ezra Pound,* edited with an introduction by T.S. Eliot. Copyright 1918, 1920, 1935 by Ezra Pound.

The New York Times "Onomatopoeia" by William Safire from *You Could Look It Up*. Copyright © 1988 by The Cobbett Corporation. Originally appeared in *The New York Times*. Reprinted by permission.

W. W. Norton & Company, Inc. "Garbage" by Ammons A.R. from *Garbage*. Copyright © 1993 by A.R. Ammons. From "Civil Disobedi-ence" reprinted from *Walden and Civil Disobedience, A Norton Critical Edition,* by Henry David Thoreau, edited by Owen Thomas. Copyright ©1966 by W. W. Norton & Company, Inc. "Who Burns for the Perfection of Paper" from *City of Coughing and Dead Radiators* by Martin Espada. Copyright © 1993 by Martin Espada. Used by permission of W. W. Norton & Company, Inc.

W. W. Norton & Company, Inc. and Adrienne Rich "In a Class-room" from *Time's Power: Poems 1985–1988* by Adrienne Rich. Copyright © 1989 by Adrienne Rich. All rights reserved. Used by permission.

Harold Ober Associates, Inc. "The Corn Planting" from *Sherwood Anderson Short Stories,* edited by Maxwell Geismar. © 1962 by Eleanor Anderson. "A Black Man Talks of Reaping" by Arna Bon-temps. Copyright © 1963 by Arna Bontemps. Reprinted by permission of Harold Ober Associates Incorporated.

Simon J. Ortiz "Hunger in New York City" from *Woven Stone* by Simon J. Ortiz. Published by University of Arizona Press, 1992 © 1976 by Simon J. Ortiz. Used by permission of Simon J. Ortiz.

Penguin Books Ltd. "Melting Snow" by Kobayashi Issa (18 lines) from THE PENGUIN BOOK OF JAPANESE VERSE translated by Geoffrey Bownas and Anthony Thwaite (Penguin Books, 1964) Trans-lation copyright © Geoffrey Bownas and Anthony Thwaite, 1964.

Plimoth Plantation Excerpt from Plimoth Plantation Web site (www.plimoth.org).

Princeton University Press From *Walden* by Henry David Thoreau. Copyright © 1971 by Princeton University Press. Used by permission of Princeton University Press.

Random House, Inc. "The Unknown Citizen," copyright 1940 & renewed 1968 by W.H. Auden, from *W.H. Auden: Collected Poems.*

"The Writer in the Family" from *Lives of the Poets* by E. L. Doctorow, copyright © 1984 by E. L. Doctorow. "Cats" from *Living Out Loud* by Anna Quindlen, copyright © 1987 by Anna Quindlen. "Race at Morning" from *Big Woods* by William Faulkner, copyright © 1955 by The Curtis Publishing Company. Used by permission of Random House, Inc.

Russell & Volkening, Inc. "Average Waves in Unprotected Waters" by Anne Tyler. Copyright © 1977 by Anne Tyler. This story originally appeared in *The New Yorker*, February 28th, 1977. Reproduced by permission of Russell & Volkening as agents for the author.

Estate of Ricardo Sanchez "i yearn" by Ricardo Sanchez. Copyright © 1975 by Ricardo Sanchez. Reprinted by permission of the Estate of Ricardo Sanchez.

Scribner, a division of Simon & Schuster, Inc. "The Far and the Near" from *Death to Morning* by Thomas Wolfe. Copyright © 1935 by Charles Scribner's Sons; copyright renewed © 1963 by Paul Gitlin. "In Another Country" from *Men Without Women* by Ernest Hemingway. Copyright 1927 by Charles Scribner's Sons. Copyright renewed 1955 by Ernest Hemingway. Reprinted with the permission of Scribner, a division of Simon & Schuster.

Scribner, a division of Simon & Schuster and The Literary Estate of Marianne Moore "Poetry" from *The Collected Poems of Marianne Moore* by Marianne Moore. Copyright © 1935 by Marianne Moore, copyright renewed © 1963 by Marianne Moore and T.S. Eliot. Used by permission of Scribner, a division of Simon & Schuster, Inc., and The Literary Estate of Marianne Moore.

Scribner, a division of Simon & Schuster and Melanie Jackson Agency, LLC "Gulf War Journal from a Woman at War" from *A Woman at War* by Molly Moore. Copyright © 1993 by Molly Moore. Used by permission of Scribner, a division of Simon & Schuster and Melanie Jackson Agency, LLC.

Simon & Schuster, Inc. from *Lonesome Dove* by Larry McMurtry. Copyright © 1985 by Larry McMurtry. Used by permission of Simon & Schuster.

Sterling Lord Literistic, Inc. "The Crisis, Number 1" by Thomas Paine from CITIZEN TOM PAINE. Copyright by Howard Fast. Used by permission of Sterling Lord Literistic, Inc.

Estate of William Stafford "Traveling Through the Dark" from *Stories That Could Be True: New and Collected Poems* by William Stafford. Copyright © 1960 by William Stafford. Used by permission.

Charles Scribner's Sons, a division of Simon & Schuster, Inc. "Winter Dreams" by F. Scott Fitzgerald, from *All The Sad Young Men*. Copyright 1922 by Frances Scott Fitzgerald Lanahan; copyright renewed 1950. "Richard Cory" from *The Children of the Night* by Edwin Arlington Robinson, published by Charles Scribner's Sons.

Syracuse University Press "The Iroquois Constitution" from *Parker on the Iroquois: Iroquois Uses of Maize and Other Food Plants; The Code of Handsome Lake; The Seneca Prophet; The Constitution of the Five Nations* by Arthur C. Parker, edited by William N. Fenton (Syracuse University Press, Syracuse, NY, 1981). Used by permission.

Rosemary Thurber and the Barbara Hogenson Agency, Inc. "The Night the Ghost Got In" copyright 1933, © 1961 by James Thurber. From *My Life and Hard Times*, published by Harper & Row. Reprinted by arrangement with Rosemary Thurber and the Barbara Hogenson Agency. All rights reserved.

University of Nebraska Press, Reprinted from the *Journals of the Lewis and Clark Expedition, volume 5*, edited by Gary E. Moulton by permission of the University of Nebraska Press. Copyright © 1988 by the University of Nebraska Press. Used by permission.

The University of North Carolina Press "To His Excellency, General Washington" and lines from "An Hymn to the Evening" from *The Poems of Phillis Wheatley* edited and with an introduction by Julian D. Mason, Jr. Copyright © 1966 by The University of North Carolina Press, renewed 1989. Used by permission of the publisher.

University of Texas Press and the author "El Corrido de Gregorio Cortez" from *With His Pistol In His Hand: A Border Ballad And Its Hero* by Americo Paredes, Copyright © 1958, renewed 1986. By permission of the author and the University of Texas Press.

USA Today and Robert N. Wiener Pro bono work headlined "Lawyers leave poor behind" by Robert N. Wiener, from *USA Today* (September 25, 2000). Copyright © 2000 by *USA Today*. Used by permission.

Viking Penguin, Inc., a division of Penguin Putnam, Inc. From "On Social Plays," copyright © 1955, 1978 by Arthur Miller, from *The Theater Essays of Arthur Miller* by Arthur Miller, edited by Robert A. Martin. From *The Crucible* by Arthur Miller, copyright 1952, 1953, 1954, renewed © 1980, 1981, 1982 by Arthur Miller. "The Turtle (Chapter 3)" from *The Grapes of Wrath* by John Steinbeck, copyright 1939, renewed © 1967 by John Steinbeck. Used by permission of Viking Penguin, a division of Penguin Putnam Inc.

Wesleyan University Press "For My Children" by Colleen McElroy from *What Madness Brought Me Here*. "Camouflaging the Chimera" by Yusef Komunyakaa from *Neon Vernacular*. "What For" by Garrett Kaoru Hongo from *Yellow Light*. Used by permission of Wesleyan University Press.

Joel White, for the Estate of E.B. White From "Here Is New York" by E.B. White from *Essays of E.B. White*.

Darryl Babe Wilson "Diamond Island: Alcatraz" by Darryl Babe Wilson. Copyright © 1991 by Darryl Babe Wilson. Reprinted by permission of the author.

Yale University Press From *Mary Chesnut's Civil War*, edited by C. Vann Woodward. Copyright © 1981 by C. Vann Woodward, Sally Bland Metts, Barbara G. Carpenter, Sally Bland Johnson, and Katherine W. Herbert. All rights reserved. Reproduced by permission of the publisher, Yale University Press.

Note: Every effort has been made to locate the copyright owner of material reprinted in this book. Omissions brought to our attention will be corrected in subsequent editions.

Mr. and Mrs. Robert Gill through the Patrons of Art and Music (1981.89); **300** Tammy Rice/The Learning Source; **302** ©Visuals Unlimited; **304** Thomas Victor; **305** *Mysterious Night*, ca. 1895, watercolor on board, 30-1/2 x 21-1/2 inches, Morris Museum of Art, Augusta, GA; **306** CORBIS-Bettmann; **309** "I at length . . . ," Edgar Allen Poe's Tales of Mystery and Imagination (London: George G. Harrap, 1935), Arthur Rackham, Print Collection, Miriam and Ira D. Wallach Division of Art, Prints and Photographs, The New York Public Library; Astor, Lenox and Tilden Foundations; **312** Ron Watts/CORBIS; **316** Steve Mohlenkamp/Index Stock Photography, Inc.; **323** ©2000 The Munch Museum/The Munch-Ellingsen Group/ Artists Rights Society (ARS), New York; **328** *The Raven*, 1845, Edmund Dulac, The Granger Collection, New York; **334** *Nathaniel Hawthorne* (detail), 1862, Emanuel Gottlieb Leutze, The National Portrait Gallery, Smithsonian Institution, Washington, D.C./Art Resource, New York; **337** New York State Historical Association, Cooperstown, New York; **340** Ron Watts/CORBIS; **344** *Cemetery*, Peter McIntyre, Courtesy of the artist; **352** The Granger Collection, New York; **356** *Captain Ahab on the deck of the Pequod*, 1930, pen and ink drawing, The Granger Collection, New York; **357** Stock Newport, Inc.; **359** CORBIS; **361** *Moby-Dick*, 1930, pen and ink drawing, The Granger Collection, New York; **362** The Whaling Museum; **364** *Moby-Dick*, 1930, pen and ink drawing, The Granger Collection, New York; **369** Culver Pictures, Inc.; **375** Phil Schermeister/CORBIS; **377**, **380** Digital Imagery ©Copyright 2001 PhotoDisc, Inc.; **382** Alex Oliveira/Globe Photos; **383** *Early Morning at Cold Spring*, 1850, oil on canvas, 60 x 48" Asher B. Durand, Collection of the Montclair Art Museum, Montclair, New Jersey; **384** ©Lee Snider; Lee Snider/CORBIS; **385** (b.) Courtesy of the Library of Congress; (t.) Hulton-Deutsch Collection/CORBIS; **386** *Ralph Waldo Emerson* (detail), Frederick Gutekunst/The National Portrait Gallery, Smithsonian Institution, Washington, D.C./Art Resource, NY; **389** *Sunset*, Frederick Edwin Church, Munson-Williams-Proctor Institute Museum of Art, Utica, New York; **393** Leonard Harris/Stock, Boston; **394** Frank Whitney/The Image Bank; **400** The Granger Collection, New York; **402** Owen Franken/PNI; **406** Burstein Collection/ CORBIS; **408** ©The Stock Market/Dan McCoy; **410** ©Lee Snider; Lee Snider/CORBIS; **417** *Walden Pond Revisited*, 1942, N.C. Wyeth, tempera, possibly mixed with other media on panel, 42 x 48" Collection of the Brandywine River Museum, Bequest of Miss Carolyn Wyeth; **418** The Granger Collection, New York; **420** *Waiting Outside No. 12*, Anonymous, Crane Kalman Gallery; **422** *Room With a Balcony*, Adolph von Menzel, Staatliche Museen Preubischer Kulturbesitz, Nationgalerie, Berlin; **426** Frederic Edwin Church, American, 1826–1900. *Twilight in the Wilderness*, 1860s. Oil on canvas, 101.6 x 162.6 cm. © The Cleveland Museum of Art, 1997, Mr. and Mrs. William H. Marlett Fund, 1965.233; **432** The Granger Collection, New York; **440** *The Lawrence Tree*, 1929, Georgia O'Keeffe, Wadsworth Atheneum, Hartford, The Ella Gallup Sumner and Mary Catlin Sumner Collection, ©1998 The Georgia O'Keeffe Foundation/Artists Rights Society (ARS), New York; **443** *The Reaper*, c.1881, Louis C. Tiffany, oil on canvas, National Academy of Design, New York City; **448–449** *Nobody Around Here Calls Me Citizen*, 1943, Robert Gwathmey, oil on canvas, H. 14-1/4" x W. 17" Collection Frederick R. Weisman Art Museum at the University of Minnesota, Minneapolis, Bequest of Hudson Walker from the Ione and Hudson Walker Collection. ©Estate of Robert Gwathmey/Licensed by VAGA, New York, NY; **449** *Langston Hughes* (detail), c.1925, Winold Reiss, The National Portrait Gallery, Smithsonian Institution, Washington, D.C./Art Resource, New York; **450** *Mandolin*, Rosa Ibarra, Courtesy of the artist; **451** Photo by M&A Productions; **454** Digital Imagery ©Copyright 2001 PhotoDisc, Inc.; **460–461** *The Fall of Richmond*, Currier & Ives, SuperStock; **461** (t.) *Portrait of Abraham Lincoln* (detail), William Willard, The National Portrait Gallery, Smithsonian Institution, Washington, D.C./Art Resource, New York, (b.) The Granger Collection, New York; **462** (all) The Granger Collection, New York; **463** (1886), (1903), (1908) The Granger Collection, New York, (1881) CORBIS-Bettmann; **464** CORBIS-Bettmann; **465** (both) Courtesy of the Library of Congress; **467** Nebraska State Historical Society; **471** *Six O'Clock, Winter*, 1912, John Sloan, The Phillips Collection; **472** *Samuel Longhorne Clemens (Mark Twain)* (detail), 1935, Frank Edwin Larson, The National Portrait Gallery, Smithsonian Institution, Washington, D.C./Art Resource, New York; **473** *Fight for the Standard*, oil on canvas, H 26 3/4 inches, W 21 1/2 inches, Wadsworth Atheneum, Hartford. The Ella Gallup Sumner and Mary Catlin Sumner Collection Fund; **474** (l.) CORBIS-Bettmann, (r.) The Granger Collection, New York; **476** Courtesy of the Library of Congress; **479** Courtesy National Archives; **480** Museum of the Confederacy, Richmond, Virginia; **481** *Young Soldier: Separate Study of a Soldier Giving Water to a Wounded Companion* (detail), 1861, Winslow Homer, Oil, gouache, black crayon on canvas, 36 x 17.5 cm., United States, 1836–1910, Cooper-Hewitt, National Museum of Design, Smithsonian Institution, Gift of Charles Savage Homer, Jr., 1912-12-110, Photo by Ken Pelka, Courtesy of Art Resource, New York; **488** Courtesy of the Library of Congress; **494** *Frederick Douglass* (detail), c. 1844, Attributed to Elisha Hammond, The National Portrait Gallery, Smithsonian Institution, Washington, D.C./Art Resource, New York; **496** *The Chimney*

Corner, 1863, Eastman Johnson, oil on cardboard, 15 1/2 x 13 in., Munson-Williams-Proctor Institute Museum of Art, Utica, New York; Gift of Edmund G. Munson, Jr.; **498** *A Home on the Mississippi*, 1871, Currier & Ives, The Museum of the City of New York, Harry T. Peters Collection; **500** Ron Watts/CORBIS; **506** CORBIS-Bettmann; **508** Superstock; **509** The Kobal Collection; **520** (l.) *Portrait of Abraham Lincoln* (detail), William Willard, The National Portrait Gallery, Smithsonian Institution, Washington, D.C./Art Resource, New York, (r.) *Robert E. Lee* (detail), 1864–1865, Edward Caledon Bruce, The National Portrait Gallery, Smithsonian Institution, Washington, D.C./Art Resource, New York; **523** CORBIS; **525** Buddy Mays/ CORBIS; **532** Courtesy of the Library of Congress; **533** *Newspapers in the Trenches '64*, William Ludwell Sheppard, Museum of the Confederacy, Richmond, Virginia, Photography by Katherine Wetzel; **534** Courtesy of the Library of Congress; **537** Courtesy of the Library of Congress; **539** Ron Watts/CORBIS; **542** Andre Jenny/Focus Group/PictureQuest; **544**, **546** The Granger Collection, New York; **547** Bettmann/CORBIS; **552** Sygma; **555** Chip Hires/Liaison International; **556** D. Hudson/ Sygma; **558** The Washington Post; **559** *The Old Stage Coach of the Plains*, 1901, Frederic Remington, oil on canvas, Amon Carter Museum, Forth Worth; **560** (b.) Corel Professional Photos CD-ROM™, (t.) Courtesy National Archives; **561** ©Bettmann/ CORBIS; **562** *Samuel Longhorne Clemens (Mark Twain)* (detail), 1935, Frank Edwin Larson, The National Portrait Gallery, Smithsonian Institution, Washington, D.C./Art Resource, New York; **564** *Paddle Steamboat* Mississippi, Shelburne Museum, Shelburne, Vermont, Photo by Ken Burris; **566** The Historic New Orleans Collection, Museum/Research Center; **569** *Mark Twain (Samuel L. Clemens) Riding the Celebrated Jumping Frog*—an English caricature, 1872, Frederic Waddy, The Granger Collection, New York; **571** The Granger Collection, New York; **572** ©Craig K. Lorenz/Photo Researchers, Inc.; **578** The Granger Collection, New York; **580** *Edge of Town*, Charles Ephraim Burchfield, The Nelson-Atkins Museum of Art, Kansas City, Missouri; **582** Corel Professional Photos CD-ROM™; **584** Ron Watts/CORBIS; **586** Esbin/Anderson/Omni-Photo Communications, Inc.; **594** *Chief Joseph* (detail), 1878, Cyrenius Hall, National Portrait Gallery, Smithsonian Institution, Washington, D.C./Art Resource, New York; **596** Kansas State Historical Society; **599** Ron Watts/ CORBIS; **600** Kansas State Historical Society; **602** National Museum of American History, Smithsonian Institution; **606** CORBIS-Bettmann; **608** Wayne Lynch/DRK Photo; **611**, **614** Corel Professional Photos CD-ROM™; **617** Annie Griffiths/DRK Photo; **618–619** CORBIS; **626** Corel Professional Photos CD-ROM™; **628** *Open Range*, 1942, Maynard Dixon, oil on canvas, 34 1/2 x 39" Museum of Western Art, Denver. #36.79. Bernard O. Milmoe, Photographer.; **630** AP/Wide World Photos; **631** *Channel to the Mills*, 1913, Edwin M. Dawes, oil on canvas, 51 x 39 1/2 in. Minneapolis Institute of Arts, anonymous gift; **632** The Granger Collection, New York; **635** *Afternoon in Piedmont (Elsie at the Window)*, c. 1911, Xavier Martínez, Collection of The Oakland Museum of California, Gift of Dr. William S. Porter; **636** Corel Professional Photos CD-ROM™; **642** ©Archive Photos; **644** *Memories*, 1885–86, William Merritt Chase, oil on canvas, Munson-Williams-Proctor Institute Museum of Art, Utica, New York; **648** Digital Imagery ©Copyright 2001 PhotoDisc, Inc.; **650** Bettmann/CORBIS; **656** The Granger Collection, New York; **658** Stock Montage, Inc.; **664** (l.) *Edwin Arlington Robinson* (detail), 1933, Thomas Richard Hood, The National Portrait Gallery, Smithsonian Institution, Washington, D.C./Art Resource, New York, (r.) *Edgar Lee Masters* (detail), 1946, Francis J. Quirk, The National Portrait Gallery, Smithsonian Institution, Washington, D.C./Art Resource, New York; **666** Horst Oesterwinter/International Stock Photography, Ltd.; **668** *The Thinker (Portrait of Louis N. Kenton, 1900)*, Thomas Eakins, The Metropolitan Museum of Art, Kennedy Fund, 1917, Copyright © 1967, 1984 by The Metropolitan Museum of Art; **670** Joel Greenstein/Omni-Photo Communications, Inc.; **674** CORBIS-Bettmann; **676** George Schreiber (1904–1977), *From Arkansas*, 1939, oil on canvas, Sheldon Swope Art Museum, Terre Haute, Indiana; **680** Robbie Jack/CORBIS; **682** The Granger Collection, New York; **688** Tim Davis/Photo Researchers, Inc.; **690** ©Julie Habel/CORBIS; **691** John Barrett/Globe Photos; **694** ©The Stock Market/José L. Peláez; **702–703** Edward Hopper, American, 1882–1967, *Nighthawks*, oil on canvas, 1942, 84.1 x 152.4 cm, Friends of American Art Collection, 1942.51, ©2000 The Art Institute of Chicago. All Rights Reserved; **704** (1915) CORBIS-Bettmann, (1919) National Archives, (1920) Bettmann/CORBIS, (1929) The Granger Collection, New York; **705** (1931) *The Persistence of Memory*, 1931, Salvador Dali, The Museum of Modern Art, New York. Given anonymously. Photograph © 2000 The Museum of Modern Art, New York, (1939) SuperStock, (1941) The Granger Collection, New York, (1945) Alfred Eisenstaedt, Life Magazine © Time Warner; **706** Culver Pictures, Inc.; **707** Museum of Connecticut History; **708** Culver Pictures, Inc.; **710** Courtesy of the Library of Congress; **712** Photographs and Prints Division, Schomburg Center for Research in Black Culture, The New York Public Library, Astor, Lenox and Tilden Foundations; **714** Historical Pictures Collection/Stock Montage, Inc.; **715** *No Place to Go*, 1935, Maynard Dixon, Oil on canvas, 25 x 30 inches. The Herald Clark Memorial Collection, Courtesy of Brigham Young University Museum of Fine Arts. All

Staff Credits

The people who made up the *Prentice Hall Literature: Timeless Voices, Timeless Themes* team—representing design services, editorial, editorial services, market research, marketing services, media resources, online services & multimedia development, production services, project office, and publishing processes—are listed below. Bold type denotes the core team members.

Susan Andariese, Rosalyn Arcilla, Laura Jane Bird, Betsy Bostwick, **Anne M. Bray,** Evonne Burgess, **Louise B. Capuano, Pam Cardiff,** Megan Chill, Ed Cordero. Laura Dershewitz, Phillip Fried, **Elaine Goldman,** Barbara Goodchild, Barbara Grant, **Rebecca Z. Graziano, Doreen Graizzaro,** Dennis Higbee, **Leanne Korszoloski,** Ellen Lees, David Liston, **Mary Luthi, George Lychock,** Gregory Lynch, Sue Lyons, **William McAllister,** Frances Medico, Gail Meyer, Jessica S. Paladini, Wendy Perri, Carolyn Carty Sapontzis, **Melissa Shustyk, Annette Simmons, Alicia Solis,** Robin Sullivan, Cynthia Sosland Summers, Lois Teesdale, **Elizabeth Torjussen, Doug Utigard,** Bernadette Walsh, Helen Young

Additional Credits

Gregory Abrom, Robert Aleman, Diane Alimena, Michele Angelucci, Gabriella Apolito, Penny Baker, Sharyn Banks, Anthony Barone, Barbara Blecher, Helen Byers, Rui Camarinha, Lorelee J. Campbell, John Carle, Cynthia Clampitt, Jaime L. Cohen, Martha Conway, Dina Curro, Nancy Dredge, Johanna Ehrmann, Josie K. Fixler, Steve Frankel, Kathy Gavilanes, Allen Gold, Michael E. Goodman, Diana Hahn, Kerry L. Harrigan, Jacki Hasko, Evan Holstrom, Beth Hyslip, Helen Issackedes, Cathy Johnson, Susan Karpin, Raegan Keida, Stephanie Kota, Mary Sue Langan, Elizabeth Letizia, Christine Mann, Vickie Menanteaux, Kathleen Mercandetti, Art Mkrtchyan, Karyl Murray, Kenneth Myett, Stefano Nese, Kim Ortell, Lissette Quinones, Erin Rehill-Seker, Patricia Rodriguez, Mildred Schulte, Adam Sherman, Mary Siener, Jan K. Singh, Diane Smith, Barbara Stufflebeem, Louis Suffredini, Lois Tatarian, Tom Thompkins, Lisa Valente, Ryan Vaarsi, Linda Westerhoff, Jeff Zoda

Prentice Hall gratefully acknowledges the following teachers who provided student models for consideration in the program.

Kate Anders, Suzanne Arkfeld, Elizabeth Bailey, Bill Brown, Diane Cappillo, Mary Chapman, Deedee Chumley, Terry Day, Cheryl Devoe, Dan Diercks, Ellen Eberly, Nancy Fahner, Terri Fields, Patty Foster, Joanne Giardino, Julie Gold, Christopher Guarraia, Dianne Hammond, Jo Higgins, Pauline Hodges, Gaye Ingram, Charlotte Jefferies, Bill Jones, Ken Kaiser, Linda Kramer, Karen Lopez, Catherine Lynn, Ashley MacDonald, Kathleen Marshall, LouAnn McCarty, Peggy Moore, Ann Okamura, Will Parker, Maureen Rippee, Tucky Roger, Terrie Saunders, Marilyn Shaw, Ken Spurlock, Mary Stevens, Sandra Sullivan, Wanda Thomas, Jennifer Watson, Amanda Wolf